WILLMINGTON'S BIBLE HANDBOOK

HAROLD L. WILLMINGTON

Tyndale House Publishers, Inc.
CAROL STREAM, ILLINOIS

Visit Tyndale's exciting Web site at www.tyndale.com

TYNDALE and Tyndale's inkwell logo are registered trademarks of Tyndale House Publishers, Inc.

Willmington's Bible Handbook

Designed by Melinda Schumacher

Edited by Bill Deckard

Additional editorial work: Kathryn Olson, Anne Goldsmith

Production coordinators: Julee Schwarzburg, Annette Taroli

Typesetter: Joyce Svensen

Print buyer: Linda Walz

Library of Congress Cataloging-in-Publication data

Willmington, H. L.
[Bible handbook]
Willmington's Bible handbook / Harold L. Willmington.
p. cm.
Includes bibliographical references and indexes.
ISBN-13: 978-0-8423-8174-1 (hardcover : alk. paper)
ISBN-10: 0-8423-8174-0 (hardcover : alk. paper)
1. Bible—Handbooks, manuals, etc. I. Title.
BS417.W487 1997
220.7—dc21 97-17459

Printed in the United States of America

12 11 10 09 08 07 06
11 10 9 8 7 6 5

For reasons known only to God, the word ***grandfather*** *is not to be found once in the Bible! But happy and honored indeed is the man who answers to this glorious name. This* ***Bible Handbook*** *is affectionately dedicated to my three grandchildren:*

Nathanael Paul Willmington, born October 28, 1989
Carissa Nicole Willmington, born April 4, 1991
Abigail Christine Willmington, born April 9, 1997

❖ CONTENTS

✣ INTRODUCTION

This *Bible Handbook* was written with two groups of readers in mind:

- Pastors, teachers, and other diligent Bible students seeking an efficient refresher course in Bible knowledge.
- Non-Christians as well as Christians new to Bible study who seek a basic introduction to God's Word.

It is the author's sincere desire that those in the second group will, through the help of this book, discover what those in the first group already know: that the Bible is the most exciting, practical, and inspirational book ever written! With this goal in mind, this handbook, unlike many other Bible handbooks, focuses on comprehensively summarizing the Bible. In a way, you could call it a "minicommentary." Chapters are subdivided into units of thought, with ample cross-references to show how each piece of divine revelation relates to the whole.

The lists and background material toward the end of the book are designed to give an overview of Scripture, again showing its remarkable unity. Please note the amount of material in this section devoted to the person and work of Jesus Christ, who is truly the focal point of all Scripture (see Eph. 1:10).

The Bible's unity sets it apart from all other religious writings. While many so-called holy books are rambling and incoherent though perhaps claiming only one author, the Bible speaks the same message from beginning to end even though it was written by at least 40 authors over some 2,000 years. The section titled "How We Got the Bible" offers clues as to how this happened, but perhaps the best explanation is 2 Peter 1:21: "It was the Holy Spirit who moved the prophets to speak from God."

Besides its unity, another hallmark of the Bible is its historical accuracy. This is highlighted throughout both sections of this *Bible Handbook,* but perhaps most strikingly in the section on archaeology. More exciting than any blockbuster movie have been the thousands of archeological discoveries that verify and bring to life the people and events we read about in Scripture.

The author has attempted to bring some of these people to life in 138 "People to Remember" stories scattered throughout the book. We hope you'll enjoy getting to know these very human Bible characters and will be able to apply and share what you learn from their good (and bad) examples.

Back to the two groups: If you're a newcomer to the Bible, may Romans 10:17 come true for you: "Faith comes from listening to this message of good news—the Good News about Christ." May your study of God's Word lead you to faith or to a renewal of your faith commitment. If you are already following Christ, may Psalm 119:105 continue to be your wonderful reality: "[God's] word is a lamp for my feet and a light for my path."

❖ NOTES TO READER

CROSS-REFERENCES

Cross-references are used extensively in this book. Scripture references are given throughout, as are references to other sections in this book. The latter are noted as "see exposition on Gen. 1:1" or something similar. References with no book abbreviation, such as "15:1-6," refer to a passage within the book being discussed in that section.

ABBREVIATIONS

OT	Old Testament
NT	New Testament
1 Chron.	1 Chronicles
2 Chron.	2 Chronicles
Col.	Colossians
1 Cor.	1 Corinthians
2 Cor.	2 Corinthians
Dan.	Daniel
Deut.	Deuteronomy
Eccles.	Ecclesiastes
Eph.	Ephesians
Exod.	Exodus
Ezek.	Ezekiel
Gal.	Galatians
Gen.	Genesis
Hab.	Habakkuk
Hag.	Haggai
Heb.	Hebrews
Hos.	Hosea
Isa.	Isaiah
Jer.	Jeremiah
Jon.	Jonah
Josh.	Joshua
Judg.	Judges
Lam.	Lamentations
Lev.	Leviticus
Mal.	Malachi
Matt.	Matthew
Mic.	Micah
Nah.	Nahum
Neh.	Nehemiah
Num.	Numbers
Obad.	Obadiah
1 Pet.	1 Peter
2 Pet.	2 Peter
Phil.	Philippians
Philem.	Philemon
Prov.	Proverbs
Ps.	Psalms
Rev.	Revelation
Rom.	Romans
1 Sam.	1 Samuel
2 Sam.	2 Samuel
Song	Song of Songs
1 Thess.	1 Thessalonians
2 Thess.	2 Thessalonians
1 Tim.	1 Timothy
2 Tim.	2 Timothy
Zech.	Zechariah
Zeph.	Zephaniah

PART I:

BIBLE SURVEY

GENESIS

? Creation
? The Flood

2090 B.C. Call of Abraham

2006 Birth of Jacob

1898 Joseph to Egypt

1876 Jacob & family to Egypt

1805 Death of Joseph

BACKGROUND

The book of Genesis traces earth's history from Creation to the death of Joseph in about 1805 B.C. Genesis has two main parts, both of which are foundational to everything else in the Bible. Its record of Creation and the early history of humanity (1–11) establishes the existence, power, and goodness of God. Its record of God's special dealings with the nation of Israel (12–50) shows his intention to establish and develop a relationship with humanity.

AUTHOR

Moses. Some believe Genesis was the work of several authors over many years. Even some who believe Moses wrote Exodus to Deuteronomy doubt that he wrote Genesis, since its events transpired long before his birth. The evidence suggests, however, that Moses did write Genesis:

- During his years in the Egyptian royal family, Moses could have become a skilled writer and historian; the author of Genesis shows a knowledge of Egyptian terms and customs (Exod. 2:1-11; Acts 7:22).
- The Bible refers to Moses as a writer (Exod. 17:14; 24:4; Deut. 31:9, 24; Luke 20:28; John 1:45). Deuteronomy 31:24–32:47 shows that he was skilled as both writer and historian.
- The unity of theme and style throughout the Pentateuch suggests a single author.
- NT and early Jewish writers viewed Moses as the author of the entire Pentateuch ("law," see John 1:45).

DATE AND LOCATION

Though the exact time Moses wrote Genesis is unknown, it was likely near the close of his first 40 years, while he was still in the Egyptian court and had access to historical documents. The chronology of 1 Kings 6:1 suggests 1446 B.C., when Moses was 80, as the approximate date of the Exodus, so he probably wrote Genesis c. 1486 B.C.

PURPOSE

- To reveal the origin and purpose of the universe, life, and humanity.
- To show the personal, relational, covenant-making nature of God.
- To record the early history of the Hebrew people.
- To begin revealing Jesus the Messiah.

UNIQUE FEATURES

- Genesis introduces the single most important issue of life, the problem of sin and evil, and begins to show the solution to that problem.
- It introduces three of the four God-given institutions foundational to human history: marriage (2), human government (see exposition on 9:1-17), and the chosen nation of Israel (12). The fourth institution, the church, is introduced in Matthew 16.
- Page for page, Genesis probably offers more unforgettable characters and stories than any other book in human history. People of all religions have benefited from these stories.
- It records the Abrahamic covenant (12:1-3), the first of the three most important unconditional covenants in the OT. The other two are
  - ➤ the Davidic covenant (2 Sam. 7:9-16)
  - ➤ the New Covenant (Jer. 31:31)

See *Biblical Covenants*, p. 820.

COMPARISON WITH OTHER BIBLE BOOKS

Revelation:

- Genesis records humanity's first rebellion against God (3:1-6); Revelation records the final rebellion (Rev. 20:7-10).
- Genesis records the entrance of sin (3:1-6); Revelation records its exit (Rev. 20:10; 21:4-8).
- Genesis records the imposition of the curse (3:9-19); Revelation records the lifting of the curse (Rev. 22:3).
- Genesis records the beginning of death (3:19); Revelation records the end of death (Rev. 21:4).
- Genesis records the creation of the present heavens and earth (1:1); Revelation records the creation of the new heavens and earth (Rev. 21:1).

Romans:

- In Genesis, Abraham is the patriarch of Israel; in Romans, he is the patriarch of all who believe (Rom. 4:16).

John, 1 John:

- All "begin at the beginning," but their beginnings are different: Genesis begins with Creation; John and 1 John begin *before* Creation, with the preexistent Word.

Galatians:

- Both show that salvation is by faith (15:6; Gal. 3:6).
- Both show God's desire to redeem all humanity (12:2-3; Gal. 3:8).

OUTLINE

GOD AND EARLY HUMANITY (1–11)
- Creation (1:1–2:3)
- The Garden of Eden (2:4-25)
- The Fall (3)
- Cain and Abel (4)
- From Adam to Noah (5)
- The Flood (6–9)
- Noah's descendants (10)
- The Tower of Babel (11:1-9)
- From Shem to Abraham (11:10-32)

GOD AND THE PATRIARCHS (12–50)
- Abraham (12:1–25:10)
  - The call of Abram (12:1-9)
  - Abram visits Egypt (12:10-20)
  - Abram and Lot separate (13)
  - Abram rescues Lot (14:1-16)
  - Melchizedek (14:17-24)
  - God's covenant with Abram (15)
  - Hagar and Ishmael (16)
  - Abram becomes Abraham (17:1-8)
  - The covenant of circumcision (17:9-14)
  - God promises Abraham a son (17:15–18:15)
  - Sodom and Gomorrah (18:16–19:29)
  - Lot and his daughters (19:30-38)
  - Abraham deceives Abimelech (20)
  - Birth of Isaac (21:1-7)
  - Hagar and Ishmael sent away (21:8-21)
  - Abraham's treaty with Abimelech (21:22-34)
  - Abraham told to offer Isaac (22)
  - Sarah dies, buried at Machpelah (23)
  - Isaac and Rebekah (24)
  - Death of Abraham (25:1-10)
- Isaac (25:11–27:46)
  - Death and genealogy of Ishmael (25:12-18)
  - Jacob and Esau (25:19-34)
  - God's promise to Isaac (26:1-5)
  - Isaac and the Philistines (26:6-35)
  - Jacob gets Esau's blessing (27)
- Jacob (28–36)
  - The stairway to heaven (28)
  - Leah and Rachel (29:1-30)
  - Jacob and his children (29:31–30:24)
  - Jacob and Laban (30:25–31:55)
  - Jacob wrestles with God (32)
  - Jacob and Esau reunited (33)

Dinah and the Shechemites (34)
Jacob returns to Bethel (35)
Genealogy of Esau (36)
Joseph (37–50)
Joseph's dreams (37:1-11)
Joseph sold into slavery (37:12-36)
Judah and Tamar (38)
Joseph and Potiphar's wife (39:1-19)
Joseph in prison (39:20–40:23)
Pharaoh's dreams (41:1-36)
Joseph, prime minister of Egypt (41:37-57)
Joseph helps, forgives brothers (42–45)
Jacob and family settle in Egypt (46–47)
Jacob's last days (48–49)
Joseph's last days (50)

GOD AND EARLY HUMANITY (1–11)

1:1 *When, who, and what?* The Bible's very first verse tells us that a supernatural being brought the universe into existence:

- When? "In the beginning . . ."
- Who? ". . . God . . ."
- What? ". . . created the heavens and the earth."

It is a simple statement of fact. While the verses that follow provide many details about God's creative activity, they do not explain it in scientific terms. Believers accept it "by faith" (Heb. 11:3). Scientists have offered several theories as to how the universe came into being. One of the more well known is the Big Bang theory—that billions of years ago the universe suddenly burst forth from a state of near-infinite density and that the results of that explosion continue today as our universe continues to expand. While the Big Bang theory does not prove the biblical creation account, it does suggest that our universe had a specific and spectacular beginning, as 1:1 states.

GENESIS 1:1 AND OTHER WORLDVIEWS. What does 1:1 say to those who interpret reality apart from a personal, infinite God?

- To the atheist it says that Creation was the work of God.
- To the polytheist it says there is only one God.
- To the pantheist it says that God is apart from and independent of his creation.
- To the evolutionist it says that the universe was created and did not evolve.
- To the materialist it says that matter is not eternal but was itself created.
- To the existentialist it says creation has a purpose.

1:2 *It was shapeless, empty, and dark when he began.* At the beginning of Creation Week, the earth was "empty, a formless mass." There was soil and water but no light. The Holy Spirit was "hovering over" this newly created world.

The Holy Spirit, third person of the Trinity, may be best known for his appearance at Pentecost (Acts 2), but he made his grand entrance here, at the very beginning of Creation. We read elsewhere that Jesus, Son of God and second person of the Trinity, took part in Creation as well (John 1:1-3; Col. 1:16; Heb. 1:2).

1:3-5 *Day One: Light and time.* Though God had already brought something

THE WONDERS OF GENESIS 1:1

1:1 Tells us what God did.
1:2–2:25 Tells us how he did it.

THIS IS A SUMMARIZATION STATEMENT

▼

"In the beginning God created the heavens and the earth."

▲

IT IS ALSO A REFUTATION STATEMENT

PHILOSOPHY REFUTED:	HOW REFUTED:
Atheism	There is a God
Polytheism	There is but one God
Pantheism	He created all things
Evolutionism	He is apart from his creation
Materialism	Matter itself was created
Existentialism	There was a purpose to creation

into existence (1:1-2), 1:3 marks the first occurrence of a phrase that will introduce each day of Creation: "Then God said . . ." God's spoken words brought everything into existence (Ps. 33:6; Heb. 11:3).

The first thing God is recorded to have spoken into existence was light—apparently a temporary light source, meant to function only until Day Four, when the sun, moon, and stars would be created. Yet even on this first day there was a division between light and darkness—which God called day and night.

"It was good" shows both the perfection of and God's satisfaction with creation. God repeated the phrase after each of the six "working days" of Creation.

1:6-8 *Day Two: Water and sky.* God created a "space between the waters," the sky, to divide earthbound water from an atmospheric canopy of water vapor.

1:9-13 *Day Three: Soil and seas, grass and trees.* God gathered all the earthbound water "into one place," and dry land emerged. This "one" place must be viewed in light of the plural "seas" (1:10). As soon as the dry ground emerged, God graced it with vegetation and flowers. While evolutionary theories see life beginning in a water-borne substance, Moses tells us that organic matter began on dry ground.

The trees yielded fruit of like "kind." This word, used in 1:12, 21, 24, 25, suggests a clear differentiation of species.

1:14-19 *Day Four: Sun, moon, and stars.* God now created special light sources, all of which serve three purposes: "signs" reminding people of God's creative work (Ps. 8:3; Rom. 1:19-20); "seasons" defining time periods so that people can plan their activities; and "lights."

1:20-23 *Day Five: Birds and fish.* Next God created the birds of the air and creatures of the sea, from the tiny hummingbird to the massive blue sperm whale.

1:24-25 *Day Six (1): Animals.* Day Six began with the creation of land animals—"livestock, small animals, and wildlife."

1:26-31 *Day Six (2): A creature like its Creator!* Day Six climaxed with the creation of humankind, made in the "image" of God (1:26). The first man was instructed to take charge over all the earth and to fill it with his own kind. (He is referred to as "man" or "the man" until 2:19, where he is called Adam.)

Human beings are in the "image" of God in that only they, among all animate beings, have the godlike characteristics of self-awareness, the ability to choose between good and evil, and the ability to relate to their Creator. To create a being able to relate to him, however, God had to give that being the freedom to reject him. Without such freedom, the being would have been a mere robot. 3:6 records the first time humans chose to exercise their freedom to reject God.

God refers to himself in the plural: "in our image" (1:26). This is the first biblical evidence for the doctrine of the Trinity: that God exists in three persons, Father, Son, and Holy Spirit. While the term *Trinity* does not appear in the Bible, various passages mention the three members of the Godhead in various combinations (11:7; Isa. 48:12-16; Matt. 28:19; John 14:26; 2 Cor. 13:13; see exposition on Eph. 1:1-14; 1 Pet. 1:2).

2:1-3 *Day Seven: Creation completed, God rests.* Having completed his work of Creation, God rested on the seventh day, establishing a weekly pattern of work and rest on which Israel's Sabbath would be based (Exod. 20:8-11). Whether believers or not, people benefit from a weekly day of rest (see Mark 2:27). Sunday, as the day of Christ's resurrection, has replaced Saturday as the Christian Sabbath. Scripture also uses the Sabbath as a symbol of eternal life (Heb. 4:1-10).

LITERAL DAYS? Were the days of Genesis 1 literal 24-hour days? People tend to answer that question in one of four ways:

- They reject the Creation account in favor of evolution.
- They see spiritual value in the biblical account but reject it as science.
- They view the days figuratively, believing that God may have used evolutionary methods to create.
- They view the days as literal 24-hour days.

Taken at face value, the biblical record suggests six 24-hour days:

- The use of numerical adjectives ("first," "second," etc.).
- The fact that each day had an "evening" and a "morning" (the Hebrew terms used in 1:5, 8, 13, 19, 23, 31).
- When Moses spoke of Creation elsewhere he assumed normal, 24-hour days (Exod. 20:11; 31:17).
- Some have suggested that the first three days of Creation may have been longer than the rest, since the sun and moon were not created till Day Four. Yet even the first three days had an evening and morning.

2:4-14 *A perfect home for the perfect couple.* God prepared a garden called Eden, situated among beautiful trees and watered by water that "came up out of the ground" (2:6) and a river with four branches. The names of two of those branches, the Hiddekel (Greek, "Tigris") and the Euphrates, suggest present-day Iraq as the Garden's location.

2:4 begins a second account of Creation, and the first of the "genealogies" that make up the rest of Genesis. 2:4–4:26 is introduced as the "account of the creation of the heavens and the earth" (2:4), and successive sections are introduced in similar fashion: "the history of the descendants of Adam" (5:1–6:8); of Noah (6:9–9:29); of the sons of Noah (10:1–11:9); of Shem (11:10-26); of Terah (11:27–25:11); of Ishmael (25:12-18); of Isaac (25:19–35:29); of Esau (36:1–37:1); and of Jacob (37:2–50:26). This systematic division suggests a concern for historical accuracy.

2:15-17 *God gives the man a job and a warning.* God told the man to take care of the Garden. He invited him to eat freely of all the trees in the Garden except for the tree of the knowledge of good and evil. If the man ate from that tree, he would "surely die."

2:18-25 *A bride from his side while he slept.* God told the man to name all the animals and gave him a name of his own, Adam (2:19). God then created from Adam's side a woman to be his companion. Adam and the woman became husband and wife, in a wedding performed by God himself.

Marriage is the first of the four God-given institutions foundational to human history (see *Unique Features*):

- God's decree that a husband and wife are "united into one" (2:24) is the *foundation* of marriage. Christ cited 2:24 word for word to explain why divorce violates God's will (Matt. 19:5).
- One reason for marriage is *propagation* (1:28).
- But marriage should also involve love—an *illustration* of Christ's love for his church (Eph. 5:25-29).

3:1-5 *The craftiest creature.* Into the perfection of Eden came Satan, speaking through a serpent (see Rev. 12:9; 20:2). This "shrewdest" of all creatures tempted Eve to disobey God by promising that, if she would eat from the forbidden tree, she would become like God.

3:6 *The first and fatal sin.* The woman ate the forbidden fruit and gave some to Adam, who also ate. Exercising their God-given right to choose, they chose to disobey God. Paul explains the consequences of this first act of human disobedience: "When Adam sinned, sin entered the entire human race. Adam's sin brought death, so death spread to everyone, for everyone sinned" (Rom. 5:12). Concerning this explanation, note:

- Through Adam's one act of disobedience, sin entered a previously perfect world.
- Sin brought with it decay and death—for plant and animal life as well as people (3:17-18; Rom. 8:20-22).
- Because of this first sin, all people are sinners.

THE GEOGRAPHY OF GENESIS 1–11

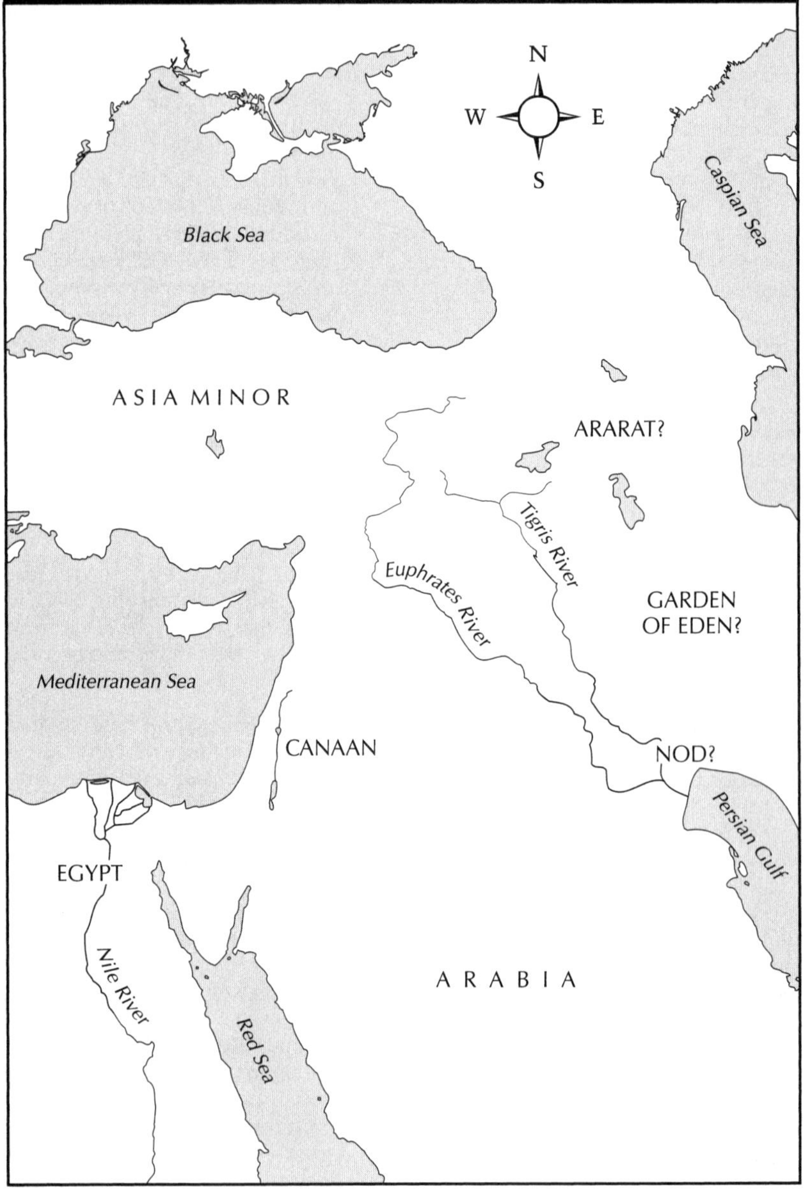

- Despite what one thinks of the biblical account of sin's origin, the simple fact is that "all have sinned" (Rom. 3:23).

This event is often called the fall of man, and Adam's action was the "original sin." Chronologically Eve ate first, but theologically Adam is declared the original sinner (Rom. 5:12; 1 Tim. 2:14). As head of the human race, Adam is held responsible for its actions.

John warned believers about three temptations: "the lust for physical pleasure, the lust for everything we see, and pride in our possessions" (1 John 2:16). Satan subjected Eve to all three:

- Eve saw that the fruit looked delicious (lust for physical pleasure);
- that it "looked so fresh" (lust for everything we see);
- and that it "would make her so wise" (pride).

Satan tempted Jesus in a similar way (see exposition on Matt. 4:1-11).

3:7-13 *The bitter fruit: Shame, fear, and excuses.* Adam and Eve had enjoyed friendship with a God who walked in the Garden (3:8). Now, at the sound of his voice, they experienced shame and fear and tried to hide. Yet he found them and asked what they had done. Adam blamed Eve, and Eve blamed the serpent, but God held all three accountable (3:14-24).

3:14 *The sentence for the crafty serpent.* God didn't bother to ask the serpent what it had done, he merely announced its punishment: For lending its body to Satan, it was cursed to crawl in the dust. Evidently serpents did not crawl before the Fall. Some scholars think they even had wings and stood upright. Isaiah 65:25 indicates that the serpent's judgment will last throughout the Millennium when the rest of the animal kingdom is at peace. Throughout the Bible the serpent is a symbol for treachery and sin (Ps. 58:3-4; Matt. 23:33).

3:15 *The sentence for the "old serpent."* Satan, the "old serpent" (Rev. 20:2), who used the snake's body to approach Adam and Eve, was doomed to defeat by Jesus Christ, the "offspring" of the woman. Satan would bruise Christ's heel—a nonfatal wound; but Christ would bruise Satan fatally, on the head. Isaiah echoes the first part of this first gospel proclamation: Jesus was "wounded and crushed for our sins" (Isa. 53:5). Paul, writing after the Cross, echoes the second part (Rom. 16:20). Even though humanity has free will, God knew we would fall and had already planned for our redemption (Eph. 1:4-5).

3:16-21 *Forgiven, but sentenced to sorrow and death.* God forgave Adam and Eve's disobedience and clothed them in the skins of animals (3:21). The death of those animals symbolizes Christ's death, which would offer all sinners the clothing of God's righteousness. (For more on righteousness as "right clothing," see exposition on 15:1-11).

Even though forgiven, Adam and Eve would suffer the consequences of their sin. The woman would suffer pain in childbirth, while the man would struggle in his attempts to grow food. Neither childbirth nor physical labor were the result of sin; they were part of God's plan (2:15). But both became harder and more painful after the Fall.

God climaxed Adam and Eve's punishment with a sentence of physical death (3:19), carrying out his earlier warning (2:17). Scripture describes two kinds of death—physical and spiritual. Both involve *separation.* Physical death is the separation of the spirit from the body; spiritual death is the separation of the sinner from the Savior (Matt. 25:41).

The Bible also describes two births: "Humans can reproduce only human life, but the Holy Spirit gives new life from heaven" (John 3:6).

- To have only one birth means to die twice: The unbeliever will suffer both physical and spiritual death (Heb. 9:27).
- To have two births (John 3:3) means to die but once: The believer will never die spiritually (John 3:16).

3:22-24 *Banished from Eden and the tree of life.* The sentence of death (3:19) became a certainty as Adam and Eve were driven from the Garden and its tree of life. This banishment involved mercy as well as judgment: Had they eaten of the tree of life, they would have lived forever in a state of sin and spiritual misery.

The "mighty angelic beings" spoken of here (Hebrew *cherubim*) are apparently a special kind of angelic being concerned with God's holiness (Exod. 25:18-22; see exposition on Ezek. 10:1-22).

4:1-15 *First family, first homicide.* Eve gave birth to Cain and Abel. Abel was a shepherd; Cain was a farmer. God refused Cain's gift of farm produce but accepted Abel's animal sacrifice. Abel's gift was offered "by faith" but Cain's was not (Heb. 11:4). Cain apparently knew what God desired and was given a second chance to make the right sacrifice (4:7). He still chose not to and, in bitterness, killed Abel.

God decreed that Cain would become a restless wanderer. Realizing that his parents would have more children (5:4) and that one of them might someday seek his life in revenge, Cain sought God's protection. God gave Cain a protective "mark." This would be a deterrent to lawlessness in the days before divinely sanctioned human government (9:1-7). God was also claiming his right to show mercy or take vengeance as he saw fit (Deut. 32:35; Rom. 9:15; Heb. 10:30).

4:16-24 *Cain's children: Gifted but godless.* Cain's descendants pioneered in music, cattle raising, and toolmaking. But Lamech's boast about his vengeance killing (4:23-24) suggests that the Cainites were no pioneers when it came to morality. Cain probably married one of his own sisters (5:4); the longevity and genetic soundness of early humanity would have made this more advisable than in our own day.

4:25-26 *Seth: "Another Abel."* Eve named her third son Seth, meaning "granted" or "appointed," because she saw him as the replacement for Abel. That Seth lived up to Eve's expectations is suggested by the religious awakening reported here. Some believe our earliest ancestors were polytheists, but 4:3-5, 26 indicates that they were monotheists.

5:1-20 *The first list of "begots."* After fathering a number of sons and daughters, Adam died at age 930. Genealogies such as in these verses were important to ancient peoples to establish family relationships, privileges, and responsibilities. The genealogies in Scripture establish the historical reality of Jesus and show that his birth was foreknown and planned by God.

Notice that the people in this genealogy lived very long lives. This could be due to the lingering beneficial effects of both humanity's and nature's unfallen state. If the earth's vapor canopy (1:7) remained intact until the Flood (7:11-24), it may have slowed the aging process by filtering the sun's ultraviolet rays.

5:21-28 *The first person to leave this life alive.* Enoch's son Methuselah lived to be 969—the oldest human on record. But Enoch himself was one of two recorded humans who never died physically. The other was Elijah (2 Kings 2:11). The Bible indicates that believers alive when Christ returns will also escape death (1 Cor. 15:51-52; 1 Thess. 4:16-17).

Enoch was a man of great faith (Heb. 11:5). He, like his great-grandson Noah "enjoyed a close relationship with God" (5:24; 6:9). Enoch was the first recorded preacher (see Jude 1:14-15).

5:29–6:7 *Noah, the "sons of God," and the "daughters of men."* Humanity had become so wicked by Noah's day that God decided to destroy them all. The wickedness apparently had something to do with the "sons of God" marrying human women. "Sons of God" may refer to the godly line of Seth, with "beautiful women of the human race" representing the ungodly line of Cain. Some say the sons of God were fallen angels.

6:8-13 *The family that found the grace of God.* Noah and his family were godly in an otherwise godless world. God warned them of his plan to destroy humanity. Long before the promise to Abraham, the giving of the law through Moses, or the coming of Christ, Noah and his family experienced grace. It seems natural to connect *law* with the OT and *grace* with the NT. A more correct contrast is that the OT shows how God in grace dealt with Israel and sinners, while the NT shows how God in grace deals with the church and sinners.

6:14-22 *Noah builds a floating zoo!* God told Noah to build a large ship to save his family from the Flood. He also told him to take one male and female from each "unclean" species and seven pairs from each "clean" species (7:2-3). For an explanation of "clean" and "unclean" animals, see exposition on Deuteronomy 14:3-21.

7:1-10 *They enter the ark and wait a week.* Construction completed, Noah brought his family and all the animals into the ark—and waited for seven days.

"Go [also translated *Come*] into the boat" (7:1) marks the first biblical invitation. Jesus renewed the invitation: "Come to me, all of you who are weary and carry heavy burdens, and I will give you rest" (Matt. 11:28). It is given again in Revelation 22:17 and will be issued one final time to all believers at the Last Judgment (Matt. 25:34).

7:11-24 *The Flood.* The Flood began with 40 days of rain; the water rose more than 20 feet above the highest peaks, destroying all human and animal life. The Flood has been the object of endless debate:

- *What triggered the Flood?* It has been suggested that a secondary source of water existed in vast pressurized subterranean reservoirs. The actual trigger to unleash these waters may have been an earthquake, which in turn would have sent immense clouds of dust skyward, condensing and precipitating the water-vapor canopy (1:7; 7:11), which today no longer exists in its pre-Flood capacity.
- *How long did the Flood last?* According to the dates given in Scripture, 371 days elapsed from Noah's entering the ark (7:7) till the day he stepped out (8:18).
- *Was the Flood really worldwide?* Both biblical and secular evidence suggest that it was:
  - ➤ *The need for the ark:* There was no dry ground anywhere on earth for refuge.
  - ➤ *The wide distribution of humankind:* Even with the most literal interpretation of Scripture—that the Flood occurred just 10 generations after Adam—there would have been at least 10 million people on earth, and their nomadic ways could have taken them far beyond the Middle East. Some estimate a pre-Flood population of more than 2 billion.
  - ➤ *Scripture's comparison of the Flood judgment and the coming fire judgment (2 Pet. 3:3-7, 10):*

HOW BIG WAS THE ARK?

- 450 feet long, 75 feet wide, 45 feet high
- Had a total deck area of 101,250 square feet (more than 21 standard college basketball courts)
- Largest ship ever built until A.D. 1884
- Nearly one-half the length of the *Queen Mary*

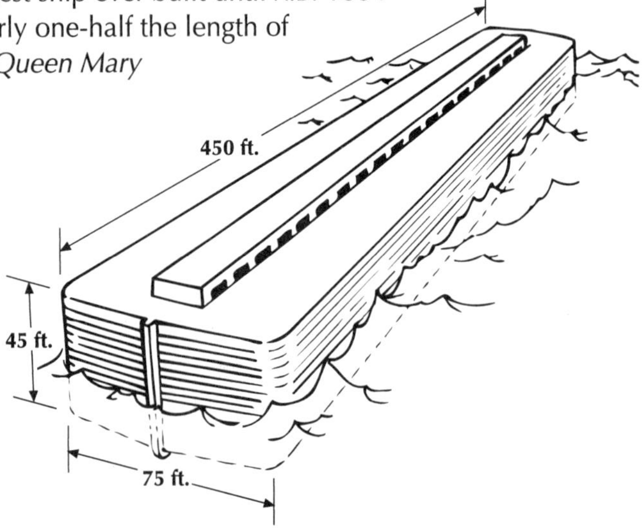

HOW DID NOAH FIND ROOM FOR ALL THE ANIMALS?

- Total animal population would not have exceeded 35,000 vertebrates
- Average size would be that of a sheep
- Modern train of 150 boxcars could carry this
- Ark had carrying capacity of over 520 boxcars!

Since the fire will be universal in scope, it is logical to conclude that the Flood was universal as well.

➤ *God's promise not to send another such flood (9:11):* If the Flood was merely local, then God lied, for there have been many extensive floods since that time.

➤ *Widespread Flood traditions:* The early aborigines of nearly every part of the world have preserved records of a great flood, suggesting that the entire earth was repopulated by Noah's descendants.

➤ *Discoveries of marine fossils on mountaintops:* How did they get there, if not by a flood that covered those mountains?

- *How could there have been room for all the animals in the ark?* The ark was approximately 450 feet long, 75 feet wide, and 45 feet high. With its three decks (6:16), it would have had a total deck area of 101,250 square feet, equal to 21 basketball courts. (See illustration on previous page.)

8:1-14 *The ark arrives at Ararat.* Nearly six months after the Flood began, the water started receding, and the ark came to rest on a mountain in the Ararat region of what is today Turkey (see *Mount Ararat,* p. 887). After another six months, an olive branch in a dove's beak signaled that the ark's passengers could safely disembark.

8:15-22 *Noah walks into a new world and worships.* Noah left the ark, built an altar, and sacrificed to God, who promised never to destroy the world again by water (9:8-17). The earth will, however, be destroyed again—by fire (2 Pet. 3:10).

9:1-17 *New rules and a rainbow.* With a world to repopulate, God reissued the mandate of 1:28: "Multiply and fill the earth." He decreed that humanity would be permitted to eat the flesh of animals. "Just as I have given you grain and vegetables" (9:3) suggests that this was not so before the Flood. But people would not be allowed to consume an animal's blood, for it is the source of life.

Death would be the penalty for shedding human blood, because humans are made "in God's image" (9:6). This law against murder represents the beginning of divinely sanctioned human government (see Rom. 13:1-4).

The post-Flood atmosphere produced a rainbow, which, God said, was a sign of his promise never again to destroy the world by water.

9:18-29 *"Cursed be Canaan."* Drunk with wine from his own vineyard, Noah lay uncovered in his tent. Ham "saw that his father was naked and went outside and told his brothers" (9:22). Shem and Japheth discreetly covered Noah with a garment. Noah reacted by pronouncing a curse on Ham's son, Canaan, while blessing the descendants of Shem and Japheth.

What was the horrible sin that prompted Noah's curse? Some believe it was homosexuality: The Hebrew language seems to suggest it; the word used for *naked* (9:22) is connected with sexual immorality in Leviticus 18; 20; Canaan's descendants were notorious for their sexual perversion (Lev. 18; see *Canaanites,* p. 862; *Ugarit,* p. 900).

10:1-32 *Noah's descendants.* The descendants of Noah's three sons are listed. Shem is described as the "ancestor of all the descendants of Eber" (10:21). These were the "Eberites," better known to us as the Hebrews or Israelites.

11:1-9 *The trouble at Babel.* Noah's descendants built the Tower of Babel for two reasons: to make a name for themselves and to assure their unity and security. They probably didn't intend the tower to reach into outer space. The Bible describes "a tower that reaches to the skies" (11:4). Many scholars believe the text should read "whose top is heaven." Among the ruins of Babylon is a tall building constructed of dried bricks in seven stages corresponding to the seven known planets, topped by a lofty tower displaying the signs of the zodiac.

God brought an end to this ambitious building project by confusing the builders' language and scattering them all over the earth—so that humanity's unity would not degenerate to the pre-Flood level of spiritual depravity.

11:10-32 *Introducing the father of the faithful.* This post-Babel genealogy traces the "descendants of Eber" (10:21) to Abram (11:27), renamed Abraham in 17:5. Abram was the tenth generation from Noah.

Abram was born c. 2165 B.C. We know nothing of his early life or of how he learned of God, except for the information given in 12:1; Joshua 24:2; and Acts 7:2. Prior to his conversion, Abram may have been a worshiper of idols (Joshua 24:2). In Abram's day, Ur was a wealthy commercial center and seaport on the Persian Gulf at the mouth of the Euphrates River. Its skyline was dominated by a ziggurat similar to the Tower of Babel and by temples to pagan deities.

GOD AND THE PATRIARCHS (12–50)

12:1-3 *Seven prophetic promises.* In about the year 2090 B.C., God called Abram to leave the comforts of his homeland and take his family to "the land that I will show you." Abram's speedy response to God's command was the first of several actions on his part that would earn him the title of "spiritual father of those who have faith" (Rom. 4:11, 16).

God made several promises to Abram—promises of seed, soil, and a Savior:

- Abram was to father a great nation *(seed);*
- God would prepare a land for that nation *(soil);*
- the entire world would be blessed by a *Savior* who would come through Abram's seed (Matt. 1:1; Gal. 3:8).

While all of Abraham's descendants—the nation of Israel—were commissioned to be a blessing to the world, because of their repeated failure to do so the promise would be fulfilled through Christ (see exposition on Isa. 41:1-20; 43:8-13).

12:4-9 *Abram sets out at 75.* Abram, now 75 years old, along with his wife, Sarai, and his nephew Lot, left Haran and made the desert journey to Canaan. Arriving there, Abram built an altar, and God, appearing to him, promised to give him the land. Then he moved on to Bethel, which means "house of God" and was to play a significant role in Israel's history.

12:10-20 *Famine in Canaan, failure in Egypt.* Abram had obeyed God and was living in the Promised Land. But there was a famine, so he left Canaan and went to Egypt. Fearful that Pharaoh would kill him in order to marry Sarai, Abram told him that Sarai was his sister. This was partly true: She was his half sister (20:12). Pharaoh made plans to marry Sarai, but God sent a plague on his house. Pharaoh rebuked Abram for his deceit, but Abram apparently didn't learn his lesson, for he would use this very ploy again (20:1-18).

13:1-4 *Back to Bethel, the place of blessing.* Abram returned from Egypt to Canaan and worshiped God at the altar he had built at Bethel.

13:5-13 *"You can have first choice."* To avoid conflict among their herdsmen, Abram allowed Lot to have first choice of grazing land. Lot selected the fertile Jordan Valley near Sodom.

13:14-18 *"Descendants as the dust of the earth."* As Abram prepared to move on to Hebron, God reaffirmed his promise: Abram's descendants would be as numerous as the dust of the earth.

14:1-16 *"They've taken Lot!"* Sodom and five other cities lost a battle with Kedorlaomer and his allies. Lot was taken captive, but Abram defeated Kedorlaomer and rescued Lot.

God would scarcely have bothered to record this pagan dogfight were it not for the four little words "They also captured Lot." Despite his behavior Lot still belonged to God, and God knows his own (2 Tim. 2:19).

14:17-24 *Melchizedek and Bera: A tale of two kings.* En route to Hebron following his victory, Abram met two kings:

THE GEOGRAPHY OF GENESIS 12–50

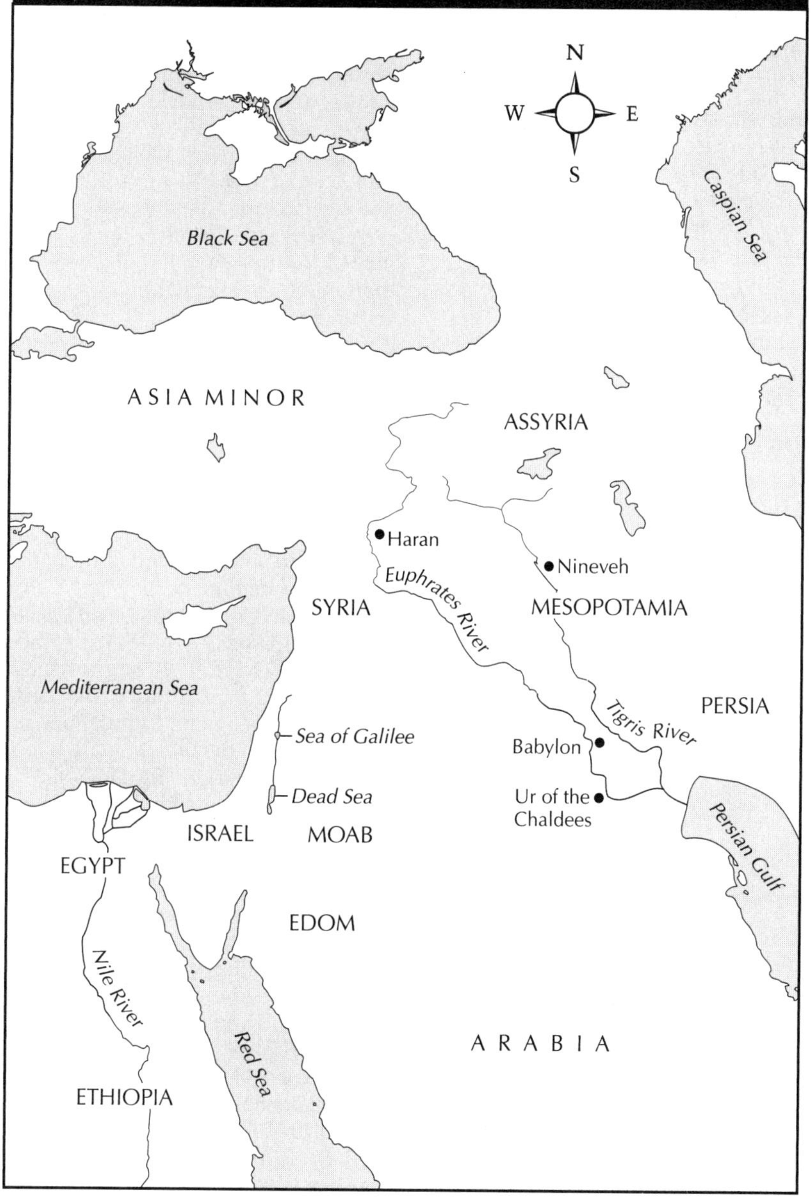

Melchizedek, king of Salem; and Bera, king of Sodom. Abram rejected Bera's offer of wealth, saying he didn't want Bera to get credit for Abram's wealth. But he did accept a gift from Melchizedek, and in turn gave him a tenth of the spoils from the war.

MELCHIZEDEK AND CHRIST.
Melchizedek, a priest (14:18) as well as a king, is mentioned again in Psalm 110:4 and Hebrews 5:6-10; 7:1-22.

- *There are three main theories concerning Melchizedek:*
  - That he was actually Noah's son Shem.
  - That he was a preincarnate appearance of Christ himself.
  - That he was simply a king of Jerusalem—*Melchizedek* literally means "king of righteousness," and Salem may be an early name for Jerusalem.
- *Melchizedek gave Abram bread and wine and blessed him. This is the first Bible mention of bread and wine, foreshadowing Christ's death.*
- *14:18 is the first biblical occurrence of the word* priest. *The three great OT offices were prophet, priest, and king:*
  - The prophet represented God to humanity (1 Kings 18:15).
  - The priest represented humanity to God (Lev. 8:1–9:24).
  - The king, under God, ruled over humanity (1 Sam. 10:1).
- *Melchizedek filled two of those offices; Christ fills all three:*
  - He was a prophet (past ministry, Matt. 21:11; Luke 7:16; John 1:18; 4:19; Heb. 1:1-2).
  - He is a priest (present ministry, Rom. 8:34; Heb. 4:14-16; 7:24-27).
  - He will be a king (future ministry, Rev. 19:11-16).

See exposition on Hebrews 7:1-28.

15:1-11 *Belief becomes righteousness.* Abram asked God if his servant Eliezer might be his heir, since the promised son had not been born. God said no, for Sarai would indeed have a son. Abram "believed the LORD, and the LORD declared him righteous because of his faith" (15:6). God validated his renewed promise to Abram through a blood covenant.

The covenant of blood is one of three kinds of legal covenants in the Bible. The others are the covenant of salt (Lev. 2:11-16; 2 Chron. 13:5) and the covenant of a sandal (Ruth 4:7-8).

A key verse for all believers, 15:6 marks the first mention of three important biblical words:

Believed.

- Abram was not the first person to believe in God, but his faith is a pattern for all believers (Rom. 4; Gal. 3:6-9; Heb. 11:8-10, 17-19).
- The Bible does not say that Abram pleased God or appeased him, as most religions require, but simply that he believed in him.

Declared. This word is also translated "reckoned" (NASB) or "accounted" (NKJV). It suggests an imputation or attribution by God. There are three main imputations or attributions in the Bible:

- The imputation of Adam's sin upon all humankind (Rom. 3:23; 5:12).
- The imputation of the sins of all humankind upon Christ (Isa. 53:5-6; 2 Cor. 5:14-21; Heb. 2:9; 1 Pet. 2:24).
- The imputation of God's righteousness upon each believing sinner (Rom. 4:6-25; Phil. 3:9; James 2:23).

Righteous. The Bible teaches that all sinners are naked before God (3:7-10; Heb. 4:13; Rev. 3:17). Some realize this and try to make their own spiritual clothes, but God looks upon such clothes as "filthy rags" (Isa. 64:6). Whenever sinners realize their nakedness and turn to God, he clothes them in his own righteousness (Isa. 61:10; Zech. 3:4; Luke 15:22).

15:12-21 *"Four centuries of slavery, then Canaan."* God gave Abram seven prophecies, all of which were fulfilled. The reference following each prophecy shows its fulfillment:

- Abram's descendants would be strangers in a foreign land (46:2-4).
- They would be servants in that land (Exod. 1:7-14).
- The servitude would last 430 years (Exod. 12:40).
- God would judge the nation that enslaved them (Exod. 7–12).
- Abram himself would be spared all of this (25:7-8).
- After four generations in Egypt, Israel would return to Canaan (Exod. 6:16-20—Moses was the fourth generation).
- Israel would come out of Egypt with great wealth (Exod. 12:35-36; Ps. 105:37).

16:1-16 *A marriage definitely not made in heaven.* Still not fully believing God's promise, the barren Sarai gave her maidservant Hagar to Abram for childbearing purposes. When Hagar became pregnant, however, Sarai's attitude changed and she drove her away.

The "angel of the LORD" met Hagar by a spring, named her unborn son, and sent her back to Sarai. Many scholars believe that OT appearances of the "angel of the LORD" are actually appearances of preincarnate Christ, though in some cases it may have been God the Father (see exposition on 17:1-8).

Hagar returned home and gave birth to Ishmael. Abram was 86 at the time.

17:1-8 *A name change at 99.* Abram, meaning "exalted father," now became Abraham, "father of many." For the fourth time God affirmed his covenant with Abraham (12:2-3, 7; 13:14-17; 15:5).

God's appearance to Abram is an example of a "theophany," a visible manifestation of the invisible God. Though God told Moses that "no one may see me and live" (Exod. 33:20), he has occasionally allowed believers to catch a glimpse of him in various forms (18:2; Exod. 24:9-18; 33:18-23; Judg. 13:17-23; Ezek. 1:26-28). Sometimes these theophanies are referred to as the "angel of the LORD" (see exposition on 16:1-16). God's ultimate self-revelation would be in the person of Jesus Christ (see exposition on John 1:14).

17:9-14 *Circumcision, the seal of the covenant.* God commanded Abraham that he and all the males of his household must be circumcised. Concerning circumcision:

- Abraham was the first man to be circumcised. This in itself was a demonstration of his faith, as circumcision renders one temporarily helpless.
- Circumcision is the sign and seal, but not the source, of God's promise: Faith in God's word is the source (15:6; Rom. 4:1-12).
- Circumcision of the flesh without cleansing the heart of sin is worthless (Deut. 10:16).
- Circumcision is not required under the New Covenant of grace (Acts 15:1-2, 28-29; Rom. 4:1-12; Gal. 5:2-6).
- Paul, however, compares circumcision to baptism (Col. 2:11-12).
- Circumcision has always been recommended for hygienic reasons.

17:15-22 *A name change at 90, the promise of a son.* God changed Sarai's name to Sarah and told her she would have a son (to be named Isaac) and would become the mother of nations.

17:23-27 *Abraham seals the covenant.* Abraham, now 99, fulfilled God's command of 17:9-14; he and all the males in his camp were circumcised.

18:1-15 *Isaac: The good news.* Once again God appeared to Abraham, who prepared food for his divine visitor and the two angels with him. God said Sarah would give birth within a year. Sarah, listening inside the tent, laughed, and God rebuked her. Sarah denied that she had laughed.

18:16-33 *Sodom: The bad news.* God told Abraham he would destroy Sodom and Gomorrah. At Abraham's request, God agreed to spare Sodom, hometown of Lot, if just 10 righteous people could be found there.

19:1-11 *A backslidden believer and the sinners of Sodom.* When the two angels came to Sodom, Lot invited them into his own home to save them from Sodom's perverse inhabitants. Soon, however, Lot's home was surrounded by Sodomites who demanded that the two angels be handed over to them for sexual purposes. Lot tried in vain to reason with them, even offering them his two virgin daughters. He tried to convince his married daughters and their husbands that Sodom was doomed, but they refused to take him seriously.

The angels had found Lot at the gate of Sodom, meaning that he may have been a public official. Note the progression of Lot's tragic fall:

- First, Lot looked longingly at Sodom (13:10).
- Then he chose the area of ground near Sodom (13:11).
- Next he pitched his tent toward Sodom (13:12).
- Then he moved right into the city (14:12).
- Finally, he gave his energies (19:1-11) and even offered his own daughters (19:8, 12-14, 30-38) to Sodom.

19:12-29 *The fire falls as the sun rises.* At daybreak, Lot and his family fled the doomed Sodom. As fire and brimstone fell, Lot's wife looked back and was instantly destroyed. From a distant highland, Abraham could see the smoke from the burning city (see *Sodom and Gomorrah,* p. 888).

Jesus used Sodom along with the Flood as illustrations of judgment (Luke 17:26-30; see also Deut. 29:23; Ezek. 16:49-50).

19:30-38 *Two sons by his own two daughters.* Having no husbands but wanting to preserve their father's name, Lot's two daughters got their father drunk, had sexual relations with him, and became pregnant. Their descendants would become the Moabites and the Ammonites, enemies of Israel.

20:1-18 *"She's my sister," he says again.* Moving south into Philistine territory, Abraham falsely introduced Sarah to King Abimelech as his sister, but God warned Abimelech not to have sexual relations with her. This was the second time Abraham had lied about Sarah (12:10-20), and again it was because he feared for his own safety should his hosts learn that the beautiful Sarah was his wife. Because of the incident, God "had stricken all the women with infertility as a warning to Abimelech for having taken Abraham's wife" (20:18). But when Abraham realized that Abimelech was acting honorably, he prayed on Abimelech's behalf, and God rescinded his judgment on the king and his land.

21:1-7 *The birth of "Laughter."* Sarah gave birth to Isaac, whose name means "he laughs." Both parents rejoiced for the baby's supernatural birth, and Sarah desired that "all who hear about this will laugh with me" (21:6).

There are at least 11 births in Scripture in which God himself intervened: Jacob and Esau (25:21); Reuben (29:31); Issachar (30:17-18); Joseph (30:22-24); Samson (Judg. 13:2-5); Obed (Ruth 4:13); Samuel (1 Sam. 1:19-20); the son of a woman from

Shunem (2 Kings 4:14-17); John the Baptist (Luke 1:5-13, 57); Jesus (Luke 1:26-38; 2:7).

21:8-21 *Sarah and Hagar: More trouble in the tent.* At Isaac's weaning ceremony, an angry Sarah saw Ishmael mock her son. She demanded that Abraham send both Ishmael and Hagar into the desert. Through an angel, God reassured Hagar of his care. Paul used the conflict between Hagar and Sarah to compare law and grace (see exposition on Gal. 4:21-31).

21:22-34 *A treaty sealed with seven lambs.* Seeing that God was with Abraham, Abimelech offered to make a treaty with him. Abraham accepted, sealing the treaty with seven lambs. (Note the similarity with 26:17-33, where Isaac signed a treaty with the Philistines.)

22:1-24 *Isaac on the altar: A close-up of Calvary.* God told Abraham to offer Isaac as a sacrifice. Abraham obediently tied Isaac to the altar, but at the last moment God commanded that Isaac be untied, and God miraculously provided a ram in Isaac's place. Because Abraham was willing to offer Isaac, God again promised to bless him (22:15-19).

When the time came to offer the sacrifice, Isaac innocently asked, "Where is the lamb?" and Abraham replied, "God will provide a lamb, my son" (22:8). This one sentence summarizes the Bible's central message—that God would give his own Son as the atonement for sin:

- "Where is the lamb?" (22:7)
- "Look! There is the Lamb of God." (John 1:29)
- "The Lamb is worthy." (Rev. 5:12)

23:1-20 *Sarah dies; Abraham buys a burial place.* Sarah died at 127, and Abraham mourned. Ephron offered to give Abraham the cave of Machpelah, near Hebron, as a family burial plot, but Abraham insisted on paying for it. Sarah (23:19), Abraham (25:9), Isaac, Rebekah, and Leah (49:31), and Jacob (50:13) would all be buried in that cave. 23:2 is the Bible's first mention of crying. The last such mention is in Revelation 5:4. But someday tears will cease forever (Rev. 21:4).

24:1-56 *"Bring back a bride!"* Abraham sent a trusted servant (possibly Eliezer, see 15:2) to his original home in northwestern Mesopotamia to find a wife for Isaac. In Mesopotamia, the servant asked God to show him a sign as to whom he should select. At that exact moment Rebekah came upon the scene. The servant told Rebekah and her family why he was there and why he knew God had selected her as Isaac's bride.

24:57-67 *The bride-to-be agrees to go.* Rebekah agreed to the servant's proposal, bid her family farewell, went with the servant to Canaan, and married Isaac.

TYPOLOGY OF CHRIST IN A COURTSHIP. Notice the typology in the story of Isaac and Rebekah:

- *Abraham* is a type of the heavenly Father, who is planning a marriage for his beloved Son (Matt. 22:2).
- *Isaac* is a type of Christ, who was offered up as a sacrifice (22; Matt. 27) and seeks his bride. Like Isaac, Christ loves his bride dearly (24:67; Eph. 5:25).
- The *servant* is a type of the Holy Spirit.
  - ➤ The servant came to Mesopotamia for one reason—to take a bride for Isaac. The Holy Spirit came at Pentecost (Acts 2) for one purpose—to gather a bride for the Son.
  - ➤ Abraham's servant gave honor to the father and son. Today the Holy Spirit gives honor to the Father and Son (John 15:26).
- *Rebekah* is a type of the church. Before anyone can be a part of

IMPORTANT PLACES IN THE STORY OF ABRAHAM

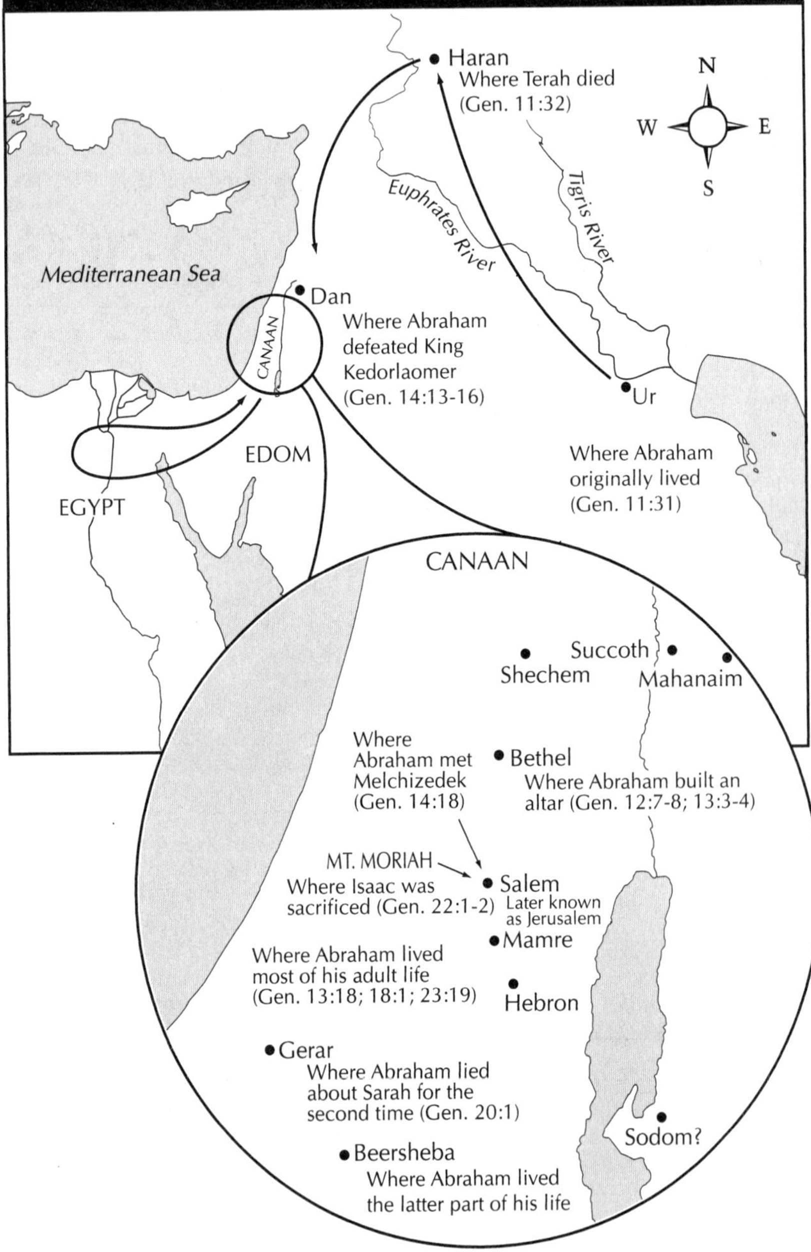

Christ's bride, he or she must answer the question Rebekah answered: "Are you willing to go with this man?" (24:58).

25:1-6 *Six sons from his third wife.* After Sarah's death Abraham married Keturah, who bore him six sons. The fourth was Midian, father of the Midianites. Centuries later, Moses would marry a Midianite woman (Exod. 2:16-21). Still later the Midianites would oppress Israel and Gideon would defeat them (Judg. 6–8).

25:7-11 *Farewell to the father of the faithful.* Abraham died at 175. Isaac and Ishmael buried him with Sarah at Machpelah.

25:12-18 *The death of Ishmael, father of Arabia.* Ishmael fathered 12 sons, who founded 12 tribes. He died at 137. Present-day Arabs claim Ishmael as their ancestor.

25:19-26 *Jacob and Esau: One birthday, two nations.* Isaac and Rebekah remained childless for 20 years. Isaac prayed for Rebekah, and she bore twins. God had told Rebekah that her two sons would become rival nations. Esau was born first, but when the second twin followed, his hand grasped Esau's heel, so they named him Jacob, meaning "he deceives" or "he grasps the heel."

25:23 introduces a theme that will recur throughout Israel's history: The older shall serve the younger. Another example is Ephraim and Manasseh (48:1-22). Younger sons in Christ's lineage include Judah, Perez, and David. Paul saw this as God's sovereign election (Rom. 9:6-13).

25:27-34 *A birthright sold for soup.* Esau became a hunter, while Jacob stayed close to home. One day Esau was hungry when he returned from the field, so he sold his birthright to Jacob for a bowl of stew. Traditionally the birthright went to the oldest son, giving him a double portion of the inheritance. To trade it away was equal to forfeiting dominance in the family.

26:1-35 *Isaac and the Philistines: Like father, like son.* During a famine God promised Isaac he would provide for him just as he had for Abraham. The famine drove Isaac to seek relief from the Philistine king Abimelech. Isaac lied to Abimelech about Rebekah, claiming she was his sister. Later, the truth came out. This Abimelech was probably the son of the Abimelech to whom Abraham had told a similar lie (20:1-18).

Isaac reexcavated some wells that had belonged to Abraham but had been filled in by the Philistines (26:17-33). The Philistines, realizing God was with Isaac, convinced him to make a treaty with them. (Note the similarity with 21:22-34, where Abraham signed a treaty with the Philistines.)

Meanwhile Esau married two Canaanite women, causing great anguish to Isaac and Rebekah.

27:1-29 *Jacob and the blessing: Right goal, wrong method.* Age 137 and assuming he would die soon, Isaac instructed Esau to prepare a meal for him, indicating that he would use the occasion to give Esau his blessing. Overhearing the conversation, Rebekah arranged for Jacob to disguise himself as Esau so that he instead might receive the blessing. The deception worked, and Jacob received the blessing. (Ironically, Isaac lived another 43 years—see 35:28.)

Rebekah was right in thinking God wanted Jacob to get the blessing (25:23), but she was wrong to take matters into her own hands. The end never justifies the means (Rom. 3:7-8).

27:30-46 *Esau vows revenge: "Death to the deceiver!"* No sooner had Jacob left with Esau's blessing than Esau returned. The deception was discovered, but it was too late: Unable to rescind the blessing, Isaac could only give Esau the "spiritual leftovers."

Esau vowed to kill Jacob. Learning of this, Rebekah arranged for Jacob to seek refuge with her brother Laban in Mesopotamia.

28:1-5 *Jacob the deceiver blessed and banished.* To protect Jacob from Esau's wrath, Isaac sent him away, reassuring him that the God who had blessed his grandfather and father would also bless him.

At this point Isaac drops out of the biblical account, even though he lived another 43 years. Isaac was not a man who dreamed dreams or conquered continents. He has been described as the mediocre son of a great father (Abraham) and the mediocre father of a great son (Jacob):

- Isaac was a submissive son, presumably willing even to be sacrificed (22:7-10) and to let someone else choose his bride (24).
- He was an affectionate and caring husband (24:67; 25:21).
- He was also indulgent, both as husband and father:
  - ➤ He had little control over Esau, who married two non-Israelite women (26:34).
  - ➤ He had little control over Rebekah, who felt free to deceive him (27:5-13).
  - ➤ He had little control over Jacob, who looked to Rebekah instead of to Isaac for authority (27:13).
- He was, nevertheless, a man of faith (22:7-10; 24:63; 25:21; 26:25; 28:1-4; Heb. 11:20).

28:6-9 *"Maybe this will make them happy."* Hoping to appease his parents' disappointment with his marriages to pagan women, Esau married his cousin Mahalath, daughter of Ishmael.

28:10-22 *Jacob and the stairway to heaven.* At Bethel, during his flight to Haran, Jacob dreamed and saw angels ascending and descending a stairway to heaven. God used the vision to reaffirm to Jacob the promises of the Abrahamic covenant. Awakening, Jacob poured oil on the rock he had used as a pillow and promised he would serve the Lord, if the Lord would meet all his needs—a selfish prayer, to say the least!

God's promise to Jacob (28:15) summarizes one of the great themes of Genesis—God's faithfulness to his chosen people despite their unfaithfulness.

29:1-14 *The woman at the well will be his wife.* Arriving in Haran, Jacob pushed aside a heavy stone covering a well, allowing some sheep to find water. He soon learned that the beautiful keeper of those sheep was his cousin Rachel. Next he met Laban, his uncle and future father-in-law.

Two other OT marriages began with a meeting at a well (24:10-28; Exod. 2:15-21).

29:15-30 *He works for one wife, gets two.* Jacob agreed to work seven years for Laban in order to marry Rachel. Following his wedding night, a furious Jacob discovered that his crafty father-in-law had given him Rachel's older and less attractive sister, Leah! Laban again promised Rachel to Jacob, providing he would observe the traditional bridal week with Leah and promise to work an additional seven years for Rachel.

29:31–30:8 *Jacob's first six sons.* Leah gave birth to Jacob's first four sons: Reuben, Simeon, Levi, and Judah. The barren and desperate Rachel gave her handmaid, Bilhah, to Jacob for childbearing purposes, resulting in the births of Dan and Naphtali.

30:9-13 *"Two can play that game": Sons seven and eight.* Leah, temporarily barren herself, offered Jacob her own servant girl, Zilpah, for childbearing. She bore him another two sons, Gad and Asher.

30:14-21 *Sons nine and ten, and a daughter.* Leah's son Reuben found some mandrake plants, which were believed to increase fertility. When Rachel saw the plants, she bargained with Leah, offering her Jacob for the night if she could have the plants. Leah agreed and as a result gave birth to Issachar. Later she bore Zebulun and a daughter, Dinah.

30:22-24 *Rachel is finally rewarded: Son eleven.* Rachel finally had a son, Joseph, who along with her later son, Benjamin (35:18), would be favored by Jacob.

Half of Jacob's sons were born to Leah, whom he never intended to marry. These included Levi, father of Israel's priesthood, and Judah, forebear of Israel's kings and of Christ.

30:25-43 *Laban's plea: "Stay, and name your price."* After Joseph's birth, Jacob decided it was time to return to Canaan. Laban begged Jacob to stay and work for him, realizing that much of his own wealth came from God's blessing on his son-in-law. Jacob agreed to stay, with one strange-sounding condition: that he could have all the speckled and spotted animals. Though the scheme was pure superstition, God blessed Jacob, and he thrived at Laban's expense.

31:1-55 *"Your father keeps cheating me. Let's leave!"* Understandably, Jacob's success aroused Laban's envy, and he began changing the terms of their agreement. Jacob decided it was time to leave Haran and return to Canaan. Without telling Laban, he and his family left under cover of night.

Learning of their departure, Laban set out in pursuit, but God warned him in a dream not to harm Jacob. Catching up with the caravan, Laban accused Jacob of stealing his household idols. Rachel had taken the idols without informing Jacob. Finally making peace, Jacob and Laban set up a pile of stones to signify that neither would cross that boundary to harm the other.

Rachel's taking the idols, like Jacob's relying on superstition, shows that even Israel's "first family" was affected by the paganism around them.

32:1-21 *"Does Esau still want to kill me?"* As Jacob led his family back to Canaan, he learned that his brother, Esau, was coming to meet him with a small army. Jacob pleaded with God to save him from Esau's wrath. Hoping to appease Esau, he sent ahead some animals as gifts.

32:22-32 *An all-night wrestling match.* As Jacob slept that night, in fear of Esau, he wrestled with God, demanding that he bless him. God put Jacob's hip out of joint and changed his name to Israel ("one who struggles with God"). Jacob named the place Peniel ("face of God"). Though he would still be known primarily as Jacob, "the deceiver," his descendants would be known by his new name.

Note these contrasts between Jacob's encounters with God at Bethel (28:10-22) and Peniel:

- God touched Jacob's heart at Bethel; at Peniel he claimed his life.
- Bethel saw Jacob's conversion and salvation; Peniel saw his consecration and sanctification.
- Bethel introduced Jacob to the peace of God; Peniel freely gave him that peace. He now possessed not only life but also abundant life (John 10:10; Rom. 5:1; Phil. 4:7).

33:1-16 *Jacob and Esau: Reunion and relief.* To Jacob's relief, his reunion with Esau was peaceful. He introduced his wives and children to Esau, and the brothers parted as friends.

33:17–34:31 *Dinah and Shechem: Rape and revenge.* Jacob purchased land near the city of Shechem, pitched his tent, and built an altar. Sometime

Important Places in the Story of Isaac, Jacob, and Joseph

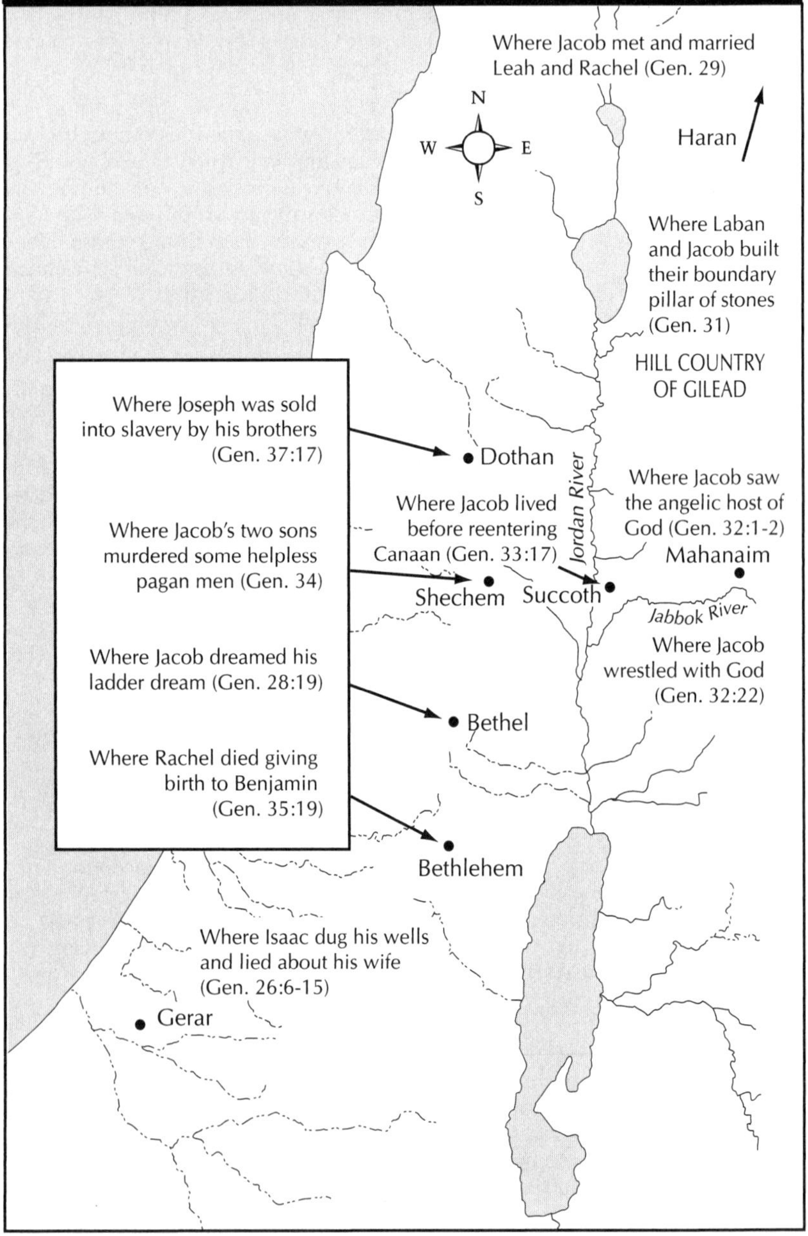

thereafter, Jacob's only daughter, Dinah, was raped by Shechem, son of Hamor. Hamor met with Jacob and tried to arrange a marriage. Learning of the rape, Dinah's brothers were enraged. They demanded that Hamor and his sons circumcise themselves before any marriage took place. As the men recovered from their circumcisions, Simeon and Levi murdered all of them. Jacob rebuked his sons, saying their actions had made him "stink" to the Canaanites.

35:1-15 *Back to Bethel and blessing again.* God told Jacob to go back to Bethel, that special place of meeting (12:6-9; 13:3-4; 28:11-19), to build an altar. Jacob instructed his family to destroy their idols, wash themselves, and put on fresh clothing in preparation for the event. At Bethel God appeared, reminding Jacob of his new name and of the Abrahamic covenant. Jacob made an offering and once again anointed the stone pillar where he had seen the stairway to heaven (28:18).

35:16-20 *Benjamin: Son of her sorrow, son of his strength.* Rachel died giving birth to Benjamin and was buried "on the way to" Bethlehem (35:19). She had named her son Ben-oni, "son of my sorrow," but Jacob named him Benjamin, "son of my right hand." Centuries later a young virgin would give birth to another baby in Bethlehem. He would be known as the "man of sorrows" (Isa. 53:3) and would be exalted to God's right hand (Heb. 1:3).

35:21-26 *Reuben's fornication.* Reuben, Jacob's oldest son, committed fornication with Bilhah, his father's concubine.

35:27-29 *Together again for their father's funeral.* Isaac died at 180. Jacob and Esau met once again as they buried him at Machpelah.

36:1-43 *Descendants of Esau.* Esau's genealogy shows he is the ancestor of the Edomites, destined to be foes of Israel (see exposition on Obadiah).

37:1-17 *Joseph despised for his dreams.* There was discord in Jacob's family. Joseph's brothers hated him because he was Jacob's favorite son and because of his dreams, in which he had seen his entire family bowing down to him.

37:18-36 *Joseph sold, Jacob deceived.* Joseph's brothers attacked him, took his prized robe, and sold him to some Ishmaelites headed for Egypt. They smeared goat's blood on the robe, allowing Jacob to conclude that Joseph had been killed by a wild beast.

In a sense, Jacob reaped what he had sown (Gal. 6:7-8): Jacob had deceived his father using a young goat's skin (27:16); now his own sons deceived him using a young goat's blood.

38:1-10 *Er and Onan: Both brothers die by divine judgment.* Judah "left home," possibly because of the family discord, and married a Canaanite. The marriage, against Israelite traditions (24:3; 28:1) and later forbidden by the law (Deut. 7:3-4), led to disaster. God judged and killed two of Judah's sons. Er died first, for unspecified reasons. Then Onan died for refusing to father a son to carry on Er's name.

Fathering children for a deceased brother was a common practice in ancient times. Known as levirate marriage, it would become a part of the law (Deut. 25:5-10).

38:11-26 *Tamar and Judah: Harlotry and hypocrisy.* Er's widow, Tamar, denied an heir by Onan, became upset when Judah refused to give her his third son in marriage. Still wanting a child, she disguised herself as a prostitute and seduced Judah. Hearing that Tamar was pregnant, Judah self-righteously ordered her to be killed—until he learned that the child was his own

THE LIFE OF JACOB

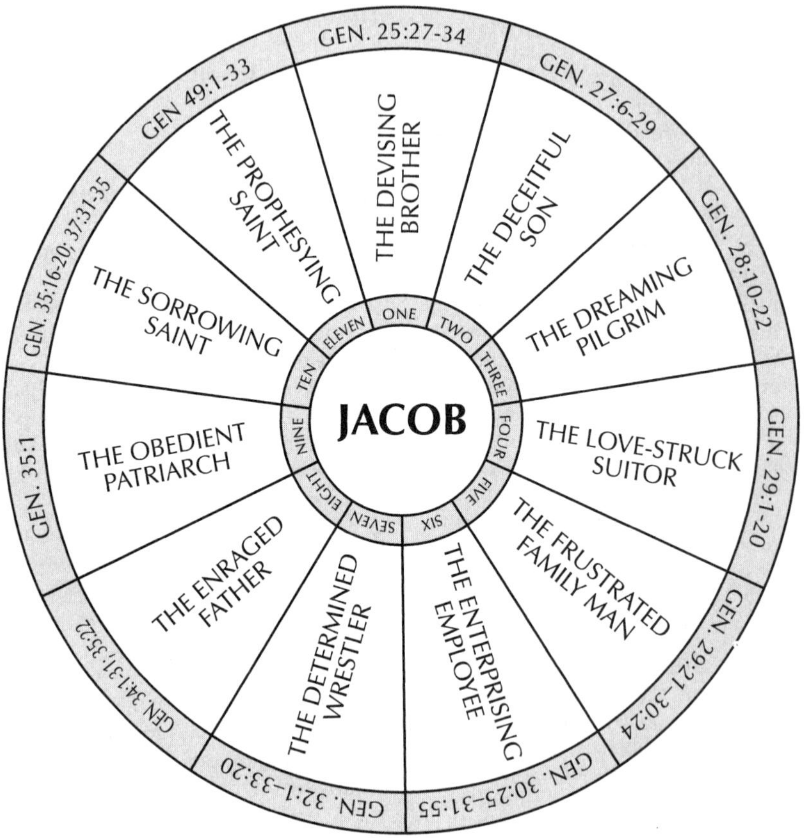

(38:24-26) and humbly confessed his sin.

38:27-30 *Another case of older vs. younger.* Tamar had twin boys. The midwife tied a scarlet thread around the wrist of Zerah, whose hand appeared first, but he drew back his hand and the other baby, Perez, was actually born first. Note that Christ's lineage included this illegitimate child, as well as Rahab the prostitute and other less-than-noble people.

39:1-18 *Joseph denies her, so she defames him.* Joseph's Ishmaelite captors sold him to Potiphar, a soldier in Pharaoh's court. Potiphar's wife tried to seduce Joseph, but he denied her advances and ran from her house. Furious at Joseph's refusal, Potiphar's wife told her husband that Joseph had raped her.

39:19-23 *Joseph prospers in prison.* Believing his wife's false accusations, Potiphar had Joseph imprisoned. But

God was with Joseph, and soon the chief jailer had put him in charge of the entire prison.

40:1-23 *A tale of two dreams.* Two of Joseph's fellow prisoners, servants to the king, had strange dreams, and Joseph correctly interpreted both of them.

41:1-36 *Joseph's 14-year forecast.* When Pharaoh had two strange dreams, Joseph was called to interpret them. The dreams, said Joseph, meant that Egypt would soon have a severe famine.

41:37-57 *Promoted from prisoner to prime minister.* Pharaoh made Joseph his prime minister, to prepare Egypt for the predicted famine. Joseph married Asenath, an Egyptian woman (41:45), and had two sons (41:50-52). He named the first one Manasseh, signifying that God had enabled him to forget the bitter past. He named the second Ephraim, signifying his fruitful present and future.

In one day Joseph, age 30, was elevated from prison to palace, but this high honor came only after many long years of imprisonment—showing the value of humility (Ps. 75:6-7; 1 Pet. 5:6).

42:1-38 *Joseph's brothers bow before him.* There was famine in Canaan as well. Jacob sent his sons to Egypt to buy food. They bowed in the presence of Egypt's chief administrator, not knowing he was Joseph, but Joseph recognized them. He gave them food and sent them home but held Simeon hostage until they would return with Benjamin. Jacob, however, refused even to consider sending Benjamin to Egypt.

43:1-34 *Benjamin brought to Egypt.* After the food brought back from the first trip ran low, Jacob was forced to send his sons, including Benjamin, back to Egypt. He sent with them many gifts for "the man" in charge of the food. Upon their return to Egypt, Joseph prepared a meal for his brothers. They were astonished when this Egyptian official seated them according to their ages. Benjamin was given five times as much as the others.

44:1-34 *A silver cup in his sack!* As the brothers left again for Canaan, Joseph had his silver cup secretly placed in Benjamin's sack. Joseph's steward stopped the brothers and, of course, found the cup. Joseph demanded that Benjamin become his personal slave for stealing the cup. A desperate Judah offered to take Benjamin's place.

45:1-28 *"I am Joseph, your brother."* Unable to contain his secret any longer, Joseph revealed himself to his brothers. He reassured them that he was not angry with them for selling him as a slave: God had a purpose for his slavery—to save the lives of many during the famine. Joseph told them to return home and bring Jacob back to Egypt. Pharaoh sent several wagons and donkeys with gifts for Jacob. At first Jacob wouldn't believe that Joseph was alive, but when he saw the wagons loaded with Egyptian treasures he was convinced.

46:1-27 *"Go to Egypt, but I'll bring you back to Canaan!"* God told Jacob that he should move to Egypt to escape the famine but that his descendants would someday return to the Promised Land. 46:8-27 lists the 66 members of Jacob's family who went with him to Egypt. Counting Joseph and his wife and two sons, 70 Israelites now lived in Egypt. It was about 1876 B.C., some 430 years before the Exodus (compare 15:13 and Exod. 12:40).

46:28–47:10 *Reunion in Goshen, presentation at the palace.* Jacob and Joseph met in Goshen. At Joseph's advice, the entire clan settled there, for it was the only part of Egypt where shepherds were not despised. Joseph then presented his father and five of his brothers to Pharaoh, and they informed him of their decision to live in Goshen.

47:11-26 *Joseph's generous tax: Only 20 percent for Pharaoh.* As the famine worsened, people were forced to use all their money, livestock, and fields to buy grain. Joseph generously arranged for them to give just one-fifth of their harvest to Pharaoh, keeping the rest for food and seed.

47:27-31 *Jacob's final request: "Bury me in Canaan."* Feeling that death was near at age 147, Jacob requested that he be buried in the cave of Machpelah in Hebron. Joseph promised to honor that request (see 50:13).

48:1-22 *The right hand on the wrong head?* As Jacob blessed Joseph's sons, he placed his right hand on the head of Ephraim, the younger, instead of on Manasseh and said that Ephraim would be greater than Manasseh. 450 years later, Moses agreed (Deut. 33:17). Israel's history would bear out both prophecies—yet another case of the older serving the younger (see 2 Chron. 25:7, where the name Ephraim stands for all of Israel's 10 northern tribes).

Jacob's adoption of Joseph's sons (48:5; 1 Chron. 5:1) gave them equal status with Jacob's other sons. Joseph's descendants through them would become two separate tribes bearing their names, confirming once again Joseph's dreams of being elevated above his brothers (37:1-11).

49:1-33 *A father foretells his family's future.* Jacob then gathered his own sons around him and prophesied concerning their descendants. From the tribe of Judah, he said, would come the Messiah himself. Jacob's predictions reflected the way each son had lived, suggesting that a person's character and actions can affect his children and grandchildren. Moses blessed the 12 tribes in similar fashion (Deut. 33).

50:1-13 *Egypt honors the Hebrew patriarch.* All Egypt observed Jacob's death. Following 70 days of mourning, an escort of Egyptian officials served as an honor guard as Jacob's body was carried back to Canaan.

50:14-21 *"Now that our father is dead, we're dead!"* Joseph's guilt-ridden brothers assumed they would be killed now that their father was dead. But Joseph reassured them that he had no such intentions, especially considering how God had brought good out of the situation.

50:22-26 *Joseph's final request: "Bury me in Canaan."* Joseph died at 110. His request for burial in Canaan would be honored, but not until centuries later (Exod. 13:19).

PEOPLE TO REMEMBER FROM GENESIS

ABRAHAM

Key Facts: Father of Hebrew nation, role model of faith (12:1-3; Rom. 4:11)
Birth: Recorded in 11:26
Father: Terah (11:26)
Brothers: Nahor, Haran (11:26)
Sister: Half sister, Sarah (20:12)
Wives: Sarah, Hagar, Keturah (11:29; 16:3; 25:1)
Sons: By Hagar: Ishmael (16:15-16); by Sarah: Isaac (21:2-3); by Keturah: Zimran, Jokshan, Medan, Midian, Ishbak, Shuah (25:1-2)
Occupation: Shepherd, landowner (13:2)

Key Events in His Life:

- Called by God (12:1-8)
- God's promise reaffirmed (13:14-18)
- His meeting with Melchizedek (14:17-24)
- His new name (17:5)
- Birth of Isaac (21:1-3)
- Told to offer Isaac (22:1-14)

Age at Death: 175 (25:7-10)

Total Bible References: 307

Key References: 11–25; Exod. 2:24; 2 Kings 13:23; Isa. 41:8; 51:1-2; John 8:39; Acts 7:1-8; Rom. 4; Gal. 3:1-18; Heb. 11:8-10, 17-19; James 2:21-23

Abraham Speaks

I still miss Sarah. She died nearly 40 years ago—that's a long time to be without someone you love. I remember when she and I packed up and left Ur. What a handsome couple we were. Of course our friends and relatives thought we were crazy. "It's bad enough to leave the comfort and safety of city life," they said. "But to head out for an unknown land at the command of some invisible God, well, that's sheer insanity!" (11:31, 12:1; Heb. 11:8)

And of course there was the day Sarah watched Isaac and me pack up and head for Mount Moriah. Neither of us could ever forget that awful day. Though she never talked about it, I know that she knew what was going on. It was the thought of actually having to kill Isaac that bothered me most. I knew God would somehow give this son of promise back to me. But the thought of actually placing him on the altar was too much to bear as we walked together up that mountain. (18:1-15; 22:1-14; Heb. 11:17-19)

I wonder how Ishmael is doing these days. The last report was that he had married an Egyptian girl and fathered 12 sons. I hope the best for them. My heart still grieves when I recall those events that forced us to go our separate ways. (21:8-21; 25:12-18)

Keturah has been a good wife to me. She has given me six healthy sons. But it is Isaac, of course, the heir of the covenant, my miracle son, who is my joy and comfort. (17:17-21; 18:14)

Again my thoughts turn to Sarah. So much has happened since the two of us left Ur. We both found the righteousness of God that we sought. We grew ever more sure that "all the families of the earth" would be blessed through the beloved son God gave back to us that day. (12:3; 15:6)

No, Sarah, it was our friends, not us, who were wrong. I know you sometimes missed the comfort and safety of big-city life—I still do at times. But God assured us all along that we would someday have a home far more substantial than anything this old world can offer—even more substantial than Ur! (Heb. 11:8-10)

Spiritual Lessons from Abraham

- Faith means obeying God even when we don't understand his revealed will (12:1-9; 22:1-18; Heb. 11:17-19).
- Following God should radically change our relationship to the world; it may even mean severing ties with friends and family (12:1; Rom. 12:2).

- Taking matters into our own hands can cause problems for ourselves and others (16:1-16; 21:8-21).
- Lying always increases, and never decreases, our problems (12:10-20).
- Righteousness comes by faith, not by works (15:6).
- Focusing on eternity will help us endure the hard times in this life (Heb. 11:8-10).

Key Verse

"Abraham believed God, so God declared him to be righteous" (Rom. 4:3; see Gen. 15:6).

ADAM

Key Fact: World's first human (1:27; 2:7)
Wife: Eve (2:20-25; 3:20)
Sons: Cain, Abel, Seth, unnamed (4:1-2, 25; 5:4)
Daughters: Unnamed (5:4)
Occupation: Farmer (2:15; 3:17-19, 23)
Age at Death: 930 (5:5)
Total Bible References: 30
Key References: 1:26–5:5; 1 Chron. 1:1; Job 31:33 (KJV); Luke 3:38; Rom. 5:12-15; 1 Cor. 15:22, 45; 1 Tim. 2:12-14

Adam Speaks

Look at them, standing there so tall and majestic, with outstretched wings and flaming swords! Glorious creatures! But I dare not approach any closer; their assignment is to keep Eve and me out of the Garden. Would we have become friends in Eden if that serpent scandal had not occurred? I'll probably never know. (3:1-24)

It doesn't seem possible that more than nine centuries have come and gone! I love to tell my descendants that Eve and I had our first child at about the same time we celebrated our first birthdays and our first wedding anniversary—that always causes some gasps of amazement!

How often I have wondered what life would be like today if we had simply obeyed God. Abel would still be alive. Cain wouldn't be out there somewhere, running from God. And life would have been so much easier for all of us. I think of all my efforts over the years to grow a garden as nice as Eden. God was certainly right when he warned about how hard it was going to be. (3:1-24; 4:16)

It is sobering to think that, while Eve and I once lived in innocence inside that beautiful Paradise, we shall soon die as sinners here on the outside. He told us we were made in his image, but look at us now! (1:26-31; 2:8-14; 3:1-24)

And yet there's still hope. Seth and his children seem to be doing well. He has certainly been a good influence on our other children. (4:25-26; 5:4)

And I know that the same gracious God who forgave and clothed us with animal skins in Eden will clothe us in the righteousness of the offspring of that future woman he talked about. And someday he'll welcome us into his eternal Eden. What more could a 930-year-old redeemed sinner ask! (3:21; Rev. 21:9–22:5)

Spiritual Lessons from Adam

- We should never forget that, however much we are affected by sin, we are created in God's image (1:26-27).
- God gave us the ability to choose between good and evil; each choice we make is important (3:6, 11-12, 16-19).
- It is impossible to hide from God (3:8).
- Sin always brings guilt (3:7), fear (3:10), and pain (3:16-19).
- Our sin can affect many lives; it could even affect the whole world (Rom. 5:12).

Key Verse

"Everyone dies because all of us are related to Adam, the first man. But all who are related to Christ, the other man, will be given new life" (1 Cor. 15:22).

CAIN

Key Facts: First child born on earth, first murderer (4:1, 8)
Birth: Recorded in 4:1
Brothers: Abel, Seth, unnamed (4:2, 25; 5:4)
Sisters: Unnamed (5:4)
Son: Enoch (4:17; not same as in 5:21-24)
Occupation: Farmer, builder (4:2-3, 17)
Total Bible References: 19
Key References: 4:1-17; Heb. 11:4; 1 John 3:11-12; Jude 1:11

Cain Speaks

No doubt about it whatsoever—I have become the richest and most powerful man in all the land of Nod! And I've done it myself, with no outside help. Abel was content to waste his life raising those miserable sheep. But not me. I abandoned the fields and built the world's first city. My descendants have also done quite well, if I do say so myself. Young Jubal is the most famous musician alive today. And Tubal-cain is known all over as a master craftsman. (4:6-22)

Yes, I've come a long way from growing vegetables. But why do I feel so frustrated and empty? Why can't I escape this bitterness of soul and enjoy myself? Will I ever stop having those terrible nightmares about the rejected offering? And God's words still haunt me: "You will be accepted if you respond in the right way. But if you refuse to respond correctly, then watch out! Sin is waiting to attack and destroy you, and you must subdue it." Why can't I get those words out of my mind? Haven't I done pretty well? A thousand curses on my brother's memory and my father's religion! I'm glad I killed Abel. What a fool he was to let God rule his life. What good did it do him? (4:3-7; Heb. 11:4)

I must admit, though, that during some of those sleepless nights I have secretly wondered if offering a lamb would have changed everything after all. But away with such emotional trash! I've made my choice, and it doesn't have anything to do with God or with sacrifices. I've made my choice, and I've done quite well.

Spiritual Lessons from Cain

- Obedience is important in our relationship with God (4:3-7; Heb.11:4).
- Envy can lead to more outward sins, even murder (4:1-8; 1 John 3:12).
- We must exercise our willpower in our fight against sin (4:7).

- Sin can have lifelong consequences (4:9-12).
- Life without God is a lonely existence (4:10-14).
- God cares about and protects even those who sin against him (4:13-15).

Key Verse
"You will be accepted if you respond in the right way. But if you refuse to respond correctly, then watch out! Sin is waiting to attack and destroy you, and you must subdue it" (4:7).

ESAU
Key Facts: Jacob's brother, father of the Edomites (25:26; 36:43)
Birth: Recorded in 25:22-28
Father: Isaac (25:21-25)
Mother: Rebekah (25:21-25)
Brother: Jacob (25:26)
Wives: Judith, Basemath, Mahalath (26:34; 28:8-9; 36:1-3)
Sons: Eliphaz, Reuel, Jeush, Jalam, Korah (36:4-5; 1 Chron. 1:35)
Occupation: Shepherd, hunter (25:27)
Key Events in His Life:
- Sold his birthright (25:27-34)
- Lost his father's blessing (27)

Total Bible References: 76
Key References: 25–28; 32–36; Mal. 1:2-3; Rom. 9:13; Heb. 12:15-17

Esau Speaks
Just look at him, riding off with his family and servants as fast as he can! Maybe he's afraid I'll change my mind. No doubt about it, I made him squirm like a desert worm. And just look at all these gifts he brought me! They almost seem like bribes. Of course, Jacob thought my men would slaughter his whole family. After all, he did cheat me out of both my birthright and my blessing. (25:27-34; 27:1-41; 32:6-20)

Strange, though—until recently I probably would have gone out of my way to kill him. Losing the birthright was bad enough. But being denied the blessing took a long time to get over. And I know he went along with my parents in disapproving of my first two wives. (Was that why my mother conspired with him? He always was her favorite.) (27:1-17)

Yet when we finally did meet, I felt no desire whatsoever to harm him. Maybe I'm mellowing in my old age. One would almost think that this invisible God Jacob claims to serve had something to do with it. (33:4-16)

Spiritual Lessons from Esau
- We should never trade spiritual treasures for earthly treasures (25:29-34; Heb. 12:16-17).
- Many of God's blessings, once missed, can never be reclaimed (27:34-38; Heb. 12:17).
- The unwise actions of children can bring grief to their parents (26:34-35).
- Sometimes nonbelievers demonstrate more forgiveness than believers (33:4).

Key Verses
"Look after each other so that none of you will miss out on the special favor of God . . . like Esau. He traded his birthright as the oldest son for a single meal. And

afterward, when he wanted his father's blessing, he was rejected. It was too late for repentance, even though he wept bitter tears" (Heb. 12:15-17).

EVE

Key Fact: World's first woman (2:21-22)
Husband: Adam
Sons: Cain, Abel, Seth, unnamed (4:1-2, 25; 5:4)
Daughters: Unnamed (5:4)
Total Bible References: 7
Key References: 2:19–4:25; 2 Cor. 11:3; 1 Tim. 2:12-14

Eve Speaks

I really need to keep accurate records of all my offspring—there must be thousands of them by now! Adam's name for me was certainly well-chosen: Eve, the "mother of all people everywhere." But at least all my descendants' mothers knew what to expect when they were born. No one else will ever experience the uncertainty of bearing the first child on earth. It was really something as Adam and I slowly realized that this child was coming from me, rather than from Adam's side the way I did! But any joy and wonder we felt about the approaching birth was ended by those terrifying last hours. And then there was the agony of seeing my firstborn kill his own brother. And now he's gone, too. (3:20–4:16)

For all my own suffering, I still feel guilty to think that, had it not been for my disobedience, none of my daughters and granddaughters would have had to suffer in having their own children. These thoughts gnaw at my soul each time I walk past Eden and see those angelic beings. What shame is mine—listening to the subtle one rather than the Holy One. To think that I really believed I could match wits with the serpent! He took me in so quickly. But, no, I'm not making excuses again—it was my fault and mine alone. And yet I, like Adam, have found forgiveness and the promise of a Redeemer. (3:1–4:8; Heb. 3:1-5)

Spiritual Lessons from Eve

- Satan can tempt us in the most unexpected ways (3:1-5).
- Each of us must bear the responsibility for our own sin; and each of us must endure the consequence of that sin (3:6, 13, 16).
- The child of God should resist the devil (James 4:7; 1 Pet. 5:9) and withstand him (Eph. 6:13-14) but never debate him (3:2-3).
- Each of us has great power to influence those around us, for good or ill (3:6).

Key Verse

"And the LORD God said, 'It is not good for the man to be alone. I will make a companion who will help him'" (2:18).

ISAAC

Key Facts: Abraham's promised son, father of Jacob (17:19; 25:21-26)
Birth: Recorded in 21:1-7
Mother: Sarah (21:2-3)
Brothers: (half brothers) Ishmael, Zimran, Jokshan, Medan, Midian, Ishbak, Shuah (16:15; 25:1-2)

Wife: Rebekah (24:67)
Sons: Esau, Jacob (25:24-26)
Occupation: Landowner (25:5)
Key Events in His Life:

- On the altar at Moriah (22:1-14)
- Marriage to Rebekah (24:1-67)
- Birth of Jacob and Esau (25:19-26)
- Gives Esau's blessing to Jacob (27:1-40)

Age at Death: 180 (35:27-29)
Total Bible References: 128
Key References: 17:5–35:29; Exod. 2:24; 2 Kings 13:23; Luke 3:34; Rom. 9:7-8; Gal. 4:28; Heb. 11:17-20

Isaac Speaks

How I hate to see Jacob leave like this. I know the guilt his mother feels. But, dear wife, don't be too hard on yourself. Most of the fault is mine. God told me that the firstborn twin would serve the younger one, but I didn't listen. (25:23; 28:1-5)

Then we both began to show partiality. Esau became my favorite and Jacob yours. One thing is painfully clear: I've never had the rapport with my sons that my father had with me; I seriously doubt that either of them would lie down on an altar at my command! (22:1-9; 25:28)

How could we have gone so wrong? We started off so well. I'm still thankful that I allowed my father's servant to pick you out for me. How delighted I was to meet you, and how good you have been to me. Wasn't it great the way God answered my prayer for children? If only we had prayed sooner! (24:1-4, 67; 25:21)

Looking back, I probably spent too much time digging wells and such things, instead of fathering my sons. You can't be blamed for all of this. No, the guilt rests on me. Now I must send Jacob away so that Esau won't kill him. (26:18-33; 27:41)

Look! Jacob is turning to wave to us one more time. I have but one hope in this hour of despair—Jehovahjireh: "The LORD Will Provide." That's the name my father gave to that special spot on Mount Moriah. God always did make provision for Abraham. Maybe he'll do the same for Abraham's heartbroken son. (22:14, KJV)

Spiritual Lessons from Isaac

- Submission can lead to great blessing, even when it seems illogical or unwise in human terms (22:9-18).
- Sometimes it is more wise to submit to the decisions of our godly parents or other authority figures than to try to do things on our own (24:1-4, 67).
- We should faithfully pray for our spouses and the other significant people and situations in our lives (24:63; 25:21; 26:25).
- Children often learn from and repeat the sins and mistakes of their parents (12:13; 20:2; 26:6-7; Num. 14:18).
- Parental favoritism can cause division in the home (27:1-38).

Key Verse

"Take your son, your only son—yes, Isaac, whom you love so much—and go to the land of Moriah. Sacrifice him there as a burnt offering on one of the mountains, which I will point out to you" (22:2).

JACOB (Israel)

Key Fact: His 12 sons founded Israel's 12 tribes (29:31–30:24; 1 Chron. 2–8)
Birth: Recorded in 25:22-26
Father: Isaac (25:21-26)
Mother: Rebekah (25:21-26)
Brother: Esau (25:25)
Wives: Leah, Rachel, Bilhah, Zilpah (29:23, 28; 30:4, 9)
Sons: By Leah: Reuben, Simeon, Levi, Judah, Issachar, Zebulun (29:32-35; 30:18-20); by Rachel: Joseph, Benjamin (30:22-24; 35:16-18); by Bilhah: Dan, Naphtali (30:5-8); by Zilpah: Gad, Asher (30:10-13).
Daughter: Dinah (30:21)
Occupation: Shepherd, rancher (29–31; 37:2)
Key Events in His Life:

- Buys Esau's birthright (25:27-34)
- Gets Esau's blessing (27:1-29)
- Vision at Bethel (28:10-22)
- Marries; begins family (29:1–30:24)
- Wrestles with God; given new name (32:24-32)
- Son Joseph sold into Egypt (37:1-36)
- Moves his family to Egypt (46:1–47:12)
- Blesses his sons (48:1–49:28)

Age at Death: 147 (47:28)
Total Bible References: 252
Key References: 25–37; 42; 45–50; Exod. 2:24; 2 Kings 13:23; Hos. 12:2-5; Matt. 22:32; Luke 3:34; Acts 3:13; 7:8-16; Heb. 11:9, 20-21

Jacob Speaks

In many ways life is easier here in Egypt than it ever was back home. More hectic perhaps, but easier. Of course it doesn't hurt when the prime minister happens to be your son! But the wide and mighty Nile can never compare with the calm, cool waters of the Jordan. Pilgrims come here from afar to gaze upon the lofty pyramids, but they are rock piles compared to the majesty of Mount Hermon. (41:38-41)

Of course at my age it matters little where one resides. A man's memories accompany him wherever he goes. And what memories are mine! How proud I am of Joseph. I did spoil that boy—but I can take precious little credit for either his political know-how or his spiritual maturity. (37:3-4; 39:7-9; 41:38-41)

I hope he'll have fewer regrets in his old age than I have in mine. But it's not all bad. Both my father and my brother have long since forgiven me for deceiving them. And I've forgiven my sons for deceiving me. They certainly did prove to be their father's sons! (25:29-34; 27:1-29; 33:4)

Sometimes I long to visit Bethel once again, where I first saw God atop the stairway with his angels, and where I promised to follow him—with a few conditions, of course! Then I'd like to stand again on Peniel's soil where we wrestled together. It was there he changed my name, you know. (28:12-22; 32:1–33:17)

But enough of the past. The present demands my attention. My 12 boys will soon gather to receive my blessing. Then I'll actually climb that heavenly stairway and be forever in God's presence. (48:8–49:28)

Spiritual Lessons from Jacob

- It is possible to pursue the right goal (25:23; Rom. 9:10-13) in the wrong way (25:29-34; 27:1-29).
- We should never place conditions on our promises to God (28:20-22).
- We should show proper respect to everyone in our life, even those for whom we don't have strong emotional feelings (29:30-32).
- We shouldn't be afraid to place all our trust in God, even in difficult times when we are tempted to take matters into our own hands (32:13-20; 33:1-4).
- Intense spiritual struggle often produces great spiritual blessing (32:24-31).
- Our own spiritual failings will be reflected in the lives of our children and others within our sphere of influence (compare 27:1-29 with 34:1-29; 35:22; 37:31-35; and 38:12-23). What we sow in our actions toward others we will reap in their actions toward us.

Key Verse

"What's more, I will be with you, and I will protect you wherever you go. I will someday bring you safely back to this land. I will be with you constantly until I have finished giving you everything I have promised" (28:15).

JOSEPH

Key Facts: Favorite son of Jacob, used his power in Egypt to rescue his family from famine (37:3; 45:7-11)
Birth: Recorded in 30:22-24
Father: Jacob (30:25)
Mother: Rachel (30:22-24)
Brothers: Benjamin (35:24). Half brothers: Reuben, Simeon, Levi, Judah, Issachar, Zebulun, Dan, Naphtali, Gad, Asher (35:23-26)
Sister: Half sister, Dinah (30:21)
Wife: Asenath (41:45)
Sons: Manasseh, Ephraim (41:51-52)
Occupation: Prime minister of Egypt (41:37-41)
Key Events in His Life:

- His dreams (37:5-10)
- Sold by his jealous brothers (37:12-28)
- Imprisoned in Egypt (39–40)
- Interprets Pharaoh's dreams (41:1-36)
- Becomes prime minister (41:37-57)
- Helps and forgives his brothers (42–45)
- Settles his family in Egypt (46:1–47:12)

Age at Death: 110 (50:22-26)
Total Bible References: 214
Key References: 37–50; Ps. 105:16-22; Acts 7:9-14; Heb. 11:22

Joseph Speaks

Perhaps someday I'll write my autobiography. I could call it *From Political Prisoner to Prime Minister*! Actually, *God's Faithfulness in a Foreign Land* would be a better title. It doesn't seem possible that I've lived in Egypt for some 93 years now. Things certainly have changed since I arrived here in chains as a 17-year-old boy. Of course I wouldn't have ended up here at all if I hadn't worn that beautiful coat so much and if I hadn't foolishly talked about those dreams. But I guess even such childish mistakes can be a part of God's plans. (37:3-19; 50:20)

The moment I stepped onto Egyptian soil it seemed that God's faithfulness really clicked in! I could have been desperate and bitter. After all, I was sold into slavery, brought to a foreign land, accused of rape, and thrown into prison. Yet even then my spirits were high. My father's dying words probably expressed it best. Let's see, what did he say? "But his bow remained strong, and his arms were strengthened by the Mighty One of Jacob." (37:27-28; 39:19-23; 49:24)

It was good to visit Canaan again, even on such a sad occasion. My father's final request was to be buried at Machpelah, along with Grandfather Isaac and Great-Grandfather Abraham. Now that I'm back in Egypt it appears that my 10 guilt-ridden brothers still need some reassurance of my forgiveness. I hope I can say something this morning to set their minds at rest once and for all. (49:29-31; 50:15-21)

Spiritual Lessons from Joseph

- The circumstances of our lives are not as important as the way we respond to them (39).
- Showing others what we have learned from God requires sensitivity as well as courage (37:5-11).
- Sin is always wrong, even in a foreign land where no one knows or cares about us (39:7-9).
- Those who live godly lives will suffer persecution (39:10-20; 2 Tim. 3:12).
- In due time, God will exalt and reward the one who honors him (41:38-44; James 4:10; 1 Pet. 5:5-6).
- God is able to use human sinfulness for his glory (50:20; Ps. 76:10).

Key Verse

"Pharaoh said, 'Who could do it better than Joseph? For he is a man who is obviously filled with the spirit of God'" (41:38).

LOT

Key Facts: Nephew of Abraham, escaped destruction of Sodom (12:4-5; 19:1-29)
Father: Haran (11:27)
Sons: Moab, Ben-ammi (19:36-38)
Daughters: Unnamed (19:14, 31-38).
Occupation: Shepherd, landowner, city official (13:5; 19:1)
Key Events in His Life:

- Moves with Abram to Canaan (11:31–12:5)
- Chooses the best land, near Sodom (13:7-12)
- Rescued from captivity by Abram (14:1-16)
- Rescued from Sodom (19:1-29)
- Commits incest (19:30-38)

Total Bible References: 34
Key References: 11–14; 19; Luke 17:28-29, 32; 2 Pet. 2:7-8

Lot Speaks
Thank God that Uncle Abraham isn't here! What on earth would he say? What could he say to a nephew whose sinfulness has resulted in the death of his wife and now the sin of incest! Would to God I had been content to be a herdsman alongside my uncle—that pilgrim of faith. (13:1-5; 19:12-38)

It was wealth and excitement that attracted me to city life. And not just any city, of course. No, I was foolish enough to choose the most depraved place around! Why, oh, why did I move there? (13:12-13; 18:20)

Even more troubling, why did I stay? Not a day went by that I was not tormented by the depravity of Sodom. In one sense it was a relief when I found myself among those marched off into slavery after that disastrous war. But once again, faithful Abraham was there for me. He showed us he could lead soldiers as well as sheep! And how I sang his praises! But, to my dying shame, the very next morning found me rushing back to Sodom. (14:12-16; 2 Pet. 2:7-8)

And now the city is no more. No doubt the fierce heat will keep the curiosity seekers away for a long time to come. So much for the sordid past. What now? Where will I go? What will I do? Merciful God! Uncle Abraham built an altar at Bethel and received your forgiveness. May you grant that same sweet forgiveness to his shame-filled nephew. (13:1-4)

Spiritual Lessons from Lot

- Never "move your tents to a place near Sodom" (13:12-13). That is, don't seek the company of ungodly people (Ps. 1).
- When you are delivered from Sodom (14:16), *don't return!*
- Spiritual compromise can injure your own soul (2 Pet. 2:8), invite the contempt of nonbelievers (19:9), and even bring immorality (19:30-38) and death to your own family and friends (19:14, 26).

Key Verses
"Lot took a long look at the fertile plains of the Jordan Valley in the direction of Zoar. The whole area was well watered everywhere. . . . Lot chose that land for himself. . . . Lot moved his tents to a place near Sodom, among the cities of the plain" (13:10-12).

NOAH

Key Fact: Helped his family survive the Flood (6–8)
Father: Lamech (5:28-29)
Brothers: Unnamed (5:30)
Sisters: Unnamed (5:30)
Sons: Shem, Ham, Japheth (5:32)
Occupation: Farmer, shipbuilder (6:14-22; 9:20)
Age at Death: 950 (9:28-29)
Total Bible References: 50
Key References: 5:28–10:32; Isa. 54:9; Ezek. 14:12-14, 19-20; Luke 3:36; 17:26-27; Heb. 11:7; 1 Pet. 3:19-20; 2 Pet. 2:5

Noah Speaks
I still get a bit uneasy when I hear thunder! But then the rainbow appears and everything is fine again. Really, I shouldn't need any reassurance. One look at that

huge empty ship up there on the mountain should remind me of God's faithfulness. (8:4; 9:13-15)

I sure needed to keep my eyes on God through all those long years of building that ark. The work itself was hard enough. But it was also hard to endure the constant harassment from my neighbors. I'm sure that huge ark was a sight to behold! But I still can't believe that none of them listened to my warnings in all those 120 years God gave them to repent. I guess things were every bit as bad as God said they were. How thankful I am that my whole family found grace in his sight and remained faithful all those years. (6:9-22; Heb. 11:7; 1 Pet. 3:19-20; 2 Pet. 2:5)

Of course things got kind of bad for me just recently. How ironic that I survived all that water but succumbed to a jar of wine! I still don't know why I did it. Maybe I just assumed nothing like that could ever happen to a man God had used so mightily. (9:20-21)

I'm almost 950, probably near the end of my life. God has blessed me with three healthy sons. Apparently Shem will carry on the faith of our fathers. Death holds no fear for me. I found grace in God's eyes on the eve of the Flood, and his grace will surely see me through the final hours. The one who remembered me back then won't forget me now. (6:8; 8:1; 9:23-26)

Spiritual Lessons from Noah

- We can walk with God (6:9), even in a generation running with the devil (6:5; 2 Pet. 2:4-9).
- One person's faith can lead to the salvation of many (6:8-9; 7:7).
- True faith expresses itself in obedience (6:22).
- Our obedience may make the disobedient feel guilty (Heb. 11:7).
- Considering the godlessness of Noah's day, the godlessness of our own day should not surprise us (6:1-8; Luke 17:27; 1 Pet. 4:12).
- Even mature believers can fall into serious sin when they let their guard down (9:20-29; 1 Cor. 9:27).

Key Verse

"Noah found favor with the LORD" (6:8).

RACHEL

Key Facts: Beloved wife of Jacob, mother of Joseph and Benjamin (29:30; 30:22-24; 35:17-18)
Father: Laban (29:16)
Sister: Leah (29:16)
Death: Recorded in 35:16-20
Total Bible References: 47
Key References: 29:6–35:20; Ruth 4:11; Jer. 31:15; Matt. 2:18

Rachel Speaks

She really is a beautiful woman. I was always more flamboyant than Leah, and Jacob took to me right away. He even worked 14 years for me—how many wives could claim that? But I think he's beginning to realize that Leah has a quiet beauty of her own—especially since she has borne him all those handsome sons. (29:17-28)

I just never could let go of my envy of her sons. Even though Jacob always spent more time with me, I longed for a happy, growing family like Leah's. Then there was the time I almost lost even Jacob's love. He thought I was blaming him for my being childless—and I suppose I was, but I was just beside myself with jealousy. (30:1-6)

Then, even after Joseph was born, I took my father's household gods, thinking they would assure the birth of that second son I wanted so bad. Imagine! We were on our way to the land of the true God my husband served, yet I was clinging to those worthless idols. (30:14; 31:34)

I try to fill my mind with these thoughts of the past, but they can hardly displace my present agony. I'm near the time to give birth, but my body tells me that something is dreadfully wrong. At least the baby will be born in Bethlehem. I've always liked that name—-"House of Bread." It has a reassuring sound. This long journey has been hard on me, but we should be there soon. (30:24; 35:16-20)

Spiritual Lessons from Rachel

- It is all too easy to turn to other people (30:1-4), or even to superstition or idolatry (30:14; 31:34) to meet our needs instead of depending on God himself.
- Envy and jealousy can harm even the best of human relationships (30:1-5).
- Envy and jealousy can cause even people who seem to have it all to want more (30:1-5).

Key Verse

"Jacob spent the next seven years working to pay for Rachel. But his love for her was so strong that it seemed to him but a few days" (29:20).

REBEKAH

Key Facts: Isaac's wife, Jacob's mother (24:67; 25:26)
Father: Bethuel (22:23)
Brother: Laban (24:29)
Sons: Esau, Jacob (25:21-26)
Total Bible References: 29
Key References: 24–27; Rom. 9:10

Rebekah Speaks

I always enjoyed meeting people and helping them however I could. How could I have known that showing hospitality to that stranger would mean an exciting new life in a far-off land! Of course it wouldn't have happened at all had God not given me the courage to say yes to his amazing offer: marriage to his master's son, whom I had never met! (24:10-67)

I guess my love for domestic things was just what Isaac needed after his mother's death. He certainly did show me a depth of love I had never before known. Not that our marriage was without its problems. We waited 20 years for those two boys of ours. And what a strange pregnancy. It actually felt as though they were struggling with each other—just like they did after they were born! Then there was the prophecy that the older would serve the younger. I wonder if that will really happen. (24:67; 25:21-23; Rom. 9:10-13)

Even though they were twins, those boys had so little in common. Esau, the robust twin, took up hunting and the outdoor life, while Jacob, my smooth, subdued one, was content to cook. I sensed trouble brewing when Isaac announced the birthright transfer. Then it literally boiled over! What on earth was I thinking when I hatched that shameful plot? (25:20-34; 27:1-35)

I see tears filling Isaac's eyes as we say good-bye to Jacob. Mine are dry, but inside there's an ocean of sorrow. Thank God Esau isn't here; he might really try to kill Jacob. I worry constantly about him. He has been so indifferent to us and to God, especially since marrying those Hittite girls. (26:34; 27:41)

But that sorrow was nothing compared to the despair I now feel watching Jacob disappear, perhaps never to return. I cling to one hope: We're sending Jacob to my homeland, where I hear there are a few people left who love and honor Abraham's God. I know how you feel, dear son. Decades ago I left my own home to marry your father here in Canaan. Now, as you travel in the opposite direction, may the same God who guided me, guide you. (28:1-5)

Spiritual Lessons from Rebekah

- A simple act of kindness can change your entire life (24:10-67).
- When we see God's will clearly, we should be prepared to act quickly and decisively (24:57-58).
- Favoritism, in the home or elsewhere, always breeds trouble (27:1-42).

Key Verse

"So they called Rebekah. 'Are you willing to go with this man?' they asked her. And she replied, 'Yes, I will go'" (24:58).

SARAH

Key Facts: Abraham's wife, Isaac's mother (11:29; 17:19)
Place of Birth: Ur of the Chaldeans (11:31)
Father: Terah (11:26; 20:12)
Brother: Half brother, Abraham (20:12)
Son: Isaac (21:1-7)
Age at Death: 127 (23:1-2)
Total Bible References: 56
Key References: 11–25; Isa. 51:1-2; Rom. 4:19; 9:9; Gal. 4:21-31; Heb. 11:11; 1 Pet. 3:4-6

Sarah Speaks

Let's see now, he'll be 37 on his next birthday, so that means I'll be 127 on mine. God told us to call him Isaac, which means "he laughs." Can you believe it? Of course there were times when we both laughed in disbelief at the promise of his birth. After all, I was 90 at the time and Abraham was 100! Perhaps that's why he was to be named Laughter—to remind us of our lack of faith and the Almighty's faithfulness! (17:17; 18:12)

Is it possible to cry over laughter? Well, I once did—that time when Abraham was commanded to take Isaac up Mount Moriah and offer him as a burnt sacrifice. But, oh, the joy when both father and son came back down that mountain! Jehovahjireh himself had provided a substitute for my Isaac, my Laughter. (22:1-2, 13-14)

How faithful God has been to the three of us in spite of our failures. I still blush to remember how I forced Abraham to marry Hagar, hoping to rearrange God's plan and adopt her son as mine. Well, never you mind, Sarah. That's all in the forgiven and forgotten past. The Lord has given you not only a son in your old age but also a new name: "Princess"—he called me Princess! (16:1-3; 17:15)

I often wonder whom Isaac will marry. Will I live to see my grandchildren? He *will* have children, you know. God has promised that our descendants will be as the dust of the earth and the stars of the heavens. Honestly now, what more could any princess desire? (13:16; 15:5)

Spiritual Lessons from Sarah

- Only heartache awaits if we try to force God's providence by our own devices (16:1-6).
- It is futile to lie to the God who sees, hears, and knows all things (18:9-15).
- A submissive spirit is very "precious to God" (1 Pet. 3:4-6).
- Even people of great faith do not always act in faith (compare Heb. 11:11 with Gen. 16:1-6; 18:9-15).

Key Verse

"Sarah conceived and bore Abraham a son in his old age, at the set time of which God had spoken to him" (21:2, NKJV).

1805 B.C.
Death of Joseph

1730
Israel enslaved in Egypt

EXODUS

BACKGROUND

After coming to Egypt to escape the famine in Canaan (Gen. 46), the Israelites endured 400 years of bitter servitude (1:1-14). God had told Abram this would happen (Gen. 15:13-21) but that after the 400 years Israel would return to Canaan as his instrument of judgment against the Canaanites ("Amorites," Gen. 15:16). Exodus records the story of how God supernaturally freed the Israelites from slavery in Egypt, formed them into a nation governed by his law, and began leading them back to their homeland in Canaan.

1526
Birth of Moses

AUTHOR

Moses.

- 1:1 indicates Exodus is a continuation of Genesis, which Moses wrote (see *Genesis: Author*).
- There are indications within the book itself of Moses' keeping written records (17:14; 24:4; 34:27).
- Moses is the only recorded eyewitness to all the events of Exodus.
- The education he received in the Egyptian royal household (2:1-11; Acts 7:22) would have prepared him as a writer and historian.
- Other Bible authors believed Moses wrote Exodus and the rest of the Pentateuch (Josh. 8:31; Luke 20:28; John 1:45).

1446
The Exodus, Law given

DATE AND LOCATION

The chronology of 1 Kings 6:1 suggests 1446 B.C. as the approximate date when the Israelites left Egypt (12:40-41). Moses may have begun recording the events of Exodus at that time, as he led the people through the wilderness of Sinai.

PURPOSE

- To continue the history of Israel begun in Genesis.
- To continue revealing the personal, relational, covenant-making nature of God.

- To show God's concern for, and power to rescue, his people.
- To provide moral, social, and spiritual laws for Israel.

UNIQUE FEATURES

- The events of Exodus mark Israel's birth as a nation:
  - ➤ Though its land had yet to be claimed, the Exodus marked the first chapter in its war of independence.
  - ➤ The giving of the law could be called its "constitutional convention."
- Exodus also marks the beginnings of Israel's Tabernacle and yearly festivals.
- The miraculous crossing of the Red Sea has been called the Resurrection of the Old Testament, since many OT authors look back on it as the prime example of God's power in Israel's history.

COMPARISON WITH OTHER BIBLE BOOKS

Leviticus:

- Exodus shows how God got his people out of Egypt. Leviticus shows how he tried to get Egypt out of his people.
- Exodus relates to Leviticus as the Gospels do to the Epistles in the NT:
  - ➤ *Exodus, Gospels:* manifestation of the Passover Lamb; *Leviticus, Epistles:* explanation of the Passover Lamb
  - ➤ *Exodus, Gospels:* God's approach to us; *Leviticus, Epistles:* our approach to God.
- In Exodus God is the Savior; in Leviticus he is the Sanctifier.
- In Exodus he spoke from Sinai; in Leviticus he spoke from the sanctuary.
- Exodus introduces leaven as one of the two great OT symbols for sin (12:15-20). Leviticus introduces the second such symbol: leprosy (Lev. 13–14).

OUTLINE

ISRAEL IN NEED OF DELIVERANCE (1)

- How Israel came to Egypt (1:1-7)
- Egypt oppresses the Israelites (1:8-22)

PREPARING FOR DELIVERANCE (2:1–7:13)

- Birth and childhood of Moses (2:1-10)
- Moses in Midian (2:11-25)
- God calls Moses at the burning bush (3:1–4:12)
- Aaron appointed to help Moses (4:13-17)
- Moses returns to Egypt (4:18-31)
- Moses and Aaron before Pharaoh (5:1-5)
- The oppression worsens (5:6–6:13)
- Genealogy of Moses and Aaron (6:14-27)
- Aaron's rod becomes a snake (6:28–7:13)

DELIVERANCE BEGINS: THE TEN PLAGUES (7:14–11:10)

- Plague 1: Waters become blood (7:14-25)
- Plague 2: Frogs (8:1-15)
- Plague 3: Gnats (8:16-19)
- Plague 4: Flies (8:20-32)

Plague 5: Livestock pestilence (9:1-7)
Plague 6: Boils (9:8-12)
Plague 7: Hail and lightning (9:13-35)
Plague 8: Locusts (10:1-20)
Plague 9: Darkness (10:21-29)
Plague 10 foretold: Death of the firstborn (11)

DELIVERANCE COMES: THE EXODUS (12:1–15:21)
Passover (12:1-28)
Plague 10: Death of the firstborn (12:29-30)
The Exodus (12:31-51)
Consecration of the firstborn (13:1-16)
Crossing the Red Sea (13:17–14:31)
Songs of victory (15:1-21)

DELIVERANCE FORGOTTEN (15:22–18:27)
The people grow discontent (15:22-27)
God sends manna and quail (16)
God sends water from a rock (17:1-7)
Israel defeats the Amalekites (17:8-16)
Jethro helps Moses (18)

THE COVENANT AT SINAI (19–31)
The covenant offered and accepted (19:1-8)
Israel prepares to hear from God (19:9-25)
The Ten Commandments (20)
Social laws (21–23)
Israel again accepts the covenant (24)
Laws of worship (25–31)

THE COVENANT BROKEN AND RENEWED (32–34)
The golden calf (32)
Moses and the glory of God (33)
The covenant renewed (34)

THE TABERNACLE (35–40)
Materials (35)
Craftsmen and furnishings (36–38)
Priestly garments (39)
Dedication (40)

ISRAEL IN NEED OF DELIVERANCE (1)

1:1-7 *Historical review: How Israel came to Egypt.* The 70 Israelites who came from Canaan to Egypt had now lived there for more than 400 years (12:40-41; Gen. 15:13), and had become great in number and wealth. Compare 1:1-5 with Genesis 46:8-27.

1:8-22 *He hasn't heard of Joseph, so he oppresses them.* After Joseph died, a new pharaoh came to power "who knew nothing about Joseph" and therefore did not care about the Israelites. He also feared them because of their numbers and power. The Egyptians tried forced labor and infanticide—construction and destruction—as means of controlling the Israelites, but God protected the Israelites and they continued to prosper.

PREPARING FOR DELIVERANCE (2:1–7:13)

2:1-10 *Released by his mother, rescued and raised by a princess.* Moses was born into the tribe of Levi. His parents' attempt to save him from infanticide led to his being raised in the household of Pharaoh.

Moses' life divides into three parts of 40 years each:

- Moses the prince of Egypt (2:1-10)
- Moses the shepherd of Midian (2:11–4:17)
- Moses the lawgiver of Israel (4:18—Deut. 34:5)

2:11-22 *Hebrew hostility sends Moses to Midian.* Moses killed an Egyptian who was mistreating a Hebrew slave. When the Israelites responded with hostility toward Moses, he feared for his life and fled to the land of the Midianites in the Sinai desert. There he married Zipporah, daughter of Jethro, and became a shepherd. The Midianites were descendants of Abraham through Midian, one of his six sons by Keturah (Gen. 25:1-2).

2:23-25 *Israel cries out, God "remembers" them.* Pharaoh's death set the stage for Moses to return to Egypt (4:19), where his people were still being oppressed. When the Israelites cried out in their distress, God "remembered" his promise to Abraham and his descendants (2:24). "Remembered" does not mean God had forgotten the Israelites. The Hebrew is closer to "concentrate on" or "act on."

3:1-10 *It burns without burning up.* As he was tending sheep, Moses saw a bush burning but not being consumed. God spoke to him out of the bush, saying Moses was to be his instrument to bring the Israelites out of Egypt and back to Canaan. Moses' unique worship experience would lead to a 40-year work experience!

3:11-12 *Called by God, Moses offers an excuse: "I'm not worthy."* Asked to deliver Israel, Moses immediately protested that he was not equal to the task. God tried to reassure him. Moses would offer three more excuses, and God would answer each one, giving him more than enough resources to lead the people and confront Pharaoh.

3:13-22 *Excuse 2: "They don't know you anymore."* Moses protested that the Israelites had wandered too far from God to take seriously God's offer to liberate them. God assured Moses of his identity: "I AM THE ONE WHO ALWAYS IS." (3:14; see also John 8:58); and of his ability to bring Israel out of Egypt. He told Moses in detail some of the things that would happen as he led Israel.

The promise that Israel would leave Egypt wealthier than they came (3:19-22) parallels Abraham's experience (Gen. 12).

4:1-9 *Excuse 3: "What if they don't believe me?"* Moses protested again: The Israelites would not believe he had God's backing. God answered this objection by teaching Moses how to perform some miracles, to show that he was with him.

4:10-17 *Excuse 4: "I can't talk very well."* Moses protested yet again, saying he was not eloquent enough to lead a nation. God grew angry at Moses' reluctance but promised to help him. He commissioned Moses' brother, Aaron, to be his spokesman: Both God from above and Aaron from his side would help Moses. Acts 7:22 is interesting in light of Moses' claim of ineloquence.

4:18-26 *Moses accepts the call and returns to Egypt.* Finally agreeing to God's direction, Moses bid Jethro farewell and returned to Egypt.

God cautioned Moses that he would "make [Pharaoh] stubborn" so that he would not let the people go. Some form of this phrase is repeated after each of the 10 plagues—sometimes stating that God hardened Pharaoh's heart, other times that Pharaoh hardened his own heart. Moses explained to Pharaoh that God was hardening his heart so that Pharaoh might see God's power (9:16). Paul saw this as an example of God's sovereignty (Rom. 9:14-18).

Moses had either neglected or refused to circumcise his son Gershom (Gen. 17:14), and as a result God "confronted Moses and was about to kill him" (4:24). Realizing the danger Moses was in, Zipporah quickly circumcised Gershom (4:25).

God regarded the entire nation of Israel as his "son" (4:22-23; see Hos. 11:1).

4:27-31 *They welcome the brothers and worship together.* Arriving in Egypt, Moses met Aaron and told him all that God had said. The two of them reported to the Israelite elders, who, as God had predicted (3:18), responded positively to the hope of liberation, and bowed in humble worship.

5:1-5 *"Let my people go."* Moses asked Pharaoh to let the Israelites go into the wilderness to worship. In essence Pharaoh replied, "I don't recognize this God, so why should I release his people?"

Pharaoh's arrogant question, "And who is the LORD?" (5:2) would be echoed by another king some 850 years later (Dan. 3:15). The first of these proud monarchs learned that "the LORD" was God of water (14:1-31); the second learned that he was God of fire (Dan. 3:16-30).

5:6-21 *"Make them sweat! No more straw!"* To show his displeasure with Moses and Aaron's request, Pharaoh increased the Israelites' workload. The Israelites blamed Moses for their greater burden. Even though the people knew their prophesied time of bondage was due to end soon (Gen. 15:13), and even though Moses had demonstrated miraculous powers to them (4:30), they did not believe. Like the modern naturalist, they were constantly needing proof.

5:22–6:13 *"I am Abraham's God, and I'll bring you back to Abraham's land."* Discouraged, Moses asked God why the promised deliverance had not yet come. God reassured him that it would eventually come.

6:14-27 *The genealogy of Moses and Aaron.* Moses interrupted his story of events in Egypt to trace his and Aaron's family history. On the importance of genealogies in the ancient world, see exposition on Gen. 5:1-20.

6:28–7:7 *"Speak to Pharaoh again."* God told Moses and Aaron to approach Pharaoh again, cautioning them again that he would "make [Pharaoh] stubborn" (4:21). Moses was now 80 years old, ready to begin the final third of his life (see exposition on 2:1-10).

7:8-13 *They match the first miracle, but not the second.* As Moses and Aaron approached Pharaoh, they backed up their divine mission with a miraculous sign. Pharaoh's magicians were able to duplicate part of Moses' miracle, but God had the last word. Paul named two of these magicians (2 Tim. 3:8).

DELIVERANCE BEGINS: THE TEN PLAGUES (7:14–11:10)

7:14-24 *Plague 1: Water becomes blood.* As Moses continued to plead with Pharaoh to let the people go, God validated his pleas with 10 devastating plagues. The plagues had a dual purpose:

- to show Israel the strength of its God
- to show Egypt the nonexistence of *its* gods. Each plague was

directed against a particular Egyptian deity.

Seven of the 10 plagues were preceded by warnings to Pharaoh. Six of those warnings included the plea, "Let my people go" (7:16; 8:1, 20; 9:1, 13; 10:3).

The first plague involved the waters of the Nile becoming blood. Although this was a severe hardship on his land, Pharaoh was unimpressed and his heart "remained hard and stubborn" after his magicians apparently duplicated the miracle.

While the tenth plague (death of the firstborn) can hardly be explained in natural terms, some scholars dismiss the first nine as seasonal occurrences common in the Nile valley. God may have used such natural means, yet the plagues were undeniably miraculous:

- It is doubtful that mere natural occurrences would have made such an impression on Pharaoh's magicians (8:19).
- The plagues affected the Egyptians but not the Israelites living in their midst (8:22-23; 9:4-7, 26; 11:7); natural phenomena have no such precise boundaries.
- Moses was able to end the plague of frogs on command (8:8-14). If his prediction of when they would die (8:10) was just a lucky guess, it was doubly lucky in that Pharaoh both initiated the request that Moses get rid of the frogs (8:8) and then set the date when he should do so (8:10).

7:25–8:15 *Plague 2: Frogs fill Egypt, from Nile to kneading bowl.* Again Moses asked Pharaoh to let the people go, threatening a plague of frogs if he refused. Pharaoh refused and the frogs came. The magicians again appeared to duplicate the plague. But when Pharaoh wanted the frogs to disappear, he turned to Moses, promising to let the Israelites go if Moses would lift the plague. Moses did so and Pharaoh broke his promise.

8:16-19 *Plague 3: Dust becomes gnats.* The third plague came without warning. Aaron struck the dust with his staff, and it became gnats. This time Pharaoh's magicians were unable to duplicate the plague. They were impressed enough to give God the credit, even in Pharaoh's presence!

8:20-32 *Plague 4: Flies! Dense swarms in every home!* The fourth plague, dense swarms of flies—perhaps a larger, bloodsucking variety—drove Pharaoh to offer two compromises: that the people could worship their God as long as they remained in Egypt; and (when that offer was refused) that they could go, but not too far. Once the plague ended, he revoked this second offer. Pharaoh would offer two more such compromises (10:10-11, 10:24-29).

As he warned Pharaoh about the plague of flies, Moses told him that there would be no flies in the area where the Israelites lived. He made it clear that God would give this miraculous protection in order that "you will know that I am the LORD."

9:1-7 *Plague 5: Fields full of dead animals.* Moses next predicted a pestilence on Egypt's livestock, again predicting that the plague would not affect the Israelites. This time Pharaoh sent his men to investigate and found that, indeed, the Israelites' animals had been spared. Still, however, "his heart remained stubborn," and he refused to let the people go.

This plague must have had grave economic and religious consequences for the Egyptians. Oxen were used for labor in the fields; camels, donkeys, and horses were used for transportation; and the bull was an object of worship.

9:8-12 *Plague 6: This time, the dust becomes boils.* The sixth plague, like the third, came without warning. And like the third it involved inorganic matter becoming organic: Ashes became dust, which became boils. Even the magicians were covered with boils and unable to duplicate the plague.

9:13-35 *Plague 7: The worst hailstorm in their history.* God's warning about the seventh plague included an explanation of why he was hardening Pharaoh's heart (see exposition on 4:18-26). Some Egyptians apparently heeded God's warning this time (9:20). The hail and lightning made this plague the worst storm in Egypt's history (9:24). The details of 9:31-32 show the historical accuracy of this account.

10:1-20 *Plague 8: Locusts! They come with the wind, they cover the sun!* The eighth plague, locusts, destroyed whatever the hail had spared. A locust is capable of eating its own weight daily, and one square mile of a swarm can contain up to 200 million locusts. "Not one green thing remained, neither tree nor plant, throughout the land of Egypt" (10:15). 10:10-11 marks the third compromise suggested by Pharaoh: The Israelites could go, but they must leave their children behind.

10:21-29 *Plague 9: "It was so dark you could feel it."* Plague nine, like plagues three and six, came without warning—a 72-hour blackout. This called into question Ra, the sun god and chief Egyptian deity, especially since Israelite homes still had light. Pharaoh suggested one last compromise: "Go," but "let your flocks and herds stay here" (10:24). Moses refused the compromise, and Pharaoh ordered him to leave his presence and never return.

11:1-10 *Plague 10 foretold: "Your firstborn will die."* Moses announced the horrible final plague: All the firstborn of Egypt would die. This was the only plague that God said would affect the Israelites as well as the Egyptians, if they failed to take the prescribed preventive measures (12:1-28).

DELIVERANCE COMES: THE EXODUS (12:1–15:21)

12:1-20 *The Passover: "Sprinkle the blood to save your life."* God gave specific instructions for how Israel's firstborn could escape the final plague. Each household was to kill an unblemished, one-year-old lamb and sprinkle its blood on the doorposts of the house. The instructions were very personal: The death angel would pass over only those houses having blood on the doorposts.

The flesh of the lamb was to be roasted and eaten along with bitter herbs and unleavened bread. The people were to "eat the food quickly," dressed for travel (12:11), apparently to show that they were ready for liberation. The unleavened bread was symbolic of their haste, which allowed no time for bread to rise (12:39). Today this meal is called seder and takes place on Passover.

Passover was to be kept "forever" as a "special festival" of their deliverance from Egypt (12:14). It was to be followed by the seven-day "Festival of Unleavened Bread" (12:15-20). The term *Passover* often applies to the entire eight days.

Passover was to begin on the fourteenth day of Abib ("this month," 12:2). God decreed that Abib was from then on to be the first month of Israel's calendar year, to commemorate their liberation from Egypt. Jews today still keep Passover on the prescribed day, but the month of Abib is now called Nisan and is the seventh month of the Jewish year, overlapping March and April. The Jewish year now begins on Rosh Hashanah, the first day of the month of Tisrai and the traditional date of Creation.

12:21-28 *Final instructions for their final hours in Egypt.* As the night of Israel's liberation approached, Moses called the elders together and told them to begin preparation for the Passover meal—and they immediately did so (12:28). During these final instructions he once again reminded them that the rite of Passover should be passed down from generation to generation as a remembrance of God's miraculous deliverance (12:24-27).

12:29-30 *Plague 10: As the firstborn die, mourning begins at midnight.* Without warning to the Egyptians, the death angel struck at midnight. The firstborn of every household died, from Pharaoh's house to the house of the lowliest servant. The Israelites followed the Passover instructions (12:28) and escaped this plague.

12:31-42 *The Exodus: They walk out with great wealth.* Following the death of the firstborn Egyptians, Pharaoh summoned Moses and told him to assemble the Israelites and leave at once. They left Goshen in the Nile delta and traveled to Succoth, some 30 miles to the southeast.

As God had promised (3:19-22), they left Egypt with great wealth, apparently because God had "caused the Egyptians to look favorably on the Israelites" (12:36). Moses especially was respected by the Egyptians (11:3). Pharaoh's words, "Give me a blessing as you leave" (12:32), suggest that even he secretly respected Moses.

After 430 years in Egypt, the 70 Israelites who had come there to escape famine had grown to 600,000 men plus women and children. They were accompanied in their Exodus by "many people who were not Israelites" (12:38).

12:43-51 *Procedures for Passover.* God gave additional instructions about the Passover meal. It was to be for Israelites only. Non-Israelites who joined them could partake, but only after being circumcised.

13:1-16 *The festival and the firstborn: Reminders.* Moses gave further instructions about the Festival of Unleavened Bread and the dedication of the firstborn. Both were to be reminders of their deliverance by God's "mighty power" (13:3, 9, 14, 16).

The stipulation that this ceremony should be "like a mark branded on your hands or your forehead" led in later centuries to the practice of male Israelites wearing phylacteries, small boxes containing Scripture, worn on the forehead and left upper arm. The boxes contained four Scriptures:

- Exodus 13:1-10
- Exodus 13:11-16
- Deuteronomy 6:4-9
- Deuteronomy 11:13-21

God had saved all Israel from bondage (13:14) and therefore the whole nation was his by right, but he claimed only the firstborn as a substitute for the whole nation (13:1-2). While firstborn animals were to be offered as a sacrifice to God, firstborn sons were to be redeemed with money (13:13, 15; see Num. 3:46-47). God would later claim the Levites as substitutes for Israel's firstborn (Num. 3:12-13, 40-47).

13:17-20 *The safer way, but not the shorter way.* The shorter route to Canaan was along the coast, but this led through the land of the Philistines, a pagan people that Israel was not spiritually mature enough to face at that time. So Israel took the long road, toward Sinai.

13:21-22 *The cloud by day, the fire by night.* God would lead his people through the desert by a "pillar of cloud" during the day and a "pillar of fire" at night. (See 1 Kings 8:10-11 for a similar manifestation of God's presence.)

14:1-14 *God hardens Pharaoh's heart, to honor himself.* As the Israelites approached the Red Sea, Pharaoh began regretting that he had lost their services as slave laborers. God hardened Pharaoh's heart one last time, and he pursued the Israelites. This last pursuit by the hard-hearted Pharaoh would fulfill God's stated purpose for hardening his heart: "That you might see my power and that my fame might spread throughout the earth" (9:16).

As Pharaoh's army closed in on them, the people again despaired and complained to Moses.

14:15-18 *"Stretch out your staff! The sea will separate!"* God told Moses that, if he would simply stretch out his staff over the Red Sea, he and the whole nation would pass through it on dry ground.

14:19-20 *The pillar of cloud: Light for Israel, dark for Egypt.* As the Egyptians approached, the pillar of cloud hid Israel from them, becoming "darkness to the Egyptians" but "lighting the Israelite camp" (14:20).

This light marks the first appearance of what would come to be known as the Shekinah, the visible indication of God's presence. This is usually referred to as "the glorious presence of the LORD" (see 16:7, 10; 24:16; 2 Chron. 5:14; 7:1; exposition on Ezek. 11:22-25; 43:1-5; Rev. 15:8). The Hebrew root of the word *Shekinah* actually means "dwelling," and describes God's choosing to dwell among his people, as he did in the Tabernacle (29:43-46).

14:21-31 *The Red Sea: Slaves delivered, soldiers drowned.* The Red Sea parted and Israel passed through it, but then the waters came together again and the Egyptian army perished. God used natural means, a "strong east wind" that "blew all that night" (14:21) to accomplish a miracle: The wind "opened up a path through the water" (14:21). "So the people of Israel walked through the sea on dry ground, with walls of water on each side!" (14:22). If the Red Sea was actually the Sea of Reeds, a papyrus marsh, as some have suggested, at least it was deep enough to cover Pharaoh's army so that all of them drowned (14:28).

15:1-21 *Songs of victory on the seashore.* Moses and the Israelites sang victory songs, recounting the miracle at the Red Sea and predicting similar successes as they reclaimed the Promised Land.

Moses' sister Miriam, who led the women in celebration, is called a "prophet" (15:20). See *Prophetesses,* p. 849, for other women who served in this way.

DELIVERANCE FORGOTTEN (15:22–18:27)

15:22-27 *Bitter waters purified, healthy bodies promised.* When the Israelites came to a place where the water was bitter they complained loudly, and God showed Moses how to make the water drinkable. He also promised that, if they would obey him, he would protect them from illness. All along their journey, whenever the Israelites encountered obstacles, God was ready to help them if only they would trust in him. Often, as here, he helped even though they didn't trust him.

16:1-36 *Murmuring, manna, and meat.* Even after their miraculous Exodus, the Israelites feared God would let them starve. They complained, and God sent manna and quail. These divine provisions would help sustain them during their 40 years in the wilderness. They would eat other food, such as animals from their herds, but the miraculous provision was needed to help sustain such a large group of people. 16:31 describes the manna.

The people were to gather twice as much manna on the sixth day of each week, since none would fall on the Sabbath (16:5, 22-30). Even when provided food with so few restrictions, they disobeyed (16:20).

17:1-7 *"First no food, now no water."* The people complained once again, this time about the lack of water. Moses struck a rock, and a supernatural stream of water came out. Water often symbolizes life and salvation in the Bible. Paul saw this event as symbolic of Christ (1 Cor. 10:1-4).

17:8-16 *He raises his hands, they win the battle.* Israel was suddenly attacked by a fierce desert people called the Amalekites, descendants of Esau (Gen. 36:12). Moses chose a young man named Joshua—who would later lead Israel into Canaan—to lead the army. Israel won (17:9-12) through divine intervention.

17:14 shows that Moses was a writer and historian.

18:1-12 *At Sinai, a warm welcome for Moses.* In June of 1446 B.C. (see *Date and Location*), Israel arrived at Mount Sinai, where they would remain for 11 months and 5 days. Moses was greeted by his father-in-law, Jethro, and his wife, Zipporah, who had returned from Egypt to her Sinai homeland. They rejoiced when told how God had freed Israel from Egypt.

18:13-27 *A wise father-in-law.* At Jethro's advice, Moses selected capable men to help him settle legal disputes.

THE COVENANT AT SINAI (19–31)

19:1-8 *God's covenant nation: "I carried you on eagle's wings."* Moses reminded the people of God's deliverance and care for them, and asked them to keep God's covenant—so that they could be his "special treasure" and "kingdom of priests." They agreed to do so. By this time, it should have been obvious to the people that the God who had rescued them from Egypt "on eagle's wings" (19:4) would keep his part of the covenant.

19:9-15 *"Get ready to hear from God."* Moses helped the people sanctify themselves in preparation for God's appearance on Mount Sinai. God told Moses to set boundaries so that no one would touch the mountain and die.

19:16-25 *God appears on Mount Sinai.* Moses and all Israel witnessed the glory of God being manifested on Mount Sinai, with shaking, fire, smoke, and the sound of a trumpet. Again God warned Moses not to let the people come too close to the mountain. Even believers are seldom prepared to approach a holy God.

20:1-17 *The Ten Commandments.* God's first words from Sinai have come to be called the Ten Commandments. The first four have to do with honoring God himself: his unique nature and demands, his name, and his day. The final six have to do with the honorable treatment of fellow humans:

1. "Do not worship any other gods besides me." God will have no rivals, whether from false religions or from otherwise good things, such as family, money, or fame, which may usurp his preeminent place in our devotion.
2. "Do not make idols of any kind, whether in the shape of birds or animals or fish." To make an idol or image of God is to try to bring God under our control. Rather, God wants us to submit to and serve him. See John 4:24.
3. "Do not misuse the name of the LORD your God." We should not use God's name in an empty or insincere way, such as by making

an oath that we cannot fulfill (Lev. 19:12).

4. "Remember to observe the Sabbath day by keeping it holy." By imitating God's creation cycle of work and rest, and setting apart one day for God alone, Israel showed its faithfulness to him.

   Under the New Covenant, believers are not obligated to keep the Sabbath. In Christ they have experienced the fulfillment of the Sabbath-rest principle by trusting in God's grace, rather than in human effort, for salvation (Heb. 4:3-10).

5. "Honor your father and mother." Children must respect their parents. Under the law, to curse one's parents was a capital offense (Lev. 20:9). Honoring them, on the other hand, brought great blessing (Exod. 20:12).
6. "Do not murder." Murder is the willful, premeditated taking of life. The law did, however, sanction killing as a defensive or punitive act (Deut. 20:10-18) and prescribed the death penalty for various sins (Lev. 20:9-16; 24:17, 23; Deut. 13:6-11; 17:2-7).
7. "Do not commit adultery." Like the taking of life or property, adultery violates an exclusive covenantal relationship. Marriage is so crucial to the social order that adultery was among those sins for which the law prescribed death (Lev. 20:10).
8. "Do not steal." Private property was to be respected. To steal from another human is essentially to steal from God, since all things ultimately belong to him (Lev. 25:23).
9. "Do not testify falsely against your neighbor." To tell a lie, especially as a witness in court when someone's life is at stake, is to despise God, the author of truth. Instead of imitating God, the liar imitates Satan, the "father of lies" (John 8:44) and "accuser" of believers (Rev. 12:10).
10. "Do not covet." To covet is to desire for yourself any person or thing that belongs to someone else.

20:18-21 *"We're afraid of him."* The events on Sinai filled Moses and the Israelites with fear (see Heb. 12:18-21). Moses assured them that God only wanted to instill in them a healthy fear, to keep them from sin.

20:22-26 *"No idols, and only one altar."* God forbade idols, but gave instructions for building a simple altar for animal sacrifices. In place of pagan idolatry, the people would have a concrete way to express their faith in the one true God.

21:1-11 *Fair labor laws.* God gave detailed laws governing social relationships (21–23). Most of these are "case" laws, beginning with "if . . ." followed by a specific example. ("Categorical" laws, by contrast, are more general and are often based on a command to "do" or "do not.") Though some of these laws may sound unjust to modern ears, they were a great improvement over the customs of the pagan cultures of that day.

First came laws protecting the rights of both masters and servants (21:1-11; see exposition on Lev. 25:35-55). Hebrew servants were to be set free every seventh (Sabbath) year.

21:12-27 *Laws concerning violence.* God's law distinguished between premeditated and unpremeditated murder, with only the former being a capital offense. The places to which the unpremeditated murderer could "run" (21:13) were the "cities of refuge" (Deut. 19:1-13). Kidnapping and assaulting one's parent were also capital offenses.

Punishments were also prescribed

THE THREEFOLD DIVISION OF THE LAW

Moral Code

1. Do not worship any other gods besides me.
2. Do not make idols of any kind, whether in the shape of birds or animals or fish.
3. Do not misuse the name of the LORD your God.
4. Remember to observe the Sabbath day by keeping it holy.
5. Honor your father and mother.
6. Do not murder.
7. Do not commit adultery.
8. Do not steal.
9. Do not testify falsely against your neighbor.
10. Do not covet.

(Exodus 20)

The Revelation from Christ
(1 Corinthians 10:4)

Spiritual Code

This section dealt with those special ordinances that foreshadowed Christ and his full redemption.
It included:

1. The seven Levitical festivals
2. The five Levitical offerings

(Exodus 35–40; Leviticus)

The Realization in Christ
(Matthew 5:17-18; Romans 10:4; 1 Corinthians 5:7)

Social Code

This section included rules governing Israel's diet, sanitation, quarantine, soil conservation, taxation, military service, marriage, childbirth, divorce, etc.
(Exodus 21–34; Leviticus)

The Regulation until Christ
(Galatians 3:24)

for lesser personal injuries. "Eye for eye, tooth for tooth" (see 21:23-25) was a restraint against escalating retaliation.

21:28-36 *"Control your animals."* Owners would be held responsible for the destructive actions of their animals. Property owners would be responsible for injuries to animals resulting from their negligence.

22:1-15 *Crimes against property.* The law also covered theft, dishonesty, and the careless destruction of property. In some cases the penalty was restitution amounting to double the loss.

22:16–23:9 *Do's and don't's, diet and devotion.* The law covered matters such as sexual relationships, sorcery, idolatry, money lending, bribery, slander, and diet. See Leviticus 11 for more detail on dietary laws. The Israelites were exhorted not to oppress foreigners, since they themselves had been "foreigners in the land of Egypt" (22:21).

23:10-13 *"Sow it in the sixth, set it aside in the seventh."* The law of the Sabbath (20:8-11) was repeated and expanded to include the land: "Let the land rest and lie fallow during the seventh year. Then let the poor among you harvest any volunteer crop that may come up."

23:14-19 *"Don't forget the three festivals."* Three times a year all Israelite males were to appear before the Lord in Jerusalem. These were part of the yearly cycle of seven festivals (Lev. 23).

23:20-33 *"I'll send an angel before you."* God's "angel" would protect the Israelites and show them the way through the wilderness, while fear and "hornets" (perhaps a pestilence or disease) would drive out the Canaanites (23:27-28). God reminded Israel once again not to make treaties with the Canaanites.

Concerning "my angel" (23:23), see exposition on Genesis 16:1-16. God said he would drive out the Canaanites "a little at a time" (23:30), so that the land would not be left desolate and become infested by wild animals (23:29).

24:1-8 *Again they agree to keep the covenant.* Moses descended Mount Sinai, read the law to Israel, put it into written form, and confirmed the covenant by building an altar and sacrificing on it. Just as they did before Moses ascended Sinai, the people again agreed to obey the law (19:8).

24:9-18 *The glory of God and the God of glory.* Moses, Aaron, Nadab and Abihu (Aaron's sons), and 70 elders went up the mountain and were allowed to see the glory of God. But only Moses was allowed to enter the cloud of God's glory. Moses stayed in the cloud for 40 days.

25:1-9 *"Take an offering and build a tabernacle."* God told Moses to build a "tabernacle," a large tent, as a place for God to dwell among Israel. All the material needed for this project was to be provided from the people themselves.

25:10-22 *The Ark of the Covenant: "This is where we'll meet."* The Ark of the Covenant was to be made of acacia wood covered with gold. It resembled a cedar chest, about four feet long and two feet high. It was to contain the stone tablets on which the Ten Commandments ("the terms of the covenant," 25:16) were written (34:28), as well as a pot of manna and Aaron's rod. Its lid, called the mercy seat, was made of solid gold and featured two gold cherubim facing each other.

The Ark was the most important item in the Tabernacle, for it was where God manifested his presence (25:22).

25:23-30 *The holy bread: "God supplies your spiritual food."* Next came instructions for a table for the "Bread of the Presence." There were 12 cakes of this bread (Lev. 24:5-9), representing the 12 tribes and showing that God was the source of their spiritual food.

25:31-40 *The golden lampstand: "God shows the way."* There was to be a lampstand made of pure gold. The lamps, fed with oil, were trimmed every morning and evening and were to burn continually (Lev. 24:2-4), as reminders that God was the source of spiritual direction. On "pattern" (25:40), see exposition on Revelation 11:15-19.

26:1-37 *The Tabernacle: Two rooms divided by one curtain.* The Tabernacle was to be constructed of gold-covered poles and crossbars, overlaid and surrounded by curtains. A veil was to separate the "Holy Place" from the "Most Holy Place" (26:33), where one item was kept—the Ark of the Covenant. The veil represents the sinless humanity of Christ (Heb. 10:20; see Matt. 27:51).

God gave specific instructions not just for the construction but also for the location of each part of and item in the Tabernacle, indicating how important it was to him.

27:1-8 *Horns to hold the sacrifice.* The bronze altar would be the first piece of furniture as one entered the Tabernacle from the east. Horns on its four corners held the animal sacrifices.

27:9-21 *A courtyard of curtains.* The courtyard surrounding the Tabernacle was 75 feet wide by 150 feet long, surrounded by linen curtains.

28:1 *"Aaron and sons will be your priests."* Aaron and his sons were to be Israel's priests, with Aaron being the first high priest. The entire tribe of Levi would later be appointed to assist the priests (Num. 18:1-2).

28:2-43 *Garments for the priests.* Aaron was to wear special clothing to separate himself from the people. The multicolored ephod, a seamless garment, had two stones—each with the names of six of Israel's tribes—attached to the shoulders. The breastplate, fastened to the ephod with gold chains, displayed 12 precious stones—one for each tribe. The high priest was to place the Urim and Thummim (meaning "lights" and "perfections") over his heart so he could always determine God's will. Golden bells were attached to his robe. A special seal on his turban said, "SET APART AS HOLY TO THE LORD" (28:36).

29:1-28 *Consecrating the priests: Water, oil, blood, and bread.* God gave detailed instructions for consecrating Aaron and his sons for their ministry: The ceremony should include washing with water, anointing with oil, sprinkling with animal blood, and an offering of bread to be "lifted up as a special gift to the LORD" (sometimes translated "wave offering") (29:23-25).

Leviticus 8 records the actual ceremony in which Aaron and his sons were consecrated. Aromas of offerings are often called pleasing to the Lord (29:18, 25, 41; see Gen. 8:21; 2 Cor. 2:15-16; Eph. 5:2; Phil. 4:18).

29:29-42 *Details of priestly dress and duties.* God then gave specific instructions regarding the clothing of priests and the sacrifices they were to perform. While God was giving instructions about the consecration and duties of Aaron as high priest, Aaron was fashioning an idol for the Israelites in the shape of a golden calf (32:1-5).

29:43-46 *"Do this for me, and I'll dwell with you."* God reminded Moses that the Tabernacle and all the ceremonies related to it were symbolic of his wish to dwell among his people. When John would later describe Christ's coming to "[live] here on earth among us" (John 1:14), he would use a Greek word suggesting that Christ literally "pitched his tent" on earth.

30:1-10 *An altar of incense for the prayers of his people.* The altar of incense would be just outside the Most Holy Place. Incense would be burned on it daily, symbolizing the prayers of God's people. The altar would also be used in the annual offering of atonement (30:10; Lev. 16:12-13).

30:11-16 *"A half-shekel for your life."* All male Israelites 20 and older were to give a half-shekel for maintenance of the Tabernacle. It was a token amount, because its true purpose was "to make atonement for yourselves." It was the same for rich and poor, showing that everyone needed atonement (38:25-28).

30:17-21 *The bronze washbasin: "Wash before you worship."* A bronze washbasin would provide water for the priests to wash their hands and feet before performing their duties. The penalty for not washing was death. Cleanliness and purification are emphasized throughout Exodus—Deuteronomy.

30:22-38 *Oil and incense for worship only.* God gave detailed instructions for making a special blend of oil and incense that was never to be used for anything besides the Tabernacle worship.

31:1-11 *Architects appointed and anointed.* God designated that Bezalel and Oholiab should lead the building of the Tabernacle (35:30–36:2). He filled them "with the Spirit of God, giving [them] great wisdom, intelligence, and skill in all kinds of crafts" (see exposition on 1 Sam. 9:27–10:8).

31:12-17 *Death to those who desecrate his day.* God ended his instructions to Moses on Mount Sinai by reminding him to keep the Sabbath. Death was the punishment for profaning it.

31:18 *The tablets of stone.* Having given his law, God gave Moses two tablets of stone containing the Ten Commandments (24:12).

THE COVENANT BROKEN AND RENEWED (32–34)

32:1-14 *The golden calf: Idolatry and immorality.* Concluding that Moses would never come down from the mountain, the people had asked Aaron for another god to lead them. Aaron fashioned a golden calf, and the Israelites worshiped it. "After this, they celebrated with feasting and drinking, and indulged themselves in pagan revelry" (32:6).

Because they worshiped the golden calf, God was ready to destroy the whole nation and start over with just Moses. Moses begged God to forgive the people, so that other nations would not accuse him of injustice and so that the promises to Abraham, Isaac, and Jacob would not be broken. God promised not to destroy them.

32:15-20 *He breaks the tablets and burns the calf.* When Moses came down from the mountain and saw the idolatry and immorality firsthand, he became enraged and threw down the stone tablets, breaking them. He melted down the golden calf, ground it to powder, mixed the powder with water, and made the people drink it.

32:21-24 *The pitiful excuse of the priest.* Confronted by Moses, Aaron refused to accept responsibility for making the golden calf. Even while God was declaring him the spiritual leader of Israel (28:1), Aaron had been giving in to peer pressure and leading the nation into sin.

32:25-29 *Who is on the Lord's side? The Levites!* Realizing how wicked the people had become, Moses called for all "who are on the LORD's side" to come to him. The sons of Levi responded, and Moses ordered them to purge the camp of those who had taken part in the idolatry.

32:30–33:23 *"Forgive them or forsake me!"* Once again Moses asked God to forgive Israel or "blot me out of the record you are keeping" (32:32). God said that he himself could no longer go with the people, because if he did he would have to punish them. Instead, he would send an angel to guide them (23:20). Moses pitched his tent far from the camp and met with God. God promised to continue leading Israel. To reassure Moses, God allowed him another glimpse of his glory (33:20-23; see Isa. 6:1-5).

Joshua continued to serve as Moses' second-in-command and was present with him in the tent (33:11).

34:1-9 *New tablets for the Ten Commandments.* Moses ascended Mount Sinai again, with new stone tablets to replace those he had broken. God appeared to him, and he bowed and worshiped, begging him once more to continue leading Israel.

As is true throughout Scripture, the attributes of God described in 34:6-7 include a balance of compassion and justice. On "punishing the children for the sins of their parents" (20:5; 34:7), see exposition on Ezekiel 18:1-18.

34:10-17 *The covenant renewed.* God told Moses he would renew his covenant with Israel. But Israel would have to do its part by avoiding the practices of the Canaanites and by keeping the law.

34:18-26 *Again, "Don't forget the festivals."* God reminded Moses once again of the importance of the regular festival days he had instituted for Israel.

34:27-28 *Two new stones for the Ten Commandments.* Moses recorded all that God said, and God inscribed the Ten Commandments on the new stone tablets. These verses provide evidence that Moses wrote Exodus (see *Author*).

34:29-35 *The glow of God on his face.* As Moses came back down the mountain, his face glowed from speaking with God, and the people were afraid of him. Covering his face with a veil, Moses reported all that God had told him on the mountain (see exposition on 2 Cor. 3:7-18).

THE TABERNACLE (35–40)

35:1-3 *The Sabbath stressed again.* Moses emphasized once more the importance of the Sabbath. Anyone found working on the Sabbath would be put to death.

35:4–36:7 *Generous help from grateful hearts.* To build the Tabernacle, Moses asked for freewill offerings of money, materials, and skills, and the people gladly responded (35:20-29). As directed (31:1-11), Moses appointed Bezalel and Oholiab to lead the project.

The people gave so generously that Moses had to issue a decree that no more be given (36:5-7). The magnitude of their generosity can be seen from the total weight of the precious metals mentioned in 36:8–39:31. Some of this would have come from their plunder of Egypt (12:35-36).

36:8–38:31 *The Tabernacle and its furnishings: Funded, fashioned, and finished.* With ample funding and willing labor, the work on the Tabernacle and its furnishings proceeded smoothly.

39:1-31 *Priestly garments: Made to order.* Garments were made for the priests, faithfully following the specified designs (28:1-42). The colors of these robes matched some of those in the Tabernacle curtains.

39:32-42 *Moses gives it his seal of approval.* When the work was completed, Moses inspected the

CONSTRUCTION OF THE TABERNACLE

Israel's House of Worship

From the wilderness of Sinai until the building of Solomon's Temple in 960 B.C.

Description and Size

- Consisted of three sections: (1) outer court (2) inner court (3) Most Holy Place
- Outer court: 150 feet long, 75 feet wide, 7 1/2 feet high
- Tent within the outer court: 45 feet long, 15 feet wide, 15 feet high
- Tent had two rooms, which were separated by a thick veil
- Eastern tent room known as the inner court or Holy Place
- Western tent room known as the Most Holy Place

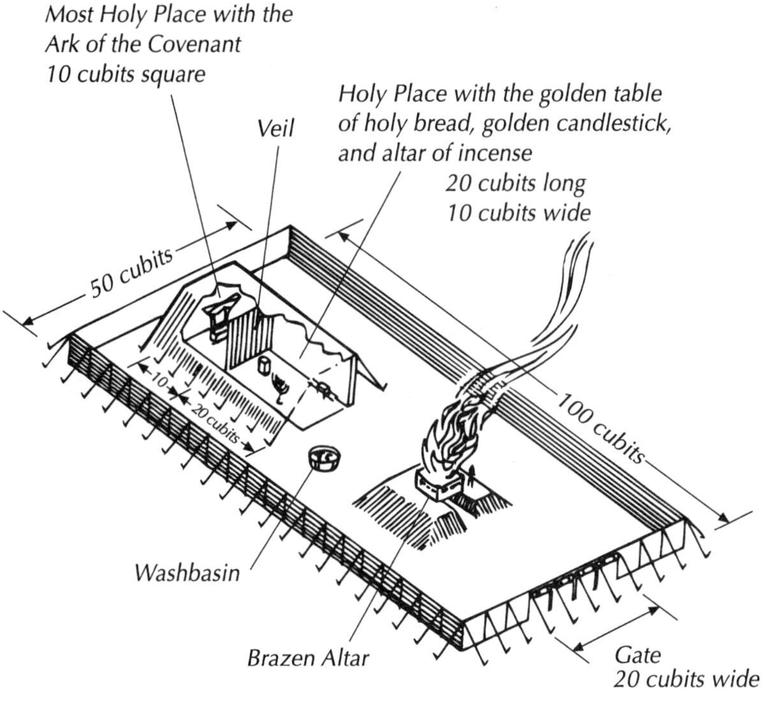

Building Materials

Gold, silver, bronze, animal cloth, acacia wood, onyx

THE FURNISHINGS OF THE TABERNACLE

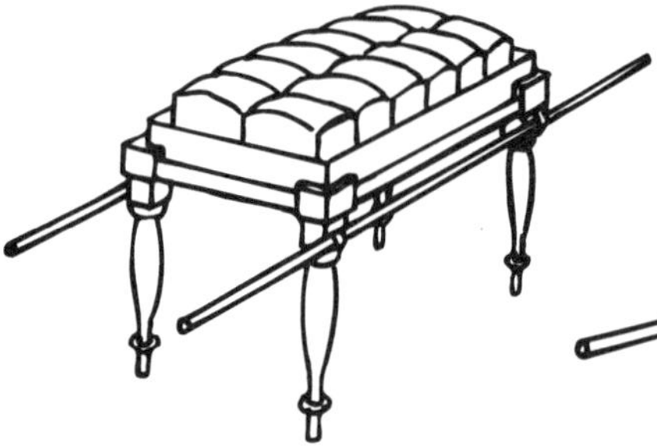

TABLE OF THE BREAD
OF THE PRESENCE

ALTAR OF INCENSE

THE ARK OF THE COVENANT

THE WASHBASIN

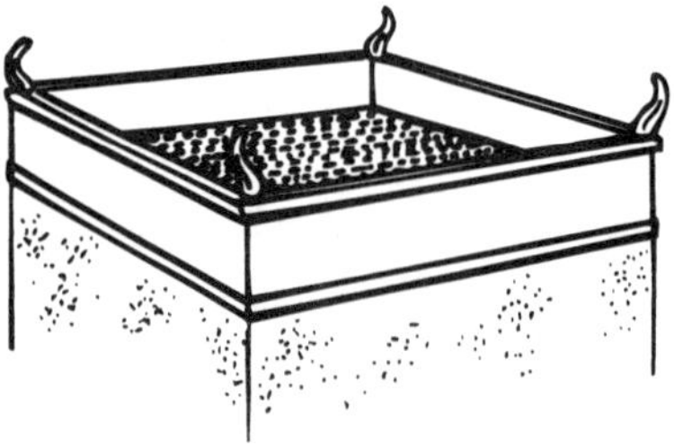

BRAZEN ALTAR

GOLDEN CANDLESTICK

Tabernacle and found it to be just as the Lord had prescribed. The Tabernacle and the priests were ready for the journey to the Promised Land.

40:1-33 *Grand opening!* The Israelites now set up the Tabernacle for the first time. A precise order was to be followed in doing so, with the Ark of the Covenant going in first, and immediately after that the veil separating it and the Most Holy Place from the rest of the Tabernacle (26:33).

This mobile place of worship would be taken down and set up many more times during 40 years of desert wandering.

40:34-38 *God's glory surrounds and saturates it.* With the Tabernacle completed and set up, God's presence filled it so much that Moses could not enter. The angel (23:20-33; 33:1-3), the cloud, and the fire (40:36-38) would guide Israel on to the Promised Land.

PEOPLE TO REMEMBER FROM EXODUS

AARON

Key Facts: Moses' older brother, Israel's first high priest (28:1; Num. 26:59).
Birth: Recorded in Num. 26:59
Father: Amram (Num. 26:59)
Mother: Jochebed (Num. 26:59)
Sister: Miriam (Num. 26:59)
Wife: Elisheba (6:23)
Sons: Nadab, Abihu, Eleazar, Ithamar (6:23)
Occupation: High priest (28:1)
Key Events in His Life:

- Appointed to speak for Moses (7:1)
- His rod becomes a serpent (7:8-13)
- Appointed high priest (28:1)
- Makes golden calf (32:2-4)
- Speaks against Moses (Num. 12)
- His rod buds (Num. 17)
- Excluded from Promised Land (Num. 20:12)

Age at Death: 123 (Num. 20:27-28; Num. 33:39)
Total Bible References: 339
Key References: 4:14—Deut. 10:6; Ps. 77:20; 105:26-45; 133; Mic. 6:4; Acts 7:40; Heb. 5:4; 7:11

Aaron Speaks

I suppose history will remember me simply as the older brother of Moses. That's all right. Perhaps Miriam will be thought of as the older sister of Aaron! (Actually, I don't think she would mind.) What awesome responsibilities God entrusted to Moses and Miriam and me. She was a prophet, I was Israel's first high priest, and Moses—well, everyone knows about Moses. Not a bad record for three Hebrew kids born outside the Promised Land. If only our parents could have known all this when they set Moses afloat on the Nile. (2:3; 15:20; 28:1-2)

Moses broke the news to me this morning: The office of high priest is to be transferred immediately to Eleazar, my third son. Actually, I had expected it for some time now. It is a good and wise decision. Both Eleazar and Ithamar have shown themselves to be trustworthy. How different they are from my two oldest boys, Nadab and Abihu. Where, oh where, did I fail them? How did it happen? What prompted them to deliberately tempt God? As always when I think of their horrible death, images of that golden calf flash across my mind. Did my own disgraceful actions contribute somehow to their death? (32; Lev. 10:1-2; Num. 20:25-26)

But I should not and will not torture myself with such thoughts. Thank God for all my memories of serving in the Tabernacle. The Ark of the Covenant is my hope and comfort. Whenever I sprinkle the blood on the altar in the Tabernacle, Israel's sins—including mine—are covered. (25:9-10, 22; Lev. 4)

I see we've reached the top of Mount Hor. Just enough time to bid farewell to Eleazar and Moses before I personally meet him who dwells in the shining cloud above the mercy seat. (25:22; Lev. 16:2; Num. 20:25-29)

Spiritual Lessons from Aaron

- As believers, we are called upon to support, honor, and pray for our leaders (17:12-13; 1 Tim. 2:1-2; Titus 3:1-2; Heb. 13:7, 17; 1 Pet. 2:13-17).
- We should be very careful about criticizing our spiritual leaders (Num. 12:1-2; 1 Tim. 5:19; James 1:19).
- We should always be on our guard against the power of peer pressure (32:1-5).
- We must take responsibility for our sin and not blame it on others (32:4, 22-24).
- We should take God's laws seriously and help those within our sphere of influence to take them seriously as well (30:9; 32:1-5; Lev. 10:1-7).

Key Verse

"Your brother, Aaron, and his sons, Nadab, Abihu, Eleazar, and Ithamar, will be set apart from the common people. They will be my priests and will minister to me" (28:1).

MOSES

Key Facts: Israel's great lawgiver, author of the Pentateuch (19–31; Luke 24:44; John 1:17; 5:46)
Birth: Recorded in 2:2
Father: Amram (6:20)
Mother: Jochebed (6:20)
Brother: Aaron (6:20)
Sister: Miriam (Num. 26:59)
Wife: Zipporah (2:21)
Sons: Gershom, Eliezer (18:2-4)
Key Events in His Life:

- Rescued from river; raised as royalty (2:3-10)
- Flees to Midian (2:11-15)
- Called to lead Israel (3–4)
- The Exodus; crossing Red Sea (12:31-42; 13:17–14:31)

- Brings water from rock (17:1-7)
- Receives law at Sinai (19–31)
- Supervises building of Tabernacle (36–40)
- Sends spies into Canaan (Num. 13)
- Announces 40 years of wandering (Num. 14:26-39)
- Forbidden to enter Canaan (Num. 20:1-13)
- Bronze serpent (Num. 21:4-9)
- Farewell address (Deut. 1–33)

Age at Death: 120 (Deut. 34:1-5, 7)
Total Bible References: 804
Key References: Exod.—Deut.; Ps. 90; 105:26-45; Isa. 63:11-13; John 1:17; Acts 7:17-44; Heb. 3:1-5; 11:23-29; Rev. 15:2-4

Moses Speaks

I really don't feel 120! My vision and hearing are as sharp as ever. The steep heights of Mount Nebo present no difficulty to my legs and lungs. How amazing to reread those words God recently told me to write: "Seventy years are given to us!" By his grace I've already exceeded my allotted time by half a century! (Deut. 34:1, 7; Ps. 90:10)

I've actually lived three lives: First there was Moses the student politician, learning all the wisdom in Egypt, preparing for a civil-service career. Then there was that terrible moment when these hands killed a man. That began my second life as a shepherd, less hectic and more reflective. And I would surely still be there today had not that bush started burning. (3:1-3, 12; Acts 7:22)

From that time on I lived "life number three"—Moses the deliverer and lawgiver. My simple nomadic existence suddenly gave way to almost continuous heart-pounding, breathtaking action—sticks becoming snakes; rivers turning to blood; frogs, gnats, flies, and locusts filling the air; and all those other horrible plagues—and the most horrific of all: the death of Egypt's firstborn. (4:2-3; 7:14–11:10; 12:29-42)

Then, the dry path in the watery sea; a fiery sign in the sky; bread falling from heaven. And then the ultimate event—the giving of God's law and a brief glimpse of him in person. (13:21-22; 14; 16:14-15; 19–31; 33:18-23)

Even now, four decades later, it all seems more fiction than fact. As I stand here on the barren slopes of Nebo, looking westward toward the land of milk and honey, once again I regret that inexcusable sin for which God has forbidden me to enter Canaan. What a staggering price I paid for my raw, uncontrolled anger! (Num. 20:10-12; Deut. 31:20)

But on to more pleasant thoughts. My people's present victories crowd out the past defeats. I have just today completed a section of God's holy record, which I trust our future generations will read. I led the past generation out of Egypt. Now I have brought their children to the very threshold of freedom in the Promised Land. God's faithfulness has far exceeded all my failures.

Dear Lord, my work is done. Allow me now to see in fullness that which I have already seen in part—your gracious and glorious self. (3:10; Deut. 31:24-26)

Spiritual Lessons from Moses

- God's way is the right choice, even though it often means denying ourselves the pleasures of this life (Heb. 11:25-26).

- There's no use in trying to excuse ourselves from God's service. He can answer all our excuses (3:11-15; 4:1-17).
- We shouldn't try to do everything ourselves. We should be willing to let others help us (18:13-26).
- Fellowship with God will bring a radiance to our lives that others will notice (33:18-23; 34:29-35).
- Moses' successful leadership was due in part to his love for those he led (32:32; see Rom. 9:1-3; 10:1).
- Moses, the world's most humble person (Num. 12:3), failed God and forfeited his place in the Promised Land because of anger (Num. 20:2-13). In the words of Paul, "If you think you are standing strong, be careful, for you, too, may fall into the same sin" (1 Cor. 10:12).
- Our goal in life should be spiritual, not worldly, success (Deut. 34:10-12; 2 Tim. 4:7).

Key Verse
"For the law was given through Moses; God's unfailing love and faithfulness came through Jesus Christ" (John 1:17).

LEVITICUS

BACKGROUND

The events in Leviticus cover about one month in 1446 B.C., following the giving of the law at Mount Sinai (Exod. 20). In Israel's earlier history, worship had been a family affair, with the head of each household acting as "priest" for his family. After God gave Israel the law and the Tabernacle, however, he designated Aaron and his descendants to be priests (Exod. 28:1), and the rest of the tribe of Levi to assist them (Num. 18:1-2). Leviticus consists mainly of instructions concerning the duties of priests and Levites.

AUTHOR

Moses (see *Genesis, Exodus: Author*). Some 50 times in Leviticus, we read words to the effect that "the LORD said to Moses." If Moses himself did not record these words from God, he must have dictated them to a scribe, in which case he would still be rightly called the author. Moses' background and training as Egyptian royalty would, however, have made him better suited than any of his contemporaries to record God's words. The NT affirms Moses as the author of Leviticus:

- The "Law" in which John says Moses wrote (John 1:45, NIV) refers to the first five books of the OT.
- Quotes from Leviticus are attributed to Moses (Rom. 10:5).

DATE AND LOCATION

Moses probably recorded the events and the directives from God shortly after they occurred, in 1446 B.C. There are clear indications in the text that Leviticus was written at Sinai (25:1; 26:46; 27:34).

PURPOSE

- To show the Israelites, freed from Egyptian bondage, how they should live as God's people. It is the same for all believers: First comes redemption, then sanctification.

***1805 B.C.* Death of Joseph**

***1446* The Exodus, Law given, events of Leviticus**

***1406* Israel enters Canaan**

***1377* Othniel, 1st judge**

***1051* Saul, 1st king**

- To instill an awareness of sin and describe what constitutes holiness in one's relationship with God. Under the law this was accomplished in large part by concrete, visual illustrations (e.g., blemishes or defects in humans or animals).
- To foreshadow the complete and perfect sacrifice of Christ by repeatedly emphasizing the complete and perfect sacrifices of animals.
- To add to the revelation of God's nature in Genesis and Exodus by focusing on his holiness.

UNIQUE FEATURES

- The phrase *the LORD said* appears more than 50 times in Leviticus—more than in any other Bible book.
- No other Bible book speaks so much of holiness. Various forms of *holy* occur more than 100 times. *Sacrifice* occurs 42 times, *priest* 189 times, and *blood* 86 times.

COMPARISON WITH OTHER BIBLE BOOKS

(See *Exodus: Comparison with Other Bible Books.*)

OUTLINE

OFFERINGS (1–7)
- To maintain fellowship (1–3)
  - Burnt offering (1)
  - Grain offering (2)
  - Peace offering (3)
- To restore fellowship (4:1–6:7)
  - Sin offering (4:1–5:13)
  - Guilt offering (5:14–6:7)
- Further regulations for the offerings (6:8–7:38)

ORDINATIONS (8–10)
- Moses consecrates Aaron and his sons (8)
- Aaron and his sons begin their priesthood (9)
- Nadab and Abihu (10)

ORDERLY LIVING (11–15)
- Uncleanness from food (11)
- Uncleanness from childbirth (12)
- Uncleanness from diseases (13–15)

OFFERINGS (16–17)
- Day of Atonement (16)
- Rules for sacrificing and eating meat (17)

ORDERLY LIVING (18–20)
- Laws of sexual morality (18)
- Various laws and penalties (19–20)

ORDINATIONS (21–22)
- Regulations for priests (21:1–22:16)
- Rules for sacrificing (22:17-33)

OFFERINGS (23–25)
- Weekly Sabbath (23:1-3)

Passover, Festival of Unleavened Bread (23:4-8)
Festival of Firstfruits (23:9-14)
Festival of Harvest (also called Pentecost) (23:15-22)
Festival of Trumpets (23:23-25)
Day of Atonement (23:26-32)
Festival of Shelters (23:33-44)
Offering of oil and bread (24:1-9)
Blasphemy (24:10-23)
Seventh year Sabbath (25:1-7, 18-22)
Fiftieth year Sabbath (Jubilee) (25:8-17, 23-55)
OBEDIENCE AND DISOBEDIENCE (26)
REDEMPTION OF TITHES AND OFFERINGS (27)

OFFERINGS (1–7)

1:1-17 *The burnt offering.* With just one verse of introduction, Moses begins Leviticus by telling the children of Israel what God "called to Moses from the Tabernacle" concerning worship. First, the burnt offering: The animal offered is to have no physical defects; the person offering it must lay his hand on its head to symbolize that its death will serve as his substitute.

2:1-16 *The grain offering.* This offering was an expression of thanksgiving for God's daily provision of food. The worshiper was to take some fine flour, pour olive oil on it, and give it to the priest, who then would burn it. No yeast or honey was allowed, but salt was always to be added. Salt, as a preservative, was a reminder of God's covenant faithfulness. Any parts of the offering not required to be burned on the altar were to be gifts for the priests.

3:1-17 *The peace offering.* The peace offering was a voluntary offering to bring about peace, or fellowship, with God. It could be a bull, cow, lamb, or goat. In each case, however, the animal had to be blemish-free, and its blood was to be sprinkled on the sides of the altar.

4:1-35 *The sin offering.* The sin offering applied to four kinds of people, all of whom had sinned unintentionally. The sacrifice differed slightly depending on whether the offender was a priest, another leader, a member of the community, or the whole nation, but in each case the sacrifice would "make atonement" for the sin (4:20, 26, 31, 35).

5:1-13 *More sin offerings.* Additional sin offerings were prescribed for three kinds of people: those who refused to tell what they knew about a crime; those who touched some unclean thing; and those who had made rash vows.

5:14–6:7 *The guilt offering.* The guilt offering differed from the sin offering in that it was to be preceded by restitution for the wrong done. Whether the sin was intentional or unintentional, the penalty was the same: full restitution plus a 20 percent penalty plus the sacrifice of a ram.

6:8–7:38 *Further regulations for the offerings.* Further regulations were given for each offering, with the section for each beginning with the phrase "These are the instructions regarding":

- burnt offering (6:9-13)
- grain offering (6:14-23)
- sin offering (6:24-30)
- guilt offering (7:1-10)
- peace offering (7:11-21)

There were also regulations concerning what was to be done with the portion of the sacrifices not actually offered. 7:22-25 specifies that the fat portions of the sacrifice were reserved for the Lord and were not for human consumption. 7:28-36 stresses the portion that was to go to the priests.

ORDINATIONS (8–10)

8:1-36 *Aaron and sons: Anointed along with the altar.* Moses interrupts his recitation of laws to report the ordination of Aaron and his sons as priests. After being clothed with priestly garments, Aaron and his sons—along with the Tabernacle and altar—were anointed with oil. A bull and ram were killed as a sin and burnt offering for Aaron and his sons. The ram's blood was smeared on the priests' right earlobes, their right thumbs, and their right big toes. A "wave offering" (see exposition on Exod. 29:1-28) was presented next. As a final act of consecration, Moses sprinkled blood and oil on Aaron and his sons.

The consecration ceremonies were to last for seven days, during which time Aaron and his sons were to remain inside the Tabernacle.

9:1-24 *At the first sacrifice: He raises his hands, and the fire falls.* As the priests began their ministry, Moses commanded the people to bring their various offerings to the altar, so that God's glory might be seen. Aaron provided the example by sacrificing a calf for his own sin. Then he blessed the people, the glory of God appeared, and the fire fell from heaven and consumed the offering (see 1 Kings 18:38).

10:1-7 *Their apostate fire brings his angry fire.* Two of Aaron's sons, Nadab and Abihu, offered unauthorized fire before the altar. Fire from God immediately consumed both of them. God permitted Israel to mourn the deaths of these two apostates, but forbade Aaron and his remaining two sons, Eleazar and Ithamar, to do so. As God's representatives, they were to identify themselves with his wrath.

10:8-11 *"No drinking while on duty."* Following the death of Nadab and Abihu, God told Aaron that, on pain of death, no priest was to drink wine or strong drink when going into the Tabernacle. This was to help them "distinguish between what is holy and what is ordinary."

10:12-20 *Their uncle is upset, till their father explains.* After reviewing some of the priestly duties with Aaron and his remaining sons, Eleazar and Ithamar, Moses became angry concerning how his nephews had conducted the sin offering. Aaron explained that they were not deliberately disobeying God, but were afraid because of what had just happened to their brothers. Moses seemed satisfied with that explanation.

ORDERLY LIVING (11–15)

11:1-47 *A special diet for a special people.* After the events of 8–10, the recitation of laws continues with a list of permitted and forbidden foods—designated here and elsewhere in Scripture as "clean" and "unclean" animals. The Israelites could eat any animal with cloven hooves that chewed its cud, or any fish that had fins and scales. 20 birds were listed that could not be eaten. If someone touched an unclean animal, he was to wash his clothes and quarantine himself for 24 hours. (see exposition on Deut. 14:3-21)

These regulations were given to keep the Israelites clean. God was holy, and he wanted his people to be holy. While the dietary laws are no longer in force (Acts 10:9-16; Mark 7:19), God still wants his people to be holy (see 1 Pet. 1:16, which quotes 11:44).

12:1-8 *Uncleanness from childbirth.* Though Scripture portrays childbirth as joyous, because of the Fall it also marks the birth of a sinner (Ps. 51:5). Therefore, the new mother was considered ceremonially unclean. If the child was male, the uncleanness lasted for seven days, the baby was circumcised on the eighth day, and the mother's time of purification would continue for another 33 days. If the baby was female, the time of uncleanness and purification was doubled.

13:1-46 *Uncleanness from leprosy.* Anyone suspected of having leprosy was to be brought to the priest for a diagnosis (see Matt. 8:1-4). Procedures were given for determining whether or not a sore was leprous. A leper had to live outside the camp and make his condition known whenever he went out in public. If the diagnosis was uncertain, the person was quarantined for seven days for a closer examination.

13:47-59 *Mildew on clothes.* Regulations were also strict concerning "infectious mildew" on clothing (13:47). If the mildew did not fade or disappear after washing, the clothes were to be burned.

14:1-32 *Ceremonial cleansing of healed lepers.* If the leper recovered, the priest would kill a clean bird and dip a living bird in its blood, sprinkling this blood seven times on the cured leper. The leper would then wash his or her clothes, bathe, and fulfill other prescribed rituals.

14:33-57 *Mildew in houses.* "Infectious mildew" in houses (14:34), or dry rot, was also viewed with great concern. The house was first to be emptied. If evidence of mildew was seen on a wall, that wall was to be removed and the other walls scraped. If the mildew disappeared, a ceremony of cleansing was performed, just as for a cured leper. If the signs continued, however, the entire house was destroyed.

15:1-33 *Sexual uncleanness.* Any genital discharge caused a man to be ceremonially unclean, along with any object or person he touched. The ceremonial cleansing lasted seven days, beginning with the man washing his clothes and bathing in running water, and ending with an offering.

In the case of women, the prescribed cleansing depended on whether or not the discharge was due to her menstrual period (15:19).

OFFERINGS (16–17)

16:1-34 *The Day of Atonement.* While various sacrifices were prescribed for various individual sins, the tenth day of the seventh month was a special day for Israel: On that day the high priest would enter the Most Holy Place and atone for the sins of the entire nation.

Aaron was not to enter the Most Holy Place except on the Day of Atonement. Before entering, he was to offer a sin offering and burnt offering for himself, then bathe and properly clothe himself (preachers need to be saved and cleansed too!).

Two goats were selected by lot, the one to be sacrificed as a sin offering and the other to serve as a "scapegoat." Aaron was to sprinkle the blood of a bull and goat seven times on the mercy seat, then lay hands on the scapegoat and confess all the sins of Israel. The scapegoat was then led outside the camp and released in the wilderness, symbolically carrying away the sins of the people.

As the priests performed the ceremonies of atonement, the people were to spend the day in quiet self-examination and humility, commemorating God's cleansing from sin.

The Day of Atonement (Hebrew *Yom Kippurim*) cleansed Israel from all their sins; the word *all* occurs nine times in chapter 16 in this regard. But the forgiveness lasted only until the next Day of Atonement (Heb. 10:3-4). Yet it looked forward to Christ's once-for-all sacrifice of himself (Heb. 7:20-28; 10:11-14). Isaiah 53:6 depicts Jesus as the scapegoat who bears away the sins of all who believe in him.

17:1-16 *Rules for sacrificing and eating meat.* To offer up animal sacrifices at any place except the Tabernacle was considered murder, resulting in excommunication for the guilty party (17:1-9). Excommunication was also the penalty for eating blood, because the life of the flesh is in the blood, and it is the blood that makes atonement for sin (17:10-14). The penalty was less severe if the person unknowingly consumed the blood of an animal that had died a natural death or had been killed by another animal (17:15-16).

ORDERLY LIVING (18–20)

18:1-30 *Laws of sexual morality.* Sexual relations were prohibited with close relatives, with the same sex, and with animals. The Canaanites practiced such things, and that was one reason why God was using the Israelites to drive them out of the land (18:24-25; see *Canaanites*, p. 862). The reward for observance of these prohibitions would be continuance of life (18:5; see Luke 10:28; Rom. 10:5). The punishment for disobedience would be expulsion from the land, just as the Canaanites were being expelled (18:28).

19:1-37 *Various laws and penalties.* Laws were given concerning obedience to parents, keeping the Sabbath, offering sacrifices in the proper manner, providing for the poor, not cheating employees, not seeking revenge, and not following heathen customs and religious rites.

The Israelites were to "be holy because I, the LORD your God, am holy" (19:2; 11:44; see 1 Pet. 1:15-16). They were also told to "love your neighbor as yourself" (19:18; see Mark 12:31).

20:1-27 *The penalty for pagan perversions.* Excommunication was the penalty for serious sexual sins. Death by stoning was the punishment for devil worship, child sacrifice, sorcery, and various sexual sins. God called upon his people to be separate from the other nations and, again, to "be holy because I, the LORD, am holy" (20:23, 26).

ORDINATIONS (21–22)

21:1–22:16 *Regulations for priests.* Rules and requirements were given for priests, including special rules for high priests. As with the animals sacrificed, the priests had to be free of physical defects. A deformed member of the priestly family could partake of food from the tabernacle (21:22) but could not perform priestly duties.

22:17-33 *Rules for sacrificing.* Animals presented as sacrifices had to be clean (11:1-47) and in prime condition, with no visible defects. The animal could not be sacrificed until it was eight days old. The mother and its offspring could not be killed on the same day.

OFFERINGS (23–25)

23:1-44 *Divinely appointed days.* This chapter outlines procedures for Israel's Sabbath and yearly festivals:

- The Sabbath, the seventh day of each week, was to be Israel's day of rest (23:1-3).
- Passover began at twilight on the 14th day of the first month; the Festival of Unleavened Bread began the next day and continued for seven days (23:4-8). Passover commemorated Israel's deliverance from Egypt; the Festival of Unleavened

Bread recalled the haste with which they had left Egypt (see exposition on Exod. 12:1-20).
- On the Festival of Firstfruits a sheaf of the first grain from the harvest was brought as a gift to the Lord (23:9-14). This festival took place the day after the Sabbath following Passover.
- The Festival of Harvest (Greek *Pentecost*) occurred 50 days after the Festival of Firstfruits; it marked the end of the harvest season and was to include a second grain offering (23:15-22).
- The Festival of Trumpets was observed on the first day of the seventh month and was announced by the loud blowing of trumpets (23:23-25). Originally seen as a call for national assembly, it came to be considered a call for national repentance.
- The Day of Atonement, the 10th day of the seventh month, was a day of fasting and sorrowful contemplation of one's sin (23:26-32; see exposition on 16:1-34).
- The Festival of Shelters was to last seven days, beginning the 15th day of the seventh month. During this joyous festival the people were to live in booths made of leafy branches to remind them of their supernatural deliverance from Egypt (23:33-44).

This was the same as the Festival of the Final Harvest (Exod. 23:16). While Pentecost marked the end of the spring harvest, the Festival of Shelters marked the end of the fall harvest.

24:1-9 *Burning the lamps and baking the bread.* Each morning and evening Aaron was to supply the golden lampstand with fresh oil and trim its wicks. Every Sabbath he was to place the 12 loaves of holy bread in two rows on the gold table (see exposition on Exod. 25:23-30), mix the loaves with incense, and burn them with fire.

Various pagan religions down through the ages have involved the offering of food to gods. But since God does not need food (Ps. 50:12-13), the holy bread had a primarily spiritual focus. While it was primarily spiritual, however, the holy bread could also be used to meet the physical needs of priests (24:9). Later, David and his men would use it to meet their own physical needs (1 Sam. 21:2-6), and still later Christ would cite David's action as an example of the proper relationship between law and compassion (Matt. 12:1-4).

24:10-16, 23 *When he cursed God, they killed him.* During a fight a young man blasphemed God's name. At God's command the witnesses stoned him (24:23).

24:17-22 *An eye for an eye: Harsh but necessary.* The "eye for eye, tooth for tooth" principle of restitution was necessary to maintain order in society. It was also a restraint against the excessive punishments typical of the ancient Near East. See exposition on Matthew 5:21-48.

25:1-34 *Respect for the land: "Give it a regular rest."* The Israelites were to work their land for six years, then allow it to lie fallow the seventh year. God reassured them that if they would obey this command, he would provide them a bumper crop during the sixth year.

Each 50th year was to be the Year of Jubilee, a time of rejoicing. The land was to remain idle and was to be returned to its original owners. Any land sold could be redeemed by the original owner until the jubilee year, when it would automatically return to him. This was to remind Israel that the land actually belonged to God, and they were only "foreigners and tenants," not permanent landowners (25:23).

25:25-28 introduces the law of the "kinsman redeemer" (or "family redeemer," see Ruth 2:20), which protected the property of the poor (see exposition on Deut. 25:5-10).

25:35-55 *The poor: Servants, not slaves.* Israel was to care for its poor, lending them money without interest. When they hired fellow Israelites, they were to treat them as working servants and not as slaves. If a poor Israelite sold himself to a rich foreigner living among them, he had the same rights as if he were working for a fellow Israelite.

Slavery in Bible times was a social and economic institution not unlike in postbiblical times. Israelites could become slaves voluntarily, for financial security or to repay a debt to a fellow Israelite (25:39); or involuntarily, as God's way of punishing their disobedience (Jer. 5:19; 17:4). Voluntary slaves could eventually earn their freedom. Enslavement of foreigners by Israelites was always involuntary, either by capture (1 Sam. 17:9), purchase from a slave market (22:11; 25:44; compare Ezek. 27:13), or birth to a slave (Gen. 17:23; Lev. 22:11).

The Bible never condoned slavery, but it recognized slavery as an economic reality and sought to regulate its practice. Israelite servants were eligible for release after six years of service (Exod. 21:2-4; Deut. 15:12-18), and at the Year of Jubilee even if they hadn't served six years (25:40). If a man died childless, a designated slave, whether Israelite or foreign, could inherit his property.

Despite such safeguards, to be a slave usually meant poverty and lack of control over one's destiny. Nevertheless, to be the slave of a great person was considered an honor; thus Moses and the prophets considered themselves "servants of God," and Paul in NT times would take pride in calling himself Christ's slave (see Rom. 6:16-22; 1 Cor. 6:20; 7:22; Phil. 1:1).

THE NINE FESTIVALS. In all, God designated nine special festivals and rest times for Israel, commemorating his work of creation and redemption:

The three kinds of Sabbath speak of God's *creative* work, coming in endless cycles of seven just as God rested on the seventh day:

- The weekly Sabbath (23:1-3; Exod. 20:8-11)
- The seventh year Sabbath (25:1-7; Exod. 23:10-11)
- The 50th year Sabbath (Jubilee) (25:8-17)

Although their full significance would be seen only after the death and resurrection of the Messiah, the other six annual festivals speak of God's *redemptive* work:

- Passover (23:4-8) speaks of Calvary (1 Cor. 5:7).
- The Festival of Firstfruits (23:9-14) foreshadows the Resurrection (1 Cor. 15:23).
- The Festival of Harvest (Pentecost) (23:15-22) would mark the coming of the Holy Spirit (Acts 2).
- The Festival of Trumpets (23:23-25) speaks of the Rapture and the Second Coming (1 Thess. 4:13-18).
- The Day of Atonement (23:26-32) speaks both of Calvary and of Israel's national restoration at the end of the Tribulation (Rev. 6–19).
- The Festival of Shelters (23:33-44) speaks of God dwelling with his people during the Millennium (Rev. 20:1-6; 21:3).

OBEDIENCE AND DISOBEDIENCE (26)

26:1-13 *The glorious results of obedience.* In return for obedience to his law,

God promised regular rains, bumper crops, and loaded-down fruit trees. He would remove all savage beasts, permitting the people to dwell safely in the land. Five of them would chase 100 of their enemies, and 100 would defeat 10,000.

The prophet Amos, writing when Israel had become a disobedient nation, foretold a restoration of these promises if Israel would repent (compare 26:5 and Amos 9:13).

26:14-46 *The grievous results of disobedience.* Disobedience would result in plagues, terror, drought, wild animals killing children and cattle, terrible famine, defeat, and scattering among the nations. But if, after their disobedience, Israel would come back to God, he would fulfill his promises to Abraham, Isaac, and Jacob, and restore the nation. (See exposition on 2 Chron. 36:15-21.)

REDEMPTION OF TITHES AND OFFERINGS (27)

27:1-29 *"What if I give it, then need it back?"* Finally, guidelines were given for the person who gave a tithe or special offering and then needed to redeem it. Because all Israelites and their possessions were God's by right (25:23; see exposition on Exod. 13:1-16), they were not to take their tithes and offerings lightly (27:10, 33). Monetary amounts were assigned for various cases, with the amounts being suited to the giver's age, gender, and ability to pay.

27:30-34 *"But remember, a tenth belongs to God."* The final verses of Leviticus deal specifically with the redemption of tithes. Moses reminded the people that a tenth of everything—including money, crops, and livestock—belongs to God.

1446 B.C.
The Exodus,
Law given

1443
Kadesh-barnea,
wilderness
wandering begins

1406
Israel
enters Canaan

NUMBERS

BACKGROUND

Having received the law at Sinai (Exodus—Leviticus), Israel prepared for their return to Canaan (1–10). After completing the short journey to the borders of Canaan, however, they rebelled against the Lord (13–14) and were condemned to 40 years of wandering in the wilderness. 15–36 records various events of those years of wandering, as the nation vacillated between spiritual success and apostasy. The book ends with Israel encamped once more within sight of the Promised Land.

AUTHOR

Moses (see *Genesis, Exodus: Author*). There are indications within the book itself that Moses is its author (1:1; 33:2). The detailed, eyewitness account could only have been provided by Moses.

DATE AND LOCATION

Since the Exodus occurred in 1446 B.C. (see *Exodus: Date and Location*), the book could not have been written until about 1406. Moses probably kept a journal of the wandering, so Numbers would actually have been written over the course of the 40 years and put into its final form in 1406.

PURPOSE

- To show that God chastens his people when they disobey.
- To foreshadow the sacrifice of Christ through symbolism such as the red heifer and the bronze serpent (19; 21).
- To continue revealing the attributes of God (Genesis—Leviticus) by showing:
  - ➤ his perseverance in covenant keeping
  - ➤ the balance between his grace and his wrathful chastening

OUTLINE

ISRAEL AT SINAI: PREPARATION (1:1–10:10)
- A census of the people (1)
- Assigning campsites around the Tabernacle (2)
- Census of Levites, their duties assigned (3–4)
- Standards for purity (5)
- Nazirites (6)
- Offerings for the Tabernacle from Israel's leaders (7)
- Dedication of the Levites (8)
- Fiery cloud, silver trumpets (9:1–10:10)

FROM SINAI TO KADESH: FRUSTRATION (10:11–20:13)
- Departure from Sinai (10:11-36)
- Complaints and solutions (11)
- Miriam and Aaron criticize Moses (12)
- Rebellion at Kadesh-barnea (13–14)
- Additional laws (15)
- Rebellion of Korah, Dathan, and Abiram (16)
- Aaron's staff buds (17)
- Duties of Levites (18)
- Purification by the ashes of a red heifer (19)
- Moses strikes the rock (20:1-13)

FROM KADESH TO MOAB: ANTICIPATION (20:14–36:13)
- Edom denies passage to Israel (20:14-21)
- Death of Aaron (20:22-29)
- Bronze serpent (21:1-9)
- Israel defeats Sihon and Og (21:10-35)
- Balak and Balaam (22–24)
- Israelites seduced by Moabites (25)
- Second census of the people (26)
- Joshua to succeed Moses (27)
- Regulations for worship and vows (28–29)
- Regulations for vows (30)
- Israel defeats the Midianites (31)
- Settlement of Transjordan tribes (32)
- Review of the wilderness journey (33)
- Settlement of Canaan described (34–36)

ISRAEL AT SINAI: PREPARATION (1:1–10:10)

1:1-46 *The first census: All able men over 20.* With Israel still at Sinai, Moses was commanded to take a census of all the men 20 years and older who could fight for Israel when they entered Canaan. He selected one man from each tribe to assist him. The total number of fighting men in the 12 tribes was 603,550, suggesting a total population of well over 2 million. (On the tribes of Ephraim and Manasseh, see exposition on Gen. 48:1-22.)

1:47-54 *"But leave out the Levites."* The Levites were excluded from the census because, as those responsible for the Tabernacle, they were not to be warriors.

2:1-34 *Tent sites for 2 million.* God wanted the Israelites to have an organized camp. Each tribe was assigned a place around the centrally positioned Tabernacle. Each tribe had a "banner" (2:2) to identify it. The men appointed to help conduct the census were appointed to lead each tribe. The tribes on each side were given specific marching orders to follow whenever the Israelites broke camp (2:9, 16, 24, 31).

3:1-4 *His two surviving sons.* With Nadab and Abihu dead because of disobedience (Lev. 10:1-7), Aaron had only two sons, Eleazar and Ithamar, to assist him as priests.

3:5-13 *"The Levites are mine, for your service."* Because he had freed the Israelites from Egypt, their firstborn males belonged to the Lord (Exod. 13:1-2, 11-16; 22:29). God now claimed all the male Levites in place of the firstborn of all the tribes and gave them to Aaron as assistants.

3:14-39 *"Now you can number the Levites."* God told Moses to number the Levites, divided into three families according to the three sons of Levi—Gershon, Kohath, and Merari (see Exod. 6:16-20; Moses and Aaron descended from Kohath). This census differed from that of the whole nation in that all Levite males one month and older were counted.

The families of Gershon were to camp near the Tabernacle to the west. They were to care for its curtains and coverings.

The families of Kohath were to camp to the south and care for the Tabernacle furnishings—the Ark of the Covenant, table, lampstand, altars, and vessels.

The families of Merari were to camp to the north and care for the framework of the Tabernacle and courtyard.

Moses, Aaron, Eleazar, and Ithamar were to pitch their tents to the east of the Tabernacle, at its entrance.

The total number of Levite males one month old and older was 22,000.

3:40-51 *Redeeming those not redeemed by Levites.* Moses now counted all the *firstborn* males of Israel *one month and older.* The total was 273 more than the total number of male Levites, who were to have been their ransom (3:5-13). Each of these 273 "extra" firstborn sons were to be redeemed with five shekels of silver.

4:1-49 *Second census of Levites: All males aged 30 to 50.* Next came a census of Levite males between ages 30 and 50, which was apparently the age-span of their official Tabernacle service. The total was 8,580.

The Kohathites were given more detailed instructions concerning care of the Tabernacle furnishings, especially of transporting them from one site to the next. Apparently Eleazar was to supervise these duties (4:16).

The Gershonites' and Merarites' duties were reiterated. Ithamar was assigned to supervise their work.

5:1-4 *"Those who are defiled must depart."* Because God's presence was with Israel, all who were ritually defiled by disease or death had to be removed from the camp until cleansed.

5:5-10 *Confession and restitution plus 20 percent.* This instruction seems to supplement Leviticus 6:1-7. Theft was to be confessed and the stolen goods returned, plus the monetary equivalent of 20 percent of their value. If the one stolen from was now deceased, the goods were given to the priest.

5:11-31 *"Is she innocent or immoral? The test will tell."* If a man suspected his wife of adultery, the priest would make her drink a special mixture of holy water and dust. Her guilt or innocence would be determined by her physical reaction to the drink. This unusual "trial by ordeal" placed justice in God's hands and protected innocent women from the false accusations of jealous husbands.

6:1-21 *The way of the Nazirite.* A Nazirite was one who voluntarily took a vow of separation to the Lord for a fixed period of time. During the days of his vow he was not to drink any strong beverage, cut his hair, or touch a corpse. When he had completed his period of separation, he was to appear before the priest with specified offerings. After his head was shaved and his hair burned, he was permitted to resume normal life.

6:22-27 *A special blessing from priest to people.* God gave Moses the words for a special blessing, speaking of security, grace, and peace, whereby the priests were to bless the people.

7:1-88 *Gifts for the Tabernacle: The legacy of the leaders.* On the day Moses finished setting up the Tabernacle, the 12 tribal leaders who assisted with the first census (1:5-15) brought an offering. (This was probably the same day mentioned in Exod. 40:17; the events of chapter 7 probably preceded those of chapter 1.)

Each leader brought an ox, for a total of 12; and each two leaders brought a wagon, for a total of six. Two of the wagons and four oxen were given to the Gershonites to help them transport the Tabernacle curtains and coverings. Four wagons and eight oxen were given to the Merarites to transport the Tabernacle boards. The Kohathites, who were to carry the Tabernacle furnishings on their shoulders (4:15; 7:9), received no oxen or wagons.

The altar of burnt offerings was dedicated over a period of 12 days (7:10-83). The description of these days is repetitious, for each day a tribal leader brought identical gifts and offerings. While the repetition may seem monotonous, it shows that God valued each gift.

7:84-86 summarizes the silver and gold offerings. The silver weighed a total of 2,400 shekels, and the gold totaled 120 shekels. 7:87-88 summarizes the leaders' sacrificial offerings.

7:89–8:4 *He hears a voice above the Ark.* Whenever Moses entered the Tabernacle, the Lord spoke to him from between the two cherubim above the mercy seat of the Ark of the Covenant. On this occasion, God gave instructions concerning the golden lampstand. This ornate, seven-branched lampstand was fashioned from a single piece of gold. The seven lamps were to light the Holy Place in the Tabernacle.

8:5-19 *Dedication of the Levites.* To be purified for service, the Levites underwent a ritual of sprinkling and shaving. Then the people laid their hands on them, and they were offered "as a special offering" (8:11), indicating that they were being substituted for the firstborn of the other tribes (3:5-13). The Levites in turn laid their hands on two bulls and made atonement for themselves.

The Levites were a gift to the priests to assist with the Tabernacle. They were also a gift to all Israel, to atone for the other tribes. By camping near the Tabernacle they prevented the other tribes from carelessly violating the Tabernacle and incurring God's wrath.

8:20-26 *Duties of the Levites.* Having been purified and dedicated to the Lord, the Levites assumed their responsibilities. 4:3 indicates that Levites began serving at age 30, while 8:24 says they could begin at 25; there may have been a five-year apprenticeship. Retirement from active service was at age 50.

9:1-14 *Passover: Instructions, extensions, but no exemptions.* A year had passed since Israel left Egypt. It was the first month of the year (roughly equivalent to March–April), and they were to observe the Passover on the 14th day, to commemorate their deliverance.

As Passover was about to begin, some men in the camp were ceremonially unclean because of contact with a corpse, and therefore could not participate. They were concerned enough to ask Moses what they should do about it. God told Moses that, when there was a legitimate reason for nonparticipation, the person could observe Passover exactly one month later. If, however, a person willfully refrained from Passover, he or she was to be excommunicated.

Foreigners could participate in Passover if they were willing to meet the same requirements as the Israelites (Exod. 12:48-49).

9:15-23 *The cloud: It moves, they move; it stops, they stop.* The Israelites journeyed through the wilderness as the pillar of cloud or fire led them (see Exod. 13:21-22; 40:34-38). When the cloud hovered over the Tabernacle, Israel remained camped. When the cloud began moving, they broke camp and followed.

10:1-10 *The several sounds of the silver trumpets.* Two silver trumpets were made for the leaders to communicate with the people. The sounding of both trumpets called the nation to gather at the Tabernacle. The sounding of one trumpet called only the leaders. Sounding "short blasts" (10:6) signaled breaking camp and resuming the journey.

FROM SINAI TO KADESH: FRUSTRATION (10:11–20:13)

10:11-36 *Departure from Sinai: The cloud moves, so they move.* On the 20th day of the second month of the second year since Egypt, the cloud began to move, so Israel broke camp and departed from Sinai.

Israel's march was as organized as its camp. Leading the march were Judah, Issachar, and Zebulun, the tribes encamped to the east of the Tabernacle. The Gershonites and Merarites followed, carrying the Tabernacle structure. Then followed Reuben, Simeon, and Gad, from the south. The Kohathites then followed, carrying the Tabernacle furnishings. Then came Ephraim, Manasseh, and Benjamin from the west, and Dan, Asher, and Naphtali from the north.

Moses invited Hobab, his Midianite brother-in-law, to accompany the Israelites.

Whenever the cloud moved (presumably in the morning), indicating Israel should break camp, the Ark set out and Moses claimed God's promises with a prayer: "Arise, O LORD, and let your enemies be scattered! Let them flee before you!" When the Ark rested (presumably in the evening), Moses prayed, "Return, O LORD, to the countless thousands of Israel!"

11:1-3 *The fire of anger falls from heaven.* No sooner had the people begun their journey than for some unspecified reason they complained. God became angry and sent a fire that consumed some of those on the outer edges of the camp. Moses prayed on their behalf, and the fire was quenched.

11:4-23 *"Oh, for the good old days of slavery!"* Tiring of the daily manna, the Israelites quickly forgot their grievous days of slavery in Egypt and remembered only the delicacies they no longer enjoyed. Moses felt overwhelmed by the complaining. He told God that the burden of providing for the people was too great, and asked God to just take his life and relieve him of his responsibilities. Instead, God instructed Moses to select 70 men to assist him. (For a similar incident, see Exod. 18:13-27.)

God promised to send the meat that the Israelites craved. He warned Moses, however, that the meat would become loathsome to them.

11:24-30 *"I only wish they were all so Spirit-filled!"* The Spirit of God fell on the 70 selected men, just as promised, and they began to prophesy. When two of them, Eldad and Medad, continued to prophesy after the others had stopped, Joshua suggested that Moses stop them. Moses refused, saying that he wished all the people would be so Spirit-filled, instead of complaining!

11:31-35 *Death at the dinner table.* God sent meat as promised—a great flock of quail. While the people were enjoying it, God sent a plague (as also promised!) and many of them died.

12:1-16 *Finding fault with the world's meekest man.* Moses' own sister and brother, Miriam and Aaron, criticized him for marrying an Ethiopian. They were also jealous of Moses' leadership role—even though he was the most humble man on earth (12:3)! God severely reprimanded them for speaking against Moses. Miriam, apparently the instigator, was struck with leprosy. Moses prayed for Miriam, and she was healed but was still required to be quarantined from the community for seven days. Israel did not proceed on its journey until Miriam's quarantine ended.

13:1-20 *At Kadesh-barnea: "Is Canaan worth taking?"* While camped at Kadesh-barnea (see 32:8), Moses chose 12 men, one from each tribe, to go into Canaan and search it out, gathering information about the people and their fortifications, the soil and its fertility and vegetation.

13:21-25 *The evidence: Two men to carry a cluster!* As a sample of Canaan's bounty, the spies brought back samples of figs and pomegranates, along with a cluster of grapes so large it took two men to carry it.

13:26–14:9 *The answer: Two say let's go, the rest say no.* After a 40-day tour through the land, the men returned to report to Israel. They all agreed that the land was good. However, 10 of them felt that the Canaanites were so strong that Israel couldn't possibly defeat them. Caleb and Joshua disagreed, urging the people to claim the land at once. The people sided with the 10 who brought the negative report.

14:10-38 *Their dues for distrust: 40 years for 40 days.* God was angry at Israel for their distrust. He threatened to destroy them all and make a greater nation from Moses and his descendants. Moses interceded for Israel, arguing that God's reputation with the Egyptians would be damaged if anything happened to Israel (compare Exod. 32:1-14). He appealed to God's mercy.

God promised to pardon Israel. However, he assured Moses that the present generation, who had witnessed his power and yet distrusted him, would die before Israel reached the Promised Land. Only Caleb and Joshua (14:29-30) would enter Canaan. God specified that the death sentence would apply only to those 20 years and older (14:29-31).

Israel had rejected a good land because they doubted God's ability to give it to them. For every day that the spies had gotten to see Canaan and yet rejected it, Israel would spend one year in the wilderness—as God waited for the present generation of disbelieving adults to die off. The 10 men who had brought the negative report, however, died immediately by a plague.

On "punishing the children for the sins of their parents" (14:18), see exposition on Ezekiel 18:1-18.

14:39-45 *They repent, but it's too late.* When the Israelites heard God's judgment against them, they confessed that they had sinned and began pre-

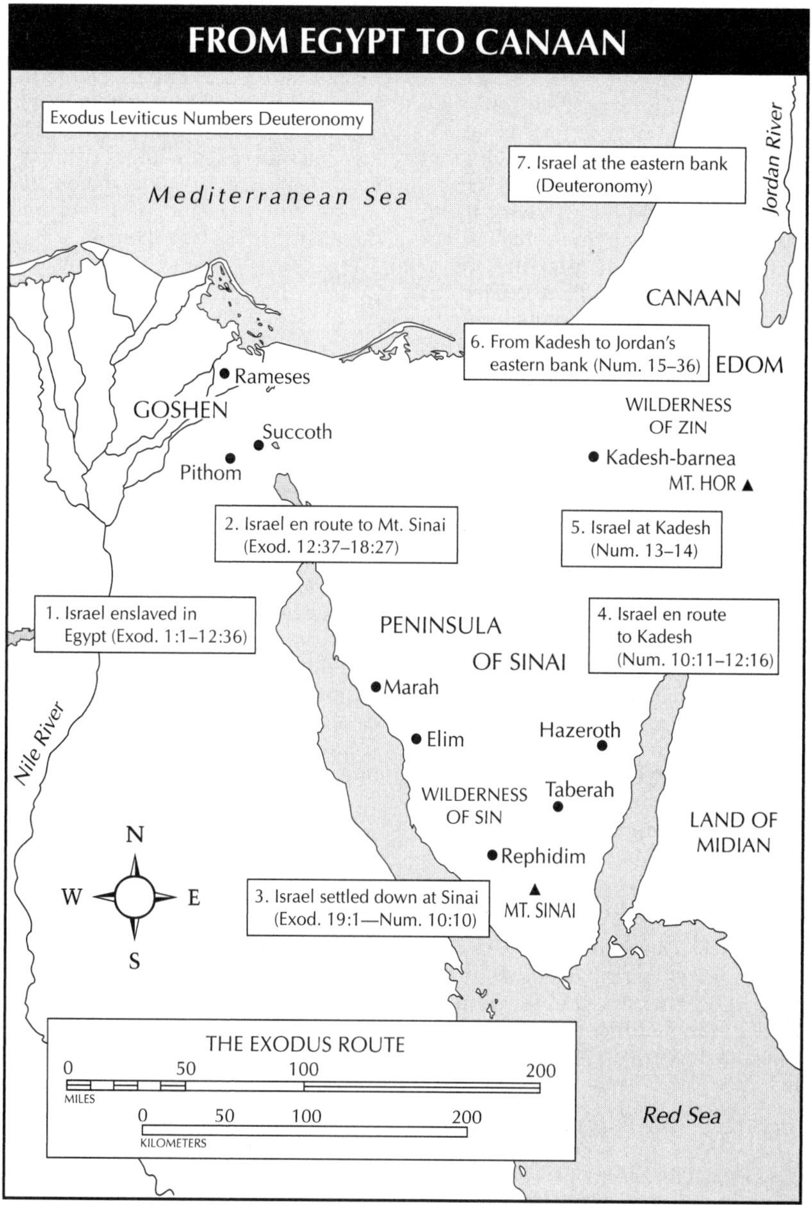
FROM EGYPT TO CANAAN
Exodus Leviticus Numbers Deuteronomy
Mediterranean Sea
7. Israel at the eastern bank (Deuteronomy)
Jordan River
CANAAN
6. From Kadesh to Jordan's eastern bank (Num. 15–36)
EDOM
Rameses
GOSHEN
Succoth
Pithom
WILDERNESS OF ZIN
Kadesh-barnea
MT. HOR
2. Israel en route to Mt. Sinai (Exod. 12:37–18:27)
5. Israel at Kadesh (Num. 13–14)
1. Israel enslaved in Egypt (Exod. 1:1–12:36)
PENINSULA OF SINAI
4. Israel en route to Kadesh (Num. 10:11–12:16)
Marah
Nile River
Elim
Hazeroth
WILDERNESS OF SIN
Taberah
LAND OF MIDIAN
N
W
E
S
Rephidim
3. Israel settled down at Sinai (Exod. 19:1—Num. 10:10)
MT. SINAI
THE EXODUS ROUTE
0
50
100
200
MILES
0
50
100
200
KILOMETERS
Red Sea

paring to move forward into Canaan. They did so in spite of Moses' warning that God would not be with them, and they were horribly humiliated by the enemy.

15:1-21 *Offerings to please the Lord.* The Lord gave instructions on how to offer grain and drink offerings with the burnt or fellowship offerings (15:1-16). These burnt offerings were to be brought for special vows, freewill offerings, or festival offerings, as a pleasing aroma to the Lord. Then he gave instructions concerning the first-fruits that were to be offered once Israel was in the Promised Land (15:17-21).

Though few historical details are given, 15:1–20:1 actually covers some 38 or 39 years, the majority of the Israelites' 40-year journey to Canaan.

15:22-29 *Offerings to appease the Lord.* Next came instructions about burnt offerings for those sinning unintentionally.

15:30-36 *When no appeasement is possible.* No sacrifice was provided for the one who sinned deliberately. That person was to be excommunicated. "Brazenly" (15:30) literally means "with a high hand." 15:32-36 records a real-life example of such deliberate sin. A man willfully violated the Sabbath by gathering sticks; in this case the Lord prescribed death by stoning.

15:37-41 *The tassels are silent reminders.* The Israelites were to attach tassels to their garments, to remind them of God's commandments and to promote meditation on those commandments.

16:1-11 *Korah, Dathan, and Abiram rebel.* Moses and Aaron were challenged by 250 of Israel's leaders who were envious of their positions of honor. The rebellion was led by Korah, a fellow Kohathite, along with Dathan and Abiram. Moses proposed that they all appear before the Lord and let *him* decide who would be the leader.

16:12-19 *The rebels' charge: "You'll destroy us in this desert."* Dathan and Abiram refused to appear before the Lord and accused Moses of failing to take them to the Promised Land. The meeting proceeded without them; the Lord displayed his glory before the whole congregation of Israel and threatened to destroy them all.

16:20-35 *The rebels' fate: Destroyed by the desert.* When Moses interceded, God instructed the congregation to withdraw from the tents of Korah, Dathan, and Abiram so that they would not die along with those rebels. After the congregation had retreated, the ground miraculously opened up and swallowed Korah, Dathan, and Abiram. The other 250 rebels were destroyed by fire.

16:36-40 *Recycled as a reminder.* God instructed Moses to take the censers of the deceased rebels and make them into sheets to cover the altar. This covering would serve as a reminder to all Israel that anyone who was not a descendant of Aaron was forbidden to offer incense to the Lord.

16:41-50 *He stands between the dead and the living.* The people blamed Moses and Aaron for the death of the rebels, so God brought a plague on the people. Moses quickly instructed Aaron to make atonement for the congregation. As Aaron stood literally "between the living and the dead" (16:48), the plague ceased, but not before 14,700 more had died.

17:1-13 *A stick grows sprouts.* Since Aaron's authority had been challenged by Korah's rebellion, God provided miraculous proof of Aaron's preeminence. A leader from each tribe was told to put his name on his staff and lay it before the Lord, along with Aaron's staff. On the next day Aaron's staff sprouted blossoms and almonds. This was a clear indication that he was God's choice to be priest and that his position was not to be contested. Moses was told to preserve Aaron's rod before the Ark of the Covenant (17:4, 10) as a reminder of this disastrous rebellion.

18:1-7 *"They, and they alone, can help you."* After once more declaring his choice of Aaron and his sons as priests, God decreed that the rest of the tribe of Levi could assist them in their work. No one else was to come near the Tabernacle to serve in any capacity, and not even the Levites were to handle the "sacred objects" (18:3).

18:8-20 *"This part is for the priests."* Since the priests would not be receiving land in Canaan, remuneration for their services was to come through the offerings. Any portions of offerings not burned on the altar were to be gifts for the priests. This, said the Lord, was to signify that "I am your inheritance and your share" (18:20).

18:21-32 *"They'll tithe to you; then you'll tithe to me."* Because the Levites would have no land in Canaan, they would receive all the tithes of Israel. From those tithes they would tithe to the Lord.

19:1-22 *The ashes of the red heifer.* For ceremonial cleansing, a red heifer was to be selected and burned outside the camp, and the ashes saved. Anyone needing cleansing would be sprinkled with the ashes mixed with water. Anyone who touched a corpse, entered the dwelling of someone who had died, or touched a grave was ceremonially unclean and was to be purified by the ashes. Anyone refusing to be purified in this manner was to be excommunicated. The heifer's red color may have represented blood.

20:1 *The death of Miriam (and her whole generation).* Moses' sister Miriam died in the first month of the 40th year of wilderness wandering, making her among the last of her disbelieving generation to die before Israel reached Canaan.

20:2-13 *He says, "Speak," but they strike instead.* Once again Israel complained about their lack of water. They felt sorry for themselves, saying it would have been better had they died in Korah's rebellion or remained in Egypt. Once before Moses had been instructed to strike a rock, and it had given water (Exod. 17:3-6). This time Moses and Aaron were told to *speak* to the rock. Instead, they angrily struck it. Their disobedience disqualified them from leading Israel into Canaan.

FROM KADESH TO MOAB: ANTICIPATION (20:14–36:13)

20:14-21 *A reasonable request rudely refused.* As Israel traveled around the southern end of the Dead Sea before turning northward, Moses asked the king of Edom (descendants of Esau) to let the Israelites pass through his land. He assured the king that Israel would not stray from the trade route and would pay for any water they used along the way. The king refused the request. For the historical consequences of this refusal, see exposition on both Jeremiah 49:7-22 and Obadiah.

20:22-29 *Aaron dies, the torch of priesthood is passed.* Warned that his death was imminent, Aaron, his son Eleazar, and Moses went up Mount Hor. There Moses removed Aaron's priestly garments and placed them on Eleazar, signifying the transfer of the priesthood from father to son. Aaron died, and Moses and Eleazar returned to the camp.

21:1-3 *Israel defeats Arad.* The king of Arad attacked Israel and took some prisoners. Israel retaliated and defeated them.

21:4-9 *A snake problem solved by a serpent!* Again the Israelites complained and God sent a plague of serpents, causing many to die. Moses was instructed to erect a bronze serpent on a pole, and all who looked upon the serpent in faith were healed. Jesus would see this as a foreshadowing of his death on the cross (John 3:14).

21:10-20 *On toward Moab.* The account of Israel's travel to the border of Moab is sketchy at best. The writer reports that further details are given in the "Book of the Wars of the LORD," which has been lost to history. When Israel came to Beer (Hebrew, "well"), the Lord gave them water. They responded in song, "Spring up, O well . . ."

21:21-30 *Israel defeats Sihon.* Israel requested permission from Sihon, king of the Amorites, to pass through his land, but he refused. Israel fought the Amorites and defeated them. The war was recounted in poetic verse (21:27-30; see similar poetry in Exod. 15:1-21; Judg. 5:1-31).

21:31-35 *Og and his men try; Og and his men die.* Og, king of Bashan, and his people tried to do what Sihon and the Amorites could not do—stop Israel. Encouraged by God, Israel had quick and complete success over Og. Though Moses' account is brief, the victory would be remembered for centuries to come (Pss. 135:10-11; 136:18-20).

22:1-20 *Balak's deal for Balaam: Cash for curses.* Israel "traveled to the plains of Moab and camped east of the Jordan River, across from Jericho," where they would remain during the rest of the events recorded in Numbers (26:3; 33:50; 35:1; 36:13). Balak, king of Moab, knew of Israel's success against the Amorites and feared what Israel might do to him. Along with the "leaders of Midian" (22:4, 7), he offered to pay Balaam, a diviner, to curse Israel. God permitted Balaam to go to Israel, but warned him to speak only the words God gave him.

22:21-35 *Which one is the real donkey?* As Balaam traveled to Israel, God caused his angel to stand in Balaam's way. Balaam didn't see the angel, but his donkey did. Twice it tried to avoid the angel, but each time Balaam beat it. The second time, the donkey spoke to Balaam, and then he saw the angel—who was about to kill him. Once again God warned Balaam to speak only the words he would give him.

22:36–24:25 *He can't curse what God has blessed.* Arriving in Israel, Balaam tried to satisfy Balak and curse Israel . . . but he blessed Israel instead! His second and third attempted curses resulted in more blessings. Balaam's final words about Israel (24:10-25) included references to a "star" and "scepter"—prophecies ultimately fulfilled by the Messiah. See exposition on Ezra 6:1-12; Jude 1:11.

25:1-18 *Israelites seduced by Moabites.* While Israel was encamped at Acacia Grove near Moab, the people engaged in immorality with Moabite women and worshiped their gods, including the Baal of Peor. God instructed Moses to have the participants in this apostasy executed. (For Balaam's key role in this apostasy, see exposition on 31:1-54.)

Despite this threat of execution, an Israelite brazenly brought a Midianite woman into his tent. Phinehas, son of Eleazar, was angered by this outrageous action and speared them both. As a reward for his zeal, Phinehas was promised an everlasting priesthood (see Josh. 24:33; Ps. 106:30-31).

God blamed the Midianites for both of these incidents and told the Israelites to take revenge upon them (25:16-18; 31:1-3).

26:1-65 *The second census of the people.* God called for a new census. Like the earlier one (1:1-54), this was to include males 20 and older who could fight. The total this time was 601,730. Since the first census, five tribes had decreased in size, and seven had increased. Overall, Israel had shrunk by almost 2,000 men.

God instructed Moses concerning distribution of land in Canaan. Larger tribes were to receive larger portions of land, and smaller tribes were to receive smaller portions.

The Levite men were counted again; they totalled 23,000—an increase of 1,000.

As 26:64-65 indicates, with the exception of Joshua and Caleb, all the adult males numbered in the first census had died in the wilderness, just as God had predicted (14:20-23, 29-32).

27:1-11 *Five determined daughters.* Zelophehad, a man from the tribe of Manasseh, died without a male heir. His daughters appealed to Moses to give them their father's inheritance in the land so that his name would not disappear from the clan. This was a unique situation; Moses brought their appeal to the Lord for his judgment. The Lord granted their request and gave Moses instructions for similar situations that might arise in the future.

27:12-14 *Permitted to look, but not to live there.* God told Moses to go up "the mountains east of the river," from where he would be able to view the Promised Land before dying. As God had told him, he would be barred from entering the land because of his disobedience (20:7-13). (Moses' actual viewing of the land and his death are not recorded until Deuteronomy 34, after his final exposition of the law. There, the place of his death is called Mount Nebo [Deut. 32:49] and Pisgah Peak [Deut. 3:27; 34:1].)

27:15-23 *"Joshua has my Spirit, so he'll succeed you."* God informed Moses that Joshua would be the one to succeed him as Israel's leader, because he was one "who has the Spirit in him" (27:18). Moses presented Joshua to Eleazar and to the whole congregation. He laid his hands on him, symbolizing the transferal of office, and publicly gave him his charge.

28:1–29:40 *Festivals and offerings: Why, what, and when.* 28–29 gives details about offerings and festivals, supplementing the instructions in Leviticus 1–7; 16–17; 23–25. The offerings are dealt with according to their frequency of observance, starting with daily and ending with yearly offerings.

30:1-16 *Regulations for vows, for him and her.* All vows made by men had to be kept. If a woman was unmarried and lived under the authority of her father, he could either approve or annul her vows. A married woman was under the authority of her husband. He could approve or annul her vows, even if they had been made before marriage.

31:1-54 *Punished for Peor: Five kings and a false prophet.* God had told Moses to take revenge against the Midianites for what had happened at Peor (25:16-18). He was to select 1,000 warriors from each tribe. The Israelites defeated the Midianites and killed their five kings.

They also killed the false prophet Balaam; although 24:25 states that Balaam returned to his home after failing to curse Israel, he had apparently joined with the Midianites. According to 31:16 and Revelation 2:14, Balaam was the one primarily to blame for Israel's apostasy at Peor.

Moses was angry when he learned that the army leaders had spared the Midianite women and children. He ordered them to kill all the male children and all the women who were not virgins and could therefore have been among those who had led Israel into sin.

Moses was instructed to divide the spoils equally among the Israelites, with one-half going to those who had fought for Israel and one-half going to the rest of the people. Israel didn't lose a single man in the battle with the Midianites. They showed their gratitude for this by bringing all the gold of the spoils to the Lord.

32:1-42 *"You can have the east, if you'll help us win the west."* The men of Reuben and Gad saw that the land Israel had already conquered east of the Jordan River was suitable for their cattle. They asked that it be given to them for their inheritance instead of land on the western side.

Moses was angry with these tribes, assuming they wanted to avoid helping the other tribes conquer Canaan. The Reubenites and Gadites protested that they did intend to help. Moses finally agreed to their request, but only after warning them that they could not return to their land until the conquest was complete.

"Half the tribe of Manasseh" chose to join Reuben and Gad east of Jordan (32:33).

33:1-49 *His journal of the journey.* Moses gave a review of Israel's travels and encampments, from the time they left Rameses in Egypt to their present campsite in the plains of Moab.

33:50-56 *The bottom line: Destroy or be destroyed.* God told Moses to warn Israel to drive out all the inhabitants of Canaan and destroy all their pagan shrines and other symbols of worship. Otherwise the people of the land would become irritants to them, and the punishment meant for the Canaanites would fall on Israel.

Pagan shrines, also called "high places," were a common feature of pagan religion in ancient times, as worshipers sought literally to get closer to their gods by being nearer to the heavens. These shrines would remain a common feature of the landscape in the Promised Land because the Israelites either failed to destroy those built by pagans or built them for their own worship (1 Kings 14:23). Even some of Israel's better kings failed to remove these vestiges of paganism (see exposition on 1 Kings 3:2-4; 15:14; 2 Kings 12:3).

34:1–35:8 *Division of Canaan described for each tribe.* God specified the boundaries of the land of the nine and a half western tribes. Moses reminded Israel that Reuben, Gad, and half of Manasseh had already been assigned land east of the Jordan. Joshua and Eleazar were to oversee the distribution of land to the 12 tribes, with one man from each tribe assisting them. The Levites were to receive 48 cities and the pasturelands around those cities (35:1-8).

35:9-34 *Cities of refuge.* Israel was to set aside six "cities of refuge"—to which those guilty of accidental manslaughter could flee from the avenger of blood. If one who had killed intentionally fled to one of these cities, he would be put to death. If the killing had resulted from sudden anger, without forethought, the congregation would decide whether it was manslaughter or murder. A murder conviction required the testimony of two witnesses (35:30). The person granted asylum had to remain in the city of refuge until the death of the high priest. Should he leave before that time, the avenger of blood could kill him and not be charged with murder.

36:1-12 *Those five determined daughters, again!* Moses had granted the request of Zelophehad's daughters to receive their father's inheritance in Canaan (27:1-11). Now, some elders of their tribe asked Moses what would happen should those daughters marry outside their tribe: Wouldn't some of their tribe's inheritance transfer to the other tribe? Moses agreed and told the five that they would have to either marry within their own tribe or lose their inheritance. All five married within their tribe.

36:13 *"By the Jordan, across from Jericho."* As Numbers ends, Moses notes once more that Israel was encamped in the plains of Moab, just across the Jordan from Jericho (22:1; 26:3; 33:50; 35:1).

❖ ❖ ❖

PEOPLE TO REMEMBER FROM NUMBERS

BALAAM

Key Fact: Tried to curse Israel (22–24)
Father: Beor (22:5)
Occupation: Diviner (22:7)
Death: Recorded in 31:8
Total Bible References: 61
Key References: 22–24; 31:16; Deut. 23:3-5; Josh. 24:9-10; Neh. 13:1-2; Mic. 6:5; 2 Pet. 2:15; Jude 1:11; Rev. 2:14

Balaam Speaks

I know what people are saying behind my back: "There goes Balaam, the best prophet money can buy!" But it could be worse: They could be talking about how a four-legged creature made a donkey out of its two-legged rider! (22:7, 22-31)

On my recent assignment in Israel, of course, I wasn't paid a cent. Talk about sheer frustration! There I was, standing on the hills of Jordan, looking out over the Israelite camp. My assignment seemed simple enough: Pronounce a curse on Israel. But that was far easier said than done! When I opened my mouth to blast out against the "chosen nation," instead of curses I heard words of blessing come forth! Well, I may have been frustrated, but those who had hired me were absolutely furious! (22–24)

But all is not lost. I was able to instigate some sexual involvement between some Israelite men and Moabite women. While I couldn't curse them, I did manage to corrupt them! In fact, rumor has it that more than 20,000 Israelites were killed by their God for this little escapade. Not a bad day's work for a prophet who never got paid! (25:1, 9; 31:16; Rev. 2:14)

But I'll have to admit to being a little worried; things are just too quiet around here. What if Israel survives all this? What if they destroy Moab as I unwillingly predicted they would? Worse still, what if they come looking for me? (31:8)

Spiritual Lessons from Balaam

- God has many ways of humbling us when we stubbornly refuse to do his will (23:22-30).
- We should not let the love of money cause us to misuse our God-given abilities (2 Pet. 2:15; Jude 1:11).
- When Satan and his servants fail to defeat us one way, they may attack us on another front (24:10; 25:1-3; 31:16; Rev. 2:14).

Key Verses
"They have wandered off the right road and followed the way of Balaam son of Beor, who loved to earn money by doing wrong. But Balaam was stopped from his mad course when his donkey rebuked him with a human voice" (2 Pet. 2:15-16).

MIRIAM
Key Facts: Moses' sister, a prophetess (26:59; Exod. 15:20)
Birth: Recorded in 26:59
Father: Amram (26:59)
Mother: Jochebed (26:59)
Brothers: Moses and Aaron (1 Chron. 6:3)
Death: Recorded in 20:1
Total Bible References: 14
Key References: 12:1-16; Exod. 2:1-10; 15:20-21; Deut. 24:9; Mic. 6:4

Miriam Speaks
Spring has finally arrived, and the desert is blooming with wildflowers. But for me it is late autumn. I know death is near. Both Aaron and Moses stopped by this morning. I felt constrained once again to express my deep regret to Moses for that shameful time when I criticized his choice of a wife and actually tried to undermine his ministry. As usual, he reassured me that he had long since forgiven me. And he reminded me of the terrible price I paid for my criticism. How could I have forgotten that! (12:1-16; 20:1)

He also reminded me that, had I not persuaded an Egyptian princess to hire our own mother to raise him, our nation might still be in Egypt rather than marching toward the Promised Land! It's truly amazing how God uses us in our human frailty—I only hid Moses because he was my little brother; but just look what has come of it! (Exod. 2:1-9)

I must remember to give Aaron my tambourine—just for safekeeping. I don't want anyone to discard it after I'm gone. After all, maybe it will wind up in a museum someday. They would probably make a sign saying something like "tambourine once played by Miriam, Israel's first prophetess." That makes me smile and feel a little better. What a story this old instrument could tell about our celebration after our supernatural escape from the Egyptians. Let's see, what were the words of that song? "I will sing to the LORD, for he has triumphed gloriously. . . ." I hope that that faithful old tambourine will be treasured for generations to come and that it will always remind our people of how God miraculously brought our nation into being. (Exod. 15:1-21)

Spiritual Lessons from Miriam

- Cain was wrong! We *are* to be our brother's keeper (Gen. 4:9). Miriam's faithful care of her infant brother assured a deliverer and lawgiver for Israel (Exod. 2:1-10). A seemingly insignificant act of concern can have far-reaching results.
- We should be careful about criticizing our leaders—especially those who look after our spiritual needs. We may not pay for such rebellion the same way Miriam did, but the results can be equally disastrous (12:1-16; Ps. 105:15; 1 Tim. 5:17, 19; Heb. 13:7, 17).

Key Verses
"Then Miriam the prophet, Aaron's sister, took a tambourine and led all the women in rhythm and dance. And Miriam sang this song: 'I will sing to the LORD, for he has triumphed gloriously; he has thrown both horse and rider into the sea'" (Exod. 15:20-21).

1446 B.C.
The Exodus, Law given

1443
Kadesh-barnea, wilderness wandering begins

1406
Israel at Jordan, events of Deuteronomy, Israel enters Canaan

DEUTERONOMY

BACKGROUND

In about 1406 B.C., having nearly completed their 40-year "sentence" of wilderness wandering (Num. 15–36) due to their rebellion at Kadesh-barnea (Num. 13–14), the Israelites were encamped "in the land of Moab east of the Jordan River" (compare 1:5 with Num. 36:13). Deuteronomy, which means "second law," is a collection of history lessons and teachings by Moses, aimed especially at those Israelites who would have been younger than 20 at the time of the Exodus (Num. 14:29-31), and therefore might never have heard a formal presentation of the law.

AUTHOR

Moses (see *Genesis, Exodus: Author*). There are indications within the book itself that Moses is its author (1:1; 4:44). The detailed eyewitness accounts and speeches attributed to Moses could only have been recorded by Moses himself or by someone working closely with him, such as Joshua. The NT specifically refers to Moses as the author of parts of Deuteronomy (Matt. 19:7 refers to 24:1-4; Luke 20:28 refers to 25:5-6).

DATE AND LOCATION

Since the Exodus took place in 1446 B.C. (see *Exodus: Date and Location*), Deuteronomy could not have been written until about 1406 B.C. Moses probably kept a journal of the wanderings, so Deuteronomy, like Numbers, would have been written over the course of the 40 years and put into its final form as Israel prepared to enter Canaan.

PURPOSE

- To give detailed instruction about God's law and his covenant with Israel:
  - Genesis tells of Israel's *election.*

  - ➤ Exodus tells of its *redemption.*
  - ➤ Leviticus tells of its *sanctification.*
  - ➤ Numbers tells of its *direction.*
  - ➤ Deuteronomy tells of its *instruction.*
- To exhort Israel to pay attention to God's instruction; the words *do, keep,* and *observe* appear 177 times in Deuteronomy.
- To show that God rewards obedience and punishes disobedience.

UNIQUE FEATURES

- As does Leviticus, Deuteronomy places great emphasis on the word of God (4:1-2, 9; 11:18-20; 12:32; 30:11-14).
- Jesus began his ministry by quoting from Deuteronomy three times in answer to three temptations by the devil:
  - ➤ Matthew 4:4 quotes 8:3.
  - ➤ Matthew 4:7 quotes 6:16.
  - ➤ Matthew 4:10 quotes 6:13.
- Key prophecies in Deuteronomy provide a basic outline for all of Israel's history:

Prophecy	*Fulfillment recorded in*
Victorious entrance into Canaan (7:2; 9:1-3; 31:3)	Joshua
Sin while in Canaan (31:16-29)	Judges—2 Kings 16; 18–24
Exile (4:26-28)	2 Kings 17; 25; Ezekiel—Daniel
Return from exile (30:1-3)	Ezra—Nehemiah

OUTLINE

SERMON ONE (1:1–4:43)
- Remembering the wilderness (1–3)
- Remembering Sinai: A call to obedience (4:1-43)

SERMON TWO (4:44–26:19)
- The Ten Commandments reviewed (4:44–5:33)
- A call for wholehearted commitment (6)
- Blessings of the chosen people (7)
- Blessings of the chosen land (8)
- Remembering the rebellions (9)
- The Ten Commandments given again (10:1-11)
- A call for wholehearted commitment stated again (10:12-22)
- Love and obedience demanded and rewarded (11)
- False religions, true worship (12)
- False prophets (13)
- Various regulations (14–15)
- Three main festivals reviewed (16:1-17)
- Various regulations (16:18–25:19)
- Stewardship obligations (26)

SERMON THREE (27–30)
- Blessings and curses (27–28)

SERMON ONE (1:1–4:43)

1:1-8 *Remembering the wilderness: Introduction.* As Deuteronomy opens, what should have been an 11-day walk (1:2) had tragically stretched into 40 years of wandering. Now, as the Israelites camped by the Jordan, ready to enter the Promised Land, Moses began a series of dynamic sermons to remind them of, and teach them about, their special relationship to God. In 1–4 he will trace their journey from Sinai to the Jordan.

1:9-18 *70 Spirit-filled assistants.* Before leaving Mount Sinai, Moses had gazed across the seemingly endless throngs of Israelites and realized he couldn't lead them alone. Following his father-in-law's advice, he appointed 70 Spirit-filled elders to assist him (Exod. 18:13-27). On OT manifestations of the Holy Spirit, see exposition on 1 Samuel 9:27–10:8.

1:19-46 *Kadesh-barnea: "You refused him, so he refused you."* Moses next recalled the disastrous Kadesh-barnea rebellion (Num. 13–14), when Israel had refused to enter Canaan. Israel's initial disobedience (1:26) led from one sin to another, but it all stemmed from their unbelief in God's promises (1:32).

Since Israel had refused God, he refused them; he barred all adult Israelites from entering Canaan (1:35, 39) and condemned them to wander in the wilderness (1:40; Num. 14:26-37).

The old saying "What goes around comes around" surely fit these disobedient people. What they sowed in refusing to enter the land they reaped by dying in the wilderness. God was offended by Israel's disbelief, so he judged them harshly.

When the death sentence was pronounced, the Israelites changed their minds, but it was too late (1:41-46; Num. 14:39-45). Many people are sorry for their sin only after they get caught.

2:1-3 *The 38 lost years of wandering.* Moses was not exaggerating when he said, "We wandered around Mount Seir for a long time." That "long time" was 38 years! In Numbers, Moses covered those 38 years in chapters 15–19, which give almost no historical detail. In Deuteronomy, he covers them in one verse!

After the 38 years, God decreed that Israel had wandered "long enough," and he directed them to "turn northward" toward Canaan.

2:4-23 *"Don't pick a fight with your relatives."* As the Israelites turned northward, God told them not to disturb those whose land they must pass through who were "your relatives"; this included the Edomites, descendants of Esau, and the Moabites and Ammonites, descendants of Lot.

2:24-37 *"But if they attack first, you can fight back."* If, however, any of those nations started a confrontation, Israel would be allowed to defend itself. When the Ammonite King Sihon attacked, Israel "conquered all his towns and completely destroyed everyone—men, women, and children" (2:34).

Why did God allow the killing of children on this and similar occasions? These children were being raised in immorality and hatred of God (see *Canaanites,* p. 862); their death before the age of accountability not only spared them a similar life of godlessness but also probably secured them a place in heaven.

3:1-11 *The man with the big bed.* Continuing north on the east side of the Jordan, Israel defeated Og, the Amorite king of Bashan (3:1-11; see exposition on Num. 21:31-35). Og was no little man. His iron bed was more than 13 feet long and 6 feet wide.

3:12-20 *The territory of the two and a half.* The tribes of Reuben, Gad, and half of Manasseh settled east of the Jordan, from the Dead Sea in the south to the Sea of Galilee in the north (Num. 32:1-42).

3:21-22 *Moses reassures his successor.* Moses recalled reassuring Joshua that, just as God had given victory over Sihon (2:30-33) and Og (3:1-3), he would be with Israel as they entered the Promised Land (Josh. 1:1-9).

3:23-29 *But for Moses, the answer was still no.* God had already told Moses he could not enter the Promised Land (Num. 20:12; 27:12-14). When Moses asked again, the answer was still no, but God graciously promised him he would get to climb Mount Pisgah for a breathtaking view of the land (34:1).

4:1-8 *Remembering Sinai: "If you want to live, keep his laws."* Having reviewed the 38 years of desert wandering, Moses took his readers back to the giving of the law at Sinai. He called them to obey the law "so that you may live" (4:1). There's a great difference between the law that came through Moses and the grace that came by Jesus Christ (John 1:17). The law said, "Obey and live; disobey and die." Grace says, "Believe and live."

4:9-14 *"And teach your children the miraculous message."* Israel was to tell their children and grandchildren about the miracles at Sinai and to teach the law revealed there.

4:15-31 *Idols should be avoided. . . .* Moses warned against idol worship, noting that the Lord is both jealous (4:24) and merciful (4:31). Israel was his property, and he was zealous toward his own as a consuming fire. If God's children turned from him to worship images or nature, he would scatter them among the nations.

4:32-40 *". . . for we have known him."* Israel alone of all people since Creation had been chosen by God, had heard him speak, and had witnessed his mighty power in delivering them from Egypt. Such gracious love demanded obedience to God's Word.

4:41-43 *Salvation cities east of Jordan.* Revenge was a popular concept among the Gentiles but was not to be allowed among God's people. To help hold this human tendency in check, God established six cities of refuge, three on the east side of Jordan and three on the west, where anyone who had committed involuntary manslaughter could take refuge until the matter was settled. The three eastern cities are named here; the western cities were named after Israel entered Canaan (19:1-13; Josh. 20:7).

SERMON TWO (4:44–26:19)

4:44-49 *Another look at the law.* Having reviewed Israel's fruitless wilderness wanderings, Moses moved on to a restating of the law. This new section begins with the statement, "This is the law" (4:44), and continues through 26:19.

5:1-27 *"First, consider the commandments."* Moses began by restating the Ten Commandments (Exod. 20) for the new generation of Israelites. He reminded them that these commandments were written on stone tablets by God himself and that Israel had promised to hear and obey all that God commanded (5:27).

5:28-33 *The rest of the rules: "Then you will live."* God took the people up on their promise to hear and obey, commanding them to hear the rest of the law and to walk in all his ways; "then you will live long and prosperous lives" (5:33).

5:31 names three parts of the law, which can be equated with three sections of Exodus:

- commands (Exod. 20:1-17)
- laws guiding community life (Exod. 21–23)
- regulations guiding worship (Exod. 25–31)

6:1-5 *The bottom line of the law.* Having exhorted the people to keep the law, Moses reminded them of God's supreme majesty and urged them to "love the LORD your God with all your heart, all your soul, and all your strength" (6:5). When a scribe asked Jesus what he considered the essence of the law, he quoted 6:5 (Matt. 22:34-40). It was the "bottom line" for ancient Israel and it is the bottom line for Christians today.

"Hear, O Israel! The LORD is our God, the LORD alone" (6:4), also translated "The LORD our God, the LORD is one," is known in Judaism as the "Shema" (Hebrew, "hear"). It is one of the four Scriptures carried in the phylacteries still used by Orthodox Jews (6:8; 11:18; see exposition on Exod. 13:1-16).

6:6-25 *Teaching, writing, and "wearing" the law.* God's Word was to be in the heart as well as in the head. Whenever possible, night or day, parents were to teach their children the Scriptures. Had the people really done this, the failures of the book of Judges would have been avoided.

For the "wearing" of the law (6:8), see 11:18 and exposition on Exodus 13:1-16.

7:1-5 *No compromise with the condemned.* The seven nations mentioned in 7:1 represented all Gentiles currently living in the Promised Land. All were to be destroyed—men, women, and children. For Israel to do less than this would be to compromise their devotion to God.

7:6-11 *". . . because he chose to love us."* The Israelites were a holy people because God had chosen them above all others. God's love for and favor toward them was based not on their worthiness but on his unconditional love.

7:12-26 *Obedience means blessing and freedom from fear.* If the people would faithfully obey God, they would be blessed in the Promised Land. They would have no reason to fear their enemies because the same mighty God who had delivered them from Egypt would eliminate the Gentile nations one by one. On 7:22, see exposition on Joshua 13:1-7.

8:1-6 *40 years of room, board, and clothing.* Throughout their 40 years of wandering, the Israelites always had adequate provision for their physical needs. One might think that the dependable refreshments of God's miraculous care and his promises of "the good land" (8:10) would have elicited obedience from God's people. Israel never had a problem believing God's Word, but they did have trouble "behaving" it.

8:7-9 *Almost like the Garden of Eden!* What glorious prospects were in store for the Israelites if only they would walk in God's ways. Canaan was beautiful and fertile, and God would supply their every need (see Rom. 8:28; Phil. 4:19).

8:10-20 *"Remember! Don't forget!"* When they finally enter the land and enjoy its bounty, Israel must not forget the God who gave it to them. Nine times in Deuteronomy Israel is warned not to forget God's faithfulness (4:9, 23, 31; 6:12; 8:11, 14, 19; 9:7; 25:19). Forgetfulness has been a problem among God's children throughout history.

9:1-3 *Israel's enemies: "They're big, but he's bigger."* Recalling the spies in Canaan (Num. 13), Moses reminded Israel that when they entered the land they would face armies humanly impossible to defeat. But human power is useless against God's promises (Phil. 4:13). With God going before his people, the enemy would quickly fall.

9:4-29 *"It's not because we're so good, but because they're so bad."* Moses emphasized that God would drive out the Canaanites because of their wickedness, not because of Israel's worthiness (see Lev. 18:24-30; *Canaanites,* p. 862; *Ugarit,* p. 900). From the time they left Egypt, the Israelites had continually provoked the Lord to wrath (9:8). He was especially grieved with their worship of the golden calf (Exod. 32). The sins of his own people are an affront to God. Moses recalled his own righteous anger over their idolatry (9:13-24).

10:1-5, 10-11 *The new stone tablets: Inscribed and stored for safekeeping.* After Moses had broken the stone tablets, God told him to prepare two more tablets, on which he inscribed the Ten Commandments once again (Exod. 34:1). He placed the new tablets in the Ark of the Covenant.

10:6-9 *Aaron's death, and an honor for Levi.* In this parenthetical note Moses recalled Aaron dying, his son Eleazar becoming high priest, and the tribe of Levi being set apart to bear the Ark of the Covenant (18:1; Num. 18:1-6).

10:12-22 *What God wants most of all.* In an impassioned plea, Moses stressed that the law was not merely an outward ritual of sacrifices and festivals; it was primarily a heart attitude, a life of respect, love, and service to God (Ps. 51:16-19).

11:1-7 *First call to obedience: For parents only.* God's call for love and obedience was directed most forcefully at the older Israelites, who had witnessed his mighty acts along the way from Egypt to Canaan. Their children, who had not fully shared those experiences, would be held less accountable (11:2; compare Luke 12:48).

11:8-17 *Second call to obedience: For everyone.* God loved the *land* of Israel even as he loved the people (11:12). His promise to bless the land, however, depended on the obedience of the people. Failure to love, obey, and serve God would bring his curse on both the people and their land (11:16-17).

11:18-21 *"Store it in your heart, share it with your children."* Israel was to teach God's Word to their children, but they would be able to do so only as they stored his Word in their own hearts (11:18-21). 11:18 describes the use of phylacteries (see exposition on Exod. 13:1-16).

11:22-32 *Blessing or judgment? "It's your call."* God's blessings on the Israelites depended on their diligently keeping the law (11:22-32). Law and grace are exact opposites. The law said, "Do and you will live"; grace says, "You have been given life; therefore do."

12:1-28 *"Destroy those altars, then build one just for me."* When they entered the land, Israel was to destroy all altars and images of false gods (12:2-4). God would choose their place of worship (12:8-11). Knowing that many of them would live far from the place he would choose, God provided for the killing of animals for food in such remote areas (12:20-28). However, all animals for sacrifice were to be brought to the designated place. (The question of killing animals in the remote areas would have come up because many Israelites ate meat only when offering sacrifices.)

12:29-32 *No addition or subtraction allowed.* God's people were not to be entrapped by the ways of the heathen nations or to inquire after their gods (12:29-32). They were neither to add to nor take away from the law (12:32; 4:2; see Rev. 22:18-19).

13:1-18 *Avoiding and punishing apostasy.* These verses reveal three things that often draw God's people into apostasy: false prophets with miraculous signs; evil influence within families; and ruthlessly persuasive men. Death by stoning was decreed for those who served other gods (13:6-11; see 17:2-5). God was so insistent that his people worship and serve him only, that he demanded the destruction of entire cities if their leaders influenced them to serve other gods (13:12-18).

14:1–15:23 *Various regulations:*

Mourning: Pagan or proper? (14:1-2). God's people were his "special treasure" and must not be involved in such heathen practices as cutting themselves or shaving their hair on behalf of the dead.

Food for the faithful (14:3-21). Most of the forbidden animals had some connection with pagan religions or were simply unfit for human consumption (Lev. 11).

Guidelines for giving to God (14:22-29). The law provided specific patterns for giving, and specified the purpose: "to teach you always to fear the LORD your God." Giving to the Lord brought blessing (14:24) and rejoicing (14:26).

Debts and the poor (15:1-11). During the seventh-year Sabbath (Lev. 25:1-7), there was to be a "rest" or cancellation of debts. This was intended to promote concern for the poor. Ideally, people would loan to the poor even though the Sabbath year (15:9) was approaching and their loan might not be repaid.

"Set him free after six years" (15:12-18). Remembering their slavery in Egypt, Israel was to release Hebrew slaves after six years (see exposition on Lev. 25:35-55). At the time of release, they were to give their slaves ample provisions for starting a new life. Slaves who chose to remain with their master were marked with a pierced ear. The Lord promised a special blessing on those who treated their slaves well.

Firstborn animals (15:19-23). To acknowledge God's provision and Israel's being his firstborn, the firstborn of the herds were to be set apart from normal use (see exposition on Exod. 13:1-16).

16:1-17 *The three main festivals reviewed.* Once a year, Israel was to celebrate its miraculous escape from Egypt. The celebration was called Passover in remembrance of the death angel passing over all the homes protected by the blood of the lamb (16:1-8; see exposition on Exod. 12:1-28).

Seven weeks after Passover and the Festival of Unleavened Bread, Israel celebrated what is variously called Pentecost, the Festival of Harvest, the Festival of Weeks, or the Day of the Firstfruits (16:9-12; Num. 28:26).

The Festival of Shelters (16:13-15), also known as the Festival of Booths, the Festival of Ingathering or Final Harvest (Exod. 23:16; 34:22), or the Festival of the Lord (Lev. 23:39, NIV), was a reminder of Israel's deliverance out of Egypt and the shelters in which they lodged before entering the Sinai desert.

All Israelite men were to appear before the Lord (16:16-17) during these three festivals.

16:18–18:14 *Various regulations:*

Judges and justice (16:18-20). The people were to appoint judges who were impartial and incorruptible.

Sacred trees and pillars (16:21-22). Worship of idols in the form of sacred trees and pillars was forbidden.

"Be sure to offer the best" (17:1). Sacrifices were to be without defect. The God of holiness and perfection refuses to accept less than our best.

Wanted: At least two witnesses (17:2-7). While idolatry was abominable to God, punishable by stoning, he ensured justice by requiring two or more witnesses for a guilty verdict.

Settling serious disputes (17:8-13). Disputes too difficult for the two parties to resolve were to be brought before the spiritual leaders and judges (Matt. 18:15-17).

Rules for kings (17:14-20). Anticipating Israel's demand for a king (1 Sam. 8:5-22), Moses gave principles to guide their selection and conduct. The primary stipulation was that the king be an Israelite (17:15).

Support of priests and Levites (18:1-8). Priests and Levites were forbidden certain privileges, such as inheriting land, in exchange for the higher honor of spiritual leadership. The people were to provide for their physical needs.

The abomination of the occult (18:9-14). Israel was to avoid Canaanite "abominations" such as child sacrifice, witchcraft, "calling up the dead," and astrology.

18:15-19 *A prophet like Moses.* Moses interrupted his recitation of laws to foretell of "a prophet like me" who would one day be raised up from among Israel and would speak with authority in God's name. Peter understood this as a reference to Christ (Acts 3:22).

18:20–25:16 *Various regulations:*

"If the prophecy fails, the prophet dies" (18:20-22). A professed prophet who spoke in the name of any god except the one true God, or whose prophecy failed to come true, was to be put to death.

Cities of refuge (19:1-13). The six cities of refuge are mentioned once again (4:41-43; see exposition on Num. 35:9-34; Josh. 20:1-9).

"Leave those landmarks alone" (19:14). Apparently the clandestine moving of a neighbor's boundary stone was a common practice in those days. As the Israelites prepared to become landowners, Moses forbade such trickery.

The penalty for perjury (19:15-21). False testimony was a serious matter; those guilty of it were to be put to death.

"If your name is on this list, go home." (20:1-9). Men who were newly betrothed or at other transition points in life were exempt from military service. The "terrified" were exempt as well, lest their lack of courage demoralize other soldiers.

Other nations: Strike a deal, or destroy? (20:10-20). Nations outside of Canaan, but within the larger territory promised to Abraham, were to be offered servanthood if they would declare peace with Israel. Otherwise, every adult male among them was to be slain. Of the nations living within Canaan, not even women and children were to be spared (20:16-17). God knew, and history would prove, that failure to "completely destroy" those wicked nations would result in his people committing their abominations (20:18).

Atonement for unsolved murders (21:1-9). When a murder was unsolved, the town nearest where the victim was found was to sacrifice a young heifer as atonement for the murder.

Marrying female captives (21:10-14). An Israelite soldier could marry a female captive, but was to follow certain rules to protect her dignity. These rules were a great improvement over how most ancient nations treated captive women.

This permission to marry non-Israelites applied only to non-Canaanite captives and did not contradict the prohibition against marrying Canaanite women (7:1-3): Canaanite women were to be killed along with their husbands and children (20:16-17).

The son of an unloved wife (21:15-17). A man with more than one wife was not to deny the rights of his firstborn son just because he was the son of an unloved wife. These instructions show that polygamy was never God's ideal for marriage.

Death to the disobedient son (21:18-23). A son who failed to honor his father and mother, continually rebelling against their discipline, was to be stoned.

Good neighbors at the Lost and Found (22:1-4). Anyone finding a lost item or injured animal was to make all reasonable efforts to restore it to its owner.

Proper dress for male and female (22:5). Dressing like the opposite sex was declared to be something the Lord detests.

Birds in the nest (22:6-7). The rules protecting nesting birds show God's concern for all life, animal as well as human.

Safety first in building plans (22:8). The safety of neighbors and visitors was to be considered when building a new home.

Separation of seed, animals, and fabrics (22:9-12). Principles of sanctity and separation applied to garden seed, animals, and garments. Fringes (tassels) were reminders of God's commandments (Num. 15:37-41).

Accusations of unchastity (22:13-21). A man falsely accusing his wife of not being a virgin when they married was to be punished and fined. If the accused wife was proved not to have been a virgin at marriage, she was to be put to death.

The seriousness of sexual sins (22:22-30). If a man and woman committed adultery, both were to be stoned. If a man raped a betrothed woman, only he was to be stoned. If he raped a virgin who was not betrothed, he was to pay a fine and marry her. The severity of these penalties shows God's intolerance for sexual sin.

Barred from the sanctuary, but not from grace (23:1-8). Whether for ceremonial or symbolic reasons, certain Israelites and proselytes from surrounding nations were not permitted to enter the sanctuary for worship. Such prohibition, however, did not deny them God's grace and forgiveness.

Sanitation on the battlefield (23:9-14). Even in battlefield conditions, sanitation was a priority.

Runaway slaves (23:15-16). Slaves who had escaped (presumably after being mistreated) were to be allowed to live in peace and were not to be forcibly returned to their master.

Ritual prostitution (23:17-18). Both male and female prostitution, common in Canaanite religion, were forbidden.

For all Israelites: Loans without interest (23:19-20). Interest could be charged to foreigners, but not to fellow Israelites.

"Pay your vows promptly." (23:21-23). Vows to the Lord were to be taken seriously and paid promptly.

Fruit from your neighbor's field (23:24-25). Produce could be eaten in a neighbor's vineyard or field, but only so much as the person could eat while there; none could be kept for later.

Restrictions on divorce and remarriage (24:1-4). God allowed divorce in some cases, but only as a means of restricting and regulating the practice. Malachi 2:16 expresses his overriding disapproval of divorce (see exposition on Matt. 19:1-12).

After the wedding, free for a year (24:5). A new husband was to be free of military and business duties for one full year, to encourage and strengthen the new couple in their mutual commitment. The military exemption applied to betrothed men as well (20:7).

Various humane rules (24:6-18). There were specific rules concerning loan collateral (24:6); kidnapping (24:7); leprosy (24:8-9); loan collection (24:10-13); payment for services (24:14-15); administration of justice (24:16); the rights of widows and orphans (24:17-18).

Produce left for gleaning (24:19-22). Israelites were to leave a portion of their harvest to be gleaned by strangers, orphans, and widows. They were to do this remembering "that you were slaves in the land of Egypt."

The 40-stripe limit (25:1-3). Criminal justice was to be equitable, with a maximum of 40 lashes to the guilty party.

"The oxen that plow should also partake" (25:4). Oxen used for treading grain should not be muzzled but should be allowed to partake of the grain. Paul applied this to the support of evangelists (1 Cor. 9:9-10).

How a brother-in-law loses his shoes (25:5-10). A widow's brother-in-law was to marry and provide for her. If he refused, the rejected widow could publicly remove his sandals and spit in his face—divinely motivated social pressure to encourage obedience! Called levirate marriage (*levir* = Latin "brother-in-law"), the practice was common in ancient cultures. Though he lived centuries before the Mosaic law, Onan was killed by God for refusing to honor this custom (Gen. 38:1-10). By contrast, Boaz honored this law (see exposition on Ruth).

Modesty on the battlefield (25:11-12). Certain immodest actions were forbidden even though they would have been good self-defense.

Honesty in business (25:13-16). Honesty and fairness were to govern business transactions.

25:17-19 *Amalek's actions: Unforgivable, unforgettable.* As the Israelites left Egypt, the Amalekites, descendants of Esau, attacked them (Exod. 17:8-16). During the battle they attacked the sickly and helpless Israelites who lagged behind (25:18). Moses reminded the people that God wanted the Amalekites utterly destroyed because of this (Exod. 17:14-16). King Saul would later lose his throne for failing to fulfill this decree (1 Sam. 15).

26:1-15 *"My firstfruits for his faithfulness."* In gratitude for deliverance, the people were to give the earliest produce of each harvest to the priest. As they did so they were to recite the details of their deliverance. Their tithes were to help Levites, strangers, orphans, and widows (26:12-15).

26:16-19 *The mutual commitment of God and his people.* Moses declared Israel's commitment to the Lord and his commandments, and God's commitment to exalt Israel as his holy people.

SERMON THREE (27–30)

27:1-26 *Blessings and curses.* Upon crossing the Jordan, the Israelites were to erect a monument containing the words of the law, followed by an altar (27:1-8). Worshiping God and obeying his Word were absolutes for Israel's life in the Promised Land.

Moses prescribed in detail a ceremony of blessing and cursing that was to take place in Canaan (27:9-26). With the priests and the Ark in the valley between, half of the tribes were to stand on Mount Gerizim and the other half on Mount Ebal. Those on Mount Gerizim would pronounce blessings for obedience. Those on Mount Ebal would pronounce a great chorus of curses on those who disobeyed the law.

Joshua, Moses' faithful successor, carried out these instructions with great precision (Josh. 8:30-35).

28:1-14 *Abundant blessings for obedience.* Military superiority (28:1-2), prosperity (28:3), physical well-being

(28:4-5), spiritual well-being (28:9), and international respect (28:10) were assured Israel if they would obey God (28:1, 12).

28:15-68 *"But disobedience will bring disaster."* Disobedience, on the other hand, would bring curses (28:15-68), including diseases, severe drought, and military defeat. Along with defeat would come despair. Everything the people put their hand to, including marriage (28:30), would prove unsuccessful. Such failure would be a clear sign of their disobedience (28:46). What a tragic downward spiral would occur—from disease to drought to defeat to despair to ultimate deportation by Gentile powers (28:48, 64)—if Israel refused to heed God's Word. And this is just what happened (see 2 Kings).

29:1-8 *His faithfulness, their fickleness: A review.* Once again God through Moses reminded Israel of the triumphs and trials they had experienced in their deliverance from Egypt. While God had been faithful, Israel had been ungrateful.

29:9-29 *A call for commitment.* With the past behind them, God called his people to renewed covenant obedience, promising to establish them and to be their God. If they broke their covenant, all the foregoing curses would be upon them. The ultimate curse would be loss of the Promised Land.

30:1-10 *"If we repent, he will restore."* Having lost their land, if Israel would then repent, God would remove all the curses and restore their land.

30:11-20 *"Life or death? It's up to you."* The law would be Israel's test, and it was very clear: It was as close as their very mouths and hearts. Though God is infinite in wisdom and power, he is very direct and simple with his people: Life and blessing would come if they loved and obeyed the Lord; death and cursing would come if they turned away to false gods. It was up to them.

THE FINAL DAYS OF MOSES (31–34)

31:1-8 *Joshua commissioned to lead.* Moses reminded the people of his old age and that God had anointed Joshua to succeed him as their leader (Num. 27:18-23). God's promise of his unfailing presence with Moses (31:6) was extended to Joshua (31:7-8, 23) and belongs to the church today (Heb. 13:5).

31:9-13 *"Read it every seven years."* Having put the entire law into written form, Moses delivered it to the priests and specified that it was to be read publicly every Sabbath year at the Festival of Shelters. Later (31:24-27), Moses instructed the priests to keep the Book of the Law beside the Ark of the Covenant.

31:14-30 *"Sing them a song of warning."* God told Moses about Israel's future apostasy and instructed him to compose a song of warning for them. The song was to celebrate the person and work of God, the demands of the law, and the penalties for breaking it. It would "stand as evidence against" the Israelites after their apostasy had led to disaster (31:21). That God's warnings came true can be seen in the book of Judges.

32:1-47 *The Song of Moses.* 32 records the song Moses was commanded to write. The prelude (32:1-3) called upon all to hear and take hold of the doctrine to be taught in the song.

The first part of the song (32:4-14) emphasized the person of God in all his perfection and justice toward Israel. He had bought them, set their bounds, protected them, and provided for them.

The second part (32:15-27) noted that, in spite of his grace and provision, Israel had taken God for granted and had forsaken and forgotten him. His response, in grieved jealousy and righteous anger, was to break his promises and determine to remove them from their land (32:26).

Part three (32:28-33) focused on Israel's inability to understand God's dealings with them.

Part four (32:34-47) was the grand finale, with God declaring his sovereignty over all, his ultimate vengeance on his adversaries, and his future mercy toward his people.

32:48-52 *Permitted to see the Promised Land.* God told Moses he would be allowed to see the Promised Land from Mount Nebo before he died (3:23-29; Num. 27:12-14). But because of his disobedience (Num. 20:7-13), he would not be allowed to enter the land.

33:1-25 *The final blessings of Moses.* As he prepared to die, Moses prepared his people for victory in Canaan by pronouncing his blessings on the 12 tribes. He spelled out the two things that would be the ultimate source of blessing in Israel: the continued presence and protection of God (33:2) and the counsel of his Word (33:3). The blessings are prophetic: Moses the statesman became Moses the prophet as he forecasted the various activities of the 12 tribes.

33:26-29 *"Underneath are his everlasting arms."* In a final crescendo of praise, Moses declared Israel a happy people because of their incomparable God, whose everlasting arms would undergird and protect them.

34:1-12 *". . . and from Mount Pisgah's lofty height . . ."* The Lord evidently prepared a clearer-than-usual day to show Moses the Promised Land from Mount Pisgah, which is the highest point of Mount Nebo. With no cloud cover, Mount Hermon, on Israel's northern border, can be seen from Pisgah.

So special was this godly man that the Lord himself secretly buried him in an unmarked grave (34:6). Though 120 years old, Moses' strength and sight were that of a young man (34:7). Moses received one of the greatest eulogies ever written (34:10-12).

DEUTERONOMY'S PORTRAIT OF GOD

THE PERSON OF GOD

"Hear, O Israel! The LORD is our God, the LORD alone" (6:4).
"Look now; I myself am he! There is no god other than me!" (32:39).

THE GREATNESS OF GOD

"The LORD your God is the God of gods and Lord of lords. He is the great God, mighty and awesome, who shows no partiality and takes no bribes" (10:17).

THE GRACE OF GOD

"I will say it again: The LORD your God is not giving you this good land because you are righteous, for you are not—you are a stubborn people" (9:6).

THE LOVE OF GOD

He loved Israel's ancestors

"Because he loved your ancestors, he chose to bless their descendants and personally brought you out of Egypt with a great display of power" (4:37).

He loved Israel

"For you are a holy people, who belong to the LORD your God. Of all the people on earth, the LORD your God has chosen you to be his own special treasure. The LORD did not choose you and lavish his love on you because you were larger or greater than other nations, for you were the smallest of all nations! It was simply because the LORD loves you, and because he was keeping the oath he had sworn to your ancestors. That is why the LORD rescued you with such amazing power from your slavery under Pharaoh in Egypt" (7:6-8).

"For the people of Israel belong to the LORD; Jacob is his special possession. He found them in a desert land, in an empty, howling wasteland. He surrounded them and watched over them; he guarded them as his most precious possession. Like an eagle that rouses her chicks and hovers over her young, so he spread his wings to take them in and carried them aloft on his pinions. The LORD alone guided them; they lived without any foreign gods" (32:9-12).

He would continue to love Israel
"He will love you and bless you and make you into a great nation. He will give you many children and give fertility to your land and your animals. When you arrive in the land he swore to give your ancestors, you will have large crops of grain, grapes, and olives, and great herds of cattle, sheep, and goats" (7:13).

THE FAITHFULNESS OF GOD

He provided for Israel in the wilderness
"The LORD your God has blessed everything you have done and has watched your every step through this great wilderness. During these forty years, the LORD your God has been with you and provided for your every need so that you lacked nothing" (2:7).

"For forty years I led you through the wilderness, yet your clothes and sandals did not wear out. You had no bread or wine or other strong drink, but he gave you food so you would know that he is the LORD your God" (29:5-6).

He did so in spite of their constant sin
"Remember how angry you made the LORD your God out in the wilderness. From the day you left Egypt until now, you have constantly rebelled against him" (9:7).

THE WILL OF GOD

"And now, Israel, what does the LORD your God require of you? He requires you to fear him, to live according to his will, to love and worship him with all your heart and soul, and to obey the LORD's commands and laws that I am giving you today for your own good" (10:12-13).

THE WORD OF GOD

His Word is clear and near
"This command I am giving you today is not too difficult for you to understand or perform. It is not up in heaven, so distant that you must ask, 'Who will go to heaven and bring it down so we can hear and obey it?' It is not beyond the sea, so far away that you must ask, 'Who will cross the sea to bring it to us so we can hear and obey it?' The message is very close at hand; it is on your lips and in your heart so that you can obey it" (30:11-14).

Don't add to it or take away from it
"And now, Israel, listen carefully to these laws and regulations that I am about to teach you. Obey them so that you may live, so you may enter and occupy the land the LORD, the God of your ancestors, is giving you. Do not add to or subtract from these commands I am giving you from the LORD your God. Just obey them" (4:1-2).

Meditate on it personally
"So commit yourselves completely to these words of mine. Tie them to your hands as a reminder, and wear them on your forehead" (11:18).

Teach it to your children
"Teach them to your children. Talk about them when you are at home and when you are away on a journey, when you are lying down and when you are getting up again. Write them on the doorposts of your house and on your gates" (11:19-20).

Put it into practice
"The message is very close at hand; it is on your lips and in your heart so that you can obey it" (30:14).

1406 B.C.
Israel
enters Canaan

1399
Joshua
completes
conquest
of Canaan

1377
Israel
in apostasy,
Othniel, 1st judge

JOSHUA

BACKGROUND

After 400 years of bondage in Egypt and 40 years of wandering in the wilderness, the people of Israel were finally ready to take possession of a land promised to them since the time of Abraham. Joshua, one of the two leaders who had remained faithful during the Kadesh-barnea rebellion (see Num. 13–14), had been chosen to lead them into Canaan (Num. 27:15-23). The book bearing Joshua's name records his conquest of Canaan (1–12), his division of the land among the tribes (13–21), and his final exhortations to Israel (22–24).

AUTHOR

In light of the many detailed eyewitness testimonies and long speeches recorded in the book of Joshua, it is likely that Joshua himself either authored or directed the writing of the vast majority of the book. The text itself demonstrates Joshua's concern for written records: He wrote a copy of the law of Moses (8:32), had geographical records compiled (18:8-9), and committed to writing the words of a covenant (24:25-26).

Some have questioned Joshua's authorship because of the book's statement concerning the "leaders who outlived" Joshua (24:31) and the frequent occurrences of the phrase "to this day," suggesting a time after Joshua's death. The best explanation is that Joshua or his scribes did in fact write the majority of the book, but that later scribes, also acting under divine inspiration, joined together the speeches, historical accounts, and geographical notes that make up the book. (In some cases "this day" is quite close to the time of Joshua, as in 6:25, which states that Rahab was alive "to this day.")

DATE AND LOCATION

Joshua died in about 1390 B.C. (see 24:29), 15 years after the conquest began. Assuming Joshua was the author, most of the book would have been written by then, most likely in Joshua's hometown of Timnath-serah or in one of the spiritual centers where priests would be found, such as Shechem (24:1) or Bethel, where the Ark would later reside (Judg. 20:26-27).

PURPOSE

Joshua teaches that God keeps his promises no matter how unlikely their fulfillment may appear. This is seen in God's *general* promise to give the land of Canaan to Israel, and in his *specific* promises to grant success in particular battles (6:2; 10:8). God's promises did not fail (21:45). The Israelites simply had to obey and step out in faith.

RECIPIENTS

Joshua was recorded primarily for all Israelites since it deals with matters such as purification, obedience to God's commands, and God's faithfulness. But it had special significance for Israel's leaders, reminding them of the consequences of not following through on God's command to completely conquer the land.

UNIQUE FEATURES

- Joshua records three memorable miracles (3:14-17; 6; 10).
- Joshua reveals that Gentiles were not necessarily excluded from God's plan under the dispensation of Mosaic law. Rahab, the Canaanite prostitute who joined the Israelites, is mentioned in three NT passages:
- Matthew 1:5 (her place in the genealogy of Christ)
  - ➤ Hebrews 11:31 (her faith)
  - ➤ James 2:25 (her good works)
- Joshua records an important Christophany, or preincarnate appearance of Christ—as the "commander of the LORD's army" (5:13-15). Christ appears in bodily form several times in the OT (see exposition on Gen. 16:1-16; exposition on Zech. 1:7-11; compare exposition on Gen. 17:1-8).

COMPARISON WITH OTHER BIBLE BOOKS

Exodus:

- Exodus records how God led his people out of the land of bondage, while Joshua tells us how God led his people into the land of blessing (see Deut. 6:23).
- Both the exit of Exodus and the entrance of Joshua involved a miraculous parting of waters—in Exodus the Red Sea; in Joshua the Jordan River.
- Both books are not just literal in their discussion of exit and entrance, but symbolic as well. Believers are spiritually taken out of "Egypt" (spiritual death) and brought into "Israel" (salvation, abundant life).

OUTLINE

INVASION: ISRAEL CLAIMS CANAAN (1:1–5:12)
- God's message to Joshua (1:1-9)
- Joshua's message to the people (1:10-18)
- Spies sent to Jericho, hidden by Rahab (2)
- Crossing the Jordan (3:1–4:18)

Encampment at Gilgal (4:19–5:12)
SUBJECTION: ISRAEL CONQUERS CANAAN (5:13–12:24)
The commander of the LORD's army (5:13-15)
The central campaign (6:1–8:29)
Jericho (6)
Ai (7:1–8:29)
Covenant renewed on Ebal and Gerizim (8:30-35)
The southern campaign (9–10)
The Gibeonite deception (9)
The sun stands still (10:1-27)
Final southern cities subdued (10:28-43)
The northern campaign (11)
List of defeated Canaanite kings (12)
DIVISION: ISRAEL COLONIZES CANAAN (13–21)
Land still to be conquered (13:1-7)
Land east of the Jordan for two and a half tribes (13:8-33)
Allotment of land west of the Jordan: Introduction (14:1-5)
Testimony of Caleb, his allotment (14:6-15)
Land for Judah (15)
Land for Joseph's descendants (16–17)
Land for the remaining seven tribes (18–19)
Cities of refuge (20)
Cities for the Levites (21)
DECISION: JOSHUA CALLS ISRAEL TO FAITH (22–24)
Joshua's exhortations (22:1–24:28)
To the eastern tribes (22)
To Israel's leaders (23)
To the whole nation (24:1-28)
Joshua's death (24:29-33)

INVASION: ISRAEL CLAIMS CANAAN (1:1–5:12)

1:1-9 *God's message to Joshua: "Obey the Book."* Moses, Israel's great leader, was dead, but Joshua, his understudy for 40 years, was ready to take the torch and lead Israel into the Promised Land. No human leader is indispensable to God.

God renewed the promise given through Moses: that all the land of Canaan on which the sole of Israel's feet would tread would belong to them (1:3; Deut. 11:24). He reminded Joshua that Israel's success in conquering Canaan would result not from any military advantage but from meditation on and obedience to the law. Only by so doing could Joshua and his people be "strong and very courageous" (1:6, 7, 9, 18) as they faced the challenge of Canaan.

Obedience brings victory. Although many interpreters of Joshua view Canaan as symbolic of heaven, it is more beneficial to see it as a symbol of God's challenge to us to walk in his perfect will.

1:10-11 *Joshua's message to the people: "Get ready to go."* Joshua appointed officers to notify the people that they should be prepared to cross the Jordan River into Canaan in just three days.

1:12–18 *Joshua's message to the eastern tribes: "This is your battle too."* Moses had permitted the tribes of Reuben and Gad, and half of Manasseh, to settle on the eastern side of the Jordan River, with the understanding that their soldiers would first cross the Jordan with the other tribes and help them conquer the Canaanites (Num. 32:1-32). Joshua reminded these tribes of their commitment to do so. They agreed to obey Joshua as they had obeyed Moses.

Both the eastern (1:13) and western (1:15) tribes viewed their new homeland as a place of "rest" from their long wilderness journey. The promise of rest in Canaan is first recorded in Deuteronomy (Deut. 3:20; 12:10; 25:19). The fulfillment of that promise comes later in Joshua's account (21:44; 23:1).

2:1-24 *Rahab, the spies, and the scarlet cord.* Two spies were sent across the Jordan into Jericho. There they found refuge and gained information in the house of Rahab the prostitute, who hid them from the local authorities and helped them escape. Admitting that her whole city was terrified of the Israelites (2:9-11; see Deut. 2:25; 11:25), Rahab requested that they show mercy to her and her family when they destroyed Jericho. The spies agreed to do so, provided that she tie a scarlet cord from her window to identify her house.

3:1-13 *Preparing to cross the Jordan.* The priests bearing the Ark of the Covenant were instructed to lead the people across the Jordan, with the people following the priests at a distance of half a mile (Hebrew "2,000 cubits"). God promised that Joshua would be exalted that day in the eyes of Israel (3:7-8), as they saw firsthand that God was with him just as he had been with Moses.

3:14-17 *Walking where water had been.* Just as promised, as soon as the feet of the priests touched the water, the Jordan began to dry up (3:14-17). Even though it was at flood stage, its waters "began piling up" 15 to 20 miles to the north while Israel crossed over on dry land. Skeptics have claimed that the waters were actually blocked by an earthquake. Yet an earthquake would not explain the sudden return of the waters (4:18). And even if an earthquake caused the stoppage, its timing was surely miraculous.

Psalm 114:3, 5 recalls Israel's miraculous crossing of the Jordan. The Lord would later allow miraculous crossings of the Jordan through both Elijah and Elisha (2 Kings 2:8, 14).

4:1-18 *Stones to serve as a sign.* 12 chosen men (3:12) gathered stones from the Jordan as a memorial of the miraculous crossing. Joshua also set up stones marking the spot in the river where the priests had stood with the Ark (4:9).

The Israelites now realized that God was working through Joshua just as he had worked through Moses, and they revered him as their new leader (4:14).

When all the Israelites had crossed the river, Joshua told the priests bearing the Ark to finish crossing as well. When they had done so, "the Jordan River flooded its banks as before."

4:19-24 *Stories around the campfire at Gilgal.* The Israelites camped at Gilgal, and Joshua built a memorial out of the 12 stones the 12 men had taken from the river. He instructed the people to teach their children the significance of the memorial: that the Lord brought them over the Jordan just as he had brought them through the Red Sea 40 years earlier. Their witness to this miracle would help make it possible "that all the nations of the earth might know the power of the LORD" (4:24).

5:1 *Pagans paralyzed by fear.* With Israel now on the west side of the river, the worst fears of the pagans were realized; they were well aware of what Israel had done to other nations in recent days (2:9-11).

5:2-9 *Circumcision: Rolling away the reproach of Egypt.* During their 39 years in the wilderness, Israel had failed to observe the Passover or to circumcise their sons. Now in the land, they observed the covenant sign (see Gen. 17:9-14); by doing so they "rolled away the shame of your slavery in Egypt" ("Gilgal" means "to roll away").

5:10-12 *First Passover in the Promised Land.* Now that the time of year was right (4:19; see Exod. 12:2-6) and the people were prepared by circumcision (see Exod. 12:48), Israel observed its first Passover in the Promised Land. Being in the Promised Land meant an abundance of food, so the manna God had supplied in the desert now ceased (see Exod. 16:4-31).

SUBJECTION: ISRAEL CONQUERS CANAAN (5:13–12:24)

5:13-15 *A man with a sword says, "Take off your sandals!"* Near Jericho, Joshua met the "commander of the LORD's army," undoubtedly a preincarnate appearance of Christ. His instructions to Joshua were similar to God's instructions to Moses in Exodus 3:1-5, and Joshua responded accordingly.

6:1-19 THE CENTRAL CAMPAIGN: *Preparing for Jericho.* As the conquest of Canaan began, the Israelites' first military target was Jericho, near Gilgal. The Lord's instructions for this first battle would test Joshua's obedience, for they were certainly unconventional by military standards: marches around the city for seven days, climaxed by a trumpet blast and great shout on the seventh—at which time, said God, Jericho's walls would collapse.

The spoils from Jericho were to be devoted entirely to the Lord (6:17-19). The city and its occupants were to be destroyed. The only exceptions were Rahab and any of her family who came to her house for protection (2:17).

6:20-27 *They shout, and the walls come down.* Israel carefully followed the instructions, and God miraculously flattened Jericho's walls. The sole survivors were Rahab and her family. As Joshua departed from the ruins of Jericho, he cursed anyone who in the future would try to rebuild the city. His curse would be literally fulfilled in the days of Ahab (compare 6:26 with 1 Kings 16:34).

7:1-15 *Achan's sin brings defeat at Ai.* 7:1 states that Achan, in direct opposition to 6:18-19, had taken some of the spoils from Jericho. Because of his sin, "the LORD was very angry with the Israelites." When a reduced number of confident Israelites proceeded on to Ai, God withheld his blessing and they were defeated.

Unaware of Achan's sin, Joshua thought God had been unfaithful to his promise. He protested that such defeats would tarnish God's reputation among the Canaanites. The Lord then revealed that the defeat had resulted from sin in the camp (7:11) and instructed Joshua to find the offender and punish him (7:13-15).

7:16-26 *They were stoned and burned for his sin.* Through the casting of lots, Achan was found to be the guilty party. When confronted with his sin, he admitted to having coveted some of the spoils, then stealing and hiding them. The stolen goods were found in his tent. Achan, his family, and his cattle were all brought to the valley of Achor (which means "trouble"—7:24-26), where they were stoned and burned. The Lord then turned from his anger against Israel (7:26).

8:1-29 *Victory at Ai.* As Israel prepared for a return visit to Ai, the Lord promised victory this time and gave permission to take the spoils. Through the clever use of an ambush, the Israelites defeated Ai.

8:30-35 *Gerizim and Ebal: Blessings and curses.* Remembering Moses' instructions (Deut. 27:2-8), Joshua led Israel to the mountains of Gerizim and Ebal, where he built an altar and engraved on it the words of the law. Also according to Moses' instructions (Deut. 11:29; 27:12-13), he led Israel in reciting the prescribed blessings and curses from the two mountains.

9:1-27 *THE SOUTHERN CAMPAIGN: Alliance by deception.* When several Amorite kings banded together to fight Israel, the Gibeonites decided to break ranks and pursue peace. They approached Israel, pretending to have traveled a great distance—their old clothes and moldy bread were "proof"—and asked Israel to become their allies. Israel was allowed to make such alliances with nations outside of Canaan, but not with nations such as Gibeon that lived within Canaan (Deut. 20:10-18).

Joshua and Israel were duped by the Gibeonites' performance. Instead of consulting the Lord, they hastily agreed to an alliance. Three days later, the Israelites learned that they had been tricked—that, rather than being from a far-off land, the Gibeonites lived only about 20 miles away. The Israelites were understandably embarrassed and angry, but since they had made the alliance under oath, they remained committed to it. They stipulated, however, that because of their trickery the Gibeonites would have to be Israel's servants (9:22-27).

10:1-11 *Alarmed by the alliance, they declare war.* When the Amorite kings learned of the Gibeonite-Israelite alliance, they were alarmed and set out to punish Gibeon, hoping to make it an object lesson to other cities that might consider making peace with Israel. Threatened by the Amorites, Gibeon reminded Joshua of their alliance and he came to their defense. The Lord confused and routed the Amorites, striking them with a hailstorm as they fled.

10:12-15 *"No day like it, before or since."* In the thick of the battle, Joshua addressed the sun and commanded it to stand still. It did so: "It did not set as on a normal day." After citing the "Book of Jasher," as corroboration for the historicity of this unique occurrence, Joshua notes, "Never before or since has there been a day like that one." Skeptics have labeled the event an eclipse or some other natural phenomenon.

10:16-27 *Cowardly kings captured in a cave.* The Amorite kings had abandoned their armies and hidden in a cave, where Joshua's men found and killed them.

10:28-43 *Final southern cities subdued.* Joshua took Israel in a sweeping campaign to the south, attacking all the cities that had sent armies against Israel and Gibeon. He succeeded in eliminating all the remaining organized resistance in southern Canaan.

11:1-15 *THE NORTHERN CAMPAIGN.* Hearing of Joshua's success in the south, the northern Canaanite kings banded together to stop him. God once again scattered the enemy, and Joshua hamstrung the horses and burned the chariots they had abandoned. The city of Hazor had been the leader of the northern coalition. Joshua burned Hazor and killed its king.

11:16-23 *Summary of the three campaigns.* As this brief summary of his conquests indicates, Joshua had now destroyed the major points of resistance throughout Canaan. It can be calculated on the basis of Caleb's brief autobiography (14:6-12) that the conquest took seven years.

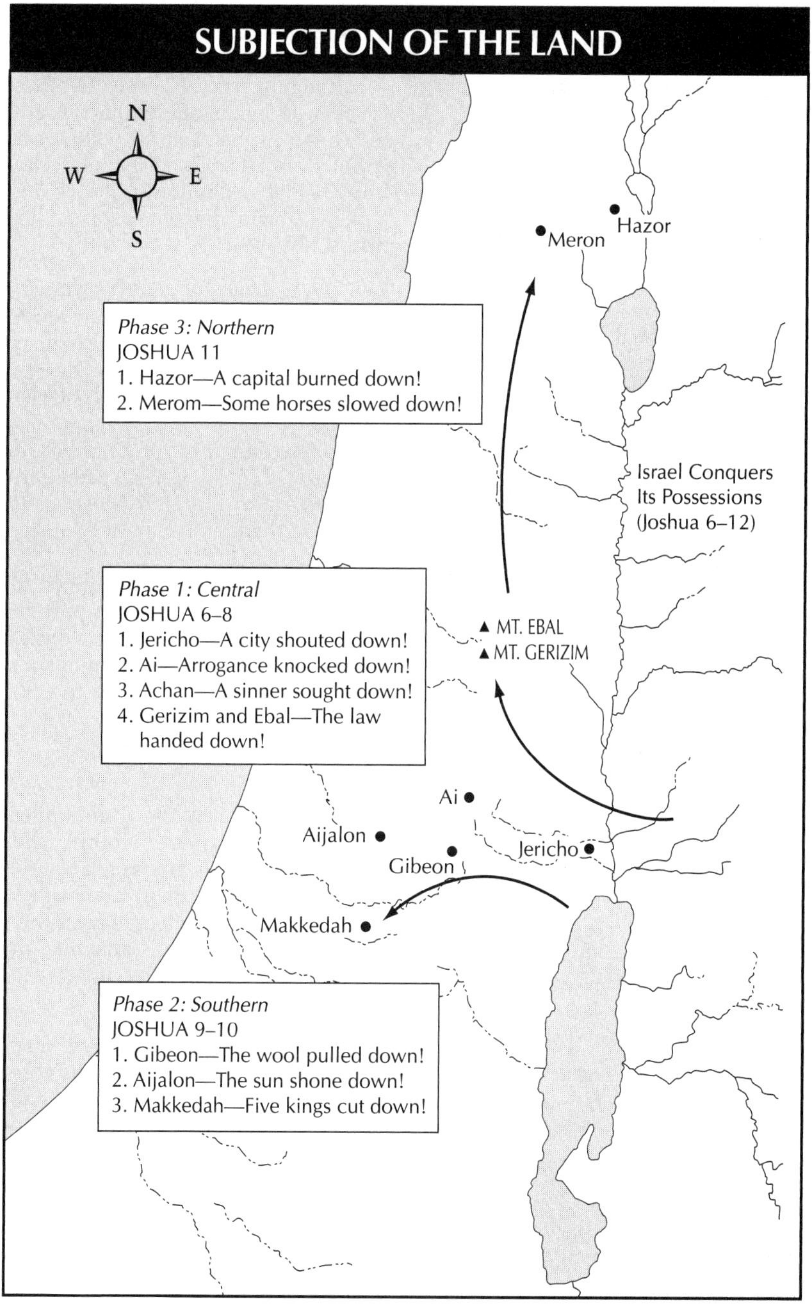
SUBJECTION OF THE LAND
N
W
E
S
Hazor
Meron
Phase 3: Northern
JOSHUA 11
1. Hazor—A capital burned down!
2. Merom—Some horses slowed down!
Israel Conquers
Its Possessions
(Joshua 6–12)
Phase 1: Central
JOSHUA 6–8
1. Jericho—A city shouted down!
2. Ai—Arrogance knocked down!
3. Achan—A sinner sought down!
4. Gerizim and Ebal—The law handed down!
MT. EBAL
MT. GERIZIM
Ai
Aijalon
Gibeon
Jericho
Makkedah
Phase 2: Southern
JOSHUA 9–10
1. Gibeon—The wool pulled down!
2. Aijalon—The sun shone down!
3. Makkedah—Five kings cut down!

12:1-24 *List of defeated Canaanite kings.* Chapter 12 lists the nations east of the Jordan defeated by Moses (12:1-6) and the nations on the west defeated by Joshua (12:7-24).

DIVISION: ISRAEL COLONIZES CANAAN (13–21)

13:1-7 *Territory still to be taken.* Though Israel now essentially controlled Canaan (11:23), there was "much land" yet to be conquered. Even though the conquest was incomplete, however, God told Joshua to begin dividing the land among the tribes. Apparently he had allowed some land to remain unconquered for a specific purpose (Deut. 7:22).

13:8-33 *Land east of Jordan for two and a half tribes.* The two and a half tribes who had already received land east of the Jordan were now told the boundaries of their inheritance (13:8-13; see Num. 32:1-33).

The Levites already knew that they would not receive any land; the Lord and the tithe of Israel were to be their inheritance (13:14; 21:1-42; Num. 18:20-24).

13:15-33 describes the precise portions of Transjordan given to each of the two and a half tribes.

14:1-5 *The land west of Jordan: "Divide it by lot."* Joshua, Eleazar, and the leaders of the tribes were to assign land to the western tribes by casting lots, the method prescribed by Moses (Num. 26:55).

14:6-15 *Very much alive at 85!* Caleb, who along with Joshua had withstood the negative report of the 10 spies (Num. 14), reminded Joshua of that event and of God's special promises to them. Still healthy at 85, Caleb was given the city of Hebron.

15:1-63 *Land for Judah.* 15:1-12, 20-63 describes the land allotted to the tribe of Judah. Jerusalem, chosen later as Israel's religious and political center (2 Sam. 5:6-12; 6:1-19), remained under the control of the Jebusites (15:63).

Having inherited Hebron (14:6-15), Caleb, a Judahite, offered his daughter Acsah in marriage to whomever could defeat Debir, a city near Hebron. Caleb's nephew Othniel defeated Debir and won Acsah as his bride (15:13-19).

16:1–17:13 *Land for Joseph's descendants.* The territory for Joseph's descendants was evidently drawn as one lot, then divided between Ephraim and the western half of Manasseh.

The five daughters of Zelophehad (see Num. 27:1-11; 36:1-12) came forward to claim the land Moses had promised them on behalf of their deceased father (17:3-6).

17:7-13 describes the land given to western Manasseh. Several important Canaanite cities near the plain of Esdraelon received special mention since Israel had so far failed to conquer them.

17:14-18 *"We need more land!"* Probably due to the presence of unconquered Canaanites, the Ephraimites and western Manasseh complained that their land was not large enough. Rather than offer them more land, Joshua gave them two options: Either clear out the remaining Canaanites or clear the areas covered by timber and live there.

18:1 *Transferring the Tabernacle from Gilgal to Shiloh.* Throughout the conquest, Israel's base of operations had been at Gilgal. Now Joshua chose a more central location, Shiloh, and erected the Tabernacle there (18:1). Shiloh would be Israel's religious and political center throughout the period of the judges.

18:2–19:48 *Land for the remaining seven tribes.* 36 men scouted out the remaining land for the seven tribes yet to

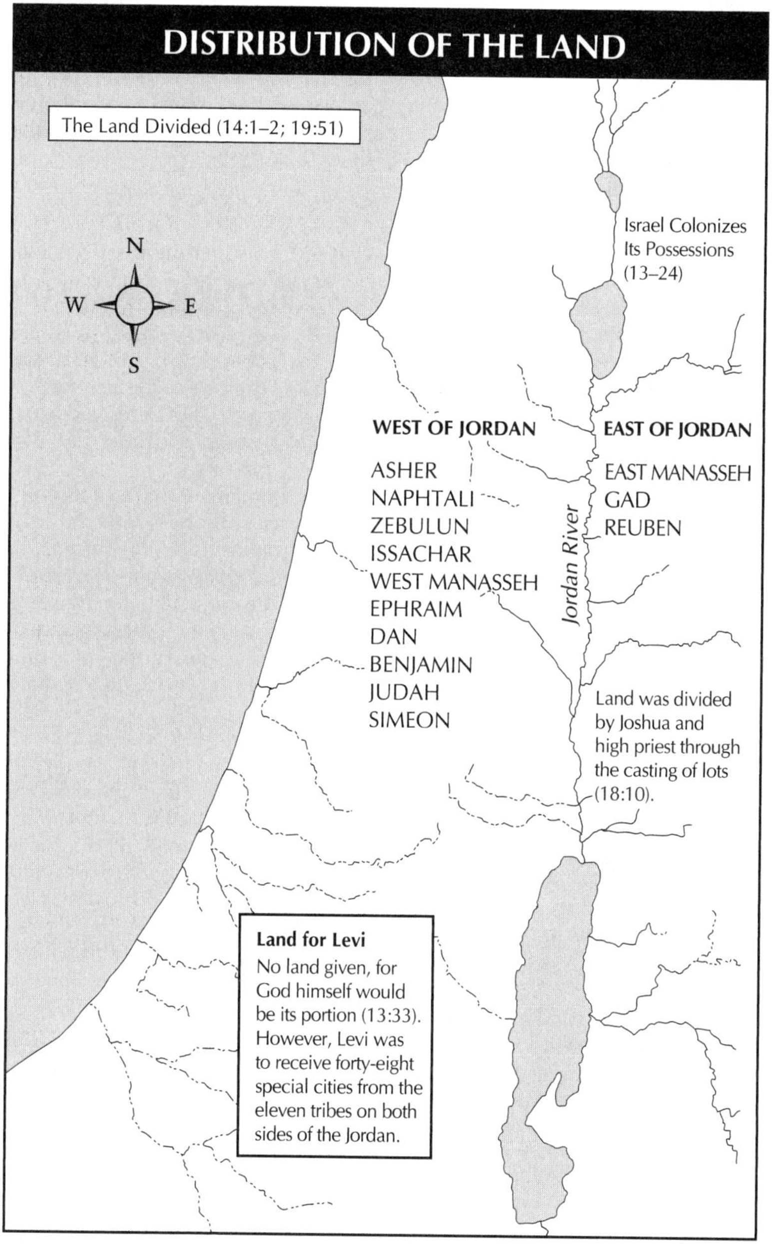

DISTRIBUTION OF THE LAND
The Land Divided (14:1–2; 19:51)
N
W
E
S
Israel Colonizes Its Possessions (13–24)
WEST OF JORDAN
ASHER
NAPHTALI
ZEBULUN
ISSACHAR
WEST MANASSEH
EPHRAIM
DAN
BENJAMIN
JUDAH
SIMEON
EAST OF JORDAN
EAST MANASSEH
GAD
REUBEN
Jordan River
Land was divided by Joshua and high priest through the casting of lots (18:10).
Land for Levi
No land given, for God himself would be its portion (13:33). However, Levi was to receive forty-eight special cities from the eleven tribes on both sides of the Jordan.

receive land. Lots were cast to assign the land. 18:11–19:48 describes the allotments for Benjamin, Simeon, Zebulun, Issachar, Asher, Naphtali, and Dan.

Judah had been assigned too much land, so Simeon was given part of it (19:9).

The tribe of Dan would not be satisfied with its allotment and would later relocate to a northern site (Judg. 18).

19:49-51 *A special allotment for the leader.* After all the tribes had received their inheritance, they honored Joshua by awarding him Timnath-serah, the city he had requested.

20:1-9 *The six cities of refuge.* Joshua appointed three cities of refuge west of the Jordan and confirmed the three Moses had already appointed in the east (see Num. 35:6-34; Deut. 4:41-43).

21:1-42 *The Levites claim their cities.* The Levites understood that they would not receive any land with the other tribes but that Moses had promised them special cities to live in (13:14; Num. 35:2-5). Joshua assigned 13 cities to the descendants of Aaron (21:4, 9-19), 10 to the other Kohathites (21:5, 20-26), 13 to the Gershonites (21:6, 27-33), and 12 to the Merarites (21:7, 34-41), for a total of 48 Levite cities.

21:43-45 *"He has kept all his promises!* With all the land assigned, Joshua offered a testimonial to God's faithfulness. He had brought the people to the land and had given them peace. "All of the good promises that the LORD had given Israel came true."

DECISION: JOSHUA CALLS ISRAEL TO FAITH (22–24)

22:1-9 *Joshua's call to faith—to the eastern tribes.* The soldiers from the two and a half eastern tribes had remained faithful to their promise to stay with the western tribes until Canaan was subdued (see 4:12-13). As they now prepared to return to their land and families east of Jordan, Joshua commended them for their loyalty, invited them to claim their share of the spoils, and admonished them to keep the law.

22:10-34 *An altar at the river causes controversy.* As the eastern warriors crossed the Jordan on their way home, they stopped to build a large altar—evidently one that could be seen from a great distance. When the western tribes heard about it, they suspected that the easterners were rebelling against the Lord and establishing a rival place of worship. They prepared for holy war.

Before actually going to war, and in accordance with the law (Deut. 13:12-15), Phinehas, son of Eleazar the priest, led a delegation to determine whether this new altar really was an act of rebellion. He passionately reminded the eastern tribes of Israel's past rebellions and God's punishments.

The eastern tribes insisted that the altar was intended not for idolatry but only for reminding their children that they worshiped the same God as the tribes living west of the Jordan (22:24-27). That explanation satisfied Phinehas and the representatives. They reported back to the western tribes, and all rejoiced that idolatry was not involved and that civil war had been averted.

23:1-16 *Joshua's call to faith—to the leaders.* Joshua reminded Israel's leaders of all they had seen God do for them. He admonished them to obey the law and separate themselves from the nations around them. He warned them that involvement with their pagan neighbors would be a snare to them. He warned that the God who had faithfully blessed them for their obedience (23:14) would just as faithfully punish them if they disobeyed (23:15-16).

"Be strong! Be very careful to follow all the instructions" (23:6) echoes God's words to Joshua before the conquest (1:6-9; see also 1:18; 10:25).

24:1-13 *Joshua's call to faith—to the whole nation.* Calling Israel to Shechem for his final recorded address, Joshua reminded them of God's goodness in calling Abraham out of his pagan environment to this land of Canaan. God had been faithful in protecting and providing for Isaac, Jacob, and Esau. He had sent Moses and Aaron to deliver Israel from Egypt. He delivered them through the Red Sea. He fought for them against the Amorites in the Transjordan and prevented Balaam from cursing them.

God had enabled them to conquer all of Canaan, central, south, and north, giving them "cities you did not build" and "vineyards and olive groves . . . you did not plant" (24:11-13).

24:14-15 *"As for me and my house . . ."* How would Israel respond to God's faithfulness? Joshua couldn't answer that question for the whole nation, but "as for me and my family," he declared, "we will serve the LORD."

24:16-28 *Their response: "We'll serve him too."* Challenged by Joshua's personal commitment, the people responded that they too would serve and obey God. Joshua made a covenant with the people and erected a stone as a reminder.

24:29-32 *The death of Joshua.* Joshua died at age 110 and was buried near his inheritance in Timnath-serah. A hero of another generation was honored as well, as the bones of Joseph were buried in Canaan as he had requested (see Gen. 50:25).

24:33 *The death of Eleazar.* Eleazar the high priest, Joshua's spiritual companion, also died and was buried.

PEOPLE TO REMEMBER FROM JOSHUA

CALEB

Key Fact: Stood with Joshua against negative report of 10 spies (Num. 14:6-9)
Father: Jephunneh (Num. 13:6)
Sons: Iru, Elah, and Naam (1 Chron. 4:15)
Daughter: Acsah (15:16)
Occupation: Soldier (14:6-14)
Total Bible References: 28
Key References: 14–15; 21:12; Num. 13–14; Judg. 1; 1 Chron. 6:56

Caleb Speaks

At long last, the burial place of Abraham and Sarah is cleansed of its pagan occupants. Mighty warriors, these sons of Anak—but their fierce fighters were no match whatsoever for my "faith fighters"! Not a bad accomplishment for an 85-year-old retired soldier! If only our people could have exercised their faith in God at Kadesh-barnea on that dark day 45 years ago. How sad and ironic that our single tribe of Judah has just defeated these "giants" who so terrified our entire nation at Kadesh-barnea. (14:6-15; Num. 13:31–14:4)

Hopefully, Othniel will remember *my* example—not theirs. I hope he'll take good care of our heritage here in Hebron. And I hope he'll take good care of Acsah. She's always been so strong-willed, as she proved once again by asking for all that extra land! I always figured it would take a good soldier to make her a suitable husband! (15:13-19)

Spiritual Lessons from Caleb

- The majority opinion is not always the right opinion (Num. 13:26-31).
- The older a Spirit-filled believer becomes, the better and braver he becomes (14:6-12).

Key Verse

"But my servant Caleb is different from the others. He has remained loyal to me, and I will bring him into the land he explored. His descendants will receive their full share of that land" (Num. 14:24).

JOSHUA

Key Facts: Moses' successor, led Israel into Promised Land (1:1-3)
Father: Nun (Exod. 33:11)
Occupation: Soldier, national leader (Exod. 17:9; Deut. 34:9)
Key Events in His Life:

- Withstands negative report of spies (Num. 14)
- Chosen to succeed Moses (Num. 27:16-23)
- Leads Israel into Canaan (3–4)
- Conquers Jericho (6)
- Renews covenant at Mount Ebal (8:30-35)
- Commands sun to stand still (10:12-14)
- Completes conquest of Canaan (11)
- Helps distribute land to 12 tribes (13–21)
- Final exhortations to Israel (22–24)

Age at Death: 110 (24:29-30)
Total Bible References: 201
Key References: 1–24; Exod. 17; 24:13; 32–33; Num. 11:26-30; 13–14; 26:65; 27:12-23; 32:11-12; Deut. 3:21-28; 31; 34:9; Judg. 2; Heb. 4:8

Joshua Speaks

"Choose today whom you will serve." That's what I said to Israel, Lord. And then Israel said to you, "We, too, will serve the LORD, for he alone is our God." (24:15-18)

I pray that they'll perform as promised.

These last three years have been rather peaceful. The only major incident was over that altar at the Jordan, but Phinehas took care of that without my help. How I have enjoyed this time of peace and quiet! It seems most of my life has been hectic and action-filled. The first 54 years were the worst, growing up in Egypt as a slave. (11:23; 22:10-34)

Then that man with his message from the burning bush came storming into town, forever changing our lives. "Let my people go!" That was his message from God. Little did I realize back then that within six months I would be not only a free man but also the appointed leader of Israel's army. What a victory we enjoyed there at the base of Sinai! It still staggers me to think of it—from slave to soldier to successor of Moses himself. (Exod. 5:1; 17:9, 13-16; Num. 27:18-23)

Caleb dropped by to see me recently. It was so good to hear his testimony. We both recalled our fateful mission from Kadesh-barnea. In fact, we even remembered our challenge to the frightened crowd: "Do not rebel against the LORD, and don't be afraid of the people of the land. They are only helpless prey to us! They have no protection, but the LORD is with us! Don't be afraid of them!" If only they had believed us then, most of those who died in the wilderness would be in Canaan today—and Caleb and I would have gotten here 40 years sooner! But they didn't believe us, so here I am, starting a new life at 110! (Num. 13–14)

"You must lead my people across the Jordan River into the land I am giving them." That's what you commanded me to do 10 years ago, Lord. And with the help of the commander of your army, that's what I've done. (1:2; 5:13-15)

Spiritual Lessons from Joshua

- Good leaders must first be good helpers (Exod. 17:8-10; 24:13; 33:11; Num. 27:16-23).
- Impossible situations provide glorious opportunities to trust God (Num. 14:6-9).
- Even the most faithful can allow fear to replace faith (7:1-9).
- Rash decisions made without prayer may be regretted (9:1-27, especially 9:14).
- We should stand up for our faith, whether or not anyone else is willing to do so; our faith can set the example for others, especially those in our own family (24:14-15).

Key Verse

"If you are unwilling to serve the LORD, then choose today whom you will serve. Would you prefer the gods your ancestors served beyond the Euphrates? Or will it be the gods of the Amorites in whose land you now live? But as for me and my family, we will serve the LORD" (24:15).

RAHAB

Key Facts: Ex-prostitute, saved lives of Israelite spies in Jericho, ancestor of Christ (2; 6; Matt. 1:5)
Husband: Salmon (Matt. 1:5)
Son: Boaz (Matt. 1:5)
Total Bible References: 8
Key References: 2; 6; Matt. 1:5; Heb. 11:31; James 2:25

Rahab Speaks

Somehow I just knew those Hebrew spies would honor their word and save me and my family on that incredible day. How can I ever forget the anxiety among my neighbors as that throng of Israelites, who had already made such a name for themselves, marched around our town for seven days? For my family, it was actually a relief when the trumpets blew and the walls came crashing down all around us! Our city and all our friends were destroyed, but as I think back on our depraved way of life, I know we had it coming. (2; 6; Deut. 9:4; Heb. 11:31; James 2:25)

I was certainly in the thick of it all—and I still bear the scars of my shameful past. No woman can sell herself like I did for so many years and remain unaffected. But things changed forever for me the moment I helped those two Hebrews and married into a Hebrew tribe. Life has been good here in Bethlehem. My husband's barley fields have produced plentifully. But the greatest blessing has been the birth of Boaz. He has turned out to be not only a wonderful son but also a wise businessman, and has taken good care of our fields. (Ruth 2:3; Matt. 1:5)

I do wish Boaz would marry and settle down. For some reason, none of the young ladies of Bethlehem have caught his eye. Surely, when the time comes, he'll pick someone from Judah and not a foreigner! But then, who's to say? Had it not been for God's grace in directing his father to choose a Canaanite girl, neither mother nor son would be here today. (Ruth 4:13-22)

Spiritual Lessons from Rahab

- Even someone seemingly far from the Lord can respond in faith when given the opportunity (2:1-22; Heb. 11:31).
- The reality of faith is proven by good works (2:1-22; James 2:24-25).
- God remembers and rewards our good works (Heb. 6:10). Rahab's ministry to the two Jewish spies afforded her a place in the genealogy of both King David and the Messiah himself (Matt. 1:5-6, 16).

Key Verse

"It was by faith that Rahab the prostitute did not die with all the others in her city who refused to obey God. For she had given a friendly welcome to the spies" (Heb. 11:31).

JUDGES

1446 B.C.
The Exodus

1406
Israel enters Canaan

1377
Othniel, 1st judge

1093
Call of Samuel

1075
Samson, last judge

1051
Saul, 1st king

BACKGROUND

Now that the Israelites were settled in the Promised Land, they began to experience the twin problems of compromise and apostasy: As they compromised on their mandate to completely eradicate the depraved Canaanites, they repeatedly fell into the idolatry and immorality of those nations. This would lead to a series of military defeats, followed by deliverance by a series of "judges." These judges were not legal administrators but strong leaders who helped the nation deal with each successive crisis.

Judges records a repeated cycle:

- sin (Israel "did what was evil in the LORD's sight": 2:11; 3:7, 12; 4:1; 6:1; 10:6; 13:1)
- servitude to pagan nations
- supplication to God
- salvation (deliverance)

Israel's moral condition grew progressively worse as the downward cycle was repeated. Each time a judge died, "the people returned to their corrupt ways, behaving worse than those who had lived before them" (2:19).

The Hebrew word translated "judge" comes from a word meaning "to exercise authority." The judges were people who used their authority to save or "deliver" Israel from oppression. Various forms of *judge* occur 20 times in the book of Judges; various forms of *deliver* occur 48 times.

AUTHOR

Unknown. Some have suggested that Samuel, considered by some to have been Israel's last judge (see 1 Sam. 7:6, 15-17; Acts 13:20), may have compiled the records of his predecessors.

DATE

The events described in Judges, from just after the death of Joshua to the beginning of the monarchy, span 335 years

(1380–1045 B.C.). The recurring observation that "in those days Israel had no king" (17:6; 18:1; 19:1; 21:25) suggests that Judges was written during the monarchy, perhaps c. 1020. This means that Samuel, who lived about 30 to 40 years into the reign of Saul, could have been its author. Concerning the NT suggestion that the period of the judges lasted some 450 years (Acts 13:20, KJV), see the NLT or NIV for that verse.

PURPOSE

- To show that the external threat of defeat by other nations is not as serious as the internal threat of moral depravity and idolatry; indeed, external threats always result from internal problems.
- To show Israel why human kingship became necessary for their nation: The Lord was to be their king, as Gideon acknowledged (8:23), but they were so wicked that human kingship became necessary. The writer sees a causal relationship between the fact that there was no king in Israel and the fact that "people did whatever seemed right in their own eyes" (17:6; 21:25).

COMPARISON WITH OTHER BIBLE BOOKS

Joshua:

- In Joshua there is strong, sustained leadership, and unity among the tribes; in Judges there is no sustained leader, and disunity among the tribes.
- In Joshua Israel takes land from the Canaanites; in Judges the Canaanites take land from Israel.
- Joshua emphasizes obedience, victory, and freedom; Judges shows disobedience, defeat, and slavery.

OUTLINE

ISRAEL'S SUBJECTION (1:1–3:8)
- The conquest of Canaan continues (1:1-26)
- Six tribes fail to conquer their land (1:27-36)
- Disobedience and its consequences (2:1–3:7)

ISRAEL'S SOLDIERS (3:8–16:31)
- Othniel (3:8-11)
- Ehud and Shamgar (3:12-31)
- Deborah and Barak (4–5)
- Gideon (6–8)
  - Gideon prepared to lead (6:11–7:15)
  - Gideon's first victory over the Midianites (7:16-25)
  - Gideon's final victory over the Midianites (8:1-21)
  - Gideon rules over Israel (8:22-35)
- Abimelech's murderous reign (9)
- Tola and Jair (10:1-5)
- The Ammonites oppress Israel (10:6-18)
- Jephthah's triumph and tragedy (11:1–12:7)
- Ibzan, Elon, and Abdon (12:8-15)
- Samson (13–16)
  - Birth of Samson (13)

Samson marries a Philistine (14)
Samson's exploits against the Philistines (15)
Samson and Delilah (16:1-22)
Death of Samson (16:23-31)
ISRAEL'S SHAME (17–21)
Micah's idolatry (17)
The Danites' idolatry and relocation (18)
The Benjamites' outrageous crime (19)
The civil war against Benjamin (20)
Reconciliation; wives for the Benjamites (21)

ISRAEL'S SUBJECTION (1:1–3:8)

1:1-26 *The conquest of Canaan continues.* The book of Judges continues the story of Israel's conquest of Canaan. Several incidents recorded in 1–2 repeat the record of Joshua.

After the death of Joshua, there was still land to be taken from the Canaanites. Judah and Simeon defeated the city of Bezek and took its king, Adoni-bezek. He was made to suffer the same torture he had inflicted on others—loss of his thumbs and big toes.

1:12-15 repeats Joshua 15:13-19, about Othniel winning the daughter of his Uncle Caleb (3:8-11).

Judah was able to conquer the major cities and mountainous region of Philistia, but the people in the valleys proved too formidable because of their iron chariots (1:16-19).

Although Judah initially took Jerusalem (1:8), it evidently regained its freedom (1:21) and remained under Jebusite control until the time of David (2 Sam. 5:6-9).

Ephraim and Manasseh were able to capture Bethel (1:22-26), an important city in patriarchal history (Gen. 28:10-19).

1:27-36 *Six tribes fail to conquer their land.* Manasseh, Ephraim, Zebulun, Asher, and Naphtali were unable to conquer important Canaanite cities. Even when they grew stronger, they didn't drive out the Canaanites but put them to forced labor instead. Dan would later choose to relocate rather than fight to claim its land (18:1-31).

2:1-6 *Warnings and weeping at Bokim.* The angel of the Lord (see exposition on Gen. 16:1-16) declared that Israel's inability to drive out all of the Canaanites was a result of its disobedience and compromise with those pagan nations. The people responded with a public display of sorrow and named the place Bokim ("weeping") to commemorate the occasion.

2:7-19 *A preview of apostasy.* The author gives a "flash-forward" summary of Israel's apostasy during the time of the judges: Although Israel obeyed the Lord while Joshua lived, after his death the new generation would serve the deities of Canaan and, as a result, would fall under Canaanite rule. Even when God sent judges to deliver Israel from oppression, they would not serve him. Instead, each generation would become increasingly more sinful (2:19).

2:20–3:7 *Intermarriage and idolatry.* God had permitted the Canaanites to remain among Israel as a test of his people's loyalty to him. Israel's association with these remaining Canaanites led to intermarriage, and intermarriage led to idolatry (3:6)—precisely what both Moses and Joshua had warned of (Deut. 7:3-4; Josh. 23:6-13).

ISRAEL'S SOLDIERS (3:8–16:31)

3:8-11 *Othniel.* Because of Israel's sin, God allowed them to be oppressed by a Mesopotamian king for eight years. Then he raised up Othniel, Caleb's nephew and son-in-law (1:12-15), who delivered Israel. The land then enjoyed 40 years of peace.

"The Spirit of the LORD came upon" Othniel (3:10). This is also said of Gideon (6:34), Jephthah (11:29), and four times concerning Samson (13:25; 14:6, 19; 15:14; see exposition on 1 Sam. 9:27–10:8.)

3:12-30 *Ehud leads with his left.* When Israel again "did what was evil," God allowed them to be oppressed for 18 years by Eglon, king of Moab. God then "raised up a man to rescue them," a Benjamite named Ehud. Entrusted to carry tribute to Eglon, Ehud used his left-handedness to conceal a dagger, with which he killed the king. He then led the Israelites in a successful battle against Moab, ushering in 80 years of peace (3:30).

3:31 *Shamgar.* Shamgar, another deliverer of Israel, killed 600 Philistines with a cattle prod.

4:1-3 *Jabin and his 900 "tanks."* The Lord "sold" Israel into the hands of the Canaanite king Jabin, who with his 900 chariots led by Sisera had a decided advantage.

4:4-16 *Deborah and Barak.* Deborah, already recognized in Israel as a prophetess, now became its judge. Barak evidently had ignored God's mandate to lead an army against the oppressing Canaanites. When Deborah reminded him of this, he agreed to go only if she would accompany him. Deborah advised Barak concerning when to fight (4:14), and the Lord caused a rout of the Canaanite army.

While Barak was somewhat overshadowed by Deborah, he is elsewhere called a deliverer of Israel (1 Sam. 12:11) and a man of faith (Heb. 11:32).

4:17-24 *Sisera seeks refuge in the wrong tent.* Sensing defeat, Sisera fled on foot and sought refuge in the tent of Jael, assuming she was a friend. Jael, however, was loyal to Israel, and while Sisera was asleep she drove a tent peg through his skull and killed him—fulfilling Deborah's prediction (4:9).

5:1-31 *Deborah and Barak sing a victory song.* After their victory, Deborah and Barak sang a song of praise to the Lord for those who had volunteered for the battle. The song called upon neighboring kings to take notice of the mighty works of God. It acknowledged Israel's hardship under Canaanite oppression and gave God all credit for the victory.

While specifically praising the tribes of Zebulun and Naphtali for their sacrificial participation (5:18), the song specifically denounced other tribes—Reuben, Dan, Asher, and "Gilead"—for not participating (5:15-17). "Gilead" probably refers to the eastern tribes of Gad and half of Manasseh.

The song acknowledged God's intervening on Israel's behalf, probably by sending a torrential rainstorm that made the battlefield too muddy and slippery for the enemies' chariots (5:20-22; see 4:7, 15).

Jael was praised (in graphic detail!) for her bravery in dealing the deathblow to Sisera (5:24-27). The song closes by imagining the emotions of Sisera's mother as she waits in vain for his return (5:28-30).

6:1-6 *Midian oppresses Israel.* Israel's continued disobedience brought an invasion by hordes of Midianites and Amalekites. For seven years they destroyed Israel's harvests. So bad was the oppression that some Israelites hid in caves (6:2).

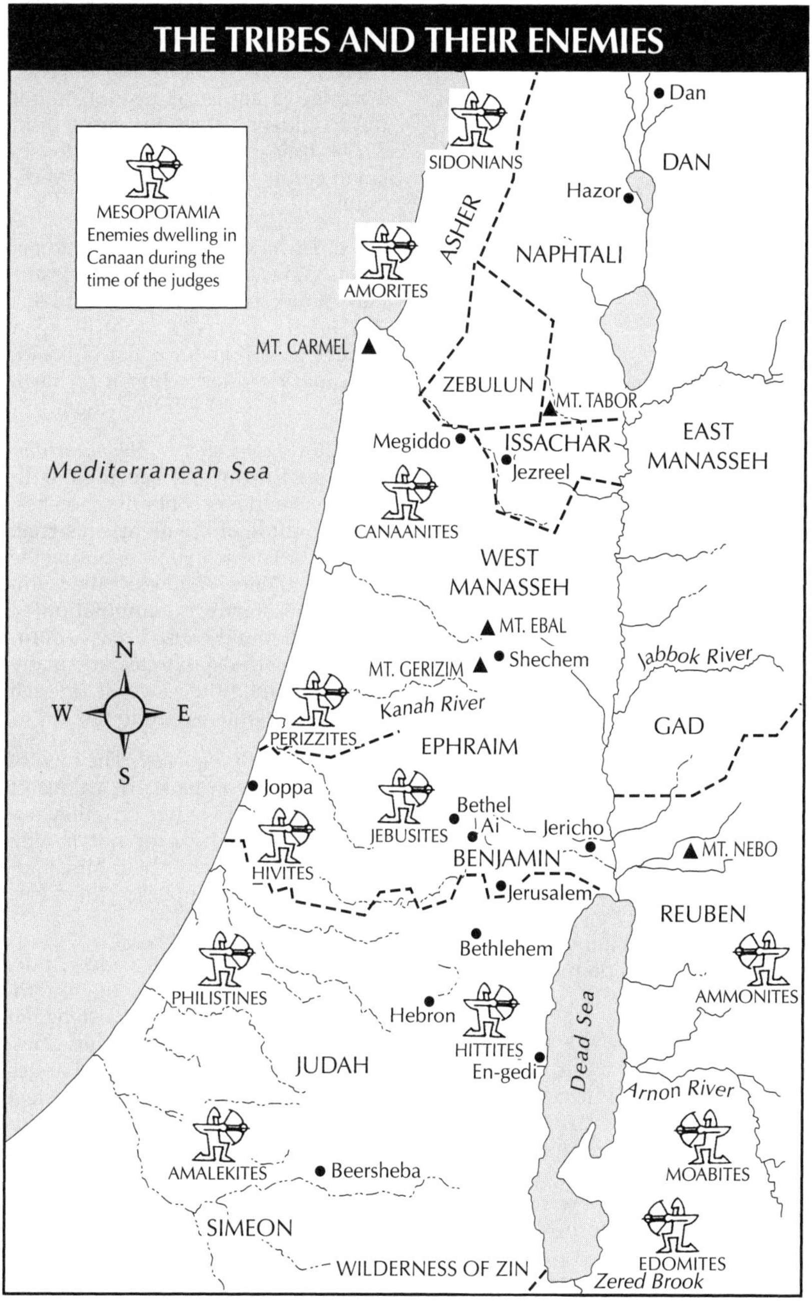

THE TRIBES AND THEIR ENEMIES
MESOPOTAMIA
Enemies dwelling in Canaan during the time of the judges
Dan
DAN
SIDONIANS
Hazor
ASHER
NAPHTALI
AMORITES
MT. CARMEL
ZEBULUN
MT. TABOR
Megiddo
ISSACHAR
EAST MANASSEH
Jezreel
Mediterranean Sea
CANAANITES
WEST MANASSEH
MT. EBAL
N
Shechem
Jabbok River
MT. GERIZIM
W
E
Kanah River
GAD
PERIZZITES
EPHRAIM
S
Joppa
Bethel
JEBUSITES
Ai
Jericho
HIVITES
BENJAMIN
MT. NEBO
Jerusalem
REUBEN
Bethlehem
PHILISTINES
Dead Sea
AMMONITES
Hebron
HITTITES
En-gedi
JUDAH
Arnon River
AMALEKITES
Beersheba
MOABITES
SIMEON
WILDERNESS OF ZIN
EDOMITES
Zered Brook

6:7-10 *"Sin brings sorrow; it's that simple."* When Israel cried out in distress to the Lord, he sent an unidentified prophet, who reminded them of God's past deliverances. God had often warned them not to worship foreign deities, but they had not obeyed. Now they were paying for their disobedience.

6:11-24 *Gideon: An unlikely leader?* The angel of the Lord confronted Gideon, a Manassehite, as he tried to salvage a little grain from the invaders by threshing in an unconventional and secret place—a winepress. To Gideon's surprise, the angel called him a "mighty hero" and instructed him to deliver Israel from the Midianites. Protesting that he was the "the least in my entire family!" (6:15), Gideon asked for a sign as reassurance of his call. When he brought an offering to the angel, the angel touched it with his staff and the offering was consumed by fire.

6:25-32 *"Let Baal defend himself."* The Lord told Gideon to tear down the pagan fertility altars belonging to his father, Joash, and build in their place an altar to the Lord. When Gideon did this, his neighbors were enraged and asked Joash to turn his son over for execution. Joash retorted that if Baal was indeed a god, they should let him defend himself. In honor of this occasion, Joash gave Gideon the name Jerubbaal (6:32; 7:1; 8:29).

6:33-35 *Gideon blows a trumpet and gathers an army.* As the armies of Midian and Amalek gathered against Israel, the Spirit of the Lord came upon Gideon. He blew a trumpet to muster an army, and his father's family responded. Messengers went to neighboring tribes to recruit additional men (6:33-35).

6:36-40 *The sign: Wet one morning, dry the next.* Through two more signs, involving a fleece, God again assured Gideon that he would deliver Israel through him.

7:1-8 *God orders some military cutbacks.* Through a series of tests, God reduced Gideon's volunteer army from 32,000 to just 300 men—ridiculously small compared to the 135,000 Midianites.

7:9-15 *His morale is boosted by a loaf of bread!* Gideon received a final assurance before battle as he overheard one Midianite warrior recounting a strange dream about a loaf of bread, and another interpreting it to mean that Gideon would destroy them.

7:16-25 *Blazing torches, blowing trumpets.* Gideon armed his men with trumpets and jars containing torches. In the middle of the night, on signal, they all broke their jars—exposing the flaming torches—and blew the trumpets. The startling combination of sight and sound caused mass confusion among the Midianites, and many of them turned their swords on each other, while others tried to flee.

8:1-3 *Gideon the diplomat.* The men of Ephraim were apparently jealous of Gideon's initial victory, and they angrily criticized him for not having called them sooner to help him. Gideon's diplomacy appeased them (see exposition on 12:1-7).

8:4-9 *"I'll be back!"* As Gideon pursued the Midianites over the Jordan, he sought food for his exhausted men at two Transjordanian Israelite cities. Fearing reprisal from the Midianites should Gideon not completely defeat them, these cities refused to help Gideon. Gideon threatened to return and punish them when his mission was accomplished.

8:10-21 *Victory and vengeance.* Most of the Midianites had already been killed; only 15,000 remained for Gideon to fight in the eastern desert. Having defeated them, he returned and took vengeance on the cities that had refused to help him.

8:22-35 *He refuses the crown, but can't resist the gold.* The Israelites wanted to make Gideon their king. He wisely rejected the offer, declaring that only God should reign over Israel. He did, however, request in return for his victory the gold earrings taken in plunder. With the gold he made some sort of image, which the people made into an object of worship. Despite this idolatry, Israel enjoyed peace for 40 years. Gideon had many wives and 70 sons.

After Gideon's death (8:32-35), Israel quickly forgot the Lord's deliverance and returned to the worship of Baal.

9:1-57 *The murderous reign of Gideon's son.* Abimelech, Gideon's son by his Shechemite concubine, aspired to be a king. Persuading his mother's relatives to support him, he hired assassins to murder his 70 half brothers, eliminating any potential competition. The murderous scheme was successful; only one of the 70 escaped. The people of Shechem declared Abimelech their king.

Jotham, the surviving half brother, told a parable that portrayed Abimelech as unfit to be king (9:7-15), and pronounced a curse on Shechem, predicting that Abimelech and the Shechemites would end up killing each other.

After Abimelech had reigned three years, there was a falling out between him and the people of Shechem. 9:24 states that God's hand was in this falling out, so that both Abimelech and the people of Shechem would pay for their crime against the 70 sons of Gideon. 9:25-57 shows God's providence at work as, true to Jotham's prediction, Abimelech and the Shechemites end up killing each other.

10:1-5 *Tola and Jair.* Tola, from the tribe of Issachar, judged Israel in some undefined capacity for 23 years. Jair, a Gileadite with 30 sons, judged for 22 years.

10:6-9 *Will they never learn? Sin brings suffering!* In spite of all their past difficulties, Israel continued to serve more and more foreign deities, and the Lord began subjecting them to oppression on two fronts—the Philistines from the west and the Ammonites from the east.

10:10-18 *"This time, you're on your own."* For the first time during the period of the judges, Israel admitted they had sinned. But God apparently knew that their repentance was not genuine, for he declared that he would no longer deliver them (10:13). He would grieve in compassion at their misery (10:16), but he would not raise up a new judge. This time Israel would have to find its own deliverer.

11:1-11 *Jephthah's testing.* Jephthah, a Manassehite, was rejected by his half brothers because his mother was a prostitute. After being driven from his home and community, however, Jephthah proved to be a capable leader. When the Ammonites threatened to attack, Jephthah's people requested that he return home to lead them.

11:12-33 *Jephthah's triumph.* After trying to negotiate with the Ammonites, Jephthah prepared for battle. Before going into battle, he made a rash vow that if the Lord would give him victory over the Ammonites, he would offer as a burnt offering "the first thing coming out of my house to greet me when I return in triumph" (11:30-31). Little is told concerning the battle except that Jephthah was victorious.

11:34-40 *Jephthah's tragedy.* To Jephthah's horror, when he returned home his only daughter was the first one to come out to greet him. Both he and his daughter agreed that he was obligated to fulfill his vow. After

THE TIME OF THE JUDGES

The action during this period centers around twelve individuals or groups of individuals.

THE ANGEL OF THE LORD . . . . . . (Judg. 2:1; 6:11; 13:3)

THE SPIRIT OF GOD . . . . (Judg. 3:10; 13:25; 14:6; 15:14)

A DISTURBING SPIRIT . . . . (Judg. 9:23)

TWELVE MILITARY REFORMERS . . . . . . (Judg. 3–8; 10–16)

A BLOODY BUTCHER . . . . (Judg. 9)

AN IDOL-WORSHIPING SON . . . . (Judg. 17–18)

A COWARDLY LEVITE . . . . (Judg. 19–20)

A MOABITE GIRL . . . . (Ruth 1–4)

AN UNDISCIPLINED PRIEST . . . . (1 Sam. 1–4)

A DEDICATED MOTHER . . . . (1 Sam. 1–2)

SOME FRUSTRATED PHILISTINES . . . . (1 Sam. 5–6)

A CIRCUIT-RIDING PREACHER . . . . (1 Sam. 7)

spending two months with her friends, she returned to her father, and he fulfilled his vow by killing her. Jephthah's actions were based on pagan traditions and would not have had God's approval.

12:1-7 *Shibboleth: Mispronounce it and you die!* As they had been with the Manassehite Gideon, the Ephraimites were jealous of the success of the Manassehite Jephthah. They accused him of not calling them to assist him when he fought the Ammonites (12:1). Jephthah was not diplomatic as Gideon had been, but bitterly scolded the Ephraimites for not coming when he *did* call them (12:2-3). Jephthah's men turned on the Ephraimites, who tried to escape across the Jordan. Those who were caught trying to cross the river were compelled to say "shibboleth" (which probably means "flowing stream"). All who pronounced it "sibboleth," using the *s* instead of the *sh* sound, were assumed to be escaping Ephraimites and were killed. *Shibboleth* has been preserved in modern times as a synonym for "password" or "test of faith."

12:8-15 *Ibzan, Elon, and Abdon.* Ibzan, a Bethlehemite with 30 sons and 30 daughters, judged Israel for seven years. Elon, from the tribe of Zebulun, judged Israel for 10 years. Abdon, from the tribe of Ephraim, judged Israel for eight years. He too had a large family—40 sons and 30 grandsons.

13:1-25 *The birth of Samson.* The angel of the Lord appeared to the barren wife of Manoah and announced that she would bear a son. She was to avoid strong drink because her son would be a Nazirite from birth (see exposition on Num. 6:1-21), with the special mission of "beginning" to deliver Israel from the Philistines (13:5, KJV, NASB, NIV). Israel would not decisively defeat the Philistines until the time of David.

A further angelic visit assured Manoah and his wife of God's supernatural involvement in their son's birth. The child Samson was born, and as he grew "the LORD blessed him" and "the Spirit of the LORD began to take hold of him" (13:24-25).

14:1-4 *His pagan wife is part of God's plan.* Samson saw a Philistine girl and wanted to marry her. His concerned parents wondered why he couldn't find an Israelite girl to marry. Samson's retort depicted the spiritual attitude of his day: "Get her for me. She is the one I want" (14:3). None of them knew, however, that this marriage was a part of God's plan to use Samson to fight the Philistines (14:4; see 13:5).

14:5-18 *The honey, the riddle, and the betrayal.* On his way to the Philistine girl's home to make wedding arrangements, Samson encountered a lion. The Spirit of the Lord empowered him to kill it. Later, when he returned that way for his wedding, he found that bees had built a honeycomb in the lion's carcass. At his wedding feast, Samson told a riddle having to do with the honeycomb, and wagered that none of the guests could solve it. (Only someone who had seen him find the honey could have solved the riddle).

The stumped Philistines threatened to burn the bride's father's house if she could not learn the answer to the riddle. After several days of tearful appeals to Samson, she learned the secret and informed the Philistine guests, who then told Samson the answer.

14:19-20 *30 die to pay his debt.* Angered by the betrayal, Samson went to another Philistine city, killed 30 men, and stripped the corpses of their clothes to pay off his riddle wager. Though Samson's actions may seem anything but spiritually motivated, "the Spirit of the LORD" (14:19) was using him "to disrupt the Philistines" (14:4).

15:1-8 *Meanwhile, his best man steals his bride!* When Samson returned to claim his wife, he was forbidden to see her. Assuming Samson had abandoned her, her father had given her in marriage to Samson's best man (14:20; 15:2)! An angry Samson, using a very unusual method, burned the ripened harvest fields and vineyards of the Philistines. When the Philistines retaliated by burning Samson's wife and her father, an even angrier Samson took revenge again, killing more Philistines.

15:9-20 *Bound by 3,000, he kills 1,000.* Some men of Judah, fearful of reprisal, persuaded Samson to let them bind him and turn him over to the Philistines. As soon as he had been turned over, however, the Spirit of the Lord enabled him to break free and he killed 1,000 more Philistines.

16:1-3 *Gaza's gates are useless against him.* A bold but careless Samson entered Gaza to visit a harlot. The Gazites tried to capture him by locking the city gates, but Samson ripped up the entire gate structure and carried it to a hill 38 miles away.

16:4-22 *But Delilah's determination does him in.* The rulers of the five main Philistine cities each promised to pay 1,100 shekels of silver to Samson's lover, Delilah, if she could find the secret to his great strength. Delilah asked Samson what his secret was. He strung her along with false answers, then, wearied by her persistence (16:16), divulged the truth: He was a Nazirite and his hair, the symbol of his separation, had never been cut.

Delilah used the information, cut his hair, and turned over a weakened Samson to the Philistines. They put out his eyes, imprisoned him, and compelled him to do hard work. There was a note of hope, however: While he was in prison, his hair began to grow again.

16:23-31 *Samson prays and pulls the house down.* When the Philistines gathered to honor their god, Dagon, they brought out the blinded Samson to entertain them. Positioning himself between two supporting pillars, he prayed for one last demonstration of strength and pulled the building down upon himself and all who were present. As Samson died, he killed even more Philistines than in all his other amazing exploits combined. Though Samson did not totally defeat the Philistines (see exposition on 13:1-25), he had fulfilled God's destiny for his life (14:4).

ISRAEL'S SHAME (17–21)

17:1-13 *A silver idol, a personal priest.* A man named Micah stole some silver from his own mother. When he returned the stolen silver, she told him she had dedicated it to the Lord and wanted him to make an idol from it. He made the image and added it to his private religious shrine, where his own son served as his personal priest.

The author of Judges interrupts this bizarre episode to note that "in those days Israel had no king, so the people did whatever seemed right in their own eyes" (17:6). He will repeat the statement verbatim as a final summary of the entire book (21:25).

An unemployed Levite wandered through Micah's region, and Micah hired him to be his personal priest in place of his son (17:7-13).

18:1-31 *"What's a nice priest like you doing in a place like this?"* Meanwhile the tribe of Dan, still unable to claim its land, decided to relocate. As they searched for a new location, they happened to encounter Micah and his personal priest. When the Danites decided to move to the northernmost region of Israel, they invited Micah's priest to accompany them (18:7-26). The Danites conquered the peaceful city of Laish and renamed it Dan after their ancestor. The city became infamous for its idolatry (18:27, 30-31).

19:1-30 *The Benjamite atrocity: "The worst crime since Egypt."* A Levite traveling with his concubine stopped in the Benjamite town of Gibeah to spend the night. When the men of the city tried to sexually assault the Levite, he gave them his concubine instead. After an entire night of brutal sexual assaults, she returned to the house where the Levite was staying and died on the doorstep. To let his fellow Israelites know of this horrendous crime, the Levite cut the woman's corpse into 12 pieces and sent them to each of the 12 tribes. All who heard of the crime agreed it was the worst they had heard of since their days in Egypt (19:30).

20:1-48 *The civil war against Benjamin.* 400,000 men from all the tribes gathered to learn the details of what the Benjamites had done to the woman. Hearing the Levite's account (which omitted his own role in surrendering her to the mob), they were unified in their resolve to punish the offenders. They demanded that Benjamin turn over the guilty men of Gibeah (20:8-13). When the Benjamites refused to do so, the 11 other tribes declared war against them.

Apparently the other 11 tribes were no more righteous than Benjamin, for Benjamin won the first two battles (20:19-25). The 11 tribes then gathered at Bethel before the Ark of the Covenant. Led by Phinehas the high priest, they wept, fasted, and offered sacrifices, and God promised victory. On the third day of battle the Benjamites were defeated, with 25,100 killed. In their zeal to win and punish, the 11 tribes turned on the Benjamite women and children as well. When the fighting ended, the only Benjamites left alive were 600 warriors who had escaped the battle.

21:1-24 *Reconciliation, wives for the Benjamites.* The 11 tribes now faced a troubling situation: They had almost destroyed an entire fellow tribe; and having vowed never to give their daughters in marriage to a Benjamite, they saw no way to save the tribe from extinction.

When it was discovered that the city of Jabesh-gilead had not joined in the war against Benjamin, the 11 tribes killed everyone in that city except for 400 virgin females, who were given as wives to 400 of the 600 surviving Benjamite warriors.

The 200 still unmarried Benjamites were granted another means of finding wives: While the men of the other tribes still would not directly give them their daughters, they were permitted to kidnap and claim as a wife any young woman who was on her way to a certain feast at Shiloh (21:16-24).

21:25 *A sad but fitting summary.* The sordid stories of Judges, which seem to grow worse as the book progresses (see 2:19), make the book's final verse a grand understatement: "In those days Israel had no king, so the people did whatever seemed right in their own eyes."

PEOPLE TO REMEMBER FROM JUDGES

DEBORAH

Key Facts: Judge, helped Barak defeat Canaanites (4–5)
Husband: Lappidoth (4:4)
Occupation: Prophetess, judge (4:4)
Total Bible References: 9
Key References: 4–5

Deborah Speaks

I often think of her, that other Deborah, whose name was given to this very palm tree under which I hold court. Perhaps I was named after her. She was a nurse; I am a prophetess. She ministered to Rebekah and Isaac; I have been called to help Barak. (4:4, 6; Gen. 24:59; 35:8)

What a sight that was, watching Barak charge down the slopes of Mount Tabor with his 10,000 troops, utterly crushing the enemy. I found myself asking, *Is this the same timid man who only a day or so ago flatly declared he would lead no army unless I went with him?* In fact I asked him, "What in the world has transformed you?" And he smiled and said, "I assumed you would know. It had nothing to do with this world. It's called faith!" (4:8, 14-15; Heb. 11:32)

I think we both felt bad about my prophecy at first, but that was before we met Jael. What a woman! Probably the words in our song of celebration said it best: "Most blessed is Jael." (4:9; 5:24)

Spiritual Lessons from Deborah

- Don't undervalue your occupation or position in life. God called an Israelite wife and mother to serve as a prophetess and to spearhead one of Israel's great military attacks (4:4-15).
- Though Deborah was right in helping Barak, we should not need another person's help to obey the clearly revealed will of God. Barak's partial obedience resulted in partial rewards (4:4-9).

Key Verses

"Deborah, the wife of Lappidoth, was a prophet who had become a judge in Israel. She would hold court under the Palm of Deborah, which stood between Ramah and Bethel in the hill country of Ephraim, and the Israelites came to her to settle their disputes. One day she sent for Barak son of Abinoam, who lived in Kedesh in the land of Naphtali. She said to him, 'This is what the LORD, the God of Israel, commands you'" (4:4-6).

EHUD

Key Facts: Judge, killed Eglon, brought peace to Israel (3:21-30)
Father: Gera (3:15)
Total Bible References: 8
Key References: 3:15–4:1

Ehud Speaks

Remember what Moses said about God's right hand saving our nation at the Red Sea—"Your right hand, O LORD, is glorious in power. Your right hand, O LORD, dashes the enemy to pieces"? (Exod. 15:6)

Well, thank God for his right hand, but I want equal time—because in our day you've seen a left-handed man save Israel! Think of it—for 18 years that fat, greedy Eglon ruled over us with a heavy hand. The nerve of some people! But no more. By God's grace and a little help from a knife and a trumpet, neither Eglon nor his 10,000 warriors will ever threaten Israel again. You should have seen his surprised look when I drew my knife with my left hand! And I wish I could have seen the look on the guards' faces when they found their king dead. They thought they had frisked me so well. Of course, by the time they found him I was long gone! I wish all those kids who used to tease me could see me now—I've still got my fast legs and my strong left arm! (3:12-30)

Spiritual Lessons from Ehud

- Ehud felt it necessary to kill Eglon for the deliverance of Israel. Christians do not live in a theocracy as the Israelites did, and Ehud's extreme solution is seldom called for, but some evils in society demand a radical response from godly people (3:21).

- God delights in choosing and using all kinds and people—male, female, black, white, young, old; despite a prejudice common in primitive cultures, God used this left-handed man for a great cause (3:15).

Key Verse
"When Israel cried out to the LORD for help, the LORD raised up a man to rescue them. His name was Ehud son of Gera, of the tribe of Benjamin, who was left-handed" (3:15).

GIDEON
Key Facts: Judge, defeated the Midianites (7:22; 8:10-12)
Father: Joash (6:11)
Sons: Abimelech, Jotham, and 68 unnamed (8:30; 9:1, 5)
Total Bible References: 40
Key References: 6–8; Heb. 11:32

Gideon Speaks
Seven bitter years of oppression because of our sin, followed by 40 blessed years of peace because of his faithfulness—what a wonderful God we serve! How little did I know about Jehovah-shalom back then. But at his command I built an altar *to* him and tore down another *for* him. (6:1, 24-25; 8:28)

300 ill-armed men pitted against 135,000 well-armed men—outnumbered 450 to one! What an uneven and unfair contest it appeared to be—and, indeed, *turned out to be* . . . for the 135,000! Courage, obedience, and faith, accompanied by trumpets, jars, torches, and shouts brought our victory. (7:6-7, 16-22; 8:10, 28; Heb. 11:32)

Dear God, please don't let the problems of the present overshadow those glories of the past. I was doing so well—proclaiming you our king, and refusing the crown. And then I started remembering all that gold, and human nature just got the best of me. That seemingly harmless gold image has become a snare and an idol for our whole nation. Merciful Lord, as you once saved us from our enemies, please now save us from ourselves! (8:22-27)

Spiritual Lessons from Gideon
- God often calls the least likely person to perform mighty acts for him (6:11-15).
- It is never wise to second-guess God's will after it has been clearly revealed (6:14-23, 36-40).
- The outcome of our spiritual battles is often dependent upon the overthrow of the "Baals" (false gods) in our lives (6:25-27).
- Even when we're outnumbered 450 to one, God can give us the victory (7:7; 8:10)!
- We should be careful of what we allow into our life, lest it become a snare to ourselves and others (8:24-27; 1 Cor. 8:9; 10:23-24, 31-33).

Key Verses
"'But Lord,' Gideon replied, 'how can I rescue Israel? My clan is the weakest in the whole tribe of Manasseh, and I am the least in my entire family!' The LORD said to him, 'I will be with you. And you will destroy the Midianites as if you were fighting against one man'" (6:15-16).

JEPHTHAH

Key Facts: Judge, defeated the Ammonites, made rash vow that he later regretted (11:30-40; 12:7)
Mother: Unnamed prostitute (11:1)
Daughter: Unnamed (11:34, 37)
Total Bible References: 28
Key References: 11:1–12:7; Heb. 11:32

Jephthah Speaks

What on earth could I have been thinking! To utter those reckless words on any occasion would be serious, but to say them on the eve of battle was sheer insanity! As if the Holy One of Israel could be bribed by a mere sacrifice. Even my wretched background is no excuse for this pitiful action. What a beautiful sight it was to watch her running to meet me, dancing joyfully to the sound of tambourines. And then it struck me like the wheel of an enemy chariot: This is my only child, my daughter—and now I must offer her up. The next two months were the most depressing and difficult of my entire life. She then returned to me, and I did to her according to my vow. O merciful God! I tearfully sought her forgiveness. Now I seek yours. (11:1-3, 29-39)

Spiritual Lessons from Jephthah

- A person's background does not in the least prevent God from working greatly in his or her life (11:1-3, 32-33; 1 Cor. 1:26-29).
- Be careful about the promises you make; be prepared to produce what you promise (11:30-40; Ps. 76:11; Eccles. 5:4-5).

Key Verses

"Jephthah made a vow to the LORD. He said, 'If you give me victory over the Ammonites, I will give to the LORD the first thing coming out of my house to greet me when I return in triumph. I will sacrifice it as a burnt offering'" (11:30-31).

PHINEHAS

Key Fact: Israel's third high priest (Exod. 28:1; Num. 20:25-26; Josh. 22:30-32)
Father: Eleazar (Exod. 6:25)
Son: Abishua (1 Chron. 6:4)
Total Bible References: 14
Key References: 20:28; Exod. 6:25; Num. 25:6-13; 31:6; Josh. 22:13-32; 24:33; Ps. 106:30

Phinehas Speaks

I can still see them: Zimri, a son of the covenant, escorting his pagan female friend, Cozbi, into the tent for sexual purposes, both of them utterly unashamed and defiant. I stood outside for a moment, gathering my thoughts concerning this incredible sight. Then I exploded with righteous indignation. Who did they think they were, snubbing their brazen noses at both God and Moses! I knew, of course, what had to be done. God's command must be obeyed: Death to all whoremongers in our camp—Israelite and pagan alike. In a moment they were dead, and the plague was over. (Num. 25:6-15)

I was also able to prevent a civil war in the days of Joshua, but not on this sad occasion. What a bloodbath! 11 tribes against Benjamin; multiplied thousands slaughtered on both sides. In fact, I'm told the tribe of Benjamin has been reduced to a mere 600 soldiers! Sin has tragically reversed the divine promise that one of us could defeat 1,000 of the enemy. Instead, we kill each other by the thousands. Forgive us, O God, for killing our own. Empower us to conquer our enemies. (20:18-48; Josh. 22:30-34; 23:10)

Spiritual Lessons from Phinehas

- Drastic situations often require drastic action. By his swift and severe judgment upon a God-defying couple, Phinehas stopped a divine plague that had already killed 24,000 people (Num. 25:6-9).
- "God blesses those who work for peace," Christ taught (Matt. 5:9). Phinehas was later a peacemaker, as his wise advice prevented a terrible intertribal war (Josh. 22:10-34).
- Sometimes, however, even the most capable and respected leaders cannot save their followers from calamity (20).

Key Verses

"Then the LORD said to Moses, 'Phinehas son of Eleazar and grandson of Aaron the priest has turned my anger away from the Israelites by displaying passionate zeal among them on my behalf. So I have stopped destroying all Israel as I had intended to do in my anger. So tell him that I am making my special covenant of peace with him. In this covenant, he and his descendants will be priests for all time, because he was zealous for his God and made atonement for the people of Israel'" (Num. 25:10-13).

SAMSON

Key Facts: Judge, known for great strength and memorable exploits in battle (14:6, 19; 15:14, 20)
Birth: Recorded in 13:2-24
Father: Manoah (13:2)
Wife: Unnamed (14:10-18)
Death: Recorded in 16:21-30
Total Bible References: 36
Key References: 13–16; Heb. 11:32

Samson Speaks

I wonder how many people are out there. By the volume of laughter there must be thousands. What a pathetic sight I must be, a half-dressed, dirty, totally blinded enemy soldier playing court jester! (16:21-25)

Obviously I didn't intend it to end this way. But then, of course, a life of sin does not exactly produce a glorious rainbow at the end of the trail. I'm sure it all began with uncontrolled lust. Not even my Nazirite vow or his mighty power on me could save me from myself. Neither Delilah nor the combined Philistine army could have conquered me from without had not the enemy from within opened the doors. Is this all I have to show after 20 years of working for Israel? (13:7, 25; 14:3, 6, 19; 15:14; 16:1)

But this is no time for remorse: The final plan is now in place, thanks to the help of this young lad. Lord God, strengthen me just this once, that I may with one blow take vengeance on the Philistines for my two eyes. Let me die with them! . . . Yes, it's working. I can feel the central pillars give way. And I hear screams instead of laughter. (15:20; 16:26-30)

Spiritual Lessons from Samson

- When should parents begin praying for their children? Long before they are born! (13:12-14).
- The Spirit of God can use us mightily in spite of our human failings (14:1-4; 16:1-3). That doesn't mean, however, that we will escape the consequences of our wrong choices (16:30).
- Casting the pearls of our faith before godless people can lead to our own spiritual blindness and slavery (16:4-21; see Matt. 7:6).
- The writer of Hebrews recalled Samson's faith (Heb. 11:32) but made no mention of his many sins—a classic example of amazing grace (Ps. 103:10-14).

Key Verse

"You will become pregnant and give birth to a son, and his hair must never be cut. For he will be dedicated to God as a Nazirite from birth. He will rescue Israel from the Philistines" (13:5).

RUTH

c. 1100 B.C.?
Events of Ruth

1093
Call of Samuel

1075
Samson, last judge

1051
Saul, 1st king

1004
David, descendant of Ruth, becomes king

BACKGROUND

Sometime shortly before 1100 B.C., during the last days of Israel's judges, an Israelite family moved to the land of Moab to escape a famine in Israel. When the father and two of his sons died, his wife returned to Israel with her Moabite daughter-in-law named Ruth. This set the stage for a beautiful story of faithfulness, love, and marriage. It is included in the Bible because from Ruth the Moabitess and her Israelite second husband, Boaz, would come Jesus the Messiah.

AUTHOR

Unknown.

DATE AND LOCATION

Though it is not known precisely when the story was recorded, it had to be at least a few generations after the events it relates, for three reasons:

- The end of the book mentions David, the great-grandson of Boaz and Ruth.
- The opening expression, "in the days when the judges ruled," implies an author who lived after that time.
- 4:7 mentions a custom "in those days" that apparently had fallen out of practice.

Ruth was probably written in Jerusalem by a court historian in the time of David or Solomon, between 1000–920 B.C.

PURPOSE

The beginning and end of Ruth reveal much about its purpose.

- The book ends with a genealogy, and the last word of the book is *David.* The primary purpose of Ruth was to document David's godly ancestry.
- A secondary purpose can be seen in the book's opening verses. After preliminary facts set the stage, the drama

opens with Naomi expressing her hope that her daughters-in-law will find "rest" or "security" after the deaths of their husbands. The same Hebrew word is found in 3:1, where again Naomi wishes "a permanent home" for Ruth, this time with a specific plan to achieve that goal. Ruth did indeed find a home in the God and people of Israel, as should all unbelievers. Ruth can be seen as representing the extension of God's grace to Gentiles.

- A final purpose was to show the wonderful, though sometimes hidden, ways in which God meets needs. Naomi was "empty" in 1:21 but had a full lap (a son) in 4:16. Note the foreshadowing of Naomi's spiritual "filling" when she was physically filled with food (3:17), as Boaz tells Ruth not to go to her mother-in-law "empty-handed," the same Hebrew word as in 1:21.

UNIQUE FEATURES

Ruth provides a marvelous illustration of redemption. The law made provision for women who, due to the death of their husband, were left without heirs and faced with the loss of their property. Both heirs (Deut. 25:5-10) and property (Lev. 25:25-28) were to be secured by a "close relative," or "kinsman redeemer" (Hebrew *goel,* 2:20; 3:9, 12-13; 4:1, 3, 6, 8, 14). This law sanctioned the ancient custom of *levirate* or "brother-in-law" marriage. Genesis 38:1-10 records an incident in which the custom was disregarded; the story of Ruth illustrates its proper application.

The kinsman redeemer had to meet three qualifications:

- he had to be a blood relative.
- he had to be willing to redeem.
- he had to be able to pay the redemption price.

The kinsman redeemer is a beautiful picture of Christ, who met all these qualifications (Gal. 4:4-5; Eph. 1:7; Heb. 2:14-15; 1 Pet. 1:18-19).

COMPARISON WITH OTHER BIBLE BOOKS

Genesis:

- Genesis, like Ruth, contains examples of God's providence. What at first seems to be coincidence often turns out to be God's plan. Joseph happened to be in the right place at the right time in Egypt, as did the servant of Abraham in Genesis 24.
- The genealogy beginning in 4:18 is similar to many such lists in Genesis and begins with the same Hebrew phrase as is found there.

Esther:

- Ruth was a Gentile who lived among Jews; Esther was a Jew who lived among Gentiles.
- Ruth married a Jew; Esther married a Gentile.
- Both Ruth and Esther had relatives to obey (for Ruth, her mother-in-law, Naomi; for Esther, her uncle Mordecai), and both were rewarded for their obedience.
- Both books contain evidence of God's providence overruling the "coincidences" of life.

OUTLINE

RUTH'S RENUNCIATION (1)
- The setting of the drama (1:1-5)
- Naomi's three commands to return (1:6-15)
- Ruth's renunciation of her people and gods (1:16-18)
- Naomi's emptiness (1:19-22)

RUTH'S REAPING (2)
- Introduction of Boaz (2:1-3)
- Boaz takes special notice of Ruth (2:4-17)
- Naomi is glad to hear of Boaz (2:18-23)

RUTH'S REQUEST (3)
- Naomi's plan (3:1-5)
- Ruth's proposal (3:6-9)
- Boaz's pledge (3:10-13)
- Ruth returns to Naomi (3:14-18)

RUTH'S REDEMPTION (4)
- Boaz confronts the nearer kinsman redeemer (4:1-8)
- Witnesses affirm Boaz as kinsman redeemer (4:9-12)
- Marriage of Boaz and Ruth; blessing of Naomi (4:13-17)
- Genealogy: From Ruth to King David (4:18-22)

RUTH'S RENUNCIATION (1)

1:1-5 *A Jewish family moves to Moab.* Elimelech and Naomi and their family moved to Moab because of a famine in Israel. Apparently at this time Moab was not hostile to Judah. The family, however, underwent even greater hardships while in Moab. First Elimelech died. Then his two sons married Moabite women and died soon afterward. The family was reduced to Naomi and her two Gentile daughters-in-law.

1:6-18 *"Your people shall be my people."* Hearing that Israel's famine had ended, Naomi decided to return there, but pleaded with both of her daughters-in-law to stay with their people and find new husbands. While Orpah reluctantly did so, Ruth could not leave her beloved mother-in-law. She declared devotion not only for Naomi but for Naomi's people and her God as well.

It is fitting that Naomi, who sought "rest" for others (1:9; 3:1, 18) while herself experiencing only unrest (1:20), should eventually find rest for herself (4:13-16).

1:19-22 *Back in Bethlehem.* Naomi and Ruth's return to Israel caused quite a stir. Feeling that her life was no longer "pleasant" (the meaning of her name), Naomi asked to be called Mara, which means "bitter" (see Exod. 15:23).

RUTH'S REAPING (2)

2:1-17 *Enter bachelor Boaz.* Boaz, a wealthy unmarried relative of Elimelech, saw Ruth gleaning in his field and, having heard of her loyalty to Naomi, treated her kindly. He gave her permission to glean indefinitely and protected her from his male workers, ordering them to leave some extra stalks for her to pick up.

2:18-23 *"Boaz, you say? Glory to God!"* When Naomi learned where Ruth had worked she rejoiced, knowing that Boaz was a "close relative" or "kinsman redeemer" (see *Unique Features*). She was well aware of the possibilities this presented for her daughter-in-law.

RUTH'S REQUEST (3)

3:1-5 *Her mission: Make a marriage.* Naomi made plans for Ruth to ask Boaz to redeem her. When Boaz retired for the night, Ruth was to lie down, "uncover" his feet, and await an opportunity to speak with him. This was apparently a local custom; though Ruth as a foreigner may have found it strange, she promised to obediently follow Naomi's instructions.

3:6-13 *"I'd love to, but there's this problem. . . ."* Ruth uncovered the feet of the sleeping Boaz, and at about midnight he awoke and was startled to find a woman there. Learning her identity and hearing her request, Boaz gladly agreed to be her kinsman redeemer. He pointed out, however, that there was a closer relative who should first be given the opportunity to fulfill that role for Ruth. If that man refused, Boaz promised, he would become Ruth's redeemer.

"Spread the corner of your covering over me" (3:9) is a figure of speech for marriage, portraying the refuge marriage provides. Upon their first meeting (2:4-13), Boaz had commended Ruth for taking "refuge" "under [the] wings" of Israel's God (2:12). The same Hebrew word is used in both verses; it can be translated *wing* or *corner (of a garment)*. Little did Boaz know that he himself would be the means through which God would protect Ruth. Ezekiel 16:8 uses the same imagery to show God's care for Israel.

3:14-18 *She returns before she can be recognized.* Ruth did not sleep *with* Boaz, but at his feet; and she arose the next morning early enough to leave without creating gossip. When she returned home and told Naomi how things had gone and of Boaz's generosity, Naomi knew that Boaz would act promptly on Ruth's behalf.

RUTH'S REDEMPTION (4)

4:1-6 *He confronts the man with the prior claim.* Even as Naomi was expressing her confidence in him, Boaz went to the town gate and approached the closer relative concerning Ruth and Naomi. The man initially agreed to redeem their land. But when Boaz mentioned that a widow went along with the land, he declined the offer, fearing an adverse effect on his own financial affairs.

The town gate was the center for social and economic life in ancient Israel. This was where news was first heard, where local and traveling merchants sold their wares in the cool shade of the town walls, where soldiers were stationed, and where legal disputes were handled.

4:7-12 *He makes a statement with his sandal.* To affirm his unwillingness to redeem Naomi and Ruth and their land, the nearer relative removed his sandal. Boaz then announced, in the presence of the assembled elders, that he would assume the duties of kinsman redeemer. They affirmed his right to do so, and pronounced a blessing on him.

As 4:7 explains, the passing of a sandal was one of many symbolic gestures or "sign acts" practiced by the Israelites. Note that, by removing his own sandal, the closer relative may have avoided the public humiliation of having his sandal forcibly removed for declining his responsibility toward Naomi and her dependents (see Deut. 25:5-10).

Footwear often symbolized ownership in Bible times. Note Psalm 60:8 (KJV), where the Lord cast his shoe over Edom, claiming his ownership of that land. Note also God's directive to Abraham, Moses, and Joshua to claim ownership of Canaan by walking on it (Gen. 13:17; Deut. 11:24; Josh. 1:3).

4:13-17 *They are married; she is blessed.* Ruth and Boaz were married and had a son. Naomi's friends saw this grandchild as a special blessing for Naomi in her bereavement.

4:18-22 *Her son: King David's grandfather.* The final verses of Ruth trace the lineage of Boaz, which would eventually produce Israel's Messiah. God did not work only through Israelites, but also through Moabites and even Canaanites (such as Rahab) who believed in him. Ruth was King David's great-grandmother, and Boaz was the son of Rahab, a Canaanite harlot (Josh. 2).

PEOPLE TO REMEMBER FROM RUTH

BOAZ

Key Facts: Married Ruth, became ancestor of Christ (4:13, 21-22; Matt. 1:5-16)
Father: Salmon (4:21)
Mother: Rahab (Matt. 1:5)
Wife: Ruth (4:13)
Son: Obed (4:13, 17)
Occupation: Farmer (2:3)
Total Bible References: 33
Key References: 2–4

Boaz Speaks

Thank God for the speedy decision of Ruth and Naomi's kinsman redeemer! I practically grabbed the sandal out of his hand before he could change his mind! No doubt about it, Ruth was well worth waiting for. All my friends would agree that I didn't exactly jump into marriage. In fact, some probably wondered if I would ever settle down. (4:6, 8)

But my mother had repeatedly urged me to choose a godly woman. Apparently she still suffered from some unpleasant memories concerning her immoral past, in spite of God's marvelous transforming grace. Of course, until that first encounter in the field, neither mother nor son could have imagined that God would select a Moabite widow to answer our prayers. (2:8; Josh. 2:1; Matt. 1:5; Heb. 11:31)

Spiritual Lessons from Boaz

- We should treat everyone kindly—even strangers—for we never know what good might come of such encounters (Heb. 13:1). Boaz showed kindness (2:5-16) and found a good wife (4:13).
- As much as he desired Ruth, Boaz acknowledged that there were certain legal responsibilities to fulfill before he could claim her (3:12-13). Emotions should not cause us to take shortcuts around divine or human laws.
- God gives his best to those who allow him to make the choice! By waiting on the Lord, Boaz found a good wife and became an ancestor of Christ (1:15-18; 2:11-12; 4:13-22).

Key Verse
"And with the land I have acquired Ruth, the Moabite widow of Mahlon, to be my wife. This way she can have a son to carry on the family name of her dead husband and to inherit the family property here in his hometown. You are all witnesses today" (4:10).

NAOMI
Key Fact: Ruth's mother-in-law (1:3-6)
Husband: Elimelech (1:2)
Sons: Mahlon and Kilion (1:2)
Total Bible References: 21
Key References: 1–4

Naomi Speaks
I probably have the dubious distinction of being the only one of my people to exchange a good name for a bad one. You probably know that my given name, Naomi, means "pleasant." But during a terrible emotional storm I changed it to Mara, meaning "bitter." Of course I was not trusting God at the time, or I would have remembered that he often does just the opposite—that is, he often changes a bad name for a good one. I remember Elimelech pointing this out to me and the boys—how God changed the name of Sarai, meaning "contentious," to Sarah, meaning "princess." He also changed Jacob, "supplanter," to Israel, "one who wrestles with God." (1:20; Gen. 17:15; 32:28)

I am anything but bitter these days, to say the least; that's why I've returned to my original name. A merciful God has indeed bestowed upon me many pleasant blessings, including a wonderful daughter-in-law and a precious grandson. Little Obed has become the light of my life. (1:16-17; 4:16-17)

Spiritual Lessons from Naomi

- We should never conclude in the hour of sorrow, as did Naomi, that "the LORD himself has caused me to suffer" (1:13). In spite of that despair, Naomi later saw that same divine hand in a much more favorable light and promptly acted upon her new understanding (2:20; 3:1-4).

Key Verse
"One day Naomi said to Ruth, 'My daughter, it's time that I found a permanent home for you, so that you will be provided for'" (3:1).

RUTH
Key Facts: David's great-grandmother, ancestor of Christ (4:13, 21-22; Matt. 1:5)
Husbands: Mahlon and Boaz (4:10-13)
Son: Obed (4:13, 17)
Total Bible References: 13
Key References: 1–4

Ruth Speaks
As I sit here watching little Obed play, my thoughts go back to those bittersweet years in Moab. Frankly, I thought my life was over when Mahlon died. How wrong I was! My wonderful life in Israel as the wife of my dear Boaz has all but erased

those memories. I knew from the moment I met Boaz that he was a very special man of God. And my life with him has certainly confirmed those first impressions. (1:5; 2:4-23; 4:13-17)

I wonder what happened to Orpah. Did she ever remarry? Did she return to her gods? I surely hope not. I have longed so often to share my faith in Jehovah God with her. (1:6-14)

Obed is becoming stronger and smarter each day. But even more important, he is from the tribe of Judah. Boaz tells me his ancestor Jacob predicted that Israel would one day have kings and that they would come from our tribe. Is it possible that I might become the mother or grandmother or even great-grandmother—of a king? Of such thoughts are dreams made. (4:6-17; Matt. 1:5)

Spiritual Lessons from Ruth

- Ruth became a believer during an hour of great sorrow (1:4-5, 16-17). Sometimes adversity is a much more faithful friend than prosperity.
- Our good deeds do not go unnoticed or unrewarded by God. Ruth's wonderful kindness to Naomi (2:11-12; 4:15) was surpassed by God's wonderful kindness to Ruth. She married the godly Boaz (4:13), became the great-grandmother of King David (4:18-22), and was included in the genealogy of Christ himself (Matt. 1:5-6, 16).

Key Verses

"Ruth replied, 'Don't ask me to leave you and turn back. I will go wherever you go and live wherever you live. Your people will be my people, and your God will be my God. I will die where you die and will be buried there. May the LORD punish me severely if I allow anything but death to separate us!'" (1:16-17).

1093 B.C.
Call of Samuel

1051
Saul,
1st king

1024
David's 1st
anointing,
Goliath

1011
Death of Saul,
David's 2nd
anointing

1 SAMUEL

BACKGROUND

1 Samuel records Israel's transition from rule by judges to rule by kings. While Samson was the last judge mentioned in the book of Judges, Samuel also "judged" Israel (7:6, 15-17; Acts 13:20); therefore the period of the judges could be said to have lasted till the coronation of Saul as Israel's first king (10). The low ebb of religious life seen in 1–10 certainly prolongs the sad note sounded at the end of the Judges account (Judg. 21:25).

Israel's next true "deliverer" or "judge" would be their second king, David (16–31), who would himself be the forebear of Israel's final great deliver, the Messiah (see 2 Sam. 7:12-17).

AUTHOR

Though Samuel was involved in producing written records (10:25), the whole of 1, 2 Samuel cannot be from him since he died (25:1) before many of the events of those books transpired. Accounts from the prophets Samuel, Nathan, and Gad were probably joined together by an unknown author (see 1 Chron. 29:29).

DATE

1, 2 Samuel were originally one book, which was later divided simply because it was too long. The events covered in the two books—from the birth of Samuel to the end of David's reign—took place 1100–971 B.C. Since the compiler did his work during the time of "the kings of Judah" (27:6), the books must date from the time of the divided kingdom and were likely completed not long after the death of Solomon (931 B.C.).

LOCATION

Samuel apparently had a school for prophets at Ramah (19:20) in the central part of Israel. Initial records about Saul and David would have been kept there. Once Jerusalem was established by David as the capital, court records began to be kept there, and this is probably where the two books were compiled.

PURPOSE

- Along with Numbers, Deuteronomy, and Judges, the books of Samuel sought to promote the "prophetic viewpoint": Obedience to God brings rewards; disobedience brings punishment.
- 1 Samuel shows the dangers of making demands on God, specifically Israel's desire to have a king just as their pagan neighbors had (8:4, 20).
- On the other hand, 1 Samuel records the fulfillment of the ancient prophecy that Israel's kings would come from the tribe of Judah (Gen. 49:8-12).

UNIQUE FEATURES

- 1 Samuel introduces Samuel, whom we might call Israel's first "professional prophet." Samuel was a circuit rider (7:15-17) and founder of several schools for prophets (10:10; 1 Kings 18:13; 2 Kings 2:3, 5; 6:1-2).
- Other highlights (and lowlights) of 1 Samuel include
  - ➤ One of Scripture's most memorable teachings on obedience (15:22) and on outward appearances vs. true worth (16:7)
  - ➤ Scripture's greatest friendship (18:1)
  - ➤ History's tallest man (17:4)
  - ➤ A desperate king of Israel consulting a witch (28:3-25)

COMPARISON WITH OTHER BIBLE BOOKS

The Saul of 1 Samuel and the Saul (Paul) of the NT:

- Both were from the tribe of Benjamin (9:1-2; Phil. 3:5); the first was tall and impressive in appearance (9:2), while the second was probably unimpressive (2 Cor. 10:10).
- The first began as God's friend and ended as God's enemy (10:6-7; 28:6); the second began as God's enemy and ended as God's friend (Acts 9:1; 2 Tim. 4:18).
- The life of the first was characterized by disobedience (13:13; 15:22-23); the life of the second was characterized by obedience (Acts 26:13-19).

OUTLINE

THE STORY OF HANNAH (1:1–2:11)

- Her sorrow (1:1-8)
- Her supplication (1:9-18)
- Her son (1:19-28)
- Her song (2:1-11)

THE STORY OF ELI (2:12–3:21)

- Eli and his sons (2:12-36)
- Eli and Samuel (3)

THE STORY OF THE ARK OF GOD (4:1–7:2)

- The Ark captured in battle (4:1-11)
- Death of Eli (4:12-22)
- The Ark removed to Philistia (5)

The Ark returned to Israel (6:1–7:2)
THE STORY OF SAMUEL (7:3–10:27)
His leadership: The covenant at Mizpah (7:3-17)
His sons' failure; Israel asks for a king (8)
His anointing of Saul (9–10)
THE STORY OF SAUL (11–15)
Saul the sovereign (11–12)
Saul the sinner (13–15)
Disobedience concerning a sacrifice (13)
Poor leadership of his troops (14)
Disobedience concerning the Amalekites (15)
THE STORY OF DAVID (16–31)
David the selected (16:1-13)
David the singer (16:14-23)
David the soldier (Goliath) (17)
David the hunted (18–26)
Saul hopes the Philistines will kill David (18)
Saul tries to capture David (19)
Jonathan warns David (20)
Saul punishes those who help David (21–22)
Saul tries to capture David at Keilah (23:1-13)
Saul tries to capture David in the wilderness (23:14-29)
David takes part of Saul's robe at En-gedi (24)
David and Abigail (25)
David takes Saul's spear and jug (26)
David the sidetracked (27–31)
David lives among the Philistines (27)
Saul and the witch at Endor (28)
The Philistines prepare to fight Israel (29)
David avenges the raid on Ziklag (30)
Death of Saul; defeat of Israel (31)

THE STORY OF HANNAH (1:1–2:11)

1:1-8 *Trouble in a two-wife family.* 1 Samuel opens with the story of a man from Ephraim named Elkanah and his two wives, Peninnah and Hannah. Elkanah favored Hannah, which made Peninnah jealous even though she had borne many children while Hannah was barren. So bad was the rivalry that Hannah sometimes became unable to eat. Elkanah tried in vain to remind Hannah how special their relationship was, asking, "You have me—isn't that better than having ten sons?" (1:8).

Like the number seven, the number 10 showed completion or special emphasis. Job, for instance, said that he was insulted "ten times" (Job 19:3) when the actual number was less than that.

1:9-11 *"Give me a son, and I'll give you my son!"* Hannah prayed about her barrenness, promising that if God would give her a son she would give him back to God for lifelong service. The pledge "as a sign the has been dedicated to the LORD, his hair will never be cut" (1:11) indicates she would dedicate him as a Nazirite (see exposition on Num. 6:1-21; Judg. 13:1-25).

As in Genesis 8:1 and Exodus 2:24, the Hebrew word sometimes translated "remember" (1:11, KJV, NIV) does not mean "to recall" but rather "to pay special attention to." Paul used the corresponding Greek verb in a similar way when he talked about remembering the poor (Gal. 2:10).

1:12-18 *"In that case, may your request be granted!"* As Hannah prayed for a son in the Tabernacle at Shiloh, Eli the priest at first thought she was drunk. Finally convinced of her sincerity, he assured Hannah that her prayers would be answered. With this reassurance, Hannah began eating again.

The NIV translates "Tabernacle" (1:9; 3:3) as "temple," and many scholars agree that the Israelites had probably erected a permanent house for the Ark by this time.

1:19-28 *A baby boy for the barren wife.* As Eli had promised, Hannah had a son, whom she named Samuel. And as *she* had promised, as soon as Samuel had been weaned she gave him back to God. Humanly speaking, it must have been the most difficult task of Hannah's life to give up such a longed-for son at such an early age.

2:1-10 *A prayer of praise from a mother of many.* Her barrenness long forgotten, Hannah offered praise to the God who had given her a son. While Elkanah had claimed to be better than 10 sons, Hannah now saw herself as a mother of "seven" (2:5), obviously a figurative expression of her great joy.

God is called a "Rock" (2:2) numerous times throughout Scripture. The image refers to the towering cliffs and outcroppings in the Judean desert. These would later be places of refuge for David when he fled from Saul, thus the prevalence of the image in the psalms he wrote.

2:11 *The high priest's helper.* Samuel "became the LORD's helper, for he assisted Eli the priest." Though he was not from the high priest's family, Samuel would turn out to be far more godly than Eli's own sons (2:12-17).

THE STORY OF ELI (2:12–3:21)

2:12-17 *His greedy and godless sons.* Eli's two sons, Hophni and Phinehas (1:3), were greedy and irreverent in their dealings with sacrifices and the people who offered them. They threatened worshipers who resisted their irreverence (2:16). They even committed immorality with women who had come to serve at the Tabernacle (2:22; see Exod. 38:8).

2:18-21 *Linen robes for her little son.* Unlike Eli's wicked sons, the young Samuel was devoted to his work in the Tabernacle. Though Hannah had truly given Samuel back to the Lord, she was allowed to assist him in his ministry by making him a new robe each year. Eli blessed Hannah each time she visited, and she bore five more children—making her the mother of at least six (see 2:5)!

Samuel was a Levite (1 Chron. 6:26, 33) and served as a priest (2:18-21; 7:5-14; 13:11). "The hill country of Ephraim" (1:1) identified his father's geographic origins.

2:22-26 *He tries to warn them, but it's too late!* Eli's sons became so notorious that everyone began reporting them to Eli. They ignored his reprimands, apparently because he had been chronically ineffectual as a father (see 3:13). Meanwhile Samuel "continued to gain favor with the LORD and with the people" (2:26).

2:27-29 *"You honor them, and dishonor him."* A prophet held Eli directly responsible for his sons' conduct.

2:30-36 *All will die before their time; two will die the same day.* The prophet went on to tell Eli that the wickedness he had allowed in his household would be severely punished. All his male descendants would die young, and the priesthood would eventually be taken from them altogether (see 1 Kings 2:27). As a sign that all this would transpire, Hophni and Phinehas would die on the same day.

3:1-9 *A call from God confirmed by Eli.* When Samuel was still very young, and Israel's spiritual condition was dark, he heard God's voice, and Eli confirmed his call as a prophet. The three calls (3:4, 6, 8) indicate God's firm intent to call Samuel; the number three, like seven and 10, stands for completion (1:1-8; 2:1-10).

3:10-21 *"What did God say?" With heavy heart he tells him.* Samuel's first assignment as a prophet was to reconfirm God's intention to bring judgment on the house of Eli. Eli coerced the reluctant Samuel to tell him the whole truth, and accepted it as God's will.

Eli's question (3:17) shows that God's judgment on him had already begun: God was no longer speaking through Eli, but through Samuel. The whole nation recognized this (3:20).

"Dan to Beersheba" (3:20, KJV, NKJV, NIV) was the traditional way of defining Israel's boundaries, though under Solomon it would extend beyond those points.

THE STORY OF THE ARK OF GOD (4:1–7:2)

4:1-11 *"The Ark will save us!" (or so they thought).* Israel fought against the Philistines and were badly defeated. Deciding that the presence of the Ark of the Covenant might improve their prospects, they brought it from Shiloh to the battlefield. When the people saw the Ark, "their shout of joy was so loud that it made the ground shake" (4:1-5). When the Philistines heard the shout and knew that the Ark had arrived in the Israelite camp, they were terror-stricken, for they had heard about the plagues in Egypt and the miraculous Red Sea crossing. Their fear became a wake-up call, however, and they defeated Israel and captured the Ark (4:6-11). The two sons of Eli were killed in the battle—both of them on the same day, precisely as prophesied (2:34).

Israel had failed to completely conquer Canaan in Joshua's day (Josh. 13:1), and the Philistines and other nations remained a threat. The Philistines held most of the coastal plain: When Israel was weak they made incursions inland; when Israel was strong they were confined to the coast.

The Ark apparently never returned to Shiloh. Some historians believe Shiloh was destroyed by the Philistines sometime after Eli's death. Nob, the "city of the priests" (22:19), apparently replaced Shiloh as Israel's center of worship.

4:12-18 *He dies of a broken neck.* When Eli heard of Israel's great defeat, his sons' deaths, and the capture of the Ark, he fell from his seat, broke his neck, and died an ignoble death.

4:19-22 *She dies of a broken heart.* When Phinehas's wife heard the news, she died in childbirth, but not before naming her son Ichabod, meaning "Where is the glory?"; for, she observed, the Ark's capture meant that "the glory has departed from Israel" (4:22).

5:1-12 *"We've got a tiger by the tail!"* When the Philistines brought the Ark home with them, two remarkable things happened: The idol of Dagon, their main deity, fell down as if worshiping the Ark; and the people were struck with illness and many died. Moving the Ark to two other cities only brought the plague to those places as well. The conclusion was obvious: The Ark must be returned to Israel (5:11)!

6:1-12 *Sent back, by superstition and science.* Asked what to do about the Ark, the Philistine priests proposed a solution that was half superstition and half scientific experiment:

- Gifts of gold, in shapes representing the plague, should go with the Ark as a "guilt offering" (6:3) to Israel's God. This offering was probably more superstition than faith.
- The Ark and gifts should be sent on a cart led by two cows that had never pulled a cart, and had been recently separated from their calves. The cows' natural inclination would be to return to their calves. Even had their calves been with them, the chances of these unbroken cows pulling the cart toward Israel would have been slim indeed. If the cows took the Ark to Israel, it would be obvious that the plague had come from Israel's God (6:9).

That the cows did take the Ark to Israel (6:10-12) was clearly God's doing since, unled by human hands, they "went straight along the road toward Beth-shemesh."

6:13–7:2 *Received, with rejoicing and regret.* As the Philistines watched from a distance (6:16), the people of Beth-shemesh received the Ark with joy. Carelessly, however, a great number of them looked inside the Ark and were struck dead (6:19; see Num. 4:20). God does not tolerate impious acts, whether committed by pagans or by believers.

Though they had rejoiced at its return, the men of Beth-shemesh were now eager to be rid of the Ark. It was taken to Kirjath-jearim, where it remained for 20 years. The brevity of the account of those 20 years (7:2) leaves the impression that the Israelites just wanted the Ark stored away somewhere so that it would do no further damage.

THE STORY OF SAMUEL (7:3–10:27)

7:3-6 *"Destroy your idols and come to Mizpah!"* Having already demonstrated spiritual leadership (see 4:1), Samuel now led a great revival at Mizpah.

7:7-14 *The enemy hears and attacks.* The Philistines probably viewed the gathering at Mizpah not as a revival but as a political and military "pep rally" that would threaten their interests, so they gathered their forces against Israel. Terrified, the Israelites urged Samuel to pray on their behalf. Samuel prayed and offered sacrifices, and the Lord delivered them miraculously, ushering in an era of peace between Israel and Philistia that would last throughout Samuel's lifetime. "Ebenezer" (7:12) means "the stone of help."

7:15-17 *Israel's first circuit-riding preacher.* From his home base at Ramah, Samuel traveled regularly to key cities in Israel. He "continued as Israel's judge for the rest of his life" (7:15). Samuel obviously had a solid ministry that made a lasting impact on Israel.

8:1-9 *"Give us a king," they cry.* Samuel made his two sons judges, but they were corrupt and dishonest. The people asked for a king, claiming distrust of Samuel's sons as their reason. Yet their own words betrayed their real motive: They wanted a king "like all the other nations" (8:5)—a word-for-word fulfillment of Moses' 300-year-old prediction (Deut. 17:14)! The Lord then showed Samuel the real reason behind Israel's desire for a king: "They don't want me to be their king any longer" (8:7).

8:10-18 *"Here's what your king will cost you."* Samuel warned the people that the institution of kingship would eventually become oppressive and a financial drain on the nation.

8:19-22 *"Give us a king," they cry again.* Despite Samuel's warnings, the people again demanded a king. Finally, the Lord directed Samuel to grant their wish.

9:1-2 *Enter Saul: The answer to their prayers?* From the description in 9:2, Saul was just the kind of king the Israelites were looking for—the tallest and most handsome man in all Israel. Saul's father, Kish, was "a rich, influential man."

9:3-26 *He looks for lost donkeys but finds a new life.* While looking for his father's lost donkeys, Saul was told that a prophet in a certain place could help him find them. That prophet turned out to be Samuel, who had been instructed to anoint Saul as Israel's first king. When Samuel declared his intention to Saul, calling him "the focus of all Israel's hopes," Saul was understandably surprised (9:20-21).

9:27–10:8 *For Saul: Anointing, three signs, and the Spirit.* In 1051 B.C., without even Saul's servants present, Samuel anointed him and proclaimed him king. Then he foretold three signs that would confirm to Saul that God had chosen him. Next, Saul would experience a special visitation of God's Spirit. After all these things had transpired, Saul was to go to Gilgal and await Samuel's arrival.

Although the Holy Spirit did not indwell believers in OT times, passages such as 10:6 indicate that God did grant special visitations of his Spirit to OT believers (see 16:13; Exod. 31:3; Num. 11:17, 25; Judg. 6:34; 14:6; Neh. 9:20; Isa. 61:1; Ezek. 2:2; Mic. 3:8).

10:9-16 *A new heart for the new king.* All the signs confirming Saul's kingship occurred that very day, just as Samuel had predicted. In addition, God "changed [Saul's] heart" to equip him for his new responsibilities as king.

The people were surprised to find Saul among the prophets (10:10-13), but God can call anyone into his service. Note the similar call of Amos, who had no background in prophecy before his call (Amos 7:14-15).

10:17-27 *"Here's your king . . . but where is he?"* Having reminded the people once more that a vote for a king was a vote against God, Samuel prepared to present Saul to them . . . but Saul was nowhere to be found—until the Lord himself exposed his hiding place (10:22). Saul's apparent reluctance was the first indication that he would not live up to the special gifts and empowerment God had given him.

While Saul surely made a strong impression on most of the people (10:23-24), not all those present were ready to accept his leadership (10:27).

THE STORY OF SAUL (11–15)

11:1-11 *Saul "rides to the rescue" at Jabesh-gilead.* When the Ammonites threatened Jabesh-gilead, the people of that city were not certain that Israel could muster an army to rescue them. Possibly because of the opposition noted in 10:27, Saul had not yet asserted his authority as king—when news of the Ammonite threat reached him, he was in the field with his cattle (11:5). As soon as he heard of the problem, however, he raised an army from all of Israel and defeated the Ammonites.

The Ammonites were one of the enemies of Israel to the east, in modern-day Jordan; the Philistines were the enemy on the west, that is, the coast; and the Arameans (Syrians) were the enemy to the north.

Symbolic acts such as the sending of parts of oxen (11:3-8) were quite common in the ancient Near East (Judg. 19:29-30). Various Israelite prophets performed similar "sign acts":

- rending clothes as a sign of mourning (2 Sam. 1:11; 2 Kings 5:7-8; Matt. 26:65)
- sprinkling ashes on one's head to show repentance (Dan. 9:3; Matt. 11:21)
- wearing a yoke to warn of impending captivity (Jer. 27:2; 28:10).

11:12-15 *Crowned again, but he won't kill his critics.* Having seen him prove himself in battle, the whole nation united to proclaim Saul king. He was gracious in victory, refusing the suggestion that he should eliminate his critics (10:27).

12:1-5 *The final words of a faithful man.* Saul's coronation was also the occasion for Samuel's "farewell address" to Israel. He began by reminding the people that having a king was their choice, not his. Then he reminded them that he, as their judge, had never oppressed them; though he didn't say so explicitly on this occasion, he had previously warned that kings *would* oppress them (8:10-22).

12:6-13 *They haven't learned the lessons of history.* Samuel then gave a brief historical review, stressing that Israel's disobedience had always brought disaster, that their repentance had always brought deliverance, and that God was their true king (see 10:19).

12:14-15 *But today, a new chance to pass the test!* Israel's sad history did not have to be repeated: If the people and their new king followed the Lord, they would have peace and prosperity; if not, then disaster would come again.

12:16-25 *A miracle to back up his message.* To add emphasis to his warnings, Samuel called on the Lord to send a rainstorm, even though it would interfere with the harvest. The Lord obliged, and the storm struck fear in the people's hearts. Having gotten their attention, Samuel warned them once more that their future prosperity would depend on obedience to their true king. Yet even in their times of disobedience, said Samuel, God would be merciful; and Samuel, for his own part, would faithfully pray for them.

13:1-7 *The Philistines prepare for war.* Saul's son Jonathan attacked a garrison of Philistines, causing the whole Philistine nation to prepare for war with Israel. The people of Israel were so terrified that they hid in caves and bushes (compare Judg. 6:2).

13:8-15 *A king with a foolish heart, a man after God's heart.* Eager for God's blessing against the Philistines, and impatient when Samuel didn't arrive to offer a sacrifice, Saul took it upon himself to act as priest. Samuel rebuked him for doing so and declared that, because of his rash and impious actions, his kingship was doomed. God would seek "a man after his own heart" to replace Saul.

This was the first of Saul's two critical failures; the second is recorded in chapter 15. Soon after that second failure, God found in David the man after his own heart (see Acts 13:22).

13:16-23 *A well-equipped enemy.* As Israel and the Philistines prepared for battle, there was a "David and Goliath" imbalance between them—with the Philistines representing Goliath! The Philistines evidently controlled the iron supplies of that region (13:19), and Israel's army had no swords (13:22). (On 13:21, see *Pim,* p. 890.)

14:1-15 *Jonathan's faith and bravery.* Convinced that God was with him, Jonathan went into the Philistine encampment with no one but his armor bearer. With a little help from an earthquake, they killed 20 enemy soldiers. Jonathan's attitude that "nothing can hinder the LORD. He can win a battle whether he has many warriors or only a few!" (14:6) recalls the story of Gideon (Judg. 7; see also 17:46-47; Zech. 4:6; Matt. 19:26).

14:16-23 *The Philistines panic; Israel prevails.* Jonathan's exploit and the earthquake threw the Philistines into confusion. Under Saul's leadership, Israel seized the opportunity and chased them farther to the west.

Saul's desire to have the Ark of the Covenant with his troops (14:18) is the first mention of the Ark since 7:2, where, after the events of 4:1–7:2, the people understandably had wanted little to do with it.

14:24-30 *Jonathan criticizes his father's curse.* Before going into battle, Saul had pronounced a curse on anyone who ate anything before the victory was won. After unwittingly violating his father's decree (14:27), Jonathan sharply criticized it, saying that a much greater victory could have been won had the people been well-fed and in good spirits. The author apparently agreed with Jonathan's criticism, noting that Saul's troops were "weary and faint" (14:24, 28, 31).

14:31-35 *Saul's law causes his soldiers to break God's law!* When they finally had a chance to eat, Saul's soldiers were so hungry that they ignored the law's decree about draining the blood before eating meat.

14:36-46 *Saved from his own father.* Saul inquired of the Lord as to whether or not he should further pursue the Philistines. Getting no answer, he assumed there was sin among his soldiers, and he promised to kill the offender. When the offender turned out to be Jonathan, he tried to kill him, but his soldiers protected Jonathan. The episode shows that Saul made rash decisions and that he was losing stature in the eyes of his people.

14:47-52 *The family and army of Saul.* Though Saul was not always faithful, he did have some notable military successes. One price of that success, however, was that he had to maintain a standing army, and he claimed for that army all the "brave and strong" men of Israel—fulfilling Samuel's warning about what a king would do (8:11).

Notable among Saul's children is Michal (14:49), who would become David's wife (18:27) and would be a pawn in the conflict between David and Saul (18:20-25; 19:11-17; 25:44). Abner (14:50), Saul's cousin and commander of his army, would be humiliated by David (26:13-16) and, after Saul's death, would lead the fight to keep the throne in Saul's family (2 Sam. 2–3).

15:1-5 *Samuel says, "Destroy them all!"* Samuel told Saul to "completely destroy" the Amalekites, sparing none of them, not even their animals. Samuel was repeating what Moses had commanded some 300 years before: The Amalekites were to be punished for their cowardly attack on helpless Israelites during the Exodus (see exposition on Exod. 17:8-16; Deut. 25:17-19).

15:6-9 *Saul says, "Let's keep their animals."* Saul killed all the Amalekites . . . except for their king and the best of their animals. While the Amalekites were destroyed because of their opposition to Israel during the Exodus, the Kenites were spared because of their kindness to Israel during that same time.

15:10-23 *"Your sin has cost you the crown."* Both the Lord and Samuel were deeply grieved at Saul's disobedience. Saul, for his part, added pride (15:12), lying (15:15), and passing the blame (15:21) to his disobedience. Calling Saul a rebel against God (15:23), Samuel declared once again that God had rejected him as king (see 13:13-14).

15:11 speaks of God "repenting" (KJV). However, Samuel says later in the chapter that God does not repent like a man does (15:29, KJV). People often live to regret decisions made hastily or with too little information. Obviously God faces neither of those problems. He does, however, change direction sometimes, simply because people change and do not always follow the path God has laid out for them.

15:22 is one of the great OT descriptions of true worship (Isa. 1:11-17; Mic. 6:6-8).

15:24-35 *"Pray for me," he requests. "It's too late," he replies.* Saul begged to be forgiven and kept in power, but Samuel rejected his plea. Samuel then finished Saul's assignment by personally killing the Amalekite king Agag.

Though God's forgiveness is unlimited, he usually allows us to face the consequences of our sin—as would also be the case with David's sins of adultery and murder (2 Sam. 11).

THE STORY OF DAVID (16–31)

16:1-13 *The youngest anointed with oil and the Spirit.* In about 1024 B.C., God instructed Samuel to pay a visit to Jesse, to proclaim one of his sons Israel's next king. God rejected the most likely candidate, declaring that he was more interested in the new king's heart than in his outward appearance (16:7); he didn't want another Saul (9:2)!

God passed by seven of Jesse's sons and settled on David, the youngest, to be his king—yet another example of the older serving the younger (see exposition on Gen. 25:19-26). David would have been about 17 at the time.

Samuel anointed David with oil (16:13). *Messiah,* the Hebrew name for Christ (John 1:41), literally means "anointed one." David was called the Lord's anointed (2 Sam. 19:21), but so was Saul (1 Sam. 24:10) and even the Persian king Cyrus (Isa. 45:1), whom God used to accomplish his purpose.

David was also anointed with the Holy Spirit (16:13), just as Saul had been (10:10).

16:14-23 *Songs to soothe the savage beast.* The Holy Spirit, which God had given Saul when he became king (see exposition on 9:27–10:8), now departed and was replaced by a "tormenting" spirit. At the recommendation of his servants, Saul sent for David, who was a musician. David's music soothed Saul; he became Saul's armor bearer and trusted friend as well (16:21). David would become a composer and lyricist as well as a musician, authoring fully half of the Psalms.

17:1-11 *"We've got a morale problem: He's 10 feet tall!"* As the Philistines and Israelites faced off on opposite hilltops, the Philistines presented their "champion" Goliath (17:4), with a winner-take-all proposition: Send your best man to fight him; whichever side loses will become slaves of the other side. The Israelites, including King Saul, were terrified at the prospect.

The detailed weights and measurements given for Goliath and his armor in the original Hebrew suggest the historical accuracy of this account. Goliath was not just six cubits or seven cubits tall—he was "six cubits and a span" (17:4, KJV). Someone had actually measured him.

17:12-22 *A delivery boy with a care package.* As the battle raged and Goliath continued taunting Israel (17:16), David was dividing his time between his duties in Saul's palace and his duties as a shepherd. Jesse sent him with some food for his older brothers who were in Saul's army.

17:23-30 *David: "Who does he think he is!" Eliab: "Who do you think you are!"* Having seen Goliath and having heard of his boasts, David expressed outrage that a "pagan Philistine" would dare say such things about God's people. But Eliab, David's oldest brother, was equally outraged that the young David would make even the slightest suggestion that he could take on Goliath. Meanwhile, despite the offer of a fabulous reward (17:25), none of Saul's men were willing to face Goliath (17:24).

17:31-37 *"He'll fall, just like the lion and bear!"* When David offered to take on Goliath, Saul was skeptical, but David's enthusiasm and stories of his boyhood feats finally won Saul over; he sent David to the task with his blessing. David had been faithful in little things; now the stage was set for greater things.

17:38-47 *Five smooth stones, and God's help.* Saul gave David his own armor, but David rejected it in favor of his more familiar sling and stones. When he encountered Goliath, the giant was disdainful of David and his sling. But David proclaimed that he would be victorious because he would fight in God's name and with his help.

Throughout his dealings with Goliath, David was guided not by a desire for personal glory but by his zeal for the Lord (17:26, 36, 45, 47).

17:48-54 *Struck by a stone, severed by a sword.* The first rock from David's sling found its target, but David took Goliath's sword and stabbed him just to make sure he was dead. Then he cut off his head. Their champion fallen, the Philistines fled. Goliath's sword would soon be in David's hand again (21:9).

17:55-58 *"Abner, whose son is that?"* Impressed by David's victory, Saul inquired about his family background. This seems strange in light of their previous relationship (16:19-23), and some scholars have suggested that some of these events may have been recorded out of their historical sequence. It could also be that Saul was preparing to honor his earlier pledge of tax exemption for the father of the man who would kill Goliath (17:25).

18:1-5 *David finds new fame and friendship.* David now became a permanent part of Saul's court, "a commander in his army," and loved by all of Saul's servants. Especially noteworthy was his new friendship with Saul's son Jonathan—a friendship that would be greatly tested in the months ahead.

18:6-9 *Bitten by the envy bug.* Saul overheard some local women praising David—at Saul's expense—and was stricken with envy. From that day on, he would be consumed with evil thoughts toward David.

18:10-16 *David grows more famous; Saul grows more fearful.* The next time David played his music for Saul, Saul tried to kill him. Realizing that God had departed from him and was protecting David, Saul banished David from his presence. As Saul grew ever more fearful of David, David grew ever more popular with the people.

18:17-30 *"The Philistines will kill him—with the help of my daughters!* Saul continued to conspire against David, even using his daughters as pawns in his deadly game. He offered first Merab, then Michal, to David, for the price of killing 1,000 Philistines. When David killed 2,000 and claimed Michal, Saul feared him all the more (18:29). Throughout this crisis David remained humble (18:18) while Saul remained envious (18:25). But while Saul's influence continued to decline (18:17, 19), David became more and more prominent (18:30).

19:1-10 *A warning from Jonathan, another spear from Saul.* Jonathan warned David that Saul was after him again. He then reminded Saul of David's heroism and exacted from him a promise not to kill David. But Saul once again tried to spear David while he was playing his music.

19:11-17 *David's wife saves his life.* Still hoping that others would help him kill David, Saul sent messengers to lie in wait at David's house. Michal discovered the plot and helped David escape.

19:18-24 *Saul seeks David, finds the Spirit instead.* David fled to Ramah, where Samuel was still carrying on his prophetic ministry. When Saul learned of it, he sent three separate delegations of soldiers to capture David. All three groups, upon arriving in Ramah, experienced religious awakenings. Finally, Saul himself went to Ramah, where he also experienced "the Spirit of God" (19:23) and temporarily abandoned his pursuit of David.

20:1-11 *"Trust me: Dad doesn't want to kill you."* David knew Saul was trying to kill him, but Jonathan thought his fears were unfounded. David proposed a test: He would miss the banquet scheduled for the following day; if Saul was angry at his absence, both he and Jonathan would know that Saul was trying to kill him. David would certainly have been missed at the banquet: The head table seated only four: Saul, Jonathan, Abner, and David.

20:12-17 *The covenant of close companions.* Before finalizing their plans for the day of the banquet, Jonathan, son of the king, and David, destined to be the next king, made a covenant of loyalty between themselves and their descendants. Once again the writer notes Jonathan's great love for David (20:17; see 18:1, 3; 19:1).

20:18-23 *The arrows will give the answer.* The plan was set: On the day of the banquet, David would be hiding in a nearby field. Once Jonathan had brought up the matter of David's absence and seen Saul's response, he would signal that response to David with three arrows. If the arrows signaled that Saul was angry, David would flee. Jonathan reminded David that even if he fled, their covenant should still be honored (20:22-23).

20:24-34 *A brush with death convinces him.* Saul was indeed angry that David didn't attend the banquet. In a rage he tried to kill Jonathan; that convinced Jonathan that David's fears were justified. Saul claimed that his anger was for the benefit of Jonathan, for as long as David lived Jonathan would not inherit the throne (20:30-31). But the weight of evidence suggests it was Saul's envy of David, not his concern for Jonathan, that fed his murderous anger.

20:35-42 *With sorrow they go their separate ways.* As David must have expected, the arrows signaled Saul's rage. He and Jonathan embraced, reaffirmed their covenant, and David embarked upon the life of a fugitive.

21:1-7 *The fugitive tells a falsehood.* Having fled to Nob, David sought food from a priest for himself and his men. He lied about his situation, evidently fearing rejection if he admitted to being a fugitive. Apparently he didn't fully trust God's revelation that he would be king.

The only food available was the holy bread, but David convinced the priest to let him eat it. Jesus would later give implicit approval to David's action, using this incident to illustrate the proper relationship between law and compassion (Matt. 12:1-4; see Lev. 24:1-9).

Saul's servant Doeg saw David at Nob (21:7) and would later reveal David's location to Saul (22:9).

21:8-15 *David the madman.* Not wanting to stay at Nob too long, David asked the priest for a sword and prepared to leave. He was given the strongest and sharpest sword in the land—Goliath's sword, which had been stored there.

David's next stop was in Philistine territory, where he sought the help of Achish, king of Gath. There, fearing he had been recognized, he pretended to be insane and apparently was escorted out of town.

Throughout his flight from Saul, David moved in and out of Philistine territory and the wilderness of the Judean hill country.

22:1-5 *The frustrated 400.* Returning to Israelite territory, David attracted the attention of his family—and some 400 derelicts and malcontents. He took his parents to Moab, the land of his ancestor Ruth, so that he could focus on his own crisis without worrying about their safety.

David then organized the 400 men into a private army and, at the direction of a prophet, moved them into Judah, which provided the protection of hills and forests.

22:6-10 *"I saw him at Nob."* Saul gave his servants a tongue-lashing for not doing more to help him capture David. Under this pressure, Doeg revealed that he had seen David at Nob and that Ahimelech the priest had helped him.

22:11-19 *The spy becomes the executioner.* Saul sent for Ahimelech and charged him with treason for helping David. Ahimelech reminded Saul of David's faithfulness (22:14) and pleaded ignorance concerning David's fugitive status, but Saul ordered the execution of Ahimelech and the 85 other priests at Nob. When Saul's servants refused to kill these holy men, he assigned the job to Doeg.

22:20-23 *"I should have known he was a spy."* One priest, Abiathar, son of Ahimelech, escaped the slaughter and brought the grim news to David. Recalling that he had seen Doeg at Nob and had known Doeg would report him to Saul, David blamed himself for the massacre. He promised to protect Abiathar against Saul.

Abiathar became David's priest (23:9) and would name his son for his slain father. This second Ahimelech would become a key adviser to David (2 Sam. 8:17).

23:1-13 *David rides to the rescue.* Having heard that the Philistines were attacking Keilah, David mustered his army and saved the city. When Saul heard David was in Keilah, he made plans to capture him, but David escaped, taking his ragtag fugitive army and "roaming the countryside" (23:13). David's deliverance of Keilah increased not only his fame but his army as well. The 400 had now grown to 600.

23:14-29 *The 600 head for the trees and caves.* David and his men found refuge in forests and caves in the wilderness of Ziph. There Jonathan secretly visited him, and they renewed their covenant (23:16-18). This would be their final meeting.

Jonathan voiced what he had likely known all along: that David was God's choice for king. And he added, "as my father is well aware" (23:17; see exposition on 24:8-22).

23:26 indicates how close Saul came to capturing David. Later, of course, David by his own choice would come much closer than this to Saul.

Ironically, David escaped Saul this time when the Philistines unexpectedly invaded (23:27), their invasion having been made possible by Saul's own foolish preoccupation with David.

24:1-7 *A funny thing happens in the cave.* Having taken care of the latest Philistine invasion, Saul heard that David was hiding in the wilderness of En-gedi. Pursuing him there, he happened to stop for a rest in the very cave where David was hiding. David's men urged him to seize this opportunity to kill Saul, but instead he merely cut off the edge of Saul's robe. He later regretted even taking such a harmless action against Saul, "the LORD's anointed one."

The hem of a robe was an important status symbol in those days. Cutting this part of the clothing was highly symbolic, explaining David's remorse.

This was the first of two times David would pass up an opportunity to kill Saul (see 26).

24:8-22 *"I just spared your life, so why do you seek mine?"* David showed Saul the severed hem of his robe as evidence that he did not intend to kill him. Saul acknowledged that David was a better man than he, and was more fit to be king. 24:20 was Saul's first official admission that David was to be king, though he knew all along that this was God's will (13:13-14; 15:28; 23:17).

Having secured David's oath of nonaggression (24:21-22), Saul called off his pursuit and went home. From this point on, Saul would vacillate between hatred for David and sorrow for that hatred. David, evidently anticipating such changes, stayed in hiding (24:22).

25:1 *The death of Samuel.* Although it is doubtful that Saul gave him any serious attention in his later years, the whole nation lamented Samuel's death.

25:2-35 *Abigail saves her stupid spouse from certain death.* David's men had shown kindness to the shepherds of Nabal, a wealthy businessman (25:7, 21). When David sought a favor from Nabal in turn, he refused and belittled David (25:10-11), and David planned revenge. When Nabal's wife, Abigail, heard what was happening, she secretly brought David a peace offering and urged him not to take revenge on her husband.

Even Nabal's wife acknowledged that he lived up to his name, which means "fool" (25:25). Abigail, by contrast, was very sensible (25:3), a fact shown by her recognition that David was destined to be king (25:28) and by the wise advice she gave him (25:29-31).

David realized the soundness of Abigail's advice and called off his retaliation against Nabal (25:32-35).

25:36-44 *Death for Nabal, a new wife for David.* When Abigail went to tell Nabal about his narrow escape from David, Nabal was in the midst of a drunken feast. When Abigail finally told him the news, he became immobilized by fear. 10 days later, the Lord himself took Nabal's life.

David saw Nabal's death as his vindication and as his opportunity to claim Nabal's beautiful and sensible widow as his wife. Meanwhile Saul reclaimed his daughter Michal, David's first wife, and gave her to another man.

26:1-25 *Spared again, while he sleeps.* Once again Saul pursued David, and once again David passed up a chance to kill him:

- This time, as before, David was held in check by his reluctance to kill "the LORD's anointed one" (26:9; see 24:6).
- This time, as before, he took evidence to show that he could have killed Saul (26:11-12, 16; see 24:4, 11).
- This time, as before, David disclaimed any desire to usurp Saul's throne (26:18-20; see 24:9-15).
- And this time, as before, the narrow escape caused Saul to repent of his efforts to kill David (26:21-25; see 24:16-22).

David's humiliation of Abner (26:13-16) could help explain Abner's later opposition to David.

27:1-12 *The man of faith has a lapse of faith.* Though Saul had once more repented of pursuing him, David still did not trust Saul. Nor apparently did he trust God to protect him, for he went once more to the Philistine city of Gath to seek the help of King Achish (see 21:10-15). Achish gave David and his men the city of Ziklag as a place of refuge.

During the year and a half he lived in Ziklag, David and his 600 men made frequent raids against mutual enemies of Philistia and Israel. David felt compelled, however, to tell the Philistines that the raids were against Israel, so that the Philistines would not think he was loyal to Saul.

28:1-2 *David? In the Philistine army?* The Philistines prepared once more to fight against Israel. Assuming that David was indeed disloyal to Saul, the Philistines recruited him for their army—and David felt he had no choice but to pretend to be on their side.

28:3-25 *Saul and the spirit of Samuel.* Terrified at the size of the Philistine army, Saul sought the Lord's help but heard no answer. In desperation he visited a medium and asked her to contact the recently deceased Samuel. Samuel appeared and predicted that the Philistines would defeat Israel and that Saul would die in battle the very next day.

Samuel made a direct connection between Saul's impending death and his disobedience to God (28:18).

All indications are that the spirit was indeed Samuel. This does not mean the Bible teaches that the dead can be contacted, just that in this instance God chose to bring Samuel back to speak to Saul. The medium's apparent fright upon seeing Samuel (28:12) suggests that even she recognized it was God's hand, not her own powers, that brought him back.

29:1-11 *The Philistines suspect and reject David.* As the Philistines prepared to fight Israel, some of their military leaders became suspicious of David. Although Achish still supported David, the majority distrusted him, so David and his men were sent back to Ziklag.

30:1-20 *Ziklag: Raid and recovery.* When David and his men arrived at Ziklag, they found that the Amalekites had destroyed the city and captured its inhabitants. David pursued the Amalekites, located and defeated them, and recovered all his people and possessions. God's providence was obvious in that "Nothing . . . small or great, son or daughter, or anything else" was lost to the Amalekites (30:19).

The people remaining in Ziklag had discussed stoning David, yet even in these terrible circumstances David found spiritual strength in his relationship with God (30:6).

30:21-31 *Generous in victory.* When David had pursued the Amalekites, 200 of his 600 men had been too exhausted and had stayed behind (30:10). Despite the protests of some of his men, he insisted that those who had stayed behind should share equally in the spoils with those who had fought.

In another display of gratitude, David sent a share of the spoils to all the cities that had helped him and his men during his prolonged flight from Saul (30:26-31).

31:1-13 *Slain as Samuel had said.* True to Samuel's prediction (28:19), the Philistines defeated Israel, and Saul and his three sons—including Jonathan—were killed. Saul asked his armor bearer to kill him so that no Philistine could claim that honor. When the armor bearer refused, Saul committed suicide.

The Philistines made a public display of Saul's body. When the men of Jabesh-gilead heard of it, they rescued the body and gave it a proper burial (31:11-13). The year was 1011 B.C., some 13 years after David had been anointed to succeed Saul.

❖ ❖ ❖

PEOPLE TO REMEMBER FROM 1 SAMUEL

ELI

Key Fact: High priest served by the young Samuel (1–4)
Sons: Hophni and Phinehas (1:3)
Age at Death: 98 (4:12-18)
Total Bible References: 33
Key References: 1–4

Eli Speaks

Why on earth did they carry the Ark to the battlefield? Did they see it as some kind of heavenly rabbit's foot to bring them luck? Oh, Hophni and Phinehas, my wicked sons! Don't you realize the futility of depending on the Ark of God when you have turned your backs against the God of the Ark? (2:22; 4:3-4)

Israel will probably lose this battle and I'm mostly to blame. I put my boys before the Lord and never really tried to restrain them. How differently they have turned out from that mighty prophet I once trained as a boy in the Tabernacle. (2:29; 3:1-9, 13)

That cry coming from the city! It must mean the messenger from the battlefield has arrived. Yes, there he is. What is the news? Merciful God! The battle is lost, my sons are dead, and the Ark has been captured! It is too much. My life is over. (4:14-18)

Spiritual Lessons from Eli

- When we judge others too quickly, we usually judge them wrongly (1:9-16; Matt. 7:1).
- Spiritual leaders need to be careful not to neglect the spiritual education of their own children. To rephrase Mark 8:36, "What shall it profit a father if he gains great spiritual stature and loses his own sons?" (2:12-17; 3:13)

Key Verses

"Then the LORD said to Samuel, 'I am about to do a shocking thing in Israel. I am going to carry out all my threats against Eli and his family. I have warned him continually that judgment is coming for his family, because his sons are blaspheming God and he hasn't disciplined them'" (3:11-13).

HANNAH

Key Fact: Mother of Samuel (1:19-20)
Husband: Elkanah (1:2)
Total Bible References: 13
Key References: 1–2

Hannah Speaks

It's true: You simply cannot out-give God! I dedicated Samuel, my firstborn, to serve God in the Tabernacle. Then, he gave me three more sons and two daughters—six healthy children! A far cry from that barren, heartbroken woman who once stood in the Tabernacle in bitterness of soul, praying for a son! Elkanah couldn't be more proud, and the once-proud Peninnah couldn't be more subdued! (1:1-11, 27-28; 2:18-21)

I trust that my Samuel has been a real help to Eli. The combined forces of advanced age, excessive weight, and two wicked sons have taken their frightful toll. It's such a contrast to see Eli's saddened face during our yearly visit to the Tabernacle, and then to see the joy-filled countenance of my son. (1:12-18, 25-26; 2:18-26; 4:18)

Did I ever teach him the words of that song his miraculous birth inspired? "My heart rejoices in the LORD! Oh, how the LORD has blessed me! Now I have an answer for my enemies, as I delight in your deliverance." (2:1)

I'm sure that Samuel knows that same kind of joy.

Spiritual Lessons from Hannah

- God often pours his richest blessings on those most despised by the world. Hannah, despised by Peninnah because she was barren (1:2, 6), bore six children, including one of Israel's greatest prophets (1:20; 2:21; 3:19-20; see Ps. 113:9).
- Hannah realized what all parents must realize: God gives us our children that we might give them back to him (1:11, 27-28).

Key Verses

"I asked the LORD to give me this child, and he has given me my request. Now I am giving him to the LORD, and he will belong to the LORD his whole life" (1:27-28).

JONATHAN

Key Facts: Saul's son, David's closest friend (14:1; 18:1-4)
Mother: Ahinoam (14:49-50)
Brothers: Eshbaal, Malkishua, Abinadab (14:49; 1 Chron. 8:33)
Sisters: Merab, Michal (14:49)
Son: Mephibosheth (2 Sam. 4:4)
Death: Recorded in 31:1-2
Total Bible References: 91
Key References: 13–20; 23:16-18; 31:1-2

Jonathan Speaks

I will die on the battlefield tomorrow along with my father and brothers. I think I already knew this in my heart, even before that bizarre event with the medium of Endor, which provoked Samuel's devastating prophecy. Well, it could be worse. I'd much rather be killed *with* my father than *by* him, which he actually tried to do two times! Unbelievable! Having your own father seek your life for eating some honey and for supporting God's anointed man! (14:26-30; 20:33; 28:19; 31:2)

How tragic that he came to regard David, my best friend, as his most bitter foe. Yet this "notorious outlaw" spared my father's life two times. It's all too much for me to sort out. (18:1-42; 24:4; 26:12; 2 Sam. 1:25-27)

No matter. Tomorrow the end will come. My only real concern is Mephibosheth. What will become of my five-year-old son? I comfort myself by remembering the covenant David and I made in the forest so many years ago. I know he'll keep his promise. (20:12-16; 23:16-18; 2 Sam. 4:4; 9:1-13)

Spiritual Lessons from Jonathan

- Real friendship often demands sacrifice. Jonathan's unwavering support of David provoked the hatred of his father, Saul (20:30), eliminated any possibility of his own future kingship (20:31), and nearly cost him his life (20:33).
- The benefits of close friendship often continue even after death. David would later honor and care for Mephibosheth, Jonathan's crippled son (2 Sam. 9:1-13; 21:7).

Key Verse

"After David had finished talking with Saul, he met Jonathan, the king's son. There was an immediate bond of love between them, and they became the best of friends" (18:1).

SAMUEL

Key Facts: Prophet and priest, anointed both Saul and David as king (3:1, 20; 9:27–10:1; 16:13)
Place of Birth: Near Mount Ephraim (1:1, 19-20)
Father: Elkanah (1:19-20)
Mother: Hannah (1:19-20)
Brothers: 3 unnamed (2:21)
Sisters: 2 unnamed (2:21)
Sons: Joel, Abijah (8:1-3)
Key Events in His Life:

- Assists Eli in ministry (2:18-21)
- Called by God; prophesies against Eli (3)
- Leads national revival (7:2-17)
- Anoints Saul as king (9–10)
- Condemns Saul for acting as priest (13:1-14)
- Condemns Saul for sparing Agag (15:10-35)
- Anoints David as king (16:4-13)
- Appears posthumously to Saul (28)

Death: Recorded in 25:1
Total Bible References: 134
Key References: 1–16; 19:18-24; 25:1; 28; Jer. 15:1; Heb. 11:32

Samuel Speaks

I should probably consider this a great honor: I'm the only person ever allowed to return to this earth after having departed from it! But the nature of my mission and message somehow dims its glory. "God has become your enemy," I tell him. "In 24 hours both you and your sons will die on the battlefield. David will inherit your kingdom!" For a moment it looks as though Saul will die right here in the witch's parlor! (25:1; 28:14-20)

Eli, Saul, and David—three men who have affected my life more than any others. The first was good but weak; the second was sullen and wicked. I wonder about the third: I hope he will prove both faithful and fruitful. (3:13; 13:14; 16:14)

My thoughts return to Saul. Would it have come to this had his mother dedicated her son to God as did mine? I can still see him standing there on the doorstep of my home in Ramah, inquiring about his father's missing donkeys. He was staggered with astonishment when I told him to forget the lost animals because he had "found" the throne of Israel. (9:1–10:1)

Oh, Saul! What went wrong? I wanted so much for you to succeed. Disobedience: I suppose that comes as close to explaining it as anything. (15:22, 35–16:1)

The old king will soon be dead. Long live the new king! *Ichabod* described Saul. By God's grace, may *Ebenezer* describe David's reign. (4:21; 7:12)

Spiritual Lessons from Samuel

- Even young children can know when God is speaking to them (3:1-10).
- A spiritually mature person will be approved by God and respected by others, as is seen in the lives of both Samuel and Jesus (2:26; Luke 2:40, 52).
- An obedient life is a productive life, as God assures that none of our works or words "fall to the ground" (3:19, KJV, NKJV, NIV).
- We should find ways to remember the good things God does for us, just as Samuel established the stone called Ebenezer to remind Israel of God's help (7:12).
- It is tragically possible for godly fathers to raise ungodly children, as did both Eli (2:12-17) and Samuel (8:1-5). See Proverbs 22:6 for the answer to this tragedy.
- It is easy, but dangerous, to judge people by outward appearances rather than by the content of their character (9:2; 13:13-14; 16:7).

Key Verses

"As Samuel grew up, the LORD was with him, and everything Samuel said was wise and helpful. All the people of Israel from one end of the land to the other knew that Samuel was confirmed as a prophet of the LORD" (3:19-20).

SAUL

Key Fact: Israel's first king (9:27–10:1)
Father: Kish (9:1-2)
Wife: Ahinoam (14:50)
Sons: Jonathan, Eshbaal, Malkishua, and Abinadab (14:49; 1 Chron. 8:33)
Daughters: Merab, Michal (14:49)
Key Events in His Life:

- Chosen as king (9–10)
- Saves Jabesh-gilead (11)
- Condemned for acting as priest (13:1-15)
- Condemned for sparing Agag (15)
- Begins hostilities toward David (18:1-16)
- Murders 85 priests for helping David (22:6-19)
- Continues pursuit of David (23:7–24:22; 26)
- Consults medium at Endor (28)
- Dies in battle (31)

Death: Recorded in 31:1-6
Total Bible References: 388
Key References: 9–31

Saul Speaks

Wretched woman! How did she escape when I purged the land of her kind? But even more wretched am I. Look at me, Israel's king, reduced to wearing strange clothes and sneaking by night to the home of a witch! Disgraceful! And it's all God's fault, of course. He refuses to counsel or comfort me. No mystery though. David was always his favorite. (13:14; 28:3, 6, 8)

I've been rejected simply for doing my own thing. Isn't that what rulers are expected to do? Incredible! Choosing a sheep tender over me! The lad has already demonstrated his weakness in twice sparing me, his mortal foe. How can a man expect to be a successful king when he can't even deal harshly with his own enemies? (13:11-12; 15:12-24; 24:4-7; 26:12)

But I must admit he is clever, being able to persuade both Samuel and my own son to join his ranks. Really, looking back, I would have been better off purging such fools as these men from the land rather than worrying about all those witches. Well, there are at least 85 religious leaders he can't count on to help him any longer. (16:12-13; 22:17-18 23:16-17)

Curses! She recognizes me! I must quickly reassure her or all is lost.

Good, she accepts my reassurances. What's that? She reports seeing an old man wearing a robe, ascending up out of the earth. Yes, it has to be Samuel! At last! Now I'll know the outcome of tomorrow's battle. Hopefully it will be a positive message. But how do I explain this sickening dread descending on me? (28:14)

Spiritual Lessons from Saul

- The Christian life is a marathon, not a 100-yard dash. Saul began well, displaying obedience (9:3-5), respect (9:7), humility (9:21), courage (11:1-11), and a forgiving spirit (11:12-13). But ultimately he failed God miserably in all these areas and many more.
- Don't try to assume a responsibility God has not given you (13:9-14).
- God values obedience more than the careful observance of religious traditions (15:22).
- The inward enemy of envy is far more dangerous than any outward enemy (18:9-12; 19:1; 20:30-31; 23:7).
- To refuse the ministry of the Holy Spirit is to invite the presence of an evil spirit (16:14).
- A life of disobedience always brings regret (26:21).
- If we reject God, he will reject us (15:23; 2 Tim. 2:12-13).

Key Verses

"How foolish!' Samuel exclaimed. 'You have disobeyed the command of the LORD your God. Had you obeyed, the LORD would have established your kingdom over Israel forever. But now your dynasty must end, for the LORD has sought out a man after his own heart. The LORD has already chosen him to be king over his people, for you have not obeyed the LORD's command'" (13:13-14).

2 SAMUEL

BACKGROUND

1 Samuel records David's rise to power as Saul fell from God's favor. 2 Samuel tells the story of David's kingship and the establishment of his royal line (3:10), through which Jesus the Messiah, the final and greatest Davidic king, would come (7:12-13; see Isa. 9:7; Luke 1:32). The book begins just before David's second anointing as king, in 1011 B.C. (see 2:4), and ends shortly before his death in 971 (see 1 Kings 2:10).

AUTHOR

(See *1 Samuel: Author.*)

DATE AND LOCATION

(See *1 Samuel: Date, Location.*)

PURPOSE

- While Judges showed Israel's need for a king and 1 Samuel showed that David was God's choice as king, 2 Samuel shows God's blessing on his chosen king. The people needed to know this in order to respect and obey the king.
- David's successors needed to be reminded of the "prophetic viewpoint": Obedience to God brings reward; disobedience brings punishment. This is clearly illustrated in God's blessings for David's obedience and punishment for his sin.

UNIQUE FEATURES

- 2 Samuel records the establishment of Jerusalem as God's Holy City.
- The law of sowing and reaping is nowhere more clearly illustrated than in the tragic results of David's sin with Bathsheba.
- While 1 Samuel records the anointing of David as king by Samuel in the presence of his family (1 Sam. 16:13),

1051 B.C.
Saul, 1st king

1011
Death of Saul, David's 2nd anointing

1004
David's 3rd anointing, king of all Israel

1002
David and Bathsheba

971
Death of David, Solomon king

931
Death of Solomon, kingdom divided

2 Samuel records the two public anointings of David as king, by the people of Judah (2:1-7) and by all 12 tribes (5:1-5).

- 2 Samuel introduces the second of the three most important OT unconditional covenants: the Davidic covenant (7:10-16; see *Biblical Covenants,* p. 820). The other two are
  - ➤ the Abrahamic covenant (Gen. 12:1-3)
  - ➤ the New Covenant (Jer. 31:31)

COMPARISON WITH OTHER BIBLE BOOKS

Ezekiel:

- While David fought to keep Israel's 12 tribes together, the Messiah foretold in Ezekiel will find no disunity among the tribes (Ezek. 37:15-22).
- Both books discuss preparations for a temple: David for Solomon's Temple; Ezekiel for the millennial Temple.

(See *1 Chronicles: Comparison with Other Bible Books.*)

OUTLINE

DAVID THE SOVEREIGN (1–10)
- David's lament for Saul and Jonathan (1)
- David anointed king over one tribe (2:1-7)
- War between David and Ishbosheth (2:8–4:12)
- David anointed king over all 12 tribes (5:1-5)
- David captures Jerusalem (5:6-16)
- David defeats the Philistines (5:17-25)
- David brings the Ark to Jerusalem (6)
- God's covenant and David's response (7)
- David's victories listed (8)
- David's kindness toward Mephibosheth (9)
- David defeats the Ammonites and Arameans (10)

DAVID THE SINNER (11)
- His sin of adultery (11:1-5)
- His sin of deceit (11:6-13)
- His sin of murder (11:14-27)

DAVID THE SUFFERER (12–20)
- First payback for David's sin: Death (12)
- Second payback: Incest (13:1-22)
- Third payback: Murder (13:23-39)
- Fourth payback: Absalom's rebellion (14–18)
- Aftermath of Absalom's rebellion (19)
- Sheba's rebellion (20)

DAVID THE STATESMAN (21)

DAVID THE SINGER (22–23)
- His song (22)
- His last words (23:1-7)
- His mighty men (23:8-39)

DAVID THE STATISTICIAN (24)

DAVID THE SOVEREIGN (1–10)

1:1-16 *His death report brings his own death.* A young Amalekite brought the news of Saul's death to David, who was in Ziklag after defeating the Amalekites. The young man claimed to have dealt the deathblow to the dying Saul, at Saul's request. After a time of mourning for Saul and Jonathan (1:11-12), David reprimanded the young man for having killed the Lord's anointed, and ordered his execution.

According to 4:10, David assumed that the young man was expecting a reward for killing Saul.

1:17-27 *A song of national mourning.* David composed and sang a song in honor of Saul and Jonathan. He expressed hope that the Philistines would not find comfort in Saul's death, then went on to praise the two men for their skill and bravery in battle (1:21-23, 25, 27), their qualities of character (1:23), and their skill as national leaders (1:24).

David reserves special laments and praises for Jonathan, with whom he had enjoyed a special friendship (1:26). His description of Saul as "gracious" was generous, considering Saul's relentless efforts to kill him (1 Sam. 18–26).

2:1-7 *David anointed by Judah.* At God's direction, David and his men and their families moved from Ziklag to Hebron. There he was proclaimed king of Judah, the tribe to which he belonged. David would later be declared king over all 12 tribes (5:1-5). When told how the men of Jabesh-gilead had rescued Saul's body, David sent them a message of gratitude.

2:8-11 *Abner crowns a counterking.* Abner, who had been commander of Saul's army, proclaimed Saul's son Ishbosheth king of all the tribes except Judah. This split between Judah and the northern tribes would become permanent after the death of Solomon. (For Abner's previous dealings with David, see 1 Sam. 17:55-58; 26:5-16.)

2:12–3:1 *A deadly game and the fight that follows.* The generals of Judah and the northern tribes arranged for 24 of their young soldiers to meet in what was either an athletic contest or serious combat. Whatever its purpose, the event proved deadly and inconclusive, with all the combatants dying.

The fight that began with 24 men soon extended to the observers. The wider fight led to 360 deaths among Ishbosheth's men but only 20 on David's side. That imbalance characterized the larger scope of the war between David and Ishbosheth, as Judah grew "stronger and stronger" while Ishbosheth's northern army grew "weaker and weaker" (3:1). God's favor was clearly upon David.

2:13 introduces Joab, David's nephew and leader of his army. Joab's brother Asahel was killed by Abner in the aftermath of the ill-fated competition (2:18-23).

3:2-5 *Sons and spouses in the first family.* While David ruled in Hebron, he had six sons by six different wives. Among these sons, Absalom and Adonijah would become key players in later family conflicts. (For a complete list of David's wives and children, see *People to Remember: David.*)

3:6-21 *An angry Abner defects to David.* When Ishbosheth accused Abner of sleeping with one of Saul's concubines, Abner was incensed, considering it a petty matter in light of all he had done for Ishbosheth. In retaliation, he offered to join David's forces against Ishbosheth, thereby turning "the entire nation of Israel" to David's side (3:12).

David agreed to the offer, with one condition: that his wife Michal, whom Saul had given to another man, be returned to him. With that condition met, Abner began encouraging the northern tribes to support David, and David gave a feast for Abner and his men.

3:22-27 *Murdered with a false motive.* As soon as Abner went home from the feast, Joab returned from a battle. Upon hearing about Abner's friendly meeting with David, Joab tried to convince David that Abner was plotting against him. Joab then killed Abner. His motive for doing so, however, was not to protect David but to avenge the death of his brother Asahel (3:30; see 2:18-23).

3:28-39 *David reacts with rage and resignation.* David was saddened and angered by the murder of Abner. He pronounced a curse on Joab and his descendants, and turned Abner's funeral into a public humiliation of Joab. David renounced the "strong" actions of Joab and his men but admitted that those actions had made him feel helpless (3:39). The people evidently approved of David's more conciliatory approach toward the former rebels (3:36-37).

4:1-12 *Benjamite brothers killed for killing their king.* Without Abner, Ishbosheth felt helpless in his war with David; even at noon on a hot day he was lying on his bed (4:5). Baanah and Rechab, who should have been especially loyal to Ishbosheth as fellow Benjamites, seized the opportunity to get on the winning side: They killed Ishbosheth and immediately reported their deed to David.

Instead of rewarding them, David had them killed, comparing their action to that of the young Amalekite who had expected a reward for killing Saul (1:1-16).

The injury to Jonathan's son Mephibosheth (4:4) would give David an opportunity to honor Jonathan's memory (9).

5:1-5 *Crowned by all 12 tribes.* With the rebellion ended, all 12 tribes came to Hebron and proclaimed David their king. Years before, Samuel had anointed David in a private ceremony (1 Sam. 16:6-13). The people knew that God had chosen David as their king and had already learned to trust him as a leader (5:2). David became king of all Israel at age 30; Jesus would begin his public ministry at the same age (Luke 3:23).

5:6-16 *Jerusalem: David's choice, and God's choice too.* Jerusalem, which Israel had failed to conquer in Joshua's time (Judg. 1:21), now fell to David and his men. David made it his capital, perhaps because of its strategic location between Judah and the northern tribes. It was apparently God's choice as well (see Deut. 12:10-11).

David's men, led by Joab (1 Chron. 11:6), took Jerusalem by entering through a water-supply tunnel (5:8). Hezekiah would later build a new tunnel, perhaps in part because the old one was obviously hard to defend (see *Warren's Shaft,* p. 891; *Hezekiah's Tunnel,* p. 893). David fortified a part of Jerusalem, called it the City of David, and "built additional fortifications around the city, starting at the Millo and working inward" (see *Millo,* p. 890).

With generous help from Hiram, king of Tyre, David built a house for himself and his growing family (5:11, 13-16). Hiram would later help Solomon build the Temple (1 Kings 5).

David's power increased (5:10; compare 3:1), and he knew that God was blessing his kingship (5:12).

5:17-25 *Success! Like raging waters and marching trees!* When the Philistines heard David had become king, they mustered their forces against him. David defeated them twice. He apparently saw God's hand in the first victory, comparing it to the bursting of a dam; the second victory was obviously miraculous, as David's men advanced to "a sound like marching feet in the tops of the balsam trees."

That the Philistine soldiers abandoned their idols in battle (5:21) suggests that even they doubted the truth of their religion.

6:1-15 *The Ark returns, after a 90-day delay.* With his throne and capital city established, David made plans to bring the Ark of the Covenant to Jerusalem. The Ark had been in the house of Abinadab for 20 years (1 Sam. 7:1-2). As Abinadab's sons, Uzzah and Ahio, transported the Ark on a cart, the people evidently followed along in celebration and worship. The variety of instruments played, and the observation that they played the instruments "with all their might" (1 Chron. 13:8), shows the significance of the event.

When the oxen stumbled, Uzzah touched the Ark to prevent it from falling. He was immediately struck dead for his "error" (KJV; "irreverent act," NIV). Even on an occasion of joy, God does not relax his standards of holiness.

Uzzah's transgression would not have happened had David insisted on transporting the Ark in the proper way (see Num. 4:1-15).

God's punishment of Uzzah made David both angry and afraid. He kept the Ark outside Jerusalem for three months but finally brought it into the city when he saw the blessings showered upon those who were keeping it (6:11-12).

6:16-23 *She doesn't appreciate his adoration, to say the least!* At the height of the celebration over the Ark, David was seen "leaping and dancing before the LORD." Michal despised him for it and accused him of exposing himself "to the servant girls like any indecent person might do!" David countered that the dance, though perhaps undignified, had been performed "before the LORD" in all humility. God showed his displeasure over Michal's criticism by making her barren (6:23).

Michal's failure to appreciate David's spontaneous worship recalls Eli's mistaken belief that the praying Hannah was drunk (1 Sam. 1:13).

6:17 is the first reference to the Tabernacle since 1 Samuel 3:3. The Tabernacle (or "temple," see exposition on 1 Sam. 1:12-18) was probably destroyed along with Shiloh (see exposition on 1 Sam. 4:1-11). David had apparently built a new Tabernacle in preparation for the Ark's return.

7:1-17 *"I don't need a bigger house, but David does."* As Israel enjoyed a time of peace, David began thinking about building a permanent home for the Ark. Nathan the prophet gave his blessing to that plan.

David used this time of rest not for self-indulgent pleasure but for meditation and plans for future ministry. Later, David would take a vacation when he should have been at war, with disastrous results (11).

The Lord reminded Nathan (7:4-7) that he had never had a permanent dwelling and still did not need one. He promised, however, to turn David's kingship into a permanent "house," with his sons succeeding him "forever" (7:13), a promise that would find its ultimate fulfillment in Christ (Isa. 9:7; Luke 1:32).

The Lord also said that David's son *would* build him a permanent dwelling. 1 Chronicles 22:7-10 gives the Lord's reason for allowing Solomon, instead of David, to build the Temple.

God's promises to David (7:10-16) are often called the Davidic covenant (see *Unique Features*).

7:18-29 *David's response: "Praise God from whom all blessings flow!"* David responded to God's promises with a prayer of humility and adoration. The eloquence of the prayer reveals David the poet, who by this time had already composed several of the psalms recorded in the book of Psalms.

8:1-18 *Success over all surrounding nations.* Chapter 8 is David's "trophy case," listing the many nations he conquered as well as the vast treasures those and other nations brought to him as tribute. Israel would attain its greatest size during the days of David and Solomon. Most of this territory was gained under David, the man of war, then fortified and defended under Solomon. 8:15-18 mentions David's main military and religious leaders. 23:8-39 gives a more complete list of his military men.

9:1-13 *"Nothing but the best for my best friend's son!"* David looked for an opportunity to show kindness to the house of Saul, to honor the memory of Jonathan and the covenant they had made (21:7; 1 Sam. 20:14-23). Informed of Jonathan's crippled son Mephibosheth (see 4:4), David sent for him and restored to him all the property that had belonged to Saul. He assigned Ziba and his family to be Mephibosheth's servants and gave Mephibosheth a place of honor in the royal court.

David had always shown kindness to the house of Saul, considering him the "the LORD's anointed one" (1:14-16; 1 Sam. 24:6; 26:11). Now, he showed the same kindness for Jonathan's sake. In like manner, God shows kindness to sinners for Jesus' sake (Eph. 1:6).

10:1-19 *Their respect ridiculed, Israel resorts to war.* When the king of Ammon died, David sent a delegation to comfort the new king. The delegates were rejected and publicly humiliated. When they realized that the Israelites were angered by what they had done, the Ammonites hired mercenaries from Syria and prepared for war. When war came, Israel won decisively. Israel's neighbors were afraid to make coalitions anymore (10:19), solidifying the victories Israel had won (8:1-14).

Concerning "sign acts" such as the shaving of the beard (10:4), see exposition on 1 Samuel 11:1-11.

DAVID THE SINNER (11)

11:1-5 *On vacation, David finds temptation.* While Israel's armies fought on two fronts, David stayed at home in Jerusalem. During one idle evening, he saw Bathsheba on her roof and arranged a sexual liaison with her. Shortly thereafter, Bathsheba notified David that she was pregnant.

11:6-13 *First he tries to trick him.* Bathsheba's husband, Uriah, was away at war. David quickly arranged to bring him home and encouraged him to sleep with his wife so that he would be the presumed father of her unborn child. Unlike David, however, Uriah refused to enjoy his wife's company while his comrades were in battle.

11:14-27 *He arranges Uriah's death and marries his widow.* When the "paternity plot" failed, David arranged for Uriah to die in battle. With Uriah dead, David married Bathsheba.

One sin often leads to another. David's lust led to adultery and murder and would plunge his family and eventually the entire nation into generations of conflict. The account of David's sin ends with the obvious: "The LORD was very displeased with what David had done" (11:27).

DAVID THE SUFFERER (12–20)

12:1-6 *"Such a man should die!"* Shortly after David's marriage to Bathsheba, the prophet Nathan told him a parable about a rich man who stole the only sheep belonging to a poor man. David was understandably enraged at the rich man's greed, saying that anyone who would do such a thing should die.

12:7-12 *"You are the man!"* Nathan applied the parable directly to David who, though he had many wives, had taken Uriah's only wife. Nathan pronounced a curse on David's house: David would suffer great personal tragedies, and his kingdom would never again know peace.

Harsher words of rebuke and punishment can hardly be imagined. God had given David so much. As with many believers, however, David had taken it all for granted.

12:13-23 *Repentance doesn't stop the retribution.* David, the man after God's own heart (Acts 13:22), repented of his sin, and his repentance was evidently sincere (12:16-17). Nonetheless, the punishments Nathan had predicted immediately began happening, with the death of David and Bathsheba's son being the first of many tragedies. When God forgives our sins, it does not necessarily mean we will escape the consequences of those sins.

12:24-25 *A baby called "Beloved."* Bathsheba bore David another son, Solomon. Through Nathan, the Lord directed that this child should also be called Jedidiah, which means "beloved of the LORD." The name would certainly prove prophetic, as Solomon enjoyed so many special blessings from God (1 Kings 2–11).

12:26-31 *Meanwhile, back on the battlefield . . .* The story now shifts back to the war with the Ammonites (11:1), which David's men were fighting while he pursued Bathsheba. At Joab's urging, David became involved in the war and helped solidify Joab's success, with the result that "all the Ammonite cities" came under Israelite control.

13:1-22 *Amnon and Tamar: From lust to loathing.* Amnon, son of David, became consumed with desire for Tamar—his half sister and Absalom's full sister. Feigning illness to be alone with Tamar, Amnon tried to seduce her. She resisted, urging him to marry her legally (13:13); but Amnon refused and raped her, after which his lust turned to loathing and he disowned her. Tamar bitterly protested Amnon's treatment of her, declaring that his disowning her was a far worse sin than the rape (13:16). She then went into mourning (13:19-20).

When David heard about it, he became angry but did nothing, possibly because of his love for Amnon, his firstborn son (3:2; 13:37), or his lingering guilt feelings concerning Bathsheba. Absalom guessed correctly what had happened, and hated Amnon because of it, but pretended to be unconcerned (13:20, 22).

13:23-33 *Retaliation for the rape.* Absalom waited two years to avenge Tamar, assuming that after so long a time Amnon would no longer be on his guard. The delay apparently worked; Amnon accepted an invitation to visit Absalom away from the king's protection, and Absalom had him killed.

13:34-39 *Absalom goes to his grandfather in Geshur.* Absalom fled to the home of his maternal grandfather, Talmai (3:3), and stayed for three years. Meanwhile David got over his mourning for Amnon and began to miss Absalom.

14:1-20 *"We'll convince the king through parable and praise."* Sensing that David secretly longed for a reunion with Absalom, Joab used deceitful means to encourage him to forgive his son. Enlisting the help of a "wise woman," he gave her a parable concerning forgiveness to tell David, hoping the story would change his mind. When the woman applied the parable directly to David (14:13) and praised his wisdom (14:17), David realized that Joab was conspiring with her to bring Absalom home.

14:21-24 *"He can come back, but he can't come home!"* Despite the underhandedness of this attempt to change his heart, David agreed that Absalom could return to Jerusalem—so long as he stayed in his own house and didn't come into David's presence. Joab promptly brought Absalom to Jerusalem.

14:25-33 *The burning barley gets his attention.* Two years after he returned to Jerusalem, Absalom still had not seen his father the king. When he tried to enlist Joab as a mediator and Joab refused, Absalom set Joab's barley field on fire. That got Joab's attention, and soon he was able to get Absalom into the king's palace, where Absalom was reunited with King David after five years of separation.

15:1-6 *Absalom goes into politics.* Absalom began building up his own personal army. He also began sowing seeds of discontent against David. As he had with Amnon, Absalom proved very crafty as he planned his own advancement. Absalom's good looks (14:25) may have helped him "steal the hearts" of Israel (15:6).

15:7-12 *"Fulfilling a vow" is the last thing on his mind.* After four years of winning support among his countrymen, Absalom set in motion a plan to take the kingship from his father. (The "four years" designated by the NLT and NIV renderings of 15:7 matches biblical chronology much better than the "forty years" of the KJV and NKJV.) In order to gather a greater following, Absalom left Jerusalem on the pretext of needing to fulfill a vow in Hebron. He gave instructions to potential followers concerning how the rebellion would begin.

Absalom also enlisted the support of Ahithophel, Bathsheba's grandfather (11:3; 23:34) and a "counselor" to David (15:12). With his plans beginning the take shape, Absalom's conspiracy against David grew ever stronger.

15:13-17 *The revolt begins; David prepares to flee.* Warned by a messenger that many were joining Absalom's rebellion, David made preparations to move his family, his private army, and his servants out of Jerusalem, leaving 10 of his concubines to look after his house.

15:18-22 *Ittai, a friend indeed.* When David noticed Ittai, a non-Jewish newcomer to Jerusalem, preparing to leave with him, he urged him to stay in the safety of Jerusalem rather than face an uncertain future with David. Ittai, however, pledged loyalty to David, proving himself more faithful to the king than many Israelites. That David referred to Absalom as "King Absalom" (15:19) suggests he assumed the rebellion would succeed.

15:23-29 *With sorrow he sends it back.* As David fled eastward from Jerusalem toward the wilderness, he told Zadok the priest to take the Ark back to Jerusalem. He knew that Jerusalem, not the battlefield, was the place for the Ark; and he trusted that, if God chose to restore him to the throne, he would once again see Jerusalem and the Ark.

15:30-37 *David's defense: A prayer and a plan.* David and his people wept as they left Jerusalem. When David learned that Ahithophel had joined Absalom's revolt, he prayed that Ahithophel would give Absalom bad advice. He then sent Hushai to Jerusalem as a spy in Absalom's court; his mission was to work against Ahithophel and to send progress reports to David.

16:1-4 *Maligning his master?* As David fled, he encountered Ziba, whom he had appointed to look after the needs of Mephibosheth (see exposition on

9:1-13). Ziba brought supplies to David and told him that Mephibosheth had stayed in Jerusalem, hoping to become king himself. Mephibosheth would later deny any such intention (19:24-30).

16:5-14 *Reviled, he refuses to retaliate.* As David and his people continued to flee, they encountered Shimei, a member of Saul's family. Shimei cursed and threw stones at David's entourage, declaring that God was punishing David for having taken the throne from Saul's family. David's men urged him to retaliate but he refused to do so. Though truly a man of war against pagan nations, David was quite lenient toward fellow Israelites who challenged his authority.

16:15-19 *Enter the spy from David's camp.* As David fled, Absalom and his people arrived in Jerusalem. Shortly thereafter, Hushai arrived and pledged loyalty to Absalom.

16:20-23 *Godless counsel from a godless counselor.* At Ahithophel's advice, Absalom publicly committed adultery with the 10 concubines David had left in his house. Ahithophel, who had a reputation for giving good advice (16:23), argued that such an outrageous act would widen the breach between David and Absalom, making Absalom's followers all the more committed to him.

17:1-14 *Disastrous counsel from David's spy.* Ahithophel went on to advise Absalom concerning battlefield tactics. Ahithophel's advice was good, using swiftness and surprise against David and his weary men. Absalom then sought a second opinion from Hushai, David's spy. Hushai recommended a slower approach, which would of course give him time to warn David. Absalom accepted Hushai's advice (17:14), perhaps because it appealed to his vanity (17:11).

17:15-22 *Forewarned and forearmed.* True to David's original plan (see exposition on 15:30-37), Hushai sent messengers warning him of Absalom's pursuit. David immediately moved his people further eastward, across the Jordan.

17:23 *The spurned adviser kills himself.* When Ahithophel realized Absalom had rejected his battle plan, he went home and hanged himself. He knew that, however the battle turned out, he was doomed: If Absalom was defeated, Ahithophel's career was over since he had sided with Absalom; if Absalom was victorious, Ahithophel's career was likewise over since Hushai's advice would have won the battle.

17:24-29 *Waiting for war, east of the Jordan.* As Absalom crossed the Jordan and pursued David, David and his people were helped by three men of that area, Shobi, Makir, and Barzillai. God continued to take care of David through unusual means. Makir had previously been an ally of the house of Saul (9:4-5). His willingness to help David suggests that the rebellion did not have wide support east of the Jordan.

Absalom made Amasa his military commander in place of Joab, who was on David's side (18:2). Amasa was David's nephew and therefore a cousin of both Joab and Absalom (see 19:13).

18:1-4 *"Better 10,000 die than you."* Knowing that Absalom's army wanted to kill him, David's people refused to let him go into battle.

18:5-18 *20,000 die, including Absalom.* David's army defeated Absalom's rebel force. 20,000 Israelites died in this civil war, making it the bloodiest of Israel's civil wars for which casualty totals are given. The battle was fought in rugged terrain, which itself claimed many lives (18:8). Absa-

THE LIFE OF DAVID

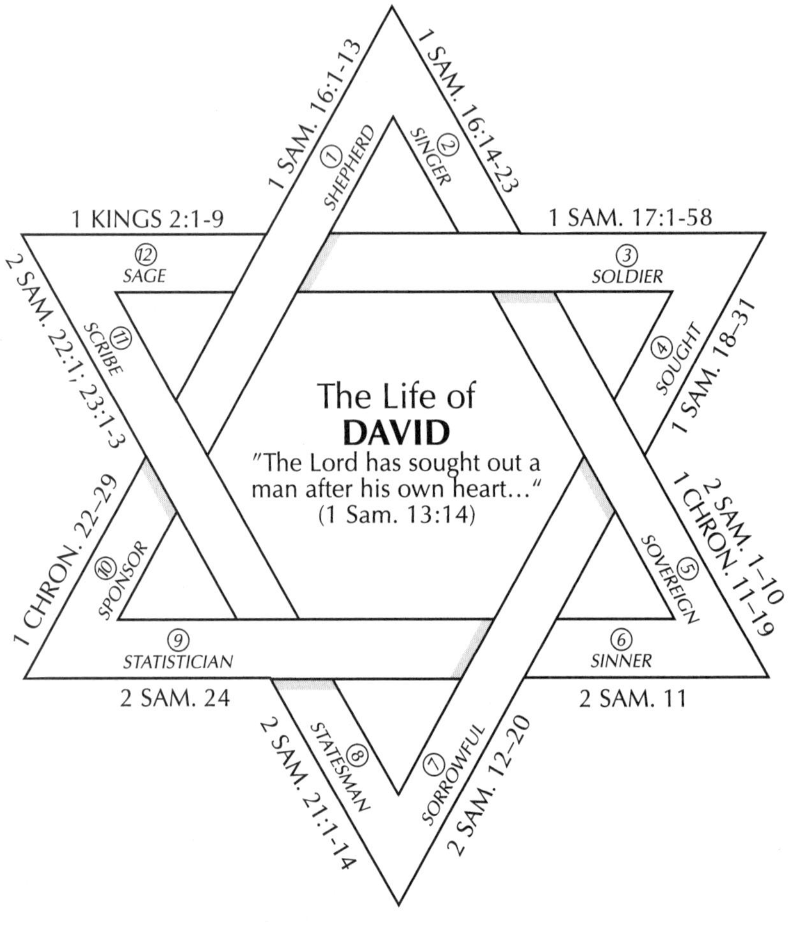

lom himself was killed after getting his hair caught in some tree branches.

David had asked his troops to show leniency toward his rebellious son (18:5). Whether or not Joab honored that request is unclear: Though he "took three daggers and plunged them into Absalom's heart" (18:14), Joab's armor bearers are credited with actually killing Absalom (18:15). In any event, the three daggers suggested Joab's hatred for Absalom.

18:19-32 *David gets the news from two reluctant runners.* News of the victory of David's forces, and of Absalom's death, came to David by way of two messengers, both of whom were reluctant to report Absalom's death (18:29, 32). Ahimaaz wanted to bring the good news of victory but not the news about Absalom (18:19-23).

18:33 *Requiem for a rebel.* David grieved greatly over Absalom, but Absalom's rebellion would not be the last (see 20:1-22).

19:1-8 *"Quit crying, and congratulate your troops!"* When Joab saw how much David grieved because of Absalom, he wisely advised the people not to publicly celebrate the victory. Realizing also, however, that resentment over David's grieving could cause another revolt (19:5-7), he wisely urged David to put his grief aside and make a public appearance, and David did so.

19:9-17 *"Why can't I go home?"* With David victorious over Absalom, most of the tribes were ready to bring him back to the throne in Jerusalem. The lone holdout was Judah, in whose territory Jerusalem was located. David won Judah's support in part by promising to make his nephew Amasa commander of his army in place of his other nephew, the competent but strong-willed Joab.

When David and his people prepared to cross the Jordan on their way home, they were met by Shimei, who earlier had cursed him (16:5-14), and by Ziba, who had accused Mephibosheth of disloyalty (16:1-4).

David was escorted across the Jordan (19:18) by people from Judah and Benjamin, the two tribes that would one day become the southern kingdom.

19:18-23 *"I'm the king; I don't need to kill him."* Shimei fell at David's feet and begged forgiveness. Abishai urged David to kill him, just as he had when Shimei had cursed David (16:9). But David was lenient toward Shimei, just as he had been when Shimei cursed him (16:10-12). David felt secure enough as king to show compassion to his enemies (19:22).

19:24-30 *"That's OK, Ziba can have my half."* Ziba had accused Mephibosheth of disloyalty to David (16:1-4), who had shown such great kindness to Mephibosheth (9). David confronted Mephibosheth about those accusations, and Mephibosheth proclaimed his innocence and his loyalty to David. When Ziba had accused Mephibosheth, David had given Ziba the rights to Mephibosheth's property. Now, not knowing whom to believe, David told the two men to divide the property equally between them. Mephibosheth, however, declined to claim his half, declaring that it was enough for him to see the king safely back on his throne.

19:31-39 *Too old for his reward.* David offered to reward Barzillai for his help during the revolt (17:27-29) by bringing him back to Jerusalem and providing for him there. Barzillai declined the offer because of his old age.

19:40-43 *10 tribes jealous of Judah.* A delegation from the 10 northern tribes complained that the one tribe of Judah was getting too much of David's attention. The people of Judah responded that they had a right to such attention because of their blood relationship to David. The northerners responded that they had a greater claim because of their greater numbers and because they had been the first to seek David's restoration after the civil war. The seeds were already being sown for the later division of the kingdom upon Solomon's death. Despite their claims of loyalty, 19:40 suggests that only half of the northern tribes fully supported David.

Because they had helped Judah return David to Jerusalem (see exposition on 19:9-12), the tribe of Benjamin, which would later join Judah as the southern kingdom, may already have been associated with Judah though not mentioned by name in this incident. However, Benjamin was not yet unanimous in its support of David (see exposition on 20:1-3).

20:1-3 *Another rebel, another rebellion.* Capitalizing on the unrest among the northern tribes and the apparent uncertainty about David among the Benjamites, Sheba declared a rebellion and won wide support.

20:4-13 *Appointed by David, assassinated by Joab.* David told Amasa to muster the army and pursue Sheba. When Amasa, who had performed poorly for Absalom, took too long in carrying out those orders, David appointed Abishai to the same task. Joab, though not commissioned to do so, also pursued Sheba. Encountering Amasa on the battlefield, Joab killed him, whereupon all of Amasa's men followed Joab. Ever zealous for David's cause, Joab was also ever ready to see death as the solution to problems.

20:14-22 *"Let's make a deal: his head for our city!"* Joab united all the tribes behind him, cornered Sheba in the city of Abel, and laid siege to the city. Not wanting their city destroyed, the people of Abel executed Sheba and delivered his head to Joab. Siege warfare was almost always a losing proposition for ancient cities, since it would be only a matter of time until the attackers were victorious.

20:23-26 *The king's cabinet.* David's main military, political, and religious leaders are listed (compare 8:15-18). Both lists must have been compiled during periods of peace, when David was able to concentrate on leading his people. Significant in this list is Joab, whose exploits had restored him to the top post in David's army.

DAVID THE STATESMAN (21)

21:1-14 *Even though dead, he causes a catastrophe.* When there was a famine in Israel, the Lord told David it had come as punishment for Saul's slaughter of the Gibeonites. Though that slaughter is not recorded in Scripture, it would have been a violation of Joshua's covenant with the Gibeonites (21:2; Josh. 9:1-15). At their request, David allowed the Gibeonites to execute seven of Saul's sons as atonement for the slaughter. Mephibosheth the son of Jonathan was spared because of David's commitment to Jonathan (21:7; see exposition on 9:1-13; 1 Sam. 20:12-23). A proper burial concluded the whole affair, and God began blessing Israel again.

21:15-22 *Four fearsome giants from Gath.* In a series of four wars, Israel defeated the Philistines four times and killed four Philistine giants, one of whom was related to Goliath. Though he was by now too old to fight effectively (21:15, 17), David participated in the first battle. His military career thus began (1 Sam. 17) and ended with a battle against a Philistine giant.

DAVID THE SINGER (22–23)

22:1-51 *The singer and his song.* David composed a song to commemorate his victories over both the house of Saul and the many pagan nations surrounding Israel. The song is repeated in Psalm 18. David's song begins and ends with references to God as a "rock" (22:3, 47). Hannah made a similar comparison (1 Sam. 2:2).

23:1-7 *Final words of the singer-warrior.* In his final words to his people, David described God's ideal king (23:3-4); noted God's faithfulness to him in spite of his failings (23:5); and, perhaps for the sake of future kings, underscored the importance of dealing with rebellion (23:6-7).

David was the "sweet psalmist of Israel" (23:1), but when the occasion demanded, he was a man of war (23:6-7).

23:8-12 *David's top three soldiers.* The writer singles out three of David's military leaders and recalls their heroic deeds. Their heroism reflects well on David himself: Leaders can often be assessed by the character of the followers they attract.

23:13-17 *Three heroes and their heroic leader.* The writer next recalls an incident from the days of David's flight from Saul: Three soldiers risked their lives to bring water to David from his favorite well; but David, to show his appreciation for the great risk they had taken, refused to drink the water.

23:18-19 *One against 300.* Abishai, known as a zealous warrior (16:9; 19:21-22; 20:6; 1 Sam. 26:5-12), was remembered especially for singlehandedly killing 300 men.

23:20-23 *He killed a lion, and men that looked like lions.* Next comes the story of Benaiah, noted for killing a lion, two "lionlike" men, and a "great Egyptian warrior."

23:24-39 *These also served.* The accounts of 23:8-23 contain cryptic references to elite groups of three as well as a group of 30 chief men (23:9, 13, 16-19, 22-23). The 37 men listed in 23:24-39 probably comprise David's elite group—his military honor roll (1 Chron. 11–12). One can imagine endless stories about these men being told and retold through the centuries as Israelites looked back upon their nation's glory days. Such true accounts also served as preventive medicine: Let no one dare raise a hand against Israel's king!

DAVID THE STATISTICIAN (24)

24:1-9 *Incited to take a census.* For some unspecified reason, the Lord became angry at Israel once again. The prior occasion implied by "again" was probably the famine of 21:1. In his anger, the Lord caused David to take a census of Israel, an act destined to displease him because it showed a lack of faith in God's ability to multiply the nation (see Gen. 15:5; 1 Chron. 27:23). It could also be that David's desire specifically to number the fighting men (24:9) was an act of disbelief in God's ability to win Israel's wars. While God had ordered a census in Israel's earlier days (Num. 1:2), with all the victories he had won, David should have by now learned to trust God. We learn elsewhere that God used Satan to incite David to take the census (1 Chron. 21:1).

Joab warned David against the census, but David ignored the warning and assigned the task to Joab himself.

The separate numbers for Israel and Judah (24:9) are one more indication of the growing rift (see exposition on 19:40-43) that would eventually result in a divided kingdom.

24:10-16 *David prescribes the plague.* Realizing that he had sinned in taking the census, David repented. The Lord chose to punish Israel anyway and offered David three choices of punishment. David chose what seemed the least destructive option, and 70,000 people died within 72 hours.

24:17-25 *He builds an altar and stops the plague.* David repented again and begged the Lord to stop the plague. God instructed him to build an altar at the threshing floor of Araunah. When Araunah offered to give the threshing floor to David, David insisted on buying it so that his sacrifice to God would not be without personal cost. David's attitude recalls that of Abraham centuries earlier when he bought the cave of Machpelah (Gen. 23:1-16). In light of ancient Near Eastern customs, the offer of the gift may in both cases have been only a formality, the seller fully expecting the buyer to insist on paying. The land purchased, David built an altar, and the plague was lifted.

❖ ❖ ❖

PEOPLE TO REMEMBER FROM 2 SAMUEL

ABNER

Key Fact: Saul's military commander (1 Sam. 14:50)
Father: Ner (1 Sam. 14:50)
Death: Recorded in 3:27
Total Bible References: 61
Key References: 2–3; 1 Sam. 14:50-51; 17:55-57; 26:5-16

Abner Speaks

Who knows? I might have been a better statesman than soldier. At any rate, we've apparently convinced him. My associates agree—the summit meeting at Hebron was a success. Of course, neither of us mentioned that embarrassing incident several years ago when he removed Saul's spear and water canteen while we were both sleeping! Believe me, the king never let me forget that! (3:20-21; 1 Sam. 26:5-16)

Well, Saul's dead now, and that idiot son of his has proven a total failure, in spite of all my efforts to make him king. I guess the last straw was when he accused me of sleeping with his father's concubine! Unbelievable! His control over the 11 tribes is deteriorating by the day, but he's more interested in my private sex life! Down with Ishbosheth! Long live David! As far as I'm concerned, he's now king over *all* Israel. I assume of course that he'll reward my support. At least he seemed pleased when I pledged to turn Ishbosheth's troops over to him. (2:8-10; 3:1, 6-11, 20-21)

What's this? A runner approaches with a message. Joab wants to meet with me back in Hebron? I guess I'll go, but I do feel some apprehension. Does David's general seek my help or my head? (3:26-27)

Spiritual Lessons from Abner

- God demands faithfulness whatever our lot in life. Abner was appointed to lead King Saul's army, but on at least two occasions failed to protect the king himself (1 Sam. 24:1-7; 26:5-16).
- We reap what we sow (Gal. 6:7). Abner helped arrange a deadly contest in which 24 young Jewish warriors ended up stabbing each other to death (2:12-16). Later he himself was stabbed to death (3:27).

Key Verses

"So everyone in Judah and Israel knew that David was not responsible for Abner's death. Then King David said to the people, 'Do you not realize that a great leader and a great man has fallen today in Israel?'" (3:37-38).

ABSALOM

Key Fact: Led rebellion against his father, David (15–18)
Birth: Recorded in 3:3
Father: David (3:2-3)
Mother: Maacah (3:3)
Brothers: 18 half brothers (1 Chron. 3:1-8), including Amnon, Adonijah, and Solomon (3:2-4; 12:24)

Sister: Tamar (13:1)
Sons: 3 unnamed (14:27)
Daughter: Tamar (14:27)
Death: Recorded in 18:9-15
Total Bible References: 108
Key References: 13–19

Absalom Speaks

What a fool I was to heed Hushai's advice instead of the sound counsel of Ahithophel. No doubt about it, the battle is lost. Our rebels were simply no match for my father's seasoned troops. (17:1-13; 18:6-8)

How unfair, for in my mind most of this mess is his fault. I was forced to kill Amnon because my father wouldn't, and then to suffer as an exile for the next three years in a foreign land. That was bad enough, but then when I returned, two years passed before he would even talk to me. If only he had chosen me to succeed him instead of Solomon! (13:28-29, 37-38; 14:28)

Well, a curse on the past. My present predicament calls for some quick thinking; if I ever get untangled I'll kill that wretched mule! Whatever caused him to run under this huge oak tree with its thick branches? And then, even worse, to keep on going and leave me hanging here in midair! (18:9)

Someone's coming! Friend or foe? My worst nightmare—it's Joab! (18:10-14)

Spiritual Lessons from Absalom

- Pride usually leads to humiliation. Absalom was especially proud of his hair, but ultimately it played a key role in his death (14:25-26; 15:1; 18:9-15; see Prov. 16:18).
- We should show proper respect to those in authority. Absalom's failure to do so contributed to his undoing (15:2-12; see Ps. 105:15).

Key Verses

"He got up early every morning and went out to the gate of the city. When people brought a case to the king for judgment, Absalom would ask where they were from, and they would tell him their tribe. Then Absalom would say, 'You've really got a strong case here! It's too bad the king doesn't have anyone to hear it. I wish I were the judge. Then people could bring their problems to me, and I would give them justice!' . . . So in this way, Absalom stole the hearts of all the people of Israel" (15:2-4, 6).

DAVID

Key Facts: Israel's greatest king, author of half of the book of Psalms
Father: Jesse (Ruth 4:17; 1 Sam. 16:1)
Brothers: Eliab, Abinadab, Shammah, Nethanel, Raddai, and Ozem (1 Sam. 17:12-13; 1 Chron. 2:13-15); 1 unnamed (the seventh of 1 Sam. 16:10)
Sisters: Zeruiah, Abigail (1 Chron. 2:16)
Wives: Michal, Ahinoam, Abigail, Maacah, Haggith, Abital, Eglah, and Bathsheba (3:2-5; 11:26-27; 1 Sam. 18:27; 1 Chron. 3:1-8)
Sons: Amnon, Kileab (also called Daniel), Absalom, Adonijah, Shephatiah, Ithream, Shimea, Shobab, Nathan, Solomon, Ibhar, Elishua, Elpelet, Nogah, Nepheg,

Japhia, Elishama, Eliada, Eliphelet (3:2-5; 5:13-16; 1 Chron. 3:1-8; 14:3-5); 1 unnamed (12:15-23)
Occupation: Shepherd, musician, songwriter, soldier, king of Judah, king of all Israel (2:1-7; 5:1-5; 23:1; 1 Sam. 16:11, 23; 18:5)
Key Events in His Life:

- Anointed king by Samuel (1 Sam. 16:12-13)
- Kills Goliath (1 Sam. 17:17-54)
- Flees from Saul (1 Sam. 19)
- Becomes king of Judah (2:1-7)
- Becomes king of all Israel (5:1-5)
- Establishes Jerusalem as capital (5:6-16)
- Brings Ark to Jerusalem (6:1-15)
- God's covenant with him (7:9-16)
- Wins many military victories (8; 10)
- Adultery with Bathsheba (11–12)
- Absalom's rebellion (15–18)
- Names Solomon his successor (1 Kings 1:28-39)

Age at Death: 70 (5:4-5; 1 Kings 2:10-11)
Total Bible References: 1,118
Key References: 1 Sam. 16—1 Kings 2; Psalms; Isa. 9:7; Jer. 30:8-9; Ezek. 37:24-25; Zech. 12:7-10; Matt. 1:1; Heb. 11:32

David Speaks

From Bethlehem, my birthplace, to Jerusalem, my capital—two locations separated by six miles and 70 years: What experiences have been mine during that span of distance and time! From the highest rooftop here in the palace I can see the Judean hills where I once tended sheep for my father. But one day Samuel the prophet visited our little town and changed my life forever. (1 Sam. 16:1-13)

Memories, memories, memories, both wonderful and wretched. The victory over Goliath; Jonathan's friendship; the coronations at Hebron; capturing Jerusalem; bringing the Ark into the city; and seeing the gratitude of Mephibosheth: Those are wonderful memories. (2:1-7; 5:1-7; 6:12-15; 9:7-8; 1 Sam. 17; 18:1)

But there was also the murder of a faithful soldier after committing adultery with his wife; the death of my infant son; the rape of my daughter by her own half brother; the murder of that half brother by *his* half brother; the rebellion of another son; that terrible census fiasco! (11; 12:18; 13:1-14, 28-29; 15:1-12; 24)

But I begged and received God's forgiveness for it all. How I love to read and reread the words he once gave me: "He has not punished us for all our sins, nor does he deal with us as we deserve. For his unfailing love toward those who fear him is as great as the height of the heavens above the earth. He has removed our rebellious acts as far away from us as the east is from the west." (Ps. 51; 103:10-12)

But now to the inventory: The materials for the Temple have been assembled and dedicated, the nation is secure from its enemies, my psalms of praise are completed, and Solomon has been anointed as my successor. I hope he will take to heart the final thoughts I have left for him and his people: "The person who rules righteously, who rules in the fear of God, he is like the light of the morning." (22:1; 23:3; 1 Chron. 29:10-27)

Spiritual Lessons from David

- If we are faithful in little things, we will be entrusted with greater responsibilities. David proved faithful in caring for his father's sheep before being called to shepherd God's flock (1 Sam. 16:11; 17:34-35; Ps. 78:70-72).
- Spiritual growth takes time. David was anointed as king by Samuel when he was about 17 years old (1 Sam. 16:12-13). He would not actually rule over all Israel, however, until many years later (5:4-5). A toadstool can spring up overnight, but mighty trees don't grow quite that fast.
- God has given each of us the necessary equipment to fight our spiritual battles; we shouldn't try to use another person's armor (1 Sam. 17:38-40).
- Dishonesty is always wrong. David's lie to Ahimelech would indirectly lead to 85 deaths (1 Sam. 21:1-9; 22:6-19).
- It's always too soon to quit: When Saul was pursuing him, David concluded that he was doomed (1 Sam. 27:1), yet history would prove otherwise.
- Heartache will be the sure result of marrying someone who does not share our love for God (6:14-23).
- Sin leads to suffering and shame, no matter how godly the sinner (12:13-23).
- God is often more concerned about our response when convicted of sin, than about the sin itself (see 11:1-17, which describes David's sin, and Ps. 51, which describes his sorrow for that sin).
- David began and ended his ministry by acknowledging the absolute sovereignty of God in the lives of his people (1 Sam. 17:46-47; 1 Chron. 29:10-15).

Key Verse

"But God removed [Saul] from the kingship and replaced him with David, a man about whom God said, 'David son of Jesse is a man after my own heart, for he will do everything I want him to'" (Acts 13:22).

971 B.C.
Death of David,
Solomon king

931
Kingdom divided,
Israel, Judah

874
Ahab king
of Israel, Elijah
begins ministry

1 KINGS

BACKGROUND

1 Kings tells the history of Israel from 971 to 852 B.C. Beginning with the final days of David's reign, it records Israel's glory days during the reign of Solomon, then the tragic civil strife that resulted in a separation between the 10 northern and two southern tribes in 931 (12). It ends with the reign of the northern king Ahaziah, where 2 Kings takes up the story.

1, 2 Kings, originally one document, *interprets* the history it reports, showing how Israel's spiritual decline led to a decline in its political fortunes (see *Purpose*).

AUTHOR

Unknown, perhaps Jeremiah (see *2 Kings: Author*). The author probably made use of court records such as *The Book of the Acts of Solomon* (11:41), *The Book of the History of the Kings of Israel* (14:19), and *The Book of the History of the Kings of Judah* (14:29).

DATE

The statement in both 1 and 2 Kings that a nationwide lack of righteousness had existed "to this day" (12:19; 2 Kings 17:23, 34, 41) suggests that most of the events of these books were recorded in the final years of the southern kingdom, c. 630–600 B.C.

LOCATION

Probably Jerusalem, considering the author's use of court records. *The History of the Kings of Israel* must have been brought to Jerusalem after the fall of the north.

PURPOSE

- Israel's kings needed to be reminded of the "prophetic" interpretation of their nation's history: Obedience to God brings reward; disobedience brings punishment (see *1 Samuel: Purpose*). This is illustrated repeatedly through the lives of Solomon and his royal successors.

- The prophetic principle applied to all Israelites as well, with the lives of the kings serving as examples.
- With its many reports of the fulfillment of specific prophecies, 1, 2 Kings has reminded believers down through the ages of the power and truth of God's Word (see exposition on the following passages: 2:26-27; 13:1-10; 15:25-32; 16:8-14, 29-34).

UNIQUE FEATURES

- 1 Kings records a great tragedy as Solomon, who was "wiser than anyone else" (4:31), gave himself over to the temptations of wealth and women (10:14–11:13).
- It records the building and dedication of Israel's first Temple, which lasted nearly four centuries (968–586 B.C.). Compare 5–8 with 2 Chronicles 2–7.
- During Solomon's reign, Israel attained its largest size ever—much larger than present-day Israel. Solomon not only solidified but also expanded the gains made by David (4:24; see exposition on 2 Sam. 8:1-18).
- 17:22 records the first of eight bodily resurrections (besides that of Christ) recorded in the Bible (see exposition on Acts 20:7-12).

COMPARISON WITH OTHER BIBLE BOOKS

(See *2 Chronicles: Comparison with Other Bible Books.*)

OUTLINE

THE TRANQUIL YEARS: THE SPIRITUAL WELFARE OF ISRAEL (1:1–11:25)
- Solomon's coronation and early triumphs (1–2)
  - Solomon's triumph over Adonijah his brother (1; 2:13-25)
  - David's charge to Solomon; his death (2:1-12)
  - Solomon's triumph over Abiathar the priest (2:26-27)
  - Solomon's triumph over Joab the general (2:28-35)
  - Solomon's triumph over Shimei the troublemaker (2:36-46)
- Solomon's talent, treasure, territory, and team (3–4)
- Solomon's Temple (5–8)
  - Preparation (5)
  - Construction (6–7)
  - Dedication (8)
- Solomon's further triumphs and treasures (9–10)
  - Triumphs and treasures described (9)
  - Treasures admired by the Queen of Sheba (10:1-13)
  - Treasures described (10:14-29)
- Solomon's transgressions and decline (11:1-25)

THE TURBULENT YEARS: THE CIVIL WARFARE OF ISRAEL (11:26–22:53)
- Jeroboam, first northern king (11:26–14:20)
  - Jeroboam rebels against Solomon (11:26-40)
  - Death of Solomon (11:41-43)
  - Jeroboam rebels against Rehoboam (12:1-15)

Jeroboam rules the 10 northern tribes (12:16–14:20)
Rehoboam, first southern king (14:21-31)
Abijam (Abijah), second southern king (15:1-8)
Asa, third southern king (15:9-24)
Nadab, Baasha, second, third northern kings (15:25–16:7)
Elah, Zimri, fourth, fifth northern kings (16:8-20)
Omri, sixth northern king (16:21-28)
Ahab, seventh northern king (16:29–22:40)
Apostasy (16:29-34)
Association with Elijah (17–19)
Association with Ben-hadad (20)
Association with Naboth (21)
Association with Jehoshaphat (22:1-40)
Jehoshaphat, fourth southern king (22:41-50)
Ahaziah, eighth northern king (22:51-53)

THE TRANQUIL YEARS: THE SPIRITUAL WELFARE OF ISRAEL (1:1–11:25)

1:1-4 *Keeping the king comfortable.* As King David approached death, his servants found a young woman to care for him and keep him warm at night. He did not, however, have sexual relations with her (1:4).

1:5-10 *Enter Adonijah, ready to rebel.* David's oldest surviving son, Adonijah, proclaimed himself king. He won the support of Joab the military leader and Abiathar the priest, but did not seek the support of Nathan the prophet or of Solomon.

Like his half brother Absalom, who had also led a rebellion (2 Sam. 15–18), Adonijah was "very handsome" (1:6).

1:11-27 *They report the rebellion to the dying David.* Bathsheba and Nathan reported Adonijah's rebellion to David, reminding him that he had chosen Solomon as his successor.

1:28-40 *"Solomon shall succeed me!"* David assured Bathsheba and Nathan that Solomon was indeed his chosen successor, and he ordered his immediate coronation. The coronation took place amid great celebration (1:38-40). Solomon rode to his coronation on David's own mule (1:33, 38), symbolizing his right to his father's throne (see 1:44). Contrary to Western culture, riding a mule was considered an honor and was customary for the inauguration of kings.

1:41-49 *The other celebration turns to panic.* As Adonijah and his followers celebrated his coronation, they heard the noise of Solomon's coronation. For fear of Solomon, everyone forsook Adonijah and went their separate ways. Had David died before proclaiming Solomon king, Adonijah's rebellion may well have succeeded.

1:50-53 *The repentant rebel is put on probation.* With his followers in mutiny, Adonijah feared Solomon and fled to the Tabernacle for protection. Solomon promised not to kill him, so long as he caused no more trouble. Solomon neither punished Adonijah nor gave him a blanket pardon—a preview of the wisdom God would later grant him.

2:1-12 *David's last words and death.* Aware that death was near, David gave Solomon some final words of advice. He urged him to keep the law, noting that God's promises to the house of David depended on this. He also urged him to punish Joab and Shimei but to show kindness to the family of Barzillai (see 2 Sam. 17:27-29; 19:31-39).

David then died, at the age of 70 (see 2 Sam. 5:4-5). 40 years (2:11) was an impressive reign; Solomon would also reign 40 years (971–931 B.C.), but few other Israelite kings would last that long.

As Solomon took over as king, the kingdom "was firmly established" (2:12).

2:13-25 *Death by the sword for his not-so-subtle stunt.* Adonijah asked Bathsheba to speak to Solomon on his behalf, asking that he be allowed to marry Abishag (see 1:1-4). Seeing this as a plot by Adonijah to regain the throne, Solomon had him put to death.

2:26-27 *Spared for David's sake.* Though he had supported Adonijah's rebellion, Solomon spared Abiathar the priest because of his long-standing loyalty to David. He did, however, remove him from the priesthood, fulfilling the curse on the house of Eli (see exposition on 1 Sam. 2:30-36).

2:28-35 *He seeks asylum at the altar, to no avail.* Joab, who had also taken part in the rebellion, sought asylum at the Tabernacle as had Adonijah (1:50). But Solomon, following his father's advice (2:5-6), had him executed. Benaiah replaced Joab as head of the army, and Zadok, from whom the Sadducees would take their name, took Abiathar's place as priest (see 2 Sam. 15:23-29). The Lord had predicted that the priest who replaced Eli's last descendant would be the first of a line of priests that would last "forever" (1 Sam. 2:35). Ezekiel's references to Zadok's descendants (Ezek. 40:46) bear this out.

2:36-46 *He disobeys, departs, and dies.* Though Shimei was not a part of Adonijah's rebellion, David warned Solomon about him (2:8-9) because of his curse against David (2 Sam. 16). Solomon confined Shimei to a limited area. When Shimei crossed the boundary, he was condemned to die.

3:1 *The first of his many wives.* Solomon made a treaty with the king of Egypt and married his daughter—the first of his many foreign wives. The prophets forbade marriage to foreign women, not because of their race, but because of their idolatry. In all likelihood these women never became true believers in God; such marriages were simply for the establishment of commercial and military alliances.

3:2-4 *He loves the Lord, but . . .* 3:1 indicates that Solomon was already planning to build a Temple for the Lord. Meanwhile the Israelites, including Solomon, were offering sacrifices at "local altars," traditionally translated "high places." While 3:2 seems to excuse this practice because they lacked a more suitable place of worship, "except that" (3:3) would suggest that it displeased God, and 1:39 suggests that the Tabernacle was still available for true believers (see exposition on Num. 33:50-56).

3:5-15 *"Name it, and it's yours!"* The Lord offered Solomon anything he desired, and Solomon asked for the wisdom to rule Israel well. He would later affirm that wisdom is preferable to wealth (Eccles. 7:11). Because he asked for wisdom and not wealth, God gave Solomon good health and great wealth as well (3:13-14). As Solomon would also later write, tangible blessings such as health and wealth often follow wisdom (Eccles. 7:11).

3:16-28 *Wisdom wins the day and saves a baby.* When two women were brought to Solomon claiming the same baby, Solomon proposed to settle the dispute by dividing the baby in half, whereupon the identity of the true mother became readily apparent.

Though Solomon's proposition may seem cruel, the successful resolution of the case won him the respect of all Israel—and a permanent place in the history of jurisprudence!

4:1-19 *His cabinet and his kitchen cabinet.* 4:1-6 lists Solomon's government, military, and religious officials. As in David's time (2 Sam. 8:15-18), the presence of such a list indicates solidity and order in the kingdom. 4:7-19 lists Solomon's 12 governors who, while surely having other responsibilities, provided food for his household. While David established Israel's capital and expanded its territory, Solomon organized its infrastructure.

4:20-28 *With peace and prosperity for all.* Both Solomon's household and the nation as a whole enjoyed peace and great prosperity during his reign. This was truly the golden age of Israel, as indicated by the building of the Temple and many other public buildings (5–7). See *Unique Features.*

4:29-34 *The depth, breadth, and fame of his wisdom.* Solomon was "wiser than anyone else." He became known throughout "all the surrounding nations," not just for his wisdom but for his knowledge of nature. 4:32 supports the Bible's claim that Solomon authored most of the proverbs in the book of Proverbs. He would also author two other biblical books, Ecclesiastes and Song of Songs.

5:1-12 *"I need your help." . . . "It's as good as done!"* Solomon asked Hiram, king of Tyre in Lebanon, to provide cedar logs for building the Temple. Hiram, who respected Solomon as a wise ruler (5:7), readily agreed and asked for gifts of food in return. Solomon began sending him yearly shipments of grain, and there was peace between the two nations. Throughout the OT, the expression "cedars of Lebanon" is synonymous with strength and grandeur (Ps. 29:5; Isa. 2:13). There are few cedars in Lebanon today, however.

5:13-18 *180,000 workers, 3,300 bosses.* Solomon relied on the conscription of some 180,000 workers, plus 3,300 supervisors, to gather the stone and timber for building the Temple. This massive use of forced labor recalls Samuel's warning about the nature of kings (see exposition on 1 Sam. 8:10-18 and 14:47-52), and resentment over the servitude would be one of the factors in the division of Israel upon Solomon's death (12:4). Note, however, that according to 2 Chronicles 2:17-18; 8:9, the 150,000 workers mentioned in 5:15 were non-Israelite residents of the land (see exposition on 9:15-25).

6:1-13 *Building Basics, Part One.* The writer gives the dimensions of Solomon's Temple and describes its floor plan. The Temple was about 90 x 30 x 45 feet high—twice the size of the Tabernacle.

As Solomon built the Temple, God renewed his covenant with Israel: He stood ready to deliver on all he had promised, if only the people would remain faithful to their side of the agreement (6:11-13).

Scholars disagree on exact dates, but if 967 B.C. is accepted as the date when construction began on the Temple, then the 480 years mentioned in 6:1 suggests 1446 B.C. as the approximate date of Israel's exodus from Egypt.

6:14-38 *Building Basics, Part Two.* The writer now focuses on the materials and ornamentation used for the Temple's interior. The interior was lined with cedar and overlaid with gold.

Special attention is given to the Most Holy Place, which would house the Ark of the Covenant. The large cherubim described in 6:23-28 would have been in addition to the cherubim on the Ark itself.

The Temple was completed seven years later, in 960 B.C. (6:37-38). It would stand for 374 years before being destroyed by the Babylonians in 586.

7:1-12 *His private and public palaces.* Solomon also built several houses for himself, including one or two residences (7:1-2), a separate house for his first wife (7:8), a more public building for his kingly duties (7:7), and a "Hall of Pillars" (7:6).

7:13-51 *The craftsman and his craft.* The work on the Temple and other buildings was supervised by Huram, a craftsman from Tyre whose mother was an Israelite (7:13-14, 40, 45). Huram's work is described in detail (7:15-50).

Besides the furnishings built by Huram, Solomon included in the Temple "all the gifts his father, David, had dedicated" (7:51). David had, of course, wanted to build the Temple himself (2 Sam. 7:1-17) and had apparently begun setting aside various items for that purpose (2 Sam. 8:11). Solomon's inclusion of these things in the Temple would have reminded the people of the legitimacy of his claim to David's throne.

8:1-11 *Transferred from Tabernacle to Temple.* The Ark of the Covenant was moved from the Tabernacle to the Temple amid a worship ceremony led by Solomon. This transfer was from one hill of Jerusalem to another—from the City of David northward to what is today known as the "Temple Mount" area.

With the Ark installed in its new home, the cloud of God's presence filled the place so much that the priests were unable to continue their duties (8:10-11), an event reminiscent of the day the Tabernacle was dedicated (Exod. 40:34-35).

8:12-21 *He begins by blessing them.* Solomon presented the Temple to the Lord (8:12-13), then blessed the assembled people. He reminded them of God's promises to Israel, symbolized by the Ark and the Temple in which it now rested.

8:22-53 *"Hear our prayers from this place!"* Solomon then turned again to pray to God. He affirmed that God is not limited to dwelling in the Temple; he still lives in heaven (8:30). Not even all of heaven can contain him (8:27).

He prayed that the nation would remain true to God, but that God would forgive them when they sinned (8:31-32) and would not let them be totally destroyed by natural disasters or wars brought on by their sin (8:35-36, 46-52).

Solomon's prayer included a plea that God's grace would extend to foreigners who expressed faith in him (8:41-43).

He ended his prayer by reminding the Lord of Israel's special relationship with him (8:53; see Exod. 19:5-6).

8:54-61 *"He is faithful, so be faithful."* Solomon then turned and spoke to the people again, urging them to remember God's faithfulness and to be faithful to him in return. 8:56 recalls the words of Joshua (Josh. 21:45; 23:14). 8:22 and 8:54, along with various descriptions in the Prophets, suggest that OT believers prayed with arms extended toward heaven, presumably facing upward with eyes open (Exod. 9:29-33; Ezra 9:5; Isa. 1:15).

8:62-66 *14 days of dedication.* The Temple was then officially dedicated, with a ceremony involving thousands of burnt offerings, followed by a feast lasting 14 days. An atmosphere of great joy prevailed. The borders of Israel mentioned in 8:65 are larger than the traditional north-to-south borders of "Dan to Beersheba" (4:25; see *Unique Features*).

SOLOMON'S TEMPLE

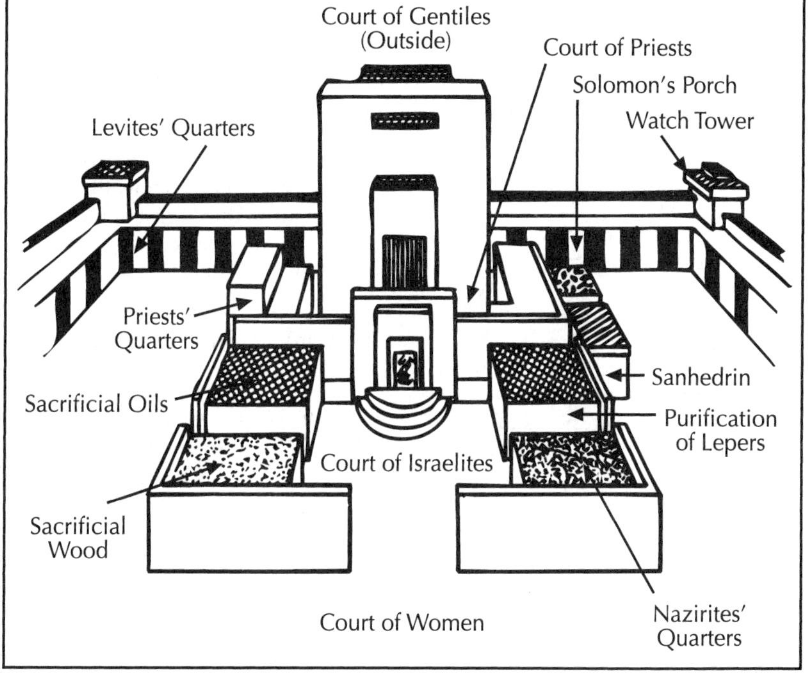

9:1-9 *"Will this Temple last? It's up to you."* God appeared to Solomon a second time (see 3:5-14), promising to bless Israel if they obeyed him, but warning that if they began following other gods, their beautiful new Temple would be destroyed. God would appear to Solomon again in 11:9-13.

9:10-14 *He doesn't like his 20 towns.* 20 years after their friendship began, Solomon gave King Hiram 20 cities in Galilee, but when Hiram went to see them he was not very impressed. Nonetheless, he gave Solomon a substantial gift of gold in return.

9:15-25 *Achievements at what price?* An account of Solomon's building projects and land acquisitions is introduced as an explanation for his extensive use of forced labor (9:15), suggesting what a sore point this had become. 9:20-22 suggests that only foreigners were conscripted (see 2 Chron. 2:17-18), but 5:13 and 11:28 indicate Israelites were enslaved as well. Whatever the situation, Solomon's labor practices were unpopular enough to help divide the kingdom (12:4).

On "the Millo" (9:15, 24), see exposition on 2 Samuel 5:6-16 and *Millo*, p. 890. On the cities mentioned in 9:15-19, see *Fortresses Built by Solomon*, p. 891. The nations mentioned in 9:20 are a painful reminder of Israel's failure to eradicate the Canaanites.

9:26-28 *Solomon the sailor.* Solomon extended his empire to the Red Sea, where he built a fleet of ships that sailed to Africa and Arabia, bringing great wealth to Israel. With Joppa already established as a port on the Mediterranean (2 Chron. 2:16), Israel now had two coasts from which to trade.

10:1-13 *"The half has not been told!"* Having heard of Solomon's great wisdom and wealth, the queen of Sheba came to visit and was astounded at what she saw.

10:14-29 *Wisest and wealthiest in the world.* Further details are given concerning Solomon's wealth, wisdom, and fame. Estimates of his net worth range from tens of millions to several billion dollars. Unfortunately, while chapter 10 marks the peak of Solomon's fame and fortune, chapter 11 will record his spiritual downfall.

11:1-8 *They turn his heart from God.* Solomon married hundreds of women, in many cases for political reasons. These marriages were in direct violation of God's will (11:2) and led Solomon to turn his heart from God and worship his wives' gods.

Just as Solomon's "political" marriages affected him spiritually as well, Israel's great prophets would proclaim that there was no such thing as merely political alliances on the national level; such alliances always had spiritual implications. To trust in the chariots of Egypt was to distrust the Lord (Isa. 30:1-3; 31:1).

11:9-13 *The price of paganism.* The Lord appeared to Solomon a third time, expressed his anger over Solomon's apostasy, and declared that the kingdom would be taken away from his family. Only one tribe would remain, "for the sake of your father, David." To turn one's heart toward other gods (11:4) is to turn one's heart away from the Lord (11:9).

11:14-25 *The adversaries begin arriving.* Soon after condemning Solomon, the Lord began raising up leaders to oppose him. Hadad (11:14-22), an Edomite who had fled an Israelite massacre, returned and caused trouble for Solomon (11:25).

While Hadad attacked from the southeast, Rezon, a Syrian, attacked from the north (11:23-25). He would cause problems throughout the rest of Solomon's reign.

Solomon knew that God used foreign nations to judge Israel (8:46), but he probably didn't expect that he would be the one to bring on such judgment.

THE TURBULENT YEARS: THE CIVIL WARFARE OF ISRAEL (11:26–22:53)

11:26-40 *A ripped-up robe brings rebellion.* Jeroboam, an "industrious" young man (11:28), had been appointed by Solomon to oversee some of his slave laborers. One day a prophet told Jeroboam about God's denunciation of Solomon. Ripping a robe into 12 pieces and giving 10 to Jeroboam, he predicted that Jeroboam would one day rule 10 of Israel's tribes. Not willing to await God's timing, Jeroboam rebelled (11:26) and fled to Egypt when Solomon tried to kill him (11:40).

11:41-43 *The death of Solomon.* Solomon died after ruling 40 years, and his son Rehoboam became king. He would reign from 931–913 B.C.

12:1-15 *A stupid reply to a sincere request.* When Jeroboam heard that Solomon was dead and Rehoboam was king, he returned from exile, gathered his followers, and petitioned Rehoboam to renounce Solomon's oppressive policies. Rehoboam's older advisers urged him to do as Jeroboam had requested. His younger friends, however, recommended that he threaten even greater oppression. Seeking to break away from his father's shadow and establish his own identity, Rehoboam took the advice of the younger men, thus hastening the division of the nation.

12:16-20 *"Down with David! Up with Israel!"* When the people heard Rehoboam's scornful response to their request, they declared their independence and made Jeroboam their king. Judah, the tribe of Rehoboam and his royal ancestors, remained loyal to him. This was the "one tribe" God had promised to the Davidic line (11:13).

The tribe of Benjamin would also remain loyal to the Davidic kings (12:21), but the southern kingdom would always be known as simply "Judah" because of the strength and religious importance of this one tribe. (Concerning Benjamin's association with Judah, see exposition on 2 Sam. 19:40-43; Ezra 1:5.)

Having entered Canaan in 1406 B.C., Israel had survived there without a king for some 350 years. Now in 931, just 120 years after getting its first king in 1051, Israel was a divided nation.

12:21-24 *"Don't fight; this is my doing."* Rehoboam gathered his fighting men and prepared for war with the 10 renegade tribes, but the Lord put a stop to those plans, saying that the division of the kingdom was his will. God had his reasons for allowing this division and did not want more needless bloodshed.

12:25-33 *A new religion for the new nation.* Jeroboam established Shechem as his headquarters. Fearing that the people would defect to Rehoboam if they went to Jerusalem to worship, Jeroboam established Dan and Bethel as alternative religious centers, complete with their own Temples, non-Levite priests, and feast day. Jeroboam would reign 931–909 B.C.

13:1-10 *His arm freezes as the altar splits.* A "man of God" came to Bethel, where Jeroboam was worshiping at his new altar. The man prophesied that disaster would befall the altar. When the prophecy was immediately validated by a supernatural sign, Jeroboam tried to befriend the man, but, following God's instructions (13:9), the man refused the hospitality and departed.

The man's prophecy (13:2) would be literally fulfilled more than 200 years later by a man named Josiah (2 Kings 23:15-16). Josiah was one of only two people in the Bible whose exact names were predicted by a prophet. The other was Cyrus, named some 100 years before his birth (Isa. 44:28).

As with all true prophets, the man from Judah was not interested in any earthly reward for his ministry (see 2 Kings 5:15-27; Acts 8:14-24).

13:11-34 *An old prophet, a young prophet, and a complacent king.* As the man of God returned home, an old prophet of Bethel heard of his prophecy, intercepted him on the road, and invited him to come back to Bethel. When the man of God refused, the old prophet falsely claimed that God was behind the invitation. The man of God accepted the invitation and was later killed by a lion for having done so. When the man of God was buried, the old prophet told his sons that, when he died, they should bury him with the man of God.

Though not specifically stated, the old prophet apparently resented the man of God's prophecy against Bethel. Yet when God actually spoke through the old prophet (13:20-24), he came to believe the prophecy against Bethel (13:32) and therefore wanted to be buried with the man of God in order to escape God's judgment on Jeroboam's false religion.

The miraculous nature of these events is underscored by the unusual behavior of the lion (13:28).

Even after these remarkable events, Jeroboam was unrepentant. The writer notes (13:33-34) that Jeroboam's downfall (14) resulted directly from his rebellious religious practices. The political fortunes of Israel, whether united or divided, were always tied to its obedience to God.

14:1-18 *He dies for his father's sins.* When Jeroboam's son Abijah became ill, he sent his wife to Ahijah, the prophet who had predicted Jeroboam's rise to power (11:29-31). Ahijah predicted that Abijah would die and that the rest of Jeroboam's male heirs would die unnatural deaths and the kingship would be taken from his family—all as judgment on Jeroboam's religious apostasy. The child died as predicted and was mourned throughout the land.

Though his people were divided, God still expected all 12 tribes to obey him. Though the Temple and the Davidic kings were in Judah, God had wanted to work through Jeroboam in the north as well.

14:19-20 *Jeroboam's record: 22 years of transgression.* Jeroboam died after reigning 22 years and was succeeded by his son Nadab. Though Jeroboam's reign was long, little is recorded about him besides his religious apostasy. For at least the next 200 years, Israelites would talk about "the evil ways of Jeroboam" (2 Kings 17:22).

14:21-31 *Meanwhile in Judah: Idolatry, immorality, and invasion.* As the 10 northern tribes sank into idolatry, the southern kingdom was not doing much better. Even with Jerusalem and the Temple in his domain, Rehoboam allowed the construction of other shrines and the immoral practices they promoted. During his reign Jerusalem was invaded and many of Solomon's treasures were taken (14:25-28). Rehoboam died and was succeeded by his son Abijam (called Abijah in 2 Chronicles).

15:1-8 *Abijam reigns (913–911), but only because of David.* Abijam reigned for three years and was as evil as his father, but God allowed him to reign and allowed his son to succeed him "for David's sake" (15:4). Abijam's reign, like Rehoboam's, saw continuous warfare between Israel and Judah (14:30; 15:6-7).

15:9-15 *He deposes his own grandmother!* Judah's next king, Asa (911–870), led a great reform. He got rid of much of the idolatry and immorality and even deposed his own grandmother because of her idolatry.

15:16-24 *A bad deal with Ben-hadad, however.* Asa was able to end the civil war with Israel, but only by making a spiritually compromising alliance with Ben-hadad, king of Syria. Asa's gift to him from the Temple treasuries was surely an affront to God (see 2 Kings 16:7-9).

Asa died after a long reign of 41 years (15:10), and his son Jehoshaphat (873–848) succeeded him. Though Asa's reign had both good and bad moments, he had laid the foundation for a spiritual revival, should Jehoshaphat want it (see 22:41-50).

15:25-32 *Nadab (Israel, 911–909): As evil as his dad.* (The focus now shifts back to the northern kingdom, until 22:41.) Nadab proved to be as evil as Jeroboam. He would also be the first and last of Jeroboam's royal heirs. After just two years, he and all his brothers were killed by Baasha, who then became king. Baasha's slaughter fulfilled the prophecy of 14:7-16.

15:33–16:7 *Baasha (Israel, 909–886): Devoured by dogs.* Baasha reigned 24 years. Though he had been God's instrument to judge the house of Jeroboam, Baasha committed the same sins and incurred the same judgment. The curse against Baasha (16:2-4) is almost identical to that against Jeroboam (14:7-11).

16:8-14 *Elah (Israel, 886–885): Killed by his charioteer.* Elah succeeded Baasha as king and reigned two years before being killed by Zimri, one of his chariot commanders, while he was drunk. Zimri also killed all the rest of Baasha's male descendants, fulfilling the prophecy of 16:3. While the Davidic dynasty survived in the south, the northern kingdom was characterized by such coups.

16:15-20 *Zimri (Israel, 885): The seven-day wonder.* When the people heard that Zimri had killed Elah, they declared Omri, the commander of the army, as their king, and besieged Zimri's palace. Realizing he was doomed, Zimri committed suicide. Zimri's death, like the deaths of five of his predecessors, was God's judgment for his sin (16:18-19).

16:21-28 *Omri (Israel, 885–873): Good builder, bad king.* After a brief power struggle, Omri became king. Omri brought some measure of stability and prosperity to Israel. He established a dynasty that would last for three generations. And he built Samaria, which would last even longer as the northern kingdom's capital. But Omri was more evil than any of his predecessors (16:25), paving the way for his notorious son Ahab.

16:29-34 *Ahab (Israel, 874–853): Godless ways, godless wife.* Ahab became king and would reign 22 years. More evil than Omri, he opened the door to total religious rebellion when he married Jezebel and began promoting the worship of her god, Baal. Other northern kings had worshiped foreign gods while claiming to give the highest honor to Jehovah. But Ahab made it clear that Baal would be the focus of his worship.

16:34 records the literal fulfillment of Joshua's curse on Jericho (Josh. 6:26).

17:1-7 *Elijah: "No rain till I say rain!"* God sent Elijah to Ahab, prophesying a long drought that could be broken only by Elijah himself. God then directed Elijah to take refuge beside a small stream, where he would have water and food. As the drought worsened, even this stream dried up.

Elijah's ability to prevent rain is shared by the two witnesses of Revelation (Rev. 11:6).

17:8-16 *Her oil and flour outlast the famine.* With his water supply gone, Elijah was directed to go to Zarephath, where a widow would provide for him. When Elijah arrived at her home, the widow's food supply was nearly gone, yet miraculously it was enough for her and her family as well as Elijah till the drought ended (compare Matt. 14:14-21; 15:32-38).

17:17-24 *A lifeless son carried upstairs; a lively son carried downstairs.* The widow's son died, but after Elijah prayed God restored him, confirming to the widow that Elijah was a prophet of God.

18:1-16 *"Tell the ruler it's going to rain!"* Elijah went to Ahab and announced the end of the drought. On his way he met Obadiah, a godly servant of Ahab. When Elijah asked Obadiah to announce his arrival to Ahab, Obadiah resisted, saying that Ahab had been looking everywhere for Elijah and that Obadiah's life would be in danger if he announced Elijah's arrival and then Elijah didn't show up. Elijah assured him that he would show up, so Obadiah reported his arrival and Ahab went out to meet him. 18:4 gives a preview of the wickedness of Jezebel.

18:17-19 *"I'm not the problem, but I'm looking at the problem!"* Ahab greeted Elijah as the "troublemaker" of Israel, an ironic greeting, to say the least, as Elijah was quick to point out. Elijah told Ahab to summon the prophets of Baal and Asherah, along with "all the people of Israel," to Mount Carmel. 18:19 presents Jezebel as the primary influence in Ahab's religious apostasy. For "Asherah," see 2 Kings 13:1-9.

18:20-30 *Will your god come through?* As the people gathered on Mount Carmel, Elijah challenged them to choose once and for all between Jehovah and Baal. When they were silent, he proposed a contest to see whose god would provide fire for a sacrifice. The people agreed that that would be a good test of true divinity. Elijah invited the prophets of Baal to go first. They prayed and performed various incantations all day, but no fire came from Baal. Elijah mocked their efforts (18:27), making Baal's failure all the more evident to the assembled crowd.

18:31-40 *He fixes the altar, prays, and the fire falls!* Elijah then repaired a broken-down Israelite altar, filled it with water, prayed, and fire came from the Lord, consuming the water as well as the sacrifice. Elijah prayed that this demonstration of God's power would turn the people's hearts back to him (18:37), and that is what happened (18:39). At Elijah's command, the people seized the prophets of Baal, and Elijah executed them.

18:41-46 *A tiny cloud, then a cloudburst.* Elijah told Ahab the drought would end. A tiny cloud appeared and soon brought heavy rainfall. Both Ahab and Elijah went down from Carmel to Jezreel, Ahab by chariot and Elijah by foot. Elijah, with divine help, outran Ahab's chariot.

19:1-8 *"I'll have your head!"* Ahab reported to Jezebel the defeat at Carmel and Elijah's slaughter of the prophets of Baal. Jezebel sent word to Elijah that she intended to kill him, and Elijah fled. After being ministered to by an angel in the wilderness, he traveled to Mount Horeb, which was either the same as Mount Sinai or close to it (Exod. 3:1; 33:6).

As did Obadiah (18:3-16), Elijah let fear overcome him. As did Jonah (Jon. 4:3), he begged God to end his life.

19:9-18 *A still, small voice, and 7,000 saints.* Confronted by God, Elijah complained that he was the only one left in Israel who had not forsaken him to worship Baal. God came to him in "the sound of a gentle whisper" (19:12), traditionally translated as a "still, small voice," assuring him that he was far from the only God-fearing Israelite (19:18). God also told Elijah to anoint Hazael as king of Syria and Jehu as king of Israel, and to anoint Elisha as his own successor as prophet (19:15-17). The new kings, along with Elisha, were to be God's instruments of judgment (19:17).

Though neither was literally anointed by Elijah, Hazael would become king of Syria after murdering Ben-hadad (2 Kings 8:15), and Jehu (not the same as the prophet mentioned in 16) would become king of Israel after Ahab's son Jehoram (2 Kings 9:1-10).

19:11-12 has been precious to believers down through the centuries who have heard God speak quietly, rather than in grand, thundering tones.

19:19-21 *From plower of soil to prophet of God.* Elijah found Elisha at work on his farm and commissioned him as a prophet. After bidding his family farewell, Elisha followed Elijah. The story of his ministry will be told in 2 Kings 2–13.

20:1-12 *"Don't count your chickens before they hatch!"* Ben-hadad, along with 32 other kings, besieged Samaria. When Ahab answered their verbal threats with sarcasm, they prepared to storm the city. Exchanges of curses and boasts (20:10-12) were common in ancient battles.

20:13-22 *The defeat of the drunks.* Ahab's army, though greatly outnumbered by the Syrians, defeated them soundly, perhaps in part because the Syrian leaders were drunk and therefore overconfident (20:16-18). The victory was also supernatural, however: God sent his prophet with instructions and encouragement (20:13-14, 22), giving Ahab one more chance to repent and recognize Yahweh as the true God. Ben-hadad escaped (20:20), but would later return.

20:23-30 *"Their gods are hillbilly gods!"* Convinced that the choice of battle site had led to their defeat because its hilly terrain favored Israel's "gods," the Syrians mounted a rematch. This time as before, however, Israel was victorious.

It was common in ancient Near Eastern polytheism to view each god or goddess as having a special sphere of power. Baal, for instance, was a god of weather and fertility. It was quite radical in this context to not only believe in just one God but to believe that he was all-powerful in all areas of influence.

20:31-34 *He foolishly befriends his bitter foe.* Seeing that they were defeated, the Syrian leaders dressed in sackcloth and begged for mercy for their king. Ahab granted their request and made a treaty with Ben-hadad. Such a treaty was totally unnecessary, for God had already revealed that Israel would defeat Syria (20:28).

20:35-43 *"You spared his life, so you'll die in his place!"* After a very realistic portrayal of the situation among his own peers (20:35-36), a prophet condemned Ahab for having failed to deal with Ben-hadad as God had commanded. The prophet's parable and Ahab's indignant response (20:39-40) recall Nathan's parable and David's response (2 Sam. 12:1-7; see also exposition on 2 Sam. 14:1-20).

21:1-4 *Not for sale, at any price!* Ahab offered to buy the vineyard of his next-door neighbor, Naboth. Naboth turned down the offer, saying he could not in good conscience sell his family's inheritance. Ahab was "angry and sullen" about Naboth's refusal. It was extremely important in Israelite culture to keep land within a family. If land ever fell to outside ownership, descendants were expected to reclaim it (see Lev. 25:25-28; Ruth 4:1-4).

21:5-16 *Jezebel's poison-pen letters.* When Jezebel learned why Ahab was so despondent, she wrote letters arranging Naboth's death. The plot was carried out, Jezebel announced Naboth's death to Ahab, and Ahab prepared to take possession of Naboth's vineyard. Jezebel's evil nature and her influence over Ahab, hinted at in 16:31; 18:4, 19, are clearly seen here.

21:17-26 *Dogs will attend their deaths.* While Ahab was on his way to the vineyard, a prophet of God was on his way there as well. Elijah confronted Ahab concerning Naboth's vineyard and prophesied that both Ahab and Jezebel would die ignoble deaths (see 22:37-40; 2 Kings 9:30-37). Ahab's greeting to Elijah on this occasion (21:20) recalls his earlier greeting (18:17).

21:27-29 *A foxhole conversion?* Faced with Elijah's dire predictions, Ahab repented and went into mourning, and the Lord promised to delay carrying out the death sentence against his family. The sentence would be carried out by Jehu (2 Kings 10:1-11). Ahab's later injustice toward Micaiah (22:26-27), his treachery toward Jehoshaphat (22:29-33), and his willful disregard of God's warning through Micaiah (see exposition on 22:13-28) show that his repentance, if truly sincere, was very short-lived.

22:1-12 *"You wouldn't like that other prophet."* Ahab invited Jehoshaphat, king of Judah, to help him free Ramoth in Gilead from Syrian control. Jehoshaphat agreed to do so but wanted to make sure it was God's will. Ahab called on 400 of his prophets, all of whom agreed they should fight. Jehoshaphat doubted their word, however, and asked Ahab to send for a "prophet of the LORD" (22:7), who could be trusted to tell the truth. Ahab admitted that there was one such prophet—Micaiah by name—but expressed hatred for Micaiah, who always prophesied against him. Ahab didn't seem to care about *why* Micaiah's prophecies were always negative.

22:13-28 *Sheep without a shepherd.* Refusing to go along with the crowd, Micaiah prophesied disaster should Ahab go to war. In calling the 400 other prophets liars (22:19-23), Micaiah had the confidence that came from doing exactly what God told him to do.

Ahab's recognition that Micaiah's initial positive prediction was false (22:15-16) suggests that Ahab may have seen through the lies of the other 400 as well. His earlier repentance (21:27-29) certainly showed that he could recognize true prophecy when he wanted to.

22:29-40 *A cowardly king, a poorly aimed arrow.* Ignoring Micaiah, Ahab and Jehoshaphat went to war with Syria. Seeking to circumvent Micaiah's prophecy, Ahab disguised himself and conspired to make Jehoshaphat the focus of enemy attention—and Jehoshaphat nearly died as a result. Finally, however, a random arrow found the disguised Ahab and killed him.

22:41-50 *Judah's king is good, for the most part.* The writer now summarizes the rest of Jehoshaphat's reign, noting that he was a good king, though he failed to continue the reforms of his father Asa as much as he could have (see exposition on 15:16-24).

22:51-53 *But Israel's next king is bad.* Ahaziah succeeded Ahab his father and reigned for two years (853–852). His evil ways were compared to Ahab, to Jezebel, and to Jeroboam. He would be followed by his brother Jehoram, who would be the final descendant of Ahab to rule. (Ahaziah's story continues in 2 Kings.)

PEOPLE TO REMEMBER FROM 1 KINGS

ABIATHAR

Key Facts: Co–high priest with Zadok, escaped bloodbath at Nob (1 Sam. 22:20-23; 1 Chron. 15:11)

Father: Ahimelech (1 Sam. 22:20)

Son: Jonathan (2 Sam. 15:27)

Total Bible References: 31

Key References: 1:5-7; 2:26-35; 1 Sam. 22:11-23; 23:6-13; 2 Sam. 15:24-29; 19:11-13

Abiathar Speaks

Solomon could have had me executed, of course, but he didn't. Had he done so it would have been ironic, for my father was executed for befriending his father! My father didn't deserve to die. I probably do. I still don't know what caused me to side with the king's enemies. (1:7; 2:26; 1 Sam. 21:1-6; 22:11-20)

At least I was loyal when I served as co–high priest under David. It was my privilege to help him when both Saul and later his own son were trying to kill him. In fact, I was the one who convinced the elders of Judah to reinstate David as their king following Absalom's rebellion. God of Israel, may I be remembered as a faithful servant under David, not as a foolish rebel against Solomon! (1 Sam. 23:6; 2 Sam. 15:24; 19:11)

Spiritual Lessons from Abiathar

- Even the most seemingly faithful friends may fail us: Abiathar displayed great loyalty to David (1 Sam. 23:6-13; 30:7; 2 Sam. 15:24-29; 19:11-13) but sided against David's son Solomon (1:7, 19, 25).
- No matter how long it takes, what God says will happen will surely happen. Abiathar's removal from the priesthood (2:26-27) fulfilled God's promise 100 years earlier to remove the house of Eli from the priesthood (1 Sam. 2:30-36).

Key Verse

"Then the king said to Abiathar the priest, 'Go back to your home in Anathoth. You deserve to die, but I will not kill you now, because you carried the Ark of the Sovereign LORD for my father, and you suffered right along with him through all his troubles'" (2:26).

AHAB

Key Fact: Allowed his wife, Jezebel, to turn him into one of Israel's worst kings (16:29-33; 21:7-15)
Father: Omri (16:28)
Wife: Jezebel (16:31)
Sons: Ahaziah, Joram (Hebrew *Jehoram*) (22:51; 2 Kings 3:1)
Daughter: Athaliah (2 Kings 8:18, 26)
Death: Recorded in 22:34-35
Total Bible References: 90
Key References: 16–22; 2 Kings 10:1-11

Ahab Speaks

At least the pain is becoming less intense. A bad sign, though—probably due to the loss of so much blood. But of course that was part of the prophecy! Elijah and Micaiah were right. The battle has been lost, and I shall soon die. It was no doubt a terrible blunder allowing my Baal-worshiping wife to turn me against Jehovah God. Where is *her* god when I need him? (16:30-33; 21:19; 22:17)

The priests on Mount Carmel must have asked the same question! Baal's silence up there was deafening, but Elijah's God responded with fire from heaven. I should have known he was the true one when I was allowed twice to defeat these same Syrians. But not this time! A curse upon my greed, and for my encouraging Jezebel to satisfy it by the murder of an innocent man. (18:26-29, 36-38; 20:13-20, 28-29; 21:1-16)

For 22 years I ruled over Israel, never allowing God a place in my heart. Now, in the hour of death, I neither ask for nor desire the relationship to change. I have rejected him; he now returns the favor.

Spiritual Lessons from Ahab

- An unbelieving spouse can help ensure an unhappy and godless life (16:31-33; 21:1-16).
- Unbelievers sometimes blame believers for their troubles: Ahab blamed Elijah (18:17); Nero blamed the Christians; Hitler blamed the Jews.
- The false gods we worship, whether literal idols or things like fame or fortune, can never answer our prayers or meet our true needs (18:26, 29).

Key Verses

"But Ahab did what was evil in the LORD's sight, even more than any of the kings before him. And as though it were not enough to live like Jeroboam, he married Jezebel, the daughter of King Ethbaal of the Sidonians, and he began to worship Baal. . . . He did more to arouse the anger of the LORD, the God of Israel, than any of the other kings of Israel before him" (1 Kings 16:30-31, 33).

ASA

Key Fact: One of Judah's best kings (15:9-15)
Father: Abijam (15:8)
Son: Jehoshaphat (22:41)
Death: Recorded in 2 Chron. 16:12-13
Total Bible References: 58
Key References: 15:8-24; 2 Chron. 14–16

Asa Speaks

My feet cause me great discomfort. For two years I have suffered. I fear the simple act of walking will soon be denied me. I suppose the prophet Hanani is laughing at me from his prison cell. Well, let him laugh as he rots away! I have no intention of releasing him. How dare he rebuke me for my warfare policies and peace treaties! (2 Chron. 16:7-12)

But even as I think about such things, my soul pains me more than my feet. Where is that love and zeal I once had for God? After all, it was through his strength that I fortified Judah's cities, built up its army, and led the people in a mighty revival! Of course who could forget the greatest moment of all, when he supernaturally struck down that massive Ethiopian army as it prepared to invade? I still recall my prayer to him as we faced our enemy: "O LORD, no one but you can help the powerless against the mighty! Help us, O LORD our God, for we trust in you alone. It is in your name that we have come against this vast horde." (15:11-13; 2 Chron. 14:6-15)

But that was all back then. Here I sit today with diseased feet and bitterness of soul.

Spiritual Lessons from Asa

- God, and God alone, can help the powerless against the mighty (2 Chron. 14:11).
- God is eager to help us, if only we seek his will (2 Chron. 16:9).
- Those who rightfully point out our sin cannot be silenced, no matter how much we ignore or persecute them (1 Chron. 16:7-10).

Key Verse

"The eyes of the LORD search the whole earth in order to strengthen those whose hearts are fully committed to him" (2 Chron. 16:9).

BATHSHEBA

Key Facts: Wife of Uriah, then David, mother of Solomon (2 Sam. 11:3, 27; 12:24)
Father: Eliam (2 Sam. 11:3)
Sons: Solomon, Nathan, Shimea, Shobab, and 1 unnamed (2 Sam. 11:27; 12:18, 24; 1 Chron. 3:5)
Total Bible References: 12
Key References: 1–2; 2 Sam. 11–12

Bathsheba Speaks

I think my son was a little upset with me for a while. But then, how was I to know his older half brother was using me to get to him? But all that has been forgotten, I'm sure. He has indeed become a good and wise king. David would have been proud. (2:1-2, 13-25; 4:29-34)

I do worry, though, over his growing interest in riches and the many pagan women he has married. Surely he must know God's views on all this. (2 Sam. 9:1-9; 10:14-29; 11:1-8)

I was taken on a special tour through the new Temple the other day. What a magnificent building! If only David, who wanted so much to build it, could have been with me! (2 Sam. 7:1-2)

I think about him constantly. What a horrible way to begin a marriage, with adultery and murder. But that was some 40 years ago. Israel's merciful God has long since forgiven both of us! I bore David five sons, four of whom are still living. I often wonder what our little first son would be doing today had he lived. Forgive us, tiny one, for our sin caused your death. (2 Sam. 11; 12:13-18; 1 Chron. 3:5; Ps. 51)

Nathan and Zadok stop by to see me regularly. I'm convinced much of David's success was because of this godly prophet-and-priest team. (1; 2 Sam. 7:1-17; 12; 15:24-37)

Death holds no fear for me. A passage from one of my husband's writings has been my daily source of comfort and assurance: "Surely your goodness and unfailing love will pursue me all the days of my life, and I will live in the house of the LORD forever." (Ps. 23:6)

Spiritual Lessons from Bathsheba

- A person should not allow his or her physical carelessness to entice a member of the opposite sex (2 Sam. 11:2-3).
- Adultery is sinful, no matter what the circumstances or how otherwise morally upright the people involved (2 Sam. 11:26-27; Acts 13:22).

Key Verses

"When Bathsheba heard that her husband was dead, she mourned for him. When the period of mourning was over, David sent for her and brought her to the palace, and she became one of his wives. Then she gave birth to a son. But the LORD was very displeased with what David had done" (2 Sam. 11:26-27).

JEROBOAM

Key Fact: First northern king of divided Israel (12:19-20)
Father: Nebat (11:26)
Mother: Zeruah (11:26)

Sons: Abijah, Nadab (14:1; 15:25)
Death: Recorded in 2 Chron. 13:20
Total Bible References: 84
Key References: 11:26–14:20; 2 Chron. 10–13

Jeroboam Speaks

In some ways I have been successful in defying Jehovah God for the entire 22 years of my reign! According to Jacob, Israel's kings were to come from the tribe of Judah. Later, Moses wrote that the priests would proceed from Levi. Finally, Solomon claimed the nation's religious center to be the city of Jerusalem. But I have dismissed all such silly requirements! (Gen. 49:10; Num. 3:11-13)

In the first place, I'm from the tribe of Ephraim, not Judah. Then, I've replaced the Levitical priests with worthless and ignorant men from other tribes. Thirdly, I've built two new religious centers, Bethel and Dan, to replace Jerusalem. Finally, adding insult to injury, I've introduced the worship of the golden calf in those two cities! (8:29; 11:26; 12:25-31)

I hate the God of David and Solomon. Thanks to him, my beautiful altar at Bethel has been destroyed and my army has been routed. But worse, what freethinker could possibly worship a deity who once refused to heal his sick son? (13:1-5; 14:1-18; 2 Chron. 13:13-19)

Yes, I've done things my way these past two decades. But although I've defied him, I'm under no delusion whatsoever that I've defeated him! In fact, to the contrary, this strange sickness that has suddenly befallen me may well be his hand of judgment. (2 Chron. 13:20)

Spiritual Lessons from Jeroboam

- Even those most blessed by God can choose to rebel against him and become the greatest of sinners (11:37-38; 14:14-16). Jeroboam's sins are mentioned 22 times in 1, 2 Kings—more than the sins of any other person in Scripture.

Key Verses

"Then the LORD will shake Israel like a reed whipped about in a stream. He will uproot the people of Israel from this good land that he gave their ancestors and will scatter them beyond the Euphrates River, for they have angered the LORD by worshiping Asherah poles. He will abandon Israel because Jeroboam sinned and made all of Israel sin along with him" (14:15-16).

JOAB

Key Facts: Commander of David's army, killed Abner, Absalom, and Amasa (2 Sam. 3:27; 8:16; 18:14; 20:10)
Mother: Zeruiah (2 Sam. 2:13)
Brothers: Abishai, Asahel (2 Sam. 2:18)
Death: Recorded in 2:28-34
Total Bible References: 138
Key References: 1–2; 2 Sam. 2–3; 10–14; 18–20; 23–24

Joab Speaks

It's a little awkward to say the least, visiting the Tabernacle for the first time, not to offer a sacrifice, but to seek protection from my enemies! Actually, I've never before felt any need for God or his sacred building. "Better a sword than a sacrifice!" That has been my philosophy. But now that death is near I realize the emptiness of this godless lifestyle. (2:28)

My heart is too old and set in its ways to change, though. It's all the fault of that idiot Adonijah! I should have known at the beginning that he was a loser—all talk and no performance. But I supported him and now it will cost me my life. (1:5-7)

If only I could have controlled Solomon the way I once controlled his father David. I highly resent all that praise he has received, while I'm totally ignored. Like it or not, he would never have accomplished what he has without my trusty sword. Of course he never forgave me for killing Abner and Absalom. Fools! They all deserved to die! But now it is my turn. (2 Sam. 3:27; 18:14)

"Joab" means "God is judge." That's the name my mother gave me. I stand here in the Tabernacle, grasping the horns of the altar with the growing fear that he indeed will soon judge me!

Someone is shouting outside, demanding my surrender. I recognize the voice—it is Benaiah the lion killer. I refuse! He'll have to come and get me! (2:34; 2 Sam. 23:20-23)

Spiritual Lessons from Joab

- Those who live by violence often die by violence (2:5, 28-34).
- Those entrusted to uphold the law (2 Sam. 8:16) must never usurp that law (1:5-7).

Key Verses

"Then the LORD will repay him for the murders of two men who were more righteous and better than he. For my father was no party to the deaths of Abner son of Ner, commander of the army of Israel, and Amasa son of Jether, commander of the army of Judah. May Joab and his descendants be forever guilty of these murders, and may the LORD grant peace to David and his descendants and to his throne forever" (2:32-33).

NATHAN

Key Facts: Prophet, condemned David for adultery and murder (2 Sam. 7:2; 12:1-15)

Total Bible References: 28

Key References: 1; 2 Sam. 7:1-17; 12:1-15

Nathan Speaks

Well, book number two is done. I'll never write as much as Moses. But I hope my biographies of David and Solomon will be helpful to future generations. In a way it's good they're both gone. Each would have been heartbroken over this tragic civil war. It crushes me just to think about it—80 years of tribal unity ruined in as many hours by an arrogant and immature young man. (12:1-19; 1 Chron. 29:29; 2 Chron. 9:29)

I felt closer to David, of course. I doubt that he would have accepted that severe rebuke from anyone but me. But his blatant sins of adultery and murder had to be condemned. I was right on target. (2 Sam. 11–12)

But there was that occasion when I gave him the wrong advice. Of course, how was I to know God had already determined that Solomon would build the Temple?

Admittedly, I had less in common with David's son. But I did name him, you know. His father called him Solomon, meaning "peace," but I named him Jedidiah, meaning "beloved of the Lord." (2 Sam. 12:24-25; 1 Chron. 28:2-6)

And I did all I could to make sure that Solomon would succeed David as king, just as he wished. God has decreed, after all, that David's descendants are to rule Israel. (1:11-27; 2 Sam. 7:12-17)

But now this! Oh, foolish, foolish Rehoboam! What have you done? Why have you done it? Where will it lead? (12:1-19)

Spiritual Lessons from Nathan

- Sometimes even the godliest counselor may unintentionally give the wrong advice (2 Sam. 7:1-5).
- A true friend will give reproof as well as affirmation, as the situation demands (2 Sam. 12:1-12; Prov. 27:6).

Key Verses

"Then Nathan said to David, 'You are that man! . . . Why, then, have you despised the word of the LORD and done this horrible deed?'" (2 Sam. 12:7, 9).

THE QUEEN OF SHEBA

Key Fact: Foreign queen who came to Israel to verify reports of Solomon's greatness (10:1-13)

Total Bible References: 9

Key References: 10:1-13; Matt. 12:42

The Queen of Sheba Speaks

As if either of us needed the presents we gave each other! But I leave Jerusalem having received more from him than I brought to him. His wealth is indeed impressive, but the wisdom he displayed is absolutely incredible. In fact I found myself sharing the burdens and secrets of my heart with him! (3:28; 4:29-31; 10:2-3, 10-13; 2 Chron. 9:13-14)

To say the least, his power and personality have overwhelmed me! Rumors concerning a king's greatness are almost always exaggerated, but in his case they don't begin to describe the glory! (10:5-7)

Spiritual Lessons from the Queen of Sheba

- Just as the queen of Sheba's skepticism turned to belief upon her firsthand experience of Solomon's wisdom and wealth, skeptics down through the centuries have been convinced when responding to the invitation to "taste and see that the LORD is good" (Ps. 34:8).
- If the queen of Sheba was willing to go to such great effort to verify the reports of Solomon's wealth, we should be even more willing to explore the spiritual wealth the Bible claims to offer (Matt. 12:42).

Key Verse

"The queen of Sheba will also rise up against this generation on judgment day and condemn it, because she came from a distant land to hear the wisdom of Solomon. And now someone greater than Solomon is here—and you refuse to listen to him" (Matt. 12:42).

REHOBOAM

Key Facts: Son of Solomon, first southern king of divided Israel (11:43–12:24)
Mother: Naamah (14:21)
Wives: 18, including Mahalath and Maacah (2 Chron. 11:18-21)
Children: Abijam, Jeush, Shemariah, Zaham, Attai, Ziza, and Shelomith are named among 28 sons and 60 daughters (2 Chron. 11:19-21)
Death: Recorded in 14:31
Total Bible References: 50
Key References: 11:43–12:27; 14:21-31

Rehoboam Speaks

It's just not fair! Both my father and grandfather lived to reach 70, and ruled over all 12 tribes—for 40 years each. But look at me, only 58, apparently at the end of my life after ruling over just two tribes. It's mostly the fault of those political idiots who advised me at Shechem. Had it not been for their stupid counsel, things no doubt would have turned out differently. If only my father had killed Jeroboam when he had the chance. Without his leadership the 10-tribe revolt probably would not have happened. (11:40; 12:1-20; 14:21)

But most of all, I blame Jehovah God. It was his prophet who encouraged Jeroboam. And he allowed the king of Egypt to embarrass me by attacking Jerusalem and carrying off many of our greatest treasures. (11:29-40; 14:25-28)

Well, for better or for worse, I've done things my way. Admittedly, at the very beginning I forsook the God of Solomon and David. It is painfully obvious now that in the final days of life he has forsaken me! (2 Chron. 12:1, 13-16)

Spiritual Lessons from Rehoboam

- "A hothead starts fights; a cool-tempered person tries to stop them" (Prov. 15:18). Scripture's most tragic example of this is seen in Rehoboam's senseless answer to Israel's northern leaders, which triggered the civil war (12:1-16).
- When seeking advice, we should value the voice of experience (12:1-16).

Key Verse

"But when Rehoboam was firmly established and strong, he abandoned the law of the LORD, and all Israel followed him in this sin" (2 Chron. 12:1).

SHIMEI

Key Fact: Cursed David during the king's retreat from Absalom's revolt (2 Sam. 16:5-13)
Father: Gera (2 Sam. 16:5)
Death: Recorded in 2:41-46
Total Bible References: 18
Key References: 1:8; 2:8-9, 36-46; 2 Sam. 16:5-13

Shimei Speaks

1,000 curses on those two miserable servants! I should have let them rot in Gath. Their attempted escape has cost me my life! Well, I suppose Solomon would have found an excuse to kill me anyway. It's common knowledge that David wanted him to punish me. (2:8-9, 36-39)

Looking back, I don't know why David didn't kill me when he had the chance those two times in the wilderness. Probably some sort of weakness on his part. If only my long-dead relative Saul were still on the throne! Whatever you might say about him, Saul knew how to deal with his enemies, including David! In fact, had he killed the son of Jesse, I would not today be standing before this pompous monarch son of his, receiving the death sentence. A plague on those two servants, on Solomon, and on the God of Israel! I hear the footsteps of Benaiah the royal executioner coming my way. (2:46; 1 Sam. 18:11; 22:18-19; 24:5-6; 26:11; 2 Sam. 16:5-13; 19:16-23)

Spiritual Lessons from Shimei

- "Whoever stubbornly refuses to accept criticism will suddenly be broken beyond repair" (Prov. 29:1). Shimei would learn that the hard way: He sinned against David (2 Sam. 16:5-8) and was twice forgiven (2 Sam. 16:9-13; 19:16-23). He would later sin against Solomon (2:36-40) and be executed (2:41-46).

Key Verses

"Remember Shimei son of Gera, the Benjaminite from Bahurim. He cursed me with a terrible curse as I was fleeing to Mahanaim. When he came down to meet me at the Jordan River, I swore by the LORD that I would not kill him. But that oath does not make him innocent. You are a wise man, and you will know how to arrange a bloody death for him" (2:8-9).

SOLOMON

Key Facts: Israel's richest king, world's wisest man (3:11-13)
Birth: Recorded in 2 Sam. 5:14
Father: David (2 Sam. 12:24)
Mother: Bathsheba (2 Sam. 12:24)
Brothers: Full brothers: Shimea, Shobab, and Nathan (1 Chron. 3:5). Half brothers: Amnon, Kileab (also called Daniel), Absalom, Adonijah, Shephatiah, Ithream, Ibhar, Elishua, Elpelet, Nogah, Nepheg, Japhia, Elishama, Eliada, and Eliphelet (2 Sam. 3:2-5; 5:13-16; 1 Chron. 3:1-8; 14:3-5)
Sister: Half sister, Tamar (2 Sam. 13:1)
Wives: Many, including Naamah (3:1; 11:3; 14:21)
Son: Rehoboam (14:21)
Key Events in His Life:

- Proclaimed king of Israel (1:28-40)
- Defeats primary opponents (2:13-46)
- Asks for wisdom, receives wealth also (3:1-15)
- Builds Temple (5–7)
- Visited by queen of Sheba (10:1-13)
- Allows wives to turn his heart from God (11:1-13)
- Faces several rebellions (11:14-40)

Death: Recorded in 11:43
Total Bible References: 297
Key References: 1–11; Neh. 13:26; Ps. 72; 127; Proverbs; Song of Songs; Ecclesiastes; Matt. 6:28-29

Solomon Speaks

"Happy is the person who finds wisdom and gains understanding." If only I had always observed those words, which I myself wrote! I wasn't born with wisdom, nor did I study or search for it. God graciously gave it to me. How peaceful and productive both the king and his kingdom were when I used my wisdom. How stressful and unsettled things became when it was ignored. (3:12; 4:24-25; 11:1-25; Prov. 3:13)

What privileges have been mine: power, fortune, fame, and honor! What opportunities God has given me: building the Temple, presiding over the greatest Passover celebration in history, and establishing Israel as a great nation. But, oh, what greed, lust, pride, and disobedience I have displayed! I allowed my life to be controlled by immorality and idolatry, through the influence of my pagan wives. Indeed, what would Moses have thought had he known one of Israel's kings would so shamefully disregard all three of the very simple commandments he laid down concerning how we should rule? (4:21, 25; 5–6; 8:62-66; 10:1, 6-8; 23; 11:1, 9; Deut. 17:14-17)

At his invitation, I once asked God for wisdom. The request pleased him and he granted it. In retrospect, perhaps I should have sought something far better, namely, a heart after God's own heart, like that of my father David. (3:4-13; 1 Sam. 13:14)

Spiritual Lessons from Solomon

- We should pray for godly wisdom (3:5-9; Prov. 4:7; James 1:5).
- God gives his best to those who allow him to make the choice! Solomon received the wisdom he asked for, plus the riches, honor, and long life he did not ask for (3:12-14).
- "How much better to get wisdom than gold!" (Prov. 16:16). While Solomon preached this, he did not always practice it (10:14, 22).
- Because we are fallen human beings, even the wisest among us can ignore the best advice. Solomon's acquisition of horses (4:26), gold (10:14), and wives (11:1-3) was a direct violation of a four-century-old piece of good advice (Deut. 17:14-17).
- One's choice of a marriage partner can have a decisive effect on one's life, for good or for ill (11:3-11).

Key Verse

"There was no king from any nation who could compare to [Solomon], and God loved him and made him king over all Israel. But even he was led into sin by his foreign wives" (Neh. 13:26).

ZADOK

Key Facts: Co–high priest with Abiathar in David's time, high priest in Solomon's time (2:35; 2 Sam. 8:17)
Father: Ahitub (1 Chron. 6:8)
Son: Ahimaaz (2 Sam. 15:27)
Total Bible References: 40
Key References: 1:8, 38-39; 2:35; 2 Sam. 8:17; 15:24-37; Ezek. 44:15

Zadok Speaks

What a wealthy, famous, and wise king he has been these past three decades. He still is rich and well known, but I fear lust and greed have all but snuffed out his wisdom. Yes, there is reason for much concern at this time, especially when one considers his successor son. I have no confidence whatever in young Rehoboam. (10:6-8; 23; 11:1-11; 12:1-15)

Oh, for the glory days of David. Life was not nearly as easy back then, but it was far more rewarding. How can I ever forget carrying the Ark of the Covenant into Jerusalem, and bringing it to David in the wilderness during Absalom's rebellion? True, of course, the son of Jesse on occasion strayed from the path of righteousness, but then he tearfully accepted Nathan's rebuke. However, it appears my words of warning to Solomon are falling on deaf ears. Dear God, I prayed for the king when his half brother tried to keep him from the throne. Now, let me intensify my efforts lest a far more deadly enemy, his own carnal nature, drive him from it. (1:8; 2 Sam. 6:15; 11–12; 15:24-29)

Spiritual Lessons from Zadok

- God rewards the faithfulness of his servants. As a reward for his faithfulness, God promised that Zadok's descendants would serve as priests in the millennial Temple (Ezek. 44:15; 48:11).

Key Verse

"The Levitical priests of the family of Zadok continued to minister faithfully in the Temple when Israel abandoned me for idols. These men will serve as my ministers. They will stand in my presence and offer the fat and blood of the sacrifices, says the Sovereign LORD" (Ezek. 44:15).

2 KINGS

BACKGROUND

2 Kings details the final years of Israel's divided kingdom, from 852 to about 560 B.C. Despite periodic revivals, spiritual conditions in both kingdoms grew steadily worse until both eventually fell—the north in 722 (17), followed 136 years later by the south in 586 (25). (See *1 Kings: Background.*)

The time span covered by 2 Kings (and 2 Chron. 22–36) saw the emergence of the first of Israel's "writing prophets" (see *Introduction to the Prophets,* p. 353).

AUTHOR

Unknown (see *1 Kings: Author*). It is possible that Jeremiah had much to do with recording the final decades of the southern kingdom, especially since he enjoyed a good relationship with Josiah. Some scholars think Jeremiah wrote all of 1, 2 Kings, though he could not have written the final chapter of 2 Kings, since he was not in exile in Babylon.

DATE AND LOCATION

See *1 Kings: Date, Location.* Chapter 25 was probably recorded in Babylon, within 30 years after the fall of Jerusalem in 586. The Jews were allowed to maintain scribal activities while in captivity.

PURPOSE

See *1 Kings: Purpose.*

UNIQUE FEATURES

- 2 Kings records the final two of three OT resurrections (4:32-37; 13:20-21; for the first, see 1 Kings 17:17-24).
- It records the second of two men in the Bible who left this earth without dying (Elijah, 2:1-18; Enoch was the first, Gen. 5:21-24).

931 B.C.
Kingdom divided, Israel, Judah

852
Elisha inherits Elijah's ministry

740
Isaiah begins ministry

722
Fall of Israel

627
Jeremiah begins ministry

586
Fall of Judah

- It records the second and third of three occasions when God rolled back the waters of the Jordan River (2:8, 14; see Josh. 3).
- It records the second OT miracle involving the rotation of the earth around the sun (20:8-11; see Josh. 10:12-14).

COMPARISON WITH OTHER BIBLE BOOKS

Isaiah:

- Both record the attack of Sennacherib and Hezekiah's illness (18:13–20:21; Isa. 36–39).

Jeremiah:

- Both record the southern kingdom's final days, its fall, and Jehoiachin's fate in Babylon (24:18–25:30; Jer. 52).

(See *2 Chronicles: Comparison with Other Bible Books.*)

OUTLINE

2 Kings continues the story of Israel's "Turbulent Years" (1 Kings 11:26–22:53; see *1 Kings: Outline*), subdividing those years into the "Splintered Kingdom" (northern vs. southern tribes) and the "Surviving Kingdom" (Judah, which survived the fall of the 10 northern tribes).

THE SPLINTERED KINGDOM (ISRAEL AND JUDAH) (1–17)
- Elijah (and Ahaziah, eighth northern king) (1)
- Elisha's ministry begins (2)
  - Authority passed; Elijah taken up (2:1-18)
  - Authority proven (2:19-25)
- Elisha and Joram (Jehoram), ninth northern king (3:1–8:15)
  - Elisha provides water (3)
  - Elisha provides resurrection (Shunammite's son) (4)
  - Elisha provides healing (Naaman) (5)
  - Elisha provides deliverance (chariots of fire) (6:1-23)
  - Elisha provides deliverance again (6:24–7:20)
  - Elisha provides a prediction (8:1-15)
- Jehoram (Joram), fifth southern king (8:16-24)
- Ahaziah, sixth southern king (8:25-29)
- Jehu, 10th northern king (9–10)
- Athaliah, seventh southern ruler (queen) (11)
- Joash (Jehoash), eighth southern king (12)
- Jehoahaz, 11th northern king (13:1-9)
- Jehoash (Joash), 12th northern king (13:10-13, 22-25)
- *Death of Elisha* (13:14-21)
- Amaziah, ninth southern king (14:1-22)
- Jeroboam II, 13th northern king (14:23-29)
- Uzziah (Azariah), 10th southern king (15:1-7)
- Zechariah and Shallum, 14th, 15th northern kings (15:8-16)
- Menahem, 16th northern king (15:17-22)
- Pekahiah and Pekah, 17th, 18th northern kings (15:23-31)

Jotham, 11th southern king (15:32-38)
Ahaz, 12th southern king (16)
Hoshea, 19th northern king; fall of northern kingdom (17)
THE SURVIVING KINGDOM (JUDAH) (18–25)
Hezekiah, 13th southern king (18–20)
His helplessness against Sennacherib (18)
His helper against Sennacherib (19)
His healing (20)
Manasseh, 14th southern king (21:1-18)
Amon, 15th southern king (21:19-26)
Josiah, 16th southern king (22:1–23:30)
Discovers the Word of God (22)
Does the work of God (23:1-30)
Jehoahaz, 17th southern king (23:31-34)
Jehoiakim, 18th southern king (23:35–24:5)
Jehoiachin, 19th southern king (24:6-16)
Zedekiah, 20th southern king, begins reign (24:17-20)
Fall of southern kingdom (25)

THE SPLINTERED KINGDOM (ISRAEL AND JUDAH) (1–17)

1:1-8 *Ahaziah (Israel, 853–852* B.C.). He has a great fall, both physically and spiritually. After briefly mentioning the rebellion of Moab against Israel (1:1; see 3:4-27), the writer resumes the story of Ahaziah (see 1 Kings 22:51-53). When Ahaziah sustained a serious injury, he sent his servants to inquire of the Canaanite god Baal-zebub concerning his prospects for recovery. Elijah intercepted Ahaziah's servants and sent word to him that, because he had sought help from Baal-zebub, he would die from his injury. Though not told the prophet's name, Ahaziah knew who it was from the content of his prophecy.

Baal is Canaanite for "lord." One of Baal's names was "Baal-zebul," which means "lord of the height," signifying his supremacy. The Israelites tried to mock Baal by changing this to the similar-sounding "Baal-zebub" (1:2), which means "lord of the flies" and suggests that Baal is really lord of nothing. The derogatory name would later be used to describe Satan (see exposition on Matt. 10:16-42). It lives on in our day in the title of the 1954 William Golding novel.

1:9-12 *Fire falls on the first two delegations.* When Ahaziah sent 50 men to summon Elijah to his palace, Elijah called down fire from heaven on them. The same fate befell a second delegation. Elijah is sometimes called the "prophet of fire" (see 2:11-12; 1 Kings 18:30-38).

1:13-18 *He says he will die, and he does.* Ahaziah sent a third delegation and this time Elijah returned to Ahaziah with them. He repeated to Ahaziah the prophecy of his death, and the prophecy was fulfilled.

2:1-8 *He follows him like his shadow.* As Elijah's ministry neared its end, in about 850 B.C., Elisha, his designated heir (1 Kings 19:16-21) reappeared as his loyal disciple. Elisha stated three times his intention to follow Elijah (2:2, 4, 6), showing his complete devotion to the task. Elijah miraculously parted the Jordan River (2:8) so that he and Elisha could cross (see 2:14; Josh. 3). 2:1 suggests that not only Elijah but also Elisha and the "group of prophets" (2:3) knew that God intended to take Elijah in a miraculous way (2:11).

2:9-11 *A fiery chariot, a whirlwind, and he's gone.* Elijah granted Elisha's request to become his "rightful successor" (Hebrew, "Let me inherit a double share of your spirit"), provided that Elisha "see" him after he was taken up into heaven. Then, in an instant, a "chariot of fire" appeared, and Elijah was taken up to heaven in a whirlwind.

2:12-18 *"Where is the Lord God of Elijah?"* Having expressed grief at Elijah's departure, Elisha received a confirmation of receiving Elijah's prophetic gift as he parted the waters of the Jordan just as Elijah had done (2:8).

Though the other prophets recognized that Elisha had received Elijah's gift, they apparently did not believe Elijah had actually been taken up to heaven and insisted on searching for him. Just as Elisha predicted, however, they did not find him.

Elisha cried out, "Where is the LORD, the God of Elijah?" (2:14). Today, however, as someone has said, the urgent cry is, "Where are the Elijahs of the Lord God?"

2:19-22 *He sweetens the waters with salt.* Elisha received further public confirmation of his prophetic gift as he miraculously purified a local water supply.

2:23-25 *Never mock a bald-headed prophet!* As Elisha began his ministry, a group of youths mocked his baldness. Elisha pronounced a curse on them, and they were mauled by bears. Disrespect for the Lord's prophet is the same as disrespect for the Lord.

3:1-12 *Joram (Jehoram) (Israel, 852–841): A march against Moab.* Joram, son of Ahab, became king of Israel when his brother Ahaziah died without a male heir (1:17). Joram was evil, but not quite so bad as his father and mother (Jezebel).

When the Moabites, whom David had conquered and made his servants (2 Sam. 8:2), rebelled against Israel, Jehoram formed an alliance with Judah and Edom to put down the rebellion. When their troops ran low on water, Jehoshaphat, the king of Judah (see 1 Kings 22:41-50), sent for Elisha.

Throughout most of 3:1–8:15, Joram is referred to simply as "the king."

3:13-27 *Fooled by water that looks like blood.* Elisha agreed to pray for water, specifying that he would do so for the sake of the good king Jehoshaphat, not for Joram. When an abundance of water covered the allies' camp, the morning sun gave it the appearance of blood. Assuming the allies had already killed each other, the Moabites struck overconfidently and were soundly defeated (see *The Moabite Stone*, p. 892).

As with the 10 plagues in Egypt (Exod. 7–12), God often used natural phenomena in miracles, but this did not make them any less miraculous. The water filled the valley at Elisha's command, apart from any apparent natural causes (3:15-20).

4:1-7 *All available vessels filled with oil.* When the widow of a fellow prophet told Elisha of her desperate financial situation, God enabled Elisha to provide for her through the miraculous multiplication of oil, recalling the similar miracle by Elijah (1 Kings 17:8-16).

4:8-17 *A son for the serving Shunammite.* A woman of Shunem began showing hospitality to Elisha whenever he passed through town. Eventually, she even set aside a special room for him. (Such hospitality for true prophets should have been common in Israel, but sadly was not.) In return for her kindness, Elisha promised the woman that she would miraculously have a son. "At that time the following year" (4:17), the son was born. The woman's humble service and genuine concern for God's prophet was duly rewarded.

4:12 introduces Elisha's servant Gehazi.

4:18-31 *But then the boy dies.* Several years later, however, the boy suddenly died. Laying her son on Elisha's bed, the woman went looking for Elisha, found him at Mount Carmel, and reported her son's death. Though he should have known Elisha was concerned for the woman, Gehazi was rude toward her until Elisha reprimanded him (4:25-27). Sent by Elisha to resurrect the son, Gehazi failed again (4:29-31).

4:32-37 *The sneezing corpse.* Arriving at the woman's home, Elisha went to his room and prayed for the boy. After sneezing seven times, the boy came back to life (see *Unique Features*).

4:38-41 *He purifies the poisoned pot.* During a time of famine, some prophets made some stew from ingredients that proved to be poisonous. When the problem was discovered, Elisha miraculously purified the stew.

4:42-44 *100 hungry men.* When someone brought Elisha a gift of bread, he instructed that it be used to feed a hungry crowd. To the people's amazement, the bread was sufficient to feed everyone. The leftovers from this feast (4:44) parallel those from Christ's feeding of the 5,000 and the 4,000 (Matt. 14:20; 15:37).

5:1-5 *A military man with a deadly disease.* When Naaman, a commander in the Aramean army, contracted leprosy, his wife's young Israelite servant girl recommended that he go to Elisha. He did so, with the blessing of his king. The servant girl had an effective ministry, even though she was young and was in Aram as a captive of war (5:2).

5:6-8 *"Send that sick soldier to me."* The Aramean king sent Naaman to the king of Israel (Joram) with a letter requesting healing. Thinking the unusual request was a pretext for a quarrel, Joram reacted with rage. Sadly, he didn't even think of consulting a prophet, but Elisha, hearing of the incident, confidently offered his services.

5:9-14 *Furious at first, he obeys and is healed.* When Elisha told Naaman he would be healed after washing seven times in the Jordan River, Naaman became furious, thinking such actions unnecessary. His servants suggested that it was the very simplicity of the prescribed action that made him so angry and that he would have readily obeyed had Elisha prescribed "some great thing." Realizing they were right, Naaman washed seven times in the Jordan and was healed.

5:15-19 *Cleansed, converted, and charitable.* Cleansed of his leprosy, Naaman, who had probably been a polytheist, expressed faith in Israel's God and offered Elisha a gift for his services (see 5:5). Elisha refused the gift, desiring only that God receive the glory (see exposition on 1 Kings 13:1-10).

5:20-27 *The grievous price of greed.* Gehazi, by contrast, saw the healing as a financial opportunity. He told Naaman that some fellow prophets had a financial need, and Naaman gave him some of the gifts he had brought. Realizing what Gehazi had done, Elisha decreed that Gehazi and all his descendants would inherit Naaman's leprosy. Gehazi's greed led him to two lies (5:22, 25) as well as a deceitful act (5:24). One sin always leads to another.

6:1-7 *It sinks like a rock but rises like a cork.* Elisha had gathered so many "student prophets" that they had to build a larger place to live. During the building project, an axhead fell into the water, but Elisha caused it to rise to the surface and it was retrieved.

6:8-12 *"OK, who's the spy?"* As the king of Aram (Syria) made plans to attack Israel, he was distressed to see the Israelites posting guards at the very place he planned to attack. He suspected there was a traitor in his ranks, but his servants recognized that the Israelites' knowledge of their plans was the supernatural work of God through Elisha.

6:13-17 *Chariots of Aram vs. chariots of fire.* The king of Aram sent "a great army with many chariots and horses" to surround Dothan, where Elisha was staying. When Elisha's servant was terrified by the Arameans, Elisha prayed on his behalf and the Lord showed him a supernatural vision of "horses and chariots of fire," confirming Elisha's assurance that Israel would be victorious against the Arameans (6:16). The vision of the fiery chariots links Elisha's ministry with that of Elijah, the prophet of fire (see 1:9-12).

6:18-23 *He leads the sightless soldiers to Samaria.* As the Arameans closed in on Elisha, God struck them blind. Elisha led the blinded soldiers to Samaria, where their sight was restored and they were set free. Elisha didn't want to kill them, only to demonstrate to them that the God of Israel was the one true God. And the Arameans must have gotten the point, because they left Israel alone for a while (6:23).

6:24-33 *Siege and famine: A deadly combination.* Sometime later, the Aramean king Ben-hadad besieged Samaria during a severe famine. Things became so bad that there was at least one reported case of cannibalism. When King Joram heard about the cannibalism, he began blaming the famine on Elisha and sought to kill him.

The incident repeated a familiar trend in ancient Israel: When things went well the prophets were not thanked, but when things went badly they were blamed.

7:1-11 *The skeptic and the lepers.* Elisha predicted that the famine would end within a day. When the king's chief servant was skeptical about his prophecy, Elisha predicted that he would not live to see the famine's end. That night some Israelite lepers ventured into the Aramean camp and found it deserted. After first keeping their discovery secret so that they could have everything left by the Arameans, they had a change of heart and reported it to the king.

The writer tells us that the Arameans had fled after the Lord supernaturally caused them to hear the sound of an attacking army and they mistakenly concluded that Israel had hired Hittite and Egyptian mercenaries. Though it was only natural for the Arameans to assume this, the prophets were very much against such alliances because they showed a lack of trust in Jehovah and because they often led to religious compromise (see Isa. 30:1-2; 31:1).

7:12-20 *While the city dines, the skeptic dies.* Joram guessed that the Arameans had only pretended to flee, hoping to ambush the Israelites when they raided their camp. But in desperation he allowed his servants to go and investigate. Finding that the Arameans had indeed fled, they plundered the camp, and the city had plenty of food, just as Elisha had predicted (7:1). The skeptical servant died, however (7:17-20), as Elisha had also predicted. The fatalism of both the lepers (7:3-4) and the king's servant (7:13) shows how desperate the situation in Samaria had become.

8:1-6 *A providential meeting in the palace.* The Shunammite woman (4:8-37) had escaped the famine when Elisha warned her to flee (8:1-2). Returning to Israel after the famine, and seeking to reclaim her land, she just happened to appear before the king at the same time as Gehazi, and Gehazi was able to intervene on her behalf—one of numerous instances in the Bible where apparent good timing is not coincidence but God's providence (see Gen. 22:13; 24:13-15; Exod. 2:3-5; Ruth 2:3; Esther 6:1-3).

Gehazi's appearance at this time suggests that the famine and the other events of 6–7 actually took place before Naaman's healing and Elisha's curse on Gehazi (5).

8:7-10 *"Tell him he'll live . . . though really he'll die."* When King Ben-hadad became ill, he heard that Elisha was in town and sent his servant Hazael to him. Elisha told Hazael that Ben-hadad would die, but Hazael should nonetheless tell him that he would live.

8:11-15 *And he does die, at Hazael's hand!* Elisha then predicted that Hazael himself would become king of Aram and would bring great suffering to Israel. Hazael then returned to Aram, told Ben-hadad he would recover, then killed him and became king in his place, fulfilling Elisha's prophecy!

8:16-24 *Jehoram (Judah, 853–841): Wicked man with a wicked wife.* Jehoram succeeded his father Jehoshaphat as king of Judah. Jehoram had married Athaliah, daughter of Ahab and Jezebel, and had become like Ahab.

During Jehoram's reign Judah lost the territory of Edom, one of a number of losses in the divided kingdom that reduced the lands won by David.

Jehoram of Judah and Jehoram of Israel, both of whom were also called Joram, ruled at approximately the same time.

8:25-29 *Ahaziah (Judah, 841): Godless son of a godless mother.* Jehoram's son Ahaziah succeeded him, and he was wicked as well. He joined forces with Joram of Israel to fight against King Hazael of Aram. Joram was injured in the battle, and Ahaziah went to Jezreel to visit him.

Throughout the turbulent years of the divided kingdom, Israel and Judah were constantly shifting between hostilities and alliances with each other.

9:1-13 *Jehu (Israel, 841–814): Anointed to avenge the victims of Ahab.* At Elisha's direction, a prophet anointed Jehu, a military leader, to succeed Jehoram as king. The prophet told him he was being made king to avenge all those killed by Ahab and Jezebel (9:7-10). His fellow soldiers enthusiastically accepted him as their king.

9:14-20 *"Who was that crazy charioteer?"* Jehu immediately began conspiring against Joram, who was still in Jezreel with Ahaziah, recovering from his wounds. As Jehu and his men arrived at Jezreel, Joram sent two messengers to inquire as to his identity and the nature of his visit. Both messengers defected to Jehu; meanwhile the watchman in the tower, observing how "recklessly" the charioteer drove, concluded it must be Jehu!

9:21-29 *He kills two kings at one time.* Joram and Ahaziah got in their chariots and went to meet Jehu. They caught up with him at Naboth's vineyard, where Jehu killed both of them.

9:30-37 *As predicted, the dogs eat her.* As Jehu entered the palace grounds in Jezreel, Jezebel called to him from a window. She obviously expected to die, for she compared Jehu to Zimri, the soldier who had slaughtered the house of Baasha (1 Kings 16:8-20). Three of Jezebel's servants threw her down from the window. When some servants later went to bury her, they found she had already been eaten by dogs, fulfilling Elijah's prophecy (see 1 Kings 21:23).

10:1-11 *70 heads in two piles.* Jehu invited the people of Israel to choose one of Ahab's 70 remaining sons to be

THE DIVIDED KINGDOM

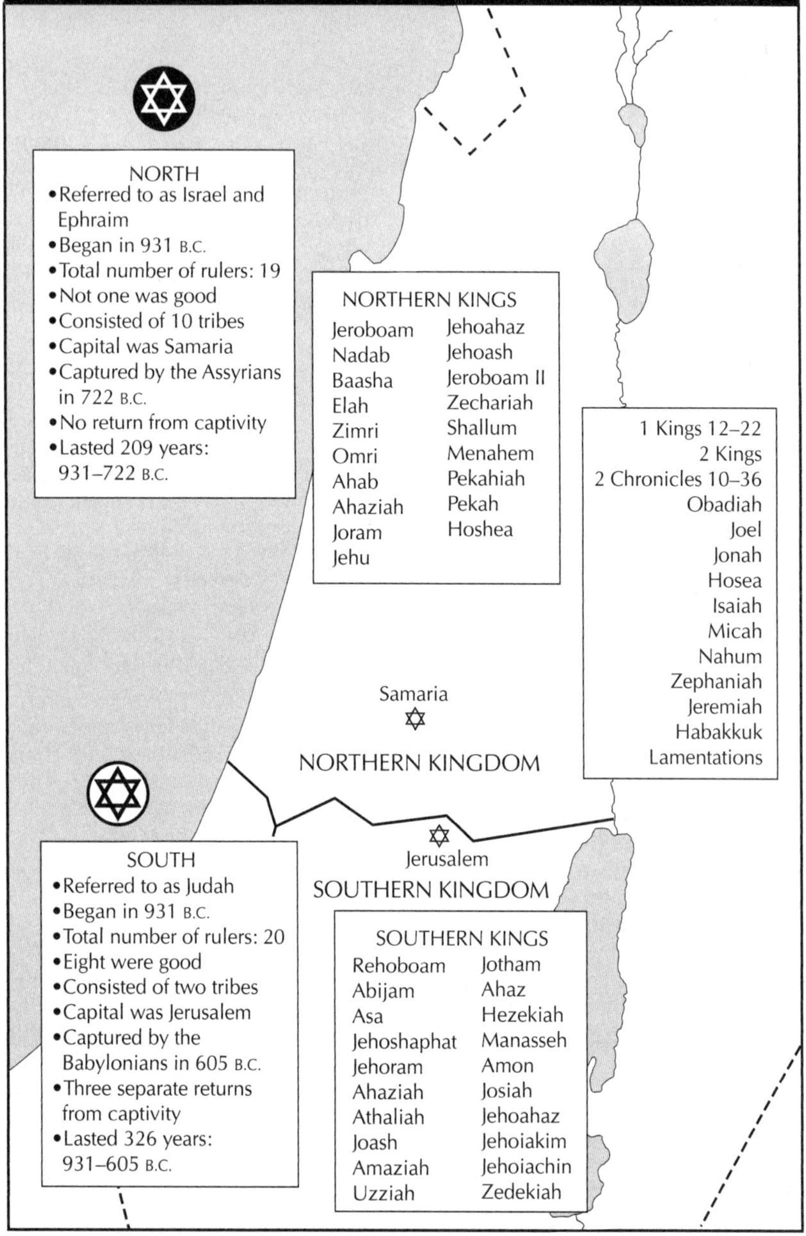

their king. When they chose to follow Jehu instead, he directed them to execute the 70 sons. The executions were promptly carried out.

10:10 is one of many examples of Scripture affirming its own trustworthiness as God's inspired Word (see 2 Tim. 3:16; 2 Peter 1:21).

The 70 sons probably included grandsons. The Hebrew word for "son" was used for any male descendant.

10:12-17 *"Come, see what I have done for the Lord!"* Jehu and his men executed 42 of Ahaziah's male relatives, then went to Samaria and killed "everyone who was left there from Ahab's family," completing God's judgment on Ahab and his family (1 Kings 21:17-24). Jehu clearly saw this purge as an act of obedience to the Lord (10:15-16).

10:18-28 *Deceived and destroyed.* With Ahab's *family* destroyed, Jehu turned his attention to Ahab's *religion*. Pretending to want to give a feast for Baal, he lured Baal worshipers from all over Israel into the temple of Baal, then slaughtered them and destroyed the temple.

10:29-36 *His anger ends with Baalism.* Unfortunately, Jehu's zeal for the Lord died down as soon as he had eradicated Ahab's Baal worship. He failed to deal with all the other evil influences dating back to Jeroboam. Nonetheless, in recognition of his purge of Baalism, God promised that Jehu's sons would succeed him; the promise, however, would extend only to the fourth generation (10:30; see 15:8-12; Hos. 1:4).

Because of Israel's continuing disobedience, God continued allowing pagan nations to regain territory that David had conquered (10:32-33). Judah was losing land as well (see exposition on 8:16-24).

By taking Israel's Transjordanian land, the Aramean king Hazael (10:32) was beginning to fulfill Elisha's prophecy concerning him (8:12; see exposition on 13:1-9).

Jehu died and Jehoahaz his son succeeded him.

11:1-3 *Athaliah (Judah, 841–835): Slayer of David's seed.* The focus now shifts back to Judah. King Ahaziah had been killed by Jehu along with the northern king Joram. When Athaliah, daughter of Ahab, wife of the southern king Jehoram, and mother of Ahaziah, saw that her only remaining son was dead, she tried to destroy all of her grandsons. Assuming she had succeeded, she proclaimed herself queen.

One royal heir, the one-year-old Joash (Jehoash), escaped the purge and was hidden during Athaliah's six-year reign.

Athaliah would be the only woman to rule by herself over either kingdom. She had been an evil influence on Ahaziah (2 Chron. 22:2) and on her other sons, whom she allowed to loot the Temple and offer its sacred objects to Baal (2 Chron. 24:7).

11:4-12 *In the seventh year they make their move.* Joash had been hidden by his aunt Jehosheba (11:2), wife of the high priest Jehoiada (2 Chron. 22:11). After Athaliah had reigned six years, Jehoiada, along with other priests and the palace guards, proclaimed Joash king.

11:13-16 *"Long live the king . . . death to the queen!"* When Athaliah heard the noise of the secretly planned coronation (11:12), she went to investigate, whereupon she was executed.

11:17-21 *A revival follows her removal.* Jehoiada then initiated a great religious revival throughout Judah. He supervised the destruction of the temple of Baal, just as Jehu had done in the north (10:25-28).

12:1-3 *Joash (Judah, 835–796): The seven-year-old survivor.* Joash began his reign at age seven. He would be a good king while under the godly influence of Jehoiada. After Jehoiada's death, however, he allowed a resurgence of paganism (2 Chron. 24:15-19), a fact alluded to in 12:3.

12:4-16 *Holes in their pockets, a hole in its lid.* Joash appointed the priests to collect money and supervise its use in making some much-needed repairs to the Temple. When after 23 years there had been little progress, Joash relieved the priests of their supervisory roles (12:6-8). Apparently they had been misappropriating the money.

The work resumed, with money being brought to a single box in the Temple, with a hole in its lid for the donations. The work then proceeded swiftly; the workmen, who were now in charge of spending the money, proved to be more trustworthy than the priests (12:14-15)!

The items mentioned in 12:13 were probably among the things stolen by Athaliah's sons (2 Chron. 24:7). They would be replaced after the rest of the Temple repairs were done (2 Chron. 24:14).

12:17-18 *A shameful bribe; he should have trusted God!* Threatened by Hazael of Syria, Joash tried to bribe him with treasures from the palace and Temple; he then fled from Jerusalem.

12:19-21 *Apostasy and assassination.* During Joash's apostasy following the death of his spiritual mentor Jehoiada, Jehoiada's son Zechariah had tried to lead a revival, and Joash had ordered him killed. Joash's own servants then killed him to avenge Zechariah's death (see 2 Chron. 24:20-25).

13:1-9 *Jehoahaz (Israel, 814–798): The evil king who prays for his people.* Meanwhile in the northern kingdom, Jehoahaz had replaced his father Jehu as king. Jehoahaz led the nation back into religious apostasy, so the Lord allowed Aram to oppress them. After Jehoahaz pleaded with God on Israel's behalf, he delivered them. Even after the deliverance, however, the people continued to sin.

"The king of Aram had killed the others like they were dust under his feet" (13:7) describes the cruelty Elisha had foreseen (8:12). The prophet Amos, writing some 50 years later, would predict God's judgment on Aram for its cruelty to Israel (see Amos 1:3-5).

13:22-23 is a flashback explaining why God delivered Israel from the Arameans during Jehoahaz's reign.

13:10-19 *Jehoash (Israel, 798–782): The evil king who befriends Elisha.* Jehoash (Joash) succeeded his father Jehoahaz and was an evil king. 13:10-13 summarizes his reign; 13:14–14:16 fills in some of the details. As Elisha neared death, Jehoash visited him and expressed sorrow over his ill health. Jehoash's lament over Elisha (13:14) echoes Elisha's own lament over Elijah (2:12).

Elisha then used a "sign act" (see exposition on 1 Sam. 11:1-11) to predict the outcome of the ongoing conflict between Israel and Aram. When, in response to Elisha's prompting, Jehoash struck the ground only three times, Elisha predicted that Israel would defeat Aram only three times and would not win a permanent victory over them.

13:20-25 *After his death: A miracle and a fulfilled prophecy.* Elisha died and was buried. Shortly thereafter, during a battle, a soldier was hastily buried alongside Elisha. When the two corpses touched, the soldier came back to life.

13:22-25 retells and adds to the story of Israel's conflict with Aram (13:3-7). Just as Elisha had predicted, Jehoash won three victories over Hazael's son Ben-hadad. These victories marked the beginning of a rise in the fortunes of the northern kingdom that would last to the reign of Jeroboam II (14:23-29). God was merciful to Israel in spite of their sins, "because of his covenant with Abraham, Isaac, and Jacob" (13:23).

14:1-7 *Amaziah (Judah, 796–767): Not the best, but a good king.* Amaziah succeeded his father Joash as king in the south. He began as a good king, seeking to follow the law (14:6), but was not as zealous as he could have been (14:3-4). Though Amaziah ruled well, he did not measure up to David (14:3). Comparison to David was reserved for Judah's best kings: Asa (1 Kings 15:11), Hezekiah (18:3), and Josiah (22:2).

14:8-22 *The price he pays for his pride.* Amaziah challenged the northern king Jehoash to war. Jehoash responded with an insulting parable, and the two went to war. Jehoash won and proceeded to destroy part of Jerusalem's wall and take some of the Temple treasures and some hostages back to Samaria. The war was completely needless, a product of Amaziah's pride (14:10; see 14:7). 14:15-22 records the deaths of both of these kings.

14:23-29 *Jeroboam II (Israel, 794–753): Jonah's king.* Jeroboam II reigned 41 years, during which time the northern kingdom gained much territory and experienced economic prosperity. Spiritually, however, both the king and his land were corrupt. Jonah began his prophetic ministry during this time. 14:25 shows that Jonah was a real person and that the book of Jonah is not fiction.

15:1-7 *Uzziah (Judah, 790–740): The sad story of a good king.* Uzziah (Azariah), like so many other kings, ruled well but failed to eradicate pagan religious practices. After he had reigned about 40 years, Uzziah offered incense in the Temple, in violation of the law (see 2 Chron. 26:16-21), and was stricken with leprosy. He spent the rest of his life in seclusion while his son Jotham oversaw the affairs of state.

During his 50-year reign, Uzziah repaired the fortifications of Jerusalem, reorganized the army, regained the Red Sea port city of Ezion-geber, and gained territory on both Israel's eastern (Edom) and western (Philistia) boundaries (see 2 Chron. 26:1-15). By this time both the south and the north had increased their boundaries to almost those of the time of Solomon (see exposition on 14:23-29). There was, however, a nation on the horizon that would put an end to the prosperity: Assyria!

15:8-12 *Zechariah (Israel, 753–752): The last of Jehu's line.* Zechariah succeeded his father, Jeroboam, and reigned just six months before being killed by Shallum, who then became king. Zechariah was the fourth and last descendant of Jehu to reign, fulfilling precisely the prediction of 10:30.

Although both Zechariah and his father, Jeroboam II, were evil, Zechariah's sins were compared not to those of his father but to those of "Jeroboam son of Nebat." The sins of this first Jeroboam were still remembered, nearly 200 years after his death (17:21-23, see 1 Kings 14:19-20).

15:13-15 *Shallum (Israel, 752): The killer is killed.* Having killed and succeeded Zechariah, Shallum reigned only one month before being killed by Menahem. After the economic and political resurgence under Jeroboam II, things were beginning to fall apart in the northern kingdom.

15:16-22 *Menahem (Israel, 752–742): He pays off King Pul.* Menahem reigned 10 years. In order to secure his throne, he attacked a rebellious city and committed atrocities against its pregnant women. Menahem paid tribute to King Pul of Assyria, also known as Tiglath-pileser, making him the first king to interact with this nation that would soon bring the northern kingdom to an end.

15:23-26 *Pekahiah (Israel, 742–740): Another short and evil reign.* Nothing is recorded of Menaham's son Pekahiah except that he was evil and was killed after two years by Pekah.

15:27-31 *Pekah (Israel, 740–732): The beginning of the end.* During the 20-year reign of Pekah, Tiglath-pileser of Assyria captured large amounts of Israel's land and took many Israelite captives—despite having been paid off earlier by King Menahem (15:19-20). More will be learned about Pekah's reign in 16:5-9.

15:32-38 *Jotham (Judah, 750–731): In general, a good king.* Jotham reigned 19 years, at approximately the same time as Pekah in the north. He was a good king, yet like many others failed to deal with the widespread religious apostasy. Isaiah, Hosea, and Micah began their prophetic ministries at about this time. 15:37 previews the events of 16:5-9.

16:1-4 *Ahaz (Judah, 735–715): He sacrifices his own son.* Ahaz, son of Jotham, rivaled the northern kings for wickedness (see 2 Chron. 28:24), even sacrificing his own son as an offering to a pagan god.

16:5-9 *A short civil war.* King Pekah of the north (see 15:27-31) had joined forces with Aram to try to stop Assyria from taking over Palestine (see 15:29). When King Ahaz of Judah refused to help them, preferring to pay Assyria not to attack him (16:7-9), Israel and Aram attacked Jerusalem but were unable to defeat it (16:5-6; see Isa. 7:1-2). Meanwhile, Assyria conquered Damascus, the capital of Syria.

16:10-20 *A heathen altar in the house of God.* As King Ahaz was in Damascus, meeting with Tiglath-pileser, a pagan altar struck his fancy. He had a replica of the altar built in Jerusalem, and decreed that this new altar should become the focus of worship. Once again, a "political" alliance had proven to be much more than merely political. God's own house was no longer his own; he had to share it with a pagan god!

17:1-4 *Hoshea (Israel, 732–722): The foolish final ruler.* After the Israel-Aram coalition (16:5) was crushed by Assyria, the new king of the northern kingdom, Hoshea, began paying tribute to Assyria. When Tiglath-pileser was succeeded by his son Shalmaneser (17:3), Hoshea withheld the tribute and appealed to Egypt for help. The Egyptians were in no position to help, however, and Hoshea soon found himself imprisoned by the Assyrians.

17:5-23 *The fall of the north, reported and explained.* In 722 B.C., Assyria captured Samaria and took the people of the northern kingdom into exile. 17:7-23 explains at great length why this happened: It happened because Israel, which had been given the land of Canaan as a judgment against the Canaanites (Deut. 9:4-5), had themselves become just as wicked as those pagans. Moreover, they had done so despite repeated warnings from the prophets (17:12-14). God would later come to the same conclusion regarding Judah (see exposition on 2 Chron. 36:15-21).

Some Israelites were left in the land (2 Chron. 30:6). Though their number is unknown, according to the rules of ancient warfare they would have been the uneducated classes—those deemed incapable of reviving the nation.

The tribe of Judah (and Benjamin; see exposition on 2 Sam. 19:40-43) escaped this judgment (17:18), yet 17:19 sounds an ominous warning about the eventual fall of the southern kingdom as well (see 25). God's greatest warning to Judah was the defeat of the northern kingdom, but Judah would not heed even this.

17:21-23 credits Jeroboam with initiating Israel's decline (see exposition on 1 Kings 14:19-20).

17:24-41 *The Samaritans: New race, new religion.* Assyria brought people from other nations to help repopulate the conquered northern kingdom. When these new inhabitants were plagued by lions, they assumed it was because they did not know how to worship "the God of the land" (17:26). Assyria sent an Israelite priest to teach them about the Lord, and over time there grew a mixture of paganism and faith in the true God. This was the beginning of the Samaritan race and religion.

THE SURVIVING KINGDOM (JUDAH) (18–25)

18:1-8 *Hezekiah (728–686): The revival ruler.* Six years before the fall of the northern kingdom, Hezekiah became coregent with King Ahaz of Judah. Then, in 715, when Hezekiah was 25 years old, Ahaz died and Hezekiah became the sole monarch and ruled for another 29 years (18:1-2). He was a great king, receiving a commendation shared only by Josiah (compare 18:5 and 23:25). Hezekiah refused to pay tribute to Assyria.

Hezekiah's reforms included destruction of the bronze serpent made by Moses centuries before (see Num. 21:4-9), which had become an object of idolatry.

18:9-12 *He sees his neighbors carried captive.* In 722 B.C., Hezekiah's sixth year as coregent, the northern kingdom fell. Though Hezekiah took proper warning from that event, apostasy loomed in Judah just one generation away.

18:13-25 *A sinful and unsuccessful attempt to appease.* In 701, 14 years after the north fell to the Assyrian king Shalmaneser, his nephew Sennacherib captured "the fortified cities of Judah" and laid siege to Jerusalem. Hezekiah tried to bribe him with treasures from the Temple (18:14-16), but Sennacherib's men soon returned, taunting Hezekiah and urging him to pledge allegiance to Assyria (18:17-25). Their taunts included mockeries against Judah's God (18:22).

Though Hezekiah's righteousness is lauded (18:3-7), his willingness to give away the Temple treasures shows that he was far from sinless.

18:26-37 *"Face it! You don't have a chance!"* Hezekiah's men asked the Assyrians to speak in Aramaic, the diplomatic language of the day, hoping that this would prevent Jerusalem's populace from becoming overly frightened by the threats. The Assyrians, of course, refused to do so, and began addressing their threats directly to the people watching from the city wall. They reminded them of how many other nations had fallen to Assyria and urged them to surrender. Again, the taunts included blasphemy against the Lord (18:30-35).

19:1-7 *Hezekiah despairs; Isaiah reassures.* In despair because of the siege, Hezekiah sent messengers to Isaiah, urging him to seek God on Judah's behalf. Isaiah replied that God had told him the Assyrian siege would fail and Sennacherib would die. With the odds so greatly in the Assyrians' favor, only a miracle could produce such an outcome.

19:8-19 *A desperate prayer for deliverance.* Sennacherib himself sent a letter to Hezekiah, once again mocking Judah and its God, and reminding him how many other nations had fallen to his Assyrian army. Hezekiah laid the letter out before the Lord and in a contrite prayer acknowledged God's greatness and uniqueness.

19:20-34 *A note from heaven's king to Assyria's king.* The Lord honored Hezekiah's humble prayer and through Isaiah issued a warning to Sennacherib: Because of his "arrogance" ("rage") against the Lord (19:28), Sennacherib and his men would be defeated and Jerusalem would be saved.

19:35-37 *An angel kills his soldiers; his sons kill him.* Soon thereafter, the "angel of the Lord" (commonly called the "death angel") put to death 185,000 Assyrian soldiers, and Sennacherib returned in defeat to Nineveh, where he himself was later killed by his own sons.

20:1-11 *The sign on the sundial means death is delayed.* When Isaiah told Hezekiah he would die soon, Hezekiah begged the Lord to spare him. The Lord promised to extend his life for 15 years and to continue sparing Jerusalem from the Assyrians. When Hezekiah asked for a sign that he would be spared, the Lord caused the sun to recede by 10 degrees on the sundial (see *Unique Features;* Isa. 38–39). It was because of Hezekiah's repentance that the Lord spared both him and the city (2 Chron. 32:26).

20:12-21 *"You showed it all? Someday they'll steal it all!"* When the king of Babylon sent messengers to Hezekiah, he foolishly showed them all the precious metals and spices in his storehouses. Isaiah predicted that, because of Hezekiah's foolish pride, Judah would someday be carried captive to Babylon. Despite Hezekiah's undeniable good qualities (18:3-7), his response to Isaiah showed great selfishness (20:19). (Concerning the tunnel Hezekiah built [20:20], see *Hezekiah's Tunnel, Siloam,* p. 893.)

21:1-9 *Manasseh (695–642): Worst of the wicked.* Hezekiah's son Manasseh became coregent with his father and succeeded him as king in 686. Manasseh was Judah's longest-reigning king and was the most wicked of any king north or south. He was more evil than even the Canaanites (21:9).

21:10-18 *To be wiped away as water from a dish.* God sent prophets to warn that, because of Manasseh's sins and the sins he influenced the people to commit, he would destroy Judah "as one wipes a dish and turns it upside down."

This wiping of the bowl and the measuring for destruction (21:13) are typical of the numerous word pictures the prophets used (see Amos 7:7-9; 8:1-3). God communicates to his people in ways they can understand, using illustrations from everyday life.

2 Chronicles 33:10-17 records that Manasseh was for a while held captive by the Assyrians in Babylon, during which time he turned to God in repentance and as a result was restored to his throne. (Assyria was still quite strong, despite its devastating losses at Jerusalem in 701.)

21:19-26 *Amon (642–640): 22 years of transgression.* Manasseh's son Amon succeeded him and ruled 22 years. As evil as his father, his own servants eventually assassinated him.

22:1-2 *Josiah (640–609): Godliest of the godly.* Amon's young son Josiah succeeded him in 640 and reigned 31 years. Josiah's reforms, sparked by his own turning to the Lord in about 632 (see 2 Chron. 34:3), were the greatest the nation had ever seen. By God's providence Assyria had become weak by this time and could no longer exercise its influence over Palestine as it had for the previous century.

Jeremiah, Nahum, Habakkuk, and Zephaniah all began their prophetic ministries during Josiah's reign.

22:3-13 *Found: The forgotten law.* Josiah, like his ancestor Joash nearly 200 years before (see exposition on 12:4-16), raised money to repair the Temple. During the repairs, in about 621, Hilkiah the high priest found a copy of the law. Upon reading the law, Josiah was appalled by how far the nation had strayed from its teachings. He asked Hilkiah to "speak to the LORD for me and for the people" concerning the law and the nation's disobedience. 23:22 underscores the extent of Israel's neglect of the law.

22:14-20 *"The nation will not die till you die!"* Hilkiah asked the prophetess Huldah for a word from the Lord concerning the rediscovered law. Huldah prophesied that the nation would suffer all the calamities prescribed in the law for their disobedience but that because Josiah had been so repentant, the calamities would not happen during his lifetime.

23:1-20 *The law is read; the revival is on.* Josiah read publicly from the law and led the nation in repentance and covenant renewal. He supervised the destruction of idolatrous shrines and objects of worship and the execution of pagan priests throughout the land.

23:15 is 1, 2 Kings' final mention of the wicked influence of Jeroboam. 23:16-18 records another tie to the time of Jeroboam, as Josiah protected the grave of the "man of God" who had prophesied against Jeroboam, and the older prophet who had recognized the truth of his words and asked to be buried with him (see 1 Kings 13).

23:21-23 *A neglected feast renewed.* Josiah commanded the people to keep the Passover, and the writer notes that "there had not been a Passover celebration like that since the time when the judges ruled in Israel." 2 Chronicles 35:1-19 gives more details about Josiah's Passover. 2 Chronicles 30 records a Passover in the time of Hezekiah, which 2 Kings does not mention. The last actual biblical occurrence of the word *Passover,* prior to the time of Hezekiah and Josiah, is Joshua 5:10-11.

23:24-27 *He was the best.* The writer gives Josiah an unconditional commendation shared only by Hezekiah (18:5). Josiah, however, surpassed even Hezekiah in the extent of his reforms. Nonetheless, God still intended to punish Judah for its sins.

Three of Josiah's sons would become kings and, tragically, all three were evil (see *People to Remember from 2 Kings: Josiah*). Though Jeremiah spoke strongly against all three of Josiah's sons, he gave Josiah high marks (Jer. 22:15-16).

23:28-30 *Killed at Megiddo.* In 612, the rising Babylonian empire had destroyed Nineveh, capital city of Israel's longtime foe, Assyria. In 609, Pharaoh Neco marched through Palestine to Carchemish on the Euphrates River to aid what was left of the Assyrians in their last-ditch effort to stop Babylon (see 2 Chron. 35:20). Josiah tried to stop Neco, since if the Egyptians were successful in forming this alliance, Judah would have been at the mercy of Egypt. Josiah was killed in the battle, and Judah began paying tribute to Egypt (23:33, 35).

Neco's expedition would itself end in disaster. The Battle of Carchemish dragged on till 605, ending with Babylon defeating both Assyria and Egypt. Babylon would then turn its attention to other conquests, including Judah (see exposition on 24:1-7).

Megiddo (23:29) is a city on the plain of Megiddo, also called the valley of Jezreel and, in the NT, Armageddon, the future site of history's last great battle (see Rev. 14:14-20; 16:13-16; 19:17-19). This large, flat area is an arrowhead-shaped plain in the northern part of Palestine, surrounded by mountains (the majority of Israel is mountains or highlands). Megiddo's flatness was a blessing to merchants and travelers, and thus trade routes went through Jezreel. The flatness and the travel routes also made it a natural meeting place for armies.

23:31-34 *Jehoahaz (609): King for 90 days.* Josiah's son Jehoahaz succeeded him, but he was not a good king like his father. He reigned only three months before being imprisoned by Pharaoh. Pharaoh gave the kingship to Eliakim, another son of Josiah, and changed his name to Jehoiakim.

23:35-37 *Jehoiakim (609–597): Vassal to Pharaoh.* At the beginning of his reign, Jehoiakim was subservient to Egypt, placing the land under heavy taxation to raise tribute for Pharaoh. The 20 years of independence under Josiah had come to an end. Idolatry came back under Jehoiakim, and Jehoiakim as well as his son Jehoiachin (24:8-20) were condemned by God through the prophet Jeremiah. Jehoiakim would become notorious for burning Jeremiah's scroll (see Jer. 36:23, 32).

24:1-7 *But then he rebels.* Under Jehoiakim, Judah eventually became subservient to two powers, Egypt and Babylon. The Egyptians, who had killed Josiah on their way to meet the Babylonians in battle, were themselves defeated once they arrived at the Euphrates River (see exposition on 23:28-30). This left the way open for Babylon to come down into Palestine in 605 B.C. They took some key leaders (including Daniel) back with them to Babylon (see Dan. 1:1-6) and made sure that Jehoiakim would remain subservient to them (see exposition on 2 Chron. 36:5-8).

Probably encouraged by yet another battle between Egypt and Babylon in 601 B.C., in which both sides sustained heavy losses, Jehoiakim rebelled against Babylon (24:1); but by the time Jehoiakim died, Babylon was firmly in control of everything east of Judah (24:7).

24:8-16 *Jehoiachin (597): 90 days till the downfall.* Jehoiakim's son Jehoiachin succeeded him as king. After he had reigned just 90 days, Babylon invaded for the second time (in 597) and took the king and his family and all the most educated people (including Ezekiel) into captivity (see Ezek. 1:2; 40:1). Jeremiah had predicted this calamity (Jer. 22:24-30).

By this time Babylon, under Nebuchadnezzar, had asserted itself as the superpower of the ancient Near East. Egypt had no hope of regaining its former power (24:7).

The Babylonians are referred to as the "Chaldeans," recalling Abraham's heritage in "Ur of the Chaldeans" (Gen. 11:28). Chaldea was the southern part of Babylonia, but its name was sometimes used for the entire area.

24:17-20 *Zedekiah (597–586): Judah's last king.* Nebuchadnezzar appointed Mattaniah, another son of Josiah, as king and changed his name to Zedekiah. He would be Judah's final king. After reigning several years as Nebuchadnezzar's puppet, Zedekiah rebelled.

25:1-7 *The blind captive is the king.* Babylon responded by laying siege to Jerusalem in 588. After enduring the siege for two years, then being abandoned by his own army, Zedekiah fled the starving city in 586, was overtaken and captured at Jericho, was presented before King Nebuchadnezzar at Riblah, and was then blinded and taken captive to Babylon.

Jeremiah the prophet played a key role in the last days of Zedekiah and his kingdom (see Jer. 21; 24; 32; 34; 37–39; 52).

Together, Jeremiah and Ezekiel made an amazing prediction about Zedekiah's fate: Jeremiah predicted that he would see the king of Babylon (Jer. 34:2-5). But Ezekiel predicted that he would not see the city of Babylon itself (Ezek. 12:13). The events of 25:6-7 fulfilled both prophecies.

25:8-21 *The Temple torched, its treasure taken.* The Babylonians raided Jerusalem a third time, destroying the Temple and the nicer homes and the city walls, and taking most of the remaining people as captives to Babylon. Some of the poor were allowed to stay and were given land (25:12; see Jer. 39:10; compare exposition on 17:5-23). They also took many of the sacred Temple vessels. These vessels would reappear in Daniel 5:2-4, where Belshazzar used them to mock Israel's God.

The Temple had been the centerpiece of Jerusalem, God's own house and the focus of Israelite worship. The Temple the Babylonians destroyed was the one Solomon had built. A second Temple would be built some 70 years later, with the encouragement of the prophets Haggai and Zechariah, by those returning to Jerusalem after exile. This second Temple, added to and refurbished in major ways, stood in Jesus' day but was destroyed by the Romans in A.D. 70. The third Temple, to be built during the Millennium, is discussed in detail by Ezekiel.

25:22-26 *Gedaliah appointed, assassinated.* Nebuchadnezzar appointed Gedaliah as governor over the Jews remaining in Jerusalem. After reigning less than three months, he was assassinated. Then, "all the people of Judah, from the least to the greatest," fled to Egypt (see Jer. 40–43).

25:27-30 *From prison to palace, after 37 years.* Meanwhile in Babylon, the captive former king Jehoiachin, having found favor with Babylon's new king, was released from prison and given a place of honor.

PEOPLE TO REMEMBER FROM 2 KINGS

AHAZ

Key Facts: 12th king of Judah, first person to hear virgin-birth prophecy (16:1; Isa. 7:11-14)
Father: Jotham (15:38)
Son: Hezekiah (16:20)
Age at Death: 36 (16:2, 20)
Total Bible References: 41
Key References: 16; Isa. 7:11-14

Ahaz Speaks

What a way to begin a reign! Admittedly, I was terrified. Two enemy nations surrounding your city—that would frighten anyone. But then Isaiah and his son met me by the aqueduct, trying to offer reassurance. Of course I refused the offer. Isaiah might have been able to sell his brand of religion to my father Jotham and grandfather Azariah, but not to *this* freethinking monarch! (15:3; 16:1-2)

Frankly, I've found it far more important to impress Tiglath-pileser than some invisible deity who calls himself the Holy One of Israel! (2 Chron. 28:16-20; Isa. 7:1-14)

I'm not an atheist, of course, just a practical man. If you must worship, do it at the altars that can help you the most. That's why I offered up burnt sacrifices to the gods of Damascus. But I didn't stop with mere animals. In the ultimate act of worship I offered up my own son as a burnt sacrifice! How many Jehovah worshipers have shown *that* kind of zeal! (16:3; 2 Chron. 28:22-23)

My grandfather reigned 52 years. Apparently, it will be my lot to do so for a brief 16 years. So be the will of the gods. I am still bothered, however, by the prophet's statement alongside that aqueduct so many years ago. I still remember it well: "Therefore the Lord himself will give you a sign: Behold, the virgin shall conceive, and bear a Son, and shall call his name Immanuel." (Isa. 7:14)

The bothersome word is the son's name, Immanuel, meaning "God with us." Will Israel's God someday indeed dwell with his people in the flesh? Is he the true God? Have I damned my soul by worshiping false gods?

Spiritual Lessons from Ahaz

- "Taste and see that the LORD is good. Oh, the joys of those who trust in him!" (Ps. 34:8). How tragic that wicked King Ahaz refused to do this, not even allowing God to show him a sign (Isa. 7:10-12).
- We can allow adversity to make us either better or bitter! Compare the better reaction (2 Cor. 12:8-10; 1 Pet. 1:7) with Ahaz's bitter response (2 Chron. 28:22-23).

Key Verses

"And when trouble came to King Ahaz, he became even more unfaithful to the LORD. He offered sacrifices to the gods of Damascus who had defeated him, for he said, 'These gods helped the kings of Aram, so they will help me, too, if I sacrifice to them.' But instead, they led to his ruin and the ruin of all Israel" (2 Chron. 28:22-23).

ATHALIAH

Key Facts: Judah's only queen, tried to kill all the royal heirs of David (11:1-3)
Father: Ahab (8:16-18, 24-26; 11:1)
Husband: Jehoram (8:16-18, 24-26; 11:1)
Son: Ahaziah (11:1)
Death: Recorded in 11:13-16
Total Bible References: 15
Key References: 8:18, 26; 11:1-20

Athaliah Speaks

That fool Jehoshaphat allowed his son Jehoram to marry me! Now I, a Baal worshiper like my mother, Jezebel, am queen over Judah. Mother would have applauded my desecration of the Jewish Temple and my blood purge against David's royal line. Curses on you, Jehu, for killing her! (8:18; 9:30-37; 11:1; 1 Kings 16:31)

I must keep an eye, however, on my own relatives—Jehosheba and her high priest husband Jehoiada. Sources tell me they may be part of a plot against me. (11:2-4; 2 Chron. 22:11)

But wait! What's this I see? A huge crowd has assembled just outside the Temple? Who are they applauding? (11:4-12)

Treason! Treason! Heads will roll for this despicable act! Jehoiada, what's this all about? What do you mean, I shall die by the sword of David? And I demand to know why you have placed a crown on the head of this six-year-old boy! (11:4-16)

Spiritual Lessons from Athaliah

- God will never allow mere mortals to defeat his plans. Athaliah mistakenly thought she had succeeded in destroying all of David's royal heirs (Christ's ancestors), but Joash survived (11:1-3; see 1 Kings 19:18; Rom. 11:1-5).
- We reap what we sow (Gal. 6:7). Athaliah, who tried to murder all the royal heirs of David, was herself executed (11:1-16).

Key Verse

"When Athaliah, the mother of King Ahaziah of Judah, learned that her son was dead, she set out to destroy the rest of the royal family" (11:1).

ELIJAH

Key Facts: Prophet, taken up to heaven without dying (2 Kings 2:1-11)

Key Events in His Life:

- Predicts drought; fed by ravens (1 Kings 17:1-7)
- Helps widow; raises her son (1 Kings 17:8-24)
- Defeats prophets of Baal (1 Kings 18:17-40)
- Ministered to in despair (1 Kings 19:1-18)
- Names Elisha as his successor (1 Kings 19:19-21)
- Condemns Ahab and Jezebel (1 Kings 21:17-24)
- Taken up to heaven (2:1-11)
- Appears at Transfiguration (Matt. 17:1-13)

Total Bible References: 95

Key References: 1 Kings 17—2 Kings 2; Mal. 4:5-6; Matt. 16:13-14; 17:1-13; James 5:17-18

Elijah Speaks

I've often wondered just how Enoch might have felt. Now I know! Did God remove him in such spectacular fashion as I am experiencing? Amazing! Who would have anticipated in their wildest dreams leaving this earth in a chariot of fire, pulled by horses of fire! (2:11; Gen. 5:24)

In a way it's fitting, though, for fire seems to have accompanied my ministry. It was God's fire that fell from heaven to consume the sacrifice on Mount Carmel. Then, who could forget witnessing that mighty wind, fearful earthquake, and roaring fire on Mount Horeb? Of course, God spoke to me in his still, small voice. Finally, I prayed down great sheets of fire to consume my enemies who were trying to arrest me. And now this, my fiery ride to glory! (1:10-12; 1 Kings 18:38; 19:12-13)

I see Elisha standing below with open mouth, taking this all in. Good! This will qualify him for that double anointing from God he requested. (2:9-12)

How ironic to remember I once rather envied that young widow's son whom God allowed me to raise from the dead, wondering if someone might do this for me when I died. He was the first person in history to be raised, you know! But now, miracle of miracles, here I am, only the second person in history to leave this life without dying! Not bad at all for a prophet who once sat beside a dried-up brook, having to depend on ravens to feed him! (1 Kings 17:1-7, 17-24)

Spiritual Lessons from Elijah

- Elijah learned, as we must learn, that the lowly "drying-brook experience" (1 Kings 17:1-7) is often necessary to prepare us for the lofty "Mount Carmel event" (1 Kings 18:20-40).
- God's provision will never fail for those who give their all to him (1 Kings 17:8-16; Matt. 6:33).
- God expects us to build the altar, gather the wood, and prepare the sacrifice (as Elijah did literally in 1 Kings 18:30-37). Then, and only then, will he send the fire of his blessings (1 Kings 18:38).
- We are never closer to defeat than following our moments of greatest victory. On Mount Carmel, Elijah stood alone against 450 priests of Baal (1 Kings 18:22). Immediately following this, however, he experienced deep despair (1 Kings 19:1-10).
- God expects us to take care of our physical needs. An empty stomach can sometimes discourage one's soul (1 Kings 19:4-7).
- God speaks more often in persistent whispers than in loud shouts (1 Kings 19:11-12).

Key Verses

"At the customary time for offering the evening sacrifice, Elijah the prophet walked up to the altar and prayed, 'O LORD, God of Abraham, Isaac, and Jacob, prove today that you are God in Israel and that I am your servant. Prove that I have done all this at your command. . . .' Immediately the fire of the LORD flashed down from heaven and burned up the young bull, the wood, the stones, and the dust. It even licked up all the water in the ditch!" (1 Kings 18:36, 38).

ELISHA

Key Facts: Prophet, Elijah's successor, performed several miracles (3–8; 1 Kings 19:16)
Father: Shaphat (1 Kings 19:16)
Total Bible References: 58
Key References: 3–8; 1 Kings 19:16-21

Elisha Speaks

I can only hope they're prepared by now to minister without me. I've done my best to provide proper instructions for these young prophets. I've also purified their water and food, fed their hungry, recovered their lost tools, and provided oil for their widows! (2:3-5, 19-22; 4:1-7, 38-44; 6:1-7)

Well, at least they won't be running around looking for this old bald head as they once did when they were trying to find Elijah. (2:15-16, 23-24)

I only hope I have been half the teacher to them that Elijah was to me. What a remarkable man! There I was, plowing with oxen, when he suddenly threw his coat on my shoulders and announced that I would be his successor! Frankly, I think he had his doubts about me, considering how I hesitated. But what could he do? God himself had commanded it! (1 Kings 19:16-21)

Funny, Elijah's final miracle was identical to my first miracle—the parting of the Jordan. We also both raised young men from the dead. (2:7-8; 13-14; 4:8-37; 1 Kings 17:17-24)

But in other ways our ministries differed. He could pray down fire from heaven, while God would allow me to feed a starving city and heal a leper. (5:10-14; 7:1, 18; 1 Kings 18:38)

Death approaches, but I feel no fear. God once sent his angels to protect me. I know he will now commission them to comfort and reassure! (6:8-18)

Spiritual Lessons from Elisha

- Seeking and following God's purpose for our lives should take precedence over family and friendship ties (compare 1 Kings 19:19-21 with Matt. 6:33; 8:21-22).
- We should live our lives in such a way that others will know we believe in God and stand for the truth. Elisha knew that if Naaman were to come to him for healing, he would become convinced "that there is a true prophet here in Israel" (5:8, 15).
- People of faith need have no fear, even when surrounded by their physical, spiritual, or financial enemies, knowing that "there are more on our side than on theirs!" (6:16; see Pss. 27:3; 34:7; Heb. 1:14).
- The influence of a godly person continues after his or her death, imparting life to others (13:20-21).

Key Verse

"When they came to the other side, Elijah said to Elisha, 'What can I do for you before I am taken away?' And Elisha replied, 'Please let me become your rightful successor'" (2:9).

HEZEKIAH

Key Facts: 13th king of Judah, saw Jerusalem saved by the death angel (2 Kings 18–19)
Father: Ahaz (16:20)
Mother: Abijah (18:2)
Wife: Hephzibah (21:1)
Son: Manasseh (20:21)
Age at Death: 54 (20:21; 18:1-2)
Total Bible References: 124
Key References: 18–20; Isa. 36–39

Hezekiah Speaks

I'll be 54 on my next birthday. Of course, had God not stepped in, I would have died at 39—but he promised me an additional 15 years! Amazing! I'm sure no other person who ever lived could retire at night with the absolute certainty he would see the sun rise on the following day. But this has been my experience. (18:1-2; 20:6)

Pride no doubt played a part in my original problem. I'll never forget the bitterness and despair that settled down on me upon hearing Isaiah's announcement concerning my death. But, oh, the joy I felt when God himself spared my life! Each time I see a sundial my heart stops to praise him! (20:11; 2 Chron. 32:24-26; Isa. 38:9-14)

How many times have I repeated those words: "You have rescued me from death and have forgiven all my sins." I do hope the psalms I wrote during that time will continue to be used in the Temple along with those of David, even after my death. (Isa. 38:17, 20)

What a glorious God we have, who saves his king from death and his Holy City from destruction! Yes, I learned about his mercy while Sennacherib learned about his terrible judgment! (19:32-37)

Spiritual Lessons from Hezekiah

- There is much in life that is good, but we are never to worship it. Rather, we are to worship the God who made it. Because the Israelites were worshiping the bronze serpent, Hezekiah was right to destroy it (18:4; see Num. 21:9).
- For 15 years Hezekiah had the assurance that when he retired at night, he would see the morning light (20:6). None of us has this promise, so we should heed the advice of James 4:13-15.
- Hezekiah foolishly and unsuccessfully tried to bribe his enemy Sennacherib (18:14-25). To the contrary, we are to resist the forces of darkness (Eph. 6:13-14; 1 Pet. 5:8-9).

Key Verses

"Hezekiah trusted in the LORD, the God of Israel. There was never another king like him in the land of Judah, either before or after his time. He remained faithful to the LORD in everything, and he carefully obeyed all the commands the LORD had given Moses" (18:5-6).

JEHOIAKIM

Key Facts: 18th king of Judah, burned Jeremiah's scroll (23:34-36; Jer. 36:23, 32)
Father: Josiah (23:34)
Mother: Zebidah (23:36)
Brothers: Johanan, Zedekiah, and Jehoahaz (Shallum) (1 Chron. 3:15)
Son: Jehoiachin (24:6)
Age at Death: 36 (23:36; Jer. 22:18-19)
Total Bible References: 41
Key References: 23:34–24:6; 2 Chron. 36:5-8; Jer. 22:13-23; 36

Jehoiakim Speaks

Look at those flames! I wonder how long it took that religious fool to write his manuscript? Well, it lasted only a few minutes in the fire! How dare he rebuke me for my lifestyle! If I decide to build a comfortable palace, that's my business. I mean, what does he expect me to do, live in a tent? (Jer. 22:13-17; 36:4, 20-23)

I should have long since killed that rabble-rouser, as I did Urijah and others who refused to bow in obedience to their king. It's bad enough being pressured by the Egyptians and Babylonians, let alone having to put up with Jeremiah's religious rantings. (23:34–24:6; Jer. 26:20-24)

Well, this will all stop when I catch him. A royal messenger hands me a report. Good! Maybe they've located him. What's that? You say he's rewritten and expanded his miserable book, predicting I will receive the burial of a donkey—and that my unlamented body will be thrown outside the gates of Jerusalem? (Jer. 22:18-19; 36:26-32)

Spiritual Lessons from Jehoiakim

- God's Word "stands firm in heaven" forever (Ps. 119:89). It was foolish for Jehoiakim to try to destroy it (Jer. 36:20-23), and it would be foolish for us as well (Isa. 40:7-8; Matt. 24:35; Luke 16:17).
- Jehoiakim lived like a wild dog, so it is only fitting that he would die like a donkey (Jer. 22:18-19).

Key Verses

"Therefore, this is the LORD's decree of punishment against King Jehoiakim, who succeeded his father, Josiah, on the throne: 'His family will not weep for him when he dies. His subjects will not even care that he is dead. He will be buried like a dead donkey—dragged out of Jerusalem and dumped outside the gate!'" (Jer. 22:18-19)

JEHOSHAPHAT

Key Facts: One of Judah's best kings, instituted nationwide program to teach the law (2 Chron. 17:1-9)
Father: Asa (1 Kings 15:24)
Mother: Azubah (1 Kings 22:42)
Sons: Jehoram, Azariah, Jehiel, Zechariah, Azariahu, Michael, and Shephatiah (2 Chron. 21:1-2)
Age at Death: 60 (1 Kings 22:42, 50)
Total Bible References: 77
Key References: 3; 1 Kings 22:41-50; 2 Chron. 17–21

Jehoshaphat Speaks

"Jehoshaphat: Judah's fourth king. Reigned 25 years. Often compromised his convictions."

I wonder. Will the royal chroniclers write such things about me? To my great shame and regret, I did compromise my beliefs several times. One time it nearly cost me my army, another time it nearly cost me my navy, and a third time I nearly lost my life. Undoubtedly my most inexcusable compromise was arranging for the marriage of my son Jehoram to Athaliah, the wicked daughter of Ahab and Jezebel. (8:16-18; 1 Kings 22:1-40; 2 Chron. 20:35-37)

But thank God there is another, brighter side to those 25 years. By his grace I was able to help bring about some degree of religious revival in Israel. I even helped start a nationwide program to teach the law to our people. (1 Kings 22:43-46; 2 Chron. 17:7-9)

Then there was that incredible battle where the heroes were singers instead of soldiers! How terrified we all were at the beginning, realizing Jerusalem was surrounded by a vast enemy alliance. But then, in response to my prayer, God answered through the mouth of Jahaziel the Levite: "Do not be afraid nor dismayed because of this great multitude, for the battle is not yours, but God's. . . . You will not need to fight in this battle. Position yourselves, stand still and see the salvation of the Lord." So there I was, on the battlefield bright and early the next morning, appointing the singers and the song: "Praise the Lord; for his mercy endures forever." What a victory was ours, and what a praise service we had in the valley of Beracah! (2 Chron. 20:1-26)

Beracah. It means blessing. Dear Lord, this one word aptly summarizes your gracious relationship with your servant. In spite of his failure and foolishness, you have bestowed upon him . . . Beracah!

Spiritual Lessons from Jehoshaphat

- There is room for great creativity in Christian ministry. When Jehoshaphat realized that some Israelites could not easily come to the Temple to hear the law read, he organized a program to take the law to them. They couldn't come to the mountain, so the mountain came to them (2 Chron. 17:7-9)!
- Even when we are totally surrounded by our spiritual enemies, we can "stand still and watch the LORD's victory" (2 Chron. 20:15-17). God is just as powerful today as he was in Jehoshaphat's day (Heb. 13:8).
- If we are not careful, the good things we achieve for the Lord can be overshadowed by the spiritual compromises we make. Jehoshaphat made foolish alliances with three wicked kings: Ahab (1 Kings 22:1-40); Ahaziah (1 Kings 22:44); and Joram (3).

Key Verses

"Jehoshaphat was a good king, following the ways of his father, Asa. He did what was pleasing in the LORD's sight. During his reign, however, he failed to remove all the pagan shrines, and the people never fully committed themselves to following the God of their ancestors" (2 Chron 20:32-33).

JEHU

Key Facts: 10th king of northern kingdom, had Jezebel and priests of Baal killed (9–10)
Father: Jehoshaphat (9:2)
Son: Jehoahaz (10:35)
Death: Recorded in 10:35
Total Bible References: 48
Key References: 9–10; 1 Kings 19:16; Hos. 1:4

Jehu Speaks

I've killed so many people in my time that death seems as common as birth or marriage. Two kings finished off in a single day—and this by a former chariot driver! Wherever you are, Elisha, your prophecy has been fulfilled! (9:1-10, 20-29)

Of course, I added a few notches on my sword just for fun. I can still hear the screaming of those miserable Baalite priests! I guess the death of that old hag Jezebel was the highlight, though. (9:30-37; 10:18-28)

Yet it's kind of strange: As accustomed as I've become to death, I'll have to admit it is a little frightening as I approach the end of my own life. One thing is certain, however: I won't need to journey to Jerusalem to worship Elisha's God; our golden calves at Bethel and Dan will give me whatever help and comfort I need. (10:29-31)

Spiritual Lessons from Jehu

- It is possible to appear outwardly to be a follower of God without truly being one. Externally, Jehu faithfully performed the revealed *will* of God

(10:30); internally, however, he was hostile toward the *person* of God (10:31; Matt. 15:7-8).

Key Verses

"The LORD said to Jehu, 'You have done well in following my instructions to destroy the family of Ahab. Because of this I will cause your descendants to be the kings of Israel down to the fourth generation.' But Jehu did not obey the law of the LORD, the God of Israel, with all his heart. He refused to turn from the sins of idolatry that Jeroboam had led Israel to commit" (10:30-31).

JEZEBEL

Key Facts: Wife of King Ahab, promoted Baal worship, tried to have Elijah killed (1 Kings 16:31; 19:1-2)
Father: Ethbaal (1 Kings 16:31)
Son: Joram (9:22)
Daughter: Athaliah (assumed to be Jezebel's daughter since we know Ahab was her father)
Death: Recorded in 9:30-37
Total Bible References: 20
Key References: 9:7-10, 21-23, 30-37; 1 Kings 16:31; 18:1-19; 19:1-3; 21:5-25

Jezebel Speaks

Just look at him down there, filled with arrogance, seated in his fancy chariot! It goes to show how far Israel has sunk, allowing this backwater wild man to be its king. I can tell my sarcasm in calling him Zimri has infuriated Jehu. Good! May Baal punish him with Zimri's fate! (9:20, 30-31; 1 Kings 16:18)

I know death is near. If only I could have succeeded in killing Elijah! Well, at least one of his miserable prophecies will fail. I won't be eaten by wild dogs! Jehu will no doubt slay me by his sword. Listen! What is he ordering his officials to do? Throw me out of this window to my death? But wait—what's that terrifying sound! The fierce growls of hungry mongrels down below! (9:32-37; 1 Kings 19:1-2; 21:23)

Spiritual Lessons from Jezebel

- There is nothing better than a godly spouse (Prov. 31:10-12), who can bring fame (Prov. 31:23) and delight (Prov. 31:28). And there is nothing worse than a godless spouse (1 Kings 16:31), who brings shame (1 Kings 21:25) and death (1 Kings 22:37-38).

Key Verse

"No one else so completely sold himself to what was evil in the LORD's sight as did Ahab, for his wife, Jezebel, influenced him" (1 Kings 21:25).

JOSIAH

Key Fact: Best (and last good) king of Judah (23:25)
Father: Amon (21:24)
Mother: Jedidah (22:1)
Wives: Hamutal (23:31; 24:18), Zebidah (23:36)
Sons: Johanan, Jehoiakim, Zedekiah, Jehoahaz (Shallum) (1 Chron. 3:15)

Age at Death: 39 (22:1; 23:28-30)
Total Bible References: 20
Key References: 21:24–23:30; 1 Kings 13:1-3; 2 Chron. 34–35; Jer. 22:15-16

Josiah Speaks
What a terrible price to pay for one single act of disobedience! God said don't go to Megiddo, but I went! I don't know why I did it. Perhaps it was foolish pride. At any rate, here I am, dying from a battle wound when I should be reigning over Judah's people in Jerusalem! (2 Chron. 35:20-24)

My sole comfort in these pain-filled final hours is this: Since I was young my heart has been wholly given over to the worship and service of Jehovah! Thoughts of those happier days now fill my mind. I remember that wonderful revival he allowed me to preside over. Then there was that glorious Passover, the greatest since the days of Samuel the prophet. (23:1-22; 2 Chron. 34:3; 35:1-19)

And who could ever forget the thrill and wonder of holding that precious copy of God's Word, accidentally discovered in the Temple (of all places!), and then later actually reading from it to my people! Merciful God, receive me now into your presence with that blessed peace you promised me through your servant Huldah. (22:8-10, 22; 23:1-3)

Spiritual Lessons from Josiah

- Josiah's birth, name, and ministry were predicted nearly three centuries in advance (compare 23:15-16 with 1 Kings 13:1-3). Actually, however, this is true for all believers as well (see Eph. 2:10)!
- Josiah rightly understood that any spiritual revival must be preceded by the reading and heeding of God's Word (23:1-22).
- Be sure the cause you are willing to die for is worth it! Josiah sacrificed his life in a battle he need not and should not have fought (2 Chron. 35:20-24).
- Godly parents do not always have godly children. All three of Josiah's sons who became king (see 1 Chron. 3:15) were evil: Jehoahaz (Shallum), 23:31-32; Jehoiakim, 23:36-37; and Zedekiah, 24:18-19.

Key Verses
"'But a beautiful palace does not make a great king! Why did your father, Josiah, reign so long? Because he was just and right in all his dealings. That is why God blessed him. He made sure that justice and help were given to the poor and needy, and everything went well for him. Isn't that what it means to know me?' asks the LORD" (Jer. 22:15-16).

MANASSEH
Key Facts: Most wicked king of Judah, later repented (21:1-17; 2 Chron. 33:10-17)
Father: Hezekiah (20:21)
Mother: Hephzibah (21:1)
Wife: Meshullemeth (21:19)
Son: Amon (21:18)
Age at Death: 67 (21:1, 18)
Total Bible References: 26
Key References: 21:1-18; 2 Chron. 33:10-20

Manasseh Speaks

"The meanest man that ever lived!" That's how my generation once looked upon me. In fact, *several* generations suffered during my 50-year-plus reign of terror! (21:1-18)

But of course that was before my imprisonment! Looking back today, I shudder to recall my wicked deeds. How incredibly sad to think the son of such a godly father would have actually sacrificed his own sons to a godless idol. The awful cries of those innocent people I slaughtered will never be silenced in my memory. Isaiah surely died thinking there was absolutely no hope for this bloody and blasphemous king. (20:21; 21:6, 16; 2 Chron. 33:2-11)

But my prayer in prison changed everything. Blessed God, allow your servant in his final years to serve the Holy One of Israel with the zeal he once had for Lucifer, son of the morning! (2 Chron. 33:12-16)

Manasseh: That's my name. "From the meanest man alive to a sinner saved by grace": That's my testimony!

Spiritual Lessons from Manasseh

- Manasseh, Judah's worst king (2 Chron. 33:1-9), was the son of Hezekiah, one of Judah's best kings (18:3-5). Parents must carefully cultivate their children as precious flowers and not carelessly allow them to grow up as poisonous weeds (see Prov. 22:6; Eph. 6:4; 2 Tim. 1:5).
- "As people sinned more and more, God's wonderful kindness became more abundant" (Rom. 5:20). Paul may well have had Manasseh in mind when he penned those words. While briefly imprisoned, this cruel and godless king repented and was gloriously saved (2 Chron. 33:11-13).

Key Verses

"But while in deep distress, Manasseh sought the LORD his God and cried out humbly to the God of his ancestors. And when he prayed, the LORD listened to him and was moved by his request for help. So the LORD let Manasseh return to Jerusalem and to his kingdom. Manasseh had finally realized that the LORD alone is God!" (2 Chron. 33:12-13).

NAAMAN

Key Fact: Cured of leprosy through Elisha's ministry (5)
Occupation: Military commander (5:1)
Total Bible References: 11
Key References: 5; Luke 4:27

Naaman Speaks

Thank God for the testimony of that faithful little Israelite servant girl. Had it not been for her I would still be just another unfortunate pagan, dying of leprosy. But here I stand with cleansed flesh and cleansed heart, before God's prophet in the land of Israel. (5:1, 3, 14, 15, 17)

"Go and wash yourself seven times in the Jordan River." That's what he told me to do. How furious I was at that moment, and also how wrong! Some of the credit for my healing must be given to those faithful servants who persuaded me to follow Elisha's simple but strange command. (5:10-13)

I now depart for my home in Aram, not as Naaman the dying warrior but as Naaman the living witness! (5:15)

Spiritual Lessons from Naaman

- Moral goodness alone will not bring salvation. Naaman was a good and brave soldier, used by God to give victory to the Aramean people, but he was also a leper and an unredeemed sinner (5:1; see John 3:1-10).
- Those who seek good advice must be humble (James 1:2; 3:13). Naaman wisely took the good advice of those around him, including a little servant girl (5:2-4) and some of his military associates (5:13).
- Salvation depends not on one's religious heritage but on a personal response of faith (Luke 4:27).
- God doesn't want a mighty demonstration of our intellect or power but rather the simple obedience that comes from faith (5:10-14).

Key Verses

"Elisha sent a messenger out to him with this message: 'Go and wash yourself seven times in the Jordan River. Then your skin will be restored, and you will be healed of leprosy.' But Naaman became angry and stalked away. 'I thought he would surely come out to meet me!' he said. 'I expected him to wave his hand over the leprosy and call on the name of the LORD his God and heal me! . . . But his officers tried to reason with him and said, 'Sir, if the prophet had told you to do some great thing, wouldn't you have done it? So you should certainly obey him when he says simply to go and wash and be cured!' So Naaman went down to the Jordan River and dipped himself seven times, as the man of God had instructed him. And his flesh became as healthy as a young child's, and he was healed!" (5:10-14).

UZZIAH (AZARIAH)

Key Facts: 10th king of Judah, violated the priesthood, stricken with leprosy (15:1-7; 2 Chron. 26)
Father: Amaziah (14:21)
Mother: Jecoliah (15:2)
Wife: Jerusha (15:33)
Son: Jotham (15:32)
Age at Death: 68 (15:2, 7)
Total Bible References: 34
Key References: 15:1-7; 2 Chron. 26

Uzziah Speaks

I hope Isaiah will preach at my funeral. I suppose he could refer to me as Judah's former king as well as a famous builder, military commander, rancher, and farmer. How difficult it has been, after having been surrounded by hundreds of court officials for more than 50 years, to now dwell totally alone, as an outcast. (15:1-7; 2 Chron. 26:9-15; Isa. 6:1)

But I have only myself to blame. I should have learned from the life of Saul. We both knew God had forbidden Israel's kings from assuming the duties of a priest. But we both disobeyed, causing the Lord to remove him from the kingship and to punish me with leprosy. (1 Sam. 13:8-14; 2 Chron. 26:16-19)

I respect the high priest Azariah for rebuking me in the Temple. I have often wondered if that terrible earthquake had anything to do with my transgression. At any rate, here I am at 68, ready to die. Zechariah has been a great comfort to me. The Lord continues to give this godly man special revelations. (2 Chron. 26:5, 17-18; Amos 1:1)

Spiritual Lessons from Uzziah

- Paul told Timothy, "Complete the ministry God has given you" (2 Tim. 4:5). Perhaps no OT person did this more fully than Uzziah. In addition to ruling his people, this king became a great builder, military leader, rancher, and farmer (2 Chron. 26:9-14). Only eternity will reveal how far we have fallen short in using our God-given gifts! (See also 1 Tim. 4:14; 2 Tim. 1:6.)
- Tragically, however, Uzziah tried to exercise a ministry forbidden to him—the priesthood. Our gifts are to be used only in obedience to God, not to feed our sinful pride (2 Chron. 26:16).
- The pride that caused Uzziah to fall also caused Satan to fall (see Isa. 14:12-15; Ezek. 28:11-17) and can cause any of us to fall as well (1 Cor. 10:12).

Key Verses

"And [Uzziah] produced machines mounted on the walls of Jerusalem, designed by brilliant men to shoot arrows and hurl stones from the towers and the corners of the wall. His fame spread far and wide, for the LORD helped him wonderfully until he became very powerful. But when he had become powerful, he also became proud, which led to his downfall. He sinned against the LORD his God by entering the sanctuary of the LORD's Temple and personally burning incense on the altar" (2 Chron. 26:15-16).

ZEDEKIAH

Key Fact: Last king of Judah (24:18; 25:1-7)
Father: Josiah (1 Chron. 3:15)
Mother: Hamutal (24:18)
Brothers: Johanan, Jehoiakim, and Jehoahaz (Shallum) (1 Chron. 3:15)
Death: Recorded in Jer. 52:11
Total Bible References: 55
Key References: 24:17–25:7; Jer. 21; 24; 32; 34; 37–39; 52

Zedekiah Speaks

Finally! We're stopping for a rest. I can hear the sound of water. It must be the rivers of Babylon. What's that the enemy soldiers are demanding? "Sing us one of those songs of Jerusalem!" Our musicians, I'm told, have refused to comply and are hanging their harps upon the willow trees near the river. That's good! I agree with the logic of their refusal. How can we sing the Lord's song in a foreign land? (Ps. 137)

What bitterness fills my soul! Here I am, at 31, a dethroned and blinded king, being led to Babylon where I shall no doubt live as a common slave. It would have been far better had Nebuchadnezzar killed me in Jerusalem as he did my sons. (24:18; 25:7)

What would David and Solomon have thought had they known their beloved city and Temple would be looted, burned, and totally destroyed? Well, at least they might have derived some comfort from Jehovah, but I have rejected him and he has probably rejected me. My future is as black and painful as these sightless eyes. (24:19; 25:8-17)

Spiritual Lessons from Zedekiah

- "With many counselors, there is safety" (Prov. 11:14). Both Jeremiah (Jer. 27:12-15; 38:17-18) and Ezekiel (Ezek. 12:12-13) tried to advise Zedekiah, but the wicked king would have none of their counsel, and therefore he found no safety.
- "A doubtful mind is as unsettled as a wave of the sea that is driven and tossed by the wind. People like that . . . can't make up their minds. They waver back and forth in everything they do" (James 1:6-8). Zedekiah was a classic example of such wavering back and forth. He tried to pressure Jeremiah into softening his message (Jer. 21:1-2), then imprisoned him (Jer. 32:2-3), then released him (Jer. 37:16-17), then imprisoned him again (Jer. 38:1-6).

Key Verses

"Go to King Zedekiah of Judah, and tell him, 'This is what the LORD, the God of Israel, says: I am about to hand this city over to the king of Babylon, and he will burn it. You will not escape his grasp but will be taken into captivity. You will stand before the king of Babylon to be judged and sentenced. Then you will be exiled to Babylon.'

"But listen to this promise from the LORD, O Zedekiah, king of Judah. This is what the LORD says: 'You will not be killed in war but will die peacefully among your people. They will burn incense in your memory, just as they did for your ancestors. They will weep for you and say, "Alas, our king is dead!" This I have decreed, says the LORD'" (Jer. 34:2-5).

A COMPARISON OF CHRONICLES AND SAMUEL—KINGS

Except for the genealogies of 1 Chronicles 1–9, the books of 1, 2 Chronicles record many of the same events recorded in the books of 2 Samuel and 1, 2 Kings:

THE TRIUMPHANT YEARS
(The Psalmist/Warrior of Israel)

The ruler:	*The record:*	
(Saul's death)	1 Sam. 31	1 Chron. 10

The ruler:	*The record:*	
David	2 Sam.	1 Chron. 11–29

The ruler:	*The record:*	
(Solomon becomes king)	1 Kings 1:1–2:12	1 Chron. 28–29

THE TRANQUIL YEARS
(The Spiritual Welfare of Israel)

The ruler:	*The record:*	
Solomon	1 Kings 2:10–11:43	2 Chron. 1–9

THE TURBULENT YEARS
(The Civil Warfare of Israel)

The Splintered Kingdom

The rulers:	*The record:*	
19 (north), 12 (south)	1 Kings 12—2 Kings 17	2 Chron. 10–28

The Surviving Kingdom (Judah)

The rulers:	*The record:*	
8 (south)	2 Kings 18–25	2 Chron. 29–36

1 CHRONICLES

BACKGROUND
See *A Comparison of Chronicles and Samuel—Kings,* p. 237.

AUTHOR
Unknown, though tradition ascribes authorship to Ezra. The book is written from a priestly point of view; Ezra was a priest as well as an important leader, and it was completed during Ezra's time. Most conservative scholars believe an unknown chronicler may have been the final editor of 1, 2 Chronicles as well as the books of Ezra and Nehemiah.

1, 2 Chronicles were originally one document. The author or authors made use of court records such as *The Book of the Kings of Israel* (9:1; see 2 Chron. 20:34), "King David's official records" (27:24), and *The Book of the Kings of Judah and Israel* (or "Israel and Judah"; cited several times in 2 Chronicles).

DATE AND LOCATION
Aside from the opening genealogy (1–9), the events of 1, 2 Chronicles—from the death of Saul to the decree of Cyrus—took place 1010–538 B.C. However, the genealogy of Zerubbabel (3:17-21) takes us beyond 538. The completed books were probably compiled in the postexilic period, about 450–430, probably in Jerusalem, where the court records were kept.

RECIPIENTS
1, 2 Chronicles was written for the second and third groups of Jews returning from exile in 457 and 445 B.C., during the time of Ezra, Nehemiah, and Malachi. These Jews needed to be encouraged in the task of rebuilding their nation. Since they were primarily from the tribe of Judah, 1 Chronicles focuses on David and 2 Chronicles focuses on his descendants, the kings of Judah.

1406 B.C.* *Israel enters Canaan

1377* *Apostasy, 1st judge

1051* *Saul king, Israel united

931* *Death of Solomon, Israel divides

722* *Fall of Israel

586* *Fall of Judah

PURPOSE

- To provide a *religious* history of Israel from the time of Saul to the return from Babylon. (1, 2 Sam. and 1, 2 Kings record the *political* history of that same period.)
- To demonstrate to the postexilic Jews, who were unstable in their faith, that God was still active and would keep his promises.
- To show to a people who had lost their Davidic kings and were now ruled by Persia that God would always be faithful to the Davidic throne (17:13-14, 24, 27) and that in the meantime the heart of the Persian king was in God's hands (2 Chron. 36:22-23).
- To show, furthermore, that while Israel waited for the Davidic kingship to be renewed, they had the legacy of David—the Temple—as the sign of God's continued blessing.

UNIQUE FEATURES

The following material is found only in 1 Chronicles and not in the parallel account of 2 Samuel:

- the genealogy of the tribes (1–9)
- extensive preparations for the return of the Ark (15–16)
- extensive preparations for the building of the Temple (22–29)
- a psalm of David (16)
- the fact that Satan encouraged David's census of Israel (21:1)

COMPARISON WITH OTHER BIBLE BOOKS

2 Samuel:

- 1 Chronicles provides details about David and his associates not given in 2 Samuel.

OUTLINE

GENEALOGY: CREATION TO END OF EXILE (1–9)
- Patriarchs (1)
- Tribes of Israel (2–7)
- Tribe of Benjamin (Saul's tribe) (8)
- Returning exiles (9:1-34)
- Saul's genealogy repeated (9:35-44)

HISTORY OF DAVID (10–29)
- Condemnation; death of Saul (10)
- David and his mighty men (11–12)
- Ark brought to Jerusalem (13–16)
- God's covenant with David (17)
- David's conquests (18–20)
- David's census (21)
- Preparations for the Temple (22)
- Organization and duties of priests and Levites (23–26)
- Organization of army and government (27)
- More preparations for the Temple (28:1–29:20)
- Solomon becomes king (29:21-25)
- Death of David (29:26-30)

GENEALOGY: CREATION TO END OF EXILE (1–9)

1:1-27 *Genealogy from Adam to Abraham.* The first nine chapters of 1 Chronicles give genealogical records, starting with Adam and ending with the Jews who returned from the Babylonian exile. In this section, which gives the genealogies from Adam to Abraham, the following specific records are given:

- From Adam to Noah's sons (1:1-4)
- Descendants of Japheth (1:5-7; see Gen. 10:2-5)
- Descendants of Ham (1:8-16; see Gen. 10:6-20)
- Descendants of Shem (1:17-27; see Gen. 10:21-31; 11:10-26)

These genealogies show that the author had access to the Genesis account and followed it closely. There are some deviations from the Genesis genealogies since the emphasis here is on David. Shem comes last since Israel came from him.

1:28-54 *Genealogy from Abraham to Jacob.* This section includes these genealogies:

- Abraham's descendants through Hagar and Keturah (1:28-33; see Gen. 25)
- Sons of Isaac (1:34)
- Sons and descendants of Esau (1:35-54; see Gen. 36)

Isaac is the last of Abraham's children mentioned, to demonstrate his significance to Israel. Isaac's sons Esau and Israel (Jacob) are identified, and Esau's descendants are listed.

2:1-2 *Sons of Jacob.* 2:1-55 gives the historical records from Jacob to David. 2:1-2 lists all 12 sons of Jacob (see Gen. 35:22-26). This both highlights the nation of Israel as a whole and introduces the line of David through Judah, one of Jacob's 12 sons.

2:3-55 *Genealogy of Judah.* The chronicler selectively chooses descendants of Perez and Zerah (2:5-8), Hezron (2:9-41), and Caleb (2:42-55) for his historical records leading up to David (2:15; see Ruth 4:18-22). The mention of Bethlehem (2:51, 54) would not go unnoticed by an Israelite interested in the history of King David. Bethlehem was the great-grandson of Caleb (whose wife's name was Ephrathah, 2:50). Apparently, the birthplace and region where David (and later Christ) was born was named after these ancestors (see Mic. 5:2).

3:1-24 *Genealogy of David.* The writer interrupts the genealogy of Judah to trace David's lineage to Zedekiah, Judah's last king (3:1-16), and then through the Babylonian exile and beyond (3:17-24). Compare Matthew 1:1-17.

4:1–8:40 *Genealogy of the sons of Jacob.* The writer now gives historical records of all 12 tribes of Israel, beginning with a resumption of Judah's genealogy:

Judah (4:1-23). Judah comes first, even though he was not Jacob's firstborn, since David came from this tribe.

Simeon (4:24-43). The genealogy of Simeon includes a note about the success of the tribe's herds on both sides of the Jordan valley (4:39-43). Simeon is mentioned right after Judah because of its assimilation into the territory of Judah during the time of Joshua (see Joshua 19:1-9).

Reuben (5:1-10). Reuben's genealogy is given within the context of the indiscretion which forced him and his line to lose the privilege of being Jacob's firstborn (Gen. 35:22). "Ruler" (5:2) refers to David.

Gad (5:11-22). Gad's genealogy highlights the tribe's settlement of the territory east of the Jordan River and north toward the Sea of Galilee.

Eastern Manasseh (5:23-26). This is the half of the tribe of Manasseh that settled east of the Jordan, north of Gad's territory (Bashan; see exposition on Num. 32:1-42). The chronicler highlights this tribe's idolatry (5:25) and their eventual capture and deportation by the Assyrians. Other than the brief note in 2 Chronicles 30:6, this is the chronicler's only reference to the fall of the northern kingdom.

Levi (6:1-30). The genealogy of the priestly tribe of Levi is based on Levi's three sons: Kohath (6:2-15), Gershon (6:17-28), and Merari (6:29-30).

The musicians' guild (6:31-48). The writer highlights the Levites whom David appointed to lead the music ministry (see 25; Neh. 12:45-47).

Aaron (6:49-53). Aaron's line is traced to Zadok, a prominent priest during the reign of David. As the writer notes, only those Levites who were descendants of Aaron could offer sacrifices to atone for Israel's sins. 6:50-53 repeats 6:4-8.

Cities of priests and Levites (6:54-81). The cities where priests and other Levites lived are listed, based on the lines of Kohath, Gershon, and Merari.

Issachar (7:1-5). 7:1-40 lists six northern tribes. 7:1-5 briefly mentions the tribe of Issachar, emphasizing its population (see Gen. 46:13; Num. 26:23-25).

Benjamin (7:6-12). The genealogy of Benjamin is listed according to three of his sons: Bela (7:7), Beker (7:8-9), and Jediael (7:10-12).

Naphtali (7:13). Just one verse is devoted to the tribe of Naphtali (see Gen. 46:24).

Western Manasseh (7:14-19). This is the half of the tribe of Manasseh that settled in Canaan, west of the Jordan (see Josh. 17).

Ephraim (7:20-29). See Numbers 26:35-37 and Joshua 16. (On the tribes of Ephraim and Manasseh, see exposition on Genesis 48:1-22.)

Asher (7:30-40). See Genesis 46:17. The tribe of Dan is not mentioned by name in the genealogies of 1–9, but it is mentioned in 12:35.

Benjamin again, featuring King Saul (8:1-40). The chronicler returns to Benjamin to give the background of its most famous son, King Saul. 8:1-33 brings the record up to Saul, and 8:33-40 lists Saul's descendants.

9:1-9 *Genealogy of the returning exiles.* 9:1-34 gives the records of those who returned to Palestine after the Babylonian captivity, completing the introductory genealogies. 9:1-9 is a general listing of returning exiles (see Neh. 11:1-9).

Along with Judah and Benjamin (the southern tribes), the writer lists people from the northern tribes of Ephraim and Manasseh as being among those who returned (see exposition on Ezra 1:5-6).

The "Temple assistants" ("Nethinims," KJV) in 9:2 were those whom David had appointed to that task (see exposition on Ezra 8:1-20).

9:10-34 *Genealogy of the returning priests and Levites.* 9:10-13 focuses on six priestly families that returned from exile, corresponding to those cited by Nehemiah (see Neh. 11:10-14). 9:14-16 lists the other Levites who returned. 9:17-27 focuses on the gatekeepers among them. Other functions of the Levites are also mentioned (see Neh. 11:15-24).

9:35-44 *Genealogy of Saul repeated.* The genealogy of Saul (see 8:29-40) is repeated, to introduce the account of Saul's death (see 10).

HISTORY OF DAVID (10–29)

10:1-7 *Saul's death: By enemy arrows and his own sword.* Saul committed suicide in 1011 B.C. by falling on his own sword, but the main cause of his death was defeat by his Philistine enemies, whose archers had wounded him (see 1 Sam. 31:1-7). His armor bearer and three sons, including David's friend Jonathan, were killed as well, fulfilling the prophecy of judgment on Saul (see 1 Sam. 28:19).

10:8-10 *His head on display in Dagon's temple.* In an act of great cruelty and pride, the Philistines mutilated Saul's body and put his head on display in the temple of Dagon their god (see 1 Sam. 31:8-10).

10:11-12 *Decent burials for all four.* The people of Jabesh-gilead, perhaps remembering Saul's rescue of their city (see 1 Sam. 11:1-11), bravely took the bodies of Saul and his sons to give them respectful burials (see 1 Sam. 31:11-13).

10:13-14 *"Here's why he died."* The chronicler attributes Saul's violent death to God himself, citing two reasons:

- his disobedience (see 1 Sam. 13:8-14; 15)
- his seeking guidance from a medium (see 1 Sam. 28:3-25)

11:1-3 *David: King over all 12!* The writer now turns to his major focus, the kingship of David. The leaders of all 12 tribes anointed David as king in 1011 B.C. in Hebron, which would be David's first capital (see 2 Sam. 5:1-5).

11:4-9 *The heathen city becomes the Holy City.* David captured Jerusalem from the Jebusites and made it his capital (2 Sam. 5:6-10). The chronicler highlights Joab's leadership in this effort, which won him the job of leading David's army.

11:10-47 *Exploits of the Three and the Thirty.* The writer recounts the feats of some of the great warriors who served David. The inner circle of leaders associated with Joab, David's commander in chief, were known as "the Three." The chronicler names Jashobeam, who killed 300 men at one time (11:11), and Eleazar, who helped David defeat the Philistines at Pas-dammim (11:12-14). The third of the three, Shammah, is mentioned in 2 Samuel 23:11-12.

Mention is also made of three warriors who had procured water for David from a well in Bethlehem when the Philistines controlled that city (11:15-19). Abishai, brother of Joab, is also noted as a particularly famous warrior (11:20-21). Then the names of many other of David's mighty men, called "the Thirty," are listed (11:22-47). These were the remaining captains in David's army (see 2 Sam. 23:8-39).

12:1-22 *They leave Saul to follow David.* Most of the warriors listed in 11 were from Judah. 12 lists warriors from a number of other tribes who had come to David's aid before he became king. The Benjamites who helped David at Ziklag (see 1 Sam. 27) are listed first (12:1-7), probably to show that even Saul's relatives were defecting to David while Saul was still alive.

Some fierce warriors from the tribe of Gad came over to David. They are described as being "as fierce as lions and as swift as deer" (12:8-15).

Other mighty warriors from the tribes of Benjamin, Judah, and Manasseh also came over to David's camp before he became king (12:16-22).

12:23-40 *They all come to Hebron to crown him king.* The story of David's anointing at Hebron (see 11:1-3) is retold, with an emphasis on the presence of armies from all 12 tribes.

13:1-7 *His first act is to bring the Ark back.* David asked that the Ark of the Covenant be brought to Jerusalem from Kiriath-jearim, where it had been kept following its return from Philistine captivity (see 1 Sam. 6:1–7:2). Unlike Saul, David had a heart for the things of God (see 2 Sam. 6:1-5).

13:8-11 *But the celebration is short-lived.* As the Ark was being brought to Jerusalem on an oxcart, it was jostled at a rough place in the road. Uzzah reached up to steady it and was struck dead by the Lord. While David's desire to bring the Ark to Jerusalem was correct, carrying it on an oxcart violated the law (see Exod. 25:13-14).

13:12-14 *It stays for a while with Obed-edom.* Becoming fearful after God's judgment on Uzzah, David placed the Ark in the home of Obed-edom for three months rather than bringing it up to Jerusalem as originally planned. God blessed Obed-edom's house because of the presence of the Ark.

14:1-2 *Selected for the sake of his people.* David realized that God had selected him to be king and that there was a divine purpose for his prominence, "for the sake of" the whole nation (see 2 Sam. 5:11-12).

14:3-7 *The king's kids.* The writer lists David's wives and the children born to him up to this time (see 2 Sam. 5:13-16). Though he was a godly man, David was also a polygamist. David's polygamy would bring discord to his own family and would be imitated with tragic consequences by his son Solomon (see 1 Kings 11:1-4).

14:8-17 *Twice they come up, twice they go down.* David's armies defeated the Philistines twice in the valley of Rephaim. This marks the beginning of David's defense of his kingdom against foreign powers (see 2 Sam. 5:17-25).

15:1-13 *"Let's make sure this mission is successful!"* Now the chronicler returns to David's attempt to bring the Ark of the Covenant back to Jerusalem. This time, David instructed his people to use the prescribed means of transportation. The Ark was to be housed in a tent, probably similar to the Tabernacle (15:1).

15:14-24 *Practicing for the big event.* David prepared the people for the celebration that would accompany the Ark's return. It would be no ordinary event, but one of worshipful celebration.

15:25-28 *They enter the city, sacrificing and singing.* As the Ark was brought into Jerusalem, there was joyous celebration, including sacrifices and singing. As the Levites carried the Ark in the correct way, "God was clearly helping" them (15:26; see 2 Sam. 6:12-15).

15:29 *But one refuses to rejoice.* Seeing David dancing as the Ark entered Jerusalem, Michal, David's wife and Saul's daughter, despised him (see 2 Sam. 6:16). It may be that she viewed this as unnecessary emotionalism. It may also have reminded her of her father's failure to give the Ark its proper place in the nation.

16:1-36 *Their assignment: Praise and pray.* As the celebration of the Ark's return continued (see 2 Sam. 6:17-19), David appointed Asaph to lead those in charge of worship. David gave Asaph and his men a song of thanksgiving to sing for the occasion. The song has parallels in the book of Psalms:

- 16:8-22 = Psalm 105:1-15
- 16:23-33 = Psalm 96
- 16:34-36 = Psalm 106:1, 47-48.

Although the passages in Psalms do not attribute the song to David, he probably composed it. Though he sang David's song on this occasion, Asaph himself is credited with composing several of the psalms in the book of Psalms.

16:37-43 *More worship assignments.* The writer gives a summary of those who served the Lord before the Ark. Asaph and his brothers are again mentioned (16:37) as well as 68 men from the family of Obed-edom, of whom two were to serve as gatekeepers. Zadok was appointed as a high priest in charge of the Tabernacle, which was located in Gibeon, six miles northwest of Jerusalem (16:39-42). Later, other priests would be designated for service in Jerusalem, where the Ark was located and where the Temple would be built (see exposition on 24:1-19).

17:1-6 *What David proposes to do for God.* David wanted to build a special place for the Ark of the Covenant, rather than housing it in a tent. Through the prophet Nathan, God told David that he would not be allowed to do this (see 2 Sam. 7:1-7).

17:7-15 *What God promises to do for David.* Although God would not allow David to build a house for him, he turned the tables and promised a "house" or dynasty for David. This Davidic covenant involved the permanent establishment of David's throne (see 2 Sam. 7:8-17).

17:16-27 *"How great thou art!"* David responded to God's covenant with him by acknowledging God's greatness and asking for his continued blessing (see 2 Sam. 7:18-29).

18:1-17 *One victory after another.* The chronicler outlines David's conquests over the Philistines to the southwest (18:1); over Moab, east of the Dead Sea (18:2); and over Syria, northeast of Israel (18:3-11). These victories helped solidify David's kingdom.

David's nephew Abishai is credited with defeating the Edomites, who lived south of the Dead Sea (18:12-13). 18:14-17 lists David's military and religious leaders and his personal aides (see 2 Sam. 8).

19:1-7 *Suspected, rejected, and ridiculed.* Up to this point David had spared Ammon, the territory due east of the Jordan River. After the death of Nahash, its king, David sent a delegation to comfort the new king, Nahash's son Hanun. Fearful of David's power and suspecting his true intentions, Hanun's men convinced him to mistreat David's delegation. Realizing that this had been a terrible mistake and that war with Israel was inevitable, Hanun hired mercenaries, including Syrians, and prepared for battle (see 2 Sam. 10:1-6).

19:8-19 *Allied to no avail.* With the help of his commanders Joab and Abishai, David defeated the Ammonite-Syrian alliance, and the Ammonites retreated to Rabbah, their capital city (see 2 Sam. 10:7-19).

20:1-3 *He captures the city and claims the crown.* Final victory over the Ammonites came the next spring, with David capturing Rabbah and wearing the Ammonite crown (see 2 Sam. 11:1; 12:26-31). The chronicler omits the story of David's sin with Bathsheba, which would have taken place between the events of 20:1 and those of 20:2-3 (see 2 Sam. 11:1–12:25).

20:4-8 *The bigger they come . . .* Conflict with the Philistines continued as David's armies fought three battles, during each of which a notable giant was killed (see 2 Sam. 21:15-22).

21:1-6 *A census inspired by Satan.* David instructed Joab and the other leaders to take a census of the nation's fighting men. Joab resisted, understanding that such an action entailed a sinful disbelief in God's ability to preserve the nation; but David would not relent, and the census was taken (see 2 Sam. 24:1-9).

The human cause of David's action was most likely pride of accomplishment. 21:1 indicates that Satan tempted David to do it, while the parallel passage (see 2 Sam. 24:1) says that God influenced the action. The apparent discrepancy is removed when one remembers that Satan is simply the unwilling servant of God and can do nothing without his permission (see Job 1:6-12).

21:7-13 *"I prefer your wrath!"* God was angered by David's census. David repented of his sin, and God gave him a choice of three punishments for the nation: three years of famine, three months of defeat by their enemies, or three days of direct punishment from God. David either chose the last of the three options or cast himself upon God's mercy (which would prove to be the third choice). David knew that God's judgment, no matter how severe, would be more merciful than human cruelty (21:13; see 2 Sam. 24:10-14).

21:14-16 *His wrath and relenting.* God's angel brought a plague on Jerusalem, and 70,000 people died before God stopped the judgment. God's "relenting" (21:15) shows that David was right in trusting his mercy, rather than falling "into human hands" (21:13). This account shows how one person's sin can impact the lives of many innocent people (see 2 Sam. 24:15-16).

21:17-30 *"Build an altar," says the angel.* David contritely asked God to judge him rather than the people, since the fault in ordering the census was his. Instead of judging him, however, God merely asked him to perform a sacrifice at a specific location, the threshing floor of Ornan. When David offered to buy Ornan's threshing floor, Ornan offered to give it to him, but David refused, saying that he couldn't offer a sacrifice to God "that [had] cost [him] nothing!" (21:24). David bought the land, offered the sacrifice, and God honored it (21:26-27; see 2 Sam. 24:17-25).

22:1-5 *David gathers the building supplies.* David began gathering materials to build "the Temple of the LORD." Although God didn't want David to actually build it (17:4), he was allowed to make the preparations.

22:6-16 *Not the soldier but the son.* David told Solomon about God's desire for a permanent place of worship and explained why God hadn't allowed him to build it: God wanted his house to be built by a man of "peace and rest" (22:9), rather than by a soldier like David who had shed much blood.

David reminded Solomon of all the preparations he had already made for the Temple (22:14-16) and expressed his hope that God would give Solomon wisdom, courage, and a pure heart as he began this important project (22:12-13).

22:17-19 *"We're at peace, so seek the Lord and build his house."* David encouraged the other leaders of Israel to help Solomon build the Temple. He assured them of God's presence and help, and pointed out that the peace God had given them made it possible for Israel to focus on seeking the Lord rather than on military preparedness.

23:1–27:34 *Organizing the kingdom.* Having effectively turned over the reins of the government to Solomon, David's last major act as king was to organize Israel's religious, military, and political life:

The Levites and their duties (23). David began by organizing the 38,000 Levites 30 years and older into three divisions, based on Levi's sons Gershon, Kohath, and Merari. 23:24-27 indicates that David lowered the age of Levite service to 20 years (see exposition on Num. 8:20-26). This lower age was evidently necessitated by the anticipated increase in the Levites' responsibilities upon the completion of the Temple (23:28-32).

Enough godly men for 24 groups (24:1-19). David next organized the priests (the Levites directly descended from Aaron). While there were apparently too few Levites overall, there were too many priests, so David organized them into 24 divisions and assigned each division to serve two weeks per year. He did this based on their lineage (24:3) through either Zadok of the house of Eleazar (son of Aaron) or Ahimelech of the house of Ithamar (son of Aaron).

It may be that the two lines were

divided between priestly duties at Gibeon, where the Tabernacle from the wilderness was located, and at Jerusalem, where the Temple would be built (see exposition on 16:37-43).

It is clear that this Davidic system of organization lasted in some form into the first century, since John the Baptist's father was "a member of the priestly order of Abijah" (compare 24:10 and Luke 1:5).

The remaining Levites (24:20-31). Levites not in the formal priestly group are listed.

The music men (25). David sought to organize the music of the Temple worship. Three groups are listed by families: the sons of Asaph (see exposition on 16:1-36), the sons of Heman, and the sons of Jeduthun. A total of 288 men were assigned musical duties. As with the priests, David established a rotation system based on selection by lot.

Guardians of the gates (26:1-19). David assigned gatekeepers for the Temple. As with the priests and the musicians, they were to be rotated by lot. All would have equal opportunity to serve.

The money men (26:20-28). Ahijah was to be the Temple's chief treasurer. The sons of Gershon were to help manage the money. Shelomoth was responsible for allocating the spoils of war.

Regional supervisors (26:29-32). Some of the Levites were appointed to manage "all matters related to the things of the LORD and the service of the king" in Israel's remote, outlying areas.

A monthly military (27:1-15). As with the priests, musicians, and other public servants, David organized his army into rotations of service. There was a commander plus 24,000 men for each month of the year.

The 12 tribal leaders (27:16-24). David placed an appropriate individual in charge of each tribe. 27:23-24 recalls the census of 21:1-7 and its disastrous results.

The king's cabinet (27:25-34). Finally, David appointed leaders for different parts of his government, such as the treasury at Jerusalem (not the Temple treasury, see 26:20) and various regional operations.

28:1-10 *A special briefing on a special building.* David's farewell address is recorded in 28:1–29:20. He began by reviewing the plans for the Temple and the history of his own desire to build it and God's redirection of those plans. He then publicly challenged Solomon to seek God with all of his heart as he began building the Temple.

28:11-19 *"Here are the blueprints from God himself!"* David publicly gave the plans for the Temple to Solomon, affirming that they came directly from God's Spirit (28:12, 19). He designated the amounts of gold to be used for various items in the Temple (28:14-18).

28:20-21 *"And here are the workers; they're at your service!"* David challenged Solomon once more to take on the building project and commended to Solomon's use the craftsmen he had assembled as well as the religious and political leaders he had organized (see 23–27).

29:1-9 *"Please assist my son."* Having challenged Solomon, David challenged the people to help him and to follow David's example in giving generously to the building of the Temple. The people responded with a generous offering.

29:10-20 *A prayer of praise by the king and his people.* David prayed a public prayer of praise and thanksgiving. He acknowledged that the gifts for the Temple were from God himself. He also prayed for Solomon's spiritual development. The people all joined David in his spirit of praise and petition (29:20).

29:21-25 *A grand welcome for the new king.* After sacrificing and feasting, Solomon was crowned king in 971 B.C. As he began his reign, he enjoyed the hearty approval of all the people. "Again they crowned David's son Solomon" (29:22) refers to Solomon's first anointing during Adonijah's rebellion (see 1 Kings 1:39), an event the chronicler omits.

29:26-30 *The passing of Israel's greatest.* After reigning 40 years, King David died "at a ripe old age, having enjoyed long life, wealth, and honor." The chronicler's summary and his mention of the various books telling about David show the purpose of this first part of his book: to honor David, Israel's greatest king, and to keep his memory alive.

2 CHRONICLES

BACKGROUND
See *A Comparison of Chronicles and Samuel—Kings,* p. 237.

AUTHOR
See *1 Chronicles: Author.*

DATE AND LOCATION
See *1 Chronicles: Date and Location.*

RECIPIENTS
See *1 Chronicles: Recipients.*

PURPOSE
See *1 Chronicles: Purpose.* 2 Chronicles shows God's continuing faithfulness to the house of David (7:17-18).

UNIQUE FEATURES
The following material is found only in 2 Chronicles and not in the parallel account of 1–2 Kings:

- the miracle at the end of Solomon's prayer (7:1-3)
- the defection of godly Levites and other northern Israelites to Judah after the civil war (11:13-17)
- the temporary humbling of Rehoboam (12:2-8, 12)
- the stoning of Zechariah (24:20-22)
- the conversion of Manasseh (33:10-17)
- various additional details about Jehoshaphat, Uzziah (Azariah), Hezekiah, and Josiah

COMPARISON WITH OTHER BIBLE BOOKS
1, 2 Kings:

- See *Unique Features.*

***971 B.C.* Solomon begins reign**

***931* Kingdom divides, Israel, Judah**

***841* Joash, last in line of David, survives purge**

***722* Fall of Israel**

***621* Discovery of Law sparks Josiah's revival**

***586* Fall of Judah, exile to Babylon**

***538* Cyrus's decree, exiles return**

Exodus:

- Among the numerous parallels between the building of the Tabernacle and the building of the Temple:
- As Bezalel was designated by name to build much of the Tabernacle (Exod. 31:2), so Solomon was designated by name to build the Temple (1 Chron. 28:6).
- Both Bezalel and Solomon were from the tribe of Judah.
- Both Bezalel and Solomon were guided by the Spirit in their work (1:1-12; Exod. 31:3).
- The glory of God appeared at the dedication of both Tabernacle and Temple (7:1; Exod. 40:34).

OUTLINE

THE REIGN OF SOLOMON (1–9)
- Solomon requests wisdom (1)
- Solomon recruits builders for the Temple (2)
- Solomon's realization of the Temple (3–4)
- Solomon receives the Ark in the Temple (5)
- Solomon reviews the Temple's construction (6:1-11)
- Solomon requests God's blessing on the Temple (6:12–7:11)
- God responds: "Will it be blessed or cursed?" (7:12-22)
- Review of Solomon's reign (8)
- Solomon receives the Queen of Sheba (9:1-12)
- Further review of Solomon's reign (9:13-31)

THE KINGS OF JUDAH (10–36)
- Rehoboam (10–12)
  - He rebuffs the northern tribes (10:1-15)
  - He faces their revolt (10:16–11:23)
  - His relapse, repentance, and restoration (12)
- Abijah (13)
- Asa (14–16)
- Jehoshaphat (17–20)
  - His advocacy of the law (17)
  - His alliance with Ahab (18)
  - His advocacy of the law renewed (19)
  - His army of singers (20)
- Jehoram (21)
- Ahaziah (22:1-9)
- Athaliah and Joash (22:10–24:27)
  - Joash survives Athaliah's purge (22:10–24:3)
  - Joash supervises the Temple repairs (24:4-14)
  - Joash succumbs to evil advisors (24:15-27)
- Amaziah (25)
- Uzziah (26)
- Jotham (27)
- Ahaz (28)
- Hezekiah (29–32)

- His consecration of the Temple (29)
- His celebration of Passover (30)
- His contributions for worship (31)
- His conflict with Assyria (32)

Manasseh (33:1-20)
Amon (33:21-25)
Josiah (34–35)

- His dedication to reform (34:1-13)
- His discovery of the law (34:14-33)
- His devotion to the Passover (35:1-19)
- His death (35:20-27)

Jehoahaz (36:1-4)
Jehoiakim (36:5-8)
Jehoiachin (36:9-10)
Zedekiah (36:11-14)
Fall of Jerusalem; decree of Cyrus (36:15-23)

THE REIGN OF SOLOMON (1–9)

1:1-6 *Solomon's gift to God at Gibeon.* Having noted the death of King David in 971 B.C. (see 1 Chron. 29:26-30), the chronicler notes once again that God "was with [Solomon] and made him very powerful" (compare 1:1 with 1 Chron. 29:25). He then reports Solomon's sacrifice of a thousand offerings at Gibeon. Though David had taken the Ark to Jerusalem and made a special housing for it (see 1 Chron 15:1), the Tabernacle remained at Gibeon.

1:7-12 *He gets what he asks for and what he doesn't ask for as well.* Following Solomon's sacrifices, God offered to give him anything he desired. Solomon asked only for the wisdom to govern his nation. Because of Solomon's wise request, God promised him great wealth as well (see Prov. 4:7; 8:11; 9:10; 1 Kings 3:5-13).

1:13-17 *God keeps his promise of gold.* Solomon's amazing acquisitions of gold, silver, horses, and chariots are cited as proof that God kept his promise to make Solomon wealthy.

2:1-2 *Wanted: 150,000 workers and 3,600 foremen.* Chapters 2–4 outline Solomon's building of the Temple. 2:1-2 shows the magnificent scope of the project: It would require 150,000 laborers and 3,600 supervisors.

2:3-10 *Furniture and fabric for food.* Solomon sought building supplies and skilled labor from Hiram, king of Tyre, in exchange for wheat, barley, wine, and olive oil. In dealing with his Tyrian friends, Solomon boldly exalted the Lord (2:5-6; see 1 Kings 5:1-7).

2:11-16 *"I'm sending you my very best!"* Hiram responded favorably to Solomon's request. He sent Huram-abi, his "master craftsman," to oversee the work (see 1 Kings 5:8-10; 7:13-14).

2:17-18 *Alien laborers.* Solomon took a census of the aliens working on the Temple project. Their total number, 150,000, matches 2:2. Apparently, Solomon used non-Israelites for most of the manual labor (see 1 Kings 5:11-18; see exposition on 1 Kings 9:15-25).

3:1-7 *Only the best for God's house.* The Temple was built on Mount Moriah, where Abraham had offered Isaac (see Gen. 22:2). It was about 90 by 30 by 45 feet high, with a front porch area attached. The outer sanctuary (the Holy Place) was decorated with gold and precious jewels (see 1 Kings 6:1-3). The work began in 967 and would be completed in 960.

3:8-14 *Even more gold for the Most Holy.* The Temple's inner sanctuary, the Most Holy Place, was even more elaborately garnished with gold. It was half the size of the outer sanctuary, the same proportion as in the Tabernacle. This new home of the Ark of the Covenant featured two gold-plated wood cherubim with wing spans of 15 feet each. The Most Holy Place was separated from the outer sanctuary by a linen curtain of colorful embroidery.

3:15-17 *Jakin and Boaz: They stand for God.* Two pillars stood outside the front of the Temple, which faced east. The southern pillar was named Jakin, meaning "he establishes"; the northern pillar was named Boaz, meaning "in him is strength." They symbolized God, who established and strengthened Israel.

4:1-10 *An altar, a washbasin, and 10 lampstands.* The Temple's huge altar (30 by 30 by 15 feet) was probably located outside the Temple, near its eastern entrance. A water tank or laver, 15 feet across, was near the altar and was used for the washing ceremonies of the priests. The 10 basins of 4:6 were for washing burnt offerings (see 1 Kings 7:23-26).

4:11-22 *A job well done!* The chronicler now gives a short summary of items built for the Temple, reminding the reader of the chief craftsman (Huram-abi, 4:11, 16) and of the one who commissioned him (Solomon, 4:16, 18; see 1 Kings 7:40-50).

5:1-14 *Israel's holiest possession comes to Israel's holiest place.* The Levites and priests moved the Ark of the Covenant from its temporary tent home into the Most Holy Place. They worshiped God, and God honored their worship by filling the Temple with his shekinah-glory cloud—a literal application of Psalm 22:3! (See exposition on Exod. 14:19-20 and exposition on Ezek. 11:22-25; 1 Kings 8:1-11.)

6:1-11 *Their king preaches . . .* Solomon then addressed the assembled people, speaking of God's past actions and promises (6:5-9) and of his making the Temple his special home on earth (6:1-2; see 1 Kings 8:12-21).

6:12-42 *. . . then he prays . . .* Solomon then prayed, kneeling on a specially built platform in front of the altar. He began by praising and acknowledging God. While he made several detailed requests on his people's behalf, the overall thrust of his prayer was the centrality of the Temple in the relationship between God and his people (see 1 Kings 8:22-53).

7:1-3 *. . . and then the fire falls!* After Solomon's prayer, fire from heaven burned up the sacrifices, signifying God's acceptance of the Temple. The people responded with worship and a sense of awe. For a similar display of fire from heaven, see 1 Kings 18:36-38.

7:4-11 *A seven-day celebration.* Next came a seven-day celebration, with continual sacrifices and singing. It extended throughout the whole nation, not just Jerusalem (7:8; see 1 Kings 8:62-66).

7:12-22 *"When they're humble, I will hear and heal!"* God appeared to Solomon a second time (see 1:7-12), promising to hear and heal the people when they humbly turn to him. He reaffirmed Solomon's inheritance of the Davidic covenant, providing he and his descendants follow the Lord (7:17-18; see 1 Kings 9:1-9). This provisional clause did not mean that the Davidic covenant as a whole was conditional, only that the inclusion in the covenant of individual kings depended on their individual obedience (see Ps. 89:3-4, 30-37).

7:14 lists four conditions for revival: humility, prayer, earnest seeking of God, and repentance.

8:1-10 *Public works of the world's wisest man.* The chronicler highlights the completion of Solomon's building projects, the beginning of his foreign conquests, and the use of non-Israelite labor for his projects (see 1 Kings 9:10-23). (See, however, exposition on 1 Kings 9:15-25.)

8:11 *Relocated for religious reasons.* Feeling that it wasn't right to live in a house where the Ark had been kept, Solomon built a new house for his wife (see 1 Kings 9:24).

8:12-16 *Strict about the sacrifices.* Solomon strictly followed Moses' prescriptions for sacrifices and David's organizational plan for Temple service (see 1 Kings 9:25).

8:17-18 *Both king and admiral.* Much of Solomon's financial success was apparently due to the development of a fleet of merchant ships for international trade (see 1 Kings 9:26-28).

9:1-12 *She comes, she sees, he conquers.* The skeptical and pagan Queen of Sheba came to Jerusalem to see for herself if Solomon lived up to his reputation. Testing Solomon's wisdom, she found it beyond what she had expected. Seeing the great buildings he had built and the riches he possessed, she honored the God who had so richly blessed him. Solomon and the Queen of Sheba exchanged many gifts before she returned home. The gold alone weighed almost 10,000 pounds (see 1 Kings 10:1-13)!

9:13-31 *The wisest and wealthiest of all.* Before recording his death, the chronicler speaks once again of Solomon's God-given wisdom and how it enabled his accumulation of such great wealth (9:22-24; see 1 Kings 10:14-29; 11:41-43).

THE KINGS OF JUDAH (10–36)

10:1-5 *"He was bad; please be better!"* Solomon's son Rehoboam succeeded him as king and ruled from 931 to 913 B.C. A delegation led by Jeroboam asked him to relax the burdens of forced labor (see exposition on 1 Kings 9:15-25) and, presumably, high taxes, which Solomon had placed upon the nation (see 1 Kings 12:1-4).

As 10:2 notes, Jeroboam had just returned from Egypt, having fled there "to escape from King Solomon." Jeroboam was one of several leaders who had opposed Solomon after his apostasy (see 1 Kings 11:14-40).

10:6-15 *"To the contrary, I'll be much worse!"* Rehoboam sought advice concerning how he should answer Jeroboam's delegation. Refusing the counsel of the older and wiser men, he followed the advice of his peers and foolishly told the delegation that he would be harsher than his father was (see 1 Kings 12:6-14). The chronicler notes that Rehoboam's ill-considered response, which would lead to the division of the kingdom, was within God's providence (10:15; see exposition on 1 Kings 11:26-40).

10:16-19 *"Then we'll be independent."* Rehoboam's decision and attitude angered the delegation and the people they represented. Jeroboam led the northern 10 tribes to declare independence from the Davidic dynasty (see 1 Kings 12:15-19).

11:1-4 *Forbidden to fight.* Quite naturally, Rehoboam began to raise an army to recover his lost territory and subjects, but the Lord stopped him through the words of a prophet, confirming once again that the division of the northern and southern kingdoms was according to God's plan (see 1 Kings 12:20-24).

11:5-23 *All in all, a good start.* Rehoboam gave up hopes of reclaiming the northern tribes but did take steps to preserve what was left of his kingdom—Judah and Benjamin. Meanwhile Jeroboam was moving swiftly to establish new religious practices for his 10 tribes, and this led many priests and Levites and other faithful northern Israelites to defect to Rehoboam (11:13-17).

Though it didn't rival that of his father, Solomon, Rehoboam's family was quite large (11:18-23).

12:1-13 *Sin brings suffering; repentance brings restoration.* Having become firmly established as king over Judah and Benjamin, Rehoboam forsook the Lord and suffered invasion by Egypt as a result. When a prophet spoke to them about their sin, however (12:5), Rehoboam and the other leaders repented, and God delivered the nation (see 1 Kings 14:25-28).

12:14-16 *The bottom line: A bad king.* The chronicler's overall assessment of Rehoboam as king is negative. Rehoboam had not followed God as had his grandfather David (see 1 Kings 14:29-31).

13:1-12 *Abijah (913–911): A sermon for the enemy.* Abijah (called Abijam in 1 Kings) succeeded his father, Rehoboam, as king. The north-south conflict that had raged throughout Rehoboam's reign (see 12:15) continued, and in one battle Abijah found himself outnumbered two to one by Jeroboam's men. Before the battle Abijah "shouted" to the northern Israelite troops (from a distance, no doubt), charging them with three sins:

- they had ignored the Davidic covenant (13:5-7)
- they were worshiping idols (13:8)
- they had expelled the legitimate priests (13:9)

Abijah then predicted that Judah, having remained faithful to God, would win the battle (13:10-12; see 1 Kings 15:1-2).

13:13-19 *Surrounded, but saved by the Lord.* Jeroboam's troops set an ambush behind Judah. The men of Judah called on the Lord and, because they did, God helped them win the battle, at the cost of a half-million northern troops (13:17).

13:20-22 *Death for one king, prosperity for the other.* Jeroboam never recovered from this great loss and died by God's hand. Abijah, on the other hand, "grew more and more powerful" and lived long enough to marry 14 wives and father 38 children.

14:1-8 *Asa (911–870): Revivalist, builder, soldier.* Chapters 14–16 record the reign of Asa, who followed his father Abijah as king of Judah. 14:1-8 summarizes Asa's positive accomplishments:

- He followed God, encouraged revival, and destroyed pagan places of worship.
- He built fortified cities to protect Judah.
- He gathered an army and kept it intact.

(see 1 Kings 15:8-12)

14:9-15 *He cries out in fear, they march out in faith.* An extremely large army of Ethiopians caused Asa to cry out to God for help; God enabled Israel to soundly defeat them.

15:1-7 *"Don't do as they did."* The prophet Azariah challenged Asa to follow the Lord fully and not allow the nation to experience the trauma of a past time—perhaps the time of the judges—when it "was without the true God" and experienced "every kind of problem" (see Judg. 21:25).

15:8-15 *Revival results in rewards.* Asa responded to Azariah's exhortation by continuing his reforms, eliminating places of false worship from the land, and encouraging the renewal of the Mosaic covenant. He even legislated death for those who refused to cooperate (15:13). God rewarded his efforts with several years of peace (15:15, 19).

15:16-19 *Even his mother is removed from office!* Asa was so serious about reform that he removed his own mother from her official position as queen mother because of her involvement in pagan religion (see 1 Kings 15:13-15). On the "pagan shrines" (or "high places," 15:17), see exposition on Numbers 33:50-56.

16:1-10 *Wrong enemy, wrong friend.* Baasha, king of northern Israel (909–886 B.C.), began building a fortress near Jerusalem, apparently to prevent his subjects from defecting to the southern kingdom. Asa responded by paying the Syrians to break their treaty with the north so that Baasha would withdraw. The plan worked, and Baasha retreated (see 1 Kings 15:17-22).

The prophet Hanani pronounced judgment on Asa's action, saying that the nation's long period of peace would now come to an end. Asa became angry and imprisoned Hanani.

16:11-14 *The tragic end of a tremendous king.* Asa contracted a foot disease and sought the help of physicians but failed to seek the Lord's help. As a result, he died (see 1 Kings 15:23). Asa's failure to consult the Lord may have stemmed in part from his bitterness following Hanani's rebuke. Though Asa began well, he did not finish well.

17:1-19 *Jehoshaphat (873–848): Taking God's word to God's people.* Jehoshaphat continued the revival begun by his father, Asa. Most notably, he sent teachers and priests throughout the land to teach the law. The people of Judah gave great wealth to their good king (17:5), and all the surrounding nations paid him tribute (17:10-11). During this time of peace and prosperity, Jehoshaphat amassed much property and a strong army (17:12-19).

18:1-3 *A wedding and a war: Two unwise alliances.* Following his early success and spiritual leadership, Jehoshaphat made two unfortunate mistakes: He arranged the marriage of his son Jehoram to the daughter of Israel's wicked king Ahab (18:1; see 21:6), and he agreed to join Ahab in battle to reclaim Ramoth-gilead from Syria (see 1 Kings 22:1-4).

18:4-5 *Four hundred say, "You'll return a conqueror!"* Jehoshaphat asked Ahab (874–853 B.C.) to seek guidance from the prophets concerning their battle plans. The prophets all encouraged them to pursue their plans (see 1 Kings 22:5-6).

18:6-22 *But one says, "You'll return a corpse!"* Jehoshaphat realized, however, that the prophets Ahab had consulted were false prophets, so he asked him to find a "prophet of the LORD." Ahab called for Micaiah, even though he disliked him because of his negative prophesies. Micaiah prophesied that, if they tried to take Ramoth-gilead, they would be defeated and Ahab would die. Despite Micaiah's further warnings (18:18-22), Ahab refused to listen (see 1 Kings 22:7-23).

18:23-27 *"Remember," he says, "you won't return!"* Micaiah also prophesied against one of the prophets, Zedekiah, who had been very dramatic in his predictions of victory (18:10). Ahab imprisoned Micaiah for his negative prophecies, but Micaiah continued his warnings even from prison (see 1 Kings 22:24-28).

18:28-32 *How foolish can a good man be!* Ahab convinced Jehoshaphat to wear his royal robes into battle, while Ahab himself wore a disguise. When the Syrians saw Jehoshaphat, they assumed he was Ahab and attacked him. Jehoshaphat cried out to God for help, and God protected him (see 1 Kings 22:29-33).

18:33-34 *A random arrow, a fulfilled prophecy.* Ahab's treacherous disguise did not prevent him from being randomly and fatally wounded in the battle, just as Micaiah had predicted (see 1 Kings 22:34-37).

19:1-11 *The other king returns and resumes his reforms.* Jehoshaphat survived the defeat and returned to Judah, where Jehu the prophet confronted him concerning his alliance with "those who hate the LORD." Evidently taking the rebuke to heart, Jehoshaphat renewed his reform efforts (see 17:1-9). He established a legal system based on the law and traveled throughout the land to encourage revival.

20:1-13 *A timely prayer at the Temple.* The movement of enemy troops against Judah caused Jehoshaphat to call for a time of national fasting and prayer. Reminding the Lord of his past faithfulness, he described the nation's present predicament and asked him to help once more.

20:14-17 *"Stand still and watch me work!"* The Lord responded by promising that he would fight for his people, and that they would not have to fight at all! They were, however, to gather for battle to watch what God would do.

20:18-24 *Success by singers instead of soldiers.* Jehoshaphat led his armies, while singers praised the Lord as they went into battle. God sent confusion to the enemy armies; they turned against each other and were all killed.

20:25-30 *A victory rally in the valley.* It took three days for the men of Judah to carry away the spoils of war. On the fourth day they held a celebration and named the valley Beracah, meaning "praise," because of what the Lord had done.

20:31-37 *Overall, an A on his report card.* The chronicler's summary of Jehoshaphat's reign highlights his following the Lord, while noting that he had failed to destroy the pagan high places. He had also tried once more to ally himself with a wicked northern king, but the Lord frustrated that venture as well (20:35-37; see 1 Kings 22:41-50).

21:1-11 *Jehoram (853–841): Killing the competition.* Jehoshaphat's son Jehoram succeeded him as king of Judah. He began his reign by killing all his brothers to eliminate any competition for the throne. The writer noted that Jehoram, though a king of Judah, "followed the example of the kings of Israel." He noted further that this was in part because of the wicked influence of his wife (21:6), Athaliah (22:2), daughter of the northern king Ahab.

Despite Jehoram's wickedness, the Lord remained faithful to his promise that David's descendants would rule over at least part of Israel's 12 tribes (21:7; see 7:17-18; 2 Sam. 7:8-17). Because of Jehoram's apostasy, Judah lost control of Edom and Libnah (21:8-11; see 2 Kings 8:16-22).

21:12-15 *Devastating words from a departed prophet . . .* Elijah the prophet had sent a message to Jehoram predicting that a plague would fall on the land and that he himself would die a painful death. These judgments would come because he had killed his brothers and led the nation into idolatry.

How this prophecy came from Elijah is unclear, since he supposedly had been taken up to heaven during the reign of Jehoram's father, Jehoshaphat (see 2 Kings 2:9-11). Some scholars assume the letter to have been prophetic. Others believe that Elijah was not taken up till after Jehoram's reign began.

21:16-20 *. . . and a devastating fulfillment.* Shortly thereafter, Elijah's prophecy was fulfilled, as invaders carried away all but one of Jehoram's sons and he himself died—to no one's sorrow. The sparing of Jehoram's youngest son (21:17) shows God's continuing faithfulness to his promise to keep David's descendants on the throne.

22:1-9 *Ahaziah (841): Like mother, like son.* As the only surviving son, Ahaziah succeeded his father, Jehoram, and continued his evil policies—in large part because of the influence of his mother, Athaliah. Thus Judah continued to be affected by the paganism which characterized the northern tribes at this time.

Ahaziah joined with the northern king Jehoram in another attempt to regain Ramoth-gilead. While visiting Jehoram later, Ahaziah was killed by Jehu, the military leader who had been anointed by God to become king of the northern kingdom in place of Ahab's descendants (see 2 Kings 8:25-29).

In some versions, Ahaziah is also called Jehoahaz (21:17) and Azariah (22:6).

22:10-12 *Athaliah (841–835): Judah's only, and deadly, queen.* Hearing that Ahaziah, her son, was dead, Athaliah tried to exterminate all his children (her own grandchildren!). Had she succeeded, God's promise to David (see 2 Sam. 7:10-16) would have failed. However, Joash survived the purge and was hidden in the Temple (see 2 Kings 11:1-3).

23:1-15 *Joash (835–896): Crowned in a careful coup.* While Athaliah reigned, Jehoiada the priest led a conspiracy to bring the young Joash to the throne and thus restore the Davidic dynasty. With their plans in place, the conspirators publicly proclaimed Joash king (23:11). When Athaliah heard the noise of the coronation ceremony, she came to investigate, whereupon she was killed (see 2 Kings 11:4-16).

23:16–24:3 *A role model for the young monarch.* As the seven-year-old Joash began his reign, Jehoiada led a revival throughout the nation. His good influence over Joash is suggested by his arranging marriages for him (24:3) and by the fact that, though Joash did well while Jehoiada lived (24:2), he would fall to evil influences after Jehoiada's death (24:17-22; see 2 Kings 11:17–12:3).

24:4-14 *His collection box brings a construction boom.* Probably through Jehoiada's influence, the young Joash ordered repairs to the Temple, which had apparently fallen into disrepair under the preceding three monarchs, especially under Athaliah, who had allowed her sons to break in and steal from it (24:7). By the time Joash reached adulthood, it had become apparent that the money intended for the repairs was not reaching Jerusalem (24:6), so Joash set up a special box in the Temple to receive offerings. That system worked much better, and the project was brought to a successful conclusion (see 2 Kings 12:1-16).

24:15-22 *When the godly exit, the godless enter.* Jehoiada, leader of the coup and counselor to the king, died at age 130 and was praised by the writer for his faithful service. With Jehoiada's good influence gone, Joash began listening to godless advisors. Despite the warnings of prophets, he allowed the reinstatement of idol worship. When Zechariah, either the son or grandson of Jehoiada, prophesied against Joash, Joash had him killed (24:20-22). As he died, Zechariah called on the Lord to exact retribution for his death.

24:23-27 *Wounded by his foes, finished off by his friends.* God allowed Syria to attack Judah as a judgment against Joash's apostasy. Joash was injured on the battlefield; then, while recovering from his wounds, he was killed by his own men in retaliation for his murder of Zechariah (see 2 Kings 12:17-21).

25:1-4 *Amaziah (796–767): Right actions, wrong attitude.* Joash's son Amaziah became king following his father's death. His first action as king was to execute those who had killed his father. The author noted that Amaziah spared the children of those men, as the law decreed. He noted that, in general, Amaziah "did what was pleasing in the LORD's sight, but not wholeheartedly" (25:2; see 2 Kings 14:1-6).

25:5-13 *"God is not with the north."* Amaziah raised an army of 300,000 from his own land of Judah and hired 100,000 mercenary soldiers from the northern kingdom. A prophet confronted him about hiring the mercenaries, declaring that God was "not with" the northern kingdom, so they were to be sent home immediately. Amaziah obediently sent the northern mercenaries home. Soon thereafter he went to battle against the Edomites (the people of Seir referred to in 25:11, 14) and was victorious. Meanwhile the mercenaries, angry at being sent home, captured some of Judah's territory (see 2 Kings 14:7).

25:14-28 *From apostasy to arrogance to assassination.* Amazingly, after defeating the Edomites, Amaziah began worshiping their gods! A prophet confronted him about this and, when Amaziah rebuffed him, predicted Amaziah's death. Soon thereafter Amaziah, overconfident after defeating the Edomites, challenged the northern king Joash to battle. Joash responded with an insulting parable (25:18), and the fight was on. The northerners defeated Amaziah and plundered Jerusalem and the Temple (25:22-24). Several years later, Amaziah was assassinated by his own people (25:25-28; see 2 Kings 14:8-20).

King Joash implied in his parable that it would be foolish for Amaziah to attack Israel. 25:20 reveals that God caused Amaziah to make this foolish choice because of his earlier foolish choice to worship the Edomite gods.

26:1-15 *Uzziah (790–740): A glorious beginning.* Uzziah followed his father, Amaziah, as king of Judah and prospered in battle and in civilian pursuits. The chronicler highlighted Uzziah's success in his many building and farming projects (26:9-10) and as a military leader and inventor (26:11-15). He underscored the connection between the king's success and his obedience to God (26:5; see 2 Kings 14:21-22; 15:1-4); in some versions, 2 Kings refers to Uzziah as Azariah—not to be confused with Azariah the chief priest (26:17).

26:5 introduces another prophet named Zechariah (see 24:20). The Bible mentions 34 men named Zechariah!

26:16-23 *The price he pays for pride.* Uzziah burned incense on the altar—an action the law reserved for priests. When Azariah the chief priest confronted him about this sin, Uzziah responded in anger, and God struck him with leprosy. He would remain a leper for the rest of his life, living in isolation while his son Jotham ran the government (see 2 Kings 15:5-7).

27:1-9 *Jotham (750–731): Good king, evil nation.* Jotham is given higher marks than his father because he respected the sanctity of the Temple. Jotham built many fortresses around the nation and defeated the Ammonites. Yet while he was winning God's approval (27:6), the people of Judah as a whole "continued in their corrupt ways" (27:2; see 2 Kings 15:32-38).

28:1-4 *Ahaz (735–715): One of Judah's very worst.* Jotham's son Ahaz failed to learn from his father's example. Instead, he was influenced by the pagan religion of the north and actively promoted it in Judah. He even sacrificed his own children to false gods (see 2 Kings 16:1-4).

28:5-8 *The price for perversion: Defeat, death, and deportation.* In response to these terrible crimes against humanity, God allowed both Syria and Israel's northern kingdom to defeat Judah. Many of the people of Judah were taken captive to the northern kingdom (see 2 Kings 16:5-6).

28:9-15 *"Don't push your victory too far!"* The prophet Oded confronted the men of Israel as they led the Judahites captive. He warned them they should not enslave their "own relatives," especially considering their own guilt before God. The northerners felt convicted and, after feeding and clothing their captives, released them.

28:16-21 *Attempts to bribe Assyria, to no avail.* Because of his terrible sins, Ahaz and his kingdom remained weak (28:19), and because of this weakness both the Philistines and the Edomites attacked them. Ahaz sought help from Assyria's king Tiglath-pileser, who had just defeated Syria on Ahaz's behalf (see 2 Kings 16:5-9). Though Ahaz paid tribute to Tiglath-pileser, however, he refused to help him this time and attacked him instead (28:20).

28:22-27 *Before he dies, he nails the Temple doors shut.* In desperation over his military defeats, Ahaz began sacrificing to the gods of Syria and destroying the objects of true worship in the Temple. (See also 2 Kings 16:10-18.) Finally, he closed the doors of the Temple and built pagan altars throughout the whole country. As with many evil kings before him, Ahaz was buried in Jerusalem but not in the royal tombs.

29:1-19 *Hezekiah (728–686): Undoing what his father had done.* Ahaz, one of Judah's worst kings, was succeeded by his son Hezekiah, who would be one of Judah's best kings (see 2 Kings 18:1-3). Hezekiah repaired the Temple doors, then selected 14 Levites to help him restore Temple worship and reverse the perversions of his father. They removed the pagan items Ahaz had brought to the Temple, presumably burning them in the Kidron Valley, and replaced the items of true worship that he had discarded. They consecrated the Temple's outer court and then the Temple itself.

29:20-30 *The grand reopening.* The Temple's reopening was marked by a time of sacrificing and singing, led by Hezekiah. Though smaller in scope, the spirit of this rededication recalls the Temple's original dedication by Solomon (6–7).

29:31-36 *Plenty of helpers, but where are the priests?* After the official sacrifices under Hezekiah's leadership, the people themselves were allowed to bring sacrifices and offerings to the priests. However, there were not enough priests to handle all who came, so the Levites had to perform more than their customary duties as assistants. By noting that the Levites were "more conscientious about purifying themselves than the priests" (29:34), the author hints that the priests may have been more involved than the Levites in false worship under Ahaz.

30:1-9 *A royal invitation to a special service.* Hezekiah invited all of Israel to come to Jerusalem and celebrate the Passover. Perhaps viewing this as an opportunity to reunify the nation, he invited those from the northern tribes who had escaped the north's fall to Assyria (30:6; see exposition on 2 Kings 17:5-23; exposition on 1 Chron. 5:23-26). Hezekiah had to delay the Passover for a month to allow the priests more time to sanctify themselves (see exposition on 29:31-36). Such a delay was allowed by the law (see Num. 9:10-11). (See also exposition on 2 Kings 23:21-23.)

30:10-12 *Some ridicule, others respond.* While most of the northern tribes rejected and even mocked King Hezekiah's invitation, some from the tribes of Asher, Manasseh, and Zebulun "humbled themselves" and agreed to attend. 30:12 indicates that the occasion brought great unity to Judah, the host tribe.

30:13-20 *Special remission for those not ready.* As they gathered for the Passover, the people began purging Jerusalem of pagan religious items—just as the priests had cleansed the Temple (see 29:16). During the Passover, the leaders realized that many of the people were ceremonially unfit to partake. Hezekiah prayed on their behalf, and God "healed the people," allowing them to partake. Even under the law, God was more interested in the heart than in outward rituals.

30:21-27 *Seven days of celebration are not enough.* The joy of the renewed Passover was so great that everyone agreed to extend it from the customary seven days to two weeks. The writer observes that this was the most remarkable event to take place in Jerusalem since the days of Solomon.

31:1 *Rejoicing leads to revival.* The Passover led to genuine revival, as the worshipers went throughout the land, destroying all symbols of paganism.

31:2-10 *Tithes, tithes, and more tithes!* Hezekiah organized the priests and reminded the people of their obligation to tithe toward the priests' support. The response was overwhelmingly positive—another sign that true revival had occurred.

31:11-21 *Levite accountants.* Hezekiah appointed Levites to receive and disburse the tithe money and other offerings.

32:1-8 *"We'll stop up the wells and stop Sennacherib!"* When Sennacherib, king of Assyria, invaded Judah and threatened Jerusalem, Hezekiah helped the people prepare for the coming battle: They organized the army; made more weapons; strengthened Jerusalem's fortifications; and stopped up the water sources outside the city, so that the enemy soldiers would have nothing to drink. Most important, Hezekiah encouraged the people in their faith (32:6-8).

32:9-19 *He scorns Judah's God in Judah's language.* A delegation from Sennacherib shouted threats to the people of Jerusalem, boasting of all the other nations that had fallen to Assyria and daring Judah's God to prove himself more powerful than the gods of those nations. Despite a request that they speak in Aramaic (see 2 Kings 18:26), the Assyrians shouted their threats in Hebrew so that their message would have its full effect on the general populace, who would not have understood Aramaic (see 2 Kings 18:17-37; Isa. 36:2-12).

32:20-21 *Death to the army, then to the king.* Encouraged by the prophet Isaiah, Hezekiah responded to Sennacherib's threats with earnest prayer. In answer, God's angel killed the entire Assyrian army. Later, Sennacherib was killed by his own sons (see 2 Kings 19; Isa. 37).

32:22-26 *Pride brings pain, humility brings healing.* Israel then enjoyed a time of peace and prosperity. The prosperity caused Hezekiah to become proud, however, and God judged him with a terminal illness while at the same time threatening the nation as well. Hezekiah then "repented of his pride," and God spared both him and the nation (see 2 Kings 20:1-11; Isa. 38).

32:27-33 *A good king fails his finals.* After recovering from his illness, Hezekiah became still more prosperous. When Babylon sent ambassadors to Hezekiah, God used the occasion to "test [Hezekiah] and to see what was really in his heart" (32:31). The 2 Kings account reports the sad results of Hezekiah's spiritual final exam: He proved to be proud and foolish (see 2 Kings 20:12-13), and selfish as well (see 2 Kings 20:14-19; Isa. 39).

Nevertheless, Hezekiah's people "honored him at his death." Unlike Israel's less admirable kings, such as Ahaz (see 28:27), Hezekiah was buried in the royal tombs.

33:1-9 *Manasseh (695–642): By any standard, the most godless of all.* Hezekiah's son Manasseh restored the pagan worship his father had eradicated. He allowed satanic practices, child sacrifices, and defamation of the Temple. His evil influence on Judah was even worse than that of the Canaanites (33:9; see 2 Kings 21:1-9).

33:10-13 *But God gets his attention!* As a judgment against Manasseh, God allowed the Assyrians to attack Judah and take Manasseh captive to Babylon. While in captivity, Manasseh repented and God forgave him and restored him to the throne.

33:14-20 *What a change conversion brings!* Manasseh demonstrated the sincerity of his conversion by rebuilding the nation's defenses, removing the idols he had built, and encouraging true worship (see 2 Kings 21:17).

33:21-25 *Amon (642–640): Like his father, corrupt; but unlike his father, unrepentant.* Manasseh's son Amon repeated the wicked deeds of his father, but, unlike his father, he never repented. Finally, his own servants assassinated him (see 2 Kings 21:18-24). Evidently, the idols Manasseh had removed from public places had not been destroyed, for Amon found them and worshiped them (33:22).

34:1-7 *Josiah (640–609): By any standard, the most godly of all.* Amon's son Josiah began his reign as a child. At age 16 he turned to God and began to purge the land of false worship (see 2 Kings 22:1-2).

34:8-13 *He resolves to repair the Temple.* At age 26, Josiah initiated an effort to repair the Temple. After the repairs under Joash some 180 years previously, and the more recent (and perhaps more minor) work under Hezekiah, the Temple had apparently been in disuse for a number of years and was again in need of repair (see 2 Kings 22:3-7) 34:6, 9 shows that many who had escaped the fall of the northern kingdom were looking to the south for leadership (see 30:6).

34:14-18 *Found: The manuscript of Moses!* During the work on the Temple, Hilkiah the priest discovered a copy of the law of Moses (the entire Pentateuch) and had it delivered to the king and read in his presence (see 2 Kings 22:8-14). This could have been the only surviving copy of the Law, perhaps hidden for safekeeping during the almost total abolition of Israelite worship by Manasseh and Amon.

34:19-28 *"Judgment will come after you're gone."* Upon hearing the law read, Josiah mourned over the sins of Israel, realizing that God was surely angry with the nation. At Josiah's direction, Hilkiah consulted the prophetess Huldah concerning Israel's fate. She replied that Israel would indeed be judged but that, because he had mourned and humbled himself, the judgment would not come during Josiah's lifetime (see 2 Kings 22:15-20).

34:29-33 *His reading plus their response brings revival.* Josiah read the law to the people, then publicly made a covenant to follow God and challenged the people to do so as well. The people responded positively, and revival spread throughout the nation (see 2 Kings 23:1-3).

35:1-19 *The greatest Passover since Samuel!* Josiah led the nation in the restoration of the Passover. More than 41,000 animals were brought for sacrifice, and the Ark was restored to its rightful place in the Temple—presumably after having been removed during the repairs. The chronicler describes this as the greatest Passover since the time of Samuel (35:18), apparently surpassing even the 14-day celebration led by Hezekiah (see 30; exposition on 2 Kings 23:21-23).

35:20-27 *A foolish fight, a fatal wound.* In 609 B.C., the Egyptian army was marching through Judah on its way to Carchemish on the Euphrates River, to help Assyria fight Nebuchadnezzar and the Babylonians. Despite Pharaoh Neco's claim that he had no quarrel with Judah and didn't want to fight them, Josiah attacked the Egyptians and was fatally wounded. He was buried amid great mourning (see 2 Kings 23:28-30). Pharaoh's march was itself doomed: Nebuchadnezzar would defeat him at Carchemish in 605 and would soon thereafter defeat Judah as well.

36:1-4 *Jehoahaz (609): Judah's king, deposed by Egypt's king.* Josiah's son Jehoahaz succeeded him but ruled only 90 days before Pharaoh Neco deposed him, forced Judah to pay tribute, and installed Jehoahaz's brother Eliakim as Judah's next king. Neco changed Eliakim's name to Jehoiakim, a further indication of Egypt's power over Judah at this time (see 2 Kings 23:31-34).

36:5-8 *Jehoiakim (609–597): Installed by Egypt, bound by Babylon.* During Jehoiakim's reign, in 605 B.C., Nebuchadnezzar took some Israelites, including Daniel, as well as some of the Temple treasures, to Babylon (see Dan. 1:1-6). Verse 6 can be translated "bound him . . . to take him to Babylon" (see NIV, KJV), which may indicate that Jehoiakim was actually allowed to remain in Judah after promising loyalty to Nebuchadnezzar. This would explain his continuing in power till 597 B.C. (see 2 Kings 23:36–24:6).

36:9-10 *Jehoiachin (597): His first and last 100 days.* Jehoiakim's son Jehoiachin succeeded him as king and ruled just 100 days (90 days, according to 2 Kings 24:8) before Nebuchadnezzar took him captive, along with many other Israelites, including Ezekiel (see 2 Kings 24:8-17; Ezek. 1:2; 40:1). The NLT, following many OT manuscripts, gives Jehoiachin's age as 18, which fits the context better than other versions that cite his age as 21.

36:11-14 *Zedekiah (597–586): Judah's foolish final king.* Zedekiah, Judah's last king before the Babylonian captivity, was evil as most of his predecessors had been and failed to repent when warned by Jeremiah (see Jer. 21:3-7). He also ignored the warnings of Nebuchadnezzar and rebelled against Babylon (see 2 Kings 24:18-20). While the chronicler's account focuses on Judah's kings, he notes that all of the nation's civil and religious leaders were becoming more and more ungodly.

36:15-21 *Judah's judgment: Jerusalem falls.* Concluding that his people were beyond repentance (36:15-16), God allowed the Babylonians to invade again. This time they brutally slaughtered many people, ransacked the Temple, burned the city, and took the survivors captive to Babylon. God had earlier come to the same conclusion with regard to the northern kingdom (see 2 Kings 17).

One reason given for this terrible judgment was the need to let the land rest, since Judah had not observed the law's requirement that the land lie fallow each seventh year (36:21). God decreed 70 years of captivity, implying that the Sabbath year had not been kept for 490 years (see Lev. 25:1-7; 26:27-43; 2 Kings 25; Jer. 29:10; exposition on Dan. 9:20-27).

36:22-23 *But after 70 years, a new era!* The chronicler ended his book optimistically, noting the decree of the Persian king Cyrus that enabled the Jews to return to Jerusalem from their captivity in Babylon (see exposition on Ezra 1:1-4).

EZRA

BACKGROUND

In 539 B.C., 66 years after the first group of Jews was taken captive to Babylon in 605 (see exposition on 2 Kings 24:1-7), the Babylonian Empire was itself overthrown by King Cyrus of Persia. One of Cyrus's first acts as Babylon's new ruler was to allow its many captives, including the Jews, to return to their homelands (see *The Cyrus Cylinder*, p. 894). The book of Ezra records the first return of Jewish exiles from Babylon in 538 and the second return in 457, when Ezra himself was among those returning. The book of Nehemiah, originally combined with Ezra, records the return of Nehemiah and his companions in 445.

See *The Return from Exile*, p. 264.

AUTHOR

Ezra and Nehemiah were both authored by Ezra, though Nehemiah's memoirs supplied much of the material for the book bearing his name:

- Ezra is clearly the subject of the first-person pronouns referring to the author of the book of Ezra (7:28; and repeatedly in 8–9). Though Nehemiah 1–7 has similar repeated usage of the first-person pronoun, Ezra could easily have compiled that book from Nehemiah's journals.
- Ezra would have had firsthand knowledge of many of the events in both books.
- Ezra—Nehemiah bears marked similarities to 1, 2 Chronicles (see *Comparison with Other Bible Books*), and there is strong traditional support for Ezra authoring Chronicles (see *1 Chronicles: Author*).

Most conservative scholars believe an unknown "chronicler" may have been the final editor of Ezra and Nehemiah as well as of 1, 2 Chronicles.

538 B.C.
Exiles return with Zerubbabel

536
Temple rebuilding begins

535
Temple rebuilding stops

520
Work resumes, through ministries of Haggai, Zechariah

516
Temple finished

473
Esther saves Jews still in Persia

457
More exiles return with Ezra

445
Nehemiah rebuilds wall

THE RETURN FROM EXILE

"The truth is that you will be in Babylon for seventy years. But then I will come and do for you all the good things I have promised, and I will bring you home again." *(Jer. 29:10)*

A CHRONOLOGY OF THE RETURN STAGE

FOREIGN KING	DATE	EVENT	SCRIPTURE	OLD TESTAMENT BOOK	LOCATION
Cyrus the Great	539–530	Conquers Babylon Issues return decree	Dan. 5; Ezra 1–3	• Ezra 1–6	
Cambyses	530–522	Not referred to in Old Testament		• Haggai	Jerusalem
Smerdis	522–520	Stops work on the Temple	Ezra 4:1-23	• Zechariah	
Darius the Great	520–486	Orders work to continue	Ezra 4:24; 6:1-22	(See Ezra 5:1; 6:14)	
Xerxes	486–465	Makes Esther his queen	Esther 1–10	• Esther	Persia
Artaxerxes	465–424	Allows Ezra to return Allows Nehemiah to return	Ezra 7–12; Nehemiah 1–13	• Ezra 7–12 • Nehemiah	Jerusalem

DATE AND LOCATION
The events of Ezra—Nehemiah cover 93 years; their compilation was probably completed in about 430 B.C. in Jerusalem.

RECIPIENTS
The Jews who returned from Babylon, including not just the two tribes of the south (Judah and Benjamin) but representatives of all 12 tribes (see exposition on 1:5-6).

PURPOSE
(Ezra—Nehemiah)

- To reassure the returning exiles that God would keep his covenant with them (Neh. 9:32) and that there was therefore "hope for Israel" (10:2).
- To demonstrate the power of prayer (Ezra 9–10; Neh. 9) and the importance

of the Word of God in times of crisis (Nehemiah makes frequent references to reading from the law).
- To show what can happen when just one person (Ezra and Nehemiah, respectively) takes a stand for the Lord.

UNIQUE FEATURES

- The Bible tells the stories of several ministry partnerships, such as Moses and Aaron, and Elijah and Elisha. Ezra—Nehemiah tells of three such teams: Zerubbabel and Jeshua; Haggai and Zechariah; and, of course, Ezra and Nehemiah.
- Ezra was one of the last OT authors and one of the first of the Jewish scribes who would preserve the OT canon.
- Ezra is one of two books in the Bible that contain a significant amount of Aramaic, a sister language to Hebrew (the other is Daniel).

COMPARISON WITH OTHER BIBLE BOOKS

Ezra—Nehemiah and 1, 2 Chronicles:

- Ezra's involvement with all four books is suggested by these similarities:
  - ➤ Both contain many lists.
  - ➤ The last two verses of 2 Chronicles (36:22-23) are identical to the first three verses of Ezra.
  - ➤ Both use similar expressions, such as "the house of God."
  - ➤ Levites and Temple assistants are prominent in both.

Ezra—Nehemiah and Haggai:

- Both compare the new Temple with the former Temple of Solomon (3:12; Hag. 2:3).
- Both speak of the guidance of the Spirit of God (Neh. 9:20; Hag. 2:5).
- Both speak of God instilling an enthusiasm in the returning exiles (1:5; Hag. 1:14).

OUTLINE

THE FIRST RETURN, UNDER ZERUBBABEL: A HISTORICAL ACCOUNT (1–6)
- Return of the exiles (1–2)
- Revival of sacrifices (3:1-6)
- Rebuilding the Temple begun (3:7-13)
- Roadblocks to the rebuilding (4)
- Rebuilding the Temple completed (5–6)

THE SECOND RETURN, UNDER EZRA: A BIOGRAPHICAL ACCOUNT (7–10)
- Royal authorization of Ezra (7)
- Remnant accompanying Ezra (8)
- Reforms enacted by Ezra (9–10)

THE FIRST RETURN, UNDER ZERUBBABEL: A HISTORICAL ACCOUNT (1–6)

1:1-4 *Cyrus proclaims what Jeremiah predicted.* (See *Background.*) Ezra begins where 2 Chronicles ended, with the issuing of Cyrus's decree allowing the Jews to return to their homeland (see *Comparison with Other Bible Books*). Cyrus's decree fulfilled Jeremiah's prophecy that the Jews would return after 70 years of captivity (Jer. 29:10; see exposition on Jer. 25:8-14).

Isaiah, prophesying earlier, had actually referred to Cyrus by name (Isa. 44:28–45:1).

1:5-6 *He gives them the desire to go.* Ezra notes that God had given many of the exiles a desire to return to their homeland. At Cyrus's suggestion, many Jews and non-Jews who chose to remain in Babylon gave generous gifts to those returning, recalling similar gifts at the time of the Exodus (Exod. 12:35-36). Although only three tribes are mentioned—Judah, Benjamin, and Levi—it is clear that representatives from all 12 tribes were among those returning:

- At the time of Israel's civil war, various people from all 12 tribes moved to Jerusalem and allied themselves with the southern kingdom (2 Chron. 11:13-17).
- Paul spoke of "the twelve tribes of Israel" (Acts 26:7) as though people from all those tribes were identifiable in his day.
- The NT mentions the tribes of Zebulun and Naphtali (Matt. 4:13-15) and Asher (Luke 2:36).
- Jesus saw his ministry as being to the entire house of Israel, not just to one or two tribes (Matt. 10:5-6).

These verses refute the claims of British Israelites, who teach that people of British descent comprise Israel's "10 lost tribes."

1:7-11 *He returns the Temple treasures.* Cyrus restored to the Jews some 5,400 gold and silver items that Nebuchadnezzar had taken from the Temple (see 2 Kings 24:13; see exposition on 2 Kings 25:8-21) and that Belshazzar had used to mock Israel's God (Dan. 5:2-4).

2:1-70 *The leaders and those they lead.* Ezra lists the families who returned from exile and introduces Zerubbabel, the grandson of Jehoiachin (3:2; 1 Chron. 3:17-19), as their political leader (see Hag. 1:1). Zerubbabel would face a difficult task in rebuilding the Temple and was often personally encouraged by God himself (Hag. 1:14; 2:4, 21, 23; Zech. 4:6-7, 9-10).

10 other leaders are listed, including Jeshua (2:2), who would be Israel's first high priest following the exile. Nehemiah (2:2) was not the same as the Nehemiah who would return to Judea 93 years later and for whom the book is named.

The people are listed in several groups: priests (2:36-42); descendants of Temple servants (also translated "Nethinim," 2:43-54; see exposition on 8:1-20); descendants of Solomon's officials (2:55-58); and various people whose Israelite identity could not be verified (2:59-63). On "sacred lots" (2:63; literally, "Urim and Thummim"), see Exodus 28:30. In all, 50,000 people and 8,000 animals made the trip from Babylon to Judea.

3:1-6 *The altar goes up despite the opposition.* The first thing Jeshua did upon arriving in Jerusalem was rebuild the altar on its prescribed site. He did so despite immediate opposition from the non-Jews now living there (3:3). Following this, the people celebrated the Festival of Shelters and began regular observance of the various sacrifices.

3:7-13 *Rejoicing and regretful remembering.* Two years after arriving in Jerusalem, and after gathering supplies, the people began rebuilding the Temple. As soon as the foundation was laid, there was a memorable dedication service: As the younger generation rejoiced, the older Jews wept, remembering Solomon's beautiful Temple, which had been much larger than the new one.

4:1-5 *"Thanks, but no thanks."* As they saw the Temple taking shape, the local people who had been opposing the Jews began offering to help them, but Zerubbabel and Jeshua wisely refused their offer. The would-be helpers then resumed their efforts to hinder the rebuilding.

4:6-16 *The poisonous pen of the pagans.* Eventually, the Israelites' opponents began writing letters of accusation to the governing authorities—an annoying practice that went on for many years. One of these letters (4:11-16) suggested that King Artaxerxes read up on Jerusalem's rebellious past and predicted that the Jews living in the rebuilt city would refuse to pay taxes.

4:17-24 *"Accusation confirmed! Cease construction immediately!"* After reviewing Jerusalem's history, Artaxerxes concluded that Jerusalem was indeed a threat to his kingdom's stability. He ordered the Jews to cease their rebuilding.

5:1-5 *Haggai and Zechariah: "Don't stop working now!"* Some 15 years later, two fearless and faithful prophets, Haggai and Zechariah, began encouraging the people to ignore the king's order and to keep on building (see Hag. 1:1, 8; Zech. 1:1). Seeing that the work was proceeding, a local delegation led by Tattenai asked the Jews who had given them the authority to build. They told Tattenai about Cyrus's decree, and he wrote a letter to King Darius concerning the matter.

Perhaps recalling the earlier discouragement, especially of the older Jews (see 3:12), God inspired Haggai at this time to help them put everything in its proper perspective, comparing the new Temple with both Solomon's Temple and the future millennial Temple:

- *Solomon's Temple:* "Is there anyone who can remember this house—the Temple—as it was before? In comparison, how does it look to you now? It must seem like nothing at all!" (Hag. 2:3).
- *The millennial Temple:* "The future glory of this Temple will be greater than its past glory, says the LORD Almighty. And in this place I will bring peace. I, the LORD Almighty, have spoken!" (Hag. 2:9).

5:6-17 *Tattenai's letter: "Did Cyrus really say that?"* Ezra records the text of Tattenai's letter to Darius: Tattenai reported the Jews' claim that Darius's predecessor, King Cyrus, had signed a decree allowing the Temple to be rebuilt. Tattenai demanded to know if Cyrus had indeed signed such a decree.

6:1-12 *Darius's reply: "Yes, he did! Let them work!"* A search in the royal archives quickly revealed Cyrus had indeed ordered the reconstruction of the Temple, just as the Jews had claimed. 6:3-5 records Cyrus's original decree; 6:6-12 records Darius's reinforcement of that decree. Darius ordered Tattenai and his men to help the Jews in any way they could.

This is but one of many biblical examples of God using the opposition of his enemies to serve his purposes. Tattenai's letter, intended to stop the rebuilding of the Temple, actually assured its completion. As the psalmist said, "Human opposition only enhances your glory" (Ps. 76:10). There are many biblical examples of this:

- Esau's wrath caused Jacob to flee to Haran, where he met Rachel (Gen. 27:41-45; 29:10-11).
- The wrath of his 11 brothers sent Joseph to Egypt as a slave; there, he became prime minister and rescued his family from famine (Gen. 37:23-28; 41:38-44; 50:20).
- When a Moabite king hired Balaam to curse Israel, the result was a beautiful prophecy about Christ (Num. 22:1-6; 24:17).
- When Haman built a gallows to hang Mordecai, he was himself hanged on it (Esther 5:12-14; 7:10).
- When an Israelite king burned a book from God, the book was

rewritten with an addition that prophesied the king's own doom (Jer. 36:20-23, 27-32).

- The crucifixion of Christ resulted in salvation for all repentant sinners (Acts 2:36).
- A Roman emperor banished the apostle John to a lonely island to prevent him from preaching the gospel; while there, John wrote Revelation (Rev. 1:9).

6:13-15 *Project completed by prayers, prophets, and the people.* Tattenai honored Darius's decree and lent his support to the rebuilding; with additional encouragement from Haggai and Zechariah, the new Temple was completed in 516 B.C., some 20 years after construction began (compare 3:8 and 6:15).

6:16-22 *Dedication and celebration.* A worship ceremony marked the completion of the Temple; priests were assigned to its service, and the Passover was celebrated. The returning exiles invited Jews who had been left behind in Palestine at the time of exile (see exposition on 2 Chron. 30:1-9) but who had now "turned from their immoral customs" (6:21) to observe Passover with them.

THE SECOND RETURN, UNDER EZRA: A BIOGRAPHICAL ACCOUNT (7–10)

7:1-10 *To Israel, to teach!* In 457 B.C., some 80 years after Zerubbabel and Jeshua had led the first group of exiles back to Jerusalem, King Artaxerxes granted Ezra permission to go there as well. Ezra's purpose in making the five-month journey was "to study and obey the law of the LORD and to teach those laws and regulations to the people of Israel" (7:9-10). Ezra's genealogy (7:1-5) shows that he was a priest; 7:6 states that he was also a respected scribe.

7:11-26 *The favor and finances of the king.* Artaxerxes issued a decree inviting other Israelites, especially priests, to go with Ezra to Israel. He gave generous provisions for the trip and urged others to do so as well. He decreed that non-Jewish authorities in the area around Judea should make every effort to help the Jews. Most amazingly of all, he instructed Ezra to make the law of Moses the law of the land and to strictly enforce it (7:25-26). Artaxerxes evidently was either renewing or maintaining the liberal policies of Cyrus (1). His generosity was motivated at least in part, however, by a desire to appease Israel's God (7:23).

7:27-28 *"Praise God from whom all blessings flow!"* Ezra recalled his prayer of thanksgiving upon hearing of the king's offer of help, and his gathering of fellow Israelites for the trip to Jerusalem.

8:1-20 *Lots of laypeople but not one Levite!* Some 1,500 people embarked on the journey with Ezra. 8:1-14 gives their genealogies. During a stopover early in the journey, Ezra discovered that there were no Levites making the trip (8:15). He quickly sent men back to Babylon to find some Levites and Temple servants. The men soon returned, with 41 priests and 220 Temple servants.

As 8:20 explains, the Temple servants (also translated "Nethinim") were people whose ancestors David had appointed to that position. Because they had non-Israelite names (2:43-54), some scholars have concluded that they may have descended from captives of war such as the Gibeonites (Josh. 9:27) or the Midianites (Num. 31:1-30), both of whom had become Israel's servants.

8:21-23 *Fasting and prayer will have to do.* As they prepared to resume their journey, Ezra and the people prayed for God's protection. Having already declared to Artaxerxes their faith that

TO BABYLON FROM JUDAH

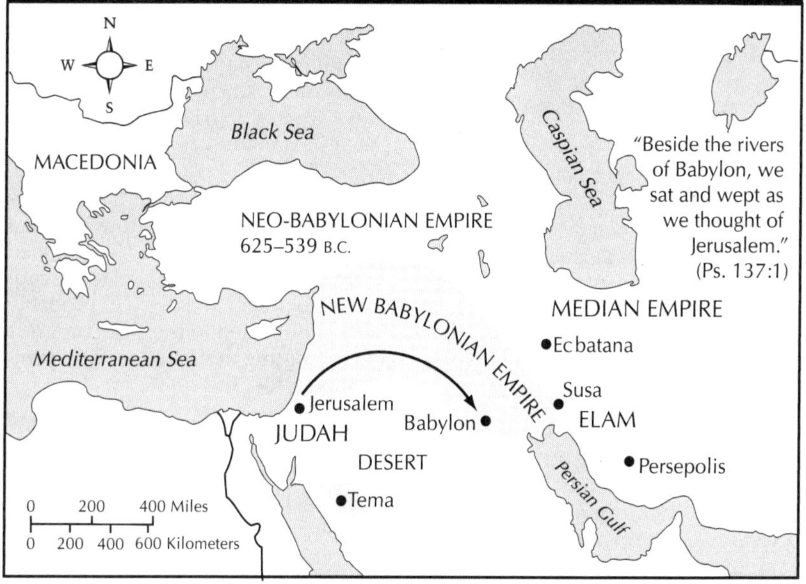

TO JUDAH FROM BABYLON

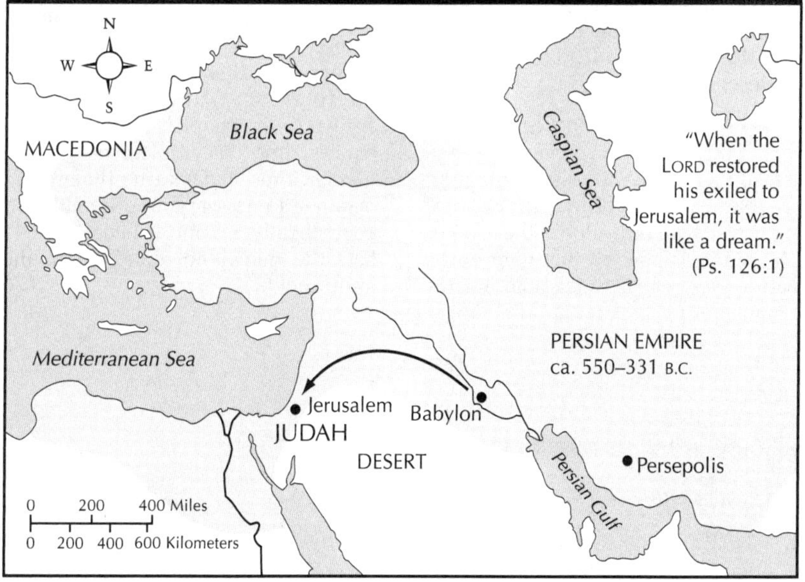

God would protect them, they were "ashamed" to ask him for an armed escort (8:22).

8:24-30 *12 entrusted to transport the treasure.* Ezra gave 12 priests the responsibility for safeguarding the treasures Artaxerxes had given for the Temple.

8:31-36 *Safe arrival, sacrifices, and support.* After what had been an 11-day delay (see 7:9; 8:31), Ezra and the people resumed their journey and arrived safely in Jerusalem, where they offered sacrifices of thanksgiving. Having received word of Artaxerxes' support for these new returnees, the non-Israelites of the region gave them their full support as well (8:36).

9:1-4 *What he hears breaks his heart.* Shortly after arriving in Jerusalem, Ezra was told that many of the Israelites already living there, including the priests, had intermarried with the Canaanites and were practicing their religion. Ezra publicly expressed his dismay at this, and many other concerned Israelites joined with him.

9:5-15 *"When will we ever learn?"* Ezra prayed, acknowledging Israel's long history of sin in spite of divine judgment, and thanking God for his many undeserved mercies.

10:1-4 *"There's still hope," says Shecaniah.* The number of people who had joined Ezra in his mourning (9:4) grew, so that "a large crowd of people" mourned with him. One of the leaders, Shecaniah, suggested that Ezra lead a nationwide reform that would include sending away the foreign wives, along with the children of these mixed marriages. He assured Ezra that such a reform would find wide support.

The "divorce" of a foreign wife would really have been considered an annulment since, according to the law, such a marriage would have been illegal anyway (see Deut. 7:1-3; Mal. 2:16).

As Moses had warned the Israelites (see Deut. 7:4), the foreign wives had turned their hearts from God. Indeed such intermarriage had led to the captivity in the first place. It probably also contributed to the slow progress on rebuilding the Temple (see exposition on 6:13-15).

10:5-9 *A call for reform, in the rain.* Having charged Israel's leaders to join him, Ezra called for all who meant business with God to assemble in Jerusalem on the twentieth day of the ninth month. In spite of a driving rain, many came and stood before Ezra.

10:10-44 *"Repent and renounce these relationships!"* Ezra challenged the men of Israel to repent of their sins and put away their foreign wives. Except for a few dissenters (10:15), the people all agreed to do this. Because of the inclement weather and the legal proceedings of such a process, Ezra agreed to the people's request for adequate time to complete the annulments. Some 90 days after the process began, all necessary annulments had been legally accomplished. 10:18-44 lists the men who took part in the annulments.

PEOPLE TO REMEMBER FROM EZRA

EZRA

Key Fact: Led the second of three returns to Jerusalem following the Babylonian captivity (7–8)

Father: Seraiah (7:1)
Occupation: Priest, scribe, teacher of the law, political leader (7:1-6, 10, 21-26)
Total Bible References: 24
Key References: 7–10; Neh. 8–12

Ezra Speaks

What a glorious eight days! I once thought my first view of Jerusalem was the highlight of my entire life, but not so! What greater joy could a Bible teacher possibly experience than standing on a platform in the city of God, publicly teaching the Word of God from daybreak till noon for a solid week? How good God is, moving the heart of a pagan king to allow me to come here in the first place. And working alongside Nehemiah these many years has been a great blessing. (7:11-26; Neh. 8:1-4, 9, 18)

Lord God of our fathers, you have permitted me to lead your people from Persia to your Holy City and to bring about a great revival among them here. The new Temple has been built, and our city walls are now complete. It is enough! Allow your prophet, priest, scribe, and Bible teacher to depart this life for the eternal one! (6:15; 7:6, 10; 8:32; 10:7-17; Neh. 6:5)

Spiritual Lessons from Ezra

- Careful preparation must precede any successful undertaking. "Ezra had determined to study and obey the law of the LORD" (7:10).
- The more we understand the holiness of God, the more we will understand the seriousness of sin. Ezra understood and mourned greatly (9).

Key Verse

"Ezra had determined to study and obey the law of the LORD and to teach those laws and regulations to the people of Israel" (Ezra 7:10).

ZERUBBABEL

Key Fact: Led the first of three returns to Jerusalem following the Babylonian captivity (2:2)
Father: Either Shealtiel (3:2) or Pedaiah (1 Chron. 3:19)
Brother: Shimei (1 Chron. 3:19)
Sons: Meshullam, Hananiah, Hashubah, Ohel, Berekiah, Hasadiah, Jushab-hesed (1 Chron. 3:19-20)
Daughter: Shelomith (1 Chron. 3:19)
Occupation: Political leader (Hag. 1:1)
Total Bible References: 26
Key References: 2:2; 3:2–5:2; Hag. 1:12–2:23; Zech. 4

Zerubbabel Speaks

It all began with that incredible announcement: "This is what King Cyrus of Persia says: The LORD, the God of heaven, has given me all the kingdoms of the earth. He has appointed me to build him a Temple at Jerusalem. . . ."

I could scarcely believe my ears! Here was a royal decree issued by King Cyrus himself! And yet I should not have been amazed, for Jeremiah predicted this very thing many years ago. But what the prophet did not predict was the fact that the Persian emperor would appoint *me* to lead them back! Little did I or any of the

50,000 who accompanied me realize the trials and triumphs that would confront us during the next 22 years. (1:1-3; Jer. 29:10)

I doubt that there was ever a stranger dedication service than ours when we finished the foundation of the new Temple. It was amazing: Half of the people were laughing for joy and the other half were weeping with sorrow! I wonder what our pagan neighbors must have thought! (3:8-13)

But that was just the beginning. I never realized the damage one slanderous letter could cause. God will someday judge Bishlam and his evil associates for their part in this wickedness. But God controlled the hand of the governor when he wrote that second letter on our behalf. What a tremendous source of reassurance the prophets Haggai, Zechariah, and the high priest Jeshua were to me during those trying days. (4:7; 5:1-17; Hag. 2:1-9)

So here we are, 22 years after leaving Persia, enjoying our completed Temple in the Holy City! No doubt about it: Zechariah's word to me back then says it all: "It is not by force nor by strength, but by my Spirit, says the LORD Almighty." (6:14-15; Zech. 4:6)

Spiritual Lessons from Zerubbabel

- "How can goodness be a partner with wickedness? How can light live with darkness?" (2 Cor. 6:14). Close relationships such as marriage cannot be shared by believers and unbelievers. For Zerubbabel, the building of the Temple was too sacred a task to share with pagans (4:1-3).
- God rewards faithfulness. Because of his zeal, Zerubbabel was promised two things:
  - ➤ He would be allowed to finish building the new Temple (Zech. 4:8-10).
  - ➤ He would be given a special ministry in the Millennium (Hag. 2:23).

Key Verses

"This is what the LORD says to Zerubbabel: It is not by force nor by strength, but by my Spirit, says the LORD Almighty. Nothing, not even a mighty mountain, will stand in Zerubbabel's way; it will flatten out before him! Then Zerubbabel will set the final stone of the Temple in place, and the people will shout: 'May God bless it! May God bless it!'" (Zech. 4:6-7).

NEHEMIAH

473 B.C.
Esther saves Jews still in Persia

457
Exiles return with Ezra

445
Nehemiah rebuilds wall

433
Nehemiah goes to Babylon on state business

432
Nehemiah returns to Jerusalem, finds problems

430
Malachi ministers to exiles

BACKGROUND

See *Ezra: Background.* The book of Nehemiah records Nehemiah's return to Jerusalem from exile in Babylon (445 B.C.), his rebuilding of Jerusalem's walls, his career as a political leader, and his temporary return to Babylon 12 years later (13:6). While Ezra was a priest and Bible teacher who focused his attention on the *purification* of the people of Jerusalem, Nehemiah was a statesman and builder (see exposition on 13:28-31) who focused his attention on their *protection.*

AUTHOR

See *Ezra: Author.* While Ezra probably compiled the book from Nehemiah's memoirs, Nehemiah obviously authored the sections directly attributed to him, including 1–7 and 13, where the first-person pronouns refer to him.

DATE AND LOCATION

See *Ezra: Date and Location.*

RECIPIENTS

See *Ezra: Recipients.*

PURPOSE

See *Ezra: Purpose.*

UNIQUE FEATURES

- Though Esther follows it in the canon, Nehemiah is chronologically the final historical book of the OT.
- Though much of its material was actually compiled by Ezra, Nehemiah is the most autobiographical of the Bible's historical books.
- Nehemiah is one of the best examples in Scripture of a

man committed to a vision and to encouraging others to join him in fulfilling that vision.

- Artaxerxes' decree (2:8) marks the official start of the 70 weeks prophesied in Daniel 9:25-27.

COMPARISON WITH OTHER BIBLE BOOKS

See *Ezra: Comparison with Other Bible Books.*

OUTLINE

NEHEMIAH REBUILDS JERUSALEM'S WALL (1:1–7:3)

- Nehemiah's response to the wall's disrepair (1)
- Nehemiah's request to rebuild the wall (2:1-10)
- Nehemiah's reconnaissance of the broken wall (2:11-20)
- Nehemiah begins rebuilding the wall (3)
- Enemies ridicule, threaten builders (4)
- Remedies for problems among the builders (5)
- Enemies resume opposition (6:1-14)
- Rebuilding completed; security reinforced (6:15–7:3)

EZRA AND NEHEMIAH REVIVE JERUSALEM'S PEOPLE (7:4–13:31)

- Registering those who returned before Nehemiah (7:4-73)
- Ezra reads the law (8)
- The reading leads to revival (9–10)
- Residents of the land listed (11:1–12:26)
- Rebuilt wall dedicated (12:27-47)
- Nehemiah's reforms (13)

NEHEMIAH REBUILDS JERUSALEM'S WALL (1:1–7:3)

1:1-4 *He hears and is heartbroken.* Nehemiah, a Jewish exile who had risen to prominence in the Persian empire (1:11), was among those who had remained in Babylon during the first and second returns of exiles to Judea. Nehemiah's brother Hanani, who had returned, came back to Babylon and reported to him that the Jews in Judea were "in great trouble and disgrace" and that Jerusalem's walls were badly in need of repair. Nehemiah was greatly distressed at the news and spent several days in fasting and prayer.

1:5-11 *His request: God's forgiveness and the king's favor.* Nehemiah confessed both his sins and those of his people. He asked God to acknowledge those among the Jews who were truly seeking him and to honor his promise to fully restore them to the land if they repented. He also asked God to grant a positive reply to a request he evidently planned to make of King Artaxerxes (1:11).

2:1-3 *He tells the king of the trouble.* Noticing one day that Nehemiah seemed depressed, King Artaxerxes asked him what was wrong, and Nehemiah told him of Jerusalem's disrepair. Nehemiah's conversation with Artaxerxes took place in Nisan, the first month of the Jewish year, four months after he had heard of Jerusalem's plight in Kislev, the ninth month of the previous Jewish year (1:1). Both events, however, are said to have taken place in the twentieth year of Artaxerxes' reign. The years of the Babylonian king's reign apparently did not coincide with those of the Hebrew calendar.

2:4-8 *The king's response: Permission to proceed.* Nehemiah requested permission to rebuild Jerusalem's walls, and Artaxerxes granted it. He also requested letters guaranteeing his safe passage and requisitioning timber to repair the city gates. The king granted these requests as well. Artaxerxes was the son of Xerxes, the Persian king who married Esther (Esther 2:16-18). 12 years before sponsoring Nehemiah, Artaxerxes had enabled Ezra's return (Ezra 7).

2:9-10 *But the provincial powers are not pleased.* Accompanied by a military escort, Nehemiah journeyed to Judea and presented his credentials to the local leaders. Two of the leaders, Sanballat and Tobiah, were "very angry" at Nehemiah's intention of helping the Jews. They would both remain bitter foes of the rebuilding effort. 4:2 suggests that Sanballat's political power may have been centered in Samaria, which had been the capital of Israel's northern kingdom. He may have feared a revival of the rivalry between Samaria and Jerusalem.

2:11-16 *Nehemiah's midnight mission.* Under cover of darkness, Nehemiah inspected the city walls, not even revealing his plans to the fellow Jews who accompanied him.

2:17-18 *The recommendation: "Rise up and rebuild!"* On the following day Nehemiah met with the Jewish leaders, told them of his mission, of God's blessing, and of the king's permission to rebuild. When he challenged them to help him, the leaders responded positively and began the work without delay.

2:19-20 *Enter the troublemaking trio.* Sanballat, Tobiah, and Geshem ridiculed the rebuilding project. Nehemiah responded by proclaiming his confidence that God would help them, and his conviction that Jerusalem belonged to the Jewish people.

3:1-32 *The builders and their bailiwicks.* Nehemiah methodically listed the people who worked on the wall, along with the section of wall each worked on. The picture given is of people from many walks of life becoming involved in the project in many different ways. Several of the people simply repaired the portion of wall adjacent to their own homes. One group was singled out as being less than zealous about their work (3:5), though the speedy completion of the project (6:15) in the face of great odds indicates that most of the people worked enthusiastically. In describing the work, Nehemiah gives the names of Jerusalem's 10 gates—the only such listing in Scripture.

4:1-6 *"Even a fox could make it fall!"* Noting the rebuilders' speedy progress (4:2), Sanballat and Tobiah once again ridiculed their efforts. Nehemiah responded with prayer. Soon, thanks to the workers' enthusiasm (4:6), the wall was half finished.

4:7-20 *Half workers, half warriors.* As the conspiracy against his workers grew ever stronger, Nehemiah continued to pray for them (4:9). Eventually, he had to begin arming them: Half of them stood guard while the other half worked. Even those doing the building were armed (4:18). Ensuring safety was made especially difficult by the fact that the workers were thinly spread out along the wall (4:19-20).

4:21-23 *Working and watching from dawn to dusk.* The sunrise-to-sunset work schedule and foregoing of creature comforts show the dedication and urgency with which the people pursued their task. The round-the-clock guards show the degree of danger they faced.

5:1-13 *Amid the fight, a family conflict.* As if the armed opposition to his building project were not enough, Nehemiah learned that some of the wealthier Israelites were taking advantage of their poorer countrymen. He severely rebuked the greedy rich at a public meeting, demanding that they begin helping the poor. They were convicted by his words and agreed to do so.

5:14-19 *A politician who pays his own way.* Nehemiah noted that he had always held himself to the same high standard he demanded of the wealthy:

- During the 12 years of his first term as governor, he took no salary and even paid the food bills for 150 of his helpers (5:14, 17-18).
- He had not only supervised the rebuilding of the walls but had also done some of the actual labor himself (5:16).
- He loaned money to needy Jews (5:10).

Nehemiah asked the Lord to remember the good he had done for Israel (5:19; see 13:14, 22, 31).

6:1-4 *Four invitations, and he refuses all four.* Four times Nehemiah's opponents invited him to meet with them at a location away from Jerusalem. Realizing these were actually plots to lure him into a trap, Nehemiah refused all four invitations, saying, in essence, "I'm doing a great work, so why should I waste my time meeting with you?"

6:5-9 *Then, an accusation: "You're trying to be king!"* Sanballat's next tactic was to send Nehemiah a letter charging that, as soon as the wall was rebuilt, he planned to proclaim himself king of Judah and rebel against Artaxerxes. He threatened to send the letter to Artaxerxes himself unless Nehemiah met with him. Once again Nehemiah refused.

6:10-14 *Then, the "Temple temptation."* Shemaiah, a false prophet, told Nehemiah that his foes were threatening to kill him and suggested that he seek sanctuary in the Temple. Nehemiah realized, however, that Shemaiah had been hired by Sanballat and Tobiah and that the offer of sanctuary was a clever attempt to discredit him in the eyes of his followers by making him violate the sanctity of the Temple.

6:15–7:3 *Its foes frustrated, the wall is finished.* Jerusalem's wall was completely rebuilt, and 10 new gates were built, in just 52 days. Judah's enemies were both frightened and humiliated, realizing that this could have been accomplished only by the power of God. Tobiah, however, through his inside connections with disloyal Jews (6:17-18; see 13:4-9), continued to make trouble. Realizing he still had foes both inside and outside the city, Nehemiah kept his round-the-clock guards on permanent duty (7:1-3).

EZRA AND NEHEMIAH REVIVE JERUSALEM'S PEOPLE (7:4–13:31)

7:4-73 *A record of those already there.* While taking a census, Nehemiah found a list of the nearly 50,000 exiles who had come to Jerusalem in the first return (Ezra 1–6). Few of these, however, had settled in Jerusalem (7:4), possibly because of its disrepair and the dangers involved in living there. Nehemiah would shortly initiate an effort to repopulate the capital (11:1-2).

8:1-12 *Public school at the Water Gate.* Ezra stood in a public square next to the Water Gate, reading from the Law each day from morning till noon. As he read, 13 Levite scholars moved among the people explaining what was being read (8:7-8). The people maintained a humble, worshipful attitude during the reading (8:5-6). When the leaders saw that the people were weeping, they encouraged them to see the occasion as one of joy rather than sorrow (8:9).

8:13-18 *Home sweet home for seven days.* As Ezra read the law, he came to the passage concerning the Festival of Shelters. Realizing that it was the time of year for this festival, the people immediately began observing it. The writer notes that this festival had not been observed since the days of Joshua—a lapse of nearly 1,000 years.

The Passover also suffered neglect throughout Israel's history (see exposition on 2 Kings 23:21-23). While Ezra records its observance by the first group of returning exiles (Ezra 6:16-22), there is no specific mention of it in Nehemiah's account. These and most other Israelite festivals should have been celebrated yearly (see *Israel's Festivals,* p. 904).

9:1-38 *The people, then Ezra, confess their sins.* As Ezra continued to read the Law, time was given for the people to respond by confessing their sins and worshiping. Ezra then led them in a prayer of confession. His prayer progresses historically:

From Creation to Canaan (9:6-21). He acknowledged God as Creator and as the one who had both founded Israel and preserved it in spite of its many sins.

From Canaan to the Return (9:22-31). He then reviewed God's faithfulness and mercy in the days of Joshua, the judges, and the kings.

Israel's present situation (9:32-38). Ezra then surveyed the present circumstances, which were not good: The people were, in essence, slaves in their own land. He ended by calling on the people to make a covenant with God (9:38).

10:1-39 *And they agree, in writing, to do better.* The people agreed to make a covenant. 10:1-27 lists the leaders who "ratified and sealed" the written covenant; 10:28-29 mentions those who gave their oral consent; and 10:30-39 gives the text of the covenant. They made a four-part vow: to avoid intermarriage with non-Israelites, to avoid profaning the Sabbath, to maintain the Temple, and to tithe faithfully.

11:1-2 *One out of 10 moves in.* With Jerusalem firmly reestablished as Israel's political and religious capital, the leaders now addressed the problem of its underpopulation (see 7:4). They decreed that a 10th of the country's population should move to Jerusalem. Though lots were cast to determine who would move there, some freely chose to do so.

11:3-24 *Who's who in Jerusalem.* Nehemiah listed the various groups of people living in Jerusalem, including the political leaders (11:3-9), priests (11:10-14), Levites (11:15-18), and gatekeepers (11:19). In some cases, he specified the jobs these people performed. Pethahiah (11:24) was Judah's representative to the Persian court.

11:25-36 *The other 90 percent.* Nehemiah then listed the cities outside Jerusalem where returned exiles were living. All of these cities were in the regions historically occupied by Judah and Benjamin.

12:1-26 *More records of priests and Levites.* Nehemiah then recorded various lists of priests and Levites who had served or were serving in Jerusalem, in some cases specifying their duties.

12:27-43 *A dedication in two directions.* Levites from throughout the land came to Jerusalem for the dedication of the new wall. Nehemiah divided the leaders into two groups and instructed them to walk in opposite directions along the wall, giving thanks, singing, and blowing trumpets as they went. The celebration could be heard for miles around (12:43).

12:44-47 *Musicians and money men.* Levites were appointed to handle the collection and distribution of tithes and to direct the music ministry. The writer nostalgically recalled the great Temple singers of David's time.

13:1-3 *"Separate from the Ammonites and Moabites."* While reading the law, the Jews discovered the ancient curse against the Ammonites and Moabites, prohibiting them from taking part in Israelite worship because of their treacheries against Israel (Deut. 23:3-4). When the people learned of this curse, "all those of mixed ancestry were immediately expelled from the assembly."

13:4-9 *"Especially from that Ammonite!"* Sometime before this, Eliashib the high priest had extended hospitality to Tobiah, one of Nehemiah's fiercest opponents, who was an Ammonite (4:3). He had provided this enemy of Israel a guest room in the Temple! Nehemiah had been in Babylon when this happened. Upon returning to Jerusalem and hearing of Tobiah's housing arrangement, he threw him and all his belongings out of the Temple and "purified" the room where he had been staying.

Nehemiah's visit to Babylon (13:6) would have fulfilled his implied promise to Artaxerxes (2:6) to return to his duties there after his mission to Jerusalem. Having returned to Babylon, Nehemiah was apparently permitted to return again to Jerusalem. The trip occurred 12 years after Nehemiah's first arrival in Jerusalem (compare 5:14 and 13:6). Nehemiah's need to report back to Babylon and Ezra's remarks about Israel's subservience (9:36-37) show Persia's continuing control over the returned exiles.

13:10-14 *Without pay, the singers can't sing.* Upon his return to Jerusalem, Nehemiah also discovered that the Levites were not receiving their rightful salaries and had therefore been forced to give up their Temple duties and resume farming to feed their families. Nehemiah took measures to assure that the tithes were properly collected and disbursed to the priests and Levites.

13:15-22 *"Don't sell on the Sabbath."* Nehemiah also noticed many people doing business on the Sabbath. He rebuked them and ordered the city gates closed from Friday evening till Saturday evening.

13:23-27 *Talk about righteous indignation!* Nehemiah also found several Jews who had intermarried with foreigners, despite their promise not to do so (10:30). He severely rebuked them, called down curses on them, and in some cases beat them and pulled out their hair!

13:28-31 *Rebuilder and reformer.* Nehemiah drove from the Temple the grandson of Eliashib the high priest, who had married Sanballat's daughter. He then proceeded to purge all foreign influences from Israel's religious life and to take further steps to organize the duties of the priests and Levites.

Nehemiah's achievements were remarkable:

- He was responsible for the rebuilding of Jerusalem's walls (1:1–7:3).
- With Ezra's help, he rebuilt Israel's social and religious life as well (7:4–13:31).

His achievements are all the more remarkable considering that Eliashib, his high priest, was closely connected with two of Israel's worst enemies (13:4, 28).

PEOPLE TO REMEMBER FROM NEHEMIAH

ARTAXERXES
Key Facts: King of Persia, allowed Ezra and Nehemiah to return to Jerusalem (2:1-8; Ezra 7)
Father: Xerxes (Ahasuerus)
Total Bible References: 9
Key References: 2:1-8; 13:6; Ezra 4:7-23; 7

Artaxerxes Speaks
Well, they're both gone now. I must be getting soft in my old age, allowing two of the best public servants a king ever had to leave and march off for some far-off land! First there was Ezra the scribe, a totally loyal and dedicated man. That's probably one of the reasons I used both my authority and my financial resources to help him in his trip to Jerusalem. But I guess an even more important reason was to honor the memory of my dead father, Xerxes. I think he would have approved. I know his queen wife, Esther, a Jewess herself, would have strongly supported my actions! (Ezra 7:6, 10-11, 13-26; Esther 1:1; 2:16-18)

But wouldn't you know it: Less than 12 years after Ezra left, Nehemiah, my chief cupbearer, approached me with a similar request—so I helped him as well. My sources tell me he has just completed his original mission, the rebuilding of the walls of his beloved city. That's wonderful! I wish nothing but the best for both Nehemiah and Ezra. Their God has indeed blessed them. Could it be that the Jehovah of Israel is the true God, just as they have always claimed? (2:1-8; 6:15)

Spiritual Lesson from Artaxerxes
- Like Artaxerxes, many nonbelievers are sympathetic to many aspects of God's cause. They should be special objects of our prayers and witness (2:1-9; Ezra 7; see Mark 12:28-34). Note especially Ezra 7:25, where Artaxerxes actually decrees the teaching of the law!

Key Verses
"Praise the LORD, the God of our ancestors, who made the king want to beautify the Temple of the LORD in Jerusalem! And praise him for demonstrating such unfailing love to me by honoring me before the king, his council, and all his mighty princes! I felt encouraged because the gracious hand of the LORD my God was on me. And I gathered some of the leaders of Israel to return with me to Jerusalem" (Ezra 7:27-28).

NEHEMIAH
Key Fact: Returned from Babylonian captivity to rebuild Jerusalem's wall (7:1)
Father: Hacaliah (1:1)
Brother: Hanani (1:2)
Total Bible References: 5
Key References: 1–7, 13

Nehemiah Speaks

Can it be that 12 years have gone by since that terrible winter day when I first learned about the plight of Jerusalem? How faithful God was, some four months later—in the springtime!—to soften the king's heart so that he sent me on my first pilgrimage to the Holy City. I'll never forget the sight of those burned and broken-down walls! (1:1-3; 2:1-16; 13:6)

Nor will I ever forget the welcome words of my fellow Jews in Jerusalem when I challenged them to help me rebuild the walls: "Good! Let's rebuild the wall!" That's what they said! And they immediately began to work. And God was so faithful, enabling us to do in just 52 days what ordinarily would have taken many years to accomplish! (2:17-18; 6:15)

Then there were the ridicule and taunts of Sanballat and Tobiah: "That stone wall would collapse if even a fox walked along the top of it!" That's what those pagans said about our wall. But not so! How strong this wall is, surrounding Jerusalem! How beautiful its 10 gates! Small wonder the utter humiliation of our foes upon its completion (3:1-31; 4:3; 6:16).

It was awesome indeed to see Ezra, that mighty scribe, standing on a platform by the Water Gate, reading and interpreting God's Word! Who could have *not* signed that covenant after hearing him! (8:1-8; 10:1-27)

Finally, there was that glorious music on dedication day. My ears still ring with the sound of those two choirs walking in opposite directions atop the wall, accompanied by cymbals, harps, lyres, and trumpets. "The joy of the LORD is your strength!" That's what I said back then. That's what I still believe today. (8:10; 12:27-40)

Spiritual Lessons from Nehemiah

- Prayer is the first and most important step in any project for God (1:4-11).
- Righteousness brings boldness (Prov. 28:1). Nehemiah dared request from the king a leave of absence that would last 12 years (2:5-8; 5:14)!
- Any group effort will succeed or fail on the strength of its leadership (2:11-18). Among Nehemiah's key leadership qualities were
  - ➤ total confidence in God (4:14);
  - ➤ faithfulness in prayer (4:4-5, 9; 6:9);
  - ➤ refusal to compromise (2:19-20);
  - ➤ willingness to share in the actual work (5:16).
- It is amazing what can be accomplished when our work is inspired by devotion to the Lord. Nehemiah guided the rebuilding effort to completion in just 52 days (6:15; see Phil. 4:13).
- Nehemiah learned that spiritual warfare requires both offensive and defensive weapons (4:13-23). See Ephesians 6:12-16 (defensive weapons) and Ephesians 6:17 (offensive weapons).

Key Verse

"Then I told them about how the gracious hand of God had been on me, and about my conversation with the king. They replied at once, 'Good! Let's rebuild the wall!' So they began the good work" (2:18).

538 B.C.
Exiles return
with Zerubbabel

473
Esther saves
Jews still in Persia

457
More exiles
return with Ezra

445
Nehemiah
rebuilds wall

ESTHER

BACKGROUND

In 486 B.C., 52 years after Cyrus had permitted Zerubbabel to lead the first group of Jewish exiles from Babylon back to Judea (Ezra 1–2), Xerxes (also called Ahasuerus) became king of the Persian Empire. In about 478, Xerxes married a Jewish exile named Esther. The book bearing her name tells the story of how Esther, because of her marriage to Xerxes, was able to defeat a plan to exterminate all Jews in the Persian Empire (which would have included those who had returned to Judea). More Jews would return to Judea during the reign of Xerxes' son Artaxerxes (Ezra 6–7; Neh. 2). Many, however, would choose to remain in Babylon and other parts of the Persian Empire.

AUTHOR

Unknown. The author's familiarity with minor details of the story and with Persian customs, in addition to his obvious sympathy with the Jewish exiles, suggests that he was probably a Jew living in Persia at the time the events of the book took place. Mordecai's journal (9:20) may have been one of his sources.

DATE AND LOCATION

The familiarity with details (see *Author*) suggests Esther was written soon after the events it records, probably c. 450 B.C., and probably in Persia.

PURPOSE

- To encourage the Jews remaining in Babylon and the rest of Persia to remain firm in their faith.
- To show those Jews who had returned to Judah that God was at work among his people outside of Judah as well.
- To demonstrate, to all believers, God's providential care for his people.

UNIQUE FEATURES

- Esther and the Song of Songs are the only two biblical books that do not mention the name of God.
- Esther records the origin of the Festival of Purim (9:16-19) and is the only biblical book to mention this festival.

COMPARISON WITH OTHER BIBLE BOOKS

See *Ruth: Comparison with Other Bible Books.*

OUTLINE

THE RISE OF ESTHER (1–2)
- The rejection of Vashti (1)
- The selection of Esther (2:1-18)
- Mordecai's detection saves the king (2:19-23)

THE LIES OF HAMAN (3–5)
- Haman's request to exterminate the Jews (3)
- Mordecai's request that Esther intervene (4)
- Esther's request that the king spare the Jews (5)

THE PRIZE OF FAITH (6–10)
- Mordecai honored for his loyalty (6)
- Haman hanged for his treachery (7)
- Mordecai promoted; his people preserved (8:1–9:17)
- Purim: Celebrating the preservation (9:18-32)
- Mordecai remembered (10)

THE RISE OF ESTHER (1–2)

1:1-8 *A six-month show of his gold and glory.* For 180 days, King Xerxes of Persia hosted the various officials of Persia's 127 provinces in the capital city of Susa, evidently seeking to impress them with his wealth and power. At the end of the six months, he gave a lavish week-long feast (1:5-8).

Though the biblical account does not state this, Xerxes may have been trying to build morale for another assault on Greece. His father, Darius the Great, had been soundly defeated by Greece at the Battle of Marathon in 490 B.C. The week-long feast occurred in 482. Xerxes would himself be defeated by Greece in 480 and 479. Despite such defeats, Xerxes controlled a vast empire, stretching from India to Ethiopia (1:1).

1:9-22 *Queen Vashti rejected for her refusal.* On the seventh day of the feast, the half-drunk king summoned Queen Vashti to appear and parade before his intoxicated guests. When she refused to do so, the angry but uncertain king consulted his lawyers, who immediately suggested he divorce her, so that her unsubmissive attitude would not be imitated by women all over Persia. Xerxes agreed and promptly divorced her.

1:19 is the book's first reference to the fact that a "law of the Persians and Medes" could not be revoked. This feature of Persian law would play a key role in the unfolding story (see exposition on 2:1-14 and on 8:1-8). Some scholars see this finality of laws as an example of the pride of the Medo-Persian civilization: They couldn't face the fact that any of their laws could possibly be wrong!

2:1-14 *A contest to name a new queen.* After his wrath had subsided, and presumably when he was again sober, Xerxes apparently regretted having divorced Vashti (2:1). Yet even the king was bound by the finality of Persian law (see 1:19). Sensing the king's regret, his aides suggested a search be made to find the most beautiful young woman in the empire, who would become the new queen. One of the contestants was a Jewish woman named Esther. Upon the advice of her cousin Mordecai, Esther kept her Jewish nationality secret.

2:15-18 *The Jewish woman wins the contest and the crown.* After a six-month course in the art of beauty and charm, Esther and the other contestants were taken to the palace. It was love at first sight for the king, and he immediately made Esther his new queen.

2:19-23 *He saved the king's life: It's in the book!* Mordecai, who had become a government official, overheard and reported a plot to kill the king. The men involved were executed, and the incident was duly recorded in the palace records.

THE LIES OF HAMAN (3–5)

3:1-11 *"Kill them all, and I'll cover the cost."* About four years later, Xerxes appointed as his prime minister a cruel and arrogant man named Haman. The king demanded that all other officials bow down to Haman, but Mordecai declared that, as a Jew, he could not do so. When Haman noticed that Mordecai refused to bow, and learned of his racial background, he became furious and asked the king to exterminate all Jews in the kingdom, pledging to personally cover any costs incurred. Xerxes agreed, saying that the royal bank would pay for the massacre. Haman decided, by casting lots (3:7), that the massacre should take place in the twelfth month of the year (he cast the lots during the first month). Xerxes apparently signed the decree without even realizing precisely what racial group he had agreed to exterminate (3:8-11)!

Haman claimed that his desire to kill the Jews arose from his concern about the security threat their insubordination might pose for the empire (3:8). But the fact that Haman was an "Agagite" (3:1) may help explain his deep hatred. Many scholars believe this means he was an Amalekite descended from King Agag, who was spared by Saul and then killed by Samuel (see 1 Sam. 15). The Amalekites had long been bitter enemies of Israel, having attacked them while they journeyed to Canaan (see Exod. 17:8-16; Deut. 25:17-19).

Although Haman had claimed he was willing to cover the costs of the massacre, his order that the Jews' possessions be plundered (3:13) suggests he was motivated in part by greed.

3:12-15 *A savage decree and a social drink.* Xerxes signed and sent to all the provinces a decree that, on the thirteenth day of the twelfth month, every Jew in the empire was to be slaughtered. Having issued this horrendous decree, the king and Haman "sat down to drink." Meanwhile, the people of Susa "fell into confusion" over the barbaric plan.

4:1-9 *"Plead for your people!"* Upon learning of the decree, Mordecai tore his clothes and stood outside the palace gate in sackcloth, mourning loudly. As Jews throughout the empire heard of the edict, they mourned as well. Hearing that her cousin was mourning, Queen Esther sent a messenger to determine the cause of his sorrow. Mordecai explained about the edict and told the messenger to urge Esther to petition the king on behalf of her people.

4:10-17 *"It could mean death, but duty demands it!"* By way of her messenger, Esther reminded Mordecai that approaching the king uninvited for any reason could mean instant death. Mordecai in turn reminded her that, even as queen of the empire, she should not expect to escape the approaching holocaust. He urged her to view her royal position as God's provision for saving his people. Convicted by Mordecai's words, Esther agreed to approach the king, soliciting her people's prayers as she did so.

Though God is not specifically mentioned in Esther, Mordecai's belief that Esther had become queen "for just such a time as this" and that "deliverance for the Jews will arise from some other place" if she didn't act (4:14), shows his firm trust in God's providence.

5:1-8 *Graciously received, to her great relief!* Much to Esther's relief, Xerxes was not offended by her unexpected visit. To the contrary, he welcomed her warmly. He asked her what she wanted, promising, "I will give it to you, even if it is half the kingdom!" Esther's only response was to invite the king, along with Haman, to a banquet later in the day. At that banquet, she refused to reveal her request unless the two men would attend a second banquet.

5:9-14 *Only one hitch to Haman's happiness.* Hearing that Esther had invited him to a second banquet, Haman was elated. On his way home, however, he once again encountered Mordecai, who once again refused to bow. At home, Haman bragged about his two banquet invitations but also complained about Mordecai. Upon the suggestion of his wife and friends, Haman had a 75-foot-high gallows built, intending the next day to ask Xerxes to hang Mordecai on it.

THE PRIZE OF FAITH (6–10)

6:1-3 *A big surprise for a sleepless king.* Unable to sleep, Xerxes ordered the historical record to be read. From it he was reminded of how Mordecai had once saved his life (see 2:19-23). He also learned, to his dismay, that Mordecai had never been rewarded for his bravery.

6:4-14 *A bigger surprise for a humiliated Haman.* At that moment Haman arrived at the palace, seeking permission to hang Mordecai. Knowing nothing of Haman's intentions, the king innocently asked his advice on how to give special honor to a deserving person. Assuming the king was referring to him, Haman recommended a lavish public procession.

Much to Haman's chagrin, the king put him in charge of the proposed procession and informed him that the honoree was Mordecai! Haman dutifully led the procession for Mordecai and returned home in humiliation. Learning of his humiliation, Haman's friends advised him to give up his vendetta against Mordecai. At that moment Haman was summoned to attend Esther's second banquet.

Even Haman's pagan friends evidently recognized a special divine blessing on the Jewish people (6:13).

7:1-10 *Esther's request and Haman's hanging.* Finally, at her second banquet for Xerxes and Haman, Esther told the king of the plot against her people and asked that the king do something to save them. When she revealed that Haman had instigated the plot, Xerxes became furious. The king's anger was further fueled by a misinterpreted coincidence (7:7-8) and by the news that Haman had built a gallows to hang Mordecai. He immediately ordered that Haman, instead, be hanged.

Xerxes' anger upon learning that Haman had instigated the plot against the Jews (7:6-7) contrasts sharply with his earlier casual attitude toward Haman's plans (3:8-15). The king may have wrongly assumed that Haman knew that Esther was a Jew and that the proposed massacre was a plot against her.

8:1-8 *"Write another decree, and I'll sign it."* When Xerxes learned of Mordecai's relationship to Esther, he appointed him to the office vacated by Haman's death. Esther then asked the king to write a second decree to annul the extermination decree. The king instructed Esther and Mordecai to write the decree themselves, indicating he would authorize whatever they wrote.

8:8 mentions once again the fact that Persian laws could not be changed (see 1:19; exposition on 2:1-14). Esther and Mordecai faced the challenge of writing a second decree that would nullify the effects of the first one. The massacre would still be carried out; it would be up to their second decree to minimize its severity!

8:9-17 *Their new decree: "Defend yourselves!"* Under Mordecai's direction, the king's scribes drew up a new decree that permitted the Jews to defend themselves against the planned massacre. Understandably, this new decree produced great joy in Jewish communities throughout the empire. The joy in the capital city was enhanced when Mordecai appeared in public in the "royal robe" of his new office (8:15).

The decree also led many non-Jews to adopt the Jewish faith (8:17). Some of these may have been sincere proselytes, convinced by one more sign of God's providence (6:13). Others may have been motivated by fear of being on the losing side (8:17).

9:1-17 *Instead of genocide, "the opposite happened."* When the day of the planned massacre arrived, rather than the enemies of the Jews overpowering them, "quite the opposite happened" (9:1), and the Jews defeated their enemies. The cause of the Jews was helped by the decision of government officials throughout the empire to side with them (9:3). This official support was due to Mordecai's rising stature in the empire (9:4). In all, the Jews killed 75,000 of their enemies, including Haman's 10 sons.

While the Jews in Susa extended the battle against their enemies to a second day (9:11-15), the Jews throughout the rest of the empire celebrated their victory (9:16-17).

The account of the massacre shows that the Jews had many enemies in the empire besides Haman (see especially 9:1, 16). Haman's prejudice (3:8) was apparently widely shared.

9:18-32 *A special festival, lest they forget.* Having completed their two days of fighting, the Jews in Susa, the capital, held their own celebration. Mordecai then decreed that his people should establish the fourteenth and fifteenth days of the month of Adar as a yearly festival to celebrate their victory. They called the festival Purim (9:26) to commemorate the fact that Haman had tried to decide their fate by the casting of lots ("purim," see 3:7). Esther wrote a letter confirming Mordecai's decree (9:29-32). Purim is still an important celebration among Jews and still includes feasting and gift-giving (9:18-19).

In addition to saving the Jews from extermination under Xerxes, Esther no doubt exercised a great influence upon her stepson Artaxerxes, who later allowed more Jews to return to Judea under Ezra and Nehemiah.

10:1-3 *Praised by his people and the Persians.* Mordecai was second in command to King Xerxes, and his wise leadership brought him great respect both among his own people and among non-Jewish Persians.

PEOPLE TO REMEMBER FROM ESTHER

ESTHER
Key Facts: Israelite exile, became queen of Persian Empire, saved her people from attempted holocaust (2:17; 7:3-6; 8:3-8)
Father: Abihail (2:15)
Husband: Xerxes (2:16-17)
Total Bible References: 55
Key References: 2; 4–9

Esther Speaks

"Who can say but that you have been elevated to the palace for just such a time as this?" That's the secret message Mordecai sent me during those dark hours. Looking back, I can see just how right he was! God had allowed a pagan king to select me as his queen so that I might be used to help save my people from their enemies. (4:14; 8:3-8)

That wicked and cruel Haman! I can understand how Moses must have felt when he withstood the onslaughts of that evil Egyptian king. Probably the turning point in all this came after that three-day fast when I risked death by entering the king's room uninvited. The relief was indescribable when he held out his golden scepter. I'll never forget the astonishment on his face when he learned I had endangered my life just to invite him to dinner! He probably didn't even think I could cook! (Exod. 5–12; 4:16–5:4)

What a wondrous series of events then took place. Who could possibly have imagined that a case of royal insomnia would help save a life and eventually a nation! Mordecai and I now join in this happy celebration here in Susa. It is the 14th of Adar, and we are calling it the festival of Purim. May this glad day always be remembered by future generations! (6:1-6; 9:18-19, 26)

Spiritual Lessons from Esther

- God had brought Esther to her place of influence in the kingdom of Persia "for just such a time as this" (4:14). Likewise, believers today have been placed in their "palaces"—their spheres of influence—in order to do "the good things [God] planned for us long ago" (Eph. 2:10).
- Truly serving others on God's behalf may mean risking our own peace and security (4:10-16).

Key Verse

"Go and gather together all the Jews of Susa and fast for me. Do not eat or drink for three days, night or day. My maids and I will do the same. And then, though it is against the law, I will go in to see the king. If I must die, I am willing to die" (4:16).

HAMAN
Key Facts: Prime minister under Xerxes, tried to exterminate the Jews (3:1-9)
Father: Hammedatha (3:1)
Wife: Zeresh (5:14)

Sons: Parshandatha, Dalphon, Aspatha, Poratha, Adalia, Aridatha, Parmashta, Arisai, Aridai, Vaizatha (9:7-10)
Death: Recorded in 7:10
Total Bible References: 52
Key References: 3–7

Haman Speaks

That stupid wife of mine! I'm in this terrible situation because of her wrong advice! Then, when it is too late to help, she comes up with the correct conclusion! A thousand curses on the God of Abraham! What a mess. How was I to know the king's miserable wife was Jewish or that he had that worthless Mordecai in mind when he asked my advice about honoring someone? (2:10; 5:14; 6:6-7, 13)

Or maybe it was the way I had thrown myself across the couch where Esther sat. Of course he totally misunderstood my intentions. I was merely pleading for my life, as any rational person would have done. (7:7-8)

Well, whatever the case, my doom is sealed. The guards have stopped now. We've arrived. I mean, who could miss it, a 75-foot-high gallows! (5:14; 7:10)

Spiritual Lessons from Haman

- God protects his people (see Gen. 12:3; Isa. 54:17):
  - ➤ Pharaoh learned that God's people could not be drowned (Exod. 14).
  - ➤ Nebuchadnezzar learned that they could not be burned (Dan. 3).
  - ➤ Darius learned that they could not be eaten by lions (Dan. 6).
  - ➤ Haman learned that they could not be hanged (5:14; 7:10).
- "Human opposition only enhances [God's] glory" (Ps. 76:10). Haman was one of several biblical people who proved the psalmist right (see exposition on Ezra 6:1-12). God can use even the opposition of his enemies to his glory (3:1-11; 9:16).
- Envy is like a cancer as it eats away at its victim (5:9-13).
- We always reap what we sow (5:14; 7:10; see Prov. 26:27; Hos. 8:7; Gal. 6:7).

Key Verses

"When Haman saw that Mordecai would not bow down or show him respect, he was filled with rage. So he decided it was not enough to lay hands on Mordecai alone. Since he had learned that Mordecai was a Jew, he decided to destroy all the Jews throughout the entire empire of Xerxes" (3:5-6).

MORDECAI

Key Facts: Israelite exile, Esther's cousin, helped her save Jews from extermination, became prime minister of Persia (2:7; 4:1-14; 10:3)
Father: Jair (2:5)
Total Bible References: 56
Key References: 2–10

Mordecai Speaks

Just think of it! As a boy I was carried from Jerusalem into captivity by a cruel empire. Now, as an old man, I serve as prime minister of the empire that defeated that first empire! (2:5-6; 8:2; 10:2; Dan. 5:30-31)

And there was that other amazing turn of events: My bitterest enemy, who tried to hang me, wound up honoring me instead—and then was hanged himself on the gallows he had built for me! (5:14; 6:6-11; 7:10)

My rise to the top began when the king—with a little help from Haman!—honored me for my courage. But it was Esther's courage that inspired us all and spurred us on to defeat our many enemies throughout the empire. (2:19-23; 4:16–5:8; 6:1-11; 7:1-4)

Still, the king seems to think I've done a good enough job both for my own people and for the rest of his constituency. He says I'll have a place in his written family history. Though I said it concerning her, perhaps both Esther and I came to the palace "for just such a time as this." (4:14; 10:1-3)

Spiritual Lessons from Mordecai

- Right actions will be rewarded, even though the reward may be delayed (2:21-23; 6:1-11).
- We should not hesitate to speak up for a worthwhile cause. Mordecai publicized his people's peril (4:1-3); solicited Esther's help (4:7-8); and, when she did not take action immediately, exhorted her to do so (4:13-14). His willingness "to say the right thing at the right time" (Prov. 15:23) helped save the nation.

Key Verses

"Mordecai sent back this reply to Esther: 'Don't think for a moment that you will escape there in the palace when all other Jews are killed. If you keep quiet at a time like this, deliverance for the Jews will arise from some other place, but you and your relatives will die. What's more, who can say but that you have been elevated to the palace for just such a time as this?'" (4:13-14)

XERXES

Key Facts: King of Persian Empire, married Esther (1:1-3; 2:15-18)
Wives: Vashti, Esther (1:9; 2:15-18)
Total Bible References: 28
Key References: 1–10; Ezra 4:6

Xerxes Speaks

What an incredible turn of events: My former prime minister was hanged from the same 75-foot-high gallows he had prepared for my present prime minister! Was all this a mere coincidence, or could it be that invisible Hebrew God working quietly behind the scenes? (4:14; 5:14; 7:10)

Well, whatever the case, Haman got just what he deserved! His prejudice, greed, and pride were bad enough, but he crossed the line by plotting against my wife! The nerve of that shifty-eyed Agagite! (3:1, 8-13; 6:6, 13; 7:6)

Apparently the Jews have survived the attempted purge. I'm glad it worked out that way. I was tricked into signing that death warrant in the first place. (3:8; 9:16)

Esther's courage continues to impress me. She is indeed what her name suggests, a bright star! I'll show my respect for her by supporting the new festival of Purim she helped institute. (2:7; 4:15–5:5; 9:26)

Mordecai has demonstrated real leadership capacity. He's been a great prime minister. Of course, had it not been for him, I'd probably be in my grave today! It will be an honor to have his name mentioned along with mine in that book they're writing about my family. (2:21-23; 3:8; 10:2)

Spiritual Lessons from Xerxes

- Careless actions can have long-term consequences. The abrupt and thoughtless actions of Xerxes cost him one wife (1:10-22) and nearly resulted in the death of his beloved second wife (2:10; 3:8-15). Act in haste; repent at leisure!
- Love is the foundation of marriage. While Xerxes was obviously not a believer, he did nevertheless love and honor Esther (2:17; 5:1-3; see Eph. 5:25; 1 Pet. 3:7).

Key Verse

"Then [Xerxes] asked her, 'What do you want, Queen Esther? What is your request? I will give it to you, even if it is half the kingdom!'" (5:3)

2090 B.C.
Call of Abraham

c. 2007?
Job

1805
Death of Joseph, end of Genesis

JOB

BACKGROUND

Job is the first of five OT books of poetry—first in both canonical and historical order. With a date as early as 2000 B.C. (the time of Abraham), Job may be the Bible's oldest book. It tells the story of Job, a righteous and wealthy man whom God allowed Satan to tempt through great suffering. Though poetic in form, Job, like the other biblical books of poetry, is firmly rooted in history. Both Ezekiel (14:14, 20) and James (5:10-11) considered Job a historical person.

AUTHOR

Unknown. Some believe Moses was the author, due to the early date and the vocabulary similar to the Pentateuch (see *Comparison with Other Bible Books*). But there is no solid evidence for this.

DATE

The early date (2000 B.C.) is suggested by such things as

- the patriarchal lifestyle seen in the book;
- the use of the ancient patriarchal name for God (*El Shaddai,* "the Almighty," used 31 times);
- the absence of any mention of Israelite history.

LOCATION

Though the "land of Uz" (1:1) is clearly outside of Israel (perhaps northern Arabia), the style and vocabulary of the Hebrew writing, as well as the mention of the Jordan River (40:23), suggest that the book was written in Israel for an Israelite audience.

PURPOSE

- To address the question of why innocent people suffer.
- To promote faith and trust in God, whose ways are higher than those of humankind (42:1-5; see Isa. 55:9).

UNIQUE FEATURES

- Because of its focus on human suffering, Job has a unique appeal to people of all religions.
- Job, like Zechariah, gives a brief glimpse of confrontations between heavenly beings.
- Job is the only biblical book to refer to what may have been dinosaurs (Hebrew "behemoth" and "Leviathan," 40:15; 41:1).

COMPARISON WITH OTHER BIBLE BOOKS

Genesis:

- Job's description of earth's early history (38:4-11) provides a complementary parallel to Genesis 1.
- Both use the Hebrew expression for "sons of God" (2; Gen. 6).
- The ancient patriarchal name for God, *El Shaddai* ("the Almighty"), occurs in Genesis and Job more than in any other biblical books.

Ecclesiastes:

- Job explores the meaning of suffering; Ecclesiastes explores the meaning of life.

OUTLINE

CRITICISMS FROM SATAN (1–2)
- Job introduced (1:1-5)
- Satan's accusations (1:6-12)
- Job's tragedy; his reaction (1:13-22)
- More accusations from Satan (2:1-6)
- More tragedy for Job; his wife and friends react (2:7-13)

CONVERSATIONS WITH FRIENDS: CYCLE 1 (3–14)
- Job's lament (3)
- Eliphaz speaks (4–5)
- Job's response (6–7)
- Bildad speaks (8)
- Job's response (9–10)
- Zophar speaks (11)
- Job's response (12–14)

CONVERSATIONS WITH FRIENDS: CYCLE 2 (15–21)
- Eliphaz speaks (15)
- Job's response (16–17)
- Bildad speaks (18)
- Job's response (19)
- Zophar speaks (20)
- Job's response (21)

CONVERSATIONS WITH FRIENDS: CYCLE 3 (22–31)
- Eliphaz speaks (22)
- Job's response (23–24)
- Bildad speaks (25)
- Job's response (26–31)

DISSERTATION BY ELIHU (32–37)
- Elihu denounces Job and his friends (32–33)
- Elihu refutes Job's complaints (34–35)
- Elihu defends God (36–37)

CONFRONTATION WITH GOD (38:1–42:6)
- God's questions for Job (38:1–40:2)
- Job's response (40:3-5)
- More questions for Job (40:6–41:34)
- Job's response (42:1-6)

CONSIDERATION FROM GOD (42:7-17)
- Spiritual restoration (42:7-9)
- Material restoration (42:10-17)

CRITICISMS FROM SATAN (1–2)

1:1-5 *Job's faith, family, and fortune.* Job was a wealthy man, blessed with a large and happy family. He had seven sons, which in the Bible signifies completeness (see 2:13, 42:8, 13). The writer emphasized Job's "blameless" character (1:1, 5), making it clear at the outset that the suffering he would soon endure was not the result of his own sin.

1:6-12 *Hell challenges heaven.* Satan appeared before the Lord and accused Job of serving God only because of the earthly benefits of doing so (1:9-11). God gave Satan permission to bring suffering into Job's life, with the only limitation being that he could not bring physical harm on Job himself (1:12).

Satan appears elsewhere in Scripture as one who makes accusations against believers (see Zech. 3:1-4; Rev. 12:10). Though he rebelled against God and was cast out of heaven (see Isa. 14:12-15; Ezek. 28:12-19), Satan apparently still has access to heaven as one of the angels (or "sons of God," 1:6, KJV, NKJV, NASB), which in this context probably included both good and evil angels.

1:13-19 *Total disaster in one day!* By means of human enemies and natural disasters, Job lost all his wealth and children.

1:20-22 *"Blessed be the name of the Lord."* Job responded to his catastrophic tragedy with great sorrow, but also with an attitude of worship and unquestioning faith in God.

2:1-8 *Can his faith survive physical suffering?* Disappointed that Job remained faithful to God, and convinced that just a little more suffering would defeat him, Satan asked permission to cause bodily suffering to Job himself. God allowed him to do so, as long as the suffering was not fatal. Shortly thereafter, Job contracted a skin disease.

2:9-10 *His helpmate is no help.* Job's wife, full of great sorrow herself, was unable to give Job any moral support. Rather, she invited him to share her bitterness toward God.

2:11-13 *Job's three friends: They come to comfort; they stay to condemn.* Three of Job's friends, Eliphaz, Bildad, and Zophar, came to visit him, hoping to offer some comfort in his grief. So great was their own grief upon seeing his suffering firsthand that they sat with him for an entire week without uttering a word. Though this silent empathy was admirable, their attitude would soon change.

CONVERSATIONS WITH FRIENDS: CYCLE 1 (3–14)

3:1-26 *JOB: "Why was I born? Why don't I die?"* With forceful poetic words, Job openly wished he had never been born, or that he could have been stillborn or died in infancy. Considering his painful and useless life, Job wondered, why didn't God just let him die (3:20-26)?

4:1-11 *ELIPHAZ: "The innocent don't suffer, therefore . . ."* Having listened to Job's anguish, Eliphaz offered a response. Acknowledging Job's stature as a spiritual leader (4:3-4), he expressed his conviction that truly innocent people simply do not suffer as Job was suffering (4:7), while evil people do suffer (4:8-11)—implying that Job was suffering because of sin.

4:12-21 *"And how could you be innocent anyway?"* Eliphaz went on to tell of a "truth" he learned during a dream: If even the angels in heaven are not totally innocent, how could any human expect to be innocent? Again, the implication was that Job was suffering because of sin.

5:1-16 *"Here's what I would do."* Having noted the futility of complaining about suffering (5:1-5), and having expressed again his belief that suffering results from sin (5:6-7), Eliphaz urged Job to repent and turn to God (5:8-16).

5:17-27 *"Don't despise his discipline."* Eliphaz promised Job that if he would simply accept his suffering as discipline from God, he would eventually be restored to health and prosperity. While this is a valid principle (see Heb. 12:5-11), Eliphaz was wrong in applying it to Job's situation.

6:1-13 *JOB'S RESPONSE: "How can you know my sorrow?"* Job responded by noting that even his bitter complaint (3) did not do justice to the depth of his personal suffering. He had as much right to complain as an animal deprived of its food (6:5-7). Death was his only remaining hope (6:8-13).

6:14-21 *Friends as dependable as dry rivers.* Job had hoped for comfort from his friends. Instead he got condemnation. They were like dried-up streams, from which a weary traveler expects water but gets only disappointment.

6:22-30 *"Show me where I'm wrong!"* Job had not asked his friends for physical or financial help, only for their sympathy. Now he asked them simply to be specific in their accusations: What specific sin had brought on his suffering?

7:1-21 *His pain and his protest.* Job saw no prospect of an end to his pain. There was no time when he could get rest from it. All hope had vanished like the clouds. Therefore, he would make his protest to God (7:11): Why was God harassing him? Why did he frighten him with bad dreams? Why was he constantly testing him? If Job had sinned, why didn't God simply forgive him and leave him alone?

8:1-7 *BILDAD: "Words like the blowing wind."* Bildad, the second friend to speak, accused Job of speaking irresponsibly. How could he possibly make such claims about his own righteousness in light of God's perfection? While Bildad's opening remarks had truth in them, he was operating under the same false premise as Eliphaz: that Job had brought his suffering on himself by his own sin.

8:8-22 *Shackles for the sinner, rewards for the righteous.* Bildad argued on the basis of history (8:8-10) and nature (8:11-19) that sin always brings punishment. The only possible conclusion was that God helps the righteous but not the wicked (8:20-22). Again, the implication was that Job must be guilty of some sin and should consider repenting.

9:1-13 *JOB'S RESPONSE: "You're right: Mere man can't argue with the Almighty."* Job acknowledged the truth of Bildad's assertion that sinful humans shouldn't question God. He offered eloquent proof of God's wisdom and power.

9:14-31 *"Even the sinless can't stand before him."* While claiming to be blameless (9:21), Job admitted that God could and would judge him anyway. Still, the misery of his present condition made him feel hopeless, and he began to claim outright that God was unfair (9:22-24).

9:32-35 *Help wanted: Someone to mediate.* Job longed for a mediator to intercede with God on his behalf (see 19:25). The NT shows that Christ was such a mediator (see 1 Tim. 2:5).

10:1-22 *Created for condemnation?* Job longed to know a reason for his suffering, thinking perhaps that such understanding would make it more palatable. He reminded God that his present suffering was inconsistent with the great care God had shown in creating him (10:8-17). He wondered why God had allowed him to be born if he knew he would one day suffer like this (10:18-22).

11:1-12 *ZOPHAR: "How dare you talk to him that way!"* Job's third friend, Zophar, was abhorred by the way Job had been talking to God. He wished that God would appear to respond to Job's foolishness and show Job that he deserved *more* judgment than he was currently receiving (11:5-6)!

11:13-20 *My counsel: "Confess your sins!"* Zophar's advice to Job was similar to that of Eliphaz and Bildad: Repent of your sin and seek God's forgiveness. Though all three comforters urged Job to admit his sins and repent, none of them had identified just what his sin might be.

12:1-12 *JOB'S RESPONSE: "A bunch of know-it-alls!"* Job's response to Zophar was actually a response to all three friends. In satirical language, he noted their pride in believing that they possessed such high knowledge. He was offended by their condescending attitude and considered himself as qualified as they in such matters (12:3-6). In fact, said Job, even animals are capable of knowing such things!

The condescending attitude of Job's friends can sometimes be seen in those who try to comfort others based on doctrinal knowledge rather than feelings of mercy.

12:13-25 *"But God is omniscient and omnipotent."* Only God is omniscient and omnipotent, said Job. Therefore, he is the only one competent to give full answers about sin, suffering, and justice.

13:1-12 *The smartest option? Silence!* Considering God's omniscience and omnipotence, said Job, his so-called comforters would do well to remain silent. They should not try to speak for God. In fact, Job seemed to expect God to judge them for doing so (13:10-11)—as he eventually did (42:7-9).

13:13-19 *"I'm right, so I'll defend myself."* Job expressed faith in God, even if the current sickness was meant for his death (13:15). Still, he expected that God would fully vindicate him (13:15-16). This section resembles a courtroom scene in which Job is pleading before the Judge.

13:20-25 *"Only spare me from these two things . . ."* Job felt that he could get a fair hearing before God, if only God would spare him of two things: the continued presence of his judging hand; and the overwhelming awareness of his majesty.

13:26-28 *God's "bitter" book.* Job wondered if perhaps God was punishing him for sins committed long ago in his youth, presumably sins he had already dealt with (see 1:5). The grand heights of 13:15 appear to have given way to a fit of depression and pessimism.

14:1-6 *Few days, full of futility.* Job acknowledged the transitory nature of human life, its difficulties, and its impurity. In light of such human frailty, couldn't God turn away his judging hand and let him rest during his few remaining days?

14:7-22 *"Will I ever be like a tree?"* If a tree is cut down, said Job, its roots can bring it back to life; but humans are not like that—once dead, they will never return to life (14:10-12). Job acknowledged the possibility of life after death (14:14-15) but didn't hold out much hope of actually seeing it. Later, in a more optimistic mood, Job would return to the question of 14:14 (see 19:25-27).

CONVERSATIONS WITH FRIENDS: CYCLE 2 (15–21)

15:1-16 *ELIPHAZ: "You're a windbag, not a wise man."* Eliphaz spoke again, castigating Job as a speaker of empty words. In Eliphaz's view, a wise man would not continue to maintain his innocence against all the evidence of judgment in his life.

15:17-35 *"The sages of the ages say the sinful suffer!"* Eliphaz asserted that wise people throughout history have believed that sin brings suffering. He cited several examples of such suffering. Of course he was doing much more than just giving a history lesson. His example of the loss of wealth (15:29), for instance, betrays his real motive: to suggest once again that Job himself is suffering because of sin.

Contrary to Eliphaz's view, the Bible teaches that wealth is not always a blessing (see Luke 16:19-31; James 5:1-6).

16:1-17 *JOB'S RESPONSE: "You call yourselves comforters?"* Job's reply to Eliphaz showed his strong disgust: his so-called friends were not comforters at all. It would be easy for him to criticize as they were doing. If the tables were turned, however, he would comfort rather than criticize (16:5). Though he continued to complain about his friends' misguided counsel, Job was apparently most angry with God himself (16:11-14).

16:18-22 *An advocate in heaven?* For a second time, and seemingly with more conviction, Job longed for a mediator to represent him before God (see exposition on 9:32-35 and 19:23-29).

17:1-9 *"The wrong will fail, the right prevail!"* Expecting to die soon, Job continued to proclaim his innocence. His three friends, on the other hand, had shown their own unrighteousness by failing to be properly appalled by his predicament (17:8).

17:10-16 *"Death is my only hope."* Job's friends had said there was hope for Job if he would repent of the sin that had supposedly brought his suffering. Job, knowing that there was no such sin, continued to see death as his only release.

18:1-21 *BILDAD: "Let's be logical: Only sinners suffer."* Bildad began his second speech by wondering aloud if Job would ever stop talking. He dismissed as illogical Job's self-centered view of his suffering, and his remarks that brute beasts knew as much as his three friends (12:3-12). Echoing Eliphaz's second speech, Bildad cited a series of misfortunes that come upon the wicked—insinuating once again that Job had sinned.

19:1-12 *JOB'S RESPONSE: "You're unfair, and so is he!"* Job accused his friends of continued cruelty and unfairness. He went on to accuse God of unfairness, giving his own list of misfortunes based on his own suffering (19:6-12).

19:13-22 *Forsaken by family and friends.* Job cried out in loneliness, observing that his family, close friends and acquaintances, young children, and servants had all forsaken him. On top of that, his own physical suffering continued. Because of these things, he pleaded for pity from his friends (19:21-22).

19:23-29 *"I know that my Redeemer lives!"* From his valley of despair, Job went to the mountaintop of faith, expressing his confidence that redemption would surely come (see exposition on 16:18-22). Seen in the context of God's complete revelation, Job's Redeemer is

- his personal Redeemer ("my," 19:25)
- a living Redeemer (19:25), foreshadowing Christ's resurrection
- the one who would, in accordance with the law, pay the price for Job's deliverance (19:25; see Lev. 25:25-55)
- a Redeemer who will be on the earth in the last days (19:25), foreshadowing Christ's second coming
- the basis for Job's personal hope of life beyond the grave (19:26; see exposition on Isa. 26:1-19)
- the one through whom God will eventually vindicate Job (19:27; see 42:10-17)

Having proclaimed his faith, Job warned his three friends of God's judgment (19:28-29; see 42:7-9).

Job expressed the hope that the story of his suffering, and his reflections on it, could be recorded for future generations (19:23-24). He could hardly have known how completely that hope would be realized!

20:1-29 *ZOPHAR: More examples, more insinuation.* Zophar began his second speech by challenging Job's right to rebuke his friends. He then followed in the footsteps of Eliphaz and Bildad by listing the sins of wicked men and the judgments brought down on them. And, like his friends, Zophar again implied that Job's suffering was God's judgment for his sin.

21:1-34 *JOB'S RESPONSE: A list of his own.* Seeking to contradict his friends' contention that the wicked are always punished for their sins in this life, Job gave examples of how evil people prosper. The wicked often live very happy lives (21:7-16). They are often honored both in life (21:31) and in death (21:32). His friends might say, in such cases, that the evil people's *children* would suffer for their parents' sins. Yet even if that were the case, the evil parents themselves would have escaped direct punishment (21:18-21). In light of such evidence, the friends' argument that only the wicked suffer is totally false (21:34).

CONVERSATIONS WITH FRIENDS: CYCLE 3 (22–31)

22:1-5 *ELIPHAZ: "I repeat: You're suffering because of your sin!"* Speaking for the third time, Eliphaz reaffirmed the philosophy that he, along with Bildad and Zophar, had been advocating all along: People suffer because of sin. If that were not the case, Eliphaz reasoned, people's good deeds would have no value to God. Furthermore, the greatness of Job's suffering showed the greatness of his sin.

22:6-20 *A suggested list of Job's sins.* Although Eliphaz did not know of any specific sins Job had committed, he offered a few possibilities, including refusal to help the needy (22:6-11) as well as a defiant attitude toward God (22:12-20).

22:21-30 *A suggested remedy: Repent!* The solution still seemed simple to Eliphaz: Job must repent of his sins and turn to God; then, he would once again enjoy God's favor. Eliphaz's assessment of Job contrasted sharply with that of God (1:8; 2:3), of the book's author (1:1), and of Job himself. Although Job did not respond immediately to Eliphaz's false charges, he would later mount a lengthy self-defense (29–31).

23:1-17 *JOB'S RESPONSE: "If I could locate him, he might listen!"* Job expressed a desire to find God and make his plea to him in person. Job was confident that such an encounter would lead to his total vindication (23:10-12). Even so, he knew that God was sovereign (23:13-14) and therefore feared meeting him (23:15-17).

24:1-17 *The godless person seems to prosper . . .* Job noted again how the ungodly prospered while God apparently ignored this unjust state of affairs.

24:18-25 *. . . but in a flash, he falls and is forgotten!* Job was confident, however, that although the wicked prospered and God seemingly ignored their misdeeds, he would eventually punish them. The basis for Job's confidence appears to be the fact that neither the righteous nor the wicked can escape death (24:20-24).

25:1-6 *BILDAD: "If the stars don't measure up, how can sinners?"* Bildad's third discourse was short and to the point: God is all-powerful, as evidenced by his "army" (25:3, perhaps angels) and by his control of the natural world ("light," 25:3). And nothing, not even the moon or stars, possesses God's purity. Therefore, how can Job justify himself—since all humans are just worms or maggots in comparison to the stars?

While Bildad's affirmation of human sinfulness was correct, his application of this argument to Job's situation missed the point of Job's question concerning why the innocent suffer.

26:1-4 *JOB'S RESPONSE: A study in sarcasm.* Job began the longest speech of the book (26–31) with a series of mocking questions that exposed Bildad (along with Eliphaz and Zophar) as insincere counselors who did not really care about the needy.

26:5-14 *Nature's majesty a mere shadow of his might.* Job declared that the greatness of creation, to which Bildad had alluded (25:5), revealed only a small portion of God's power (26:14). God would later use creation as perhaps the best illustration of his own power (38–41).

27:1-6 *Job's vow: To serve in spite of suffering.* In another high point of faith, Job promised to maintain his integrity and declare his innocence even when his suffering might be viewed as a judgment from God.

27:7-23 *A warning to his friends.* Job then called for God's judgment on his enemies (27:7) and illustrated the ways God might judge them (27:8-23). Undoubtedly he had his three so-called friends in mind.

28:1-28 *Fear brings wisdom to the woeful.* Job then returned to meditating on the inability of humans to fully comprehend God's ways (see Isa. 55:8-9). Humans do have great technological abilities (28:1-11). In spite of such abilities, however, they cannot find or purchase wisdom because it is hidden (28:20-21). Only God possesses perfect wisdom. In light of that fact, humans who want wisdom should have a healthy fear of God (28:28; see Prov. 1:7; 9:10).

Applying this teaching to Job's situation, the sufferer must follow God in spite of his or her suffering, since only God fully understands what is going on.

29:1-25 *Once respected for who he was and what he did . . .* Job began a lengthy self-defense, recalling the good old days when he was respected by all who knew him. That respect was inspired both by his good character (29:1-11) and by his many good deeds (29:12-25).

30:1-14 *. . . but now despised even by the despicable!* In sharp contrast to the respect he once enjoyed, now Job was scorned even by "outcasts."

30:15-31 *Unending pain, unanswered prayers.* Job's emotional affliction and physical pain led him to pray for relief. But God did not seem to hear (30:15-20). Once again he challenged God, speaking of his supposed cruelty to the innocent Job (30:21-31).

31:1-40 *"If I have sinned, punish me!"* Job named a long list of sins, inviting his enemies to determine whether he had committed any of them, and then, if he had, to mete out the appropriate punishment. Job's own list of hypothetical sins is more extensive than Eliphaz's earlier list of false charges (see exposition on 22:6-20). His confidence in his innocence is seen in his wish that his enemies would have written down his alleged crimes so that he could deal with them one by one (31:35-37).

DISSERTATION BY ELIHU (32–37)

32:1-22 *Enter Elihu, an angry young man.* Elihu, who was younger than Job and his three friends, had apparently been listening to their debate. Now he joined in, expressing anger at the four older men and arrogantly noting that older men were not always wise—thus his decision to join in the debate (32:5-9). Elihu was angry at Job for trying to vindicate himself but was even more angry with Job's three friends for condemning Job without having convinced him that he was wrong (32:3, 10-15). Because they had failed to make their case, Elihu felt that he should now offer his own opinion (32:16-22).

33:1-7 *"I'll be your mediator."* Elihu expressed confidence in his own God-given wisdom and assured Job that he would give him a fair hearing and would help him make his case before God.

33:8-13 *Job's sin? Not actions, but attitude.* Elihu contended that Job had sinned, not in any action, but in his attitude toward God, namely his accusations of God's cruelty in spite of his innocence (see 13:24-27; 19:11; 27:1-6). Elihu was partly right about this. However, he had totally ignored the original question of the debate: Did sin cause Job's suffering? (Job's sinful *attitude* had arisen *after* his suffering, not before it.)

33:14-30 *"He speaks in many ways."* In response to Job's claim that God had been silent in the midst of his suffering (13:24), Elihu asserted that God does speak—through dreams or visions (33:14-18), through physical pain (33:19-22), and through angels (33:23). If Job would respond to these messages from God, he would regain his health and happiness (33:24-30).

33:31–34:4 *"Speak up, or listen and learn!"* Elihu invited Job to respond to his comments or, if he had no response, to keep on listening. He invited Job's three friends to do the same.

34:5-9 *"Here's what he said . . ."* Elihu summed up Job's two main complaints against God: that God is unjust (34:5-6) and that righteousness does not pay (34:9). He would answer the first complaint in the rest of chapter 34 and the second in chapter 35.

34:10-37 *"The creature cannot condemn his Creator!"* In answer to Job's claim that God is unjust, Elihu, like the three friends, defended God's justice. Also like the three friends, he assumed that Job had sinned (34:36-37) since God would not allow the innocent to suffer (see 36:7). He confidently asserted that other wise men agreed with his assessment: Job was being foolish and was rebelling against God (34:34-37).

While Elihu assumed that Job had sinned, he did not accuse him of any specific sins, nor did he dwell on Job's sinfulness as the cause of his suffering, as the first three debaters had done. Elihu focused, rather, on the value of suffering for moral instruction (see exposition on 36:5-23).

35:1-16 *"Righteousness or rebellion: He notices neither."* Next, Elihu addressed the second part of Job's complaint: that his present suffering showed there was no benefit in righteous living (35:1-3). Elihu responded that human actions, whether good or bad, have no effect on God (35:6-7), therefore Job should not expect any quick answers from him. His only option was to "wait" in faith (35:14).

Numerous Scriptures on both God's love and his anger call into question Elihu's view of a God unaffected by human actions (see Gen. 6:3-6; Matt. 23:37; 2 Pet. 3:9).

36:1-4 *"I've got all the answers, so listen!"* Claiming to have "well-rounded knowledge," Elihu again encouraged Job and his friends to listen carefully as he "defended" God.

36:5-23 *"Let him teach you in tribulation!"* Elihu asserted that God used tribulation and trouble as a teaching tool to drive the ungodly to repentance. He suggested that Job had been slow to learn this lesson (36:16-23) and encouraged him not to let his bitterness lead him to sin (36:21).

While God does sometimes use suffering to bring us to repentance (see Heb. 12:5-11), the Bible clearly teaches that suffering is not always the result of sin or of God's desire to discipline (see *Spiritual Lessons from Job*).

36:24–37:24 *"Who can know the Unknowable?"* Rather than becoming bitter, said Elihu, Job should learn to praise God for the greatness of his creation. Elihu proceeded to do just that, speaking of God's majesty and mystery. He challenged Job to explain various natural phenomena (37:14-22) and concluded that God is unknowable (37:23-24).

CONFRONTATION WITH GOD (38:1–42:6)

38:1 *GOD SPEAKS: Answers in a whirlwind.* Now that Job, Eliphaz, Bildad, Zophar, and Elihu had finished their discussions, God spoke. Rather than addressing the question at hand—Why do the innocent suffer?—God answered more with his awesome presence ("from the whirlwind") than with his words. He pointed again and again to the wonders of his creation and to the inability of humans to fully know him (see Isa. 55:9).

38:2-11 *"Where were you when I made the earth?"* God declared that Job had spoken "ignorant words." He then began a series of rhetorical questions to show Job how little he knew about the world. For one thing, Job knew little about the creation of the world since he had not been there at the time (38:4-7).

38:12-38 *"How well do you know the heavens and the earth?"* Did Job know what caused light and darkness (38:19-20), what the dimensions of the earth were (38:18), or what caused various weather patterns (38:22-30)? What about stars and clouds (38:31-38)? Job's response to all of this should have been to acknowledge God's dominion over all (38:33).

Though Job did not understand the causes behind these natural phenomena, God spoke to him as one well acquainted with the basic facts of creation and laws of nature.

38:39–39:30 *"What about my animals?"* Closer to home, God now quizzed Job about his knowledge of various animals:

"Do they need you?" (38:39–39:8) First mentioned were lions, birds, mountain goats, deer, and wild donkeys, all of which give birth, raise their young, and generally go about their lives without human help. The implication is that God's supremacy is above man's dominion.

"Can you tame them?" (39:9-12) How could Job presume to challenge God when he couldn't even tame the wild ox, one of God's lesser creatures?

"How do you explain this one?" (39:13-18) God asked Job to examine the strange features of the ostrich: a bird that couldn't fly, often destroyed its own young, seemed rather stupid, yet could run faster than a horse. Could Job have ever designed such an animal?

"Can you control the horse or the hawk?" (39:19-30) Creatures as diverse as the mighty horse and soaring birds of prey reflect the majesty of their Creator and live their lives outside of human control.

40:1-2 *"Can you answer any of those questions?"* As he had done at the beginning of his discourse (38:2-3), God issued a challenge to Job: If Job wanted to accuse God of wrongdoing in allowing his suffering, he should be prepared to answer the questions God had posed concerning the wonder of his creation.

40:3-5 *JOB'S RESPONSE: "I've talked too much already!"* Job acknowledged his insignificance compared to God. In a gesture of contrition, he put his hand over his mouth and ceased his complaints.

40:6-14 *GOD SPEAKS AGAIN: Only God can criticize God!* The Lord continued his challenge of Job, questioning his ability to judge his fellow humans, much less his Maker.

40:15-24 *By the way, what about the behemoth?* God then described the behemoth, apparently the largest land animal of its day (40:19). How could Job question God, since he could not design such a creature? Various scholars have identified the behemoth as

- a real animal still existing today, such as the hippopotamus (this theory is reflected in the NLT's rendering)
- a real but extinct animal, such as a dinosaur
- a mythical animal, such as a dragon

In light of its immensity (40:17-20), it seems most likely that the behemoth was a dinosaur-type creature. Job's apparent firsthand knowledge of the behemoth would thus imply that humans and dinosaurs coexisted. Since evolutionary theory precludes such a possibility, scholars who believe in evolution usually assert that the behemoth was a smaller, still-existent animal. That the behemoth was a real animal and not some mythical creature can be seen from the context: Having described real animals as proof of his majesty, why would God climax his argument by describing an imaginary being?

41:1-34 *Can you catch and control Leviathan?* Having presented his greatest land creature as proof of his power, God then presented his greatest sea creature, Leviathan. If Job could not create a behemoth or Leviathan, how could he presume to complain against one who could? Like the behemoth, Leviathan has been variously identified as

- a sea creature still existing today, such as the crocodile or whale
- an aquatic dinosaur
- a mythical creature, such as a sea serpent or dragon

The biblical description makes it most likely that Leviathan was an aquatic dinosaur-type creature. To identify Leviathan as a still-existent creature woefully ignores its bizarre description. Though the term "Leviathan" can be traced to Canaanite traditions about a mythical sea monster, and though the text does appear to describe a malevolent dragonlike creature (41:14-21, 34), the existence of a mythical name does not imply that such a creature was not real. On the contrary, the ubiquitous legends of dragons suggest a basis in reality. Psalm 104:25-26 names Leviathan as one of many real sea creatures. So also here, Leviathan should be taken as literally as all the other animals in the preceding chapters.

42:1-6 *JOB'S RESPONSE: "I had heard, now I see!"* Having seen his glory as never before, Job humbly repented of his complaints against God.

CONSIDERATION FROM GOD (42:7-17)

42:7-9 *A sacrifice for their false advice.* Because of their false counsel, God commanded Eliphaz, Bildad, and Zophar to offer sacrifices and to allow Job to serve as their priest and pray for them.

42:10-17 *Restored health, double the wealth, and more!* Because he repented, God restored Job to health and gave him double his original wealth. He gave him as many sons and daughters as he had had before and allowed him to live another 140 years.

In the end, God never gave a reason for Job's suffering. Rather, he showed that he was sovereign over all circumstances of life, whether good or bad. His restoration of Job's wealth and well-being was a wonderful demonstration of that sovereignty (see Ps. 23).

❖ ❖ ❖

PEOPLE TO REMEMBER FROM JOB

JOB

Key Facts: Accused by Satan before God, allowed to suffer greatly, eventually restored (1:9-12; 2:2-8; 42:10)

Wife: Unnamed (2:9)

Sons: 14 unnamed (1:2; 42:13)

Daughters: Jemimah, Keziah, Keren-happuch, and 3 unnamed (1:2; 42:13-14)

Occupation: Rancher (1:3)

Total Bible References: 56

Key References: 1–42; Ezek. 14:14, 20; James 5:11

Job Speaks

"The LORD gave me everything I had, and the LORD has taken it away. Praise the name of the LORD!" That was my testimony at the very beginning. Now, safe on the other side of that pain-wracked, despair-filled period, I would say it like this:

"The LORD gave, the LORD has taken away, and the LORD has given again; praise the name of the LORD!" (1:21)

For so he has! I suffered the loss of my fortune, my family, my health, and the goodwill of my friends. But now my wealth has been doubled and my health restored. Ten children have been added to my family, and my once false friends are now true companions once more. (1:13-19; 2:7-8, 11; 42:7, 9, 10-15)

How tragically ironic, though, that agonizing time! I sought desperately to see God, but he desired that I first see myself as the sinner I really was. When that finally happened, the grief turned to gladness. What a glorious God! (23:3; 40:3-4; 42:5-6)

Even though he gave me an additional 140 years, I know I must soon die. But no matter. My assurance back then is my comfort today: "I know that my Redeemer lives, and that he will stand upon the earth at last. And after my body has decayed, yet in my body I will see God!" (19:25-26; 42:16-17).

Spiritual Lessons from Job

- Job was both a righteous and a rich man (1:1-3). It is possible to be both. However, see Matthew 19:23-26.
- It is reassuring to know that Satan must obtain permission from God himself before he can tempt a believer (1:6-12; 2:1-6). Furthermore, God determines the boundaries of each trial, for he knows just how much each of us can bear (see 1 Cor. 10:13).
- Job's three friends claimed that his suffering was the result of his sin (4:7-8; 8:20), but God rebuked them for this erroneous teaching (42:7; see John 9:1-3). In reality, Job was allowed to suffer to accomplish several things:
  - ➤ to answer Satan's accusations (1:9-11; 2:4-5)
  - ➤ to teach Job about God's sovereignty (42:1-5)
  - ➤ to make Job more aware of his own sinfulness (compare 29; 31 with 40:4; 42:6)

God allows suffering for other reasons as well:

- ➤ He may use it to teach us (Heb. 12:5-11). Even Christ, though sinless, learned from his suffering (Heb. 5:8).
- ➤ He may allow it so that our lives will be a testimony to others of our faith in spite of suffering (John 9:1-3).
- ➤ Sometimes we bring suffering on ourselves.
- ➤ Sometimes the suffering is just a part of life in a fallen world, the fault of no one in particular (see Rom. 8:18-39).

Key Verses

"For examples of patience in suffering, look at the prophets who spoke in the name of the Lord. We give great honor to those who endure under suffering. Job is an example of a man who endured patiently. From his experience we see how the Lord's plan finally ended in good, for he is full of tenderness and mercy" (James 5:10-11).

PSALMS

BACKGROUND

The book of Psalms is a collection of poems and songs written by various Israelites over a period of about 900 years (see *Date*). Most of the psalms were obviously meant for public worship, while others seem more suitable for private worship or reflection.

Psalms is divided into five "books" (see *Outline*), each ending with a similar doxology. Many scholars believe this division reflects the historical development of the Psalms, with Books One and Two being compiled during or shortly after the time of David, Books Three and Four being added after Israel's fall, and Book Five coming after the return from exile. Others have seen in the division an effort to match Israel's five books of Law with five books of praise.

The Psalms deal with a wide variety of themes and historical events (see *Purpose,* below, and *A Topical Overview of the Psalms,* p. 327). Most of the psalms include titles, some of which explain their purpose or historical background.

AUTHOR

Many of the psalms mention their authors by name:

- David, king of Israel, authored at least half of the psalms; 73 are ascribed to him within the psalm, and two others are credited to him in the NT (2, see Acts 4:25-26; and 95, see Heb. 4:7).
- Either Asaph, a Levite in charge of worship music in the Tabernacle (1 Chron. 15:16-17), or one of his descendants authored at least 12 psalms (50; 73–83).
- The "descendants of Korah," the priest who led a rebellion against Moses (Num. 16), authored at least 12 psalms. Psalm 88 lists Heman the Ezrahite (see 1 Chron. 6:33) as an author along with them.
- Solomon, king of Israel, wrote Psalms 72 and 127.

1406 B.C.? Moses writes Psalm 90

1041 Birth of David, shepherd, musician, king, psalmist

538 Israel returns from exile (Ps. 126?)

- Moses, Israel's lawgiver and deliverer, authored the oldest psalm, 90.
- Some scholars have suggested King Hezekiah as author of the unattributed "songs of ascents."
- Ethan the Ezrahite wrote at least one psalm (89).
- 34 of the psalms are unattributed.

DATE

The Psalms were written over a period of about 900 years, from the time of Moses (90, written about 1405 B.C.) to the time of Israel's return from Babylonian exile (126, 147–150, written c. 500 B.C.).

PURPOSE

The purpose of the various psalms differs somewhat, depending on the author and the occasion of writing:

- Almost all of the psalms in some way called the believer's attention to some characteristic of God and the role he plays or should play in the believer's life. These may be expressions of either public or private worship.
- Many of the psalms taught Israel about God's work in their history (see "Special-Event Psalms" in *A Topical Overview of the Psalms,* p. 328). As the *Overview* illustrates, the psalms taught about many other issues of faith as well. (Paul saw Christian hymns as well as OT psalms as teaching tools—see Eph. 5:19.)
- The original purpose of many psalms is overshadowed by their messianic prophecies (see "Messianic Psalms" in the *Topical Overview*).
- Several psalms, such as 6, 32, and 51, are prayers of personal confession and repentance.
- Many psalms, such as 7, 35, 55, and 109, are "imprecatory," calling on God to punish the wicked. While the violent language of these psalms may sometimes seem out of keeping with a God of grace and love, the following should be kept in mind:
  - The hatred expressed reflected concern over violation of God's laws, not personal grievances.
  - The psalmists were right in expressing these things to God in prayer rather than seeking their own vengeance (see Deut. 32:35; Rom. 12:19).
  - The psalmists were motivated as much by concern for the victims of sin as by hatred for the sinners themselves (see 10:8-10).
  - Though the psalmists prayed against their enemies, they prayed *for* them as well (see 9:20 and exposition on 35).
  - Even NT writers, with their more complete knowledge of grace, pronounced curses on people under certain circumstances (see Gal. 1:8-9; 2 Pet. 2:12).

UNIQUE FEATURES

- With its devotional emphasis, Psalms is one of the most personal of all Bible books as it focuses on the relationship between God and the believer.
- Psalms is the most messianic of OT books and is second only to Isaiah for the number of times it is quoted in the NT. Jesus quoted from it at both the

beginning and the end of his earthly ministry (69:9, see John 2:17; 31:5, see Luke 23:46).

- Notable individual psalms include
  - the most beloved and widely quoted OT chapter (23),
  - the most vivid description of God's omnipresence, omnipotence, and omniscience (139),
  - the Bible's longest (119) and shortest (117) chapters,
  - the Bible's most personal prayer of confession (51).

COMPARISON WITH OTHER BIBLE BOOKS

1, 2 Samuel:

- Both recount key events in the life of David (see "Events in the life of David" in the *Topical Overview,* p. 329).

Isaiah:

- Both speak of Christ's suffering on the cross (22:6-18; 69:20-21; Isa. 52:13–53:12).
- Both speak of the restoration of God's people through the Messiah (14:7; 53:6; Isa. 49:6).
- Both speak of Christ's judging the nations (2:8-9; 72; 96:13; 110:6; Isa. 2:4; 11:4; 42:1, 4).
- Both speak of Christ's eternal reign (18:50; 45:6; 102:26; Isa. 51:6-8; 60:20).

The Pentateuch:
See *Background.*

OUTLINE

BOOK ONE (1–41)
BOOK TWO (42–72)
BOOK THREE (73–89)
BOOK FOUR (90–106)
BOOK FIVE (107–150)

BOOK ONE (1–41)

Psalm 1 *Fruitful trees, useless chaff.* The person who delights in God's Word and lives by its precepts will prosper (1:1-3); the ungodly will be condemned (1:4-6).

Psalm 2 *Rebels unite, but the Son will reign.* National leaders throughout history have rebelled against God and promoted ungodliness, but God merely laughs at their feeble attempts to defeat him (2:1-4). Meanwhile, he has set in motion his plan to give all kingdoms of the earth to his Son (2:5-9; see Heb. 1:5-9, which applies it to Christ). Those kings who choose to honor the Son will be blessed; those who reject him will perish (2:10-12; see Joel 3:9-11; Zech. 14:2; Rev. 6:15-17; 17:14).

Psalm 3 *"Now for a good night's sleep!"* When his son Absalom rebelled (2 Sam. 15), David's friends advised him to expect no help from God (3:1-2). Yet David declared his faith in God and looked to him for help (3:3-4). With this assurance he could lie down in peace, though 10,000 enemies surrounded him (3:5-8).

Psalm 4 *Set apart with joyful heart.* In spite of occasional distress and opposition from the ungodly, the upright believer can rejoice, knowing that he or she occupies a special place in the heart of God. (Compare 4:4 and Eph. 4:26.)

Psalm 5 *"Destroy the godless; deliver the godly!"* As he prayed in the morning (5:1-3; see 55:17), David declared his loyalty to God (5:2), expressed his concern about all the ungodly people around him (5:4-6), and prayed that God would deliver him from their evil control (5:8-12).

Psalm 6 *"He has heard me! Let my enemies depart!"* Weary both in body and spirit, David prayed earnestly for deliverance (6:1-7). Then, confident that the Lord had heard his pleas, he addressed his enemies, telling them to leave him alone (6:8-10).

Psalm 7 *"Rise up, Lord, and save the righteous!"* Describing his enemies as ravenous lions, David rhetorically asked the Lord if there was some sin in his life that had brought on their attacks (7:1-5). Then he answered his own question, declaring his innocence and calling on God to judge his enemies and vindicate the righteous (7:6-13). He noted how often the schemes of the ungodly backfire on them (7:14-16). This theme—that we reap what we sow—appears often in Psalms and elsewhere in Scripture (see 9:16; 35:7-8; 140:5-10; Esther 9:25; Gal. 6:7-8).

Psalm 8 *Mortals and the Milky Way.* As David contemplated the majesty of creation, he expressed amazement that God would even bother with such insignificant creatures as mortals (8:1-4). What's more, God has given humans a significant place in the universe as the caretakers of his creation (8:5-9; see Gen. 1:28). As God's glory is seen in the created order, it is also seen in the praise of children (8:2), which in its simplicity confounds God's enemies (see Matt. 21:15-16; 1 Cor. 1:27-29).

Psalm 9 *The eternal Helper of the helpless.* David praised God for preserving and protecting the righteous and destroying the very memory of the ungodly (9:3-16). He prayed that God would cause the nations to fear him so that they would repent and be spared eternal punishment (9:17-20).

"The grave" (9:17) is *Sheol* in Hebrew and in various English Bible versions is translated either "hell," "Sheol," "the Pit," or "the grave." Various NT versions translate it "hell" or "Hades" (see exposition on Luke 16:9-31). It is the place of the dead, both righteous and unrighteous (see 16:10), where the weary find peace and rest (Job 3:17, 22). God would in due time rescue his people from Sheol (16:10). Sheol has no relationship to the various Greek words translated "hell" in the NT. (See exposition on Eccles. 9:1-8.)

Psalm 10 *"Why do you allow injustice?"* The psalmist asked one of life's most perplexing questions: Why does God permit the godless to persecute the godly (10:1-11)? He reminded the Lord of his past faithfulness in delivering the oppressed and urged him to do so once again (10:12-18).

Psalm 11 *The faithful need not flee.* David's friends had urged him to flee from his oppressors, but he saw no need to do so, since he had committed his soul to God, who was still "in his holy Temple" and would still deal justly with both the righteous and the ungodly.

Psalm 12 *Few good people, and becoming fewer!* David lamented the dwindling number of virtuous people (12:1-4) but expressed confidence that the Lord, through the power of his word, would preserve the righteous who must live in such a godless society (12:5-8).

Psalm 13 *"How long, O Lord?"* How long, David asked, would God allow evil to triumph over him (13:1-4)? He answered his own question, expressing faith that God would deliver him (13:5-6).

Psalm 14 *God's final triumph over godless fools.* David expressed utter contempt for those who deny God's existence (14:1; see 53:1). He noted the sad spiritual state of humankind (14:2-3; see Rom. 3:10-12), expressed wonder that they did not see how God favored the righteous (14:4-6), and longed for the day when God would bring final victory to his people (14:7; see Ezek. 11:17).

The word *salvation* (14:7) occurs frequently in the Psalms. While Christians define salvation primarily as deliverance from sin, the psalmists would have understood it primarily in its OT sense of deliverance from earthly danger.

Psalm 15 *"Who may dwell on your holy hill?"* What kind of person, asked David, could expect to enjoy fellowship with God? Such a person would be loyal to God and his people (15:4) and would be just and generous in all his or her human relationships.

Psalm 16 *"No God but you!"* David expressed his love for God and his people (16:1-3) and vowed not even to mention the names of the pagan gods (16:4). He expressed his appreciation for God's providence in his life (16:5-9) and his confidence that the blessings would continue (16:10-11). Both Peter and Paul saw 16:10 as a prophecy of Christ's resurrection (see Acts 2:27-28; 13:35).

Psalm 17 *"Keep me as the apple of your eye."* Reminding God of his sincere efforts to live a godly life, David asked him to hear his prayer (17:1-6). He asked for protection from and triumph over his enemies (17:7-14) and expressed confidence that God would answer his prayers and would resurrect him after death (17:15; see exposition on Isa. 26:1-19).

Psalm 18 *A lifetime of victory.* Toward the end of his life, David praised God for having delivered him from all his enemies, especially from Saul (see parallel passage, 2 Sam. 22).

"He thundered from heaven" (18:1-19). David praised God for delivering him (18:1-3), then described that deliverance with breathtaking imagery; God had drawn David "out of deep waters" and led him to a place of safety.

"He has rewarded my righteousness!" (18:20-29). David saw God's faithfulness to him as the just reward for his own faithfulness to God. He, rather than his devious enemies (18:26-27), had been rewarded.

What a glorious God! (18:30-50). David resumed his praise of the God who had protected, empowered, and led him, giving him victory over all his enemies. David's victories were substantial indeed (see 2 Sam. 8:1-14; 10:19), but they would be only a foretaste of Christ's victory over all nations of the earth (see 2:8; Isa. 52:15; 1 Cor. 15:24; Phil. 2:10-11).

Psalm 19 *Silent, written, and spoken witnesses.* David expressed wonder at how the sun, moon, and stars bear witness to the awesome glory of God (19:1-6). Even more wonderful, however, is God's revealed word, which is to be savored more than gold or tasty food (19:7-11). David prayed that his study of God's Law would keep him from sin, so that he, too, would be a suitable witness to his Lord (19:12-14).

Psalm 20 *"Some trust in chariots. . . ."* The priests prayed that God would protect King David, granting him all his desires, including success over his enemies (20:1-5). David then expressed his own confidence that God would grant victory—through supernatural means (20:6-9).

Psalm 21 *A victory won, and more to come.* David praised God for a military victory and the peace, prosperity, and honor that had followed (21:1-7), and expressed his trust that God would continue to help him defeat his enemies, who were also God's enemies (21:8-13).

Psalm 22 *Forsaken, for now . . .* Feeling forsaken by God and despised by fellow humans (22:1-8), David pleaded with God to deliver him (22:9-21) and promised to publicly praise him for the deliverance (22:22-26). He foresaw a time when the whole earth would worship God and participate in his kingdom (22:27-31). NT writers and even Christ himself saw in this psalm many prophecies concerning Christ:

- His incarnation would enable him to minister to other humans and to become the perfect sacrifice for their sins (22:22; Heb. 2:12, 17).
- At his crucifixion, his garments would be divided and gambled for (22:18; Matt. 27:35).
- On the cross he would
  - echo David's cry of anguish (22:1; Matt. 27:46)
  - be ridiculed (22:7-8; Matt. 27:42-43)
  - suffer the piercing of his hands and feet (22:16; Luke 24:39-40)
  - be publicly stared at (22:13, 17; Matt. 27:39, 47)
- In general, 22:1-26 foreshadows Christ's crucifixion and resurrection, while 22:27-31 foreshadows his millennial reign (see exposition on Philippians 2:9-11).

Psalm 23 *My shepherd in life, in death, and forever.* David described God as his shepherd:

- In *life,* the Lord had provided for his every need, giving him rest, guidance, and strength.
- As he approached *death,* he could count on God's comforting presence.
- After death, David would live with his wonderful shepherd *forever.*

Psalm 24 *Who may go up with the King of glory?* Noting God's greatness as King of the earth, David described the kind of person who might be invited to ascend with this King to his royal city to enjoy fellowship with him. Such a person would be godly in his or her relationships both with God and with fellow humans (24:4). David then imagined the triumphant reception as the King entered his royal city (24:7-10). One can imagine the angelic hosts reciting David's grand poetry as Christ entered heaven following his death and resurrection (see Acts 1:9-11).

Psalm 25 *"Save, guide, forgive."* David asked the Lord for deliverance, guidance, and forgiveness. He asked God to overlook the sins of his youth, looking at him instead through eyes of mercy and forgiveness (25:1-7). David expressed his belief that God does, indeed, deliver, guide, and forgive those who fear him (25:8-15). He ended with another plea for deliverance from both outward enemies and inward affliction and that God would protect his people (25:16-22).

Psalm 26 *Separated from sin and to God.* David proclaimed his innocence before the Lord and his desire to serve him and testify of his goodness. He asked the Lord to help him fulfill that desire.

Psalm 27 *Confidence amid the conflict.* David had found that the person who lives his life daily in the presence of God, gazing upon his beauty, has no need to fear (27:1-6). He asked the Lord for mercy and expressed confidence that such mercy would always be there, even if his own parents should abandon him (27:7-10). He asked for guidance and deliverance and encouraged himself to be patient and courageous, knowing that God would always help him (27:11-14).

Psalm 28 *His reliable rock.* Addressing the Lord as his "rock," David prayed that God would punish the ungodly (28:1-5), and he thanked him for his gracious protection. God had filled his heart with singing and had given him strength and victory (28:6-9).

The writers of Scripture, especially the psalmists, often refer to the Lord as a "rock" (see 18:2; 42:9; 61:2; 95:1; Deut. 32:15, 18, 30; 1 Sam. 2:2; 2 Sam. 22:47; 1 Cor. 10:4).

Psalm 29 *The sovereign sound of his voice.* David compared God's majestic and mighty voice to a thunderstorm, which breaks down the cedars of Lebanon and shakes the mountains and wilderness (29:1-10). He called on this mighty God to give his people strength and peace.

Psalm 30 *Overconfident . . . overwhelmed . . . overjoyed.* In a time of prosperity, David had become overconfident (30:6). When illness came, he was overwhelmed (30:1-5, 7-10). Then came the healing, and his mourning turned to joy.

Psalm 31 *Praise for protection and peace.* In a time of great adversity, David asked God to deliver him (31:1-5). He was confident that God would help him (31:6-8, 14-18) but nonetheless confessed that he was afraid (31:9-13). He then moved beyond his doubts (31:22), praising God for his protection and peace and urging others to share his renewed sense of trust in God (31:23-24).

"I entrust my spirit into your hand" (31:5) may have been a familiar prayer for David in battlefield situations. Christ would pray that prayer once, not as a cry of desperation, but as a shout of victory (see Luke 23:46).

Psalm 32 *"Thank God, I'm forgiven!"* David described the peace and joy he had felt after confessing his sins (32:1-2) and contrasted it with the misery and frustration he had endured before confessing (32:3-5). He urged others to follow his example of honesty before God; rather than being like a beast of burden that has to be harnessed into submission, humans can choose to be led by the gentle touch of God's hand (32:6-11).

Psalm 33 *Victory through worship, not warfare.* David called on all righteous people to praise God, whose words are truth, who spoke all things into existence, and who controls history (33:1-11). The nation that follows this God is blessed, for he will protect it as the best-equipped army could not. Victory is assured not by a nation's warriors but through its worshipers (33:12-22).

Psalm 34 *"Just put him to the test."* David acknowledged the Lord's continued blessing and protection (34:1-7) and urged others to put him to the test, assuring them they would find him to be a good God who provides for his children and protects them from all danger (34:8-22).

The protection of the "angel of the LORD" (34:7) recalls the experience of Elisha and his servant (2 Kings 6:15-17). The promise of 34:20 was literally fulfilled as Christ hung on the cross (John 19:32-36).

Psalm 35 *"I'll give you glory in the Great Assembly!"* David pleaded for God's help against enemies who had attacked him without any just cause (35:7), promising that when victory came, he would publicly praise him for it (35:9-10, 18, 28). Shortly before his death, David did offer such public praise for military victories (see 1 Chron. 29:10-15).

Though David now prayed *against* his enemies, he had also prayed *for* them in their hour of need (35:12-14). Christ commanded prayer for enemies (Matt. 5:43-48) and taught it by example (Luke 23:34), as did Stephen (Acts 7:60) and Paul (2 Tim. 4:16).

Psalm 36 *Sleepless sinners, satisfied saints.* God gave David a revelation concerning ungodly people: They are so godless, self-centered, and deceitful that they lie awake at night hatching evil plots (36:1-4). The righteous, on the other hand, enjoy abundant blessings from God (36:5-9), who is both the life and light of humankind (36:9). David prayed for continued blessings and protection from the ungodly (36:10-12).

Psalm 37 *Prosperous sinners, poor saints.* David encouraged his hearers not to be distressed by all the wealthy sinners around them, who often tried to do them harm:

Frustrated or fruitful? (37:1-8) Though evildoers may seem to prosper (37:7, 16), they will ultimately fail (37:2), while those who trust God, though seemingly not as prosperous (37:16), will find justice and the desires of their heart.

Laughed at or lifted up? (37:9-33) God laughs at the ungodly, for he knows their judgment is coming (37:13). Meanwhile, he enables the "gentle and lowly" to "possess the land" (37:11, 22; see Matt. 5:5), however much the ungodly seek to harm them (37:12-17). Even though a righteous person may suffer a temporary setback, he will not be permanently defeated (37:23-24).

Destroyed or delivered? (37:34-40) Once more David urged his hearers to patiently seek God's way: Proud and evil people would be cut down like trees, while the righteous would enjoy peace and deliverance.

Compare Psalms 49 and 73.

Psalm 38 *Sin, suffering, supplication.* David was suffering great physical distress because of some sin he had committed (38:1-8). Both friends and relatives were keeping their distance (38:11). Rather than trying to excuse his sin (38:13-14), David confessed it and cried out to God for deliverance (38:9-10, 15-22).

Psalm 39 *"Remove my sickness. I'm only a shadow!"* Having tried in vain to keep silent about his suffering (39:1-3), David asked God to impress upon him both the brevity and uncertainty of human life (39:4-9). Feeling that he had suffered enough for his sin, he asked God to cease disciplining him, for he was but a pilgrim passing through this earth (39:10-13). Moses, writing five centuries before David, expressed similar thoughts (90:12).

Psalm 40 *Double trouble demands double deliverance.* David thanked God for lifting him out of "the pit of despair," setting him "on solid ground," and giving him "a new song" (40:1-3). He pledged himself to serve and speak for God (40:4-10).

Recognizing, however, that his sins were "more numerous than the hairs on my head" (40:12), David prayed once more that God would come quickly to his aid (40:13-17).

Christ shared David's delight in doing God's will (40:6-8; see Heb. 10:4-7).

Psalm 41 *"He helps those who help the helpless."* David declared that the Lord would bless and honor those who ministered to the poor and weak (41:1-3). He then told the Lord of his own need for healing and deliverance from his enemies (41:4-9) and asked him to come to his aid (41:10-12).

The close friend who had turned against David (41:9) may have been Absalom (see 2 Sam. 15:4-12) or Ahithophel (see 2 Sam. 16:15, 20-23), but Christ saw in David's lament a prophecy of his own betrayal by Judas (see John 13:18).

41:13 is apparently the doxology for the psalms comprising Book One.

BOOK TWO (42–72)

Psalm 42 *Hope in God, part 1.* As he grieved and his enemies taunted him, the psalmist, one of the "descendants of Korah," longed for God like a thirsty deer seeks water (42:1-4). As he pondered his desperate situation, he realized that the only solution was to "hope in God" (42:5, 11).

Psalm 43 *Hope in God, part 2.* In what appears to be a continuation of Psalm 42, the psalmist expressed his feeling that God had forsaken him. He prayed that God's light and truth would both illuminate and instruct him, allowing him to "hope in God."

Psalm 44 *"Why don't you do it again, Lord?"* The psalmist had heard how God freed Israel from Egypt (44:1-3) and expressed the hope that God would once again "command victories" for his people (44:4-8). Yet in reality, it seemed as though God not only had rejected his people but was actually fighting against them! They had been scattered to the wind and were ridiculed by the nations (44:9-16). The psalmist was even more perplexed because he was not aware of any great sin among the people. Why would God withhold victory from those who were trying to honor him? He pleaded with God to awake from his apparent sleep and help his people (44:17-26).

Psalm 45 *Praise for a groom, advice for a bride.* The psalmist praised the bridegroom at a royal wedding for both his military skill and his spiritual leadership (45:1-9). He then urged the bride, evidently from another land, to transfer her loyalty from her own people to her husband's people (45:10-15). He closed with a benediction of praise to the king (45:16-17).

This psalm may actually describe two weddings: The wedding of Solomon to Pharaoh's daughter (1 Kings 3:1), and the future wedding of Christ to his church (2 Cor. 11:2; Eph. 5:31-32; Rev. 19:6-9). Both call for a transfer of loyalties!

45:6-7 is quoted in Hebrews 1:8-9, where God the Father addresses God the Son as his divine equal.

Psalm 46 *Jerusalem's divine citizen.* God is the believer's refuge in every storm of life (46:1-3). He dwells among his people, therefore they are joyful, secure, and victorious (46:4-11).

Psalm 47 *Pride of Jacob, God of Abraham.* The worship leader called on Israel to praise their God, who would lead them to victory. God had personally selected the choicest blessings for Jacob (Israel) and had received the worship of nations as the God of Abraham.

Psalm 48 *Celebrating the city of God.* Jerusalem was a great city because God dwelled within it (48:1-3). Realizing God's place in the city, a visit to Jerusalem by foreign kings brought both admiration and fear (48:4-8). The psalmist invited the people of Jerusalem to walk around their beautiful city, counting its towers and viewing its palaces (48:9-13), and he encouraged them to preserve their faith for future generations (48:9-11, 13-14).

Psalm 49 *How much silver to save a soul?* The psalmist argued that the wealthy of this world were really worse off than the poor: The wealthy trust in their wealth but die anyway, just like animals (49:12, 20). No amount of money can save their souls (49:7-8; see Matt. 16:26). The righteous are the real winners, for they "will rule over" the wealthy in the afterlife (49:14). Therefore there is no reason to envy or fear the rich (49:16-20; see 37; 73; James 5:1-5).

Psalm 50 *The Judge in his courtroom.* Someday, said Asaph, the great Judge of the universe will appear in glory to evaluate the deeds of his people (50:1-6). As he judges their worship, he will not be concerned primarily about the correctness of their sacrifices, for all animals are his anyway; rather, he will be concerned with their obedience (50:7-23).

Psalm 51 *A sinning saint pleads for mercy.* David pleaded for God's mercy, acknowledging that he had sinned (51:1-6; see 2 Sam. 11). He longed for cleansing (51:7) and for the restored joy (51:12), renewed ministry (51:13), and heartfelt praise (51:15) that would surely follow. He understood that God desired repentance, not sacrifice (51:16-17). He believed that if God would forgive and restore him, it would bring revival to the whole nation (51:18-19).

Psalm 52 *A prediction of retribution.* David expressed righteous indignation at a man the title identifies as Doeg, who betrayed David and killed 85 priests and their families at Nob (1 Sam. 22). David predicted that God would make Doeg a public example of his wrath (52:5-7), while he himself would become like a productive olive tree (52:8).

Psalm 53 *"No, not one."* God had scanned the entire human race and found that none were righteous (53:1-3). David recognized that this indicated a heart problem, not a head problem (53:1; see 14:1). He longed for God's kingdom to be established on this sin-filled earth (53:6).

Psalm 53 is very similar to Psalm 14 and may have been a revision of that earlier psalm. Paul quoted these psalms to show the depravity of the human race and its desperate need for salvation (Rom. 3:10-12).

Psalm 54 *"Their brutality will boomerang!"* David sought divine deliverance from "strangers" the title identifies as the Ziphites, who betrayed him to Saul when he hid among them (see 1 Sam. 23:14-24). Confident that God was on his side and would repay his enemies (54:4-5), David praised God for victory.

Psalm 55 *"Oh, for the wings of a dove!"* Distressed by the constant plots and persecution of his enemies, David longed to escape to some far-off desert place (55:1-8). He called on God to destroy the conspirators, one of whom had been his close friend (55:9-15). Even as he expressed his faith in God's deliverance (55:16-19, 22), he couldn't forget the cruelty of his friend's betrayal (55:20-21, 23).

Psalm 56 *God keeps his tears in a bottle.* David felt himself to be in danger all day long from his foes, who slandered him and hid beside the trail to ambush him (56:1-2, 5-6). Nonetheless, he trusted in God, who kept a careful record of his every sorrow and had always come to his rescue.

Psalm 57 *Safe from the lions, in the shadow of God's wings.* As David hid from Saul in a cave (see 1 Sam. 24:3), he began each anxious day by playing his harp and singing songs of praise (57:7-11), expressing his confidence that God would save him (57:3).

Psalm 58 *"Turn these serpents into snails!"* David rebuked certain unjust religious or political leaders, who in their very lifestyles were as dangerous as snakes (58:1-5). He asked God to judge them and render them as powerless as "snails that dissolve into slime" (58:6-8). He expressed confidence that God would punish these evildoers and reward the righteous (58:9-11).

Psalm 59 *"They're back! Please help!"* David sought God's protection from his many enemies, who were attacking him repeatedly (59:6, 14). He was confident that God would defeat them and asked that, instead of killing them, God would let them live on in defeat as an object lesson to other opponents (59:11).

Psalm 60 *"Lord, you have hurt us; now heal us!"* Seeing his people defeated due to God's displeasure, David prayed that God would restore them (60:1-3). He was confident that if Israel would truly march under God's banner (60:4), the very one who had cast them off (60:10) would lead them to victory (60:12) over all their enemies (60:8-9).

Psalm 61 *A high rock of refuge.* Feeling overwhelmed, David sought refuge in the "rock" of God's strength (61:1-2; see exposition on 28). His past experience of this refuge (61:3-7) encouraged him to keep putting his trust in God. Despite the constant dangers David faced, God did "add many years to the life of the king" (61:6), prolonging his life to the 70 years promised by Scripture (see 90:10; 2 Sam. 5:4).

Psalm 62 *Weightless warriors and a rock of refuge.* As David's enemies conspired to dethrone him (62:4; see 2 Sam. 15; 20), he found refuge in God (62:1-3). He had learned that from God's perspective, his seemingly powerful enemies were no more than mere vapor (62:9). On the other hand, he had learned to trust in God as "a rock where no enemy can reach me" (62:7), and he wanted his readers to learn such trust as well (62:8).

Psalm 63 *Desiring the Lord in a dry land.* While hiding from King Saul in the wilderness (1 Sam. 21–26), David longed to spend time with God in his sanctuary (63:1-2). Memories of that sanctuary filled his mind as he lay awake at night thinking of God and his faithfulness (63:3-8). He regained his assurance that God would uphold his cause and defeat his enemies (63:9-11).

Psalm 64 *"His arrows will avenge me!"* David prayed for God's protection against an especially vicious and cunning group of conspirators, who spewed bitter words like arrows and congratulated themselves on their perfect schemes (64:1-6). David knew that God would shoot his own arrows, causing their very cleverness to be their undoing (64:8). Their defeat would bring great fear to other would-be rebels and great rejoicing to all the righteous (64:9-10).

Psalm 65 *He hears! He forgives! He satisfies!* God hears those who pray to him; he forgives them and provides abundantly for them (65:1-4). They can only respond by praising him for his great power (65:5-8) and provision (65:9-13).

Psalm 66 *Flood and fire: To purify, not punish.* The psalmist praised God for his great works (66:1-4), specifically for his salvation of Israel at the Red Sea (66:5-7; see Exod. 14). God had subjected his people to many painful ordeals—both flood and fire—not to punish but to purify them (66:8-12). While in great difficulty, the psalmist had promised God many offerings. He now kept his vows as he witnessed to his hearers about God's great mercy (66:13-20).

Psalm 67 *"Bless the Lord, and he will bless our land."* Israel should praise their God, because of his righteous rule over the land (67:1-5). If they would do this, God would bless them with rich harvests (67:6-7), which would be a testimony to all nations (67:2, 7).

Psalm 68 *The march of the Almighty.* David praised God for both his power and his goodness. He "rides the clouds" but also is a "father to the fatherless" (68:1-6). David recalled the Lord's mighty power and miraculous provision throughout his nation's history (68:7-27) and asked God to continue defeating their enemies (68:28-31).

"Bashan" (68:15) probably refers to Mount Hermon, while "Mount Zion, where God has chosen to live," (68:16) is Jerusalem. The prophecy of 68:29 was fulfilled during the time of Solomon (see 1 Kings 10) and will be fulfilled again during the millennial reign of Christ (see Isa. 60:3-6).

Psalm 69 *"Pull me out of this mire!"* Both David's own sins and the attacks of his enemies had caused him terrible and continuous grief (69:1-5); he was sinking in the "mire" (69:2, 14). Yet he felt that he was suffering primarily because of his loyalty to God (69:6-12). He called on God to rescue him and defeat his enemies (69:13-29). He expressed confidence that deliverance would come (69:30-36) and that this would be a powerful testimony to the whole nation (69:32-33; on 69:31, see 1 Sam. 15:22).

Psalm 69 is rich in prophecies about Christ and comparisons between David and Christ:

- Both were hated without cause (69:4; John 15:25).
- Both were misunderstood by their families (69:8; 1 Sam. 17:28; John 7:5).
- Both displayed great zeal for God (69:9; 2 Sam. 6:14-15; John 2:17).
- Though it was probably metaphorical in David's case, Christ was literally offered sour wine (or vinegar) for his thirst (69:21; Matt. 27:48).

Psalm 70 *Praise and an SOS.* Surrounded by his enemies, David offered up an urgent prayer for deliverance, taking time to praise God while doing so. To acknowledge and adore God in the hour of trouble is to be rescued and restored by him.

Psalm 71 *His help in youth and in old age.* "I've trusted you, O LORD, from childhood," David prayed. "Now, in my old age, don't set me aside. Don't abandon me when my strength is failing." David was saying, in effect, "Take care of this old man, so that I might declare your power to the next generation!" (71:1-18). Though always in danger, David knew God would answer this prayer. Therefore, he would continue to praise God and testify concerning his justice, goodness, and forgiveness (71:19-24).

Psalm 72 *The king and the King.* Solomon asked the Lord for wisdom so that during his reign the poor would receive justice (72:2-7). He would reign over a vast empire (72:8-11), which would be characterized by peace, justice, and prosperity, bringing universal and everlasting fame to its king (72:12-17).

Though many of the things Solomon predicted would become true of his own reign (1 Kings 10:23), they refer ultimately to the millennial reign of Christ (see Luke 1:30-33). Many of the psalm's themes are echoed in Isaiah's description of the Messiah (Isa. 2:4; 9:7; 11:4; 32:1; 49:23).

72:18-19 is apparently the doxology for the psalms comprising Book Two.

Books One and Two contain 56 of the 75 psalms attributed to David and may have been compiled during or shortly after David's lifetime (see *Background*). The compilers of these books would not have known that later generations would include other psalms of David in the three later books, thus the remark of 72:20.

BOOK THREE (73–89)

Psalm 73 *Envy in the city; answers in the sanctuary.* Asaph wondered why God allowed so many ungodly people to accumulate great fortunes, enjoy good health, and live long lives (73:1-12). But that was only half the problem, for all too often exactly the opposite was true of godly people

(73:13-15). While worshiping one day, he realized that the ungodly were not so well off after all, since they were destined for eternal destruction (73:16-20). With this new understanding, he worshiped enthusiastically, declaring that he desired nothing on earth besides his relationship with God (73:21-28). "Leading me to a glorious destiny" (73:24) suggests that Asaph looked forward to life after death (see exposition on Isa. 26:1-19; see 37; 49).

Psalm 74 *"How could this have happened?"* A descendant of Asaph, apparently his namesake, looked back on the destruction of Jerusalem and wondered how God could have let it happen (74:1, 10-11). He asked God to remember his people during this time of calamity (74:2, 19-21) and to take measures to defeat the enemy and restore the honor of his name (74:10-23). Surely the one who created the world and divided the Red Sea could handle the present situation (74:12-17)! The psalmist's question (74:1) was answered in 2 Chronicles 36:14-16.

Psalm 75 *God promotes and punishes.* Asaph thanked God for his sovereign judgment: He elevates one and deposes another according to his will. God will, in his own time and way, destroy the ungodly and exalt the righteous.

Psalm 76 *More majestic than the mountains.* The everlasting mountains cannot compare to God's glory, nor the most powerful army to his strength (76:1-10). In light of God's character, his people are to fulfill their promises to honor and serve him (76:11-12). On "human opposition only enhances your glory" (76:10), see exposition on Ezra 6:1-12.

Psalm 77 *The good old days.* In a time of great distress, Asaph recalled "the good old days" and wondered why God had seemingly forgotten his people (77:1-9). Rather than dwell on the depressing present, however, he chose to find comfort in God's mighty acts in times past, such as the Red Sea crossing (77:16-20).

Psalm 78 *A history lesson.* Recalling perhaps the admonition of Deuteronomy 4:9, Asaph was determined to pass on to Israel's next generation some of the lessons he had learned from history. He didn't want to be like some former generations, who had forgotten those lessons and therefore had been defeated (78:1-11):

The more they received, the more they rebelled (78:12-33)! Asaph recalled the amazing things God had done for his people, such as the plagues in Egypt (78:12) and his provisions during their journey to the Promised Land. Sadly, however, God's bounty had been rewarded by ingratitude and rebellion (78:17-20, 30-33). Therefore, God sentenced them to "failure" as they wandered in the desert (78:33; see Num. 14:29-30, 35).

Retribution, repentance, rebellion: A vicious cycle (78:34-41). Whenever God would discipline his people they would repent (78:34-35), yet soon they would rebel again (78:36-37), and he, being "merciful," would forgive them again (78:38). This cycle was repeated many times (78:38, 40-41; see Num. 14:22).

"They rebelled because they didn't remember" (78:42-64). Asaph stressed once again that Israel kept rebelling because they kept forgetting God's marvelous deeds, such as the plagues in Egypt (78:42-51), his guidance and provision in the wilderness (78:52-54), and the conquest of Canaan (78:55). After all this, they continued to test his patience.

A loving shepherd for his sheep (78:65-72). Asaph, who lived in David's time, saw David's kingship as another example of God's grace. He ended his psalm with high hopes that the wandering sheep of Israel would follow this king who had a shepherd's heart.

Psalm 79 *"Cleanse our iniquities, consume our enemies!"* Asaph's namesake (see exposition on 74) lamented the terrible destruction of God's city, his Temple, and his people (see 2 Chron. 36:15-19). He prayed that God would forgive and restore his people and destroy their enemies, for the honor of his name.

Psalm 80 *A shepherd and his vineyard?* Asaph appealed to Israel's great shepherd to save his people, whom he was disciplining by allowing them to be dishonored by their neighbors (80:1-7). Switching metaphors, Asaph spoke of Israel as a vine that God had carefully planted, but had now allowed to be harvested and even destroyed by passersby and animals (80:8-16; see Isa. 5:1-10). Once again, he called on God to restore his people.

Psalm 81 *Sin spoils the celebration.* During one of Israel's regular festivals, Asaph exhorted the people to praise God for his acts of national deliverance (81:1-7). He lamented, however, the people's constant sin, reminding them of the blessings that could have been had they only obeyed (81:8-16; see Matt. 23:37; Luke 19:41-42).

Psalm 82 *He judges the judges.* God, the judge of all the world, called on human judges to stop favoring the ungodly and defend the poor and helpless. God had elevated those judges to lofty positions, calling them "gods" (see John 10:34), yet they would be judged as surely as the lowliest person.

Psalm 83 *Crush their conspiracy!* Asaph spoke to the Lord concerning several nations that had formed a conspiracy against Israel (83:1-8). He called on him to do to those nations as he did to various other nations in times past so that those nations, too, would realize that Israel's God is the true and only God (83:16, 18).

Psalm 84 *From the valley of sorrow to the home of the sparrow.* The psalmist longed to enter the Temple courtyard and find sweet refuge near the altar, as the sparrows and swallows had done (84:1-4). He imagined the thoughts of pilgrims as the Lord helped them through the valley of sorrow and they grew ever stronger as they approached the palace (84:5-7; see 23:4). Finally, he contemplated again the joy of just 24 hours in God's presence, even as a lowly doorkeeper (84:8-12).

Psalm 85 *"Revive us again!"* Having thanked God for forgiveness of sins (85:1-3), the psalmist prayed that God would revive his people and set aside his anger so that Israel might once again have cause to rejoice (85:4-7). He then expressed confidence that the Lord would indeed bless the land (see Hab. 3:2).

Psalm 86 *Wanted: Holiness, strength, and a sign.* Having acknowledged God's greatness and mercy (86:1-7) and that he alone is God (86:8-10), David asked the Lord for moral instruction (86:11-13), for supernatural strength (86:16), and for a sign to reassure him amid all his enemies (86:14-15, 17).

Psalm 87 *A blessing just to be born there!* Jerusalem is praised as the most blessed of all cities. Someday the highest imaginable honor will be to have been born in Jerusalem.

Psalm 88 *In the depths of deepest despair.* Heman the Ezrahite expressed to God a deep despair that had plagued him all his life and had brought him great physical distress, even though he had prayed often about it (88:1-9). Mustering what little faith he had left, he wondered if God would rescue him before it was forever too late (88:10-14). Despite this flicker of hope, he ended on a note of total pessimism as he returned to reciting his troubles (88:15-18).

Psalm 89 *God's covenant with David.* Ethan the Ezrahite wrote in celebration of God's everlasting covenant with David and his descendants (89:1-4; see 2 Sam. 7:10-16; Luke 1:30-33).

Glorious for who he is and what he does (89:5-18). He began by praising God for his faithfulness, power, and sovereignty over creation (89:5-13). He praised God for perfectly balancing love and truth, which walk before him as attendants (89:14-18).

David's reign to remain, regardless (89:19-37). God had promised David that his enemies would all be defeated and his descendants would rule forever (89:19-29). God would keep this promise no matter how much David or his descendants might sin (89:30-37).

But has he changed his mind (89:38-52)? Noting the current state of affairs in Israel, however, Ethan wondered if God had broken his covenant with David (89:38-51).

89:52 could be seen either as an upbeat ending to Ethan's psalm, matching his earlier optimism, or as a doxology for all the psalms of Book Three.

BOOK FOUR (90–106)

Psalm 90 *Wisdom for a brief life.* Book Four begins with a psalm by Moses, probably the oldest of all the psalms. Moses wrote of the stark contrast between God's eternality and humankind's short life span, which, due to the effects of sin, is often spent in emptiness and pain (90:1-11). Moses asked God to give his people the wisdom to make their brief lives happy and productive (90:12-17).

Psalm 91 *The shadow of the Almighty.* God will provide protection, reassurance, and warmth to anyone willing to trust him (91:1-6). He will protect believers from every conceivable danger (91:7-13). The psalm ends in the words of God himself, promising deliverance and long life to all who "call on" him (91:14-16).

When the devil quoted 91:12 to Christ in the wilderness, Christ corrected his misapplication of its promise by quoting another Scripture (see Matt. 4:6-7; Deut. 6:16).

Psalm 92 *Like bulls and cedars.* For the believer, it is a joy to praise God for his

- kindness in the morning and faithfulness in the evening (92:1-4);
- omnipotence and omniscience (92:5);
- victories over the ungodly (92:6-9);
- and for the victories of the righteous, to whom he gives the strength of a bull and the might of the cedars of Lebanon (92:10-15).

Psalm 93 *The splendor and statutes of God.* All creation speaks of the greatness of God. He is the eternal King, robed in majesty and strength, and his creation reflects those attributes (93:1-4). His laws, likewise, are firmly established and unchanging (93:5).

Psalm 94 *How firm a foundation!* The psalmist called on God to judge the ungodly, who were persecuting his people while proudly declaring that God couldn't see their evil deeds (94:1-7). He pointed out the folly of such insolence (94:8-11) and the joy awaiting the godly: Whenever his foot began to slip (94:18), he would find peace, mercy, victory, comfort, and security on the firm foundation of God's word (94:12-22). Meanwhile, proud sinners would only find God's wrath and judgment (94:23).

Psalm 95 *Better to worship than to wander!* Israel was called to bow the knee in worship before their great King, Creator, and Shepherd (95:1-7). They were admonished to have soft hearts and not to be like the Israelites during the Exodus, who rebelled against God and were condemned to 40 years of restless wandering (95:8-11).

Psalm 96 *Idols and the Infinite.* The psalmist invited all creation to praise God, who is above all gods (96:1-6). He invited all nations to acknowledge God's glory and uniqueness, to bring offerings to him, and to give testimony to his name (96:7-10). He called on all nature to worship him and to look forward to the day when he would come at last to bring justice to the earth (96:11-13).

Psalm 97 *When his fire goes forth, the mountains melt!* All creation bears witness to God's righteousness (97:1-6). All who love the Lord should rejoice in his power and justice and should stand against the forces of evil (97:7-12).

Psalm 98 *Joy to the world!* As the psalm's title indicates, the psalmist praised God for both his salvation (98:1-6) and his righteous judgment (98:7-9). He imagined all creation joining with him in his praise. Isaac Watts based his famous hymn "Joy to the World" on this psalm.

Psalm 99 *Three satisfied customers.* God, who is supreme above all rulers of the earth, is to be worshiped for his holiness, justice, and forgiveness. When Moses, Aaron, and Samuel called to him for help, he answered them (99:6-7). He forgave them, even when he had to discipline them (99:8).

Psalm 100 *Creator and Shepherd.* The psalmist called on the people to come joyfully into God's presence, knowing that he is both their Creator and their Good Shepherd and that his goodness, love, and faithfulness will last forever.

Psalm 101 *The company we keep.* David committed himself to personal integrity (101:1-2) and promised to support those with high moral standards and to oppose the ungodly (101:3-8). He vowed not even to entertain in his home those who are proud, selfish, or slanderous.

Psalm 102 *An end to his suffering in sight.* With his health broken, his heart sick, and his enemies attacking, the psalmist begged God to intervene (102:1-11). He expressed hope in Jerusalem's Messiah, who would hear the cry of his people and city (102:12-22) and would put off the old clothing of this present heaven and earth and create all things new (102:23-28; see Isa. 65:17-18; Rev. 21:1).

Psalm 103 *"Don't forget to praise him!"* Remember what God has done, said David: He forgives sins, heals diseases, redeems lives, satisfies desires, and renews our youth (103:1-5). He executes justice but also displays great compassion, for he knows our frailties (103:6-18). All things everywhere—his angels and "everything he has created," including humans—should praise this great God (103:19-22; see 148).

Psalm 104 *"What a wondrous world he has made!"* God's power and glory are seen in natural phenomena (104:1-4), such as the universal Flood (104:5-9). Creation also shows God's compassion as he satisfies the hunger and thirst of both humans and animals and provides light and darkness to order their lives (104:10-30). Praise is the only fitting response to such wonder (104:31-35).

Psalm 105 *History 105: God's faithfulness.* The writer called on Israel to thank and praise God for his marvelous works (105:1-5). He reminded them of their national history, noting God's faithfulness to his covenant with Abraham (105:6-15). God had been faithful in providing salvation through Joseph (105:16-24) and through the miracles during Moses' ministry:

- the 10 plagues (105:25-38; Exod. 7–12)
- the cloudy and fiery pillar (105:39; Exod. 13:21)
- the deliverance from Egypt (105:37; Exod. 14)
- the manna (105:40; Exod. 16)
- the water from the rock (105:41; Exod. 17)

Finally, God had given them the Promised Land (105:43-45), fulfilling his promise to Abraham (105:42; see Gen. 17:1-6).

Psalm 106 *History 106: Israel's unfaithfulness.* In an apparent continuation of Psalm 105, the writer once again called the nation to praise God (106:1-5). He then reviewed their history again, focusing this time on their own unfaithfulness as seen, for instance, in

- the Red Sea crossing (106:6-12; Exod. 14:10-12, 21-30)
- the rebellion of Korah, Dathan, and Abiram (106:16-18; Num. 16:31-33)
- the golden calf (106:19-23; Exod. 32:1-4)
- Moses' striking the rock (106:32-33; Num. 20:2-13)
- their compromises with the Canaanites during the time of the judges (106:34-46)

Despite this repeated unfaithfulness, the Lord had saved his people again and again (106:43), both to defend his own honor (106:8) and to show his mercy (106:44-46). The writer ended his history lesson by asking God to deliver his people once again (106:47).

106:48 is apparently the doxology for the psalms comprising Book Four.

BOOK FIVE (107–150)

Psalm 107 *Gathered from around the globe.* The psalmist called on the redeemed to acknowledge their Redeemer (107:1-3). He told four stories of lostness and redemption, beginning at 107:4, 10, 17, and 23, each ending with the same plea: "Let them praise the LORD for his great love and for all his wonderful deeds to them." The stories seem to describe Israel's history, with Israel sinning (107:11, 17) and God punishing them but then delivering them because of his love.

The psalm ends with another two images of desolation and redemption (107:33-38 and 107:39-43).

"He has gathered the exiles from many lands" (107:3) suggests that this psalm was composed after Israel's return from exile, making it a fitting first psalm of this final book, which many believe was compiled after the exile (see *Background*). Israel's regathering was, of course, only a dim foreshadowing of the great regathering the Messiah will bring about in the last days (see Matt. 24:31).

Psalm 108 *Confident of his help in conflict.* David could praise God with a "confident" heart because of his confidence in him (108:1-5). He prayed for God's help in battle (108:6-9), sure that the one who had cast them off (108:11) would now lead them to victory (108:13) over all their enemies (108:8-9). Israel needed God's aid, for they knew that human help was worthless (108:12).

This psalm appears to combine material from two earlier psalms (57:7-11 and 60:5-12).

Psalm 109 *"Give them a taste of their own medicine!"* David prayed that God would punish those who were persecuting him (109:1-5) and that the punishment they received would match the grief they had caused him and many others (109:6-20). Describing again his own embattled condition, David urged God to deal with his enemies in a way that would unmistakably demonstrate his great power (109:21-31). On 109:8, see Acts 1:20.

Psalm 110 *A Messiah like Melchizedek.* David spoke of "my Lord," to whom God would give a place at his right hand, while giving him victory over all his enemies and making him "a priest forever in the line of Melchizedek." The book of Hebrews reveals this "Lord" to be Jesus Christ (see Heb. 5:6, 10; 6:20; 7:11-19; see exposition on Gen. 14:17-24).

Peter quoted 110:1 at Pentecost, affirming that David had the Messiah in mind when he wrote those words (see Acts 2:34-35).

Psalm 111 *Praise for his power and precepts.* The psalmist praised God for his mighty and miraculous works (111:1-6); God fed his people in the wilderness and led them into the Promised Land (111:5-6). He also praised God for his law. All 613 OT commandments are faithful, just, and trustworthy (111:7-10).

Psalm 112 *The family that fears God.* This psalm says that people who fear the Lord will, along with their families, enjoy both financial and spiritual prosperity (112:1-9). The godless, meanwhile, will look on with envy (112:10).

Psalm 113 *Sunrise-to-sunset praise.* The believer is to praise God's name during every waking hour (113:1-4). Indeed, who else is like God, who is enthroned in the heavens yet stoops down to help the poor and needy (113:5-9)?

Psalm 114 *Two partings for his special people!* Though they were already his chosen people (see Gen. 12:1-3), when God led the Israelites out of Egypt they became his nation in a more special way (114:1-2). The Red Sea parted to let them out of bondage; the Jordan parted to let them into their Promised Land (114:3-8). God will do whatever it takes to get us where he wants us to be.

Psalm 115 *Impotent gods, omnipotent God.* The psalmist compared the idols of the nations with Israel's God and called on all Israelites to worship their God only. Idols have mouths, eyes, ears, noses, hands, and feet, but only the true God can speak, see, hear, smell, feel, and walk (115:1-13).

Psalm 116 *Death had him surrounded!* Death was staring the psalmist in the face when God stepped in and saved him (116:3-12). He praised God for this timely protection (116:1-2, 13-19).

Psalm 117 *Who should praise him? Why?* This shortest chapter of the Bible calls on all the world to praise God for his unfailing love and faithfulness.

Psalm 118 *"He has become my salvation!"* Even if the psalmist was surrounded by all nations of the earth, he was confident that the Lord would save him and that he would see a great victory celebration (118:1-21). He praised God in words the NT applies to the Messiah:

- "The stone rejected by the builders has now become the cornerstone" (118:22; see Matt. 21:42; 1 Pet. 2:6-8).
- "Bless the one who comes in the name of the LORD" (118:26; see Mark 11:9).

Psalm 119 *God's word in the believer's life.* Psalm 119 is devoted entirely to praise of God's word and its role in the life of the believer. The psalm is an amazing acrostic poem in which each of the verses in each of 22 eight-verse segments begins with the same letter of the Hebrew alphabet, thus covering all 22 Hebrew letters. For instance, verses 1 through 8 each begin with *aleph,* verses 9 through 16 each begin with *beth,* and so forth.

The other unique feature of the psalm is its repeated use of nine different words to describe God's revelation. These appear in random order and with differing frequency.

Joy in his judgments (119:1-8). Those who keep God's law "with all their hearts" are assured of great blessing.

Purity in his precepts (119:9-16). "How can a young person stay pure?" By "hiding" God's word in his or her heart—studying, meditating on, and even memorizing Scripture.

Security in his statutes (119:17-24). Amid persecution, the psalmist felt like a stranger in the world but found comfort in God's word.

Deliverance in his decrees (119:25-32). Lying "in the dust, completely discouraged," the psalmist knew that deliverance from his sinful nature would come as the Lord helped him understand his laws.

Worth in his word (119:33-40). If the psalmist could truly learn God's law and keep from desiring the "worthless things" of this life, then he would find delight, revival, and reassurance.

Liberty in his law (119:41-48). The person who trusts in God's word will "walk in freedom," fearing no one and even speaking of his or her faith "to kings."

Comfort in his commands (119:49-56). Because the psalmist had kept God's laws (119:55-56), they were a comfort in the hour of pain and persecution.

Meeting with God at midnight (119:57-64). The psalmist declared his loyalty to God and his word: God was his portion; he was loyal to God's people (119:63); he hurried, "without lingering," to keep God's commandments, even arising at midnight to spend time with the Lord.

"Thank God for my affliction!" (119:65-72). The psalmist's affliction was a good thing (119:65, 68, 71) because it had turned him from his wayward life back to God and his word (119:67).

"You did it because you loved me!" (119:73-80). Again the writer expressed his belief that God had afflicted him for his own spiritual good, because it had turned him to his word.

Worn out like a wineskin (119:81-88). Though worn out by persecution, the psalmist was also wearing himself out seeking comfort in God's word (119:81-82)!

Forever standing firm in the heavens (119:89-96). As surely as the earth itself endures, so also will God's word stand firm (119:89-91). The psalmist hoped God's word would bring that same endurance to his own life (119:92-96).

Wiser than his enemies, instructors, and elders (119:97-104). The psalmist had surpassed all his associates in wisdom (119:98-100) because he studied and practiced God's law (119:99-100).

A lamp and a light (119:105-112). God's word offered the psalmist both illumination and inspiration. Though his enemies always threatened, God's word was his heritage and joy (119:111).

Depart, all you double-minded! (119:113-120). The psalmist would separate himself *from* the ungodly that he might separate himself *to* God's word (119:113, 115).

A time for action! (119:121-128). While pleading for mercy for himself as a lover of God's law, the psalmist implored God to exercise justice against those who disregarded God's law.

"Easily understood, even by the uneducated!" (119:129-136). Even the "simple" can become wise through God's word. The writer "panted" for more of this wisdom (119:131; see 42:1) and expressed great sorrow over the widespread disobedience to God's law.

The Scriptures in the time of storm (119:137-144). Though consumed with anguish over the wickedness around him (119:139), the psalmist found delight in God's word (119:143).

Delighting in them day and night

(119:145-152). Though many sinful people were near him, the psalmist found the Lord near as well (119:150-151) as he arose before dawn and stayed awake at night contemplating the Scriptures.

Error-free and eternal (119:153-160). Amid persecution, the true believer can trust in a God whose words are totally trustworthy and will not change (119:160).

"I pray seven times a day!" (119:161-168). In spite of persecution, the psalmist found peace and hope (119:165-166) through his faithful and frequent practice of prayer.

"Come seek me," said the straying sheep to the Shepherd! (119:169-176). Confessing that he had gone astray, the psalmist declared that, nonetheless, he had not forgotten God's word, and he hoped that God would seek him (119:176) and would hear, help, and save him (119:169-170, 173-174).

Psalm 120 *"I prefer peace; they want war!"* Describing himself as being "for peace," the psalmist prayed for deliverance from his neighbors, all of whom seemed to want war.

Psalms 120–134 are titled "songs for the ascent to Jerusalem." Though the origin of this term is not known, these psalms may have been sung by pilgrims "ascending" to Jerusalem to worship at the Temple. If the 10 "songs" that are anonymous were authored by Hezekiah (see *Author*), these psalms may have had another purpose.

Psalm 121 *Kept safe by the Creator of stars*. The psalmist was confident of being protected 24 hours a day by the very God "who made the heavens and the earth!"

Psalm 122 *"If you pray for this place, may you prosper!"* Having come to Jerusalem to worship, the psalmist admired the city, prayed for its peace and prosperity, and invited others to do so as well, asking the Lord to bless those who so prayed.

Psalm 123 *Humbly seeking his heavenly hand*. Feeling the contempt of the rich and proud around him, the psalmist expressed humility before God, looking to him for help as a servant would look to his or her master.

Psalm 124 *Had he not helped, what would have happened?* Without the Lord, Israel would have been "swallowed alive" by its enemies (124:1-5). The psalmist praised God for his protection.

Psalm 125 *A mountain surrounded by mountains*. Those who trust God are as unmovable as a mountain (125:1) and are surrounded by the even greater mountains of the Lord's presence (125:2). With this assurance, the psalmist was sure that God would overcome all evil (125:3-5).

Psalm 126 *Rejoicing at their return*. The psalmist rejoiced with some people freed from captivity (126:1-3) but also apparently prayed for those still held captive (126:4-6). Many scholars have seen in this a description of Israel's first return from Babylonian exile (Ezra 1–3), following which they still faced much opposition as they tried to rebuild the Temple (Ezra 4–6).

Psalm 127 *Big houses, many children*. The person who builds without God's support labors in vain; the person who builds with God's support experiences his blessings even as he rests from his work. Likewise, he can experience the blessing of many children, who will protect him from his enemies as he gets older.

Psalm 128 *A fruitful vine and young olive trees*. The psalmist wished prosperous employment and a happy home to all who obeyed God's will.

Psalm 129 *Down often, but never out!* Israel had been persecuted many times but never totally destroyed

(129:1-4). The writer asked God to destroy Israel's enemies just as grass withers when it sprouts in the shallow soil on an ancient Mideastern housetop. Some scholars see in 129:3 a prophecy of the scourging Christ endured before his crucifixion (see John 19:1).

Psalm 130 *There's hope! He doesn't keep score!* Sure that God was not interested in keeping a record of sins, the psalmist eagerly awaited his forgiveness and urged all Israel to share his confident "hope in the LORD."

Psalm 131 *"Be still, my soul."* David stood before God in quiet, humble contemplation, as a child before its mother, making God the focus of his hope and trust and urging his hearers to do likewise.

Psalm 132 *David's promise to God; God's promise to David.* The psalmist recalled David's promise to build a house for the Lord (132:1-5; see 2 Sam. 7:1-3) and the return of the Ark to Jerusalem prior to that time (132:6-7; see 2 Sam. 6). He then recalled the Lord's response to David's promise, as he promised to build David an everlasting house (132:11-18; see 2 Sam. 7:4-16).

Psalm 133 *Fragrant like oil and dew.* David found in fragrant anointing oil and the dew on a mountain two fitting pictures of the blessedness of unity.

Psalm 134 *Worship him, all his servants!* The Songs of Ascents end with an exhortation to all who serve the Lord to praise him as well.

Psalm 135 *The bottom line: He lives; they don't.* The psalmist called the people to praise the Lord for his mighty works in history (135:4, 8-14) and in creation (135:5-7). The true God made his people, while the false gods were made *by* their people (135:15-18; see 115:4-8).

Psalm 136 *Thank him for Creation and redemption.* God is praised for his work in Creation (136:1-9) and redemption (136:10-26), with each successive recitation of his miraculous deeds calling forth the repeated response: "His faithful love endures forever."

Psalm 137 *Hanging up their silent harps.* An exile from Israel described the sorrow he and fellow exiles felt as they reached Babylon (137:1-6; see 2 Kings 25). He prayed that God would severely punish their captors (137:7-9).

Psalm 138 *"All kings would praise you if only . . ."* David declared that surely all kings of the earth will praise God when they hear the truth about him (138:4-5). All kings of the earth, in fact all people both small and great, saved and unsaved, *will* someday bow before the King of kings (see Phil. 2:10-11; Rev. 5:13)!

Psalm 139 *A great king, amazed by a great God.* David praised God because God is

- *omniscient:* He knows our thoughts, our words, and our ways (139:1-6, 17-18),
- *omnipresent:* His presence is felt in heaven, at the hour of death, in the most remote places, and in the darkest of nights (139:7-12),
- *omnipotent:* He forms the delicate and complex human body within the mother's womb (139:13-16).

David then called on the Lord to apply all his divine qualities to eradicating the ungodly people of the earth (139:19-22). At the same time, he invited divine scrutiny of his own life and asked for the Lord's continued guidance (139:23-24).

Psalm 140 *"Free me, capture them!"* David prayed that he would be delivered from slanderous enemies who planned to entrap him (140:1-5) and that they would become trapped by their own plots (140:6-11). Knowing God's goodness, he was sure that justice would prevail (140:12-13).

Psalm 141 *"Remove me from the rebellious; rebuke me by the righteous!"* David prayed for inward sanctification (141:3-4) and for outward separation from the ungodly (141:4). He invited the rebuke of righteous people; when it is needed, said David, such rebuke is like "soothing medicine" (141:5).

Psalm 142 *Refuge, rescue, and release.* Overwhelmed and all alone (142:1-4), David was sure that God would hear his cry for refuge, rescue, and release (142:5-7).

Psalm 143 *Deliver! Guide! Revive!* Crushed by his enemies, David longed for time alone with God (143:3-6) and for a victory such as God had brought Israel in "the days of old" (143:5; see 77:5). He prayed for deliverance and for spiritual guidance and revival (143:7-12).

Psalm 144 *A "passing shadow" prays for paradise.* Noting the greatness of God and the insignificance of humans (144:3-4), David asked for God's divine help against his human enemies (144:5-7). He envisioned a time of perfect peace and prosperity, with healthy children and livestock, and acknowledged that such a paradise could come only from God (144:12-15).

Psalm 145 *His majesty, might, and mercy.* David praised God for his mighty acts (145:1-7), his mercy (145:8-9), his everlasting kingdom (145:10-13), his compassion (145:14-16), and his mercy, provision, and protection (145:17-21). Perhaps David's praise was for the benefit of his son Solomon (see 145:4; compare Deut. 4:9; 6:7; Isa. 38:19).

Psalm 146 *"Trust him who is all and does all!"* Do not put your faith in humans, who will soon die (146:3-4). Rather, trust the Lord, who created the universe and who defends the oppressed, feeds the hungry, restores sight to the blind, and protects the helpless (146:5-10).

Psalm 147 *Creator and Redeemer.* The same God who heals hurting hearts also numbers and names the stars (147:4-6). The same God who sustains all of nature (147:7-18) has also revealed himself in a special way to his chosen people (147:19-20). God is both Creator and Redeemer, and takes special delight in those who hope for his redemption (147:11).

Psalm 148 *Recruiting a choir from heaven and earth.* The psalmist enlisted all the heavenly hosts (148:1-6) and everything on earth, both animate and inanimate (148:7-12), to praise the Lord.

Psalm 149 *With a song and a sword.* Israel was to joyfully exalt the person of God while at the same time exacting punishment from God on nations that rejected him.

Psalm 150 *"Let everything praise him!"* This last psalm calls God's people, along with "everything that lives," to praise him—with the voice plus any available musical instrument. Psalm 150 in its entirety is apparently the doxology for the psalms comprising Book Five.

A TOPICAL OVERVIEW OF THE PSALMS

ATTRIBUTES OF GOD PSALMS

The following are just a few of the Psalms' descriptions of God:

- Eternality (90; 102)
- Glory (96; 113)
- Goodness (27; 107)
- Holiness (99)
- Justice (75; 82; 94)
- Majesty (18; 93; 97)
- Mercy (86; 136)
- Omnipotence (18; 33; 76; 146)
- Omnipresence (139)
- Omniscience (139; 147)
- Providential care (65; 104)
- Unfailing Love (36)
- Uniqueness (115; 135)

MESSIANIC PSALMS

Passages from the Psalms reveal many things about the coming Messiah, including his

- Creative power (102:25-27; John 1:3, 10; Heb. 1:10-12)
- Obedience to the Father (40:6-8; Heb. 10:5-7)
- Zeal for the Father (69:9; John 2:17)
- Faithfulness as a shepherd (23; John 10)
- Rejection by Israel (118:22-23; Matt. 21:42)
- Praise by little children (8:2; Matt. 21:16)
- Betrayal by a friend:
  - the treachery of Judas (41:9; 55:12-14; Matt. 26:47-50; John 13:18)
  - the tragedy of Judas (69:25; 109:6-8; Acts 1:18-20)
- Slander by false witnesses (27:12; 109:2-3; Matt. 26:59-61)
- Suffering and death:
  - forsaken by God (22:6-8; Matt. 27:39-43)
  - ridiculed (22:6-8; Matt. 27:39-43)

- beaten (129:3; John 19:1)
- prayed for his enemies (109:4; Luke 23:34)
- hands and feet pierced (22:16; Luke 24:39-40)
- given sour wine to drink (69:21; Matt. 27:34, 48)
- garments gambled for (22:18; Matt. 27:35)
- none of his bones broken (34:20; John 19:36)

Resurrection (16:8-11; Matt. 28:1-6; Acts 2:25-32; 13:35)
Ascension (68:18; Luke 24:50-51; Eph. 4:8)
Victorious entrance into heaven (24:7-10; Rev. 7:9-12)
High Priestly work (110:1, 4; Matt. 22:44; Heb. 5:6; 7:17)
Marriage to the church:

- description of the bridegroom (45:2, 6-8; Luke 4:22; Heb. 1:8-9)
- description of the bride (45:9, 13-15; Rev. 19:7-9)

Destruction of the heathen (2:1-9; Acts 4:25-26; Rev. 6:12-17)
Millennial reign (45:6; 72:17; 98:4-9; Heb. 1:8; Rev. 11:15)

RELATIONSHIP PSALMS

The Shepherd and his flock (22–24)

The Good Shepherd (22) describes the sacrifice of Christ—his past work (John 10:11)

The Great Shepherd (23) describes the sufficiency of Christ—his present work (Heb. 13:20-21)

The Chief Shepherd (24) describes the sovereignty of Christ—his future work (1 Pet. 5:4)

The Son and his Father (2, 40, 45, 102, 110)

Five conversations between God the Father and God the Son are recorded in these five psalms relating to

- his role at Creation (102:25-27; Heb. 1:10-12)—words of the Father to the Son
- his earthly obedience (40:6-8; Heb. 10:5-9)—words of the Son to the Father
- his anointing (45:6-7; Heb. 1:8-9)—words of the Father to the Son
- his eternal priesthood (110:1, 4; Heb. 7:17, 21)—words of the Father to the Son
- his victory at Armageddon (2:6-9; Rev. 2:27)—words of the Father and Son to each other

SPECIAL-EVENT PSALMS

Events in Israel's history

Departure from Egypt and arrival in Canaan (114; Exod. 12–14; Josh. 1–3)
Sin at Kadesh-barnea (90; Num. 13–14)
Marriage of King Solomon (45; 1 Kings 3:1)
Death angel deliverance of Jerusalem (48, 67, 121; 2 Kings 19; Isa. 37)
Destruction of Jerusalem by Nebuchadnezzar (74, 79, 80; 2 Kings 25; 2 Chron. 36)

- Babylonian captivity (137; 2 Kings 25; 2 Chron. 36)
- Return from Babylonian captivity:
  - Praise by the returning remnant (126; Ezra 1–2)
  - Prayer by the returning remnant (85; Ezra 3–5)
- Dedication of the second Temple (92; Ezra 6)

Events in the life of David

- Living in Saul's court (11; 1 Sam. 18)
- Saved from Saul by Michal (59; 1 Sam. 19:11-18)
- Fleeing from Saul (63, 143; 1 Sam. 19–31)
- Escape from Achish (34, 56; 1 Sam. 21)
- Slaughter of priests at Nob (52; 1 Sam. 22:17-23)
- Living in cave of Adullam (57, 142; 1 Sam. 22)
- Betrayal by Ziphites (54; 1 Sam. 23)
- End of Saul's efforts to kill him (18; 1 Sam. 26–31; see 2 Sam. 22)
- Return of Ark to Jerusalem (15, 24, 68, 132; 2 Sam. 6)
- Joab's victory over Edomites (60; 2 Sam. 8)
- Establishment of David's kingdom (21; 2 Sam. 8)
- Sin with Bathsheba (32, 51; 2 Sam. 11–12)
- Flight from Absalom (3, 4, 35, 41; 2 Sam. 15–18)
- Cursed by Shimei ("Cush") (7; 2 Sam. 16:5-14)
- Dedication of building materials for Temple (30; 1 Chron. 29)
- Coronation of Solomon (72; 1 Chron. 29:21-25)

Future events

- Tribulation (46; Matt. 24; Rev. 6–19)
- Millennium (47, 98; Rev. 20)

c. 971 B.C.
Solomon granted wisdom, writes many proverbs

960
Solomon completes Temple

931
Death of Solomon

PROVERBS

BACKGROUND

The book of Proverbs is a collection of proverbs and wise sayings brought together for the purpose of imparting wisdom (see exposition on 1:1-7). Some of the proverbs deal with serious moral issues, while others are simply observations and advice about everyday life, such as one might expect from a person with the broad interests of King Solomon (see 1 Kings 4:32-33). The proverbs tend to be brief and memorable, easily learned and applied.

Proverbs focuses on the difference between the *wisdom* that results from belief in God and the *folly* that results from denial of his existence. It describes the fate of the "fool" (see exposition on 12:1), who, because he has deliberately rejected God (see Ps. 14:1; Rom. 1:18-23), becomes one of "the wicked" (see exposition on 4:10-19). As the wicked fool moves ever further from God, he moves further from wisdom and common sense as well. By contrast, the wise person realizes God exists and has a healthy "fear" of God's authority (see exposition on 1:1-7). He or she realizes, therefore, that right and wrong actions have consequences. Such awareness of how the world works leads to a happy and satisfying life.

AUTHOR

Proverbs includes wise sayings from several authors, with the vast majority coming from Solomon, who had asked the Lord for wisdom instead of wealth (see 1 Kings 3:5-9):

- *Solomon:* Proverbs is divided into seven sections (see *Outline*). 1:1 suggests that Solomon may have authored the entire first section (1–9), although that verse may be an introduction to the book as a whole (Solomon may have compiled the entire book). The second major section (10:1–22:16) is directly attributed to Solomon, as is

the fourth (25–29). Proverbs probably includes at least 800 of Solomon's 3,000 proverbs (see 1 Kings 4:32).
- Solomon may also have written many of the proverbs in the third section, the "Words of the Wise" (22:17–24:34), whose compiler and authors are anonymous. Many scholars also assume he wrote the final section, the tribute to the worthy woman (31:10-31).
- *Agur,* apparently a non-Israelite, is credited with the proverbs of the fifth section (30).
- *Lemuel* authored the sixth section (31:1-9). He was a king (31:1), presumably a non-Israelite. Some scholars believe, however, that Lemuel was actually Solomon.

DATE

Solomon reigned 970–930 B.C. The "advisers of King Hezekiah" (25:1) would have lived some 200 years after Solomon. Dates for the anonymous collection and the collections of Agur and Lemuel are unknown.

PURPOSE

Proverbs seems in large part to be addressed to those who are "simple," who have not yet made up their mind between the way of wisdom and the way of folly (see exposition on 14:15, 18). It seeks to impart to them the wisdom that comes from the "fear of the LORD" (see exposition on 1:1-7) and to show them how to apply that wisdom to life.

COMPARISON WITH OTHER BIBLE BOOKS

Genesis—Deuteronomy:
- While the books of law outline God's laws and specify blessings for obedience and punishments for disobedience, Proverbs presents righteous behavior as being in the best interest of the individual since it leads to the best kind of life.

Job:
- Both praise wisdom (1:1-9; Job 28:12-28).
- Both show that wise and righteous people are not always rewarded with health and wealth (see exposition on 15:6, 16-17; Job 1–2).

Psalms:
- Both contrast the righteous with the wicked (numerous proverbs; Ps. 1; 37).
- Both emphasize the "fear of the LORD" (1:7; 9:10; 16:6; Ps. 111:10; 112:1; 128).

Ecclesiastes:
- Both praise wisdom (1:1-9; Eccles. 9:14-18).
- Both despise the "fool" (numerous proverbs; Eccles. 10).
- Both emphasize the "fear of the LORD" (1:7; 9:10; 16:6; Eccles. 12:13).
- Both contain practical instructions (see exposition on 27:23-27; parts of Eccles. 5; 7).
- Both affirm that all people are sinners (20:9; Eccles. 7:20).

OUTLINE

A CALL TO PURSUE WISDOM (1–9)
PROVERBS OF SOLOMON (10:1–22:16)
WORDS OF THE WISE (22:17–24:34)
MORE PROVERBS OF SOLOMON (25–29)
THE WISDOM OF AGUR (30)
THE WORDS OF LEMUEL (31:1-9)
THE WORTHY WOMAN (31:10-31)

A CALL TO PURSUE WISDOM (1–9)

1:1-7 *"Here's why we're writing this book."* The first verse of Proverbs identifies it as "the proverbs of Solomon" (however, see *Author*). 1:2-7 states the book's purpose: to impart wisdom. Wisdom in Proverbs is not intellectual knowledge but "skill" (1:5, RSV) in handling the issues of everyday life. This skill is based above all on a healthy fear of God. This fear or respect for God

- "is the beginning of knowledge" or "wisdom" (1:7; see 9:10; Job 28:28)
- imparts confidence and life (14:26-27; 19:23)
- produces contentment (15:16)
- saves from evil (16:6)
- brings riches and honor (22:4)

1:2-7 is a fitting introduction to the entire book. With its offer of instruction to "young people" (1:4), it may also be seen as an introduction to the book's first section (1–9).

1:8-9 *"Listen to them, too."* The "fear of the LORD" (1:7) must be followed by a deep respect for the advice of one's parents. The writer put this advice in the mouth of a father who, in 1:8–9:18, would take his son on a walk through the city streets, showing him the scenes of everyday life and exhorting him to seek wisdom instead of folly. Ten exhortations are introduced with the words "my child" and followed by commands such as "pay attention" or "listen carefully." The child was to heed the advice of wisdom, which is personified in several ways:

- a street vendor or prophetess calling out at the city gate (1:20-33; 8:1-21, 32-36)
- a master architect helping in God's creation (8:22-31)
- a sister (7:4)
- a noble lady offering good instruction (3:13-18; 4:6-9; 9:1-6)

The son is to reject the temptations of the

- "immoral woman" (2:16-19; 5:3-14; 7:5-23)
- "adulterous woman" (2:16; 6:24-35)
- "woman named Folly" (9:13-18)

The personifications are for the most part women, traditionally referred to as "Dame Wisdom" and "Dame Folly."

1:10-19 *"Just say no!"* The father wanted to impart his experience to his child. He hoped that his child would always choose the path of righteousness and purity.

1:20-33 *Calling out like a street vendor.* Personifying wisdom as a vendor offering her wares, the father warned his child not to ignore her advice. If wisdom called out and the child refused to listen (1:24-27), the child would one day call out, only to have wisdom refuse to hear him (1:28-33; see 8:1-11).

2:1-9 *Seek and you will find.* If the child would diligently seek wisdom (2:1-4), he would find it—and righteousness as well—for true wisdom comes from God (2:5-9).

2:10-22 *Insured against iniquity and immorality.* Wisdom would deliver from evil and keep those who love her on the right track. Specifically, it would keep the young man from the immoral woman (2:16-22), whose seductions always lead to death (2:18; see 5:3-14).

3:1-10 *Trust in him, tithe to him.* The child would be rewarded with a long and peaceful life (3:1-4, 7-8) if he would trust in God and acknowledge him (3:5-6; 28:26) and give him the "best part" of his wealth, as the law required (3:9-10).

3:11-12 *Correction means satisfaction.* If the child wanted to enjoy health, wealth, and a long life (3:13-18), he should accept his father's correction (3:11-12). Such correction can and should be administered in love (3:12; see 13:1, 24).

3:13-18 *A treasure and a tree of life.* Wisdom is pictured as a noble lady who is more precious than silver or gold or rubies, and is a "tree of life." Throughout Proverbs, wisdom is compared to precious jewels and metals (see 8:10-11; 16:16; 20:15). The "tree of life" image recurs as well (see 11:30; 15:4; compare Ps. 1:3).

3:19-20 *"By wisdom he made the world."* By wisdom God created the world (3:19) and by wisdom he sustains it (3:20; see 8:22-31; Ps. 104:24).

3:21-26 *Safety, confidence, and sweet sleep.* The wise person will find protection from harm by day and secure sleep at night, both a result of the confidence wisdom brings (3:26).

3:27-35 *"Do unto others . . ."* The wise person will be kind and generous (3:27-30; see James 3:17). He or she will not be envious of the wicked (3:31-33; see 23:17-18; 24:1, 19-20; Ps. 37) but rather will be humble (3:34-35; see James 4:6).

4:1-9 *"Listen to me as I listened to him."* The father exhorted his child to learn wisdom from him, even as he had learned it from his own father. Wisdom is personified as a woman who should be embraced, exalted, and not forsaken.

4:10-19 *The right path, the light path.* The father had led his child on the paths of wisdom. Now it was up to the child to choose that path, which would lead to ever increasing joy and light (4:18; see 15:24), rather than the path of the wicked (4:14), which would lead only to deeper darkness (4:19).

Proverbs mentions "the wicked" nearly a hundred times. These are the "fools" who, because of their rejection of God and the wisdom he offers, have become more and more hopeless in their sinful rebellion (see *Background*).

4:20-27 *The bottom line: Guard your heart.* All the father's instructions and wise sayings would do no good unless the child would guard his or her heart (4:23). This means involving the intellect as well as the emotions in the quest for righteousness. The "heart" produces not just feelings but also understanding (see 2:2).

5:1-14 *"Don't even pass by her door!"* No matter how seductive the immoral woman may appear, the wise young man should avoid her at all costs, not even going near her door (5:8). If he gives in to her, she will destroy everything he has worked for in life (5:9-14; see 22:14).

5:15-23 *One wife for one life.* The father affirmed, in beautiful poetry, the sanctity and joy of marriage (see 18:22).

6:1-5 *"If you've been too generous, admit it!"* If a person overextends himself or herself in showing generosity, he or she should not be afraid to humbly admit the mistake and ask to be freed from the obligation. Several proverbs warn against unwisely cosigning for the debts of others (see 11:15; 17:18; 22:26-27).

6:6-11 *Lazy people, lowly ants.* Diligence like that of the ant will ensure prosperity. Just a little laziness, on the other hand, can become habitual and result in financial ruin and a wasted life (see 10:4-5; 12:24, 27; 14:23; 19:15-16; 20:4, 13; 24:30-34). Even someone who greatly desires wealth can end up in poverty because of laziness (21:25-26; see 13:4). (See exposition on 26:13-16.)

6:12-19 *God's "Bottom Seven" list.* The wicked person is insincere and deceitful in everything he does (6:12-15). Seven characteristics of such people are singled out as particularly displeasing to God (6:16-19). 6:13 describes some of the body language people of ancient times may have used to communicate evil intentions (see 10:10; 16:30).

6:20-35 *Fornication's fruit: Disease, dishonor, death.* Returning to the theme of 5:1-23, the father again urged his son to listen to his advice, particularly regarding the seductions of evil women (6:24-35). The man who is seduced "is an utter fool" (6:32), "scoop[s] fire into his lap" (6:27), suffers "wounds and constant disgrace" (6:33), and "destroys his own soul" (6:32).

7:1-27 *Like a spider seducing a fly!* Urging his son once again to "write" his commands "deep within your heart" (to internalize them), the father issued further warnings about immoral women. He described an aimless young man who was easy prey to the wayward woman's flattery and aggressiveness.

8:1-11 *The call of wisdom.* Having described the seductions of the adulteress, who boldly sought her prey "in the streets and markets" (7:11-12), the father described wisdom as a prophetess standing in a prominent place near the city gates, loudly proclaiming her worth. In contrast to the fleeting pleasures offered by the adulteress, wisdom offers things of lasting value. City gates were the center of social and economic life in Bible times and were therefore a favorite place for merchants, politicians, and prophets.

8:12-21 *The worth and availability of wisdom.* Wisdom gives understanding and strength (8:14), as well as riches and honor (8:18-21). It enables kings to rule well (8:15-16). Best of all, there are no prerequisites to gaining wisdom except earnestly desiring it (8:17; see Matt. 7:7). Though wisdom tends to make its possessor wealthy (8:18, 21), it produces other fruit that is "better than the purest gold" (8:19).

8:22-31 *The person of wisdom.* Wisdom is described as an "architect" or "master craftsman" (8:30) who assisted God in creating the world. Because of other passages describing his important role in Creation, scholars tend to view these verses as a description of Christ (see John 1:1-3; Col. 1:15-17).

8:32-36 *The rewards of wisdom.* To find wisdom is to find life. To despise wisdom is to wrong one's own soul and to love death.

9:1-6 *The banquet of wisdom.* Wisdom is again presented as a noble lady offering instruction (see 3:13-18). Having prepared a banquet, she invites "those without good judgment" to feast on her life-giving teachings.

9:7-12 *The reaction to wisdom.* When the voice of wisdom offers advice, wise people and scoffers respond very differently. Wise people welcome the advice and become still wiser (9:9); scoffers despise the person giving the advice (9:7-8). The difference between these two kinds of people is that the wise person fears the Lord (9:10; see 1:7; Job 28:28).

9:13-18 *The enemy of wisdom.* Having described "Dame Wisdom," the father ended his admonition by again describing "Dame Folly," who was obviously the exact opposite of everything Dame Wisdom stood for. For instance, while Wisdom counseled the young man to drink from his own well (5:15)—that is, to be faithful to his wife—Folly declared that "stolen water is refreshing" (9:17).

PROVERBS OF SOLOMON (10:1–22:16)

Except for 1–9, most of the book of Proverbs consists of short, disconnected proverbs, many of which touch on similar themes. While each proverb offers valuable insights into skillful living (see exposition on 1:1-7) and deserves careful study, the present exposition can only cover representative sections and give references to parallel passages.

10:1-7 *The wise and foolish children.* Solomon noted the stark contrasts between the wise child, who is a joy to his parents, and the foolish child, who brings them grief (see 17:21, 25; 19:13; 23:24-25).

10:19 *Are your lips sealed?* It is unwise to speak too hastily or openly (see 15:28; 17:27-28; 21:23; 29:20), especially when you are angry (see 12:16; 19:11; 29:11; James 1:19).

10:22-32 *Rewards for the right, ruin for the wrong.* Solomon drew several contrasts between the righteous, who will eventually receive the desires of their heart, and the wicked, who will come to sudden ruin (see 11:19, 23; 12:7, 21; 13:21; 15:6; 17:20; 28:18; 29:1).

11:1 *Calibrate those scales!* God is concerned with honesty in the marketplace. The law of Moses demanded honest measurements in "length, weight, or volume" (Lev. 19:35-36). For instance, a dishonest Israelite merchant may have taken a weight that he knew weighed one pound and written a higher or lower weight on it, depending on whether he was using it for buying or selling (see 16:11; 20:10, 23). Likewise, a person buying land may have secretly moved a boundary marker in order to increase the size of his property (see 22:28; 23:10-11). Modern technology has produced many advancements in such theft by deception.

11:4-9 *Dollars won't help on that day.* Money cannot buy righteousness in God's economy. For "day of judgment," see exposition on Isa. 2:5–4:1.

11:5-6, 8 *Caught in their own trap.* While the righteous are delivered, the wicked are often ensnared by their own evil devices (see 28:10). For other biblical examples of God's turning evil intentions to his own glory, see exposition on Ezra 6:1-12.

11:10-11 *The upright uphold the city.* Righteous citizens are truly a blessing and should be recognized as such (see 14:34).

11:14 *Get a second—and third—opinion.* When making an important decision, it is wise to get advice from several sources (see 15:22; 24:6).

11:22 *A gold ring in a pig's snout.* Spiritual traits such as modesty are more important than physical beauty.

11:24-26 *The ironies of greed and generosity.* Generous people end up receiving more than they give, while stingy people lose what they try to keep (see 13:7; 19:17; 21:13; 22:9; 2 Cor. 6:10; James 2:5).

11:27-31 *Your inheritance: Trees or wind?* "The godly are like trees that bear life-giving fruit," while "those who bring trouble on their families inherit only the wind." Throughout Proverbs, Solomon and the other wise men expressed confidence that good would ultimately triumph over evil (see 10:25; 12:3, 7, 12; 14:11; 29:16). Proverbs' frequent use of tree images ("tree," "foliage," "roots") for the righteous recalls Psalm 1.

12:1 *Do you hate school?* A wise person loves learning from others (see 10:8; 15:31-33; 19:20), while "fools think they need no advice" and therefore see no need for instruction or correction (see 12:15; 13:18; 16:25; Judg. 21:25). The fool's unrealistically high self-esteem comes from his or her rejection of God, which leads to wickedness and a lack of understanding of the common-sense issues of life (see *Background* and exposition on 26:1-12).

13:20 *Choose your friends wisely.* People tend to become like the people with whom they associate. One should be especially careful of forming close friendships with "fools," or with angry or evil people (see 22:24-25; 24:1; 29:24). It is only natural for good and evil people to avoid each other's company (see 29:27; Ps. 1:1; 1 Cor. 15:33).

13:22 *"Your gold will go to the godly."* Wealth gained dishonestly often ends up benefiting the godly poor rather than the ungodly rich who accumulated it (see 28:8; Eccles. 2:26).

14:1 *Destroying your own home.* The foolish person will destroy even those things most precious to him or her.

14:12 *"But it seemed so right."* Decisions that seem right, humanly speaking, may be totally wrong by God's standards. Human nature, aided by the work of Satan, can make darkness appear as light (see 2 Cor. 11:14). Believers should always compare their own thoughts with Scripture (see 16:1-3; 21:2; 24:12).

14:15, 18 *Simple today, a fool tomorrow.* The position of the "simple" person, the "naive" bystander (14:15, NASB), is not neutral but extremely precarious, for he or she is in the process of becoming a fool (14:18; see *Purpose*).

14:20-21 *"They don't have friends, so be their friend."* Solomon had noticed that the rich tend to be much more popular than the poor (14:20); he urged believers not to practice such discrimination (14:21). Many Proverbs, like 14:20, are simply observations about the realities of life, rather than statements of moral truth (see *Background*). For instance, 14:20 does not mean a poor person will *never* have friends.

18:23 and 19:4, 7 offer similar observations about discrimination against the poor, while 28:27 issues a similar admonition against such discrimination.

16:14-15, 20:14, 21:14, and 22:7 are other examples of observation proverbs.

14:27 *When fear is a fountain of life.* "The advice of the wise is a life-giving fountain," as is "fear of the LORD" (13:13-14). Those who seek life outside the law will find only death. (See 10:27; 19:16, 23; 28:14.)

14:31 *Protector of the poor.* God identifies with the poor and views as a personal reproach any oppression or mockery of them (see 17:5; 19:17; 21:13). He establishes their property rights (see 15:25; 23:10-11) and pleads their cause (22:22-23).

15:1-2, 4, 7 *Your word power.* Words have great power to either heal or hurt (see 12:18; 16:24). They can "bring life and health" (15:4), "lead to life" (10:11), or be "as lovely as golden apples" (25:11). Used wrongly, words can crush the spirit (15:4), "pierce like a sword" (12:18, NIV), and bring death (18:21). (See 12:17-19, 22-23; on gossip, see exposition on 26:17-28.)

While the proximity of two proverbs does not necessarily imply a connection, the affirmation of God's omnipresence (15:3) reminds us that he hears our every word. We cannot conceal gossip or foolish talk from God by moving to a private place or lowering our voice (see Ps. 139:7-12).

15:6, 16-17 *Do the righteous always prosper?* 15:6 declares that "there is treasure in the house of the godly." 15:16-17 makes it clear, however, that this is not always the case. Yet when the righteous experience hard times, they can be assured that a life of poverty in godly surroundings is better than a life of wealth amid ungodliness (see 16:8; 17:1; 19:1; 28:6).

15:8-9 *Heartless worship.* The mere offering of a sacrifice means nothing to the Lord unless the worshiper's heart is right. The cost-free prayer of the upright is worth far more than the expensive animal sacrifice of the wicked (see 21:27).

15:13, 15 *Better than medicine.* As modern-day health professionals are discovering, the emotions play a key role in physical well-being (see 15:30; 17:22).

16:18-19 *Pride and prosperity.* Pride leads to humiliation, while humility brings honor (see 11:2; 18:12; 22:4; 29:23). It is better to be humble and poor than proud and rich. The OT repeatedly presents pride and idolatry as the sins most dangerous to God's children.

16:31 *Gray hair: A badge of honor, if . . .* Older people have earned a "crown of glory," if they have lived a godly life (see 20:29).

17:8 *Bribers, beware!* Solomon noted several times in Proverbs the things that can be accomplished by a timely gift or bribe (see 18:16; 21:14). Yet even though this is the way ungodly people do things, God condemns bribery (see 17:23).

17:13, 15, 26 *No plea bargains, please!* Like other Bible authors, Solomon took issue with those who, out of favoritism, condemn the innocent or acquit the guilty (see 18:5; 24:23-25; 28:21; Exod. 23:7; Isa. 5:23).

17:14 *Anyone can start a quarrel. . . .* It takes very little effort to start an argument but much effort to prevent or stop one (see 20:3).

17:16 *Always a waste.* A fool will squander opportunities to gain both wisdom and wealth (see 21:20).

18:8 *To gossip or not to gossip?* Gossip is a universal temptation; it is like "dainty morsels." The wise person will not gossip, choosing rather to conceal the tempting information (see 11:13). He or she conceals it out of love (see 10:12), knowing the great damage gossip can do (see 16:28; 17:9; 1 Pet. 4:8).

18:13, 17 *Listen to both sides.* It is unwise to form an opinion before hearing both sides of an issue.

18:18 *Gambling or divine guidance?* Solomon viewed the casting of lots not as gambling but as trust in God's overruling providence (see 16:33). When the apostles chose Matthias, their casting of lots was preceded with prayer (see Acts 1:24-26; see also Lev. 16:8; Esther 3:7; Jon. 1:7.)

18:24 *The best of all brothers!* Friendship ties can be even closer than family ties and can provide opportunities for mutual edification and correction (see 27:6, 17). Yet Solomon also acknowledged the great worth of blood relationships (see 17:17).

20:9 *The answer? Nobody!* "Is anyone righteous?" Solomon answered the question in the negative (see 1 Kings 8:46; Eccles. 7:20), as did David (Ps. 14:1-3), Paul (Rom. 3:10), and John (1 John 1:8).

20:17, 21 *Don't get rich too quickly!* Wealth gained dishonestly, or too quickly, will bring misery (see 13:11;

21:5-6; 28:20, 22; 1 Tim. 6:9-10). By contrast, "people who work hard sleep well" (Eccles. 5:12).

20:19 *Don't fall for flattery!* The wise person will not be taken in by flattery, knowing that it can often be a trap (29:5). Rather, he or she will value honest criticism (28:23). (See Rom. 16:18.)

20:20 *No light for the rebel.* Just as great blessing is promised to those who honor their parents (see Eph. 6:2-3), those who dishonor them will suffer severely (see Exod. 21:17). Evil people are portrayed as being "snuffed out" also in 13:9 and 24:20.

21:3 *He watches the worshiper, not the worship.* God valued purity of heart and justice in social relationships more than correctness in worship, even under the OT sacrificial system (see 21:27; 24:11-12; 1 Sam. 15:22; Ps. 50:7-15; Isa. 1:11, 17; 58:1-12).

21:9, 19 *Sometimes it's simpler to be single!* A life of singleness and poverty is preferable to marriage to a disagreeable spouse (see 19:13; 25:24; 27:15-16).

21:17 *Love pleasure, lose your treasure.* The hedonist, like the lazy person (see exposition on 6:6-11), will end in poverty (see 23:20-21; 28:19).

21:22 *Right vs. might.* Wisdom will eventually win the day over military strength (see 24:5-6; Eccles. 7:19).

21:30-31 *Lord of all!* No amount of human thought, planning (21:30), or action (21:31) can negate God's sovereign will. Ultimate justice will come from him (21:31; see 29:26). Even kings are subject to God (21:1).

22:1 *A good name.* A good name is to be preferred over all the riches of the world (see Eccles. 7:1).

22:2 *The common bond of rich and poor.* Solomon's admonitions to respect those who live in poverty (see 14:31 and exposition on 14:20-21) were grounded in the realization that all humans have the same Creator (see 29:13; Job 31:13-15; Gal. 3:28).

22:6 *If you love them, train them.* If children are diligently trained, they will remember and benefit from that training. If left to themselves (see 29:15), their inexperience can lead them into foolish mistakes with lifelong consequences (22:15). They should be trained and disciplined while there is still hope (see 19:18) of saving them (see 23:13-14; Ps. 9). The well-disciplined child will be a delight to his or her parents (see 29:17). (See exposition on 3:11-12; Deut. 6:6-7; Eph. 6:4; Heb. 12:7.)

WORDS OF THE WISE (22:17–24:34)

22:17-21 *"Here's what I want you to know."* The anonymous compiler of this third collection of Proverbs invited the reader to "apply your heart" to his sayings, which are "filled with advice and knowledge."

22:29 *The pursuit of excellence.* Success will come to those who pursue excellence in their work, while "lazy people" (10:4) or those who talk instead of work (see 14:23) will not succeed.

23:1-5 *When a ruler invites you to dinner.* Dinner at a ruler's house calls for avoiding gluttony and being wary of the host's ulterior motives (23:1-3). When in such situations, one would do well to heed the perspective on wealth that follows (23:4-5).

23:6-8 *When a miser invites you to dinner.* A dinner invitation from a miser is just as well turned down; your efforts at friendship will be wasted on him or her.

23:15-28 *Watch out for wine and wicked women.* As in 1:8–9:18, the writer addressed his child, urging him to seek godly wisdom (23:15-18, 22-25) and to avoid the company of drunkards and gluttons (23:19-21) and immoral women (23:26-28).

23:29-35 *It sparkles. . . . It stings.* Alcoholic beverages may be appealing to the senses (23:31), but as these graphic illustrations show, they are a hindrance to wisdom and can cause great physical and emotional harm (see 20:1).

24:3-4 *The house that wisdom built.* The practice of wisdom produces a full and satisfying life, which may or may not include material prosperity (see exposition on 8:12-21 and on 15:6, 16-17).

24:11-12 *Rescue the perishing!* Pretended ignorance (24:12) is no excuse for failing to speak up for the victims of violence and injustice (see exposition on 21:3).

24:15-20 *Down seven times, but not out!* No matter how often a righteous person is seemingly defeated, he or she will always recover. The wicked person, however, will fall and not recover (24:15-16).

The righteous should not, however, rejoice over the misfortunes of the wicked (24:17; see Job 31:29; 1 Cor. 13:6). Such rejoicing could turn God's wrath away from the sinner and against the righteous (24:18; see 17:5).

Even when the wicked person prospers, he or she is not to be envied, for, in terms of eternity, "the evil have no future" (24:19-20).

24:21-22 *A wise rebel?* Even though political rebellions may seem to have legitimate causes (see 28:2), the wise person will tend to avoid getting involved in them, choosing rather to trust in God's providence over human affairs (see exposition on 21:30-31; Rom. 13:1-7; 1 Pet. 2:13-17).

24:29 *The Rule was always Golden!* Rather than return evil for evil, OT believers were to trust God to bring about justice for them (see 20:22; Deut. 32:35; Rom. 12:17-21). The NT states this principle positively as the "Golden Rule" (see Matt. 7:12; 5:39; 7:12).

MORE PROVERBS OF SOLOMON (25:1–29:27)

25:1 *Copied by Hezekiah.* A second collection of proverbs attributed to Solomon begins with the note that they were compiled by "the advisers of King Hezekiah."

25:2-7 *In the corridors of power.* Speaking no doubt from experience, Solomon offered observations concerning those who seek to influence kings. Even though it is easier to know the mind of a king than to know the mind of God (25:2), they are still somewhat mysterious (25:3). Those who seek an audience with a king should do so with the greatest humility (25:6-7; see 27:2; Luke 14:7-11). Meanwhile, the king himself must be very careful about whose advice he listens to, for there will be no shortage of unsavory characters seeking his influence (25:4-5; see 20:26).

25:8-10 *Be slow to sue.* It is better to settle disputes in private than to risk public humiliation (see Matt. 18:15).

25:16-17 *Moderation in all things.* Whether the subject is food or friendship, one should never overdo a good thing.

25:18 *When words are deadly weapons.* Three warlike similes describe the harm that can be done by the false witness; such liars deserve severe punishment (see 19:5, 9; 21:28).

25:21-22 *Kindness, not combat.* Whenever possible, an enemy is to be treated kindly. As with the prohibition of vengeance (see exposition on 24:29), the NT is not the only place that teaches love for one's enemy (see Exod. 23:4-5; Matt. 5:43-45; Rom. 12:20-21).

25:28 *How high are your walls?* A person with no self-control exposes himself or herself to all kinds of danger, just like an ancient city with no walls (see 14:29; 16:32; 19:11).

26:1-12 *Facts on the fool.* The fool (see *Background*) is described from several perspectives. He is unworthy of honor but very worthy of a good beating (26:1, 3; see 19:29). He is useless for any practical endeavor (26:6-8). Efforts to reform him are hopeless (26:11). (See 17:10, 12; 23:9.)

26:4-5 does not have to be seen as a contradiction: While one generally should not engage in useless dialogue with a fool, sometimes it may be necessary to do so, so that he won't think his worthless arguments are beyond challenge.

26:13-16 *Which one is the laziest?* After drawing three caricatures of lazy people, Solomon contemptuously noted that even such sloths are wise in their own eyes (see exposition on 6:6-11).

26:17-28 *Misuses of the mouth.* Solomon condemned the insensitive practical joker (26:18-19) and the flatterer (26:28), along with the hypocrite (26:23-26), liar (26:28), troublemaker (26:17, 21), and gossip (26:20, 22) for their misuses of the gift of speech.

27:14 *"Hold it down out there!"* Some observation proverbs (see exposition on 14:20-21) appear to take a lighter view of life, or at least to look at serious issues in a more philosophical way (see 25:19). Others deal with familiar emotions not necessarily related to any moral issue (see 13:12; 14:10, 13; 25:20, 25).

27:23-27 *Work now, enjoy later.* The person who is punctual and diligent in his or her work will, in due time, enjoy the fruit of that work (compare 24:27 and 28:19).

28:1 *What are they afraid of?* While a guilty conscience breeds irrational fear, a clear conscience produces self-confidence. Furthermore, good people have far fewer enemies than do the wicked (see 16:7).

28:11 *The emperor's new clothes.* Wealth can give a person an unrealistically high opinion of himself or herself. It is part of the "lure of wealth" (Matt. 13:22). Meanwhile, a perceptive poor person "sees through" the deceived rich person (28:11, NASB).

28:13 *Confession or cover-up?* Honest confession of sin is always better than any attempt to conceal an unpleasant truth (see Job 31:33; Ps. 32:3-5; 1 John 1:9).

28:15-16 *The use and abuse of power.* Kings have great power for good or ill (see 28:28; 29:2, 4) and will be rewarded according to how they use that power (28:16; see 29:14). They should remember that, though many seek their favor, God will have the last say (see 29:26). (See 16:14-15; 19:12; exposition on 25:2-7 and on 31:1-9)

29:18 *Needed: Leaders from the Lord.* Without good spiritual leadership, people tend to fall deeply into sin (see Exod. 32:25; Judg. 21:25; 1 Sam. 3:1; Amos 8:11-12; Mark 6:34; Heb. 13:17).

THE WISDOM OF AGUR (30)

30:1-4 *"I know so little about the Lord."* Agur introduced the collection of his wise sayings by acknowledging his own lack of knowledge and wisdom concerning the ways of God. 30:4 recalls Job 38–41, where the Lord convinced Job of *his* lack of such knowledge.

30:5-6 *Absolutely accurate: No additions allowed!* Agur declared that God's words were "true" and that humans should not add to them. This is the OT counterpart to Revelation 22:18-19—the Bible's affirmation that its message and even its very words are completely trustworthy.

30:7-10 *Not too rich, not too poor.* Agur sought a happy medium between wealth and poverty so that he would not fall prey to the temptations associated with either extreme.

30:11-31 *"Amazing in three . . . or four . . . ways."* Having expressed amazement at the God of creation (see 30:4), Agur made several observations about the humans and animals that populate God's world. Since the number three expresses completion, his repeatedly making four observations instead of just three implies that he could have listed many more:

Four kinds of sinners (30:11-14). Agur singled out four kinds of people for special rebuke: Those who disrespect their parents, hypocrites, the proud, and the greedy. (On "devouring" the poor, see Ps. 14:4; Amos 8:4.)

Four unsatisfied things (30:15-16). Agur had seen many things—and people—as insatiable as leeches.

Four fantastic things (30:18-19). Agur expressed wonder at three natural and one human phenomena. The mixture of human and nonhuman examples both here and in 30:15-16 suggests that Agur found the human examples by far the most amazing.

Four unbearable things (30:21-23). People given positions or honors they don't deserve become unbearable to those over whom they have power (see 19:10).

Four small, smart, strong things (30:24-28). Even the seemingly least significant members of the animal kingdom can teach us wisdom, since they, like us, were created by God.

Four things that march like a monarch (30:29-31). The list of "stately monarchs," like the two lists of 30:15-19, contains three nonhuman examples and one human example.

30:32-33 *"Keep calm and quiet!"* Perhaps thinking still of the "king as he leads his army" (30:31), Agur issued a final call for patience and humility.

THE WORDS OF LEMUEL (31:1-9)

31:1-7 *"Abstain from adultery and alcohol."* Lemuel, identified by some as Solomon, advised kings to abstain from alcoholic drink and from immoral sexual relationships (see 23:19-28). Both are hindrances to the wisdom rulers need.

31:8-9 *"Defend the defenseless."* On the positive side, kings should have a special concern for the poor and the defenseless—as does the Lord (see exposition on 14:31).

THE WORTHY WOMAN (31:10-31)

31:10-31 *The worthy woman.* The writer, assumed by many to be Solomon, described a woman who was a good wife (31:10-12, 23, 28); a caring mother (31:15, 21, 27-28); a vital part of her community's social and economic life (31:13, 16-20, 23-24); and, in general, an honorable person (31:25-31; see 12:4; 18:22; 19:14).

c. 971 B.C.
Solomon granted wisdom

960
Solomon completes Temple

c. 935?
Solomon writes Ecclesiastes (after apostasy?)

931
Death of Solomon

ECCLESIASTES

BACKGROUND

The wise King Solomon (see *Author*), who shared his God-given wisdom in Proverbs, focused in Ecclesiastes on the meaning of life in an imperfect, fallen world. Though Solomon's faith in God shows through at key places (see 3:14; 5:7; 8:12; 12:8, 13), he seems for the most part to leave God out of the equation, declaring again and again that life is meaningless. A thorough reading of the book suggests, however, that Solomon's purpose was to show how utterly meaningless life is *apart from God.*

The word *vanity,* translated "meaningless" by the NLT and NIV, appears 29 times and sets the tone of despair that pervades Ecclesiastes. The phrase "under the sun" appears 27 times and suggests that Solomon was making his case for despair based only on evidence from the natural world.

As the outline suggests, Solomon dealt with the problem of life's apparent meaninglessness in four stages:

- He stated his "belief" that life is meaningless (1:1-11).
- He offered evidence for that belief, showing how his and other people's efforts to find meaning in life yielded only despair (1:12–6:12).
- He offered advice about how to cope with a meaningless world (7:1–12:8).
- Having hinted at his own belief in God, he concluded by stating that meaning *can* be found through faith in and obedience to God (12:9-14).

Ecclesiastes appears to be the work of a Solomon made older and wiser by the unforeseeable misfortunes of life and by his own serious mistakes in spite of his great wisdom (see exposition on 5:8-12; 1 Kings 11:1-13). Ecclesiastes, which means "teacher" or "preacher," was Solomon's pen name for this book as well as the book's title (1:1).

AUTHOR

Solomon:

- He is "King David's son, who ruled in Jerusalem" (1:1).
- The description of the author's wealth and variety of experiences fits what we know of Solomon.
- The book's great wisdom fits Solomon, who received wisdom as a gift from God (see 1 Kings 3:1-13) and authored numerous proverbs (see 1 Kings 4:29-34).

DATE AND LOCATION

Ecclesiastes was likely written in the latter years of Solomon's life, c. 935 B.C. (see *Background*), in Jerusalem (1:1).

PURPOSE

See *Background.*

UNIQUE FEATURES

- Because of its focus on the meaning of life, Ecclesiastes has a unique appeal to people of all religions.
- The repetitions of *vanity* and *under the sun* (see *Background*) constitute the most prominent emphasis of a single word or phrase in any biblical book.

COMPARISON WITH OTHER BIBLE BOOKS

See *Job; Proverbs: Comparison with Other Bible Books*

OUTLINE

LIFE IS MEANINGLESS: THE PROBLEM (1:1-11)
LIFE IS MEANINGLESS: THE PROOF (1:12–6:12)
LIFE IN A MEANINGLESS WORLD (7:1–12:8)
THE BIRTH OF A MEANINGFUL LIFE (12:9-14)

LIFE IS MEANINGLESS: THE PROBLEM (1:1-11)

1:1-11 *"Nothing matters! All is meaningless!"* Solomon began his discourse on life by declaring, "Everything is meaningless" (1:2; see 12:8; Ps. 39:5-6). He illustrated this meaninglessness from the realms of nature (1:1-7) and human experience (1:8-11). Sunrises and sunsets come and go. The winds blow and the rivers flow, but for no apparent purpose. The human experience could be summarized as, "Been there, done that!"

LIFE IS MEANINGLESS: THE PROOF (1:12–6:12)

1:12-18 *He decides to find out for himself.* With his privileged position as a wise and wealthy king, Solomon felt able—and compelled—to discover whether life was indeed as meaningless as his own experience suggested.

2:1-3 *"It's party time!"* Solomon had sought meaning through the pursuit of pleasure but quickly concluded that such a pursuit was worthless. Pleasure would never satisfy people's greatest need—the need for peace and purpose.

2:4-11 *Creature comforts by the cartload.* Solomon had then tried to plug the hole in his soul by inaugurating great public works projects, by amassing a great fortune, and by further seeking to satisfy his every desire. He concluded, "But as I looked at everything I had worked so hard to accomplish, it was all so meaningless. It was like chasing the wind" (2:11).

2:12-17 *Wisdom is better, but not for long.* Solomon meditated on the relative merits of wisdom and folly. Though the wise person was obviously better than the fool, as light is superior to darkness, there was a fatal flaw: Both the wise and the foolish alike would soon die and be forgotten.

2:18-23 *"The worthless will inherit your wealth."* Though wise people and fools are equal in death, in a way the wise person's lot is worse because the wealth he or she has accumulated through wisdom might end up, after his or her death, in the hands of a fool!

2:24-26 *"So enjoy it now!"* Since you can't take it with you and a fool may inherit your wealth, Solomon concluded, you might as well enjoy it to the fullest while you can.

3:1-8 *You name it, there's a time for it!* Solomon listed some 28 "times" in the calendars of humanity. With the exception of the first two—the time of their birth and death—people for the most part control the timing of these events.

3:9-15 *Eternity in our hearts, but creatures of time.* God has given humans some concept of eternity, but they are still creatures of time. God alone is eternal, controlling both past and future. The bottom line for humans, said Solomon, is to fear God (3:14; see 5:7; 8:12; 12:13), to be happy (3:12), and to enjoy God's gifts (3:12-13; see 5:18-19; 8:15).

3:16-22 *No better than animals?* Solomon noted the evil and injustice in the world and expressed confidence that God would, in his own time, judge all things. Till then, however, humans sometimes seem no better than animals, with both breathing the same air, eating the same food, and dying similar deaths.

4:1-3 *The best fate? To have never existed!* Considering all the suffering in the world, Solomon concluded, the dead are more fortunate than the living, and those never born are most fortunate of all!

4:4-8 *Envy and the economy.* Envy drives people to work needlessly hard to accumulate the things they covet. (Someone has described this process as buying things we don't need with money we don't have to impress people we don't like!)

4:9-12 *Two are better, and three is best!* God created humans to function as social, not solitary, creatures (see Gen. 2:18).

4:13-16 *Success quickly turns sour.* Success is never permanent, as exemplified by the poor youth who wins the people's hearts away from the old monarch, only to fall into disfavor himself.

5:1-7 *"Watch your words, but keep your vows!"* Solomon cautioned against making rash vows but also asserted that once a vow is made it must be fulfilled (see Deut. 23:21-23; Judg. 11:29-40).

5:8-12 *Trickle-down dishonesty.* Bribery and corruption, Solomon sadly observed, often begin at the very top with the king, and then affect all the officials who surround him. In sharp contrast to this elite but corrupt world is the common working man, who is poor but at peace with himself.

There is some indication that Solomon himself may have been guilty of corruption later in his reign (see 1 Kings 12:1-4).

5:13-17 *Gone with the wind.* Solomon had seen people hurt by risky investments gone sour, which naturally confirmed his conviction of life's meaninglessness. Jesus spoke of a better kind of investment that yields a guaranteed 100 percent return! (See Matt. 6:19-21; 19:29.)

5:18-20 *"Do your best, enjoy the rest!"* In light of life's brevity, said Solomon, the best philosophy is to work hard, enjoy the fruits of that work, and not think too much about life's brevity but leave such matters to God (see exposition on 9:9-12).

6:1-6 *Wealth without health.* Another of life's unfortunate ironies is that people often become wealthy only when they no longer have the physical capacity to enjoy their wealth (6:1-2). Likewise, the person who is rich in children but does not enjoy them would be better off not to have been born (6:3-6).

6:7-9 *A bird in the hand . . .* Humans labor to satisfy their desires, yet those desires are never satisfied (6:7). Those are happiest who are content with what they have (6:9).

6:10-12 *Has the past determined the present?* In light of God's overwhelming sovereignty (6:10; see Job 9:32), Solomon seemed somewhat fatalistic about the ability of mere humans to affect their own lives. His apparent fatalism should, however, be interpreted in light of his later encouragement of his readers to exercise their free will (12:9-14).

LIFE IN A MEANINGLESS WORLD (7:1–12:8)

Even if life has no meaning, one should live wisely. Solomon tried to promote such wisdom.

7:1-4 *Better a funeral than a festival!* The death of a friend causes us to take inventory of our own life and to confront our mortality. As someone has said, "Only one life; 'twill soon be past. Only what's done for Christ will last."

7:5-26 *The fruits of the fool and the way of the wise.* Much of Solomon's advice in 7–11 is in the form of proverbs:

- "It is better to be criticized by a wise person than to be praised by a fool" (7:5).
- Wisdom is better than wealth (7:11-12).
- The wise person avoids extremes (7:16-17).
- Wisdom is better than military power (7:19).
- The wise person avoids sexual immorality (7:26).

7:27–8:1 *One in a thousand?* Solomon had found few who exhibited true wisdom (see Prov. 20:9). His apparent prejudice against women (7:28) should be judged in light of Proverbs 31:10-31 and the Song of Songs. The few who are wise can be identified by their shining faces (8:1; see Prov. 3:13-18; 4:18).

8:2-9 *Obey the king!* The wise person in this imperfect world will be obedient to established civil authority, trusting God to bring about final justice (8:6; see exposition on Prov. 24:21-22 and on Rom. 13:1-7). Such submission makes sense in light of our inability to foresee the future (8:7-8; see James 4:13-15).

8:10-17 *What if he commits a hundred crimes?* Though the wicked often seem to go unpunished in this life, their day of judgment will surely come (see Acts 17:31; Rev. 20:11-15). Rather than try to figure out such mysteries (8:16-17), one should simply enjoy life and trust God's providence (8:15; see 2:24; 3:12-13; 5:18; 9:7).

9:1-8 *"Better a live dog than a dead lion!"* Even though life seems unfair, and the righteous die just as quickly as the wicked (9:1-3), in the final analysis life has tremendous advantages over death. Only the living can hope, aspire, plan, and enjoy life's many rewards.

Solomon's statement that "the dead know nothing" (9:5) should be interpreted in light of his later statement that "the spirit will return to God" (12:7). To Christians who understand eternal life in light of Christ's resurrection, OT statements about the afterlife often seem inadequate. However, the OT saints were not without hope of life beyond the grave (see exposition on Isa. 26:1-19).

9:9-12 *"Enjoy! It's later than you think!"* Because life can end so unexpectedly (9:11-12), one should enjoy the pleasure (9:9) and fulfillment (9:10) it affords (see exposition on 5:18-20; Job 7:6-7; Ps. 102:3; 103:14-16; James 4:13-15).

9:13-18 *Wisdom, though good, is often forgotten.* Though wisdom is superior to folly, few appreciate it, as exemplified by a wise man who saved his city and was then forgotten.

10:1-20 *Sometimes it seems that nothing goes right!* This imperfect world is full of perils: Dig a well and you may fall into it. Demolish a wall and you may be bitten by a snake. Work in a quarry and you risk being crushed by stones. And as always, the fool talks nonsense (10:11-15), and even those in authority may not be trustworthy (10:16-20). In such a world, it is wise to be cautious and even a little pessimistic.

11:1-6 *Risks and returns.* Life in an imperfect world involves taking risks and investing generously (see Luke 6:38). The person who waits for perfect conditions never accomplishes anything (11:4), but the person who steps out in faith (11:5) and works hard (11:6) will find great reward.

11:7-10 *Enjoyment now, but judgment later.* As a person enjoys the fruit of hard work, he or she should remember that death and judgment will surely come (see Heb. 9:27).

12:1-8 *"Young person, prepare for old age!"* Solomon warned the young among his readers to be prepared for old age, when all the joys of youth (see 11:9) would be just a memory. The best way to prepare for that difficult time is to love God and live for him today (12:1). Without such a commitment of faith, life would end as it began, without meaning or purpose (12:8; see 1:2).

THE BIRTH OF A MEANINGFUL LIFE (12:9-14)

12:9-14 *In a nutshell: Fear and obey him.* After confidently affirming the inspiration of his message and urging his readers to take it very seriously (12:9-12), Solomon summed up what he had learned from his quest for life's meaning: The only way one can make sense of life is to "fear God and obey his commands" (12:13; see 3:14; 5:7; 8:12; Prov. 1:7; 9:10).

c. 971 B.C.
Solomon, marries 1st wife

c. 950?
Solomon writes Song of Songs (before numerous wives?)

931
Death of Solomon

SONG OF SONGS

BACKGROUND

The Song of Songs, also called the Song of Solomon, is a collection of love poems between a husband and wife, with occasional sections attributed to friends or relatives who shared in the couple's happiness. The personal pronouns in the original text suggest the identities of the various speakers, and though they occasionally differ, several modern English translations provide subheads in an effort to identify those speakers.

The poems describe the couple's courtship and marriage, though it is not entirely clear at what point the marriage took place (see exposition on 4:16–5:1).

In explicit but tasteful and beautiful imagery, Song of Songs celebrates both the emotional and physical aspects of marriage.

AUTHOR

Solomon (1:1). Though Solomon eventually had a thousand wives and concubines (see 1 Kings 11:3), he could have written Song of Songs early in his life, before his sinful polygamy.

Some scholars have suggested that 1:1–3:5 describes the woman's true love, a peasant shepherd, while the rest of the book describes Solomon's using his kingly position to steal the woman away from the shepherd. Most recent scholarship, however, sees Solomon as the sole male protagonist throughout. Some have suggested he may have disguised himself as a shepherd to see whether the woman would love him without knowing his true kingly identity.

Of the 1,005 songs Solomon composed (see 1 Kings 4:32), this was his "song of songs" (1:1), his very best.

DATE AND LOCATION

About 950 B.C., in Jerusalem.

PURPOSE

- *The review:* Song of Songs demonstrates the love that should exist between a husband and wife.
- *The preview:* Christians through the ages have seen the book as an illustration of Christ's love for his bride, the church.

UNIQUE FEATURES

- Song of Songs is unique among Bible books for its intimate look at sexual love.
- It is one of only two Bible books that do not mention the name of God (the other is Esther).

COMPARISON WITH OTHER BIBLE BOOKS

Proverbs:

- Both use water metaphors to describe women (4:15; Prov. 5:15-18).
- Both use the gazelle or doe as an illustration of gracefulness (2:7, 9, 17; Prov. 5:19).
- Money can buy neither love (8:7) nor wisdom (Prov. 3:13-15; 8:10-11).
- The voice of love in Song of Songs is similar to the voice of the prophetess (Dame Wisdom) in Proverbs 8:1–9:12. Both voices draw people in powerful ways.

Ecclesiastes:

- While Ecclesiastes describes Solomon's vain search for happiness, Song of Songs tells of at least one time, perhaps early in his kingship, when he did find it.

OUTLINE

ACT ONE: SERENADED BY A SHEPHERD (1:1–3:5)
ACT TWO: MARRIED TO A MONARCH (3:6–8:4)
CONCLUSION: THE WONDER OF WEDDED LOVE (8:5-14)

ACT ONE: SERENADED BY A SHEPHERD (1:1–3:5)

1:1–2:2 *"You light up my life!"* The female lead of the story, a Shulamite (see 6:13), joyfully described her lover and her love for him (1:2-4, 7), then described herself (1:5-6). Her friends, the "young women of Jerusalem" (see 2:7), shared in her joy (1:4).

The Shulamite had been forced to work in her brothers' vineyard but had neglected her own vineyard, meaning she had been unable to adequately care for herself (1:6).

The Shulamite asked the shepherd where she could find him (1:7); he invited her to come to him, praised her beauty (1:8), and they traded further words of mutual admiration (1:9–2:2).

The Shulamite described herself as the "rose of Sharon" (2:1). Sharon was a coastal wasteland characterized by scrub oak forests and swamps. But amid this ugliness were beautiful roses. The shepherd agreed with this metaphor of contrast, calling the Shulamite a "lily among thorns" (2:2).

2:3-7 *Expressions of love, public and private.* The Shulamite recalled the shepherd's expressions of love both in public (2:4-5) and in private (2:3, 6). She declared to her friends what would become the dominant theme of the book: Love cannot be bought or forced and shouldn't be prematurely aroused (2:7; see 3:5; 8:4, 6-7).

2:8-17 *"The voice of my beloved."* The Shulamite recalled the shepherd's tender words, perhaps a marriage proposal (2:8-13). The shepherd responded with more tender words (2:14), and the Shulamite responded in kind (2:16-17).

This interpretation follows the NIV assignment of section headings; in the orginal Hebrew, the speaker in each case is not always clear. Because of the reference to predators in the vineyard in 2:15, the NLT assigns that verse to the young women of Jerusalem. The NKJV assigns it to the Shulamite's brothers.

3:1-5 *Her midnight mission.* The Shulamite dreamed that she had lost her lover, but after searching diligently she found him.

ACT TWO: MARRIED TO A MONARCH (3:6–8:4)

3:6-11 *Coming in splendor with 60 soldiers.* The bride described Solomon in all his kingly majesty, accompanied by his royal bodyguard, coming to Jerusalem for their wedding.

4:1-15 *His praise: "Like doves, goats, and sheep."* Solomon praised his bride and expressed his love for her in similes drawn from nature and rural life (compare 6:4-10; 7:1-9).

4:16–5:1 *Her response: "Come to your garden!"* The bride replied with similar word pictures, inviting Solomon to consummate their marriage. The marriage was consummated, followed by great celebration. (Some commentators see the marriage taking place later, between 6:4–8:14.)

5:2-8 *She opens the door, but he is gone.* Solomon's wife dreamed of his knocking on her door at night, then disappearing. After trying to find him, she asked her friends to help in her search.

5:9–6:3 *"Why is he better than others? I'm glad you asked!"* The Shulamite's friends asked what was so special about Solomon that she would want so badly to find him (5:9). She responded with lavish words of praise that form a counterpart to Solomon's praise of her (5:10-16; see 4:1-15). The friends inquired further about Solomon's whereabouts, and she suggested looking in his garden (6:1-3).

6:4–7:9 *Their reunion brings more praise.* Having been reunited with her, Solomon once again praised his wife (6:4-10); she responded (6:11-12); and he resumed his expressions of admiration (7:1-9).

7:10–8:4 *"And now for the honeymoon!"* The Shulamite asked Solomon to take her away to the "fields" and "vineyards," where she would give him her love. She expressed her desire for a closer relationship with him (8:1-3) but acknowledged once again that love must not be prematurely aroused (8:4; see 2:7; 3:5).

CONCLUSION: THE WONDER OF WEDDED LOVE (8:5-14)

8:5-7 *Floods cannot quench it.* As she and Solomon returned from their honeymoon, the Shulamite spoke of the power of love and the jealousy it can cause. Love cannot be bought, it cannot be easily extinguished, and it should never be treated flippantly.

8:8-9 *"But what about our little sister?"* The Shulamite's brothers expressed concern about their little sister and promised to protect her from premature sexual advances, whether she proved to be chaste or promiscuous. (Hebrew, "If she is a wall [i.e., reserved], we will build battlements of silver on her; but if she is a door [i.e., overly outgoing], we will surround her with panels of cedar.")

8:10-14 *His vineyard, her vineyard.* Alluding to Solomon's literal vineyard, the Shulamite declared that she had faithfully kept the vineyard of her body for Solomon alone and invited him once more to partake of it (8:10-12). Solomon asked her to sing to him, and she responded (8:13-14).

INTRODUCTION TO THE PROPHETS

The OT concludes with 17 books of prophecy, beginning with Isaiah. These represent the ministries of 16 men of God who warned, exhorted, and encouraged a divided Israel and Judah in the troubled 400-year period of their decline, downfall, exile, and restoration:

Event or Person(s)	***Date(s)***	***Historical Record***
Israel and Judah divide	931 B.C.	1 Kings 12
Elijah and Elisha (major "nonwriting" prophets)	875–800	1 Kings 17—2 Kings 13
The 16 "writing" prophets (Isaiah—Malachi)	850–450	2 Kings 8—Nehemiah

The OT canon divides the prophetic books into the four longer or "major" prophets (including Lamentations), which are in chronological order, followed by the 12 "minor" prophets, whose chronology is less exact. Following are the approximate dates of each prophet's ministry:

Obadiah (850–840 B.C.)
Joel (835–796)
Jonah (790–760)
Amos (760–750)
Hosea (760–720)
Isaiah (740–690)
Micah (740–690)
Fall of northern kingdom (Israel) (722)
Nahum (630–612)
Zephaniah (632–621)
Habakkuk (612–605)
Jeremiah (627–580)
Fall of southern kingdom (Judah), exile (586)
Lamentations (586)
Ezekiel (592–570)
Daniel (580–536)
First return of exiles from Babylon (538)

Haggai (520)
Zechariah (520–480)
Second and third returns from Babylon (457 and 445)
Malachi (430)

The prophets' immediate concern was the present and the "near future"—the religious, moral, and political issues facing their contemporaries. But they were inspired by God to also foretell things concerning the "far future"—the coming of Jesus Christ the Messiah, his provision for salvation, and his ushering in of God's everlasting kingdom.

The dual focus on the near and far future, coupled with the prophets' often poetic style and their concern with the events of their own day, can make the interpretation of their writings somewhat challenging for readers from a different time and culture.

ISAIAH

BACKGROUND

When Isaiah began his ministry in about 740 B.C., Israel was at a crisis point in its history. Assyria, its menacing neighbor to the northeast, was well on its way to becoming the dominant force in the ancient Near East. Both the northern and southern kingdoms were tempted to form political alliances either with or against Assyria. Meanwhile, both Israel and Judah were suffering the devastating fruits of religious and moral compromise. God commissioned Isaiah to call Israel and Judah to repent of their sins and unbelief and to trust him alone for both personal salvation and national deliverance. 12:2 summarizes this overall theme: "See, God has come to save me. I will trust in him and not be afraid."

In 1–35 Isaiah spoke to a nation awaiting God's judgment, which would come in 722 (during Isaiah's ministry) for the northern kingdom and in 586 (100 years after Isaiah's time) for the southern kingdom. He assured both kingdoms that, though judgment would surely come, God would deliver the faithful "remnant" of his people (see exposition on 10:20-23). Then, at history's end, he would make a reunited Israel the center of a redeemed world where all nations would live together in peace. 1–35 includes several hints of a Messiah who would one day offer salvation to Israel and the whole world.

In 36–39 Isaiah cited the contemporary example of King Hezekiah, who trusted God and saw his kingdom miraculously delivered from Assyria in 701.

In 40–66 Isaiah shifted his focus to after the fall, speaking words of comfort and hope to the Jews who would be exiled to Babylon. He predicted their return from exile and revealed more fully the coming Messiah, whom he now presented as God's chosen "Servant." This Servant would take over the failed mission of God's other "servant," the nation of Israel (see exposition on 41:1-20).

931 B.C. *Kingdom divides, Israel, Judah*

874 *Ahab, Elijah*

740 *Isaiah begins ministry*

722 *Fall of Israel*

701 *Death angel strikes Assyrians*

690 *Isaiah ends ministry*

627 *Jeremiah begins ministry*

586 *Fall of Judah*

The term *Messiah* does not appear in Isaiah. Messiah means "anointed one" and speaks of Israel's hope for an eternal successor to King David who would deliver their nation once for all. Therefore, while the actual term does not appear in Isaiah, the concept it expresses fills the entire book (see exposition on the following passages: 4:2-6; 9:1-7; 11:1–12:6). *Christ* is the Greek equivalent of Messiah.

In his prophecies relating to the climax of human history and the restoration of Israel, Isaiah introduces many themes repeated in later Bible books, especially Revelation:

- History's climax will begin with the "day of the LORD," a time of worldwide suffering and judgment on all of God's enemies (see 13:9-13; exposition on 2:5–4:1 and on 24:1-23). Commonly referred to as the Tribulation, this period of time is described in detail in Revelation 6–19. (See *The Great Tribulation,* p. 379, and exposition on the following passages: Dan. 9:20-27; Joel 2:28-32; Matt. 24; 1 Thess. 5:1-11; 2 Thess. 1:1–2:12; 2 Pet. 3:8-13.)
- At the end of the Tribulation, Christ will return to earth and defeat his enemies at Armageddon (34; 63–64; see Rev. 14:14-20; 16:13-16; 19:11-21).
- After his victory over all his foes, Christ will gather the faithful remnant of Israel, judge all faithless Israelites, and usher in the "Millennium," his thousand-year reign as the final Davidic king, when believers from all nations will come to Jerusalem and live together in peace (see Rev. 20:1-6 and *The Millennium,* p. 379). Isaiah gives several descriptions of the Millennium, including:
  - 11:1-9
  - 29:17-24
  - 30:18-33
  - 32:1-20
  - 35:1-10
  - 54:1-8
  - 60–62
  - 65:17-25
  - 66:5-13
- Isaiah also gives a glimpse of the "new heavens and a new earth" that will follow the Millennium (65:17; 66:22; see 2 Pet. 3:13; Rev. 21:1–22:5).

AUTHOR

Isaiah the prophet. Commonly acknowledged as the "Prince of the Prophets" because of his exquisite literary style, Isaiah has also been called the "St. Paul of the Old Testament" because of his methodical presentation of humankind's problem of sin and God's answer of salvation. Isaiah may have been related to Judah's royal family.

Because of the shift in mood and audience between 1–39 and 40–66, some have suggested separate authors for the two sections. Strong evidence points, however, to a single author:

- The commonsense understanding of the statement of authorship (1:1) is that it applies to all 66 chapters.
- The same style, vocabulary, and figures of speech occur in both sections.

- NT writers attribute both sections to Isaiah (see John 12:37-41; Matt. 3:3; 4:14-16; Rom. 9:27-29; 10:16).
- One of the Dead Sea Scrolls includes the entire text of Isaiah, with no break between chapters 39 and 40 (see *The Dead Sea Scrolls,* p. 901).

DATE AND LOCATION

Isaiah prophesied from 740 B.C., the year of King Uzziah's death (6:1), until about 690, during Hezekiah's reign. His recorded visions cover much of that time span and are not always in chronological order. For instance, though it presumably preceded all his visions, Isaiah did not record his prophetic "call" until chapter 6. His ministry was probably, for the most part, in Jerusalem.

PURPOSE

- See *Background.*
- To warn about the danger of alliances with pagan nations and worship of their gods.
- To warn of judgment, encourage repentance, and promise forgiveness and restoration.
- To teach about God's attributes (see *Isaiah and the Attributes of God,* p. 378).
- To foretell the coming of Messiah.

UNIQUE FEATURES

- 52:13–53:12 stands out as the clearest OT gospel presentation.
- Isaiah is a treasury of information about the attributes of God (see *Isaiah and the Attributes of God,* p. 378).
- Isaiah is the OT book most often quoted in the NT. (Psalms is the second most quoted. Both are quoted twice as often as Genesis and Exodus, their closest competitors.) Isaiah and Psalms provide most of the OT prophecies of details of Christ's crucifixion. Isaiah gives the only OT prophecy of his virgin birth (7:14).
- Of the 33 occurrences of the word *salvation* in the prophets, 26 are in Isaiah.

COMPARISON WITH OTHER BIBLE BOOKS

The entire Bible:

- Isaiah has 66 chapters; the Bible has 66 books. Isaiah's two main sections, with 39 chapters in the first and 27 in the second, mirror the Bible's two sections, with 39 and 27 books. The first section of Isaiah covers the history and sinfulness of Israel, as does the OT; the second section of Isaiah covers the person and ministry of the Messiah, as does the NT.
- Both Isaiah and the Bible end with descriptions of the new heavens and earth (see 65:17; 66:22; Rev. 21:1–22:5).

All other OT prophets:

- Virtually every prophet after Isaiah quotes from or interacts with his prophecies, though none of them mention him by name (see especially Micah, Nahum, Habakkuk, Zephaniah, Zechariah, Hosea).

OUTLINE

JUDGMENT ON GOD'S FAITHLESS SERVANT (1–39)
- God's complaint against Judah (1)
- Judah's fall and restoration (2–4)
- Judgment on God's vineyard (5)
- Isaiah's prophetic call (6)
- Destruction by Assyria; salvation by Messiah (7:1–9:7)
- Judgment on the northern kingdom (9:8–10:4)
- Destruction of Assyria; salvation by Messiah (10:5–12:6)
- Judgment on other nations: Examples for Israel (13–23)
  - Babylon (13:1–14:23)
  - Assyria (14:24-27)
  - Philistia (14:28-32)
  - Moab (15–16)
  - Damascus (17)
  - Ethiopia (18)
  - Egypt (19)
  - Egypt and Ethiopia (20)
  - Babylon (21:1-10)
  - Edom and Arabia (21:11-17)
  - Jerusalem (22)
  - Tyre and Sidon (23)
- Universal judgment (24–27)
  - God's ultimate triumph over evil (24–25)
  - His ultimate exaltation of Israel (26–27)
- Judging and restoring Israel (28–33)
  - Sin, judgment, and restoration (28–29)
  - The choice: Egypt or the Lord (30–31)
  - God's reign over a restored Israel (32–33)
- Universal judgment (34–35)
  - Edom an example of judgment (34)
  - The redeemed will rejoice (35)
- Deliverance of Hezekiah: An example for Israel (36–39)
  - Siege (36)
  - Salvation (37)
  - Sickness and healing (38)
  - Stupidity (39)

COMFORT FROM GOD'S FAITHFUL SERVANT (40–66)
- Predictions of peace (40–48)
  - After judging, God will comfort his people (40)
  - God will deliver his people (41)
  - Introducing God's Faithful Servant (42)
  - God's love for his servant Israel (43)
  - God's superiority over idols (44–45)
  - God's superiority over Babylon (46–47)
  - God will deliver his people (48)

- The Prince of Peace (49–57)
  - Messiah's mission (49)
  - Messiah's obedience (50)
  - Preparing for salvation (51:1–52:12)
  - Messiah's suffering (52:13–53:12)
  - Messiah's mission accomplished (54)
  - A call to accept Messiah (55)
  - Salvation for Gentiles (56:1-8)
  - Grace for Israel's wicked leaders (56:9–57:21)
- Prescriptions for peace (58–66)
  - Hypocrisy and true worship (58)
  - Sin and repentance (59)
  - Zion's glory (60)
  - Zion's restoration (61–62)
  - Judgment and salvation (63–64)
  - Glimpses of eternity (65–66)

JUDGMENT ON GOD'S FAITHLESS SERVANT (1–39)

1:1-20 *Dumber than donkeys, sinful as Sodom, but ripe for repentance.* The first part of Isaiah's prophecy (1–12) was directed at Israel's southern kingdom of Judah. They were like rebellious children, and further discipline seemed useless (1:5). They seemed to care less about their God than an ox cared about its master (1:3). They thought that mere keeping of the ceremonial laws would appease God (1:10-15), when they should have realized that God was more concerned with morality and justice (1:16-17; see 58). They were as guilty before God as Sodom and Gomorrah (1:9-10), yet if they would repent, God would forgive them (1:18-20). On the few who were spared (1:9), also referred to as the "remnant" (10:21), see exposition on 10:20-23.

1:21-31 *"The faithful city is an unfaithful woman."* Isaiah lamented over Jerusalem, which had degenerated from a religious capital to a capital of sin and injustice (1:21-23). But God intended to purge his holy city and restore its former purity (1:24-31).

2:1-4 *Learning worship instead of war.* Isaiah foresaw a time when all people of the earth will be at peace and will come to Jerusalem to worship Israel's God and keep its law—a time commonly known as the Millennium, the thousand-year reign of Christ (see *Background,* above; and *The Millennium,* p. 379).

Worship in the Millennium will take place at the "Temple of the God of Israel" (2:3). Ezekiel 40–48 describes this restored Temple (see *Facts on the Millennial Temple,* p. 423).

2:4 is inscribed on the foundation of the United Nations headquarters in New York. It will become a reality, however, only in the Millennium (see 65:25). Until that day, the opposite situation predicted by Joel 3:9-10 will exist (see Mic. 4:3).

2:5–4:1 *When people crawl and cringe in caves.* Because the Israelites were still so corrupt (2:6-9), the Millennium foretold in 2:1-4 would be delayed till after the terrible "day of the LORD" (see 13:9), when God will "shake the earth" in judgment (2:21; see exposition on 24:1-23 and 64:1-12; Joel 3:16; Hag. 2:6, 21; Heb. 12:26-27).

The "day of the LORD" in Scripture

refers to God's supernatural intervention in human history, usually with reference to events that will take place at the end of time. Most often, it relates to the "Tribulation" preceding the second coming of Christ (see *Background;* 13:6, 9; exposition on Dan. 9:20-27; Joel 2:1, 11, 31; Amos 5:18; Zeph. 1:7-8, 14, 18; 2 Pet. 3:10; Rev. 6–19). Sometimes, as in Amos 9:11, it has in view the restoration of Israel that will follow the Tribulation. In Amos 9:11 and other passages it is referred to simply as "that day." The NT speaks of "that day when Christ Jesus comes back again" (see exposition on Phil. 1:1-6).

3:1–4:1 offers more details of the coming Tribulation. It is a picture of political and social chaos, where children replace rulers (3:4), there is much poverty and suffering (3:6-7), and war destroys so many men that women welcome polygamy to ensure their security (4:1).

4:2-6 *Freed from fire, defended by cloud and fire.* After the devastating judgment in which God "will wash the moral filth" of Jerusalem (4:4), those "who have survived the destruction of Jerusalem" (4:3) will enjoy a time of peace and prosperity (4:2). They will be watched over by the Lord in the same way he protected Israel during their desert wanderings (4:5-6).

The "branch" is the Messiah, who will spring up out of the "stump" of Jesse (11:1) and bring new life to Israel (see Jer. 23:5; 33:15; Zech. 3:8; 6:12). He is the promised "seed" or "descendant" of David (Jesse's son), whose kingdom will last "forever" (see 2 Sam. 7:12-13). (See exposition on 11:1–12:6.)

5:1-23 *The fruit of his vineyard: Nothing but wickedness.* Judah had become like a vineyard bearing inferior fruit; therefore God would destroy it (5:1-7). He would destroy the wealthy but selfish landowners (5:8-10), the godless hedonists (5:11-19, 22), the proud (5:21; see Prov. 3:7), and those who promote injustice (5:20, 23).

Proper knowledge of God (5:13) includes both cognitive and experiential knowledge. One can "know" how to get to a city by being told directions, or by having been there many times already. It is the latter sense in which Judah did not know God: They had no ongoing relationship with him.

The people were so wicked that Sheol ("the grave"), the place of the dead (see exposition on Ps. 9), was "licking its chops in anticipation" of them (5:14).

5:24-30 *"Attention all nations: They're yours for the taking!"* Because of the wicked fruit of his vineyard Judah, God would allow any and all nations to conquer Judah at will. And when God issued that invitation, Judah's enemies would be swift to respond and quick to conquer (5:26-30).

6:1-7 *While they sing "Holy," he cries "Unclean!"* Isaiah described his call as a prophet, which occurred in the last year of King Uzziah of Judah. His call came during a vision in which he "saw the Lord," an experience shared by few other humans (OT examples: Moses in Exod. 33:18-23; Ezekiel in Ezek. 1; and Daniel in Dan. 7:9-14). As he watched the angels worship in heaven, Isaiah felt overwhelmed by his own sinfulness (see exposition on Gen. 17:1-8 and on John 1:15-18).

Threefold repetition in Hebrew can indicate a superlative—the best on the continuum of good-better-best. Thus "holy, holy, holy" (6:3) simply means "most holy."

6:8-13 *He hears the voice and volunteers.* God expressed his desire for a prophetic messenger, and Isaiah immediately volunteered. God warned him that the people of Judah would be unresponsive to his message and that most of them would die in their sin, with just a "stump" remaining to act as a "seed" for new life (6:13; see exposition on 10:20-23).

7:1-9 *"Those two has-beens have had it!"* Aram and the northern kingdom of Israel had formed an alliance against Assyria, to the north and east of Aram. When they asked King Ahaz of Judah (735–715 B.C.) to join them, he refused, and they attacked him (7:1-2; see exposition on 2 Kings 16). God sent Isaiah and his son Shear-jashub to reassure Ahaz that God himself would defeat the kings of Aram and Israel, whom he dismissed as "two burned-out embers" (7:4).

Shear-jashub literally means "a remnant will return," a name obviously intended to encourage King Ahaz (see exposition on 10:20-23). Isaiah would soon have another son with a symbolic name (see 8:1-4).

7:10-16 *Immediate sign rejected, ultimate sign revealed!* God invited Ahaz to test him by asking for a sign, but Ahaz refused. He pretended to refuse out of humility, but in truth he did so out of unbelief (7:10-13). Isaiah then predicted that "the virgin will conceive a child! She will give birth to a son and will call him Immanuel—'God is with us'" (7:14), and that, before the child was old enough "to choose what is right and reject what is wrong . . . the two kings you fear so much . . . will both be dead" (7:15-16).

This prophecy would have a double fulfillment:

- Isaiah's wife would soon have another son, and before he had come of age (compare 7:16 and 8:4), both Aram's and Israel's northern kingdoms would have fallen to Assyria (see 2 Kings 17:6).
- The prophecy was ultimately fulfilled in the virgin birth of Christ (see Matt. 1:22-23). The Hebrew word *almah* (which can also mean "young maiden") is translated in this passage as *parthenos* ("virgin") by the Greek Septuagint (*parthenos* is also translated "virgin" in Matt. 1:23).

7:17-25 *"Then they'll turn on you!"* Having refused God's help against Aram (Syria) and Israel, Ahaz formed an alliance with Assyria against those two nations (see 2 Kings 16:7-9). Now Isaiah warned that, once Assyria had defeated Aram and the northern kingdom (in 722 B.C.), this nation Ahaz had chosen to trust would attack his nation as well (which in fact they did in 701).

The shaving of the head and beard by their enemies (7:20) was considered a shame and was done voluntarily only as a sign of mourning (see 15:2).

8:1-4 *Why such a long name?* A son was born to Isaiah (see 7:14) and named Maher-shalal-hash-baz, which means "swift to plunder and quick to spoil." His very name foretold the fall of the northern kingdom; it fell in 722 B.C., just 13 years after Ahaz became king and, as predicted, before the son would have come of age (see exposition on 7:10-16). The name would serve as a warning to Judah as well (see 7:17).

8:5-10 *If not the stream of Shiloah, then the flood of Euphrates!* Because Judah had rejected God (Hebrew, "the gently flowing waters of Shiloah") and had chosen instead to trust in human leaders, God would bring upon it the wrath of Assyria—"a mighty flood from the Euphrates River" (8:7-8).

Shiloah was probably Jerusalem's water supply. The image may have occurred to Isaiah as he encountered King Ahaz "at the end of the aqueduct" (7:3). Those who "rejoiced" in the leaders of Israel and Aram probably included northern Israelites and rebellious southerners.

8:11-22 *The choice: Fear them, or fear and trust God.* As they faced the difficult days ahead, the people of Judah should honor and fear and hope in God (8:13, 17) rather than fear human leaders (8:12). They should heed the law (8:16, 20) rather than look to "mediums and psychics" for guidance (8:19). If they would trust God, he would keep them safe (8:14). If they did not trust him, the one who had been their "Rock" (see exposition on 1 Sam. 2:1-10) would become "a stone that causes people to stumble" (8:14; see Jer. 6:21; Luke 2:34; Rom. 9:33; 1 Pet. 2:8).

Whenever the people began to doubt God's predictions of the trouble ahead and the hope to follow, the names of Isaiah's two sons were there as signs for them (8:18).

9:1-7 *The light of God in the land of darkness.* The devastation of Israel by Assyria would eventually give way to an era of universal peace. Indeed, the very region of Israel where the Assyrian armies first brought darkness and death (9:1) would be the first to experience this new day (9:2). As the NT reveals, that new day of hope would be the advent of Christ the Messiah, the promised Son (9:6-7; see Matt. 28:18; Luke 1:32-33; 2:11).

9:7 reaffirms God's promise to David in 2 Sam. 7:13 (see exposition on 1:1–12:6; see also 7:14).

As Matthew pointed out in his Gospel, the region of Israel referred to in 9:1 was indeed the first to rejoice in the light (9:2) brought by the preaching of Christ (see Matt. 4:12-16).

9:6 gives several names for the promised Son:

- "Wonderful Counselor" (see 28:29; Rom. 11:34)
- "Mighty God," "Everlasting Father" (see John 1:1-3)
- "Prince of Peace" (see Luke 2:14; John 14:27; Acts 10:36; Rom. 5:1-10; Eph. 2:14-18; Heb. 7:2)

9:8–10:4 *No punishment enough for his prideful people.* Because it had so thoroughly rejected God (see exposition on 2 Kings 17:5-23), had promoted injustice (10:1-4), and had pridefully failed to repent in spite of his discipline (9:9-10), God would totally destroy Israel's northern kingdom. A foreboding refrain declared that no amount of punishment could satisfy his anger, for "his fist is still poised to strike" (9:12, 17, 21; 10:4). The judgment on sinners (9:8–10:4) contrasts sharply with the hope of the righteous (9:1-7).

10:5-19 *Death to the proud destroyer!* The Assyrians were used by God to destroy the northern kingdom in 722 B.C., and they boasted that they would soon destroy Jerusalem as well (10:9-11). But God had other plans: He would destroy Assyria because, out of pride (10:12-15), it would go far beyond its mandate against Israel (10:5-11).

Assyria would in fact suffer a stunning defeat when it marched against Jerusalem in 701 (see 37:36-38). Then, in 612, Nineveh, its capital, would fall to Babylon, and in 605 it would suffer final defeat by Babylon at the Battle of Carchemish (see 33:1). Babylon would be used by God to lead Judah into captivity in 586. Then, as the wheels of divine justice continued to turn, Babylon itself would be defeated by the Persian king Cyrus in 539, as predicted by Isaiah (see 45:1 and exposition on 13:1-22) and Habakkuk (Hab. 2:5-17).

10:20-23 *The redeemed and returning remnant.* When Israel was judged, a "remnant" of Israelites would be spared and would return to God. The Bible often speaks of such a remnant—Israelites who have either remained faithful to God or have survived a national defeat (see 1:9; 6:13; 11:11; 2 Chron. 30:6; Jer. 40:11, 15; Zeph. 3:13; Zech. 8:6; Rom. 9:27; 11:5).

10:24-34 *Felled in a flash, like a mighty fir.* Just as he had defeated Israel's foes in times past (10:24-27), the Lord would defeat the Assyrians once they had served his purpose against Israel. The proud and mighty Assyria would be cut down as easily as one cuts down a large tree (10:33-34). Height (10:33) is often a symbol of pride in the Bible (see 14:13-14).

11:1–12:6 *The stump, the Branch, and the glorious fruit.* Continuing the tree images of 10:33-34, Isaiah predicted that the stump remaining of Judah would produce a "branch" (see 4:2; 6:13; 53:2), which NT references confirm to be Christ (see Rev. 5:5). Isaiah also notes here that "the Spirit of the LORD will rest on" this Branch, a prediction that was fulfilled during the baptism of Christ (11:2; see John 1:32).

Christ will usher in a Millennium of peace and justice in which all nature as well as humans will share (11:1-9; see 29:17-24; 30:18-33; 32; 35; 65:17-25; Rom. 8:18-22; Rev. 20:1-6). During the Millennium, God will once again gather the faithful remnant of Israel to its homeland (11:11-12). The 12 tribes will be at peace with each other (11:13) and will be "a banner of salvation to all the world" (11:10-12), calling them to worship the one true God (12). The Millennium, and the "new heavens and new earth" that will follow (see exposition on 65:17–66:24), will fulfill God's promise to David that one of his royal descendants will reign forever (see 9:7; 2 Sam. 7:13).

12:2 is a theme verse for much of Isaiah: Trust in God, not in foreign alliances, for salvation. It echoes two other great faith verses: Genesis 15:6 and Hebrews 11:6.

13:1-22 *Babylon: From wonder to wasteland.* As a warning to Israel, Isaiah issued a series of prophecies against specific nations (13–23). If God would judge these pagan nations, how much more severely would he judge his own people, who had received his special revelation! (See Rom. 2:12-24.)

Isaiah began with a prophecy concerning Babylon (see also 21:1-10), which after conquering Judah would itself be destroyed by Persia (one of the "countries far away," 13:5). This greatest of all cities of its time would become a desert (13:19-22).

13:9-13 seems to look farther into the future, to the end times when God will "shake" heaven and earth (see exposition on the following passages: 2:5–4:1; 24:1-23; 64:1-12).

14:1-23 *The fall of a king and an angel.* When the Israelites were freed from bondage and returned to their homeland, they would gloat over the fall of their oppressor Babylon (14:1-4). Many scholars see in Israel's "taunt" (14:4-23) a reference both to the humiliating fall of Babylon's king and to Satan's fall from heaven. Such a view gains credence from the similar passage in Ezekiel 28:11-19, which also seems to describe an angelic being who, because of pride, was cast out of heaven (see also Luke 10:18). Whether or not Satan's fall is in view, he would have at least influenced the *king's* fall; and the fatal "I wills" of 14:13-14 are characteristic of Satan's efforts to promote self-worship (see Gen. 3:1-5).

14:24-27 *Assyria: Disaster before its final defeat.* Though Assyria would ultimately fall to Babylon in 605 B.C., this prophecy refers to its defeat on the "mountains" (14:25) of Israel in 701 when the "angel of the LORD" killed 185,000 of its men (see 37:36-38; 2 Kings 19).

14:28-32 *Philistia: "Don't rejoice! His son will be worse!"* Isaiah warned the Philistines not to rejoice in the death of King Shalmaneser of Assyria, for his son would be worse than he. God intended to destroy Philistia while his own people dwelt in safety (14:30,

32). The fact that King Ahaz died in the year of this prophecy (14:28) was merely coincidental; he was not the king referred to in 14:29.

15:1–16:14 *Moab: Invasion, pride, and fall.* Israel's neighbor Moab would be invaded, and her people would become refugees (15:5-7). Despite his compassion, God would bring additional suffering upon these desperate refugees (15:9). Israel would offer them asylum (16:3-5), but out of pride they would refuse the offer and ultimately fall (16:6-14).

The Moabites had close ties with the Israelites (see Gen. 19:31-38; Ruth 4:10, 18-22) but had always opposed them, spiritually as well as politically (see Num. 25; Judg. 3:12-14; 1 Sam. 14:47; 2 Sam. 8:2, 11-12; 2 Kings 3). Perhaps in part because of these family ties, Isaiah wept over their fate (15:5; 16:7, 9, 11).

The Lord declared that Moab's day of reckoning would come within three years (16:14). It came right on schedule, with an invasion by Assyria in 732 B.C.

17:1-14 *Damascus and Israel: Partners in crime, partners in punishment.* The northern kingdom of Israel (referred to as "Ephraim" in some translations) and Damascus, the capital of Aram, had been allies against Judah. For this they would suffer together (17:1-3). Both would be besieged and deported by Assyria (see 2 Kings 15:29; 17:6). Israel was singled out for special rebuke since they had forsaken their Rock (17:10; see exposition on 1 Sam. 2:1-10). Then Assyria itself would be judged (17:12-14; see exposition on 10:5-19).

18:1-7 *Ethiopia: "You'll bring gifts then but not now."* Ethiopia had sent ambassadors to Judah (18:1-2), seeking to form an alliance with them against Assyria. But Isaiah sent them home (18:2), assuring them that God would deal with Assyria in his own good time (18:4-6) in a way so dramatic that the whole world would see it (18:3). Then, during the Millennium, Ethiopia, like the rest of the world, *would* bring gifts to the Lord in Jerusalem (18:7).

19:1-25 *Egypt: Their water and wisdom will disappear.* Because of its idolatry and witchcraft (19:1, 3), Egypt would see its usually wise leaders fail (19:3), leading to civil strife (19:2). They would suffer foreign invasion (19:4) and a catastrophic natural disaster as the Nile dried up (19:5-15). Even tiny Judah would be a threat to the humbled Egypt (19:16-17).

During the Millennium, after God has disciplined Egypt, he will graciously heal her (19:18-25). Egypt and Assyria (present-day Iraq) will be "connected by a highway," allowing both nations to freely travel to Jerusalem to worship God (19:23-25). In all of ancient times, Egypt and Assyria (earlier Mesopotamia) were natural enemies; their coming together will be equivalent to the wolf and the lamb living in harmony (see 11:6).

20:1-6 *Egypt, Ethiopia, and Isaiah: Naked in public.* Despite their hope for restoration (see 18:7; 19:23-25), for the present both Ethiopia and Egypt must face the humiliation of God's judgment—as acted out for them by Isaiah. Assyria temporarily took control of Egypt in 663 B.C.

21:1-10 *Babylon: Fallen and broken.* Looking some 150–200 years into the future, Isaiah foresaw Babylon's fall to Persia ("Elamites," 21:2) in 539 B.C. Yet, though he rejoiced at its fall (21:9), the horror of it all made him ill (21:3; see also 13:1–14:23).

21:11-17 *No freedom for Edom—or Arabia.* While the morning of victory was coming for Assyria, the night of defeat (21:12) was coming for both Edom (Seir) and Arabia, both of which would try in vain to stop Assyria (see 34:5-17).

22:1-14 *Jerusalem: Sorrow for the celebrating city.* While Jerusalem celebrated their rescue by the death angel in 701 B.C. (see 37:36-38; 2 Kings 19), Isaiah recalled that narrow escape with sadness, for the people had exhibited self-reliance (22:8-11) and hedonistic fatalism (22:13) rather than repentance (22:12) and trust in God (22:11). Isaiah predicted judgment for this godlessness (22:14).

Though Jeremiah is called the weeping prophet, Isaiah also wept, both for Israel and for other nations (22:4; see 15:5; 16:7, 9, 11).

22:15-25 *A proud politician and a good one gone bad.* Isaiah condemned Shebna, a proud public official, and predicted that he would be replaced by Eliakim (22:19-20; see 36:3 for the apparent fulfillment). Eliakim would be like a father to the people (22:20-23), until he too would be judged (22:22-25). The kind of authority given temporarily to Eliakim would be righteously and permanently exercised by Christ (22:22; see exposition on Rev. 3:7-13).

23:1-18 *Tyre and Sidon: Their ships will cease to sail.* Tyre and Sidon had become powerful through international trade. They had also become proud (23:9) and were major purveyors of godlessness (23:17). When they were conquered, all their trading partners would mourn (23:1-7). After 70 years they would be restored, only to resume their godless influence on the world (23:15-17; see Matt. 11:21-22). Concerning Tyre's ultimate fate, see exposition on Ezekiel 26:7-21.

God made it clear that it was he—not any earthly power—who was judging Tyre and Sidon (23:9). And he would continue to use them for his own purposes. Their ill-gotten gain would ultimately benefit the righteous (23:18; see exposition on Prov. 13:22).

24:1-23 *On Judgment Day: Tottering like a tent.* Having warned several specific nations (see 13–23), Isaiah now spoke in broader terms about God's ultimate triumph over evil (24–25) and exaltation of Israel (see 26–27). He began by describing a future time of universal suffering and devastation (24:1-13), sent by God because all humankind had transgressed his laws (24:5). A few will escape this judgment, just as a few olives or grapes can be gleaned after the harvest (24:13), and they will rejoice (24:14-16; see exposition on 10:20-23), but for most of humankind there will be only judgment (24:16-23). The earth will shake. It will "stagger" like a "drunkard" and "tremble" like "a tent in a storm"—clearly a description of the Tribulation.

Out of this terrible devastation, however, will come the glorious light of Christ in his millennial kingdom (24:23; see 60:19-20; Rev. 21:23; 22:5).

Because of its description of the Tribulation and Millennium, 24–27 is often called "Isaiah's Apocalypse." (*Apocalypse* is Greek for "revelation"; the book of Revelation also describes the Tribulation and Millennium.)

25:1-12 *Death for the proud, dinner for the patient.* Isaiah praised God for his great and final triumph over evil. God will destroy the proud foreign nations (25:2-5, 10-12) and the power of suffering and death (25:7-8), and in their place will prepare a banquet (25:6) for all who have waited patiently for his salvation (25:9). The precious promise of 25:8 is restated twice in Revelation (see Rev. 7:17; 21:4).

26:1-19 *A song of souls set free.* The redeemed, those who have waited patiently for the Lord (25:9; 26:8) and have trusted in him (26:3-4; see 12:2), will praise the God who has brought down the "arrogant city" of human pride (26:5) and has given them a "strong" city (26:1) filled with peace (26:12). The pain of childbirth (26:16-18) will lead to a glorious resurrection

(26:19). For other comparisons of spiritual struggle to childbirth, see 13:8; 42:14; John 16:21; Gal. 4:19.

26:19 is one of the few, but nonetheless strong, evidences that OT believers had a hope of life beyond the grave (see exposition on Job 19:23-29; Ps. 17:15; 73:24; exposition on Eccles. 9:1-8; exposition on Dan. 12:1-4; compare Gen. 22:5 with Heb. 11:19).

26:20–27:13 *A vineyard revived.* Isaiah invited the righteous to take shelter until the wrath of God's judgment had passed (26:20–27:1). Then they could rejoice as Israel, God's vineyard (see 5:1-7), was restored to his care and protection (26:1-11).

While the repetition of the phrase "in that day" (27:1, 2, 13) may indicate that all of chapter 27 refers to Israel's restoration in the end times, some scholars see 27:12-13 as referring to that event in a special way. Isaiah's dual focus on both the near and the far future (see *Introduction to the Prophets*, p. 353) can cause confusion, especially when he talks about the return of the remnant, since the return of ancient days will be repeated in the end times (see exposition on 54:1-17).

28:1-29 *Israel: Drunk in the face of destruction.* Having described God's final judgment on all humankind and his restoration of Israel (24–27), Isaiah again issued words of judgment, this time focusing on Israel itself (28–33). While destruction loomed at its door (28:2-3), Israel had degenerated into drunken dissipation (28:1-8). Even its leaders were drunk (28:7). They had reduced the law to a set of rules (28:7-13). They had "struck a bargain to avoid death," trusting their security to human alliances rather than to God (28:15).

But God would annul their covenant (28:18). Just as the natural world exhibits cause and effect, Israel's sins would lead to a harvest of judgment (28:19-29).

In place of their covenant with death, God offered his people the "cornerstone" of messianic hope (28:16; see 8:14; Matt. 21:42; Rom. 9:33; 10:11; 1 Pet. 2:4-8).

Because Israel would not learn from God in their own language, he would speak to them in a language they couldn't understand (28:11)—that is, the Assyrians would "speak to" them about God's wrath by invading them! Paul would later quote this passage to explain how the gift of tongues is a sign of judgment to nonbelievers (see 1 Cor. 14:20-22).

29:1-16 *Israel: Asleep in the face of salvation.* Because of its sin, Jerusalem ("Ariel") would be destroyed (29:1-4), but as quickly as the nations conquered it, their apparent victories would come to nothing (29:5-8). Despite such promises of salvation, a "spirit of deep sleep" prevailed over Israel, and it scarcely realized what God was undertaking on its behalf (29:9-12). God's people were practicing an outward form of religion, but their hearts were far from him (29:13; see Ezek. 33:31; Matt. 15:8-9).

29:17-24 *Israel: Finally awake to its Maker.* With the coming of the messianic kingdom, Israel's desert will bloom, its fields will produce bumper crops, and those who had been deaf and blind to God's law (29:9-12) will finally appreciate all that God had done for them.

30:1-17 *"Don't look for allies in Egypt!"* Rather than trusting in God alone, some of Israel's leaders looked to Egypt as a possible ally (30:1-7), even pressuring the prophets to agree with them (30:8-11). Such misplaced trust would bring only humiliation and defeat (30:3, 12-14). Since they had trusted in horses rather than in God, by horses they would be defeated (30:15-17).

Concerning the danger of foreign alliances, see exposition on 1 Kings

11:1-8 and on 2 Kings 16:10-20. Human nature wants to hear "nice things" (30:10), not demands of holiness (30:11).

30:18-33 *Another look at the Millennium.* Just as God's faithful remnant was waiting for him to act on its behalf (see 25:9; 26:8), God was patiently waiting to bless it (30:18). This blessing will come in the Millennium (30:19-26; compare 29:17-24). The Millennium will be preceded by the destruction of God's foes (30:27-33). (As 30:31 indicates, this passage also foretells the destruction of Assyria.)

31:1-9 *"Forsake the horses; return to the Holy One!"* If Israel persisted in looking to Egypt and its horses instead of to God for help, Israel and Egypt would perish together (31:1-3; see 30:1-7, 15-17). God would defend his people just as surely as a bird defends its nest (31:4-5), therefore Israel should return to him (31:6).

32:1-20 *The coming King will reign in righteousness.* Once more Isaiah called his contemporaries to look beyond their present troubles to the triumphant Messiah, who would put an end to all injustice and usher in an age of peace. In Messiah's day, God's Spirit would be "poured down upon us from heaven" (32:15; see Joel 2:28-32; Acts 2:16-21). It would be a time of renewal and bounty (32:15; see 29:17-24).

33:1-16 *When the destroyers are destroyed . . .* When Assyria had ceased plundering its neighbors, it would itself be plundered (33:1-4; see exposition on 10:5-19). Meanwhile God's people would dwell in his kingdom (33:5-6). Even though Assyria was terrifying Israel and other nations (33:7-9), God would soon show it his might (33:10-12). Only those who pursued justice and righteousness would survive his judgment (33:13-16).

33:17-24 *. . . you'll behold the king in his beauty!* The faithful remnant would soon see their "king in all his splendor" (33:17). Gone would be the terror of the strange-sounding Assyrians (33:19). They would see a Jerusalem finally at peace, with God as its judge, lawgiver, and king (33:22).

34:1-17 *Edom: An example of judgment.* Having discussed God's judgment on and restoration of Israel (28–33), Isaiah once again broadened his focus to God's final judgment on all nations that had opposed his chosen people, singling out Edom as an example of divine wrath (34:5-17; see 21:11-12). Many scholars see 34 as a description of Armageddon.

35:1-10 *Healing and a holy highway.* In a pattern familiar by now, Isaiah followed his description of Edom's judgment with a description of the Millennium. Both nature and redeemed humanity will experience restoration (35:5-7). The redeemed will return to Zion on the "Highway of Holiness" and will find "everlasting joy" (35:8-10; see 51:11).

36:1-22 *Hezekiah under siege.* Having again and again urged Israel to trust its God rather than foreign alliances, Isaiah recounted an inspiring story from Israel's recent history to show that God could indeed be trusted. The story, which concerns King Hezekiah, covers 36–39 and is parallel, often word-for-word, to the account of the story in 2 Kings 18–20.

After destroying the fortified cities around Jerusalem, the Assyrian King Sennacherib threatened Jerusalem itself in 701 B.C. (the latter days of Isaiah's ministry). Sennacherib's men boasted publicly about their king's recent victories and questioned God's ability to save Israel. As a result, Israel's leaders were demoralized (36:22).

37:1-38 *Hezekiah and Isaiah see their city saved.* When Hezekiah heard of Sennacherib's siege and his blasphemous boasts, he asked Isaiah to seek God on

Israel's behalf. Isaiah delivered three words from the Lord concerning the situation:

Message 1: "Don't worry, he's doomed" (37:5-20). Isaiah assured the frightened Hezekiah that Sennacherib's siege would not succeed; that, in fact, Sennacherib himself would soon return home and be killed (37:5-7). Meanwhile, the Assyrians continued to mock the Israelites and their God (37:8-13). Sennacherib sent a threatening message to Hezekiah, and Hezekiah "spread it out before the LORD" and prayed about it (37:14-20).

Message 2: Sennacherib's rise and ruin (37:21-29). Isaiah spoke next concerning Sennacherib: It was the God of Israel who had permitted his past victories. But now, because of his sin and arrogance, the God of Israel would punish him.

Message 3: "Neither army nor arrows will enter the city" (37:30-35). Isaiah then spoke directly to the people of Jerusalem: The Assyrians would not enter their city. God would save Jerusalem for his name's sake and for the sake of his covenant with David.

The messages fulfilled: Jerusalem saved (37:36-38). Jerusalem was delivered as the "angel of the LORD" miraculously destroyed the Assyrian army. Sennacherib returned home in defeat and, sometime later, was killed by his own sons.

38:1-22 *Hezekiah's sickness and healing.* Told that he would soon die, Hezekiah cried out to God; God healed him and promised to add 15 years to his life. Hezekiah wrote a song of praise to commemorate the miraculous event (38:9-20).

39:1-8 *Hezekiah's stupidity and selfishness.* When envoys from Babylon visited Hezekiah, he proudly showed them all his wealth. Isaiah rebuked him for this, predicting that Babylon would someday return and take Israel's wealth and its people as well. Hezekiah's response (39:8) reveals great selfishness in this otherwise good king.

COMFORT FROM GOD'S FAITHFUL SERVANT (40–66)

40:1-11 *The grief ends, the glory begins.* Having focused on God's judgment of Israel and other nations (1–39), Isaiah shifted his emphasis to God's desire to bring his people a new era of peace and comfort (40–66). While in 1–39 Isaiah looked ahead to Jerusalem's fall, the viewpoint of 40–66 is after the fall, predicting the Israelites' return from exile, and beyond that the coming of Messiah and the final great return of exiles in the Millennium.

Their "sad days" (or "warfare") having ended, God was ready at last to "comfort" his people (40:1-2). A forerunner proclaimed God's triumphant approach (40:3-5) and declared the trustworthiness of his word (40:8). Israel's great and powerful God would care for them as tenderly as a shepherd (40:9-11).

40:12-26 *"Their gods can't speak, ours created the stars!"* Isaiah expressed amazement at the God who is omnipotent (40:12, 15-17), omniscient (40:13-14), incomparable (40:15-20; 45:5-6), and the eternal Creator of everything bound by time (40:21-26). It is ludicrous to compare him with false gods (40:18-20; see exposition on 44:6-28).

40:27-31 *Running like deer, flying like eagles.* Those who "wait" for their almighty God (see 25:9; 26:8, KJV) will themselves experience supernatural strength.

41:1-20 *An emancipator from the east.* Calling Israel and all nations into his courtroom, God foretold the coming of the Persian king Cyrus as his instrument of judgment against Babylon (41:1-7; see 44:28; see exposition on 45:1-13). He encouraged his people—who would by then be captives in Babylon—not to fear this great warrior from the east (41:8-10), for God would use him to defeat all their enemies and restore Israel to its former glory (41:11-20).

Throughout Isaiah's prophecy, both the nation of Israel (41:8-9) and the coming Messiah are called God's "servant." Israel had been commissioned to serve God as his witness to the world but had failed in that mission (see 42:18-19; see exposition on 43:8-13). Therefore, God had commissioned a new Servant (see exposition on 42:1-17).

41:21-29 *No other gods can make these claims!* The Lord challenged all idolaters to present their case (41:21) and offer some evidence for the validity of their gods. He challenged them to find another god who could prophesy as the Lord could and mentioned again the coming of Cyrus (41:25). God does not shrink from any evidence for other gods, since he knows such evidence is nonexistent (see 44:6-28).

42:1-17 *"Behold! My Servant!"* God announced the advent of his chosen "servant," whom he would send to establish justice on earth (42:1-4). God then spoke directly to the servant, commissioning him for his task (42:5-9). This servant, Jesus Christ the Messiah, would bring justice and light to the Gentiles (42:1, 6; see 9:2; Luke 2:32).

This passage contains the first of Isaiah's four "servant songs" about the Messiah, who would

- bring justice and light to the Gentiles (42:1-9)
- restore Israel and bring salvation to all people (49:1-7)
- be obedient in suffering (50:4-9)
- be rejected by humankind but exalted by God (52:13–53:12)

Though Christ would bring about justice, he would not do so by force (42:3-4; see John 18:36).

Isaiah called on all creation to praise God for the victory he would bring about through his servant (42:10-13). Then God himself spoke, comparing his preparations for the servant's reign to the pain of childbirth (42:14-17; compare Matt. 24:8).

42:18-25 *The other servant: Blind to his works, deaf to his word.* In sharp contrast to Christ the obedient servant (42:1-17) was the nation of Israel, presented here as a deaf, blind, and disobedient servant who had failed to fulfill its divine destiny (see exposition on 43:8-13).

43:1-7 *Surviving the fire, gathered from afar.* Despite their disobedience, God loved his people Israel and would redeem them. His promise to gather them "from the distant corners of the earth" (43:6) recalls references to Israel's "remnant" (see exposition on 10:20-23).

43:8-13 *"You are my witnesses."* Recalling the rebuke of 42:18-19, God called on his blind and deaf servant Israel to declare to the assembled nations the truth concerning his mighty acts on Israel's behalf.

God had chosen Israel to be his "witnesses" to the world (43:10). He told Abraham that the whole world would be blessed through his descendants (see Gen. 12:1-3). The mandate to be witnesses was repeated as they crossed the Jordan into Canaan (see Josh. 4:21-24). Solomon sensed something of the importance of that commission when he prayed for all the foreigners who would visit the Temple (see 1 Kings 8:41-43). But for the most part Israel failed in its mission, becoming just like its pagan neighbors (see exposition on 2 Kings 17:5-23 and on 2 Chron. 36:15-21).

Christians, like Israel, are to be witnesses of God's mighty acts of salvation (compare 43:10 and Acts 1:8).

43:14-28 *When he rescues and forgives, they forget.* For Israel's sake, God would destroy Babylon and deliver Israel from captivity (43:14-21). Even so, Israel would keep on taking God's blessings for granted (43:22-24) . . . and he would keep on forgiving them (43:25)—yet they would still be held accountable (43:26-28). Those most blessed are often the most ungrateful.

44:1-5 *His water for their soil, his spirit for their sons.* God assured Israel that he had chosen them and would continue to bless them. He added, "I will pour out my Spirit and my blessings on your children" (44:3; see Jer. 31:31-34; Ezek. 36:26-27; Joel 2:28-32; Acts 2:16-21). God makes plans for his servants even from the womb (44:2; see 46:3; 49:1; Ps. 139:13).

44:6-28 *The God who helps vs. gods who must be helped.* Having declared God's glory and uniqueness, Isaiah painted a detailed and almost comical picture of idols, which were totally at the mercy of those who made and worshiped them (44:9-20; see exposition on the following passages: 40:12-26; 41:21-29; 46:1-13; Jer. 10:1-18). He called on Israel to return to the one true God, who had redeemed them and would continue to do so (44:21-28).

Isaiah predicted, by name, a pagan king not to be born until 150 years later, through whom God would deliver his people from captivity in Babylon (44:28; see exposition on 45:1-13).

45:1-13 *Cyrus: For God's glory and Jacob's good.* The Lord addressed the future king Cyrus, declaring that it was he who would make Cyrus great (45:1-3). But he would do this for the sake of Israel (45:4) and for his own glory (45:5-8). He declared his divine prerogative to use Cyrus to restore Jerusalem and free "my captive people" from Babylon (45:9-13).

45:14-25 *"Every knee shall bow!"* God declared that all people will one day acknowledge his power (45:14), and Isaiah echoed his words, affirming that there is only one God, who is supremely worth worshiping (45:15-17). God spoke again, declaring himself to be the Creator and the only true God (45:18-21). He invited all people to turn to him (45:22) and declared that one day "every knee will bow" to him (45:23; see Rom. 14:11; Phil. 2:10). At that time, his enemies will be ashamed and his own people will be justified (45:24-25; see exposition on 66:1-24).

46:1-13 *"You carry your gods, ours carries us!"* The discussion of Cyrus's victories on God's behalf led to thoughts of Babylon's idols, who had to be carried by their worshipers and were therefore obviously powerless to save them (46:1-2). While Babylon carried their gods, Israel's God carried them (46:3-4)! While the Babylonians lavished gold on their helpless gods (46:5-7; compare 44:9-20), Israel's mighty God controlled all of history. By calling in Cyrus—the "bird of prey from the east"—he would destroy Babylon and free its Israelite captives (46:8-13).

47:1-15 *From queen of kingdoms to childless contempt.* Isaiah foresaw the fall of Babylon, the proud "queen of kingdoms" (47:1-5). God had let his people fall into Babylon's hands for discipline, but instead of simply disciplining them Babylon "showed them no mercy" (47:6). Because of this cruelty, and her pride and idolatry (47:8-10), Babylon would become the very thing she despised (47:8-9); widowhood and childlessness were a disgrace in ancient times (see 4:1; 54:1). Babylon's religion would be powerless to save it (47:12-15).

48:1-16 *He tells them ahead of time: "I'll save you!"* God had always known that his people would repeatedly forsake him (48:1-2). Therefore he had always told them ahead of time what he was going to do, so that they could not credit those events to their idols (48:5) or to some natural cause (48:7). God would save his people, in spite of their wickedness, so that no false god could be credited with defeating his chosen ones (48:9-11). In fact, he would soon defeat Babylon on their behalf; and once more, he was telling them ahead of time so that they would know it was he who was doing this for them (48:12-16)!

48:17-22 *Liberation Day!* Having expressed his love for them, God prophetically signaled the day of his people's liberation from Babylon. He pictured their salvation as an escape from a desert to a land of abundant water (see 12).

49:1-13 *A servant prepared to save.* In the second of four "servant songs," God's chosen servant spoke of his mission. God had prepared him from the womb to bring Israel back to him and to "bring my salvation" (49:6) to all the world (49:1-7). The servant then reviewed God's promises to himself and Israel. God would help his servant in his mission of liberating Israel (49:8-9). He would gather the remnant of his people and give them comfort and prosperity (49:9-13).

49:14-26 *"Has God forgotten you? Certainly not!"* In response to the Israelite exiles' concern that God had forgotten them, the servant promised that they would soon be restored to their homeland, where they would experience such growth that their boundaries would seem too small (49:14-21). Their restoration would involve a reversal of sorts, as their captors became their captives (49:22-26)—the situation that will exist in the Millennium (see 60:10, 14; 61:5). Not only is God aware of his people, he also cares deeply for them (49:15-16).

50:1-11 *Two servants: Light and darkness.* God's faithless servant Israel had failed him, not because he had "divorced" them, but because they had in effect divorced him (50:1-3). By contrast, God's faithful servant would humbly learn from him (50:4-5). He would willingly endure persecution because he trusted in God and wanted so much to do his will (50:6-9; see Matt. 26:67; 27:26, 30). Israel must choose: They could walk in God's light (50:10), or in the light of their own campfires (50:11), which was really darkness (50:10).

51:1–52:12 *"Prepare yourselves for salvation!"* Having introduced the Servant Messiah, Isaiah reassured the Israelite captives that they would soon be free. His words also foreshadow the coming of Messiah and the final great liberation of the faithful in God's everlasting kingdom.

Isaiah urged his hearers to give their full attention to his important message: They were to "listen" (51:1, 4, 7), "wake up" (51:17; 52:1), and then respond by immediately leaving sinful Babylon (52:11-12).

Just as God had blessed Abraham, he would "comfort Israel" (51:1-3), making its wilderness "as beautiful as Eden" (51:3; see 29:17-24). He would bring everlasting salvation and justice to all people (51:4-8).

Isaiah called on the Lord to bring about a second Exodus, as the nation he had led out of Egypt would now be led out of Babylon (51:9-11; see 63:11-14). He also looked further into the future, to the "everlasting joy" of the Millennium (see 35:10).

The Lord agreed that he, who had created all things, could certainly free his people from exile (51:12-16). He would soon transfer his wrath from Israel to their oppressors (51:17-23).

Once more Isaiah called Israel to prepare for their liberation, for God would soon free them from Babylon (52:1-10), and they should be ready to flee (52:11-12).

Compare 52:7 and Romans 10:15.

52:13–53:12 *His suffering brings salvation.* Isaiah's fourth and final Servant song focused on the Servant's suffering and death for the sins of Israel and all humanity. NT quotations show clearly that these verses refer to Christ (see Matt. 8:17; Luke 22:37; John 12:37-38; Acts 8:26-35; Rom. 4:25; 10:15-16; 15:21; 1 Pet. 1:2; 2:24-25; see *Old Testament Prophecies about Christ,* p. 838.) Christ would accomplish his mission, and God would highly exalt him while humanity stood speechless before his beaten and bleeding form (52:13-15). He would be counted as nothing because of his lowly background, rejected because of his message, and acquainted with grief because of his earthly mission (53:1-3).

While Christ was punished for the sins of all humanity, many onlookers would assume he was dying for his own crimes (53:4-6). His fellow Jews, in particular, would feel that his death was justifiable punishment for his supposed blasphemy (see John 5:18; 10:33; 19:7).

53:6 is the "all" verse, beginning and ending with *all:* All need a Savior, and Christ offers salvation to all.

Though sinless (53:9), Christ would make no attempt to defend himself as he was led to die for others' sins (53:7-8; see Matt. 26:63; 27:12-14). God fully intended this seeming injustice to take place, since Christ would be the final, perfect offering for the sins of all (53:10-12; see Luke 22:37; John 1:29; Rom. 5:18-19; 2 Cor. 5:21).

Having allowed him to die, God would then raise Christ from the dead and allow him to see that his mission had been accomplished (53:11-12; see Phil. 2:5-11).

54:1-17 *His "mission accomplished" means peace.* Because the Servant would fulfill his mission, Israel could be assured that its punishment for sin was complete; it could now look forward to a time of peace and prosperity (54:1-8). Just as God had honored his covenant with Noah, he would honor his "covenant of blessing" with Israel (54:9-10). While Israel would see the results of Christ's work in part as it returned from exile, the full results will not be seen until the final great return from exile of all redeemed humanity in the Millennium (see exposition on 26:20–27:13).

55:1-13 *Accept his salvation!* Because the Servant had accomplished his mission, all who were thirsty were invited to drink from the waters of salvation (55:1; see exposition on 48:17-21; John 4:13-14; Rev. 22:17). There was a sense of urgency: "Seek the LORD while you can find him. Call on him now while he is near" (55:6; see Heb. 3:13). All were welcome, but they would have to forsake their pride (55:8-9) and their wicked ways (55:7). Those who would do so would find great joy (55:10-13).

Besides being an admonition against pride, 55:9 is a comfort to those who suffer or are unsure of God's plan for them. Likewise 55:11 gives reassurance to faithful witnesses unsure of their ability to adequately proclaim God's truth.

56:1-8 *A house of prayer for Gentiles too!* Maintaining his sense of expectancy about the Messiah and his kingdom, Isaiah turned his attention from the exiles in Babylon (40–55) to the Jews still living in Canaan (56–66). (See 63:18, which suggests a historical context after the Temple's destruction but before its restoration.) Jewish believers were to accept social outcasts, such as eunuchs, as full members of God's family. Likewise they were to accept any foreigners who chose to "commit themselves to the LORD" (56:3). God's Temple was "for all nations" (56:7). He desired to "bring" to himself Gentiles as well as Jews (56:8; see John 10:16).

Concerning the place of Gentiles in God's plan, see Amos 9:11-12; Acts

CHRIST IN ISAIAH

ONE
His Incarnation
7:14; 9:6

TWO
His Youth in Nazareth
7:15; 11:1-2; 53:2

THREE
His Relationship with the Father
42:1; 50:4-5

FOUR
His Miracles
35:5-6

FIVE
His Message
61:1-2

SIX
His Specific Ministry to the Gentiles
9:1-2

SEVEN
His Gracious Ministry to All
42:2-3

EIGHT
His Suffering and Death
50:6; 52:14; 53:1-10

NINE
His Resurrection, Ascension, and Exaltation
52:13; 53:10-12

TEN
His Millennial Reign
9:7; 11:3-5; 32:1; 33:22
42:4-7; 49:1-12; 59:16-21

11:1-18; 15:16-17; Romans 4:9-16; Galatians 3:7-9; and exposition on the following passages: 43:8-13; 60:1-22; 65:1-16; 66:18-21; Ephesians 2:11–3:13.

56:9–57:21 *Grace for Israel's wicked leaders.* As the whole world awaited salvation, Israel's leaders were either drunk or asleep, failing in their duties as leaders and witnesses (56:9–57:2; see 42:18-25). To their insensitivity they added idolatry and immorality (57:3-10). Yet God had not given up on them. If any of these backsliders (57:17) would trust the Lord (57:13) and humble themselves (57:15), God would "not fight against" them forever (57:16) but would heal and lead them (57:18). For those who persisted in their wickedness, however, there would be "no peace" (57:21; see 48:22).

58:1-5 *Fruitless fasting, pointless praying.* In the final chapters of his written prophecy (58–66), Isaiah spoke again of the judgment and salvation of God and spelled out clearly the conditions for taking part in his salvation. Isaiah called to account those who went through the motions of religious observance (58:1-3) while at the same time committing sin and promoting injustice (58:3-5; see 1:10-17; Prov. 21:3).

58:6-14 *God helps those who help others.* The kind of worship God desires includes a sincere effort to promote morality and help the poor and oppressed (58:6-7, 9-10). It also means setting aside the Sabbath as a time to delight in the Lord rather than pursuing earthly pleasures (58:13). This kind of worship will bring health and joy and satisfying fellowship with God. (See Matt. 23:23.) The poor and oppressed are always close to God's heart (see Deut. 24:14; Prov. 14:31; Jer. 5:28; Amos 2:6-7; 5:11; Matt. 19:21; Luke 1:52-53; 7:22; Gal. 2:10).

59:1-21 *God helps the hopeless sinner.* Israel's sins had separated them from God. Isaiah described their sins (59:3-8) and, speaking for the people, acknowledged that the accusations were true (59:9-15). They were guilty of both unrighteousness and injustice. Their sins had left them blind and hopeless (59:9-11). God would judge their sins (59:15-19), but there was hope for any who would repent (59:20-21).

Alienation between a person and God is always the fault of that person, not of God (59:1-2). The covenant referred to in 59:21 is the New Covenant (see Jer. 31:31-34).

60:1-22 *Rise and shine!* For all who repent and turn to God—whether Jew or Gentile—there is the bright prospect of his millennial kingdom. The remnant of Israel, as well as many believing Gentiles with all their great wealth, will come to the restored Jerusalem to live and worship. Israel's former enemies will now bow down to them and work for them (60:10, 14). Righteousness will prevail (60:21), there will be no war (60:18), and the city gates will always be open, welcoming all foreigners (60:11; compare Rev. 21:25-26). God himself will be the city's source of light (60:19-20; compare Rev. 21:23; 22:5). All this will be final and eternal proof to Israel that "I, the LORD, am your Savior" (60:16).

In the light of God's grace, none of his children are insignificant (60:22).

61:1-11 *A Messiah of comfort . . . and vengeance.* Messiah spoke, declaring he would take vengeance on God's enemies and bring comfort to his people. This is a concise summary of the mission of Christ. He brought comfort and salvation at his first coming, and therefore quoted part of 61:1-2 during his earthly ministry (see Luke 4:18-19). He said nothing of taking vengeance on God's enemies (also in 61:2) at that time, for that part of his mission will not be fulfilled till he returns triumphant at the end of time (see 9:6-7; 1 Cor. 15:24-26; Rev. 17:14).

In the Millennium, Israel will receive "beauty for ashes" and "clothing of salvation" (61:3, 10). They will all receive the "double portion" of the firstborn son (61:7). Israel will at last fulfill its destiny as a nation of priests (61:6; see Exod. 19:6; compare exposition on 42:18-25), while its former enemies serve it (61:5).

God considered the entire Israelite nation his "firstborn" (see Exod. 4:22; Jer. 31:9).

62:1-12 *Note the new name: Beulah.* Isaiah would not rest till he saw his prophecy of glory for Israel fulfilled (62:1); he placed "watchmen" on Jerusalem's walls who shared his concern (62:6-7). He was fully confident that Zion's day of salvation would come (62:11), the day when her name would be changed from Forsaken and Desolate to Hephzibah ("my delight is in her") and Beulah ("married" or "cared for"). God himself would be her husband (62:4-5, 12; see Rev. 21:2).

63:1-19 *Questions for the warrior, questions for God.* As a blood-soaked warrior approached, a watchman asked his identity. He identified himself as the one who all alone had conquered Israel's foes and was ready to redeem his people (63:1-6). Isaiah responded with praise for the God who throughout history had shown grace toward his people, no matter how often they rebelled against him (63:7-9).

When he recalled the Exodus, however, Isaiah wondered why God had not yet delivered his people once again (63:11-17), and begged him to do so quickly (63:17-19; see 51:9-11).

63:1-6 can be seen as foreshadowing Christ's second coming and victory at Armageddon (see Rev. 14:18-20; 19:11-21). On "winepress" (63:3), compare Joel 3:13; Revelation 14:18-19; 19:15.

64:1-12 *The consuming fire of the coming Christ.* Isaiah continued his plea for God to act, in language that foreshadows Christ's second coming. That last great event will be heralded by a shaking of the earth (64:1; see 2:5–4:1; Heb. 12:18-29) similar to the shaking of Sinai at the giving of the law (64:3; see Exod. 19:18; Heb. 12:26). The image of fire (64:2) also links these two great events (see Exod. 24:17; Heb. 12:29).

Isaiah realized that the awesome God (64:4) could hardly tolerate his people's sin. The sin had long been practiced (64:5), and its effects ran deep (64:6-7; see Jer. 17:9; Rom. 3:10). Nonetheless, the prophet called in faith for God to forgive and restore (64:8-12).

65:1-16 *The pagans respond but not his people.* As God held out his hand to his own people Israel, they continued in their rebellion (65:2-4, 6), even while many non-Israelites were seeking him (65:1). God would punish his people (65:6-7, 11-12) but would preserve a faithful remnant, whom he would bless (65:8-10). He contrasted the happy fate of his "servants" to that of his enemies (65:13-14).

65:17-25 *New heavens and a new earth!* God will one day create "new heavens and a new earth." The former creation, with all its pain and suffering and death, will be forgotten forever. While 65:17 and 66:22 mention the new heavens and earth (see Rev. 21:1–22:5), and some features of 65–66 seem to have this time period in view, the suggestion of 65:20 that death will not yet be totally destroyed leads many scholars to conclude that 65–66 speaks mainly of the Millennium (see Rev. 20:1-6).

66:1-24 *Two eternities from which to choose.* God desires the fellowship of those who truly believe in him (66:1-2). Yet such are hard to find; most "choose their own ways," and therefore their worship is an abomination (66:3). Since they have refused to trust in God (see 12:2), God will bring on them the very calamities they fear (66:4).

Meanwhile those who have been ridiculed for their faith will be vindicated as, all at once, Israel is reborn (66:5-9). Jerusalem's inhabitants will rejoice, for they will enjoy abundant provisions and "peace . . . like a river" (66:10-13).

While the redeemed have fellowship with their Lord during the Millennium, God's enemies will be experiencing his wrath (66:17). All people of the world will have the opportunity to choose for or against the Lord, as the faithful remnant of Israel "will declare [God's] glory to the nations" (66:18-21; see exposition on 45:14-25). The redeemed will experience their reward forever (66:22-23), as will those who have rejected God (66:24).

PEOPLE TO REMEMBER FROM ISAIAH

ISAIAH

Key Facts: Prince of Prophets, arguably the greatest of OT prophets
Father: Amoz (38:1)

Wife: Unnamed (8:3)
Sons: Shear-jashub, Maher-shalal-hash-baz (7:3; 8:1)
Total Bible References: 53
Key References: 1–66; 2 Kings 19–20; Matt. 3:3; 8:17; 12:17-21; Rom. 10:16, 20

Isaiah Speaks

If my count is correct, Manasseh is Judah's 14th ruler. This means I have prophesied during the days of more than one-third of Judah's kings. I received my call during the year Uzziah died. Then came Jotham, followed by young Ahaz. (6:1)

How frightened Ahaz was when we first met. Well, I tried to reassure him, but he wouldn't listen. That was just the beginning, of course, for he went from simple unbelief to unspeakable devil worship, even sacrificing his own sons! No one mourned his death! (7:1-2; 11-12; 2 Kings 16:3; 2 Chron. 28:27)

Then there was his remarkable son, Hezekiah, who was the exact opposite. What memories his 29-year reign invoke. Who could ever forget that darkest of nights when we were hopelessly surrounded by one of the cruelest and most powerful enemies of our time, the Assyrians! At God's direction, I reassured Hezekiah that not one soldier's foot nor even an enemy arrow would intrude into our beloved city. (37:33-35)

How well we all remember the cries of anguish the next morning, coming from what was left of the enemy troops when they discovered 185,000 of their fellow soldiers lying dead in heaps all around our city walls! (37:36)

But Hezekiah is gone, replaced by his son Manasseh. In spite of having such an exemplary father, Manasseh has turned out even worse than his despicable *grandfather.* In fact, friends tell me he plans to silence me soon! [According to tradition, and based on the apocryphal "Ascension of Isaiah," Isaiah was executed by being sawn in two during the dark times mentioned in 2 Kings 21:16 (see Heb. 11:37).]

What glorious revelations God has given me concerning Israel's future Messiah: I've been allowed to write about his birth, his death, his resurrection, and his eternal reign! (7:14; 9:6-7; 52:13; 53:1-11; 60:1-6)

I began my ministry more than 40 years ago saying, "Here am I; send me." I now conclude with, "Here am I! Receive me to yourself." (6:8, KJV)

Spiritual Lessons from Isaiah

- The brighter the light of God's glory, the darker the shadow of my sin (6:1-5; see Luke 5:8; Rev. 1:17).
- Isaiah *volunteered* for God's service before being *drafted* (6:8; see 1 Sam. 3:1-10; Rom. 12:1-2).
- Cleansing is achieved only through confession (6:5-7; see Ps. 32:5; 51:1-4, 7).

Key Verse

"Then I heard the Lord asking, 'Whom should I send as a messenger to my people? Who will go for us?' And I said, 'Lord, I'll go! Send me'" (6:8).

SENNACHERIB

Key Facts: King of Assyria; army destroyed by death angel (2 Kings 18:13; 19:32-35)
Father: Sargon II
Sons: Adrammelech, Sharezer, Esarhaddon (37:38)

Death: Recorded in 2 Kings 19:37
Total Bible References: 13
Key References: 36–37; 2 Kings 18–19

Sennacherib Speaks

I stand here in the temple of Nisroch at Nineveh, demanding that my god tell me what went wrong! Of course I'm referring to that fateful and frightful military campaign 20 years ago! My army has never been the same. Obviously, losing 185,000 soldiers in a single night by some invisible hand has taken a terrible toll on both commander and troops! (37:36)

The march was so successful at first. I sacked Babylon, subdued both Aram and Philistia, and destroyed the Jewish stronghold at Lachish. But then we came to Jerusalem. At the time, I wrote in my diary that I had trapped Hezekiah in his city "like a bird in a cage." And quite honestly, I had every reason to believe the weak king of Judah would quickly surrender—after all, he had sent me that huge bribe while I was destroying Lachish. (2 Kings 18:14-16; 2 Chron. 32:9-15)

But then Hezekiah changed his mind. Probably that religious fanatic Isaiah got to him. Oh, mighty Nisroch, why did you allow the Judean God Jehovah to defeat both you and me?

What's that disturbance I hear? How dare anyone interrupt the king during his time of worship! But wait! Two figures approach me with drawn swords! It is my two sons! (37:37-38)

Spiritual Lessons from Sennacherib

- The person who laughs *at* God or his people may eventually be laughed at *by* God (see 2 Kings 18:22, 33-35; 19:20-21; Ps. 2:1-5).
- Sennacherib's fatal mistake was to assume that Israel's God was only as powerless as his own false gods (see 2 Kings 19:10-13).
- Hezekiah was saved *from* the sword after worshiping the true God (see 2 Kings 19:14-19, 32-35); Sennacherib was slain *by* the sword while worshiping his false god (see 2 Kings 19:36-37).

Key Verses

"And this is what the LORD says about the king of Assyria: His armies will not enter Jerusalem to shoot their arrows. They will not march outside its gates with their shields and build banks of earth against its walls. The king will return to his own country by the road on which he came. He will not enter this city, says the LORD. For my own honor and for the sake of my servant David, I will defend it" (37:33-35).

ISAIAH: PRINCE OF PROPHETS

INDEX TO SELECTED TOPICS IN ISAIAH

ISAIAH AND THE ATTRIBUTES OF GOD

- Eternality (40:28; 63:16)
- Faithfulness (25:1; 49:7)
- Gentleness (40:11)
- Glory (40:3-5; 42:8; 59:19)
- Goodness (58:8-14)
- Grace (43:22-28; 48:17-22; 49:14-18; 55:1-9; 57:16-21; 63:7-8)
- Holiness (6:3; 57:15)
- Justice (56:1-8)
- Long-suffering (42:14; 65:2)
- Mercy (40:1-2)
- Omnipotence (31:4-5, 8-9; 40:9-10, 12; 42:5; 64:1-4)
- Omniscience (28:23-29; 40:13-14; 41:21-24; 42:9)
- Sovereignty (40:15-17, 21-27; 41:1-4; 44:6-20, 24-27; 45:7-12, 14-15; 46:1-4, 6-8; 66:1-2)
- Trinity (48:16; 63:9-10)
- Uniqueness (40:18-20; 46:5, 9-12; 48:12-13)
- Word (40:6-8; 55:10-13)
- Wrath (1:28-31; 30:27-28; 33:14-16; 63:11-15, 17-19)

ISAIAH AND THE MESSIAH

THE LAMB

His incarnation

- Born of a virgin (7:14)
- Both God and man (9:6)
- Descended from David (9:7; 11:1)

His relationship with the Father

- Prepared by the Father (49:1-2)
- Named by the Father (9:6)
- Loved by the Father (42:1)

Empowered by the Father (50:4; 61:10-11)
Commissioned by the Father (42:6-7; 49:3-7)
Reassured by the Father (49:8-9; 50:7-9)
Obedient to the Father (50:5)

His relationship with the Holy Spirit
The power (11:2)
The preaching (61:1-3)

His relationship with Israel
Its illumination (9:1-2)
Its foundation (28:16)

His relationship with the Gentiles
Revealing salvation (42:6-7)
Receiving adoration (11:10)

His gracious ministry
Not a fanatic (42:2)
Not a faultfinder (42:3)
Not a failure (43:4)

His crucifixion
Its origin (Who caused his death?)
His foes (all sinners) (53:3-6)
His Father! (53:6, 10)
Its ordeal (50:6; 52:14)
Its outcome (53:5-9, 11-12)

THE LION

His exaltation (52:13)

His millennial reign
Its nature (11:3-5)
Its extent and duration (9:7)
Its meaning to Israel (59:20-21)
Its meaning to Gentiles (52:15)
Its meaning to sinners (59:16-18)

ISAIAH AND THE END TIMES

THE GREAT TRIBULATION

Its reasons
Pride (2:10-17; 13:11)
Idolatry (2:18)
Lawlessness (24:5)

Its results
Divine plagues on the skies (13:10, 13)
Divine plagues on the soil (13:9; 24:1, 19-20)
Divine plagues on sinners
The fear of sinners during the Tribulation (2:19-22; 13:6-8; 24:17-18)
The "fewness" of sinners following the Tribulation (13:12; 24:2-4, 6-13)

THE MILLENNIUM

The millennial king
Jesus the glorious and beautiful (28:5-6; 33:17)

- Jesus the righteous (32:1-4)
- Jesus the light-giver (24:23; 60:19-20)

The millennial kingdom

- Israel in the Millennium
  - Its citizens purified (4:4; 66:19-21)
  - Its country glorified (60:1-18)
  - Its capital magnified (2:1-3; 4:2-6; 33:5-6, 20-23; 52:1-10; 62; 65:18-19; 66:10-14)
- Gentile nations
  - Wars will cease (2:4; 9:5)
  - Worship will begin (11:10)
- The needy in the Millennium
  - Deaf and blind will hear and see (29:18; 35:5)
  - Lame and mute will walk and talk (35:6)
  - Humble and poor will rejoice (29:19)
  - Sick will be healed (33:24)
  - Captives will go free (52:11-12)
  - Ignorant will learn (29:24)
  - Sorrowful will sing (30:29-33; 35:10; 42:10-17; 65:19)
  - Godless will vanish (29:20-21; 32:5-8)
  - Fearful will be unafraid (29:22-23; 35:3-4)
  - Petitioners will be heard (65:24)
  - Dying will live (25:8; 65:20)
- Nature in the Millennium
  - Plant life (29:17; 30:23-25; 32:15-20; 35:1-2, 7; 65:21-23)
  - Animal life (11:6-9; 65:25)

JEREMIAH

BACKGROUND

Jeremiah began his prophetic ministry in 627 B.C., nearly 100 years after the northern kingdom of Israel fell to Assyria in 722 and some 60 years after the end of Isaiah's ministry. Assyria had dominated Judah for much of those 100 years but was now at the end of its glory days. Babylon, the rising new superpower, would conquer Assyria in 605 and Judah in 586.

In about 632, the young King Josiah had begun seriously to seek God's will (see 2 Chron. 34:3). Then in 621 a long-forgotten copy of the law of Moses was discovered, leading to a nationwide religious awakening (see 2 Kings 22–23). But by the time of Jeremiah's first prophetic messages (2–6), still during Josiah's reign, the revival had all but ended.

Josiah was killed in an ill-conceived battle with Egypt in 609 (see exposition on 2 Kings 23:28-30), and Judah came under Egyptian control. Josiah's son Jehoahaz had succeeded him, but Egypt deposed him after just 90 days and made his brother Jehoiakim their puppet king (see exposition on 2 Kings 23:31-34). Egypt was defeated by Babylon in 605, and Judah came under Babylonian domination.

By 601 the Babylonians had withdrawn from Judah, and Jehoiakim turned to his former Egyptian masters as allies against Babylon (2 Kings 24:1). The Babylonians returned in 597, just after Jehoiakim's death, and captured Jerusalem. They took Jehoiakim's son Jehoiachin captive to Babylon after he had reigned only 90 days (see exposition on 2 Kings 24:8-16), and installed Zedekiah, another son of Josiah, as their puppet. Egypt urged Zedekiah to become its ally against Babylon.

Much of Jeremiah's ministry had to do with showing his fellow Israelites that their oppression and coming defeat by Babylon were God's way of calling them to repentance and faith (see exposition on 27:1-22). Because of that conviction, he opposed any alliance with Egypt—or with any other nation, for

***627 B.C.* Jeremiah begins ministry**

***608* Jeremiah's Temple sermon, imprisonment**

***605* Judah's 1st deportation to Babylon**

***597* 2nd deportation**

***593* Jeremiah's yoke sermon**

***c. 586* Jeremiah in cistern, Jerusalem falls, Jeremiah to Egypt**

***581* Jeremiah's last prophecy**

that matter—earning himself the hatred of "patriotic" Israelites who saw Egypt as their only hope. Like Isaiah before him, Jeremiah longed for a nation that trusted in God alone (see *Isaiah: Background*).

Jeremiah predicted that, in any event, Egypt would provide little help against Babylon. Zedekiah finally sided with Egypt, and when Babylon attacked in 587 and again in 586, Egypt floundered and Jerusalem fell (see 2 Kings 25), just as Jeremiah had predicted. Ironically, Jeremiah was then coerced to flee to the very Egypt whose help he had opposed (43:5-7).

Jeremiah's book is a collection of prophecies given at various times in his life. Though they are not all in chronological order, approximate dates can be determined by the kings named (see *Outline*).

Shortly after Jerusalem's destruction, Jeremiah recorded his thoughts about that event in the book of Lamentations.

AUTHOR

Jeremiah, whose prophecies were recorded by his secretary, Baruch (see 36:4, 32) and collected by an unknown compiler:

- Jeremiah is referred to numerous times in language that implies his authorship (1:1, 4).
- Daniel referred to him as author of the passages concerning the 70 years of exile (25:11-12; 29:10; Dan. 9:2).
- Matthew names Jeremiah as author of two quotes from the book of Jeremiah (Matt. 2:17-18; 27:9-10).

As Baruch noted, Jeremiah's actual words end at 51:64; chapter 52—especially 52:31-34, which reflects a time well into the exile—may have been added by a disciple of Jeremiah. (Note that 52:31, 33 speaks of "Jehoiachin," who elsewhere in Jeremiah, in some translations, is called Jeconiah or Coniah.) Chapter 52 is almost identical to 2 Kings 24:18–25:30.

From the text of his book, we know more about Jeremiah's personal life than about any other prophet. Sometimes known as the prophet of doom, he had few friends and many enemies. Also known as the weeping prophet, he mourned continually for his people and land (see 4:19; 8:21; 9:1; 10:19).

The OT mentions eight other Jeremiahs, including two others mentioned in this book (35:3; 52:1).

DATE AND LOCATION

See *Background.* Jeremiah ministered from about 627 B.C. (see 25:3) to about 581 (see exposition on 44:1-14), mainly in Jerusalem (see 22:1-2; 29:1; and other passages where he speaks with various kings). The date of compilation is unknown.

PURPOSE

Jeremiah proclaimed God's word concerning five areas:

- God: To proclaim that God created and controls everything (see 10:12-16; 32:26-27).
- Sin: To show that the seriousness of Judah's sin demanded divine punishment.
- God's remedy for sin: To introduce the radical, once-for-all solution to sin—the divine gift of a new heart (31:31-34; 33:6-9).

- God's person to provide the remedy: To predict the renewal of the Davidic kingship by the coming Messiah (the "Branch," 23; 33), who would save Israel from its sins (23:6; 33:16).
- God's plan for redeemed humanity: The Messiah will one day establish his millennial kingdom (see *Isaiah: Background*), free from the curse of sin and death (see 23:1-8; 30:9; 33:14-18). In Jeremiah, as in Isaiah, prophecies of a return from exile have two great future events in mind: the return of the Jews from Babylon, and redeemed humanity's return to God in the Millennium (see 30:10-11 and exposition on Isa. 26:20–27:13).

UNIQUE FEATURES

- Jeremiah was the most persecuted OT prophet.
- He was the only prophet forbidden to pray for his nation (see exposition on 7:16-27).
- He was the only prophet to record an eyewitness account of Jerusalem's fall (39; see Lam.).
- Jeremiah contains the Bible's most extended and detailed prophecies about Babylon, mentioning it 164 times—more than in all the rest of the Bible. The apostle John would give the name Babylon to the city of the Antichrist (Rev. 17–18).
- Jeremiah referred to another prophet, Micah, by name (26:18). Jeremiah himself was referred to by Daniel (Dan. 9:2). Though many of the prophets were contemporaries, only one other writing prophet, Daniel, was mentioned by name in print by a fellow prophet (Ezek. 14:14, 20; 28:3). Likewise the prophetic books make only one mention by name of a major nonwriting prophet (Elijah, Mal. 4:5).
- Jeremiah records the last of the three most important OT unconditional covenants (see *Biblical Covenants,* p. 820):
  - ➤ the Abrahamic covenant (Gen. 12:1-3)
  - ➤ the Davidic covenant (2 Sam. 7:10-16)
  - ➤ the New Covenant (31:31)

COMPARISON WITH OTHER BIBLE BOOKS

Other prophets:

- Jeremiah was a contemporary of Habakkuk and shared some of his concerns. Parallels can also be seen with Micah and Haggai, as noted in the *Comparison* sections for their books. Obadiah 1:1-9 parallels Jeremiah 49:7-22.

OUTLINE

(Approximate dates indicate breaks in time sequence.)

JEREMIAH'S CALL (1)[627 B.C.]

JEREMIAH'S MINISTRY TO JUDAH (2–45)

  Calls to repentance (2–6)[626–615]

  The Temple and idolatry (7–10)[608]

  The broken covenant (11–12)

  Warnings of doom (13:1–15:16)[605–590]

  Jeremiah's sorrow and singleness (15:17–16:9)

Further warnings (16:10–17:27)
The potter and the jar (18:1–20:6)
Jeremiah's anguish (20:7-18)
Warnings to kings (21–22)
The Branch of righteousness (23:1-8)
Warnings about false prophets (23:9-40)
The vision of figs (24)[597–586]
The cup of God's wrath (25)[605]
Jeremiah imprisoned (26)[608]
Jeremiah urges submission to Babylon (27–29)[593]
The sign of the yoke (27)
Hananiah's reaction (28)
Warning the exiles about false prophets (29)
The New Covenant (30–31)[589–587]
Jeremiah buys a field (32)
The Branch of righteousness (33)
Zedekiah and the slaves (34)
The Recabites (35)[c. 607]
Jeremiah's scroll (36)[605]
Jeremiah imprisoned and kept in a cistern (37–38)[587–586]
Jerusalem falls (39)
Jeremiah, Gedaliah, and Johanan (40–41)[586–585]
The remaining Jews flee to Egypt (42:1–43:7)
Jeremiah's ministry in Egypt (43:8–44:30)
A prophecy for Baruch (45)[605]
WARNINGS TO THE NATIONS (46–51)[605–585]
Egypt (46)
Philistia (47)
Moab (48)
Ammon (49:1-6)
Edom (49:7-22)
Damascus (49:23-27)
Kedar and Hazor (49:28-33)
Elam (49:34-39)
Babylon (50–51)
HISTORICAL POSTSCRIPT (52)[586–560]

JEREMIAH'S CALL (1)

1:1-10 *Set apart before his birth.* Jeremiah began his book by noting that his ministry extended from the 13th year of Josiah (627 B.C.) until "the people of Jerusalem were taken away as captives" (586). His ministry would actually extend longer, possibly to about 581 (see exposition on 44:1-14). Long before Jeremiah's birth, God had decided Jeremiah would be a prophet. Despite Jeremiah's reluctance and fear (1:6-8), God gave him a difficult assignment (1:10) and promised his divine help (1:7-9).

1:11-19 *A branch and a boiling pot.* To confirm his calling of the frightened Jeremiah, God gave him two visions:

The almond branch (1:11-12), which blooms late, spoke of a judgment long overdue, ready to burst forth. The pot of boiling water "tipping from the north" revealed that God would pour the wrath of Babylon upon Israel (1:13-15). God encouraged Jeremiah to boldly prophesy these things, even though Israel would actively oppose him.

JEREMIAH'S MINISTRY TO JUDAH (2–45)

2:1-19 *God's bride becomes the lions' dinner.* Jeremiah began his first message (2:1–3:5), given during Josiah's reign (see 3:6), by recalling the days when the Israelites had been devoted to their Lord, as a bride to her husband (2:1-3). Regrettably, they no longer displayed such love. They had committed sins of commission, serving idols; and sins of omission, forsaking their true God (2:4-13). Such backsliding had brought the enemy upon the northern kingdom like hungry lions devouring their prey, and the same thing could happen to Judah (2:14-19).

2:20-37 *"The strongest soap cannot remove this stain!"* God's people had chased after foreign gods as an adulterer pursues an affair, as an animal in mating season (2:20-25). They had collected as many foreign gods as there were cities in Judah (2:28; see 11:13) and had forgotten the one true God (2:32). Despite the obvious evidence of their sin (2:33-34), they claimed innocence (2:23, 33). No human effort could wash away such great sin (2:22). The only remedy was national humiliation through military defeat (2:37).

As it had throughout its history, Israel sought security in political alliances rather than in God alone (2:17-19, 36-37). Jeremiah warned that such alliances would prove futile (2:36-37), just as they had in Isaiah's time. Both Assyria and Egypt would soon be defeated by Babylon. Jeremiah, like Isaiah, saw a strong connection between foreign alliances and religious apostasy (2:19; see exposition on the following passages: Isa. 30:1-17; 1 Kings 11:1-8; 2 Kings 16:10-20).

3:1-5 *"If you'll return, I'll overlook my law."* Though he had every right to condemn them for "prostituting" themselves with false gods, and though his law said a man could not take back his divorced wife if she had married another man, God wanted his unfaithful children to return to him.

3:6-11 *The sad story of two sinful sisters.* Jeremiah began the second of his two messages during Josiah's reign (3:6–6:30) by again reminding the people of the fall of the northern kingdom. "Treacherous" Judah was worse than her "faithless" sister Israel because Judah had failed to learn from Israel's fall.

3:12–4:4 *The glad offer of a grieved but gracious Father.* If they would acknowledge their sin, God would forgive both Israel and Judah (3:12-14), and would bring them from exile to his everlasting kingdom (3:14-18). In the Millennium (see *Purpose*), the shadow of religious observance surrounding the Ark will be replaced by the substance of the Messiah himself. This present age will be forgotten in the light of his presence (3:16; see Isa. 65:17). Having made his offer, God once again called his children to repent (3:19–4:4).

4:5-31 *Devastated by his own decree of doom.* With growing urgency, Jeremiah declared that a "lion" from the "north" (Babylon) was already preparing to invade Judah (4:5-9). Once more he called on Judah to repent (4:14). In anguish and with pounding heart he described a fruitful land of Judah turned into a wilderness (4:19-31).

5:1-9 *The price of reprieve: Just one who is righteous.* With biting irony, God promised to pardon the whole nation if just one person could be found who sought truth and practiced justice (5:1-2). Jeremiah searched in vain for such a person (5:3-5) and concluded that God's threatened punishment would be well deserved (5:6-9).

5:10-19 *"You served their gods; now you'll serve* them!" Because Israel had ignored God's efforts to discipline them (5:10-13), he would bring Babylon against them (5:14-17). Because they had worshiped foreign gods in their own land, they would now serve a foreign nation in another land (5:18-19). Judah would be exiled, not totally destroyed (5:18; see 4:27).

5:20-31 *The oceans obey him, but his people do not.* The oceans remained in their ordained place, obeying their Creator, but God's people had chosen otherwise (5:22-25). Did not God have the right to punish such rebellion? (5:29). As in all of Scripture, the poor and fatherless are high on the list of God's concerns (5:28; see exposition on Isa. 58:6-14).

6:1-9 *Run, Benjamin, run!* As his message drew to a close, Jeremiah warned his own tribe, Benjamin, to prepare to flee the advancing Babylonians. He painted a grim scene of the coming invasion. Worst of all, it was the Lord himself who would lead this army against his own people (6:6-9)! "The Lord disciplines those he loves" (Heb. 12:6).

6:10-21 *No shame, no peace.* Jeremiah repeated the charges against Judah: They were all sinful, "from the least to the greatest" (6:13). Their prophets and priests were promising peace (6:14; see 8:11), but where there is unashamed wickedness, there can be no peace (6:15). God had called his people to "ask for the old paths," where they could have found peace, but they had refused to do so (6:16, KJV; see 18:15). Therefore, their only prospect was judgment (6:18-21; see exposition on Ezek. 13:1-23). On "obstacles" (6:21), see exposition on Isaiah 8:11-22.

6:22-30 *"'Rejected silver'—that's what they'll call us."* In one last effort to bring about repentance, Jeremiah described again the cruelty of the coming invasion. If the Israelites didn't repent, God would reject them as one rejects inferior silver (6:27-30).

7:1-15 *"You think he won't destroy it? Look at Shiloh!"* Shortly after the death of Josiah in 609 B.C., after Egypt had deposed Jehoahaz and made Jehoiakim king, Jeremiah spoke concerning Judah's insincere worship in the Temple (7:1–8:3, often called his Temple sermon). The people of Judah falsely assumed that, since God's Temple was there, God would not destroy Jerusalem (7:1-4). But Jeremiah exposed the hypocrisy of standing before God in the Temple while living in sin at home. They need only visit Shiloh, where God had allowed the Tabernacle to be destroyed and the Ark to be captured (see 1 Sam. 4), to know that he would not hesitate to destroy Jerusalem as well.

Some scholars see 7:4 as Jeremiah's expression of cynicism concerning the revival that had taken place under Josiah (see *Background*). The chronicler noted, however, that Jeremiah mourned Josiah's death (2 Chron. 35:25).

Jesus would apply 7:11 to the false worship of his day (see Matt. 21:13).

7:16-27 *The prophet should pray no more.* God told Jeremiah to cease praying for Judah: Since they had turned a deaf ear to God, he would turn a deaf ear to them. In such a case it is useless to pray (7:16; see 11:14; 14:11; 1 John 5:16). Since the day God brought them out of Egypt, Israel had disobeyed him (7:17-26). Jeremiah could be sure that they would disobey him as well (7:27).

7:28–8:3 *"Shave your head in shame, sinful city!"* Because of the seriousness of their sin and because of the great suffering soon to come upon them, it would be fitting for the Israelites to shave their heads in mourning (7:28-34; see 47:5; 48:37). In the coming judgment, the bones of the dead would be exhumed and exposed to the very elements they once worshiped (8:1-3).

The people had brought pagan altars into the Temple (7:30; see 2 Kings 21:5) and were even sacrificing their children to foreign gods (see 19:4-6; Isa. 30:33). This horror was taking place at Topheth, in the valley of the son of Hinnom, or Gehenna, on the southern edge of Jerusalem. By NT times, the name of Gehenna was synonymous with hell, and it is translated as such 12 times in the NT (see Matt. 5:22; James 3:6).

8:4-17 *"The birds know more than my people!"* Jeremiah's Temple sermon was followed by a series of prophecies about sin and judgment (8:4–10:25). While birds followed their God-given instincts, God's people failed to heed his law (8:4-9), therefore he would punish them (8:10-13). Because they were not ashamed of their sin, he would bring great shame on them (8:12). They would be overrun by their enemies (8:14-17).

8:18–9:2 *No medicine? No doctors?* Burdened by Judah's plight, Jeremiah pleaded with the Lord to heal them (8:18-22) and wept for the doomed cities (9:1-2). Yet as the prophet pleaded his people's case (8:18-19), God merely repeated the charges against them (8:19). Jeremiah was willing to journey as far as Gilead to find a cure (see Gen. 37:25). God would eventually go much farther than Gilead to find a permanent cure for sin (see 23:6; 31:31-34).

9:3-16 *Why all this suffering? For all their sin!* The Lord spoke again of Judah's sin, focusing this time on dishonesty in interpersonal relationships (9:3-8). Then he asked a rhetorical question: "Should I not punish them for this?" (9:9). Again Jeremiah lamented Judah's coming destruction (9:10), and again God pronounced its doom and spelled out the cause of that doom: "because my people have abandoned the instructions I gave them; they have refused to obey my law" (9:13).

9:17-26 *A call to sorrow.* The Lord called on all Judah to publicly mourn their approaching doom (9:17-22). They would be punished in the same way God would punish a sinful Gentile nation (9:25-26). But the punishment would be for their ultimate good, as Jews and Gentiles alike would come to know their God (9:23-24). On 9:24, see 1 Corinthians 1:31; on 9:26, see Romans 2:28.

10:1-18 *Worshiping the worthless.* Denying the true, living, eternal Creator God for false, dead, temporal idols is surely the height of insanity, said Jeremiah. His picture of workmen building the very gods they would later worship recalls Isaiah's similar sarcasm (see exposition on Isa. 44:6-28).

10:19-25 *"Have mercy! We're only human!"* Once again Jeremiah fell into deep depression as he contemplated Judah's coming judgment (10:19-22). He pleaded with God to be merciful to his people (10:24), who were, after all, only human (10:23), and to reserve his most severe judgment for the Gentiles who had persecuted them. On 10:23, see Proverbs 16:1; 20:24.

11:1-10 *"Remember the Exodus? and the law?"* In a message perhaps delivered in connection with the rediscovered law (see 2 Kings 22–23), Jeremiah reminded the people of their historic disregard for that law and of their ingratitude for deliverance from the slavery of Egypt.

11:11-17 *Again he says, "No more prayer!"* Considering their sin and ingratitude, the time for praying for Judah had ended (11:14), and the time for punishment had come. Judah had as many gods as cities (11:13), but none of them could even hear, much less save Judah from God's judgment.

11:18-23 *"We hate the message; let's kill the messenger!"* The people of Jeremiah's hometown threatened to kill him if he didn't stop prophesying. Jeremiah cried out to the Lord, who declared that none of Jeremiah's opponents would survive the coming invasion.

12:1-17 *How long? Not much longer!* Perplexed by the continuing prosperity of the wicked, Jeremiah asked the Lord how long he would delay their day of reckoning (12:1-4). God replied that because of Judah's great sin, the "sword of the LORD" would quickly destroy them (12:5-13). God would "uproot" both Judah and its evil neighbors from their lands but would then restore them all, providing they kept his law (12:14-17). Concerning the fate of these Gentile neighbor nations, see 46–49. On the prosperity of the wicked, see exposition on Psalm 37.

13:1-27 *Signs of the times.* Jeremiah gave five warnings concerning the coming destruction:

Rotted and ruined, just like Judah (13:1-11). At God's direction, Jeremiah acted out an object lesson concerning Israel's sin: Just as his linen belt was rendered useless (13:1-7), so Judah had become useless to God.

A different kind of wine (13:12-14). When Jeremiah said, "All your wineskins will be full of wine," the people assumed he was talking of prosperity. But he declared that God would fill Judah's leaders with drunkenness and then destroy them.

"Humble yourselves while you can see" (13:15-17). Judah should humbly seek God, before the darkness of foreign invasion overtook them.

Even the king should humble himself (13:18-19). Jeremiah called on Judah's king and queen to fall before God in humility, for their kingdom would soon fall. This was probably the young king Jehoiachin (Jeconiah), who ruled just 90 days before being taken captive in 597 B.C.; and his mother, Nehushta (see 29:2; 2 Kings 24:8).

Judah stop sinning? Impossible! (13:20-27). Judah's punishment was inevitable because its moral condition was hopeless. It was as impossible for Judah to cease sinning as for a human or animal to change skin color. God would address this impossible situation in 31:31-34.

14:1-12 *"No rain, and here's the reason."* Prolonged drought had brought famine in Judah. Already spiritually dry, they were now physically dry as well (14:1-6). They repented (14:7-9), but God turned a deaf ear, once more ordering Jeremiah not to even pray for them; the drought was the just punishment for their sin (14:10-12). From its earliest history, drought was part of the prescribed curse on Israel for not following God (see Lev. 26:14-20).

14:13–15:9 *"Spare them? Not even for Samuel's sake!"* Jeremiah observed that many prophets were promising peace. God replied that he had not authorized those prophets and that both they and the people would perish (14:13-16). Both Jeremiah (14:17-18) and the people (14:19-22) again pleaded for the drought to end. But the Lord was determined to carry out his intentions to punish his people. He would not spare them, even if Moses and Samuel, two of Israel's godliest men, were to plead their case (15:1). Such would be the coming judgment that there would be "more widows than the grains of sand along the seashore" (15:8). Even a mother of seven would be childless (15:9).

15:10-21 *"You have let me down!"* Overwhelmed by the opposition to his message, Jeremiah regretted the day of his birth, but God reassured him that he would be vindicated (15:10-11). God spoke again of the coming judgment (15:12-14), and Jeremiah urged him to bring that judgment swiftly so that, after all his lonely suffering, he would be vindicated as a prophet. He accused God of letting him down, being "as uncertain as a seasonal brook," by not bringing swift judgment (15:15-18).

With mild rebuke, God assured Jeremiah that he would succeed in his prophetic ministry (15:20-21), but only if he would focus on the Lord and on his ministry instead of letting his opponents upset him (15:19).

16:1-9 *No wife for Jeremiah.* God told Jeremiah not to marry (16:1-2) nor to take part in community life (16:8). By abstaining from such pleasures, he would bear witness that the devastation to come would include the disruption of all such normal practices.

16:10-21 *Repayment now, restoration and revival later.* While the deliverance from Egypt was supernatural, even more miraculous would be the day when God would bring his people home from Babylon, the land of the north (16:14-15). But first, God would have to "punish them doubly for all their sins" (16:18), making them fair game for Gentile "fishermen" and "hunters" (16:16-17). Jeremiah rejoiced that Gentile idolaters would someday acknowledge the one true God (16:19-20), and God assured him that this would indeed happen.

The second exodus of 16:14-15 may foreshadow the final great regathering of all nations in the Millennium (see exposition on Isa. 54:1-17).

17:1-8 *Trusting in everything but God.* Judah's sin was indelibly inscribed on their stubborn hearts; therefore, God would punish them (17:1-4). If they would only trust God, they would flourish like a well-watered tree (17:7-8; see Ps. 1; Isa. 12:2; 30:18). They were trusting in mere human alliances and therefore had become like wilted shrubs in the desert, fruitless and barren (17:5-6; see exposition on 2:20-37).

17:9-13 *The great deceiver.* Judah's refusal to trust God was but one example of the utter depravity of the human heart (17:9: see Isa. 64:6-7; Rom. 3:10). God was Israel's only hope; there was no hope for those who rejected him (17:13).

17:14-18 *"Remember your message, and your messenger!"* Jeremiah pleaded for vindication and for his own safety. He had no desire to see Judah destroyed (17:16). On the other hand, he prayed for swift judgment on all who mocked his prophesies (17:18) and asked why those prophecies had not yet come true (17:15).

17:19-27 *Observe it and live; ignore it and die.* Judah was challenged to hear God's word and cease doing business on the Sabbath. Keeping the Sabbath would mean remaining in the land. Ignoring it would bring destruction (see exposition on Neh. 13:15-22).

18:1-17 *Too late to reshape it?* Jeremiah watched a potter reshape a flawed pot into something better. God declared that he, like a potter, had sovereign control over Israel, to shape or reshape it as he pleased. Even though he had decreed judgment, he could easily change plans if Judah repented (18:1-10). Jeremiah relayed the offer to the men of Judah, but they declined, saying they were too sinful to repent (18:11-12).

God expressed dismay at his people. They had forsaken the "cold, flowing streams" of godliness for the "muddy paths of sin"; therefore he would have to judge them (18:13-17).

18:18-23 *"We can't shut him up, so we'll shut him out!"* Unable to silence Jeremiah, his enemies plotted to slander and ostracize him. Jeremiah asked God to bring them to justice.

19:1-15 *The sign of the smashed jar.* At God's instruction, Jeremiah took some of Judah's elders to the Valley of Hinnom (see exposition on 7:28–8:3), where he smashed an earthen jar as a sign of judgment. Returning to Jerusalem, he repeated the message.

20:1-6 *Magor-missabib: Fear on every side.* Angered by Jeremiah's prophecies, Pashhur the priest persecuted him. Jeremiah responded by giving the priest a name prophetic of the approaching terror (20:3-6).

20:7-18 *"I'd quit if I could, but I can't."* Jeremiah complained again about the way he was being ridiculed. His tormentors had applied to him the name he had given Pashhur (20:3, 10). Jeremiah wanted to give up his ministry but felt compelled to continue (20:9). He praised God for his mighty presence (20:11-13), yet lamented the day of his birth.

21:1-10 *Deliverance? Yes, but not the kind they want.* In about 588 B.C., shortly before Jerusalem's fall, King Zedekiah asked Jeremiah to pray for deliverance from Nebuchadnezzar and the Babylonians (21:1-2). Jeremiah replied that, quite to the contrary, God would deliver the king and his people *to* the Babylonians (21:3-10). God had offered his people the way of life, but they had chosen the way of death. Death would come at the hands of Babylon. All who would save themselves should defect to Babylon (21:8-10). Jeremiah had given similar warnings at least twice already (see 24 and exposition on 27:1-22).

37:1-10 records a similar request for prayer by Zedekiah at about the same time.

As elsewhere in Scripture, Jeremiah refers to the people of Babylon as the "Chaldeans" (see exposition on 2 Kings 24:8-16).

21:11–22:30 *Warnings fit for a king.* Jeremiah recorded a series of prophecies to various kings of his time in Judah:

Promote justice or prepare for judgment (21:11–22:9). Kings should pursue justice. The alternative is fiery judgment.

Death in a distant land (22:10-12). Jehoahaz (Shallum), Josiah's evil son and first successor, had been taken captive to Egypt in 609 B.C. after reigning just 90 days. Jeremiah predicted he would die there (see 2 Kings 23:31-34).

A donkey's death (22:13-23). Unlike his righteous father Josiah (22:15-16), Jehoiakim (609–597) had lived in selfish luxury. He would be given the burial of a donkey (22:19).

Deposed and discarded (22:24-30). Because of his sin, Jehoiakim's son Jehoiachin (also called Coniah and Jeconiah) would be discarded like a broken dish (22:28). Even if he were a valued ring, his fate would be the same (22:24). Jehoiachin was deposed and exiled in 597 after reigning just 90 days (see exposition on 2 Kings 24:8-16); and, just as Jeremiah prophesied (22:30), none of his sons succeeded him. (He was succeeded by Zedekiah, his uncle.)

23:1-8 *Careless shepherds vs. the Good Shepherd.* Israel's spiritual and political shepherds had failed to take care of their flock; therefore the flock had been scattered. But God would regather them, under new and better leaders (23:1-4). God would raise up a descendant of David, a "righteous Branch," to "do what is just and right throughout the land" (23:5-6; see

33:15-16; see exposition on Isa. 4:2-6). This will take place in the Millennium (see exposition on 16:10-21).

23:9-40 *Their flowery words vs. his fiery word.* Jeremiah warned that many of Judah's prophets and priests were "ungodly, wicked men" (23:9-12). The prophets got their messages from foreign gods and promoted ungodliness (23:13-15). They promised peace to everyone, even "those who stubbornly follow their own evil desires" (23:16-17; see 6:14; Judg. 21:25).

False prophets and priests would reap the whirlwind of God's fury (23:18-20), for they had spoken boldly even though God did not send them. If they had truly been speaking for God, they would have promoted morality (23:21-22). God was well aware of what they were doing (23:23-24).

God's true word was "like fire" (23:29). The false prophets, by contrast, spoke glib words based either on dreams or on the thoughts of other false prophets and tried to pass those off as God's word (23:25-32). What's more, they made light of Jeremiah's message of doom (23:33-38). Therefore, God would judge them (23:39-40). Their so-called dreams would become nightmares!

24:1-10 *Two figs, two fates.* Sometime during the reign of Zedekiah (597–586 B.C.), after Jehoiachin and many of Judah's elite (including Ezekiel) had been led captive to Babylon in 597 (see Ezek. 40:1), Jeremiah saw a vision of two baskets of figs, one good and one rotten. The good represented the Jews taken captive in 597. God would protect them and bring them back to faith in him. The bad figs were those who remained in Jerusalem or had fled to Egypt. They would be scattered throughout the earth, to be consumed by "the sword, the famine, and pestilence." (See exposition on 27:1-22.) On "hearts that will recognize me" (24:7), see exposition on 31:31-34.

25:1-7 *"I've been warning you for 23 years . . ."* Jeremiah's record of his ministry now jumps back to 605 B.C., the "fourth year of Jehoiakim's reign." He reminded the people that for 23 years (since about 627) he had been warning them to turn from their evil ways. Other prophets had warned them as well. Any punishment God now brought upon them would therefore be justified.

25:8-14 *"Now about the next 70 years . . ."* Because of Judah's sin, God would use his "deputy," the Babylonian king Nebuchadnezzar, to punish them. Then, after 70 years of captivity, they would be set free and Babylon itself would be destroyed (25:12; see 29:10; 2 Chron. 36:22-23; Dan. 5).

Nebuchadnezzar came to power in 605 B.C. and led the first group of Israelites captive that same year. Babylon would be conquered in 539, nearly 70 years later, by the Persian king Cyrus. The first exiles returned in 538, roughly 70 years after the first captives went to Babylon. Some scholars, however, date the 70 years of the captivity from 586, the date of the third and final deportation, to 516 when the new Temple was completed by the returned exiles (see Zech. 1:12).

Just as Nebuchadnezzar was God's "deputy" to judge Israel, so Cyrus would be his "anointed one" (Isa. 45:1) to judge Babylon on Israel's behalf.

25:15-38 *God's wrath: One cup for all nations.* God gave Jeremiah the "cup of the LORD's fury" (Isa. 51:17; see Rev. 14:10) to pour in judgment on Judah and all other nations that rejected him (25:15-29). If God would punish his own people, no other nation should expect to escape (25:29). The "day of the LORD," the last great period of judgment on all nations, commonly referred to as the Tribulation, is identified here as "that day" (25:30-38; see *Isaiah: Background*).

26:1-6 *Temples, like Tabernacles, can be destroyed.* 26:1-24 records the events surrounding Jeremiah's Temple sermon (7:1–8:3) at the beginning of Jehoiakim's reign (c. 608 B.C.). 26:1-6 reiterates God's instruction for Jeremiah to "stand out in front of the Temple of the LORD" to deliver the sermon (26:2; see 7:2). Jeremiah was to warn that the Temple, just like the Tabernacle before it, would come under God's judgment.

26:7-24 *Prophets can be destroyed too.* Having heard his warning about the Temple, the priests, prophets, and people cried out for Jeremiah's blood and reported his sermon to the authorities (26:7-11). Jeremiah warned them that he was speaking on God's behalf and called on them to repent (26:12-15). The authorities recommended clemency, recalling how King Hezekiah had heeded Micah's warning and Jerusalem had been spared (26:16-19; compare 26:18-19 and Mic. 3:12). Uriah, a prophet contemporary with Jeremiah, had been killed by Jehoiakim (26:20-23). Jeremiah himself was spared this time (26:24) but was surely aware of the peril of his profession.

27:1-22 *He wears a yoke to warn the people.* The story now jumps from 608 to 593 B.C. (see 28:1). Nebuchadnezzar had become king of Babylon in 605. He had taken many Israelites captive in 605 and 597 and had deposed Jehoiakim's successor, Jehoiachin, replacing him with Zedekiah. Zedekiah had done Nebuchadnezzar's bidding at first but then began conspiring with other nations to overthrow Babylon (27:3). (The KJV follows most Hebrew manuscripts and names Jehoiakim instead of Zedekiah in 27:1.)

In response to Zedekiah's conspiracy against Babylon, Jeremiah put a yoke around his neck and declared to the assembled nations that it was God's sovereign will that they all serve Babylon (27:4-6) until such time as Babylon itself was judged (27:7). To resist serving Babylon would mean certain destruction by "war, famine, and disease" (27:8).

Jeremiah then delivered the same warning to Zedekiah himself (27:12-15) and to all the Israelites (27:16-22). He warned all three audiences against the false prophets who were encouraging rebellion. A similar warning, given about the same time, is recorded in 24.

28:1-17 *The prophecy and death of Hananiah the liar.* In the same year as the events of chapter 27, the prophet Hananiah predicted that the Israelites taken captive to Babylon in 605 and 597 would be home within two years (28:1-4). Jeremiah expressed his sincere hope that the exiles' stay in Babylon would indeed be brief (28:5-6); yet, based on what God had said, he was skeptical of Hananiah's positive outlook (28:7-8). He reiterated the ancient test of all such prophecies: The prophet is from the Lord only if his or her prophecy comes true (28:9; see Deut. 18:20-22).

Hananiah repeated his prophecy of peace, breaking Jeremiah's yoke for emphasis (28:10-11). Jeremiah responded that, because of his false prophecy, Hananiah would die within the year (28:12-16). Two months later, he was dead (28:17).

Hananiah's specific word of hope for Jehoiachin (28:4) was contradicted by Jeremiah (see exposition on 22:24-30). Jeremiah's version proved to be right (see 52:31-34).

29:1-14 *"Be good citizens; then he'll bring you home."* Having heard that false prophets among the exiles in Babylon were also predicting their early release, Jeremiah sent them a letter of correction and encouragement. He warned that the exile would last a long time but encouraged them to approach that time with a positive attitude and to become productive, peace-loving members of Babylonian society (29:1-9). The exile would last 70 years; then God would bring them back to Judah (29:10-14; see exposition on 25:8-14).

Jeremiah's letter may have been sent to Babylon in 593 B.C., at the same time he sent the scroll of his prophecy against Babylon, when Zedekiah was summoned to appear there (see 51:59). The promises of 29:11-14 have been precious to believers down through the ages.

29:15-32 *False prophets will be punished.* Jeremiah's letter continued with warnings against false prophets and dire predictions of the fate of those who had ignored earlier warnings and stayed in Jerusalem (29:15-23). Singled out for special rebuke was Shemaiah, an exile who had sent a letter to the leaders in Jerusalem urging them to silence Jeremiah (29:24-32). He and all other false prophets would be severely punished.

30:1-11 *Jacob's trouble, Messiah's triumph.* It was the last months before Jerusalem's fall in 586 B.C. Zedekiah had revolted against Babylon in about 590–589 (see 52:1-3). Babylon had begun besieging Jerusalem in 588 (see 52:4). Famine and pestilence raged throughout Judah (see 52:6), and Jeremiah languished in prison (see 32:1-2). Amid this crisis, Jeremiah prophesied concerning God's ultimate plans for his people (30–33). At the end of earthly history, God will bring both the northern and southern kingdoms back from captivity (30:1-3). First, however, will come the "time of trouble for my people Israel," which most scholars identify with the Tribulation (30:4-7). But in "that day" (30:7-8; see 25:15-38), Jacob (the nation of Israel) will be saved out of his trouble by a future King David, who is Christ the Messiah (30:9; see 2 Sam. 7:12-16 and exposition on Isa. 11:1–12:6 and Luke 1:69).

God would "discipline" his people but would not "destroy" them. Rather, he would "save" them "from distant lands," bringing them back from exile (30:10-11). This return would take place both in the historical context of that day and in the end times (see *Purpose*).

30:12-24 *Problem, prescription, and promise.* Judah's sin problem was "incurable" (30:12-14). God's judgment was the only possible prescription (30:15). After judgment, however, Judah would be restored (30:16-17) and Jerusalem would be rebuilt (30:18-22). 30:23-24 echoes the warning of 23:19-20.

31:1-14 *What a day that will be!* As a shepherd gathers his sheep (31:10), God will one day restore Israel to its land. Like a loving Father (31:1, 9), he will "draw" them back from captivity (31:3). It will be a time of rejoicing and prosperity.

31:15-25 *"I hear your weeping."* God was aware of his people's great suffering at the hand of Babylon, here symbolized by their deportation from Ramah (31:15; see 40:1). He heard their cries of repentance (31:18-19) and promised to restore them to their land (31:16-17, 20-25). Matthew would see in the deportation a foreshadowing of the slaughter at Bethlehem after Christ's birth (see Matt. 2:16-18).

31:26-30 *Was it a dream?* With the amazement of one who awakens from a pleasant dream (31:26), Jeremiah again noted God's promise of restoration (31:27-30). As he had destroyed Israel for its sins, he would now build it up again (31:28; see 1:10). The future time of renewal would be a time of individual responsibility before God (31:29-30; see exposition on Ezek. 18:1-18).

31:31-34 *A covenant written on hearts.* The Lord then made an amazing announcement: "The day will come . . . when I will make a new covenant with the people of Israel and Judah" (31:31). This covenant would be unlike the present Mosaic covenant (31:32), in that God would "write" it on his people's hearts (31:33). It would bring about a new kind of relationship with God and a permanent remission of sin (31:34). While the NT clearly identifies this New Covenant as God's promise of forgiveness through the death of Christ on the cross, it will be offered to Israel in a special way during the Millennium (see exposition on Rom. 11:11-32 and on Heb. 8:1-13; see also *Biblical Covenants,* p. 820; Isa. 59:20-21; Ezek. 16:60-63; 37:26-28).

31:35-40 *A future as sure as the sun and moon.* With the last of his people headed for exile, God promised they would never cease to be a nation. The promise was as dependable as the

THE NEW COVENANT

✡ **Location**
The book of Jeremiah
(31:31-34)

✡ **Recipients**
The whole house of Israel

✡ **Nature**
Israel to receive new hearts from God
(24:7; 32:39)

✡ **Superiority**
It will be immutable and unconditional

✡ **Time Period**
After the Tribulation and during the Millennium

✡ **Basis**
The grace of God and the death of Christ
(Hebrews 8:8-12)

✡ **Mediator**
Jesus Christ!
(30:9; 33:15-18)

patterns of nature (31:35-37). Citing specific landmarks within Jerusalem, God promised that his Holy City would one day be rebuilt (31:38-40).

32:1-15 *Jeremiah buys a field.* It was now 587 B.C. Jerusalem was under siege (see 39:1; 52:4), and "Jeremiah was imprisoned in the courtyard of the guard in the royal palace" (32:2). Jeremiah had warned Zedekiah that he would be defeated by Nebuchadnezzar and would be taken captive to Babylon, and Zedekiah had responded by imprisoning Jeremiah (32:1-5). At God's direction, Jeremiah purchased a field in his hometown, which by then was already occupied by Babylon (32:6-12). To show his confidence that his descendants would someday regain the land, he took great care to preserve the deed (32:13-15).

Jeremiah's actual incarceration in the "courtyard of the guard" is recorded in 37:21. While he was imprisoned, Jeremiah trusted his business affairs to Baruch (32:11-12), his personal secretary (see 36:4; 45).

32:16-25 *"Lord, why did I buy that field?"* Jeremiah had unquestioningly obeyed God's command to buy the field. As he praised God (32:16-24), he admitted to being perplexed as to why God had told him to make such a purchase (32:25). On "children suffer for their parents' sins" (32:18) see exposition on Ezek. 18:1-18.

32:26-44 *"Because someday you'll all buy fields again."* The Lord replied that, though Israel's sin had provoked him to give their land to Babylon (32:26-35), he would one day restore it to them and they would prosper (32:36-44); fields would once again be bought, just as Jeremiah had bought his field (32:43-44). Again God promised a new covenant (32:38-40).

33:1-13 *"Great and mighty things! Just ask me!"* As Jeremiah's imprisonment dragged on, God's word came to him again. Just as the sovereign God had created all things, he was able to restore his people to their land and give them prosperity (33:4-13), causing all nations to praise him (33:9).

33:14-26 *"The LORD is our righteousness!"* Once again God promised to send a Messiah to restore David's throne and save Israel from its foes. Israel would then say, "The LORD is our righteousness!" For by his death he would make his people righteous (33:16; see 23:5-6; 1 Cor. 1:30; 2 Cor. 5:21). The promise of Messiah (33:15, 17) and the restoration of both Israel and Judah (33:25-26) were as certain as the laws of nature.

34:1-7 *"You'll be captured and carried off but not killed."* As Babylon and all its allies closed in on Jerusalem (34:1, 6-7), Jeremiah warned Zedekiah that all efforts against Nebuchadnezzar would be futile. Even the king would be exiled to Babylon, though he would be allowed to die in peace (see 52:11). 2 Kings 25:6-7 fulfills both Jeremiah's prophecy that Zedekiah would see Nebuchadnezzar (34:2-5) and Ezekiel's prophecy that he would not see Babylon itself (see Ezek. 12:13).

34:8-22 *"You didn't free them, so he won't free you!"* The law of Moses decreed that Hebrew slaves should be freed after six years (34:13-14; see Lev. 25:39-46; Deut. 15:12). Israel had not observed this law (34:14) until very recently, when King Zedekiah had decreed that they do so (34:8-10). The reform had been short-lived, however, and the people had reenslaved their fellow Israelites (34:11). God decreed, therefore, that the whole nation would become slaves to Babylon (34:12-22). Because they had not freed their slaves, Israel would be "free"—free to die (34:17)!

35:1-11 *The Recabites: Faithful to their father.* The story now jumps back in time to the days of Jehoiakim (c. 607

B.C.). At God's direction, Jeremiah offered wine to a group of Recabites, a nomadic tribe that had sought protection from Israel against Babylon. True to the teaching of their ancestor Jonadab, the Recabites refused the wine (35:1-11). Jonadab lived nearly 250 years before this time (see 2 Kings 10:15-16, 23).

35:12-19 *The Israelites: Unfaithful to their Father.* Unlike the Recabites, Israel had been unfaithful to its Father. Therefore Israel would be judged (35:17), while the Recabites would go free (35:18-19).

36:1-19 *Baruch records and reads the words.* In about 605 B.C., Jeremiah's secretary, Baruch, recorded all of Jeremiah's prophecies concerning Israel and Judah. Because Jeremiah had been barred from entering the Temple area, he directed Baruch to go there and read the scroll in public (36:1-10). He hoped that Judah would repent (36:3, 7). When Baruch read the scroll to the palace officials, they were terrified. Suspecting that the king would be displeased when they showed him the scroll, they urged Baruch and Jeremiah to hide.

36:20-32 *Jehoiakim hears, hates, and burns the words.* As feared, Jehoiakim rejected Jeremiah's words, burned the scroll, and demanded the prophet's arrest—but the Lord hid and protected him (36:20-26). Jeremiah then rewrote the scroll, adding more words of judgment: Because of his contempt for God's Word, Jehoiakim would die in disgrace (see exposition on 22:13-23) and none of his sons would succeed him (36:30).

37:1-10 *The king's new idea: Prayer.* The narrative now jumps ahead again to the last months before Jerusalem's fall, prior to Jeremiah's imprisonment (37:4). As suggested by Jeremiah's prophecy (see 36:30), Jehoiakim's son Jehoiachin had reigned only 90 days before being led captive to Babylon along with many of Judah's best and brightest. Zedekiah, installed on the throne by Nebuchadnezzar (37:1), had reigned for about 10 years and had consistently rejected Jeremiah's warnings (37:2; see 21:1-10; 24; 27). Hoping now to win God's favor, Zedekiah asked Jeremiah to pray for the nation (37:3). 21:1-10 records a similar request for prayer by Zedekiah at about the same time. When Egypt came to Judah's aid (37:5), the Babylonians temporarily lifted their siege, but Jeremiah predicted that the Egyptians would soon retreat and Babylon would return and destroy Jerusalem (37:6-10).

37:11-21 *The prophet's new home: Prison.* During the time when Babylon had retreated from Jerusalem because of the Egyptian threat (37:5), Jeremiah ventured three miles northeast of Jerusalem to his hometown, Anathoth, which was apparently in Babylonian hands, to claim some personal property (37:11-12). Falsely accused of defecting to the enemy, he was imprisoned (37:13-15). In prison he was secretly consulted by Zedekiah, who publicly opposed him. Jeremiah again warned Zedekiah that he would be captured (37:17). He also defended his track record as a prophet and begged to be moved from the "dungeon" (37:16, 18-20). Zedekiah relented and moved Jeremiah to the "courtyard of the guard" (37:21), from where he would later make a second, divinely directed purchase of property in Anathoth (32).

38:1-13 *His second new home: A cistern.* Because he kept on advocating defection to the Babylonians (see exposition on 27:1-22), some government officials imprisoned Jeremiah in an underground cistern (38:1-6). Zedekiah did nothing to prevent this from happening (38:5). Later, however, at the suggestion of a royal official named Ebed-melech, Zedekiah ordered that Jeremiah be taken out of the cistern (38:7-13).

38:14-28 *"Tell me the truth and I won't kill you!"* Once again under Zedekiah's protection (38:14-16), Jeremiah implored him to save himself and the city by surrendering to Babylon; not to do so would mean disaster (38:17-18). When Zedekiah expressed reservations about this advice (38:19), Jeremiah repeated the advice and the warning (38:20-23). Zedekiah asked Jeremiah to keep their meeting a secret, and Jeremiah did so (38:24-27). Jeremiah would remain in the courtyard of the guard until Jerusalem's fall (38:28).

39:1-10 *Jerusalem destroyed, Judah exiled.* The time of God's judgment had come. Having been under siege for about a year and a half, Jerusalem was invaded by Nebuchadnezzar's army (39:1-3). Zedekiah and his men fled but were captured. Zedekiah was blinded and led captive to Babylon (39:4-7). Jerusalem was then destroyed, and the rest of the people were led captive—except for the poor, who were allowed to remain and occupy some of the property of those taken captive (39:8-10; see 2 Kings 25; Lamentations).

39:11-18 *Jeremiah released, Ebed-melech rewarded.* Jeremiah had been taken captive along with the rest of the people to Ramah, about five miles north of Jerusalem and evidently a staging area for the trip to Babylon (see 40:1 and exposition on 31:15-25). He was then released and put in the care of Gedaliah, the Israelite who had been appointed by Nebuchadnezzar as governor over the Jews remaining in Judah (39:11-14; see 40:5). Jeremiah told Ebed-melech, who had escaped the destruction, that his escape was a divine reward for his earlier intervention on Jeremiah's behalf (39:15-18; see 38:7-13). Gedaliah's father, Ahikam, had also protected Jeremiah (see 26:24).

40:1-12 *The good government of Gedaliah.* The story of Jeremiah's capture is told (40:1), and the story of his release and coming to live with Gedaliah is retold (40:2-6). The poor who had been left in the land came to Gedaliah for encouragement and direction (40:7-8). He encouraged them to live peaceably in the land and be loyal to Babylon (40:9-10). Many Israelites who had fled from Nebuchadnezzar to nearby countries returned and felt secure under Gedaliah's brief rule (40:11-12).

40:13–41:18 *Gedaliah assassinated.* The Ammonites, perhaps coveting Judean land, commissioned Ishmael, a member of Judah's royal family, to murder Gedaliah. When Johanan told Gedaliah of the plot, he refused to believe it (40:13-16), yet he was assassinated—less than three months after taking office (41:1-3). Having tasted blood, for no apparent reason Ishmael and his men then killed 70 fellow Israelites on their way to Jerusalem to mourn the pillaged Temple (41:4-9). Ishmael tried to take the entire population of Mizpah (presumably including Jeremiah) back to Ammon, but Johanan rescued them (41:10-15).

Fearing that Babylon would take vengeance for Gedaliah's death, the surviving Israelites fled toward Egypt but stopped for a while near Bethlehem (41:16-18).

42:1-22 *God's word: "Don't go to Egypt."* Johanan asked Jeremiah to seek divine guidance as to what he and his people should do. They promised to do whatever the Lord said, whether they liked it or not (42:1-6). The Lord said they should remain in Judah. If they remained, he would end their punishment and would protect and prosper them; if they disobeyed and fled to Egypt, they would die (42:7-22).

43:1-7 *Judah's response: "We're going anyway."* Still fearing reprisal from Babylon, the people accused Jeremiah of conspiring against them by telling them to remain in Judah. Under Johanan's leadership, they fled to Egypt, taking Jeremiah and Baruch with them.

43:8-13 *The sign of the hidden rocks.* Soon after Jeremiah and his fellow Israelites arrived in Egypt, Jeremiah prophesied—using large rocks as visual aids—that Babylon would invade Egypt as well. Faithless Judah would find no refuge in Egypt.

44:1-14 *Idolaters in Judah, idolaters in Egypt.* Perhaps some five years after Jerusalem's fall, Jeremiah gave his last prophecy to the Jews in Egypt. Just as their fathers had served false gods in Canaan (44:1-6), they were proudly worshiping Egyptian gods (44:7-10). Therefore, though they had fled to Egypt, they would not escape God's wrath (44:11-14).

44:15-30 *No to God, yes to Ishtar.* The people unanimously rejected Jeremiah's warning: Crediting past prosperity to their foreign gods, they stated proudly that they would continue their idolatry. The "Queen of Heaven" (44:17; see 7:18) was probably Ishtar, the Babylonian goddess of love.

Jeremiah reminded his people that idolatry had brought on God's wrath and the fall of Jerusalem (44:20-23). Because they were persisting in idolatry, God would destroy them in Egypt (44:24-27), with only a small remnant escaping (44:28). As a sign of their own final judgment, Pharaoh Hophra of Egypt, under whom they had found refuge, would himself fall (44:30; see 46:13-26). Hophra was deposed and killed in 569 B.C., after a serious military defeat. About a year later, Nebuchadnezzar's armies invaded and defeated Egypt.

45:1-5 *Baruch rebuked.* The narrative now jumps back to about 605 B.C., after Baruch had recorded the scroll which Jehoiakim would destroy (see 36:4-8). Baruch had apparently sought career advancement (45:5), only to find himself associated with the despised Jeremiah. God reminded Baruch that the present order of society was doomed; he would be well advised to seek God's glory, not his own.

WARNINGS TO THE NATIONS (46–51)

46:1-28 *Egypt: Defeated and doomed for more defeat.* 46–51 includes prophecies from various times in Jeremiah's ministry, against various nations that had opposed Israel. First called to account was Egypt. Jeremiah ridiculed the mighty Egypt for its defeat at Carchemish (46:1-12) and predicted a future defeat by Babylon (46:13-26). Their great Pharaoh would be derided by his own troops for making much noise but having no power (46:17). (Pharaoh had made loud claims of his ability to defeat Babylon but had never made good on those claims.) Meanwhile, Israelite exiles in Egypt and other foreign lands would be rescued by their God (46:27-28).

47:1-7 *Philistia: God's sword won't be silent.* Sometime before Pharaoh's march northward in 609 B.C. (47:1; see 2 Kings 23:29-34), Jeremiah prophesied that Philistia, long-time hater of the Jews, would be destroyed by an enemy from the north, meaning Babylon. God's sword of judgment could not be silent until Israel's ancient foe was destroyed (47:6-7).

48:1-47 *Moab: The wings of death.* Moab and Ammon, the two nations resulting from Lot's incest with his daughters, were under an ancient curse because of their ill treatment of Israel (see exposition on Neh. 13:1-3). Moab, once proud and self-sufficient (48:17), would be shamed (48:1). Though the Moabites were given "wings" to flee their attackers (48:9), Babylon would spread its wings of death over them (48:40). The Moabites, like the Philistines, would shave their heads in sorrow (48:37; see 47:5).

Moab did, indeed, cease to be a nation after its destruction by Babylon. During the Millennium, however, it will be restored (48:47).

49:1-6 *Ammon: "Give back the land!"* The self-trusting Ammonites would be destroyed, but like the Moabites, they would be restored during the Millennium (49:6). Their destruction would allow Israel to reclaim the territory Ammon had taken (49:1-2). Molech (Hebrew *Milcom*) the Ammonite god, like Chemosh the Moabite god, would be "exiled" along with his worshipers (49:3; see 48:7). The name of Ammon survives as present-day Amman, capital of Jordan.

49:7-22 *Edom: Punished for pride and prejudice.* Edom, southeast of Judah, would be judged for its pride (49:16). It would not escape judgment (49:10), especially considering that many innocent people had already suffered as God's wrath was poured out (49:12). Amid the destruction, however, God would care for the widows and orphans (49:11).

The Edomites, descendants of Esau, denied passage to Israel as they journeyed toward Canaan (see exposition on Num. 20:14-21). Subsequently, they had either helped or failed to resist various nations that attacked Israel, climaxing in their apparent refusal to help when Judah fell in 586 B.C. (see Ezek. 35:5).

49:7-22 parallels Obadiah 1:1-9, which probably refers to an earlier time when Edom failed to help their Israelite brothers.

49:23-39 *Damascus, Kedar, Hazor, and Elam.* Syria, whose capital was Damascus (49:23-27), had been both ally and enemy to Israel. It fell to Assyria in Isaiah's time, and in Jeremiah's time was controlled by Babylon. God would "start a fire" in Damascus. The fulfillment of this prophecy is unknown.

Kedar and Hazor (49:28-33), nomadic peoples to the east, wealthy and with no enemies to fear, would be destroyed by Babylon as well.

The Elamites (49:34-39), famous as archers, would have their bows broken by God. But they, like the Moabites and Ammonites, would participate in the Millennium (49:39).

50:1–51:64 *Babylon: Her time will come.* In 593 B.C. (51:59), Jeremiah wrote a lengthy prophecy against Babylon, most recent oppressor of Israel. Though God had told his people to submit to Babylon as his instrument of judgment, Babylon was sinful too and would be judged:

"Flee, and you'll find compassion" (50:1-20). Babylon was doomed for destruction (50:1-3; see exposition on 25:8-14) at a future time that would also be a time of repentance among the Israelite exiles (50:4-7). The exiles should be ready to escape that day of great destruction (50:8-10). Babylon was to be destroyed because of the pleasure it took in punishing God's people (50:11-18; see exposition on Isa. 47:1-15). By contrast, God would show Israel great compassion (50:19-20). 50:5, 20 echoes the New Covenant (31:31-34).

A broken hammer, a feeble king (50:21-46). Babylon, the "mightiest hammer in all the earth," would be "broken and shattered" by God (50:23). Its destruction would be celebrated by the returned exiles in Jerusalem (50:28). While punishing Babylon for its pride (50:29-32), God would come to the defense of his people (50:33-34). Because of its idolatry (50:38), Babylon's destruction would be as thorough as that of Sodom and Gomorrah (50:40). Babylon's king would be rendered feeble by news of the impending destruction (50:43).

Babylon's idols vs. Israel's Creator God (51:1-19). Babylon would be destroyed for its treatment of Israel and Judah, for God would not forsake his people (51:1-5), who should therefore be ready to flee when judgment comes (51:6). Babylon's sin had affected the whole world (51:7), but now, at the command of the sovereign God (51:15-16, 19), both Babylon and her idols would be destroyed (51:17-18). John echoes 51:13 in his description of "Babylon the Great" in Revelation (see Rev. 17:1, 15).

Babylon's armies vs. God's battle-ax (51:20-44). God had used Babylon to punish his people and the surrounding nations, but they had gone too far in their destruction (51:24-25). God would now use his "battle-ax," Cyrus of Persia, to punish Babylon (51:20-23). He calls on other nations to join the fight against Babylon (50:27-33). They would free all the nations Babylon had "swallowed" (51:34, 44).

"Flee quickly; her destruction is sure" (51:45-58). Israel could begin preparing to flee, with the full assurance that God would destroy Babylon—to the great joy of all the righteous in heaven and on earth.

"Read it; then throw it in the river!" (51:59-64). Jeremiah wrote his prophecy against Babylon on a scroll and gave it to Seraiah, brother of Baruch (see 32:12), to be taken to Babylon. Seraiah was to read the prophecy in public, then tie a rock to it and throw it in the river, symbolizing Babylon's destruction.

The letter was sent in 593 B.C., after two groups of Jews had already been taken captive to Babylon in 605 and 597 B.C. Zedekiah had been summoned to Babylon, and Seraiah went with him as his "quartermaster." (See exposition on 29:1-14.)

HISTORICAL POSTSCRIPT (52)

52:1-11 *Purged from his presence.* Sometime after Jerusalem's fall, an unknown writer or compiler (see *Author*) reflected on the events surrounding Judah's last days. (See 2 Kings 24:18–25:30.)

Zedekiah would be the last in a long line of evil kings who, along with the nation as a whole, had provoked God's anger. When Zedekiah ignored Jeremiah's advice and rebelled against Babylon, God used the occasion to finally "banish" Judah "from his presence" (52:1-3). Having effectively controlled Judah since coming to the throne in 605, Nebuchadnezzar laid siege against Jerusalem in 588. After a year and a half of siege and starvation, the walls were penetrated and Zedekiah and his army fled (52:4-7). Zedekiah was captured, blinded, and imprisoned in Babylon till his death (52:8-11).

52:12-23 *They burn the beloved city.* A month and a day after penetrating Jerusalem's walls, the Babylonians burned the Temple and "all the important buildings," broke down the city walls, and led captive most of the remaining people (52:12-16). They took the gold, silver, and bronze furnishings from the burned Temple and carried them to Babylon.

52:24-34 *Leaders killed, captives counted, a king released.* As Judah was led captive, several of its leaders were executed (52:24-27). Nebuchadnezzar took a total of 4,600 captives (plus women and children) in three deportations. If the time spans given do not include the king's inaugural year of 605 B.C., they would correspond to 597, 586, and 581. The deportation of 581 may have been part of the reprisal anticipated by the Jews who fled to Egypt after the assassination of Gedaliah (see exposition on 43:1-7).

The book ends on a hopeful note: King Jehoiachin, taken captive in 597, was released in 560 and treated with kindness for the rest of his life. (He would have been 55 in 560; there is no record of him among the returning exiles, 22 years later.)

PEOPLE TO REMEMBER FROM JEREMIAH

JEREMIAH

Key Fact: Prophet to Judah during its last days
Father: Hilkiah (1:1)
Total Bible References: 134
Key References: 1–52; 2 Chron. 35:25; 36:11; Ezra 1:1; Dan. 9:2; Matt. 2:17-18; 27:9-10

Jeremiah Speaks

"Before you were born I set you apart and appointed you as my spokesman to the world." How long has it been since he spoke those words to me as a young priest in my hometown of Anathoth? At least 40 years! With a little shame I recall my first reaction to that divine call: I declined it on the basis of my youth and lack of knowledge. But he quickly answered both objections: "Don't say that. . . . See, I have put my words in your mouth!" (1:5-7, 9)

Now I find myself in a foreign country, brought here against my will. I said 40 years, but it seems 40 lifetimes. I've written two books (the second actually an expansion of the first, which was burned by an unappreciative reader). (43:5-7; 36:2, 23, 28)

Maybe I should write a third book and call it *Heads of State I Have Known.* Let's see, that would include Josiah, Jehoiakim, Jehoiachin, Zedekiah, Nebuchadnezzar, Gedaliah, and Johanan! Five kings and two governors—quite an impressive list! If I wrote such a book, I should probably include in it all my prophecies concerning those key leaders. (13:18-19; 36:29; 37:16-17; 39:11-12; 40:6; 42:1-2; 2 Chron. 35:25)

I don't weep over Jerusalem anymore. There is no need to. But I am deeply grieved over the deplorable paganism my people have fallen into here in Egypt. When will we ever learn? It was for this kind of abomination that God destroyed our country in the first place. (9:1; 44:1-30)

I often wonder, *Would things have been different had not the godly Josiah been killed?* I still mourn for him. (2 Chron. 35:23-25)

Often, as I sit here by myself at sunset looking north to the beloved but now destroyed Holy City, my heart is overwhelmed with loneliness and pain. But then I'm reminded of those thrilling words God gave me right after its destruction: "I still dare to hope when I remember this: The unfailing love of the LORD never ends! By his mercies we have been kept from complete destruction. Great is his faithfulness; his mercies begin afresh each day." (Lam. 3:21-23)

Spiritual Lessons from Jeremiah

- There is no excuse for not pursuing God's will for our lives. Moses pleaded *infirmity* for not obeying God (Exod. 4:10); Jeremiah pleaded *immaturity* (1:6). In both cases, God overruled their objections, promising that he would put his very words in their mouths (compare 1:7-9 with Exod. 4:11-12).
- God forbade Jeremiah to marry (16:2) but commanded Hosea to take a wife (Hos. 1:2). We must all find God's unique will for our lives (see 1 Cor. 7:7).
- Paul desired to "know Christ and experience the mighty power that raised him from the dead," to "learn what it means to suffer with him, sharing in his death" (Phil. 3:10). Jeremiah experienced such fellowship centuries before Paul wrote those words. Note the similarities between the sufferings of Jeremiah and of Jesus; both were
  - ➤ Persecuted or rejected by
    - their families (12:6; John 7:5)
    - their hometowns (11:21-23; Luke 4:16-29)
    - religious leaders (20:1-3; John 7:45-52)
    - political leaders (38:4-6; Luke 13:31-32)
  - ➤ Accused of treason (37:11-15; Luke 23:1-2)
  - ➤ Ridiculed (20:7-8; Luke 23:11)
- Even amid such suffering, however, God is faithful (Lam. 3:21-23).

Key Verses

"'O Sovereign LORD,' I said, 'I can't speak for you! I'm too young!' 'Don't say that,' the LORD replied, 'for you must go wherever I send you and say whatever I tell you. And don't be afraid of the people, for I will be with you and take care of you. I, the LORD, have spoken!'" (1:6-8).

627 B.C.
Jeremiah begins ministry

LAMENTATIONS

BACKGROUND

Jerusalem had been destroyed by the armies of Babylon (see 2 Kings 25; Jer. 39). Having warned Judah for 40 years of the inevitable approach of this tragic event, Jeremiah put his tears into words once more as he lamented the destruction of Jerusalem and the Temple.

c. 586
Jerusalem falls, Jeremiah's lament

581
Jeremiah's last prophecy

AUTHOR

Jeremiah (see *Jeremiah: Author*):

- Lamentations has marked similarities with the book of Jeremiah:
  - ➤ The Hebrew phrases "daughter of Zion," "daughter of my people," and similar phrases are used to refer to Israel about 20 times in each book.
  - ➤ The author of each book describes his tears as streams of water (1:16, Jer. 9:1).
  - ➤ The author of each book tells of being confined in a pit (3:53; Jer. 37:16; 38:6).
  - ➤ Both books describe signs of sinfulness found on the "skirts" (1:9, KJV; Jer. 2:34; 13:22, 26).
- The author was apparently an eyewitness to the destruction of Jerusalem, which fits what is known about Jeremiah.
- The suffering of the author of Lamentations (3; especially 3:53) fits what is known from the book of Jeremiah about Jeremiah's suffering.
- Jeremiah was known in Israel as a writer of laments (2 Chron. 35:25). (The Septuagint, other Greek manuscripts, and the KJV call the book the "Lamentations of Jeremiah.")

DATE AND LOCATION

The emotional intensity of the book suggests a date soon after Jerusalem's fall in 586 B.C. Its eyewitness nature suggests a location near the burning city, perhaps in Jeremiah's hometown of Anathoth, in the staging area at Ramah (see exposition on Jer. 39:11-18), or in the home of a friend.

PURPOSE

To discuss issues related to Jerusalem's destruction:

- Jerusalem was destroyed because of Judah's sin (1:8-9, 18; 4:13-16).
- But God had not abandoned his people; he was still faithful (3:21-33) and would restore them (5:19-22) if they would repent (3:40-42).

UNIQUE FEATURES

- Each of the first four chapters of Lamentations is an acrostic poem. In 1, 2, and 4, each of the 22 verses begins with a successive letter of the Greek alphabet. In chapter 3, every third of the 66 verses begins with successive Greek letters. Though chapter 5 has 22 verses as well, it does not follow the acrostic pattern.
- Though other Bible books contain laments (see 2 Sam. 1:17-27; Job 3), only Lamentations is composed entirely in this literary style.

OUTLINE

THE PROVOCATION AGAINST GOD (1)
THE PUNISHMENT FROM GOD (2)
THE SORROWFUL PROPHET OF GOD (3)
THE SUFFERING PEOPLE OF GOD (4)
THE PRAYER TO GOD (5)

THE PROVOCATION AGAINST GOD (1)

1:1-11 *Desolate because of sin.* Jeremiah surveyed the scene of Jerusalem's desolation and mourned for her. Once a great city, Jerusalem was now leveled, lonely, and empty, her people having been taken away as slaves. The very roads to Jerusalem mourned because no one traveled them anymore on their way to the feasts (1:4). While Judah's enemies prospered, Judah could only dream of her past glory (1:5, 7). Worst of all, foreigners had entered the Temple (1:10). All this had happened because of Judah's sin (1:8-9).

1:12-19 *"Has there ever been such suffering?"* The people of Jerusalem cried out to the surrounding world to take note of their great suffering, acknowledging it was because of their sin (1:12-16). Jeremiah acknowledged his people's anguish (1:17) and once again recorded their cry of confession (1:18-21). They asked God to judge their enemies as well, just as he had promised to do (see Jer. 46–51).

THE PUNISHMENT FROM GOD (2)

2:1-9 *"He has become our enemy!"* Though he used Babylon as his instrument of judgment, Jeremiah knew it was God himself who had brought this great calamity upon both his holy city and his Temple. In his anger with Judah, he had become "like an enemy" to them.

2:10-22 *Sorrowful people, sinful prophets, sovereign God.* Jeremiah joined the people in mourning their tragedy (2:10-13) and reminded them that the false prophets, instead of promoting righteousness, had led the way to destruction (2:14; see Jer. 23; 29). Now Judah had become the laughingstock of her enemies (2:15-16; see 1:7). Yet, no matter how great their suffering (2:18-22), they had to acknowledge that God had sovereignly fulfilled his purpose in punishing their sin (2:17).

THE SORROWFUL PROPHET OF GOD (3)

3:1-20 *Beloved friend or bitter foe?* Speaking for his people, Jeremiah discussed the painful experience of being afflicted and broken by God.

3:21-39 *Yet his favor and faithfulness never fail!* Despite his anguish, Jeremiah humbly recalled the unfailing mercies and great faithfulness of God (3:21-24). God is good to all who "wait for him and seek him" (3:25; see Isa. 25:9; 40:27-31).

3:40-66 *Repentance and a torrent of tears.* Including himself in the admission of rebellion, Jeremiah called the people to repentance and renewal (3:40-47). He committed himself to keep praying, pleading, and weeping until the Lord looked upon his people's plight and judged their persecutors (3:48-66).

THE SUFFERING PEOPLE OF GOD (4)

4:1-16 *God's people punished more than Sodom.* Jeremiah surveyed the calamity in Jerusalem and declared it worse than the punishment meted out to Sodom (4:1-6). Even the healthiest people saw their bodies shriveled in starvation (4:7-8). Some had even resorted to cannibalism (4:10). All this was because of their sin (4:13).

4:17-22 *Abandoned by their allies and their own king.* Jerusalem could not be saved by an ally as strong as Egypt (4:17; see Jer. 2:20-37; 37:5-7), nor even by their own king (4:20). As the Babylonian army closed in, there was no escape (4:18-19). Judah's punishment would someday end, however; then Edom, which had promoted Judah's downfall, would be punished as well (4:21-22).

THE PRAYER TO GOD (5)

5:1-22 *"Restore us, for we have suffered greatly!"* Jeremiah described the humiliation and suffering of his enslaved people (5:1-18), acknowledging that it was because of their sin (5:16). In a great crescendo of praise to the God of renewal, he called out for an end to divine judgment (5:19-22).

EZEKIEL

605 B.C.
Daniel with 1st exiles to Babylon

597
Ezekiel in 2nd exile

592
Ezekiel begins ministry, in Babylon

586
Fall of Judah

581-580
Jeremiah's last prophecy, Daniel begins ministry

570
Ezekiel's last prophecy

BACKGROUND

Ezekiel, a priest, was among the 10,000 Jews taken captive to Babylon along with King Jehoiachin in 597 B.C. An earlier exile, which included Daniel, had occurred in 605, and another group would be exiled in 586, when Jerusalem fell.

In about 592, the "fifth year of King Jehoiachin's captivity" (1:2) and six years before Jerusalem's final doom, the Lord called Ezekiel to prophesy to the still rebellious exiles in Babylon (3:1-7). Ezekiel's ministry in Babylon overlapped the latter part of Jeremiah's ministry in Jerusalem; Ezekiel probably began his ministry soon after Jeremiah's letter to the captives arrived in 593 (see exposition on Jer. 29).

Ezekiel's ministry covered at least 22 years, from 592 to 570 (compare 1:2 and 29:17). His recorded prophecies come from two distinct periods of his ministry:

- From 592 B.C. till about 585 B.C., shortly after Jerusalem's fall, he prophesied concerning that event (1–24), God's judgment on other nations (25–32), and God's future plans for Israel (33–39).
- Then, after several years of silence, he again prophesied concerning God's plans for Israel (40–48). While Ezekiel, like Isaiah, had in view both the restoration of 538 and the final great return during the Millennium, he focused primarily on the Millennium.

AUTHOR

See *Background.* The book claims Ezekiel as its author (1:1-3). It is written from a priestly point of view, which fits Ezekiel. Nearly 90 times in the book, the Lord addresses Ezekiel as "son of man" (see exposition on Dan. 7:9-14).

DATE

See *Background* and *Unique Features.* The date and circumstance of compilation of Ezekiel's prophecies is unknown.

LOCATION

Ezekiel apparently lived in his own private dwelling among the exiles in a place called Tel-abib, by the Kebar River, about 50 miles south of Babylon (1:1; 3:15, 24).

PURPOSE

To explain to the captive Jews in Babylon:

- that their captivity and the destruction of their homeland had resulted from their rebellion against God and their lack of true holiness
- that God, in his mercy, intended to restore them to true holiness; they would be a new and holy people, living in a new and holy city and worshiping in a new and holy Temple

UNIQUE FEATURES

- Ezekiel employs more visions, visual-aid attention grabbers (like shaving the head), and word pictures than any other OT writer. He tells six parables (15; 16; 17:1-21; 17:22-24; 19:1-9; 23).
- Like Haggai, he gives precise dates for his prophecies, underscoring their historical accuracy. Except for the "thirtieth year" noted in 1:1, these dates are calculated from the exile of Ezekiel and Jehoiachin in 597. (Using 586 as the date of Jerusalem's fall, a date of 597 for Ezekiel's exile can be calculated from the information given in 40:1.)

COMPARISON WITH OTHER BIBLE BOOKS

2 Samuel

- While 2 Samuel presents King David and God's covenant with him, Ezekiel speaks of David—or one of his descendants—ruling in some way in the Millennium (34:23; 37:24; some interpret this figuratively as the Messiah).
- In 2 Samuel, David fought to keep the 12 tribes together; during the Millennium, there will be no such disunity (37:15-28).
- Both discuss preparations for a Temple, 2 Samuel for Solomon's Temple and Ezekiel for the millennial Temple.

Haggai

- Both speak of the millennial Temple (40–42; Hag. 2:9).
- Both speak of an earthquake or a "shaking" in Israel (38:19; Hag. 2:6).

Revelation:

- Both Ezekiel and John saw visions of future events.
- Both Ezekiel (2:8–3:3) and John (Rev. 10) were instructed to swallow a scroll containing words they were to proclaim.
- Gog and Magog (38–39) provide the imagery for John's description of the final rebellion of God's enemies (Rev. 20:8).
- John's vision of the New Jerusalem and the River of Life (Rev. 21:1–22:5)

has marked similarities to some of Ezekiel's visions of the millennial city (48:30-35) and the river flowing out of its Temple (47:1-12).

OUTLINE

PRESENTING THE PROPHET OF GOD (1–3)
- The vision of God: Creatures, chariots, wheels (1)
- The voice of God: Ezekiel's call (2–3)

JUDGING THE NATION OF GOD (4–24)
- Symbols of the siege (4–5)
- Sermons on the judgment (6–7)
- Scenes of sin at the Temple (8–11)
- Signs, sermons, and stories of judgment (12–24)
  - The baggage and the trembling (12)
  - False prophets and idolaters (13–14)
  - The fruitless vine (15)
  - The adulterous woman (16)
  - The two eagles (17)
  - The sour grapes (18)
  - The lions and the vine (19)
  - Israel's repeated rebellions (20)
  - The sword of judgment (21)
  - The furnace of judgment (22)
  - The two adulterous sisters (23)
  - The boiling pot (24:1-14)
  - The symbolic death of Ezekiel's wife (24:15-27)

JUDGING THE ENEMIES OF GOD (25–32)
- Ammon, Moab, Edom, and Philistia (25)
- Tyre (26:1–28:19)
- Sidon (28:20-26)
- Egypt (29–32)

PRESENTING THE SHEPHERD OF GOD (33–34)
- The watchman (33)
- The worthless shepherds (34:1-10)
- The worthy Shepherd (34:11-31)

RESTORING THE NATION OF GOD (35–37)
- Preparation for restoration: Edom destroyed (35)
- Explanation of restoration: Land and hearts renewed (36)
- Vision of restoration: Dry bones rejoined (37)

DEMONSTRATING THE WRATH OF GOD (38–39)
- Invasion of Gog and Magog (38)
- Victory over Gog and Magog (39)

REVEALING THE MILLENNIUM OF GOD (40–48)
- The millennial Temple (40–42)
- God's glory in the millennial Temple (43:1-5)
- Worship in the millennial Temple (43:6–46:24)
- The millennial river (47:1-12)
- The millennial land (47:13–48:35)

PRESENTING THE PROPHET OF GOD (1–3)

1:1-3 *His eventful 30th year.* Ezekiel noted that the vision that began his prophetic ministry occurred in about 592 B.C., five years after he, along with King Jehoiachin and others, had been taken captive in 597 (compare 1:2 with 40:1). "Of my thirtieth year" probably refers to Ezekiel's age. As a priest, this would have been the normal age for him to begin his ministry.

1:4-21 *Cherubs and wheels with the speed of light.* Amid a whirlwind and fiery cloud, Ezekiel saw four "living beings," each with four faces, empowered by the "spirit," moving "like flashes of lightning" (1:4-14). These heavenly beings moved in tandem with four earthbound "wheels," also subject to the movings of the spirit (1:15-21). Repeated words and phrases such as "like," "as if," and "awesome" suggest that Ezekiel was struggling to describe an indescribable scene. The living beings are later identified as cherubim (see exposition on 10:1-22).

1:22-28 *The firmament and the Being above it.* Above the living beings and the wheels was a vast, crystal-like expanse, and from above the expanse came a sound "like the shouting of a mighty army" (1:22-25). Ezekiel saw someone resembling a man, surrounded by the appearance of a rainbow, on a sapphirelike throne. He recognized it as the Lord himself and fell on his face in worship.

2:1-7 *His mission: Reach the rebels.* God spoke to Ezekiel (1:28), commissioning him to preach to the rebellious, stubborn Israelites, even if they wouldn't listen (2:1-7). God assured Ezekiel that even if they didn't heed his words they would know he had been divinely sent (2:5). On "the Spirit came into me" (2:2) see exposition on 1 Samuel 9:27–10:8.

2:8–3:15 *First assignment: Swallow this scroll and go.* In the vision, God handed Ezekiel a scroll, filled with words of lamentation and woe, and told him to eat it—signifying that he, unlike Israel, was receptive to God's word (2:8). Again he told Ezekiel to take his word to the captives in Babylon and warned that they would not be receptive (2). Ezekiel, however, would be strengthened to withstand them by the word of God he had symbolically received into his heart (3:8-10). As the vision ended, Ezekiel found himself among the exiles (3:12-15). For seven days he remained "overwhelmed" (3:15) by his encounter with God.

Though the words on the scroll were bitter (2:10), the scroll tasted sweet to Ezekiel (3:3). Nonetheless, as he began his mission he felt bitter and angry—an understandable reaction as this sensitive priest considered the sinfulness of his people (3:14).

3:16-21 *A watchman to warn the wicked . . .* The Lord commissioned Ezekiel to be a "watchman" for Israel, to warn them when their sin invited God's judgment. If Ezekiel failed to give such warnings, God would hold him responsible (see exposition on 33:1-9).

3:22-27 *. . . but speechless till God says speak.* God appeared to Ezekiel in another amazing vision, instructing him to remain in his own house in order to avoid danger from his opponents. He would be unable to speak unless the Lord allowed him to, thus ensuring that he would speak only God's message and not his own. This restriction on Ezekiel's speech would last until Jerusalem fell (see 33:22).

JUDGING THE NATION OF GOD (4–24)

4:1-17 *A brick, a meager meal, and a prostrate prophet.* God instructed Ezekiel to draw a map of Jerusalem on a large, flat tablet of soft clay. Then, using other visual aids, he was to act out the Babylonian siege against Jerusalem, showing the impossibility of escape from judgment (see 2 Kings 24–25; Jer. 39; 52). He was apparently to perform this object lesson daily while lying on his side (4:4-8). For 390 days he was to lie on his left side, representing the sins of Israel, the northern kingdom. Then he was to lie on his right side for 40 days, representing the sins of Judah. While the exact meaning of the two numbers is not given, they equal the 430 years of Egyptian captivity (see Exod. 12:40-41). The greater time for Israel signified its greater sin.

While on his side, acting out the siege, Ezekiel was to eat a special kind of bread, baked over dried cow dung, symbolizing the famine conditions of Jerusalem's last days (4:9-17). God had originally instructed Ezekiel to use human waste as fuel (4:12). As a priest, Ezekiel knew the law concerning such things (see Deut. 23:12-14), so he protested the assignment and God relented, allowing him to use cow dung instead. The Lord's point in prescribing human waste had been to signify Israel's pollution by pagan nations in the exile (4:13).

5:1-17 *A haircut burned, divided, and scattered.* Ezekiel shaved his head and beard and divided the hair into three parts. One part he burned, one he cut up with a sword, and one he scattered to the wind (5:2), symbolizing Judah's triple doom of famine and disease, death in war, and exile (5:12). God had set Judah "at the center of the nations" (5:5) as a witness to them (see exposition on Isa. 43:8-13). Since they had failed in that mission, they would be punished in an unusually harsh way (5:9) as a lesson to the other nations (5:15).

6:1-14 *A message to the mountains.* Facing the mountains of Israel, Ezekiel prophesied that the whole land would be laid waste (6:1-7). When that happened, Israel would "know that I am the LORD" (6:7, 10, 13). Showing mercy even in judgment, God promised that a remnant of the nation would be spared from death and scattered throughout the world (6:8-10). Ezekiel was to stamp his feet and clap his hands to get the people's attention concerning this prophecy (6:11). The mountains were apparently addressed because they were the center of idol worship in Israel (6:3, 13).

7:1-27 *Starvation, sword, and sacrilege.* Ezekiel repeatedly warned that judgment would soon come upon the land (7:1-13). It would come upon the whole land (7:2), and there would be no escape (7:9). Everyday activities like buying and selling would cease (7:12). Those outside the walls would be killed by the approaching armies, while those confined to the cities by the siege would die of famine and disease (7:14-18). Disease would make the people too weak to fight (7:14, 17).

Not only would the invading armies destroy the city and nation, they would defile the Temple, showing that God's favor was no longer with the nation (7:19-27).

8:1-18 *Tears for Tammuz—in the Temple!* 14 months after his ministry began, in about 591 B.C., Ezekiel was transported in a vision from Babylon to the Temple in Jerusalem, where he saw many things that deeply alarmed and offended him (8–11). Just north of the altar gate he saw an idol (8:5). Uncovering a secret inner room, he saw its walls covered with idolatrous drawings, and elders worshiping them (8:6-12). Looking farther, he saw women weeping for Tammuz, a Babylonian deity, and 25 men worshiping the sun (8:13-16). God's response to all this idolatry was to promise no pity or escape for the nation (8:17-18).

9:1-11 *Sinners slain, mourners marked and spared.* As the vision continued, God summoned six angelic executioners to the Temple area. He commanded one of them to put a special protective mark on all those who still mourned over the sin and idolatry Ezekiel had just seen (9:1-4). This done, the other men followed after him and killed all those without the mark, beginning with the religious leaders in the Temple (9:5-7). Ezekiel begged the Lord to spare some of the people, but he refused to do so.

As this was taking place, the "glory of the God of Israel" had begun to move toward the Temple door (9:3; see Exod. 14:19-20; 1 Kings 8:1-11).

10:1-22 *The glory cloud pauses, then moves.* The being who had marked those to be spared now prepared to spread the coals of God's wrath over the city (10:1-2, 6-8). Meanwhile the glory cloud paused at the Temple door (10:3-4), perhaps signifying that, though God had decided to judge his people, his ultimate desire was to remain with them.

Ezekiel described his vision in detail, noting that it was the same as the vision he had received at the beginning of his ministry (10:9-17; see chap. 1) and that the "living beings" and the "cherubim" were one and the same (10:15, 20). The glory cloud then moved from the Temple to the eastern gate.

Cherubim are among the highest of angelic beings (see exposition on 28:11-19; exposition on Gen. 3:22-24; Rev. 4:6-8). Golden carvings of cherubim were placed over the mercy seat of the Ark of the Covenant (see Exod. 25:18-22), which represented the actual throne of God as seen here by Ezekiel. Apparently one of the responsibilities of the cherubim is to carry God's throne.

11:1-13 *No protection for false prophets.* The Lord brought Ezekiel to 25 men at the eastern Temple gate, including Pelatiah and other leaders, and identified them as those who had been giving false assurances of Jerusalem's security (11:1-3). Comparing Jerusalem to a cooking pot that protects the meat within it, they confidently declared, "Is it not a good time to build houses?" (11:3). Ezekiel responded that only those of their own people whom they had killed would be protected by Jerusalem's walls (11:7). The leaders themselves would be led out of the city and killed (11:7-12; see Jer. 52:24-27). As if to underscore Ezekiel's warning, Pelatiah died even as Ezekiel spoke (11:13).

The leaders' false sense of security may have come in part from their having survived the invasions of 605 and 597 B.C. (see 2 Kings 24:8-16).

11:14-21 *New hearts for the exiles.* Apparently these ungodly leaders were saying that those taken captive in 605 and 597 B.C. (such as Daniel, and Ezekiel himself) were under God's judgment and therefore should be rejected (11:15). God declared that, quite to the contrary, he would give those exiles his special protection (11:16) and would eventually restore all believing Israelites to their homeland, giving them "tender hearts" (or "hearts of flesh") in place of their "hearts of stone" (11:17-20; see exposition on Jer. 31:31-34). The self-confident Jerusalemites, on the other hand, may find themselves under God's judgment (11:21).

11:22-25 *Suddenly the glory is gone.* As Ezekiel's vision of the Temple ended, the glory cloud of the Lord moved from the city to the Mount of Olives. God had finally removed his special presence from his people, preparing the way for judgment. (43:1-5 promises that God's glory will return to Israel during the Millennium.) (See exposition on the following passages: Exod. 14:19-20; 2 Chron. 5:1-14; Matt. 17:1-9.)

The spirit then led Ezekiel back to Babylon, where he told the captives of his visions of Jerusalem.

12:1-16 *"Pack your bags, and dig a tunnel!"* At God's command, Ezekiel packed his belongings, dug a hole through the city wall in Tel-abib, and went out through the hole, covering his face as though blind as he went (12:1-7). Ezekiel was to explain to the exiles that his actions symbolized the hurried departure of a future group of exiles from Jerusalem, and the blinding of King Zedekiah (12:8-16; see 2 Kings 25:1-7).

Zedekiah's departure from Jerusalem would transpire just as predicted (12:12; see 2 Kings 25:4). 2 Kings 25:6-7 fulfills both Ezekiel's prophecy that Zedekiah would not see Babylon (12:13), and Jeremiah's prophecy that he *would* see Nebuchadnezzar (see Jer. 34:2-5).

12:17-20 *His last meal?* In another symbolic act, Ezekiel trembled while he ate, portraying the anxiety of Jerusalem's last days.

12:21-28 *Life goes on?* Having heard many prophecies, both true and false, about Judah's future, many Israelites had become cynical, thinking they would never come true (12:22, 27). Ezekiel was to warn, however, that the time had come for the fulfillment of all true prophecies (12:23-25, 28).

13:1-23 *"They're not builders! They're desert foxes!"* God condemned the prophets who had falsely promised peace (13:10, 16; see exposition on Jer. 6:10-21) while doing nothing to repair the "whitewashed wall" of Israel's moral depravity (13:5, 10-16). Such prophets were as useless as jackals (13:4), content to live in decaying ruins. Also to be condemned were the false women prophets, who practiced sorcery (13:17-23). Their wrong advice was hurting the righteous and helping the wicked (13:22; see Exod. 23:7; Prov. 24:23-25; Isa. 5:23).

14:1-11 *The leaders: Most lawless of all.* Recognizing him to be a prophet, some of the elders in exile came to Ezekiel for advice. God refused to speak through Ezekiel on their behalf because, though they claimed to be seeking the Lord, he knew they were idolaters (14:3-4, 7). God called on them to repent (14:6) but foresaw only certain judgment (14:5). Still, his ultimate desire was for Israel to be his people once again (14:11).

14:12-23 *Not even for Noah!* God declared he would not spare the land of Israel even if such righteous men as Noah, Daniel, and Job were living there. He would spare those three men, but no one else. The nation had already crossed over the line and must be judged. God would, however, spare a remnant of the faithful, who would then be a great comfort to Ezekiel and would help him see that God's judgment on Judah had been just (14:22-23).

It is interesting that Daniel, a fellow captive with Ezekiel and only about 35 at this time, was as well known for his righteousness as were Noah and Job.

15:1-8 *"No fruit? Throw it in the fire!"* In a parable, the Lord compared Israel to a vine. The only value of a vine is to bear fruit. It is not good for building (too crooked), for furniture (too soft), or even for fuel (it burns too rapidly). Because Israel had borne no fruit (see exposition on Isa. 43:8-13), it would be burned as refuse. Christians, likewise, must bear fruit (see John 15:1-8). The vine was a common OT symbol for Israel (see Ps. 80:8-18; Isa. 27:2-4; Jer. 12:10-11).

16:1-14 *Israel the orphan and beautiful wife.* The Lord compared Israel to a baby girl found abandoned in a field—which represents God's finding Israel in bondage in Egypt. God adopted the ragged little girl and raised her as his own, finally entering into a marriage covenant with her (16:8), representing his giving Israel the law at Sinai. God dressed his wife in beautiful clothes and jewels (16:10-14), representing the nation's glory days under David and Solomon.

16:15-43 *Israel the proud harlot.* Sadly, Israel the wife soon became proud and spurned the love of God her husband, turning instead to play the harlot with foreign gods. All the wealth God had given her was now offered to her foreign lovers (16:17-19). She was actually worse than a harlot, in that she paid her lovers rather than their paying her (16:31-34). God would allow Israel to be abused and defeated by the very nations with whose gods she had committed spiritual adultery (16:35-43).

16:44-63 *Sinful as Sodom, but still he'll save her.* It was obvious to everyone, said the Lord, that Israel was just as wicked as the nations around her. They were as sinful as their pagan forebears (16:45), as sinful as the fallen northern kingdom (Samaria) that they despised (16:46, 51-52), even as sinful as Sodom (16:46-50). God would one day restore Judah (16:60-63) but only after he had restored those other nations (16:53-55)! Then God would make a new covenant with his people, which would include atonement for all their sins (16:60-63; see Jer. 31:31-34; Rom. 11:27; Heb. 8:8-12).

17:1-24 *Two eagles and a cedar.* Ezekiel told a parable with three major players: A first eagle, large and powerful, took the top of a cedar tree and carried it to a faraway land. Seed from the tree was planted, and a vine began to grow; as it grew it turned toward the first eagle. A second eagle then appeared, and the vine turned toward it instead (17:1-10). Ezekiel applied the parable to Zedekiah's breaking of his covenant with Nebuchadnezzar (17:11-21). Nebuchadnezzar had taken captive the "topmost shoot" of Israel's "cedar tree"—the best and brightest of her citizens—in 605 and 597 B.C. He had placed Zedekiah on the throne and God, through Jeremiah (see Jer. 27), had told Zedekiah to be loyal to that alliance for the protection of his people. But Zedekiah ignored that sound advice and broke the covenant by allying with Egypt (the second eagle) against Babylon (17:15).

God considered this treason against himself (17:20) and declared that Egypt would prove useless as an ally (17:17; see Jer. 37:5-7). He also declared that Zedekiah would die in Babylon (17:16; see Jer. 52:11).

God would, however, preserve a "tender shoot" from the top of the tree and replant it in Israel (17:22-24). This "tender shoot," sometimes called the "Branch," represents Jesus the Messiah (see Isa. 11:1; 53:2; Jer. 23:5; Zech 3:8).

18:1-18 *Sour grapes and souls that sin.* Reciting a popular saying of the day, some Israelites were blaming their present suffering on the sins of their fathers, represented by "sour grapes" (18:2; see Jer. 31:29-30). God declared that, contrary to this popular wisdom, people were responsible for their own sins (18:4). He gave several examples of sin and responsibility, implying that the present generation could not blame their problems on past generations (18:5-18).

The Bible states elsewhere that God punishes "the children for the sins of their parents to the third and fourth generations" (see Exod. 20:5; Jer. 32:18), which would seem to imply that children suffer for the sins of their parents. These passages may, however, simply mean that children tend to follow their parents' example (see exposition on 20:1-32).

18:19-32 *When the bad turn good and the good turn bad.* Not only are people individually responsible for their sins (18:19-20), but repentance is always an option, even for the most wicked (18:21-23). However, God warned, the righteous person who backslides will be judged (18:24). He defended the rightness of his proclamation regarding personal responsibility (18:25-29) and issued the call once more: Repent and live (18:30-32). God takes no pleasure in the death of the ungodly (18:23, 32; see 2 Pet. 3:9). (See exposition on 33:10-20.)

19:1-14 *Young lions and a strong vine.* Ezekiel lamented Israel's fate, comparing her to a lioness and a vine. The lioness lost two of her cubs to trappers. The first cub (19:3-4) probably represents Jehoahaz, who was taken captive to Egypt in 609 B.C. (see 2 Kings 23:31-34). The other cub may have been either Jehoiachin, taken to Babylon in 597 (see 2 Kings 24:8-15), or Zedekiah, who would be taken there in 586 (see 2 Kings 24:18).

Ezekiel then compared Israel to a vine that was destined to be thoroughly uprooted and destroyed by a desert wind (19:10-14)—probably a reference to the final Babylonian invasion. Some scholars see either the entire vine, or at least its "branches" (19:12), as a reference to Zedekiah.

20:1-32 *Following their parents' example.* God told Ezekiel to remind Israel of the "loathsome . . . actions of their ancestors" (20:1-4): When God had announced his plans to deliver Israel from Egypt, he commanded them to forsake Egypt's false religion. They failed to do so, yet "to protect the honor of [his] name," he kept his promise and delivered them anyway (20:5-10).

During their wilderness journey, God provided for the Israelites' spiritual and physical needs, even though they still rebelled (20:10-26). Even after entering the Promised Land (20:27-29) and right up to the present day (20:30-32), Israel had persisted in religious apostasy despite God's goodness. Therefore, God would no longer hear their prayers (20:31).

20:33-44 *"Then you'll finally recognize me!"* The day would come when God would reclaim his people from exile,

SIX PARABLES IN EZEKIEL

1. ***A fruitless vine (15:1-8)***
2. ***The adopted girl who became a harlot (16:1-63)***
3. ***The two eagles (17:1-21)***
4. ***The tender twig (17:22-24)***
5. ***The lioness and her cubs (19:1-9)***
6. ***The two harlot sisters (23:1-49)***

weed out those among them who still rebelled, and bring them back to their homeland. Then, they would repent of their sins (20:43) and would "know that I am the LORD" (20:38, 42, 44).

20:45-49 *A forest fire and a weary audience.* Ezekiel's next prophecy of destruction used the imagery of a forest fire. Ezekiel noted that his audience was growing tired of his frequent use of parables.

21:1-32 *Swords, groans, strikes, and livers.* Using the imagery of a drawn sword, the Lord declared that complete destruction would come upon Judah and Israel. Ezekiel was to call attention to this warning with audible groans—no doubt further alienating an audience weary of his unusual preaching style (21:6-7; see 20:49)! Once again God warned of the sharpened sword of approaching judgment (21:8-13), this time instructing Ezekiel to "clap [his] hands vigorously" to accentuate the message (21:14-17; see 6:11).

The Babylonians would consult magical signs, including an animal liver, to decide whether to attack Jerusalem or Ammon and would on that basis choose Jerusalem (21:18-23). God is sovereign even over the misguided religious practices of nonbelievers. In the coming destruction, the Davidic monarchy would be overthrown (21:24-27) and would remain so until the coming of Messiah (21:27). Although the omens had guided Nebuchadnezzar to Jerusalem rather than to Ammon, Ammon would not escape judgment (21:28-32).

22:1-22 *Jerusalem: Crime capital of the world!* Jerusalem had become infamous for all the killings taking place there and had become odious to God because of its idolatry (22:1-5). The kings had led the way in the crime wave, freely using their high position to kill whomever they pleased (22:6; see 2 Kings 24:3-4) and to take advantage of people in other ways as well (22:7-12). They would be punished (22:13-16). Jerusalem itself would become a fiery furnace to purify them (22:17-22).

22:23-31 *And no one even cares!* It seemed that all of Israel's leaders were hopeless sinners. While the priests profaned the Temple and ignored the Sabbath, political leaders took bribes, prophets spoke falsely, and the people committed robbery and mistreated the poor (22:26-29). Not one righteous person could be found to stand in the "gap" in Judah's broken moral defenses (22:30).

23:1-49 *The sins of the two sisters.* In still another parable, Samaria and Jerusalem were portrayed as two sisters who were prostitutes. The whole nation had been involved in spiritual prostitution in Egypt before the Exodus (see Lev. 17:7). The northern kingdom, having never really repented of its sins in Egypt, would later become allied both politically and spiritually with Assyria (23:5-10). On political ties leading to spiritual compromise, see exposition on 1 Kings 11:1-8 and on 2 Kings 16:10-20.

Judah became worse than her northern sister, prostituting herself to Assyria and Babylon, then rejecting Babylon and returning to her first illicit lover—Egypt (23:11-21). Judah would be judged by her spurned lovers (23:22-30). Because Judah's sin was the same as that of the northern kingdom, she would suffer the same punishment (23:31-35).

Both north and south would be judged for their gross paganism (23:36-39; see 2 Kings 21:1-9). Rather than waiting for the pagans to come to them, they had invited their influence (23:40-41). They deserved the punishment prescribed by the law for both prostitutes and religious apostates (23:46-47; see Deut. 13:6-11; 22:22-30).

24:1-14 *The pot will boil, and boil, and boil.* On the very day that Babylon began its final siege of Jerusalem, God told Ezekiel to fill a pot of boiling water with the best meats and to cook it till the flesh fell off the bones. He then threw out all the meat and allowed the pot to bake itself dry to eliminate the remaining impurities. Likewise would the fires of the Babylonian siege cleanse Jerusalem of her moral impurity.

24:15-24 *Tearless at his own wife's funeral!* On that same day, God informed Ezekiel that his beloved wife would die the following day, but that he should show no grief over her death. When Ezekiel's wife died and his fellow exiles noticed his lack of grief, he explained that God was not grieving over the approaching death of Jerusalem, and neither should they (24:20-24).

24:25-27 *"You'll hear the news and speak again."* When Jerusalem actually fell, a special messenger would be sent to Babylon to inform Ezekiel. At that time, Ezekiel's impaired speech would become normal again (24:25-27; see 3:26; 33:21-22).

JUDGING THE ENEMIES OF GOD (25–32)

25:1-7 *Ammon: From glee and derision to gloom and doom.* Ezekiel prophesied against several nations involved in Israel's history (25–32). Though recorded together, the prophecies were given at various times. Ammon, east of the Jordan and north of Moab, had shown devilish glee over Jerusalem's destruction, so it would be destroyed as well. (See exposition on Jer. 49:1-6.)

25:8-11 *Moab: From scornful looks to scorched landscape.* The Moabites had scorned Israel's claims to be God's special people. Their cities would be wiped out, and then they would acknowledge Israel's God. (See exposition on Jer. 48:1-47.)

25:12-14 *Edom: Death to the pitiless butchers.* Because the Edomites had butchered helpless Israelites during the Babylonian invasion, they would be completely destroyed. (See exposition on Jer. 49:7-22.)

25:15-17 *Philistia: The "old hatred."* The Philistines, Israel's ancient foes, would also be destroyed. (See exposition on Jer. 47:1-7.)

26:1-6 *Tyre: From net worth to net spreading.* As soon as the people of Tyre heard of Jerusalem's fall, they rejoiced: As the premier sea traders of their day, they were eager to "become wealthy" with the spoils of Jerusalem and to take over Judah's "rich trade routes" (26:1-2). This commercial capital would itself be plundered. Invading armies would "scrape away its soil," making it "a bare rock . . . a place for fishermen to spread their nets" (26:3-6).

26:7-21 *Details of Tyre's destruction.* The Lord declared specifically that Nebuchadnezzar would destroy Tyre (26:7-11), and that in fact happened in 572 B.C. The amazing fulfillment of 26:12-14 would come 240 years later: Part of Tyre was on an island, and that part survived the 572 assault. In 332, however, Alexander the Great completed Tyre's destruction by using the debris from 572 to build a causeway to the island, which he then destroyed! Tyre has never been rebuilt, and in fact remains to this day a place for local fishermen to dry their nets! Tyre's horrible fate would cause her former trading partners to fear and mourn (26:15-21). (See exposition on Isa. 23:1-18.)

27:1-36 *His lamentation for Tyre.* Ezekiel lamented Tyre's fate, comparing Tyre to a ship. Goods from many lands had made Tyre one of the most beautiful cities in the known world

(27:1-9). 23 nations had traded with Tyre (27:12-24). Yet the mighty ship of Tyre would finally sink (27:25-36).

28:1-10 *The king of Tyre: Deluded by success.* Tyre's king was proud of his nation's success. He attributed much of that success to his own wisdom, even considering himself a god (28:1-5). But the true and only God would judge him (28:6-10). 28:3 is another indication of Daniel's fame, even as a young man (see exposition on 14:12-23).

28:11-19 *The real king of Tyre.* As Ezekiel continued to describe God's judgment against the king of Tyre, he spoke in terms that many Bible scholars see as a picture of the fall of Satan. Like the king of Tyre, Satan became too proud of himself and was therefore judged. From being the "mighty angelic guardian," the most beautiful of all God's creatures (28:12-15), he came to "a terrible end" and "all who knew [him were] appalled at [his] fate" (28:19). (See exposition on Isa. 14:1-23.)

28:20-26 *Sidon: Destroyed like her sister.* Sidon, a coastal commercial center about 20 miles north of Tyre, would be destroyed as well (28:20-23). With its hostile neighbors destroyed, Israel would return to its homeland and live in peace (28:24-26).

29:1-7 *Egypt: Pulled from the Nile for nonsupport.* In a prophecy given a year before the one against Tyre, Ezekiel dealt with Egypt, the superpower to the south (29–32; compare exposition on Jer. 46). Pharaoh, the proud "monster" and ruler of the Nile, would be pulled from his river kingdom and left on dry land to be devoured by beasts and birds (29:1-5). The judgment would come because, after enticing Judah into an alliance against Babylon, Pharaoh would fail to support them (29:6-7; see Jer. 37:5-10).

29:8-16 *Egypt's desolation and restoration.* Because of their king's pride (29:3, 9), Egypt would be desolate and uninhabited for 40 years as its people went into exile (29:8-12). Egypt would then be restored to its land but would never again be a major world power (29:13-15). As future Israelites observed lowly Egypt, they would be amazed that they had ever looked to it for protection (29:16).

29:17–30:19 *"Egypt will pay Babylon for Tyre!"* Seventeen years later, in 570 B.C.—two years after Babylon had defeated Tyre—Ezekiel prophesied again concerning Egypt. God told Ezekiel that since Nebuchadnezzar had done God's will by defeating Tyre, and since his men had gained few spoils from their victory, God would allow them to conquer and plunder Egypt. Judah would be encouraged by the fulfillment of God's judgment on Egypt (29:21). The Babylonians had laid siege against Tyre for 13 years, from 585 until they finally defeated them in 572, during which time the seafaring Tyrians probably shipped their wealth to their many seaport colonies.

Ezekiel went on to foretell the details of Egypt's destruction (30:1-19). Egypt's current pharaoh was deposed and killed in 569, and Babylon invaded in about 568.

Though placed amid his other prophecies against Egypt, 29:17–30:19 was Ezekiel's latest recorded prophecy, coming in 570, two years later than the prophecy of 40–48.

30:20-26 *Egypt's arms broken.* Ezekiel now recorded an earlier prophecy about Egypt, given in 586 B.C. God would break Pharaoh's arms, preventing him from even holding a sword. Meanwhile Nebuchadnezzar's arms would be strengthened, so that his sword (his armies) would be successful.

31:1-18 *"Remember that great cedar?"* Two months later God spoke again, with an object lesson for the proud Pharaoh: Assyria had once been as great as Egypt. Indeed, Assyria the great "cedar" was the envy of all the other trees in the forest. Even the trees of Eden paled by comparison (31:1-9). Because of Assyria's pride, God allowed foreign armies to destroy her (31:10-17). Egypt, which was also a beautiful tree, would likewise be cut down (31:18).

32:1-16 *Not a young lion, but an old crocodile.* About a year and a half later, after Jerusalem had fallen, Ezekiel lamented the coming destruction of Egypt, outlining the trouble and dismay that was sure to come. Pharaoh may have imagined himself a strong young lion, but God preferred a more truly Egyptian analogy: Like a crocodile too old to fight back, Pharaoh would be pulled from the Nile and left to die on dry land (32:2-6; see exposition on 29:1-7).

32:17-32 *When Egypt joins the nations in hell.* About two weeks later, Ezekiel offered a final lament for Egypt. Pharaoh and his beloved nation would be consigned to "the pit" (32:18; see 26:20; 28:8; 31:16-17), or "the grave" (32:27), along with many other "outcasts" (or "the uncircumcised"). On the OT view of hell, see exposition on Psalm 9.

PRESENTING THE SHEPHERD OF GOD (33–34)

33:1-9 *The watchman, again.* In a message given either just before or just after Jerusalem fell, God stressed once again the duties of the watchman to warn people of their sin—a duty which by now Ezekiel had faithfully fulfilled (see 3:16-21).

33:10-20 *The good, the bad, and the repentant.* For those who sincerely despair over their sin, it is never too late to repent (33:10-11). God does not delight in judging his people (33:11). Past righteousness won't save those who sin; past unrighteousness won't condemn those who repent (33:12-20; see exposition on 18:19-32).

33:21-22 *He hears the news and speaks again.* As God had promised (see 24:26), a messenger arrived in Tel-abib to tell Ezekiel that Jerusalem had fallen. As God had also promised (see 24:27), Ezekiel then regained his normal faculty of speech. (Jerusalem had fallen in December of 586 B.C.; the messenger arrived in Babylon about 10 months later.)

33:23-29 *"Abraham possessed it, but you're no Abraham!"* Favorably comparing themselves to Abraham, the Jews remaining in Israel after its fall were confident that the land was theirs to keep. But their ongoing sins meant that they, too, would be judged (33:23-29).

33:30-33 *"Yes, he was a prophet."* Meanwhile, the exiles in Babylon were politely listening to Ezekiel but failing to heed his warnings. God assured Ezekiel that, as his prophecies came true, they would realize that "a prophet has been among them."

34:1-31 *Fat shepherds, scrawny sheep, and a Good Shepherd.* God indicted Israel's religious and political leaders, who cared more about themselves than about their people; they were like healthy shepherds watching over sickly sheep (34:1-6) or like strong sheep taking advantage of weaker sheep (34:17-19). As a result, their flock had been scattered (34:5-6).

God would judge these uncaring shepherds (34:7-10, 20) and would himself become their loving Shepherd (34:11-16). He would "set one shepherd over them, even [his] servant David," who would be "a prince" among them (34:23-24) and would also be their shepherd (34:25-31). Ezekiel would make several more references to this prince, especially in 45–46.

This "prince" who is also a "shepherd" has been variously identified as Christ, as someone else from the line of David, or as a resurrected David himself (see 37:25). Christ's identity as the "good shepherd" (John 10:11-16) suggests that Ezekiel was referring to him. On the other hand, the reference to this shepherd's "sons" (46:16) and the rules laid down for his conduct (45:9–46:18) suggest someone other than Christ.

On 34:17, 22, see exposition on Matthew 25:31-46.

RESTORING THE NATION OF GOD (35–37)

35:1-15 *"You want blood? I'll give you blood!"* To prepare the way for a restored Israel, its enemies would be destroyed. Mount Seir (Edom—see 35:15) is given as an example of those enemies. The Edomites descended from Jacob's brother, Esau, and had a "continual hatred" for Israel (35:5; see exposition on Jer. 49:7-22). The climax of their hatred came as they helped Babylon destroy Jerusalem in 586 B.C. (35:5). Since they evidently liked blood, said the Lord, he would give them more blood (35:6). Edom had rejoiced at Israel's downfall; the whole world would rejoice when Edom fell (35:14-15; see Mal. 1:2-5).

36:1-15 *"Build bigger barns! You'll need them!"* Because they had delighted in and benefited from Judah's downfall, God would bring shame upon Edom and Israel's other enemies (36:1-7). Meanwhile the Israelites will one day receive material blessings beyond measure (36:8-15).

36:16-38 *"You'll also need a new heart."* God had driven Israel from its land because their sins had dishonored his name (36:16-19). Yet even in exile they continued to dishonor him (36:20). Therefore, not so much for their sake as for his own name's sake, he will one day restore them to their land, give them a new heart, and put his spirit within them, enabling them to obey him (36:21-28; see exposition on Jer. 31:31-34).

While this promise will be fulfilled for the entire nation of Israel during the Millennium, its fulfillment is foreshadowed by the Spirit's indwelling of all believers in Christ.

37:1-28 *Israel's dry bones restored.* In a vision, Ezekiel saw a valley filled with dry bones. God instructed him to prophesy to the bones, after which they would come to life (37:1-6). Ezekiel spoke as commanded, and the bones came together but had no life in them (37:7-8). He spoke again, and the breath of the Lord came into the bones, and they became "a great army" (37:9-10). God explained that the dry bones represented the scattered Jewish exiles. One day he will gather them from their "graves of exile" and bring them back to their homeland (37:11-12). He will breathe his Spirit into them, bringing spiritual renewal (37:13-14).

Ezekiel was then told to join two sticks together and explain that this meant Israel and Judah would one day be reunited under one king, "my servant David" (37:15-28; see exposition on 34:1-31).

Following the establishment of the state of Israel in 1948, many Christians have come to interpret 37:7-10 as a two-part prophecy: The physical restoration of Israel (37:7-8) occurred in 1948; the spiritual restoration (37:9-10) awaits Christ's second coming.

DEMONSTRATING THE WRATH OF GOD (38–39)

38:1-23 *God and the godless Gog.* The Lord then described a future attack on the restored Israel by an array of enemy nations (38–39), led by "Gog of the land of Magog" (38:2). These nations would join together to attack peace-loving Israel (38:8-16). God warned, however, that he would use their attack on his people to bring glory to himself (38:16-17), defeating them with natural forces and mutiny (38:18-23).

References to a restored Israel (38:11, 14) and to the "distant future" (38:8, 16) suggest that the defeat of Gog will come during the Great Tribulation in the end times. Some identify it with Armageddon, at the end of the Tribulation (see Rev. 14:14-20; 16:13-16; 19:17-19). The book of Revelation mentions an attack by "Gog and Magog" at the end of the Millennium, which follows the Tribulation (see Rev. 20:8). Since many OT prophecies have dual fulfillments, Ezekiel could have had both events in view.

While some of Gog's coconspirators (38:5-6) can be identified as modern-day enemies of Israel, the nationality of Gog himself is not clear. References to "Rosh" (38:2-3, NASB) and the "distant north" (38:15) lead some to see a Russian connection. Josephus identified Magog with the area north and northeast of the Black Sea now occupied by Russia and other former Soviet nations.

39:1-20 *When Magog falls, the birds will feast.* God will "drive" Magog to its battle against Israel but will then bring sudden defeat upon it, bringing glory to his name (39:1-8). So great will be the slaughter, it will take seven years to burn all the weapons and seven months to bury the dead (39:9-16). Scavenging animals will have a feast (39:17-20; see Rev. 19:17-21).

39:21-29 *"All nations will know me."* Following Magog's defeat, Israel and all nations will acknowledge God (39:21-24). Ezekiel repeated God's promise to restore Israel to their land and to pour out his Spirit upon them (39:25-29).

REVEALING THE MILLENNIUM OF GOD (40–48)

40:1-4 *The man with the measuring rod.* Ezekiel ended his book with a vision he saw in 572 B.C. describing life in the Millennium (40–48), which will center around the restored Temple. As his vision began, he encountered an angelic messenger with a measuring rod, with which he would proceed to measure the Temple in great detail. Ezekiel was to note carefully what he saw and report it to Israel. (Though Ezekiel would have given these Temple plans to his fellow exiles before they returned to Judah, there is no indication that they used them in rebuilding the Temple at that time.)

40:5-46 *Measuring the Temple courtyards.* The angel began the tour of this future Temple by measuring the wall surrounding it. Taking to heart the admonition to pay close attention, Ezekiel noted that the measuring rod was six cubits long, but that each cubit was actually a cubit and a handbreadth, making the rod about 10.5 feet long (40:5). The wall around the Temple courtyard will be one rod high and one rod wide. Ezekiel described the inner and outer courtyards and the various rooms and alcoves surrounding the Temple, including areas for preparing sacrifices (40:38-43) and rooms for singers and priests (40:44-46). There will be gates into the outer and inner courtyards on all four sides. Between the Temple and the western wall will be a large building of an unspecified nature (41:12).

40:47–41:26 *Measuring the Temple.* The inner courtyard, in front of the Temple, will be 100 long cubits (175 feet) square. In the center of this courtyard will be the altar (see exposition on 43:13-27). Then comes the Temple, with its "foyer" (40:48-49), its sanctuary or Holy Place (41:1-3), and the Most Holy Place (41:4). Surrounding the Holy Place and the Most Holy Place on three sides are three floors of 30 rooms each, which will probably be used for storage. On each side of these rooms will be a wall, six cubits (10.5 feet) thick on the first floor. As each successive level of rooms becomes wider, the wall will become thinner (41:5-11; compare 1 Kings 6:5-6).

Ezekiel described the Temple's interior decorations (41:21-26). Apparently the only furniture inside the Temple will be the altar of incense (41:22).

42:1-20 *Other buildings and the big picture.* On the north and south sides of the Temple proper will be more priests' chambers, where the Temple garments are to be stored and the sacred portion of the sacrifices eaten (42:1-14).

The angel then took Ezekiel out through the east gate and measured the entire Temple area (42:15-20). The KJV and NKJV give the overall dimensions as 500 rods, or one mile square, in 42:15-19, but in 42:20 give the dimensions as 500 *cubits* or 875 feet square, which matches the dimensions previously given. The NLT and NIV avoid this apparent contradiction by following the Septuagint, which gives the dimensions as 500 cubits (875 feet) throughout 42:15-20. The Temple area can be visualized, then, as being about the length of three football fields on each side.

43:1-5 *Suddenly, his glory returns!* The glory cloud of God, which earlier had departed from the Temple through the eastern gate (10:19; 11:23), now returned through the same gate to take up residence in the Temple (43:1-5). The departure of God's glory will not be permanent.

43:6-12 *"I want to dwell with them, if only . . ."* Having returned to his millennial Temple, the Lord declared that the Temple symbolized his desire to dwell with his people forever, if only they would recognize his holiness and cease profaning his name (43:6-9). Ezekiel was to teach the people everything he had learned in his vision, with the hope that this would lead them to true and lasting repentance (43:10-12).

43:13-27 *The altar and its sacrifices.* God then described the altar and the ceremony of sacrifices related to it, which closely resemble those originally prescribed by the law.

Why there will be sacrifices in the Millennium is not clear, considering the all-sufficiency of Christ's sacrifice for sin (see Heb. 10:11-18). Perhaps they will be a memorial of God's great work of salvation through Christ, to show

- the holiness of God
- the seriousness of sin
- the costliness of salvation
- the necessity of new birth

While sacrifices could serve such a commemorative purpose during the Millennium, this passage has led many scholars to conclude that Ezekiel's millennial Temple represents only a figurative shadow—shown to him in language he could understand—of the New Jerusalem described by John in Revelation 21:1–22:5. The fact that the New Jerusalem will have no Temple would seem to support this view. Other scholars believe, however, that the "new heaven and a new earth" described by John will follow the Millennium, thus allowing for a literal Temple during the Millennium itself.

44:1-3 *The eastern gate: Do not open.* The Lord then brought Ezekiel to the eastern gate of the Temple and declared that it must remain closed, since that was the gate through which he had entered the Temple. Perhaps this was meant to be a guarantee that God's glory would never again leave his people. Special privileges regarding

FACTS ON THE MILLENNIAL TEMPLE—Ezekiel 40–48

Its Biblical Order

1. The Tabernacle of Moses (Exod. 40). Dates: 1444–1100 B.C.
2. The Temple of Solomon (1 Kings 6). Dates: 959–586 B.C.
3. The Temple of Zerubbabel (Ezra 5). Note: This was later greatly enlarged by Herod (see John 2). Dates: 516 B.C.–A.D. 70
4. The temple of Christ's body (John 2). Dates: 4 B.C.–A.D. 30
5. The spiritual temple, the church (Acts 2). Dates: Pentecost—Rapture
6. The tribulational Temple (Rev. 11). Dates: Rapture—Armageddon
7. The millennial Temple (Ezek. 40–48)

Its Purpose

- To provide a place for the glory cloud of God (44:4)
- To provide a center for the King of glory (43:7)

Its Prince

- Not Christ (45:22; 46:16)
- Perhaps someone from the line of David

Its Unique Features

- No veil
- No table of holy bread
- No lampstands
- No Ark of the Covenant
- East gate to be closed (44:2)

Its Sacrifices (Isa. 56:7; 60:7; Jer. 33:18; Zech. 14:16-21)

- A reminder to all of the necessity of the new birth
- An object lesson of the costliness of salvation
- An example of the awfulness of sin
- An illustration of the holiness of God

Its River (47:1-12)

- The source: Proceeding from beneath the Temple
- The course: Flows to Dead Sea and Mediterranean Sea
- The force: Waters deep enough to swim in

Its Glory Cloud

- It came through the eastern gate into the Temple (43:1-5).

Its City

- Circumference: Six miles (48:35)
- Name: The millennial Jerusalem will be named "Yahweh Shammah," meaning "The LORD Is There" (48:35).

the eastern gate were granted to the "prince" (see exposition on 34:1-31).

44:4-31 *Millennial priests? Only those zealous Zadokites!* Specific rules will govern who can enter the Temple. Non-Israelites who do not love the Lord will be absolutely excluded (44:4-9). Levites, because of their long history of unfaithfulness, will be allowed to minister to the people, but "they may not approach [God] to minister as priests. They may not touch any of [his] holy things or the holy offerings" (44:10-14). Only the sons of Zadok, who had remained faithful during Israel's times of rebellion, will serve as priests (44:15-31; see 1 Kings 2:28-35). They will teach the people about ritual holiness (44:23), will be judges (44:24), and will receive no land in the millennial kingdom, relying on offerings for their support (44:28-31).

Gentiles will acknowledge God as Lord (see 36:23; 38:23) and will be full participants in his ultimate plan of salvation (see exposition on Isa. 56:1-8).

45:1-8 *Special soil.* A parcel of land surrounding the Temple, about eight miles square, will be set aside for priests and Levites (45:1-5), for the city of Jerusalem (45:6), and for the prince (45:7-8).

45:9–46:18 *Religious rules for prince and people.* Ezekiel described various duties of the millennial prince and his people. The princes should set an example of honesty and fairness in financial matters (45:9-12). The people are to give the prince a portion—much less than a tithe—to maintain the Temple (45:13-17). As in the law, the bull used for the offering of atonement must be without blemish, recalling Christ's perfect sacrifice (45:18-20). The Passover and the Festival of Shelters will both be celebrated during the Millennium (45:21-25), as will the Sabbath and other festival days (46:1-11).

While the outer eastern gate to the Temple area will be kept shut (see 44:1), the inner eastern gate will be opened on the Sabbath so that the prince can observe the sacrifices (46:1-8). After he leaves, the gate will remain open till sunset. When he makes a freewill offering, however, the gate will be closed as soon as he leaves (46:12).

On crowded feast days, the people—including the prince—are to leave through the gate opposite to where they entered, presumably to avoid congestion (46:9-10).

The prince is to follow strict guidelines concerning his personal wealth and is forbidden to exploit his people (46:16-18).

46:19-24 *Kitchens for priests and people.* In a passage that would seem to fit better following 42:14, Ezekiel described two kitchens close to the Temple, reserved for preparing the priests' sacrifices (46:19-20); and four kitchens in the corners of the outer courtyard, for the sacrifices of the people (46:21-24).

47:1-12 *A river of life and healing.* A river of water deep enough to swim in will flow out of the Temple to the east into the Kidron Valley and on to the sea (presumably the Dead Sea). It will give life to trees along its banks, which will in turn provide nourishment and healing. The apostle John would describe a similar river in his vision of the New Jerusalem (see Rev. 22:1-2).

47:13–48:29 *Territory for the tribes and Temple.* God then defined the geography of Israel's restored land, which was to be a permanent inheritance for them and for "the foreigners who have joined you" (47:22-23). The land will extend from the Mediterranean Sea on the west to the Dead Sea on the east, and from north of Sidon in Lebanon to Kadesh in the south (47:15-20). He specified the territories of the 12 tribes (48:1-7, 23-29), which will surround the territory set aside for Jerusalem, the Temple, and the lands of priests and Levites (48:8-22).

48:30-35 *The city's name: The Lord Is There.* Ezekiel's recorded prophecies end with a last glimpse of restored Jerusalem, a four-square city, 1.5 miles long on each side, with 12 gates, each named for one of Israel's 12 tribes (compare Rev. 21:12-14). Because of God's permanent presence within its walls, the city will be named, "The LORD Is There."

PEOPLE TO REMEMBER FROM EZEKIEL

EZEKIEL

Key Fact: Prophesied from exile in Babylon concerning the reason for Israel's fall and its hope for the future
Father: Buzi (1:3)
Wife: Unnamed (24:18)
Occupation: Priest and prophet (1:3; 2:3-4)
Total Bible References: 93
Key References: 1–48

Ezekiel Speaks

My wife and I were newlyweds when Nebuchadnezzar took us away from our homeland as captives. How good it was to see Daniel, who had suffered the same fate some eight years earlier. God has certainly elevated him; as I write this he holds a position second only to the king himself. (1:1; Dan. 1:1-6; 6:1-3)

I was only 25 upon arriving in Babylon. Then, five years later, beside the Kebar River, the Lord called me into full-time service. A watchman on the wall! That was to be my assignment. What an ordination ceremony it turned out to be, with angelic cherubim in attendance! (1:3-28; 3:17; 10:1; 40:1)

My wife was so proud of me. How we loved each other! She was the dearest thing on earth to me. Then, seven years later, with no warning, God suddenly removed her! I still remember those dreadful words: "Son of man, I am going to take away your dearest treasure. Suddenly she will die." And as if that were not hard enough, he forbade me to give even a hint of my unbearable sorrow! With a heavy heart, the next morning I told the people what was going to happen. Then, after what was certainly the longest and most anxious day of my life, my precious wife died. Yet with God's help the next day at her funeral, I restrained my emotions just as he had commanded. (24:15-18)

God then consoled my broken heart, explaining that all this was to be a sign to my people in Babylon, for on the very day of her funeral, Nebuchadnezzar's armies were laying siege to Jerusalem! In other words, the joy of my people's lives—their Holy City—would be removed just as my joy had been removed. (24:1, 15-27; 33:21-22)

In reality, of course, my supernatural visit to the Temple had already shown me the need for divine judgment. The blasphemy and filth occurring right in the house of God had sunk to a new low! And then, to my horror, I witnessed the departure of God's glory cloud. (8:1-16; 10:1-19; 11:23)

I know I shall die here in Babylon, a lonely widower. But God has not left me without hope. Through the visions he gives me, the grievous past gives way to the glorious future. Think of it: All of our foes will be defeated, and we shall be resurrected, redeemed, and returned to the Promised Land! (34:28-29; 36:24-25)

Then a beautiful new Temple will be built, with a life-giving river flowing from it, purifying the Dead Sea and causing the Jordan valley to blossom as a rose! Then, Jerusalem will be elevated and will become the worship center of the world! (40–42; 47:1-12; 48:30-35; Isa. 35:1-2)

But to me, the most exciting vision was the one showing the return of God's glory cloud through the eastern gate, never again to depart! (43:1-5)

Spiritual Lessons from Ezekiel

- Ezekiel was commissioned to be a watchman, warning his people of impending danger; as Christians, we have the same commission (3:16-21; 1 Tim. 4:1-3, 6; Heb. 13:17).
- He faithfully and fearlessly proclaimed God's word to a hard-hearted and rebellious people (2:3-4) in spite of great personal difficulties and heartache:
  - ➤ He had been taken from his homeland as a captive (1:1; see Ps. 137:1-6).
  - ➤ His beloved wife suddenly died (24:15-18).
  - ➤ For a long time, he was unable to exercise his faculty of speech in a normal way (3:26; 24:27; 33:21-22).
- But Ezekiel had learned what Paul would learn—what we should learn today: "[God's] gracious favor is all you need. [God's] power works best in your weakness" (2 Cor. 12:9).
- Ezekiel learned from the very beginning how to feed on God's Word (3:1-3). We should seek spiritual nourishment from the same source (2 Tim. 2:15; 3:14-17).

Key Verses

"Then he added, 'Son of man, let all my words sink deep into your own heart first. Listen to them carefully for yourself. Then go to your people in exile and say to them, "This is what the Sovereign LORD says!" Do this whether they listen to you or not'" (3:10-11).

DANIEL

BACKGROUND

During Nebuchadnezzar's first raid on Jerusalem in 605 B.C., he took several of its foremost citizens captive to Babylon. Among these was a teenager named Daniel (1:1-6; see 2 Kings 24:1). Soon after he arrived in Babylon, Daniel was selected for service in the royal court. He excelled in that role and soon rose to a position second only to the king (2:48). Such was Daniel's reputation and influence that, when Babylon fell to Medo-Persia in 539, Daniel occupied the number two position under the new rulers as well (6:1-3).

While distinguishing himself in the governmental affairs of Babylonia and Persia, Daniel remained unswervingly faithful to the God of Israel. His book records the effects of his life and prophecies on Babylonian and Persian royalty (1–7), and his prophecies concerning Israel's place in world events down through the ages (8–12). Daniel recorded most of 1–7 (specifically, 2:4–7:28) in Aramaic, the trade language of the Babylonian Empire. The prophecies of 8–12, however, are in the Hebrew of their target audience.

Daniel's amazing prophecies, with their specifically stated applications, have been called the key to understanding all of biblical prophecy.

Daniel's early ministry overlapped that of the older Ezekiel, who was taken captive to Babylon in 597 and lived about 50 miles south of Babylon. Though there is no record of the two men ever having met, Ezekiel had apparently heard of this famous young Hebrew (see Ezek. 14:14, 20; 28:3).

Daniel's final prophecies (10–12) came after the first group of Jewish exiles returned to Judah in 538. There is no record of Daniel himself having ever returned. Many Jews remained in Persia well beyond the time of Daniel. The Jewish queen Esther may have been inspired by Daniel's life and prophecies as she rescued the Jews of Persia from extermination in about 473.

605 B.C.
Daniel with 1st exiles to Babylon

586
Fall of Judah

580
Daniel begins ministry

570
Ezekiel's last prophecy

539
Babylon falls, exiles freed, Daniel in lion's den

536
Daniel's last prophecy

Still later, in 457 and 445, two more groups of exiles would return to Judea, under Ezra and Nehemiah.

AUTHOR

Daniel is named as the author both internally (8:1; 9:2; 10:2) and externally (Matt. 24:15).

DATE AND LOCATION

Daniel's book records events from his life during the reigns of the Babylonian kings Nebuchadnezzar (605–562 B.C.) and Belshazzar (553–539), and during the first years of Persian rule under Darius and Cyrus. The first verses of chapters 2; 7; 8; 9; and 10 cite specific dates (the writings are not recorded in strict chronological order—see *Outline*). His writings would have been compiled sometime shortly after the last one (10–12) was finished, c. 536.

PURPOSE

- To proclaim God's sovereign control over human affairs (5:21), a lesson pagans needed to learn and Jews needed to remember as they faced life with no human king.
- To provide examples of believers who stood up for their God even in the face of death—examples greatly needed by the Jewish captives in pagan Babylon.

UNIQUE FEATURES

- Daniel has more to say about the Tribulation and the Antichrist than any other OT book.
- Daniel 11 includes a greater number of prophecies already fulfilled than any other single chapter in the Bible.
- Daniel refers to another prophet, Jeremiah, by name (9:2; see *Jeremiah: Unique Features*).
- 9:25-26 marks the only OT occurrence of the Hebrew term *Messiah* ("Anointed One") (see *Isaiah: Background*).
- In the original Aramiac, 7:13 uses the term "Son of man." This term occurs several times in the OT, mainly in Ezekiel, referring to Ezekiel himself. It also occurs many times in the NT in reference to Christ. Daniel's use of it is the only clearly messianic OT occurrence.
- Daniel is the only OT book to mention angels by name:
  - ➤ Gabriel, who interpreted visions for Daniel (8:16; 9:21) and would later announce Christ's birth to Mary (Luke 1:19, 26)
  - ➤ Michael the "archangel," seen here and elsewhere in Scripture as a spiritual warrior and defender of believers (10:13, 21; 12:1; Jude 1:9; Rev. 12:7-9)

Except for the fallen angel Lucifer (Isa. 14:12, KJV, NKJV), Gabriel and Michael are the only two angels mentioned by name in all of Scripture.

COMPARISON WITH OTHER BIBLE BOOKS

Revelation:

- There are so many parallels between Daniel and Revelation that seminaries often include them in the same course:
  - ➤ Both mention an earthly kingdom becoming God's everlasting kingdom (2:44; Rev. 11:15).
  - ➤ Both use the word *times* for units of years (7:25; 12:7; Rev. 12:14).
  - ➤ Both mention the ministry of the angel Michael (see *Unique Features*).
  - ➤ Both speak of a book containing the names of the righteous (12:1; Rev. 20:12).
  - ➤ Both speak of 10 kingdoms (2:41; 7:24; Rev. 17:12).

OUTLINE

(Note gaps and breaks in time sequence.)

GOD'S MAN IN BABYLON (1–7)
- Daniel's preparation (1) [605 B.C.]
- Nebuchadnezzar's dream (2) [604?]
- The fiery furnace (3) [c. 585?]
- Nebuchadnezzar's humiliation (4) [c. 565?]
- The handwriting on the wall (5) [539]
- The lions' den (6) [539]
- Four kingdoms and the Son of Man (7) [553]

GOD'S PROPHET FOR ISRAEL (8–12)
- The ram, the goat, and the little horn (8) [549]
- Daniel's prayer and the 70 weeks (9) [539]
- Israel's tribulation and triumph (10–12) [536]

GOD'S MAN IN BABYLON (1–7)

1:1-7 *The best of Israel's talent and treasure.* When Nebuchadnezzar besieged Jerusalem in 605 B.C., he plundered the Temple and took captive many from among the Jewish royalty and nobility, including Daniel (see *Background*). After arriving in Babylon, Daniel and three others were immediately groomed for service to the king.

The course of study prescribed for Daniel and his friends and the new names they were given indicate Nebuchadnezzar's desire to indoctrinate them in Babylonian ways. The very fact of their being chosen for leadership, however, probably means that Nebuchadnezzar saw some value in respecting the culture of the peoples he conquered. He may have sent some of the men from this "training school" back to their homelands to govern those left behind.

Note that Daniel's amazing ministry in Babylon began when the Lord "gave" Nebuchadnezzar victory over Judah (1:2). Jeremiah would later come to understand it to be God's will that Israel submit to Babylon as God's instrument of judgment (see exposition on Jer. 27:1-22).

1:8-16 *The Israelite Fabulous Four.* When presented with the king's prescribed diet, Daniel and his friends asked to be excused from eating the rich Babylonian food. Their mentor begged them to reconsider, fearing that their health would suffer and he would be accused of negligence. Daniel proposed that he let them try a meager vegetarian diet for 10 days. They did so, and after the 10 days were healthier than the trainees who had followed the king's diet. Daniel had feared being defiled by the Babylonian food (1:8), which could have involved one or more of the following:

- It may have been offered to pagan gods.
- It may have been unclean according to Jewish dietary laws (see Lev. 11).
- Eating at the king's table would have implied unconditional loyalty to him and his empire. Table fellowship was a serious matter in Bible times (see Matt. 9:9-13).

1:17-21 *The reward for their resolution.* God rewarded the four men's stand of faith by granting them supernatural wisdom and elevating them in the eyes of the king, who gave them choice positions of service.

2:1-23 *"Can you guess what I dreamed?"* Soon after Daniel's arrival in Babylon, Nebuchadnezzar had a terrifying dream. He asked his court magicians not just to interpret the dream but to actually tell him what he had dreamed. When the magicians were unable to do this, he called for the execution of all the "wise men" of Babylon (2:1-13). Because they were numbered among the wise men, Daniel and his friends faced execution, but through his wisdom Daniel was able to buy some time (2:14-16). God gave Daniel insight into the dream. Daniel thanked him and praised his sovereignty over human affairs (2:17-23).

2:24-28 *"I can't, but he can and has!"* Having pleaded for clemency for the doomed wise men (2:24), Daniel received an audience with the king. When asked if he could reveal the dream and its interpretation, Daniel gave God full credit for the interpretation he was about to give.

2:29-35 *A statue smashed by a stone.* Having noted that the king's dream would be fulfilled "in the future" (2:28-29; see exposition on Ezek. 38:1-23), Daniel described the dream. The king had seen a statue with a head of gold, chest and arms of silver, belly and thighs of bronze, legs of iron, and feet of both iron and clay. A stone cut "by supernatural means" had struck the feet, toppling the entire image.

2:36-45 *The meaning of the nightmare.* Daniel declared that the statue's gold head represented Nebuchadnezzar (2:38). After Babylon fell, an "inferior" kingdom of silver would arise. This kingdom clearly refers to Medo-Persia (see exposition on 7:15-28). Just as the statue's arms of silver were joined by its chest of silver, so the Medes and Persians had been joined by Cyrus to defeat Babylon.

After Medo-Persia would come a kingdom of "bronze," which would "rule the world"—clearly a reference to Greece (see 8:21 and exposition on 7:15-28).

Then would come a fourth kingdom, which "will smash and crush all previous empires." This kingdom, represented by the iron of the legs and the iron and clay of the feet, would divide into 10 "toes," some of which "will be as strong as iron, and others as weak as clay." There would apparently be some effort to unite the 10 toes of this kingdom, composed of the two naturally separate elements, but the effort would fail (2:41-43). It would seem most logical to interpret this fourth kingdom as Rome, which followed Greece (see exposition on 7:15-28).

"During the reigns of those kings," God would establish a kingdom that would destroy all the other kingdoms and would "stand forever." The rock cut "by supernatural means" (2:44-45) represented this triumphant, everlasting kingdom. While the other kingdoms were composed of dead minerals, this final kingdom was a living stone; it would grow into a great mountain, filling the whole earth (see 2:35).

2:46-49 *"Your God is the greatest!"* Though he may not have understood the full import of Daniel's interpretation, the fact that Daniel knew his dream convinced Nebuchadnezzar that Daniel's God was truly the "God of gods." So impressed was he that he gave Daniel a position second only to himself.

Daniel's earlier reference to Nebuchadnezzar as the "king over many kings" (2:37) should be seen not as irreverence but merely as a common way of forming a superlative in Hebrew. He was simply acknowledging Nebuchadnezzar as the greatest earthly king of his day (compare Ezek. 26:7). Even Nebuchadnezzar, at this point, acknowledged the true King over all earthly kings (2:47; see 1 Tim. 6:15; Rev. 17:14; 19:16).

3:1-18 *The choice: Bow down or burn up.* Apparently forgetting his acknowledgment of the one true God (see 2:47), Nebuchadnezzar made a statue of gold and commanded that it be worshiped. Those who did not do so would be cast into a fiery furnace (3:1-6). When the signal was given to worship the statue, Daniel's three friends, Shadrach, Meshach, and Abednego, refused to do so (3:7-12). Furious over their refusal, Nebuchadnezzar gave them one last chance to bow down to the statue, and once again they refused. They declared their faith that God could save them from the furnace and that they would obey God even if he did not save them (3:13-18).

The dimensions of the statue (6 cubits wide by 60 cubits high) followed the Babylonian numerical system, which was based on 6 rather than 10. Modern units of measure such as 60 minutes in an hour and 360 degrees in a circle have Babylonian origins. During their exile in Babylon, Israel adopted Babylonian month names for their calendar. The measurements of time involved in Daniel's visions of the Tribulation (see exposition on 9:20-27) suggest they adopted the 360-day Babylonian year as well.

3:19-30 *The fourth man in the furnace.* Daniel's three friends were thrown into the furnace, which had been made so hot that even the men who threw them in were killed by the heat. Soon, however, Nebuchadnezzar saw the men walking amid the flames and noticed a fourth man with them, whom he acknowledged as a "divine being" (3:19-25). Nebuchadnezzar called the men out of the furnace and, upon noticing that they showed no trace of injury from the fire, once again acknowledged the one true God (3:26-30).

The fourth person in the furnace was "like the Son of God" (3:25, KJV, NKJV) or "like a divine being" (NLT). Though Nebuchadnezzar could not have known of Christ, the Son of God, Christian scholars through the ages have believed it was he, in a preincarnate manifestation, who helped Daniel's friends, just as he had helped Hagar (see exposition on Gen. 16:1-16) and Joshua (see exposition on Josh. 5:13-15).

4:1-18 *A tree standing tall and proud.* Daniel next recorded a story about King Nebuchadnezzar, told in the king's own words. The king began by praising God (4:1-3), then told of events that had led to a spiritual renewal in his life. He had had another troubling dream. When none of his magicians could interpret it, he called again for Daniel (4:4-9). In his dream, Nebuchadnezzar had seen a tree so large it dominated the entire earth. Yet, despite its obvious importance, an order came from heaven to cut the tree down and chop off its branches, leaving only a stump (4:10-15). The

A STATUE AND A STONE

DANIEL 2

HEAD: **GOLD**
WORLD POWER:
BABYLON 606–539 B.C.

CHEST AND ARMS: **SILVER**
WORLD POWER:
PERSIA 539–331 B.C.

BELLY AND THIGHS: **BRONZE**
WORLD POWER:
GREECE 331–323 B.C.

LEGS AND FEET: **IRON and CLAY**
WORLD POWER:
ROME 322 B.C. – A.D. 476 FUTURE

In Daniel 7 the same four nations are described, but from a heavenly view, which looks upon them as four wild animals.

World Power	Description
Babylon	Lion
Persia	Bear
Greece	Leopard
Rome	Monster

dream image then became personified, as it was ordered that, for seven years (or "periods of time"), "he" would be exposed to the elements of nature and would become like a wild beast (4:15-16). All this would happen so that he would acknowledge God's sovereignty (4:17).

4:19-27 *A prophet struck silent.* Realizing the terrible truth the dream revealed, Daniel "was overcome for a time, aghast" (4:19). The dream, he said, meant that Nebuchadnezzar would be driven from human society and would live like an animal till he truly acknowledged God (4:20-25). The fact that the stump was spared, however, meant that Nebuchadnezzar's kingdom would be restored to him when he repented (4:26). Daniel urged the proud king to repent right away to avoid this awful judgment (4:27).

4:28-33 *A king cut down to size.* A year went by after the dream and Nebuchadnezzar had not repented. Then one day as he was congratulating himself on the splendor of his capital city, the promised judgment fell, and Nebuchadnezzar spent seven years living in the wilderness as a wild beast. 4:34 suggests this involved his becoming insane.

Though skeptics used to question it, most scholars now agree that Nebuchadnezzar was truly the one who "built" Babylon (4:30), in that it was his amazing palaces and temples—including the famous hanging gardens—that put Babylon on the map. Excavations indicate that Babylon's walls were 350 feet high and 87 feet thick, and were guarded by 250 watchtowers!

4:34-37 *A king with uplifted eyes.* After seven years of this ordeal, Nebuchadnezzar "looked up to heaven," regained his sanity, began praising God, and was restored to his kingdom as God had promised. Nebuchadnezzar apparently saw his experience as a lesson in humility (4:37). Compare exposition on Isaiah 10:24-34; see also Isaiah 2:12-13.

5:1-4 *Drunks drinking from the wrong cups.* In 539 B.C., more than 20 years after Nebuchadnezzar's death, King Belshazzar gave a great feast, during which he and his guests mocked the God of Israel by drinking to their pagan gods using cups taken from Israel's Temple (see 1:2; 2 Chron. 36:7). They would soon regret their mockery!

The fact that Babylon was invaded that very night (5:30-31) means it is quite possible that Belshazzar and his fellow party-goers were aware that the Persian army was at their gates; they may have assumed that their city, with its amazing walls, was immune to invasion.

Concerning the identity of Belshazzar, see *The Nabonidus Chronicles,* p. 894. Nebuchadnezzar was Belshazzar's "father" only in the broader sense of that word in Hebrew and Aramaic.

5:5-12 *"The words on the wall . . ."* During the feast, Belshazzar suddenly saw a man's fingers writing on the palace wall. Frightened, he asked his astrologers to interpret the words, but they were unable to do so (5:5-9). The queen then told him of Daniel, still renowned from the days of Nebuchadnezzar (5:10-12).

Skeptical scholars have suggested that perhaps the writing on the wall was the shadow of a clerk at work in the kitchen, mistaken as supernatural by the drunken revelers. It seems unlikely, however, that such a misperception would have gone uncorrected. Whatever the source of the writing, Daniel's interpretation of its meaning quickly came true.

The inability of the astrologers and magicians to help either Belshazzar or Nebuchadnezzar recalls the similar failures of Pharaoh's magicians (see Exod. 8:18-19).

5:13-29 *". . . mean your kingdom will fall."* Belshazzar offered Daniel the number three position in the kingdom if he could interpret the handwriting. Daniel declined the reward but agreed to give the interpretation (5:13-17). First, however, he reminded Belshazzar of Nebuchadnezzar's pride and subsequent humiliation and pointed out that Belshazzar's mocking the God of Israel (see 5:1-4) showed that he had learned nothing from Nebuchadnezzar's experience (5:18-23).

The handwriting, said Daniel, meant that God had judged Belshazzar and that his kingdom would fall to the Medes and Persians (5:24-28). The actual inscription, *mene, mene, tekel, parsin,* can mean "numbered, numbered, weighed, and divided"—thus Daniel's interpretation. The words can also refer to weights: *Mene* denotes a quantity of 60, presumably 60 shekels in this case; *tekel* is another form of the word *shekel; parsin* is a form of the word *half,* presumably a half-shekel in this case. It is interesting that the weights were given in descending order, suggesting Babylon's downfall.

5:30-31 *The swift fulfillment.* Belshazzar kept his promise to reward Daniel, but that very night the Medo-Persians invaded, Belshazzar was killed, and Darius the Mede became Babylon's new king. This fulfilled numerous biblical predictions of Babylon's fall, including Isaiah 13:17-22 and Jeremiah 50–51.

Confirming the biblical account, the Greek historian Herodotus wrote that the Medo-Persian army surprised the Babylonians by lowering the level of the Euphrates River on the outskirts of the city, thereby passing under its walls. The surprise element was enhanced, wrote Herodotus, by the fact that Babylon's leaders were engaged in some sort of celebration—apparently a reference to Belshazzar's feast.

One of the great mysteries of biblical history is the identity of "Darius the Mede" (5:31; 6:1, 28), the first Medo-Persian ruler of Babylon (c. 539). This Darius is mentioned nowhere else in all of recorded history. Some scholars believe he was an ally of Cyrus, who ruled Babylon until Cyrus himself took over. Others believe he was Cyrus himself. 6:28 has been used to support both sides in this debate: Some believe that the original Aramaic of the passage may read, ". . . in the reign of Darius, that is, the reign of Cyrus." Others cite the reference to "Cyrus the Persian" as the author's attempt to differentiate him from Darius the Mede. If Darius was someone other than Cyrus, his reign was brief, since it was Cyrus who issued the decree for the exiles' return in 538. Darius the Mede is not to be confused with the later Darius the Great (521–486), who encouraged the rebuilding of the Temple (see Ezra 5:1–6:15).

6:1-9 *Daniel despised, Darius deceived.* As soon as Darius took control of Babylon, Daniel became one of his top three advisors and was soon in line to be chief of that elite group (6:1-3). This made some of the other leaders jealous, and they conspired against him. Finding no way to blackmail Daniel, they convinced the king to pass a law that they assumed Daniel, because of his religion, would not obey: The law stated that no one in the kingdom could pray to anyone except the king! Perhaps out of pride, the king signed the decree. On the finality of Medo-Persian laws (6:8), see exposition on Esther 1:9-22.

6:10-15 *Faithful Daniel, remorseful Darius.* Hearing of the king's outrageous decree, Daniel prayed as usual and was immediately exposed by the watchful conspirators (6:10-13). Darius then regretted his decree and tried to set Daniel free. Those efforts having failed, he resigned himself to the fact that Daniel would die. The "room" in which Daniel prayed (6:10) was probably an upper chamber whose windows were kept open for air circulation. Daniel had "always" practiced rigorous spiritual disciplines, a quality of character already seen in his response to the royal diet (see 1:5-8).

6:16-28 *Lions and the lion-hearted.* As Daniel was thrown into the lions' den, Darius expressed confidence that God would deliver him. When the anxious king returned to the den the next morning, he found Daniel alive and praising God for protecting him (6:19-23). The king threw Daniel's accusers to the lions and issued a decree that Daniel's God should be honored throughout the empire (6:24-27; compare 3:29; 4:34-35). Once again, Daniel was in favor with Babylon's ruler (6:28).

7:1-8 *Godless kingdoms . . .* The Aramaic half of Daniel (see *Background*) ends with a vision of future Gentile kingdoms, similar to the vision of the statue (see 2:1-45). Daniel saw four beasts come up from the sea, one after the other:

- a winged lion, which then became human
- a bear "rearing up on one side"
- a leopard with four wings and four heads
- a dreadful fourth beast, unrecognizable as any known animal, which devoured everything with its "iron teeth"

The fourth beast had 10 horns and then sprouted another little horn that wrenched out three of the other horns and "was boasting arrogantly."

7:9-14 *. . . and the kingdom of God.* Daniel then saw a vision of God on his throne, surrounded by tens of thousands of angels, ready to open the "books" of judgment (7:9-10; compare Rev. 20:11-15). God destroyed the fourth beast, with its boastful horn. He took away the "authority" of the other three beasts but spared their lives. Then, "someone who looked like a man" or, as it is traditionally rendered, "one like a son of man" (7:13; see *Unique Features*) came "with the clouds of heaven" to God, who gave him an everlasting, universal kingdom (7:13-14).

The Aramaic term "Ancient of Days," describing God, appears only here in Scripture (7:9, 13, 22). Daniel's glimpse of God on his throne, however, recalls the similar experiences of Isaiah (see Isa. 6:1-7) and Ezekiel (see Ezek. 1).

7:15-28 *"What do these things mean?"* An angel explained that the four beasts represented "four kingdoms that will arise from the earth" (7:17). However, history's final great kingdom (7:14) will belong to God's people (7:18).

The angel was not as specific in identifying the four beasts as Daniel had been in identifying the statue's gold head as Nebuchadnezzar. However, the kingdoms represented by each beast can be identified by comparing them with other information contained in Daniel, especially the descriptions in the vision of the statue (see 2:1-45) and the precise identifications in the vision of the ram and goat in the next chapter (see 8:1-14):

- The first beast's lion-to-human transformation (7:4) may refer to Nebuchadnezzar's recovery from insanity (4:28-37).
- The bear with the upraised side (7:5) corresponds to the ram with two horns, one of which was longer than the other (8:3). Gabriel clearly identified this as the Medo-Persian coalition (8:20), in which Persia was the dominant partner.
- The leopard with four wings and heads (7:6) corresponds to the goat whose broken horn became four horns. Gabriel identified this as Greece (8:21).

Greece became four kingdoms after the death of Alexander the Great.

- The 10 horns of the fourth beast parallel the 10 toes on the statue's feet (2:41), suggesting that it, too, represents Rome (see exposition on 2:36-45).

Daniel asked the angel to explain more thoroughly the dreadful fourth beast and its blasphemous little horn, which he saw "waging war against the holy people" (7:19-22). The angel explained that this beast represented a fourth kingdom so much more evil as to be "different from all the others." The little horn was an especially evil ruler who would persecute believers but would eventually be defeated by God, whose kingdom would last forever (7:24-27).

This little horn is generally identified with the Antichrist spoken of in the NT writings of John and alluded to by other names elsewhere in Scripture (see exposition on the following passages: 8:15-27; 9:20-27; 11:36-45; 2 Thess. 2:1-12; 1 John 4:1-6; Rev. 13:1-10).

On "a time, times, and half a time," see exposition on 9:20-27.

GOD'S PROPHET FOR ISRAEL (8–12)

8:1-4 *"I'm the greatest," says the ram.* Having told of events in his life as a Babylonian public servant, and visions related to those events (1–7), Daniel then related several visions specifically concerning Israel and its place in world history (8–12). The first of these came in 549 B.C. Though it marks the first of Daniel's Hebrew visions (see *Background*), 8:1 suggests a connection between the vision of 8:1-14 and that of 7:1-14, given four years previously.

While the visions of 2:1-45 and 7:1-14 deal with four successive world empires, 8:1-14 deals with the middle two of those empires—Medo-Persia and Greece—and focuses mainly on a Greek ruler commonly identified as Antiochus Epiphanes. The kingdom Gabriel will later identify as Medo-Persia (8:20) is described as a ram with two horns, one longer than the other (8:3). The longer horn is Persia, the stronger half of the coalition (see exposition on 7:15-28). The ram would do "as it pleased," expanding westward at will.

8:5-14 *"You're history," says the goat.* The kingdom that Gabriel will later identify as Greece (8:21) is described as a goat that would come from the west and defeat the ram (8:5-7). This goat had a large horn (8:5), which later broke off and was replaced by four horns (8:8; compare 7:6). Out of one of these horns would grow a "small horn" (8:9), which would become dominant over many nations, including Israel (the "glorious land," 8:9); would exalt himself to divine status; and would try to prevent Israel from worshiping God (8:10-12). Daniel was told that this sacrilege would last 2,300 days (8:13-14).

8:15-27 *The who and when of the ram, goat, and horns.* Gabriel explained that the vision of the ram and goat referred to "the time of the end" (8:15-19; see 8:26), but he proceeded to give it a more contemporary meaning as well (8:20-26). The ram was Medo-Persia, and the goat was Greece. The goat's one large horn would logically represent Alexander the Great, whose kingdom was broken into four kingdoms (the four horns of 8:22) upon his death. The "small horn" (8:9; see 7:8) would be an extremely wicked king who would "devastate the holy people" (8:24) and even challenge the "Prince of princes," at which point he would be supernaturally defeated (8:25). This king would evidently seem well-intentioned at first (see exposition on 11:21-45), then, "when they [felt] secure, he [would] destroy many" (8:25, NIV). Gabriel also verified the 2,300-day duration of this evil king's reign.

While the description of this king seems clearly to be a foreshadowing of the Antichrist (see exposition on 1 John 4:1-6), his tie with the heirs of Alexander the Great leads most scholars to also identify him with Antiochus Epiphanes, who plundered the Temple and desecrated it by setting up a pagan shrine and offering a pig on the altar. Antiochus was anti-Semitic to the core, murdering more than 40,000 in three days and selling an equal number into slavery. Antiochus began his anti-Jewish campaign on September 6, 171 B.C., and continued until December 25, 165, when Judas Maccabeus restored true worship to the Temple (recorded in the apocryphal book of 1 Maccabees). This accounts for the 2,300 days of 8:14.

9:1-2 *"He said 70 years! It's almost time!"* From reading the writings of Jeremiah (see Jer. 25:11-12; 29:10), Daniel had concluded that Israel's time of captivity in Babylon was about to end. If the years of captivity are counted from 605 B.C., when Daniel was taken to Babylon (see exposition on Jer. 25:8-14), they would have been complete in 535, only two or three years after Daniel wrote these words ("in the first year of the reign of Darius," 9:1). The first group of exiles actually returned sooner than that, in 538.

9:3-19 *The prophet's prayer: "Renew and restore us."* Anticipating the momentous change in his people's fortunes, and overwhelmed by God's faithfulness, Daniel prayed a prayer of lamentation, repentance, and petition. He identified himself with the sins and unworthiness of his people (compare Ezra 9:5-7; Neh. 1:4-7).

9:20-27 *The secret of the 70 sevens.* As Daniel pondered the meaning of Jeremiah's prophecies (see 9:1-2) and of the visions revealed to him several years previously (7–8), God once again sent Gabriel to help him understand their meaning (9:20-23). Gabriel spoke of six things (9:24) that will have been accomplished for Israel at the end of "seventy sets of seven":

- The first three of these (9:24) have to do with a final resolution of Israel's sin problem.
- The second three (9:24) relate to the ushering in of an everlasting kingdom, characterized by "everlasting righteousness."

Bible scholars through the ages have seen 9:24 as a description of Christ's atonement for sin at Calvary and of his everlasting reign. Christ's work of salvation will, according to this interpretation, reach its fulfillment after three stages of prophecy—expressed as periods of weeks—have been fulfilled. Scholars generally agree that each "set of seven" (also translated "week") in this passage represents a "week of years," or seven years:

- 49 years after "the command is given to rebuild Jerusalem" (9:25), which occurred in about 444 or 445 B.C. (see Neh. 2:8), the work of rebuilding would be completed.
- After another "sixty-two sets of seven," or 434 years, "the Anointed One will be killed, appearing to have accomplished nothing" (9:26). It seems clear that this refers to Christ's death—which occurred 434 years later.
- There will be one more period of time before the ushering in of Messiah's everlasting kingdom—a period of "one set of seven," or seven years (9:26-27). This will be a time of great suffering and sacrilege, ruled over by an evil prince. This prince will at first seem well intentioned, making a "treaty" (or "covenant") with his subjects.

Then, "after half this time," that is, after three and a half years, "he will put an end to the sacrifices and offerings," "set up a sacrilegious object," and bring about great suffering. This final week is generally seen as the Great Tribulation, and the "ruler" of 9:26 as the Antichrist:

- The ruler's abrupt change of policy (9:27) corresponds with the about-face of Antiochus Epiphanes, the prototype of the Antichrist (see exposition on 8:15-27 and on 11:21-45). Scripture indicates elsewhere that the Antichrist will at first seem sympathetic to God's people (see 2 Thess. 2:3, 11; 1 John 2:18-19, 22; 4:1-6; 2 John 1:7).
- The three-and-a-half-year second half of the prince's reign matches other descriptions of the time-span of the second half of the Antichrist's reign:
- "A time, times, and half a time" (see 7:25; 12:7; Rev. 12:14), that is, a year plus two years plus half a year
  - 1,260 days (see Rev. 11:3), or three and a half 360-day years
  - 42 months (see Rev. 11:2; 13:5)

Though the entire final seven-year "week" is usually referred to as the Tribulation, in the most technical sense only the second three and a half years would qualify for this designation, since only then will the Antichrist shed his peacemaker facade and become a ruthless persecutor.

- The time gap between the 69th and 70th weeks that this interpretation necessitates could represent the "church age." As an OT prophet, Daniel's concern would have been God's special dealings with Israel; his prophecy would not have included the years between Calvary and the end times.

The Hebrew word that many Bible versions translate "week" (9:24) is actually *seven;* therefore, 9:24 literally reads "70 sevens." That the 70 sevens is actually 70 "weeks of years," or 490 years, seems logical in light of Jeremiah's earlier prophecies concerning the exile: The exile was to last 70 years (see Jer. 25:11-12; 29:10), which, according to the chronicler, would make up for the 490 years during which Israel had failed to observe the Sabbath year (see 2 Chron. 36:21; Lev. 25:2-5; 26:34-35, 43). Except for the gap between the 69th and 70th years, the 490 years leading up to Israel's exile will be equaled by 490 years leading up to its final triumph.

10:1–11:1 *"I'm here to help. . . . Sorry I'm late!"* Shortly after the first group of Jews had returned to Jerusalem in 538 B.C., Daniel, remaining in Babylon, had another vision of the future. (Daniel would have been at least 85 by this time.) The vision was terrifying and emotionally draining (10:7-9). An angel told Daniel that he had been sent to explain the vision (10:14) but had been opposed in his mission by the "spirit prince of the kingdom of Persia" (10:13). This being, whom most commentators understand to be a fallen angel, was in turn opposed and overcome by the good angel Michael (10:13). Daniel then saw another heavenly being (10:16), to whom he expressed his sense of awe and humility in light of the vision he had seen (10:15-17). This second being spoke also of having fought against the "spirit prince of Persia" and of his association with Michael (10:18–11:1), and again promised to explain the vision to Daniel (10:19-21). Some scholars see the angel of 10:5 as a preincarnate appearance of Christ (see exposition on 3:19-30).

11:2-20 *A chronology of godless kings.* The angel then explained Daniel's terrifying vision: Persia's day of glory would climax with a king who would challenge the rising Greek Empire (11:2). Then would come a "mighty king" whose empire would be divided and given to four kings unrelated to him (11:3-4), evidently another reference to Alexander (see 7:6; 8:5-8, 21-22). 11:5-20 describes prolonged warfare between Alexander's generals Ptolemy of Egypt ("king of the south," 11:5) and Seleucus of Syria ("king of the north," 11:6). Antiochus III, a descendant of Seleucus, lost a great battle with Egypt but eventually defeated it (11:10-20). Both he and his successor oppressed Israel, the "glorious land" (11:16, 20).

11:21-35 *A chronology of Antiochus Epiphanes.* The Seleucid Empire (Syria) would then be seized by intrigue by a "despicable man" known to secular history as Antiochus IV or Antiochus Epiphanes, who would at first behave peaceably toward his subjects (11:24) but would then "take over the Temple fortress, polluting the sanctuary, putting a stop to the daily sacrifices, and setting up the sacrilegious object that causes desecration" (11:31; see exposition on 8:15-27).

11:36-45 *A chronology of the Antichrist.* Just as 8:15-27 apparently describes both Antiochus Epiphanes and the future Antichrist, 11:21-45 seems to describe both as well, with 11:36 marking the transition from the former to the latter. (Note that, according to 11:40, the king of 11:36 is neither the king of the north nor the king of the south, which allows the possibility of his being the Antichrist.) During the second half of the Tribulation, the Antichrist will do battle against Israel and many nations but will finally be defeated—apparently a reference to Armageddon (11:40-45; see Rev. 19:11-21).

Once again, as in 9:26, Daniel's vision skips over the church age, focusing only on God's dealings with Israel.

12:1-4 *"The worst is yet to come, but then they'll understand."* The angel warned Daniel that the Tribulation will be a time of unprecedented suffering (see Jer. 30:7). Yet Michael the archangel will watch over Israel, and the righteous will be delivered. Those already dead will be resurrected, "some to everlasting life" and some to "everlasting contempt." At that time, people will finally understand Daniel's prophecies.

12:2 is the OT's clearest teaching on the resurrection and afterlife (see exposition on Isa. 26:1-19) and the only OT passage differentiating between the destiny of the righteous and the unrighteous (see Rev. 20:4-6, 11-15; exposition on John 5:24-30 and on 1 Cor. 15:20-28). See also 12:13.

12:5-13 *"How long?" Two interesting answers.* Two more heavenly beings appeared and asked the angel how long it would take for the visions to be fulfilled. The angel replied that "a time, times, and half a time," or three and a half years (see exposition on 9:20-27) after Israel has been shattered, "all these things will have happened"—evidently meaning that the Antichrist himself will be defeated (compare 11:45).

Confused by the visions, Daniel asked the angel to explain them further (12:8). The angel reassured Daniel that these things would not happen until "the time of the end" (12:9) and that God would resurrect him at the end of time (12:13). Yet he also left Daniel two more cryptic references to time to ponder:

- From the time when the Antichrist turns against Israel and desecrates its worship, there will be 1,290 days (12:11)—30 days longer than the 1,260 days (three and a half 360-day years) of Revelation 11:3. The extra 30 days may allow for the judgment at the end of the Tribulation (see Ezek. 34:17, 22; Matt. 25:31-46).

- The angel then suggested that the final half of the Tribulation will last 1,335 days—another 45 days longer than the 1,290 days of 12:11! Since those who "wait" for the full 1,335 days will be "blessed," this may represent the time at which Christ's millennial reign begins (see *Isaiah: Background*).

❖ ❖ ❖

PEOPLE TO REMEMBER FROM DANIEL

BELSHAZZAR

Key Facts: King of Babylon, recipient of handwriting on wall
Total Bible References: 8
Key References: 5

Belshazzar Speaks

Those stupid soldiers—running around outside, trying to get in! How do they expect to breach these high walls! They may not realize the walls are also 87 feet thick—and that we're watching them from dozens of watchtowers! Go home and stop wasting your time!

Ah, the banquet hall! It's awfully loud in there. I guess that means everyone is having a good time! Must be at least a thousand of them. Well, time for my big announcement . . .

Leaders of Babylon! The purpose of this state dinner is two-fold: First, to show our contempt for those Persian troops outside; and second, to ridicule the Judean God who humbled Nebuchadnezzar. You have before you some of the actual gold and silver vessels taken from the Jewish Temple, all filled with wine. Now join me in a special toast, praising our gods with the sacred cups of Jehovah! (5:2-4, 20)

But wait, what's happening? The hall has suddenly become deathly silent. Why are my guests gasping in horror? What's that? . . . A hand? . . . writing on the wall above me! Quick . . . I must control myself . . . and this crowd. . . .

"Whoever can read this writing and tell me what it means will be dressed in purple robes of royal honor and will wear a gold chain around his neck. He will become the third-highest ruler in the kingdom!" (5:5-7)

My magicians and astrologers shake their heads in fear. They can't read it! Now, a message from the queen mother. Daniel the prophet can, she says! Then go and get Daniel immediately! I'll offer him the same bribe—third ruler in the kingdom! (5:8-16)

Now, what's this? Daniel refuses my gifts? How dare he publicly rebuke me for my pride! I would rebuke *him,* but then that writing hand might strike me dead! (5:17-23)

Wonderful! He's going to tell me the message of the writing . . . without cost—just one more public humiliation for me!

Am I hearing him right, or is this horrible fear affecting my mind? He tells me the Judean "God has numbered the days of [my] reign and has brought it to an end." He says it will be given to the Persians! But how can they possibly breach our defenses? (5:24-28)

What's that? Enemy soldiers are now inside the city! Marduk has been defeated by Jehovah! I'm doomed! (5:30-31)

Spiritual Lessons from Belshazzar

This wicked king would learn four important lessons but would learn all of them too late:

- Mere humans cannot ridicule almighty God without paying a frightful price (5:1-4, 30).
- In crisis situations, solutions will most likely come from godly people (5:7-17).
- Those who fail to learn from the past end up repeating it (5:18-23).
- Those who seek their own glory in this life may find themselves suddenly humiliated by God (5:25-28). Those who seek God's glory in this life will one day receive a "crown" from him (see 2 Tim. 4:6-8).

Key Verses

"You are his successor, O Belshazzar, and you knew all this, yet you have not humbled yourself. For you have defied the Lord of heaven. . . . So God has sent this hand to write a message. This is the message that was written: MENE, MENE, TEKEL, PARSIN. This is what these words mean: *Mene* means 'numbered'—God has numbered the days of your reign and has brought it to an end. *Tekel* means 'weighed'—you have been weighed on the balances and have failed the test. *Parsin* means 'divided'—your kingdom has been divided and given to the Medes and Persians" (5:22-28).

DANIEL

Key Facts: Israelite exile, prime minister in Babylon, prophet (1:1-6; 2:48-49; 5:10-12; 6:1-3)

Total Bible References: 87

Key References: 1–12; Ezek. 14:14; Matt. 24:15

Daniel Speaks

I wish them God's blessings as they leave for Jerusalem, all 50,000 of them! With Zerubbabel leading them, they're in good hands. God has not told me to leave, so I shall remain here. (Ezra 1:1-5; 2:2, 64)

How different Jerusalem must have become since I last saw it as a young man some 67 years ago. So much has happened during that time. Solomon's Temple has been destroyed and the Holy City burned. Both Nebuchadnezzar and Belshazzar are dead, and the Persians now rule the Middle East. (1:1-6; 5:30; 2 Kings 25:1-10)

Of course I warned both Nebuchadnezzar and Belshazzar of this takeover by Persia. Cyrus probably doesn't know it, but I also predicted that his empire will fall to the Greeks . . . and theirs to the Romans! What a series of glorified dogfights! (2:39-43; 5:26-28; 7:6)

How faithful God has been to his people during our long captivity, proving he is indeed Lord of both fire and wild beasts. He has honored me personally through the many visions he gave our people through me. Some of those dreams actually made me physically ill. Of course, God's judgment on sin is never a pleasant matter. That's why so much pain and bloodshed still lies ahead. (3:24-25; 6:22; 8:27; 10:7-8; 12:1)

Yet I depart this life peaceful and confident, knowing there will arise after those four brutal kingdoms a blessed fifth and final one, ruled over by the Messiah himself. I described this glorious reign to both Nebuchadnezzar and Belshazzar:

"I saw someone who looked like a man coming with the clouds of heaven. He approached the Ancient One and was led into his presence. He was given authority, honor, and royal power over all the nations of the world, so that people of every race and nation and language would obey him. His rule is eternal—it will never end. His kingdom will never be destroyed." (7:13-14; 2:44)

Spiritual Lessons from Daniel

- While godliness is not always valued by nonbelievers, in Daniel's case his high spiritual standards actually led to political success (1:8-21).
- Daniel refused payment from Belshazzar for proclaiming his God-given message; the truth is not for sale! (5:17; compare Gen. 14:21-23)
- We should pray in the good times as well as in the bad times; Daniel was praying even before he was faced with the threat of the lions' den (6:10).
- When praying about the sins of others, we should confess our own sins as well (9:3-4; see Ezra 9:5-7; Neh. 1:4-7).
- God does not always answer all our questions (12:8-13; see John 21:21-22; Acts 1:6-7).

Key Verse

"This man Daniel, whom the king named Belteshazzar, has a sharp mind and is filled with divine knowledge and understanding. He can interpret dreams, explain riddles, and solve difficult problems. Call for Daniel, and he will tell you what the writing means" (5:12).

DARIUS

Key Facts: Persian king, tricked into putting Daniel into the lions' den (6:12-16)
Total Bible References: 8
Key References: 5:31–6:28

Darius Speaks

No doubt about it, he's the greatest and most unique person I've ever met. How well I remember our first encounter: There he stood, like a spiritual rock amid the overturned tables, crushed wine vessels, and the panic-filled mob rushing about aimlessly in that chaotic banquet hall. Well, I decided right then and there that he would be the one to oversee this new outpost of our kingdom. (5:5–6:3)

Little did I realize, though, the insane envy this would create in the minds of certain petty politicians. I still bristle with anger when recalling their vicious plan to throw him to the lions by my own command. Well, the big cats had their feast, but with a different menu than they had planned! (6:4-9, 24)

I'm not a religious man, but perhaps the God of Daniel deserves closer consideration. None of our gods would ever protect us like Daniel's God protected him. I wonder if that angel was the same one that helped me during the first year of my reign? Whatever the future, my decree speaks for itself: "I decree that everyone throughout my kingdom should tremble with fear before the God of Daniel. For he is the living God." (6:22, 26; 11:1)

Spiritual Lessons from Darius

- Be wary of flattery (6:1-8).
- As the adage says, "Act in haste; repent at leisure." If you act rashly, without thinking, you are likely to later regret it (6:9-14).

Key Verses

"Then King Darius sent this message to the people of every race and nation and language throughout the world: 'Peace and prosperity to you! I decree that everyone throughout my kingdom should tremble with fear before the God of Daniel. For he is the living God, and he will endure forever. His kingdom will never be destroyed, and his rule will never end. He rescues and saves his people; he performs miraculous signs and wonders in the heavens and on earth. He has rescued Daniel from the power of the lions'" (6:25-27).

NEBUCHADNEZZAR

Key Facts: King of Babylon, founder of neo-Babylonian empire (3; 4:30; 2 Kings 24:1)
Father: Nabopolassar
Total Bible References: 91
Key References: 1–4; 2 Kings 24–25; Jer. 21–52

Nebuchadnezzar Speaks

"O King Nebuchadnezzar, please listen to me. Stop sinning and do what is right. Break from your wicked past by being merciful to the poor." (4:27)

Stinging words indeed! How they shocked and offended me! Of course, Daniel was absolutely the only person in the entire kingdom who would have dared rebuke me like that—and not have forfeited his head in the process! I've condemned people to death for far less! (2:1-13)

But I owe both my sanity and my salvation to Daniel's God. Could Marduk have revealed my dreams, or would he have been able to protect his followers in a furnace of fire? To ask the question is to answer it. (2:28; 3:26-30)

But the Hebrew God did both! How ironic to think that I once burned his city, destroyed his Temple, and carried into captivity thousands of his loyal worshipers—fine people such as Daniel, Shadrach, Meshach, Abednego, and Ezekiel. Who could have possibly known back then that someday their God would become my God! (1:1-6; 2 Kings 25:1-10; Ezek. 40:1)

But the fourth man in the fire and those seven years of insanity were more than sufficient to convince me that Jehovah is Lord of lords! (3:25; 4:3, 25, 33, 37)

Spiritual Lessons from Nebuchadnezzar

- People who can't make up their minds "waver back and forth in everything they do" (James 1:7-8). Nebuchadnezzar was like that in his initial treatment of the Jews, trying both to bow down and worship them (2:46) and to burn them (3:20-21).

- This double-mindedness may have resulted from his uncontrollable fury (2:12; 3:19) and great pride (4:30).
- "But as people sinned more and more, God's wonderful kindness became more abundant" (Rom. 5:20). There is strong evidence that Nebuchadnezzar became a believer (4:1-3, 34-37).

Key Verse
"Now I, Nebuchadnezzar, praise and glorify and honor the King of heaven. All his acts are just and true, and he is able to humble those who are proud" (4:37).

HOSEA

BACKGROUND

The reign of Jeroboam II in Israel's northern kingdom (793–753 B.C.) was the "golden age" of the north, with great military successes and a thriving economy. Spiritually, however, the nation did not do so well. Hosea began his prophetic ministry near the end of Jeroboam's reign, and during most of his 40 years of ministry things only became worse, climaxing in Israel's fall in 722 (see 2 Kings 17). Four of Israel's final six kings assassinated their predecessors ("one murder after another," 4:2). As the last prophet before Israel's fall, Hosea pleaded with his people to turn to God and be saved. He warned of Israel's coming judgment but also of its final restoration. He has been called "the prophet of immediate doom and eventual hope."

In obedience to an unusual instruction from God, Hosea married a prostitute and, as could be expected, endured her unfaithfulness in marriage (1–3). The lessons he learned from his marriage helped him address the issue of Israel's unfaithfulness to God (4–14).

Hosea's ministry overlapped that of Amos and the first half of the ministries of Isaiah and Micah.

AUTHOR

Hosea's mission was to the northern kingdom, and he was probably from that area as well. His many illustrations drawn from agriculture suggest he may have been a farmer. His name means "salvation."

DATE AND LOCATION

Hosea's ministry probably began c. 760 B.C. and ended c. 720, two years after the northern kingdom's fall. It is likely that he is one who escaped (see exposition on 2 Chron. 30:1-9). He may have fled to the southern kingdom and completed his writings there.

931 B.C. Kingdom divides, Israel, Judah

760 Hosea begins ministry

740 Isaiah begins ministry

722 Fall of Israel

720 Hosea's last prophecy

586 Fall of Judah

RECIPIENTS
Though he mentions Judah as well, Hosea addressed his prophecies primarily to the northern kingdom, which he often referred to as "Ephraim," the dominant tribe.

PURPOSE
To warn of God's impending judgment on Israel while showing the balance between his justice and his love:
- God's *love* does not mean he can forget sin. Sin must be punished.
- On the other hand, God's *justice* does not mean that he desires to completely end his relationship with his "wife" (Israel). God constantly tries to draw Israel back to himself. Even in the wake of judgment he will preserve a remnant.

UNIQUE FEATURES
- Hosea was the only prophet from the northern kingdom who recorded his prophecies (though Jonah was from the north, the book of Jonah is primarily a narrative about him, not by him).
- He was the only prophet to minister to the northern kingdom right up to its fall. He has been called "the deathbed prophet of Israel."

COMPARISON WITH OTHER BIBLE BOOKS
Isaiah:
- Both used the illustration of a husband and wife to portray God and Israel (2:19; Isa. 54:5).
- Both Hosea and Isaiah had children with symbolic names (1:4, 6, 9; Isa. 7:3; 8:3-4, 18).
- Both called God the "Holy One," a rare title for God outside of Isaiah (11:9, 12; about 30 times in Isaiah).

OUTLINE
A CASE STUDY IN ADULTERY: GOMER (1–3)
A CASE STUDY IN ADULTERY: ISRAEL (4–14)
  The charges against Israel (4–7)
  The coming judgment of Israel (8–10)
  The final restoration of Israel (11–14)

A CASE STUDY IN ADULTERY: GOMER (1–3)

1:1-2 *The prophet and the prostitute: A marriage made in heaven?* God instructed Hosea to marry a prostitute, who would then bear him "children . . . born to [him] from other men" (1:2). The text of Hosea, along with other Bible books, suggests some reasons for this most unusual directive:

- *The experiential reason:* Marriage to an unfaithful wife would help Hosea understand God's anguish over his people's spiritual fornication. God often compared his relationship to Israel to a marriage (see 2:19; Isa. 62:5; Jer. 3:14), and its frequent apostasy to adultery or prostitution (1:2; see 4:12; Isa. 1:21; Jer. 3:1).

- *The illustrative reason:* Hosea's marriage would provide a real-life example of his message to Israel (1:2; see 3:1).
- *The prophetic reason:* God would direct Hosea to give his children names describing the future punishment and eventual restoration of Israel.

1:3-9 *Tragic names for their children.* Hosea married Gomer, and she bore him three children, to each of whom God gave a prophetic name:

- Jezreel, their first son, would remind Israel that God would soon punish Jehu's dynasty for the brutal murders he committed at Jezreel. While Jehu's destruction of Ahab's family was commended by the Lord (see 2 Kings 10:30-31), Jehu's wholesale slaughter of many others apparently went beyond the Lord's intent.
- The daughter's name, Lo-ruhamah, meant "not loved" and had a double significance:
  - ➤ God's compassion for Israel, the northern kingdom, had come to an end; its judgment was imminent.
  - ➤ However, God still had compassion for Judah, the southern kingdom, and would deliver it through supernatural means (see 2 Kings 19).
- Their second son's name, Lo-ammi, means "not my people." This was not a denial of God's unconditional covenant with Abraham (see Gen. 12:1-3). That covenant continues to the present day, unchanged though as yet unfulfilled (1:10–2:1; see Rom. 11:1-2). God was speaking through Lo-ammi to those Israelites who, while related to Abraham physically, were not related to him or his God spiritually.

1:10–2:1 *Better names someday.* Looking beyond his coming judgment on Israel, the Lord promised that the judgment would someday be reversed, and Israel would be loved (Ruhamah) and would become his people (Ammi) once again. They would be "like the sands of the seashore" in number (1:10; see Gen. 22:17). This, of course, will happen when Israel repents and receives a new heart (see exposition on Jer. 31:31-34).

Paul explicitly applied the promise of 1:10 to Gentiles as well as Jews (see Rom. 9:23-25; 1 Pet. 2:10).

2:2-5 *"Try to reason with your mother!"* Looking beyond Hosea's personal domestic tragedy, God charged Israel, his wife, with adultery, and urged "her" believing children to call her to repentance. Just as Gomer had sought "food and drink . . . clothing of wool and linen" from other men, Israel had sought spiritual sustenance from false gods.

2:6-13 *"I'll try anything to keep her from sin!"* Both God and Hosea tried desperately to keep their "wife" from sin, thinking she would surely come to her senses (2:6-7). Surely she would come to realize that her true blessings came from her true husband, not from her adulterous lovers (2:8). Just as the Israelites at Sinai had taken their God-given wealth and made the golden calf, so the Israelites of Hosea's day were using their God-given wealth to worship Baal (2:8).

Hosea (like God) was prepared to go to great lengths to bring his wife back to her rightful place. He would deprive her of her luxuries, expose her before her lovers, and remove every occasion of joy from her life. Hopefully then, instead of finding her deviation satisfying, she would realize that her sin had consequences (2:9-13).

2:14-23 *Her story will have a happy ending!* If Gomer and Israel would deal with their sin, they would find restoration and joy (2:14-17). "In that coming day," referring to the end of human history (see exposition on Isa. 2:5–4:1), Israel's restoration will result in the lifting of the curse from nature (2:18, 21-23; see Rom. 8:19-22). Warfare will end (2:18; see Isa. 2:4). The people will once again own the Lord as their God, in fulfillment of the New Covenant (see Jer. 31:31-34). The tragedy that had befallen both Gomer and the nation Israel will be completely reversed. That new day (2:21-23) will be better even than the days of Israel's youth (2:15). The names of Hosea's children will change to their positive meanings of "love" and "my people" (2:23). Even Jezreel will be known not as bloodshed but as its positive meaning: "God plants" (2:22).

3:1-5 *The power of love and hope.* God told Hosea to reclaim Gomer from her life of adultery, as an example of his love for adulterous Israel. Hosea literally bought his wife back and begged her to stay with him. He saw their loveless marriage as a symbol of Israel, which would for "a long time" be committed neither to idolatry nor to God (3:4). Yet he was confident that Israel would one day return to its rightful husband (3:5).

The price Hosea paid to redeem Gomer indicates the depth to which she had sunk. The usual price for a slave was 30 shekels of silver (see Exod. 21:32), but he paid only 15 for Gomer. Barley was considered fit only for animals.

Hosea's vision of a religionless Israel (3:4) seems prophetic of the agnosticism common among many Jews today, who are committed neither to their own nor any other religious tradition. Yet in God's appointed time, Israel will come to its senses and experience a national regeneration (3:5; see Jer. 31:31-34). Then, they will "return to the LORD their God and to David's descendant, their king," that is, Christ the Son of David.

A CASE STUDY IN ADULTERY: ISRAEL (4–14)

4:1-3 *The indictment against Israel.* Having experienced the unfaithfulness of his own wife (1–3), Hosea spoke to Israel about its unfaithfulness to God (4–14). Hosea charged Israel with having totally forsaken God and having therefore become hopelessly immoral. This had brought great suffering on the whole nation. Sin affects not only the human sinner but animate and inanimate creation as well (4:3).

4:4-10 *Like priests, like people!* All Israel was guilty before God. When God sent them priests to reveal his will, they only argued with them (4:4). Therefore they would "stumble" even in broad daylight (4:5). Because they had willfully rejected knowledge of God, he would reject them as his witnesses to the world (4:6; see exposition on Isa. 43:8-13). Both laypeople and priests had become hopelessly corrupt, feeding off each other's sin. God would bring their false religion to naught (4:7-10).

Humanity's problem is not a lack of information about God but willful rejection of the abundant information available. Just as both people and priest encouraged each other's sin in Hosea's time, churches today often call pastors who will be like them rather than help them to be like God.

4:11-19 *Idolatry, intoxication, immorality: Substitutes for truth.* Because Israel had strayed from its true God (4:12), it had become involved in idolatry, drunkenness, and depraved sexual sins. Israel ("Ephraim," 13:12) was beyond hope and should be left alone (compare exposition on Jer. 7:16-27). The people of Judah were warned against associating with their northern relatives (4:15). Israel's decision to reject God was futile and would ultimately bring judgment (4:19). Those who reject God always seek a substitute to fill the resulting void.

5:1-7 *Sins too great, sacrifices too late.* Though Israel and its leaders had not ignored God, their spiritual defection and adultery did not escape God's notice. Try as they might to hide their true condition, God saw them for what they were (5:1-3). They were enslaved by their sins (5:4-5). Judah shared in Israel's sin and would also share in its judgment (5:5). When they came to the end of themselves and finally sought God with their religious formality, they would not find him, for he would have withdrawn himself from them (5:6).

5:8-15 *He'll strike like a lion, then he'll retire.* Hosea called on the ram's horn to sound the warning of judgment. Again he noted the willful nature of Israel's sin (5:11). "Determined to worship idols" (5:11) recalls Jeroboam's blatantly rejecting the Aaronic priesthood, installing his own priests, and setting up golden calves at Dan and Bethel (see exposition on 1 Kings 12:25-33).

Israel's decay would be rapid, like that caused by a moth; Judah would decay more gradually, like dry rot (5:12). Judgment would fall on the southern kingdom 136 years after it fell on the north, but it would be equally certain for both (5:13-14). When destruction came, God would withdraw from his people, allowing their well-deserved punishment to bring them to repentance (5:15).

6:1-3 *Looking ahead to the Millennium.* Hosea looked beyond the Assyrian and Babylonian captivities, to the day when Israel as a nation will be converted (see Jer. 31:31-34) and God will set up his millennial kingdom. A remnant of Israelites, both northern and southern, would repent during and after the Assyrian and Babylonian captivities (see exposition on Isa. 10:20-23); but at the end of time, the entire nation will turn to God (see Rom. 11:26-27).

6:4-11 *What should he do to them?* Throughout their centuries of spiritual vacillation, God had often confronted Israel and Judah through his priests and prophets (6:4-6). But just like Adam, they deliberately disobeyed (6:7). Thus the Lord's rhetorical question: "What should I do with you?" (6:4). Judah would fare no better in judgment than Israel, for it had committed the same sins (6:11). Judah would have ample opportunity to learn from the northern kingdom's fall, but tragically would not (see exposition on Jer. 3:6-11; on 6:6, see 1 Sam. 15:22; Matt. 9:13; 12:7).

7:1-10 *God and his unwilling patient.* God wanted to heal Israel's spiritual disease, but Israel wasn't interested (7:1-3). Like a hot oven, the people were consumed with sexual passion (7:4-7). In dividing its loyalties between God and its pagan neighbors, Israel was like a half-baked cake, burned on one side by the overheated oven (7:8-10).

7:11-16 *Choosing the wrong friends.* Like a silly dove, Israel tried to play Egypt and Assyria against each other through political alliances, while failing to trust in God as its true security (see *Isaiah: Background* and exposition on Isa. 30:1-17). God would see to it, therefore, that both nations would turn against them (7:12, 16; see 2 Kings 17).

8:1-14 *They'll reap more than they sow!* Israel's sin was so great that no eleventh-hour repentance could save it (8:2-3). Israel had sown the seed of its own defeat and would reap much more than it had sown (8:7). God would sweep them away in judgment, and the blessings that should have been theirs would be "swallowed up" by their conquerors (8:7-8). God had wanted Israel for himself, but they had "sold themselves" to foreign lovers and followed pagan religions (8:9-14). Judgment must surely come to both Israel and Judah.

Though Judah's final defeat would not come till 586 B.C.—136 years after Israel's fall to Assyria in 722—the Assyrian king Sennacherib would invade Judah in 701 and destroy all of the fortified cities except Jerusalem, which would be miraculously spared (8:14; see 1:7; 2 Kings 18:13–19:37).

On Samaria's "calf" (8:5), see 1 Kings 12:25-33. Israel would figuratively return to the bondage of "Egypt" (8:13), though this time in Assyria.

9:1-9 *Their sentence: Exile in Assyria.* Because the people of Israel had behaved "like prostitutes" with foreign gods (9:1-2), they would be exiled to "Egypt," that is, Assyria (9:3-6). Israel's sin had so completely warped their spiritual discernment that they considered God's true prophets to be insane fools (9:7-8). They had become as depraved as the men who committed the unspeakable atrocity at Gibeah (9:9; see Judg. 19).

9:10-14 *Their curse: Barren wombs.* Like a caring father, the Lord looked back to the time when Israel became a nation, portraying it as grapes in the wilderness and the firstfruit of a fig tree. Israel had been a pleasure to God as he anticipated their growth (9:10). Now, in his anger, he pronounced a curse on the entire process of procreation and child rearing (9:10-14). To people of that day, barrenness was the worst of all curses. The prophet could wish no greater judgment on Israel.

9:15-17 *From Gilgal to exile.* Citing Gilgal as a symbol of Israel's sin, God cursed the nation once more with barrenness and exile. They would become "wanderers, homeless among the nations." Gilgal was a place of idol worship (see 12:11; Amos 4:4) and was also the place where Israel had made Saul its first king (see 1 Sam. 11:14-15), doubly signifying Israel's rejection of God, its true King.

Though a few people from the northern tribes would escape to Judah when Israel fell and some would remain in the land (see exposition on 2 Chron. 30:1-9), the majority would never return from exile. Yet these 10 "lost tribes" are known to God (see James 1:1; Rev. 7:4-8), and in his time they will all be restored (see exposition on Jer. 31:31-34 and on Ezek. 37:1-28).

10:1-8 *The more it received, the more it rebelled.* The more God had blessed Israel, the more they had used those blessings to finance their paganism, but God would break down their pagan altars (10:1-2). Neither their king nor their idols could save them; in shame and desperation they would call on the mountains to cover them (10:3-8; see Luke 23:30; Rev. 6:16). Recalling again the atrocity at Gibeah (10:9; see 9:9), the Lord implied that the present generation was as depraved as the wicked men of Gibeah (see Judg. 19–20). Comparing Israel to a "trained heifer," he declared that, though he had made their work enjoyable, he would now subject them to harsh discipline (10:11).

10:12-15 *Want to reap love? Sow righteousness!* Israel could find mercy instead of judgment, if only they would repent and seek righteousness. God called on them to repent right away (10:12). Otherwise, the only option was judgment (10:13-15).

11:1-7 *Their tragic journey: From Egypt to Canaan . . . to Assyria.* God spoke tenderly of his deep love for Israel, comparing it to the love of a father for a disobedient child. He had "taught Israel how to walk," that is, revealed his will to them. He "took care of" them and "stooped to feed" them. He had remained faithful though they were faithless. Now, despite his great reluctance to do so (11:8), he must punish them—this time with exile in Assyria instead of Egypt (11:5; see 8:13; 9:3).

Matthew applied 11:1 to Christ (see Matt. 2:15). God called both Israel and Jesus his son (see Exod. 4:22-23), and both lived for a while in Egypt. Matthew's use of the passage shows the beautiful identification of the Son of God with the historical people of God. Both had a unique relationship with the Father.

11:8-11 *Punished with regret, restored with rejoicing.* Though the Israelites deserved their punishment, God, as a loving Father, was reluctant to bring it about (11:8-9). Therefore, even as he was preparing their punishment, he was also preparing their everlasting salvation (11:10-11). He will "roar like a lion," summoning them from their lands of captivity (compare Isa. 11:12; 43:5-6; Ezek. 37:12). They will return like a flock of birds—not like the silly doves of 7:11, but "trembling" with a proper sense of awe before their Redeemer, who will restore them to their land.

11:12–12:6 *"Back to Bethel!"* Israel was seeking spiritual life from idolatry, which was as hot and dry as the desert wind (11:12–12:1). Though Judah, compared to Israel, was still walking with God (11:12), it too had forgotten its source of life. Jacob, who even in the womb had "wrestled" with Esau for the blessing of the firstborn (see Gen. 25:26) and had later more literally wrestled a blessing from God (see Gen. 32:22-32), had found at Bethel the place of true worship and blessing (see Gen. 28:10-22). God implied that his people should return to Bethel for a face-to-face encounter with him.

In calling them back to Bethel, God had in view Bethel as it had been in Jacob's time, not Bethel as it had become—a place of idolatry (see 5:8-15; 10:15; Amos 4:4; 5:5).

12:7-14 *But they prefer gold to God!* Israel was interested only in getting rich through trade with its pagan neighbors (12:7-8). God had shown Israel his love and faithfulness by sending his prophets time and again to call them back to himself (12:9-10). But instead of being thankful to God for his protection, Israel had provoked him by pursuing materialism and idolatry. Therefore God must punish them; they will reap the harvest of the sin they have sown.

13:1-3 *Once like champions, now like chaff.* When Israel ("Ephraim") had been obedient to God, the whole world respected them (13:1). But as they descended into idolatry, they had lost that influence and were now no more powerful than dew or chaff. Though Israel may still have appeared to be prosperous, its days were numbered and it would pass away.

13:4-14 *From rejection, to rejection, to restoration.* God had saved Israel from Egypt only to find that, once they were secure, they rejected him (13:4-6). Therefore God must reject them (see 14:4-7), but eventually he will restore them (see 14:4-7). Ultimately, Israel's defection will result not in the death of the nation but in the death of death itself (13:14; compare 1 Cor. 15:55)!

13:15-16 *Judgment like the desert wind.* Again using the figure of the hot east wind, Hosea warned of Israel's imminent judgment. It would be a time of unspeakable suffering.

14:1-8 *"Return, and he will redeem!"* One last time Hosea urged his nation to repent and humbly return to God (14:1-3) and noted God's words of welcome to his repentant people (14:4-8). Even though Israel's sin would bring about its downfall, it was not beyond the scope of God's redeeming grace. No matter how serious had been their sin-sickness, their healing and restoration would be complete. Their sin had made them the targets of God's wrath and judgment. Their repentance would make them the objects of his love (14:4). Restoration would be possible because they would have dealt with their sin and idolatry (14:8). Because their sin had been dealt with, their fruit would be pleasing to God (14:8).

14:9 *The wise will walk in his path!* Those in fellowship with God would understand what Hosea had written. Those who resisted God would not understand and would be judged.

PEOPLE TO REMEMBER FROM HOSEA

HOSEA

Key Facts: Prophet, told by God to marry a prostitute (1:2)
Father: Beeri (1:1)
Wife: Gomer (1:2-3)
Sons: Jezreel, Lo-ammi (1:4, 9)
Daughter: Lo-ruhamah (1:6)
Total Bible References: 4
Key References: 1–14; Rom. 9:25

Hosea Speaks

She's gone again! In spite of the pleading from Jezreel, she's gone! In spite of all my attempts to keep her home, she's gone again! Why, oh, why did he order me to marry a prostitute? As I could have predicted, she's been nothing but unfaithful ever since the wedding. (1:2; 2:5-6)

But even more disturbing was his command just yesterday: "Go and get your wife again. Bring her back to you and love her, even though she loves adultery." (3:1)

I reminded the Lord that this was a violation of his own Word, but he told me to find her anyway. Of course I did what he ordered. I found Gomer in the slave market, where she had been dumped by her lovers. I was able to redeem her for 15 shekels of silver and five bushels of barley and some wine—not much of a price for a human being, however sinful! (3:2)

Time and again I have asked the reason for all this, but of course the answer is obvious: My miserable marriage has served as a sensational illustration of the marriage between God and his unfaithful wife, Israel. His wife, like mine, is notorious for sharing her bed with pagan idols. So in some small way I can sympathize with him. Jehovah's hurt is my hurt. My pain is his pain. (4:12)

Well, whatever my suffering, I count it an honor to serve as his prophet, for ours is the privilege of knowing the future. I know how God's troubled marriage will end. His wife will repent and be fully restored. As he has said, "I will heal you of your idolatry and faithlessness, and my love will know no bounds, for my anger will be gone forever!" (14:4)

That's what the future holds for his marriage. I'm not so sure about mine.

Spiritual Lessons from Hosea

- Though God's calling Hosea to marry a prostitute was very unusual and was for a specific prophetic purpose, he may sometimes call us to do things that seem illogical or unproductive by human standards. When so called, we should readily obey. Abraham's willingness to offer Isaac is another example of such obedience (see Gen. 22:1-2).
- In a day of easy divorce, Hosea's efforts to win back his unfaithful wife provide a much-needed good example. The law provided for divorce (see Deut. 24:1) but only "as a concession to [Israel's] hard-hearted wickedness" (Matt. 19:8). Divorce is never the best option, even in cases of sexual infidelity.
- Though God disciplines us, he is also eager to forgive. God ordered Hosea to give his children names with meanings suggesting judgment (1:4, 6, 9) but later gave a redeeming interpretation to those names (1:10–2:1, 23). (See also Ps. 103:9; Rom. 9:25.)

Key Verse

"Go and marry a prostitute, so some of her children will be born to you from other men. This will illustrate the way my people have been untrue to me, openly committing adultery against the LORD by worshiping other gods" (1:2).

JOEL

BACKGROUND

Perhaps during the reign of Joash (835–796 B.C., see *Date*), a terrible plague of locusts struck Judah. The prophet Joel called his people to repentance and pleaded with God to end the plague. Yet he saw in the disaster a foreshadowing of a far greater future plague: God's final judgment on sin in the Great Tribulation. Looking still farther into the future, he also saw the blessings of the Millennium. Assuming he wrote during Joash's reign, Joel was among the earliest of the writing prophets (see *Introduction to the Prophets,* p. 353).

AUTHOR

Nothing is known about Joel except his father's name (1:1) and his familiarity with Jerusalem (see *Location*).

DATE

Determining the date of this book is difficult because Joel names no Israelite kings. It is apparent, however, that he was an early prophet:

- Joel's order of placement within the 12 minor prophets would suggest a date before 800 B.C., since these books are in roughly chronological order.
- There are thematic similarities with other prophets of this era such as Amos and Isaiah (see *Comparison with Other Bible Books*).

LOCATION

Joel ministered to the southern kingdom of Judah, as seen by his references to that area:

- the "Temple of the LORD" (1:9, 14)
- "Zion" (a hill in Jerusalem, mentioned seven times)
- several references to Judah and Jerusalem

931 B.C. ***Kingdom divides, Israel, Judah***

836 ***Joash becomes king, Joel begins ministry?***

796 ***Joash's reign ends, Joel's ministry ends?***

740 ***Isaiah begins ministry***

722 ***Fall of Israel***

586 ***Fall of Judah***

PURPOSE

See *Background.*

COMPARISON WITH OTHER BIBLE BOOKS

Amos:

- Both speak of mountains "dripping" with wine (3:18; Amos 9:13).
- Both say that the Lord will "roar" from Zion (3:16; Amos 1:2).
- Both declare that the day of the Lord will be dark, not light (2:2, 10, 31; 3:15; Amos 5:18, 20).

Isaiah:

- Both proclaim that "the day of the LORD" is at hand (1:15; Isa. 13:6) and that it is a day when the sun and moon will not give light (2:10; 3:15; Isa. 13:10).
- Both speak of the pouring out of God's Spirit (2:28; Isa. 32:15; 44:3).
- Joel spoke of beating "plowshares into swords" in preparation for Armageddon (3:10). Isaiah, writing some 100 years later, reversed the saying and made it an image of millennial peace (Isa. 2:4; see Mic. 4:3).

OUTLINE

THE PRESENT DEVASTATION (1)
THE FUTURE TRIBULATION (2:1-17)
  Devastation (2:1-11)
  Deliverance (2:12-17)
THE FUTURE RESTORATION (2:18–3:21)
  Restoration and the Day of Christ (Millennium) (2:18-27)
  The Day of Pentecost (2:28-32)
  The Day of Christ (Millennium), continued (3:1-21)
    The destruction of sinners (3:1-17)
    The delight of saints (3:18-21)

THE PRESENT DEVASTATION (1)

1:1-12 *The ultimate locust plague.* God called Joel to prophesy following a severe locust plague. A mighty "army of locusts" (1:6) had stripped the entire land of produce, the worst possible calamity for a nation largely dependent on agriculture. This unprecedented disaster (1:2) had robbed the people of their joy (1:12). Even the drunkards sorrowed because the locusts had deprived them of their wine (1:5).

In contrast with God's disobedient people, the lowly locust always does his will. God used the locust, among other things, to judge Egypt (see Exod. 10:1-20). Moses later prophesied that God would use locusts, among other things, to punish his people if they were disobedient (see Deut. 28:38, 42). Now that prophecy was fulfilled.

1:13-20 *The ultimate response: Fast and pray!* Joel called for a national time of mourning, during which all the people would gather in the Temple and seek God's help. Joel saw the plague as a foreshadowing of "the day of the LORD," which was "on the way" and which would be a time of "destruction" (1:15).

THE FUTURE TRIBULATION (2:1-17)

2:1-11 *Single-minded locusts, inescapable judgment.* Joel called for the alarm to be sounded, warning Judah of the approaching day of the Lord (2:1, 11). That judgment, like the present plague, would be unique in its devastation, as emphasized by ominous figures such as "thick clouds and deep blackness," "fire," faces "pale with fright," and a "quaking" earth and "trembling" heavens. Judah's Eden-like countryside would become a desolate wilderness. Both the locusts and the future human invaders were single-mindedly bent on Judah's total destruction: As instruments of God's determined will (2:11), their march was orderly and unstoppable (2:7).

Concerning the "day of the LORD," often referred to as the "Tribulation," see *Isaiah: Background* and exposition on Isaiah 2:5–4:1.

2:12-17 *"But there's still time to turn!"* Joel called the people to repent, in hopes that God would remove the plague. He called for the trumpet to be blown a second time, to gather the people together so that the priests could intercede for them.

God "is eager not to punish" (2:13; see Exod. 34:6; Jer. 18:8; Amos 7:3, 6; exposition on Jon. 3:1-10.). His judgments are therapeutic, not punitive. They are designed to bring his people to repentance (see 2 Pet. 3:9). God is "not easily angered" (2:13; see Neh. 9:17; Ps. 103:8; Jon. 4:2; Nah. 1:3), and we should be slow to anger as well (see Prov. 15:18; 19:11; James 1:19).

Joel appealed to God to save the people of Judah so that their enemies would not doubt his ability to do so (2:17). Other OT saints urged God thus to act "for his name's sake" (see Num. 14:13-16; Ps. 42:10; 79:10). Even the Lord himself declared this as one of his motives for rescuing his people (see Isa. 37:35; 45:4-6; Ezek. 20:5-9; 36:22-36).

THE FUTURE RESTORATION (2:18–3:21)

2:18-27 *After plague and repentance, a land of plenty!* When his people have repented, God will have pity on them. He will remove and destroy the locust army. He will care for their land, restore their crops, and remove their reproach among the nations. He will make up to the people all that they have lost, and at last they will recognize him as their God.

The permanence of this restoration ("never," 2:26) and the people's seemingly permanent conversion (2:27) suggest that this passage also looks ahead to the Millennium, when the promise of Jeremiah 31:31-34 will be fully realized.

2:28-32 *His Spirit for all who seek it!* Sometime "after" this, God will "pour out [his] Spirit upon all people" (2:28; see Isa. 32:15; 44:3; Ezek. 39:29). All humanity, male and female, the high and the lowly alike, will be eligible to receive the Spirit (2:28-29). The only qualification will be a right relationship with the Lord (2:32).

The outpouring of the Holy Spirit will be accompanied by signs and wonders in nature, all in preparation for the great day of the Lord (2:30-31). It will move people to seek salvation and deliverance from judgment (2:32).

Peter saw the miraculous signs and outpouring of the Spirit at Pentecost as a fulfillment of this prophecy (see Acts 2:1-21). Evangelical scholars generally agree that Scripture promises another such outpouring at the end of the Tribulation, which will usher in the Millennium. On OT manifestations of the Holy Spirit, see exposition on 1 Samuel 9:27–10:8.

3:1-10 *The armies in the valley.* When God is ready to restore his people to their land (3:1, 7), he will gather all the nations that have violated them to the valley of Jehoshaphat, where he will judge them (3:2). God taunted his enemies and urged them to come and fight him (3:10), having already declared that all their efforts and preparation will be futile: They will not escape God's judgment; they will be as helpless before God as Israel was before them (3:4).

3:11-14 *The verdict in the valley.* Once more, God invited the nations to the valley of Jehoshaphat, declaring that the time was ripe for judgment (compare 3:13 with Isa. 63:1-6; Rev. 14:18-20; 19:15.) The "valley of decision" (3:14) is another name for the valley of Jehoshaphat, which means "the LORD judges" (3:2, 12). The multitudes in this valley will not be invited to make a decision for God. Rather, God himself will have already made the decision—to judge them.

3:11-17 is generally regarded as describing the Battle of Armageddon at the end of the Tribulation (see exposition on 2:1-11).

3:15-21 *The verdict for Israel.* Announced by momentous signs in nature, God will deliver his people. The day of the Lord will have accomplished three things for them:

- All of Judah's enemies (represented by Egypt and Edom, 3:19) will be permanently destroyed.
- Judah and Jerusalem will be permanently established as the homeland of God's people (3:20).
- They will experience national repentance and regeneration (3:17, 21).

Everything God promised the nation in the New Covenant (see Jer. 31:31-34) will be realized—because God will be personally present in Zion to guarantee it (3:17, 21).

❖ ❖ ❖

PEOPLE TO REMEMBER FROM JOEL

JOEL

Key Facts: Prophet, used locust plague to illustrate the coming Great Tribulation
Father: Pethuel (1:1)
Total Bible References: 2
Key References: 1–3; Acts 2:16

Joel Speaks

No doubt about it, we have just experienced the worst locust plague in Israel's history. Hopefully, the season of prayer and fasting I called for has resulted in the necessary repentance. What an object lesson these insects have been, however, sent not only to chasten but also to illustrate the final battle, when human warriors will invade and devastate our land. (1:1-4, 14-20)

What a dreadful day that will be! My hand trembled as I wrote of it: "I will cause wonders in the heavens and on the earth—blood and fire and pillars of smoke. The sun will be turned into darkness, and the moon will turn bloodred before that great and terrible day of the LORD arrives." (2:1-2, 30-31)

But my fears melted into peace and joy when he revealed how the story will end: "In that day the mountains will drip with sweet wine, and the hills will flow with milk. Water will fill the dry streambeds of Judah, and a fountain will burst forth from the LORD's Temple." (3:18)

All in all, I would say that the good news resulting from this plague far outweighs the bad!

Spiritual Lesson from Joel

- Joel effectively used a current event of his day, a terrible locust plague, to illustrate and warn about a future event, the Tribulation (2:1-11; 3:9-16). Jesus often used a similar method of teaching (see Luke 13:1-5; 18:18-27; 21:1-4). We, too, can draw lessons from everyday life to help others learn spiritual truths.

Key Verse

"And anyone who calls on the name of the LORD will be saved" (2:32).

AMOS

BACKGROUND

The reign of Jeroboam II in Israel's northern kingdom had been the "golden age" of the north, with great military successes and a thriving economy. Spiritually, however, the nation did not do so well. Toward the end of Jeroboam's reign, God called Amos, from the southern kingdom, to head north with a message of exhortation and judgment for Israel. As a southerner, Amos was not very welcome in the north (see 7:12-13), yet he stood his ground, knowing that God had called him.

Although there is no evidence that the two men ever met, Amos would have been a contemporary of Hosea, another prophet to the northern kingdom.

AUTHOR

Amos, a shepherd (1:1; 7:14-15) from Tekoa, a small hilltop town overlooking the Dead Sea, 10 miles south of Jerusalem.

DATE AND LOCATION

1:1 states that Amos prophesied during the reigns of Jeroboam II (793–753 B.C.) and the southern king Uzziah (Azariah, 790–740), and that God's message came to him "two years before the earthquake." Josephus dates this earthquake at the time of Uzziah's apostasy, c. 750 (see exposition on 2 Kings 15:1-7).

Amos prophesied at Bethel, where Jeroboam had erected one of his golden calves (see exposition on 1 Kings 12:25-33). He may have ministered at the north's capital city of Samaria as well. His prophecies were probably compiled and recorded at Bethel, Jerusalem, or Tekoa, perhaps shortly after the earthquake.

RECIPIENTS

Although Amos was concerned about the whole house of Jacob (3:1, 13), his message was mainly for the northern kingdom, especially those associated with its idol worship at Bethel (7).

***931 B.C.* Kingdom divides, Israel, Judah**

***c. 750* Amos prophesies, mentions earthquake**

***722* Fall of Israel**

***586* Fall of Judah**

***c. 500* Zechariah mentions earthquake of Amos' day**

PURPOSE

To call Israel to repent of

- outward actions such as violence, social injustice, and idolatry
- inward attitudes such as pride and heartless worship

Amid his denunciations, Amos proclaimed the coming messianic age.

UNIQUE FEATURES

- Amos is the only OT prophet called from one part of the divided kingdom to prophecy in the other part.
- Perhaps more than any other OT prophet, Amos shows that an effective minister of God does not need any prescribed level of education or social status; he or she needs only a call from God (7:14-15).

COMPARISON WITH OTHER BIBLE BOOKS

See *Joel: Comparison with Other Bible Books.*

OUTLINE

THE BAD NEWS: EIGHT PROPHECIES (1–2)
THE BAD NEWS: THREE SERMONS (3–6)
    Punishment for iniquity (3)
    Israel's lack of repentance (4)
    A lament for Israel (5–6)
THE BAD NEWS: FIVE VISIONS (7:1–9:10)
    The locusts, fire, and plumb line (7:1-9)
    The attack on Amos (7:10-17)
    The ripe fruit (8)
    God standing at the altar (9:1-10)
THE GOOD NEWS (9:11-15)

THE BAD NEWS: EIGHT PROPHECIES (1–2)

1:1-2 *"These nations will be judged."* Amos, a shepherd from Judah, introduced his prophecies concerning eight different nations (1:3–2:16) by describing God's awesome presence as he called those nations to account. The earthquake (see *Date*) was memorable not only to Amos but also to Zechariah, writing more than 200 years later (see Zech. 14:4-5)! Thoughts of the earthquake may also have been natural as Amos thought back on his prophecies of judgment.

1:3-5 *Syria: Payday for the "threshers."* Syria, represented by Damascus, its capital, was to be judged because of its excessive cruelty in conquering Gilead, the area east of the Jordan occupied by Reuben, Gad, and the half-tribe of Manasseh. It had apparently used iron implements of war to literally "thresh" the Israelite soldiers. This had taken place during the reign of Jehoahaz (814–798 B.C.; see 2 Kings 10:32-33; 13:3-7). Damascus would be conquered and exiled by Assyria some 20 years after Amos's prophecy, in 732 (see 2 Kings 16:9).

1:6-8 *Philistia: Death to the slave traders.* Philistia had invaded Judah during the reign of Jehoram (853–841 B.C.), about 100 years before Amos, and had taken its people captive (see 2 Chron. 21:16-17). They had sold some prisoners to the Edomites and some to Phoenicians, who in turn sold them to the Greeks (see Joel 3:4-6). Historically, their death sentence (1:8) would be carried out by Assyria from 734 to 701.

1:9-10 *Phoenicia: Death to the promise breakers.* Phoenicia (Tyre), partner in Philistia's slave trade, had sold Israelite captives to Greece and Edom. Its crime was more heinous than Philistia's because it had broken its "treaty of brotherhood" with Israel (see 1 Kings 5:1-12). Phoenicia's judgment was carried out by Nebuchadnezzar (see exposition on Ezek. 26–28).

1:11-12 *Edom: Punished for pursuing his brother.* The Edomites, descendants of Esau and therefore closely related to Israel, had been "unrelenting in their anger" toward Jacob's descendants (see 2 Chron. 28:17; exposition on Ezek. 35:1-15; Obadiah) and would be judged.

1:13-15 *Ammon: Burned for their atrocities.* Ammon had committed terrible atrocities against Judah. God promised the fire of complete and inescapable judgment, a judgment that would be carried out a century and a half later by Nebuchadnezzar (see exposition on Jer. 49:1-6).

2:1-3 *Moab: Extermination for desecration.* The Moabites had shown unreasonable wrath when they desecrated the body of the royal heir of Edom (see 2 Kings 3:26-27). God's judgment on them would be carried out when Nebuchadnezzar swallowed them up and they passed out of existence as a nation (see exposition on Jer. 48:1-47).

2:4-5 *Judah: No favoritism for his favorites.* Turning to his own people, God declared judgment on Judah for taking his favor for granted. His judgment would be carried out by Babylon in 586 B.C. (see 2 Kings 25).

2:6-16 *Israel: The "main event."* Having pronounced judgment on all the surrounding nations, including Judah, the Lord confronted the real target of his wrath: the northern kingdom of Israel. Israel had flagrantly violated God's law (2:6-8), had taken his favor for granted (2:9-12), and therefore must be judged (2:13-16). Judgment would be realized in 722 B.C.—just 30 years away—when the people would be carried into a captivity from which they would never return.

THE BAD NEWS: THREE SERMONS (3–6)

3:1-8 *Much given, much required.* Amos addressed three sermons to Israel, each prefaced by the exhortation to listen (3:1; see 4:1; 5:1). The people of Israel had enjoyed a covenant relationship with God unknown by any other nation in history. Because of this unique privilege, their punishment would be all the greater, for how could God continue to "walk" with them when they were walking in a different direction (3:1-3)?

The judgment to befall Israel would follow the natural laws of cause and effect (3:4-6). The cause was Israel's sins. The effect would be God's judgment. Amos the farmer was merely God's messenger (3:7-8).

Judah, as part of Israel's "entire family" (3:1), would also be judged—but a century and a half later.

3:9-15 *Prosecuted before a pagan jury.* God, as prosecuting attorney, invited Philistia and Egypt to form the jury as he presented his case against Israel (3:9-10). Neither the people's worship centers nor their ill-gotten possessions (3:10, 14-15) would deter God from avenging their oppression of the poor and helpless (3:9-11). God's judgment would be severe, but he would spare a remnant (3:12), through whom his messianic plans for Israel would be realized. Not even its sin would deter God from his ultimate plans to restore Israel! (See 2 Chron. 30:1-9.)

4:1-3 *Herded like cattle into captivity.* The wealthy women of Samaria, addressed as "fat cows," maintained their luxury by urging their husbands to oppress the poor. God's judgment would be sudden and severe, fitting their crimes. Bashan, east of Galilee, had lush pastures and was known for its fine cattle.

4:4-5 *Worship today, judgment tomorrow.* God mockingly invited the people of Israel to worship, though their worship, being insincere and selfish, would only compound their sins. Halfhearted worship salves the conscience but condemns the soul. Bethel and Gilgal were apparently the two most notorious centers of idol worship (4:4; see 5:5).

4:6-13 *"Prepare to meet your God!"* Any one of the many calamities God had brought on Israel should have been enough to produce repentance, yet they had had no such effect (4:6-11). Israel must therefore prepare to meet its God, not in salvation or revival, but in judgment (4:12-13). Israel would be helpless before him, for he is the sovereign, omnipotent, omniscient, omnipresent God. "Cleanness of teeth" (4:6, KJV) was a euphemism for hunger.

5:1-9 *The Sovereign you're sinning against.* Because of its sins, Israel was in sad shape, and judgment was imminent (5:1-3). Yet judgment could be avoided: Three times God extended a gracious invitation for Israel to repent (5:4, 6, 14-15). The gravity of its sin stood in stark contrast to the greatness of the one against whom Israel had sinned—the eternal God, maker and sustainer of heaven and earth, who certainly could bring about sudden and inescapable judgment (5:8-9).

5:10-15 *"Hate the bad, love the good, save your life!"* Israel's leaders had oppressed the poor, and this had not escaped God's notice (5:10-13). The oppressors would soon find themselves thrown out of the very houses they had built with their ill-gotten wealth (5:11-12). They could avert this judgment, however, if only they would "do what is good and run from evil" (5:14-15).

5:16-20 *From lion to bear (bad to worse!).* Amos's third sermon ended with pronouncements of woe against Israel (5:18; see 6:1, 3). Some falsely pious Israelites claimed to long for the future "day of the LORD," not realizing that the judgment to be experienced then will be even worse than the coming judgment by Assyria. One might escape the Assyrians, but none will escape the final judgment. It will be like escaping a lion only to encounter a bear! On the "day of the LORD," see exposition on 9:11-15 as well as exposition on Isaiah 2:5–4:1 and on Joel 2:1-11.

5:21-27 *"I hate your hypocrisy!"* God expressed utter distaste for Israel's halfhearted worship (5:21-23), accompanied as it was by social injustice (5:24). Israel had displayed such hypocrisy since its very birth in Egypt. Therefore it would go into captivity.

6:1-14 *The self-indulgent: First to be enslaved.* A special woe was pronounced against the wealthy of both Judah ("Jerusalem") and Israel ("Samaria"). Both had sunk to gross depths of self-indulgence. Both were due for a great surprise: God's judgment would overtake them. They had been prominent in their sin and self-indulgence; now they would be prominent in the exile, being "the first to be led away as captives" (6:7).

In their wealth and pride (6:1, 8), God's people had refused to trust him (6:2, 12-13). Now judgment would come, to rich and poor alike (6:11). Just as sin had covered the entire land, destruction would spread from north to south (6:14). So many would die that cremation—a rare practice in Israel—would be necessary to keep disease from spreading (6:10).

THE BAD NEWS: FIVE VISIONS (7:1–9:10)

7:1-6 *The power of prayer: Stopping locusts and fire!* Amos described some visions concerning Israel. When God showed him a swarm of locusts descending on sinful Israel, Amos realized how hopeless was his people's condition. He pleaded with God to spare them from this disaster, and God relented (see exposition on Joel 2:12-17). A vision of fire brought the same alarm from Amos and the same mercy from God.

7:7-9 *What the plumb line shows.* God then showed Amos a plumb line, which revealed that, measured against God's law, Israel was way out of line. It had escaped the judgments of locusts and fire (7:1-6), but now the time for judgment had come.

7:10-11 *Amaziah to Jeroboam: "He's saying terrible things!"* Responding perhaps to Amos's vision of the plumb line, Amaziah, a priest of the idolatrous shrine at Bethel, falsely accused Amos of conspiring against Jeroboam, of acting treasonously, and of upsetting an otherwise peaceful land. While the "dynasty of King Jeroboam" (his son Zechariah) died by the sword just as Amos had predicted (7:9; see 2 Kings 15:8-10), Jeroboam himself died a natural death (see 2 Kings 14:29), unlike Amaziah's misrepresentation of Amos's words (7:11).

7:12-13 *Amaziah to Amos: "Go home!"* Evidently unable to get the king to arrest Amos, Amaziah attacked him himself, ordering him to leave Israel and return to Judah, where he had come from. In so doing he unwittingly spoke the truth about Bethel: Because it had become a center of false worship, it truly was the house of Jeroboam rather than the "house of God," as its name implied.

7:14-17 *Amos to Amaziah: "I'll say even worse things!"* Ignoring Amaziah's threats, Amos recalled his humble origins and continued to boldly prophesy—against Israel and against Amaziah personally: Amaziah's wife would become a harlot, his children would be slain, he would die as a captive in Assyria, and the entire nation would be exiled.

8:1-10 *Sorrow and suffering in the basket.* Amos saw a basket of ripe summer fruit, signifying that Israel was ripe for destruction (8:1-3). So many would die that the burial crews would go about their gruesome task in stunned silence (8:3). The Lord would not overlook the wrongs heaped on the poor and oppressed by wealthy Israelites (8:4-7). The land would be struck by an earthquake (8:8), and there would be unusual phenomena in the heavens (8:9). Their normal happy festivities would become times of deep mourning, like those of parents mourning the death of an only son (8:10).

8:11-14 *Worse than a famine of food.* Once in captivity, the Israelites would experience a famine worse than any physical privation: For centuries they had shown contempt for God and rejected his prophets; now they would not be able to hear the words of the Lord even if they should want to.

9:1-10 *No escape—except the righteous few.* Amos then saw God confronting the idolatrous worshipers at Bethel, declaring that none would escape his wrath. God's patience had reached its limit (9:1-4). The sovereign God, who governs phenomena such as earthquakes and floods (9:5-6), could surely judge a nation like Israel (9:7-8). Yet he would not totally destroy it but would "sift" the people into exile, then separate the good from the bad among those exiles (9:8-10).

THE GOOD NEWS (9:11-15)

9:11-15 *But then, glorious restoration!* The dark present of Israel's defection would not deter God from his ultimate plans for Israel. "In that day," at the end of human history (9:11; see exposition on Isa. 2:5–4:1), God will repair the damage done to the nation and make it as good as new! Israel's ultimate restoration will include

- a renewed Davidic dynasty (9:11; see Acts 15:16)
- exaltation over the nations (9:11-12)
- conversion of the Gentiles (9:12; see Acts 15:17)
- agricultural abundance (9:13-14; see Joel 3:18)
- rebuilding of devastated cities (9:14)
- return to its own land, never to be captive again (9:15)

What a glorious future against such a dark background!

❖ ❖ ❖

PEOPLE TO REMEMBER FROM AMOS

AMOS

Key Fact: Prophet from Judah to Israel

Occupation: Herdsman, fruit grower, prophet (7:14-15)

Total Bible References: 7

Key References: 1–9

Amos Speaks

He first spoke to me on that hillside overlooking Tekoa as I tended my sheep. He instructed me to pay a visit to my northern relatives and denounce their sins as well as the sins of Judah and six pagan nations. All would be severely punished. That in itself was awesome, but those five accompanying visions were almost overwhelming! They seemed to appear without pause, like so many flashes of lightning. (1:1–3:3)

All five visions dealt with God's judgment. What a relief when the locust plague and that all-consuming fire were both averted because of his grace. But this would not be the case with the remaining three. Of course, the vision that caused the most difficulty for me personally was that of the plumb line. He talked about "testing his people with a plumb line," then went on to say he would "bring the dynasty of King Jeroboam to a sudden end." (7:1-9)

Needless to say, this kind of talk against Jeroboam infuriated his puppy-dog priest at Bethel. He demanded that I go back home and prophesy in Judah! Well, I quickly responded to this religious phony. I pointed out that although I was not an official prophet, nor even the son of a prophet, I would nevertheless oblige him by a few choice predictions. I warned him that, as a result of his godlessness, his wife would become a harlot, his land would be confiscated, and he himself would die as a captive in a foreign land. What a miserable future he faces! (7:12-17)

But it will all have a happy ending, as God revealed to me on that little hillside: "I will bring my exiled people of Israel back from distant lands, and they will rebuild their ruined cities and live in them again. . . . Then they will never be uprooted again." (9:14-15)

Spiritual Lesson from Amos

- God used a theologically untrained "layman" as one of his most effective prophets (7:14). Usefulness in God's service has more to do with the condition of the heart than with natural abilities or professional credentials (see Matt. 11:25; Acts 4:13; 1 Cor. 1:27). As far as God is concerned, the two greatest "abilities" are availability and dependability! (See Isa. 6:8; 1 Cor. 4:1-2.)

Key Verse

"Prepare to meet your God as he comes in judgment, you people of Israel!" (4:12).

OBADIAH

BACKGROUND

The Edomites, descendants of Esau and therefore closely related to Israel, were nonetheless her longtime bitter foes (see Gen. 27; 2 Kings 14:7; 16:6; 2 Chron. 28:17; Amos 1:6, 9; and exposition on the following passages: Num. 20:14-21; Jer. 49:7-22; Ezek. 35:1-15; Mal. 1:2-5). Obadiah predicted God's judgment against them. The Edomites lived in the high mountains southeast of Israel, and Obadiah saw in this geography a picture of Edom's pride and sense of self-sufficiency. The ancient city of Petra in Jordan, famous for its palaces carved into sandstone cliffs, is widely identified as the biblical Sela, in Edomite territory (see 2 Kings 14:7).

AUTHOR

Obadiah (1:1). Biographical details unknown.

DATE

Since no Israelite kings are mentioned, dating is uncertain. Obadiah spoke of the invasion of Jerusalem by pagan nations, including Edom (1:11-14). Though this may refer to Jerusalem's final fall in 586 B.C., it more likely refers to the sack of Jerusalem by the Philistines and Arabs in the ninth century B.C. (2 Chron. 21:16-17), placing Obadiah at about 850–840 and making him the earliest writing prophet of the OT, just before Joel (see *Introduction to the Prophets,* p. 353).

One support for this early date is Jeremiah's apparent quote from Obadiah (compare 1:1-9 and Jer. 49:7-22). Jeremiah applied Obadiah's words to events surrounding Judah's fall in 586, more than a century after Obadiah's time.

PURPOSE

- To predict the fall of Edom.
- In a larger sense, to predict judgment against any person or nation consumed with pride.

***931 B.C.* Kingdom divides, Israel, Judah**

***874* Ahab, Elijah**

***c. 850* Obadiah predicts Edom's fall**

***740* Isaiah begins ministry**

***722* Fall of Israel**

***586* Fall of Judah, Edom**

- To show that God, who will restore Israel, is the ultimate sovereign of the world.

UNIQUE FEATURE

- Obadiah contains the OT's most detailed prophecy about the relationship between the descendants of Esau and those of Jacob, a topic that appears repeatedly throughout the OT (see *Background*).

COMPARISON WITH OTHER BIBLE BOOKS

Jeremiah:

- 1:1-9 is virtually identical to Jeremiah 49:7-22 (see *Date*).

Joel:

- Writing a short while later, Joel, like Obadiah, spoke of Edom's violence against Judah (1:10; Joel 3:19).
- Both speak of pagan nations "casting lots" for God's chosen people and city (1:11; Joel 3:3).
- Both speak of pagan nations receiving their just deserts for mistreating Israel (1:15; Joel 3:4, 7).
- Both speak of the "day of the LORD" (1:15; Joel 1:15; 2:1; 3:14).
- Both speak of people on Mount Zion escaping destruction (1:17; Joel 2:32).

OUTLINE

EDOM: REMOVED BY GOD (1:1-16)
  Their proud heart (1:1-9)
  Their treacherous hand (1:10-14)
  Their punished head (1:15-16)
JACOB: RESTORED BY GOD (1:17-21)

EDOM: REMOVED BY GOD (1:1-16)

1:1-4 *"Put her down for her pride."* The proud nation of Edom would be destroyed (1:1-4). All the surrounding nations would be invited to take part in its destruction (1:1). Edom was smug and secure in its mountain fortress (1:3), which could be reached by only one donkey rider at a time through a narrow pass. In their pride, the Edomites had overlooked their most worthy opponent—the Lord (1:4).

1:5-7 *Their enemy: God. Their allies: None.* If thieves or grape gatherers had invaded Edom, they would only have taken as much as they could carry out (1:5). But the invaders directed by God would leave nothing (1:6). Edom would be dumbfounded when even their allies turned against them (1:7).

1:8-9 *Stupid wise men, helpless mighty men.* Edom, noted for its wise men, would be no match for God's wrath (1:8). The defection of Edom's allies would take the wise men by surprise (1:7). Nor would mighty warriors be able to save Edom (1:9).

1:10-14 *"Here's why: You betrayed your brothers."* Edom was to be "destroyed completely" for betraying its brother, Jacob (1:10). Edom had failed to help the Israelites when their land was invaded (1:11). Edom had even rejoiced at Judah's calamity (1:12) and joined in the looting following its defeat (1:13). Worse still, Edom took captive those survivors of Judah who sought refuge in its territory (1:14).

The cruel betrayal that Obadiah described would be repeated by Edom more than a century later when Judah fell to Babylon, prompting Jeremiah's apparent application of Obadiah's words to that later event (see *Date*).

1:15-16 *"Now it's your turn!"* Edom's treachery against Judah would be returned in full measure "on your own heads." They had drunk in celebration during Jerusalem's destruction, but soon they would drink of God's wrath, as would all of Judah's enemies on the day of the Lord (1:15; see *Isaiah: Background* and exposition on Isa. 2:5–4:1). Edom would be defeated by Nebuchadnezzar at about the same time he defeated Judah, in 586 B.C.; but while Judah would be restored after 70 years, Edom would never return to its homeland—a fate confirmed 400 years after Obadiah's time by the prophet Malachi (see Mal. 1:2-5) and by subsequent secular history.

JACOB: RESTORED BY GOD (1:17-21)

1:17-21 *"They'll have the whole land."* Obadiah's dark words of destruction for Edom concluded with bright words of promise for Israel. The land from which Edom was evicted will not remain uninhabited: It, along with Judah's other enemies, will be occupied by a reunited Israel in the Millennium. The nation of Israel will be restored completely. Regardless of how widely they may be dispersed (1:19-20), God's plan for the restoration of his people will not be frustrated.

❖ ❖ ❖

PEOPLE TO REMEMBER FROM OBADIAH

OBADIAH

Key Facts: Prophet, predicted destruction of Edom
Total Bible References: 1

Obadiah Speaks

It's difficult to understand and even more difficult not to become bitter. We were treated like dogs, not by some foreign pagan enemy, but by our own blood relatives. There they were, descendants of Isaac through Esau, inflicting great suffering on us, the children of Isaac through Jacob! (1:10; Gen. 25:25-26)

Why did the Edomites desert us in our time of need, standing aloof, refusing to lift a finger to help? And as if that were not enough, they actually mocked us and even helped our enemies loot our cities! Then they stood at the crossroads, both killing and enslaving those of us who tried to escape! (1:11-14)

No, in spite of all this, I must not become bitter! In fact, there is no need for me to be angry, for God himself has vowed to severely punish these proud cliff dwellers and to gloriously restore our nation. (1:3-4, 17-21)

Spiritual Lesson from Obadiah

- "Pride goes before destruction, and haughtiness before a fall" (Prov. 16:18). Edom serves as a classic example of this proverb (1:3-4). Because of its pride, Edom would "fall," never to rise again (1:15-16; see exposition on Isa. 14:1-23 and on Ezek. 28:11-19).

Key Verses

"Everyone on the mountains of Edom will be cut down in the slaughter. And why? Because of the violence you did to your close relatives in Israel. Now you will be destroyed completely and filled with shame forever. For you deserted your relatives in Israel during their time of greatest need. You stood aloof, refusing to lift a finger to help when foreign invaders carried off their wealth and cast lots to divide up Jerusalem. You acted as though you were one of Israel's enemies" (1:9-11).

JONAH

c. 790 B.C.? Jonah predicts success for Jeroboam II

c. 750 Jonah preaches, Nineveh repents

722 Assyria (Nineveh) conquers Israel

701 Death angel strikes Assyrians

612 Fall of Nineveh

586 Fall of Judah

BACKGROUND

Jeroboam II, king of Israel's northern kingdom from 794–753 B.C., was not only Israel's longest-reigning king but also one of its most successful, expanding Israel's borders back to what they had been more than 200 years before in the time of David and Solomon (see 2 Kings 14:23-29). At the same time, however, Assyria was growing in strength and pushing its way southward toward Israel, which it would conquer in 722. Jonah, from the northern town of Gath-hepher, had been used by God to predict Jeroboam's military successes (2 Kings 14:25). Now, however, the Lord had another mission for him: to travel to Nineveh, the capital of Assyria, and call that mighty and threatening nation to repentance. Although Nineveh would repent at Jonah's preaching, its conquering of Israel some 30 years later suggests the revival did not endure. Nineveh would itself fall in 612.

AUTHOR

Jonah. Though many have questioned the historicity of this greatest of all fish stories, there is ample evidence that Jonah was a real historical person:

- The Jonah of 2 Kings 14:25 was, like the Jonah of 1:1, a prophet and the "son of Amittai."
- Jesus considered Jonah a real, historical person (Matt. 12:39-41; 16:4; Luke 11:29-32).
- The book of Jonah is presented as history, with actual people and place-names given.

Although the book of Jonah is actually a book *about* Jonah (see *Unique Features*), and someone else may have done the actual writing, Jonah is rightfully considered its author since he alone would have had knowledge of all the events recorded.

DATE

The language of 2 Kings 14:25 suggests that Jonah was a contemporary of Jeroboam II, and the events reported in his book were most likely recorded soon after they occurred (794–753 B.C.).

RECIPIENTS

Since Jonah was from the northern kingdom, the book is usually considered to have been written to the north. Since Assyria was clearly a threat to both kingdoms, however, Jonah's story would have been interesting reading for all Israelites.

PURPOSE

Jonah is not the story of a man and a fish. Rather, it is the story of a man and his God. It has much to teach about the personal relationship between God and believers:

- Jonah was nationalistic in his faith, but God wanted him to see that God's compassion extends to non-Israelites as well (4:11).
- Jonah's nationalistic zeal was probably selfish, as he saw Assyria as a threat to Israel's prosperity. God wanted to show Jonah that compassion for sinners was more important than prosperity.
- Jonah was selfish on an individual level as well. If he could not control world events, at least he would try to control his shade plant (4:5-10)! God sought here as well to counter Jonah's attitude of control and anger.

UNIQUE FEATURES

- Except for one short sentence (3:4), the book of Jonah is actually a book *about* Jonah's prophetic ministry, rather than a record of his actual prophecies.
- Jonah, like Habakkuk, consists largely of a dialogue between God and the prophet.

COMPARISON WITH OTHER BIBLE BOOKS

Acts:

- Both tell of a missionary call to reach Gentiles, and both had a "Joppa connection":
  - ➤ God called Jonah to minister to Gentiles, and he at first refused, fleeing from Joppa (1).
  - ➤ While Peter was in Joppa, God called him to minister to Gentiles, and he obeyed (Acts 10).

OUTLINE

JONAH'S PROTEST; GOD'S PATIENCE (1)
JONAH'S PRAYER; GOD'S POWER (2)
JONAH'S PREACHING; GOD'S PARDON (3)
JONAH'S POUTING; GOD'S PITY (4)

JONAH'S PROTEST; GOD'S PATIENCE (1)

1:1-3 *God says go, the prophet says no.* The Lord called Jonah to preach to Nineveh, capital of Assyria. Jonah, however, "got up and went in the opposite direction in order to get away from the LORD." He boarded a ship heading for Tarshish, probably a seaport in Spain. God had commanded Jonah to go 600 miles to the east; he fled more than 1,200 miles to the west.

1:4-17 *A storm at sea—and he is its cause and cure!* Soon after Jonah's ship set sail, God sent a great storm that threatened to wreck it (1:4-5). After the sailors had called in vain on their gods, they implored Jonah to call on his God, whom he had told them about (1:6, 10). Then, by casting lots, they determined that Jonah's fleeing from his God had caused the storm (1:7-10). Jonah told them the storm would cease if they would throw him overboard. After desperately trying to reach land, and begging mercy and forgiveness from God, they threw Jonah overboard. The storm stopped at once, and Jonah was swallowed by "a great fish" (1:11-17).

Through the failure of their own gods (1:5) and the faithful witness of Jonah (1:9-10), the pagan sailors came to believe in the God of Israel (1:14, 16). Jonah's calm amid the storm (1:5) and his willingness to accept responsibility for the situation (1:12) were probably strong testimonies as well. Jonah knew that, at worst, his being thrown into the sea would deliver these innocent men from God's wrath; and at best, God would miraculously deliver him.

Though secular history offers examples of sailors being swallowed by large fish and surviving, the fish that swallowed Jonah was specially prepared by God for this purpose (1:17). On casting lots to learn God's will, see exposition on Proverbs 18:18.

JONAH'S PRAYER; GOD'S POWER (2)

2:1-10 *Inside the fish: Fearful but forgiven.* Inside the fish, Jonah was in great despair. Yet when he realized that God had miraculously saved him from drowning (2:6), he prayed and repented of his rebellion and acknowledged God as the only source of salvation (2:7-9). Jonah's dire circumstances had accomplished their purpose: to cause him to turn to the Lord and throw himself completely on his mercy (2:2). Having done this, Jonah was confident that God would restore him to normal life (2:9).

The fish deposited Jonah onto dry land (2:10). Unlike his unwilling passenger, the fish obeyed its sovereign God. Jonah's memory of being entangled in seaweed and seeing underwater mountains (2:5-6) shows the truth of his story.

JONAH'S PREACHING; GOD'S PARDON (3)

3:1-10 *A second chance for Jonah and Nineveh.* Having rescued him from the great fish, God again told Jonah to go to Nineveh, and this time he obeyed. He proclaimed that Nineveh would be overthrown in 40 days (3:1-4). In what must have been history's greatest revival, the whole city of Nineveh—"from the greatest to the least"—responded positively to his warning. Even the king, who had led Assyria in its wickedness, now became its leader in repentance (3:5-9). In response, God relented from destroying Nineveh (3:10).

Humanly speaking, God relented. That does not mean, however, that he changed his intentions toward the Ninevites. Rather, they changed their attitude toward him, and on the basis of that change, God could deal with them in grace rather than in judgment. See exposition on Joel 2:12-17.

JONAH'S TRAVELS

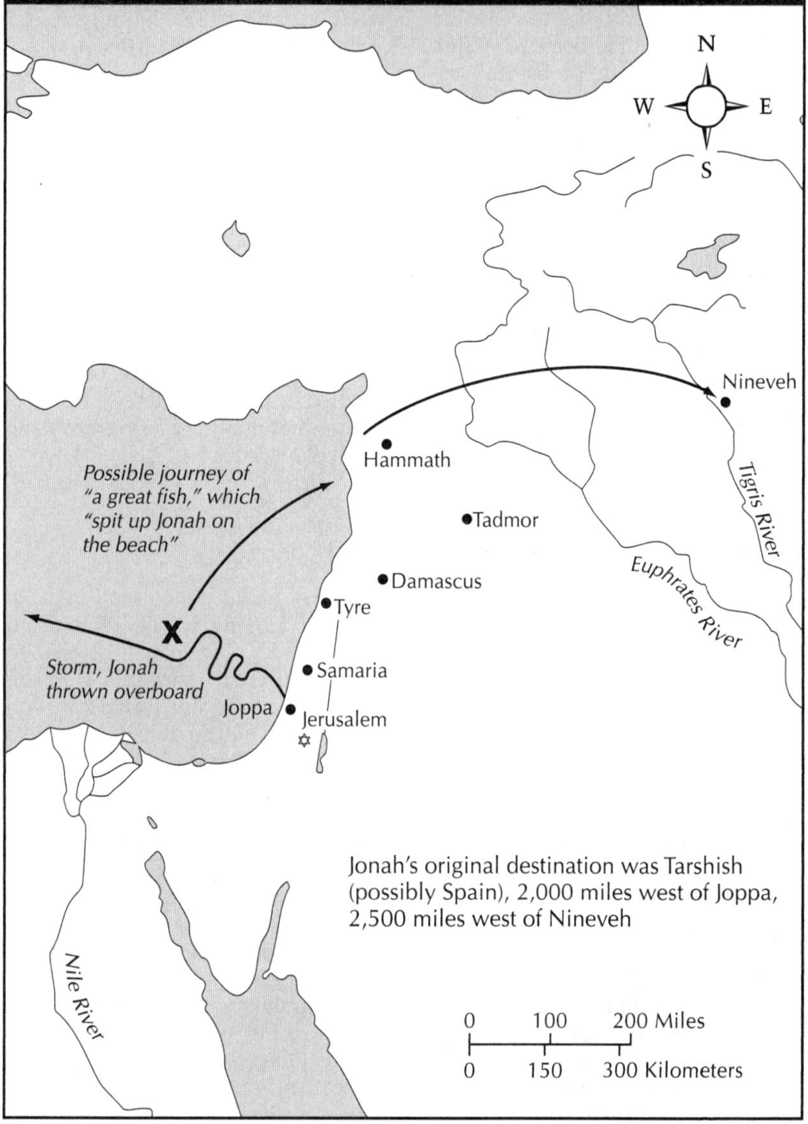

JONAH'S POUTING; GOD'S PITY (4)

4:1-4 *They're forgiven, he's furious!* When Jonah saw that God had spared Nineveh, he became depressed and angry, and God gently reproved him. Jonah's original *fear* that Nineveh might repent (4:2) betrayed his intense hatred of the Assyrians, probably the result of a misguided Jewish nationalism. Jonah had held onto this racial hatred even though he knew it was radically different from God's attitude (4:2).

4:5-11 *A weed, a worm, an east wind, and grace.* Still bitter, Jonah camped outside Nineveh, hoping that God would change his mind again and destroy the city. Still concerned about his prophet, God caused a large plant to grow to shelter Jonah from the hot sun. Then he caused a worm to destroy the plant, exposing Jonah to the heat and plunging him once more into self-pity (4:5-8).

God then confronted Jonah once again: If Jonah was so concerned about the death of a soulless plant, why shouldn't God be concerned about the souls of the Ninevites (4:9-11)?

The 120,000 undiscerning people of 4:11 may have represented all the Ninevites, who lacked knowledge of God, or it may have included just the children still too young to distinguish one hand from another. Historians estimate Nineveh's population at 600,000 at the time of its fall in 612 B.C.—a reasonable figure, considering its 60-mile circumference (3:3).

The fact that Jonah included 4:11 in his report shows that he had been brought once more to repentance and, in the end, agreed with God that Nineveh should be spared.

The worm (4:7), like the great fish (1:17), answered its Creator's call and performed its prophetic service.

PEOPLE TO REMEMBER FROM JONAH

JONAH

Key Facts: Prophet, survived being swallowed by a fish, preached in Nineveh
Father: Amittai (1:1; 2 Kings 14:25)
Total Bible References: 27
Key References: 1–4; 2 Kings 14:25; Matt. 12:39-41; 16:4; Luke 11:29-32

Jonah Speaks

He asked me how I was feeling. I responded, "Absolutely furious but not in the least surprised!" I just knew he might do something like this! Mind you, I wasn't denying the need for mercy and grace, but this occasion, I felt, demanded wrath and judgment. To think I endured a terrible storm and my horrifying confinement in the stomach of that sea monster only to see these pagan savages cry out and escape their deserved punishment! (1:4-17; 3:5-10; 4:2, 9)

Actually, I had hoped that the people of Nineveh would just ignore my preaching, so that God would rain down his fire on them just as he did on Sodom! Of course, Abraham did at least pray for Sodom. But Nineveh is different. So, here I sit on the hillside in the hot sun overlooking the city, frustrated and furious! Lord, if you really intend to save those savages, then kill me! I'd rather be dead! (4:3, 5, 8; Gen. 18:23-33; 19:24)

But wait, he now reminds me of the many innocent children who will perish if his fire does fall! Maybe I should rethink this whole business. . . . (4:11)

Spiritual Lessons from Jonah

- You cannot hide from God (1:3, 17). This is true for both believers (Ps. 139:7-12) and unbelievers (Amos 9:2-3).
- Sometimes the disobedience and sin of a believer brings suffering upon unbelievers (1:12; see also Gen. 12:17; 20:9; 26:10).
- Keep your vows to God (2:9) so that he won't find it necessary to bring a "whale experience" into your life!
- Our God is the God of the second chance (3:1), as Mark would later find out (see Acts 13:13; 15:36-38; 2 Tim. 4:11).
- Jonah spoke the truth (3), but not in love as Paul directs us to do (Eph. 4:15).
- God has mercy on every part of his creation, including nonhuman creatures (4:11).

Key Verse

"Nineveh has more than 120,000 people living in spiritual darkness, not to mention all the animals. Shouldn't I feel sorry for such a great city?" (4:11).

MICAH

BACKGROUND
About 10–20 years before the northern kingdom of Israel fell to Assyria in 722 B.C., Micah was called to prophesy to both the northern and southern kingdoms. Judah itself would barely escape destruction by Assyria in 701.

AUTHOR
Micah was from Moresheth in Judah, about 20 miles southwest of Jerusalem. His identity is verified by Jeremiah, who quoted him and named his hometown (compare 1:1; 3:12; Jer. 26:18).

DATE
Micah prophesied during the reigns of Jotham, Ahaz, and Hezekiah (1:1), c. 740–690, the same time span as Isaiah's ministry (see *Introduction to the Prophets,* p. 353).

RECIPIENTS
Micah prophesied concerning both the northern and southern kingdoms (1:1), but since he was from the south and mentioned only southern kings (1:1), it is generally assumed that his ministry was primarily to Judah.

PURPOSE
- To pronounce judgment for continual apostasy and insincere religious observance (3:8; 6:6-7).
- To show that true faith has practical manifestations, such as social justice and honesty in business (6:8).
- To proclaim God's ultimate plans for his people (2:12-13; 7:11-20).

UNIQUE FEATURES
- Micah is unique for the number and precision of his prophecies:

c. 740 B.C.
Micah, Isaiah begin ministries

722
Fall of Israel

701
Death angel strikes Assyrians

c. 690
Micah, Isaiah end ministries

586
Fall of Judah

538
1st exiles return

- ➤ the fall of the northern kingdom (1:6-7)
- ➤ the invasion of Judah by Sennacherib in 701 B.C. (1:9, 12)
- ➤ the destruction of Jerusalem and the Temple (3:12)
- ➤ Judah's Babylonian captivity (4:10)
- ➤ Judah's return from captivity (4:10)
- ➤ the exact name of Christ's birthplace (5:2)
- He was one of the few writing prophets referred to by name by another prophet (see *Jeremiah: Unique Features*).

COMPARISON WITH OTHER BIBLE BOOKS

Isaiah:

- Micah and Isaiah share one significant parallel passage (4:1-3; Isa. 2:2-4). These two contemporaries may have borrowed from Joel, an earlier prophet (see Joel 3:10, the opposite of Micah and Isaiah's message).
- Both prophets used nakedness to emphasize their message (1:8; Isa. 20:2).
- Both spoke of people coming to Israel from Assyria and Egypt (the two extremes of the ancient Near East) in the messianic age (7:12; Isa. 19:23-25).

Jeremiah:

- Jeremiah, writing more than a century later, quoted 3:12 (Jer. 26:18).
- Both spoke of greedy prophets and priests (3:11; Jer. 6:13), as well as of prophets who falsely promise peace (3:5; Jer. 6:14).
- Both spoke of a remnant of Israelites upon whom God will show mercy (7:18-20; Jer. 23:3; 44:28).

OUTLINE

DENUNCIATION OF ISRAEL (1–3)
  Judgment of Samaria (1)
  Why Israel is being judged (2)
  Judgment of Jerusalem (3)
CONSOLATION FOR ISRAEL (4–7)
  Prophesying Israel's restoration (4–5)
    The eternal kingdom (4)
    The eternal king (5:1-6)
    A kingdom triumphant and holy (5:7-15)
  Pleading for Israel's repentance (6)
  Israel's darkness (7:1-10)
  Israel's dawn (7:11-20)

DENUNCIATION OF ISRAEL (1–3)

1:1-7 *The divine indictment.* After noting that his prophecies concerned both Samaria and Jerusalem (capitals of the northern and southern kingdoms), Micah summoned all the earth to hear God's case against his people. His judgment would be catastrophic, as indicated by the figures of earthquakes, volcanoes, and flash floods (1:4). God would judge his people because of their idolatry. Their capital cities, rather than leading them in righteousness, had led them into sin (1:5).

Israel would be judged first (1:6-7; see 2 Kings 17); Judah's judgment would come 130 years later (see 2 Kings 25). Both nations had violated the first commandment (see Exod. 20:3-6), but God would purge the land of all traces of idolatry.

1:8-16 *Mourning like a wild animal.* Micah would strip himself naked and mourn loudly over his nation's coming destruction. Israel's idolatry had spread south to Judah (1:13), therefore Samaria's devastation would spill over into Judah (1:9). This was fulfilled when Sennacherib swept through the northern kingdom and on through northern Judah, right up to the very gates of Jerusalem before being miraculously stopped by the death angel (1:9, 12; see 2 Kings 18–19).

Even Micah's hometown would be affected (1:14; see 1:1). The people would express their sorrow by the extreme measure of shaving their heads (1:16; see exposition on Isa. 7:17-25).

2:1-5 *Plotting at night, sinning at sunrise.* God's judgment was justified by Israel's sin. The nation's leaders spent their nights scheming ways to deprive the poor of their property (2:1-2). God would give their ill-gotten land to foreigners (2:3-5). The nocturnal scheming (2:1) recalls Ahab's night of sullen plotting against Naboth (see 1 Kings 21:1-7).

2:6-11 *"We don't like that kind of talk!"* Many opposed Micah's message of doom (2:6). If they had been living righteously, they would have had nothing to fear from God (2:7). But they were violating the poor, the innocent, the widows and orphans—all special objects of God's care—and therefore they would be judged (2:8-10). The only prophets Israel would listen to were those who shared in their sin and therefore would not condemn them (2:11; see 2 Tim. 4:3-4).

2:12-13 *But then, the Lord will lead them back.* Micah's dark picture of judgment gave way to a bright picture of restoration—a restoration to be realized when Jesus returns to the earth and leads his "sheep" into his millennial kingdom (see *Isaiah: Background*).

3:1-4 *"They're eating my people alive!"* Because Israel's rulers had brutally oppressed the people (3:1-3), God would abandon them when the foreign armies invaded (3:4). Because they had hid their eyes from injustice, God would hide his face from them, refusing to even look at them.

This would happen "in times of trouble" (3:4; see exposition on Isa. 2:5–4:1), which in this case refers to the judgments of 722 and 586 B.C. (compare 3:4 with Jer. 11:11).

3:5-8 *Prophets for sale.* Prophets, like rulers, had violated the trust of their office. Instead of seeking to please God and deliver his message of judgment, they had given the more desirable promises of peace to those who fed them. They would seal their own doom when their false promises failed to materialize. They would show their shame and mourning openly by the traditional gesture of covering their face up to the nose (3:7; compare Lev. 13:45; Ezek. 24:17). Micah, by contrast, could authoritatively proclaim the bitter truth because he was strengthened by God's Spirit (3:8).

3:9-12 *"Jerusalem will fall, and it's all your fault!"* Emboldened by God's Spirit (3:8), Micah warned of the coming judgment. Judah's leaders had made the nation great but in the process had made its citizens miserable. Therefore, their glorious city of Jerusalem would be plowed up like fields and its buildings reduced to rock piles—a fate similar to that of Samaria (see 1:6-7). Jeremiah's book of Lamentations records in painful detail the literal fulfillment of 3:12.

CONSOLATION FOR ISRAEL (4–7)

4:1-8 *His righteous reign in Zion.* Looking ahead again to the "last days" (see exposition on Ezek. 38:1-23), Micah saw a time when God's millennial kingdom will be supreme and all nations of the earth will be spontaneously and irresistibly drawn to it. It will be a time of unprecedented peace and prosperity (4:1-3; compare Isa. 2:2-4). People will dwell in safety and security, and Israel will be at peace with its God (4:4-5).

God will regather his people from around the globe and, in the person of God the Son, Jesus Christ, will reign over them (4:6-7). Jerusalem will be restored to its former greatness.

4:9-13 *Present pain, future prize.* For the present, Judah would suffer exile (4:9-10), but its suffering would be like birth pangs (4:9) leading to a return from exile (4:10) and—looking further ahead—the glorious messianic kingdom (4:11-13).

The nations that will come against Israel at the end of time will not realize that they have been brought together by God so that he can destroy them in one final massive confrontation, which elsewhere in Scripture is called Armageddon (4:11-13; see *Isaiah: Background*). Micah's naming of Babylon as Judah's captor is remarkable: In his day it was not a dominant world power.

5:1-6 *From the house of bread, the bread of life!* Though Judah's last human king would be defeated (5:1; see 2 Kings 25), out of the lowly town of Bethlehem would come Jesus the Messiah, Israel's true king. He had already existed "from the distant past" (5:2), but in God's time he would come to earth, defeat the forces of evil, and establish his millennial kingdom (5:2-6).

Bethlehem means "house of bread." Jesus would call himself the "bread of life" (John 6:48). Assyria (5:6; see 7:12) and Babylon (see 4:10) represent all of Israel's enemies.

5:7-15 *Like the dew, like a lion.* During the Millennium, Israel will be a source of blessing to all righteous Gentiles (5:7). To those who persist in unbelief, however, it will be like a lion enforcing Messiah's rule (5:8). Every enemy will be defeated (5:9). Israel's triumph will come, however, only after God has stripped it of all human military resources (5:10-11) and all false religion (5:12-15).

6:1-5 *His case against them.* Calling inanimate creation as an impartial witness, God invited Israel to present its case against him (6:1), then prepared to present his own case against them (6:2; compare 1:2). With cutting irony, he asked his people whether he had exhausted their patience with all his goodness to them (6:3-5). Against this background of God's faithfulness, Israel's sin was all the more serious.

6:6-8 *One simple requirement.* Speaking for his people, Micah asked rhetorically whether he could secure God's favor by various kinds of sacrifice (6:6-7). But God had already answered that question: He wanted to see humility, justice, and mercy, demonstrating hearts inclined toward him (6:8; see Deut. 6:5; 10:12; 30:15-16).

6:9-12 *But they lack that requirement.* Micah then called on the wise to heed God's warning of judgment (6:9). Unfortunately, there was ample evidence that few Israelites were among the wise. Treasures gained by dishonest means filled their houses (6:10). Their deeds of injustice showed that their hearts were not right with God, therefore his wrath must fall.

6:13-16 *Let the judgment begin!* Because Israel had sinned, God must judge them. Their judgment would be a time of great suffering and frustration (6:13-15). All attempts to escape would be futile (6:14). Israel had walked in the ways of Omri and his son Ahab, the most wicked of their kings.

7:1-7 *A good man is hard to find!* Micah bemoaned Israel's sad moral condition. He found "not one fair-minded person" among them (7:2; compare Isa. 57:1; Ps. 14:3; Rom. 3:10-12). So deep was Israel's sin that it had disrupted all interpersonal relationships (7:5-6). It was just like the days of the judges (see Judg. 21:25). Amid this turmoil, Micah had complete confidence in God (7:7).

7:8-10 *Israel: Down but not out!* Speaking for his nation, Micah accepted full responsibility for the sin that had brought judgment (7:9) and declared that Israel would rise again from the depths of that judgment (7:8). Israel's enemies would witness this restoration and would no longer be able to taunt them, for they themselves would experience a judgment from which they would not recover (7:10).

7:11-13 *Bigger and better than ever!* When Israel is restored, its borders will be greater than ever (7:11-12). This was partially realized in the return from Babylon but will be ultimately fulfilled in the Millennium, when Israel's borders will stretch from Assyria to "the towns of Egypt" (7:12). In the meantime, however, Israel must be purged of its sin (7:13).

7:14-20 *And for his people: Total forgiveness!* Micah asked God to meet the needs of his people and protect them from danger (7:14). In response, God promised to do miracles for his people just as he did when delivering them from Egypt (7:15). Israel's enemies will be defeated, not because of the greatness of the nation, but because of the greatness of their God (7:16-17). Israel's God is unique, for he will forgive them of their sins, once and for all. Their sins will not deter him from his plans to regenerate them (7:18-19). He will keep his unconditional covenants with Abraham (see Gen. 12:1-3), David (see 2 Sam. 7), and Jeremiah (see Jer. 31:31-34).

PEOPLE TO REMEMBER FROM MICAH

MICAH

Key Facts: Prophet, predicted Christ's birthplace (5:2; Matt. 2:6)
Total Bible References: 2
Key References: 1–7; Jer. 26:18

Micah Speaks

Am I the only true prophet left? Are all the rest godless liars? I sometimes feel as Elijah must have felt! Both our leaders and those they lead seem to have forsaken God. It's harder to find honest people than to glean grapes or figs after all the fruit pickers have been there! (3:1, 5-8; 7:1-2; 1 Kings 19:10)

Who would have thought the time would come when your worst enemies would be in your own household! But thank God this will not be so forever. God has told me of a day when "the Temple of the LORD in Jerusalem will become the most important place on earth," when people even from among our present enemies will say, "Come, let us go up to the mountain of the LORD." It will be a time of peace, when they will "beat their swords into plowshares and their spears into pruning hooks." (4:1-3; 7:5-6)

I received this amazing message from God here in Moresheth, a two-day journey from Jerusalem, about the time Isaiah heard the same words in the Holy City itself. But it's even more thrilling to compare what he has revealed to each of us concerning the future Messiah. Isaiah predicted *how* he will be born, and I have had the privilege of revealing *where* he'll be born! Indeed, "Where is another God like you?" (1:1; 5:2; 7:18; Isa. 2:2-4; 7:14).

Spiritual Lessons from Micah

- When we, as Christians, seek to help people or to share God's Word with them, it is comforting to know we can be empowered by God's Holy Spirit. Micah had this assurance (3:8), as did Paul (1 Cor. 2:1-4; see John 14:15-17).
- Adversity is often God's way of both disciplining us and bringing greater purity into our lives (7:9; see Ps. 119:67, 71; Heb. 12:5-11).

Key Verse

"O people, the LORD has already told you what is good, and this is what he requires: to do what is right, to love mercy, and to walk humbly with your God" (6:8).

NAHUM

BACKGROUND

The end of the seventh century B.C. was an exciting time for Judah, as the great reformer Josiah (640–609) ruled in Jerusalem. Over this time of blessing, however, loomed the threat of invasion by Assyria. Nineveh, Assyria's capital, had been the site of a great revival in Jonah's day, nearly 150 years before in about 750 (Jonah 3:4-10). But the revival had faded quickly, and Assyria destroyed Israel's northern kingdom in 722 and nearly destroyed Judah in 701. Now Assyria had set its sights on Judah once again, so God called Nahum to proclaim his final judgment against Nineveh.

Nineveh's doom would come soon after Nahum's warnings, when the rising Babylonian empire defeated it in 612. Babylon would go on to win victories against Judah in 605 and 597, finally defeating it in 586.

Zephaniah and Jeremiah were Nahum's contemporaries.

AUTHOR

Nahum. Biographical details unknown. Even the location of his hometown, Elkosh (1:1), is uncertain.

DATE

The fall of Thebes (also called "No-amon," 3:8), which occurred in 663 B.C., had already taken place by Nahum's time. Assuming that Nineveh's fall in 612 (the focus of Nahum's prophecy) was yet to come, Nahum's ministry would be dated sometime between those two events. The zeal for feasts and vows (1:15) may indicate a time after Josiah's reforms had reached their climax with the rediscovery of the law in 621.

RECIPIENTS

Though Nahum focused on Assyria, his prophecy was addressed to his own people, who had suffered long under Assyria and were now invited to rejoice at its approaching destruction (1:15).

c. 750 B.C.
Jonah preaches, Nineveh repents

722
Nineveh (Assyria) conquers Israel

627
Jeremiah begins ministry

621
Law rediscovered, Nahum predicts Nineveh's fall?

612
Fall of Nineveh

586
Fall of Judah

PURPOSE

- To announce Nineveh's doom, but in a larger sense to affirm that God punishes all sin. Though he is "slow to get angry," he will not let wickedness go unpunished (1:3).
- To affirm God's sovereign control over history. Nineveh's destruction was not coincidence or simply the transition from one human empire to another. It was the direct result of God's judgment.
- To assure Judah that God cares for his own.

UNIQUE FEATURES

- Nahum is our major source of information concerning the destruction of Assyria. Other prophets focusing on the doom of particular nations include: Isaiah (Assyria and Babylon); Jeremiah (Babylon); Obadiah (Edom); Zephaniah (Judah); Ezekiel (Egypt); and Daniel (Babylon and Persia).
- Nahum and Obadiah were the only OT prophets who pronounced doom on a pagan nation without also mentioning the sins of Israel.
- Nahum documents the cruelty of Assyria, which has been called the arch villain of the OT, more ruthless by far than Israel's other foes.

COMPARISON WITH OTHER BIBLE BOOKS

Isaiah and Romans:

- Nahum spoke of a messenger on the mountains, bringing the good news of deliverance from Assyria (1:15):
  - ➤ Isaiah, writing some 100 years before Nahum, used similar words to describe the good news of deliverance from Babylonian exile (Isa. 40:9; 52:7).
  - ➤ Paul, writing some 700 years later, used similar words to describe deliverance from sin through the good news of Jesus (Rom. 10:15).

OUTLINE

WHO WILL DESTROY NINEVEH? (1)
HOW WILL HE DESTROY NINEVEH? (2)
WHY WILL HE DESTROY NINEVEH? (3:1-7)
WHEN WILL HE DESTROY NINEVEH? (3:8-19)

WHO WILL DESTROY NINEVEH? (1)

1:1-7 *The God of Judah, that's who!* Nahum began his prophecy against Nineveh by describing the God who intended to destroy that oppressive nation. He is

- a jealous God, taking vengeance on his enemies (1:2)
- a patient God, slow to anger (1:3)
- a God of power whom none can resist (1:3-6)
- a good God, a refuge to those who love him (1:7)

The God of Judah is certainly capable of executing his judgment against Nineveh.

1:8-14 *"And it's no use resisting."* Any resistance Nineveh might muster against the Lord would be futile (1:8-9, 11). Though they may have succeeded in the past against God's people (see 2 Kings 17–19), they would not succeed this time (1:9). They would be destroyed in a flash, like dry stubble (1:10). God addressed Israel, promising Assyria's destruction (1:12-13), then turned his attention back to Assyria, vowing that he was "preparing a grave" for them (1:14).

1:15 *Wonderful news! They've been wiped out!* Nineveh's doom and Sennacherib's death would be good news for Judah. They would be able to go about their peaceful endeavors without fear. The prophecy had been partially fulfilled many years before, in 701 B.C., when God had forced Sennacherib to lift his siege of Jerusalem (see 2 Kings 18–19). Its final fulfillment would come with Nineveh's destruction in 612.

HOW WILL HE DESTROY NINEVEH? (2)

2:1-7 *"Attention, Nineveh: You're next!"* Nahum warned Nineveh to prepare for an attack (2:1). They had taken Israel into captivity and had ravaged Judah (2:2); now it was their turn to be ravaged. Nahum accurately foresaw the red-robed Medo-Babylonian army, whose chariots, according to secular historians, had sharp implements attached to their wheels, giving the appearance of torches or lightning as the sunlight reflected off the rotating blades (2:3-4). The drunken defenders were taken totally by surprise and were helpless before this great army (2:5-7).

It is unclear to archaeologists how the attackers used Nineveh's extensive waterways to invade. They either

- opened the floodgates and flooded the city, causing its foundations to crumble, as 2:6 might suggest,
- or they drained the waterways (see 2:8) and entered through the exposed walls.

2:8-10 *The city stripped of silver.* Nineveh had been a center of power for more than 300 years, but that was about to end. The attackers would leave Nineveh completely void of its treasures, most of which had been taken from its own victims such as Israel. Ninevites were in a state of disbelieving grief and shock. The unimaginable had happened.

2:11-13 *The vicious lion will be the victim.* Comparing Nineveh to a mighty lion, Nahum foresaw a time when there would be no trace of his den. Though it would not happen for another 20 years, Nahum viewed Nineveh's destruction as an accomplished fact. God had given the word; it was as good as done. History records that armies later marched over the site of Nineveh without realizing it had ever been there. Assyria would learn the bitter lesson that to oppose Israel is to seal one's own doom (see Gen. 12:3).

WHY WILL HE DESTROY NINEVEH? (3:1-7)

3:1-7 *How and why it will fall.* Amid horrifying descriptions of Nineveh's fall, Nahum listed some of the sins that had brought it down (3:1, 4). Nineveh would receive what it had given: cruelty without mercy. Nineveh had an estimated population of 600,000 at the time of its fall. So many of them were slain that the few survivors stumbled over the corpses (3:3).

WHEN WILL HE DESTROY NINEVEH? (3:8-19)

3:8-13 *What goes around, comes around.* God had used Assyria to bring judgment on the Egyptian city of Thebes (3:8-10), but Assyria had been unnecessarily cruel in the process (3:10). Now, Nineveh would be as helpless before God's judgment as Thebes had been before Assyria. Its outposts of defense would fall, just like fruit shaken from a tree (3:12-13). The "ripe figs" (3:12) may also suggest the imminence of Nineveh's fall.

3:14-18 *They'll flee like locusts, never to return.* Nahum mockingly urged the Ninevites to prepare for a long siege (3:14), knowing full well that the invading army was at hand and such preparations would be too late (3:15). The swarms of people descending daily on Nineveh to seek wealth would flee like locusts before the sun when the invaders came (3:15-17). Nineveh's people would be scattered, never to return (3:18). Assyria would reap what it had sown (see 2 Kings 17:24).

3:19 *A fatal wound, a fitting end.* The news of Nineveh's fall would cause great rejoicing in Judah and the many other nations it had oppressed.

PEOPLE TO REMEMBER FROM NAHUM

NAHUM

Key Facts: Prophet, predicted destruction of Nineveh
Total Bible References: 1 (1:1)
Key References: 1–3

Nahum Speaks

I wonder if the city is as huge and magnificent as everyone claims. At least the last prophet assigned to it had the opportunity to actually hold a revival within its massive walls. But it's been nearly 150 years since Jonah thundered out his message. I'm sure I'll never see Nineveh, however much I proclaim its doom to its former victims here in Israel. (1:1-3; Jonah 3:3-4)

What an incredibly wicked city it must be, filled with immorality, bloodshed, lies, and unspeakable cruelty! Well, at least they can't complain of no warning when it finally does happen. Our God is "slow to get angry." But apparently Nineveh has crossed the line of his patience, thus sealing its doom. (1:3; 3:1-4, 6, 10)

I wonder if ever a prophet received such graphic descriptions of a city's destruction as have been given me—the shields flashing in the sunlight, scarlet-clad enemy troops advancing with raised swords, glittering chariots pulled by prancing steeds rushing down the streets, angry torrents of water wiping out everything in their wake, and the panic-filled people staggering like drunkards in their final death throes of agony! It's too bad for them that Jonah's revival didn't last. (2:3–3:18)

Spiritual Lessons from Nahum

- When speaking out on moral issues, we should maintain Nahum's balanced perspective:
  - ➤ He rebuked the sinners (1:2).
  - ➤ He reassured the saints (1:7, 15).

Key Verses

"The LORD is good. When trouble comes, he is a strong refuge. And he knows everyone who trusts in him. But he sweeps away his enemies in an overwhelming flood. He pursues his foes into the darkness of night" (1:7-8).

HABAKKUK

BACKGROUND
Israel's northern kingdom had fallen to Assyria in 722 B.C., leaving only the tiny southern kingdom of Judah in the Promised Land. In 612, Assyria was itself conquered by Babylon, the new masters of the ancient Near East. Now, Babylon was threatening to invade Judah. Even worse, the reforms of the good King Josiah, begun in 621, were losing their influence, and Judah's spiritual condition was at an all-time low (see 1:2-4). Into this situation came Habakkuk, recording for his people what God taught him about his coming judgment of both Judah and Babylon, his sovereignty over human affairs, and his loving faithfulness toward his own.

AUTHOR
Habakkuk (1:1) was apparently a Levite with experience in the music ministry of the Temple (3:1, 19).

DATE
The prominence of Babylon in Habakkuk indicates a post–612 B.C. date, but Babylon apparently had not yet invaded Judah, placing the book before 605. Though no kings are mentioned, the nation's sad spiritual condition suggests a date near the end of Josiah's reign, perhaps after the wicked Jehoiakim replaced him in 609 (see 2 Chron. 36:8; Jer. 22:18-19).

RECIPIENTS
Habakkuk probably focused his ministry on the "just" among Judeans (2:4) rather than on the wicked (1:2-4), upon whom he wished only swift judgment.

PURPOSE
- To announce that
  - the sinful in Judah will be punished
  - though Babylon will be God's instrument for punishing Judah, it too will be punished in due time

621 B.C. *Rediscovery of Law sparks Josiah's revival*

612 *Fall of Nineveh*

c. 609 *Josiah dies, Habakkuk prophesies*

605 *Babylon's 1st invasion of Judah*

586 *Fall of Judah*

538 *1st exiles return*

  - ➤ God will preserve Judah's faithful remnant (2:4)
- To help Habakkuk himself (as well as his readers) be patient with God's sovereign working in history

UNIQUE FEATURES

- Habakkuk is the only OT book consisting entirely of a dialogue between God and a human individual. (Parts of Jonah, Job, and a few other books feature such dialogues.) All other prophetic books consist mainly of records of the prophets' preaching.
- Habakkuk and Jeremiah were the last prophets to the southern kingdom before the Babylonian captivity—thus Habakkuk's 11th-hour explanations as to why God was using the Babylonians and whether or not a remnant would survive.
- Habakkuk saw one of the greatest manifestations of God's glory recorded in Scripture (3:3-15).

COMPARISON WITH OTHER BIBLE BOOKS

Isaiah:

- Both taunt the proud Babylonians (2:6-20; Isa. 14).
- Both include "woes" (2:6, 9, 12, 15, 19; Isa. 5:8-23 and other scattered occurrences).
- Both speak of the "righteous" or the "just" who trust in the Lord (2:4; Isa. 26:1-10).
- Both record a theophany, a visible manifestation of God (3; Isa. 6).

New Testament:

- The NT quotes 2:4 three times, each time with a slightly different emphasis:
  - ➤ "the righteous" (Rom. 1:17)
  - ➤ "will live" (Gal. 3:11)
  - ➤ "by faith" (Heb. 10:38)

OUTLINE

THE DOUBTS (1–2)

Question: Why does Judah go unpunished? (1:1-4)
Answer: Judah will be punished (1:5-11)
Question: Will pagans be allowed to punish Judah? (1:12-17)
Answer: Yes, but they too will be punished (2)

THE SHOUTS (3)

Words of praise (3:1-15)
Words of fear and faith (3:16-19)

THE DOUBTS (1–2)

1:1-4 *"I'm confused!"* Habakkuk began his book with a question for the Lord: For many years he had observed Judah's worsening moral condition and had asked God to intervene, yet God had seemingly ignored the situation. Would God do nothing about Judah's great wickedness?

1:5-11 *"Don't worry, I'm doing something about it."* God replied that, even as Habakkuk made his inquiry, he was preparing Babylon (also called the Chaldeans, 1:6) to bring judgment against Judah (1:5-6), just as he had used them to judge many other nations, including Assyria and Egypt (1:7-11).

Being only human, Habakkuk had suffered from tunnel vision as he considered Judah's situation. God invited him to "look at the nations" (1:5) and view the world through God's eyes. From that viewpoint, all nations both great and small are merely tools in God's hands (1:5-6).

1:12-17 *"Now I'm really confused!"* Surprised that God was planning to use wicked Babylon to judge his own people, Habakkuk reminded the Lord of his righteousness (1:12-13) and of Babylon's brutality (1:14-17). Rather than questioning God outright, Habakkuk simply presented the facts as he saw them and left it up to God to answer his unspoken question: Why should *they* punish *us?*

2:1-4 *On the watchtower: "The just shall live by faith."* Taking up a position in the "watchtower," Habakkuk waited humbly and patiently for God's answer (2:1). God answered, instructing Habakkuk to write down his words plainly so that those who read them could quickly relay them to others (2:2). The message would not be totally fulfilled right away, but the "righteous" would wait in faith for its fulfillment (2:3-4).

2:5-17 *Betrayed by their drunken pride.* The Chaldeans were drunk with wine and with power. They went on their military forays for the sheer thrill of it, "never satisfied," gathering up "many nations and peoples" (2:5). Though they would be temporarily victorious over Judah and other nations, eventually they would fall, and their former victims would then ridicule them, as God illustrated with four "woes" (2:6, 9, 12, 15). Those they had oppressed would rise up against them (2:6-8). Their great cities, built by bloodshed, would not be enough to protect them (2:9-13), for God would ultimately triumph (2:14). They had made other nations "drunk" with their violence; now they would get a taste of their own drink (2:15-17).

2:18-20 *Their helpless idols, his holy Temple.* The Chaldeans would make the fatal mistake of trusting in their gods, which were nothing but mute, lifeless, helpless idols (2:18-19; compare exposition on Isa. 44:6-28). Israel's God, by contrast, sat securely in his heaven. Not only could he talk: He had already spoken! The only sensible thing for humans to do is to be silent and listen to him!

THE SHOUTS (3)

3:1-15 *His song of salvation.* Habakkuk responded to God's revelation concerning Judah and Babylon with a prayer evidently intended to be set to music. The original Hebrew and several translations include the term *Shigionoth,* which is similar to the term *Shiggaion* that appears in the title of Psalm 7 (the NLT does not include this word, but it conveys the idea of music: "A psalm of David, which he sang to the LORD . . ."). The term *Selah,* common in the psalms, also occurs three times in this passage.

Calling on God to act quickly but with mercy (3:2), Habakkuk recalled God's past actions on Israel's behalf:

First stanza: God's glory (3:3-4). Seeing what was apparently a theophany (see exposition on Gen. 17:1-8), Habakkuk likened God's glory to the brilliance of light rays emanating from the sun—an ever-present reminder of the glory and majesty of the only true God.

Second stanza: God's power (3:5-11). Throughout Israel's history—at the Exodus, in the wilderness, at the Jordan, during the days of Joshua—God had delivered them by his mighty power, and his power was fearsome to behold!

Third stanza: God's judgment (3:12-15). Just as God delivered his people from the Red Sea, so he would deliver them from the flood of the Chaldeans. Once again, however, God's judgment was presented as nothing to be taken lightly.

***3:16-19** The singer's reaction: Fear and faith.* Habakkuk had invited God to begin his judgment (3:1-2). Having been reminded of what happened whenever God judged (3:5-15), he now trembled with fear (3:16). Still, having seen things from God's perspective, he could respond in submission, praise, and trust (3:17-19). God would see his people through the coming crisis.

The benefit of prayer is not that it changes God, but that it changes the one who prays!

PEOPLE TO REMEMBER FROM HABAKKUK

HABAKKUK

Key Fact: Prophet who said "the righteous will live by their faith" (2:4)

Occupation: Prophet, musician (1:1; 3:1, 19)

Total Bible References: 2

Key References: 1–3

Habakkuk Speaks

Let me just make one final notation to the choir director, so that they'll be sure to use stringed instruments when they sing this song. (3:19)

There, my composition is finished. I wonder how it will sound when sung by that marvelous Levitical choir. Actually, I wonder if they'll even want to sing it! One thing is sure—they won't be bored with the lyrics! Some of the stanzas resemble a funeral dirge, while others will probably come across like a glorious chorus of hallelujahs. (1:2-4; 2:14; 2 Chron. 29:30)

But that's just how I've felt while writing it. I've experienced both frustration and faith. There was the frustration of witnessing both the growing cancer of moral decay among our own people and the growing Babylonian threat from without. (1:4, 6)

Then he assured me that judgment would fall upon both the Babylonians and the rebels within our own ranks. He would use Babylon to discipline us but then, in his own time, would deal with Babylon as well. (1:7-11; 2:5-6)

How well I recall that day when I reached the end of my rope trying to figure out his will. I vowed to wait until I understood just what God had in mind. Then came his answer: "The righteous will live by their faith." So simple, but it made everything just sort of fall into place. Yes, our matchless God knows what he is doing. It's up to us to wait on his perfect timing, and live by faith. (2:1, 4)

Spiritual Lessons from Habakkuk

- Habakkuk has been called the Doubting Thomas of the Old Testament (1:1-3, 13), yet his glorious statement on faith (the exact opposite of doubt) is

quoted three times in the NT. The obvious lesson? God uses us in spite of ourselves!
- No matter how dark and desperate our circumstance, we can "rejoice in the LORD," as did Habakkuk (3:18-19).

Key Verse
"The righteous will live by their faith" (2:4).

ZEPHANIAH

686 B.C
Death of Hezekiah, ancestor of Zephaniah

632
Josiah turns to Lord, Zephaniah begins ministry?

621
Law rediscovered, Zephaniah ends ministry?

586
Fall of Judah

BACKGROUND

After the enlightened reign of Hezekiah (728–686 B.C.), Judah had endured 55 years under two of its worst kings, Manasseh and Amon, before Josiah was made king at age eight in 640. As he grew into adulthood, Josiah proved to be the most godly of Judah's kings. He experienced a personal spiritual awakening in 632 at age 16 (2 Chron. 34:3), and after the law was rediscovered in 621, he led a nationwide revival (2 Chron. 34:14-18, 29-33).

Despite Josiah's reforms and the initial positive response of the people (2 Kings 23:3), many in Judah remained lukewarm in their faith. Into this situation came Zephaniah, warning of the impending invasion by Babylon and of the "day of the LORD," the final and universal judgment at the end of human history (1:1–3:7). Looking still further into God's plans for his people, he foretold Judah's return from Babylon and the final, triumphant page of human history, the glorious millennial kingdom of God (3:8-20).

Nahum and Jeremiah were Zephaniah's contemporaries.

AUTHOR

Descended from King Hezekiah (1:1) and therefore related to Josiah, Zephaniah may well have influenced the young king as he sought the Lord and tried to promote spiritual revival.

DATE

While Zephaniah's ministry is said only to have taken place in the days of Josiah (1:1), it may well have been during the years between the beginning of Josiah's personal awakening (632 B.C.) and the onset of his more public revival efforts in 621.

LOCATION

Apparently Jerusalem, since it is mentioned often (1:4, 10, 12).

PURPOSE

- To warn of the coming "day of the LORD" and correct misconceptions about it. Many Israelites thought it would be a day for rejoicing, but Zephaniah revealed that idolatrous Israelites were considered God's enemies just as the Canaanites had been. It is not nationality but spirituality that counts.
- To hold out hope for a remnant that will survive God's judgment (3:9-20).

UNIQUE FEATURES

- The expression "the day of the LORD" is found more times in Zephaniah than in any other Bible book. As explained in *Isaiah: Background* and the exposition on Isaiah 2:5–4:1, the term can refer to any time God intervenes in history in a supernatural way, though most often it refers to judgment, particularly the Great Tribulation at history's end. Zephaniah used the term to refer to both the Babylonian invasion and the end times.

COMPARISON WITH OTHER BIBLE BOOKS

Genesis:

- Both speak of God's cutting off humankind from the face of the earth (1:3; Gen. 6:7).
- Genesis recorded the beginning of Moab and Ammon (Gen. 19:36-38); Zephaniah foretold their end (2:8-11). The fathers of these two nations were born to Lot through incest soon after the destruction of Sodom and Gomorrah. Zephaniah compared that event to the impending destruction of Moab and Ammon.
- Genesis recorded God's resting after Creation (Gen. 2:2-3); Zephaniah predicted God's resting again after completing his work of redemption (3:17, KJV).

OUTLINE

A SAD DAY COMING (1:1–3:8)
  Judah and Jerusalem judged (1:1–2:3)
  Enemy nations judged (2:4-15)
  Judah and Jerusalem judged (3:1-8)
A GLAD DAY COMING (3:9-20)

A SAD DAY COMING (1:1–3:8)

1:1-13 *Introducing: The day of the Lord.* After establishing his identity (1:1; see *Author*) and divine mission, Zephaniah lost no time in warning of an approaching time of universal judgment, the "day of the LORD" (1:7; see *Unique Features*). This terrible day would involve worldwide destruction (1:2-3), but Zephaniah began by focusing mainly on one nation: idolatrous Judah (1:4-9). God had "prepared" his people as a "sacrifice" for Babylon, his "guests" (1:7, KJV)! No one, no matter how high or low, would escape (1:8-9). All would suffer (1:10-13). Till judgment began, Judah would be spiritually complacent (1:12).

Concerning "all who avoid stepping on the threshold" (1:9, NIV), see 1 Samuel 5:1-5. Tradition holds that Nebuchadnezzar's army entered

Jerusalem through the Fish Gate (1:10), known today as the Damascus Gate, on the city's north side.

1:14-18 *A most dreadful day!* The day of the Lord would be a dark and terrible day, from which neither Judah's mighty men (1:14) nor its wealth (1:18) could save it. The bodies of the dead would be cast aside as refuse because there would be no one left to bury them (1:17). The land "will be devoured" by a God jealous because of his people's forsaking him for idols (1:18; see 1:4-5).

2:1-3 *Calling Judah to repent.* Amid his dire forecast of doom, Zephaniah held out some hope of escape to any who would repent and turn to God. But time was at a premium: They would need to repent "before judgment begins." The only way to turn a nation to God is to turn its citizens—one by one—to God.

2:4-15 *Judgment in all directions.* God's wrath upon Judah would overflow to its enemies at all points of the compass:

Judgment to the west: Philistia (2:4-7). The great cities of Philistia would be destroyed. They would become pasture land—for the faithful remnant of Judah!

Judgment to the east: Moab and Ammon (2:8-11). Moab and Ammon would share the fate of Sodom and Gomorrah (see *Comparison with Other Bible Books*). Their land, too, would ultimately become Judah's possession. Someday, God will destroy all vestiges of idolatry and, even in the remotest parts of the earth, he alone will be worshiped (2:10-11).

Judgment to the south: Ethiopia (2:12). Ethiopia would also be judged. Ethiopia ruled Egypt from 720 to 654 B.C., so Egypt was probably included in this indictment.

Judgment to the north: Assyria (2:13-15). Assyria, proud world leaders for nearly 300 years (2:15), would experience sudden and complete destruction. The beautiful city of Nineveh would become a place fit only for wild beasts. Observers would express scorn and contempt at its memory. (See exposition on the book of Nahum.)

3:1-7 *He was there, but no one noticed.* Having pronounced judgment on all four sides, Zephaniah zeroed in on his true target: Judah. The sins of the surrounding nations had "polluted" Jerusalem. Its princes, judges, prophets, and priests were all guilty of violating their trusts to enrich themselves (3:1-4). Despite Jerusalem's sins, God, through his faithful prophets, had maintained a witness within its walls, yet still they had shamelessly pursued their sinful ways (3:5). God had punished Judah's pagan neighbors, hoping Judah would learn from it, but they did not (3:6-7).

3:8 *"Wait for Armageddon."* God called the faithful among his people to "be patient" for the day when he will "accuse these evil nations." He will destroy them with "the fire of [his] jealousy" (compare 1:18). A comparison with other Bible references to such a gathering suggests this describes the final great battle of Armageddon (see exposition on Mic. 4:9-13).

A GLAD DAY COMING (3:9-20)

3:9-13 *Godliness will bring peace.* After the defeat of his foes, God will "purify the lips of all people," purging them of the vocabulary of idolatry, so that they can worship him (3:9). He will also purify and restore his people, and they will dwell in peace and be in fellowship with him and with all humankind (3:10-13). Because they are spiritually right they will be physically secure.

3:14-20 *They'll be moved out, then he'll move in.* Once the Promised Land is rid of God's enemies, God himself will resettle his people there and dwell among them. It will be a time of healing, peace, and joy. The restoration of Judah following the Babylonian captivity was only a partial fulfillment of this promise. Its ultimate fulfillment will come when Jesus returns to earth and establishes his millennial kingdom.

PEOPLE TO REMEMBER FROM ZEPHANIAH

ZEPHANIAH

Key Facts: Prophet, spoke of the "day of the LORD" more often than any other OT prophet
Total Bible References: 1 (1:1)
Key References: 1–3

Zephaniah Speaks

My great-great-grandfather once escaped the wrath of his enemies, but we will not! Perhaps the ministry of godly Isaiah prompted the Lord to save Jerusalem in the days of Hezekiah. But there will be no stay of execution this time. Hopefully, those few among us who still love God will look to him for protection in those frightful hours of judgment. (1:2-4; 2:3; Isa. 37:21-36)

What terrible words his Spirit has directed me to employ in describing our deplorable spiritual condition: I had to describe my beloved Jerusalem as being rebellious and polluted and oppressing. I described our political leaders as savage lions and wolves devouring dead carcasses, and our prophets and priests as rebellious and polluted just like the city itself. (3:1-4)

Horrible words, shameful thoughts, that should never appear in one's vocabulary referring to our once holy city! But there is hope! Grief will someday turn to glory. The Lord himself, the true king of Israel, will sanctify both our lips and our language, so that once again we—and all the rest of the nations—can call on his name and serve him as we should. (3:9, 15)

Spiritual Lessons from Zephaniah

- The Bible urges us to sing praises to God (see Ps. 30:4; Eph. 5:18-19). Too often in our times of need we substitute sighing for singing. However, the entire Trinity sings:
  - The Father sings (3:17).
  - The Son sings (see Matt. 26:30; Heb. 2:12).
  - The Holy Spirit sings (see 1 Cor. 14:15).
- Zephaniah exhorts us to clean up our conversation in light of the Lord's approaching return (3:9, see Eph. 4:29-31; 5:4).

Key Verse

"Beg the LORD to save you—all you who are humble, all you who uphold justice. Walk humbly and do what is right. Perhaps even yet the LORD will protect you from his anger on that day of destruction" (2:3).

HAGGAI

538 B.C. Exiles return with Zerubbabel

535 Temple rebuilding stops

520 Work resumes, through ministries of Haggai, Zechariah

516 Temple finished

473 Esther saves Jews still in Persia

457 More exiles return with Ezra

445 Nehemiah rebuilds wall

BACKGROUND

The first group of Jews returned from Babylonian exile in 538 B.C. (Ezra 1), and in 536 began rebuilding the Temple (Ezra 3:8-13). In about 535, however, deeply discouraged and under intense opposition, their work had ground to a halt (Ezra 4:24). 15 years later, in 520, God raised up Haggai and Zechariah to encourage them in the rebuilding and in personal holiness.

AUTHOR

Both Haggai and Zechariah are named by Ezra (Ezra 5:1; 6:14). Like Nehemiah, who would come to Jerusalem much later to rebuild its walls, Haggai was a man of action: After the Temple had sat unfinished for 15 years, it took Haggai just 23 days to inspire the people to resume the work. (The work would finally be completed in about 515—see Ezra 6:15.)

DATE

1:1 dates Haggai's ministry in "the second year of King Darius's reign," or 520 B.C. (compare Ezra 4:24). The book can be divided into three separate prophecies, each given on a specified day of that year:

- First prophecy (1): first day of sixth month, Elul (August–September) (1:1)
- Second prophecy (2:1-9): 21st day of seventh month, Tishri (September–October) (2:1)
- Third prophecy (2:10-23): 24th day of ninth month, Chislev (November–December) (2:10, 20)

Haggai probably recorded his prophecies soon after giving them.

RECIPIENTS

The Jews who had returned from exile in 538 B.C.

PURPOSE

- To encourage the rebuilding of the Temple.
- To give instruction in holiness.
- To show God's faithfulness.

UNIQUE FEATURES

- Haggai's writings, like Ezekiel's, are very precisely dated (see *Date*).
- Haggai is notable for his frequent use of the phrase "this is what the LORD Almighty says" and similar phrases (some 25 occurrences), emphasizing the seriousness of his message and the fact that God was still speaking to his people in the postexilic era.

COMPARISON WITH OTHER BIBLE BOOKS

Ezekiel:

- Both speak of the millennial Temple (2:9; Ezek. 40–42).
- Both speak of a "shaking" of the land of Israel (2:6; Ezek. 38:19).
- Both have special names for the Messiah:
  - in Ezekiel, "David" (Ezek. 37:24; though this could be a reference to a literally resurrected King David)
  - in Haggai, "Zerubbabel" (2:23)

Jeremiah:

- Both include significant prophecies involving a signet ring, the symbol of royal authority:
  - Jeremiah spoke of King Jehoiachin as a signet ring that God would cast away (Jer. 22:24), symbolizing the end of the Davidic kings.
  - In Haggai, the signet ring was taken up again and put back on the Lord's hand, signifying that the Messiah ("Zerubbabel") will be the last and greatest Davidic king (2:23).

OUTLINE

HIS WORD IN AUGUST: PERFORM (1)
- The call (1:1-11)
- The response (1:12-15)

HIS WORD IN OCTOBER: BE PATIENT (2:1-9)

HIS WORD IN DECEMBER: PONDER (2:10-23)
- Judah's contamination (2:10-14)
- God's determination (2:15-19)
- The Great Tribulation (2:20-22)
- Zerubbabel's elevation (2:23)

HIS WORD IN AUGUST: PERFORM (1)

1:1-4 *"The right time for ours, the wrong time for his!"* In August of 520 B.C. (see *Date*), God spoke to Haggai, expressing concern that the returned exiles were delaying the Temple's rebuilding (1:1-2). Haggai relayed God's concern to the people, rebuking them for having built luxurious homes for themselves while the Temple lay in ruins (1:3-4).

1:5-11 *"The more you get, the less you have. Why is that?"* Haggai challenged the people to take stock of their situation: They had worked hard with comparatively little result (1:5-6, 9-10) because they had left God out of their lives (1:9). The current drought was God's way of getting their attention (1:11). These Jews had not learned a secret Christ would teach: that God's richest blessings come to those who seek first his kingdom (see Matt. 6:33). They did not realize that blessings from God depend on obedience to God. No Temple, no blessing.

1:12-15 *With three mighty men, the building begins.* After a delay of 15 years (see *Background*), it took just 23 days (1:15) for Haggai, with the help of Zerubbabel the governor and Joshua the high priest, to restart the Temple reconstruction. God had "sparked the enthusiasm" of these three men (1:14), and the people followed their lead. Great things can be accomplished when God's people are in obedience to and in fellowship with him (1:12).

Ezra's account of the rebuilding suggests that, besides encouraging the builders on God's behalf (see Ezra 5:1, 6:14), both Haggai and Zechariah actually helped with the manual labor (see Ezra 5:2). (Joshua is called "Jeshua" in Ezra's account.)

HIS WORD IN OCTOBER: BE PATIENT (2:1-9)

2:1-9 *Smaller, yes, but far more glorious!* In the months following the resumption of reconstruction, the Lord gave Haggai messages of encouragement for the builders. Perhaps recalling the discouragement that had helped end the earlier efforts (see Ezra 3:12), Haggai acknowledged that this second Temple would lack the grandeur of Solomon's Temple (2:3) but gave assurance that God was with them (2:4-5) and that he had great plans for this new Temple (2:6-9). The description of the new Temple is generally seen as a foreshadowing of the millennial Temple as well (see Ezek. 40–42).

Nearly 70 years had passed since the destruction of Solomon's Temple; though only the oldest would have remembered it, they would surely have described it often to their children while in exile.

HIS WORD IN DECEMBER: PONDER (2:10-23)

2:10-14 *Sin is highly contagious.* Two months later, Haggai spoke of the need for holiness. With rhetorical questions, he showed that a ceremonially holy object cannot transfer its holiness to another object (2:12), but an *unclean* object contaminates everything it touches (2:13; see Lev. 22:4-6; Num. 19:11). The people should be very concerned about the effects of their personal sins on the nation (2:14). Common sense teaches the same lesson: A healthy person cannot communicate his or her health to a dying person, but a dying person can spread contagion to the healthy.

2:15-19 *As the Temple goes up, the blessings come down.* In the past, because of their sin, Israel had experienced hardship (2:15-17). Yet God was determined to bless them, and now that they had obeyed him and begun rebuilding his Temple, the blessings would come (2:18-19).

2:20-23 *"Tell the governor great honor awaits him!"* Haggai's final word of encouragement was to Zerubbabel, political leader of the returned exiles. To Zerubbabel went the honor of comparison to Israel's Messiah: After the Great Tribulation at the end of history (2:21-22; see 2:6; *Isaiah: Background;* exposition on Isa. 2:5–4:1), the

Messiah—here called Zerubbabel—will be given the honor and authority embodied in the signet ring (see *Comparison with Other Bible Books*).

❖ ❖ ❖

PEOPLE TO REMEMBER FROM HAGGAI

HAGGAI

Key Facts: Prophet, helped lead Israel in rebuilding the Temple (1:1-8; Ezra 5:1)
Total Bible References: 11
Key References: 1–2; Ezra 5:1; 6:14

Haggai Speaks

One fact is clear: My little book has indeed been inspired by God, as I tried to note as often as possible. Hopefully, future priests and Levites will recognize this as they ponder and proclaim its truths. Maybe they'll call it, "Haggai's Tale of Three Temples," for so it is. The people came up with such miserable excuses for not getting started right away in rebuilding the Temple: "It isn't time yet," they said! Obviously, however, the real reasons for their inaction were unconcern, laziness, and greed! Well, I quickly reminded them that the crop failures, droughts, and hardships we had all experienced were simply God's way of punishing such wickedness. (1:1-6, 9-11)

Of course the Lord then called us to action, instructing us to go to the mountains and gather materials to rebuild his house. And that's exactly what we did! Now, after that inexcusable delay of 15 years, our people have once again begun the rebuilding. (1:8, 12-14)

To be sure, this Temple will be far smaller than Solomon's. I recall the keen disappointment of our people as this "second Temple" began to take shape. But how thrilling it was to reveal to them God's plans for a massive and magnificent third Temple, to be built by Messiah himself, which will far exceed the beauty and size of the first two Temples combined! All the nations of the earth will come to this Temple, and he will fill it with his glory! (2:3-4, 7-9; Ezra 3:12)

Spiritual Lessons from Haggai

- We should seek to build God's kingdom rather than our own (1:2-8; see Matt. 6:25-34).
- As Christians, we should never long for the good old days, for the best days are yet to come (2:3-9)!

Key Verse

"I will shake all the nations, and the treasures of all the nations will come to this Temple. I will fill this place with glory, says the LORD Almighty" (2:7).

ZECHARIAH

BACKGROUND
See *Haggai: Background.*

AUTHOR
Zechariah (1:1), who along with Haggai encouraged the rebuilding of the Temple (see Ezra 5:1; 6:14). Zechariah was a priest as well as a prophet. His grandfather was Iddo (1:1), a priest who returned from the exile with Zerubbabel (Neh. 12:4). Apparently Zechariah succeeded his grandfather as head of that priestly family (Neh. 12:16). Zechariah would later be martyred on the Temple grounds (Matt. 23:35). The Bible mentions 34 men named Zechariah!

DATE
The prophecies of 1–8 probably would have been given between 520 B.C., when Zechariah and Haggai began encouraging the rebuilding of the Temple, and 515, when the rebuilding was completed. His final prophecies (9–14) are from later, probably about 480.

RECIPIENTS
See *Haggai: Recipients.*

PURPOSE
- To encourage the rebuilding of the Temple.
- To give instruction in holiness (rebuilt lives would result in a rebuilt Temple!).
- To provide specific information concerning both the first and second coming of Christ.

UNIQUE FEATURES
- For its length, Zechariah
  - ➤ gives more Christ-centered prophecies than any other OT book (with the exception of Isaiah)

535 B.C.
Temple rebuilding stops

520
Work resumes, through ministries of Haggai, Zechariah

516
Temple finished

c. 480
Zechariah's later prophecies

473
Esther saves Jews still in Persia

457
More exiles return with Ezra

- is quoted from or alluded to by other Bible books more than any other OT book

COMPARISON WITH OTHER BIBLE BOOKS

Isaiah:

- Zechariah uses the title "LORD Almighty" (or "LORD of hosts") as does Isaiah.
- Both use similar names and images for the Messiah:
  - "servant" (3:8; Isa. 42:1; 52:13; 53:11)
  - "Branch" (3:8; Isa. 11:1)
  - "stone" (3:9; Isa. 8:14; 28:16)
- Both speak of the nations going up to Jerusalem to worship in the messianic age (14:16; Isa. 2:2-4).
- Both speak of the "day of the LORD," or "that day," referring to God's intervention in human history at the end of time (2:11; 3:10; 14:1; see *Isaiah: Background;* exposition on Isa. 2:5–4:1).

Revelation:

- Among numerous comparisons,
  - both speak of measuring Jerusalem (2:1-2; Rev. 21:15).
  - each has its own special team of two witnesses, both of which are presented in connection with olive trees and lampstands (4:11-14; Rev. 11:3-4).
  - both mention "Babylon" as the center of wickedness (Hebrew *Shinar,* 5:11; Rev. 18).

OUTLINE

VISIONS AND QUESTIONS (1–8)
- A call to repentance (1:1-6)
- Visions in the night (1:7–6:8)
  - The rider on the red horse (1:7-17)
  - The four horns and four blacksmiths (1:18-21)
  - The man with the measuring line (2)
  - The clothing of Jeshua the high priest (3)
  - The golden lampstand and two olive trees (4)
  - The flying scroll (5:1-4)
  - The woman in the basket (5:5-11)
  - The four chariots (6:1-8)
- The crowning of Jeshua (6:9-15)
- Questions about fasting (7)
- Israel's bright future (8)

THE NATIONS AND THE MESSIAH (9–14)
- Messiah's first advent and rejection (9–11)
  - Israel's enemies judged (9:1-8)
  - Messiah's first and second coming (9:9-10)
  - Israel triumphant (9:11-17)
  - Messiah, the Shepherd of Israel (10)
  - Israel's rejection of Messiah (11)
- Messiah's second advent and acceptance (12–14)

Judah triumphant and repentant (12)
Judah cleansed, Messiah crucified (13)
Judah's final conflict and triumph (14)

VISIONS AND QUESTIONS (1–8)

1:1-6 *"Don't do what they did!"* Two months after Haggai first encouraged the returned exiles to resume their work on the Temple (compare 1:1 and Hag. 1:1), Zechariah urged them to learn from their nation's history and not repeat the errors of their fathers. God had called their fathers to repent and they had refused; therefore, God had sent them into exile.

Like Haggai, Zechariah not only encouraged the rebuilding effort but evidently helped with the manual labor as well (see Ezra 5:2).

1:7-11 *Horses and men among the myrtles.* Zechariah recorded a series of eight visions (1:7–6:8), which offered reassurance to those rebuilding the Temple. In some cases these visions also foretold Israel's final triumph in the end times.

In his first vision Zechariah saw several horsemen in a grove of myrtle trees, who reported that "the whole earth is at peace"—indicating that there was nothing to hinder the Jews from rebuilding the Temple (see 1:16). Zechariah encountered two angels in this vision:

- the "angel who was talking with me" (1:9, 13, 19, etc.)
- the "angel of the LORD" (1:11), who was the man on the horse (1:8) and the preincarnate Christ. This Angel appears throughout the OT, constantly on patrol as he intervenes to bring to reality God's plan for the ages (see exposition on Gen. 16:1-16).

1:12-13 *Prayer of the Son to the Father.* The angel (the second person of the Trinity) interceded with the "LORD Almighty" (the first person of the Trinity), asking him to keep his promise of restoration just as he had kept his promise of judgment. The Lord Almighty responded positively. On "seventy years," see exposition on Jeremiah 25:8-14.

1:14-17 *Proclamation of the Son for the Father.* The angel declared God's love for Israel (1:14); his anger for the nations which, though instruments of his wrath, had exceeded their mission against Israel (1:15); his earnest desire to rebuild Jerusalem and the Temple, making it once again his earthly dwelling (1:16-17).

1:18-21 *Four will enslave, four will save.* Zechariah saw four horns, representing the nations that had helped destroy and disperse Israel, followed by four blacksmiths, representing the nations that would punish Israel's oppressors. Once again, the implied message was that Israel was now free from oppression and therefore free to rebuild the Temple.

Some scholars believe the four horns/blacksmiths represent all the surrounding nations from all four points of the compass (compare exposition on Zeph. 2:4-15). Others believe they represent the major world empires, including those yet future, such as Rome, and culminating in Christ's millennial kingdom (see Dan. 2; 7).

2:1-13 *"Can this small city contain its fantastic future?"* Zephaniah saw a man measuring Jerusalem. An angel declared that Jerusalem would soon overflow its walls, but that God would be a "wall of fire" protecting all its inhabitants (2:1-5). The angel of the Lord ("me," 2:8) called on the Israelites still in exile to flee their lands of captivity, for God would judge those nations (2:6-9). During the Millennium, when God comes to dwell with his people, all nations will be invited to join them (2:10-12). The only fitting response to this revelation is silence before God (2:13; compare Hab. 2:20; Zeph. 1:7).

Many of those remaining in Babylon (2:7) would return to Judah with Ezra in 457 B.C. or with Nehemiah in 445. The "apple" of the eye (2:8, KJV) is the pupil, the eye's central part, which thus represents the person or thing most cherished.

OT prophets consistently prophesied that Gentiles will be included in the millennial kingdom, in fulfillment of the universal aspects of the Abrahamic covenant (2:11; see Gen. 12:3; see exposition on Isa. 56:1-8). However, this will in no way diminish Israel's prominence or special relationship to God. They will still be his "inheritance" (2:12).

3:1-5 *Satan: "Condemn him!" The Savior: "Cleanse him!"* As Jeshua the high priest ministered before the angel of the Lord, Satan opposed him (3:1; compare Job 1:6-11; Rev. 12:10), and the angel (the preincarnate Christ) came to his defense (3:2). He commanded his angels to remove Jeshua's filthy garments and clothe him in costly apparel. This is a beautiful illustration of justification—God taking the believer's sin and replacing it with his righteousness.

3:6-10 *The issue of sin: Settled in a single day!* The angel promised Jeshua that, if he would keep his life and ministry pure, he would magnify his earthly ministry and even give him a place in God's future plans (3:6-7). Jeshua would also be a sign of the coming Messiah, the "servant" or "Branch," who by his death on the cross would literally put an end to sin "in a single day" (3:9). Still further in the future will come his millennial kingdom, where all will live in peace, each under his or her own "vine and . . . fig tree" (3:10, KJV; see Isa. 36:16; Mic. 4:4).

The Branch signifies Christ's descent in the Davidic line in fulfillment of the Davidic covenant (see 2 Sam. 7:8-16). It particularly emphasizes his humanity, springing from the root of Jesse (see Isa. 11:1). The work of Jeshua and every other Israelite priest prefigured the priesthood of Christ (see Heb. 7:11–8:6).

4:1-14 *Where does all that oil come from?* Zechariah saw a vision of a lampstand with seven lamps, each with seven pipes providing its oil, which flowed from two olive trees (4:1-3). This abundant supply of oil represented the power of the Holy Spirit, which would help Zerubbabel finish rebuilding the Temple (4:4-6). Though the project had remained unfinished for 15 years (535–520 B.C.) and might therefore seem like a "mountain" to Zerubbabel (4:7), by the power of God's Spirit it would be finished (4:8-9), to the great joy of all Israel (4:10), even those who had "despised" this new Temple as a "small beginning" (4:10; see Ezra 3:12; Hag. 2:3).

The two olive trees that gave the abundant supply of oil represented Zerubbabel the governor and Jeshua the priest, the two men "anointed" to lead the returned exiles (4:11-14). To the Israel of the future they represent God's universal blessing to all nations through the ministry of the Spirit and the coming of Messiah, who combines in himself the offices of priest and king.

5:1-4 *That speeding scroll in the sky.* Zechariah saw a giant scroll (the law) flying through the sky, signifying to both present and future Israel that God is quite capable of removing sin from their land in order to fulfill his plans for them.

5:5-11 *A wicked woman in a (wicker?) basket.* Zechariah then saw a woman whom he was told personified Wickedness. She was thrust into a basket and carried away to Babylon (Hebrew

ZECHARIAH 3–5

THE CONFRONTATION IN HEAVEN (3:1-10)

The Charge —	The wearing of filthy garments
The Charged —	Jeshua and the people of Jerusalem
The Prosecutor —	Satan
The Defender —	The Branch—called this four times in the Old Testament:
	• The Branch of David (Isa. 11:1; Jer. 23:5; 33:15) Gospel fulfillment—Matthew
Jeshua Cleansed and Reassured	• My Servant, the Branch (Zech. 3:8) Gospel fulfillment—Mark
	• The man Branch (Zech. 6:12) Gospel fulfillment—Luke
	• The Branch of Jehovah (Isa. 4:2) Gospel fulfillment—John

THE GOLDEN LAMPSTAND AND THE TWO OLIVE TREES (4:1-14)

Historical meaning	May refer to the anointed team of Zerubbabel and Jeshua
Prophetic meaning	May refer to the anointed team of Elijah and Moses (See Rev. 11:3-12)

THE FLYING SCROLL (5:1-4)

Meaning	God's judgment upon the land. Humankind had broken God's entire moral law.	
Reason	Sin of swearing	Against God
	Sin of stealing	Against man

Shinar). Like the previous vision, this symbolized God's ability simply and efficiently to remove all sin from Israel—implying once more that there should be nothing to hinder the rebuilding of the Temple. To the Israel of the end times the vision reveals that God will one day remove all sin and evil from the world and rule over his redeemed people.

6:1-8 *Swing low, sweet chariots!* In his final vision of the night, Zechariah saw four chariots drawn by horses of various colors, coming from heaven and going "back and forth across the earth," by which action they "vented the anger of [God's] Spirit," especially concerning the "north." This suggests that Babylon had been finally and completely judged, and therefore the people should not be deterred from their rebuilding of the Temple. To the Israel of the future the vision indicates that God has judged all potential enemies of Messiah's universal reign.

6:9-15 *A crown for the chief carpenter.* The Lord told Zechariah to make a crown for Jeshua the high priest and to crown him, while proclaiming him king as well as head of the reconstruction effort (6:9-13). Afterward, the crown would be kept in the Temple as a memorial (6:14). The ceremony looks beyond the coronation of Jeshua to the coming of Messiah, the "Branch" (6:12; see 3:8), who not only will build the millennial Temple but will unite the offices of priest and king in himself. Those from "distant lands," the Gentiles, will be invited to help build this last great Temple (6:15; see exposition on 2:1-13).

7:1-7 *"What about our fifth-month fast?"* Two years later (compare 7:1 and 1:7), some of the returned Jews began wondering whether they should continue keeping a yearly fast in the fifth month, instituted during the captivity to commemorate the destruction of the Temple. Now that the captivity was over and the Temple was being rebuilt, was not the fast meaningless (7:1-3)? The Lord responded by asking whether those fasts were really a time of focusing on him or just an excuse for feasting (7:4-6). If their forefathers had obeyed him in the first place, they would never have needed those self-imposed fasts (7:7).

In answering their question, God also mentioned a fast in the seventh month commemorating the assassination of Gedaliah, governor of Judea after its fall (see 2 Kings 25:25). God would later give further instructions concerning both of these fasts (see 8:19).

7:8-14 *"Don't be like your fathers!"* Zechariah called on the people to show the reality of their faith by pursuing "true justice" (7:8-10, NIV). Because past generations had stubbornly refused to do this, they lost their land and were led captive (7:11-14). Our treatment of the people in our lives is indicative of the depth of our relationship with God.

8:1-17 *A city and nation blessed!* Zechariah relayed a series of encouraging words from God—to be fully realized only in the Millennium—concerning Israel's glorious future:

- God deeply loves Israel (8:2).
- He will dwell in Jerusalem (8:3).
- He will provide security for Jerusalem, so that both children and the elderly can lead happy lives (8:4-5).
- He will restore his people (8:6-8).
- The Temple reconstruction will be completed (8:9).
- The land will be secure and prosperous (8:10-15).
- Israel will be a blessing to other nations (8:13-15).

Having pronounced these blessings, Zechariah once more called the nation to obedience and justice (8:16-17; see 7:8-10).

8:18-19 *"They're feasts, not fasts!"* Without any direct command from God, the exiles had instituted four yearly fasts to commemorate tragic events in their history (see exposition on 7:1-7). God now told them to replace these demonstrations of false piety commemorating God's chastisement, with cheerful feasts of love and joy that look forward to his blessings.

The fast of the 10th month memorialized the beginning of Nebuchadnezzar's siege against Jerusalem in 588 B.C. (see 2 Kings 25:1), while the fourth-month observance recalled his breach of the city wall in 586 (see 2 Kings 25:3-4). Many Jews today, especially the Orthodox, still celebrate these four occasions as fasts.

8:20-23 *"We've heard! He's with you!"* Israel's prosperity in the Millennium will attract people from all nations who have heard of God's goodness to his people. Israel will at last be a blessing to all the world (see Gen. 12:1-3).

THE NATIONS AND THE MESSIAH (9–14)

9:1-8 *Judgment for Israel's enemies.* In 9–14, probably written much later than 1–8, Zechariah offers glimpses of Israel's coming Messiah and the bright future he will usher in for his people. 9–11 focuses mainly on his first advent, while 12–14 looks at his second advent and millennial kingdom.

All nations that had opposed Israel would be judged. Syria, Tyre, and Philistia are mentioned as representative of those enemies. The proud Tyre would ultimately be destroyed by Alexander the Great (9:2-4; see 9:13; Ezek. 26:7-21). Philistia would be purged, restored, and ultimately incorporated into Israel during the Millennium (9:4-7). The people of Israel, however, would be protected from all of the ravages of Alexander the Great by God's personal protection (9:8).

Josephus records the absorption of Philistia into Israel after their defeat by Alexander. "Him who passes by and him who returns" (9:8, NKJV) matches the exploits of Alexander, who spared Israel on his way to Egypt and again on his return.

9:9-10 *His first and second coming.* Israel was to rejoice at the coming of its King—not Alexander, but Messiah—who would come first in humility (9:9) and later in exaltation (9:10). Both would be occasions of great joy for Israel. At his second coming, he will set up his universal kingdom, banish the implements of warfare, and enforce universal peace.

9:11-17 *From downtrodden to triumphant.* God promised to save Israel from all its enemies. Those still in exile need not fear, for God would remember his blood covenant with Abraham (9:11-12; see Gen. 12:1-3; 15:9-18). He would protect them from the future Greek empire (9:13). This promise would be kept during the days of the Maccabees in the second century B.C., but its ultimate fulfillment will be when Messiah comes to earth to set up his kingdom. A glorious future lay ahead for God's people. They had been helpless before their enemies, like sheep amid wolves. Now they would be like crown jewels lifted up as a trophy to display their value to God (9:14-17).

10:1-12 *The true Shepherd regathers his flock.* Israel's false shepherds ("household gods" and "fortune-tellers") had led them astray, and therefore they were judged (10:2). Messiah, their true Shepherd, will make Israel invincible, more than equal to any military force that may come against them (10:3-5). He will gather them from exile (10:6-8), and they will experience the national regeneration promised by the New Covenant (10:9; see Jer. 31:31-34).

The fact that exiles from both the northern ("Ephraim") and southern kingdoms (10:6, 7, 10) will be regathered indicates that Zechariah had the Millennium in view. In that day, Israel will occupy the land from the Euphrates River to the Nile, in fulfillment of the Abrahamic covenant (10:11-12; see Gen. 15:18).

11:1-14 *The true Shepherd rejected by his flock.* There will come a time, however, when Israel will once again suffer great devastation (11:1-3) because of their rejection of Messiah (11:4-14). Zechariah symbolically "cared for" the flock of Israel, who were doomed for slaughter because of their rejection of Messiah (11:4-6). Zechariah called his shepherd's staffs "Beauty" and "Bands" (KJV) or "Favor" and "Union" (11:7, NLT, NIV), symbolizing Messiah's mission—to draw the nation to himself and to protect and bind them to himself and each other. Having been rejected by Israel's false shepherds, Messiah rejected them as well (11:8), breaking one of his staffs to symbolize breaking his covenant with them (11:9-11). They showed their valuation of him by the wages they offered him: 30 pieces of silver, the price of the most lowly slave (11:12-13; see Matt. 27:3-10). He responded by breaking his other staff, symbolizing the breaking of Israel's unity (11:14). Israel was indeed torn apart by internal strife after its rejection of Christ, leading to its conquest by Rome in A.D. 70, as predicted in 11:1-3.

11:15-17 *One final false shepherd.* Having rejected their true Shepherd, Israel would be ruled by a "worthless shepherd" (11:15-16), the Antichrist of the Great Tribulation (see exposition on 2 Thess. 2:1-12 and on 1 John 4:1-6). He will not, however, escape God's judgment (11:17).

12:1-9 *Judah triumphant.* "On that day," all nations of the earth will come against Judah, but Judah will prevail against them (12:1-7) in such a remarkable way that God's divine intervention will be evident to all (12:5). Judah will seem as overpowering as fire is to the wood or grain it burns (12:6). Judah will be as effective as in the time of David, when the angel of the Lord went before his army (12:8-9).

12:10-14 *Judah repentant.* In those last days, the Holy Spirit will accomplish the regeneration of Israel (see Jer. 31:31-34) and will cause them to receive the Messiah whom they had previously rejected. The Israel of the Millennium will sorrow personally and nationally for what the Israel of Jesus' first advent did to him (see John 19:37).

13:1 *Judah cleansed at the fountain.* Just as all Israel will one day express sorrow for their sin (see 12:10-14), so also they will all have access to a fountain of cleansing (13:1). The fountain, of course, is Messiah himself, who took the sins of the people upon himself. It is his sacrifice that makes the regeneration promised by the New Covenant (see Jer. 31:31-34) a reality.

13:2-6 *Judah cleansed of false prophets.* All idolatry and every false religion will be cleansed from the people and the land (13:2). False prophets will receive the death penalty demanded by the law (13:3; see Deut. 13:6-10). Even their claims of innocence will not save them (13:4-6).

13:7-9 *Shepherd smitten, sheep scattered.* Israel's true shepherd will be stricken and his flock will be scattered. Later, during the Tribulation, the Antichrist will kill two-thirds of Israel. The one-third who survive will populate the millennial kingdom. The stricken shepherd is both God ("my partner") and human ("the man"). Jesus would see this prophecy fulfilled as his disciples literally "scattered" from him just before he was "struck" down at Calvary (see Matt. 26:31).

14:1-5 *Tribulation and triumph.* On the "day of the LORD," here referring to Armageddon, Jerusalem will be sacked and half of its people taken captive (14:1-2). Christ himself will then come to fight for Israel. He will stand on the Mount of Olives, which will split from east to west, allowing the remaining Jerusalemites to flee (14:3-5). Then the triumphant Christ will establish his thousand-year kingdom (14:5).

14:6-8 *Definitely a different kind of day!* The establishment of Christ's kingdom will be marked by great changes in nature, with the cycle of day and night becoming one "continuous day" (14:6-7). Waters will flow from Jerusalem to the east and west, symbolizing spiritual purification and refreshment for all the world (14:8; compare Ezek. 47:1-12; Rev. 22:1-2).

14:9-11 *King over his creation!* Messiah's reign will be universal, and he will be universally worshiped. Jerusalem will be rebuilt and restored to its former glory. Its inhabitants will dwell in safety because all sin will have been eradicated.

14:12-15 *History's most horrible plague.* Judah's enemies will literally rot away from a plague. Chaos will reign as they fight each other. The spoils of these battles will go to Judah.

14:16-19 *No worship, no water!* The Festival of Shelters will be reinstituted in the millennial kingdom, because it foreshadowed the things that will have been realized at that time (see Lev. 23:33-44; Rev. 21:3). Failure to participate in it will be punished by drought. The people of the Millennium will be regenerated, not glorified. They will still have their sin natures and will experience God's discipline whenever necessary.

14:20-21 *"Holiness to the Lord."* In the Millennium, the distinction between secular and sacred will be erased. Even ordinary household items will be considered holy.

❖ ❖ ❖

PEOPLE TO REMEMBER FROM ZECHARIAH

ZECHARIAH

Key Fact: Prophet who had much to say about Christ

Father: Berekiah (1:1)

Death: Recorded in Matt. 23:35

Total Bible References: 6

Key References: 1–14; Ezra 5:1; Matt. 23:35

Zechariah Speaks

The 24th of Shebat—what a night that was! Those visions from heaven descended on me like a spring cloudburst. I saw horses, horns, craftsmen, measuring lines, chariots, olive trees, flying scrolls, and baskets! Perhaps the most vivid vision was that of Jeshua standing before God, accused by Satan and defended by the Messiah! (1:7-8, 18, 20; 2:1; 3:1; 4:3; 5:1, 6; 6:1)

At that time I thought absolutely nothing could surpass all this. But it was just a prelude to the revelations I had several years later. Think of it: After his triumphal entry the coming Messiah will be betrayed for 30 pieces of silver and will actually be killed by his own people—our people! Then, later, he will return to the Mount of Olives, defeat his enemies, be recognized by Israel, and set up his glorious kingdom! (7:1; 9:9; 11:12-13; 12:10-14; 14:1-4, 9)

What a time that will be, when even such ordinary things as the bells on our horses will be considered holy to the Lord! (14:20-21)

Spiritual Lessons from Zechariah

- Satan is always actively resisting God's people (3:1; see Job 1:6; Luke 22:31; Rev. 12:10). But Christ, on our behalf, is always resisting his efforts (3:2-5; see Luke 22:32).
- We must rely on the power of the Holy Spirit in all that we do (4:6; see John 15:4-5).

Key Verse

"Rejoice greatly, O people of Zion! Shout in triumph, O people of Jerusalem! Look, your king is coming to you. He is righteous and victorious, yet he is humble, riding on a donkey—even on a donkey's colt" (9:9).

MALACHI

BACKGROUND

With encouragement from the prophets Haggai and Zechariah, the first group of Jews to return from captivity had finished rebuilding the Temple in about 516 B.C. As the second and third waves of exiles returned in 457 and 445, Ezra and Nehemiah led the nation in spiritual revival. In about 432, Nehemiah returned to Babylon for a while, and when he returned to Jerusalem found that spiritual conditions had deteriorated (see Neh. 13). It is generally thought that Malachi ministered at about this time, reminding the people of God's love for them, calling them to repentance, warning of judgment, and foretelling great blessings for those whose hearts were right.

AUTHOR

Malachi (1:1). Biographical details unknown. His name means "my messenger" and appears in 3:1 in translation.

DATE

About 430 B.C. (see *Background*).

PURPOSE

- To rebuke the profaning of that which is holy.
- To rebuke the abuse of proper human relationships.
- To announce both the judgment and the blessing of the coming "day of the LORD."

UNIQUE FEATURES

- For its length, Malachi includes more questions (some 25) than any other book in the Bible—including perhaps the most famous one: "Will a man rob God?" (3:8, KJV).
- It contains the most famous OT passage on giving (3:8-10).

538 B.C.
1st exiles return to Judah

430
Malachi ministers to returned exiles

c. 300
OT canon complete, accepted

c. 146
Rise of Rome

5
Birth of Christ

COMPARISON WITH OTHER BIBLE BOOKS

Revelation:

- Both Malachi and Revelation, the last books in their respective Testaments, conclude with warnings (4:6; Rev. 22:18-19).
- Both mention Elijah as a witness to Christ's advent:
  - ➤ The mention of Elijah in 4:5 probably refers to both John the Baptist at Christ's first advent and Elijah himself at the second advent (see below).
  - ➤ Revelation 11:3-6 seems to indicate that Elijah will be one of the two witnesses before Christ's second coming.

The entire Bible:

- Chapter 4 looks back at the OT and forward to the NT:
  - ➤ 4:4 looks back to Moses and the law.
  - ➤ 4:5-6 looks forward to Christ and his kingdom. Though 4:5 in its primary sense applies to Christ's second coming, it was fulfilled in a secondary sense at his first coming by John the Baptist. There is no better link between OT and NT than these last three verses of the last book of the OT.

OUTLINE

GOD'S LOVE STATED (1:1-5)
GOD'S LOVE SCORNED (1:6–3:18)
  The priests' contempt for God (1:6-14)
  The priests' contempt for the priesthood (2:1-9)
  The people's contempt for marriage (2:10-17)
  The coming of John the Baptist and Christ (3:1-5)
  Robbing from God? (3:6-12)
  No benefit from godliness? (3:13-15)
  The benefits of godliness (3:16-18)
GOD'S LOVE SHOWN (4)

GOD'S LOVE STATED (1:1-5)

1:1-5 *Israel loved and preferred.* Malachi began his prophecy by declaring God's love for Israel, something Israel had doubted (1:2). God's love was clearly seen in his preference for Israel, descendants of Jacob, over Edom, descendants of Esau (1:2-5; see Gen. 25:23; Rom. 9:10-13). God's choice was made not on the basis of the intrinsic worth of the two men, but on the basis of his sovereign purpose. See exposition on Obadiah.

GOD'S LOVE SCORNED (1:6–3:18)

1:6-14 *"Try giving them to the governor!"* Having established God's love for Israel, Malachi showed several ways in which Israel had scorned his love (1:6–3:18). The priests had "despised" God by offering unacceptable sacrifices in direct violation of the law (1:6-8; see Deut. 15:21). They were treating God in a way that they would not dare treat a human leader (1:8). Malachi called on them to either repent (1:9) or cease their offerings altogether (1:10). By their polluted sacrifices and empty formalism they demonstrated their contempt for God (1:12-14). On the other hand, the day is coming when God's name will be exalted among the Gentiles (1:11).

2:1-9 *Unfaithful priests.* Malachi continued his rebuke of the priests. God would "bring a terrible curse" upon them and their descendants (2:1-3) because they had broken their covenant with him, by which he had promised blessing to the priesthood for its obedience and a curse for its disobedience (2:4-5; see Num. 25:10-13; Neh. 13:29). The priests should have been exemplary in their walk with the Lord and truthful in their teaching so that the people would have a proper example (2:5-7). But they had failed in this mission (2:8-9).

2:10-17 *Unfaithful husbands.* Israelite men, though claiming God as their Father, were profaning his institution of marriage by divorcing their wives and marrying foreign women. By doing so they broke their covenant with their first wife and committed violence against her (2:16) by depriving her of the protection marriage afforded.

While the law apparently allowed divorce in some cases (see exposition on Deut. 24:1-4), 2:16 expresses God's firm disapproval of the practice (see exposition on Matt. 19:1-12). Neither divorce nor polygamy has ever been God's plan. They are not good bases on which to rear godly families, for they violate the marriage covenant (2:15). Marriage problems always indicate underlying spiritual problems (2:10, 13-14).

Not only had the Israelites tried to make their evil ways seem good through their insincere piety (2:13-14); they mistook God's slowness in judgment for his approval of their evil ways (2:17). Such thinking "wearied" God, but he would graciously respond by sending the Messiah (see 3:1-5).

3:1 *The messenger and the Messenger.* The Lord says he will send his "messenger" (3:1), a word applied by three NT writers to John the Baptist (see Matt. 11:10; Mark 1:2; Luke 7:27). He will prepare the way for the "God of justice" whom they seek (2:17), Jesus Christ, who will "suddenly come to his Temple" as the "messenger of the covenant" (see Jer. 31:31-34).

3:2-5 *Some purified, others punished.* When the Messiah comes, he will exercise the judgment for which Israel longed (see 2:17), but it won't be against the heathen: He will judge the godless of Israel, especially priests (3:2-3). A cleansed priesthood will minister effectively to a cleansed nation (3:3-4). Sorcerers, adulterers, liars, and oppressors will be judged (3:5).

3:6-12 *"Stop stealing and I'll start supplying."* God declared his unchanging love for Israel and invited them to return to him (3:6-7), then discussed tithes and offerings as one way they could do so (3:8-12). They had withheld a part of their offerings, for what they considered to be good reasons (3:10). But by doing so they were renouncing God's sovereign authority. In robbing God, they had robbed themselves of his blessing and provision. The remedy? Render to God that which is rightfully his and trust him to supply their needs. They could never out-give him (3:10)!

3:13-15 *No gain from godliness?* Many in Israel had adopted a worldly perspective. To them it seemed that God favored the wicked while the godly reaped no tangible benefits from their godliness (compare Ps. 37; 73; Matt. 6:19-34; 1 Tim. 6:6).

3:16-18 *The world's most wonderful diary.* Amid Israel's spiritual decline was a remnant of people drawn together by obedience to the Lord. God not only listened to their worship but also, figuratively speaking, wrote their names in his "scroll of remembrance." God would bring them safely through the Tribulation and make them his special treasure. God always keeps before himself the names of those in fellowship with him.

GOD'S LOVE SHOWN (4)

4:1-3 *Fire of judgment, Sun of Righteousness.* "The day of judgment is coming"—that is, the Great Tribulation—when all the wicked in Israel will be utterly destroyed. The righteous, on the other hand, will bask in the warmth of the "Sun of Righteousness," Jesus the Messiah (compare Luke 1:78).

4:4-6 *"Remember Moses, prepare for Elijah!"* Malachi ended his prophecy by urging Israel to keep the law, and to look forward to the coming of Christ and the establishment of his kingdom. The promised Elijah is best understood as John the Baptist (see Matt. 11:13-14). While he was not Elijah literally, he did the work of Elijah, even as Malachi himself had done. (See *Comparison with Other Bible Books.*)

PEOPLE TO REMEMBER FROM MALACHI

MALACHI
Key Fact: Last recorded prophet to Israel (1:1)
Total Bible References: 1 (1:1)
Key References: 1–4

Malachi Speaks

At God's leading, I began my prophecy by speaking of Jacob and Esau, and concluded it with references to Moses and Elijah. The sad truth is that my people resemble Esau more than any of the other three! (1:2; 4:4-5)

Like Esau, we have despised our birthright. We have both insulted and cheated our great King. (1:8, 14; 3:8; Gen. 25:34)

Yet he still loves us and actually records our devotion to him in a special book of remembrance. Amazing! But even more thrilling, he views us as precious jewels, to be carefully gathered and preserved. (1:2; 3:16-17)

As I understand the divine plan, Elijah will help prepare for this glorious future day, when "the Sun of righteousness will rise with healing in his wings!" (4:2, 5-6)

Spiritual Lessons from Malachi

- "Jesus loves me, this I know, for the Bible tells me so!" OT saints often doubted this (1:2; see Gen. 42:36; Lam. 3:1-19). But the fact remains: God really does love us! (See Jer. 31:3; John 3:16; Eph. 2:4.)
- The only offerings acceptable to God are those that are both "living" (Rom. 12:1) and loving (1:6-9).
- Think and speak good things about God, so that your devotion for him will be recorded in his special diary (3:16)!

Key Verse

"'Look! I am sending my messenger, and he will prepare the way before me. Then the Lord you are seeking will suddenly come to his Temple. The messenger of the covenant, whom you look for so eagerly, is surely coming,' says the LORD Almighty" (3:1).

IMPORTANT EVENTS BETWEEN THE TESTAMENTS

334 B.C.	—	Alexander crosses the Hellespont
331 B.C.	—	Alexander defeats the Persians
323 B.C.	—	Alexander dies at age thirty-two in Babylon
250 B.C.	—	The translation of the Septuagint
214 B.C.	—	The Great Wall of China begun
175 B.C.	—	Apocryphal literature completed
169 B.C.	—	Epiphanes defiles the Temple on December 15
166 B.C.	—	The revolt of the Maccabees
165 B.C.	—	The cleansing of the Temple on December 25
146 B.C.	—	Destruction of Carthage by Rome and the end of the Punic Wars
63 B.C.	—	Pompey conquers Jerusalem
44 B.C.	—	Julius Caesar is assassinated in March
37 B.C.	—	Herod is appointed to govern Jerusalem
20 B.C.	—	The rebuilding and enlargement of the Temple

5 B.C.
Birth of Christ

A.D. 8
Visits Temple, age 12

26
Begins ministry

28
Chooses 12

29
Feeds 5,000, Death of John the Baptist

30
Death, resurrection, ascension

MATTHEW

BACKGROUND

As Malachi, last of the OT prophets, passed from the scene (c. 400 B.C.), Judea was a tiny province of returned Jewish exiles living in relative peace within the Persian Empire. When Alexander the Great made Persia a part of his Greek Empire (c. 333), things continued to be relatively peaceful for Israel. Greece even facilitated the translation of the OT into Greek (the Septuagint) c. 250.

The Greek Empire was divided into four parts following Alexander's death. Israel was dominated by the part centered in Egypt (the Ptolemies) until 198, at which time it came under the control of the Seleucids of Syria. In 171, the Seleucid ruler Antiochus Epiphanes began a cruel anti-Jewish crusade in which he killed tens of thousands of Jews and desecrated the Temple (see exposition on Dan. 8:15-27) before being defeated by the Jews in 165 (recorded in the apocryphal book of 1 Maccabees).

In the last 150 years before Christ, Rome gradually displaced Greece's four successor kingdoms as the dominant world power. By 64 B.C., Rome controlled Palestine. Beginning about 40, Rome allowed the Edomite Herods to govern the area. With the Middle Eastern world relatively at peace under Rome, and with Greek having become the common language of much of the empire, the "right time" (Gal. 4:4) had come for God to introduce his Messiah.

Matthew is one of four accounts of the life, death, and resurrection of this Messiah, Jesus of Nazareth. These first four books of the NT are called the Gospels, meaning "good news." Matthew, Mark, and Luke are often called the "synoptic" Gospels because they tell Christ's story from similar points of view (see *Mark: Date and Location*).

While Christ was on earth, he and his disciples evangelized mainly among their fellow Jews, though their ministry did attract many Gentiles as well. Before his ascension, Christ made it clear that Gentiles were to hear the gospel as well (see 28:19; Acts 1:8). The book of Acts records the disciples' enthusiastic response as they took the Good News throughout the Roman Empire. In his letter to the Romans, Paul explained how this universal proclamation of Christ fulfilled God's ultimate intention that all nations would be blessed and would come to faith in him through Israel, his chosen people (see Gen. 12:1-3).

AUTHOR

Matthew, also known as Levi (Mark 2:14), a tax collector (9:9) who became an apostle (10:3).

DATE

Uncertain. Some date it in the early 50s A.D., while others date in the mid-60s. See *Mark: Date and Location.*

RECIPIENTS

Jews living in Palestine.

PURPOSE

Matthew wrote some 20 years after Christ's death and resurrection. The Jewish nation as a whole had summarily rejected Jesus as their Messiah. Matthew knew that they would soon face the destruction of their very national and religious life (24:1-2). Meanwhile they endured the oppressive yoke of Rome with no relief in sight. Matthew took his pen in hand to reintroduce Jesus to the Jews and to show that he was truly what he claimed to be, the Messiah, King of Israel. He pointed to the future when Jesus would return to the earth and set up his Kingdom and realize all the promises made to the patriarchs and Israel. Until that time, Jesus' followers should give themselves to making and baptizing disciples and teaching them the things that Jesus taught (28:19-20).

UNIQUE FEATURES

- Matthew is the only Gospel containing the word *church* (16:18; 18:17).
- Matthew records five great sermons by Jesus:
  - The Sermon on the Mount (5–7)
  - The sending of the 12 (10)
  - The parables of the Kingdom (13)
  - The seven woes on scribes and Pharisees (23)
  - The Olivet discourse on the end times (24–25)
- Matthew is the most systematic Gospel, grouping together similar things such as discourses, parables, and miracles.
- Matthew emphasizes final rewards and punishments. The words *judgment, hell, fire, hypocrite,* or *woe* are found on almost every page.

COMPARISON WITH OTHER BIBLE BOOKS

Mark:

- Matthew presents Jesus as King; Mark presents him as Servant.

THE FOURFOLD GOSPEL ACCOUNT

	MATTHEW	MARK	LUKE	JOHN
PORTRAIT OF CHRIST	King and Lionlike	Servant and Oxlike	Perfect Person and Like Us	Mighty God and Eaglelike
ANGELIC REMINDER Rev. 4; Ezek.1	First Creature Lionlike	Second Creature Oxlike	Third Creature Personlike	Fourth Creature Eaglelike
STYLE OF WRITER	Teacher	Preacher	Historian	Theologian
EMPHASIS BY WRITER	His sermons	His miracles	His parables	His doctrines
CULTURE OF ORIGINAL READERS	Jews 	Romans 	Greeks 	The World 
GENEALOGICAL RECORD	Yes Matthew 1:1-17	No	Yes Luke 3:23-38	No
Reason	A king must have one.	A servant needs none.	A perfect person should have one.	God has none.
Root	Traces the regal line of David through his son Solomon		Traces the physical line of David though another son, Nathan	
Fruit	Leads to Joseph, the legal stepfather of Jesus		Leads to Mary, the physical mother of Jesus	
PLACE OF MAIN ACTION	Capernaum in Galilee			Jerusalem in Judea
TWOFOLD DIVISION	Synoptic Gospels—stress the humanity of Christ			Fourth Gospel stresses the deity of Christ

Luke:

- Matthew emphasizes Jesus' rejection; Luke emphasizes his acceptance.

Luke and John:

- Matthew (and Mark) present Jesus as the victim of the crucifixion; Luke and John present him as the victor.

Revelation:

Matthew 24 helps explain the seal judgments of Revelation 6:1–8:1.

OUTLINE

INTRODUCTION OF THE KING (1–4)
- His genealogy: Earthly lineage (1:1-17)
- His birth: Heavenly descent (1:18-25)
- Infancy and childhood (2)
- Baptism (3)
- Temptation in the wilderness (4:1-11)
- His ministry begins; calls four disciples (4:12-25)

PROCLAMATIONS OF THE KING: THE SERMON ON THE MOUNT (5–7)
- The Beatitudes (5:1-12)
- Salt and light (5:13-16)
- The law and the gospel (5:17-48)
- Giving, prayer, fasting (6:1-18)
- Money and worry (6:19-34)
- Judging and being judged (7:1-6)
- Asking, seeking, knocking (7:7-11)
- The Golden Rule (7:12)
- The two ways (7:13-29)

POWER OF THE KING (8–10)
- Healings (8:1-17)
- Leaving all to follow Christ (8:18-22)
- Calming the sea (8:23-27)
- Demons and pigs (8:28-34)
- Power to forgive sins (9:1-8)
- The call of Matthew (9:9-13)
- Fasting and feasting; the old and new (9:14-17)
- Healings (9:18-38)
- Selecting and sending the 12 (10)

OPPOSITION TO THE KING (11–12)
- Delegation from John the Baptist (11:1-19)
- Opposition from various cities (11:20-30)
- Opposition from Pharisees (12)

PARABLES OF THE KING (13)
- Sower and seed (13:1-9, 18-23)
- The purpose of his parables (13:10-17)
- Wheat and weeds (13:24-30, 36-43)
- Mustard seed (13:31-32)

- Yeast (13:33-35)
- Treasure (13:44)
- Pearl of great price (13:45-46)
- Dragnet (13:47-50)
- Treasures old and new (13:51-52)
- Opposition in Christ's hometown (13:53-58)

REVELATIONS OF THE KING TO HIS OWN (14:1–16:12)

- Death of John the Baptist (14:1-12)
- Feeding 5,000; walking on water (14:13-36)
- Warnings about Pharisees (15:1-20)
- Healings (15:21-31)
- Feeding 4,000 (15:32-39)
- Warnings about Pharisees (16:1-12)

INSTRUCTIONS OF THE KING TO HIS OWN (16:13–20:34)

- Peter's confession (16:13-20)
- Christ's first prediction of his death (16:21-28)
- Transfiguration (17:1-13)
- Disciples fail to heal a demoniac (17:14-21)
- Christ's second prediction of his death (17:22-23)
- Payment of the Temple tax (17:24-27)
- Children and the Kingdom (18:1-14)
- Conflicts in the church (18:15-20)
- Forgiveness; the unforgiving servant (18:21-35)
- Divorce (19:1-12)
- Children and the Kingdom (19:13-15)
- The rich young ruler (19:16-30)
- Workers in the vineyard (20:1-16)
- Christ's third prediction of his death (20:17-19)
- Greatness in the Kingdom (20:20-28)
- Jesus heals two blind men (20:29-34)

PRESENTATION AND REJECTION OF THE KING (21–23)

- Triumphal Entry (21:1-11)
- Cleansing the Temple (21:12-17)
- Cursing the fig tree (21:18-22)
- Parables on Israel's rejection of Christ (21:23–22:14)
- Paying taxes to Caesar (22:15-22)
- Confrontation with Sadducees (22:23-33)
- Greatest commandment (22:34-40)
- Is Christ the son of David? (22:41-46)
- Seven woes on scribes and Pharisees (23)

PREDICTIONS OF THE KING: THE OLIVET DISCOURSE (24–25)

- Jerusalem's fall; Christ's return (24)
- Ten bridesmaids; three servants (25:1-30)
- Sheep and goats (25:31-46)

DEATH AND RESURRECTION OF THE KING (26–28)

- Plot of priests and scribes (26:1-5)
- Anointing by Mary (26:6-13)

Judas plans betrayal (26:14-16)
Observance of Passover; Lord's Supper (26:17-30)
Jesus predicts Peter's denial (26:31-35)
Gethsemane (26:36-46)
Christ's arrest (26:47-56)
Trials; Peter's denial (26:57–27:31)
Crucifixion, burial (27:32-66)
Resurrection (28)

INTRODUCTION OF THE KING (1–4)

NOTE: In the comments that follow, cross-references to parallel passages in the other Gospels are given in square brackets. Italics within brackets, such as [*Mark 5:1-20;* Luke 8:26-39], indicate that you will find a more complete discussion of the passage in question in the exposition for that reference.

1:1-17 *From Abraham the friend of God to Christ the Son of God.* Matthew began his Gospel account with the genealogy of Jesus through his earthly father, Joseph. The genealogy goes back through King David to Abraham. Abraham, David, and Christ are all mentioned at the end of the genealogy as well as at the beginning. This shows that Jesus

- is legal heir to the throne of Israel (Davidic covenant, see 2 Sam. 7:4-16);
- fulfills God's promise that all nations would be blessed through Abraham (Abrahamic covenant, see Gen. 12:3). [Luke 3:23-38]

The genealogy mentions four women other than Mary—an unusual feature in genealogies of that day. While many of Christ's male ancestors were far less than noble, the inclusion of these four women especially shows God's grace and sovereignty in choosing through whom he will work:

- Tamar (see Gen. 38:13-30), Rahab (see Josh. 2:1), and Bathsheba (see 2 Sam. 11:1-5) had either committed sexual sin or been victims of it.
- Ruth was a Gentile (see Ruth 1:4).

1:18-25 *Good news for a troubled fiancé.* Joseph, engaged to Mary, learned that she was pregnant even though they had not had sexual relations. Assuming that she had been unfaithful to him, but being a "just" man, Joseph considered divorcing her quietly to avoid exposing her to public shame. However, an angel revealed to him the supernatural origin of Mary's pregnancy and that Mary's son would be the Messiah (see Isa. 7:14). With this reassurance, Joseph married Mary but refrained from sexual relations with her until Jesus was born.

Note that divorce could end an engagement as well as a marriage (1:19, NIV).

2:1-12 *"We three kings of Orient are!"* As Micah (see Mic. 5:2) had predicted, Jesus was born in Bethlehem. About two years later (compare 2:7, 16), "wise men" led by a star came to see him. When they inquired about the "king of the Jews," Herod became very concerned. When informed that prophecy indicated the young king had been born in Bethlehem (2:4-6), Herod determined when the event had occurred, directed the wise men to Bethlehem, and pretended to want to know when they found the child so that he could "worship" him.

Guided once more by the star, the

wise men found Jesus, offered gifts to him, and, being warned not to inform Herod of the baby's whereabouts, returned home.

The wise men were probably astronomers. Tradition says there were three of them—probably because of the three gifts. The myrrh, used to embalm, may have signified the ultimate reason for Christ's birth. The star was probably supernatural, since it apparently disappeared for a while, necessitating their asking directions from Herod.

2:13-15 *Their prophetic move to Egypt.* Warned by an angel that Herod would try to kill Jesus, Joseph fled with Mary and Jesus to Egypt, fulfilling an OT prophecy (see exposition on Hosea 11:1-7). Jesus would retrace the life of the nation of Israel, which took refuge in Egypt and later returned to possess Canaan.

2:16-18 *The massacre they escaped.* Realizing the wise men had fled without leading him to the infant king, Herod became enraged and killed all the male children in Bethlehem up to age two, hoping thereby to kill Jesus (compare 2:16 with 2:7). The event reminded Matthew of Jeremiah's lament for the Israelite exiles (see exposition on Jer. 31:15-25). Herod's bloody rampage was in keeping with what history reveals of this cruel man who would later order the execution of his wife and three of his sons.

2:19-23 *More directions from an angel.* For the third time an angel appeared to Joseph, this time telling him that Herod was dead so he and his family could return to Israel. A fourth dream warned them to go to the Galilean town of Nazareth instead of Judea because of potential problems with Herod's son Archelaus. This, says Matthew, fulfilled the OT prophecy that the Messiah would be called a Nazarene. The prophetic reference is unclear, though it may involve the "rod" that would come up from "the stem of Jesse" (Isa. 11:1, KJV). *Nazarene* may be related to *netzer,* meaning "rod." This would be in harmony with Matthew's emphasis on Christ's Davidic lineage. Or Matthew may have intended a more general reference to Christ's lowly nature (see Zech. 9:9; John 1:46).

3:1-12 *"Repent, bear fruit, and be baptized."* The story now moves forward 28 years to John the Baptist, who had been designated to prepare the way for Christ (3:3; see Isa. 40:3-5; Luke 1:13-17, 76). John appeared as a strange prophet in the desert of Judea. His odd clothing of camel's hair may have reminded the people of Elijah (see 2 Kings 1:8), while his diet of locusts (3:4) may have helped him identify with the poor. Many responded to John's message (3:5).

His message had two points:

- Repent (3:2).
- Prepare for the Kingdom of Heaven (3:2) and the Messiah (3:3), of whom the prophets had spoken (3:3).

The people's response was likewise twofold: confession of sin and baptism in the Jordan River (3:5-6). Many of the religious leaders, however, received a stern warning from John: They must demonstrate true repentance before he would baptize them (3:7-8). Mere descent from Abraham would not save them (3:9-10).

The coming Messiah, said John, would baptize not just with water but with the Holy Spirit and fire (3:11-12; see Acts 1:5; 2:1-4). Fire speaks of the Spirit's work in judgment (see John 16:8-11). [Mark 1:1-8; Luke 3:1-20; John 1:6-27]

3:13-17 *"But why should I baptize you?"* John the Baptist obediently baptized Jesus, while acknowledging that he needed to be cleansed by Jesus, and not the other way around. Both the Father and the Spirit signalled their approval of Christ's action (compare 17:5). [Mark 1:9-11; Luke 3:21-22; John 1:31-34]

Jesus was not baptized to be saved, for he did not need salvation. The text suggests several purposes for his baptism:

- to identify with John's proclamation of his coming
- to show John that he was in fact the Messiah (see John 1:33)
- to signal the beginning of his messianic ministry
- to identify himself as a priest of Israel (see Lev. 8:6)
- to provide an example for believers to follow
- to demonstrate the involvement and approval of the other persons of the Trinity in his ministry. In fact, the baptism of Jesus gives one of the clearest illustrations of the doctrine of the Trinity (see exposition on Gen. 1:26-31), with
  - ➤ the Father speaking from heaven (3:17)
  - ➤ the Son coming out of the water (3:16)
  - ➤ the Holy Spirit descending from heaven (3:16)
- Various theologians have promoted a "modalistic" view of the Trinity, with God taking one form at a time. But at Christ's baptism all three persons of the Trinity appeared at once.

4:1-11 *Passing the temptation test.* Following his baptism, Jesus was led into the desert by the Holy Spirit (who had come upon him at his baptism) to be tempted by the devil. Unlike Adam and Eve (see exposition on Gen. 3:6), Jesus successfully resisted Satan, showing himself qualified, as the spotless Lamb of God, to be the perfect sacrifice for sin (see John 1:29). In his temptations, Jesus overcame three categories of sin (compare 1 John 2:16):

- By refusing to satisfy his hunger by turning stones into bread, he conquered the lust for physical pleasure.
- By rejecting Satan's dare to jump from the top of the Temple, he conquered pride in one's possessions.
- By turning down Satan's offer of the kingdoms of the world, he conquered the lust for everything one sees.

Jesus responded to each temptation by quoting Scripture, showing his own familiarity with Scripture and setting an example for believers who are tempted. [Mark 1:12-13; Luke 4:1-13]

4:12-17 *The light of deity in the land of darkness.* Hearing that John the Baptist was in prison, Jesus left Judea for Galilee. Galilee encompassed the tribal territories of Zebulun and Naphtali, so Jesus' living there fulfilled the prophecy that their land would be honored by the dawning of a great light (4:15-16; see Isa. 9:1-2). Christ's message was identical to that of John the Baptist: Repent, because God's rule through the Messiah is drawing near (4:17). [Mark 1:14-15; Luke 3:19-20]

4:18-22 *Fishermen become fishers of men.* Jesus called his first four disciples, all of whom were fishermen. With the call came a promise: They would learn how to "fish for people." All four responded to Christ without hesitation. [Mark 1:16-20; Luke 5:1-11]

4:23-25 *A balm in Galilee.* Jesus traveled throughout Galilee, teaching in the synagogues, preaching, healing, and casting out demons. Word spread and he attracted large crowds from all over Israel and nearby areas. Jews began meeting in synagogues sometime after the destruction of Solomon's Temple in 586 B.C. Never intended to replace Temple worship, they were primarily for teaching and prayer.

PROCLAMATIONS OF THE KING: THE SERMON ON THE MOUNT (5–7)

5:1-12 *A bushel full of blessings.* Commonly called the Sermon on the Mount, 5–7 includes many memorable teachings of Christ. Though it sets forth principles that will become universal only during the Millennium, Jesus expected believers of his own day and ours as well to follow those principles. 5:1-12 has been called the "Beatitudes"—eight sayings that speak of blessings or happiness. Genuine happiness, said Jesus, comes from

- recognizing your need for God (spiritual poverty) (5:3)
- mourning over your sin (5:4)
- submitting to divine authority (5:5)
- desiring justice or righteousness (5:6)
- showing mercy (5:7)
- maintaining a pure heart (5:8)
- working for peace (5:9)
- rejoicing in the face of persecution (5:10-12)

[Luke 6:20-49]

5:13-16 *Shining light and seasoning salt.* Christians are to be "salt" and "light" for God. Salt was used in that day to prevent corruption, provide flavor, and promote thirst. Likewise, Christians are to stand against moral corruption; show the "flavor" of God's grace; and promote a thirst for salvation. As the light of the world, Christians are to live as well as proclaim the truth of Christ (see Phil. 2:14-15) so that others will come to know him (5:16).

5:17-20 *The Son of God and the law of God.* Christ's purpose was not to abolish the law but to fulfill it. The law would outlast heaven and earth. Every command, even what the KJV refers to as the "jots" and "tittles" (smallest letters and least strokes of a pen) are therefore significant. Christ's disciples must be more righteous than even the Pharisees—a standard that cannot be met apart from his work on our behalf (see Rom. 3:21-22).

5:21-48 *"It was said . . . but now I say . . ."* Having declared his utmost regard for the law, Jesus proceeded to show how the law's true intent went far beyond the superficial interpretation of the Pharisees. He dealt with several issues, highlighting each with a variation of "It once was said . . . but now I say . . ." The law forbade murder, but Jesus condemned anger as the root cause of murder. No gift is acceptable to God if the giver is harboring unresolved anger (5:21-26). Likewise adultery begins with a lustful heart. Lust can destroy the soul. It should be dealt with quickly (5:27-30).

A misapplication of the law had led to a liberal attitude toward divorce (5:31; see Deut. 24:1-4). Once again, Jesus called for allegiance to a higher standard (5:32; see exposition on 19:1-12).

While the law allowed the use of vows and oaths (see Lev. 19:12; Num. 30:2; Deut. 23:21-23), an honest person should not have to rely on them to back up his or her word (5:33-37; see James 5:12). The Mosaic principle of an eye for an eye was often misapplied as a license for revenge (5:38; see exposition on Lev. 24:17-22). Instead, nonresistance to evil (5:39), going the extra mile (5:40-41), and love for enemies (5:43-48) should distinguish Christian behavior.

6:1-18 *The right and wrong way to give, pray, and fast.* Doing good deeds (6:1-4), praying (6:5-15), and fasting (6:16-18) are best done in secret, to avoid spiritual pride.

6:9-13, commonly called the Lord's Prayer, is really the disciples' prayer, a guide for believers' prayers. It is not to be repeated over and over (6:7-8). Instead, it gives principles for communicating with God. Its words demonstrate

- faith in God (6:9)
- worship of God (6:9)
- expectation from God (6:10)
- submission to God (6:10)
- petition for ourselves (6:11)
- confession of sins (6:12)
- dependence on God's grace (6:12)
- compassion for others (6:12)
- dependence on God's power (6:13)
- acknowledgment of God's sovereignty (6:13)

6:5-6 does not forbid all public prayers, since Jesus and his disciples prayed publicly (see 11:25; Luke 3:21; John 17).

6:19-24 *The only bank that's fully insured.* Earthly treasure is insecure and corruptible, while eternal treasure is secure and incorruptible (6:19-20). Christians should focus on the latter, to produce a heart for eternal things (6:20-21). Greed can infect a person's entire life (6:21-23). One must choose either God or money; both cannot be served at the same time (6:24).

6:25-34 *The answer to anxiety.* For the believer, worry and anxiety are pointless. God feeds the birds and clothes the flowers (6:26, 28), and he loves and values us much more than them (6:26, 30). Worrying does not solve anything (6:27). Instead of worry, we should demonstrate faith by seeking God and trusting him to meet our needs (6:33-34).

7:1-6 *Those who judge risk judgment.* The person who judges risks being judged by the same measuring stick (7:1-2) and often exhibits the same sin for which he or she condemns others (7:3-4). Only after dealing with one's own sin can one have the spiritual insight to help other sinners (7:5). God alone can judge; still, it is the duty of Christians to speak out against sin (see 7:15-20 and exposition on 1 Cor. 5:9–6:11) and to exercise wisdom in dealing with those who reject the truth (7:6).

7:7-11 *Ask God, and he'll answer!* Believers should never hesitate to seek God's richest blessings (7:7-8), for God's generosity toward his children far exceeds our human understanding of generosity (7:9-11).

7:12 *All rules lead to one rule.* We should treat others the way we want to be treated. If we follow this principle, often called the Golden Rule, we can be confident that we are keeping God's law (compare exposition on 22:34-40; Gal. 5:13-15).

7:13-27 *Four looks at the two ways.* As the Sermon on the Mount came to a close, Jesus drew four contrasts between those who accept and those who reject him:

The road less traveled (7:13-14). The highway to destruction is wide and well traveled. The gateway to life is narrow and little used. More people will miss eternal life than find it.

Only two kinds of trees (7:15-20). Many who claim to speak in God's name are false prophets. The true prophet's life will back up his or her message. Compare 7:17-19 and 12:33.

Not all who profess possess (7:21-23). It is one thing to profess to know and serve God (7:21-22); it is quite another to be known by God (7:23). Those accepted by God are those who do his will by receiving his Son (see John 6:28-29).

Foundations firm and flimsy (7:24-27). Those who put Christ's words into practice build on a solid foundation. Those who hear the truth but fail to apply it build on sand (compare James 1:22). The storms of life will demonstrate which direction one has chosen.

7:28-29 *"This teacher is different!"* The people were amazed at the authoritative tone of Jesus' teaching. He was so different from the scribes, who could only cite the authority of earlier teachers to bolster their opinions.

POWER OF THE KING (8–10)

8:1-4 *A leper healed.* Immediately after finishing his teachings on the mountain, Jesus encountered a leper, healed him, and instructed him to tell no one about being healed—the first of several times Jesus would request such secrecy. The healed leper was to present himself to the priest for cleansing (see Lev. 14:1-32). Matthew would later explain why Jesus shunned publicity (see exposition on 12:15-21). The parallel accounts of Mark and Luke reveal, however, that the leper ignored Christ's directions and freely told others of his healing, as would many others who were instructed not to tell (see 9:30-31; Mark 7:36). [Mark 1:40-45; Luke 5:12-16]

8:5-13 *More faithful than his own people?* A Roman centurion asked Jesus to heal his servant. Jesus granted the healing and commended this Gentile's faith while condemning Israel's unbelief (8:10-12). *[Luke 7:1-10]*

8:14-17 *One healing leads to many more.* Jesus healed Peter's mother-in-law, prompting many more sick and demon-possessed people to seek healing. Matthew's reference to Isaiah 53:4 has led many to believe that physical healing is as much a part of Christ's atonement as is deliverance from sin. While sickness and death are, indeed, a result of sin and will eventually be eradicated by Christ's atonement for sin, both Scripture (see 1 Cor. 15:51-54; Rev. 21:4) and experience attest that this will not be accomplished in full until Christ's second coming. [Mark 1:29-34; Luke 4:38-44]

Note that Peter, claimed as Roman Catholicism's first pope, was married.

8:18-22 *Only the sold-out need apply.* Jesus challenged the dedication of two would-be disciples. Neither loss of physical comfort nor interruption of family ties are valid reasons to delay following Christ. [Luke 9:57-62]

8:23-27 *"Even the wind and sea obey him!"* While Christ was with his disciples on the Sea of Galilee, a storm threatened to overturn their boat, but at Christ's command it subsided. Evidently God used this experience to test the disciples' faith (8:26). They were duly impressed by Christ's control of nature (8:27). [Mark 4:35-41; *Luke 8:22-25*]

8:28-34 *A frightening miracle.* On the other side of Galilee, Jesus was confronted by two demon-possessed men. The remarkable cure Jesus performed frightened the people of the region. [*Mark 5:1-20;* Luke 8:26-39]

9:1-8 *"Be forgiven!" "Be healed!" Which is easier?* When some scribes accused Jesus of blasphemy for forgiving the sins of a paralytic, Jesus demonstrated his authority and power to forgive sins by causing the man to walk. The onlookers were amazed. [*Mark 2:1-12;* Luke 5:17-26]

9:9-13 *From tax agent to apostle.* Matthew noted his own call to discipleship, which was followed by a confrontation between Jesus and the Pharisees for his associating with Matthew's unsavory friends. Tax collectors were not liked in Jesus' day any more than in our day! They were categorized with "sinners" (9:10-11). Jesus used this occasion to stress that he had come as a physician to heal sinners. He rejected the Pharisees' practice of personal separation from undesirable people, which gave them little opportunity to make converts. [Mark 2:13-17; Luke 5:27-32]

9:14-17 *Why fast when you can feast?* When asked why his disciples did not fast, Jesus replied that as long as he was physically present with them, they should celebrate (9:14-15). He had come not merely to patch up or reform a legalistic Judaism but to bring about something new (9:16-17): salvation by grace through faith. [*Mark 2:18-22;* Luke 5:33-39]

9:18-26 *The hem of his garment, the touch of his hand.* While Jesus was on his way to visit a ruler whose daughter was ill, a woman with a hemorrhage touched his clothing and was healed. Jesus then proceeded to the ruler's house and resurrected the ruler's daughter, who had died during the delay. As a result, his fame spread far and wide. [*Mark 5:21-43;* Luke 8:40-56]

9:27-31 *Two faithful and grateful blind men.* Two blind men cried out for mercy, using the messianic title "Son of David." Acknowledging their faith, Jesus restored their sight. As in the case of the leper (see 8:1-4; Mark 1:45), the blind men ignored Christ's instructions not to publicize their healing.

9:32-34 *One miracle, two responses.* Jesus healed a man unable to speak because of demon possession. The healing brought two very different responses:
- The crowds marveled.
- The Pharisees attributed the healing to Satan.

This incident shows the ability of Satan and his demons to inflict physical suffering on humans, though this never happens outside of God's sovereign will (see exposition on Job 1:6-12; 2:1-8).

9:35-38 *Sheep without shepherds, grain without reapers.* As Jesus continued his preaching and healing, he felt deep concern for the multitudes without spiritual leadership. He explained to his disciples that many were ready to be "harvested" for the Kingdom.

10:1-15 *The call and commissioning of the 12.* Jesus selected 12 of his followers to be "apostles" (10:2) and gave them a specific mission: to proclaim to Israel the advent of their Messiah and his Kingdom (10:6-7). They were not, at this time, to evangelize Gentiles or even Samaritans (10:5). Jesus gave them the authority to heal disease and cast out demons (10:8). They were to take no money or extra supplies but to live by faith, depending on the goodness of those who responded to their ministry (10:9-10) while symbolically warning those who rejected them (10:11-15). [Mark 3:13-19; 6:7-13; Luke 6:12-16; 9:1-6]

Apostle means "messenger." Although it is usually a technical designation for the 12, the NT also applies the term to missionaries in general (see Rom. 16:7) and to Jesus himself (see Heb. 3:1).

10:16-42 *The call and commissioning of all disciples.* Christ's further instructions to the 12 apply to his disciples throughout history. Some of his words seem prophetic of the intense suffering of the faithful during the Tribulation (see 10:23). Disciples are to be prepared for persecution (10:16-26, 34-36), single-mindedly devoted to Christ (10:37-38), and bold in their witness for him (10:27-33). Those who kindly receive them will be rewarded (10:40-42).

"Beelzebub" (10:25, KJV), derived from the name of a Canaanite deity (see exposition on 2 Kings 1:1-8), was a common Jewish name for Satan.

OPPOSITION TO THE KING (11–12)

11:1-19 *Reassuring the peerless prophet.* John the Baptist, chained in a dark dungeon, probably with little food or water, was evidently having doubts about the one he had proclaimed as the Lamb of God, so he sent his disciples to ask Jesus if he truly was the Messiah (11:1-3; see John 1:29). Jesus' response contained only encouragement for John, and no rebuke (11:4-6). He went on to commend John's ministry and validate it on the basis of OT prophecy (11:7-15) and to chide the fickle crowd for their inconsistent responses to John and himself (11:16-19). *[Luke 7:18-35]*

Christ's commendation of the doubting John shows that intellectual doubts need not necessarily affect one's relationship with Christ. Christ understands human frailty (see 26:41). The inconsistency of the crowd shows the folly of always trying to please everyone.

11:20-24 *Three cities condemned for complacency.* Jesus singled out the three cities where he had performed most of his miracles and severely rebuked them for their lack of response. Their fate will be worse even than that of Sodom. [*Luke 10:13-16*]

11:25-27 *Hidden from the haughty, shown to the humble.* Jesus thanked his heavenly Father for favoring the humble in his revelation of truth (11:25-26). The truth about God comes only by revelation (11:27); therefore, those who are proud of their own learning, such as the Jewish leaders of Jesus' day, are unable to see truths that even little children can see.

11:28-30 *The trade-off: Burdens for blessings.* Describing himself as meek and lowly, Jesus invited all who so desired to come to him for rest. Those who are weary, especially under the burden of sin, will find that Christ is an easy taskmaster. This is the only self-description of Christ in Scripture.

12:1-8 *Lord of the Sabbath.* The Pharisees criticized Christ's disciples for picking grain on the Sabbath, considering this a violation of the law. Jesus cited two OT examples to show that it was not necessary to interpret the law so strictly:

- David and his men ate consecrated Temple bread because of hunger (12:3-4; see exposition on 1 Sam. 21:1-7).
- Priests work on the Sabbath without violating the law (12:5).

Actually the Pharisees were basing their criticism, not on the law itself, but on rabbinic interpretations of the law. Moving beyond legal precedents, Jesus made two other important points:

- God's overriding desire for mercy should guide any interpretation of the law (12:7; see 9:13; 1 Sam. 15:22; Hos. 6:6)
- As Lord of the Sabbath, Jesus had the right to define its true meaning.

[Mark 2:23-28; Luke 6:1-5]

12:9-14 *Healing on the Sabbath . . . in the synagogue!* Having declared himself Lord of the Sabbath, Jesus defied the Pharisees by healing on the Sabbath right in their synagogue, pointing out that even a Pharisee would rescue an endangered sheep on the Sabbath. Irate at Christ's actions, the Pharisees began to plot his death. [Mark 3:1-6; Luke 6:6-11] Compare Luke 13:10-17; 14:1-6.

12:15-21 *The Servant of God, quietly serving.* Jesus withdrew from the area, but many followed him and he "healed all the sick among them." Once again he warned those healed not to publicize their healing (see 8:1-4; 9:27-31; 16:20; 17:9). Christ's reticence reminded Matthew of Isaiah 42:1-4, which predicted that the true Messiah would not openly battle his enemies but would quietly do his work as God's Servant (12:18-21). His quiet ministry would, however, lead to victory (12:20). While the leaders of his own people were rejecting him, Christ would fulfill Isaiah's prophecy by extending the gospel to Gentiles (12:18, 21; see 28:19). [Mark 3:6-12]

12:22-30 *How can a divided kingdom survive?* When Jesus healed a blind and mute man, there was again a sharply divided response (12:22-24; compare 9:32-34):

- The crowds began to suspect that Jesus was indeed the promised Messiah.
- The Pharisees attributed his healing power to Satan.

To the Pharisees' charges Jesus responded that

- if he were to heal by Satan's power, Satan would be defeating his own purposes (12:25-26).
- they would have to make the same charge against their own Jewish exorcists (12:27).
- the miracle surely showed God's power over Satan (12:28), for how could one destroy a work of Satan such as illness before first "tying him up"? (12:29).

All who would join Christ in his battle against Satan must be very clear about whose side they are on (12:30). [Mark 3:20-30; Luke 11:14-23]

12:31-32 *Slandering the Spirit: The unforgivable sin.* In crediting to Satan the works Christ performed by the Holy Spirit, the Pharisees had committed an unforgivable sin. While this particular sin may have been possible only when Christ was physically present on earth, in a broader sense there is no hope left for anyone who persistently rejects the convicting work of the Spirit (see exposition on Heb. 10:26-31). [Mark 3:28-30]

12:33-37 *Bad roots, bad fruits.* The Pharisees' evil words, said Jesus, only revealed the evil in their hearts. Even our idle and careless words will be judged, since they reflect our hearts.

12:38-42 *Their judges: A prophet, a city, and a queen.* Although they had already seen Jesus perform many miracles, the Pharisees sought one more sign from him to prove his messianic claims. Chastising them for their persistent unbelief, Jesus reminded them of Jonah's miraculous escape from the great fish, and in a veiled prophecy compared that to his own approaching death and resurrection. In judgment, these self-righteous Pharisees will be found wanting in the presence of Gentiles who exhibit true faith. [Luke 11:29-32]

12:43-45 *Reformation minus regeneration means condemnation.* Perhaps recalling the many he had cleansed of demons, Jesus noted that such cleansing is useless unless it leads to a filling with the Holy Spirit. [Luke 11:24-26]

12:46-50 *The real family of God.* When Jesus heard that members of his biological family were looking for him, he used the occasion to teach that those who accept him as Messiah can enjoy a relationship with him that transcends earthly ties. [Mark 3:31-35; Luke 8:19-21]

PARABLES OF THE KING (13)

13:1-9, 18-23 *The sower, seed, and soils.* Following his rejection by the Jewish leaders, Jesus taught his disciples about the Kingdom of Heaven. In the first parable, a sower (Christ) cast seed (the Word of God) upon four kinds of soil (human hearts). Jesus later explained the significance of each soil (13:18-23), showing that entrance into God's Kingdom is a matter of individual response. [Mark 4:1-20; Luke 8:4-15]

13:10-17 *The purpose of his parables.* While telling the parable of the sower, Jesus paused to explain why he employed such symbolism in his teaching. Though the meaning of his explanation has been much debated, apparently Jesus intended his simple word pictures to confirm people in their response to him: Those inclined to believe found the parables an encouragement to their faith; those inclined to reject Christ would be confirmed in their unbelief, just as

Isaiah had predicted (13:14-15; see Isa. 6:9-10). However, see exposition on Mark 4:21-25.

13:24-30, 36-43 *Satan's weeds in the Savior's field.* A sower (Christ) sowed good seed (believers) in the field (the world). An enemy (the devil) sowed tares (unbelievers) in the same field. Both grew together and were hardly distinguishable until the harvest (judgment). Only God knows the hearts of those who profess faith in him.

13:31-32 *Like the mighty mustard seed.* The Kingdom of Heaven, said Jesus, would be like a tiny mustard seed, which grows into a plant 15 feet high. God's Kingdom would start out small but spread to encompass the whole world. [Mark 4:30-32; Luke 13:18-19]

13:33-35 *Yeast and the Kingdom of Heaven.* The Kingdom of Heaven is like yeast, a very little of which quickly affects a large amount of dough. Scholars interpret this parable in one of two ways:

- The yeast represents the Kingdom's positive influence on society, or
- the yeast represents the pervasive evil that the Kingdom must combat.

While yeast may indeed represent good in this context, it generally represents evil in the Bible (see 16:6; 1 Cor. 5:6-8; Gal. 5:9). [Luke 13:20-21]

Matthew noted again Christ's use of parables, seeing in it a fulfillment of prophecy (13:34-35; see 13:14-15; Ps. 78:2).

13:44-46 *Finding a fortune, on land and sea.* Two brief parables described people selling all they had to purchase a treasure. Two interpretations have been offered:

- The treasures are the Kingdom, and the eager buyers are believers who recognize its great worth, or
- the treasures are Israel or the church, and the buyer is Christ, who gave his all to purchase them.

The second view corresponds with frequent OT references to Israel as God's special treasure (see Exod. 19:5; Deut. 14:2; Ps. 135:4).

13:47-50 *Sorting out a sea catch.* Just as a fishing net catches both good and bad fish, there will be many associated with the Kingdom who are not true believers. Only at judgment will their true identity become known (compare exposition on 13:24-30, 36-43).

13:51-52 *A trained man and his treasure.* Jesus ended his parables by comparing the person who understood them to a person who values things both old and new, signifying that the truths revealed before Christ's time should be treasured along with the truths Christ revealed (compare exposition on 5:17-20).

13:53-58 *No hometown hero!* Though the people in Christ's hometown were impressed by his teaching, their knowledge of his humble roots caused them to despise and reject his messianic claims. [Mark 6:1-6] Luke tells about an earlier rejection of Christ at Nazareth (Luke 4:16-30).

REVELATIONS OF THE KING TO HIS OWN (14:1–16:12)

14:1-12 *Her dance brings his death.* In a flashback, Matthew told how John the Baptist had been imprisoned and martyred. John had rebuked Herod (Antipas) for marrying Herodias, wife of his still-living brother Philip. Herodias's persistence and her daughter's enticing dance persuaded Herod, against his better judgment, to execute John (14:3-12). When Herod later heard of Christ's miracles, his guilty conscience convinced him it was John the Baptist risen from the dead (14:1-2). [*Mark 6:14-29;* Luke 9:7-9]

14:13-21 *History's greatest fish fry.* Surrounded by a hungry crowd of more than 5,000, Jesus miraculously provided food for them. This is the only miracle of Jesus recorded in all four Gospels. [Mark 6:30-44; Luke 9:10-17; *John 6:1-13*]

14:22-33 *The wind, the water, and two walkers.* When Christ's disciples were caught at sea in a storm, he came to help them, walking on the water. When Peter tried to walk on water as well, he struggled with a lack of faith and began to sink. His prayer, "Save me, Lord!" is arguably the shortest and most direct prayer in the Bible! [Mark 6:45-52; *John 6:16-21*]

14:34-36 *Healed by the hem of his garment.* The people of Gennesaret displayed great faith, and Christ healed many of them through a mere touch of his garments. [Mark 6:53-56]

15:1-20 *Honor from their lips, hostility in their hearts.* When the Pharisees criticized Jesus' disciples for ignoring religious tradition, Jesus accused them of violating the spirit of the law by keeping back from their parents things supposedly dedicated to God. They were like the hypocrites Isaiah described, who talk about God but do not walk with him (15:7-9; see Isa. 29:13).

Jesus explained that it is the heart, not external activities, that determines a person's spirituality (15:10-11, 15-20). Told that the Pharisees, as the obvious targets of this teaching, were offended, Jesus warned his disciples to avoid them lest they be adversely affected by these "blind guides" (15:12-14). [Mark 7:1-23]

15:21-31 *Healing: For Gentiles too!* As Jesus visited a Gentile area, a Canaanite woman begged him to heal her daughter. Jesus responded first with silence, then declared that his mission was only to Israel (15:24; compare 10:5-6). When the woman continued to seek his help, he stressed again that his mission was to Jews only. When she still persisted, he commended her faith and granted the healing.

Christ's seemingly insensitive and contemptuous comparison of Gentiles to dogs must have been said with irony or to test the woman's faith, considering that

- he had at this time deliberately left Jewish territory to visit a Gentile area (15:21).
- he healed other Gentiles (see 8:5-13, 28-34).
- on several occasions he compared Israel's lack of faith to the great faith of Gentiles (see 8:11-13).
- though his mission as Israel's Messiah was indeed for Jews first (see 10:5-6; Acts 1:8; Rom. 1:16), the Bible also makes it clear that salvation is for all humankind (see 2:1-12; 12:18, 21; Acts 1:8; 11:1-18; Rom. 1:16; see exposition on 16:17-20; 21:28-32; and on Isa. 56:1-8).

Note that the Gentile woman used the messianic title "Son of David" (15:22) and worshiped Christ (15:25).

Going back to Galilee, Jesus performed many more miracles, resulting in glory to God (15:29-31). [Mark 7:24-37]

15:32-39 *History's second greatest fish fry.* Again Jesus miraculously provided food for a large crowd, this time more than 4,000. [*Mark 8:1-9*]

16:1-12 *Signs of the times, yeast of the Pharisees.* Once again the Pharisees (joined by the Sadducees) asked for a sign, and once again Jesus rebuked them and reminded them of Jonah (compare exposition on 12:38-42). They could predict the weather but failed to understand the person and work of Jesus (16:1-4).

A little later, perhaps recalling the

discussion about signs, Jesus warned his disciples to be on guard against the "yeast" (or leaven) of the Pharisees and Sadducees. When the disciples took him too literally, Jesus explained that he was talking about the Pharisees' legalistic teachings (16:5-12). On the symbolism of yeast, see exposition on 13:33-35. [Mark 8:10-21]

INSTRUCTIONS OF THE KING TO HIS OWN (16:13–20:34)

16:13-16 *"But what do you think of me?"* Jesus asked his disciples who the people thought he was, and they gave various answers. Then he asked them for their own opinion, and Peter boldly proclaimed him to be the Christ, the promised Messiah. [Mark 8:27-30; Luke 9:18-21]

Why were there so many rumors about Christ's identity?

- The belief that he was John the Baptist may have been Herod's influence (see 14:2).
- Elijah's return was predicted by Malachi (see Mal. 4:5-6).
- The apocryphal book of 2 Esdras predicted the return of Isaiah and Jeremiah (see 2 Esd. 2:18). Many Jews believed that the prophets would rise again at the Messiah's coming.

16:17-20 *"Upon which rock?"* Jesus pronounced a blessing on Peter, declaring that only by divine revelation could he have made his confession (16:16). Jesus then foretold the founding of his church (16:18; see Acts 2). He said, "You are Peter, and upon this rock I will build my church" (16:18). Some have interpreted this to mean that Peter was the foundation of Christ's church. The wordplay in Greek shows, however, that Christ himself is the foundation:

- "You are Peter [*petros,* a little stone]"
- "and upon this rock [*petra,* massive rock] I will build my church." Peter's own confession (16:16) identified Christ as the church's true foundation (compare 1 Cor. 3:11; 1 Pet. 2:4-8).

The "gates of Hades" or "hell" may refer to death, which has no hold over those in Christ (see 1 Cor. 15:51-57; 1 Thess. 4:13-18; and exposition on Ps. 9).

Christ gave Peter the "keys of the Kingdom" (16:19), which may have been prophetic of his leading role in opening God's Kingdom to Israel (see Acts 2:36-42), to the Samaritans (see Acts 8:14-17), and to the Gentiles (see Acts 10). If his possession of the keys is closely tied to his further role of "locking" and "opening" (16:19), it may have something to do with a role of church leadership (compare 18:15-20, where this principle is discussed again).

"Will be locked [or opened] in heaven" means not that God bows to human authority but that the actions of a Spirit-led Christian leader carry with them the awesome authority of heaven itself. To properly understand Peter's role in the church, it is important to note that the authority given here to Peter was later given to all the apostles (see 18:18).

Again Christ commanded secrecy (16:20; see exposition on 12:15-21).

16:21-23 *"But we won't let you die!"* Though he had already alluded to his death indirectly, Jesus now began discussing it openly (see 17:22-23; 20:17-19). Peter rebuked him, saying he and the other disciples would never let him die. Jesus in turn rebuked Peter, even calling him "Satan," for only Satan would suggest that Jesus avoid the Cross. [Mark 8:31-33]

16:24-28 *Lost and found: Someone's life.* Jesus spoke of the sacrifices that lay ahead for his disciples. Salvation is free, but discipleship costs everything. Yet only the self-sacrificing disciple will truly "find" his or her life. 16:28 probably refers to the Transfiguration (17:1-2). [Mark 8:34–9:1; see Luke 9:23-27]

17:1-9 *Once again: "This is my beloved Son!"* On a mountain with Peter, James, and John, Jesus was transfigured. His face and clothing shone with a light from within, and for the second time (see 3:17) the voice of God the Father identified him as God the Son. [*Mark 9:2-13;* Luke 9:28-36]

The glory seen in the transfigured Christ was the same glory cloud that shone in both the Tabernacle (see Exod. 40) and the Temple (see 1 Kings 8). It was later withdrawn because of Israel's sin (see Ezek. 10–11) but then returned to confirm Christ's birth to the shepherds (see Luke 2:9) and to receive Christ at his ascension (see Acts 1:9). Stephen would see God's glory (see Acts 7:55), as would Paul (see Acts 9:3) and John (see Rev. 1:16). At Christ's second coming this glory will be revealed to the whole world (see 25:31-32).

Again Jesus discouraged publicity (17:9; see 16:20 and exposition on 12:15-21).

17:10-13 *Will Elijah return?* Having seen Moses and Elijah with Christ at the Transfiguration (17:3-4), the disciples asked him about the prophecy that Elijah would precede the Messiah (see Mal. 4:5-6). Christ's response was twofold:

- Elijah had already come figuratively in the similar ministry of John the Baptist (17:12-13).
- Elijah will indeed come, as Malachi predicted, "to set everything in order" (17:11). This will happen before the Second Coming (see exposition on Rev. 11:1-14).

In another sense, of course, by appearing at the Transfiguration, Elijah did literally come in association with Christ's first coming.

17:14-21 *Little prayer, little power.* When the disciples failed to heal a demon-possessed boy (compare 10:8), Christ did the healing and then explained that their unbelief and lack of prayer had prevented their success. [*Mark 9:14-29;* Luke 9:37-42]

17:22-23 *Another prediction of his death.* Once again (see 16:21; 20:17-19) Jesus predicted his death and resurrection, causing the disciples great sorrow. [Mark 9:30-32; Luke 9:43-45]

17:24-27 *Fishing for tax money.* When asked if he paid the Temple tax (see Exod. 30:13), Jesus claimed exemption since he was the Son of God, the Temple's owner (compare 12:6). Nevertheless, to maintain a good testimony, he miraculously produced the money to pay the tax.

18:1-14 *Lambs in God's Kingdom.* When the disciples asked Jesus who was greatest in his Kingdom, he used a little child as an object lesson: Only with childlike faith can one enter the Kingdom. No one in the Kingdom is greater that anyone else—all are on equal ground. Concerning children, Jesus also stressed that

- judgment awaits any who cause them to sin (18:6)
- they are not to be looked down upon (18:10)
- God desires their salvation (18:14; see 1 Tim. 2:4)

We cannot always avoid temptation, but we should make every effort to do so (18:7-9). While we need not literally mutilate ourselves, Christ's overstatement shows the seriousness of sin.

Jesus extended his concern for children to all who are lost (18:11-14). God's greatest joy is the redemption of one lost person. [Mark 9:33-50; Luke 9:46-50; 15:3-7]

18:15-20 *Three steps to conflict resolution.* Jesus prescribed a three-step

LAND OF THE GOSPELS

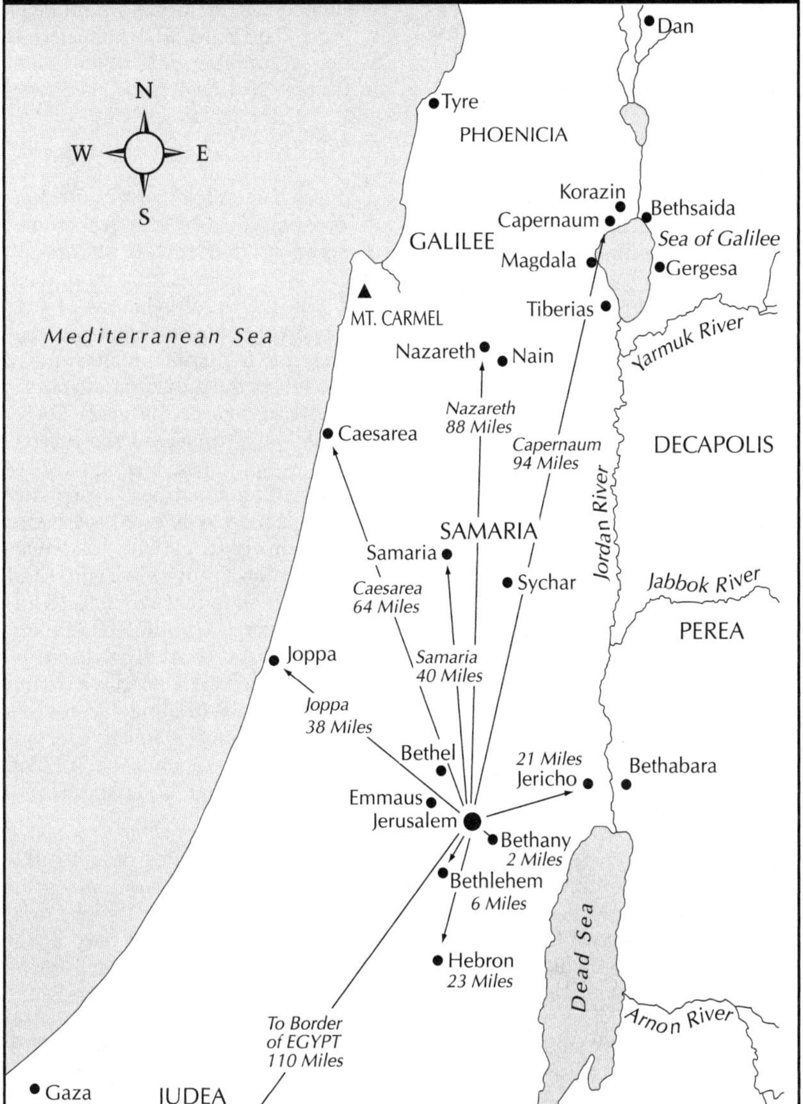

method for resolving conflicts among believers:

1. The person who is offended must go to the person offending (who may not even realize a wrong has been done) and talk about the problem (18:15).
2. If the offender does not respond, the offended one is to take one or two others to be witnesses of the confrontation and to help determine who is right (18:16).
3. If the offender still does not respond (assuming he or she is truly in the wrong), the matter is to be brought before the whole church for a decision. If the offender still refuses to repent, he or she is to be considered an unbeliever and not part of the church family (18:17).

Jesus promised God's guidance and authority (18:18-19) and his own loving presence (18:20) with any who seek his will in such situations. On 18:18, see the discussion of 16:19 in the exposition on 16:17-20. Compare also the exposition on 1 Corinthians 5:1-8 and on 2 Thessalonians 3:6-15.

18:21-35 *Forgiveness taught and illustrated.* Peter asked Jesus if he should forgive someone seven times, probably thinking this a generous plan since it exceeded the traditional rabbinic requirement of three times (and that was only in special cases!). Jesus replied that forgiveness should be unconditional and unlimited, and illustrated with a parable: A king forgave his servant (probably a tax-collecting governor over one of his provinces) for having mishandled a large amount of money. The servant then tried to extract a very small sum from his own creditors. Christians, completely forgiven by God, should never fail to forgive (18:35). [Luke 17:3-4]

19:1-12 *One husband, one wife—for life.* When some Pharisees asked about grounds for divorce, Jesus initially ignored their question and reaffirmed God's original ideal for marriage (19:1-6; see Gen. 1:27; 2:24). When they pressed the issue, citing Moses' apparent allowance of divorce (19:7; see Deut. 24:1-4), Jesus again reaffirmed God's ideal, noting that Moses' permission was "a concession to [their] hard-hearted wickedness" and that divorce was wrong for any reason other than sexual immorality (19:8-9).

Moses had stated that a man could divorce his wife if he "discovers something about her that is shameful" (Deut. 24:1). In Jesus' day there were two opposing interpretations of this. Followers of Rabbi Shammai held that this referred to marital unfaithfulness, and that was the only grounds for divorce. Followers of the more liberal Rabbi Hillel emphasized the preceding clause, "suppose a man . . . discovers something about her," essentially allowing a man to divorce his wife for any reason. Jesus clearly sided with the more conservative view (19:9) and went on to state that remarriage following divorce constituted adultery (compare Deut. 24:4). The disciples' surprise at Christ's strict views on marriage (19:10-12) underscores his overriding concern for its permanence. (See 5:31-32; Rom. 7:1-3; 1 Cor. 7:10-16.) [Mark 10:1-12; Luke 16:18]

19:13-15 *"For of such is the Kingdom of Heaven."* The disciples tried to prevent some parents from bringing their children to Jesus for blessing. Jesus rebuked them and once again (compare 18:1-6) used the occasion as an object lesson: Entrance to the Kingdom requires childlike humility. [Mark 10:13-16; Luke 18:15-17] It is interesting that Christ's teaching on divorce was followed by this encounter with children, the ones most hurt by divorce.

19:16-30 *Forsake your silver! Follow the Savior!* A rich young man came to Jesus, seeking eternal life but believing he could gain it simply by adding to his good deeds and moral achievements (19:16-20). Jesus suggested several commandments he might try keeping, not to imply that these would bring salvation, but to start him thinking about his sin (19:17-19). Then he focused on the one thing that *would* save the young man: surrendering his wealth and following Christ (19:21). Unfortunately, the man couldn't give up his wealth and pride (19:22; compare 18:3-4).

Jesus used the man's rejection of salvation to teach about the perils of earthly wealth (19:23-26). Riches can give a false self-confidence, making it hard to humbly depend on God. And yet "with God" even the rich can be saved (19:26).

The disciples, of course, had already given up their earthly wealth to follow Christ, thus Peter's question: "What will we get out of it?" (19:27). Jesus taught that, in his coming Kingdom, his 12 apostles would rule with him over Israel and would have great wealth. This would, in fact, be the happy lot of all faithful believers (19:29; see Rev. 20:6; 22:5).

Christ ended his teaching on wealth with a warning: Those with great wealth in this world, who refuse to forsake it, will not be nearly so prominent in the world to come (19:30). [Mark 10:17-31; Luke 18:18-30]

20:1-16 *Different hours, same wages?* Christ told a parable about a landowner who paid the same wages to all his workers even though they had done vastly different amounts of work. God has the sovereign right to reward us for our work as he sees fit. Anything he gives us, whether small or great, is a gift of grace and is more than we deserve.

20:17-19 *Still another death prediction.* For the third time (see 16:21; 17:22-23), Jesus predicted his death and resurrection, though his disciples probably still did not fully comprehend what he was saying. [Mark 10:32-34; Luke 18:31-34]

20:20-28 *How to be great in God's eyes.* When the mother of James and John misguidedly sought places of honor for her sons, Jesus used the occasion to teach that true greatness means following his example of

- willingness to suffer (20:22-23)
- willingness to serve (20:24-28)

Christ's warning that his apostles would suffer for his sake (20:23) was fulfilled. All of them experienced great trials, and all except John suffered violent deaths. [Mark 10:35-45]

20:29-34 *Sight restored on the Jericho road.* As Jesus left Jericho one day, pleas from two blind men gave him another opportunity to show his healing compassion. [Mark 10:46-52; Luke 18:35-43]

PRESENTATION AND REJECTION OF THE KING (21–23)

21:1-11 *"Here comes our King!"* Having miraculously located a colt, Jesus rode it into Jerusalem in literal fulfillment of Zechariah 9:9. The crowds responded enthusiastically, laying tree branches and even their own clothes as a red carpet to welcome him, and proclaiming him as their Messiah. [Mark 11:1-11; Luke 19:28-40; John 12:12-19] This event, generally called the Triumphal Entry, is often seen as Christ's formal presentation as King of Israel. It came on the Sunday before his crucifixion and is celebrated today as Palm Sunday, so named because presumably many of the "branches" (21:8) would have been from palm trees. *Hosanna* (21:9) means "save now."

21:12-17 *A place of prayer, not a refuge of robbers.* Probably the next day, Jesus entered the large outer court of the

JERUSALEM IN THE TIME OF JESUS

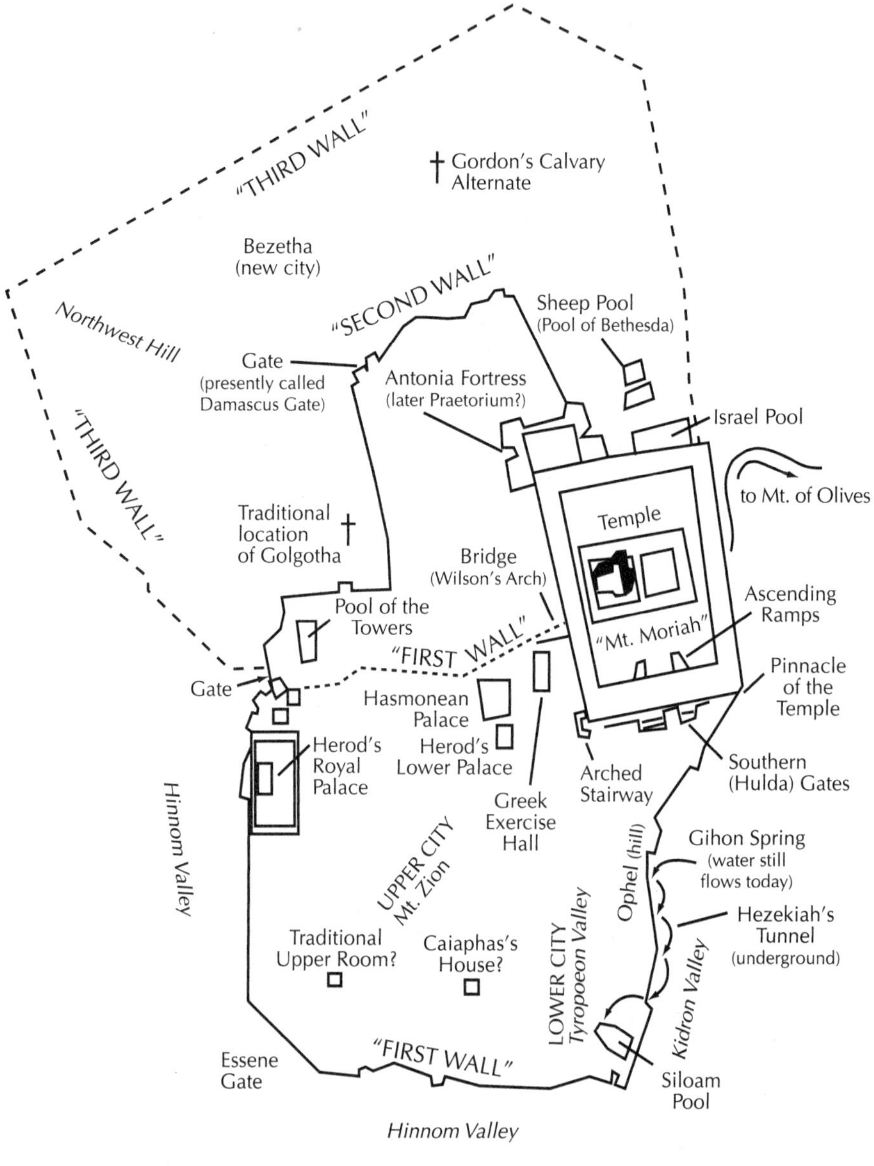

Temple and physically forced the money changers to leave (21:12-13). The money changers were there to accommodate the priests, who often made money by selling items needed for the Temple rituals. Jesus considered this contrary to the spirit of Isaiah 56:7, which called the Temple a "place of prayer." The scene reminded him of Jeremiah's criticism of Temple merchants in his own day (21:13; see Jer. 7:11). [Mark 11:15-19; *Luke 19:45-48;* John 2:13-17 relates a similar but earlier incident]

When the Pharisees became irritated at some children singing Christ's praises, Jesus quoted Psalm 8:2, affirming again that God's Kingdom is for those of childlike faith (21:14-17).

21:18-22 *Fruitless tree, fruitless nation.* The next morning, as Jesus entered Jerusalem, he looked for figs on a fig tree and, finding none, cursed it and made it wither. Though he did not say so at the time, it is apparent that his cursing of the tree foretold the setting aside of fruitless Israel as the gospel was offered to Gentiles, as seen by comparing this event with

- the parable of the fruitless fig tree (see Luke 13:6-9)
- the parables and teachings immediately following this event (see 21:28–22:14), all of which have to do with Israel's rejection of Christ and the Gentiles' inclusion in the Kingdom

When his disciples marveled at the fig tree's fate, Jesus assured them that they too would perform such wonders—possibly a prediction of the overwhelming Jewish response to the gospel on and following Pentecost. [*Mark 11:12-14, 20-24*]

21:23-27 *Two unanswered questions.* The Jewish leaders asked Jesus about the source of his authority for performing miracles. He responded by asking them about the source of John the Baptist's authority. When they refused to answer his question, he refused to answer theirs. [Mark 11:27-33; *Luke 20:1-8*]

21:28-32 *"I won't!" but he did; "I will!" but he didn't.* Jesus told a story about two sons who reversed roles: One said he would do what his father told him, but he did not. The other said he would *not* obey his father, but later he did. The first son was a picture of Israel, who had acknowledged God but then forsook him. The second symbolized the Gentiles, who had been aliens from God but would now receive him.

21:33-46 *The vicious vinedressers.* The next parable focused again on Israel and its rejection of God. The first part of the parable (21:33-37) is historical:

- The landowner (God) planted a vineyard and turned it over to tenant farmers (Israel) (21:33-34; see Isa. 5:1-7).
- The landowner sent his servants (the prophets) to get fruit from the vineyard, and they were badly treated (21:35-36).
- Finally the landowner sent his son, thinking the vinedressers would respect him (21:37).

The parable then turned prophetic: The wicked vinedressers killed the landowner's son (21:38-39)—a prophecy that would be fulfilled in less than a week!

When Jesus asked how they thought the landowner would punish those wicked vinedressers, the Pharisees, not yet realizing the parable was against them, replied that the vinedressers would be killed (21:40-41). When Jesus then made it clear that he had spoken the parable against the Pharisees and that God's Kingdom would be taken from them and given to the Gentiles (21:42-44), they began seeking ways to kill him but were afraid to because of his popularity (21:45-46). [*Mark 12:1-12;* Luke 20:9-19]

22:1-14 *Plenty of guests, but one with no garment.* Continuing the theme of Israel's rejection of him, Christ told a parable comparing God's millennial Kingdom to a royal wedding. All the king's friends were invited to attend, but they refused to come (22:1-3). After his second invitation was also spurned, the king ordered their city burned (22:4-7) and invited social outcasts to come in their place (22:8-9). These newly invited guests responded well, although one of them was banished from the banquet for being improperly attired (22:10-14).

The burning of the city may foretell Jerusalem's destruction in A.D. 70. The replacement guests obviously represent Gentiles. The exclusion of the one ill-attired guest shows the importance of personal choice in responding to the gospel. At royal weddings in that culture each guest would have been provided with a wedding garment bearing the royal imprint. Refusal to wear this garment was a terrible insult. [Luke 14:15-24]

22:15-22 *"Pray your prayers, and pay your taxes!"* Unable to kill Jesus (see 21:45-46), the Pharisees began trying to ridicule him (22:15). First, they sent the Herodians to ask him if it was right to pay taxes to Caesar. If Jesus had said it was not lawful, the Romans would have been mad. If Jesus had said it was lawful, he might have been labeled a traitor to his own nation. Taking a coin with Caesar's picture on it, Jesus wisely responded that Jews should give to Caesar what was his (the tax) and give to God what was his (worship and obedience). Believers are to pay taxes, even to an evil government. [Mark 12:13-17; Luke 20:20-26]

22:23-33 *A silly story of seven spouses.* The Sadducees, who didn't believe in angels or in the resurrection of the dead (see Acts 23:8), tried to trick Jesus with a hypothetical story and question: A man married a woman and then died. His brother married her and died as well, and so on through seven brothers. Which one would be her husband after the resurrection? Jesus' answer addressed the Sadducees' denials of both angels and resurrection:

- Resurrected people will not have marital relationships but will in that respect be like angels (22:30).
- There will indeed be a resurrection, for God called himself the God of the patriarchs after they had died, meaning they will someday live again (22:31-32; see Exod. 3:6).

The Sadducees' root problem, said Jesus, was their ignorance of the Scriptures and the power of God (22:29). Once again the crowds marveled at his wisdom (22:33). [Mark 12:18-27; Luke 20:27-40]

22:34-40 *The bottom line? Love God and your neighbor!* The Pharisees tried again to entrap Jesus, asking him which was the greatest law. Jesus cited two Mosaic teachings:

- Love God with your whole heart (see Deut. 6:5).
- Love your neighbor as yourself (see Lev. 19:18).

Undeniably, anyone who observes these two principles will keep the whole law. Once again Christ had silenced his critics. See exposition on Galatians 5:13-15 and on 1 John 3–4. [Mark 12:28-34; *Luke 10:25-37*]

22:41-46 *How can David's son be David's God?* Jesus now asked a question of the Pharisees: They accepted Psalm 110 as a prediction of the Messiah, yet they considered that he would be a merely human descendant of David (22:42). If that were the case, asked Jesus, why did David refer to him as "Lord" (Ps. 110:1)? Both the deity and humanity of the Messiah are taught clearly in the OT (see

Isa. 7:14; 9:6), but the leaders could not see it. Jesus had finally silenced his critics once and for all (22:46). [Mark 12:35-37; Luke 20:41-44]

23:1-36 *Woes for the hypocrites.* While warning his followers about the scribes and Pharisees, Jesus issued a series of woes against them, calling them hypocrites because they

- were inconsistent in their words and deeds (23:1-3)
- imposed on others non-scriptural traditions that they themselves found burdensome (23:4)
- sought human praise for their religiosity (23:5-7)
- hindered those who would follow Christ (23:13)
- cheated poor widows (23:14)
- prayed insincere prayers (23:14)
- taught others their evil ways (23:15)
- obscured the spirit of the law with legalism (23:16-24)
- were inwardly corrupt while looking good on the outside (23:25-28)
- were repeating the sins of past generations (23:29-35)

[Luke 11:37-54]

23:37-39 *Chicks rejecting their mother hen?* Jesus wept over the people of Jerusalem, who had rejected him. They would now be set aside until the "complete number of Gentiles" (Rom. 11:25) had come into the Kingdom, but would then be gloriously restored (23:39; see Jer. 31:31-34; Rom. 11:26-27). Compare Luke 13:34-35.

PREDICTIONS OF THE KING: THE OLIVET DISCOURSE (24–25)

24:1-20 *"The beginning of the horrors to come."* As Jesus left the Temple area on the Tuesday before his crucifixion, he predicted the Temple's destruction (24:1-2). As he and his disciples reached the Mount of Olives, they asked him to explain his prediction (24:3), asking specifically whether there would be a sign to signal his return and "the end of the world." His reply (24:4–25:46), often called the Olivet Discourse, answers these questions and stresses the need for vigilance and faithfulness as we await Christ's return.

Jesus described the "beginning of the horrors to come" (24:8), often seen as the first three and a half years of the seven-year Tribulation (24:4-20; see *Isaiah: Background* and the exposition on Isa. 2:5–4:1). During this time there will be false messiahs and prophets (24:4-5, 11); wars and anxiety (24:6-7); famines and earthquakes (24:7); persecution of believers (24:9); apostasy (24:10, 12); increased wickedness (24:12); worldwide evangelization (24:14); and the desecration of the rebuilt Temple by the Antichrist (24:15; see Dan. 11:31 and 12:11; and exposition on Dan. 9:20-27 and 1 John 4:1-6). When this happens, all who are able should flee for their lives (24:16-20). [Mark 13:1-18; Luke 21:5-22] See Revelation 6.

24:21-26 *"Unless that time of calamity is shortened . . ."* After the Antichrist desecrates the Temple (24:15), exactly at the midpoint of the Tribulation (see Dan. 9:27), there will come a time of distress unlike anything in previous human history (24:21). This time will be so horrible that, if it were to continue unchecked, everyone would die (24:22). During this time false messiahs and prophets will continue to deceive with great miracles (24:23-26). Some scholars reserve the term *Tribulation* for this second three-and-a-half-year period, after the Antichrist has shed his peacemaker facade (see exposition on Dan. 9:20-27 and on 2 Thess. 2:1-12). [Mark 13:19-23; Luke 21:23-24]

24:27-31 *The coming of the King in the clouds.* Christ's second coming will be preceded by cosmic signs: darkened sun and moon, falling stars, and shaking planets (24:29). Then Christ will descend to earth out of the clouds (24:30). This event will happen quickly and visibly, like lightning across the sky (24:27). A trumpet call will send angels to gather the saved from throughout the earth (24:31). This refers not to the rapture of the church, which will occur before the Tribulation (see exposition on 1 Thess. 4:13-18), but to the actual coming of Christ to earth about seven years later at the end of the Tribulation, at which time he will inaugurate his millennial Kingdom (see exposition on Rev. 20:1-6). [Mark 13:24-27; Luke 21:25-28]

24:32-36 *What the fig tree teaches.* Perhaps recalling the question of when these things would occur (see 24:3), Jesus said that just as the buds on a fig tree announce summer so also the disciples would know Christ's prophecies were about to be fulfilled "when [they saw] the events [he] described beginning to happen" (24:33).

Since Israel was often described as figs or a fig tree (see exposition on 21:18-22; Jer. 24; Joel 1:7), many scholars today see the rebirth of Israel as a harbinger of the end times. Others interpret "generation" (24:34) as "race," meaning that the Jewish race will survive till Christ returns. Either interpretation must take into account Christ's claim that even he does not know the exact date (24:36; see Mark 13:32). [Mark 13:28-32; Luke 21:29-33]

24:37-41 *Just like Noah's flood!* Prior to Christ's second coming, life will be going on as normal, just as in Noah's day. Then the wicked will suddenly be destroyed, just as in Noah's day. The ones "taken" (24:40-41) are the wicked, who will be removed from earth before the millennial Kingdom begins.

24:42-51 *Watch, wait, and work.* Believers are to be watchful (24:42-44) and faithful (24:45-51) as they await Christ's return. [Mark 13:33-37; Luke 21:34-36]

25:1-13 *Faithful and foolish virgins.* 10 virgins (representing Israel) went to meet a bridegroom (representing Jesus, their Messiah). Five were prepared and were invited to the wedding. The other five were unprepared and were excluded. The lesson: Be prepared, for no one knows when Christ will return (25:13).

25:14-30 *Faithful and foolish servants.* Three servants were given money to take care of for their master (25:14-15). The two who were good stewards were commended and rewarded (25:19-23), while the one who had not done well was condemned (25:24-30). We should be faithful with what Jesus has entrusted to us during his absence (compare exposition on Luke 19:11-27).

25:31-46 *Separating sheep from goats.* At the end of the Tribulation, Christ will gather "all the nations" (25:32) before him for judgment. They will be judged on the basis of how they treated Christ's "brothers and sisters" (25:40). The good works are not the basis but the proof of salvation—note that neither the sheep nor the goats were aware of their good works or lack thereof (25:37-39, 44). Christ's "brothers and sisters" probably refers in this context to Jewish people during the Tribulation, though the principle applies to the treatment of believers, both Jewish and Gentile, in all ages.

DEATH AND RESURRECTION OF THE KING (26–28)

26:1-5 *"Let's kill him! . . . after the Passover."* Jesus again predicted his betrayal and death, now just two days away (26:1-2). Meanwhile the Jewish leaders plotted to kill him, though they planned to put it off till after the Passover since the large crowds in town for the feast were probably still sympathetic to him (see 21:46) and might cause a riot (26:5). [Mark 14:1-2; Luke 22:1-2]

26:6-13 *They protest his anointing.* While Jesus was in Bethany, Mary anointed him with perfume worth a year's wages. When the disciples expressed outrage at her extravagance, Jesus commended her proper sense of values and noted that her actions foretold his death. Though Christ had spoken often of his approaching death, Mary was apparently the only one to take him seriously. John's account identifies the woman as Mary, sister of Lazarus (see John 12:1-8), and records the incident in its correct historical order, on the day before the Triumphal Entry. [Mark 14:3-9; Luke 7:36-50 records an earlier similar incident]

26:14-16 *The betrayer makes his bargain.* In exchange for 30 pieces of silver, Judas agreed to betray Jesus to the chief priests and immediately began looking for an opportunity to do so. The betrayal price was an exact fulfillment of prophecy (see Zech. 11:12-13). [Mark 14:10-11; Luke 22:1-6]

26:17-25 *The spy comes to supper.* On Thursday (the "first day" of the festival), Christ's disciples prepared for the Passover (26:17-19) and that night gathered with him to partake (26:20-25). During the meal, he predicted that Judas would betray him. [Mark 14:12-21; *Luke 22:7-16;* John 13:1-30]

Christ's secretive instructions (26:18) were probably an effort to hide his whereabouts from Judas as long as possible.

The Passover meal traditionally included lamb, unleavened bread, wine, bitter herbs, and a sauce made of dried dates, raisins, vinegar, wine, and spices.

26:26-30 *"This is my body. . . . This is my blood."* During the Passover, the celebration of the Old Covenant, Jesus, who by his death would become the perfect "Passover Lamb" (1 Cor. 5:7), took bread and wine from the table and instituted what would become known as the Lord's Supper, a meal symbolic of the New Covenant (see exposition on 1 Cor. 11:17-34). [Mark 14:22-26; Luke 22:17-23]

26:31-35 *"Nonsense! We'll never forsake you!"* When Christ predicted that all of his disciples would abandon him in his hour of need, they all steadfastly denied that they would. Eventually, however, they all did (see 26:56, 69-75). [Mark 14:27-31; Luke 22:31-34; John 13:36-38]

26:36-46 *Then they sleep while he struggles.* After the Passover meal, Jesus and his disciples went to the Garden of Gethsemane. While Jesus prayed, in bitter agony, his disciples slept, awakening only when Jesus announced the arrival of Judas and his coconspirators (26:46). The writer of Hebrews would later describe Jesus' mental anguish in Gethsemane (see Heb. 5:7). [Mark 14:32-42; *Luke 22:39-46;* John 18:1]

26:47-56 *A Savior betrayed and abandoned.* Judas came with an armed mob and betrayed Jesus with a kiss (26:47-50). Peter responded with armed violence (26:51; see John 18:10), but Jesus remained in control of the situation, stating that this latest turn of events was necessary. God's plan of salvation (see exposition on Dan. 9:20-27) must be carried out, including the death of the Messiah (see Dan. 9:26). Unlike the calm and composed Jesus, the disciples all panicked and fled. [Mark 14:43-52; Luke 22:47-53; John 18:1-11]

26:57-68 *A godly King before godless rulers.* Jesus was taken to the high priest, who, along with the other assembled leaders, sought false testimony against him (26:57-61). At first Jesus refused to respond to the false charges, but then he affirmed that he was the Messiah and warned that he would one day return in judgment (26:62-64). At that the leaders agreed that he was guilty of blasphemy and should be killed (26:65-66). They proceeded to beat and ridicule him (26:67-68). [Mark 14:53-65; John 18:12-14, 19-24] On 26:61, see 27:40 and exposition on John 2:18-22.

26:69-75 *Bold denials, bitter regrets.* Having followed Jesus from afar (26:58), Peter was waiting outside the high priest's chambers. Given three opportunities to speak up for Jesus, he instead denied knowing him, even cursing and swearing to bolster his denials (26:72, 74). When the rooster crowed, Peter remembered Christ's prediction (see 26:34), realized how far he had fallen from his lofty claims of loyalty, and wept bitterly (26:75). [Mark 14:66-72; Luke 22:54-62; John 18:15-18, 25-27]

27:1-2 *Their next step: Permission from Pilate.* After abusing Jesus and deciding he should die, the Jewish leaders took him to Pontius Pilate, the Roman governor. [Mark 15:1; Luke 23:1; John 18:28] Ironically, they did not have the authority to do the one thing they most wanted to do: kill Jesus. For this they needed permission from a Gentile.

Judea had become so troublesome to Rome that it had sent its own governors there to help the Herods keep order. This sometimes led to jurisdictional disputes, as seen in Luke's account of the interactions between Herod and Pilate during Christ's trials (see Luke 23:1-12). Pilate's washing of his hands (see exposition on 27:15-26) may have been in part an expression of frustration with his volatile post of duty.

27:3-10 *Judas: Remorse but no repentance.* When Judas realized that Jesus was actually going to die, he returned the betrayal price and hanged himself. Like Peter, Judas felt remorse. But while Peter's remorse led to repentance and restoration (see John 20:1-10; 21:15-18; Acts 2:14-40), Judas's remorse led only to death (see 2 Cor. 7:10). [Acts 1:16-19]

27:11-14 *A silent Savior.* As Jesus stood before Pilate, the Jewish leaders renewed their accusations while he remained silent, much to Pilate's amazement. [Mark 15:1-5; Luke 23:1-5; *John 18:28-38*]

27:15-26 *"Your choice: Redeemer or robber?"* After he had sent Jesus to Herod and Herod had returned him (see Luke 23:6-12), Pilate reminded the Jewish leaders of his custom of releasing one prisoner at Passover as a goodwill gesture. Given the choice between Jesus and Barabbas, a common criminal, they chose Barabbas and called for Jesus to be crucified (27:15-22). Pilate symbolically "washed his hands" of the matter and, when the people eagerly accepted full responsibility for Jesus' fate, released him to the soldiers to be crucified (27:20-26).

Within less than a week, the Jewish leaders had successfully turned the crowds from ardent supporters to bitter opponents of Jesus. Barabbas means "son of the father"—a beautiful picture of salvation as Christ, the true Son of the Father, died instead of Barabbas. [Mark 15:6-15; Luke 23:13-25; John 18:39-40]

27:27-31 *Ridiculed by the Roman soldiers.* Pilate's soldiers mocked Jesus, crowning him with thorns, putting a reed in his hand as his "scepter," and pretending to acknowledge him as King of the Jews. Then they led him to be crucified. [Mark 15:16-20; John 19:1-16]

27:32-50 *The Crucifixion.* Arriving at Golgotha, the soldiers crucified Jesus. They cast lots for his clothing (27:35; see Ps. 22:18) and placed a sign over his head mocking him as "King of the

Jews" (27:37; see exposition on John 19:19-22). The crowds, the religious leaders, and even the robbers crucified with him likewise mocked him, challenging him to vindicate his messianic claims by saving himself (27:38-44).

That Friday, from noon till 3 P.M., a supernatural darkness covered the land. Then, foregoing his usual tender designation of "Father," Jesus called out in agony to God, and at 3 P.M., he died (27:46-50). As he asked why God had forsaken him (27:46; see Ps. 22:1), Jesus was enduring God's judgment for the whole world (see Isa. 53:6; 2 Cor. 5:21). [Mark 15:21-41; *Luke 23:33-46;* John 19:17-30]

27:51-56 *Fearful signs follow his death.* At the moment of Christ's death, an earthquake tore apart the curtain dividing the Temple's Holy Place from its Most Holy Place, indicating that Christ's work had accomplished free access into God's presence (see Heb. 10:19-20). The earthquake also opened many graves, and many long-dead people made public appearances. These signs convinced at least one Roman soldier of Christ's deity (27:54).

Matthew noted that several women who were friends of Jesus watched "from a distance" (27:55-56). John's account places himself and Mary the mother of Jesus closer to the cross (see John 19:25-27), making John the only apostle known to have witnessed the crucifixion.

27:57-61 *"I'll bury him in my tomb."* Joseph of Arimathea, a rich disciple of Christ, took his body, put it in his own tomb, and placed a large, disklike stone over the entrance. Mary Magdalene and Mary the mother of James and Joseph (27:61; see 27:56) sat watch at the tomb. [Mark 15:42-47; Luke 23:50-56; John 19:38-42] Christ's crucifixion with thieves fulfilled the first part of Isaiah 53:9. His burial in a rich man's grave fulfilled the rest of that verse and vindicated his sinlessness.

27:62-66 *"Seal the tomb so he can't escape!"* Recalling Christ's prediction that he would rise from the dead, and fearing his disciples would steal his body to perpetuate this hoax, the priests and Pharisees, with Rome's help, sealed the tomb and posted a guard.

28:1-10 *"He's alive! He's alive!"* Just before dawn on the first day of the week (Sunday), as the two Marys returned to check on the tomb, an earthquake rumbled, and an angel rolled the stone away from the tomb. He declared that Jesus had risen from the dead, and invited the women to view the empty tomb (28:1-6). He told them to tell the disciples to meet Jesus in Galilee (28:7). While on their way to report this wonderful news, the women encountered Jesus himself—the first of his post-Resurrection appearances (see *Key Events in the Life of Christ,* p. 830). [*Mark 16:1-11; Luke 24:1-10; John 20:1-18*]

28:11-15 *The soldiers tell, then sell, the truth.* When the guards reported what had happened at the tomb, the Jewish elders bribed them to change their story and say that Christ's disciples had stolen his body. Matthew noted that, at the time of his writing, 20 years later, this false version of events was still widely accepted among non-Christian Jews.

28:16-20 *Promising his power and presence.* While appearing to a large number of his disciples (perhaps the 500 mentioned in 1 Cor. 15:6), Jesus instructed them to lead people to faith in Christ, baptize them in water, and teach them the things he had taught. As they did this they would have his power and presence. This final instruction from the Lord has come to be called the great commission and has been the marching order of the church down through the ages. [Mark 16:15-18; Luke 24:46-48; John 17:18; 20:21; Acts 1:8]

❖ ❖ ❖

PEOPLE TO REMEMBER FROM MATTHEW

ANDREW

Key Facts: Apostle, brought his brother Peter to Christ (John 1:40-42)
Father: John (John 1:42)
Occupation: Fisherman, apostle (Mark 1:16-17)
Total Bible References: 12
Key References: 4:18-20; John 1:35-42; 6:8-9; 12:20-22

Andrew Speaks

Here I am in Greece—a long way from Galilee—awaiting death by crucifixion. Really, though, I'm not in the least surprised about all this. After all, both John, my first master, and Jesus, my Messiah, died terrible deaths. (14:10; John 1:40)

I wonder if Peter is still in Babylon. Well, wherever he is, my big brother is no doubt stirring up the dust for Jesus! What a privilege it was to introduce him to the Savior. (John 1:42)

As I await certain death I often think of my days as a fisherman. Of course that's what I was doing when Jesus called me. Then I vividly recall that incredible time when, despite my doubts, he fed more than 5,000 hungry people—to say nothing of 12 hungry disciples!—with just five loaves and two small fish. (4:18-20; John 6:8-9)

Such memories comfort me. Yesterday he met my physical needs. I have every confidence that today and tomorrow he will provide for my spiritual needs as well.

Spiritual Lessons from Andrew

- Andrew didn't permit his loyalty to a human leader to keep him from following Christ (John 1:35-37). See 1 Corinthians 1:10-17 for some who did.
- Unlike Cain, Andrew knew that he was truly his brother's keeper and that his first responsibility was to introduce his brother to Christ (John 1:40-41; see Gen. 4:9).
- No matter how little we are able to give the Lord, he can make it adequate for his purposes (John 6:8-13).

Key Verses

"Andrew, Simon Peter's brother, was one of these men who had heard what John said and then followed Jesus. The first thing Andrew did was to find his brother, Simon, and tell him, 'We have found the Messiah' . . . Then Andrew brought Simon to meet Jesus" (John 1:40-42).

BARABBAS

Key Fact: Criminal set free in place of Christ (27:16-21)
Total Bible References: 11
Key Reference: 27:16-21

Barabbas Speaks

At first I thought it was either a mistake or some cruel joke. After all, it isn't every day that someone convicted of murder, robbery, and rebellion is suddenly set free by the Romans—especially if that scoundrel happens to be Jewish! (Mark 15:7; Luke 23:19; John 18:40)

But I soon discovered it was true! Seems the crowd preferred me over one who claimed to be the Messiah himself! I'll admit it sickened me to watch him being beaten and crucified. But it was even more amazing to hear him actually pray for his tormentors on the cross. I just don't know. Maybe that Roman soldier was right after all. (27:21, 54; Luke 23:34)

Spiritual Lessons from Barabbas

- Barabbas benefited from the goodness of God, but did he experience the grace of God? It is tragically possible to experience the one but not the other (see John 5:8-9, 14).

Key Verses

"So when the governor asked again, 'Which of these two do you want me to release to you?' the crowd shouted back their reply: 'Barabbas!' 'But if I release Barabbas,' Pilate asked them, 'what should I do with Jesus who is called the Messiah?' And they all shouted, 'Crucify him!'" (27:21-22).

CAIAPHAS

Key Fact: High priest who plotted Christ's death (26:3-4)
Total Bible References: 9
Key References: 26:3-4, 57-68; Mark 14:53-65; Luke 3:2; John 11:49-53; 18:24, 28; Acts 4:1-22; 5:17-40

Caiaphas Speaks

Incredible! Absolutely incredible! Look at them, barely able to walk after that severe beating, but what are they doing? Laughing and singing, of all things! Gamaliel, no doubt, gave us the correct counsel, but I wonder. Should I have killed them as originally planned? Probably not. I mean, that kind of treatment certainly didn't work on their founder, whom I arranged to have executed. (John 11:49-53; Acts 5:17-18, 33-41)

Rumors still abound that he rose from the dead. In fact, that cursed resurrection doctrine is the main theme preached by his fanatical followers! (Acts 2:24; 3:15; 4:10)

Yes, I led the plot to kill him. But what else could I have done? It was either this self-proclaimed Messiah or our entire religious and political system! Well, what's done is done. (John 11:47-50)

But I am still greatly troubled at the memory of our last meeting, especially his answer to my question as to whether he was the Son of God. He said, "I am, and you will see me, the Son of Man, sitting at God's right hand in the place of power and coming back on the clouds of heaven." What did he mean by that? What if he really was the Son of God? (Mark 14:61-62)

Spiritual Lessons from Caiaphas

- How sad that those who should know Christ best often understand him least. This was indeed the case with Caiaphas (26:62-65; John 11:49-52), as with all false religious leaders (7:21-23; 1 Tim. 4:1-2; 2 Tim. 3:5; 4:3-4; 2 Pet. 2:1; 3:16).

- If nonbelievers say, "Don't speak of Christ" (Acts 4:6-18), our response should be, "We must speak of him!" (Acts 4:19-22)

Key Verses

"And one of them, Caiaphas, who was high priest that year, said, 'How can you be so stupid? Why should the whole nation be destroyed? Let this one man die for the people'" (John 11:49-50).

HEROD ANTIPAS

Key Facts: Tetrarch of Galilee and Perea, ordered John the Baptist beheaded (14:1-12)
Father: Herod the Great
Brother: Philip (14:3)
Wife: Herodias (14:3)
Total Bible References: 27
Key References: 14:1-12; Mark 6:14-29; Luke 13:31-33; 23:7-16

Herod Antipas Speaks

Jesus of Nazareth was sent to me as a self-proclaimed king, but I turned him into a clown! Serves him right! How dare he refuse to answer my questions! (Luke 23:8-11)

Besides, rumor has it he's been guilty of bad-mouthing me. What is it with these Hebrew prophets? I ended up putting one such prophet to death for meddling in my affairs—even though I didn't really want to. (Mark 6:14-29; Luke 13:31-33)

But this one troubles me even more. In fact, I thought at first he was a reincarnation of John! Well, whoever and whatever he is, this Galilean will probably suffer a similar fate. I think Pilate will cave in to Jewish pressure and kill him. (14:1-2; Luke 23:7-12)

At any rate, at least one positive thing has come out of all this: The governor and I are now good friends! (Luke 23:12)

Spiritual Lessons from Herod Antipas

- We may try to silence those who call attention to our sins (14:3-12), but we cannot silence our own guilt (14:1-2; 1 Kings 22:7-28).
- One sin always leads to another. Herod's lust would trap him into taking John's life (14:3-12; James 3:5).
- One's spouse can have a tremendous effect on one's spiritual welfare, for good (1 Cor. 7:14; 1 Pet. 3:1-2) or for ill (Mark 6:18-20).
- Close friendships can result from either mutual faith in Christ (Acts 2:44-45; 4:32; 1 John 1:7) or mutual rejection of him (Luke 23:12).

Key Verses

"Herod would have executed John, but he was afraid of a riot, because all the people believed John was a prophet. But at a birthday party for Herod, Herodias's daughter performed a dance that greatly pleased him, so he promised with an oath to give her anything she wanted. At her mother's urging, the girl asked, 'I want the head of John the Baptist on a tray!' The king was sorry, but because of his oath and because he didn't want to back down in front of his guests, he issued the necessary orders" (14:5-9).

HEROD THE GREAT

Key Facts: Tetrarch of Judea, tried to murder the infant Jesus (2:1-18)
Father: Herod Antipater
Sons: Archelaus (2:22), Herod Antipas (14:1), Herod Philip (14:3)
Total Bible References: 9
Key Reference: 2:1-18

Herod the Great Speaks

My soldiers tell me they took another route home. Mark my word, when I locate and kill that miserable little infant they called the King of the Jews, those traveling astronomers will suffer my wrath also! In fact, the Jewish leaders who sent them to Bethlehem in the first place deserve to be punished! What a country to be ruler over! I mean, where else would a powerful monarch feel threatened by a silly story about a star and a baby king? (2:2-6, 12)

The report has just reached me. All those male babies in Bethlehem have been killed. Good! Wait a minute! What do you mean, with one exception? Curses! I'm told a carpenter, his wife, and his infant son escaped to Egypt! Could he be the one? Ridiculous! The whole story is absurd in the first place! And yet . . . (2:14, 16)

Spiritual Lessons from Herod the Great

- Human leaders should realize that God is ultimately in charge (Dan. 4:25), and they have only the authority he chooses to give them (Rom. 13:1). Any attempt to oppose him (Ps. 2:2) will fail in the end.

Key Verses

"Herod was furious when he learned that the wise men had outwitted him. He sent soldiers to kill all the boys in and around Bethlehem who were two years old and under, because the wise men had told him the star first appeared to them about two years earlier. Herod's brutal action fulfilled the prophecy of Jeremiah: 'A cry of anguish is heard in Ramah—weeping and mourning unrestrained. Rachel weeps for her children, refusing to be comforted—for they are dead'" (2:16-18).

JAMES (SON OF ZEBEDEE)

Key Fact: First apostle to be martyred (Acts 12:2)
Father: Zebedee (4:21)
Mother: Mary (Mark 15:40)
Brother: John (4:21)
Occupation: Fisherman, apostle
Total Bible References: 19
Key References: 4:21-22; 17:1-6; 20:20-28; Luke 9:51-56; Acts 1:13; 12:2

James Speaks

I've gone from contented fisherman in Galilee to condemned felon here in Jerusalem. And my crime? Preaching the resurrection of Israel's Messiah! It's Passover time. Little did I suspect some 16 Passovers ago that it would all end this way. Of course, Jesus did warn that some of us would die. (10:16-21; Acts 12:3)

Who could ever forget that sunny day by the sea when the four of us were called into full-time service? There were eventually 12 of us, but for some reason John, Peter, and I were allowed to see and hear things that none of the others saw: up on that mountain, filled with fear, almost blinded by the light, meeting with Moses and Elijah; and, most incredible of all, hearing the voice of the Father himself. (4:21-22; 17:1-6)

Glorious days, but also some moments of regret. How selfish to ask that John and I be given seats of highest honor in his Kingdom. And later, even worse, seeking fire from heaven to consume some Samaritans. Oh, how we were shamed by his rebuke, as he stated what should have been so obvious: He had come not to destroy his enemies but to save them! (20:20-28; Luke 9:51-56)

He would, of course, later die for our sins. And now I'm ready to die for his matchless name. Come do your worst, Herod! (Acts 12:1-2)

Spiritual Lessons from James

- "Much is required from those to whom much is given" (Luke 12:48). James, along with Peter and John, was permitted to witness things not seen by the other apostles (17:1; Mark 5:37; 14:33). But twice this favored follower displayed wrong attitudes (Mark 10:35-37; Luke 9:51-54). Have you been blessed by God in special ways? How have you responded in your love for him and for others (see Eph. 4:1; 1 Thess. 2:12)?
- James died a martyr's death (Acts 12:2), while according to tradition his brother John died in peace at a ripe old age. God's will for others may be totally different than his plan for you (John 21:17-22).

Key Verses

"When James and John heard about it, they said to Jesus, 'Lord, should we order down fire from heaven to burn them up?' But Jesus turned and rebuked them. So they went on to another village" (Luke 9:54-56).

JOHN (THE APOSTLE)

Key Facts: Perhaps the apostle closest to Christ, authored five NT books

Father: Zebedee (4:21)

Mother: Mary (Mark 15:40)

Brother: James (4:21)

Occupation: Fisherman, apostle

Total Bible References: 42

Key References: 4:21-22; 17:1-13; 20:20-28; Mark 5:37-42; Luke 9:51-56; John 1:29, 35-39; 19:25-27; 21:20-22; Acts 3:1-8; 8:14-17; Rev. 1:9-18

John Speaks

From the Jordan River to the Isle of Patmos, 70 years and five books later! What a life I've had! (John 1:35; Rev. 1:9)

I remember John the Baptist calling him the "Lamb of God who takes away the sin of the world." Well, Andrew and I immediately left John to spend the day with this Sin Bearer. That turned out to be the first step toward full-time service. The final step toward our new life would come on the Sea of Galilee. There we were fishing, the four of us—Andrew, Peter, my brother James, and myself—when he called out from the shoreline, calling us to follow him and saying he would show us how to fish for people. Well, we did and he has! (4:18-22; John 1:29, 36-39)

The seven decades since then have seen their share of both glory and grief. That amazing day on the mountain, the raising of that little girl, the healing of that lame man at the Temple, the crusade in Samaria—those were the glory events. (17:1-3; Mark 5:37-42; Acts 3:1-8; 8:14)

But my partisan pride, my efforts at self-promotion, and my downright vindictive spirit—those things brought only grief. Perhaps the most embarrassing were my two recent attempts to worship an angel. (20:20-28; Mark 9:38-41; Luke 9:51-56; Rev. 19:10; 22:8-9)

Apostle, elder, author, and prophet: These offices God has entrusted to me. My brother James, my former master John, along with Peter and Paul, my dear friends, are all gone now, each of them dying martyrs' deaths. I wonder, will I join their ranks? (10:2; 14:10; Acts 12:1-2; 2 Tim. 4:6; 2 Pet. 1:14; 2 John 1; 3 John 1; Rev. 1:3)

The Savior once told Peter it was none of his business what happened to me. It's really none of my business either. Whatever he wills is fine. (John 21:20-23)

What great honors he has given me, to have been so close to him and now to see him in his ascended glory and to actually have the privilege of describing for all believers our future home—that shining city among the stars! I only hope that the kind of love I learned of from our Lord will be a reality in the lives of all his disciples as they await his return. (John 13:23; 1 John 4:7-10; Rev. 1:10-18; 21:1-4, 10-27)

Spiritual Lessons from John

- God chooses and uses whomever he will, regardless of the person's natural abilities or social background. Even though John was a theologically untrained fisherman, God used him to explain three important truths about Christ: his deity (John 1:1-5), humanity (1 John 1:1-2), and sovereignty (Rev. 11:15; 19:11-16).
- Though he was the disciple closest to Jesus, John once coveted even greater honor, for which Jesus gently rebuked him (Mark 10:35-40). We should be content with what we have (Phil. 4:11; 1 Tim. 6:8; Heb. 13:5). God will determine when and how to exalt us (Ps. 75:6-7; 1 Pet. 5:5-6).
- Believe it or not, God's grace transcends denominational boundaries (Mark 9:38-41)!
- It is all too easy to give to God's servants—such as pastors or other people of influence in our lives—the honor and even worship that God alone deserves. Even John was guilty of this sort of idolatry (4:10; Col. 2:18; Rev. 19:10; 22:8-9).
- Love for God and for others is a distinguishing mark of all true Christians (1 John 2:3-11; 3:4-18; 4:7–5:3).

Key Verses

"Dear friends, let us continue to love one another, for love comes from God. Anyone who loves is born of God and knows God. But anyone who does not love does not know God—for God is love. God showed how much he loved us by sending his only Son into the world so that we might have eternal life through him. This is real love. It is not that we loved God, but that he loved us and sent his Son as a sacrifice to take away our sins" (1 John 4:7-10).

JOHN THE BAPTIST

Key Facts: Prepared the way for Christ, baptized him (3)
Birth: Recorded in Luke 1:57

Father: Zechariah (Luke 1:5-13)
Mother: Elizabeth (Luke 1:5-13)
Occupation: Prophet, evangelist
Key Events in His Life:

- Announces Christ's coming (3:1-12)
- Baptizes Christ (3:13-17)
- Inquires about Christ's authenticity (11:1-6)
- Beheaded by Herod Antipas (14:1-12)

Age at Death: 35 (recorded in 14:10)
Total Bible References: 90
Key References: 3; 11:1-6; 14:1-12; Acts 19:4

John the Baptist Speaks

At least Herod allowed my disciples to visit me here in prison today. That's a lot more than his wife would have done. They came right after returning from their mission for me. Thank God my misgivings were totally unjustified. Their report literally thrilled my soul: "He's the one, John. No doubt about it whatsoever. We watched in amazement as he gave sight to the blind, hearing to the deaf, mobility to the cripple, and, most incredible of all, life to the dead!" (11:1-6)

I thanked them again and again and bade them a final farewell. We all realized this would be our last meeting. I know it will be just a matter of time until she has my head. I am feared and hated by both the king and the queen—for my crime of denouncing their shameful sin. (14:5; Mark 6:18-19)

It's so hot and oppressive down here by the Dead Sea. How I miss the cool waters of the Jordan, where I once baptized so many, including the very one my disciples just reported about. (3:13-16)

Chained here in the darkness, I often wonder if I have lived up to the lofty predictions made about me by that angel and by my father. Or, perhaps even more significant, what about those written by Isaiah and Malachi? (3:1-3; 11:10; Luke 1:13-17, 76-79)

God will be my judge, of course. But this one thing I know: Even in the hour of death, he must increase while I must decrease, for he's the one who will take away our sin. (John 1:29; 3:30)

Footsteps outside the dungeon door . . . They're coming for me. Someone said that today is Herod's birthday party. Apparently I've been invited. (14:6)

Spiritual Lessons from John the Baptist

- The gospel message is always far more important than the gospel messenger (John 1:19-37; 3:22-36). A preacher's true spirituality is demonstrated when the crowds bypass him to hear another.
- John's message concerning repentance and right living never varied, whether his listeners consisted of the masses (Luke 3:10-11), religious leaders (Matt. 3:7-10), tax collectors (Luke 3:12-13), soldiers (Luke 3:14), or the king and queen themselves (Mark 6:17-18).
- Jesus gently reassured a troubled and imprisoned John that he was indeed Israel's Messiah (11:2-6). He will comfort and assure us today concerning our doubts and fears. He knows that we are only human and will have such doubts from time to time (Ps. 103:11-14).

Key Verse
"Isaiah had spoken of John when he said, 'He is a voice shouting in the wilderness: "Prepare a pathway for the Lord's coming! Make a straight road for him!"'" (3:3).

JOSEPH
Key Fact: Legal father of Christ (1:18-20; Luke 2:4-5)
Father: Jacob (1:16)
Wife: Mary (1:18-20; Luke 2:4-5)
Sons: James, Joseph, Simon, Judas (13:55)
Daughters: Unnamed (13:56)
Occupation: Carpenter
Total Bible References: 16
Key References: 1:18–2:23; Luke 2; 3:23

Joseph Speaks
It grieves me that in spite of our efforts they still look on him with disdain. Admittedly, both his mother and I have struggled throughout the years to even partly understand that incredible series of events. Who, indeed, could grasp the fact that my wife, while still a virgin, would give birth to the Messiah himself? But that's exactly what happened. (1:18-25; John 7:3-5)

Jesus and Immanuel! Those were to be his names, as announced by an angel to both Mary and me; the names mean "Savior" and "God with us." But neither his half brothers nor our hometown people will accept this! They simply shake their heads when we recount the story of the wondrous star and those visits by shepherds and astronomers. (1:21-23; 2:1-2; Mark 6:3; Luke 2:15; 4:29; John 7:3-5).

He has left my carpenter shop to perform the Father's work, just as he predicted he would when he was a young boy. I am told John the Nazirite has recently baptized him. What will happen next? Only he and his true Father can answer that question! (3:13-15; Luke 1:15; 2:41-50)

Spiritual Lessons from Joseph
- Joseph provides a marvelous example of obedience: God told him to wed Mary (1:24), and he did. God then instructed him to move his family to Egypt (2:13-14), and he did. Finally, God commanded him to return to Israel (2:19-21), and he did.

Key Verses
"Joseph, her fiancé, being a just man, decided to break the engagement quietly, so as not to disgrace her publicly. As he considered this, he fell asleep, and an angel of the Lord appeared to him in a dream. 'Joseph, son of David,' the angel said, 'do not be afraid to go ahead with your marriage to Mary. For the child within her has been conceived by the Holy Spirit'" (1:19-20).

JUDAS ISCARIOT
Key Facts: Apostle, betrayed Christ (Luke 22:3-4)
Total Bible References: 22
Key References: 26:47-50; 27:3-10; John 6:70-71; 12:4-6; 13:2; Acts 1:15-25

Judas Iscariot Speaks

Hypercritical and uncaring idiots! Actually, I didn't really expect any help from those religious leaders. Maybe I just wanted to be reassured I'd done the right thing. (27:3-4)

Of course I knew differently. My action was wrong. I was aware of it at the time, and I feel great remorse right now. Frankly, I still don't know why Jesus chose me in the first place. He seemed to sense right from the beginning that my heart was not with him. Certainly I had little in common with those 11 crude and uneducated men who also joined the cause. (10:2-4; 27:4; John 6:70-71)

Actually, though, why did I agree to sign up? Probably because I thought he just might be the powerful political leader we were all looking for, the one who would throw off the Roman yoke and declare himself king! Of course that would have made me a very powerful and rich man! (John 6:14-15)

But no, to the contrary, he seemed only interested in associating with sinners and sick people! Nor, apparently, did he believe in rewarding us with generous salaries! Frankly, I really resented that. In fact, this forced me, as treasurer for the group, to secretly transfer funds to my own account. (10:9-10; John 12:6)

In my mind the turning point was the Triumphal Entry, which would have provided the perfect opportunity to seize power and be proclaimed king. But what did our would-be Messiah do instead? He cried over Jerusalem! Well, that did it! I determined right then to get out as fast as possible with as much as possible. (Luke 19:41-44; John 12:12-16; 13:2)

Now that I see him being brought to trial, I realize there must be more to this remarkable man than I had admitted. I have obviously betrayed an innocent man. Meanwhile, I have no prospects for employment and no real friends to turn to. . . . There is but one course of action left. . . . (27:1-5)

Spiritual Lessons from Judas Iscariot

- People in rebellion against God prefer darkness to the light, the better to hide their sin (John 3:20). The closer Judas came to the light, the darker the shadow he cast—first as a thief (John 12:6), then as a hypocrite (Matt. 26:21-25), and finally as a traitor (26:14-16; Luke 22:48).
- Seemingly sincere Christians, even those in positions of trust, may not necessarily be what they appear to be (26:21-25; see 7:15-23; 2 Cor. 11:13-15).
- Remorse without true repentance is worthless (27:3-10).

Key Verses

"And even as he said this, Judas, one of the twelve disciples, arrived with a mob that was armed with swords and clubs. They had been sent out by the leading priests and other leaders of the people. Judas had given them a prearranged signal: 'You will know which one to arrest when I go over and give him the kiss of greeting.' So Judas came straight to Jesus. 'Greetings, Teacher!' he exclaimed and gave him the kiss. Jesus said, 'My friend, go ahead and do what you have come for.' Then the others grabbed Jesus and arrested him" (26:47-50).

MARY (MOTHER OF JESUS)

Key Fact: Gave birth to Jesus (Luke 2:7)
Husband: Joseph (1:18-20; Luke 2:4-5)

Sons: Jesus, James, Joseph, Simon, Judas (13:55; Luke 2:7)
Daughters: Unnamed (13:56)
Key Events in Her Life:

- Christ's birth and childhood (Luke 1:26–2:52)
- Witnesses Christ's first miracle (John 2:1-12)
- Learns of Christ's "true family" (Luke 8:19-21)
- Observes crucifixion (John 19:25-27)
- Among his first disciples (Acts 1:13-14)

Total Bible References: 19
Key References: 1:18–2:23; Luke 1:26–2:52; 8:19-21; John 2:1-12; 19:25-27; Acts 1:13-14

Mary Speaks

How wonderful this time of prayer has been! Kneeling here in this upper room I think of Joseph. If only he could have lived to see the day. He would have certainly stood alongside me at the cross and then shared my joy over the empty tomb. (John 19:25; Acts 1:13-14)

I know the relief that would have been his concerning the conversion of his other sons. Of course, it was that glorious resurrection appearance to James that opened their eyes. But who knows, perhaps he is aware of all these things anyway. (Acts 1:14; 1 Cor. 15:7; James 1:1; Jude 1:1)

What memories are mine. The angelic announcement. The shepherds and those very interesting men from the Far East. Simeon's strange prophecy—which now I understand all too well! The Temple episode when Jesus was but 12. And that wedding of all weddings in Cana. (2:11; Luke 1:28-35; 2:15-16, 34-35, 46-50; John 2:1-10)

John has been so kind, providing for my every need as he was instructed to do. I think I'm beginning to understand the special attachment my Son felt for him. (John 19:25-27)

But enough of memories. Back to prayer: Dear Father, how can a mere mortal even begin to thank you for the priceless privilege of giving birth to the world's blessed Redeemer? As I once helped raise him, accept my vow to totally serve him till the day of my death. My prayer to you as a young virgin in Nazareth is still my prayer today: I am the Lord's servant, and I am willing to accept whatever he wants! (Luke 1:38; 2:7, 40, 51-52)

People are beginning to move about. Apparently the prayer session is over. I see Simon Peter standing to his feet, ready to address us. I must give him my undivided attention. (Acts 1:15)

Spiritual Lessons from Mary

- God pronounced special favor on Mary (Luke 1:30), and he will favor us if we emulate her spiritual qualities:
  - ➤ She was totally submitted to God (Luke 1:38).
  - ➤ She had hidden God's Word in her heart, as is seen in her song of praise (Luke 1:46-55), where she quoted from at least 15 OT sources!
- When problems arise, we should check with Jesus first, as did Mary (John 2:3). Then we should be ready and willing to do whatever he tells us to do (John 2:5).

- Like Paul and Barnabas (Acts 15:25-26), Mary had truly risked her life for the sake of Christ:
  - ➤ She endured a difficult and dangerous journey to accomplish his birth (Luke 2:4-7).
  - ➤ She exposed herself to hostility, ridicule, and possible death at Calvary to watch him die (John 19:25-27).
- The Bible presents Mary as a worshiper of her son Jesus, not as an object of worship herself. In the upper room, she was among those praying (Acts 1:14).

Key Verse

"Mary responded, 'I am the Lord's servant, and I am willing to accept whatever he wants'" (Luke 1:38).

PETER

Key Facts: Prominent apostle, authored two NT books
Father: John (John 1:42)
Brother: Andrew (John 1:40)
Wife: Unnamed (8:14)
Occupation: Fisherman, apostle (4:18-20)
Key Events in His Life:

- Called by Christ (4:18-20)
- Tries to walk on water (14:28-31)
- Publicly confesses Christ (16:16-18)
- Witnesses Transfiguration (17:1-8)
- Denies Christ before crucifixion (26:69-75)
- Exhorted by resurrected Christ (John 21:15-22)
- Preaches at Pentecost (Acts 2)
- Proclaims gospel in Samaria (Acts 8:14)
- Sees vision, evangelizes Gentiles (Acts 10)
- Jailed for preaching; freed miraculously (Acts 12:1-10)
- At Jerusalem Council (Acts 15)
- Writes 2 NT books

Total Bible References: 183
Key References: 4:18-20; 14:28-31; 16:16-19; 17:1-8; 26:69-75; John 6:68-69; 21:15-22; Acts 2; 10–12; 15; 1 Cor. 15:5; Gal. 2:11-13; 1, 2 Pet.

Peter Speaks

35 years ago, Jesus told me that someday I would be led where I didn't want to go. I have the feeling that his prophecy will come true any day now. God will allow Nero to do what he once prohibited Herod Antipas from doing. (John 21:18-19; Acts 12:1-10; 1 Pet. 1:14)

It would be so good to see my brother Andrew once more, but he's somewhere in Greece. I wonder where Paul is these days? How thankful I am for those two men. My brother introduced me to the Savior, and Paul was a trusted fellow evangelist. I say "trusted" in part because of that one time when he didn't hesitate to correct me when I became too legalistic. (John 1:42; Gal. 2:11-12)

At my first encounter with Christ, on the shore of Galilee, he told me to catch some fish. At our last encounter, on the very same spot, he told me to feed his sheep. By his grace I've been able to obey both commands. At Pentecost, he allowed me to snare 3,000 "fish." Later, through these two letters, I have tried, with God's help, to feed his sheep. (Luke 5:10; John 21:15-17; Acts 2:41; 1 Pet. 2:2-3)

Whenever I recall the beautiful Galilean countryside I think of my shining moment, when I was privileged to publicly confess my belief that Jesus was indeed the Son of the living God. But then I also recall how, shortly thereafter, he had to severely rebuke me for trying to stand in the way of his ultimate mission as God's Son—to die for our sins. (16:16, 21-23)

Then came that darkest moment of all, when I forsook and actually denied him in public! In fact, to my horror he overheard those curses, then turned and looked at me. Never will I forget the sad gaze that penetrated my very soul. (Mark 14:50, 71; Luke 22:61-62; John 18:25-27)

But then, wonder of wonders, following his crucifixion and resurrection he personally appeared to me. Events seemed to move at lightning speed after that: his ascension, the excitement of Pentecost, the humbling experience of being used by him to heal the sick—and even one dear old saint whom we saw come back to life through his power. (Luke 24:34; Acts 1:9-11; 2:1-4; 3:1-8; 9:32-41; 1 Cor. 15:5)

There's probably nothing, of course, that can stop my approaching death. I hear they often do it by crucifixion here in Rome. When I think of all my Lord has done for me—and all he has forgiven me of—I hardly feel worthy to die in the same way he died. That's why I've made my special request. . . .

Spiritual Lessons from Peter

- The more clearly we see our Savior, the more clearly we see our sin. Both Isaiah (Isa. 6:1-5) and Peter (Luke 5:8; 22:54-62) experienced this. According to tradition, when Peter was martyred for his faith, he asked to be crucified upside down, feeling unworthy to die in the same way his Lord had died.
- God doesn't need our advice or correction. Peter tried three times to change the Lord's mind but was himself promptly corrected each time (16:21-23; Mark 14:27-31; John 13:6-9; see also Isa. 40:13; Rom. 11:33-36).
- As Peter learned one night on a stormy sea, only by looking to Jesus can we stand firm (14:22-33; Heb. 12:2).
- It is more important to seek God's will for our own life (Eph. 2:10) than to be concerned about his plans for someone else (John 21:20-22).
- God shows no partiality on the basis of race or class (Rom. 2:11), and neither should we. Even though Peter acknowledged this (Acts 10:34), he did not always live up to the truth he knew (Gal. 2:11-14).
- Peter was an eyewitness of Christ's earthly ministry, including his glorious Transfiguration (17:1-8). Yet though he greatly valued that remarkable experience (2 Pet. 1:16-18), he seemed to value even more the written Word of God that it confirmed (2 Pet. 1:19-21). None of us today share Peter's firsthand knowledge of Christ during his earthly ministry. But we can share his encounter with Christ through his Word (2 Tim. 3:16-17; 1 Pet. 1:23-25; 2:2-3).

Key Verses

"At this point many of his disciples turned away and deserted him. Then Jesus turned to the Twelve and asked, 'Are you going to leave, too?' Simon Peter replied,

'Lord, to whom would we go? You alone have the words that give eternal life. We believe them, and we know you are the Holy One of God'" (John 6:66-69).

PILATE

Key Facts: Governor of Palestine, condemned Jesus to death (27:2-26)
Total Bible References: 53
Key References: 27:2-26, 57-66

Pilate Speaks

I can't believe it! Yet another request concerning this would-be king of the Jews. Will it ever end? Even after his death it continues. First two followers desired his lifeless body. Now his enemies are demanding that I secure his tomb. (27:62-66; John 19:38-39)

Actually, I thought the situation would end when I sent him off to Herod. But that was just the beginning, for I no sooner turned around than there he was again, standing in my court. Strange case to say the least. He must have been the only man in this entire insane country more hated by the people than myself. And that's saying quite a lot! They have literally despised me since the day I slaughtered a bunch of them along with their animal sacrifices. But I have never understood their fierce animosity toward this Jesus. Certainly he didn't seem to be a threat to anyone. (27:21-25; Luke 13:1; 23:6-7, 11)

I probably should have listened to my wife and set him free, regardless of their protests. Amazing, though, that they chose Barabbas, that wretched creature, over this mild-mannered man. (27:19; Luke 23:18-19)

This Jesus told me he was a King, but not of this world. He also claimed to be the very source of truth itself. Well, I ordered him severely beaten, attempting to appease the people's taste for blood and thereby save his life, but all to no avail. At any rate, I washed my hands of his innocent blood. (27:24; John 18:36–19:5)

Strange, though, I still feel uncomfortable and uncertain—even unclean—over the whole episode. His friends desired the body, and I granted their request. His foes now demand that I secure the tomb, which shall be done. Surely this will end the matter forever. What more can he do, rise up from the dead?

Spiritual Lessons from Pilate

- We should always give due consideration to the advice of friends (Prov. 11:14). Pilate ignored his wife's advice to his own peril (27:19).
- Pilate tried to be neutral concerning Christ (27:24), but Christ does not allow such neutrality (12:30).
- When confronted with the very embodiment of truth (John 14:6), Pilate expressed contempt for the very possibility of knowing the truth (John 18:38), as do so many today (see 2 Tim. 3:7; 4:3-4; 2 Pet. 3:16).

Key Verses

"Pilate saw that he wasn't getting anywhere and that a riot was developing. So he sent for a bowl of water and washed his hands before the crowd, saying, 'I am innocent of the blood of this man. The responsibility is yours!' And all the people yelled back, 'We will take responsibility for his death—we and our children!' So Pilate released Barabbas to them. He ordered Jesus flogged with a lead-tipped whip, then turned him over to the Roman soldiers to crucify him." (27:24-26).

MARK

BACKGROUND
See *Matthew: Background.*

AUTHOR
Tradition holds that John Mark, who apparently was brought to the Lord by Peter (1 Pet. 5:13), wrote this Gospel using Peter's sermons as his main source. Thus, Mark lets us see Jesus through Peter's eyes. Mark, the unfaithful servant who deserted Paul on his first missionary journey (Acts 15:37-39), apparently was faithful in his service with Peter and was therefore chosen to write this Gospel of the obedient Servant (see *Purpose*). Some translations of Acts 13:5, 13 refer to John Mark simply as John. Peter stayed in the home of Mark's mother after his release from prison (Acts 12:12).

DATE AND LOCATION
About A.D. 57–59. Irenaeus said Mark was written after the deaths of Peter and Paul, c. 67–68, but both Clement of Alexandria and Origen placed it during Peter's lifetime, saying that Peter helped in its production and approved its use by the church. There is wide agreement that Mark's record of Peter's sermons was one of the "eyewitness" accounts Luke used in writing Luke and Acts (see Luke 1:1-4; Acts 1:1). Since Acts ends with Paul still in prison before his first release in 62, Mark must have been written before that time. Most scholars agree that Matthew used Mark as a source as well.

Matthew, Mark, and Luke are often called the "synoptic" Gospels (see *Matthew: Background*). Only about 30 verses in Mark contain accounts not paralleled in either Matthew or Luke. As any casual reader will realize, however, while Matthew and Luke may have borrowed from Mark, they each tell the stories in their own unique way, often adding details Mark

5 B.C.
Birth of Christ

A.D. 8
Visits Temple, age 12

26
Begins ministry

28
Chooses 12

29
Feeds 5,000, Death of John the Baptist

30
Death, resurrection, ascension

omitted. And Mark himself includes many details and insights the other two omit.

Most church fathers agree that Mark wrote his Gospel from Rome. Colossians 4:10 places him in Rome with Paul c. 61.

RECIPIENTS

Gentile Roman Christians, as indicated by

- Mark's portrait of Jesus as a man of action, which would have fit the Roman mind-set
- its frequent transliteration (instead of translation) of Latin words ("denarius," 12:15; "Praetorium," 15:16)
- its scarcity of OT quotations
- its explanations of Jewish words (3:17; 5:41; 7:11, 34; 14:36) and customs (7:3; 14:12; 15:42)
- its omission of parables meaningful mainly to Jews, such as the Good Samaritan and the pharisee and tax collector

PURPOSE

The Christians of Rome had come early to a personal knowledge of Jesus Christ and had had a vibrant testimony for him (Rom. 1:8), but would soon face persecution. Mark, as a good pastor, provided them a fresh and exciting biographical portrait of Jesus. He presented Jesus as the perfectly obedient Servant of God and showed what it would mean to be his disciple. Christ's obedience would cost him his life, but his life and message would be vindicated by his resurrection and ascension.

COMPARISON WITH OTHER BIBLE BOOKS

Isaiah:

- Both present Christ as the Servant of God.

Luke and John:

- Mark (and Matthew) present Jesus as victim of the cross, while Luke and John present him as victor over the cross.

John:

- Both emphasize the power of miracles.

OUTLINE

INTRODUCING GOD'S OBEDIENT SERVANT (1:1-13)
- John the Baptist (1:1-8)
- Christ's baptism (1:9-11)
- Temptation (1:12-13)

THE SERVANT'S GALILEAN MINISTRY (1:14–9:50)
- Four disciples called (1:14-20)
- Healings and exorcisms (1:21-45)
- Conflict with religious leaders (2:1–3:6)
- Selecting the 12 (3:7-19)
- Conflict with religious leaders (3:20-35)

- Parables of the Kingdom (4:1-34)
  - Sower and seed (4:1-20)
  - Hidden light (4:21-25)
  - Growing seed, mustard seed (4:26-34)
- Calming the sea (4:35-41)
- Demons and pigs (5:1-20)
- Jairus's daughter and an ill woman (5:21-43)
- Rejection at Nazareth (6:1-6)
- Sending the 12 (6:7-13)
- Death of John the Baptist (6:14-29)
- Feeding 5,000 (6:30-44)
- Walking on water (6:45-52)
- Healings (6:53-56)
- Warnings about Pharisees (7:1-23)
- Healings (7:24-37)
- Feeding 4,000 (8:1-9)
- Warnings about Pharisees (8:10-21)
- Healing a blind man (8:22-26)
- Ministry near Caesarea Philippi (8:27–9:29)
  - Peter's confession (8:27-30)
  - Christ's first prediction of his death (8:31–9:1)
  - Transfiguration (9:2-13)
  - Disciples fail to heal demoniac (9:14-29)
- Ministry in Galilee (9:30-50)
  - Christ's second prediction of his death (9:30-32)
  - Children and the Kingdom (9:33-37)
  - Christ forbids partisanship (9:38-41)
  - Children; danger of hell (9:42-50)

THE SERVANT'S JOURNEY TO JERUSALEM (10)

- Ministry in Perea and Judea (10:1-45)
  - Divorce (10:1-12)
  - Children and the Kingdom (10:13-16)
  - Rich young ruler (10:17-31)
  - Christ's third prediction of his death (10:32-34)
  - Greatness in the Kingdom (10:35-45)
- Ministry near Jerusalem (10:46-52)

THE SERVANT'S MINISTRY IN JERUSALEM (11–13)

- Triumphal Entry (11:1-11)
- Cursing the fig tree (11:12-14)
- Cleansing the Temple (11:15-19)
- The lesson of the fig tree (11:20-24)
- Forgiveness (11:25-26)
- Christ's authority questioned (11:27-33)
- Parable of the wicked farmer (12:1-12)
- Question about paying taxes to Caesar (12:13-17)
- Question about resurrection (12:18-27)
- Question about the greatest commandment (12:28-34)

Question about the son of David (12:35-37)
Denunciation of the scribes (12:38-40)
The widow's offering (12:41-44)
The Olivet discourse (13)

THE SERVANT'S DEATH AND RESURRECTION (14–16)

Plot of priests and scribes (14:1-2)
Anointing by Mary (14:3-9)
Judas plans betrayal (14:10-11)
Observance of Passover; Lord's Supper (14:12-26)
Jesus predicts Peter's denial (14:27-31)
Gethsemane (14:32-42)
Christ's arrest (14:43-52)
Trials; Peter's denial (14:53–15:20)
Crucifixion; burial (15:21-47)
Resurrection (16)

INTRODUCING GOD'S OBEDIENT SERVANT (1:1-13)

NOTE: In the comments that follow, cross-references to parallel passages in the other Gospels are given in square brackets. Italics within brackets, such as [*Matt. 4:1-11;* Luke 4:1-13], indicate that you will find a more complete discussion of the passage in question in the exposition for that reference.

1:1-8 *The messenger Malachi promised.* Bypassing any mention of Christ's birth, which had no direct bearing on his main theme (see *Purpose*), Mark began his Gospel account with the ministry of John the Baptist. John prepared the way for Christ, as both Isaiah (see Isa. 40:3) and Malachi (see Mal. 3:1) had promised. His baptizing ministry attracted large crowds, yet he spoke of one who would baptize with the Holy Spirit, not just with symbolic water. [Matt. 3:1-12; Luke 3:1-20; John 1:6-8, 15-37]

1:9-11 *He sees a dove and hears a voice.* John baptized Jesus, and God the Father confirmed Jesus' identity as his Son by sending the Holy Spirit in the form of a dove and speaking audibly from heaven. [Matt. 3:13-17; Luke 3:21-22]

1:12-13 *Attacked by Satan, assisted by angels.* The Holy Spirit led Christ into the wilderness, where he was tempted by Satan. [*Matt. 4:1-11;* Luke 4:1-13]

THE SERVANT'S GALILEAN MINISTRY (1:14–9:50)

1:14-15 *"It's time to repent and receive!"* Jesus began his ministry with a message of repentance and faith. People must receive the Good News ("gospel") that he had come to earth to deal with their sin. [Matt. 4:12-17; Luke 4:14-15]

1:16-20 *Forsaking their fish, they follow.* Jesus called Simon Peter, his brother Andrew, and the brothers James and John to leave their lives as fishermen and follow him. Three of these men—Peter, James, and John—would become the inner circle of Christ's 12 apostles (see 9:2). [Matt. 4:18-22; Luke 5:1-11; John 1:35-49]

1:21-28 *The demons know him!* Jesus taught in a synagogue, and the people were impressed by his authoritative style (1:21-22; compare Matt. 7:28-29). Jesus encountered a man possessed by a demon, who recognized him as the Son of God (see James 2:19). He exorcized the demon. Mark emphasizes the warfare between Jesus and demons. [Luke 4:31-37]

1:29-34 *The healing of the hostess.* Jesus healed Peter's mother-in-law, and she responded by serving him and his disciples. Hearing of the healing, many others came for healing as well. [Matt. 8:14-17; Luke 4:38-44]

1:35-45 *His first preaching tour begins.* After a special time of prayer in the early morning hours, Jesus embarked on a preaching tour of Galilee. When he healed a leper, it created such a stir that he began avoiding places where there would be large crowds. Mark noted that Jesus healed out of compassion—not just to show his power. [*Matt. 8:1-4;* Luke 4:42-44; 5:12-16] On Christ's desire for secrecy (see 1:34, 44; 3:12), see exposition on Matthew 12:15-21.

2:1-12 *"Doors blocked? Try the roof!"* At a house in Capernaum Jesus drew such a crowd that the doorway was impassable. Assessing the situation, some friends lowered a paralytic through the roof, and Jesus declared that his sins were forgiven (2:5). When the scribes accused him of blasphemy, he validated his right to forgive sins by healing the man. Jesus responded not to the paralytic's faith but to the faith of his energetic and loving friends. His forgiveness was an act of pure grace, since the man had not asked for it. [Matt. 9:1-8; Luke 5:16-26]

2:13-17 *The testimony of a tax collector.* Jesus invited Levi (Matthew), a despised tax collector, to follow him, and Levi obeyed without hesitation. Much to the dismay of the Pharisees, Jesus then had dinner with Levi and his unsavory friends. [*Matt. 9:9-13;* Luke 5:27-32]

2:18-22 *"Don't they believe in fasting?"* Usually at odds with each other, the Pharisees and John's disciples jointly criticized Christ's disciples for not fasting. Christ replied that while he was with them they should enjoy his presence—symbolized by feasting. After he was gone, fasting would be a necessary spiritual discipline.

Realizing this was a radical new concept to Jewish believers, Jesus metaphorically explained his mission's relationship to the law (2:21-22). Though he had come to fulfill the law (see Matt. 5:17-18), the fulfillment itself would be a transformation into something new. A New Covenant would replace the Old Covenant (see Heb. 8:1–10:18). [*Matt. 9:14-17;* Luke 5:33-39]

2:23-28 *The Sabbath: Blessing or burden?* When the Pharisees accused his disciples of profaning the Sabbath, Jesus challenged their legalism, saying that God meant the Sabbath to be a blessing, not a burden. [*Matt. 12:1-8;* Luke 6:1-5]

3:1-6 *The Sabbath: Healing or hurting?* After the argument about the Sabbath (2:23-28), the Pharisees watched to see if Jesus would heal on the Sabbath. After scolding them for being more interested in their legalism than in helping people, Jesus healed a man, and the Pharisees began plotting his death. 3:5 is the only biblical reference to Christ being angry. [Matt. 12:9-14; Luke 6:6-11]

3:7-12 *A genuine faith healer.* Jesus withdrew from the area, but huge crowds followed him. He healed many who merely touched him, and cast out many demons. [Matt. 12:15-21; Luke 6:17-19]

3:13-19 *The King's cabinet.* Jesus appointed 12 disciples—elsewhere called "apostles" (Matt. 10:2)—to be his special assistants. They were to go forth to preach and heal as he did. Of special note (compare 1:16-20) are Peter, who was the first listed, and James and John, who were given the nickname "Sons of Thunder," probably in reference to their fiery personalities (see Matt. 10:2). [Matt. 10:1-4; Luke 6:12-16]

3:20-30 *Their unforgivable accusation.* When the scribes accused Jesus of doing his wonders through Satan's power (3:22), he declared their accusation unforgivable (3:28-29). [*Matt. 12:31-32;* Luke 11:14-22]

3:31-35 *Are you related to him?* Confronted by his earthly family, Jesus declared that his real family is made up of those who do God's will. John, in his Gospel, explains that faith is the key to doing God's will (John 6:28-29). [Matt. 12:46-50; Luke 8:19-21]

4:1-20 *Four receive, but only one retains.* Jesus told a parable about four kinds of soil (4:1-9), representing four kinds of hearts that receive God's word (4:13-20). Only one kind of heart receives it in a way that produces genuine fruit. [*Matt. 13:1-9, 18-23;* Luke 8:4-15]

Jesus taught in parables to confirm people in their response to him: To those who believed, more mysteries would be revealed; to those who rejected him, the parables would only bring greater misunderstanding (4:10-12; see exposition on Matt. 13:10-17).

4:21-25 *Lessons from a lamp.* Rhetorically, Christ asked whether a lamp should be hidden or displayed openly, then declared that everything now hidden will someday be revealed (4:21-22). There are two possible interpretations:

- We must be bold in proclaiming the gospel.
- The truth will eventually be obvious to everyone (compare 4:10-12).

With either interpretation, the personal application is the same: All will be accountable for how they respond to Christ. Those who accept the message (and share it) will be blessed; those who reject it will lose everything (4:23-25). [Luke 8:16-18] (For Christ's other uses of the lamp image, see Matt. 5:15-16; Luke 11:33-36.)

4:26-34 *A growing seed, a growing Kingdom.* The growth of God's Kingdom, like the growth of a seed of grain, involves a progressive unfolding of God's plan. Though it may grow in imperceptible ways, it will someday produce a glorious harvest. This is the only parable unique to Mark. Jesus also compared the Kingdom's growth to that of a mustard seed (4:30-32). [*Matt. 13:31-32;* Luke 13:18-19]

4:35-41 *"What manner of man is this?"* When a storm threatened the disciples' boat, Jesus calmed it, to their great amazement. [*Matt. 8:23-27;* Luke 8:22-25]

5:1-20 *From maniac to missionary.* Jesus and his disciples crossed the Sea of Galilee from west to east and landed in the Gentile region of Gadara. There they were confronted by a wild, bleeding, shrieking maniac. The demons who inhabited the man demonstrated their presence by forcing him to live naked in a graveyard. They invested him with supernormal strength and made him self-destructive. Aware that Jesus was the Son of God and that they themselves were condemned, the demons requested to be sent into nearby swine—perhaps in an effort to kill Jesus and his disciples with the wild animals or to turn the community against Jesus by destroying the pigs (5:12). The pigs did, in fact, die, and the people begged Jesus to leave (5:13-17). But as the healed maniac began telling his story, the response was more positive (5:18-20).

This is the Bible's most vivid description of demon possession. A "legion" (5:9) equals about 6,000. [Matt. 8:28-34; Luke 8:26-39]

5:21-43 *A 12-year-old grief resolved, a 12-year-old girl restored.* On his way to heal the daughter of a Jewish official named Jairus, Jesus was interrupted by a destitute woman who also needed healing. In both cases human help was not sufficient, and in both cases faith was the key to their healing (5:23, 28). [Matt. 9:18-26; Luke 8:40-56]

6:1-6 *The mystery of the carpenter's Son.* When Jesus visited his hometown, the people rejected him because of his humble origins, even though they were impressed by his teaching. Their use of the title "son of Mary" (6:3) was probably derogatory, since in Jewish culture a man was never referred to as his mother's son, even if she was a widow. By not mentioning Joseph, they were probably intimating that there was a real question concerning who his father was. If they had heard anything of Christ's supernatural origin (see Isa. 7:14; Matt. 1:18), they had chosen not to believe it. [Matt. 13:53-58] Luke tells about an earlier rejection of Christ at Nazareth (Luke 4:16-30).

6:7-13 *Assignments for the King's cabinet.* The apostles Christ had chosen (see 3:13-19) were now sent out to proclaim the gospel and to heal. [*Matt. 10:1-15;* Luke 9:1-6)

6:14-29 *Herod, Herodias, and a bold young prophet.* When John the Baptist criticized Herod for marrying his brother's wife, it set in motion a chain of events that led to Herod's killing him (6:17-29), after which Herod was haunted by a guilty conscience (6:14-16). See exposition on Matthew 14:1-12. To Matthew's account, Mark adds a note concerning Herodias's desire to have John killed and Herod's reluctance to do so (6:19-20). [Luke 9:7-9]

6:30-32 *A spiritual retreat.* After his disciples reported on their first preaching tour (see 6:12-13), Jesus called for a time of rest even though the crowds were still pressing in on them. Rest is important, even amid a fruitful ministry.

6:33-44 *Loaves, fish, and a hungry crowd.* When the crowds interrupted the retreat, Jesus taught them, then miraculously fed the crowd of 5,000 men plus their families. [Matt. 14:13-21; Luke 9:10-17; *John 6:1-13*]

6:45-52 *A storm, a sinking ship, and a Savior.* When Christ's disciples were caught at sea in a storm, he came to help them, walking on the water. Mark emphasized the disciples' slowness to recognize either this amazing event or the feeding of the 5,000 as miracles (6:49, 52). [Matt. 14:22-33; *John 6:16-21*] Assuming that Mark based his book on Peter's sermons (see *Author*), it is interesting that he omitted any mention of Peter's unsuccessful attempt at water walking (see Matt. 14:28-31).

6:53-56 *Just a touch of faith.* As Jesus ventured into Gennesaret, northwest of Galilee, people came from everywhere and were healed merely by touching him. As in 5:25-43, it was the touch plus their faith that healed them. [Matt. 14:34-36]

7:1-23 *When tradition and law collide.* When the Pharisees criticized Jesus' disciples for eating with unwashed hands (7:1-5), Jesus reminded them that such regulations were from their oral traditions and not from the law itself (7:6-8). He showed how they allowed rabbinical teachings to negate the law (7:9-13). He condemned this abuse of God's clearly revealed Word. He explained to the onlookers and his disciples that evil comes from the heart, not from external things like food (7:14-23). *[Matt. 15:1-20]*

7:24-37 *To the Gentiles and back.* Coming to the region of Tyre and Sidon, north of Israel in present-day Lebanon, Jesus healed the daughter of a persistent Gentile woman, even though his ministry at this time was primarily to Israel (7:24-30). He then returned to Galilee, where his healing of a deaf mute caused onlookers to exclaim, "Everything he does is wonderful." *[Matt. 15:21-31]*

8:1-9 *Loaves, fish, and a slightly smaller hungry crowd.* As large crowds continued to follow Jesus, he was moved by compassion and miraculously fed them. The crowd numbered 4,000 men, plus women and children (see Matt. 15:38). This incident shows three things about Christ:

- his compassionate heart (8:2-3)
- his popularity at that time in his ministry (8:1; but compare 15:6-15)
- God the Father's endorsement, through his superabundant provision, of God the Son's ministry (8:5-8)

[Matt. 15:32-39]

8:10-21 *Signs and leaven.* When the Pharisees again sought proof of Christ's messianic credentials (compare exposition on Matt. 12:38-42), he rebuked them and used the occasion to warn the disciples against their false teaching, which spread like leaven and corrupted whatever it touched. [*Matt. 16:1-12*]

8:22-26 *A two-part miracle.* In Bethsaida, north of Galilee, Jesus healed a blind man, first enabling him to see people who looked "like trees walking around," then restoring his sight completely. This is the only recorded miracle of Christ that took place in two stages—though Creation, another miracle in which Christ participated (see John 1:1-3), took place in stages as well (see Gen. 1). This is also the only miracle found exclusively in Mark. Sometimes we, like the blind man, need a second touch by Jesus in order to see things from his perspective.

8:27-33 *"You're the Christ . . . but you'll never die!"* When Jesus asked his disciples what others were saying about his ministry and identity, they reported the various opinions they had heard. When he asked their own opinion, Peter identified him as the Messiah (8:27-30). However, Peter was not beyond the influence of Satan, as shown by Jesus' rebuke of his declaration that Jesus could never die (8:31-33). [*Matt. 16:13-23;* Luke 9:18-22]

8:34–9:1 *Minor gains, major loss.* Those who seek worldly wealth may risk losing eternal life. [Matt. 16:24-28; *Luke 9:23-27*]

9:2-13 *Brighter than the noonday sun.* Taking Peter, James, and John up a mountain, Jesus was transfigured in their presence, becoming white with a supernatural brightness. Moses and Elijah, representing the OT law and prophets, appeared with Jesus and were recognized by the disciples. Peter thoughtlessly suggested building three shelters or tabernacles for them (perhaps the Festival of Shelters was being celebrated at the time). God spoke from heaven, acknowledging his Son as he had at Jesus' baptism (see Matt. 3:17). Peter never forgot this significant event (see 2 Pet. 1:16-18). [Matt. 17:1-9; Luke 9:28-36]

The Greek word for *transfigure* is *metamorphoo,* from which we get *metamorphosis.* In his Transfiguration Jesus revealed his eternal glory, which during his earthly ministry was covered and contained by his fleshly body. The disciples were given a foretaste of the glorious Kingdom of God, just as Jesus had promised (9:1). What was promised by the Transfiguration became a real possibility for believers when Jesus died on the cross: At that moment, the veil of the Temple (Christ's flesh; see Heb. 10:19-20), was torn asunder (was sacrificed; see 15:37-38), giving believers access to the Most Holy Place (the glorious Kingdom of God). On 9:9-13, see Matthew 17:10-13.

9:14-29 *Believing but not believing.* A man reported to Christ that his disciples had been unable to cast a demon out of his son (9:14-18). Expressing dismay at their lack of faith, Christ asked the man whether *he* believed he could help him. When the man expressed tentative faith, Christ healed his son (9:19-27), then explained to his disciples why they had been unable to heal (9:28-29). Like the boy's father (9:24), Christians can find themselves having faith in Christ but needing his help to trust him more. [Matt. 17:14-21; Luke 9:37-42]

9:30-32 *A second prediction of his death.* For the second time (see 8:31-33), Jesus predicted his death and resurrection, much to the disciples' dismay. [Matt. 17:22-23; Luke 9:43-45]

9:33-37 *"I'm the greatest!"* Knowing that his arrogant disciples had argued among themselves about who was the greatest, Jesus taught that the greatest is the one who serves. He suggested ministry to children as one path to such greatness. [*Matt. 18:1-14;* Luke 9:46-48]

9:38-41 *"If he's not fighting us, he's for us!"* When the disciples forbade someone not working directly with them to cast out demons in Christ's name, Christ corrected them. He did not care if those doing his work were in his particular ministry group. Believers should befriend all who confess Christ, regardless of denominational labels. [Luke 9:49-50]

9:42-50 *The horrors of hell.* Returning to the theme of ministry to children (see 9:33-37), Jesus spoke of the severe punishment befitting any who would harm them. He went on to describe hell as a horrible place that should be avoided at all cost. [Matt. 18:6-9] Jesus taught the literal reality of hell, where torment is horrible, fire is real, and punishment is everlasting (see exposition on Luke 16:19-31).

On 9:49, see NLT. Jesus encouraged the disciples to be like salt amid a corrupt world (9:50; see exposition on Matt. 5:13-16).

THE SERVANT'S JOURNEY TO JERUSALEM (10)

10:1-12 *Marriage, divorce, and God's ideal.* Having already visited Jerusalem at least once (see John 2:13-17), Jesus now began his final journey to the city where he would die. When some Pharisees asked him about divorce, he stressed God's original ideal for marriage. [*Matt. 19:1-12;* Luke 16:18]

10:13-16 *"Jesus loves me, this I know."* Christ's love for children is seen in his displeasure with the disciples when they kept children from him. [*Matt. 19:13-15;* Luke 18:15-17]

10:17-31 *So close and yet so far.* When a rich young ruler asked Jesus how he could earn salvation, Jesus told him, but his great possessions kept him from responding (10:17-22). Jesus used the sad incident as an object lesson for his disciples: Wealth can keep you from seeing your need for God (10:23-27). However, both present blessings and eternal life belong to those who forsake all for Christ (10:28-31). [*Matt. 19:16-30;* Luke 18:18-30]

10:32-34 *Death, yes, but also resurrection.* As Jesus and his disciples neared Jerusalem, the disciples apparently had a foreboding of the troubles to come, so Jesus for the third time explained that he would die but would also rise again. [Matt. 20:17-19; Luke 18:31-34]

10:35-45 *"Sorry, my Father assigns those positions!"* In answer to James and John's request for places of honor in God's Kingdom, Jesus taught that true greatness comes by serving, not by seeking special positions of authority. The Father assigns such positions. [*Matt. 20:20-28*]

Jesus used the ordinance of baptism as a metaphor of his approaching death and predicted that his disciples would be martyred as well (10:38-39; see Luke 12:50).

10:46-52 *Blind Bartimaeus.* As Jesus entered Jericho he encountered Bartimaeus, a blind beggar. Despite efforts to keep him quiet, Bartimaeus called out to Jesus, Jesus healed him, and he became his disciple. This is the only time a person healed by Christ is named. Matthew's account mentions two blind men. [Matt. 20:29-34; Luke 18:35-43]

THE SERVANT'S MINISTRY IN JERUSALEM (11–13)

11:1-11 *A ticker-tape parade for their hero.* Less than a week before he would be crucified, Jesus made a triumphant entrance into Jerusalem, marking the height of his popularity. Much of the crowd viewed him as the Messiah-King. [*Matt. 21:1-11;* Luke 19:28-40; John 12:12-19] Later that night Jesus visited the Temple (11:11), perhaps setting the stage for his actions the following day (see 11:15-19).

11:12-14 *A figless fig tree.* Seeing a barren fig tree, Jesus cursed it, using it as an object lesson concerning Israel. *[Matt. 21:18-22]* Israel had been given much but had borne no spiritual fruit. Thus, the Kingdom was going to be taken from it and given to the Gentiles (see Matt. 21:42-43). Paul would later write at length on this theme using the imagery of the olive tree (see Rom. 9–11).

Even though the Passover was "too early in the season" (11:13), this particular kind of fig tree usually bore an early crop of fruit even before its leaves appeared, so Jesus was right in concluding that it was barren (see 11:20-21).

11:15-19 *Throwing out the Temple thieves.* Jesus drove the merchants from the Temple, proclaiming that it should be a place of prayer, not of commerce. This aroused the ire of the scribes and priests. [*Matt. 21:12-17;* Luke 19:45-48; John 2:13-16 records an earlier, similar incident]

11:20-24 *Faith that withers fig trees and moves mountains.* The next day, Jesus' disciples noticed that the fig tree he had cursed (see 11:14) had withered (11:20-21). Jesus told them that they, too, could perform such wonders through prayer based on sincere faith (11:22-24). [*Matt. 21:18-22*]

11:25-26 *Forgive and be forgiven.* Jesus went on to speak of forgiveness. It is totally inconsistent for those who have been forgiven by God to hold grudges against anyone.

11:27-33 *The trappers trap themselves.* The Jewish leaders' effort to trap Jesus with a question about the source of his authority backfired when he asked them about the source of John the Baptist's authority. The real issue was that the Jewish leaders were fearful of losing their *own* authority. [Matt. 21:23-27; *Luke 20:1-8*]

12:1-12 *From maligned stone to main stone.* In the parable of the vineyard owner, Jesus showed the historical truth that Israel had killed and rejected past prophets, and the prophetic truth that Israel would soon kill and reject the Son of God. This rejected stone would, however, become the chief cornerstone of God's Kingdom (12:10-11; see Ps. 118:22-23; Acts 4:5-12; 1 Pet. 2:4-8) [*Matt. 21:33-46;* Luke 20:9-19]

12:13-17 *Honor both God and government?* The Herodians, a political group from the family of Herod and loyal to Rome, joined the Pharisees in trying to trap Jesus on the issue of paying taxes. In a masterful way, Jesus taught that responsibilities to

God were not contradictory to civic duties. [*Matt. 22:15-22;* Luke 20:20-26]

12:18-27 *An intellectual but ignorant question.* When the Sadducees raised a hypothetical question concerning the afterlife, which they didn't even believe in (12:18-23), Jesus pointed out that their root problem was ignorance of Scripture and God's power (12:24-27). [*Matt. 22:23-33;* Luke 20:27-40]

12:28-34 *Not far from the Kingdom.* When a scribe asked Jesus what laws were foremost, Jesus highlighted two principles: Love God, and love others. [*Matt. 22:34-40; Luke 10:25-37*] When the scribe enthusiastically endorsed his answer, Jesus told him he was on the right track in his search for God. With his obviously wise answer, Jesus effectively silenced his critics (12:34).

12:35-37 *David's son is God's Son!* Jesus pointed out that if the scribes acknowledged Christ to be the son of David, they must also, based on Psalm 110:1, acknowledge him to be the Son of God. [*Matt. 22:41-46;* Luke 20:41-44]

12:38-40 *Steer clear of those sinful scribes!* Jesus warned his followers against the religious leaders, whose outward spirituality was pretense, while in their everyday lives they displayed pride and lack of love. [Matt. 23:1-7]

12:41-44 *When a mite is more than much.* A poor widow put in the Temple treasury "two mites" (KJV), worth hardly anything. Jesus commended her, pointing out that her gift was proportionately far greater than the gifts of the rich. [Luke 21:1-4]

13:1-18 *Foretelling tribulation.* Jesus predicted that the marvelous and enormous Temple—restored and expanded by Herod the Great—would be totally destroyed (13:1-2). He and the disciples then went to the Mount of Olives, where, in response to their question, he gave some glimpses of the future and called his disciples to faithfulness (the Olivet discourse, 13:5-37). He began by describing the first half of the coming Tribulation, which will be marked by deceptive false messiahs, wars, earthquakes, and persecution (13:5-13). Then will come a pivotal time, marked by the "sacrilegious object that causes desecration," at which point all who are able should flee for their lives (13:14-18). [*Matt. 24:1-20;* Luke 21:5-22]

13:19-23 *All but the elect will be deceived.* The last half of the Tribulation period will be highlighted by such affliction that, but for God's grace, the whole world would be destroyed and by such deception from Satan and Antichrist that virtually the whole world will be fooled into following them. [*Matt. 24:21-26;* Luke 21:23-24]

13:24-27 *A dark sun, a bright Son.* Just prior to Christ's glorious return, there will be frightening cosmic changes. [*Matt. 24:27-31;* Luke 21:25-28]

13:28-37 *Don't ask when, just be ready.* Just as blossoms on the fig tree signal summer, the beginning of these signs will show that Christ's return is near (13:28-31). [*Matt. 24:32-36;* Luke 21:29-33] In light of all these prophecies, Jesus urged his disciples to watch and pray since no one knows when the Lord will return. Even the Son of God in his humanity did not know (13:32-37). [*Matt. 24:42-51;* Luke 21:34-38]

THE SERVANT'S DEATH AND RESURRECTION (14–16)

14:1-2 *"When it's convenient, we'll kill him!"* The Jewish authorities began plotting Christ's death—cautiously, because the public was on his side. [*Matt. 26:1-5;* Luke 22:1-2]

14:3-9 *Extravagantly anointed.* When Mary, sister of Martha and Lazarus, anointed Jesus with precious oil, the disciples rebuked her for her extravagance, but Jesus commended her. *Christ* (Greek) and *Messiah,* its Hebrew equivalent, mean "anointed one" (14:3-9). [*Matt. 26:6-13; John 12:1-8*]

14:10-11 *Every man has his price.* Judas offered to betray Jesus to the chief priests. They offered to pay him a small amount, and he immediately began looking for the opportunity to betray Christ. [*Matt. 26:14-16;* Luke 22:1-6]

14:12-21 *Passover and a sad prediction.* As Jesus shared the Passover meal with his disciples, he predicted that one of them would betray him, saying it would have been better for that man never to have been born. [*Matt. 26:17-25;* Luke 22:7-16, 21-23; John 13:18-19]

14:22-26 *The blood of the new covenant.* Jesus used the elements of wine and bread to symbolize his approaching death, which would establish a New Covenant between God and his people. Even at this time of great distress, Jesus and his disciples took time to worship (14:26). [*Matt. 26:26-30;* Luke 22:17-23; John 13:12-30]

14:27-31 *When the shepherd's away, the sheep will stray.* Having said that one of his disciples would betray him (14:18), Jesus now predicted that all of them—especially Peter—would forsake him. All of the disciples—especially Peter—denied that they would do so. [*Matt. 26:31-35;* Luke 22:31-34; John 13:36-38]

14:32-42 *His grief in Gethsemane.* Deeply depressed as he contemplated his approaching death, Jesus expressed his anguish to God. Meanwhile the disciples, missing the significance of what was going on, slept soundly. [Matt. 26:36-46; *Luke 22:39-46;* John 18:1]

14:43-52 *While one betrays, the others abandon.* Fulfilling Christ's predictions (14:18, 27; see Matt. 26:25), Judas led the authorities to Jesus to arrest him, and the 11 other disciples fled to safety. [*Matt. 26:47-56;* Luke 22:47-53; John 18:1-11)

14:53-65 *"Are you the Messiah?" . . . "I am!"* During his hasty trial before Caiaphas the high priest, Jesus initially did not respond to false witnesses. However, when Caiaphas asked directly, he affirmed that he was the Messiah. *[Matt. 26:57-68;* Luke 22:63-71; *John 18:12-14, 19-24]*

14:66-72 *Three times, just as predicted.* In a specific fulfillment of Christ's prediction (14:30), Peter denied him three times. [Matt. 26:69-75; Luke 22:54-62; John 18:15-18, 25-27]

15:1-5 *"Are you the King of the Jews?"* Because the Jews had no authority to condemn Jesus to death, they brought him before Pilate, the Roman governor. Jesus affirmed once again that he was King of the Jews. [*Matt. 27:1-2;* Luke 23:1-5; John 18:28-38]

15:6-15 *"Free the murderer! Kill the Messiah!"* After Pilate had sent Jesus to Herod and Herod had sent him back (see Luke 23:6-12), Pilate offered the Jews their customary right to call for the release of a prisoner on the Sabbath, thinking they would choose Jesus. Instead they chose a common criminal. [*Matt. 27:15-26;* Luke 23:13-25; John 18:39-40]

15:16-20 *"Hail, King of the Jews!"* The Roman soldiers mocked Jesus with a crown of thorns, a purple robe, and feigned worship, then delivered him to be crucified. [Matt. 27:27-31; *John 19:1-16*]

15:21-23 *Simon of Cyrene.* A man named Simon from Cyrene (present-day Libya) was compelled to carry Christ's cross the final distance to Calvary. [Matt. 27:32; Luke 23:26]

15:24-41 *"Down at the cross where my Savior died."* As Christ was crucified, the soldiers and crowds continued to

THE FINAL DAYS OF CHRIST'S MINISTRY

SATURDAY	SUNDAY	MONDAY	TUESDAY	WEDNESDAY	THURSDAY	FRIDAY
Anointed by Mary (John 12:1-11)	The Triumphal Entry (John 12:12-19)	2nd Temple Cleansing (Matt. 21:12-17) Cursing of the Fig Tree (Matt. 21:18-22)	Confrontation with the Pharisees: ——— About His Authority (Matt. 21:23-27) ——— About Paying of Tribute (Matt. 22:15-22) ——— About the Resurrection (Matt. 22:23-33) ——— About the Greatest Command-ment (Matt. 22:34-40) ——— Denunciation of the Pharisees (Matt. 23) ——— Request by the Greeks (John 12:20-50) ——— Mt. Olivet Discourse (Matt. 24–25)	DAY OF SILENCE	Preparation for the Passover (Mark 14:12-16) Events in the Upper Room (John 13–14; Matt. 26:20-35) On Route to Gethsemane (John 15–16) The Great High Priestly Prayer (John 17) In Gethsemane (Matt. 26:36-56) Final Pre-Calvary Miracle (Luke 22:51)	UNFAIR TRIALS AND CRUCIFIXION Matt. 27; Mark 15; Luke 23; John 18

ridicule him (15:24-32). Finally, at about 3 P.M., he died, as a few of his followers looked on from afar. *[Matt. 27:33-56; Luke 23:33-49; John 19:17-37]*

15:42-47 *Buried, but not for long!* Joseph of Arimathea, a member of the Sanhedrin (15:43) but also a secret Christian (see John 19:38), buried Christ's body in his own tomb. The burial was done in haste, without proper preparation of the body, because it was Friday and the Sabbath officially began at 6 P.M. (see exposition on Luke 23:50-56 and on John 19:38-42). The entombment, like the burial, would be very brief. [Matt. 27:57-61]

16:1-11 *A surprise for the sorrowing women.* When three women came to the tomb early Sunday morning to finish anointing Christ's body for burial, they were amazed to find the stone covering rolled away. When an angel told them that Jesus had been raised from the dead, their immediate response was fear (16:1-8). Soon, however, Jesus himself appeared to Mary Magdalene (16:9-11; see exposition on John 20:11-18). [*Matt. 28:1-10; Luke 24:1-10; John 20:1-18*]

16:12-14 *"Why couldn't you believe?"* Jesus appeared to two disciples walking in the country (compare exposition on Luke 24:13-32) and to "the eleven" later that day. He rebuked them for not having believed the resurrection reports. "Eleven" is probably figurative, since Thomas was not present (see exposition on John 20:19-23, 24-29).

16:15-18 *Their mission, his miracles.* Christ summarized the mission of his followers: They were to evangelize the whole world, understanding that those who rejected the gospel faced eternal death. *[Matt. 28:16-20]* Jesus granted miraculous powers to protect these early believers and to confirm their message.

16:19-20 *He ascends; their mission begins.* Jesus ascended to heaven and took his rightful place at God's right hand, in fulfillment of prophecy (see Ps. 110:1; Eph. 1:20), and the disciples immediately began proclaiming the gospel. [Luke 24:50-53]

❖ ❖ ❖

PEOPLE TO REMEMBER FROM MARK

BARTIMAEUS

Key Fact: Blind beggar healed by Christ (10:46, 52)
Father: Timaeus (10:46)
Total Bible References: 1

Bartimaeus Speaks

Of course I'd heard how God caused our city's walls to fall in Joshua's day. But I never dreamed that one day another miracle would take place near those very walls—and that I would be right in the middle of the action! (Josh. 6:20)

I couldn't see him as he walked by, but the sound of his voice was more than enough. "What do you want me to do for you?" he asked. And as you can probably imagine, I asked him to give sight to my eyes. (10:51)

I'm sure the noisy crowd that had gathered celebrated that miracle. But no one except a poor blind beggar who now sees and need not beg can even remotely understand the joy that results when the Son of David passes by. (10:47-48)

Spiritual Lessons from Bartimaeus

- He refused to be silenced by those who sought to dampen his enthusiasm for Christ (10:48).
- He asked the right person (Christ) for the right thing (mercy and healing) at the right time (10:47, 51).

Key Verse

"'What do you want me to do for you?' Jesus asked. 'Teacher,' the blind man said, 'I want to see!'" (10:51).

JAIRUS

Key Fact: Jesus resurrected his daughter (5:21-43)
Total Bible References: 2
Key Reference: 5:21-43

Jairus Speaks

I must have experienced every possible human emotion during the past few hours. First, desperation because my only daughter was dying. But then, there was hope. Jesus himself agreed to come and minister to her. This, however, was followed by frustration and a little anger when he stopped to heal someone else. That was, of course, all well and good, but didn't he realize my little 12-year-old girl was at the point of death? (5:23-34)

Well, frustration turned to shock and grief when I was told she had died. But then, the slightest ray of hope: As we entered my house, Jesus assured me that he would somehow restore her. The final emotions were those of amazement and unspeakable joy when he raised her from the dead. What a story I have to tell! (5:35-43)

Spiritual Lessons from Jairus

- God's purpose and timing in answering our prayers does not always match our view of how things should be done. His will for Jairus involved both a *what* and a *when* (5:21-43).

Key Verses

"While he was still speaking to her, messengers arrived from Jairus's home with the message, 'Your daughter is dead. There's no use troubling the Teacher now.' But Jesus ignored their comments and said to Jairus, 'Don't be afraid. Just trust me'" (5:35-36).

JOHN MARK

Key Facts: Evangelist, authored Gospel of Mark
Mother: Mary (Acts 12:12)
Uncle: Barnabas (Col. 4:10, KJV)
Total Bible References: 10
Key References: Acts 12:12, 25; 13:5, 13; 15:36-41; 2 Tim. 4:11; 1 Pet. 5:13

John Mark Speaks

"If you try to keep your life for yourself, you will lose it. But if you give up your life for my sake and for the sake of the Good News, you will find true life." Wonderful words of comfort these are on the eve of my execution here in Alexandria. Of course, I could not possibly have known, as I recorded those words of my Master, just how precious they would become to me. Well, like Peter and Paul, I am soon to "find true life" by giving up my life. What a glorious paradox! (8:35; 2 Tim. 4:6; 2 Pet. 1:14)

What an incredible influence Peter and Paul have had on my life. To my shame I failed Paul during our first encounter, but I was able to make up for it during his imprisonments. My days spent serving under Peter in Babylon have proven invaluable. In a few short hours it will all be over. (Acts 13:13; Col. 4:10; 2 Tim. 4:11; Philem. 1:24; 1 Pet. 5:13)

Lord Jesus, you told us to take your Good News to all the world, and that's just what I've tried to do. Now, as I leave this old sinful world, accept me into that glorious new world of righteousness, which you promised the prophet centuries before my birth! (16:15; Isa. 65:17)

Spiritual Lessons from John Mark

- Our God is the God of the second chance. Compare Acts 13:13; 15:36-41 with 2 Timothy 4:11. See also Jonah 1:3; 3:1-3.

Key Verse

"Bring Mark with you when you come, for he will be helpful to me" (2 Tim. 4:11).

LUKE

BACKGROUND
See *Matthew: Background.*

AUTHOR
Luke, a physician (Col. 4:14) who traveled with Paul (see *Acts: Author*) and was the only one who remained with him during his second imprisonment (2 Tim. 4:11). Luke knew Philemon personally (Philem. 1:23-24). He was the only Gentile to write any portion of Scripture. A historian of outstanding literary skill, Luke is widely considered one of the greatest writers of all time. The author's interest in medical matters (4:38; 14:2) and attention to detail (3:1-2) lend support to "Dr. Luke's" authorship (see exposition on 9:28-36 and on 22:54-62). As Mark wrote his Gospel under Peter's influence, Luke wrote under Paul's influence.

Luke also wrote the book of Acts. Together, Luke's two books are longer than all 13 books Paul is known to have written. (Both Luke and Paul have been suggested as possible authors of Hebrews.)

DATE
The only clue lies in the probable date of Acts, which is a sequel to Luke (see *Acts: Date*). Since Acts ends with Paul still in prison before his first release in A.D. 62, we can assume that Luke was written before that date, probably c. 58–60.

RECIPIENTS
Luke addressed both his Gospel and Acts to Theophilus, of whom nothing else is known. Luke called him "most honorable Theophilus" (1:1), from which we may guess that he was of high social status. Apparently he was also a believer (1:4). Beyond Theophilus, the Gospel was written with a Greek readership in mind. With their emphasis on the pursuit of excellence, Greeks

***5 B.C.* Birth of Christ**

***A.D. 8* Visits Temple, age 12**

***26* Begins ministry**

***28* Chooses 12**

***29* Feeds 5,000, Death of John the Baptist**

***30* Death, resurrection, ascension**

would have been attracted to Luke's presentation of Christ as an exemplary human being.

PURPOSE

- To confirm the faith of Theophilus, showing that the faith he had placed in Jesus rested on firm historical ground
- To present Jesus to Gentiles as the Son of Man who, though rejected by Israel, had come to save all humankind

UNIQUE FEATURES

- Luke is the product of exhaustive research (1:1-3).
- It is the most thorough of the Gospels concerning events surrounding Christ's birth (1–2).
- It is a "Gospel of song," containing five great songs and three angelic benedictions (1–2).
- Luke shows a special interest in women (1–2; 8:1-3; 10:38-42; 23:27-28), the poor (7:11-13; 14:12-14; 16:19-31; 21:1-4), and children (2:39-52; 9:46-48; 18:15-17).

COMPARISON WITH OTHER BIBLE BOOKS

Ezekiel:

- The expression "son of man" occurs some 90 times in Ezekiel, whose author was the representative of Israel with whom God was dealing. In Luke, Jesus, the Son of Man, is God's representative.

Matthew:

- Matthew is the Gospel of sad rejection of Jesus the Messiah; Luke is the Gospel of glad acceptance of Jesus the Son of Man.

Matthew, Mark, and John:

- While Luke, like Matthew, probably used Mark as one of his sources, more than half of the material in Luke (see much of 9:51–19:27) is found in no other Gospel.
- Luke contains by far the most complete account of Christ's family background, birth, and childhood.

Acts and Hebrews:

- Whether or not Luke authored Hebrews, his Gospel can be considered the first volume of a trilogy:
  - ➤ Luke: Christ's earthly ministry
  - ➤ Acts: His ministry through his church
  - ➤ Hebrews: His High Priestly ministry

OUTLINE

THE SON OF MAN IDENTIFIES WITH HUMANKIND (1:1–4:13)

Prologue (1:1-4)
Births of John the Baptist and Christ foretold (1:5-80)
Birth of Christ (2:1-7)

- Healing, teaching at Pharisee's house (14:1-24)
- Taking up your cross (14:25-35)
- Lost sheep, coin, and son (15)
- Unjust steward (16:1-18)
- Rich man and Lazarus (16:19-31)
- Offenses, forgiveness, service (17:1-10)
- 10 lepers (17:11-19)
- Predictions of end times (17:20-37)
- Persistent widow (18:1-8)
- Pharisee and tax collector (18:9-14)
- Blessing the children (18:15-17)
- Rich young ruler (18:18-30)
- Third death prediction (18:31-34)
- Blind Bartimaeus (18:35-43)
- Zacchaeus (19:1-10)
- 10 servants (19:11-27)

THE SON OF MAN SUFFERS FOR HUMANKIND (19:28–23:56)

- Sunday: Triumphal Entry (19:28-44)
- Monday: Cleansing the Temple (19:45-48)
- Tuesday (20:1–22:6)
  - Debates with religious leaders (20)
  - Predictions of Jerusalem's fall and the end times (21)
  - Judas plans betrayal (22:1-6)
- Thursday (22:7-46)
  - Observance of Passover; Lord's Supper (22:7-38)
  - Gethsemane (22:39-46)
- Friday (22:47–23:56)
  - Betrayal; arrest (22:47-53)
  - Peter's denials (22:54-62)
  - Christ on trial (22:63–23:25)
  - Crucifixion; burial (23:26-56)

THE SON OF MAN CONFIRMED BEFORE HUMANKIND (24)

- Resurrection (24:1-12)
- Appearance on road to Emmaus (24:13-32)
- Appearance to disciples (24:33-49)
- Ascension (24:50-53)

THE SON OF MAN IDENTIFIES WITH HUMANKIND (1:1–4:13)

NOTE: In the comments that follow, cross-references to parallel passages in the other Gospels are given in square brackets. Italics within brackets, such as [*Matt. 3:1-12;* Mark 1:1-8], indicate that you will find a more complete discussion of the passage in question in the exposition for that reference.

1:1-4 *"This will bring you up to date."* Luke began his account by noting that many had already drawn up a narrative of Christ's life. Having done extensive research, including interviews with eyewitnesses, he proposed to do the same.

1:5-25 *The angel's amazing announcement.* The angel Gabriel appeared to a godly priest named Zechariah, whose wife, Elizabeth, was barren. He announced that a child would be born to the aged couple, and this child's ministry would be like Elijah's, preparing the way of the Lord (1:5-17). When Zechariah expressed doubt at this amazing prediction, the angel struck him dumb (1:18-22). Sometime later, the prophecy was fulfilled (1:23-25).

1:26-38 *A more amazing announcement.* Six months later, Gabriel appeared to a virgin named Mary, engaged to a man named Joseph. She would have a child while still a virgin. The child would be named Jesus and would be Israel's long-awaited Messiah (1:26-33). The angel explained the miraculous nature of this conception, and to substantiate his amazing prediction, he told Mary that her relative Elizabeth, though old and barren, had also miraculously conceived (1:34-37). Mary expressed her willingness to bear the child.

1:39-45 *The two expectant mothers meet.* As would have been natural because of their blood relationship, Mary visited Elizabeth as the time for John's birth drew near. Having been told that her son would introduce the Messiah, and having felt him leap in her womb when Mary arrived, Elizabeth confirmed to Mary that her child was indeed the Messiah.

1:46-56 *A song of praise from Scripture.* Mary offered praise to God, in language based on Hannah's song after Samuel's birth (see 1 Sam. 2:1-10). Mary's song, often called the Magnificat, spoke of what God had done and would do in her life (1:46-49) and in the life of her nation (1:50-55). Mary spoke of God's concern for the poor and humble, a theme prevalent in OT prophecy (see exposition on Isa. 58:6-14) and in Christ's ministry (see 7:22; 14:12-14).

1:57-80 *"Read my note: His name is John!"* When John was born, Zechariah, resisting family pressure and obeying God, named him John. Immediately his voice returned, and he glorified God, predicting the coming of Messiah (1:57-75) and his son's key role in introducing him (1:76-79). As John grew up, he chose to live "in the wilderness" (1:80; compare 3:2-4).

2:1-7 *Mary has a little Lamb!* Because Caesar had decreed that all citizens of his empire should go to their birthplaces to register for taxation, Joseph and Mary had to go to Bethlehem. While they were there, Jesus was born, fulfilling a prophecy about his birthplace (see Mic. 5:2). Idealized in nativity scenes, the "manger" in which the infant Jesus was placed was a feeding trough for animals.

2:8-20 *The shepherds: Worshiping and witnessing.* An angel announced Christ's birth to some shepherds. They speedily came to Bethlehem and, having found him, worshiped God and "told everyone" the supernatural message they had heard concerning him.

2:21-24 *Two turtledoves for the Lamb of God.* According to the law (see Lev. 12:2-8), Mary offered the sacrifice for purification after childbirth. Apparently the parents of the true "Lamb of God" couldn't even afford a lamb for the sacrifice, and therefore offered two turtledoves (see Lev. 12:8). As a firstborn son, Jesus was dedicated to the Lord (see Exod. 13:2, 12, 15).

2:25-38 *Two elderly Israelites consoled by his coming.* A prophet named Simeon (2:25-35) and a prophetess named Anna (2:36-38) testified to the identity of the infant Christ. Both were elderly, and Anna was a widow. God had told Simeon, who was waiting for "the Messiah to come and rescue Israel," that he would see the Messiah before he died. Anna told "everyone who had been waiting for the promised King" that their Redeemer had come.

2:39-52 *Growing in grace, teaching in the Temple.* Briefly summarizing Christ's early boyhood (2:39-40), Luke related a remarkable incident from his 12th year. On one trip to Jerusalem, Joseph and Mary lost track of where Jesus was. After much searching they were surprised to find him sitting among the teachers in the Temple. His ability to discuss the law with these men pointed to the special nature of this young man. His statement that he was to be doing his heavenly Father's business pointed to his understanding that he was the Son of God.

The young Jesus grew in mental, physical, spiritual, and social maturity (2:39-40, 51-52). Meanwhile, Mary quietly observed and thought about this son who was obedient to her even while preparing for his special mission in life (2:51).

3:1-22 *"Prepare the way of the Lord!"* About 18 years after the young Jesus visited the Temple, John began preaching in preparation for the beginning of Jesus' public ministry. His message included hope for the spiritually hungry (3:3-6) but a stern warning to the unrepentant (3:7-18). Jews could not consider themselves accepted by God simply because they were Abraham's children. Good deeds must demonstrate their true repentance. [*Matt. 3:1-12;* Mark 1:1-8; John 1:6-8, 15-34]

When John directed his preaching at Herod, the result was imprisonment (3:19-20). [Matt. 14:3-4; Mark 6:17-18]

Luke added a brief note about Christ's baptism by John (3:21-22). [*Matt. 3:13-17;* Mark 1:9-11; John 1:31-34]

Note the careful details of Luke the historian (3:1-2).

3:23-38 *From the Son of God to the son of God.* Luke paused from his narrative to give Christ's genealogy. While Matthew traced Christ's lineage through Joseph, his legal father (see Matt. 1:1-17), Luke traced it through Mary, beginning with Mary's father, Heli. (Men in ancient times often regarded their sons-in-law as their own sons.) The lineages of Mary and Joseph converge at King David (compare 3:31 with Matt. 1:6).

The genealogy ends with Adam, the "son of God" (3:38). Jesus, the "last Adam" (see 1 Cor. 15:45) and perfect Son of God, came to undo the devastation brought upon humanity by the first Adam.

4:1-13 *Light confronts darkness.* When Jesus encountered Satan in the wilderness, his reliance on Scripture defeated Satan's efforts to misapply it. [*Matt. 4:1-11;* Mark 1:12-13]

THE SON OF MAN MINISTERS TO HUMANKIND (4:14–9:50)

4:14-15 *A popular preacher in Galilee.* Having helped Jesus through the confrontation with Satan, God's Spirit now led him on his first preaching tour, in Galilee, where his fame spread quickly. [Matt. 4:12-17; Mark 1:14-15]

4:16-30 *"I'm the one Isaiah spoke of!"* In Nazareth, his hometown, Jesus went to the synagogue. As he read from Isaiah about divine deliverance (see Isa. 61:1-2), the people gave him their undivided attention (4:16-20). However, when he applied the passage to himself (4:21-24) and then suggested that God wanted to help Gentiles as well as Jews (4:25-27), they threw him out of town and tried to kill him, but Jesus miraculously escaped (4:28-30).

Jesus stopped his reading of Isaiah with the words "the time of the Lord's favor has come" (4:19), and didn't read the next phrase, "and with it, the day of God's anger against their enemies" (Isa. 61:2). The "time of the Lord's favor" refers to his first coming, while the "day of God's anger" relates to his Second Coming.

Jesus had faithfully attended synagogue services while growing up in Nazareth (4:16). He would be rejected again by the people of his hometown (see Matt. 13:53-58; Mark 6:1-6).

4:31-37 *The testimony of a demon.* The people of Capernaum were "amazed" at the authority with which Christ taught. One listener was demon possessed, and the demon cried out, correctly identifying Christ as the "Holy One sent from God." Christ's exorcism of the demon caused his fame to spread all the more. [Mark 1:21-28] "Authority" (4:32) probably refers in part to Christ's logical and insightful understanding of the OT.

4:38-44 *Healing them all.* Jesus healed Peter's mother-in-law and later that day healed many more people, as the demons once again identified him as the Messiah. Only with great difficulty was he able to leave that area and preach elsewhere. Christ's ability to heal all diseases contrasts sharply with so-called faith healers today, who sometimes refuse to deal with hard cases. [*Matt. 8:14-17;* Mark 1:29-34]

5:1-11 *"Launch out into the deep."* When Jesus borrowed the boat of a fisherman named Peter to use as a "pulpit," he learned that Peter and the other fishermen were having a bad day of fishing. He gave them advice that led to a massive catch. Confronted by this miracle, Peter recognized Christ's deity and his own sinfulness, and he, along with James and John, left the fishing trade to follow Jesus and "fish for people" (5:10). [Matt. 4:18-22; Mark 1:16-20; John 1:35-42 records Jesus' earlier encounter with Peter and Andrew]

5:12-16 *"I will!"* Jesus healed a leper and told him to tell no one of the healing, but to present himself to the priest for ceremonial cleansing. [Matt. 8:1-4; Mark 1:40-45] On Christ's secrecy (5:14), see exposition on Matt. 12:15-21.

5:17-26 *Power to forgive, power to heal.* Some men went to great lengths to bring a friend to Jesus for healing. Jesus forgave the man's sins and, when the Pharisees accused him of blasphemy, proved his deity by healing the man. [Matt. 9:1-8; *Mark 2:1-12*]

5:27-32 *Dinner with sinners.* Christ called Levi (Matthew) to follow him, then dined with him and his fellow tax collectors. When the Pharisees criticized his choice of company, Jesus rejected their separatism and expressed his desire to reach out to those in spiritual need. [*Matt. 9:9-13;* Mark 2:13-17]

5:33-39 *"They're having too much fun!"* Asked why his disciples didn't fast, Jesus declared that his presence with them called for celebration, not mourning (5:33-35). With two parables, he showed that he represented a new phase in what God was doing on earth (5:36-39). [*Matt. 9:14-17; Mark 2:18-22*]

6:1-5 *"They're only doing what David did!"* When his disciples were criticized for "working" on the Sabbath, Jesus defended them on the basis of historical precedent (6:3-4) and his own authority (6:5). [*Matt. 12:1-8;* Mark 2:23-28]

6:6-11 *Healer of hands and hearts.* Jesus healed on the Sabbath, contrary to Pharisaic tradition but in accord with God's desire to save life and do good. The coldhearted Pharisees began plotting against him. [Matt. 12:9-14; Mark 3:1-6]

6:12-16 *A dozen will do it!* After an all-night prayer vigil, Jesus chose 12 of his disciples to be his special "apostles," so named because they were sent out to represent his Kingdom. [*Matt. 10:1-15;* Mark 3:13-19]

6:17-19 *Transformed by his touch.* Followed by huge crowds, Jesus healed them all as "power went out from him" (6:19; see exposition on 8:40-56).

6:20-23 *The highway to happiness.* Luke recorded various teachings of Jesus (6:20-49), some of which are from the Sermon on the Mount (Matt. 5–7). Jesus said his followers can be truly blessed, or happy, even when they are poor and hungry, in sorrow, or being persecuted. [Matt. 5:3-12]

6:24-45 *More concepts of the Kingdom:*

- Those who trust wealth will someday wish they had trusted God (6:24-25; see 12:13-21; James 5:1-3).
- Human popularity may indicate divine disapproval (6:26; see John 15:19).
- Love your enemies (6:27-36). [Matt. 5:38-48; 7:12]
- Forgive, don't judge (6:37, 41-42). [Matt. 7:1-5]
- Generosity brings material blessings (6:38).
- Spiritually blind leaders (such as Pharisees) produce spiritually blind followers (6:39; see Matt. 15:12-14).
- Actions reveal the condition of the heart (6:43-45; see Matt. 7:16-20; 12:34-35).

6:46-49 *One house prevails; the other fails.* Like a house with a deep foundation, those who obey Christ will withstand the ravages of life. Those who hear but don't obey can only expect ruin. [Matt. 7:24-27]

7:1-10 *He makes the Messiah marvel.* A Roman centurion asked Jesus to heal his servant. Jesus granted the healing and commended the faith of this Gentile, who understood:

- that Israel's God was the one true God (7:5)
- that he was unworthy of this God (7:6)
- that Christ's healing power was limitless (7:7)
- that he needed to trust and obey authority (7:8)

The Bible records only one other occasion when Jesus marveled at a person's faith, and that person was also a Gentile (see exposition on Matt. 15:21-31). As for Israel, Jesus could marvel only at its tragic unbelief (7:9; see Mark 6:6). [Matt. 8:5-13]

7:11-17 *"Young man, arise!"* Moved with compassion, Jesus raised a widow's only son—the first of three persons he raised from the dead (see 8:54-56; John 11:43-44). Technically, all three were *resuscitated,* not resurrected, since all three eventually died again. Jesus was the first to rise from the dead never to die again (see Col. 1:18; Rev. 1:5).

7:18-35 *"You're the one, right?"* When, from his prison cell, John the Baptist heard reports of Jesus' miracles, he sent two of his disciples to question him about his identity. He had proclaimed that Jesus was the Lamb of God (see John 1:29). Now, perhaps because of his suffering, he was losing that confidence. Jesus responded compassionately to John's doubts, citing his miracles as proof of his Messiahship (7:21-23). Jesus then spoke about John and his ministry:

- He was the prophesied forerunner of Christ (7:26-27; see Isa. 40:3; Mal. 3:1).
- He was the greatest of all prophets, but even the least in God's Kingdom is greater than he (7:28). Whether this refers to living after the Cross, or partaking in the millennial Kingdom, the truth stated is the same.

Luke noted that even "the unjust tax collectors" had responded to

John's ministry, while the religious leaders had not (7:28-30; compare 5:32). *[Matt. 11:1-19]*

7:36-50 *Forgiveness and love: One leads to the other.* As Jesus dined in the home of Simon the Pharisee, a woman known to be a sinner began washing his feet and weeping in sorrow for her sins (7:36-38). When Simon reacted with disdain, Jesus told a parable about a money lender who forgave two debts, one large and one small. He applied the story to the sinful woman and Simon:

- Repentance leads to forgiveness from God, resulting in affection for Christ—as the woman had shown.
- No repentance leads to no forgiveness, resulting in no affection for Christ—as shown by Simon.

Note Simon's surprise that Jesus allowed this sinner to touch him (7:39; compare exposition on 5:27-32). Matthew, Mark, and John record a later, similar incident (see Matt. 26:6-13).

8:1-3 *Their savings support the Savior.* Luke noted that several women, including some such as Mary Magdalene, whom Jesus had healed, followed him and helped support him financially. One of these was the wife of a Herodian official, suggesting the extent of Christ's influence.

8:4-15 *Sower, seed, and soil.* Jesus described the response to his message with the illustration of seed in various kinds of soil. [*Matt. 13:1-9, 18-23;* Mark 4:1-20]

8:16-18 *Learning from a lampstand.* Using the image of a lamp, Jesus declared that those who accept his message and share it will be blessed by God, while those who reject it will lose everything. *[Mark 4:21-25]*

8:19-21 *Membership requirements for God's family.* When Jesus heard that his earthly mother and brothers were looking for him, he taught that his true family consisted of those who hear God's Word and obey it. [Matt. 12:46-50; Mark 3:31-35]

8:22-25 *A Savior asleep in a storm.* When a storm threatened the disciples' boat, Christ calmed it, to their great amazement. The incident shows Christ's human nature, as he grew tired and fell asleep; and his divine nature, as he took control of the weather. The Greek word for this storm refers to something of hurricane proportion. The Sea of Galilee is susceptible to sudden, violent storms as cool air from the Mediterranean is drawn down through the narrow mountain passes, clashing with the hot, humid air over the sea. [*Matt. 8:23-27;* Mark 4:35-41]

8:26-39 *"Tell what God has done for you!"* Jesus cast out demons from a madman in Gadara. The demons identified Jesus as the Son of God, and Jesus sent them into a herd of swine, causing great concern among the local people (8:34-37) but also opening doors for the gospel (8:38-39). [Matt. 8:28-34; *Mark 5:1-20*]

Luke noted that the demons begged Christ not to send them into the "Bottomless Pit" (8:31), apparently referring to the place where Satan and his demons will be confined during the Millennium (see Rev. 20:1-3). The demons knew of their coming judgment and were in no hurry to go there!

This is the first of two miracles of Christ that, humanly speaking, had destructive results (compare Matt. 21:19).

8:40-56 *"Who touched me?"* As Jesus went to Jairus's house to heal his daughter, he encountered another woman in need of healing. He healed her, then proceeded to Jairus's house. Jairus's daughter had already died, but Jesus raised her. [Matt. 9:18-26; Mark 5:21-43] Jesus' feeling "healing power go out" from him may indicate that, in his humanity, his healing ministry had left him exhausted.

9:1-6 *Assignments for the apostles.* The apostles Christ had chosen (6:12-16) were now sent out to proclaim the gospel and to heal. [*Matt. 10:1-15;* Mark 6:7-13]

9:7-9 *"I beheaded John, so who is this?"* When Herod heard of Christ's miracles, at first his guilty conscience had led him to believe he was a resurrected John the Baptist (9:7-8; compare Matt. 14:1-2). He now tried to shake that delusion and sought to meet Christ the wonder-worker (9:9). He *would* eventually meet Christ, during his trial (see 23:6-12).

9:10-17 *Food for 5,000 and their families.* Soon after the apostles returned from their first official mission (9:6), they found themselves surrounded by 5,000 hungry men—plus perhaps 15,000 women and children—and Jesus miraculously provided for them. [Matt. 14:13-21; Mark 6:33-44; *John 6:1-13*]

9:18-22 *"Some say this, some say that, but I say . . ."* While others speculated about the identity of Jesus, Peter correctly recognized him as the Christ, the Messiah sent by God. Jesus warned them to tell no one, and for the first time told them plainly that he would be killed and resurrected. [*Matt. 16:13-23;* Mark 8:27-33]

9:23-27 *Discipleship means denial and devotion.* Jesus taught that those who truly follow him must deny their own life and desires and pursue *his* life and desires instead (9:23-25). True discipleship means total devotion to Christ (9:26). Anything less will bring shame at the Second Coming. [Matt. 16:24-28; Mark 8:34–9:1]

9:28-36 *A glimpse of his Kingdom glory.* While his three inner-circle disciples watched, Jesus was transfigured, giving them a foretaste of the glory he will have in his Kingdom. [Matt. 17:1-9; *Mark 9:2-13*] Of the three who wrote of this event, only Luke the doctor noted that the disciples either had been sleeping or were falling asleep (9:32), suggesting that the Transfiguration may have occurred at night.

9:37-42 *The only Son heals an only son.* When Christ's disciples failed to heal a demon-possessed boy, Christ did the healing, then explained that unbelief and lack of prayer had prevented their success. [Matt. 17:14-21; *Mark 9:14-29*] It is interesting that, just after God had acknowledged Christ as his only begotten Son (9:35), Christ healed an only son (9:38).

9:43-45 *Confused about Calvary.* Christ's second prediction of his death was met by the disciples' disbelief and lack of perception. [*Matt. 17:22-23;* Mark 9:30-32]

9:46-48 *Servanthood leads to sainthood.* In one of the great paradoxes of the Christian faith, Jesus showed that true greatness comes from being insignificant in the eyes of the world. [*Matt. 18:1-14;* Mark 9:33-37]

9:49-50 *"You mean God accepts other denominations? Amazing!"* Jesus rebuked sectarianism by accepting all ministry done in his name. *[Mark 9:38-41]*

THE SON OF MAN REJECTED BY HUMANKIND (9:51–19:27)

9:51-56 *Some "Bad Samaritans."* Knowing his death was near, Jesus "resolutely set out for Jerusalem" (9:51). His arrival there is recorded in 19:28. The events and teachings of 9:51–19:27 may not all have occurred on this final journey. Many of these events and teachings are reported only by Luke. Mark covers this final journey in just one chapter (Mark 10).

When poorly received by a village

of Samaria, the disciples showed their prejudice by urging Jesus to destroy the village (9:51-54). Without commenting on the worthiness of those particular Samaritans, Jesus noted that he had come to save life, not destroy it.

9:57-62 *Qualifications for the Kingdom.* When three would-be disciples approached Jesus, he challenged them to give up the comforts of life and the warmth of family ties. Following Jesus involves radical commitment. [Matt. 8:18-22]

10:1-12 *The 12 joined by the 70.* Having commissioned his 12 apostles (9:1-6), Jesus now sent out 70 more followers to evangelize (10:9). His instructions were similar to those for the 12 (10:4-12; compare Matt. 10:1-15), except that this time he didn't forbid evangelizing Gentiles.

10:13-16 *These cities had their chance.* Jesus pronounced a curse on three cities that had been indifferent to his ministry. His comparison of their eternal fate to that of Tyre and Sidon (10:14) suggests that there will be degrees of punishment in hell (see exposition on 12:41-48). [Matt. 11:20-24]

10:17-24 *The Savior rejoices with the 70.* Jesus rejoiced with his 70 new ambassadors as they reported great success, but reminded them that the true reason for joy is not power in ministry but the promise of eternal life.

10:25-37 *Your neighbor? Anyone you can help!* When a lawyer asked Jesus which laws were foremost, he highlighted two principles: Love God, and love your neighbor. Perhaps seeking a loophole in these broad and demanding principles, the lawyer sought to define "neighbor" in the narrowest possible sense (10:29). Jesus responded with the parable of the Good Samaritan (10:30-37), teaching that a neighbor is anyone we can help (10:36-37). (Compare Matt. 22:34-40; Mark 12:28-34.)

10:38-42 *Worship or work: Which comes first?* When Jesus visited Mary and Martha, sisters of Lazarus (see John 11:1-2), Mary worshiped Jesus and learned from him while Martha busily did housework. When Martha complained, Jesus corrected her, saying that Mary had the right priorities. Worship of God should always precede work for him. Work is good, but we must not let the good become the enemy of the best.

11:1-4 *"Lord, teach us to pray."* Luke gave a shortened version of Christ's model prayer for his disciples (Matt. 6:9-13).

11:5-13 *"Blessed are the persistent."* Just as persistence pays off in human affairs (such as a friend seeking help at midnight—11:5-8), it pays off in spiritual matters as well. If we diligently ask, seek, and knock on God's door in prayer (11:9-10), he, being so much more generous than the best earthly father, will answer us (11:11-13). (In the Greek, 11:9 reads, "keep on asking . . ." etc., as reflected in the NLT.)

11:14-23 *By whose power?* When Jesus healed a demoniac boy, the crowds marveled but the Pharisees privately conjectured that Jesus himself had demonic powers (11:14-16). Jesus showed the illogic of their thinking. [*Matt. 12:22-30;* Mark 3:20-30]

11:24-28 *Seven spirits and a well-swept house.* This parable shows that spirituality takes not just the absence of evil but the vital presence of God. [Matt. 12:43-45] A bystander's blessing on Jesus' mother brought from him a blessing on all who obey him (11:27-28; compare 8:19-21).

11:29-32 *A single sign for the sinful seekers.* When some people insincerely requested proof of his messianic claims (see 11:16), Jesus declared them evil for having made such a request: Christ's miracles should have been sufficient proof of his claims. He gave them one more sign: the example of Jonah. *[Matt. 12:38-42]*

11:33-36 *Be sure the sunshine reaches the soul.* In two more brief parables, Jesus taught the need to share the light of truth (11:33; see Matt. 5:14-16) and to let it fill one's own life (11:34-36).

11:37-54 *Condemning corrupt leaders: Part 1.* Fittingly, Luke followed the parable of the lighted lamp with Jesus' condemnation of the Pharisees, who were inwardly dark and unclean (11:39-40). Jesus gave examples of their hypocrisy (11:42-46, 52) and pointed out how they were carrying on a long tradition of misguided religious zeal among Israel's leaders (11:47-51). *[Matt. 23:1-36]* "From the murder of Abel to the murder of Zechariah" (11:51) shows the historic scope of resistance to God's righteous ones, from the first such person killed (see Gen. 4:8) to the last, going by the order of the Hebrew OT canon (see 2 Chron. 24:20-21).

12:1-3 *Condemning corrupt leaders: Part 2.* Having condemned the religious leaders to their faces, Christ then warned the onlookers against imitating their hypocrisy. The true condition of their hearts would one day be clear to all. [Matt. 16:6-12; Mark 8:14-21]

12:4-12 *Warnings to the wise:*
- We should fear God, who holds our eternal destiny in his hands (12:4-5).
- God cares about every detail of our lives (12:6-7).
- Jesus will deny those who deny him (12:8-9).
- Blasphemy against the Holy Spirit is unforgivable (12:10; see exposition on Matt. 12:31-32).
- God's Spirit will guide us in times of trial (12:11-12).

12:13-21 *A fool in a fix.* Confronted by two greedy brothers, Jesus spoke of the danger of materialism and told a story about a man who felt secure in his great wealth but was really a fool (12:20) because he
- thought he could satisfy his eternal soul with perishable goods
- smugly assumed he would live to a ripe old age
- was totally self-centered (note the many first-person singular pronouns)

This marks the only occasion in the Bible when God himself called an individual a fool.

12:22-34 *Ravens and lilies.* Believers should never be anxious over material needs, but rather should trust God's provision and seek spiritual wealth. *[Matt. 6:25-34]*

12:35-40 *When least expected . . .* We should expectantly await Christ's second coming. It will be at an unknown time, just as a thief comes without warning. *[Matt. 24:37–25:30]*

12:41-48 *Limited knowledge, limited punishment; full knowledge, full punishment.* Jesus contrasted the fates of a faithful and an unfaithful servant (12:42-47), and of two unfaithful servants—one who knew his master's will and one who did not (12:45-48). The one who knowingly disobeyed would receive greater punishment. (Compare exposition on 10:13-16; Lev. 5:14-19.)

12:49-59 *Divisions good and bad.* Jesus desired to accomplish his mission, which included the "baptism" of death (12:49-50; see exposition on Mark 10:35-45). The nature and importance of his mission would always bring division in this present age. Even family members would bitterly differ over him (12:51-53). In everyday conflicts, however, peace should be the goal (12:57-59; see Matt. 5:25-

26). On 12:54-56, see exposition on Matthew 16:1-12.

13:1-5 *Anyone can die, so everyone should repent!* When told of an atrocity Pilate had committed, Jesus spoke of life's uncertainty. Death is impartial. It can strike both the good and the bad without warning. Therefore all must repent, lest they suffer both physical and spiritual death.

13:6-9 *"Give it one more year."* As a fig tree must produce fruit or face destruction, so believers must produce repentance or face judgment (compare Matt. 21:18-22; Mark 11:12-14, 20-24).

13:10-17 *Another Sabbath healing.* Once again Jesus healed on the Sabbath, and once again a religious leader became irate. Christ silenced him by showing his hypocrisy (compare 6:6-11; 14:1-6; Matt. 12:9-14).

13:18-21 *Seeds and leaven.* God's Kingdom will grow steadily and with amazing results, just as a tiny mustard seed becomes a mighty tree and a little leaven affects a lot of dough. [*Matt. 13:31-35;* Mark 4:30-32]

13:22-30 *Traveling and teaching.* As Jesus and his disciples continued toward Jerusalem, he spoke of eternal life:

- More people will be lost than saved (13:23-24).
- Those who depend on good deeds for salvation will be lost (13:25-27).
- Many Gentiles will be saved while many Jews will be lost (13:28-30).

13:31-33 *Herod the fox.* Some Pharisees, apparently sent by Herod himself, pretended to warn Jesus that he should leave the area or face death by Herod's men. Ignoring their false threats, Jesus declared that nothing would detract him from his planned itinerary, which called for continuing toward Jerusalem (where death, on his own terms, awaited).

13:34-35 *"O Jerusalem, Jerusalem!"* Jesus wept for the people of Jerusalem, expressing his love for them but also knowing they had rejected him and must be judged (compare 19:41-44; Matt. 23:37-39).

14:1-6 *It's always the right time to do good!* Once again Jesus healed on the Sabbath, and again he pointed out the hypocrisy of the Pharisees, who would rescue an animal on the holy day but objected to helping humans (compare 13:10-17). "The people were watching him closely" (14:1) suggests that the Pharisees had brought in the sick man in an effort to entrap Jesus. A Pharisee normally would have avoided a person with an unsightly disease like this.

14:7-14 *On being a winner at a banquet dinner.* Noticing that the Pharisee's dinner guests were competing for the best seats, Jesus warned of the perils of seeking the limelight: Self-exaltation leads to dishonor; humility leads to honor (14:7-11). He spoke of eternal rewards for those who favor the poor (14:12-14; see exposition on 1:46-56). The Bible offers little support to the view that health and wealth are signs of God's favor.

14:15-24 *Refusers and responders.* In another parable, Jesus told of a man who, when his friends turned down his dinner invitation, filled his banquet hall with social outcasts. While the parable speaks primarily of Israel's rejection of God and the subsequent call of the Gentiles, it can also be applied to individual response to the gospel. *[Matt. 22:1-14]*

14:25-35 *The priority of discipleship.* Jesus stressed the need for total commitment to him:

- We must love him so much that our love for family seems

almost like hatred by comparison (14:25-27). [Matt. 10:37-39]

- We must count the cost before making our commitment (14:28-33). Discipleship is not an easy road.
- We should be a good influence on others (14:34-35). *[Matt. 5:13-16]*

15:1-32 *Parables of the lost.* When the Pharisees complained about Jesus' associating with people of ill repute, he told three parables about God's love for the lost:

One vs. 99 (15:3-7). Like a good shepherd, God rejoices more over the salvation of the lost than over those who are already safely in his Kingdom. [Matt. 18:12-14]

"I found it!" (15:8-10). Like a woman looking for a lost coin, God goes to great lengths to search for lost souls.

When one repents, the other resents (15:11-32). In the parable of the Prodigal Son, the younger, rebellious son quickly consumed his inheritance, then humbly repented and returned home, where he was welcomed by his father. His elder brother, who had not rebelled, resented this gracious reception:

- The prodigal son represents the sinner who realizes his or her spiritual poverty (15:17) and turns to God (15:18-19).
- The father represents God, who rejoices whenever a sinner repents (15:32).
- The elder son probably symbolizes the religious leaders, who resented Jesus' inclusion of those they rejected (15:29-30; compare 15:1-2).

16:1-13 *The shrewd steward.* Jesus told about a dishonest accountant who, hearing he would be fired, quickly reduced the accounts of his master's debtors, so that they would befriend him when he became jobless. The man's boss grudgingly admitted he had been very shrewd. The application of the parable seems to be threefold:

- We are God's stewards, using the wealth he has given but really owning nothing.
- Someday God will check our bookkeeping!
- In light of this, we are to use wisely the resources he has entrusted to us.

16:14-18 *"I know your greedy hearts."* When the money-loving Pharisees derided Jesus' statement about serving God and money, Jesus assured them that God saw their inward greed (16:13-15). He went on to talk about his high regard for the law, which the Pharisees pretended to uphold even while rejecting the one who fulfilled it. On 16:18, see exposition on Matthew 19:1-12.

16:19-31 *When Hades petitions paradise.* When an ungodly rich man and a beggar, Lazarus, died, they experienced a role-reversal, with Lazarus going to a place of comfort and the rich man going to a place of torment. The rich man, who had treated Lazarus unkindly in life, found, in death, that it was too late to repent (16:23-26). It was too late even for his like-minded brothers, who had resisted God to the point of no return (16:27-31).

Many try to dismiss this graphic description of the afterlife as merely a story—saying, for instance, that the "flames" (16:24) are not literal. Some scholars, however, believe the story may be factual, since no other parable names characters. Whether parable or narrative, as the very words of Christ it must be taken seriously. Several important truths emerge:

- In the OT, Hades (16:23) referred to the place of the dead whether saved or lost (see exposition on Ps. 9); in the NT, the place of the dead who are saved is also called "Abraham's bosom" (16:23) and "paradise" (23:43).

- The story reveals at least three things about the dead:
  - ➤ They are not simply annihilated.
  - ➤ They are not unconscious ("soul sleep"), but are fully awake and alert (see Matt. 17:3; Rev. 6:9-11).
  - ➤ They have physical bodies of some sort (16:24).
- People don't reject God for lack of evidence, but because they willfully refuse to believe (16:27-31).
- The story should not be seen as a blanket condemnation of wealth or glorification of poverty, but rather as a reprimand to people such as the Pharisees who see wealth as a reward for godliness. The Bible doesn't present wealth itself as a vice, nor poverty as a virtue; but teaches a balanced view (see 11:3; Prov. 30:8-9; 1 Tim. 6:6-8).

17:1-6 *Forgiveness and faith.* It is human nature for people to offend each other (17:1), but such offenses are still a serious matter (17:1-2). Offenses among Christians call for confrontation and forgiveness (17:3-4). This requires faith, which the disciples realized they needed more of (17:5-6). [Matt. 18:1-6, 15-35]

17:7-10 *When our best is the least.* When we serve God, we are not doing him a favor, for we owe all to him and deserve far less than he gives.

17:11-19 *"Where are the nine?"* When Jesus healed 10 lepers, only one—a Samaritan—thanked him (compare exposition on 7:7-10). Not all who receive physical healing receive spiritual healing.

17:20-21 *When and where is the Kingdom?* The Pharisees asked Jesus when the Kingdom of God would come, and he taught that it would not be fully revealed outwardly in this present age. However, in the person of the King, the Lord Jesus, the Kingdom was "within" or "among" them (17:21). "Within you" cannot mean "in your hearts," since Jesus was talking to the ungodly Pharisees.

17:22-37 *Preludes to the Second Coming.* Turning to his disciples, Jesus discussed the events of the end times, preceding his triumphant return to establish his Kingdom:

- He would soon leave them but would one day return suddenly, just as judgment came quickly upon Noah's generation and Sodom (17:22, 26-32).
- Only those who have given their lives to God will be ready for that day (17:33); unbelievers will be taken away to judgment (17:34-37).

[Matt. 24]

18:1-8 *Persistence prevails.* Through constant inquiries, a widow persuaded a wicked judge to deal with her adversaries. If a wicked earthly judge could be so moved, said Jesus, how much more will our benevolent heavenly Father respond to our persistent prayers.

18:9-14 *The haughty and the humble.* While an arrogant Pharisee compared himself favorably to others, a tax collector admitted his spiritual poverty and sought mercy. Jesus declared the tax collector more righteous than the Pharisee.

18:15-17 *"Red and yellow, black and white . . ."* Christ's love for children was seen in his willingness to take time for them despite the disciples' protests. The faith of children is the model for all who would come to God. [Matt. 19:13-15; Mark 10:13-16]

18:18-30 *Rich man, poor choice.* A rich young ruler asked Christ how to find eternal life but could not accept Christ's answer (18:22-23). In his wealth and self-righteousness (18:20-21), he didn't see his spiritual need. Christ grieved over his response and spoke of the perils of wealth and the rewards for those willing to give it up and follow him. [*Matt. 19:16-30;* Mark 10:17-31]

18:31-34 *An unthinkable forecast.* For the third time, Jesus spoke clearly of his coming death and resurrection, yet the disciples still did not understand. [Matt. 20:17-19; Mark 10:32-34]

18:35-43 *"Your faith has made you well."* When a blind man called out in faith, Jesus healed him, and he became a disciple. [Matt. 20:29-34; *Mark 10:46-52*]

19:1-10 *A short man, a tall tree, and a seeking Savior.* When Jesus visited Jericho, Zacchaeus, a tax collector, made an extra effort to see him. Jesus noticed him and invited himself to his house, resulting in his salvation. As one who had grown wealthy by oppressing his own people, Zacchaeus was small not just in stature but in the estimation of others. Yet God had mercy on him, and the immediate evidence of his repentance (19:8) probably helped improve his reputation in Jericho.

19:11-27 *Two good investments, one miserable excuse.* Jesus told a parable showing how we should occupy ourselves in the time between his first and second comings: Just as the 10 servants were to invest their master's money, we are to "invest" our abilities and opportunities. Both this parable and a similar one (Matt. 25:14-30) emphasize three things:

- the divine source of our abilities
- the importance of our dependability in using them
- our future accountability for how we used them

THE SON OF MAN SUFFERS FOR HUMANKIND (19:28–23:56)

19:28-40 *Israel's King . . . on a colt!* Less than a week before they would crucify him, the people of Jerusalem welcomed Jesus with great enthusiasm. On his last entrance into the Holy City during his earthly ministry, Israel's true King rode, not in a chariot or on a charging stallion, but on a donkey. At the Second Coming, he will ride a white horse as a conqueror (see Rev. 19:11-16). [*Matt. 21:1-11;* Mark 11:1-11; John 12:12-19]

19:41-44 *"If only you had known . . ."* Once again Jesus wept over unrepentant Jerusalem and predicted its destruction (compare 13:34-35).

19:45-48 *"Take your business elsewhere!"* Jesus drove the money changers from the Temple area. John recorded a cleansing of the Temple earlier in his ministry (John 2:13-17), and he may well have done this whenever he came to Jerusalem. The money changers probably hated to see him coming and knew his message ahead of time: God's house is to be a place of prayer, not profit. [*Matt. 21:12-17;* Mark 11:15-19]

20:1-8 *"Let me ask you a question."* In the first of several confrontations during Christ's last week, some religious leaders questioned the source of his authority—part of the continuing debate over whether Jesus was from God or was doing his marvelous miracles by the power of Satan (see exposition on 11:14-23). Jesus answered their question with a question: "Did John's baptism come from heaven, or was it merely human?" The question surprised and trapped the Jewish leaders: If they denied John's divine authority, they were in danger from the many bystanders who revered him; if they admitted it, they would have to explain why they had rejected John. So they refused to answer Christ's question, and he refused to answer theirs. [*Matt. 21:23-27;* Mark 11:27-33]

While the Pharisees' theological concerns had some merit, their ultimate concern was the potential loss of their own positions of authority if the people followed Christ.

Answering a question with a question is a good debating technique, one Jesus used often (see 6:1-3; 10:25-26; 18:18-19).

20:9-19 *Employees kill their employer's son.* In the parable of the vineyard owner, Jesus showed that Israel had rejected and killed past prophets and would soon reject and kill God's Son. This rejected stone would, however, become the chief cornerstone of God's Kingdom. [*Matt. 21:33-46;* Mark 12:1-12]

20:20-26 *His answer brings silence.* With a question about taxes, the deceptive Jewish leaders tried to trick Jesus into getting either the Jewish masses or the Roman government mad at him. In a masterful way, Jesus taught that responsibilities to God did not negate civic duties. [*Matt. 22:15-22;* Mark 12:13-17]

20:27-40 *God of the living, not of the dead.* When the Sadducees raised a hypothetical question concerning the afterlife, which they didn't even believe in (20:27-33), Jesus pointed out that their root problem was ignorance of Scripture and of God's power (20:34-38). [*Matt. 22:23-33;* Mark 12:18-27]

20:41-44 *Proving his deity from David.* Jesus used Psalm 110:1 to show that he, the Messiah, was David's son and David's Lord at the same time. The only way that can be is through the Incarnation—God the Son becoming human. [*Matt. 22:41-46;* Mark 12:35-40]

20:45-47 *Public piety, private greed.* Jesus warned his followers about the hypocritical scribes, who publicly displayed self-righteousness while at the same time mistreating the poor (compare Matt. 23:1-7).

21:1-4 *A poor woman's rich gift.* Jesus declared a widow who gave less than a penny to be more generous than those who gave much without personal sacrifice. [Mark 12:41-44]

21:5-28 *Predictions of destruction before triumph.* Jesus predicted that the Temple would be literally and completely destroyed (21:5-6). The disciples asked when this would happen, and in his answer (the Olivet discourse, 21:8-38) he apparently intermingled "signs of the times" concerning the destruction of Jerusalem in A.D. 70 (see 21:20-24) with descriptions of the Tribulation just prior to the Second Coming (21:8-19, 25-38). [*Matt. 24:1-31;* Mark 13:1-27]

21:29-33 *A tip-off from the trees.* Just as the fig tree's buds show that summer is near, the beginning of these signs will show that Christ's return is near. [*Matt. 24:32-36;* Mark 13:28-31]

21:34-38 *"Look out! Look up!"* Christians should watch, pray, and live worthy lives so that they won't be caught unprepared when he comes again. [Matt. 24:37-51; Mark 13:32-37]

22:1-6 *Selling his Savior and his soul.* Even as Israel's holiest day drew near, the Jewish leaders were concerned only with their plot against Jesus. Judas came to their aid by promising to deliver him for a price. The text also notes that Satan entered into Judas. Nowhere else in the Bible is Satan said to have directly possessed a person, without the assistance of his demons. [*Matt. 26:14-16;* Mark 14:1-2, 10-11]

22:7-16 *"Follow that man with the water jug."* Jesus sent Peter and John to find a place, traditionally called the upper room (22:12), where they would eat the Passover meal, and later that night they met to share the meal. It was probably in this room that some other key events occurred:

- Christ's appearance to 10 of his apostles on the first Easter night (see John 20:19) and again a week later (see John 20:24-26)
- the prayer meeting and business meeting preceding Pentecost (see Acts 1:12-26)
- the baptism of the Holy Spirit (see Acts 2:1-4)

The room may have been in the home of John Mark's mother (see Acts 12:12). [*Matt. 26:17-25;* Mark 14:12-21]

22:17-23 *"Do this in remembrance of me."* Near the end of the Passover meal, Jesus instituted the Lord's Supper—the sharing of bread and wine, which represent Christ's death to institute the New Covenant (22:19-20). The Lord's Supper is sometimes called the Eucharist, from the Greek word for giving thanks (22:19). It is also called Communion, to emphasize the fellowship believers have with each other and with Christ (see 1 Cor. 10:16).

Jesus then predicted that he would be betrayed by one of his disciples (22:21-22). Apparently Judas had played his role of deceit well enough to fool the other disciples (22:23). [*Matt. 26:26-30;* Mark 14:22-26; John 13:1-30]

22:24-30 *"Serve others as I have served you."* When the disciples began arguing about which of them was the greatest, Jesus taught them to express greatness through servanthood (compare 9:46-48; Matt. 20:20-28; Mark 9:33-37; 10:35-45; John 13:1-17). He assured them, however, that they would indeed have prominent places in God's Kingdom (22:28-30; compare Matt. 19:27-30; Mark 10:28-31).

The behavior of the apostles seems not just childish but also rather callous, so soon after the Passover and Lord's Supper, and after hearing Jesus say that one of them would betray him. Yet God would use these all-too-human men to change the course of history.

22:31-34 *Christ, Satan, and Peter: A cosmic struggle.* Jesus predicted Peter's denial, and when Peter protested, he gave specific details as to how and when it would happen (22:34; see 22:54-62). The devil had asked permission to test Peter, just as he had with Job (see Job 1–2). Peter may have had this incident in mind when later he wrote vividly concerning the devil (see 1 Pet. 5:8-9). [Matt. 26:31-35; Mark 14:27-31; John 13:36-38] Just as Jesus had prayed for Peter (22:32), he still prays for all believers (see Rom. 8:34; Heb. 7:25; 9:24; 1 John 2:1) .

22:35-38 *Preparing for the final days.* As his crucifixion drew near, Jesus tried to prepare his disciples for the increased opposition they would face. The "sword," if intended literally, would have been for protection only (compare John 18:11, 36).

22:39-46 *"Not my will, but yours."* While Jesus prayed in the Garden of Gethsemane, his disciples slept. Jesus fully intended to endure the cross in obedience to the Father's will, but he would have gladly forgone it had there been another way to save humankind (22:42). The "cup" represents the sins of all humanity, which Jesus would "drink" as he literally became sin for the world. [Matt. 26:36-46; Mark 14:32-42]

22:47-53 *Arrested, but still in control.* Judas entered the garden with an armed mob and betrayed Jesus to them. Peter swung his sword and cut off a man's ear, but Jesus immediately healed the man. How remarkable that at a moment of great agony he demonstrated such compassion. Jesus' words and actions showed that he was completely in control of the situation (22:52-53). [Matt. 26:47-54; Mark 14:43-48; John 18:1-11]

22:54-62 *A rooster's crow, and a look from the Lord.* Jesus was arrested and brought before the high priest, while Peter followed at a distance. Peter denied three times that he even knew Jesus, after which the rooster crowed and he was filled with remorse. Luke adds the detail that, just when the rooster crowed, Jesus looked at Peter (22:61). [Matt. 26:69-75; Mark 14:66-72; John 18:15-18, 25-27] Luke does not say much about Jesus' first trial before the high priest, focusing on Peter's denial instead (see exposition on Matt. 26:57-68).

22:63-71 *"He says he's the Son of God."* Jesus was taken before the whole Sanhedrin, the body of ruling Jewish elders, whom he scolded for their unbelief while affirming his own identity as both Son of Man (22:69) and Son of God (22:70). Assuming this to be blasphemy, the rulers were ready to hand him over to be crucified (22:71). [Matt. 26:59-68; 27:1; Mark 14:55-65; 15:1; John 18:19-24]

23:1-5 *A tax evader? A rebel?* Since only Rome could condemn anyone to death, the Jewish leaders took Jesus to Pilate and accused him of subversion, on two false grounds:

- that he forbade paying taxes (a direct lie; compare exposition on 20:20-26)
- that he had proclaimed himself king (a half-truth; compare John 18:36)

Pilate apparently saw through both charges and refused to condemn him. [Matt. 27:1-2, 11-14; Mark 15:1-5; John 18:28-38]

23:6-12 *Brought together by their common enemy.* Because Jesus was a Galilean, Pilate saw an opportunity to pass responsibility for his fate to Herod, who had jurisdiction over Galilee. Herod, though glad to have finally met this worker of miracles (compare 23:8 with 9:9), apparently lost interest when no miracles were forthcoming. He allowed his soldiers to abuse Jesus, then sent him back to Pilate. Herod and Pilate "had been enemies before," probably because they were competing to rule the same territory (see exposition on Matt. 27:1-2), but their mutual dislike of Christ finally brought them together (23:12).

23:13-25 *"I find no fault with him."* Pilate pronounced Jesus innocent and offered to release him according to a Sabbath custom (23:13-17; see Matt. 27:15). But the crowd, led by the chief priests and rulers, cried out for his crucifixion, and after three tries to change their minds, Pilate gave in and sentenced him to death. The account shows Pilate's weakness and the strong influence the Jews exerted over him. [*Matt. 27:15-26;* Mark 15:6-15; John 18:38–19:16]

23:26-32 *"Weep for yourselves."* As they led Jesus to Calvary, there were many in the crowd who were on his side. As they wept for him, he told them their mourning was misplaced: The loss was not his, but the nation's, for in the days ahead Israel would suffer greatly.

23:33-38 *The Crucifixion.* Jesus was crucified between two criminals. As the soldiers and people mocked him, he asked God to forgive them. They placed a sign above him calling him the King of the Jews. From the Roman point of view this was mockery of both Christ and the Jews. From God's point of view, it was the truth. [*Matt. 27:33-43;* Mark 15:22-32; *John 19:19-22*]

23:39-43 *"Lord, remember me . . ."* While one of the thieves joined in mocking Jesus, the other recognized him for who he was and begged for

THE CRUCIFIXION OF CHRIST

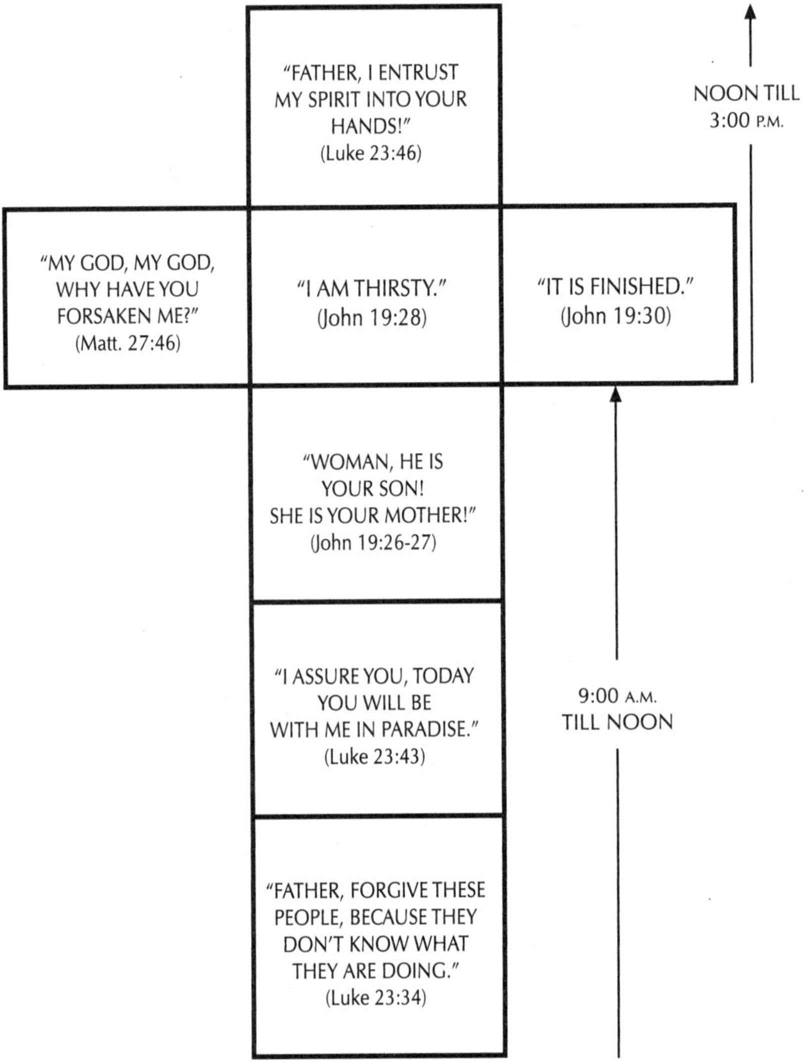

forgiveness. Jesus assured him that, when he died, he would have eternal salvation. This is truly a case of deathbed repentance and faith, with the thief having no opportunity to be baptized or perform any good deeds to earn heaven. [Matt. 27:44; Mark 15:32]

23:44-49 *At his death: Signs and responses.* As Jesus died, a combination of several miraculous signs brought a variety of emotional responses from the onlookers. [*Matt. 27:45-56;* Mark 15:33-41; John 19:28-30]

23:50-56 *A hasty burial, to keep the Sabbath.* Joseph, a member of the Sanhedrin who had not consented to Christ's death, secured permission to give him an honorable burial. The burial took place quickly, because of the need to remove the body from the cross before the Sabbath started at sundown on Friday. Some women noted the location of the tomb and made plans to give him a proper anointing after the Sabbath. [Matt. 27:57-61; Mark 15:42-47; John 19:38-42]

THE SON OF MAN CONFIRMED BEFORE HUMANKIND (24)

24:1-12 *His resurrection, their reactions.* Early Sunday morning, as the women came to finish anointing Christ's body, they found the tomb empty, and two angels told them he had risen from the dead. When they told the disciples, the initial reaction was disbelief. Peter then went to the tomb himself and verified their report. [*Matt. 28:1-10; Mark 16:1-11; John 20:1-18*] The disciples' initial skepticism and their sudden transformation into bold evangelists (Acts 1–4) are solid proof that Jesus did indeed rise from the dead.

24:13-32 *A resurrection Bible study: From Moses to Malachi.* Jesus appeared to two disciples on the road to Emmaus, near Jerusalem. Supernaturally prevented from recognizing him (24:16), they told Jesus of the crucifixion and the rumored resurrection as if he were a total stranger (24:17-24). Jesus then showed them how the entire OT foretold those events (24:25-27). Later that night, he revealed to them his true identify (24:28-32). [Mark 16:12-13]

24:33-43 *"Does a spirit eat?"* The disciples who had seen Jesus at Emmaus went to Jerusalem and reported to the disciples that they, and Peter, had seen him. Just then, Jesus appeared among them and tried to convince them that he was not just an apparition: His resurrected body had flesh and bone, ate food, and still bore the marks of his crucifixion (compare John 20:25-27) but was not subject to material laws, since he had appeared to them out of nowhere. [Mark 16:14; John 20:19-25]

24:44-49 *Another Bible study, and an assignment.* Jesus reminded the disciples of his teachings concerning his death and resurrection (see exposition on 9:43-45), then explained the OT prophecies concerning him. He commissioned them to take this gospel to all nations and promised an outpouring of the Holy Spirit to enable them for the task (24:47-49; compare Matt. 28:19-20; Mark 16:15-18; John 17:18; Acts 1:4-8).

The illumination of Scripture that Christ provided his disciples (24:45) is available to believers today through the indwelling Holy Spirit (see John 16:13; 1 Cor. 2:13-16).

24:50-53 *One final blessing, then he's gone!* Leading the disciples a couple miles outside Jerusalem, to Bethany, Jesus pronounced a blessing on them and ascended to heaven. They returned to Jerusalem and worshiped him in the Temple. [Mark 16:19-20; Acts 1:9-11] Luke would continue his historical account in the book of Acts.

❖ ❖ ❖

PEOPLE TO REMEMBER FROM LUKE

CLEOPAS

Key Fact: Encountered risen Christ near Emmaus
Total Bible References: 1
Key Reference: 24:13-35

Cleopas Speaks

I should have known who he was right from the beginning! No one else could have expounded the Scriptures to us as he did. Imagine, summarizing all the books from Genesis to Malachi during a brief seven-mile walk! (24:13, 15-16, 27)

At least we had the good sense to invite him in for a meal. What a supper that turned out to be! Everything seemed to happen at once. He had just blessed and broken the bread, causing us somehow to recognize him. But at that very instant, he disappeared! (24:29-31)

Well, within the hour we were headed back to Jerusalem with this glorious news. And would you believe that we had no sooner shared all this with the apostles in the upper room when he appeared again out of nowhere! Once again, he ate something and taught us the Scriptures. (24:33-46)

Spiritual Lessons from Cleopas

- Failure to regularly read and apply God's Word can leave us in the dark concerning how God is working in our lives and in the lives of others (24:24-27).
- For God's children, Bible study should be a heartwarming experience, not a drudgery (see 24:32).

Key Verse

"Didn't our hearts feel strangely warm as he talked with us on the road and explained the Scriptures to us?" (24:32).

ELIZABETH

Key Fact: Mother of John the Baptist (1:13)
Husband: Zechariah (1:5)
Total Bible References: 9
Key Reference: 1:1-58

Elizabeth Speaks

They wanted to name our child after his father. This was natural, of course, but we both refused. I voiced my objection while my poor husband had to write his. Zechariah had already been chastened by God's special messenger, and he had no intention of letting that happen again. So we told our relatives the baby would be called John, not Zechariah. (1:18-20, 59-64)

All our relatives kept wondering what kind of person our little John would be. And I silently agreed. Think of it: He was born of an older, barren woman; named by an angel; predicted to be a Nazirite; controlled by the Spirit while still in the womb; and commissioned to be the Messiah's forerunner. What manner of child, indeed! (1:7, 13, 15, 17, 41, 66, 76)

Spiritual Lessons from Elizabeth

- Elizabeth didn't let the burden of her barrenness and the public disgrace it brought (1:25) affect her zeal for the Lord (1:6).
- She encouraged her young cousin Mary during what was surely a difficult time in both of their lives (1:36, 39-45).
- She obeyed God in spite of the contrary advice of friends and family (1:57-60).

Key Verses

"But the angel said, 'Don't be afraid, Zechariah! For God has heard your prayer, and your wife, Elizabeth, will bear you a son! And you are to name him John. You will have great joy and gladness, and many will rejoice with you at his birth'" (1:13-14).

LUKE

Key Facts: Traveling companion of Paul, authored Luke and Acts
Occupation: Physician (Col. 4:14)
Total Bible References: 41
Key References: 1:3; Acts 16:10-40; 20:7-12; 27; Col. 4:14; 2 Tim. 4:11; Philem. 1:24

Luke Speaks

Paul was put to death this morning. Timothy, John Mark, and I spent the day together sharing, praying, and discussing the life of this incredible man! Thank God they both got here in time and were able to visit with Paul during the final days. I know their presence helped ease some of the pain he felt when many others abandoned him. (2 Tim. 4:6, 9-11, 16)

He especially enjoyed seeing Mark once again. What a contrast between their first and final encounters. Mark has indeed become the man Paul described as being useful for his ministry. (Acts 13:13; 2 Tim. 4:11)

Both Mark and Timothy have known Paul longer than I. He and I first met when he came to Troas some 16 years ago. An unusual meeting too, for God called me into full-time service through the vision he gave to Paul! (Acts 12:25; 16:1, 8-10)

What memories fill my mind: the events in Philippi, the raising of Eutychus, that miserable sea voyage to Rome, Paul's first and second imprisonments in Rome. (Acts 16:11-40; 20:7-12; 27; 28:16; 2 Tim. 1:8)

Timothy and Mark must leave soon to continue their ministries for Christ. Both were gracious in their remarks concerning my two books. Hopefully, these writings will prove helpful to the entire body of Christ. I am suddenly reminded I must contact Theophilus again, to bring him up to date on current events. (1:3; Acts 1:1)

Spiritual Lessons from Luke

- Luke was very desirous that his friend Theophilus (perhaps a new convert) rightly understand the ministry of both the Son of God (1:1-4) and God the Holy Spirit (Acts 1:1-8). We too should want to help our friends grow in their knowledge of God.

- Luke first carefully researched the life of Christ (1:3), and then the Holy Spirit inspired the very words he wrote about him. Whatever work he calls us to, God expects us to do our part and then he will do his.

Key Verses
"Most honorable Theophilus: Many people have written accounts about the events that took place among us. They used as their source material the reports circulating among us from the early disciples and other eyewitnesses of what God has done in fulfillment of his promises. Having carefully investigated all of these accounts from the beginning, I have decided to write a careful summary for you, to reassure you of the truth of all you were taught" (1:1-4).

SIMEON
Key Fact: Blessed the infant Jesus in the Temple (2:25-35)
Total Bible References: 2
Key Reference: 2:25-35

Simeon Speaks
I stand quietly here with Anna at the Temple entrance, both of us filled with joy and wonder as we watch them leave. What a truly caring and unique family. Caring because of the love demonstrated by the husband for his wife and baby. Unique because of the nature of this baby. Indeed, what a day this has been for us, to see and actually hold the Lord's Christ, the Gentile's light and Israel's glory. (2:25-26, 28, 32, 36; Matt. 1:19)

Both Joseph and Mary seemed amazed at my prophecies concerning their child, and well they should have been. What other life has been destined at birth to cause either the rise or fall of every Israelite! (2:33-34)

Blessed Holy Spirit, you have kept your promise in allowing me to see Israel's Consolation. I now am ready to depart this earthly life for the eternal one! (2:25-26)

I believe I speak for my friend Anna as well! (2:36-38)

Spiritual Lessons from Simeon

- With great expectation Simeon awaited the first coming of Christ (2:25-26). With equally great expectation we should look forward to his second coming (1 Thess. 1:10; 5:4-6; James 5:8).

Key Verses
"Lord, now I can die in peace! As you promised me, I have seen the Savior you have given to all people. He is a light to reveal God to the nations, and he is the glory of your people Israel!" (2:29-32).

ZACCHAEUS
Key Fact: Climbed tree to see Christ
Occupation: Tax collector
Total Bible References: 3
Key Reference: 19:1-10

Zacchaeus Speaks
Yes, that one single encounter back then cost me half my wealth plus full and compounded restitution for my many past dishonest deals. Looking back, was it

worth it? It was indeed! I mean, how much of that silver would it have taken to cleanse my soul? And besides, I may be less wealthy now, but now that I'm in God's family I have a lot more truly close friends. (19:8-9)

Think of it, because of my faith he called me a son of Abraham! Thank God for that sycamore tree! (19:9)

Spiritual Lessons from Zacchaeus

- Zacchaeus did not allow his sin, size, or silver to keep him from the Savior (19:1-4).
- Zacchaeus's sincere repentance made him truly a "new person" in Christ (see 2 Cor. 5:17), as exhibited by his promising to give half of his goods to the poor and a fourfold restoration to anyone he may have cheated (19:8; see Exod. 22:1; 2 Sam. 12:6).
- Zacchaeus's fourfold testimony concerning Jesus in his day can be (and should be) our testimony today:
  - ➤ He sees me (19:5).
  - ➤ He knows me (he called him by name) (19:5).
  - ➤ He loves me (he desired his fellowship) (19:5).
  - ➤ He forgives me (19:9).

Key Verses

"Meanwhile, Zacchaeus stood there and said to the Lord, 'I will give half my wealth to the poor, Lord, and if I have overcharged people on their taxes, I will give them back four times as much!' Jesus responded, 'Salvation has come to this home today, for this man has shown himself to be a son of Abraham. And I, the Son of Man, have come to seek and save those like him who are lost'" (19:8-10).

ZECHARIAH

Key Fact: Father of John the Baptist (1:13)
Wife: Elizabeth (1:5)
Occupation: Priest (1:5)
Total Bible References: 8
Key References: 1:5-23, 59-79

Zechariah Speaks

He left us today, our Nazirite son, for the Judean desert. That lonely and desolate place is no doubt the ideal spot for him to begin spiritual preparation for his ministry. (1:14-15; 3:1-2)

And what a ministry it will be. Think of it, serving as the Messiah's forerunner and ministering like a modern Elijah, bringing many people to the Lord. (Matt. 3:4-6; 11:14; John 1:23)

To think that Elizabeth and I once despaired of ever having a child, never dreaming God would answer our prayer in such an incredible way. Gabriel's words in the Temple still ring in my ears: "He will be filled with the Holy Spirit, even before his birth." So he was, and so he shall be! (1:7, 13, 15, 19, 80)

Spiritual Lessons from Zechariah

- Zechariah was in the right place, doing the right thing in the right way with a right heart, when God appeared to bless him (1:5-6, 8-9).

- Sometimes those who pray the most earnestly (1:13) are the most surprised when God answers their prayers (1:18-20). For a similar incident, see Acts 12:5-16.

Key Verses

"Then his father, Zechariah, was filled with the Holy Spirit and gave this prophecy: 'Praise the Lord, the God of Israel, because he has visited his people and redeemed them. He has sent us a mighty Savior from the royal line of his servant David'" (1:67-69).

5 B.C.
Birth of Christ

A.D. 26
Begins ministry

27
Talks with Nicodemus

28
Chooses 12

29
Feeds 5,000, raises Lazarus

30
Death, resurrection, ascension

JOHN

BACKGROUND

See *Matthew: Background.*

AUTHOR

Though the text gives no name, the consistent testimony of the early church is that the author is John, the beloved disciple (21:20-25) and early church leader (Gal. 2:9). The eyewitness quality of the Gospel confirms this. John also authored the three letters bearing his name and Revelation.

DATE

Early church fathers believed it was written in John's old age, probably A.D. 85–95, some 20 years after the Synoptics. John's five books were the last NT books written.

LOCATION AND RECIPIENTS

Eusebius says John lived in Ephesus after Paul founded the church there. From there he conducted a kind of home-missions ministry. His Gospel and letters were a part of that ministry.

PURPOSE

While the synoptic Gospels focused on the historical facts of Jesus' life, John interpreted those facts to show that Jesus was, indeed, the Messiah, the Son of God and Savior of the world. He sought to instill faith in his readers (20:30-31).

UNIQUE FEATURES

- While omitting many of the miracles reported in the synoptic Gospels, John chose seven, apparently to help show that Jesus is the Messiah:
  - changing water to wine (2:1-11)
  - healing the nobleman's son (4:46-54)
  - healing the lame man at Bethesda (5:1-18)

- ➤ feeding 5,000 (6:5-14)
- ➤ walking on water (6:16-21)
- ➤ healing the blind man (9:1-7)
- ➤ raising Lazarus (11:1-45)
- He also recorded seven occasions when Jesus bore witness to his Messiahship:
  - ➤ "I am the bread of life" (6:35).
  - ➤ "I am the light of the world" (8:12).
  - ➤ "I am the gate" (10:7).
  - ➤ "I am the good shepherd" (10:11, 14).
  - ➤ "I am the resurrection and the life" (11:25).
  - ➤ "I am the way, the truth, and the life" (14:6).
  - ➤ "I am the true vine" (15:1).

COMPARISON WITH OTHER BIBLE BOOKS

The Synoptics (Matthew, Mark, and Luke):

- The Synoptics are primarily historical; John is primarily theological and interpretative, omitting many key historical facts:
  - ➤ Jesus' genealogy and birth
  - ➤ his baptism and temptation
  - ➤ his Galilean and Perean ministries
  - ➤ his healing of demoniacs
  - ➤ his parables
  - ➤ the Transfiguration
  - ➤ the Lord's Supper
  - ➤ Gethsemane
  - ➤ the Ascension
- Instead, John focuses on:
  - ➤ Christ's early ministry in Judea and Jerusalem; while the Synoptics record only one visit to Jerusalem, John mentions four (2:13-25; 5; 7:10–10:39; 12–19).
  - ➤ his contacts and private conversations with individuals (see 3:1-21; 4:1-26)
  - ➤ his ministry to the disciples (see 13–17)
- John and the Synoptics supplement each other concerning the events of the "Last Supper":
  - ➤ If we had only the Synoptics, we would know nothing of the washing of feet (13).
  - ➤ If we had only John, we would know nothing of the institution of the Lord's Supper (Matt. 26:26-30).

1 John:

- John's Gospel was written to lead people to faith in Christ (20:30-31); the epistle was written to confirm believers in their faith (1 John 5:13).

Revelation:

- John's Gospel presents the ministry of Jesus of Nazareth on earth; Revelation presents the ministry of the exalted Jesus from heaven.

OUTLINE

JESUS THE ETERNAL SON OF GOD (1:1-18)
- His existence from the beginning (1:1-5)
- The witness of John the Baptist (1:6-8)
- The witness of the Light (1:9-13)
- The incarnation of the Light (1:14-18)

JESUS THE EARTHLY SON OF GOD (1:19–18:11)
- His early ministry (1:19–4:54)
  - Baptism (1:19-34)
  - First disciples (1:35-51)
  - Changing water to wine (2:1-11)
  - First cleansing of the Temple (2:12-25)
  - Nicodemus; the new birth (3:1-21)
  - Testimony of John the Baptist (3:22-36)
  - Woman at the well (4:1-42)
  - Healing the government official's son (4:43-54)
- His ministry in Jerusalem (5)
  - Healing the lame man at Bethesda (5:1-18)
  - Teachings (5:19-47)
- His Ministry in Galilee (6:1–7:9)
  - Feeding 5,000; walking on water (6:1-21)
  - Bread of Life (6:22–7:9)
- His return to Jerusalem (7:10–10:42)
  - Debates and discourses (7:10-53)
  - Woman taken in adultery (8:1-11)
  - Light of the World (8:12-30)
  - Abraham's children (8:31-59)
  - Healing the blind man (9)
  - Good Shepherd (10)
- His ministry at Bethany (11:1–12:11)
  - Lazarus raised (11)
  - Anointing by Mary (12:1-11)
- His ministry's conclusion (12:12-50)
  - Triumphal Entry (12:12-19)
  - Teachings (12:20-50)
- Preparing his disciples for his death (13–17)
  - Washing his disciples' feet (13)
  - Heaven; the Holy Spirit (14)
  - Vine and branches (15:1-17)
  - Persecution; the Holy Spirit (15:18–16:33)
  - Prayer for his disciples (17)
- His arrest (18:1-11)

JESUS THE EXECUTED SON OF GOD (18:12–19:42)
- His religious trial (18:12-27)
- His civil trial (18:28–19:16)
- His crucifixion (19:17-37)

His burial (19:38-42)
JESUS THE EXALTED SON OF GOD (20:1–21:25)
His empty tomb (20:1-10)
His postresurrection appearances (20:11–21:25)
To Mary (20:11-18)
To his disciples (20:19-23)
To Thomas (20:24-31)
By the Sea of Galilee (21)

JESUS THE ETERNAL SON OF GOD (1:1-18)

NOTE: In the comments that follow, cross-references to parallel passages in the other Gospels are given in square brackets. Italics within brackets, such as [*Matt. 26:6-13; Mark 14:3-9*], indicate that you will find a more complete discussion of the passage in question in the exposition for that reference.

1:1-5 *The wonderful works of the Word.* Often considered the most profound passage in all of Scripture, the first five verses of John's Gospel introduce Jesus Christ as the eternal Son of God. 1:1 affirms three great truths concerning him:
- His eternality: "In the beginning the Word already existed."
- His personality: "He was with God."
- His deity: "He was God."

"Word" is the Greek word *logos,* used frequently throughout the Greek NT and other literature of the day. It can mean message, word, concept, expression, or speech. Greek philosophers used the term, as did Philo, the first-century Jewish philosopher. However, John used it in a unique way, to teach that Jesus was the embodiment or expression of all that God is (compare exposition on Col. 1:15-23).

1:2-5 expands on 1:1:
- Jesus Christ was with the Father in eternity past (1:2).
- As a part of the Godhead, he was the Creator (1:3).
- He is both the light and life of all humankind (1:4).
- The darkness of the fallen world could not "extinguish" his light (1:5).

John's prologue establishes his special interest in showing that Jesus of Nazareth truly was the Son of God (see *Purpose*). These opening verses help establish the Bible's unique teaching that God is a Trinity (see exposition on Gen. 1:26-31).

1:6-8 *A witness for the Word.* John noted God's special commissioning of John the Baptist to introduce Jesus the Messiah. Samuel was the first pre-Christian Israelite prophet, and John was the last: Samuel introduced Israel's first King (1 Sam. 10); John presented its eternal King (1:29).

1:9-13 *Both rejected and received.* Though Jesus had created the world, when he was born, the world did not recognize him. Even his own people rejected him. There were however (and still are!) some who "accepted" him, and by so doing they became children of God. To accept Jesus means to believe in him (1:12). Birth into God's family (1:13) does not happen because of "physical birth," reformation ("human passion"), or by the actions of one's Christian parents ("human . . . plan"). Salvation is a supernatural new birth that can only be accomplished by God. "Gives light to everyone" (1:9) does not imply universal salvation, only universal revelation of truth (compare 16:8-11).

1:14 *When God becomes human.* Recalling perhaps his three years of ministry with Jesus, John expressed wonder at the fact that God the Son came from heaven to earth and lived as a human. This is commonly called the Incarnation—literally, the taking on of flesh, from *carnis,* Latin for "flesh" (see Col. 2:9). John had seen Jesus' divine glory, especially at the Transfiguration (see Matt. 17:1-9), but in many other ways as well. Jesus embodied God's grace and truth (compare 14:6). On "lived . . . among us," see exposition on Exodus 29:43-46.

1:15-18 *Not law, but grace.* John recalled the message of John the Baptist concerning Christ's greatness. Christ did not come to give a new law, but to proclaim and by his sacrificial death make possible God's grace, which is God doing for humans what they cannot do for themselves. Though several OT saints "saw" God (see Isa. 6:1-7), none had seen his essential nature. This was disclosed only in and through Jesus (see 14:8-9).

JESUS THE EARTHLY SON OF GOD (1:19–18:11)

1:19-28 *Is he Christ? Elijah? The Prophet?* When people began wondering if John the Baptist was the long-awaited Messiah, they inquired of him, and he denied any such claim. He quoted Isaiah's predictions of both the Messiah and his own humble role in preparing the way for him (1:23; see Isa. 40:3). When they pressed him further concerning why he baptized, he again humbly spoke of someone "right here in the crowd" (1:26) who truly was the Messiah. On "Elijah" (1:25), see Malachi 3:1; 4:4-6 and exposition on Matthew 17:10-13. The "Prophet" (1:25), predicted by Moses (see Deut. 18:15), was none other than Christ himself (see Acts 3:22).

1:29-34 *"Behold! The Lamb of God!"* Jesus came to be baptized by John, and John clearly identified him as
- the person who, as the sacrificial Lamb of God, would make final atonement for sin (1:29)
- the eternal Messiah (1:30)
- the one who would baptize "with the Holy Spirit," as shown by the Spirit's descending upon him as a dove (1:32-33). John's own practice of water baptism was but a shadow of Christ's Spirit baptism (1:33).
- the Son of God (1:34)

[Matt. 3:13-17; Mark 1:9-11; Luke 3:21-22]

1:35-42 *"We have found the Messiah!"* On John's recommendation, two of his disciples began to follow Jesus. One of them, Andrew, brought his brother Simon to Jesus. Jesus renamed him Cephas, a transliteration of the Aramaic word for "stone," which the NT usually renders in Greek as Peter. This name would prove prophetic of Peter's leadership among the disciples and in the early church. The synoptic Gospels record a later encounter when these brothers became Christ's disciples (see Matt. 4:18-20).

1:43-51 *"He is Jesus of Nazareth!"* In similar fashion to Andrew (1:41-42), Philip led his brother Nathanael to Jesus, testifying that he was the Messiah. Hearing that this Jesus was from Nazareth, Nathanael was skeptical (1:46), but a display of Jesus' omniscience was enough to change his mind (1:48-51). Nathanael probably knew the prophecy that the Messiah would be born in Bethlehem (see Mic. 5:2), so the mention of Nazareth probably confused him (see exposition on Luke 2:1-7). He probably had a low view of Nazareth, which housed the Roman garrison for northern Galilee, making "Nazarene" a term of utter contempt among Jews.

2:1-11 *Wonderful wine for the wedding.* A wedding in Cana provided the occasion for Jesus' earliest recorded miracle (see 2:11). When the host ran out of wine, Jesus turned water into wine of extraordinary quality, to everyone's amazement. The wedding feast probably lasted a week, as in the cases of Jacob (see Gen. 29:27) and Samson (see Judg. 14:17). Running out of wine during such a long feast could be a serious problem.

Jesus' statement to Mary (2:4) was not crude or uncaring. The NLT translates it "How does that concern you and me?" "Wine" (Greek *oinos,* 2:3, etc.) can refer to either grape juice (see Matt. 9:17) or fermented wine (see Eph. 5:18). Either way, the passage should not be seen as a license for the use of alcohol.

2:12-17 *Zeal for his Father's house.* In Jerusalem for the Passover, Jesus was distraught to find money changers doing business in the Temple, and he drove them out, reminding his disciples of one of David's psalms (see Ps. 69:9). Jesus would "cleanse" the Temple at least once more (see exposition on Luke 19:45-48).

2:18-22 *"You'll do what in just three days?"* Jesus went on to predict that "this temple" would be destroyed and rebuilt in just three days. Knowing how long Herod had spent building the Temple, the Jews were incredulous (2:18-20). Some three years later, at his crucifixion, they would use this seemingly outlandish boast to ridicule Christ (see Matt. 26:61; 27:40). As John noted, however, Christ was speaking not of the Temple but of his body, as the disciples would realize after his resurrection (2:21-22).

2:23-25 *Believers? Not really.* Jesus knew that many of the Jews who professed to believe in him had only a superficial faith, relating to his miracles and not to his deeper ministry of deliverance from sin. John would later come back to this theme of "unbelieving believers" (see 6:22-66; 8:31-59).

3:1-21 *"For God so loved the world."* Perhaps fearful of his colleagues, a Pharisee named Nicodemus came to Jesus at night, seeking deeper spiritual truth from this miracle worker. Jesus cut short any philosophical discussion, declaring that salvation required being "born again" (3:3; compare exposition on 1:9-13). When Nicodemus seemed confused and spoke of physical birth, Jesus explained that this new birth was spiritual in nature (3:4-7). To the human understanding it is like the wind, whose origin and destination are a mystery (3:8). When Nicodemus was still confused, Jesus reminded him that the OT spoke of the need for a new birth (3:9-10; see exposition on the following passages: Jer. 31:31-34; Ezek. 11:14-21; 36:16-38; Joel 2:28-32).

Jesus claimed his right to speak with authority (3:11-13), as Nicodemus should have realized, having seen his miracles (see 3:2). He reminded Nicodemus of the time when a lifted-up serpent saved Israel from a plague (see exposition on Num. 21:4-9), and predicted that his own approaching death would in like manner bring spiritual healing to all who believed in him (3:14-16).

Presenting the gospel in a nutshell, 3:16 clarifies

- the source of the gospel: God's love, demonstrated in the giving of his only Son to die on the cross
- the beneficiaries of the gospel: "everyone who believes"
- the required response: simple faith in Jesus (see 6:29)
- the importance of that response: Those who believe will live for-

- ever; those who do not believe will perish.

Jesus continued to stress the importance of the gospel and of responding to it in faith (3:17-21). All are born sinners and are condemned until they accept Jesus, the cure for sin (3:18).

Jesus said we must be "born of water and the Spirit" (3:5). While "born of . . . the Spirit" seems clearly to mean regeneration by the power of the Holy Spirit, scholars take various views on "born of water." Some say it means that baptism is essential for salvation, but that would seem to contradict 3:15-16, which makes it clear that salvation is by faith alone. More likely, it refers to one of three things:

- the breaking of water during physical birth
- the cleansing by God's written Word in the new birth (compare 4:14; Ps. 119:9; Eph. 5:25-26; Titus 3:5)
- the cleansing by the Spirit in the new birth; that is, "water" and "Spirit" are really talking about the same thing (compare Ezek. 36:25-27)

Either on this occasion or later, Nicodemus believed in Christ (see 7:45-52; 19:38-42).

3:22-36 *"He must increase, I must decrease."* When Jesus and his disciples began baptizing people near where John was baptizing, and attracting large crowds, John's disciples expressed concern about the situation (3:22-26), but John responded in words of admiration and worship of Christ (3:27-36). He was quite willing to let Jesus get all the glory (3:30).

4:1-4 *A shortcut through Samaria . . .* Not wishing to be pitted against John in a baptismal contest (4:1), Jesus left Judea for Galilee. He went there by the shortest route, straight through Samaria (4:4), even though most Jews took a longer route to avoid that despised region (see exposition on 2 Kings 17:24-41).

4:5-26 *. . . brings living water to a Samaritan.* Arriving in the Samaritan town of Sychar, Jesus encountered a woman at a public well. When he asked her for a drink, she was surprised that he would speak to any woman in public (see 4:27), let alone a Samaritan woman (4:7-9). Thus having her full attention, Jesus was able to point her to

- the possibility of spiritual refreshment and eternal life (4:10, 13-14)
- her need for both (4:16-24)
- the fact that he himself was the source of both (4:26)

4:27-42 *The soul winner from Sychar.* After her conversation with Jesus, the excited Samaritan woman went back to Sychar and told everyone what he had said to her (4:27-29). Many of them came to meet Jesus (4:30) and believed in him, not just as a miracle worker but as the Messiah (4:39-42). Meanwhile, Jesus exhorted his disciples concerning the importance of their ministry (4:31-38).

4:43-54 *The nobleman's son.* After two days in Sychar, Jesus came to Galilee, where he was well received (4:43-45). When a nobleman sought healing for his son, Jesus pronounced the son healed without actually seeing him. When the nobleman heard that his son had recovered at the exact time of Jesus' pronouncement, he and his whole family believed (4:46-54).

5:1-9 *He misses the stirring, but gets his healing.* Back in Jerusalem on a Sabbath, Jesus visited the pool of Bethesda. Many sick people were gathered there, believing it to provide healing periodically when an angel stirred its waters. According to local tradition, only the first one in the water after each stirring would be healed. When a sick man explained to Jesus that he was never able to reach the water first, Jesus healed him—a perfect picture of spiritual healing that comes only through faith and not by self-effort.

5:10-23 *Sabbath breaker and blasphemer?* When the Jewish leaders realized Jesus had healed the man on the Sabbath, they began persecuting and plotting to kill him (5:10-16). When Jesus spoke of God as his own Father, their hatred grew more intense (5:17-18). Jesus spoke of his oneness with the Father and their shared purposes in relating to humankind (5:19-23).

Jesus told the healed man to sin no more, lest he end up physically worse than before being healed (5:14), implying that, in this case, the suffering had resulted from specific sins. However, not all sickness results from specific sins (compare 9:1-3).

5:24-30 *Two resurrections: The good and the bad.* Jesus proclaimed the gospel in the simplest of terms: Faith in him brings assurance of eternal life (5:24). The Greek verb tense of "have already passed" implies this is a permanent, accomplished fact (compare 3:16-18). He went on to describe two important periods of time in God's dealings with people:

- "The time is coming, in fact it is here . . ." (5:25-27) points to the time when people will be able to receive Christ and be spiritually regenerated. This time period, the church age, has lasted two millennia so far.
- The second "time" that is "coming" (5:28-30) refers to the future resurrection of the dead, which will occur in two parts (5:29). The saved will be raised, and then 1,000 years later the wicked will be raised for the final judgment (compare Dan. 12:2; Rev. 20:4-5).

5:31-47 *Four witnesses to the living Word.* Jesus offered four "witnesses" to validate his identity as the Son of God:

- God the Father (5:31-32, 37-38)
- John the Baptist (5:33-35)
- his own miraculous signs (5:36)
- OT Scripture (5:39-47)

The Jews, however, had failed to believe the testimony of these witnesses (5:37-47; see 1:26-34).

6:1-13 *"Feed all 20,000? No way!"* Jesus miraculously fed perhaps as many as 20,000 people—counting women and children—despite the disciples' skepticism about feeding so many with the meager supplies on hand. Various scholars have suggested at least five reasons for this miracle:

- to show his concern for physical as well as spiritual needs
- to strengthen the disciples' faith
- to prove his messianic claims; the Jews had a tradition that the Messiah would feed them just as Moses had done (see Deut. 18:15; Ezek. 34:14)
- to show the value of small things when given to him
- to illustrate God's faithfulness (see Matt. 6:31-33)

[Matt. 14:13-21; Mark 6:33-44; Luke 9:10-17]

6:14-15 *His purpose: Not a crown but a cross.* When many in the crowd rightly recognized Jesus as the Messiah, they tried to make him their earthly king. Knowing, however, that such was not God's plan, Jesus withdrew from them to spend some time alone in prayer, as he often did (see Luke 5:16).

6:16-21 *Walking in wind and wild waves.* As Jesus prayed alone, his disciples were rowing their boat across the Sea of Galilee to Capernaum when a storm arose. Jesus appeared to them walking on the water. This was not some flippant show of his power. He had seen their dilemma from the mountain where he was praying and went to their rescue.

[Matt. 14:22-33; Mark 6:45-52] The storm must have been very intense to frighten these men, most of whom had dealt often with Galilee's treacherous waters (see exposition on Luke 8:22-25).

6:22-40 *"I am the bread of life."* The next day those present at the miraculous feeding went to Capernaum looking for Jesus (6:22-24). When they found him, he accused them of seeking him only because he had fed them, and urged them instead to seek spiritual blessings (6:25-27). When they expressed a desire to please God, he said that the only thing they needed to do was to believe in him (6:28-29; compare 1 John 5:4-5). When they asked for a sign comparable to manna, Jesus said that he himself was the "bread of life," who could satisfy their spiritual hunger and give them everlasting life (6:30-40). Jesus' remarks should have reminded the people of his provision of physical bread, proving he could fill their spiritual needs as well.

It is interesting that Jesus spoke those words in the synagogue in Capernaum (see 6:59), whose ruins include an engraving of a pot of manna. 6:35 is the first of Christ's seven "I am" statements in John (see *Unique Features*). On 6:37, see exposition on 1 Peter 1:1-2.

6:41-59 *Confusion about the Bread of Life.* Knowing Jesus' earthly family, the Jews were offended by his claims to be the "bread of life" (6:41-42). Jesus responded that only those granted faith by God could understand and respond to him, but those who did respond would find everlasting life (6:43-50). Prophesying his sacrificial death, Jesus then declared that his very flesh was the bread of life (6:51) and that only by in some way "eating" his flesh and "drinking" his blood could anyone have everlasting life (6:53-58). Jesus' words caused much confusion among his listeners (6:52), who may have forgotten that he was speaking symbolically of their need to believe on him (see 6:47).

Much controversy surrounds these verses. They led ancient Rome to accuse Christians of cannibalism. And they seem to support the doctrine of transubstantiation—that the bread and wine of Communion actually become the body and blood of Christ. But 6:47 and 6:63 underscore the intended spiritual application: Eating Christ's body and drinking his blood simply mean accepting his sacrifice on the cross.

6:60-66 *Rejecting the Bread of Life.* Not only the Jewish leaders (see 6:41-42, 52), but even some of Christ's disciples (not including the 12—see 6:67-69) found his "bread of life" teaching difficult and therefore ceased to follow him. Jesus made it clear, however, that true spiritual life could be found only in him. It is noteworthy that this mass defection came so soon after an amazing miracle (6:1-13).

6:67-71 *Accepting the Bread of Life.* Jesus asked his disciples if they too intended to desert him. Peter responded by affirming their belief that Jesus was the only source of eternal life. This was one of two noteworthy times when Peter eloquently declared faith in Christ on behalf of all the disciples (see Matt. 16:16). He would be their spokesman at Pentecost as well (see Acts 2). 6:64, 70-71 reveals for the first time that Jesus knew one of the 12 would betray him.

7:1-9 *The hostility of his half brothers.* When opposition in Judea drove Jesus back to Galilee, he encountered hostility there as well—from his own half brothers (other sons of Joseph and Mary). Though they initially rejected his messianic claims (7:5), two of them—James and Jude—later came to faith, as seen by the NT books that bear their names. Assuming their conversions occurred after the Resurrection (see 1 Cor. 15:7), they are a dramatic testimony to the historical reality of that event. (See Matt. 13:55.)

7:10-13 *Devout man or deceiver?* As Jesus went again to Jerusalem, there was much discussion among the masses as to whether he was a good man or a master deceiver (7:10-13). Though many of the leaders wanted to kill him (see 5:10-16), they dared not even debate with him for fear that the people would be on his side (7:13).

7:14-24 *"If you can destroy on the Sabbath, why can't I heal?"* When Jesus again taught in the Temple, the people were amazed at his level of scholarship, considering his lack of formal education (7:14-15). Jesus said that anyone sincerely seeking God could understand the truth (7:16-18). He then exposed a contradiction in their approach to the law: They were willing on the Sabbath to circumcise, which involved destruction of flesh, but objected when Jesus *restored* flesh in a Sabbath healing (7:19-24; see exposition on 5:10-23).

7:25-31 *"How could anyone match his miracles!"* Even in Jerusalem, people rejected Jesus because they knew his human origins and believed that the Messiah would be more mysterious in nature (7:25-27; compare 6:42). Jesus said that they *knew* he was the Messiah, whether they admitted it or not (7:28-29). Others in the crowd did believe, concluding that no one could possibly perform more miracles than Jesus had performed (7:31). Through all the confusion, God was protecting his Son so that he could complete his mission (7:30).

7:32-36 *Is he going to the Gentiles?* When the religious leaders sent soldiers to arrest Jesus, he declared that he would soon be returning to "the one who sent me" and that none of them would be able to follow him there. Not understanding what he meant, they speculated that he was planning to leave Israel and preach to the Gentiles.

7:37-39 *Watered by the Spirit.* On the last day of the Festival of Shelters (see 7:2; Lev. 23), Jesus invited the people to accept him for salvation and for filling with the "living water" of the Holy Spirit (compare 4:14; Acts 2:2-4). The "Scripture" Jesus referred to (7:38) may have been Psalm 78:15-16, which would have been appropriate for the Festival of Shelters, since it recalled the wilderness wanderings.

7:40-53 *"Don't tell us you're his disciple!"* The people were divided and confused in their opinions about Christ, yet there was still apparently enough support for him that no one dared arrest him (7:40-44). When the chief priests asked the soldiers they had sent (7:32) why they hadn't arrested Jesus, they expressed admiration for him. The priests pointed out that only the ignorant masses—and none of the educated leaders—were following him (7:45-49). Nicodemus then spoke up for Jesus and was sharply rebuked by his fellow Pharisees (7:50-53).

On Nicodemus's faith, see 3:1-21; 19:38-42. 7:46 shows that people were impressed by Jesus' authoritative teaching as well as his miracles. 7:52 shows the regional prejudice of Jews living in Judea (compare 1:46).

8:1-11 *The Word writes words on the ground.* The scribes and Pharisees brought a woman caught in adultery to Jesus in an effort to entrap him (8:6):

- If he told them to stone her according to the law of Moses, the Roman authorities might have been irritated since only they could execute criminals.
- If he told them to forgive her, he would appear to go against the law.

Pretending not to hear their accusations, Jesus knelt and wrote on the ground, then declared that whoever among them was sinless could initiate the stoning. When all the men had left, probably due to guilty consciences, Jesus forgave the woman and urged her to mend her ways—showing the wonderful balance between God's grace and human responsibility.

The Pharisees' verbal allegiance to the law (8:5) was hypocritical, since in bringing the woman to Jesus they themselves had broken the law:

- Jesus was not the proper authority (humanly speaking) to officiate at a trial.
- They had failed to also bring for stoning the man caught with her (see Lev. 20:10; Deut. 22:22-24).

No one knows what Jesus wrote on the ground, but some have suggested it was the names of those among the Pharisees who themselves had committed adultery.

8:12-20 *"Who says you're the 'light of the world'?"* Turning again to the Pharisees, Jesus declared himself to be the "light of the world" (8:12; see 1:5-9). When they responded that his testimony about himself was invalid, since he had no corroborating witness (8:13), Jesus said that he did have such a witness—"my Father" (8:14-18). Apparently the Pharisees thought he was referring to an earthly father (8:19). Even amid such heated confrontations, God's hand of protection was upon Jesus (8:20; see 7:30).

8:21-30 *"Someday you'll understand!"* When Jesus again told the Pharisees that he would soon be "going away" from them (compare exposition on 7:32-36), they wondered whether he was going to kill himself (8:21-22). Jesus warned them that if they didn't believe in him they would die in their sins (8:21, 23-24). When he again claimed the truth of his message, they still did not comprehend what he was saying (8:25-27). He said that everything he had been saying would make sense after they had crucified him (8:28-29).

While Jesus' words of reprimand may sound boastful or uncaring at times, Scripture makes it clear that the Pharisees and others who chose to reject him had been given ample evidence to believe:

- his miracles and acts of compassion
- his remarkable prophetic gift (see 4:19, 29)
- his irrefutable teachings (see 7:46; Matt. 22:46)
- his faultless character (8:29; see Acts 10:38)

Even as he scolded the Jews for their unbelief, "many . . . believed in him" (8:30).

8:31-36 *The slavery of sin, the freedom of the Son.* Jesus urged the Jews who had believed in him to "keep obeying my teachings" (also translated "abide in my word"). Doing so would establish them in the truth, which in turn would give them true freedom. When they misunderstood the kind of freedom Jesus meant, he explained that he meant freedom from sin. It is the nature of sin to enslave; it is the nature of truth to set free. And only in God's Word can real truth and freedom be found.

The Jews' statement about never having been enslaved was wrong even in physical terms: They conveniently forgot their enslavement in Egypt and Babylon.

8:37-59 *"Will the real seed of Abraham please stand?"* Jesus continued speaking, presumably to those in the crowd either still disbelieving or uncertain in their professed faith (compare "you are trying to kill me" in 8:37 with 8:30-31). Jesus declared that they sought to kill him, not because they were descendants of Abraham, but because they were children of the Devil (8:37-47). To be a physical descendant of Abraham does not qualify one as his spiritual descendant.

As the irate crowd hurled accusations at Jesus, he continued to claim divine authority (8:48-55). He went so far as to claim to have lived before Abraham, and then even applied to himself a description of eternality with which God the Father had described himself (8:58; see Exod. 3:14). It is no wonder that, at this point, the unbelieving Jews tried to stone him. Whatever one might say about Jesus' being a great moral teacher, his claim of deity leaves room for only one of three responses:

- he was a lunatic,
- he was a liar,
- or he was truly God, just as he claimed to be.

9:1-7 *When the Light gives sight.* When his disciples wondered whose sin had caused a man's blindness, Jesus said he had been born blind so that "the power of God could be seen in him" (9:3). Then, once more declaring himself to be the light of the world (9:5; see 8:12), Jesus told the man he could be healed by washing in the pool of Siloam. The man did so and was healed. This is the only recorded time Jesus required anyone to do anything other than believe in order to be healed.

The disciples and apparently the Pharisees as well believed that suffering results from personal sin (9:2, 34; see exposition on 5:10-23). Some rabbis even taught that a baby could sin in its mother's womb. Although the issue is complicated, since the consequences of parents' actions can profoundly affect the lives of their children (see exposition on Ezek. 18:1-18), Jesus made it clear that suffering does not always result from sin (9:3).

9:8-41 *When those with sight refuse the Light.* When word began to spread concerning this healing, the formerly blind man told his skeptical friends that "the man they call Jesus" had healed him (9:8-12). When the friends brought the man to the Pharisees, they said that Jesus could not be from God since he had healed on the Sabbath (9:13-17). Then, they decided that the man had not really been blind at all! (9:18)

The man's parents confirmed that he had been blind but, out of fear of the Pharisees, claimed not to know who had healed him (9:19-23). When the Pharisees again quizzed the healed man, he stuck to his story and gave eloquent testimony to Jesus, and the Pharisees threw him out of the synagogue (9:24-34). When Jesus heard what had happened, he found the healed man and identified himself as the Son of God, whereupon the man worshiped him (9:35-39).

When some listening Pharisees sarcastically asked Jesus if he considered them also to be blind, he stated the paradox that permeates the story: Those claiming the most spiritual sight are often the most spiritually blind (9:40-41).

Note the progression in the blind man's perception of Jesus: from seeing him as an ordinary man (9:11) to realizing he was a prophet (9:17) to worshiping him as Lord (9:38). How tragic, however, that the man's seeing parents apparently refused the light of Christ because they preferred the approval of the Pharisees (9:22; see 12:42-43; Prov. 29:25).

10:1-10 *The Shepherd gives life to his sheep.* Having again rebuked the Pharisees for their unbelief, Jesus presented himself as a "good shepherd" (10:1-30). He began by talking of how he selects and ministers to his flock (10:1-10). Several truths are highlighted in these verses:

- Jesus is the only true Shepherd; all other religions or ways of coming to God are false (10:1-2).

- Both the "gatekeeper" and the sheep recognize Jesus as the true Shepherd (10:3-5; compare 1:29; 4:29).
- Jesus has a close relationship with his sheep, unlike other religious leaders (10:3-5; compare Ps. 23).
- Jesus is the way to salvation (10:9) and to sanctification (10:10). Some have suggested that "life" (10:10) speaks of the peace *with* God that comes with salvation (see Rom. 5:1), while the life we can have "in all its fullness" (or "more abundantly") speaks of the peace *of* God that comes with sanctification (see exposition on 17:6-19; Phil. 4:7).

10:11-18 *The Shepherd gives his life for his sheep.* Using the image of a shepherd who is willing to give his life to protect his sheep, Jesus predicted his own substitutionary death on the cross. The decision to lay down his life was his own but was worked out in his relationship with the heavenly Father (10:15, 17-18). Jesus also predicted his resurrection (10:18). (See also Heb. 13:20; 1 Pet. 5:4.)

10:19-21 *Messiah or madman?* As on previous occasions, Jesus' teaching caused division among his listeners (see 7:43; 9:16). Some accused him of being demon possessed or insane. Others remembered the miracles and hoped he really was the Messiah.

10:22-30 *"My sheep hear my voice."* Once again the Jews asked Jesus whether or not he was the Messiah (10:22-24), and he replied that he had affirmed his Messiahship many times already, both by his words and by his works (10:25). Those who believed (the sheep) had heard and had begun to follow him (10:27), while those who didn't believe had not (10:26). To the believers, Jesus promised an eternal life that they could never lose (10:28; see 2 Cor. 1:19-22; Eph. 1:13-14; 1 Pet. 1:3-5; and exposition on Rom. 8:31-39). It was guaranteed by both the Father and the Son, who, said Jesus, are one (8:29-30).

The Good Shepherd sermon took place during the Festival of Dedication (10:22), which commemorated the rededication and cleansing of the Temple following its defilement by Antiochus Epiphanes 170 years before Christ (see *Matthew: Background*). It is celebrated today as Hanukkah.

10:31-33 *"He says he's the Son of God? Stone him!"* Hearing Jesus claim to be one with God, the Jews tried to stone him. While some today might say Jesus was speaking of a vague spiritual unity with God, the Jews understood his words as a claim of deity and, considering it blasphemy, prepared for the appropriate response (see Lev. 24:16).

10:34-42 *"If you don't believe my words, believe my works."* Jesus asserted that, even if the Jews couldn't accept his claims of deity, the miracles he had performed should be sufficient grounds for faith. When he again referred to his deity, however (10:38), they again tried to seize him. He escaped, and ministered beyond the Jordan (10:39-42). Note Christ's affirmation of the OT's authority and inerrancy (10:35). On "You are gods" (10:34-35), see exposition on Psalm 82.

11:1-5 *"He's sick. Can you help him?"* When Mary and Martha notified Jesus that Lazarus was sick, Jesus told his disciples that the illness would bring glory to God.

11:6-16 *"He's dead. I'll go and raise him!"* Though Jesus had a deep affection for this family from Bethany, he remained where he was for two days (11:6, see NLT, NIV). When he finally announced his plans to go to Judea, where Bethany was located, his disciples tried to discourage him, remembering previous trouble there. Jesus then told them that Lazarus was dead but that he intended to raise him (11:7-15).

The deliberate two-day delay (11:6) may have been in response to a Jewish superstition that a person's spirit hovered over the body for three days after death and that resurrection during that time was at least remotely possible. Jesus wanted to be sure that there could be no such erroneous explanation for his raising of Lazarus.

Death for the believer is a peaceful sleep (11:11; see Acts 7:60; 1 Cor. 15:6; 1 Thess. 4:13). However, it is not an unconscious "soul sleep" (see exposition on Luke 16:19-31). 11:14 shows Christ's omniscience.

11:17-37 *"I am the resurrection and the life."* When Jesus arrived at Bethany, Lazarus had been dead for four days. When Martha expressed regret that Jesus hadn't arrived in time to heal Lazarus, but confidence that he would one day live again (11:17-24), Jesus hinted that Lazarus might be living again very soon (11:25-27).

Jesus then saw Mary, who also expressed regret over his delay but didn't share Martha's hope of resurrection (11:32). During a previous encounter with Christ, it had been Mary who demonstrated the greater faith (see Luke 10:38-42).

As Jesus watched Mary weep, he too was moved to tears and was "deeply troubled." The Greek word used here is *embrim*, suggesting anger. It is translated "scolded" in Mark 14:5. This suggests Christ's grief and anger over death itself, the tragic result of Adam's sin (see Rom. 5:12).

11:38-44 *"Trust me! Remove that rock!"* Jesus asked for the stone to be removed from the grave entrance, despite the fact that Lazarus's body would have begun to decay. He then offered thanks to God and called for Lazarus to come out of the tomb, and Lazarus came out, still bound in his grave clothes (see exposition on Luke 7:11-17).

11:45-57 *"This destroyer of death must die!"* There were two responses to the resurrection of Lazarus: Many believed on Jesus (11:45), while the Jewish leaders intensified their efforts to destroy this giver of life (11:46-53). Meanwhile Jesus retreated to be alone with his disciples, even as his enemies in Jerusalem continued to look for him (11:54-57).

Note that the Jewish leaders were concerned primarily with maintaining their own positions of power (11:47-48). When Caiaphas suggested killing Christ as the best way to do this, he was unwittingly being used by God to predict Christ's death and the salvation it would bring (11:49-52).

12:1-8 *While one anoints, another complains.* Less than a week before his death, Jesus was once again in the home of his friends Lazarus, Mary, and Martha. As they shared a meal, Mary took expensive perfume and anointed Jesus (12:1-3). Judas complained that she should have given the money to them to give to the poor. Judas's motive in saying this was greed, since he, as treasurer for the group, could have embezzled from her gift (12:4-6). As he had done before (see Luke 10:42), Jesus commended Mary's proper sense of values. [*Matt. 26:6-13;* Mark 14:3-9]

12:9-11 *"He'll die again!"* Since many were being converted by the resurrection of Lazarus, the priests began plotting to kill him as well as Jesus!

12:12-19 *Joy and consternation at his coming.* The next day, Jesus and his disciples entered Jerusalem for Passover week, to the great joy of the huge crowds who had come there just to see him (12:12-13). This caused his enemies much alarm (12:19). [*Matt. 21:1-11;* Mark 11:1-10; Luke 19:29-38]

12:20-22 *"Sir, we would see Jesus."* When some Greeks sought an audience with Jesus, they approached the apostle Philip, possibly because he had a Greek name. Philip and Andrew spoke to Jesus about them, displaying again their heart for evangelism (see 1:40-42, 45-46).

12:23-26 *"It's time to plant the grain of wheat."* While the Greeks may have expected Jesus to talk about his triumphant reception at Jerusalem's gate, instead he spoke symbolically of his fast-approaching death. Just as a grain of wheat must be planted and die to produce more wheat, Jesus must now die to give spiritual life to all who believe in him (12:23-24). Likewise, his followers must die to their own lives to produce the fruit of God's Kingdom. If they do so, they will be richly rewarded in due time (12:25-26).

12:27-30 *His voice reassures his Son.* As Jesus contemplated his approaching crucifixion, God the Father audibly spoke words of comfort to him. The people mistook it as either an angel or thunder.

12:31-36 *His crucifixion, Satan's condemnation.* Jesus explained that his crucifixion would mean salvation for people from all nations but would mean judgment for Satan, the "prince of this world" (12:31). When the people again showed their lack of understanding, Jesus encouraged them to believe in him while he was still with them (12:32-36).

12:37-41 *Isaiah and Israel's blindness.* Thinking about Israel's incredible unwillingness to follow their Messiah, John recalled two prophecies of Isaiah that suggested that their rejection of Christ would lead to even greater spiritual blindness (see Isa. 6:10; 53:1).

12:42-43 *The case of the cowardly chief rulers.* Many Jewish leaders accepted Jesus but refused to confess him publicly, for fear that they would be banished from the synagogue.

12:44-50 *Not to destroy but to deliver.* Jesus, the Light of the World, was sent by the Father to save the world, not to condemn it (12:47). The world did not need to be condemned, because it was already condemned (see 3:18).

13:1-17 *The Creator cleanses his creatures' feet.* John now wrote about Christ's last Passover with his disciples (13–17). Aware that his greatest conflict was upon him, Christ nevertheless showed selfless love to the very end, even though one of his inner circle had already decided to betray him (13:1-2).

To show what it means to serve (13:15), Jesus washed his disciples' feet. Peter felt uncomfortable with the situation and initially refused the offer, but soon changed his mind (13:8-9).

Jesus said his disciples were already "bathed" (Greek *louo,* to bathe completely) and only needed to have their feet washed (Greek *nipto,* to splash; 13:10). The picture is of getting one's feet dirty while returning from a public bath, thus needing to wash them again at home. Likewise, a sinner who repents is forever clean (see Heb. 10:1-12), though on occasion he or she may become defiled by sin and require a "nipto" cleansing (see 1 John 1:9).

13:18-30 *Naming his betrayer.* Even as he enjoyed fellowship with his disciples, Jesus told them that one of them would soon betray him (13:18-21), then revealed that Judas was the betrayer. Apparently, however, the disciples didn't understand what he had said (13:22-29). Satan now went beyond influencing Judas (13:2) to possessing him (13:27).

13:31-38 *"Your love will show them my love."* Now that the wheels were in motion for his betrayal and death, Jesus spoke again of his departure and gave a parting exhortation to his disciples: They were to love each other as he had loved them, in order to help others be saved. When Peter said he was willing to die for Christ, Christ predicted that, though Peter eventually *would* die for him (13:36), in the immediate future he would deny him (13:38).

14:1-4 *Preparing a place in the Father's palace.* Before ending the Passover evening with prayer (see 17), Jesus taught on many important themes (14–16). He began with words of comfort (14:1-4) in light of the previous prediction of his death and Peter's denial. He would prepare a place in heaven for all believers and would one day return for them (14:1-3). Jesus assured them that they knew full well where he was going and how to get there (14:4). 14:3 is the only reference to the Rapture in all of the Gospels (see exposition on 1 Thess. 4:13-18).

14:5-6 *"I am the way."* When Thomas protested that he did not know where Jesus was going or how to get there, Jesus responded that he himself was the way. Jesus claimed to be the only way to God, not just one way among many.

14:7-15 *"Show us the Father."* When Philip asked for a revelation of God, Jesus replied that to see and hear from him was to see and hear from God, for he did nothing except at God's direction (14:7-10). Jesus promised to answer the disciples' prayers and exhorted them to prove their love for him by obedience (14:13-15).

14:16-26 *"The Comforter is coming!"* Jesus promised to send "another Counselor" ("Comforter," KJV), the Holy Spirit, who will live with his disciples forever (14:16) and will help them understand the truth (14:17, 26). Obedience is also a key to understanding the truth (14:21), and love is the key to obedience (14:23-24). On the baptism of the Holy Spirit, see exposition on 1 Cor. 12:12-31.

14:27-31 *His gift of peace.* Jesus promised a peace that transcends earthly circumstances (14:27), and encouraged the troubled disciples to rejoice that he would soon be with his heavenly Father again (14:28-31).

15:1-8 *Fruit, more fruit, much fruit.* Jesus is the vine, and believers are the branches. For a branch to bear fruit it must have been cleansed by the Father (salvation, 15:3) and must then abide in the Son (discipleship, 15:4-11). Committed believers will progress from fruit to more fruit to much fruit (15:2, 5, 8). However, if a branch fails to bear fruit, it is rejected and cast aside (15:2, 6). Various scholars suggest that these rejected branches represent Christians who

- lose their salvation; but this would contradict many other Scriptures (see exposition on 10:22-30)
- are no longer useful to God because of habitual sin
- commit the "sin that leads to death" mentioned in 1 John 5:16, in which case the "burning" (15:6) may refer to the *"bema"* judgment of believers (see exposition on 1 Cor. 3:10-17)
- are merely professing Christians, who are finally severed from their superficial connection with Christ (as had already happened with Judas)

15:9-17 *The fruit of obedience: Love and joy.* If we obey Christ, we will abide in his love and will have true joy (15:9-11). With Christ as our example, and secure in our friendship with him, we are to love each other (15:12-17).

15:18–16:5 *The promise of persecution.* Those who hate Christians do so because of their hatred for Christ (15:18-

25). There is no logical explanation for such hatred, since they have seen ample evidence of Christ's deity (15:22-25). Amid persecution, God will send the Holy Spirit (see 14:16-17), who will help believers bear witness to Christ in spite of the persecution (15:26-27). Jesus warned of persecution so that his disciples would be ready for it (16:1-5).

16:6-11 *The third person's threefold work for the lost.* Noticing his disciples' sorrow (16:6), Jesus spoke again of the Holy Spirit, the third person of the Trinity. It was necessary for Jesus to go to heaven so that this Counselor could come (16:7). This does not mean that the Holy Spirit had no ministry in the world up to that time but that his ministry would now expand and intensify. The Greek for "Counselor" (KJV, "Comforter") is a legal term for one who defends a case in court.

16:12-15 will describe the Spirit's ministry of comforting believers. 16:6-11, however, describes his role in "discomforting" the unsaved. He shows them their spiritual need in three areas:

- He shows them that they have refused to admit their *sin* and their need for salvation (16:9).
- He reminds them of Christ's perfect *righteousness.* Christ's righteousness constantly bothered the Jewish leaders; when Jesus returned to heaven, the Spirit took over that "bothering ministry" (16:10).
- The Spirit shows the absolute necessity of God's *judgment* on sin. The best example of this is how Satan (the "prince of this world") has been defeated through Christ's death and resurrection (16:11).

16:12-15 *The third person's threefold work for the saved.* The "comforting" ministry of the Spirit is for believers:

- He teaches the truth (16:13). At first this probably came through prophecies, but then through the written Scriptures that still guide believers today. These truths are from the Father (16:15). See exposition on Romans 8:5-17.
- He reveals the future (16:13).
- He glorifies Jesus (16:14). He does not glorify himself, as some current teachings might suggest.

16:16-33 *First the pain, then the prize.* Jesus told his disciples about all the suffering that he (and they) would go through in the days ahead, before his final triumph at the Second Coming. He compared it to a woman going through labor (16:21), with her intense pain followed by great joy when the child is born.

17:1-5 *Jesus prays for himself.* Jesus ended the Passover evening by praying for himself (17:1-5), his apostles (17:6-19), and his church (17:20-26). Praying for himself, he told God the Father that he had completed his mission on earth, and asked to be restored to his former glory.

17:1-26 has been called Christ's "High Priestly Prayer." It might also be more accurate to call this prayer, rather than Matthew 6:9-13, the "Lord's" Prayer.

Christ refers to God repeatedly as "Father" (17:1, 5, 11, 21, 24-25), a title rare in the OT. The prayer also contains two expansions of that title found nowhere else in Scripture (17:11, 25).

17:6-19 *Jesus prays for the 11.* Jesus told the Father what he had done in relation to his apostles. He had

- told them about the Father (17:6)
- conveyed the Father's Word to them (17:8, 14)
- kept them from spiritual apostasy (17:12)
- sent them into the world (17:18)

- set an example of holiness for them (17:19)

On behalf of the apostles, he asked God to

- protect them in a world hostile to God (17:11, 15)
- unify them (17:11). They would have enough enemies in the world, without fighting each other!
- fill them with joy (17:13)
- sanctify them: setting them apart *for* special use to God and setting them apart *from* the sinful world. The primary means of sanctification is the truth of God's Word (17:17; see exposition on Heb. 10:1-18).

As in all his prayers, Jesus knew God would answer him (see 11:42). Jesus constantly prayed for his apostles. He prayed for them before he chose them (see Luke 6:12-13); during his earthly ministry (see Matt. 14:23); here at the end of his earthly ministry; and in heaven today (see Rom. 8:34; Heb. 7:25).

17:20-26 *Jesus prays for his church.* For those who would become believers after the Ascension (17:20), Jesus prayed

- that they might have spiritual unity (17:21-22)
- that they might be spiritually mature (17:23). Maturity and unity go hand in hand.
- that they might behold his glory (17:24)

These prayers will ultimately be answered at Christ's second coming, when the church will become all it was intended to be.

18:1-11 *"Whom are you seeking? . . . I am he!"* Jesus and the disciples went from Jerusalem to the Garden of Gethsemane, where he prayed in agony (18:1; see exposition on Matt. 26:36-46). Judas, knowing where they were, took a band of soldiers to get Jesus. Perhaps Jesus saw the torches and the group of men coming from Jerusalem as he prayed. In any case, he had foreknowledge of the coming events and actually went out to meet the soldiers (18:4). He didn't hesitate to identify himself, since he knew his time had come (18:4-9).

In an effort to defend Jesus, Peter drew his sword and cut off the ear of Malchus, a servant of the high priest (18:10-11). Jesus reproved Peter for his lack of spiritual understanding. [Matt. 26:36-56; Mark 14:32-52; *Luke 22:39-53*]

That John knew Malchus's name suggests that John was acquainted with the high priest's household; thus, the "other disciple" (18:15) may have been John himself (compare 13:23).

JESUS THE EXECUTED SON OF GOD (18:12–19:42)

18:12-14, 19-24 *The sinless High Priest before a sinful high priest.* Jesus was arrested and taken to Annas, father-in-law of the high priest Caiaphas. Apparently Annas interrogated him (18:13, 19-23) before he was taken to Caiaphas (18:24). (The synoptic Gospels do not record the questioning by Annas, but do record a trial before the entire Sanhedrin, which John omits—see Luke 22:66–23:1. None of the Gospels give much detail about the trial before Caiaphas.)

Christ's trials, both religious and civil (18:12–19:16), were all clandestine, with no due process, violating the spirit of both Jewish and Roman law.

Note that both Annas and Caiaphas are called "high priest" (18:13, 19, 24). Although high priests generally held their position for life, Rome had interfered with that tradition. Annas, the former high priest, still had power, albeit without Roman recognition. [Matt. 26:57-68; Mark 14:53-65; Luke 22:63-71]

18:15-18, 25-27 *He warms himself, then wrongs his Savior.* As Jesus was being questioned by the high priests, Peter denied his association with him (18:15-18). Later, while warming himself at a fire, Peter's attack on Malchus came back to haunt him as one of Malchus's relatives recognized him. Again Peter denied knowing Christ, and just then the rooster crowed. [Matt. 26:69-75; Mark 14:66-72; Luke 22:54-62]

It is unclear whether John, who apparently was with Peter (18:15; see exposition on 18:1-11), was also accused of following Jesus. The young woman keeping the door knew John and let Peter in with him (18:16). In any event, John's loyalty to the Lord is shown by his presence at the cross (19:26-27).

18:28-38 *A Jewish king and a Roman governor.* The Jewish leaders took Jesus to Pilate and accused him of being a "criminal" (18:30). Reluctantly, Pilate began interrogating him. In answer to Pilate's direct question (18:33), Jesus identified himself as King of the Jews (18:37) but made Pilate think about his own understanding of what that meant (18:34-36). Jesus said his Kingdom was "not of this world" (18:36), so Pilate should not have felt threatened by it. [Matt. 27:2, 11-14; Mark 15:1-5; Luke 23:1-7, 13-15]

When Jesus claimed to represent the truth, Pilate wondered aloud, "What is truth?" (18:37-38). The question remained unanswered as Pilate left, though Jesus had already answered it (18:37). Rejection of the possibility of absolute truth means rejection of Jesus, who claimed to embody the truth (see 14:6).

18:39-40 *"Kill the Messiah! Release the murderer!"* After Pilate had sent Jesus to Herod, and Herod had sent him back to Pilate (see exposition on Luke 23:6-12), according to a Passover custom Pilate offered to release a Jewish prisoner. The crowd chose Barabbas, a thief and murderer, instead of Jesus. [Matt. 27:15-21; Mark 15:6-15; Luke 23:13-25]

19:1-3 *Mocked by the military.* The Roman soldiers mocked Christ with a crown of thorns and a purple robe, shouting in jest, "Hail, King of the Jews!" while they beat him (19:2-3). All of this followed the formal scourging, a beating with a leather whip with small pieces of rocks, glass, and metal to produce more suffering (19:1). [Matt. 27:27-30; Mark 15:16-18]

19:4-7 *"Death to the pseudo Son of God!"* Pilate presented Jesus to the crowd arrayed in the mock royal attire, but pronounced him innocent. The chief priests responded with shouts to crucify him, using their concern for the law as the excuse for his murder. [Matt. 27:22-26; Mark 15:12-15; Luke 23:20-25]

19:8-11 *Final efforts to release him.* Having been warned by his wife that there was something special about Jesus (see Matt. 27:19), and having now heard of his claim of deity (19:7), Pilate became afraid and told Jesus he wanted to release him (19:8-10). When Jesus refused to answer Pilate's questions, Pilate reminded him of his authority to kill him, but Jesus responded that all authority is in God's control. He said that the Jewish leaders, more than Pilate, were to blame for his impending death.

19:12-16 *"We have no king but Caesar!"* Pilate tried again to release Jesus, but the Jewish leaders successfully pitted loyalty to Jesus against loyalty to Caesar, even themselves claiming to be Caesar's loyal subjects. Pilate finally gave in to them, and they led Jesus away to be crucified.

How ironic that the Jews, who for both cultural and religious reasons stubbornly refused to worship

Caesar, now called him their king—in the presence of their own true King!

Pilate's de facto condemnation of Jesus was just one more violation of Roman law (see exposition on 18:12-14, 19-24), since he had declared him innocent (see 18:38; 19:4, 6).

19:17-18 *The Savior on the cross.* Jesus was taken to the place of execution and crucified as a common criminal. [Matt. 27:32-50; Mark 15:21-41; Luke 23:26-46]

19:19-22 *The sign above the cross.* Pilate placed a sign on the cross above Jesus, stating that he was the King of the Jews. Though he had seen the political necessity of condemning Jesus, in making this sign Pilate was mocking the Jewish leaders, who were understandably upset by it (19:21). Meanwhile, the thousands who were in Jerusalem for the Passover were able to read the truth about Jesus, whether they understood it or not! (19:20).

19:23-24 *The soldiers beneath the cross.* As was often the case in executions, the soldiers divided Christ's clothes among themselves. His outer coat could not be divided, so they cast lots for it, fulfilling Psalm 22:18.

19:25 *The women near the cross.* Three women, all named Mary, stood by the cross as Jesus was crucified: his mother; her sister, also named Mary; and Mary Magdalene.

19:26-27 *His concern from the cross.* Also at the cross was the apostle John. Jesus told John to look after his mother and told her to regard John as her son.

19:28-30 *"It is finished!"* As death neared, Jesus was given sour wine to drink, fulfilling the prophecy of Psalm 69:21. As he died, he cried out, "It is finished," marking the completion of his atoning work for the sins of the world. In the original the words mean, "It is forever done."

19:31-37 *A pierced side, but no broken bones.* Because the next day was a Sabbath, the Jews wanted to remove Jesus and the two thieves from the cross before sundown. Usually the soldiers would break the legs of the dying men to hasten the end. But Jesus was already dead, so this was not done. A Roman soldier did pierce his side, and both water and blood came out. This may indicate that Jesus literally suffered a broken heart on the cross. It certainly shows that he was actually dead. Both the piercing of Christ's side and the decision not to break his bones fulfilled prophecy (see Ps. 34:20; Zech. 12:10).

19:38-42 *Secret saints on a mission of mercy.* Nicodemus and Joseph of Arimathea took the body of Jesus, wrapped it for burial, and placed it in a nearby tomb. [Matt. 27:57-61; Mark 15:42-47; Luke 23:50-56] On Nicodemus, see exposition on 3:1-21.

JESUS THE EXALTED SON OF GOD (20:1–21:25)

20:1-10 *The sprint to the sepulcher.* On Sunday morning, Mary Magdalene went to the tomb and, seeing that the stone had been rolled away, concluded that someone had stolen Christ's body. She told Peter and John, and they ran to the tomb and saw that it was empty. All they saw were the linen wrappings lying there as if a body had been inside. The Resurrection had occurred without the grave clothes even being unwound!

After making this amazing discovery, the disciples returned home, having not yet connected it with any prophecies of Christ's resurrection (20:9-10).

20:11-18 *She is the first.* Apparently, after Peter and John went home Mary Magdalene remained weeping outside the empty tomb. Jesus appeared to her (making her the first to see him after the Resurrection), but she did not recognize him—probably due to her crying, the dimness of the early morning light, and the fact that she was not expecting to see him. However, when Jesus said her name (20:16), she knew it was he. Jesus then told her not to "cling" to him (the Greek indicates she was draped around his feet) but rather to go and tell the disciples that he was risen—which she promptly did.

Matthew's account seems to indicate that Jesus first appeared to Mary Magdalene and another Mary at the same time (see Matt. 28:1, 9). However, Mark indicates that there was a third woman, Salome, at the tomb (see Mark 16:1). Evidently, when the other Mary and Salome (as well as Peter and John) left the tomb (see Matt. 28:8), Mary Magdalene lingered behind just long enough to catch the first glimpse of Jesus.

20:19-23 *He shows them his hands and side.* In what was probably his fifth appearance after the Resurrection, Jesus appeared to the apostles in the upper room on Sunday evening. The only one of the 11 not there was Thomas. Jesus showed them his hands and side, apparently with the crucifixion markings still there, to prove his identity. He gave them instructions to go out just as the Father had sent him, to preach and minister. He imparted the Holy Spirit to them (20:22) in preparation for the fullness of the Spirit's coming on Pentecost (see Acts 2).

20:24-29 *Why we call him "Doubting Thomas."* When the 10 apostles who had seen Jesus told Thomas, he refused to believe unless he could see Jesus for himself (20:24-25). The next Sunday evening Jesus appeared to all 11, including Thomas. Jesus asked Thomas to touch the nail prints in his hand and the wound from the spear in his side. Apparently God had left these in Jesus' resurrection body as proof of his identity. Thomas responded by acknowledging Jesus as God in the flesh (20:28).

20:30-31 *The background and basis for John's book.* John stated his reason for writing: to record the miraculous signs Jesus did in order to help his readers believe that Jesus is the Messiah and thereby receive eternal life through him. He noted, however, that Jesus did many other miracles as well.

21:1-14 *The very first Christian businessmen's breakfast.* In a comfortable setting by the Sea of Galilee, Jesus made a special postresurrection appearance to seven of the 11 apostles. Having returned to their former trade of fishing, the apostles had fished all night in vain (compare Luke 5:1-6). At dawn's first light, they saw Jesus on the shore but didn't recognize him. When Jesus told them to cast their net on the right side of the boat, they brought in a large haul of fish. The spiritually perceptive John recognized that the stranger was Jesus. The impetuous Peter immediately swam to shore to be with him. Jesus then fixed breakfast for them as they enjoyed fellowship together.

21:15-19 *"Of course, I love you! What more can I say?"* Jesus singled out Peter for a special leadership assignment (21:15-17). In asking Peter if he loved him, Jesus used the word *agape,* sacrificial love, while Peter's response was only *phileo,* or brotherly love. This was perhaps humility on Peter's part, as he bitterly recalled having denied the Lord. The third time Jesus asked Peter if he loved him, he too used *phileo,* graciously meeting Peter at his level of ability to respond. The seriousness of his charge to Peter, however, did not change. In fact, Jesus told Peter that he would mature to self-sacrificing love and would one day give his life for his Lord (21:18). He then repeated the very first command he had ever given Peter: "Follow me" (Matt. 4:19).

21:20-23 *"But what about John?"* Having been told he would be martyred, Peter naturally wondered what would happen to John. Jesus said that was not for him to know: He should concern himself only with God's will for *his* life. Jesus hinted that John would not die a martyr's death, which started a rumor that John would never die at all. Tradition says John was the last living apostle and died of old age.

21:24-25 *"There's too much to ever tell!"* In closing, John affirmed the truth of his account and commented once again on the impossibility of adequately recording everything Jesus did in his earthly ministry (compare 20:30).

PEOPLE TO REMEMBER FROM JOHN

MARTHA

Key Facts: Sister of Lazarus and Mary, worked while Mary worshiped
Total Bible References: 12
Key References: 11:1-44; Luke 10:38-42

Martha Speaks

It's still difficult to take it all in! One day Lazarus was lying in a grave, and the next day he was enjoying himself at supper alongside our honored guest. (11:17; 12:1-2)

"I am the resurrection and the life. Those who believe in me, even though they die like everyone else, will live again." That's what Jesus said to me in the hour of my grief. I assured him that I did believe in him. But oh, how weak my faith was back then. In fact, I actually protested his command to remove the gravestone. Well, my reluctance soon turned to rejoicing when my dead and supposedly decaying brother walked out of his grave! (11:25, 27, 39, 44)

How well I recall that other time when my sister and I entertained the Savior. To my shame, I was so intent in preparing the best possible meal that I left him sitting in the next room! Well, he gently but firmly brought this fact to my attention. So now, on this unforgettable day, after serving in the kitchen for him, I'm determined to spend some quality time with him! (12:1-2; Luke 10:38-42)

Spiritual Lessons from Martha

- As Martha learned, Christ must first minister *to us* if we are to effectively minister *for him* (Luke 10:38-42).
- The greatest truths about Christ are often revealed during times of suffering (11:21-27).
- The most comforting words one believer can say to another grieving believer are those whispered by Martha to Mary: "The Teacher is here and wants to see you" (11:28).
- If we want to see the glory of God (11:40), we must believe and obey the God of glory (11:38-39).

Key Verses

"But the Lord said to her, 'My dear Martha, you are so upset over all these details! There is really only one thing worth being concerned about. Mary has discovered it—and I won't take it away from her'" (Luke 10:41-42).

MARY MAGDALENE

Key Facts: Former demoniac, first to see the resurrected Christ (Mark 16:9)

Total Bible References: 15

Key References: 19:25; 20:11-18; Matt. 27:55-56; Luke 8:2; 24:1-12

Mary Magdalene Speaks

He's gone! Disappearing as quickly and mysteriously as he appeared! But no matter, he's alive! Both my head and heart are still spinning. It's not easy to go from the depths of sorrow to the heights of joy in the span of a breath! He simply said my name, but that was enough. (20:11-18)

My happiness, however, is tempered by just a taint of shame. Why didn't we believe him when he spoke of his suffering and death and resurrection? I especially have no excuse, for did he not free me from seven wicked spirits? (Matt. 20:17-19; Luke 8:2; 24:1-12)

Perhaps my faith would have been stronger had I not seen him die. But I don't think so. Love and loyalty drew me there. But again, no matter—he has defeated death! I must hurry and report all this to the others, as he has commanded! (19:25; 20:17; Luke 24:10)

Spiritual Lessons from Mary Magdalene

- You can give without loving (see Matt. 6:1-2), but you cannot love without giving (compare 20:11-18 with Luke 8:1-3). "Wherever your treasure is, there your heart and thoughts will also be" (Matt. 6:21).
- Unable to believe (or perhaps even understand) Christ's prophecies about his resurrection (Matt. 16:21; 17:22-23), a brokenhearted Mary lingered by the empty tomb, weeping (20:11). Sometimes love is stronger even than great faith (1 Cor. 13:13).

Key Verse

"It was early on Sunday morning when Jesus rose from the dead, and the first person who saw him was Mary Magdalene, the woman from whom he had cast out seven demons" (Mark 16:9).

MARY (SISTER OF MARTHA AND LAZARUS)

Key Facts: Listened to Christ's teachings (Luke 10:38-42), anointed him with precious oil (12:1-8)

Total Bible References: 11

Key References: 11:1–12:8; Luke 10:38-42

Mary Speaks

I only meant it as an act of love! Certainly the last thing I had in mind was to minimize the plight of the poor. Admittedly though, their criticism hurt me, especially the bitter and sarcastic words of Judas. (12:3-5)

But the Master approved, and that's all that really matters. He said that my act of devotion would be remembered whenever and wherever the gospel is preached. He also said it would serve as a preparation for his burial. How it grieves me that he may soon be taken from us, but after all, I suppose that's what the gospel is all about. (12:7; Matt. 26:13; Luke 10:39)

Spiritual Lessons from Mary

- We learn from both Mary and Martha that we should never let the "if only's" of our past (11:21, 32) blind us to the blessings God has planned for our future (11:25, 44).
- Like King David, Mary refused to offer her Savior anything that was not of great value (12:3; see 1 Chron. 21:24).

Key Verses

"But the Lord said to her, 'My dear Martha, you are so upset over all these details! There is really only one thing worth being concerned about. Mary has discovered it—and I won't take it away from her'" (Luke 10:41-42).

NICODEMUS

Key Facts: Came to Christ by night, discussed the new birth (3:1-21)
Occupation: Religious leader (3:1)
Total Bible References: 5
Key References: 3:1-21; 7:50-51; 19:38-42

Nicodemus Speaks

Had only our faith been stronger, Joseph and I might not have invested in 100 pounds of expensive burial ointment! After all, he did repeatedly say his tomb would be needed only temporarily! You would think a well-known Bible teacher should have known this. But to my shame, back then I was even confused about the new birth experience. (2:19; 3:4, 10; 19:39)

Now, I understand his strange words to me on that dark night—about his being lifted up as was the serpent by Moses. He was indeed lifted up—by a cross! But then he rose from the dead, and now his disciples tell me he has ascended into heaven from the Mount of Olives. (3:2, 14; Acts 1:9-12)

And the purpose for all this? I think his words during that midnight conversation say it best: "For God so loved the world that he gave his only Son, so that everyone who believes in him will not perish but have eternal life." (3:16)

Spiritual Lessons from Nicodemus

- Even though Nicodemus at first had honest doubts (see 3:9), he was nevertheless a sincere seeker of truth (3:1-2), unlike others whom Jesus rightly perceived to be insincere (2:23-25). While sincerity alone cannot save, it is the first step toward salvation (compare Mark 12:34).
- However one might fault Nicodemus for coming to Christ by night (3:1) instead of more boldly in broad daylight, the important thing is that he came.
- Few people show more misunderstanding about concepts such as grace and the new birth than do religious people (3:1, 10).
- Nicodemus confused spiritual birth with natural birth (3:4). Being born in a Christian home does not make one a Christian. God has many children (1:12) but no grandchildren (3:3).

- Unlike other Jewish religious leaders, Nicodemus did not allow the scorn of his peers to keep him from following Christ (compare 12:42 with 7:50-51; 19:38-39).

Key Verses

"'What do you mean?' exclaimed Nicodemus. 'How can an old man go back into his mother's womb and be born again?' Jesus replied, 'The truth is, no one can enter the Kingdom of God without being born of water and the Spirit'" (3:4-5).

PHILIP (THE APOSTLE)

Key Facts: Apostle, brought Nathanael to Christ (1:45-46)
Total Bible References: 16
Key References: 1:43-46; 6:5-7; 12:20-22; 14:8-9; Acts 1:13

Philip Speaks

I'll never forget that day when I asked him to "show us the Father." I knew immediately from the look on his face that my request was misguided. Probably I was so fascinated by hearing that voice from heaven that I actually wanted to see him. I still blush with shame, however, when recalling the Savior's sad response: "Philip, don't you even yet know who I am, even after all the time I have been with you? Anyone who has seen me has seen the Father!" (12:20-21, 28; 14:8-9)

What a wonderful Messiah we have, who could miraculously supply food for thousands—even if certain of his disciples doubted his ability to do so! Now that he has ascended, I know that he will keep his promise to fill our spiritual hunger as well. (6:7, 35)

Spiritual Lessons from Philip

- "Has the LORD redeemed you? Then speak out!" (Ps. 107:2). Upon his conversion, Philip immediately began telling others about Jesus (1:43-45).
- "Taste and see that the LORD is good" (Ps. 34:8). Instead of arguing the subject of salvation, Philip wisely advised a skeptical Nathanael to "come and see" (1:46).
- Is Christ an all-sufficient or an insufficient Savior? Sometimes when we are nearly overwhelmed by the sheer magnitude of a problem, we are tempted to wonder, as did Philip (6:5-7). But our God is able (see Eph. 3:20; Phil. 4:19).
- "Sir, we want to meet Jesus" (12:20-22). This request, addressed to Philip by some Greek Gentiles, indicates that they knew he had a special relationship with the Savior. Can this be said of us? See Matthew 5:13-16; Acts 6:15; 2 Corinthians 3:17-18.

Key Verses

"Philip went off to look for Nathanael and told him, 'We have found the very person Moses and the prophets wrote about! His name is Jesus, the son of Joseph from Nazareth.' 'Nazareth!' exclaimed Nathanael. 'Can anything good come from there?' 'Just come and see for yourself,' Philip said" (1:45-46).

THOMAS

Key Facts: Apostle, doubted resurrection till he saw the risen Christ (20:24-29)
Brother: Unnamed (20:24)

Total Bible References: 15
Key References: 11:16; 14:1-5; 20:24-29

Thomas Speaks

Hopefully this time I'm in the right place doing the right thing. I mean, he did say he would meet us here sometime after he rose from the dead. . . . (21:1-2; Matt. 26:32; 28:7)

Admittedly, I've been totally confused concerning this very idea of resurrection. I think it all began when the Master announced his intention to raise Lazarus from the dead. My response to him still embarrasses me. With regrettable sarcasm, I said, "Let's go, too—and die with Jesus." I didn't just question his power to raise Lazarus—I even doubted his ability to protect us from all the hostile people around Bethany. (11:1-16)

Then there was that event in the upper room prior to his death, when he talked about heaven and I once again displayed my ignorance. (14:1-5)

Of course the final shame occurred due to my absence in the upper room following his resurrection, when he appeared to the others. When they told me they had seen him, I refused to believe it unless I could see living proof, in the flesh. (20:19-25)

Well, I certainly got my living proof! And my response that time was something I will never be ashamed of: I fell at his feet in worship! (20:28)

Such memories fill my mind as we sit here in our boats, hoping our nets will yield some fish. He said he'd meet us here . . . Could that be him, standing on the shore? I can hardly see through this early morning mist. . . . (21:1-5)

Spiritual Lessons from Thomas

- Thomas, like many believers today, apparently had just enough faith to make him miserable (11:16). We can avoid such misery by praying regularly (Jude 1:20-21), studying God's Word (Rom. 10:17), and faithfully putting into practice the things we learn from Jesus (2 Pet. 1:5-8).
- Some Christians are frustrated because they have not had the remarkable spiritual experiences that others have had or claim to have had. Jesus pronounced a special blessing on all who remain faithful to Jesus even when there seems to be little tangible proof of his presence (see 20:29).

Key Verse

"Then Jesus told [Thomas], 'You believe because you have seen me. Blessed are those who haven't seen me and believe anyway'" (20:29).

THE TEN RESURRECTION APPEARANCES OF CHRIST

FIRST DAY

1. To Mary Magdalene in the Garden
Mark 16:9-10; John 20:11-18

2. To the Women Returning from the Tomb
Matt. 28:9-10

3. To Two Followers on the Emmaus Road
Luke 24:13-32; Mark 16:12-13

4. To Peter in Jerusalem
Luke 24:34; 1Cor. 15:5

5. To Ten of His Apostles in the Upper Room
Luke 24:36-43; John 20:19-23

REMAINING 39 DAYS

6. To the Eleven in the Upper Room
John 20:24-29

7. To Seven Apostles by the Sea of Galilee
John 21:1-24

8. To the Eleven and 500 Believers on Mt. Tabor
Matt. 28:16-20; 1Cor. 15:6

9. To James, His Half Brother in Jerusalem
1 Cor. 15:7

10. To the Eleven on Mt. Olivet
Luke 24:44-50

ACTS

BACKGROUND
See *Author.* Having recorded the life, death, and resurrection of Jesus in the Gospel bearing his name, Luke now told of the works of the risen, ascended, and glorified Christ through his church. Acts shows the dramatic spread of Christianity from Jerusalem to Judea, to Samaria, to Rome, and "to the ends of the earth" (1:8).

AUTHOR
The unanimous testimony of the early church is that the author is Luke, beloved physician and author of Luke (see *Luke: Author*). This is supported by the similarity in the inscriptions of the two books (Luke 1:1-4; Acts 1:1-5) and by their similarity in character, style, and language. Acts continues the history given in Luke's Gospel. It is widely agreed that Luke, who accompanied Paul on some of his journeys (Col. 4:14; 2 Tim. 4:11; Philem. 1:24), modestly referred to himself in this book as part of the "we" of the missionary band (see 16:10-18; 20:5–21:18; 27:1–28:16).

DATE
Probably A.D. 60–62, since it ends before Paul's release from prison in 62 and makes no mention of the Neronian persecutions that began in 64.

RECIPIENTS
See *Luke: Recipients.*

PURPOSE
- To record early church history and show that the gospel message is based on historical fact
- To show that the gospel applies to all nations and classes of people

A.D. 30 ***Ascension, Pentecost***

35 ***Paul"s conversion***

40 ***Cornelius's Conversion***

47 ***Paul begins 1st missionary Journey***

49–50 ***Jerusalem Council, Paul begins 2nd journey***

60 ***Paul imprisoned in Rome***

UNIQUE FEATURES

- Acts can be called a tale of three cities, as it traces the spread of Christianity from Jerusalem to Rome through Antioch of Syria.
- It can also be called a tale of three continents—Africa, Asia, and Europe.
- It is a book of prayer, recording 18 prayer meetings.
- It is a book of revival, recording nine revivals.
- It is a book of preaching, recording 18 sermons.

COMPARISON WITH OTHER BIBLE BOOKS

Matthew, Mark, and Luke:

- In Acts the door of faith is opened to Jews, Romans, and Greeks. The three synoptic Gospels opened the door of faith to
  - ➤ Jews (Matthew)
  - ➤ Romans (Mark)
  - ➤ Greeks (Luke)

Luke and Hebrews:
See *Luke: Comparison with Other Bible Books.*

The Gospels:

- The Gospels present the work of Christ in humiliation; Acts presents the work of Christ in exaltation.
- The Gospels tell how Jesus came to earth to take upon himself a human body; Acts tells how the Holy Spirit took upon himself a human body, the church.

The Gospels and Epistles:

- Acts is the connecting link between Gospels and Epistles: the sequel to the Gospels, the basis of the Epistles.

The Pauline Epistles:

- Acts provides the historical background of all of Paul's epistles except 1, 2 Timothy and Titus (see exposition on 28:30-31).

OUTLINE

THE WITNESS IN JERUSALEM (1–7)
- Prologue (1:1-5)
- Christ's final instructions; the Ascension (1:6-11)
- In the upper room (1:12-26)
- Birth of church at Pentecost (2)
- Growth of church in Jerusalem (3:1–6:7)
  - Healing the lame man (3)
  - Persecution begins (4)
  - Ananias and Sapphira (5:1-11)
  - Signs and wonders (5:12-16)
  - Persecution resumes (5:17-42)
  - First deacons (6:1-7)
- Martyrdom of Stephen (6:8–7:60)

THE WITNESS IN JUDEA AND SAMARIA (8:1–9:31)
- Persecution resumes, aided by Saul (8:1-3)

Ministry of Philip (8:4-40)
Conversion of Saul (9:1-31)
THE WITNESS TO THE ENDS OF THE EARTH (9:32–28:31)
The church extends to Antioch (9:32–12:24)
Aeneas, Dorcas healed (9:32-43)
Conversion of Cornelius; church's response (10:1–11:18)
The church at Antioch of Syria (11:19-30)
Peter imprisoned and released (12:1-24)
The church extends to Asia Minor (12:25–16:5)
Paul's first missionary journey (12:25–14:28)
The missionaries appointed (12:25–13:3)
Cyprus (13:4-13)
Antioch of Pisidia (13:14-52)
Iconium, Lystra, Derbe (14)
Jerusalem Council (15:1-35)
Paul's new missionary team (15:36–16:5)
The church extends to the Aegean (16:6–21:30)
Paul's second missionary journey (16:6–18:22)
Macedonian call (16:6-10)
Philippi (16:11-40)
Thessalonica, Berea (17:1-15)
Athens (17:16-34)
Corinth (18:1-17)
Return home (18:18-22)
Paul's third missionary journey (18:23–21:30)
Ephesus (18:23–19:41)
Greece (20:1-6)
Troas (20:7-12)
Paul meets with Ephesian elders at Miletus (20:13-38)
Paul returns home, is arrested (21:1-30)
The church extends to Rome (21:31–28:31)
Paul's defense and trials (21:31–26:32)
Before Lysias and the Jewish mob (21:31–22:29)
Before the Sanhedrin (22:30–23:10)
Paul taken to Caesarea (23:11-35)
Before Felix (24)
Before Festus (25)
Before Agrippa (26)
Paul's voyage to Rome (27:1–28:16)
Imprisonment in Rome (28:17-31)

THE WITNESS IN JERUSALEM (1–7)

1:1-5 *The final 40 days.* Luke began this sequel to his Gospel by explaining to his friend Theophilus the interaction between Christ and his apostles during the 40 days from the Resurrection to the Ascension. Christ told them to wait in Jerusalem for the promised Holy Spirit.

1:6-9 *Commission and cloud.* Christ commissioned the disciples to be his witnesses throughout the world and promised that the Holy Spirit would give them the power to do so (see exposition on 1 Cor. 12:12-31). A cloud then transported him to heaven. 1:8 could be seen as a sort of divine outline for the book of Acts (see *Outline*):

- Witnessing in Jerusalem (1–7)
- Witnessing in Judea and Samaria (8:1–9:31)
- Witnessing to the end of the earth (9:32–28:31)

1:10-11 *Just think of it: This same Jesus!* Two men told the disciples that Jesus would one day return:

- Christ's departure to heaven was personal, as will be his return (see 1 Thess. 4:16).
- His going was visible, as will be his return (see Rev. 1:7).
- His going was from the Mount of Olives, as will be his return (see Zech. 14:4).

These two "men" may have been either humans (like Moses and Elijah, see Matt. 17:3) or angels (compare Luke 24:4 and John 20:12).

1:12-14 *Praying with one accord.* Following Christ's ascension, some of the believers met in the upper room (see exposition on Luke 22:7-16) for a special extended prayer session. Besides the 11 apostles, there were

- "several other women" who had followed Jesus from Galilee, including Joanna, wife of Herod's steward (Luke 8:3); Mary and Martha (John 11); Mary (mother of James the Less, Mark 15:40); Mary Magdalene (Mark 16:9); Salome (Mark 15:40); and Susanna (Luke 8:3)
- Mary the mother of Jesus (her final appearance)
- Jesus' half brothers (Matt. 13:55; Mark 6:3), who had been unbelievers during his earthly ministry (John 7:3-5) but were now believers. Two of these are thought to have written the NT epistles of James and Jude.

1:15-26 *The disciples call a business meeting.* Reminding his fellow apostles of the OT Scriptures predicting the defection of Judas (see Ps. 41:9; 69:25; 109:8), Peter led them in choosing Matthias to replace him. Peter stated two requirements for apostleship: to have followed Christ throughout his ministry, and to have witnessed his resurrection (1:21-22).

Though only 120 disciples were present in the upper room (1:15), there were by this time many more disciples as well (see 1 Cor. 15:6).

2:1-13 *Wind, fire, tongues, and the Spirit.* On the day of the Jewish Festival of Pentecost (see exposition on Lev. 23:1-44), a sound "like the roaring of a mighty windstorm" brought the promised filling of the Holy Spirit (2:4; see 1:4-5; John 14:16; and exposition on 1 Cor. 12:12-31), evidenced by the ability to "speak with other tongues." Jews from all over the world who were in Jerusalem for Pentecost heard the apostles speaking in their own languages, leading some to be amazed and others to conclude that they were drunk (2:5-13)—though drunkenness has never been known to give one the ability to speak other languages coherently!

This is the first of only four biblical instances of speaking in tongues (for the others, see 10:46; 19:6; 1 Cor. 14). The generally accepted date for this Pentecost is A.D. 30 (see *Dates of Selected Bible Events*, p. 816).

2:14-21 *"Joel predicted this!"* Standing with the other 11 apostles, Peter boldly declared that the phenomenon of speaking in other languages was not due to drunkenness, but was a fulfillment of Joel's prophecy concerning the visitation of God's Spirit (see exposition on Joel 2:28-32). While Pentecost did fulfill most of that prophecy, its ultimate fulfillment will come in connection with the "day of the Lord" (2:20; see exposition on Isa.

2:5–4:1). Concerning the dual fulfillment of biblical prophecy, see *Introduction to the Prophets*, p. 353.

2:22-36 *"We killed him, but God raised him."* Peter then spoke to the crowd about Christ's death and resurrection. Though Christ had been morally blameless and performed many signs showing his deity, the Jews crucified him (2:22-23). God knew, however, that this would happen, as seen in the prophecies it fulfilled (2:25-28; see Ps. 16:8-11), and in the fact that God raised Jesus from the dead—to which all the apostles could bear witness (2:24, 32). The tongues phenomenon, said Peter, proved that Jesus had ascended to his rightful place in heaven and had sent the Holy Spirit as promised (2:33-35). The conclusion: Jesus is "both Lord and Messiah!" (2:36).

2:37-41 *What an altar call!* When the invitation was given, roughly 3,000 people repented, accepted Christ, and were baptized—the first instance of the convicting ministry of the Holy Spirit promised by Jesus (see 8:12, 36; 9:18; 16:30; John 16:8-9). Acts records several instances of believers' being baptized following their conversion: the Samaritans (see 8:12), the Ethiopian (see 8:36), Saul (see 9:18), Cornelius (see 10:47-48), Lydia (see 16:15), the Philippian jailer and his family (see 16:33).

2:42-47 *"Commonism," not communism.* The new believers met for worship, fellowship, and teaching on a daily basis. "Many miraculous signs and wonders" confirmed their faith. They sold their possessions and shared with those in need. Though definitely not communism, this system of mutual ownership might be called "commonism." Note the difference: Commonism says, "What's mine is yours," while communism says, "What's yours is mine." This financial experiment was temporary; it had its problems (see 5:1-11; 6:1) and soon failed (see 2 Thess. 3:7-10).

3:1-10 *Running and rejoicing beside the Beautiful Gate.* Peter and John healed a man who had been lame since birth. He leapt to his feet and praised God, amazing the onlookers. Perhaps they recalled Isaiah's wonderful prophecy about such healing (see Isa. 35:6).

3:11-26 *"He did it! Believe in him!"* Peter quickly gave God the credit for the miracle (3:11-12, 16), while reminding the people of their part in Christ's crucifixion and God's part in his resurrection (3:13-15, 17-18). He urged them to repent, that they might be saved and might receive "times of refreshing" from the Lord as they awaited Christ's second coming (3:19-21). He reminded them that they were the children of the prophets and should therefore be ready to accept the very one spoken of by those prophets (3:22-26).

4:1-4 *Opposition and growth.* As Peter and John continued to speak following the healing of the lame man, some Jewish leaders came upon the scene, expressed great alarm at the rapid increase of believers, and arrested Peter and John. Nonetheless, the church continued to grow. The KJV suggests that about 5,000 men became believers at this time, while most other translations suggest that the number of disciples "totaled" about 5,000 by this time. Even with this latter interpretation, since it includes only men, the total number of believers could have been as much as 10,000–20,000. Such growth was nothing less than supernatural. See also 5:14; 6:7.

4:5-12 *"We did it in the strength of the stone."* When asked by the Sanhedrin how the lame man had been healed, Peter replied that he was healed through the power of Jesus, whom they had crucified. Jesus was the "stone" they had rejected, just as the psalmist had prophesied (see Ps. 118:22; see Mark 12:10-11; 1 Pet. 2:4-8).

Peter's boldness before this hostile audience confirmed a promise of Christ (see Matt. 10:16-20) and probably influenced Peter's later advice (see 1 Pet. 3:15).

4:13-18 *"You cannot preach his name!"* Unable to deny that the lame man had been healed, the Jewish leaders nevertheless forbade the apostles to speak about Jesus. Judging from their earlier attempt to conceal the fact of the Resurrection (see Matt. 28:11-15), there is little doubt that the Jewish leaders would have denied this healing if they could have—but the healed man was standing there before them, so they couldn't deny it!

Besides Matthew 28:11-15, there is no biblical record of the Jewish leaders ever trying to deny the Resurrection.

Just as there was no argument against this healing, there is no argument against the evidence of a transformed life.

4:19-22 *"But we must preach his name!"* The apostles' reply to the Jewish leaders' gag order was instant and final: We must proclaim what we have seen and heard. They were not going to obey the commands of mere humans when they conflicted with the commands of God. Fearing the reaction of the crowd if they beat them, the leaders again threatened Peter and John and released them.

4:23-31 *A prayer for courage.* The apostles, joined by other disciples, prayed for courage in the face of such opposition, reminding themselves of David's prophecy of bitter hostility against the Son of God (see Ps. 2). The Holy Spirit shook the building where they were praying.

4:32-37 *Great power, great grace, great giving.* As the apostles continued to bear witness to the Resurrection, the believers continued to share with each other (compare 2:44), even selling their property to contribute to the common purse. (4:32-35). One of many making such a sacrifice was Barnabas, so named because of his gift of encouragement (4:36-37). Barnabas would become a key figure in the church's missionary outreach (see 9:26-27; 11–15).

5:1-11 *They lie, then they die.* Ananias and his wife, Sapphira, were struck dead by God for lying about a gift to the church. Their fate recalls that of Achan (see Josh. 7:10-26):

- Satan used Achan as well as Ananias and Sapphira to attack God's people from within the camp.
- The sin of all three involved greed and lying.
- All three were confronted and condemned by God's chief spokesperson at the time.
- All three were killed for their sin.
- All three served as examples to the people (5:11; see Josh. 22:20; 1 Cor. 10:1-6).

5:12-16 *The sick, the signs, and Peter's shadow.* As the church grew, the apostles continued their miracle-working ministry. Many believed that even the touch of Peter's shadow would heal them, and all who had such faith were healed.

5:17-28 *An angel and an empty prison.* Alarmed again by the church's rapid growth, the Jewish leaders put the apostles in prison, but they were soon released by an angel and continued preaching (5:17-21). When the leaders realized what had happened, they again ordered the apostles to cease preaching (5:22-28). This is the first of three miraculous prison releases in Acts (see 12:6-10; 16:26-27). It also marks the first of six angelic appearances in Acts (see 8:26; 10:3, 22; 12:7; 12:23; 27:23).

5:29-32 *"We must obey our Lord!"* Again the apostles refused to stop preaching (see exposition on 4:19-22), saying, "We must obey God rather than human authority" (5:29). Peter believed in law and order (see 1 Pet. 2:13-14), but this time followed God's higher law.

5:33-42 *Great advice from Gamaliel.* Recalling some recent popular uprisings, a member of the Sanhedrin named Gamaliel advised the leaders to leave the disciples alone: Their ultimate success or failure would show whether or not they had God's approval (5:33-39). The other members agreed and, after again threatening and beating the apostles, they let them go. The apostles rejoiced that God had counted them worthy to suffer for him, and continued to witness (5:40-42).

6:1-7 *Seven servants of God.* Following a problem in the church concerning the distribution of food, the 12 selected seven Spirit-anointed men to handle future problems. Among the seven were Stephen and Philip. The Hellenists (6:1) were Jews, mainly from outside of Palestine, who had adopted Greek culture. Laying on of hands (6:6) was done for various reasons in Bible times:

- as a benediction (see Matt. 19:13, 15; Gen. 48:14-20)
- for healing (see Mark 5:23; 6:5)
- to impart the Holy Spirit (see 8:17, 19; 9:17)
- for ordination (6:6; see 13:3; Num. 8:9-10; 1 Tim. 4:14; 2 Tim. 1:6)

6:8-15 *The man with the face of an angel.* Stephen was confronted by Jews from a certain synagogue. Unable to withstand his Spirit-anointed wisdom, they accused him of blasphemy and had him arrested. To the amazement of his tormentors, he stood before the Sanhedrin with an angelic glow upon his face.

7:1-53 *History 101: Stiff-necked fathers and sons.* When asked if the charge of blasphemy against him was true, Stephen answered with what amounted to a lesson in Israelite history. He showed how Israel had repeatedly resisted the people God sent to save them (7:2-50), culminating in their rejection of Christ (7:51-53).

7:54-60 *"Lord, forgive them."* As he was being stoned, Stephen saw Jesus standing at God's right hand and asked him to forgive his executioners. Saul, who would later, as Paul, become the leading missionary of the early church, assisted in Stephen's stoning (7:58; see 8:1).

Stephen was the first of three people to see Jesus after his ascension (7:55; see 9:3-6; Rev. 1:10; 12-16). Note that Stephen saw Jesus standing at God's right hand. This is the only reference to the Savior standing (after the Ascension) until the book of Revelation. In all other descriptions he is said to be seated (see 2:34; Matt. 26:64; Eph. 1:20; Col. 3:1; Heb. 1:3; 13; 8:1; 10:12). Perhaps our Lord rises to welcome his saints home.

THE WITNESS IN JUDEA AND SAMARIA (8:1–9:31)

8:1-3 *Enter Saul, scatterer of sheep.* Saul, who had held the clothes of those stoning Stephen (7:58), now helped launch a full-scale persecution of believers.

8:4-8 *The Greater Samaritan Crusade.* Philip the Evangelist, one of those appointed to serve the church (6:5), went to Samaria (see 1:8), where he performed many miracles and proclaimed the gospel, with many responding.

8:9-25 *"The Spirit's power cannot be bought!"* A Samaritan named Simon, who had once attracted large crowds with his sorcery, responded to the

OUTREACH OF THE APOSTLES

OPERATION HOLY LAND

CHAPTERS 1–12

The Greater Jerusalem Crusade

Headed Up by

PETER THE FISHERMAN

Assisted by

JOHN, STEPHEN, and PHILIP

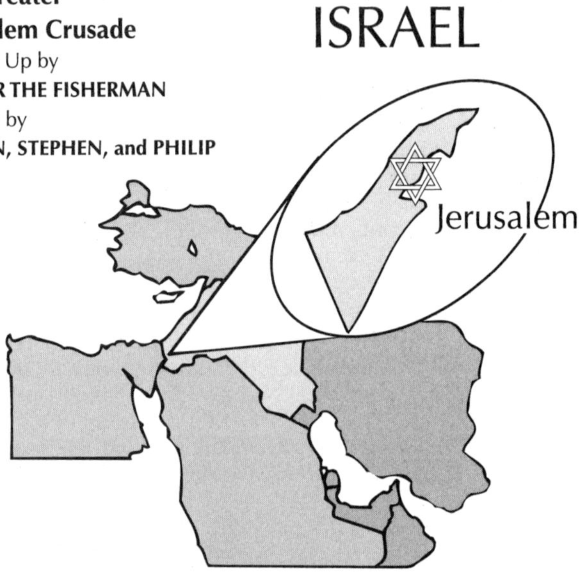

OPERATION WHOLE EARTH

CHAPTERS 13–28

The Global Crusade

Headed Up by

PAUL THE TENTMAKER

Assisted by

BARNABAS, SILAS, MARK TIMOTHY, and LUKE

gospel (8:9-13). When Peter and John came to Samaria to impart the Holy Spirit to the new believers (8:14-17), Simon saw the manifestations of the Spirit and offered to pay the apostles for that power (8:18-19). Peter promptly set him straight (8:20-24). Peter and John then returned to Jerusalem, preaching in many Samaritan villages on the way (8:25). Simon's action has given us the word *simony,* the buying and selling of religious rights and offices.

8:26-40 *"How can I understand it?"* Philip was led by the Spirit from Samaria to the Gaza Desert, where he encountered an Ethiopian eunuch (a royal official) in his chariot, reading Isaiah 53. When Philip explained the gospel based on that passage, the eunuch believed and was baptized.

The eunuch's question (8:31) reflects the tragic condition of lost sinners: How can they understand God's will unless someone guides them (see Rom. 10:13-15)? Philip was able to respond to his need and lead him to Christ based on Scripture (8:35; compare Luke 24:27-32, 45). 8:35 tells, in a nutshell, why the Bible was written.

9:1-19 *Blinded, that he might see.* One day in the year 35, about five years after Pentecost, Saul was on a mission to persecute Christians in Damascus when he was knocked from his horse and blinded by a heavenly light. Jesus appeared to him, asking why he was fighting so hard against him (9:1-5). Saul was taken to Damascus, where God commissioned a timid believer named Ananias to heal his blindness, assuring him that Saul had been chosen to take the gospel to the Gentiles (9:6-16). Having been healed, Saul was baptized (9:17-18).

Several times in Acts, the church is described as "the Way" (9:2; see 19:9, 23; 22:4; 24:14, 22).

9:20-31 *From persecutor to persecuted.* The newly converted Saul persuasively preached Christ in the Damascus synagogue, to the amazement of all who had known him as an enemy of Christ (9:20-22). Learning of a plot against his life, Saul escaped to Jerusalem, where Barnabas assured the Christians that he had been genuinely converted (9:23-27). Soon however, people in Jerusalem were trying to kill him, so he returned to Tarsus, his hometown (9:28-31). The year was A.D. 38, three years after his conversion (see exposition on Gal. 1:13-24).

THE WITNESS TO THE ENDS OF THE EARTH (9:32–28:31)

9:32-43 *Alive at her own funeral!* Meanwhile in Jerusalem, Peter healed Aeneas, resulting in many conversions (9:32-35). He then resurrected Dorcas (9:36-43), and many more came to faith.

10:1-33 *Sincere seeker, reluctant witness.* About 10 years after Pentecost, in the year A.D. 40, an angel appeared to Cornelius, a Gentile military man who was sincerely seeking God. The angel told him a man named Peter would show him how to find God, and Cornelius immediately sent for Peter (10:1-8).

Meanwhile at Joppa, Peter, unaware of all this, saw a vision in which he was told to eat some animals that the law classified as unclean (see Lev. 11:1-47). In the vision he refused to do so, and God rebuked him for his disobedience (10:9-16). At that moment the three men sent by Cornelius arrived, and Peter went with them back to Cornelius (10:17-23).

When they met, Peter and Cornelius shared with each other the amazing circumstances that had brought them together (10:24-33). Peter explained how the vision had helped him overcome his prejudice against Gentiles (10:28-29), and Cornelius expressed his eagerness to hear whatever Peter might have to say as God's spokesman (10:33).

Peter's initial reply concerning the unclean animals (10:14) is a great contradiction. If God is "Lord," one cannot say no to him.

10:34-43 *Cornelius gets a gospel summary.* Knowing that Cornelius had heard reports of Christ's earthly ministry (10:37-38), Peter gave personal testimony to the truth of those reports, especially the fact of his resurrection (10:39-41), then declared that Christ's resurrection made salvation possible for all who believe in him, whether Jew or Gentile (10:42-43).

10:44-48 *Baptized by the Spirit and in water.* At that moment God's Spirit fell upon Cornelius and all his household, regenerating them and causing them to speak in tongues, whereupon Peter baptized them. Cornelius's conversion is the third of three great conversion stories in Acts involving descendants of each of Noah's sons:

- the Ethiopian eunuch, descendant of Ham
- Saul, descendant of Shem
- Cornelius, descendant of Japheth

11:1-18 *Convinced of God's grace.* When the legalistic Jewish Christians in Jerusalem complained about Peter's association with the Gentile Cornelius (11:1-3), Peter carefully explained his vision (11:4-10), God's revelation to Cornelius (11:11-14), and the confirming sign of the Holy Spirit (11:15-17). This convinced the Jewish believers that God had indeed offered salvation to both Jews and Gentiles.

11:19-30 *Barnabas and Saul help a young church grow.* When a new church was formed in Antioch, Barnabas was sent by the Jerusalem church to help it. He in turn brought Saul from Tarsus (11:25-26; see 9:28-31) to help him. It was here in Antioch that believers were first called Christians—one of only three times this term occurs in the Bible (see 26:28; 1 Pet. 4:16). Having been told by the prophet Agabus that there would be a famine in Jerusalem, the Christians in Antioch sent gifts with Barnabas and Saul to those in Jerusalem (see exposition on 20:1-6).

12:1-17 *"Wake up, Peter! It's a jail break!"* Trying to earn the favor of the Jewish religious leaders, Herod Agrippa executed James the apostle and then put Peter in prison, planning to kill him as well (12:1-4). When believers prayed, God sent an angel to release Peter from prison (12:5-11). When Peter then tried to join the people who had been praying for him, he had difficulty convincing them that he was indeed alive (12:12-17). We shouldn't be surprised when God answers our prayers!

On the eve of his scheduled execution Peter was sound asleep (12:6), perhaps remembering Christ's promise that he would live to be an old man (see John 21:18).

12:18-24 *The penalty for blasphemy.* Unable to find his escaped prisoner, Herod went to his palace in Caesarea. Shortly thereafter, God struck him dead for allowing people to worship him.

12:25–13:3 *The first international missionaries.* Barnabas and Saul (Paul, see 13:9) returned from their mission of mercy in Jerusalem (see 11:27-30) to their home church at Antioch, taking with them John Mark (see *Mark: Author*). The Holy Spirit indicated to the church that they should dedicate Barnabas and Paul "for the special work I have for them" (13:2). This first of Paul's missionary journeys began in the year A.D. 47, some 12 years after his conversion. Concerning those 12 years, see exposition on Galatians 1:13-24.

13:4-12 *When one is blinded, the other believes.* The missionaries' first stop was Paphos on the island of Cyprus. When they witnessed to Sergius Paulus, the governor, a sorcerer named Bar-Jesus opposed them and was struck blind, which helped lead Sergius Paulus to faith. Beginning with 13:9, Saul was known by his Gentile name, Paul, perhaps to help him identify with the Gentile world.

13:13 *Mark quits the team.* The missionaries left Cyprus and sailed to Perga in Pamphylia, part of present-day Turkey. For some reason John Mark left Paul and Barnabas and returned to Jerusalem. While Barnabas had helped get Paul started in his ministry (see 9:27; 11:25-26) and had apparently been the dominant member of the missionary team (see 12:25; 13:2), "Paul and those with him" (13:13) suggests that Paul now became the leader.

13:14-41 *Paul's first recorded sermon.* Arriving in Antioch of Pisidia, Paul was invited to speak at the synagogue (13:14-15). After briefly overviewing Israel's history from the Exodus to David (13:16-22), Paul identified Jesus as David's promised seed (13:23), who had been killed by the Jews in Jerusalem (13:24-29) but was then raised from the dead, just as David had predicted (13:30-37; see Ps. 16:10). Paul explained that, through his resurrected Son, God was offering forgiveness of sins—something the law could not provide (13:38-41).

13:42-52 *"You've had your chance; now it's their turn."* Many Jews responded to the gospel (13:42-43). However, when Paul's next audience included many Gentiles, the Jews began opposing him (13:44-45). Citing God's ancient evangelistic charge to Israel (see exposition on Isa. 43:8-13 and 56:1-8), Paul and Barnabas preached to the Gentiles, and many responded, leading the Jews to expel them from the city (13:46-52).

14:1-6 *The Greater Iconium Crusade.* Going next to Iconium, in Galatia, Paul again spoke in the synagogue, and many responded, both Jews and Greeks. Once again the unbelieving Jews opposed him, and he and Barnabas had to flee.

14:7-18 *"Honest! I'm Paul, not Hermes."* At Lystra, also in Galatia, Paul healed a crippled man, causing the people to worship him and Barnabas as the gods Zeus and Hermes (14:8-13). They tried to point the awestruck crowd to the one true God, but found it difficult to do so (14:14-18).

The eagerness of even the priest of Jupiter to worship Paul and Barnabas may be explained by the Roman poet Ovid's report of an ancient myth: When Zeus and Hermes visited this area disguised as mortals, everyone turned them away except one old couple, resulting in a flood that drowned everyone except this couple. The crowd's worship may have been an effort to avoid a repetition of that event.

14:19-20 *Stoned and left for dead, or so they think.* Thanks to some troublemaking Jews, the same crowd that had tried to worship Paul now tried to kill him, but Paul survived and went back into Lystra to preach, then went to Derbe.

14:21-28 *Discipling the new churches.* Paul and Barnabas then retraced their steps, discipling and encouraging the new converts in each city, and appointing elders (14:21-25). Then, after two years on the road, they returned to their home church in Antioch and reported their great success among the Gentiles. Paul probably wrote his letter to the Galatians, his earliest known letter, at this time.

15:1-12 *Saved by grace or by circumcision?* Some Christians came from

PAUL'S FIRST MISSIONARY TRIP

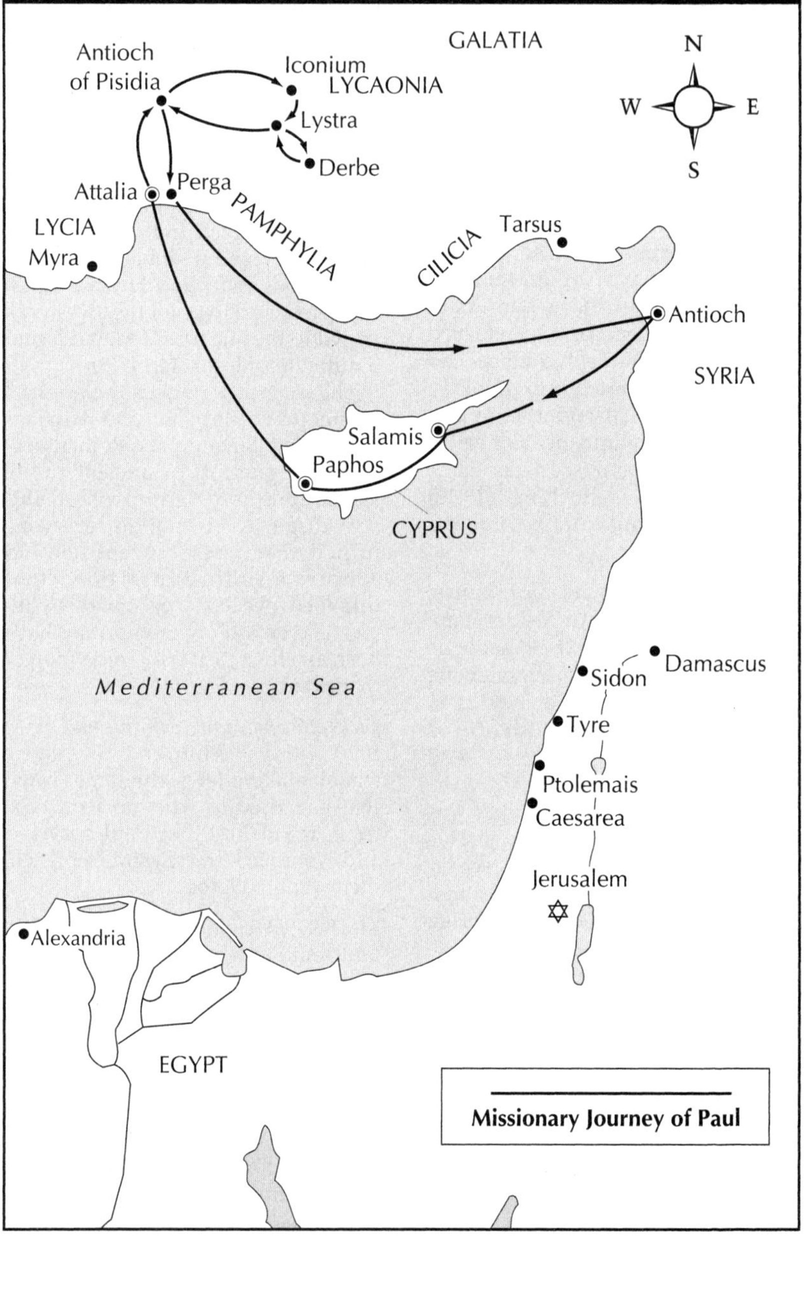

Judea to Antioch and taught that circumcision was necessary for salvation. Paul and Barnabas opposed this heresy and were sent by the church to Jerusalem to settle the matter with church leaders there (15:1-5).

At Jerusalem, Peter reminded the assembled leaders that he had personally led Gentiles to Christ (see 10:24-48) totally apart from the law. His conclusion: Why burden them with the yoke of a law that no Jew had ever kept? Why not acknowledge that Gentile Christians, just like Jewish Christians, are saved by grace alone (15:6-11)? Paul and Barnabas then told of the many Gentiles God had saved during their missionary trip.

15:13-21 *James declares the decision.* After a time of silence, James spoke up. He reminded the council of Peter's report of Gentile faith and that Amos the prophet had predicted God would save the Gentiles by grace (see Amos 9:11-12). He then announced the decision, which apparently had been reached by consensus: Circumcision would not be forced upon saved Gentiles, but they should be encouraged to refrain from unclean food and from sexual immorality.

The decision was announced not by Peter but by James, pastor of the Jerusalem church. Nowhere in early church history is Peter seen exercising official authority over the other apostles.

The decision (directed by the Holy Spirit—15:28) showed great wisdom in that it avoided unduly offending unsaved Jews (see 1 Cor. 10:32-33).

15:22-35 *A special letter to all the churches.* The leaders wrote a letter to Gentile churches announcing their decision (15:22-29). Judas and Silas took the letter to Antioch, where Silas remained, ministering with Paul and Barnabas.

15:36-41 *They disagree, divide, and double!* As they prepared for a second missionary journey, Barnabas wanted to include Mark, but Paul, remembering Mark's defection, refused, so the team split. Paul chose Silas and began ministering to nearby churches, while Barnabas took Mark and left for Cyprus. Happily, Paul was later reconciled to both Barnabas (see 1 Cor. 9:6) and John Mark (see Col. 4:10; 2 Tim. 4:11; Philem. 1:24). This is the last mention of Barnabas in Acts.

16:1-5 *Timothy joins the team.* At Lystra, a young man named Timothy, whose mother and grandmother were godly Jewish women (see 2 Tim. 1:5) but whose father was a nonbelieving Greek, joined Paul and Silas as they continued delivering the letter from the Jerusalem Council to churches in the area.

16:6-10 *Two noes, then a go.* Twice the Holy Spirit forbade Paul to preach in certain areas. Finally, in a vision at Troas, God led the team westward toward Macedonia. "We" (16:10) indicates that Luke had now joined Paul, Silas, and Timothy.

16:11-15 *The first European Christian.* The team sailed to Philippi in Macedonia, where they attended a prayer meeting beside a river. A businesswoman named Lydia, along with her entire household, was saved and baptized.

16:16-24 *When she is freed, they are bound.* Paul freed a demon-possessed girl but incurred the wrath of her masters, who had grown rich from her fortune-telling. They instigated the arrest, beating, and imprisonment of the missionaries.

16:25-34 *Songs in the prison, the gospel in a nutshell.* In the inner dungeon with their backs bleeding, Paul and Silas sang praises to God, and God sent a violent earthquake that opened all the prison doors and loosened the prisoners' chains (16:25-29). Fearing that his prisoners had escaped, the jailer drew his sword to kill himself, but Paul assured him they were all still there. Paul explained the gospel to the jailer, and he and his entire household believed in Christ and were baptized (16:30-34). The prisoners' singing recalls Christ's singing on the eve of his crucifixion (see Matt. 26:30).

16:35-40 *"We demand an apology."* Learning that Paul and Silas were Roman citizens and should not have been beaten, the frightened Philippian officials apologized and begged them to leave town.

17:1-9 *A three-week revival brings trouble.* In Thessalonica, Paul led both Jews and Greeks to Christ (17:1-4). As usual, however, some Jews stirred up trouble, accusing the apostles of turning "the world upside down" and defying Roman law.

17:10-15 *Berean Bible students.* Paul and Silas left Thessalonica by night for Berea, where they found the people more interested in the Scriptures than those in Thessalonica. Once again Paul's stay was cut short because of trouble with the Jews. Leaving Berea, he headed for Athens.

17:16-21 *The preacher and the philosophers.* After a lively encounter with Epicurean and Stoic philosophers in Athens, Paul was invited to discuss Jesus and his resurrection at their public forum, called the Areopagus or "Mars' hill" (17:22, KJV). The followers of Epicurus (341–270 B.C.) believed that while God existed, he had no interest in humankind, and the main purpose of life was pleasure. The Stoics believed God was the world's soul, and life's goal was to rise above all things, showing no emotional response to either pain or pleasure. Both groups took a dim view of Paul's theology, calling him a "babbler" (Greek *spermologos*, 17:18, which described birds making their nests).

17:22-34 *Paul's message from Mars Hill.* Paul began his address to the philosophers by mentioning all the altars he had seen in Athens, each bearing the name of a different false deity. Recalling one altar dedicated "To an Unknown God," he presented to them the true God, Creator and Controller of all things, final Judge of all humanity, and Redeemer of all who would repent (17:22-31). When Paul climaxed his sermon by telling of Christ's resurrection, some of his hearers believed, others mocked, and some weren't persuaded but still had an open mind (17:32-34).

18:1-6 *The testimony of the tentmakers.* Going next to Corinth, Paul was delighted to meet two wonderful believers, a Jewish man named Aquila and his wife, Priscilla, who were, like Paul, tentmakers by trade. He worked with them while evangelizing regularly in the synagogue. After opposition from the Jews, he again turned to the Gentiles (18:6; compare 13:46).

Aquila and Priscilla are mentioned six times in the NT. Having come to Corinth from Rome (18:2), they later accompanied Paul to Ephesus (18:18-19), where they discipled Apollos (18:24-28) and hosted a church in their home (see 1 Cor. 16:19). Still later they apparently returned to Rome (see Rom. 16:3-5). Catacomb inscriptions hint that Priscilla was from a distinguished Roman family.

At this time Paul probably wrote his first letter to the Thessalonians, whom he had just visited (17:1-9). He wrote his second letter to them about three months later.

18:7-17 *Great fishing in Corinth.* From his new headquarters in a Gentile home next door to the synagogue, Paul continued preaching. Crispus, leader of the synagogue, and his entire household were converted and baptized, along with many others

PAUL'S SECOND MISSIONARY TRIP

(18:7-8). Having received special reassurance in a vision, Paul remained in Corinth for a year and six months (18:9-11). During that time Sosthenes, a new leader of the synagogue, tried to have Paul beaten and imprisoned, but was himself beaten by an angry Gentile mob after the governor refused to hear the case.

18:18-22 *A quick trip to Jerusalem.* Accompanied by Aquila and Priscilla, Paul left Corinth for Jerusalem. He had apparently taken a Nazirite vow (18:18) and needed to visit the Temple to complete it (18:21; see Num. 6:1-21). He left his tentmaker friends in Ephesus, promising to return and minister with them if God so willed. From Jerusalem Paul returned to Antioch.

18:23 *On the road again, for the third time.* After a brief report to his home church, Paul embarked on his third missionary journey, which would take him back to Ephesus (19:1).

18:24-28 *The rest of the story.* In Ephesus, Aquila and Priscilla met a powerful Bible teacher named Apollos, whose knowledge of the gospel was limited to the message of John the Baptist. This godly couple explained to Apollos "the way of God more accurately" (18:26), whereupon he went to Achaia and boldly proclaimed Christ.

19:1-10 *Paul's two-year Bible school.* Having passed through Galatia and Phrygia (see 18:23; 19:1), Paul arrived back at Ephesus, where he led some disciples of John the Baptist to a fuller understanding of the gospel, just as Aquila and Priscilla had done for Apollos. Paul then spent two years teaching in a private school, reaching many from all over that area.

19:11-20 *The sick get better; some books get burned.* God gave Paul great power to heal people and cast out demons, but when some local exorcists tried to imitate Paul, a demon-possessed man attacked them! News of this event brought about a revival, with many converts burning their occult books.

19:21-22 *He resolves to see Rome.* As Paul's time in Ephesus drew to a close, he spoke of his hope to someday minister in Rome—a hope that would be fulfilled, though not in the way he might have hoped (see 27–28). Paul probably wrote his first letter to Corinth at about this time, three years after his ministry there (see 18:1-17).

19:23-41 *Demetrius, Diana, and discord.* Paul faced one more crisis before ending his lengthy stay at Ephesus. Demetrius, a craftsman who sold silver shrines of the Greek goddess Diana, instigated his fellow shrine merchants to lead a riot against Paul, charging that his preaching had hurt their sale of shrines (19:23-28). An angry and confused crowd soon filled the amphitheater and held a two-hour-long "Diana rally" (19:29-34). Only when an official warned them that their rioting might bring about Roman punishment did cooler heads prevail.

The temple of Diana was one of the seven wonders of the ancient world (19:27). The image in the temple was of a woman with many breasts, signifying nature's fertility. The original stone from which the image had been carved was believed to have fallen from heaven (19:35), leading some historians to believe it may have been a meteorite.

20:1-6 *From Ephesus to Troas.* Immediately following the uproar over Diana, Paul sailed to Greece, where he spent three months strengthening the believers and collecting an offering for the poor in Jerusalem (see 11:27-30; 24:17; Rom. 15:25-26; 1 Cor. 16:1-4; 2 Cor. 8–9; Gal. 2:8). When he was ready to return home to Syria, a plot by the Jews caused him to change his

PAUL'S THIRD MISSIONARY TRIP

plans and go through Macedonia. Several men joined Paul, including Luke ("us," 20:5), who with Paul soon joined the others at Troas—back on the Asian side of the Aegean.

Paul probably wrote 2 Corinthians, followed by Romans, at about this time.

20:7-12 *He sits on a wall and has a great fall.* While Paul was preaching in Troas, a young man named Eutychus fell asleep on a windowsill and fell to his death. To everyone's amazement and joy, Paul raised him from the dead. Besides the resurrection of Christ and of those raised following his crucifixion (see Matt. 27:53), the raising of Eutychus is the last of eight resurrections in the Bible:

- widow's son raised by Elijah (see 1 Kings 17:22)
- Shunammite's son raised by Elisha (see 2 Kings 4:35)
- man raised by Elisha (see 2 Kings 13:21)
- widow's son raised by Jesus (see Luke 7:14-15)
- Jairus's daughter raised by Jesus (see Luke 8:54-55)
- Lazarus raised by Jesus (see John 11:44)
- Dorcas raised by Peter (see 9:40)
- Eutychus raised by Paul (20:12)

20:13-38 *Passing the torch of testimony.* Having decided against a stopover at Ephesus so that he could get to Jerusalem for Pentecost, Paul sent for the Ephesian elders from Miletus (20:13-17). Paul reviewed his ministry among them (20:18-21, 26-27, 32-35), challenged them to feed and lead God's flock (20:28), warned concerning false teachers that would arise among them (20:29-31), and spoke of the dangers he sensed awaiting him in Jerusalem (20:22-25). Paul and the elders then prayed together and bid each other an emotional farewell.

Paul had spoken of God's grace both "publicly [and] in [their] homes" (20:20). The world's greatest theologian was also a great soul winner. Christ's teaching about the blessedness of giving, which Paul quotes (20:35), is not found in any of the Gospels (see John 21:25). Christ's life, of course, perfectly exemplified such giving (see 2 Cor. 8:9; Eph. 5:2; Phil. 2:5-8).

21:1-14 *Warnings fall on Paul's deaf ears.* Paul and his companions sailed from Miletus to Tyre, where some Spirit-anointed believers tried to warn him not to go to Jerusalem; he ignored their warnings and continued his journey (21:1-6). At Caesarea they stayed with Philip (see 6:5) and his four unmarried daughters, all of whom were prophetesses (see *Prophetesses,* p. 849). While in Caesarea, Paul was again warned against going to Jerusalem, this time by Agabus (21:10; see 11:28). Still, he was determined to go, despite the danger.

21:15-30 *Back in Jerusalem, a failed attempt to appease.* In the year A.D. 57, Paul and his companions, along with some disciples from Caesarea, arrived in Jerusalem and met with James and the other elders to report on their work among the Gentiles (21:15-19). The elders told Paul that some Jewish Christians were accusing him of trying to turn Jewish Christians in other nations away from the law. They suggested that, to dispel those rumors, Paul should take a special vow and visit the Temple, and Paul did so (21:19-26). Rather than appeasing the Jews, however, Paul's gesture only added fuel to the fire as he was falsely accused of bringing Gentiles into the Temple. A mob seized him and removed him from the Temple (21:27-30).

21:31-40 *Rescued by a Roman.* The mob was about to kill Paul when he was rescued by Claudius Lysias, commander of the Roman garrison (23:26). Learning more about Paul in a private meeting, Lysias allowed him to address his tormentors.

22:1-21 *"This is my story."* Defending himself before the angry crowd, Paul reviewed his background and Jewish theological training (22:3), his earlier persecution of Christians (22:4-5), his conversion to Christ (22:6-20), and his call to evangelize the Gentiles (22:21).

22:22-29 *"Do what you want, but I'm a citizen."* When Paul mentioned the Gentiles, the crowd became unruly again, and Lysias had Paul bound and whipped. When Paul revealed that he was a Roman citizen, Lysias became fearful, for he had almost broken Roman law by scourging a citizen (compare exposition on 16:35-40).

22:30–23:10 *Another confrontation, another confinement.* Unclear about the exact charges the Jews had brought against Paul, Lysias arranged another confrontation between Paul and his accusers (22:30). When Paul spoke, Ananias the high priest ordered his assistants to slap him. Paul called Ananias a disparaging term, not knowing he was the high priest. Upon learning of his identity, Paul apologized (23:1-5). Paul successfully divided the assembled leaders on the issue of resurrection, but the resulting uproar was so serious that Lysias once again took Paul into custody—for his own protection (23:6-10).

23:11 *"Yes, Paul, you'll go to Rome."* As Paul sat in prison that night, Jesus appeared and reassured him that this trouble would result in his taking the gospel to Rome—which Paul had longed to do (see 19:21; Rom. 1:13). (Until this divine reassurance, he probably had just been hoping to get out of Jerusalem alive—see Rom. 15:31-32.)

23:12-22 *40 frustrated (and hungry!) men.* More than 40 Jewish men conspired against Paul and took a vow to neither eat nor drink till they had killed him (23:12-15). Paul's nephew learned of the plot and, at Paul's instruction, reported it to Lysias. There is no record as to when those 40 men ate again!

23:23-35 *The midnight ride of the revered Paul.* Lysias sent Paul that very night to Caesarea, center of Roman government, protected by a small army. He sent with him a letter to Felix, Roman governor of Judea, explaining the charges against Paul.

24:1-9 *Charges by the prosecution.* The Jewish religious leaders, along with a lawyer named Tertullus, came to Caesarea to press charges against Paul. After flattering Felix (24:2-3), Tertullus falsely accused Paul of inciting riots against both the Jewish religion and the Roman government, and of profaning the Temple by bringing in a Gentile. He described Paul as a leader of the "Nazarenes," a term used only here of believers in Jesus of Nazareth.

24:10-21 *Answers by the defendant.* Paul pleaded innocent to the riot charges (24:10-13), proclaimed his loyalty to his Jewish heritage (24:14-17), and pointed out that his original accusers hadn't even bothered to press charges (24:18-19). He freely admitted, however, that he was a believer in Jesus and his resurrection (24:14-15), which, said Paul, was the real reason for the trial (24:20-21).

24:22-27 *A more convenient season?* Realizing there was no evidence against Paul, Felix put him under house arrest until Lysias arrived, instructing the guards to treat him gently (24:22-23). In the following days, Felix was deeply affected by Paul's preaching but refused to respond (24:24-25). Two years later, when Festus replaced Felix as governor, Paul was still being detained.

25:1-12 *"Let Nero decide my case."* When Festus visited Jerusalem, the Jews tried to persuade him to bring Paul there, secretly planning to kill him en route (25:1-3). Festus refused but invited them to return with him to Caesarea, where they again brought their false charges against Paul, all of which he refuted (25:4-8). Wanting to curry favor with his Jewish subjects, Festus invited Paul to go to Jerusalem to stand trial. Paul wisely refused. Having spent two years in prison without ever being convicted, he demanded his right as a Roman citizen and appealed to Caesar, and Festus granted his appeal.

The Caesar to whom Paul appealed was Nero, who had begun his reign about five years previously in A.D. 54. Nero's early reign was peaceful and gave no hint of the cruelties to follow.

25:13-27 *"I'd like to meet this man!"* When Herod Agrippa II and his sister Bernice (who reportedly was also his mistress) paid a visit to Festus, he told Agrippa about Paul's case (25:13-21), and Agrippa expressed a desire to hear from this famous prisoner (25:22). Festus eagerly brought Paul before the king, hoping that Agrippa could help him decide what to tell Nero concerning the charges against Paul (25:23-27).

Herod Agrippa II, son of the Agrippa who died for blasphemy (12:20-24), was the last of the Herodian dynasty. He sided with Rome when it destroyed Jerusalem in A.D. 70.

26:1-23 *"Here's the whole story, King Agrippa."* Defending himself before Agrippa, Paul spoke of his loyalty to the law of Moses, asserting that his accusers knew of this though they wouldn't admit it (26:1-5). He then went right to the heart of the matter: The Jews were opposing him because of his belief in Christ (26:6-8). And indeed he himself had violently opposed Christ (26:9-11) until Christ appeared to him, calling him to faith and commissioning him to preach the gospel (26:12-18).

Paul then summarized his ministry among Jews and Gentiles, saying it was for this ministry, not for the many false charges, that he was on trial (26:19-21). Again he proclaimed that Christ, in fulfillment of the OT, had brought hope of eternal life to both Jews and Gentiles (26:22-23; see 26:7-8). Paul knew that Agrippa was well versed in Jewish customs and Scriptures (26:3, 26).

26:24-32 *Almost persuaded?* Festus interrupted Paul's discourse, calling him insane. Paul denied that charge and called on Agrippa to vouch for his interpretation of Scripture (26:24-27). Agrippa replied that he was almost "persuaded" (KJV) by Paul's presentation but then proceeded to dismiss the case, noting that he would gladly have set Paul free, had he not appealed to Caesar. In Greek, 26:28 reads, "In short, you are trying to persuade me to be a Christian," suggesting that Agrippa considered Paul presumptuous to think he could so easily convert him.

27:1-12 *Smooth sailing at first.* In the year 59, Paul was at last headed for Rome, albeit as a prisoner. The voyage was smooth at first (27:1-6), but then they encountered several days of rough sailing before arriving safely at the port of Fair Havens (27:7-8). Ignoring Paul's warning about the dangers of continuing the voyage at that time of year, they prepared to sail to Crete (27:9-12). Though not recorded in Scripture, Paul had apparently been in three previous shipwrecks (see 2 Cor. 11:25).

27:13-20 *But then the storm.* Soon after leaving Crete, Paul's ship was struck by hurricane-force winds. The crew tried everything to stay afloat, but the storm raged many days till all hope was gone.

27:21-44 *"Don't worry, we'll all survive!"* After several days of storm, Paul told the crew God had reassured him that, because he wanted to get Paul safely to Rome, everyone on the ship would survive the storm, even though they would run aground on an island (27:21-26). And that is exactly what happened (27:27-44). Meanwhile, Paul's faith encouraged the others as they prepared for shipwreck (27:33-37).

28:1-10 *Ministry on Malta.* Paul and his fellow shipwreck victims learned that they had run aground on Malta, just south of Italy. When Paul survived the bite of a poisonous snake, the people looked upon him as a god (28:1-6). When he then healed the governor's father, many others came to him and were healed—and presumably heard the gospel.

28:11-16 *Rome at last!* After three months on Malta, Paul finally sailed to Rome, where he was warmly welcomed by fellow believers. He was permitted to live on his own, with just one soldier to guard him. It was A.D. 60, some 25 years after his conversion.

28:17-29 *"Isaiah was right, as always."* Paul met with the local Jewish leaders and explained how, because of his teaching about the Messiah, the Jews in Jerusalem had falsely accused him, leading him to appeal to Caesar (28:17-20). He used the OT to explain the gospel (28:21-23). Some accepted the message, others rejected it, bringing to Paul's mind Isaiah's sad prophecy concerning Israel's unbelief (28:26-27; see Isa. 6:9-10). As Paul's listeners drifted away, arguing about his message, he declared that what they had rejected the Gentiles would accept (28:28-29).

28:30-31 *Under arrest, but free to preach.* For the next two years, as Paul awaited trial before Caesar, he was free to preach the gospel from his home—apparently with great results (see Phil. 1:12-14; 4:22). During this time he wrote his letters to the Ephesians, Philippians, Colossians, and to Philemon.

Paul was apparently freed after those two years (see Philem. 1:22), then imprisoned again sometime later. He probably wrote 1 Timothy and Titus after his first release, with his final book, 2 Timothy, being written during his second imprisonment, as he awaited certain death (see 2 Tim. 1:8, 16; 4:6-12). According to tradition, he was executed by decapitation in about A.D. 67–68.

PEOPLE TO REMEMBER FROM ACTS

APOLLOS

Key Facts: Gifted evangelist, discipled by Aquila and Priscilla
Total Bible References: 10
Key References: 18:24–19:1; 1 Cor. 3:6

Apollos Speaks

I saw them as they entered the synagogue and quietly sat down, this Jewish man and his Gentile wife. They were an interesting couple. Were they seekers? Scoffers? Whatever the case, I hoped my sermon would help instruct them concerning the great truths of the faith. Little did I dream, however, that it would be just the opposite. Thank God for Aquila and Priscilla!

"Apollos," they said, "we want to fill you in regarding events following John the Baptist's ministry." (18:24-26)

I sat there spellbound, hearing the details of Messiah's death, resurrection, and ascension, and the miracle at Pentecost. What doors of service all this would open, preparing the way for a visit to Greece, where God anointed my preaching to strengthen the body of Christ there, especially in the church at Corinth. (18:27–19:1)

I have now been able to minister full circle, from Alexandria in the south, to Ephesus in the north, and Greece in the west. Who else but Paul himself could boast of this? However, I dare not forget how the great apostle put his and my ministries into their proper perspective: "My job was to plant the seed in your hearts, and Apollos watered it, but it was God, not we, who made it grow." (1 Cor. 3:6)

Spiritual Lessons from Apollos

- The person who would teach others must first be willing to be taught, as was Apollos (18:24-26).
- The gift of teaching is not limited to professional pastors or others with theological education. Aquila and Priscilla were tentmakers (18:2-3, 26). We should learn from whomever we can.

Key Verses

"When Priscilla and Aquila heard [Apollos] preaching boldly in the synagogue, they took him aside and explained the way of God more accurately. Apollos had been thinking about going to Achaia, and the brothers and sisters in Ephesus encouraged him in this. They wrote to the believers in Achaia, asking them to welcome him. When he arrived there, he proved to be of great benefit to those who, by God's grace, had believed. He refuted all the Jews with powerful arguments in public debate. Using the Scriptures, he explained to them, 'The Messiah you are looking for is Jesus'" (18:26-28).

AQUILA AND PRISCILLA

Key Fact: Fellow tentmakers who worked with, assisted, and encouraged Paul (18:1-3)

Total Bible References: 6

Key References: 18:1-3, 24-26; 1 Cor. 16:19

Aquila and Priscilla Speak

We just heard the news. Paul has been martyred in Rome by Nero. How tender to learn that we were in his thoughts right up to the very end. (2 Tim. 4:6-7, 19)

What glorious memories Paul's very name evokes. Had it not been for our expulsion from Rome, we would probably never even have met the great apostle. Wonderful ways of God, bringing together three believers who shared the same trade and the same desire for ministry! (18:1-3)

But the miracle continued, for we sailed with him from Corinth to Ephesus just in time to meet Apollos, whom we were able to help to a better understanding of the faith. How gratifying it has been to hear of his effective ministry in the years since then. (18:18, 24-25)

For our part, we'll just go on making tents, always available when God chooses to use us again.

Spiritual Lessons from Aquila and Priscilla

- This dedicated couple, tentmakers by trade (18:2-3), was greatly used by God to minister to both Apollos (18:24-28) and Paul (Rom. 16:3-4; 2 Tim. 4:19). In fact, they converted their house into a church (1 Cor. 16:19). Never downplay or underestimate your lot in life.

Key Verse

"When Priscilla and Aquila heard [Apollos] preaching boldly in the synagogue, they took him aside and explained the way of God more accurately" (18:26).

BARNABAS

Key Fact: Paul's trusted missionary colleague
Total Bible References: 30
Key References: 4:36; 9:26-27; 11–15; Gal. 2:11-14

Barnabas Speaks

The church continues to grow here in Antioch just as it did at the beginning. How wonderful it was back then to see all that spiritual excitement, especially among the new converts. What a privilege to help in the spiritual growth of the church. Then there was that hurried northern trip to select a man as my assistant in the church, one Saul of Tarsus. (11:21-25)

"Christians"—"Christ Ones." That's what the unbelievers nicknamed us back then. What a wonderful time of prayer and worship we had with the other prophets and teachers in Antioch. Of course, it was during one of those glorious sessions that God's Spirit called both Saul and me to the mission field. The next two years would forever change my life, giving me a worldwide view of the need to proclaim the Good News. (11:26; 13–14)

I still wonder who was right concerning our disagreement. Whatever the case, God used that unpleasant event to double his missionary personnel! (15:36-40)

Paul is often in my thoughts. He's now a prisoner in Rome. How thankful I am John Mark is there ministering to him. (28:16, 30; Col. 4:10)

God's commission to us on the eve of our first missionary journey still burns in my heart after all these years: "I have made you a light to the Gentiles, to bring salvation to the farthest corners of the earth." Until my dying day I intend to do just that. (13:47)

Spiritual Lessons from Barnabas

- There's one in every crowd! Barnabas was known and loved in the Jerusalem church as "Son of Encouragement" (4:36). He used to the full his spiritual gift of encouraging others (Rom. 12:6-8; 2 Tim. 1:6).
- Sometimes the greatest blessing one believer can give another is to give him or her the benefit of the doubt. Barnabas did this for both Paul (9:26-27) and John Mark (15:36-39).
- Faithfulness, like charity, begins at home. After Barnabas had proven himself in his home church (Jerusalem, 4:36-37), God used him in many churches (see 11:22-26; 13:5-6, 14; 14:1, 6).
- Even our greatest spiritual strengths can fail when our guard is down. Usually a spokesman for the church's fledgling mission to the Gentiles (15:12), on at least one occasion Barnabas was affected by anti-Gentile sentiment

(Gal. 2:11-13). "When the danger least thou fearest, then the tempter's snare is nearest."

Key Verses
"When [Barnabas] arrived and saw this proof of God's favor, he was filled with joy, and he encouraged the believers to stay true to the Lord. Barnabas was a good man, full of the Holy Spirit and strong in faith. And large numbers of people were brought to the Lord" (Acts 11:23-24).

CORNELIUS
Key Fact: Roman military officer led to Christ by Peter
Total Bible References: 10
Key Reference: 10:1-48

Cornelius Speaks
The dispatch from Rome arrived this morning: Due to my age, I am being retired immediately from military duty. While at first I felt some regret at the news, my overall feeling is great relief. For years I have served Caesar with pride, zeal, and devotion. But now I am free to serve my beloved Savior with that same faithfulness.

How often have I thanked God for Simon Peter. Had it not been for him, this old soldier would probably have degenerated into a callous and corrupt ex–military man, like so many of my army associates. How strange are God's ways. I feared him and gave liberally to his cause without even knowing him. And then that heavenly messenger appeared! "Send some men down to Joppa to find a man named Simon Peter," he said. Amazing! I'm probably one of the very few Gentiles to have ever seen an angel. (10:1-6)

To say I was impressed with Peter would be an understatement. I tried to worship the man! What a blunder! But then Peter related how God had had to straighten out some things in *his* life, which made me feel better. (10:25, 28)

Peter then told me and my family and friends all about the wonderful ministry of Christ, his death, and his resurrection. (10:34-43)

At that instant God's Spirit fell upon us in an unforgettable experience of his presence. Peter baptized us, and then he was gone. (10:44-48)

Well, all that was decades ago. But Peter's message has long since become my rally cry to all I meet: "He is the one all the prophets testified about, saying that everyone who believes in him will have their sins forgiven through his name." (10:43)

Now that I'm retired, I can share that Good News full-time!

Spiritual Lessons from Cornelius

- God directs the steps of unbelievers who are sincerely seeking him (10:1-8; see John 6:44; 16:7-11).
- Sometimes, however, God has to prepare the hearts of human soul winners to reach out to those who are seeking (10:9-22).

Key Verses
"One afternoon about three o'clock, he had a vision in which he saw an angel of God coming toward him. 'Cornelius!' the angel said. Cornelius stared at him in terror. 'What is it, sir?' he asked the angel. And the angel replied, 'Your prayers and

gifts to the poor have not gone unnoticed by God! Now send some men down to Joppa to find a man named Simon Peter. He is staying with Simon, a leatherworker who lives near the shore. Ask him to come and visit you'" (10:3-6).

FELIX

Key Facts: Roman governor, heard Jewish leaders' case against Paul
Total Bible References: 8
Key References: 23:23–24:27

Felix Speaks

Maybe I shouldn't have left Paul in chains. Well, he's Festus's worry now. Frankly, I was hoping to secure some bribe money from him and then let him go. It was so evident during the trial that those Jerusalem Jews and their slick lawyer had absolutely no case whatsoever against Paul. (24:1, 26-27)

Paul's defense was a masterpiece. And his sermon a few days later had a tremendous effect on both me and my wife. I'm ashamed to admit his words about coming judgment so unnerved me that I promptly dismissed him, promising to continue the discussion at a more convenient time. But of course that time never came. (24:10-25)

Spiritual Lessons from Felix

- Though evidently convicted by Paul's preaching, Felix refused to respond, claiming that he would reconsider at a "more convenient" time (24:25). As far as Scripture records, that more convenient time never came. God cannot save a person yesterday, and by tomorrow the heart now open may be forever closed. The only "convenient" day to accept Christ is today! (See Luke 12:20; 2 Cor. 6:2; Heb. 3:7-8.)

Key Verses

"A few days later Felix came with his wife, Drusilla, who was Jewish. Sending for Paul, they listened as he told them about faith in Christ Jesus. As he reasoned with them about righteousness and self-control and the judgment to come, Felix was terrified. 'Go away for now,' he replied. 'When it is more convenient, I'll call for you again'" (24:24-25).

FESTUS

Key Facts: Roman governor after Felix, also heard Jewish leaders' case against Paul
Total Bible References: 13
Key References: 24:27–26:32

Festus Speaks

Paul set sail for Rome today. A fascinating man indeed. Was he really mentally unbalanced as I accused him of being in the heat of the moment? Probably not, but what can you say about someone who claims he saw and heard a dead man speak from out of a bright light! (26:13-18, 24; 27:1-2)

Strange that he was so hated by his own religious peers. The idiots! They thought I could be tricked into helping them kill him. (25:1-5)

No doubt about it, both Agrippa and Bernice were impressed with Paul. I still wonder, however, just what Agrippa had in mind when he responded to him. Were his words an attempt to ridicule the prisoner? Or was there a hint that Paul's message was getting through to him? (25:23; 26:28)

Well, whatever, here's one Roman governor who couldn't be taken in by a smooth-talking Jewish evangelist. But a sobering thought remains: If he wasn't insane, what power on earth could have caused him to suffer all those things—and perhaps now the loss of life itself—simply to propagate the memory of an obscure dead man?

Spiritual Lessons from Festus

- Christians may be ridiculed for their faith whether they present it in a scholarly way or in plain, everyday language. Peter and John were obviously uneducated (4:13), while Paul was scorned for his great intelligence (26:24).

Key Verses

"Suddenly, Festus shouted, 'Paul, you are insane. Too much study has made you crazy!' But Paul replied, 'I am not insane, Most Excellent Festus. I am speaking the sober truth'" (26:24-25).

JAMES (HALF BROTHER OF CHRIST)

Key Facts: Pastored church at Jerusalem, authored NT book bearing his name
Father: Joseph (Matt. 13:54-56)
Mother: Mary (Matt. 13:54-56)
Brothers: Joseph, Simon, Judas; (half brother) Jesus (Matt. 13:55)
Occupation: Pastor
Total Bible References: 11
Key References: 1:14; 15:13; 21:18; Matt. 13:55-57; John 7:1-8; 1 Cor. 15:7; James

James Speaks

"Old Camel Knees" they call me, because of all the hours I spend kneeling in prayer. But I don't mind, for it's meant to be a compliment. It seems there is so much to talk to God about. Perhaps, though, my praying days are numbered. The high priest issued his final warning. Either I deny Jesus or be thrown from the pinnacle of the Temple into the Kidron Valley and be finished off by stoning!

Of course, I cannot and will not recant. Years ago, growing up in Nazareth, I would probably have been more than willing to denounce my older half brother for his messianic claims. How insane we were back then, my brothers and sisters and I, not realizing that he was totally different from us. To my everlasting shame I allowed our mother to stand alone at the cross, unsupported by any of us. Frankly, I experienced no great sorrow at his death. (Matt. 13:55-57; John 7:1-8; 19:25)

But, oh, what a difference a day can bring. On that glorious Resurrection Sunday the Crucified One actually appeared to me. (1 Cor. 15:7)

Of course, nothing has been the same since. Thank God that Jude, my youngest brother, has also embraced the faith. We both pray that Joseph, Simon, and our sisters will do the same. (Jude 1)

What a joy—and what a job!—to pastor the great assembly of believers in Jerusalem. I often think of that all-important meeting our church hosted. It was my privilege to announce the decision: The Jewish rite of circumcision would not be forced upon Gentiles who believe. Word has just reached me that Paul has been released from his Roman imprisonment. Praise God! He and Peter were our star witnesses in that council. (15:4, 7-12, 19; Philem. 1:22)

Hopefully, both Jewish and Gentile readers have been helped by my letter. In this dark hour I am suddenly reminded of a precious promise he directed me to write: "God blesses the people who patiently endure testing. Afterward they will receive the crown of life that God has promised to those who love him." (James 1:12)

Spiritual Lessons from James

- Familiarity often does breed contempt. Even though born of the same mother as Jesus (Matt. 13:54-56) and raised in the same home, James grew up as a skeptical unbeliever (John 7:5).
- Though James in his letter (written c. A.D. 45) taught against all kinds of prejudice (James 2:9), some years later he himself showed such prejudice (Gal. 2:11-14). We should practice what we preach (Rom. 2:21-22).

Key Verse

"Then he was seen by James and later by all the apostles" (1 Cor. 15:7).

PAUL

Key Facts: Apostle, authored 13 of the 27 NT books, may have authored Hebrews
Father: Unnamed (23:6)
Sister: Unnamed (23:16)
Occupation: Tentmaker, apostle (18:1-3; Eph. 3:6-8)
Key Events in His Life:

- Educated as a Pharisee (see 22:3)
- Persecutes Christians (7:58; 8:1-3)
- Converted (9:1-31)
- In Damascus and Arabia (Gal. 1:17)
- In Jerusalem with Barnabas (9:26-27; Gal. 1:18)
- Works at Antioch with Barnabas (11:25-26)
- On first journey, stoned at Lystra (14:8-19)
- Jerusalem Council (15; Gal. 2:1)
- On second journey, joined by Timothy (16:1-3)
- Macedonian call (16:9)
- With philosophers in Athens (17:16-33)
- On third journey, two-plus years in Ephesus (19)
- Farewell to Ephesian elders (20:17-35)
- Arrested in Jerusalem (21:27)
- Taken into Roman custody (22:24)
- Appeals to Caesar (25:10)
- Survives shipwreck; arrives in Rome (27–28)
- Under house arrest; ministers in Rome (28:30-31)
- Released after two years (?) (see Philem. 1:22)
- Imprisoned again (?) (see 2 Tim. 1:8)
- Senses that death is near (2 Tim. 4:6-8)

Total Bible References: 180
Key References: 8–28; Romans—Philemon

Paul Speaks

"An old man!" That's how I described myself to Philemon. And that was 10 years ago! I'd have to think back another 20 years to arrive at the time God called me. He said that I would be a "chosen instrument" to take his name to "the Gentiles and to kings, as well as to the people of Israel" and that I would suffer greatly for his name's sake. (9:10-16; Philem. 1:9)

How precise that prophecy has proven to be! I've often meditated on each part of it: Of course the main thrust of my missionary work has been "to the Gentiles." I have proclaimed him to Greeks and Romans and Asians; to business people and soldiers; to idolaters and philosophers. (14:8-19; 16:11-15; 17:16-34; Rom. 11:13; Phil. 1:12-14)

"And to kings!" There I was, in chains, preaching Christ at Caesarea before Felix, Festus, and King Agrippa himself! (24–26)

"As well as to the people of Israel!" Oh, how my heart has ached for Israel! Of course, I did have the opportunity to proclaim the Messiah before my people at Antioch, Jerusalem, and Rome, and many other places besides. (13:14-15, 38-39; 22; 28:16-18, 30-31; Rom. 9:1-3; 10:1)

Then what he said about suffering: No doubt about it, this old body bears ugly scars from numerous battles and beatings. But as I once reminded some Roman believers, what we suffer down here is not worthy to compare with the glory awaiting us up there. (Rom. 8:18; 2 Cor. 11:24-28; Gal. 6:17)

Hopefully both Timothy and Mark will be able to arrive before they come to get me. How much these two have meant to me. Timothy I consider my spiritual son, and Mark proved to be such a help during my previous imprisonment. God has certainly turned him around since our first trip. (15:36-40; Col. 4:10; 2 Tim. 1:2; 4:6, 9, 11; Philem. 1:24)

I know he will be heartbroken, however, to learn that Demas has forsaken me, as have many others. But that faithful one who first confronted me outside Damascus so many years ago has never for a single moment forsaken me. I think of that dark night in Jerusalem when he reassured me. Later, as I stood on a sinking ship in the midst of a frightful storm, he again came to me. And now, during the most trying time of my life, he continues to stand by me. (9:1-6; 23:11; 27:23-24; 2 Tim. 4:10, 16-17)

I have fought the good fight; I have finished the race; I have kept the faith. This is my final testimony. And my final expectation? I know that the Lord has reserved for me a crown of righteousness. So do your worst, Nero! You cannot kill that which cannot be killed. Your cruel sword will simply validate my passport into the portals of eternal glory. (2 Tim. 4:7-8)

Spiritual Lessons from Paul

- "Christ Jesus came into the world to save sinners—and I was the worst of them all" (1 Tim. 1:15). Do you feel that you have sinned too much to be saved? According to the world's worst sinner, this is impossible. Prior to his conversion, Paul relentlessly persecuted Christians (7:58; 8:1-3; 9:1-18; 22:5, 19; 26:10-11; Gal. 1:13), yet God's grace was sufficient to save him.
- To mistreat another Christian is to mistreat Christ himself. Christ identifies with his disciples (9:4; see Matt. 25:31-45; Col. 1:18).

- Paul spoke of "knowing" Christ and "the mighty power that raised him from the dead" (Phil. 3:10). But if we want to experience this power, we must be prepared to pay the price: "to suffer with him" (Phil. 3:10; see also 2 Cor. 1:5; 1 Pet. 4:13). Paul both began (9:16) and ended (2 Tim. 4:6, 16-17) his ministry by suffering.
- Paul and Barnabas were ministering *to* the Lord when they were called to minister *for* the Lord (13:2). The first involves praise and worship, while the second has to do with proclamation and witness. God wants both from us.
- No matter how unresponsive people may be when we present the gospel, we can do so with the confidence that "many people here in this city" belong to God (18:9-10). While some may scoff, there are many others whose hearts he has prepared to hear.
- At least eight times, Paul offered himself as a role model, exhorting his readers to follow him as he followed Christ (see 1 Cor. 4:16; 11:1, Gal. 4:12; Phil. 3:17; 4:9; 1 Thess. 1:5-6; 2:10; 2 Thess. 3:7-9). Are we able to offer ourselves as role models?
- Paul (2 Tim. 4:7), like Jesus (John 17:4) and unlike Belshazzar (Dan. 5:26-27), could testify at the end of life that he had successfully finished his course. We should work to make that our testimony as well.

Key Verse

"To me, to live is Christ, and to die is gain" (Phil. 1:21, NKJV).

PHILIP (THE EVANGELIST)

Key Facts: Evangelist, presented gospel to an Ethiopian royal official
Total Bible References: 16
Key References: 6:5; 8:5-8, 26-40; 21:8-15

Philip Speaks

What a privilege it was to meet and entertain in our own home the great apostle Paul himself! In addition to having wonderful fellowship, we found much in common with him. He has functioned as an evangelist over the years, as have I. He is a recognized prophet, as are my four daughters. He began his ministry as an associate in a local church, as did I. (6:1-5; 8:5; 11:25-26; 13:1; 21:8-9)

We bade him Godspeed this morning. It is obvious he plans to head straight for Jerusalem, in spite of Agabus's somber warning. At any rate, God's will be done. That was our parting prayer for him. Hopefully, that is his prayer for us as well. (21:10-15)

Paul's departure reminded me again of the day I watched that newly converted Ethiopian disappear into the dusty distance toward his homeland. Whenever God brings him to mind I pray for him. Dear long lost friend, how I hope your thrilling confession back there beside that oasis continues to be your daily testimony: "I believe that Jesus Christ is the Son of God." (8:26-39)

Spiritual Lessons from Philip

- God used Philip mightily in a citywide evangelistic crusade (8:5-8), but not before he had proven himself to be a faithful, Spirit-anointed servant in his local church (6:3-6). See Matthew 25:23.
- Ever sensitive to the Spirit's leading, Philip left his successful preaching

campaign in Samaria (8:5) to reach one man in the desert of Gaza (8:26-39). Likewise, if you truly seek his will, God will "guide you along the best pathway for your life" (Ps. 32:8).
- "Children are a gift from the LORD" (Ps. 127:3). "Teach your children to choose the right path" (Prov. 22:6). Philip acknowledged the truth of the psalm and acted upon the admonition of the proverb, raising four godly daughters (21:8-9).

Key Verse
"So Philip began with this same Scripture and then used many others to tell him the Good News about Jesus" (8:35).

SILAS (SILVANUS)
Key Fact: Paul's associate on his second missionary journey
Total Bible References: 13
Key References: 15:22–18:22; 2 Cor. 1:19; 1 Pet. 5:12

Silas Speaks
"Asked of God." That's the meaning of the name my parents gave me. And looking back, it does seem that God has had his hand upon my life. He has certainly blessed me, allowing me to help proclaim the gospel in other lands. And what a team leader Timothy and I had—the great apostle Paul himself. (15:40; 16:29-32)

While I had already experienced some danger and hardship for Christ's name, I don't believe anything could have prepared me for what would occur at Philippi. Among other things, we suffered satanic opposition, followed by being arrested, beaten, and imprisoned. So, what did we do? We sang his praises! And what did God do? He sent an earthquake! No wonder the news spread that we were turning the world upside down! (15:26; 16:16-26; 17:6)

In retrospect, I especially enjoyed the brief ministry Timothy and I had in Berea. Nowhere else did I find believers so devoted to the Scriptures! (17:10-14)

My earthly father called me "Asked of God." Hopefully, someday my heavenly Father will call me "Approved by God."

Spiritual Lessons from Silas
- Just as Aaron and Hur held up Moses' hands during the battle with the Amalekites (Exod. 17:12), Silas ministered to Paul during his second missionary journey (15:40–18:22). Christian leaders today often voice their need for godly Silases to help hold up their hands in ministry.

Key Verses
"So it seemed good to us, having unanimously agreed on our decision, to send you these official representatives, along with our beloved Barnabas and Paul, who have risked their lives for the sake of our Lord Jesus Christ. So we are sending Judas and Silas to tell you what we have decided concerning your question" (15:25-27).

STEPHEN
Key Fact: First recorded Christian martyr
Occupation: Deacon, evangelist
Death: Recorded in 7:60

Total Bible References: 7
Key References: 6:3–7:60

Stephen Speaks

I often wondered what it would be like to see his glory as did Peter, James, and John on that mountain. Or, for that matter, to have witnessed his resurrected glory along with Mary Magdalene, Cleopas, and the apostles. Now I see it, and the sight is indescribable! (7:55-56; Matt. 17:1-2; Luke 24:18-48; John 20:16-18)

It all began so innocently, with my appointment as an official servant in our local church. What wondrous days followed, as God empowered both my witness and works for him. Many new converts were added to the church, including a large number of Jewish priests. But one day my preaching antagonized a group from the synagogue and the battle was on! They accused me of blaspheming both Moses and God. What a ridiculous charge! (6:3, 7-11)

"The face of an angel" is how they described my appearance during the trial. "Heathen at heart and deaf to the truth" is how I described them at the end of the trial. (6:15; 7:51)

The pain is becoming intense, but my mind is perfectly clear! Suddenly I am filled with a great desire to pray for my tormentors as Christ once did for his! For some reason my heart goes out to that young man caring for the coats of those who stone me. (7:58, 60; Luke 23:34)

It is enough! "Lord Jesus, receive my spirit." (7:59; Luke 23:46)

Spiritual Lessons from Stephen

- Stephen began his message by speaking of the God of glory (7:1) and concluded by seeing the glory of God (7:55). The first, when faithfully done, will always give birth to the second.
- "Love your enemies! Pray for those who persecute you!" (Matt. 5:44). Following his master's example (Luke 23:34), the dying Stephen forgave those who were stoning him (7:60). What would we have done?

Key Verses

"And as they stoned him, Stephen prayed, 'Lord Jesus, receive my spirit.' And he fell to his knees, shouting, 'Lord, don't charge them with this sin!' And with that, he died" (7:59-60).

THE EPISTLES OF PAUL

First Missionary Trip	None			
Furlough	**Galatians** from Antioch Autumn A.D. 49			
Second Missionary Trip	**1 Thessalonians** from Corinth Summer A.D. 51	**2 Thessalonians** from Corinth Summer A.D. 51		
Third Missionary Trip	**1 Corinthians** from Ephesus Spring A.D. 56	**2 Corinthians** from Macedonia October A.D. 56	**Romans** from Corinth Winter A.D. 56/57	
First Imprisonment	**Ephesians** from Rome Autumn A.D. 60	**Colossians** from Rome Autumn A.D. 61	**Philemon** from Rome Autumn A.D. 61	**Philippians** from Rome Early Spring A.D. 62
Release	**1 Timothy** from Macedonia Autumn A.D. 62	**Titus** from Asia Minor Summer A.D. 66		
Final Imprisonment	**2 Timothy** from Rome Autumn A.D. 67			

A.D. 35
Paul's conversion

c. 54
Paul desires to visit Rome

57
Paul writes Romans

60
Paul imprisoned in Rome

c. 67
Paul martyred

ROMANS

BACKGROUND

In Paul's day, all roads literally led to Rome. It was the heart of the Roman Empire, and Paul had long desired to visit the city (Acts 19:21) but, after nearly 10 years of missionary travels (see *Date and Location*), had been unable to do so (1:13). Paul hoped that, once he made it to Rome, the Christians there would help him take the gospel to the western edge of the empire (15:28). When Paul learned that Phoebe, from the Corinth area (16:1), was going to Rome on business, he sent this letter with her, to share his vision with the believers in Rome and hopefully to enlist them in his missionary cause. Paul himself would not make it to Rome until about three years later, when he arrived there as a prisoner of Rome and lived under house arrest (Acts 28).

Paul also saw this letter as an opportunity to help the Roman believers become better grounded in the essential principles of their faith (see *Purpose*).

All of Paul's letters were delivered by friends. The Roman postal system was for government business only.

AUTHOR

Paul, the great apostle to the Gentiles. Born Saul in the Cilician city of Tarsus, Paul was Jewish by birth, Roman by citizenship, and Greek by culture. Educated as a Pharisee, he was dramatically converted to Christ (Acts 9; 22; 26) and became the foremost evangelist as well as the foremost theologian of the early church. Luke tells the story of Paul's life and ministry in Acts. Paul himself explains the faith in Christ that propelled that ministry in his 13 letters (Romans—Philemon). Some scholars believe he also wrote Hebrews.

DATE AND LOCATION

Late winter of A.D. 57 or early spring of 58, about 22 years after Paul's conversion, during the last three months of his third missionary journey while he was in Greece (Acts 20:3), just prior to returning to Jerusalem with an offering for the poor (15:26). More specifically, he was probably in Corinth, staying in the home of Gaius (16:23; 1 Cor. 1:14).

RECIPIENTS

Romans is addressed to "those who have been called to belong to Jesus Christ . . . in Rome" (1:6-7). There were small groups of believers meeting all over the city (16:3-5, 10-11, 14-15). Paul's personal greetings to many of them (16:3-16) suggest Paul had led them to Christ in other cities, and then, probably for economic reasons, they had relocated to the empire's capital city.

PURPOSE

- To announce his plans to visit the Christians in Rome, and to enlist support in his mission (15:24, 28-29)
- To teach the fundamental doctrine of salvation in order to fortify them against the Judaizers (1–8)
- To explain the unbelief of Israel and vindicate God's faithfulness in his dealings with that nation (9–11)
- To give practical instruction in Christian living (12–16)

UNIQUE FEATURES

- Romans is the most complete summary of Christian doctrine. If all of the Bible were lost except Romans, scarcely any fundamental doctrine would be lacking.
- As he explained the gospel in Romans, Paul quoted from the OT more often than in all his 12 other letters combined—showing how important the OT is to understanding the gospel.

COMPARISON WITH OTHER BIBLE BOOKS

Genesis:

- In Genesis, Abraham is the patriarch of Israel; in Romans he is the patriarch of all who believe (4:16).

Galatians:

- Galatians, with its discussion of justification by faith, could be called "Romans in shorthand."

James:

- Romans shows the *root* of salvation: faith alone. James shows the *fruit* of salvation: good works.

OUTLINE

GOD'S RIGHTEOUSNESS REVEALED (1:1-17)
  Salutation (1:1-7)
  Paul and the church in Rome (1:8-17)
GOD'S RIGHTEOUSNESS IMPUTED (JUSTIFICATION) (1:18–5:21)
  Universal need for justification (1:18–3:20)

God's provision of justification (3:21-31)
OT illustrations of justification (4)
Certainty of justification (5:1-11)
Universal effectiveness of justification (5:12-21)

GOD'S RIGHTEOUSNESS IMPARTED (SANCTIFICATION; GLORIFICATION) (6–8)
Questions about sanctification (6)
Identified with Christ (6:1-14)
Enslaved to righteousness (6:15-23)
New relationship in sanctification: free from law (7)
New power in sanctification: The Holy Spirit (8:1-17)
Present sufferings, future glory (8:18-39)

GOD'S RIGHTEOUSNESS TOWARD ISRAEL (9–11)
Israel's rejection (9–10)
The positive outcome of Israel's rejection (11)

GOD'S RIGHTEOUSNESS APPLIED (12:1–15:13)
The principle of righteousness (12:1-2)
Applications of righteousness (12:3–15:13)
In church and community (12:3-21)
Toward government (13:1-7)
In social relationships (13:8-14)
In matters of opinion (14:1–15:13)

GOD'S RIGHTEOUSNESS PROPAGATED (15:14–16:27)
Paul's purpose in writing; his plans (15:14-33)
Greetings, warning, benediction (16)

GOD'S RIGHTEOUSNESS REVEALED (1:1-17)

1:1-7 *A messenger and his Messiah.* Paul began by identifying himself as a messenger (apostle) and slave of Christ (1:1), then quickly shifted the focus to Christ, showing that his Messiahship was confirmed both by the OT (1:2-3) and by his resurrection (1:4). Paul spoke again of his apostolic calling, reminding his readers that they, too, had been called by God (1:5-6). He then greeted them in a phrase with which he prefaced each of his 13 epistles: "May grace and peace be yours from God our Father and the Lord Jesus Christ." Peter used the same greeting in both of his letters, as did John in one of his (see 2 John 1:3).

Grace precedes peace. There can be no peace apart from grace (see 5:1; Isa. 57:21; Jer. 6:14; Luke 7:50). Grace is the unmerited favor of God toward sinners. Someone has suggested that the spelling of the English word *grace* offers a key to its meaning: It is "**G**od's **R**ighteousness **A**t **C**hrist's **E**xpense" (see 5:20; 1 Cor. 15:10; Eph. 2:8-9; 2 Pet. 3:18). While grace is often thought of as a NT concept, it is a prevalent theme in the OT as well, beginning with Noah's finding grace in God's sight (see exposition on Gen. 6:8-13) and continuing throughout the history of God's dealing with his people (often expressed in words other than grace, see Ps. 103:10-14; Isa. 55:1-9; 63:7-8).

While Paul had not been a follower of Christ during his earthly ministry as were the other apostles (see exposition on Acts 1:15-26), like them he had seen the risen Lord (see 1 Cor. 9:1; 15:8-9) and had been chosen by Christ himself (compare 9:15 and John 6:70). No one should enter the ministry unless called by God (see John 15:16; Matt. 9:38).

Paul described himself as "chosen by God . . . to preach his good news." The term used for "chosen" can also be translated "set apart" or "separated." Paul actually experienced three specific "separations" in his life:

- at his birth (see Gal. 1:15; compare Isa. 49:1; Jer. 1:5)
- at his conversion (see Acts 9:15)
- at his call to missionary service (see Acts 13:1-2)

1:8-15 *Praises, prayers, plans.* The testimony of the churches in Rome was known throughout the empire (1:8), resulting in Paul's great desire (1:9) to visit them and encourage them in their faith (1:10-15). Having received God's mercy, Paul felt indebted to all who had not yet had that opportunity (1:14-15).

Paul's prayer to go to Rome was later answered by God but not in the way he might have expected (see Acts 27–28). Rome would be a fitting climax to Paul's adventures in the great world capitals of his day.

- He had preached at Jerusalem, the religious center of the world, where he was mobbed (see Acts 21:31; 22:22-23).
- He had preached at Athens, the intellectual center of the world, where he was mocked (see Acts 17:32).
- And when he finally preached in Rome, the political center, he would be martyred (see 2 Tim. 4:6).

1:16-17 *Proclaiming God's power.* Paul's motivation in proclaiming the gospel was knowing that God will save everyone who believes it, both Jews and Gentiles. The gospel reveals God's righteousness, which sinners can appropriate by faith. Only through faith can one be justified in God's sight (1:17; see Hab. 2:4 and *Habakkuk: Comparison with Other Bible Books*).

GOD'S RIGHTEOUSNESS IMPUTED (JUSTIFICATION) (1:18–5:21)

1:18-32 *Denial of God brings defilement of self.* Paul spoke of God's justifiable anger toward a human race that has suppressed the truth about him because of their preference for unrighteousness. Both conscience (1:19) and nature (1:20) clearly reveal God. God does not reap wrath where he has not sown knowledge (compare Ps. 19:1-3; Isa. 40:26; Acts 14:17; 17:22-29). Humankind as a whole neither acknowledges God nor thanks him for his creation and grace (1:21). Therefore, God has allowed them to become fools (1:21-23) and to sink into idolatry and moral depravity (1:24-32; compare Prov. 1:24-31). Such people know the seriousness of their crimes (1:32); nonetheless, they continue and even encourage others to join them.

Notice the devastating results of unthankfulness (1:21). Surely unthankfulness was the root cause of the fall of both Lucifer and Adam. The ultimate cure for pride is not humility but thanksgiving. A thankful person is automatically a humble person (see Phil. 4:6; 1 Thess. 5:18).

These God-denying, unthankful people became fools while thinking they were wise (1:22). The Greek for "became utter fools" is *moraino,* root of our English word *moron.* This rebellion against God's truth was the beginning of human philosophy, an ill-applied term since it means "love of wisdom" (see Acts 17:18-21; 1 Cor. 1:18-21; 1 Tim. 6:20; 2 Tim. 3:6-7; 4:3-4).

2:1-10 *Condemn another, condemn yourself.* Paul knew that many of his readers would immediately pass judgment on the people he had just described (see 1:18-32). If, however, such readers would reflect on their own lives, they would realize that they were guilty of some of the same sins (2:1). Paul's description fit all humanity. All were subject to God's righteous judgment, incurring either his honor or his wrath (2:2-10).

2:11-16 *All will be judged, by God's law or by theirs.* Judgment would apply to Jews and Gentiles alike. Both would be judged by their law: For Jews, the law of Moses (especially the Ten Commandments); for Gentiles, the law that God had written on their own conscience.

2:17-29 *"The problem? You don't practice what you preach."* Many Jews boasted of their superior knowledge of God (2:17-20), but such knowledge was useless unless correctly applied (2:21-24). The circumcised Jew who disobeyed the law was worse off than the uncircumcised Gentile who kept it (2:25-27). True membership in God's family is a matter of heart attitude, not of physical birth or ritual purity (2:28-29; see Deut. 6:1-5; 10:16; 1 Chron. 28:9-10.)

3:1-4 *"Do Jews have any advantage?"* If both Jews and Gentiles are equally guilty before God, some might ask, what is the advantage of being a Jew (3:1; see Deut. 4:32-38)? The Jews had great advantage, said Paul, in that God's Word was first revealed to them (3:2). Even if some rejected that revelation, God would keep his promises to them (3:3-4). Human sin serves only to emphasize God's righteousness. Paul would later speak more fully of the advantages of a Jewish heritage (see 9:4-5).

3:5-8 *"So let's sin, to God's glory!"* Other readers might object that if human sin shows God's righteousness, it seems unfair for God to judge the sinner who, after all, is adding to his glory. Paul dismisses this objection outright: If God can't judge, then he is less than God.

3:9-20 *High treason against the King of kings.* Quoting several OT psalms, Paul continued to assert that all God's creatures, both Jew and Gentile, sin against their Creator. No one is righteous (3:10-12). Rather, they speak (3:13-14) and do (3:15-17) many ungodly things, with no apparent fear of judgment (3:18). Such awareness of sin should humble us before God (3:19); the law, far from justifying us, only makes us more aware of our sin (3:20). See Psalm 14:1-3; Jeremiah 17:9.

3:21-26 *The Just justifies the unjust.* The righteousness that could not be had through the law is, however, available through faith in Christ (3:21-24), whose blood is the sufficient offering for the sins of all humanity (3:25-26). Because the perfect sacrifice has been offered, God can still be "just," or righteous, even while declaring righteous those who don't deserve it but who have faith in Christ (3:26).

As required by the law (3:21; see Deut. 19:15), Christ's Messiahship was validated by two witnesses:

- the law, through the symbolism of the Temple priesthood and offerings (see Luke 24:25-27; John 5:46)
- the prophets, in their many predictions of Christ (see Isa. 53; see Luke 24:25-27; 1 Pet. 1:10-11)

3:27-31 *No boasting allowed.* Because salvation is by grace through faith in Christ, no one can claim to have done anything to earn it (3:27-28). This applies to both Jew and Gentile (3:29-30). Rather than making the law void, however, grace actually establishes it, since the law's purpose was to show the need for grace (3:31; see 3:20).

4:1-12 *"We found it apart from the law."* Abraham believed God and was therefore looked upon as righteous

(4:1-4), even before he was circumcised (4:9-12). Circumcision was the seal of his salvation, but faith was its source. He was declared righteous because of his faith. (For the three great instances of this type of imputation or attribution by God in salvation history, see exposition on Gen. 15:1-11.)

Likewise David, finding that no obedience to the law could rid him of his terrible guilt, threw himself completely upon God's grace (4:5-8; see Ps. 32; 51).

4:13-25 *Good News for Abraham and us.* God's promise to Abraham and his descendants was based not on the law but on faith (4:13), for the law can only bring condemnation (4:14-15). Because the promise is based on faith, it is available to all who, because of their faith in Christ, are Abraham's true offspring (4:16-25). Because we have believed God's promise of salvation, we have received God's righteousness, just as Abraham did.

5:1-5 *Faith's fantastic fruits.* Having been justified by faith, we have peace with and access to God; the joyful hope of seeing God's glory; blessed assurance from God amid suffering; and the indwelling presence of the Holy Spirit.

5:6-11 *When, why, and how this happens.* We have the gift of salvation and peace with God because, when we were totally helpless sinners, God in his love sent Christ to die for us.

5:12-21 *Two men, two acts, two results.* Just as Adam's disobedience brought sin and death to the world (5:12, 18), Christ's obedience brought righteousness and life (5:18-21). In a long parenthetical statement (5:13-17), Paul highlighted the contrast between Adam and Christ:

- Because of the sin of one man, Adam, every human has experienced both physical and spiritual death (see Gen. 3:19; Eph. 2:1).
- Because of the righteousness of one man, Jesus Christ, every human can experience eternal life (see 1 Cor. 15:22).

Paul explained once again how the law brings not righteousness but awareness of sin (5:20; compare 3:20); the more we are aware of sin, the more we can cast ourselves on God's grace.

GOD'S RIGHTEOUSNESS IMPARTED (SANCTIFICATION; GLORIFICATION) (6–8)

6:1-14 *The cross and the empty tomb: We were there!* Having declared the glory of God's grace (5:20), Paul again brought up the possible objection: Why not sin more, to receive more grace (6:1; compare exposition on 3:5-8)? Again he refuted that heresy in the strongest possible terms (6:2-23). As exemplified by baptism (6:3-4), we were both crucified with Christ and raised with him, which means that, just as death has no more power over him, sin should have no power over us (6:5-7). Because we have died with Christ, we also have the assurance of new and eternal life through his resurrection (6:4, 8-10). We should want to live in the reality of that new life, serving God instead of sin (6:11-14; see Eph. 4:22-24; Col. 3:9-10).

Paul presented sin as a cruel tyrant, taxing his subjects beyond all endurance. The only way to be freed from this tyrant is to die to him (6:7), which is exactly what we do in coming to Christ (6:2-6).

6:15-23 *Two slaves, two wages.* Paul repeated the preposterous question of 6:1, asking why people would want to be a slave to sin when they could be God's slave instead (6:15-20). Slavery to sin leads to eternal death, while slavery to God's righteousness leads to eternal life (6:21-23).

Our enslavement to righteousness should involve the goal of holiness (6:19), or "sanctification" (NASB). Concerning the past and present aspects of sanctification, see exposition on Hebrews 10:1-18.

The "wages of sin" is spiritual death, which means separation from God and suffering throughout all eternity in the lake of fire (6:23; see Rev. 20:11-15). If God's justice is to prevail (see 3:4, 26), the greatest crime of all (rejection of him) can only be punished by the greatest penalty of all.

7:1-6 *Freed at last, from bondage to blessing.* In a further effort to illustrate our freedom in Christ, Paul compared the law, with its tendency to make us want to sin (7:5), to a demanding husband. As long as the husband lives, his wife is bound to him; when he dies, she is free to marry another. Likewise, the law and the sinful desires it arouses have no more claim over the believer; he or she is now free to be united with Christ (7:4; compare John 3:29; Eph. 5:25-27; Rev. 21:2).

7:7-25 *Sin and the Savior struggle for his soul.* Again a hypothetical question: If the law makes a person want to sin (7:5), is the law itself sinful (7:7)? No, said Paul: The problem is not with the law that reveals sin, but with the sin itself, which uses the law to incite people to sin (7:7-11). The law in itself is not evil but "holy and right and good" (7:12):

- It is holy because it came from God.
- It is right because it justly condemns the sinner.
- It is good because it leads the sinner to Christ (see Gal. 3:24).

The law is ineffective in defeating sin (see 3:20) only because of the weakness of fallen humanity (7:14-23). Herein is the real problem: When Paul wanted to do good, he didn't, and when he tried not to do evil, he did. The finest football coach would lose every game if he had an inferior team. The only possible response to Paul's dilemma is despair (7:24), and the only answer to that despair is Christ (7:25).

As Paul wrote 7:7-11, he may have recalled his bar mitzvah as a Jewish boy, when he formally took on himself the solemn responsibilities of the law. Gone were the carefree days of childhood; he was now accountable to God for his actions.

8:1-4 *To those in Christ, no condemnation!* Expanding on 7:25, Paul explained that Jesus Christ has done for us what the law of Moses could never do: He has delivered us from the law of sin and death. We can experience this freedom from sin as we walk in the power of his Spirit. Paul did not say that there is no fault or sin or imperfection, but that because of Christ there is no condemnation. Note also the time element: There is *now* no condemnation.

8:5-17 *Adopted by God, controlled by his Spirit.* Our sinful nature tries to make us focus on our fleshly desires, which lead only to death. The indwelling Spirit, on the other hand, tries to take control of our sinful flesh and to lead us to life (8:5-12). If we allow God's Spirit to control us, we will find eternal life (8:13). The Spirit leads us (8:14) and assures us of our salvation (8:16). As God's adopted children, we have the right to call him by the term of endearment Paul used: "Abba, Father" (8:14-16). If in this life we are his children, even when that involves suffering, we can be assured that someday we will share in his glory (8:17). See exposition on John 16:12-15. On "adoption" (8:15), see exposition on Galatians 3:26–4:7.

8:18-25 *Today's grief, tomorrow's glory: No comparison!* Paul looked at the thorns, storms, floods, famine, sin,

THREE TYPES CONFRONT THE LAW

The Spiritual Person and the Law (Rom. 7:1-6)

- In relationship to the law
- In relationship to the Savior

The spiritual person is DELIVERED from the law!

The Natural Person and the Law (Rom. 7:7-13)

- The law and God
- The law and sin

The natural person is DOOMED by the law!

The Carnal Person and the Law (Rom. 7:14-25)

• Any attempt to keep the law will lead to carnality.
• No attempt to keep the law can lead to spirituality.

The carnal person is DEFEATED by the law!

sickness, and death that characterize the fallen world, and declared that they aren't even worth comparing to the glorious future awaiting God's people. Meanwhile, however, the whole creation "groans" together with us (8:19-23) as we await our day of liberation. Our final victory over sin and death will be a victory for all creation as well. Unlike the rest of humankind and creation, however, believers have the indwelling Holy Spirit as an assurance of their future glory (8:23-25; see Eph. 1:13-14).

8:26-27 *That inward groan of God.* The indwelling Spirit both prays for us and helps us in our prayer life. Just as fallen nature and believers "groan" (8:22-23), even God's Holy Spirit groans as he shares our struggles. "Help" implies, however, that even as we lean on the Spirit we must do our share.

8:28-30 *How can everything turn out good?* Because God foreknew us and has predestined us for salvation, conformed us to Christ, called us, justified us, and promised to glorify us (8:29-30), we can be assured that "everything" will "work together" for our good (8:28). Note two things this does not mean:

- It does not mean that all things in and of themselves are good, only that they *work together* for good. Joseph understood this (see Gen. 50:20), though his father did not (see Gen. 42:36). (See also Ps. 76:10.)
- This promise is not for everyone, only for those who love God and have answered his call. But for these it is an all-inclusive promise, covering the good and the bad, the bright and the dark, the sweet and the bitter, the easy and the hard, the happy and the sad. The promise can be depended on in prosperity and poverty, in health and sickness, in calm and storm, in life and in death.

8:31-39 *Security in the Savior.* The fact that God would take the radical step of giving his only Son for us should assure us that, if we accept his salvation, nothing in all the universe can separate us from him or from the things he has promised (see exposition on John 10:22-30).

GOD'S RIGHTEOUSNESS TOWARD ISRAEL (9–11)

9:1-5 *His anguish for Israel.* Paul now addressed another issue: If God is so perfectly just and righteous in all his dealings with humans (see 3:4, 26), what about his dealings with his own people Israel? As was true wherever Paul preached, many Jews in Rome, both Christian and non-Christian, would wonder if the gospel meant that God had abandoned Israel (see Acts 28:28-29). Paul dealt with this important issue at great length (9–11). He began by expressing his great anguish over Israel's rejection of its Messiah, saying he was willing himself to be forever damned if that would save his people (compare Exod. 32:31-32; Matt. 23:37). On 9:3-5, see exposition on 3:1-4.

9:6-13 *Two kinds of descendants.* God's desire to extend salvation to the Gentiles should not be surprising, for not all of Abraham's physical descendants are among his spiritual children. God chose some and rejected others.

9:14-29 *What does God do? Anything he wants to!* If God thus chooses some and rejects others, is he being unfair (9:14)? "Of course not!" says Paul, giving the example of Pharaoh, whom God raised up and then destroyed, all in order to bring glory to himself (9:14-18; see Exod. 4:21; 33:19). But how can God condemn someone he has not predestined for salvation (9:19)? Such a question hardly even deserves an answer, said Paul, for God has the right to choose one and reject another just as a potter has the right to shape his clay as he sees fit (9:20-23). He has the right to choose both Jews and Gentiles, just as Hosea predicted he would (9:24-26; see Hos. 1:10; 2:23). Even the ultimate salvation of Israel will be only by his grace (9:27-29; see Isa. 10:22-23; 28:22).

This difficult passage must be balanced by some of Paul's other statements in Romans, such as

- God is absolutely impartial (see 2:11; 10:12).
- He will save all who ask him (see 10:13).

The relationship between predestination and free will has perplexed scholars for ages (see exposition on 1 Pet. 1:1-2). Concerning the present passage, note that Paul did not say that God made the clay as it was but that he worked with it as it was (compare Jer. 18:1-6; Isa. 45:9; 64:6-8). The "objects of his judgment" are "fit only for destruction." This last statement has also been translated "prepared for destruction," but it is important to note that in the original Greek, "prepared" is in the middle voice, meaning "to prepare oneself." On the other hand, God himself prepared the "objects of his mercy" for "glory." This difference in verb tense suggests that destruction is the deserved destination of sinners, while glory is the undeserved destination of the saved.

9:30-33 *So where are we now?* Paul reminded his readers of the current state of affairs: Many Gentiles, with no religious background, were accepting Christ, while many Jews, with all the benefits of their religious heritage, were rejecting him. Why? Because they had sought righteousness by works, not by faith. And when they saw their Messiah on a cross, not a throne, they couldn't accept him.

10:1-4 *Paul's supreme desire.* Speaking again of his anguish over Israel's unbelief (compare 9:1-5), Paul expressed his desire that his people abandon their pursuit of righteousness based on the law and instead accept the righteousness Christ offers. Christ is indeed the "end" of the OT law (10:4; see Gal. 3:24; Col. 2:14; Heb. 7:11-19).

10:5-13 *It's so simple: Faith plus nothing equals righteousness.* While the person seeking salvation through the law would be forever trying to keep it (10:5), the salvation Christ offers is not in some unattainable place; it as near as our hearts and mouths (10:6-12). Anyone who calls upon the name of the Lord will be saved (10:13). Paul had earlier shown that everyone is lost (1:18–3:20). He now repeats the good news of 3:21-31: Everyone can be saved! The "anyone" of 10:13 echoes the "everyone" of John 3:16.

10:14-21 *"We must tell them, but they must listen."* Human witnesses are needed to proclaim the gospel (10:14-15), but those who hear must respond, as Israel had failed to do time and time again (10:16-21).

11:1-10 *A remnant guaranteed by grace.* Once again Paul asked what many of his Jewish readers were asking: Has God rejected his own people (compare exposition on 9:1-5)? Certainly not, said Paul. He offered as proof himself (11:1) along with many other Jews of his day who had accepted Christ (11:5-6; see Acts 6:7). Even in one of the worst times of Israel's history, when Elijah thought all was hopeless, many Israelites had remained faithful (11:2-4). A few Jews had found salvation (11:7; see exposition on 1 Pet. 1:1-2). Unfortunately, however, most remained blinded by legalism (11:8-10; see Ps. 69:22-23; Isa. 29:10, 13; compare 2 Cor. 4:4; Eph.

4:18). OT prophecy spoke often on the "remnant" of faithful Israelites (see exposition on Isa. 10:20-23).

11:11-12 *Jewish rejection, Gentile blessing.* Now that Israel had rejected Christ, was it without hope? "Of course not!" said Paul. Its rejection has resulted in salvation for many Gentiles. Someday Israel will accept God's salvation (see 11:26), and that will result in even greater riches for all the world. This time of greater riches is the Millennium, in which Israel and many Gentiles will participate (see *Isaiah: Background*).

11:13-32 *Jews and Gentiles: Two olive trees.* Paul explained more fully the amazing divine plan hinted at in 11:11-12. He compared the unbelieving Jews to branches that God had broken off from Israel, the olive tree he had cultivated (11:24) for so many centuries. The Gentile Christians are like branches from a "wild olive tree" (11:17) that have been grafted into the cultivated tree. Someday, after all the Gentiles predestined for salvation (the "complete number," 11:25) have been grafted into the tree of Israel, "all Israel will be saved" (11:26), just as God had promised (see Isa. 29:17-24; 59:20-21; Jer. 31:31-34). On "mystery" (11:25), see exposition on Colossians 1:24-29.

11:33-36 *"Only God could know and do all this!"* Marvelling at the wisdom of God's age-old plan to save both Jews and Gentiles, Paul ended his discussion of that plan with a great outpouring of praise.

GOD'S RIGHTEOUSNESS APPLIED (12:1–15:13)

12:1-2 *Transformed, not conformed.* Having described the inward condition of the believer who has received God's righteousness (1–8), Paul urged such believers to live in a way that outwardly reflects their inward state (12:1–15:13). Rather than being conformed to the patterns of this world, Christians are to be transformed by offering their bodies and minds to God. "Transform" is *metamorpheo* in Greek, from which we get "metamorphosis," a change such as that of a caterpillar becoming a butterfly. The same word described Christ's transfiguration (see Matt. 17:2; 2 Cor. 3:18; 1 Pet. 1:14-16; 1 John 2:15.)

Living in a world hostile to God, daily "changing the way you think" (renewing your mind) through Bible study and prayer is the Christian's only safeguard (12:2; compare 1 Cor. 9:24-27; Eph. 4:23; Col. 3:10).

12:3-8 *Serving righteously in the church.* Christians should realistically assess the gifts God has given them, then use those gifts as a part of Christ's body, the church (see exposition on Eph. 1:15-23).

12:9-16 *Behaving righteously toward each other.* Christian relationships should be open and honest, characterized by love, humility, patience, and generosity.

12:17-21 *Behaving righteously toward one's foes.* Christians should make every effort to be at peace with their enemies, striving to win others to Christ by showing his love.

13:1-7 *Saints and the state.* Believers should obey civil laws, for human government has been established by God to help maintain social order (see exposition on Gen. 9:1-17). Such obedience includes cheerfully paying taxes (13:6-7).

13:8-10 *Love and the law.* The person filled with God's righteousness will be characterized by love, which is the summation of God's law (see exposition on Matt. 22:34-40).

13:11-14 *Time to wake up, shape up, look up!* Paul's teaching about faith should motivate Christians to "wake up"

FOUR "BUILDINGS" IN ROMANS

The Courthouse of Law
(Rom. 1–5)

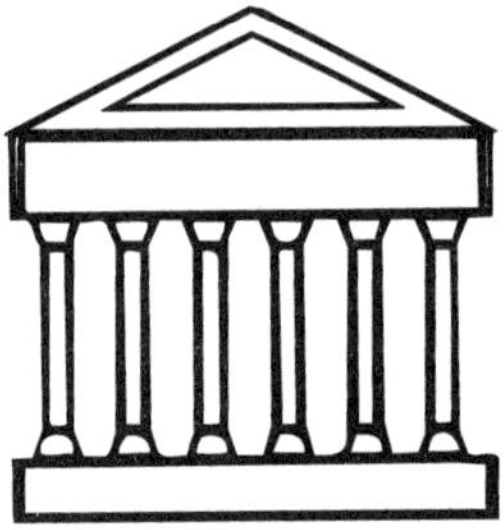

GOD'S WRATH

- Condemnation
- Justification

The Power Plant of Grace
(Rom. 6–8)

GOD'S WAY

- Sanctification
- Preservation

The Synagogue of Israel
(Rom. 9–11)

GOD'S WISDOM

- Explanation
- Vindication

The Temple of God
(Rom. 12–16)

GOD'S WILL

- Transformation
- Exhortation

and seek victory over sin, for the Lord's return is near.

14:1–15:4 *Don't judge diets or days.* Christians should not feel bound by religious traditions or regulations not clearly commanded by God. On the other hand, we must not offend those who observe such things (14:1-7). All that we do should be done with thanksgiving and praise to God, mindful that he will someday judge us (14:8-12). We should try to be a stepping stone of faith for others, rather than a stumbling block or an obstacle (14:13). We should not destroy what God is doing in another person's life just for the sake of winning a minor theological debate (14:14-21). Nor should we ever violate our own conscience (14:22-23). On 14:11, see Isaiah 45:23; Philippians 2:10-11.

The strong, mature Christian is to be tolerant toward the weak, immature believer—out of love, not out of a desire to display one's own spiritual maturity (15:1-4). Paul cited Christ's example of selfless service, as prophesied by David (15:3; see Ps. 69:9), then went on to comment on the value of OT Scripture (15:4).

15:5-13 *Jews and Gentiles: One mind, one mouth.* The goal of tolerance among believers is that they might be unified in glorifying God (15:5-7, 13). It is especially important that Jewish and Gentile Christians be united, for Christ came to save both Jews and Gentiles (15:8-12), as foretold by David (see 2 Sam. 22:50), Moses (see Deut. 32:21), an anonymous psalmist (see Ps. 117:1), and Isaiah (see Isa. 11:10).

GOD'S RIGHTEOUSNESS PROPAGATED (15:14–16:27)

15:14-33 *In closing: His plans and prayers.* As Paul's letter drew to a close, he assured the Roman believers of his confidence in their faith (15:14-15) and reviewed his ministry to the Gentiles, the urgency of which had so far prevented his coming to Rome (15:16-22). He then spoke of his desire to visit them on his way to Spain, after he had delivered the offering from Macedonia and Achaia to Jerusalem (15:23-29; see exposition on Acts 20:1-6). He asked them to pray that God would protect him from the unbelievers in Jerusalem and that he would eventually make it to Rome (15:30-33). There would be great irony in God's answer to this prayer: Paul was in fact arrested by the unbelievers in Jerusalem (see Acts 21:27-30), but this led eventually to his ministry among the believers in Rome (see Acts 27–28).

16:1-16 *"Give my greetings to . . ."* Paul had apparently entrusted his letter to Phoebe, a faithful Christian woman, for delivery to Rome (16:1-2; see *Background*). Concerning Priscilla and Aquila (16:3-5), see exposition on Acts 18:1-6. Including this faithful couple, Paul sent personal greetings to no less than 26 Christian friends living in Rome (16:3-16; see *Recipients*). The list included both Jews and Gentiles, men and women, rich and poor—showing the gospel's universal appeal.

16:17-20 *Troublemaker alert!* Without naming names, Paul warned about troublemakers and false teachers in the church. On the crushing of Satan, see Revelation 20:1-3, 10.

16:21-27 *"He is able to keep you."* After sending greetings from his coworkers, including Timothy, Paul closed by committing the Roman believers to Christ's keeping power, which is the gospel itself. On God's secret plan, traditionally translated "mystery" (16:25), see exposition on Ephesians 3:1-13 and on Colossians 1:24-29.

1 CORINTHIANS

BACKGROUND

Paul had written an earlier letter (now lost) to the Corinthians (5:9), addressing the problem of fornication among church members. He had also received a letter from them, asking his opinion on various issues (7:1). That letter had been delivered by Stephanas, Fortunatus, and Achaicus (16:17), who undoubtedly had told Paul of the deteriorating conditions at Corinth. Paul wrote this letter to answer the Corinthians' questions and address problems in the church (7:1) and to tell them of his plans to visit them (16:5-9). That visit probably took place when Paul was later in Greece (Acts 20:3), staying at the home of Gaius in Corinth (see 1:14; Rom. 16:23).

AUTHOR

Paul (1:1; 16:21; see *Romans: Author*).

DATE AND LOCATION

Having spent a year and a half in Corinth (Acts 18:1-17), Paul spent most of the next three years in Ephesus (Acts 19:1-10; 20:31). He probably wrote 1 Corinthians near the end of his time in Ephesus, c. A.D. 56.

RECIPIENTS

The church at Corinth, where Paul had ministered while working with Priscilla and Aquila as a tentmaker (4:12; Acts 18:1-17; 2 Cor. 11:9; 12:13).

PURPOSE

- To address problems in the church (1–6)
- To answer their questions (7:1–16:4); the answer to each question is introduced with the conjunction *de,* often translated *now* (7:1, 25; 8:1; 11:2, 17; 12:1; 15:12; 16:1)
- To tell them of his plans to visit them (16:5-9)

A.D. 35
Paul's conversion

52
Paul in Corinth on 2nd journey

56
Paul writes 1 Cor., lost letter, 2 Cor.

57
Paul in Corinth on 3rd journey

60
Paul imprisoned in Rome

c. 67
Paul martyred

UNIQUE FEATURES

- 1 Corinthians reveals more about the character of the early church than any other of Paul's letters.
- It is one of the most practical of all the NT epistles, offering advice both tender and severe.
- It condemns both theological and social partisanship (1–4; 11:17-22).
- It includes the Bible's most extensive discussion of spiritual gifts (12–14) and of Christ's resurrection (15).

COMPARISON WITH OTHER BIBLE BOOKS

Romans:

- Romans lays the foundation for all NT teaching on salvation; 1 Corinthians lays the foundation of all NT teaching on church life.

Romans and Galatians:

- Romans and Galatians are the foundation for Christian doctrine; 1, 2 Corinthians are the foundation for Christian ethics.

Ephesians:

- Both emphasize Christian unity.

OUTLINE

DIVISIONS IN THE CHURCH (1–4)
- Salutation, introduction (1:1-9)
- The fact of divisions (1:10-17)
- The reason for divisions (1:18–4:21)
  - Misunderstanding the church's message (1:18–3:4)
  - Misunderstanding the church's ministry (3:5–4:21)

DISORDERS IN THE CHURCH (5–6)
- Excommunication (5)
- Lawsuits (6:1-8)
- Loose morals (6:9-20)

DIFFICULTIES IN THE CHURCH (7:1–16:4)
- Marriage (7)
- Things offered to idols (8:1–11:1)
  - Concern for those less mature (8)
  - Willingness to give up freedom (9)
  - Danger of pagan feasts (10:1–11:1)
- Public worship (11:2-16)
- The Lord's Supper (11:17-34)
- Spiritual gifts (12–14)
  - Various kinds of gifts (12:1-11)
  - Purpose of gifts (12:12-31)
  - Supremacy of love (13)
  - Superiority of prophecy over tongues (14:1-25)
  - Using gifts in worship (14:26-40)
- The resurrection (15)

DIVISIONS IN THE CHURCH (1–4)

1:1-9 *All the spiritual gifts* . . . After a brief greeting to the Corinthians (1:1-3), Paul began his letter on a positive note, expressing his thanks to God for their many spiritual gifts, and his confidence that God would continue to bless them.

1:10-17 . . . *but no spiritual growth.* However great their spiritual blessings, the Corinthians had some problems. Paul dealt first of all with their divisions and quarreling. They had begun following various leaders, apparently based in part on who had baptized those in each faction. Paul pleaded for unity on the basis of their common faith in Christ (1:13), reminding them of the simplicity of the gospel, which has very little to do with the human wisdom they so much admired (1:17).

Recognizing that one of the factions centered on him, Paul didn't hesitate to single out his own fan club for special rebuke (1:12-13).

"Christ didn't send me to baptize, but to preach the Good News" (1:17) is probably the strongest biblical argument against the view that one must be baptized to be saved. Paul did not say that Christ had forbidden him to baptize, for the apostle often did baptize his converts (see Acts 16:15, 33; 18:8; 19:5). Rather, he simply said that baptism is not a part of the basic gospel message (the content of which he later defined—see 15:1, 3-4).

1:18-25 *His wisdom vs. human wisdom.* Not only is the gospel simple (see 1:17), many consider it "foolish" (1:18). This should not be surprising, since countless centuries of human wisdom have failed to bring anyone closer to God (1:19-21). Jewish scholars looked for supernatural signs, while the scholars of Greece pursued knowledge for its own sake—and both misunderstood the gospel in its simplicity (1:22-23). Those who were called, however, responded in faith and were saved (1:18, 24). The gospel's very simplicity shows how much wiser the Creator is than any of his creatures (1:25).

Jesus used simple logic and his understanding of human nature to "destroy human wisdom" (1:19; 3:19; see Matt. 21:23-27; 22:15-22; John 8:1-11).

1:26-31 *High and mighty vs. humble and meek.* Reminding the Corinthians of their humble origins (1:26), Paul said God made the gospel simple so that people would focus on and give glory to Christ, not themselves. Paul did not say "not any" wise, powerful, or wealthy people come to faith, but that "not many" such people do (1:26, KJV). John Wesley was often helped by Lady Huntington, of English nobility. This gracious woman who gave so much of her time, talent, and treasure to Christ would often testify: "I am only going to heaven through the letter *M*. How thankful I am that Paul did not say that not *any* noble are called. Therefore, I am only going to heaven through the letter *M*."

Pride was a main cause of the Corinthians' inappropriate loyalty to their various leaders (4:6, 19), thus Paul's focus on their humble past (1:26).

2:1-5 *The simplicity of his message.* Though he was well-educated (see Acts 22:3), Paul had presented the gospel to the Corinthians with simplicity, focusing on the person of

Christ, so that his hearers would put their faith in Christ, not in him.

2:6-16 *Wisdom for the spiritual, not the natural.* The gospel, in all its simplicity, is true wisdom—which the rulers of this world rejected when they crucified Christ (2:6-8). The Holy Spirit has revealed these precious truths of redemption to those who believe. In people's natural state (2:14), without the Spirit's help, such wisdom is unattainable. The natural person "can't understand" God's truth; he or she is totally unable to comprehend it (compare Acts 8:31). Such a person therefore concludes that the truth is "foolishness" (2:14; see Acts 17:18, 32; 26:24). The spiritual person (2:15), on the other hand, can understand these things (2:15; see 2 Tim. 2:15), because he or she is controlled by the Spirit (see Gal. 5:16, 25). Believers "have the mind of Christ" (2:16). This is true of all believers (see 2 Cor. 5:17), though each believer personally has to choose to experience it to the full (see Phil. 2:5).

3:1-4 *Those crybaby Christians.* Paul lamented that because they were immature and worldly ("carnal," KJV), he could not share deeper truths with the Corinthians. *Carnal* comes from the Greek for "flesh." Paul's description of these Corinthians helps define the term:

- They were helpless, like newborn infants. "Infants" conveys weakness, immaturity, and inexperience (compare Gal. 4:3; Eph. 4:14; 2 Pet. 1:9).
- They were unable to receive anything but milk (3:2), which also suggests either infancy or infirmity (see Heb. 5:11-14; 1 Pet. 2:2).
- They behaved like "people who don't belong to the Lord." Someone has suggested that Christians should ask themselves, "If I were arrested and charged with being a Christian, would there be enough evidence to convict me?" Apparently some of these Corinthians would have gotten off scot-free!

The Corinthians' exaltation of human leaders was a symptom of their carnality.

3:5-9 *"Exalt the Grower, not the sower."* Paul urged them once again not to exalt human leaders. God alone deserves the credit for the growth of his Kingdom. Apparently at Corinth, Paul had done the initial "planting" of evangelism while Apollos had done the "watering" of discipleship.

3:10-17 *Will your house survive the fire?* Thinking of his own work as a builder of the church (3:10-11), Paul reminded his readers that they too are each working on a "building" of Christian service. At the judgment seat of Christ, the fire of his discernment will test the worth of each building (3:12-15). Many of those in Corinth should be seriously concerned about the condition of their spiritual buildings (3:16-17).

Scholars generally agree that this passage describes the *"bema"* judgment, so named because it takes place at the "judgment seat" (Greek, *bema*) of Christ (see 4:1-5; Rom. 14:10; 2 Cor. 5:10):

- This judgment will not determine a person's salvation; that is determined in this life, on the basis of whether or not he or she has trusted Christ ("The builders themselves will be saved, but like someone escaping through a wall of flames," 3:15). Nor will it in any way mete out punishment for sins committed either before or after salvation; though "loss" and "a wall of flames" (3:15) might seem to suggest punishment, such punishment of believers is without scriptural basis.

- The key to understanding the *bema* judgment is in 4:2: God's "managers" or "stewards" must be faithful (compare 1 Pet. 4:10). Just as a manager is answerable to his supervisor, someday all managers will stand before him and give account for the way they have fulfilled their responsibilities.

There was actually a courtroom in Corinth called the *bema*, where the judge sat on a high seat.

3:18-23 *The path to wisdom? Foolishness!* The person who would become wise must become a fool! That is, he or she must come to realize that all worldly philosophy is useless in God's sight and that the wisdom of the ages is found in Christ (see Job 5:13; Ps. 94:11).

4:1-5 *Servants should be consistent, not critical.* Paul refused to pass judgment on the quality of his or anyone else's work for Christ, realizing that Christ would someday do this at the *bema* judgment seat (see exposition on 3:10-17). Until then, as a servant of Christ, his job was to remain faithful.

4:6-13 *"How would you like to live like us!"* Paul had used himself and Apollos as examples of the need to be humble stewards (4:6; see 3:5-6), but he wanted to make sure the Corinthians knew he was directing his remarks at them (see 3:6-7). With mild sarcasm, he contrasted the Corinthians' lot in life with his and Timothy's. While the Corinthians were living comfortably, Paul and Timothy suffered great hardship. While the Corinthians were congratulating each other on their wisdom, Paul and Timothy were being made fools for Christ's sake (4:10).

Paul reminded them that while in Corinth, he had supported himself through manual labor (4:12; see *Recipients;* compare 1 Thess. 1:9).

4:14-21 *Clenched fist or open hand?* Paul was not writing such harsh words to shame the Corinthians but rather, as their spiritual father, to warn them and urge them to follow him (4:14-16). He had sent Timothy to minister to them and would soon be there himself. Whether that visit would be pleasant or painful was up to them.

DISORDERS IN THE CHURCH (5–6)

5:1-8 *Immorality and indifference: Paul's solution.* As the proud Corinthians doted on their favorite leaders (5:2; see 4:6), they were tolerating an unthinkable sin within their church: A man was sexually involved with his father's wife (5:1-2). Paul told them to excommunicate this man, hopefully to bring him to repentance (5:3-5) and to keep him from leading others astray (5:6-8).

Paul described the excommunication as delivering the man into Satan's hands, "for the destruction of the flesh" (5:5). To paraphrase: "If this fellow is having so much fun in his sin, then remove him entirely from your fellowship and let Satan kick him around a little. Let him taste what it's like to face a hostile world without the prayers and ministry of the church." Paul was later forced to take similar action against two other people (see 1 Tim. 1:19-20; see also exposition on Matt. 18:15-20 and on 2 Thess. 3:6-15).

The Greek for sexual immorality (5:1; "fornication," KJV) is *porneia*, root word of "pornography." Paul used this word 17 times in his writings, 11 of those times in 1 Corinthians.

5:9-13 *The habitually sinning saint.* Any Christian who willfully persists in sin should be avoided until he or she repents. While the church is not called to police society, it is responsible to judge and deal strongly with its own members.

6:1-11 *Suing saints, behaving like sinners.* If possible, arguments between believers should be settled out of court with the help of other believers (6:1-6). Indeed, it would be better to silently suffer a wrong than to make the matter a legal issue (6:7). Paul reminded the Corinthians of the depraved lives many of them had led before conversion, and urged them now to live in the reality of their sanctified state (6:8-11). Some translations use the word *saint* in 6:1-2; this simply refers to one who has been "sanctified" (6:11, KJV) or "set apart" (6:11). Throughout Scripture the term describes believers (see exposition on Heb. 10:1-18).

Paul is not condemning the court system as an institution, for he himself had used it (see Acts 25:10-11). On Christians "judging" the world (6:2), see Matthew 19:28; on the judgment of angels (6:3), see 2 Peter 2:4.

6:12-13 *Permitted, but not profitable.* Those "set apart" by God (6:11) should not allow themselves to be controlled even by things that may be morally neutral, such as good food.

6:13-20 *The gravity of sexual sin.* As believers, our bodies are a part of Christ, the very temple of the Holy Spirit, making physical involvement in sin all the more serious. Considering the gravity of sexual sin, the only proper response when tempted is to "run away" (6:18; see 2 Tim. 2:22). Paul also advised running away from idolatry (see 10:14) and materialism (see 1 Tim. 6:10-11).

DIFFICULTIES IN THE CHURCH (7:1–16:4)

7:1-9 *Celibacy or marriage? Both are good.* Paul now turned to "the questions you asked in your letter" (7:1; see *Background*). Celibacy is honorable, said Paul, but realistically most people should marry, if only to avoid sexual temptation (7:1-2, 6-9). Even within marriage, both partners should guard against extramarital affairs by fulfilling their marital duties to each other (7:3-5). Each should regard his or her body as belonging to the other (7:4).

7:10-16 *"What if my spouse is not saved?"* A Christian married to a non-Christian should make every effort to keep the marriage together, for the sake of the children and in hopes of winning the spouse to Christ. If the believer leaves the marriage, he or she must not remarry (7:11). Some interpreters believe, however, that 7:15 allows the believing partner to remarry should the unbelieving partner initiate a divorce.

7:17-24 *God's will, before and after his call.* Assuming no sin is involved, the new believer is to continue in his or her established lifestyle, focusing on serving the Lord in that situation. For example, Jewish and Gentile believers should be content with being either Jewish or Gentile. Likewise a person of lower social status should be content with that status (however, see 12:13). On slavery, see *Philemon: Background.*

7:25-40 *Is singleness superior?* The believers at Corinth were apparently undergoing some kind of crisis (7:26). For this reason, and to encourage greater devotion to God (7:32-35), Paul tried to discourage those who were single from rushing into marriage. However, if both partners felt that marriage was God's will for them, they should marry. A widow was free to marry, as long as she married another believer (7:39-40).

8:1-13 *On food offered to idols: Freedom vs. sensitivity.* The Corinthians were divided as to whether it was permissible to eat meat that had previously been offered to an idol. Paul agreed with those who felt this was permissible, since idols have no real power (8:4-6). Nonetheless, he urged the more mature believers to avoid offending those whose consciences were bothered by the practice (8:1-3, 7-13). They should relate to these "weaker" believers (8:11-12; see Rom. 14:1) on the basis of love, not on the basis of their superior knowledge (8:1-3). The bottom line was be a help, not a hindrance, to these less mature Christians (8:9-13).

Human knowledge tends to "make us feel important" or puffed up, while love always "builds up" (8:1). Expressions relating to bragging or boasting occur six times in 1 Corinthians (see 4:6, 18-19; 5:2; 8:1; 13:4), always in connection with knowledge. See exposition on Colossians 2:4-10.

9:1-18 *"For the gospel, I give up my rights."* Having called on the more mature Corinthians to give up some of their rights (see 8), Paul reminded them of all the rights *he* had given up for his ministry. He had the right to financial support (9:6-14) but had given it up for testimony's sake, and because for him, proclaiming the gospel was a labor of love (9:15-18; see exposition on 4:6-13). Perhaps someone at Corinth had accused him of preaching for money.

9:19-23 *As many as possible, by any means possible.* Though Paul's self-support kept him from being "bound to obey people" (9:19), he still considered himself the "servant of everyone" (9:19; compare 9:16; Rom. 1:14), and therefore was ready to use all possible means to win people to Christ. For example:

- To reach Jews, he did things such as circumcising Timothy in Lystra (see Acts 16:1-3) and using Aramaic to address a mob in Jerusalem (see Acts 22:2).
- To relate to Gentiles, he stood while preaching in a synagogue (see Acts 13:16), though Jewish teachers usually sat (see Luke 4:20; John 8:2). At Mars' hill, he quoted from Greek literature (see Acts 17).
- He preached (see Rom. 14:1; 15:1) and practiced (see 8:13) tolerance of immature believers.

9:24-27 *"Run the race! Fight the fight!"* Paul was committed not only to winning the lost (9:19-23) but also to pleasing God. He saw life as a sort of "spiritual Olympics" and sought to win the prize of God's approval. He urged the Corinthians to guard against any sin that might disqualify them. "Disqualified" (9:27) is *adokimos* in Greek; its positive form appears as "approved" in 2 Timothy 2:15. For Paul's report on the end of his spiritual race, see 2 Timothy 4:7.

10:1-13 *Lessons from the history book.* The ancient Israelites enjoyed God's supernatural signs and spiritual blessings, but all to no avail, for their hearts were not right before him (10:1-5). The tragedies that befell them were recorded as object lessons and warnings to us, lest we also fall (10:6-11). We should always be on guard against temptation, trusting God to help us resist it (10:12-13).

10:14-22 *The tables of Satan and the Savior.* While eating food sacrificed to idols may be morally neutral (see 8), involvement in pagan festivities, however minimal, is inconsistent with participation in Christian worship. One simply cannot drink and eat at both the Lord's table and the Devil's table.

10:23–11:1 *Freedom and the law of love.* Just because something may be permissible for the Christian, that does not mean he or she should do it. The law of love asks two questions:

- Does the proposed action help or hinder the spiritual growth of others? (10:23-24)

- Will it bring glory to God? (10:31)

In practical terms, Paul advised eating whatever one is offered, unless anyone present objects (10:27-28).

11:2-16 *Commands concerning head and hair.* Because of the divine order in creation (11:2-3, 8-9), there are different behaviors appropriate to men and women in public worship (11:4-10). This does not, however, mean they are unequal, for as the facts of life demonstrate, they depend greatly on each other (11:11-12). Men are not to cover their heads, for they are "God's glory, made in God's own image" (11:7). Women, on the other hand, are to wear head coverings to demonstrate submission to their husbands (11:7, 10). Nature itself, said Paul, showed the correctness of his instructions on this matter (11:13-16). See 14:26-40.

On a woman being responsible to her husband (11:3), see exposition on Eph. 5:22-33. The reference to angels (11:10) has led some to believe that worshipers may share their pews with angels (see Eph. 3:10; 1 Tim. 5:21; Heb. 1:14; 1 Pet. 1:12)!

11:17-34 *Trouble at the Lord's Table.* The Lord's Supper had become for the Corinthians a social occasion exposing the class differences in the church (11:17-22). Paul reminded them of the purpose and historical roots of this memorial meal (11:23-26) and showed how to restore it to its intended function (11:27-34). The Lord's Supper gives the believer

- a look backward to the Cross (11:26)
- a look inward at the conscience (11:28)
- a look forward to the crown (11:26)

Paul cautioned against partaking of the Lord's Supper "unworthily" (11:27). To do so brings God's judgment, resulting in illness or even death (11:28-30). It is a serious occasion, not a social event (11:31-34). At least two groups of people are disqualified from partaking of the Lord's Supper:

- the unsaved sinner, who may qualify by obeying John 3:16
- the unclean saint, who may qualify by obeying 1 John 1:9

12:1-11 *Many gifts from one Spirit.* Mindful of the Corinthians' pagan background, Paul discussed the purpose and nature of spiritual gifts (12–14), so that they would not be deceived by false prophets claiming to speak for God (12:1-3). He began by explaining just what spiritual gifts are (12:4-11). A spiritual gift is a supernatural ability given to the believer at the time of salvation (12:7; see Eph. 4:7-13). Paul listed 13 such gifts in this chapter (12:8-10, 28), indicating that

- each believer has at least one spiritual gift (12:7, 11)
- no believer possesses all the gifts (12:29-30)

Spiritual gifts have two main purposes:

- to edify the saints (14:4)
- to glorify the Savior (14:2)

But like all good things, they can easily be abused:

- They can be abused in action:
  - ➤ refusing to use a gift (see 14:1, 12, 23)
  - ➤ not using the gift in love (see 13:1)
- They can be abused in attitude:
  - ➤ envy (see 12:15-16)
  - ➤ pride (see 12:21)

12:12-31 *Designed to be a body.* Spiritual gifts are to be used within the context of the church, enabling it to function efficiently, like a human body (see exposition on Eph. 1:15-23). As in a human body, each church member has a different but important function. Neither a human body nor a church body can be effective unless all its members work in harmony. The Holy Spirit baptizes the new believer, making him or her a member of the church, the body of Christ (12:13), and empowering him or her for righteous living and witness (12:13; see Matt. 3:11; John 14:16-17; Acts 1:8; 2:4; Rom. 8; Gal. 5:22-25; Eph. 4:4-16; 5:18; see also *God the Holy Spirit*, p. 812).

13:1-13 *Worthless without love.* Any spiritual gift, no matter how well used, is worthless without love (13:1-3). Love is the basis of all human virtues, expressing itself in many outward qualities of character and enduring when all else fails (13:4-10). Motivated by love, we should lay aside childish talk and actions and act like mature believers, awaiting the day when perfection will come (13:11-12). Faith, hope, and love are the most enduring of all human virtues, but even among these, love is the greatest (13:13) because

- love is the root of faith and hope
- while faith and hope are largely personal, love is focused on others
- love is the very essence of God himself (see 1 John 4:8)

14:1-19 *Tongues are good, but prophecy is better.* In public worship, the gift of prophecy is far more beneficial than the gift of tongues, for prophecy edifies the whole church, not just the individual; and unlike tongues, prophecy needs no interpretation. The goal should be worship that involves both the spirit and the understanding (14:15).

Though usually connected with foretelling the future, prophecy can include any activity that proclaims (we might say "forthtells") the will of God for his people. The "prophet" of 12:29 has the gift of discerning and imparting truth on God's behalf.

14:20-25 *Let them hear it in their own language!* Urging the Corinthians to seek spiritual maturity, Paul recalled how God had used a foreign language as a sign of judgment against Israel (see Isa. 28) and noted how much better it would be for unbelievers to hear the gospel in an intelligible language.

14:26-40 *Order in the church.* All believers should participate in public meetings of the church (14:26). Since the goal of such meetings is mutual edification (14:26), however, certain rules should be followed (14:27-40):

- No gift, either tongues or prophecy, is to be exercised by more than one person at the same time, and all public statements should be judged (14:27, 29-32).
- If someone speaks in tongues, there must be an interpretation (14:28).
- Women should "be silent" in the meetings (14:34-35).

On the silence of women, it should be noted that Paul had earlier spoken of women who pray and prophesy, presumably in public (see 11:5). Some scholars suggest that Paul limited the participation of women only in situations where church doctrine was being judged (14:29; see exposition on 1 Tim. 2:8-15). Others explain the seeming contradiction between 11:5 and 14:34 in terms of Paul's overriding concern for bringing order to a church in confusion (see 14:33).

Whatever Paul's view may have been toward the role of women in public church meetings, he clearly valued them as his equals in church ministry, as seen by

- his high regard for and dependence on both Priscilla and Aquila (see exposition on Acts 18:1-6)
- his association with the four daughters of Philip, all of whom prophesied (see Acts 21:8-10)
- his greetings to many women in Rome, suggesting their

- importance in the church (see Rom. 16:1-16)

See exposition on Galatians 3:26–4:7.

15:1-4 *The gospel in a nutshell.* Paul reviewed the basic gospel message, which is the historical fact of the death, burial, and resurrection of Christ, the "wonderful message" on which our faith is built. Christ was not a martyr dying for his faith, but a Savior dying for our sins. He did not say, "I am finished," but "It is finished."

All three persons of the Trinity (see exposition on Gen. 1:26-31) were instrumental in bringing about Christ's death and resurrection:

- the Father (see John 3:16; Acts 2:24)
- the Son (see John 10:11, 18)
- the Holy Spirit (see Rom. 1:4; Heb. 9:14)

15:5-11 *"He's alive, and here's the proof!"* Paul cited two proofs for Christ's resurrection:

- His many postresurrection appearances (see *Key Events in the Life of Christ*, p. 830), of which Paul listed six, including his appearance to him (15:5-8)
- The amazing fact of Paul's own salvation (15:8-11)

15:12-19 *"If he isn't, we're doomed!"* Some at Corinth questioned the very possibility of resurrection. Paul stressed that the Christian faith rests solely on Christ's resurrection. If that resurrection didn't happen, then those who believe in it are surely the most "miserable" of all people; more important, they are still in the grip of sin and death.

15:20-28 *The resurrection, the reviewing stand, and the reign.* Christ's resurrection is only the first of many that will follow. Just as Adam's sin brought death to the whole human race, Christ's resurrection brings the possibility of everlasting life (15:20-22; see exposition on Rom. 5:12-21). The coming resurrections will take place in a particular "order" (15:23), a military term referring to troops marching by rank, as in a parade:

- Christ's resurrection leads the parade, for it was the first of its kind. All those previously raised (see exposition on Acts 20:7-12) died again; Christ was the first to be raised to immortality. He was the "first of all who will rise from the dead" (see Col. 1:18).
- Next come the "troops" of the Rapture resurrection (15:23; see exposition on 15:50-58 and on 1 Thess. 4:13-18).
- Then comes the "end," which will include the resurrection of OT and Tribulation saints (15:24; see Dan. 12:2 and exposition on Rev. 20:1-6), ushering in Christ's eternal reign (15:24-28).
- Not mentioned here but implied in Revelation 20:6 is a second resurrection, after the Millennium and Satan's final rebellion, of the unrepentant who will then stand before God in the Great White Throne Judgment (see John 5:29; see exposition on Rev. 20:1-6; 20:11-15).

15:29-34 *Exhortations in light of the empty tomb.* If the Resurrection never happened, said Paul, we might as well quit making sacrifices for Christ and dedicate our lives to pleasure (15:30-32). But since he *has* been raised, we should pursue holiness (15:33-34).

Though Paul did not endorse baptism for the dead, he pointed out that the practice (evidently existent in Corinth) is meaningless if there is no resurrection (15:29). There is no biblical support for baptism for the dead. To die lost is to remain forever lost (see Luke 16:19-31; Heb. 9:27).

15:35-38 *Like a grain of wheat.* Paul didn't say exactly how God will raise the dead and what we will look like when raised. Instead he compared it to the apparent death and resurrection of a grain of wheat, leading to several thrilling conclusions:

- Our resurrected body will be more glorious than our present one, just as a plant is more glorious than its seed (15:37).
- The old body, like a grain of wheat, must die to be changed (15:36; compare John 12:24). Death will not really kill the believer, but simply release his or her new body.
- The new body keeps its identity (15:38; see 13:12).

15:39-49 *Earthly vs. eternal.* Our resurrected body will differ from our mortal body as much as animal flesh differs from human flesh; as much as the sun differs from the moon; for the one is spiritual while the other is merely natural (15:39-44). We inherited our natural body from Adam but will receive our eternal body from Christ (15:45-49).

15:50-58 *Then death will die!* At the time of the Rapture (see exposition on 1 Thess. 4:13-18), both the dead and the living will be changed in a flash. Bodies dead and decaying will become incorruptible; bodies still living but mortal will become immortal (15:50-53). Jesus will complete his triumph over death (15:54-57; 15:26). With this assurance, believers should "be strong and steady" (15:58).

The death of death itself will destroy the last of humanity's five natural enemies (15:26):

- the world (see Gal. 1:4; James 4:4; 1 John 2:15)
- the flesh (see Rom. 7:18; 8:8; Gal. 5:17; 1 John 2:16)
- the Devil (see Matt. 13:39; Eph. 6:11)
- spiritual death (see John 5:24; 8:51; Rev. 2:11)
- physical death (see Ps. 55:4; Heb. 2:15)

On "the law gives sin its power," see exposition on Romans 3:9-20. On "secret" or "mystery" (15:51), see exposition on Colossians 1:24-29.

16:1-4 *"Finally, about that offering . . ."* Paul urged the Corinthians to regularly set money aside to help him collect an offering for needy believers in Jerusalem (see exposition on Acts 20:1-6). In his next letter to them, he would devote much more time to this (see 2 Cor. 8–9).

DILIGENCE IN THE CHURCH (16:5-24)

16:5-12 *"Here are our schedules."* Paul was trying to arrange his schedule so that he could spend an extended time at Corinth (16:5-9). Meanwhile, Timothy would visit them. Perhaps because of Timothy's youth (see 1 Tim. 4:12), Paul urged them to treat him with respect (16:10-11). Apollos did not feel it was God's will for him to visit Corinth at that time, possibly because of all the troubles they were going through.

16:13-18 *"Thank God for people like Stephanas."* Paul exhorted the believers to greater faith and love, singling out Stephanas as an example they should follow.

16:19-24 *Anathema and Maranatha.* Paul sent greetings from the Christians in Ephesus, especially Aquila and Priscilla, whom he had met in Corinth (see exposition on Acts 18:1-6). He pronounced a curse on Christ's enemies and a blessing on his followers. "Cursed" (16:22) is anathema, or "fitted for destruction" (see Rom. 9:3; Gal. 1:8-9). "Our Lord, come!" is Maranatha, literally, "the Lord comes" (see Phil. 4:5; Rev. 22:20).

2 CORINTHIANS

BACKGROUND

2 Corinthians is actually Paul's fourth letter to the Corinthian church. The first letter, dealing with the problem of fornication in the church, has been lost (1 Cor. 5:9). The second letter (our 1 Corinthians) dealt with various problems he had become aware of. Paul wrote a third letter to the church at Corinth that was harsh and disciplinary in nature (see 2:3-4; 7:8-9). This letter has been lost as well; but according to a report Paul received from Titus, it apparently accomplished its purpose (7:6-8), leading Paul to write this fourth letter (2 Cor.), in which he comforted those who had gotten themselves right with God (1–9) and strongly defended his apostleship against some who were opposing his authority (10–13).

AUTHOR

Paul (1:1; 10:1; see *Romans: Author*).

DATE

A.D. 56, about six months after Paul wrote 1 Corinthians (see *1 Corinthians: Date and Location*).

LOCATION

Paul left Ephesus in the spring of 56 (after writing 1 Corinthians) and was bound for Troas, where he hoped to meet Titus and get a report from Corinth (2:12-13). Failing to find Titus there, he continued on to Macedonia (Acts 20:1), where he did meet Titus and heard from him about the situation in Corinth, whereupon he wrote this letter.

RECIPIENTS

See *1 Corinthians: Recipients.*

A.D. 35
Paul's conversion

52
Paul in Corinth on 2nd journey

56
Paul writes 1 Cor., lost letter, 2 Cor.

57
Paul in Corinth on 3rd journey

60
Paul imprisoned in Rome

c. 67
Paul martyred

PURPOSE

- To explain why his plans for another visit to Corinth had changed (1:12–2:4)
- To instruct concerning the restoration of an offending brother (2:5-11)
- To express his joy over the revival in the church as a result of his harsh letter (2:12-13; 7:15-16)
- To discuss his motivation for ministry and to defend himself against his opponents (2:12–6:10; 10–13)
- To encourage holiness (6:11–7:16)
- To encourage generous giving (8–9)

UNIQUE FEATURES

- 2 Corinthians is the most autobiographical of Paul's letters, giving an intimate view of his personal life and ministry.
- It is the least doctrinal of his letters, with the possible exception of Philemon. Yet it contains deep doctrinal truths (3–8, especially 5).
- It gives insights into the character and tactics of false teachers and of Satan.

COMPARISON WITH OTHER BIBLE BOOKS

Romans:

- Romans is primarily doctrinal and secondarily practical; 2 Corinthians is primarily practical and secondarily doctrinal.
- Romans is the most systematic, and 2 Corinthians the least systematic, of Paul's letters.

Galatians and Hebrews:

- 2 Corinthians emphasizes the New Covenant, as do Galatians and Hebrews.

OUTLINE

PAUL EXPLAINS HIS ACTIONS (1:1–2:11)
- Salutation (1:1-2)
- His sufferings in Ephesus (1:3-11)
- His change in plans (1:12–2:4)
- His recommendation concerning the offender (2:5-11)

PAUL DEFENDS HIS MINISTRY (2:12–7:16)
- The fragrance of Christ (2:12-17)
- His calling from God (3:1–6:10)
  - His letters of recommendation (3:1-6)
  - The glory of his message (3:7-18)
  - His sincerity and suffering (4)
  - His assurance (5:1-10)
  - His ministry of reconciliation (5:11-21)
  - His faithfulness amid suffering (6:1-10)
- His challenge to the Corinthians (6:11–7:16)
  - Exhortations to holiness (6:11–7:1)
  - Gratitude for their growth (7:2-16)

PAUL EXPLAINS THE COLLECTION (8–9)
- Examples of giving (8:1-9)

Encouragement to give (8:10-15)
Arrangements for the collection (8:16–9:5)
Benefits of giving (9:6-15)
PAUL DEFENDS HIS AUTHORITY (10–13)
His power in Christ (10)
Comparison with false apostles (11:1–12:13)
Plans, exhortations, benediction (12:14–13:14)

PAUL EXPLAINS HIS ACTIONS (1:1–2:11)

1:1-7 *Comforted to comfort.* Paul began with thanksgiving to the "God who comforts us," who enabled him to extend comfort to the Corinthians whether he himself was in comfort or in suffering. *Comfort* in Greek combines two words: *para* (alongside) and *kaleo* (to call). To comfort is to answer someone's call, to walk alongside, to cheer, guide, and defend that person. Its noun form, *parakleiton,* was often used of a legal counsel or "advocate" in a trial (see 1 John 2:1). Paul's comforting of the Corinthians helped establish them in their salvation (1:6). Paul would come back to the theme of comfort at the end of the letter (see 13:11).

Each member of the Trinity is a Comforter:

- Father (1:3; see Isa. 49:13)
- Son (see Isa. 61:2; John 14:1; 2 Thess. 2:16)
- Holy Spirit (the "Counselor"—John 14:16, 26; 15:26; 16:7)

Fellowship with God is the remedy for the suffering of all who, like David, have looked for comforters but found none (see Ps. 69:20).

1:8-11 *"He delivered me from death!"* Paul reported having undergone a time of great despair, increasing his sense of dependence on God. Many, including the Corinthians, had prayed for him during that time. Like Abraham, he had trusted in a God who was able to raise the dead (1:9; see Heb. 11:17-19).

1:12–2:4 *"I changed my plans. It's as simple as that."* Paul could write with a clear conscience, knowing that his testimony among the Corinthians had been godly and consistent (1:12-14). He was not double-minded as some had apparently assumed (1:17-18). He had originally planned to visit them en route to Macedonia (1:15-16).

Paul interrupted his explanation of his change of plans to speak of God's faithfulness regarding our salvation, sanctification, and eternal security (1:19-22; see exposition on John 10:22-30).

He then resumed his explanation: If he had come to Corinth when he originally planned to, it would have been with a severe rebuke. He wanted to wait till the visit could be one of joy (1:23–2:2). He had, however, written to them concerning many problems (2:3-4; see *Background*). 2:1 may indicate he had paid an unpleasant visit to Corinth before writing his third letter (compare 13:1).

2:5-11 *"Restore the repentant, lest Satan reclaim him."* Paul had told the church to excommunicate an unrepentant man due to his immorality (see exposition on 1 Cor. 5:1-8). They had done so; the man had repented; but they had refused to forgive him. Paul urged them to do so, to protect both him and themselves from further temptation.

PAUL DEFENDS HIS MINISTRY (2:12–7:16)

2:12-17 *The savor of life, the smell of death.* Recalling his anguish over not finding

Titus in Troas (2:12-13), Paul offered thanks to God, who assures believers of victory regardless of when or where problems arise (2:14). Paul likened his ministry to a Roman victory parade, during which the successful general (Jesus) would lead both conquerors (the saved) and captives (the unsaved) to their respective destinies (2:14). From the parade would ascend the fragrance of burning incense. To the captives, it was the smell of death; to the conquerors it was the savor of life (2:15-16). He defended his apostleship against charges that he was doing it for material gain (2:17; see 1:12; 11:9; 12:13; exposition on 1 Cor. 4:6-13 and 9:1-18).

The presence of truth brings both life and death. Joseph's presence in prison was death for the baker but life for the butler (see Gen. 40). Christ's presence on the cross meant death for one thief but life for the other (see Luke 23:39-43).

3:1-6 *Real-life letters of recommendation.* Though Paul was beginning to defend himself (see 2:17), he didn't need to do so, nor did he need letters of recommendation; all the recommendation he needed was breathing and walking about in the lives of his converts. The legalistic Judaizing teachers who plagued Paul's work (see exposition on 11:16-33) carried impressive letters of introduction from Jerusalem (3:1). Prior to his conversion, Paul had done the same (see Acts 9:2). Now, his testimonials were

- *personal:* "Your lives are a letter"
- *permanent:* "written in our hearts"
- and *public:* "everyone can read it" (3:2-3).

3:7-18 *The story of two glories.* Paul contrasted the temporary glory of the law of Moses, which brought the knowledge of sin and death (3:7; see Rom. 3:20; 7:10), with the eternal glory of God's New Covenant of grace (see Heb. 8:7-13), which brings the power of inward transformation (3:18). When Moses brought the law down from Sinai he wore a veil over his face, so that the people would not be frightened (see Exod. 34:29-35), but also, said Paul, so that they could not see how the law's glory was fading (3:7, 13). The New Covenant of grace is superior to the law, for its glory, given by Christ, will never fade (3:8-11, 16-18). Sadly, today, as in Paul's day, a veil still blinds the eyes of most Israelites concerning their Messiah (3:14-15).

God's goal is to make us "more and more like him," traditionally translated "from glory to glory" (3:18). This process will last throughout all eternity, but he wants to begin it now!

4:1-6 *Preaching in the light.* Again Paul proclaimed his sincerity as an evangelist (4:1-2; see 1:12-14; 2:17), unlike other so-called evangelists and even Satan himself, who try to deceive (4:2-4). While Satan aims his light at the eyes, blinding his followers, God directs his light at the heart and feet, to indwell and guide (4:3-6).

4:7 *Priceless treasure, perishable vessels.* Believers carry the "treasure" of the gospel in the "perishable containers" of their mortal bodies. One of the world's largest (108.3 carats) and most famous diamonds, presented to Queen Victoria in 1850, is displayed against a simple black cloth inside a bullet-proof case in the Tower of London. The black background brings out by contrast the diamond's dazzling glory. Likewise, God has entrusted his most prized treasure to us.

4:8-18 *Spiritual success through suffering.* Paul had suffered many hardships, being often knocked down but never knocked out (4:8-10), allowing him to demonstrate God's power and presence in his weak and decaying body (4:11-15). The conclusion: The grief down here is nothing compared to the glory we'll know up there (4:16-18).

CHARACTERISTICS OF THE GOSPEL MINISTRY

Triumphant (2 Cor. 2:14–6:18)
Sincere (2 Cor. 2:17)
Approved (2 Cor. 3:1-3)
Dependent (2 Cor. 3:4-5)
Superior (2 Cor. 3:6-18)
Open (2 Cor. 4:2)
Satanically Opposed (2 Cor. 4:3-4)
Christ-honoring (2 Cor. 4:5-7)
Suffering (2 Cor. 4:8-18)
Confident (2 Cor. 5:1-9)
Compelling (2 Cor. 5:10-17)
Representative (2 Cor. 5:18-21)
Blameless (2 Cor. 6:1-7)
Paradoxical (2 Cor. 6:8-10)
Separated (2 Cor. 6:11-18)

5:1-10 *The believer's new body.* By faith believers know that, when their present body dies, they will be given an eternal body, made and guaranteed by God (5:1-8). With this assurance, they live to please God, knowing that someday they will stand before him in judgment (5:9-10; see exposition on 1 Cor. 3:10-17).

5:11-21 *Representing the Savior, reconciling the sinner.* Mindful that God would someday judge him (5:11; see 5:10) and compelled by Christ's love (5:14), Paul was eager to proclaim the gospel (5:11-16). We are ambassadors for Christ, pleading with the unsaved to receive his offer and be reconciled by his grace (5:17-21). Christians, like ambassadors, are

- citizens of the state they represent (see Phil. 3:20; Col. 3:1-2)
- chosen for the assignment (see John 15:16)
- called home before war is declared (see 1 Thess. 1:10; 4:13–5:10)

6:1-10 *"Keep the faith, just as I have."* Paul pleaded with the Corinthians not to toss aside the gospel but to accept it and remain faithful while God's door of welcome was still open (6:1-2; see Isa. 49:8). Paul had himself been faithful in spite of terrible trials and hardships and was thus used by God to accomplish many wonderful things, including establishing the church in Corinth (6:3-10).

6:11–7:1 *Some keys to fellowship.* Despite all his sufferings, Paul had shared his very heart with the Corinthians; he urged them to respond in kind (6:11-13). If they would get serious about living holy lives, separating themselves from all wrongful ties with unbelievers, then God would be able to have the kind of fellowship he desired with them (6:14-18). In light of God's desire for their fellowship, the Corinthians should turn from all uncleanness and live in wholesome fear of him.

7:2-7 *Found: Titus, with a happy tale!* Again Paul spoke of his openness toward the Corinthians (7:2-4); and again he demonstrated that openness by telling of the panic attack that led him from Troas to Macedonia in search of Titus (7:5; see 2:12-13), and of his joy upon finally finding Titus and hearing the good news from Corinth (7:6-7).

7:8-16 *A letter both sad and glad.* Referring again to his harsh letter to the Corinthians (see 2:3-4), Paul recalled how distressed he had felt as he wrote those words of rebuke. His sorrow had turned to joy, however, when Titus reported that the letter had caused them to repent and seek revival. They had shown the type of sorrow that produces true repentance, rather than the "sorrow without repentance" that leads only to deeper despair (7:10).

PAUL EXPLAINS THE COLLECTION (8–9)

8:1-8 *The Macedonian example of giving.* Paul then spoke of the offering he was taking for the famine-stricken church in Jerusalem (8–9; see exposition on Acts 20:1-6). He began by pointing to the wonderful example of the Macedonian believers who, after dedicating themselves to God and in the midst of great hardship, had collected a large offering. He urged the Corinthians to do likewise (8:7-8).

8:9 *Christ's example.* Of course, history's greatest example of sacrificial love was Christ himself. Though rich beyond imagination, he chose to become poor to make us spiritually rich. He became what he was not (poor), that we might become what we were not (rich). The sinless Son of God became the Son of Man so that sinful sons of men might become sons of God.

8:10-15 *"Finish what you started!"* The Corinthians had begun an offering for Jerusalem a year previously but had lapsed. Paul urged them to resume their effort, not feeling they had to give more than they were able, but simply doing their fair share.

8:16–9:5 *"I've bragged about you, so don't let me down."* Paul would send Titus and two other men, who could be depended on to collect and deliver their gifts (8:16-24). He was sending them ahead of time so that the Corinthians would have their gifts ready when he arrived (9:5). Paul had told the church in Macedonia that the Corinthians had already begun an offering (8:10); he hoped Titus's early visit would encourage them to intensify their efforts and not let him down (9:1-4; compare 1 Cor. 16:2).

9:6-15 *Sow much, reap much; sow little, reap little.* Paul spoke of the blessedness of giving (9:6; see Luke 6:38; Acts 20:35), of how giving should be done in the church, and of the results of generous giving:

- Rules for giving:
  - Each individual must decide the amount he or she gives (9:7).
  - All giving should come from the heart (9:7).

- Results of giving:
  - ➤ God will meet the needs of the giver (9:8-11).
  - ➤ The giving will meet the real needs of others (9:12).
  - ➤ The recipients will praise God and pray for the giver (9:12-14).

PAUL DEFENDS HIS AUTHORITY (10–13)

10:1-6 *My weapons of war.* Turning his attention to those at Corinth who were challenging his authority (see 11:5, 13), Paul defended himself against their attacks (10–13). Though Paul and his ministry partners may not have been as impressive in person as were his opponents (10:1-2), he had on his side the full armor of God (compare Eph. 6:13), which could knock down the Devil's strongholds, refute arrogant arguments, and change rebellious hearts. In defeating Satan, one cannot simply fight fire with fire; one must use blood—the blood of Christ (see Rev. 12:11)!

10:7-11 *"Don't be fooled by outward appearances."* Calling attention to Paul's mild demeanor, his enemies sought to belittle him by pointing out that, while his letters seemed weighty and forceful, in person he was unimpressive and was a poor public speaker (10:7-10). Paul assured them that on his next visit he would be as stern in person as he had been in his letters (10:11).

10:12-18 *The only basis for boasting.* Paul's enemies had been trying to win followers by comparing themselves to each other and to Paul (10:12-14), whose work they were trying to claim as their own (10:15-16). Paul, however, would seek only God's approval (10:17-18).

11:1-4 *"I will boast because I'm jealous!"* Moved by "the jealousy of God himself," born of his desire to keep the Corinthians faithful, Paul asked them to allow him for a moment the "foolishness" (11:1; 11:16-19; 12:11) of comparing himself to his opponents (11:5–12:13). Jealousy is not the same as envy. Jealousy is the desire to possess one's own things. It is a good and natural trait, if kept in proper bounds. Envy is the desire to possess the things of another. This is always wrong.

11:5-15 *Paul and the apostate apostles.* Paul began his comparison of himself to his opponents by noting that, though not as gifted in public speaking as they were, he was just as knowledgeable (11:5-6). He had ministered to the Corinthians without charge (11:7-9; see 12:13, 16; Acts 18:1-17; 1 Cor. 4:12), unlike his opponents (see 11:16-21). He made such comparisons not out of pride but out of fear that these "false apostles," empowered by Satan himself, would lead the Corinthians astray, thus frustrating God's grace and Paul's ministry (11:10-15).

11:16-21 *"Why do you let them exploit you?"* The Corinthian believers had allowed the godless false apostles to make them their spiritual slaves, taking everything they owned and shamelessly exploiting them. Being made "slaves" (11:20) may refer both to financial exploitation and to the legalism promoted by these Judaizers (see exposition on 11:22-33 and on the book of Galatians).

11:22-33 *"All right, let's compare credentials."* Paul had everything the false teachers bragged about and more. If they boasted of their Jewish heritage, he could do so much more (11:22; compare Acts 22:3; Phil. 3:4-6). If they boasted of their ministry, he could boast of a ministry validated by incredible sufferings both physical and emotional (11:23-32). This passage provides our most complete account of Paul's hardships.

12:1-6 *A close encounter in the third heaven.* Modestly speaking in the third person (12:2), Paul related a vision God granted him of paradise, where he heard, saw, and experienced things too glorious to express in human words.

12:7-10 *Thorns and grace.* Following his ecstatic experience (12:1-6), God allowed Satan to severely afflict Paul, lest he become proud. After repeatedly asking God to remove the affliction, Paul finally learned to thank God for it, realizing how much it had taught him about the sufficiency of grace.

Some scholars believe Paul's "thorn in the flesh" was chronic ophthalmia, a disease of the eyes not too painful but at times repulsive to the onlooker. The onset of Paul's ailment, 14 years before this time (12:2), would have coincided with his entrance into Galatia, which had been occasioned by some sort of physical infirmity (Gal. 4:13-15; 6:11).

12:7 is Paul's fifth reference to Satan in this letter. From these five mentions we learn several things about the Devil:

- his *title:* "the god of this evil world" (4:4)
- his *tactics:* to take advantage of (see 2:11), inflict suffering on (12:7, compare Job 1–2), and blind unbelievers (see 4:4)
- his *treachery:* disguising himself as an angel of light (see 11:14)
- his *trustees:* false teachers (see 11:15)

12:11-13 *"Only a true apostle could do what I did."* Paul had felt compelled to show the superiority of his ministry to that of the false apostles only because the Corinthians themselves had failed to see it. His ministry differed from that of the false teachers in that it was confirmed by miracles and was free of greed.

12:14-21 *"Ready or not, I'm on my way!"* Once again Paul announced his proposed visit (12:14). Once again he reminded the Corinthians that ministry, not money, had been and would be his only purpose; neither he nor Titus nor any other coworker had taken advantage of them—nor would they ever do so (12:14-19). He expressed concern for their speedy repentance and reformation (12:20-21).

13:1-14 *Third time's the charm?* By the authority of Christ, Paul again urged the Corinthians to seriously assess their spiritual situation. He hoped his next visit would establish two things: that he was truly an apostle and that they were truly believers (13:1-10). He closed with a brief benediction (13:11-13). On "third time" (13:1), see exposition on 1:12–2:4.

GALATIANS

BACKGROUND

As Paul planted churches among the Gentiles of Galatia, other teachers came along and tried to convince the new believers that, to be truly saved, they had to keep the law. These "Judaizers" sought to discredit not only Paul's message but also his very claim to be an apostle. In Galatians, Paul vindicated both his apostleship (1–2) and his message (3–6), showing convincingly that salvation is by God's grace through faith, apart from works of the law.

AUTHOR

Paul (1:1; 5:2; see *Romans: Author*).

DATE, LOCATION, AND RECIPIENTS

Different opinions about the date of this letter are influenced by differing interpretations of the letter's recipients. The letter is addressed to "the churches of Galatia" (1:2). In Paul's day, Galatia referred to two different areas:

- Geographically, it referred to a northerly region Paul visited on his second missionary journey (Acts 16:6; 18:23).
- Politically, it referred to a Roman province that, in addition to geographical Galatia, took in more southerly regions including Iconium, Lystra, and Derbe, which Paul visited on his first journey (Acts 13:14–14:24) and revisited on his second (16:1-6) and third journeys (18:23).

If 2:1 refers to the Jerusalem Council (Acts 15), then Paul may have written this letter to the churches of southern Galatia just after that event, with the issue of law and grace fresh on his mind. That would give Galatians a date of about A.D. 49, making it the earliest of Paul's letters.

A.D. 35 ***Paul's conversion***

47 ***Paul in Galatia on 1st journey***

49 ***Jerusalem Council, Paul writes Galatians***

c. 51 ***Paul in Galatia on 2nd journey***

53 ***Paul in Galatia on 3rd journey***

60 ***Paul imprisoned in Rome***

c. 67 ***Paul martyred***

PURPOSE

- To vindicate Paul's apostleship and message, both of which the Judaizers had questioned
- To show that God's righteousness (justification) can be received by faith alone apart from the law
- To discuss the meaning of Christian liberty and show that it does not mean freedom to sin

UNIQUE FEATURES

- Galatians is the most severe of Paul's letters, offering no words of commendation.
- The doctrine of justification by faith is stated more emphatically in Galatians than in any other of Paul's letters—more so even than in Romans.
- Galatians gives an unusual amount of history for a letter. 1:18 and 2:1 give crucial clues to the chronology of Paul's life.
- Galatians is a letter of striking contrasts:
  - ➤ flesh and works vs. the Spirit and his fruit
  - ➤ the world vs. the Cross
  - ➤ circumcision vs. the new creation
  - ➤ faith vs. law
- Paul usually used an amanuensis (secretary) in writing his letters, but he wrote at least part and perhaps all of Galatians by his own hand (6:11).

COMPARISON WITH OTHER BIBLE BOOKS

Romans:

- Galatians has been called a shorthand version of Romans, which Paul wrote nearly 10 years later; Galatians discusses controversially what Romans discusses systematically.

2 Corinthians:

- Paul's defense of his apostleship (1–2) is somewhat parallel to the entire book of 2 Corinthians.

Hebrews:

- Both Hebrews and Galatians talk about the New Covenant's superiority to the Old.

OUTLINE

PAUL'S DEFENSE (1–2)
- Salutation and prologue (1:1-10)
- Proposition (1:11-12)
- Proofs (1:13–2:21)

FAITH AND LAW (3–4)
- The principle of faith vs. law (3:1–4:7)
- A plea for faith vs. law (4:8-20)
- A picture of faith vs. law (4:21-31)

CHRISTIAN LIBERTY (5–6)

Liberty, not law (5:1-12)
Liberty, not license (5:13-26)
Liberty in service (6:1-10)
Concluding remarks (6:11-18)

PAUL'S DEFENSE (1–2)

1:1-5 *Greetings of grace from a true apostle.* Stressing the validity of his apostleship, Paul greeted the Galatian believers in the name of the God of grace. The twin emphases of these opening verses—Paul's authority and God's grace—signal Paul's two main concerns in this letter.

1:6-10 *"Not even if an angel tells you!"* Paul was amazed that many of the Galatians, having received salvation by grace, had so quickly been persuaded by the Judaizers' "different" gospel of salvation by works (1:6-7). Paul urged them to reject this false gospel, even if an angel should proclaim it.

The Judaizers' message was a "different" gospel (1:6), which in Greek is *heteros* (root for "heterodoxy") meaning "another of a different kind." There is only one true gospel—the gospel of God's grace.

"Curse" (1:9) is *anathema* in Greek (see Rom. 9:3; 1 Cor. 12:3).

1:11-12 *"Let me tell you how I got it."* The gospel Paul preached was not of human origin, as the Judaizers were claiming; he had received it directly from Christ himself. Christ's direct revelation to Paul began on the road to Damascus (see Acts 9). Paul later made at least two references to information imparted directly to him by the Lord (see 1 Cor. 11:23; 15:3-4).

1:13-24 *His eventful early years.* Having claimed divine authority for his message (1:11-12), Paul set out to prove that claim (1:13–2:21). He began by telling of his youthful zeal for Judaism and persecution of Christians—a story he often told for its dramatic portrayal of God's grace (1:13-14; see Acts 22:1-16; 26:1-20; 1 Tim. 1:12-16).

He then reviewed his experiences following conversion. He had spent time in Arabia and Damascus (1:15-17), after which he briefly visited Jerusalem (1:18) before leaving again for Gentile areas (1:19-24). Throughout this travelogue, Paul emphasized how little contact he had had with other apostles, thus supporting his claim of direct revelation (1:12).

Paul's first official visit to Jerusalem as a Christian occurred three years after his conversion (1:18; see Acts 9:26-28). If the 14 years prior to the next Jerusalem visit here reported (2:1) includes the three years of 1:18, it would coincide with the date of the Jerusalem Council (see *Date, Location, and Recipients*). If 2:1 does in fact refer to the Jerusalem Council, Paul's trip to Jerusalem with famine relief (see Acts 11:27-30) is omitted here.

Paul had been called to his mission before his birth (1:15-16). The Bible records at least two other instances of divine calls to the unborn (see Jer. 1:4-10; Luke 1:15-17).

2:1-5 *Circumcision? Not for Titus.* While Paul was in Jerusalem, some legalistic believers had demanded that his Gentile companion Titus be circumcised, but Paul, taking a firm stand for the sufficiency of the gospel, had refused to bow to their pressure.

2:6-10 *Blessings on his Gentile mission.* When the church leaders and apostles in Jerusalem realized how God had blessed Paul's outreach to Gentiles, they commended his work, requesting only that he ask Gentile believers to help the famine-stricken Jewish

Christians (see exposition on Acts 20:1-6).

2:11-21 *The tentmaker rebukes the fisherman.* On one occasion, both Peter and Barnabas had hypocritically refused fellowship with Gentile believers, for which Paul strongly rebuked them (2:11-14). Nothing must be allowed to dilute the truth of salvation by grace alone (2:15-21). Peter's hypocrisy was especially surprising, considering his pioneering role in Gentile evangelism (see Acts 10).

FAITH AND LAW (3–4)

3:1-9 *Foolish pagans or Abraham's children?* Paul rebuked the Gentile Galatians for ignoring their salvation and freedom in Christ while trying to obey the Jewish law (3:1-5). The Judaizers may have promised to make them children of Abraham, but they could be true sons of Abraham only if they, like he, were saved by faith alone (3:6-9; see exposition on Gen. 15:1-11 and on Rom. 4:1-12).

3:10-14 *The law curses; the Cross cleanses.* No one can be justified by the law, for the breaking of just one law brings God's curse (3:10, 12; see James 2:10). On the other hand, anyone who so desires can be justified by faith in Christ, who through his death on the cross accepted the law's curse on our behalf (3:11, 13-14). The law is like a chain, which is entirely broken when just one link is severed. On "the just shall live by faith" (3:11, KJV), see *Habakkuk: Comparison with Other Bible Books.*

3:15-18 *A covenant confirmed centuries before the commandments.* God's promise to Abraham, fulfilled in Christ, preceded the Mosaic law by hundreds of years. Since salvation through faith was therefore offered long before the law, salvation would continue to be given to all who believed.

The 430 years Paul spoke of (3:17) was the duration of Israel's enslavement in Egypt (see Gen. 15:13; Exod. 12:40; Acts 7:6). God's original promise to Abraham (see Gen. 12:3) actually preceded Sinai by some 640 years.

3:19-25 *The law was our teacher.* If salvation comes through faith, one might ask, why did God give the law? He gave it as a "teacher" to guide sinful people until the Savior came (3:24). But with Christ's coming, the tutor's role ended (3:25). 3:19 is one of several references to the involvement of angels in giving the law (see Deut. 33:2, NASB; Ps. 68:17; Acts 7:53; Heb. 2:2).

3:26–4:7 *God's grown-up children.* Believers in Christ are no longer children in need of a tutor, but full-grown sons and daughters of God. For all practical purposes, children have no more freedom than slaves (4:1). But there are significant advantages to being an adult son or daughter:

- Servants have a master, while sons and daughters have a father.
- Servants obey out of law and fear, while sons and daughters obey out of liberty and love.
- Servants have no inheritance, while sons and daughters can expect to inherit all things.

While Jesus was God's "only son" (John 3:16), Christians become God's children by adoption (4:5). As adopted children, we can affectionately call God "Abba, Father" (4:6; compare Rom. 8:15). Our adoption is secure, for God "chose" us for it (see Eph. 1:4-5).

Paul's teachings elsewhere on the role of women in the church (see exposition on 1 Cor. 14:26-40 and on 1 Tim. 2:8-15) should be interpreted in light of his view of the equality of men and women in Christ (3:28), a revolutionary concept in Paul's day. Christ transcends not only gender differences but racial and social differences as well. On "the right time" (4:4), see exposition on Ephesians 1:7-12.

4:8-11 *"Don't abandon sonship for servanthood!"* Having been freed from the spiritual slavery of paganism, the Galatians had become enslaved to the observance of Jewish feasts and traditions. This, said Paul, was sheer insanity. He feared that his ministry of grace among them had been in vain.

4:12-20 *From dearest friend to worst enemy?* Paul begged the Galatians to remember the happy fellowship they once enjoyed with Paul, when their love saw him through a time of physical affliction (4:12-15; see exposition on 2 Cor. 12:7-10). Did they now hate him for telling them the truth (4:16)? Their real enemies, said Paul, were the legalistic false teachers (4:17-18). Speaking as their spiritual mother, Paul described his letter as an effort to give them rebirth into God's grace (4:19-20).

4:21-31 *Hagar and Sarah, law and grace.* Paul presented Hagar and Sarah, with their sons Ishmael and Isaac, as types of the contrast between the bondage of legalism and the liberty of grace. Hagar, like those who depend on the law, was a slave; and her son, who was naturally born, was also a slave. Sarah, like those who depend on grace, was free; and her son, whose birth was miraculous, was Abraham's heir (4:21-27; see Gen. 16:1–18:15; 21:1-21).

Christians, like Isaac, are the true heirs of God's promise to Abraham (4:28, 31). Just as Sarah asked Abraham to "get rid of that servant," Christians should have no desire to be in bondage to the law (4:30; see Gen. 21:10). Just as Ishmael persecuted Isaac, the Judaizers were persecuting Paul (4:29; see Gen. 21:8-9).

CHRISTIAN LIBERTY (5–6)

5:1-12 *Dependence on law means denial of grace.* Paul again pleaded with the Galatians not to forsake the way of grace for the way of law. If a person submits to circumcision, he is obligated to keep all the other laws as well. God's grace, by contrast, demands only our faith (5:1-6). Like leaven, false teachings such as legalism can spread quickly through a church (5:7-9). Paul had strong words for anyone who would spread such false teaching (5:10-12).

While the phrase "fallen away from God's grace" is often used to describe someone who has adopted a sinful lifestyle, Paul used it to describe those who had regressed into legalism (5:4).

5:13-15 *The bottom line: Love.* While the Galatians needed to be warned against legalism, they also needed to be warned against an opposite danger: lawlessness. Freedom in Christ should not become a license to sin (compare exposition on Rom. 6:15-23). Rather, it should motivate brotherly love and a willingness to serve. The whole law is summed up in the command to love (see exposition on Matt. 22:34-40).

5:16-21 *The wicked works of the flesh.* Lawlessness can best be avoided by living "according to your new life in the Holy Spirit" (traditionally translated "walking in the Spirit"). As Paul would later show in his letter to Rome, lawlessness cannot be avoided simply by trying to follow the law, for the flesh is at war with the Spirit, leaving us helpless (5:17), and the law tends to arouse our sinful desires (see exposition on Rom. 7:1-25). Paul listed several specific "desires of [the] sinful nature" or "works of the flesh."

5:22-26 *The wonderful works of the Spirit.* Paul then listed various manifestations of the "fruit" of the Holy Spirit that one can practice with no fear of transgressing any law. Believers in Christ have "crucified" the desires of the sinful nature (5:24; see 2:20; Rom. 6:6) and should seek to live in the reality of that fact (5:25; see Rom. 8:4-5).

6:1-6 *Bear each other's burdens.* An appreciation of freedom in Christ should motivate the believer to a life of service (compare 5:6, 13). We should bear each other's burdens, especially the burden of past sin, which should be dealt with in a spirit of compassion and humility. Meanwhile, we should take responsibility for our own actions (6:4-5). Those who are taught God's Word should help their teachers financially (6:6).

6:7-10 *What you sow is what you reap, only more.* If we sow to the flesh, we will reap death. If we sow to the Spirit, we will reap life. We should always be diligent in sowing to the Spirit, that is, in doing good works and practicing the fruit of the Spirit.

6:11-18 *Not circumcision but a new creation.* Paul had written this letter in his own hand, using "large letters" perhaps because of an eye problem (see exposition on 4:12-20 and on 2 Cor. 12:7-10). The Judaizers, said Paul, were motivated by pride and unwillingness to suffer for Christ. Paul, however, would continue proclaiming the gospel that brought Jews and Gentiles together as "new and different people," no matter how he might have to suffer because of that sometimes unpopular message.

Paul ended his letter as he had begun it, proclaiming the genuineness of his apostleship (compare 6:17 and 1:1).

EPHESIANS

A.D. 35
Paul's conversion

52
Paul in Ephesus on 2nd journey

54–57
Paul in Ephesus on 3rd journey

60–62
Paul imprisoned, in Rome writes Ephesians

c. 67
Paul martyred

BACKGROUND

Next to Rome, Ephesus was the most important city Paul visited on his missionary journeys. The main city of the Roman province of Asia, it was a populous port city, important as a center for commerce, religion, and politics. It had two great architectural wonders, the temple of Diana and a 50,000-seat theater (Acts 19:29). It also had a stadium or race course that often hosted fights between men and wild beasts (see 1 Cor. 9:24-25; 15:32—words written from Ephesus).

Paul visited Ephesus during his second journey, a visit cut short by his haste to return to Jerusalem (Acts 18:19-21). He visited again on his third journey and remained there for three years (Acts 19–20). He later sent Timothy to Ephesus as his representative. After Paul's death, the apostle John made Ephesus his headquarters until his death, by which time the Ephesian church had "fallen from [its] first love" (Rev. 2:1-7).

AUTHOR

Paul (1:1; 3:1; see *Romans: Author*).

DATE AND LOCATION

Paul was in prison when he wrote this letter (3:1; 4:1; 6:20). If these remarks refer to his imprisonment in Caesarea (Acts 24:27), the letter would have been written about A.D. 57–59. If they refer to his imprisonment in Rome (Acts 28:30), which is more likely, the letter was written about 60–62. Since he expressed no hope of release, it was probably just after his coming to Rome, while he was imprisoned in his own rented house (Acts 28:30).

RECIPIENTS

The words "in Ephesus" (1:1) are missing in some important Greek manuscripts. This, coupled with the fact that there are no personal greetings in the letter and no specific church problem is addressed, has given rise to the idea that Ephesians was originally a cyclical letter, intended for circulation among the seven churches of Asia Minor (Rev. 2–3). However, the majority of extant Greek manuscripts do include "in Ephesus," and none of those manuscripts indicate any other destination. Ephesians may have been intended as a cyclical letter, being first sent to Ephesus, the main city of Asia, where Paul had made his headquarters as he ministered throughout the region (Acts 19:10). Having received a good report about these churches (1:15), and hearing that Tychicus (6:21) was ready to make a trip to Ephesus, Paul seized the opportunity to send a letter.

PURPOSE

- To teach about the church as the body of Christ, composed of both Jewish and Gentile believers
- To exhort believers to conduct themselves properly toward one another because of their oneness in Christ
- To equip them for spiritual warfare

UNIQUE FEATURES

- Ephesians addresses no specific church problem.
- It is one of the least personal of Paul's letters. There is almost no personal greeting, and only two personal names appear: Paul and Tychicus.
- In the original Greek, 1:3-14 is the longest sentence in the Bible.
- The phrase "in the heavenly realms" occurs five times here (1:3, 20; 2:6; 3:10; 6:12), and nowhere else in Scripture.
- Paul used three great figures of speech to illustrate our union with Christ:
  - ➤ building (2:21-22)
  - ➤ body (1:22-23; 4:15)
  - ➤ bride (5:25-32)

COMPARISON WITH OTHER BIBLE BOOKS

Joshua:

- Joshua deals with the conquest and possession of the Promised Land, the "earthly realms"; Ephesians deals with our taking possession of our promised "heavenly realms" (see exposition on 1:1-6).

Colossians:

- The content of 78 of the 155 verses in Ephesians is repeated in Colossians with only slight differences; 78 out of the 95 verses in Colossians resemble Ephesians:
  - ➤ Both epistles stress the relationship between Christ the head and the church his body.
  - ➤ Ephesians emphasizes the body, while Colossians emphasizes the head.

Philippians, Colossians, 2 Timothy, Philemon:

- Like these epistles, Ephesians was written while Paul was in prison in Rome, with 2 Timothy coming during his second imprisonment when death was near.

OUTLINE

CALLING THE CHURCH OUT OF THE WORLD (1–3)
- Salutation (1:1-2)
- Praise for God's redemption (1:3-14)
- Awareness of redemption (1:15-23)
- Saved by grace (2:1-10)
- United by grace (2:11-22)
- United as equals (3)

THE CHURCH'S CONDUCT IN THE WORLD (4–6)
- In unity (4:1-16)
- In righteousness (4:17-32)
- In holiness (5:1-21)
- In marriage (5:22-33)
- In family and household (6:1-9)
- Amid conflict (6:10-20)
- Conclusion (6:21-24)

CALLING THE CHURCH OUT OF THE WORLD (1–3)

1:1-14 *The Trinity and our salvation.* Paul praised the work of all three members of the Godhead in bringing about our salvation (1:3-14). This is one of the Bible's clearest teachings on the Trinity (see exposition on Gen. 1:26-31):

Chosen by the Father in the past (1:1-6). God chose us for salvation and sanctification before the creation of the world and has given us "every spiritual blessing in the heavenly realms." "Heavenly realms" simply describes our experience of the reality of salvation. On "predestined" (1:5, KJV, NIV), see 1 Peter 1:1-2. On "adoption," see exposition on Galatians 3:26–4:7. On sanctification, see exposition on Hebrews 10:1-18.

Redeemed by the Son in the present (1:7-12). In the person of Jesus Christ, God has redeemed us through his blood shed at Calvary (1:7-8). Calvary was the final fulfillment of God's mysterious, ages-long plan of salvation (1:9-11; see exposition on 3:1-13), in which believers are privileged to participate (1:12).

Oikonomia, the Greek for "dispensation" (1:10, KJV), occurs elsewhere with a meaning referring to stewardship or management, as in Luke 16:2-4, 1 Corinthians 9:17, and Colossians 1:25. The school of Bible interpretation known as *dispensationalism* views the world as a household run by God. God "dispenses" or administers the affairs of his "household world" in various stages of revelation (see *Biblical Dispensations,* p. 821). Christ, as the very focal point of all these stages, was born "in the dispensation of the fullness of times" (KJV) or "at the right time"—a time that was right in terms of both the divine plan and the human condition (see *Matthew: Background;* Gal. 4:4).

Sealed by the Spirit forever (1:13-14). At the time of salvation, the Holy Spirit "seals" or "identifies" the believer, "guaranteeing" his or her salvation. This seal image suggests several things about the believer's relationship to God:

- The believer is owned by God (see 1 Cor. 6:19-20; 2 Tim. 2:19).
- he or she is eternally secure (see 4:30; see exposition on John 10:22-30).
- Salvation is a completed transaction (see Jer. 32:9-10; John 17:4; 19:30).

The Holy Spirit is "promised," for

Christ promised his coming (1:13; see John 14:16-17; 16:7, 13; Acts 1:4-5).

1:15-23 *Understanding the Trinity and our salvation.* Having heard of the Ephesians' faithfulness, Paul thanked God for them and prayed that God would show them just who Christ is, what he has done for believers, and who they are in him. Christ is the head of the church, which is his "body" (1:22-23). The NT often describes the church as the body of Christ (see 4:7-11; Rom. 12:5; 1 Cor. 12:6; see exposition on Col. 2:4–3:4). On being "filled" by Christ (1:23; 3:19), see exposition on Colossians 1:15-23.

2:1-10 *Transformed from transgressors to trophies.* We were lost in sin and under God's curse (2:1-3), but now by grace we have been saved and given a place in God's eternal plan (2:4-7). This salvation is "a gift from God" given "by his special favor" (2:8). God's "special favor" is also referred to as grace, and it describes God's part in offering salvation apart from any requirement to keep the law. "When you believed" describes faith, our part in accepting that offer. It is *apart* from works (2:9) but is also *for* the good works God created us to do (2:10).

The Greek for "masterpiece" or "workmanship" (2:10) is *poema,* from which we get *poem.* God has two treasured poems:

- the poem of creation (see Rom. 1:20; Rev. 4:11)
- the poem of salvation (2:10; see Rev. 5:9-10)

2:11-22 *From aliens to family members.* Gentiles, once alienated from Israel and from God, are now joined to both by the blood of Christ, who has removed the wall of separation represented by the law and has joined Jew and Gentile together into "one people" with direct access to God (2:11-18). Gentiles, once strangers, can now be members of God's household, living stones in his holy Temple, of which Christ is the chief cornerstone (2:19-22; see 1 Pet. 2:4-5).

Jesus "ended" the law "by his death" (2:15) by fulfilling it (see Matt. 5:17). He fulfilled it when he died on the cross for our sins, thus bringing the law to an end (see Rom. 10:4).

3:1-13 *"Let me tell you a secret."* God made known to Paul a "secret plan," or mystery, hidden for ages (3:1-5): that Gentiles would now have the same opportunity as Jews for salvation (3:6). Both would be "part of the same body," namely, the body of Christ (see exposition on 1:15-23). Gentiles could be saved before Christ, but only by becoming Jews (see Isa. 56:1-8). See exposition on Colossians 1:24-29. This joining of Jew and Gentile into the one body of Christ would complete the revelation of God's plan to the unseen realm of angels and demons (see 1:21; see exposition on 6:10-17). It was a sort of school in which they could learn about his grace (3:8-12; see 1 Pet. 1:10-12).

3:14-21 *The dimensions of his love.* Paul asked God to help his people grow stronger in their faith and better understand the full extent of his love for them (3:14-19). He ended this first half of his letter with praise to a God well able to do just that (3:20-21).

THE CHURCH'S CONDUCT IN THE WORLD (4–6)

4:1-6 *Maintaining the unity.* Having been united by their faith in Christ, believers should want to prove themselves worthy of their new condition. They should be at peace with each other (4:1-3), remembering all that they have in common (4:4-6).

4:7-16 *The Giver and the goal of his gifts.* When Christ ascended to heaven, he distributed a wealth of spiritual gifts to his followers (4:7-11) to enable them to minister together as his body on earth (see exposition on 1:15-23)

THE BOOK OF EPHESIANS: The Church of the Living God

Chapter 1

Likened to a Body

"And the church is his body; it is filled by Christ, who fills everything everywhere with his presence" (1:23).

- Wrought and planned by the Father (1:1-6)
- Bought and purchased by the Son (1:7-12)
- Taught and protected by the Spirit (1:13-14)

Chapter 2

Likened to a Temple

"We who believe are carefully joined together, becoming a holy temple for the Lord" (2:21).

Chapter 3

Likened to a Mystery

"God himself revealed his secret [mystery] to me" (3:3).

Results of this mystery

- Believers have access to the throne of God
- Believers are strengthened by the Spirit of God
- Believers can know the love of God
- Believers can request the power of God
- Believers can display the glory of God

Chapter 4

Likened to a New Person

"Until we come to such unity in our faith and knowledge of God's Son that we will be mature and full grown in the Lord, measuring up to the full stature of Christ" (4:13).

"You must display a new nature because you are a new person, created in God's likeness—righteous, holy, and true" (4:24).

Chapter 5

Likened to a Bride

"And you husbands must love your wives with the same love Christ showed the church" (5:25).

The bride is to be

- Separated
- Spirit-filled
- Singing
- Single-minded
- Submissive and circumspect

Chapter 6

Likened to a Soldier

"Put on all of God's armor so that you will be able to stand firm against all the strategies and tricks of the Devil" (6:11).

A. Children and parents (6:1-4)
  - As a soldier, the child is to obey the parents.
  - As a commander, the parent is to discipline and instruct the children.

B. Servants and masters (6:5-9)

and to bring each believer to spiritual maturity (4:12-16).

4:17-32 *Walk the new walk, talk the new talk.* Gentile Christians should "throw off" their pagan past and instead display a way of life in keeping with their new nature in Christ (4:17-24; see Rom. 12:2). Paul offered specific guidelines relating to things such as dishonesty, anger, stealing, and misuse of the tongue (4:25-29, 31-32). Such wrong actions bring grief to the Holy Spirit, who is the permanent houseguest of every believer (4:30).

5:1-13 *Walk in holiness.* We are to imitate God, to love as Christ loved, and to avoid immoral action and language (5:1-5). We are not to keep company with the godless but instead are to expose their sin, both by our godly example and by direct reproof (5:6-13).

5:14-21 *Walk in readiness.* As we pursue holiness, we are to be alert, making the most of every opportunity, for we live in difficult days (5:14-17). Rather than indulging fleshly appetites, we should seek the spiritual refreshment available in the fellowship of the church (5:18-21).

5:22-33 *A word to wives and husbands.* Just as Christ is the head of the church (see exposition on 1:15-23), a husband is the head of his wife. Therefore, women should submit to their husbands "as [they] do to the Lord" (5:22-24). Just as Christ loves the church, husbands should love their wives (5:25). A husband's love for his wife, like Christ's love for his church, should be sacrificial (5:25-29) and intimate (5:30-33).

6:1-4 *"Children, obey. Fathers, don't provoke."* Children are to obey their parents (6:1), who are responsible for their spiritual welfare (6:4). Obedient children will be blessed (6:2-3; see Exod. 20:12). Fathers are to use their authority with love, lest they make their children angry and resentful (6:4).

6:5-9 *Both slaves and masters serve Christ.* Whatever our station in life, slave (6:5-8) or master (6:9), we should treat others as we would treat Christ, the master of us all.

6:10-17 *His armor against our adversary.* Reminding us of the might of our adversary the Devil, Paul urged us to use all the resources of God against him. These include the confidence of our right standing before God ("righteousness," "salvation"), as well as the truth of God's Word.

Whatever specific roles the "evil rulers" or "powers of darkness" play in his army, Satan is powerful and resourceful (6:11-12). The believer is never told to attack the Devil, but the believer is told to withstand and resist him (6:11, 13-14; see 1 Pet. 5:8-9):

- When tempted to do wrong, we should flee as Joseph did (see Gen. 39:7-23).
- But when attacked by Satan for doing right, we should stand firm as Daniel's friends did (see Dan. 3:1-25).

Someone has observed that as pilgrims we walk, as witnesses we talk, as contenders we run, but as fighters we stand.

6:18-20 *One final weapon: Prayer.* Our spiritual warfare should always include prayer, for ourselves and for others (6:18). Paul asked for prayer for himself, that he might find the right words for witnessing (6:19-20). As we pray we must also "stay alert" to our spiritual enemy (6:18; see 1 Pet. 5:8). Christians are often told to stay alert or to be ready (see Matt. 26:41; Luke 12:37-40; Acts 20:31; 1 Thess. 5:6; 2 Tim. 4:5; 1 Pet. 4:7; Rev. 3:2; 16:15).

6:21-24 *"He'll bring you up to date."* Paul closed by noting that Tychicus would have the latest news concerning his ministry. Then, as usual, he wished his recipients peace and grace.

PHILIPPIANS

A.D. 35
Paul's conversion

c. 51
Paul in Philippi on 2nd journey

57
Paul in Philippi on 3rd journey

60–62
Paul imprisoned in Rome, writes Philippians

c. 67
Paul martyred

BACKGROUND

Paul, now in Rome under house arrest, had founded the Philippian church during his second missionary journey (Acts 16:11-40). The believers at Philippi, the main city of Macedonia, had assisted in Paul's support while he was at Thessalonica and Corinth (4:15-16; 2 Cor. 11:9). Upon hearing of his imprisonment, they sent Epaphroditus to Rome with another financial gift, which was probably what enabled Paul to live in his own rented house (Acts 28:30) rather than in jail. While in Rome, Epaphroditus became ill and nearly died (2:27). When he recovered, Paul used the occasion of his return to Philippi to send this letter, essentially a thank-you note for their gift.

AUTHOR

Paul (1:1; 3:4-6; see *Romans: Author*).

DATE AND LOCATION

Since Paul seemed confident of either acquittal or release from prison (1:19, 25; 2:24; see Philem. 1:22), he probably wrote Philippians toward the end of his time of house arrest, c. A.D. 61, about a year after he wrote Ephesians and Colossians.

PURPOSE

- To thank the Philippian believers for their financial help
- To address problems in the Philippian church, especially the rivalry between two prominent women, Euodia and Syntyche
- To refute the teachings of the Judaizers (3:1-3) and of some who were going to the opposite extreme, perhaps advocating a total disregard for law or a hedonistic lifestyle (3:18-19)

UNIQUE FEATURES

- Philippians is the most personal of Paul's letters to churches, with more than 100 first-person pronouns in its four short chapters.
- It is a letter of joy (see *Outline*).
- It contains one of the Bible's most often-quoted passages on the person of Christ (2:5-11).
- It contains no direct quotations from the OT.
- It is the only letter of Paul in which he mentions church officers in the salutation (1:1).

COMPARISON WITH OTHER BIBLE BOOKS

Ephesians, Colossians, Philemon, 2 Timothy:

- All were written during Paul's imprisonments.

2 Corinthians, 2 Timothy, Philemon:

- These, with Philippians, are Paul's most personal letters.

OUTLINE

REJOICING IN CHRIST'S SERVICE (1)
- Salutation; appreciation for the Philippians (1:1-11)
- The progress of the gospel (1:12-26)
- Exhortation to faith and courage (1:27-30)

REJOICING IN CHRIST'S SELFLESSNESS (2)
- Christ's selflessness (2:1-11)
- Imitating Christ's selflessness (2:12-18)
- Two imitators of Christ's selflessness (2:19-30)

REJOICING IN CHRIST'S SUFFERINGS (3)
- The power of his death and resurrection (3:1-11)
- The purpose of his death and resurrection (3:12-21)

REJOICING IN CHRIST'S SUFFICIENCY (4)
- Rejoicing in his peace (4:1-9)
- Rejoicing in his power (4:10-13)
- Rejoicing in his provision (4:14-23)

REJOICING IN CHRIST'S SERVICE (1)

1:1-6 *Our confidence in his completion.* Paul expressed his thanks to God for the believers at Philippi (1:3-5) and his confidence that God would continue the work of sanctification he had begun in them (1:6; see exposition on Heb. 10:1-18). God never starts something he doesn't finish; Paul was confident that the Philippians were secure in their salvation "until . . . that day when Jesus Christ comes back again" (1:6; compare 1:10; 2:16; 1 Cor. 1:8). See also exposition on Isaiah 2:5–4:1.

1:7-11 *"Only God knows how much you mean to me."* Paul felt a deep affection for this particular church, which had helped him so much (1:7-8; see *Background*). He prayed that they would grow in knowledge, wisdom, and righteousness.

1:12-18 *Want to reach hundreds? Go to jail!* Paul rejoiced that, far from hindering his ministry, his imprisonment had actually enhanced it. Apparently even some of the soldiers guarding him had come to faith (1:12-13). For different reasons, both friends and foes of Paul had stepped up their preaching activities following his imprisonment. Some of his timid believer friends had been jolted into greater boldness (1:14). Others, perhaps jealous of the impact of this newcomer to Rome, were stepping up their evangelistic outreach "out of jealousy" (1:15-17). Whatever the motivation, Paul rejoiced that the gospel was being heard (1:18). He knew, as did Asaph the psalmist, that "human opposition only enhances [God's] glory" (Ps. 76:10; see exposition on Ezra 6:1-12).

1:19-26 *"To be here or not to be here: That is the question."* Though apparently confident that he would soon be released from prison (1:19, 25), Paul's first choice would have been to die and be with Christ (1:23). His sense of duty, however, required him to remain here on earth (1:24). Whatever happened, Paul's overriding desire was that his life "always honor Christ" (1:20). While death would be "better" for Paul, his goal in continuing to live was summed up in one word: *Christ* (1:21).

1:27-30 *Wonderful news! You get to suffer for him!* Paul exhorted the Philippians to be steadfast in their faith and bold before their enemies, counting it a privilege to suffer for Christ. Suffering is promised to all true believers (see 2 Tim. 3:12).

REJOICING IN CHRIST'S SELFLESSNESS (2)

2:1-4 *Blessings* from *Christ* for *others.* Those who have been blessed in Christ should want to pass those blessings on to others. To concentrate on others, not on ourselves, is an important step in Christian growth.

2:5-8 *What Christ did for us: Humiliation.* Christ is the supreme example of selflessness. When the mighty Son of God became the lowly Son of Man, he did several things:

- He left heaven's glory for earth's poverty (see John 17:5; 2 Cor. 8:9).
- He "made himself nothing," or "emptied" himself (2:7).
  - ➤ He did not lay aside his deity. He was, is, and ever shall be the Son of God (see John 1:1; Col. 1:15; 2:9).
  - ➤ He did, for a while, hide his heavenly fame in an earthly frame. Even though he retained every single attribute of deity while on earth, he surrendered the independent exercise of those divine characteristics (compare Mark 9:12 and Rom. 15:3).
- He "appeared in human form" (2:7-8; see John 1:14; Rom. 8:3; Gal. 4:4; Heb. 2:14, 17). This simple fact can hardly be grasped by the human mind. The infinite, holy Creator suddenly came into the world in the likeness of his creatures. One might compare that to a human king voluntarily becoming a peasant. But a better comparison would be a human king becoming a lowly ant—though even that comparison would be inadequate!
- He "took the humble position of a slave" (2:7). He did not come as a mighty human king or philosopher, but as a lowly servant.
- He "humbled himself" (2:8):
  - ➤ He talked our language, wore our clothes, ate our food, breathed our air, and endured our vicious treatment. Contrast Christ's humble statement in the Garden of Gethsemane (see Matt. 26:39,

42) with the statement of arrogance that many scholars attribute to Satan (see Isa. 14:13-14).
  - ➤ Christ's ultimate humiliation came as he allowed himself to be killed (2:8; see Matt. 26:39; John 10:18; Heb. 5:8; 12:2). And this was not just any death but "a criminal's death on a cross," the worst kind of death both physically and judicially (see Ps. 22; Isa. 53; Gal. 3:13).

2:9-11 *What God did for Christ: Exaltation.* Because Christ humbly gave himself for our sins
- God has "raised him up to the heights of heaven" (2:9; see Isa. 52:13; John 17:1; Acts 2:33; Heb. 2:9).
- He has been given a name (a position and place of authority) above all other names (2:9; see Eph. 1:20; Heb. 1:4).
- Someday (2:10-11) he will be acknowledged as Lord by everyone:
  - ➤ "in heaven" (angels)
  - ➤ "on earth" (human saints and sinners)
  - ➤ and "under the earth" (demons)

See Psalm 22:27-28; Isaiah 45:23; 66:23; Romans 14:11; Revelation 15:4. On Christ's millennial reign, see *Isaiah: Background.*

2:12-18 *"Do it because God is doing it for you."* Christians are to "put into action God's saving work in [their] lives," knowing that God himself is at work within them (2:12-13). God gives us both the desire and the ability to serve him. As we do this, we will "shine brightly" before unbelievers (2:14-16; see Matt. 5:14-16).

2:19-30 *Two tremendous spiritual soldiers.* Paul hoped soon to send Timothy to minister to the Philippians. He commended him to them as one who displayed something of the servant heart of Christ (2:19-24). Epaphroditus was also an example of selflessness (2:25-30).

REJOICING IN CHRIST'S SUFFERINGS (3)

3:1-11 *The choice: Circumcision or Christ.* Paul warned against the Judaizers who wanted to "mutilate," that is, circumcise them. Christians, he declared, are the ones who are truly circumcised (3:1-3; see Rom. 2:29; 9:6-8; Gal. 6:14-15). Few, if any, could match Paul's credentials as a Jew (3:4-6), yet he considered those credentials nothing in light of God's new revelation of salvation and eternal life through Christ (3:7-11).

Many Christians want the first half of 3:10, "to really know Christ and experience the mighty power that raised him from the dead," but show little interest in the second half: to "learn what it means to suffer with him, sharing in his death." But these go hand in hand, as saints throughout the ages can attest (see Rom. 8:17).

3:12-16 *"No, I'm not there yet, but I'm on my way."* Paul wasn't perfect in his walk with the Lord, but he looked toward that day (in Christ's eternal Kingdom) when he would be. While perfection is not possible in this life, we should strive for spiritual maturity.

3:17-19 *"Follow me, not them."* Thinking of both this letter and the times he had taught the Philippians in person, Paul urged them to follow his example and teachings, and not those who, because of their wrong teaching, were actually "enemies of the cross of Christ." Paul probably had in mind both the legalizers (3:2) and the hedonists or antinomianists (meaning those "against law") whom he described in these verses.

3:20-21 *The new you.* As an antidote to hedonism, Paul reminded them of the promised resurrection, when our lowly bodies will be transformed and we will be citizens of Christ's eternal Kingdom.

REJOICING IN CHRIST'S SUFFICIENCY (4)

4:1-3 *Love expressed, love needed.* Paul expressed again his great affection for the Philippians (see exposition on 1:7-11), then asked a mature believer in the church to help reconcile two quarreling women.

4:4-7 *The peace of God: Precious and protective.* Christians should be joyous and even-tempered (4:4-5). Instead of being anxious, they should be at peace (4:6-7). The peace of God (4:7) comes through prayer and transcends all understanding. Paul gave two golden rules for those who seek such peace:

- "Don't worry about anything" (4:6). The KJV translates this as "Be careful for nothing." The Greek word used here for *worry* or *careful* describes being pulled in different directions. It is not reasonable concern but panic (see Ps. 55:22; 1 Pet. 5:7).
- "Pray about everything" (4:6). Our prayers should be both definite and devotional. It has been said that there are only two things the Christian should not worry about:
  - ➤ those things he or she can change, in which case *perspiration* is the answer;
  - ➤ those things he or she cannot change, in which case *supplication* is the answer.

All Christians enjoy peace *with* God (see Rom. 5:1), but only those who have successfully substituted prayer for care can enjoy the peace *of* God, a peace that

- guards our hearts, protecting us from wrong feelings;
- guards our minds, protecting us from wrong thinking (4:7).

Contrary to the popular saying, prayer does not always change things. But sincere prayer does always change us, by protecting against those things that can drive us to despair (see Isa. 26:3; 2 Cor. 10:5).

4:8-9 *The real power of positive thinking.* Another key to peace is focusing our thoughts on positive things. We can do this in no better way than by focusing on the things we have learned from Paul concerning the person and work of Christ.

4:10-13 *Content and strong in feast and famine.* Because Christ abided in and empowered him (4:13), Paul could be content in any and all circumstances. There are two kinds of Christians:

- Thermometer Christians, whose satisfaction is totally dependent on circumstances: They simply register the prevailing spiritual temperature.
- Thermostat Christians, whose satisfaction is totally independent of circumstances. Not only are they not affected by circumstances, they themselves help shape those circumstances.

4:14-23 *"By the way, thanks for the care package!"* Paul acknowledged the latest gift from the Philippians (4:10, 14) and recalled all their past generosities (4:15-16; see *Background*), adding that his main source of joy was the efforts and thoughts behind those gifts (4:17-18). He assured them of blessings in return and committed them to God's grace. The greetings from people in Caesar's household (4:22) show how effectively Paul had proclaimed the gospel from his involuntary confinement (compare 1:12-13).

A.D. 35
Paul's conversion

c. 55–58
Paul in Ephesus, Epaphras in Colosse

60–62
Paul imprisoned in Rome, writes Colossians

c. 67
Paul martyred

COLOSSIANS

BACKGROUND

The Colossian church was probably founded by Epaphras (1:7; 4:12-13) as the result of Paul's work in Ephesus (A.D. 55–58; Acts 19). With Paul now under house arrest in Rome (4:3, 10, 18; Acts 28:30-31), Epaphras visited him and told him of heresies plaguing the Colossians. Paul wrote this letter to warn them against those false teachings that on the one hand obscured the majesty and glory of Christ (1:15; 2:8) and on the other hand introduced asceticism (2:16-23). The false teaching was a mixture of ceremonial Judaism (2:16) and oriental theosophy (2:18) that opposed the simplicity and freedom of the gospel and vital union with Christ the risen Lord (2:19; 3:1). It was probably an early form of Gnosticism. See exposition on 2:4-10.

AUTHOR

Paul (1:1, 23; 4:18; see *Romans: Author*).

DATE

A.D. 60–61, about the same time Paul wrote Ephesians.

RECIPIENTS

Christians in Colosse, 100 miles east of Ephesus, whom Paul had never personally visited (1:4, 7-8; 2:1). Colossian believers apparently met in at least two different homes, those of Nympha (4:15) and of Philemon. Paul's letter to Philemon mentions a church meeting in his home (Philem. 1:2). That he lived in Colosse is suggested by the mentions of Archippus (4:17; see exposition on Philem. 1:1-3) and Onesimus (4:9; Philem. 1:8-16) in both letters.

PURPOSE

- To tell the Colossians of Paul's care for them and concern for their spiritual development and to relay ministry-related information (1:1-12; 4:7-18)
- To present Jesus Christ as preeminent in all things (1:13-29) and to warn against any heresy that would distract from that preeminence (2)
- To encourage holiness (3:1–4:6)

UNIQUE FEATURES

- Colossians is the most Christological of Paul's letters, containing the Bible's sharpest picture of Christ's preeminence (1:14-22).
- It contains the Bible's strongest warning against the dangers of human philosophy (2:8).
- The shorter form of Paul's benediction, characteristic of his later letters, occurs for the first time here (4:18; 1 Tim. 6:21; 2 Tim. 4:22; Titus 3:15).

COMPARISON WITH OTHER BIBLE BOOKS

Galatians:

- Galatians combats national exclusivism; Colossians combats intellectual exclusivism.

Ephesians:

See *Ephesians: Comparison with Other Bible Books.*

Ephesians, Philemon, Philippians, and 2 Timothy:

- Paul wrote these and Colossians from prison.

1 John:

- Both combat the problems of empty ritualism and of humanistic philosophies such as Gnosticism.

OUTLINE

THE PERSON AND WORK OF CHRIST (1:1–2:3)
- Salutation; thanksgiving for Colossians (1:1-8)
- Prayer for the Colossians (1:9-14)
- Christ's character (1:15-23)
- Paul's sufferings for Christ (1:24–2:3)

THE BETTER WAY OF CHRIST (2:4–3:4)
- Better than philosophy (2:4-10)
- Better than legalism (2:11-17)
- Better than mysticism (2:18-19)
- Better than asceticism (2:20-23)
- Focusing on Christ (3:1-4)

PRACTICING THE LIFE OF CHRIST (3:5–4:18)
- In personal life (3:5-17)
- In household life (3:18–4:1)
- In witnessing (4:2-6)
- Greetings; final instructions (4:7-18)

THE PERSON AND WORK OF CHRIST (1:1–2:3)

1:1-8 *"Thank God for your testimony!"* Though he had not personally worked with the Colossians (see 2:1), Paul commended them for their faith in God and love for the saints of God, of which he had heard from Epaphras.

1:9-14 *"Now let me pray for you."* Paul prayed that they would find God's perfect will, which included personal holiness, fruitfulness, and power in their Christian lives (1:9-12). This was all possible because of God's mighty act of redemption on their behalf through Jesus Christ (1:13-14).

1:15-23 *The preeminence of the preeminent one.* Christ "is first in everything" because he "existed before everything else began" (1:17).

- He is the very "image" of God (1:15). The Greek signifies not that he is simply like God but that he is God, for the very "fullness" of God dwells in him (1:19; see 2:9; Eph. 1:23; 3:19; 4:13).
- He created all things in heaven and on earth for his glory, and continues to hold it all together (1:16-17).
- He is the head of the church (1:18). Concerning "first of all who will rise from the dead" (1:18), see exposition on 1 Corinthians 15:20-28.
- He is in the process of reconciling everything in the universe to himself (1:20). That is, he is bringing all things into a right relationship with the Father. This does not mean that everyone will be reconciled to God (universalism), but anyone who so desires can be (1:21-23). This reconciliation began at the Cross and will be complete at the sound of the seventh trumpet (see Rev. 11:15).

1:24-29 *The Gentile mystery (and other mysteries).* Paul saw his present suffering (1:24-25) as a partnership in Christ's sufferings (see 2 Cor. 1:5) and as an important part of his ministry to believers (see 2 Cor. 12:15). That ministry involved proclaiming a message that had been "kept secret for centuries and generations past," namely, that Christ would now indwell believing Gentiles as well as believing Jews (1:27; see 4:3; Rom. 11:25; 16:25; Eph. 3:1-13; 6:19).

The Greek word used in 1:26 is the word for *mystery,* and that is how it has traditionally been translated. However, Paul always used the term to describe not some mystical experience but various parts of God's plan that had been previously hidden and had now been revealed (see 2:2, 9; 1 Cor. 2:7-8; 15:51; Eph. 5:32; 2 Thess. 2:7; 1 Tim. 3:16; for other NT occurrences, see Matt. 13:11; Rev. 1:20; 10:7; 17:5).

"What remains of Christ's sufferings" (1:24) does not mean that Christ's suffering was inadequate to save. It may mean that Paul's sufferings provided a more immediate testimony for his contemporaries. Or "Christ's sufferings" may mean afflictions that Christians suffer for Christ.

2:1-3 *"My deep concern for you . . ."* Paul's suffering for the Colossians was internal as well as external, as he earnestly desired that both they and the Laodiceans—and all other believers whom he did not know personally—would come to full maturity in Christ and would be knit together by strong ties of love. This they could do by abiding in Christ, who embodies "all the treasures of wisdom and knowledge."

THE BETTER WAY OF CHRIST (2:4–3:4)

2:4-10 *Wily words vs. completeness in Christ.* Lest the Colossians be fooled by the smooth talk of false teachers (2:4–3:4), Paul reminded them of the foundations of their faith (2:4-7). Though human philosophy might sound good, the Colossians had in Christ all the divine revelation they would ever need (2:8-10; see 2:3), for he is fully God (see exposition on 1:15-23).

The non-Christian teaching Paul was concerned about was probably an early form of Gnosticism. Gnostics taught dualism: that God was good while all matter was evil. Salvation for Gnostics came only through a vast series of spiritual intermediaries, whom the chosen few could approach through a specially revealed knowledge. Gnostics called these intermediaries the "fullness" of God. Paul taught that Christ himself, by himself, constituted this fullness (see 3:10 and exposition on 1:15-23). Various Gnostic teachings are reflected throughout Colossians, such as their angel worship (see 2:18) and asceticism (see 2:21). Paul's concern with Gnosticism may be reflected in other letters as well (see 1 Cor. 2:6-8; 8:1; 13:8; 1 Tim. 1:4; 4:3; 6:20). Gnosticism was probably a key element in the heresies John would later describe as the "spirit of the Antichrist" (see exposition on 1 John 4:1-6).

2:11-17 *"The charges against you have been dropped!"* Paul now turned his attention to the Judaizers. Even uncircumcised Gentiles are declared forgiven when they turn to Christ (2:11-13), for by fulfilling the law, Christ has done away with the need to be justified on the basis of law (2:14; see exposition on Eph. 2:11-22). Christ's fulfilling of the law and his triumph over death have removed Satan's power to accuse us—a power that was based on the law's power to condemn us (2:15; see exposition on Rom. 4:13-25 and on 8:1-4). Therefore the Judaizers had no right to judge the Gentile Colossians.

The believer's baptism (2:12) symbolizes the baptism of the Holy Spirit that places one into the church, the body of Christ (see exposition on 1 Cor. 12:12-31). On "with him you were raised," compare Ephesians 2:5-6.

2:18-19 *"Avoid those who adore angels."* Those who promote the worship of angels (see exposition on 2:4-10) are cheating believers out of their right to direct access to the Father through Christ.

2:20-23 *"Avoid advocates of asceticism."* Paul warned also against the false humility (2:18, 23) of an asceticism that could have been connected with either Jewish legalism or Gnosticism. Such teaching may seem moral and religious, but it cannot change the heart, and that is where real change must begin.

3:1-4 *Our heavenly focus.* Paul's warnings against false teachings (see 2:4-23) and his exhortations to holiness (3:5–4:6) are connected by a call to shift our focus from earthly things to all that we now have and will someday have in Christ.

PRACTICING THE LIFE OF CHRIST (3:5–4:18)

3:5-17 *What to wear, what not to wear.* Believers should "get rid of" the worldly clothes of sin that they wore before conversion (3:5-11) and clothe themselves with righteousness and love (3:12-15). This process can be greatly aided by Bible study, worship, and Christian fellowship (3:16-17). On "God chose you to be the holy people whom he loves" (3:12), see exposition on 1 Peter 1:1-2.

3:18–4:1 *Rules for the roles.* Paul discussed behaviors appropriate in various human relationships (see exposition on Eph. 5:22–6:9).

4:2-6 *"We can both have a great witness!"* Paul requested prayer that God would provide "many opportunities" for the gospel even from the confines of his house arrest (4:2-4). Meanwhile, he exhorted the Colossians to behave wisely toward nonbelievers so that they too might be effective witnesses.

4:7-18 *"From all of us to all of you . . ."* Paul sent greetings from several Christian friends and coworkers (4:7-15) and instructed the Colossians to exchange letters from him with the church at Laodicea (see exposition on Rev. 3:14-22). Some have suggested that the letter in the possession of the Laodiceans may have been Ephesians (see *Ephesians: Recipients*).

1 THESSALONIANS

BACKGROUND

Paul ministered in Thessalonica for about a month on his second missionary journey (Acts 17:2). The ministry was very successful (1:9), though the unbelieving Jews stirred up the unbelieving Gentiles, resulting ultimately in Paul's leaving town by night and going on to Berea (Acts 17:5-10). The hostile Thessalonian Jews followed Paul to Berea and caused trouble there as well, so Paul went on to Athens (Acts 17:11-15). Paul was concerned for the believers who he had left behind in Thessalonica, so he sent Timothy back to check on them (3:1-2). Meanwhile, Paul went on to Corinth, where Timothy rejoined him (3:6; Acts 18:5) and gave a glowing report of the Thessalonians' spiritual growth, steadfastness, and love for him. Paul wrote this letter to express his joy over the good report, to encourage them in their spiritual growth, and to answer their question concerning what would happen to Christians who had died (4:13-18).

AUTHOR

Paul (1:1; 2:18; see *Romans: Author*).

DATE AND LOCATION

C. A.D. 51, shortly after Timothy rejoined Paul in Corinth, making it the second earliest of Paul's letters (after Galatians).

RECIPIENTS

The Christians of Thessalonica, mainly Gentiles, though there were some Jews as well (Acts 17:4-5). Their city was the central station and largest city on the Egnatian Way, the Roman highway connecting the Adriatic and Aegean Seas. Paul established three churches—Philippi, Thessalonica, and Berea—along this road.

A.D. 35
Paul's conversion

51
Paul in Thessalonica on 2nd journey, writes 1,2 Thess.

57
Paul in Thessalonica on 3rd journey

60
Paul imprisoned in Rome

c. 67
Paul martyred

PURPOSE

- To commend the Thessalonians for their steadfastness amid persecution
- To defend himself against criticism of his conduct during his stay at Thessalonica (2:1-16)
- To explain his absence from them (2:17-20)
- To explain Timothy's visit to them (3)
- To give instruction on personal and corporate Christian living (4:1-12; 5:12-28)
- To explain events related to Christ's second coming (4:13–5:11)

UNIQUE FEATURES

- 1 Thessalonians tells more about Christ's second coming than any other of Paul's letters. It gives the Bible's most detailed description of the Rapture (4:13-18).
- It contains no quotations from, and few allusions to, the OT.
- It is one of the most easily understood of Paul's letters.

COMPARISON WITH OTHER BIBLE BOOKS

1 Corinthians:

- 1 Corinthians 15 explains the involvement of living believers in the Rapture; 1 Thessalonians explains how deceased believers will be involved.

Philippians and Philemon:

- These along with 1 Thessalonians are the most nonpolemical of Paul's letters.

2 Thessalonians:

- 1 Thessalonians explains why deceased believers will not miss out on the Rapture; 2 Thessalonians explains why believers will not be involved in the Tribulation.

OUTLINE

COMMENDATION AND EXPLANATION (1–3)
- Salutation; commendation (1)
- Paul defends his ministry (2:1-16)
- He explains his absence (2:17-20)
- He explains Timothy's mission (3)

EXHORTATION (4–5)
- Personal conduct (4:1-12)
- The Rapture (4:13-18)
- The day of the Lord (5:1-11)
- Conduct in the church (5:12-24)
- Concluding charges; benediction (5:25-28)

COMMENDATION AND EXPLANATION (1–3)

1:1-10 *Grateful for their good example.* Paul thanked God for the Christians at Thessalonica who, despite great suffering, had become examples to believers throughout Greece, both in personal conduct and in evangelistic zeal. 1:9-10 expands Paul's description of the Thessalonians in 1:3:

- Their "faithful work" involved turning from idolatry to the one true God.
- Their "loving deeds" involved serving the one true God.
- Their "continual anticipation" involved their expectant waiting for Christ's return.

God's Word is effective no matter how ineffective or unworthy the messenger (see Isa. 55:11; Phil. 1:15-18), but how much better when the spokespersons and the Scriptures are in perfect harmony, so that the Word goes forth "with power," with the authority of the Holy Spirit (1:5).

Concerning being chosen (1:4), see exposition on 1 Peter 1:1-2.

2:1-12 *No flattery, no bad finances.* Paul reminded the Thessalonians that he had been sincere and straightforward with them, working night and day at a secular job to earn his own keep (2:9; compare exposition on 1 Cor. 4:6-13). He had been very caring and personal, like a mother or a father (2:7-8, 11; compare 1 Cor. 4:14; 2 Cor. 6:13; Gal. 4:18-19). 1:10 shows three key dimensions to Paul's ministry:

- Spiritually, he was "pure."
- Socially, he was "honest" with the Thessalonians.
- Personally, he was "faultless."

2:13-16 *"They've always opposed their God."* Once more Paul commended his readers for their ready response to the gospel, especially considering how much the unbelieving Jews had opposed both Paul and them. Paul reminded them of how consistently the Jews had opposed Christ and the gospel:

- They had "killed their own prophets, and . . . the Lord Jesus" (2:15; see Acts 2:22-23; 5:30; 7:52).
- They had "persecuted us" (2:15).
- They "opposed everyone," trying to hinder Paul's Gentile outreach (2:15-16; see Acts 13:50; 14:19; 17:5; 18:12).

Such strong language has led some to call Paul anti-Semitic. Yet Paul was proud of his own Jewish heritage (see Acts 22:3; Phil. 3:4-5), and his great heart practically bled for the conversion of his beloved nation (see Rom. 9:1-3; 10:1).

Israel's continuing "to pile up their sins" (2:16) would bring God's "anger" but will ultimately lead to salvation for Jews and Gentiles alike (see exposition on Rom. 9–11).

2:17-20 *"Frankly, I was stopped by Satan."* Paul had tried several times to revisit the Thessalonians but was always hindered by Satan. His absence from them only increased his desire to see them, for they were his "reward and crown." Perhaps Paul saw Satan's hand in the relentless harassment of his Jewish opponents (see *Background*).

3:1-13 *Timothy's welcome report.* Upon arriving in Athens, Paul, knowing that the Thessalonians were suffering (3:3), "could stand it no longer" (3:1), so he urgently sent for Timothy (see Acts 17:15) and dispatched him to Thessalonica to check up on them (3:2, 5). Timothy had just rejoined Paul, now in Corinth, with the welcome news that the Thessalonians' faith in God and love for Paul was as strong as ever (3:6-8; see Acts 18:5). Paul responded with thanksgiving, expressing again his desire to see them and encouraging them to greater love and holiness (3:9-13).

EXHORTATION (4–5)

4:1-8 *God's perfect plan for all his people.* God's will for the Thessalonians was that they would "be holy," often translated "sanctification." This refers to a daily growing in grace and maturing in the faith (4:3; see 5:23-24; see exposition on Heb. 10:1-18). They were to be monogamous, relating to their spouses honorably, not out of lust. God has just one will for sinners: that they be saved (see 1 Tim. 2:4; 2 Pet. 3:9). And he has just one will for believers: that they be sanctified (4:3).

4:9-12 *"Mind your own business; earn your own keep."* Christians are to love each other and lead "quiet" lives. They are to be diligent workers, not just to pay their bills but so that unbelievers will trust and respect them.

4:13-18 *"Don't worry, they'll be first!"* Paul now answered a question that apparently had bothered the Thessalonians. When he was among them (see Acts 17) he had doubtless spoken of Christ's one day returning to establish his millennial Kingdom, and they probably viewed this event as being just around the corner. But since Paul's departure, a number of the Thessalonian believers had died. Did this mean they would miss out on Christ's return? Paul assured them that, quite to the contrary, when Christ returned to meet his faithful ones "in the air," he would first resurrect and gather to himself those already dead (4:15). This will be the second of the three end-times resurrections (see exposition on 1 Cor. 15:20-28).

The midair encounter of Christ and his living saints is generally called the "Rapture," from the Latin word *rapio,* meaning "to seize" ("caught up," 4:17). See exposition on 1 Cor. 15:50-58.

5:1-11 *Prepared for the thief?* Not only will all believers, dead and alive, participate in the Rapture, but by God's grace all will avoid the terrible "day of the Lord" that will follow (see *Isaiah: Background* and exposition on Joel 2:28-32). Often called the Great Tribulation, that day will come unexpectedly during a time of false peace, bringing destruction upon all unbelievers (5:1-3). But while unbelievers will be too deeply mired in their sin to be ready for this judgment (5:4-7), believers will be ready, wearing their armor of faith, watching for Christ's return (5:5-11).

Christ's second coming is often compared to a thief coming in the night (5:2, 4; see Luke 12:39; 2 Pet. 3:10; Rev. 3:3; 16:15). The analogy stresses the suddenness of his return and the need for our watchfulness as we await it. Compare 5:8 with Ephesians 6:10-17.

5:12-28 *"You do your part, and God will do his."* As he concluded his letter, Paul gave several exhortations (5:12-22), assuring the Thessalonians that God was ready to bless them and keep them "blameless" till Christ's return (5:23-24). He closed by charging them to read this letter to everyone in the church. Concerning the various exhortations:

- Because of their crucial ministry, church leaders should be held in the highest regard (5:12-13).
- In the Greek, 5:16 (not John 11:35) is the Bible's shortest verse. It is often, however, one of the hardest to keep.
- The best cure for pride is not humility (which can lead to false piety) but thankfulness (5:18; see exposition on Rom. 1:18-32). As someone has suggested:
  - Be careful for nothing.
  - Be prayerful in everything.
  - Be thankful for anything.
- There are two common ways that believers can fail in their relationship with the Holy Spirit:

- ➤ by "stifling" him (5:19), which involves not doing what he wants us to do
- ➤ by "bringing sorrow" to him (see Eph. 4:30), which means doing what he does not want us to do
- 5:23 has been a main support for the doctrine of "trichotomy," that humans are threefold beings, with a spirit, soul, and body. Whatever Paul may have meant, he was praying that God would thoroughly sanctify each individual believer.
- It is interesting that, though the original Greek text did not have chapter divisions, each of the book's five chapters ends with a reference to the Second Coming:
  - ➤ see 1:10, relating to salvation
  - ➤ see 2:19-20 and 3:13, relating to faithful service
  - ➤ see 4:17-18, relating to sorrow
  - ➤ 5:23, relating to sanctification

A.D. 35
Paul's conversion

51
Paul in Thessalonica on 2nd journey, writes 1, 2 Thess.

57
Paul in Thessalonica on 3rd journey

60
Paul imprisoned in Rome

c. 67
Paul martyred

2 THESSALONIANS

BACKGROUND

In his first letter to the Thessalonians, Paul wrote concerning the involvement of deceased believers in the Rapture, and about the terrible "day of the Lord" (the Tribulation) that would follow the Rapture (see *1 Thessalonians: Background* and exposition on 1 Thess. 4:13–5:11). Mistaking their present persecution for the dark days of which Paul wrote, the Thessalonians concluded that they had missed the Rapture and were now enduring the Tribulation—a misunderstanding perhaps reinforced by false teachers (2:2). Paul wrote this second letter to show them that their hard times did not constitute the Tribulation and to assure them of the far better things in store for them as believers.

AUTHOR

Paul (1:1; 3:17; see *Romans: Author*).

DATE AND LOCATION

C. A.D. 51, from Corinth, one to three months after 1 Thessalonians.

RECIPIENTS

See *1 Thessalonians: Recipients.*

PURPOSE

- To assure the Thessalonians that the Tribulation was not already taking place (1:1–2:12)
- To show that Christ's second advent would deliver them from their persecutions and result in the judgment of their enemies (1:5-12)
- To instruct them on church discipline (3:6-15)

UNIQUE FEATURES

- 2 Thessalonians gives the Bible's most detailed description of the Antichrist (2:1-12).

OUTLINE

THE DAY OF THE LORD: ENCOURAGEMENT (1)
THE DAY OF THE LORD: INSTRUCTION (2:1-12)
THE DAY OF THE LORD: EXHORTATION (2:13–3:18)

THE DAY OF THE LORD: ENCOURAGEMENT (1)

1:1-12 *Future justice, future judgment.* Paul thanked God for the Thessalonian believers, who were persevering amid persecution (1:3-4). That persecution, said Paul, simply showed that they were right in God's sight while their persecutors were wrong. When Christ returned, their persecutors would be punished while they themselves would be revealed to be true children of God (1:5-10). Paul prayed that they would continue to be "worthy" of such suffering and would be a glorious testimony to their Lord (1:11-12).

Paul gave these assurances in response to their misunderstanding about the "day of the Lord" of which he had spoken in 1 Thessalonians (see *Background*). Concerning the day of the Lord (also called "that day," 1:10; see 2:3), see *Isaiah: Background* and exposition on Isaiah 2:5–4:1. Christ would "appear from heaven" preceding that day—an event separate from the Rapture (see exposition on 1 Thess. 4:13-18).

God's judgment will fall on two categories of sinners (1:8):

- "Those who don't know God," probably those who have never heard the gospel but do have the witness of both conscience and nature and are therefore without excuse (see Rom. 1:18-20; 2:12-16).
- "Those who refuse to obey the Good News of our Lord Jesus."

THE DAY OF THE LORD: INSTRUCTION (2:1-12)

2:1-12 *The rise and fall of the Antichrist.* Paul assured the worried Thessalonians that the day of the Lord had not yet come, and urged them to ignore anyone claiming otherwise (2:1-2). Before the day of the Lord can begin, there will first be "a great rebellion" (2:3; see 1 Tim. 4:1-3; 2 Tim. 3:1-5; 4:3-4) and the advent of "the man of lawlessness," the Antichrist (2:3-10). The "great rebellion" probably refers to a time following the Rapture, when the absence of the church will allow free reign to the godless. Thus, though the faithful Thessalonians were undergoing terrible persecution, it was not the Tribulation, and they had not missed the Rapture.

The Antichrist, an agent of Satan himself (2:9), also called the "one who brings destruction" (2:3) and the "man of lawlessness" (2:3, 8-9), will try to usurp the place of God (2:4) and will be allowed by God to further lead astray those who have already rejected him (2:11-12). After a brief reign, the Antichrist will be destroyed by God (2:8).

While many have tried to identify the Antichrist, this and other Bible passages make only two things certain: his rise and his utter defeat. Key Bible passages on the Antichrist include Daniel 9:20-27; 11:36-45; 12:5-13; Zechariah 11:15-17; 1 John 4:1-6; Revelations 13:1-10.

The "lawlessness" that will usher in the Antichrist's reign is already present in the world but is being held in check by the one "who is holding it back" (2:7), probably meaning the Holy Spirit (see John 16:8-11).

"God will send great deception upon them" (2:11) shows God's sovereignty over his enemies (see Gen. 50:20; Exod. 4:21; Judg. 9:23; 1 Kings 22:19-23) but in no way suggests that he condones evil (see James 1:13-14).

THE DAY OF THE LORD: EXHORTATION (2:13–3:18)

2:13-17 *Chosen by him, standing firm for him.* Having explained that they had not missed the Rapture, Paul offered additional encouragement and exhortation. Assured of salvation, they should "stand firm" for the Lord. While Paul felt great affection for the Thessalonians, he apparently agreed with Luke's assessment that they lacked the zeal of the Bereans (see Acts 17:10-11). Concerning their being "chosen" and "called . . . to salvation," see exposition on 1 Peter 1:1-2.

3:1-5 *"Pray for me; I'll pray for you."* Paul asked for prayer for the fruitfulness of his ministry and for deliverance from his enemies. But his prayer request quickly became a prayer for the Thessalonians, that God would continue to build them up in love and perseverance.

3:6-15 *Dealing with the lazy and the lawless.* Christians who live "idle lives" should be strongly admonished, even separated from the fellowship of the church if that is necessary to bring them to repentance. Even amid such harsh discipline, however, the offending person should be treated as a brother or sister (3:15). Elsewhere in Scripture, both Jesus and Paul prescribed total excommunication if the offender persisted in sin and unrepentance (see exposition on Matt. 18:15-20 and on 1 Cor. 5:1-8).

Paul was concerned about reports that some of the Thessalonians were not earning their own living. He admonished them to do so, offering his own hard work as an example (3:7-9; see 1 Thess. 2:9; compare exposition on 1 Cor. 4:6-13).

3:16-18 *"Take note of my handwriting!"* Paul noted that, while he dictated the body of his letters to an assistant, here as in all his letters he was adding a salutation in his own hand, as a sign of the letter's authenticity (see Rom. 16:22; 1 Cor. 16:21; Col. 4:18).

A.D. 35
Paul's conversion

1 TIMOTHY

c. 51
Timothy joins Paul on 2nd journey

BACKGROUND

Chronological and biographical details in 1 Timothy, 2 Timothy, and Titus suggest that Paul wrote these three letters after being released from house arrest in Rome (see *Date and Location*). The letters are traditionally called the "Pastoral Epistles" because in them Paul, perhaps sensing death was near, focused on laying a firm foundation for the churches he had established.

60–64
Paul imprisoned, released, writes 1 Timothy

c. 67
Paul martyred

On his second missionary journey Paul had met Timothy, a young man of Greek and Jewish heritage (Acts 16:1-3) who had been brought up with a solid knowledge of Scripture (2 Tim. 3:15). Timothy became Paul's disciple and trusted assistant and would remain so right up to the time of his death (see 2 Tim. 4). Though Timothy was apparently shy and retiring (4:12; 1 Cor. 16:11), Paul had left him in Ephesus as his personal representative (1:3). He wrote this letter to instruct Timothy in that work (3:15).

AUTHOR

Paul (1:1; see 2:7; see *Romans: Author*).

DATE AND LOCATION

Paul's travel notes in 1 Timothy through Titus (1:3; 2 Tim. 1:17; 4:9, 13, 20; Titus 1:5; 3:12) do not match any events in Acts. This plus Paul's sense of impending death in 2 Timothy suggests the following chronology for Paul's later years:

- He was released from the house arrest that had begun in Acts 28:30-31.
- He traveled and evangelized widely, as reflected in the travel notes cited above.
- He was then arrested again:
  - ➤ The 2 Timothy travel notes suggest an emergency situation (2 Tim. 1:17; 4:9, 13, 20).

➤ Several comments in 2 Timothy reflect prison life (2 Tim. 1:8; 2:9; 4:6-22).
- He was then martyred. Paul expected this in 2 Timothy, and tradition strongly suggests it.

1 Timothy was probably the first of the three letters, being written A.D. 62–64 from Macedonia (1:3). Titus was written a little later, with 2 Timothy coming three to five years later.

PURPOSE

- To encourage Timothy in his faith (1)
- To instruct him concerning church organization (2–3)
- To instruct him concerning personal conduct (4–6)

UNIQUE FEATURES

- 1 Timothy is one of the best Bible resources on church organization.
- It emphasizes "right teaching" (1:10) but is primarily practical rather than doctrinal.

COMPARISON WITH OTHER BIBLE BOOKS

Colossians and 1 John:
- All deal with the Gnostic heresy.

2 Timothy and Titus:
- All reflect Paul's pastoral concern for churches.

2 Thessalonians 2; 2 Timothy 3; 2 Peter 2; and Jude:
- These, along with 1 Timothy 4, warn of apostasy.

OUTLINE

FIGHTING THE GOOD FIGHT (1)
- Salutation (1:1-2)
- Warning about false teachers (1:3-11)
- Paul's testimony (1:12-17)
- Timothy encouraged in the fight (1:18-20)

PREPARING CHURCHES FOR THE GOOD FIGHT (2–3)
- Exhortation to prayer (2:1-7)
- Women in the church (2:8-15)
- Leaders for the church (3)
  - Bishops (3:1-7)
  - Deacons (3:8-13)
  - The mystery of godliness (3:14-16)

PREPARING PASTORS FOR THE GOOD FIGHT (4–6)
- Warning of apostasy (4:1-11)
- Exhortation to leadership (4:12-16)
- Respect for all; care for widows (5:1-16)
- Honoring and supporting elders (5:17-20)
- Advice on leadership, health (5:21-25)
- Christian bond servants (6:1-2)

False teachers; greed; contentment (6:3-10)
The good fight of faith (6:11-16)
Proper use of wealth (6:17-19)
Conclusion (6:20-21)

FIGHTING THE GOOD FIGHT (1)

1:1-2 *His trusted child.* Paul addressed this letter to Timothy, "my true child in the faith" (see 2 Tim. 1:2; 2:1). Paul's affection for Timothy was perhaps all the greater if, as is likely, he had no natural children.

1:3-11 *False professors of the law; the true purpose for the law.* Paul had left Timothy in Ephesus to help disciple the believers there (1:3; see 3:15). One major concern was the influence of the Judaizers (see exposition on Gal. 1–4), who were trying to force other Christians to obey the law without even understanding it themselves (1:3-7). The law was given to expose sinners (1:9-10; see Rom. 3:20; 5:20), not to burden believers (1:4-5, 8).

1:12-17 *"What I was, what he did, what I now am."* Even more than any Judaizing heretic, Paul himself had once blasphemed the gospel and persecuted believers. Paul viewed his subsequent salvation as a prime example of God's grace (1:14-16). He spoke of it often (see Acts 22; 26; Gal. 1–2; Phil. 3), and thousands through the ages have been led to Christ by his story.

1:18-20 *Spiritual sons, sinking ships.* Paul charged Timothy to "fight well in the Lord's battles" (compare 6:12), thus avoiding the spiritual "shipwreck" others had suffered. On "turned them over to Satan," see exposition on 1 Corinthians 5:1-8. On the heresy that earned Hymenaeus this punishment, see 2 Timothy 2:17-18. Prophecies had been made concerning Timothy's future ministry (1:18), perhaps by the elders who commissioned him (4:14).

PREPARING CHURCHES FOR THE GOOD FIGHT (2–3)

2:1-7 *Pray for peace and for the gospel.* We are to pray for everyone, including those in authority, so that we might live in peace (2:1-2). But the main purpose of our prayers is that the gospel may go forth unhindered, for Jesus is the only Mediator between God and humankind (2:3-7).

2:8-15 *Men and women in the church.* Men should seek to maintain an atmosphere of holiness and unity in the church (2:8). Women should concentrate on developing inward, spiritual beauty (2:9-10). They should "wear decent and appropriate clothing and not draw attention to themselves" (2:9). They should "listen and learn quietly and submissively" (2:11). They may have various teaching roles in the church (see exposition on 1 Cor. 14:26-40) but not those involving authority over men (2:12). Paul gave two reasons for this:

- the order of creation (2:13; see 1 Cor. 11:8-9)
- the order of transgression (2:14)

Women will be "saved through childbearing" and faithfulness (2:15). There are many suggested interpretations for this statement:

- That though pain in childbirth was one result of humanity's original sin (2:14; see Gen. 3:16), God gives special protection in that ordeal to Christian women.
- That by being homemakers, women will be saved from the corruption of society.
- That by being homemakers instead of church leaders, they will avoid being judged as teachers of heresy.

- Since the original Greek reads "*the* childbearing," some suggest Paul was referring to the birth of Christ.

Paul's teachings on the role of women in the church should be seen in light of his recognition of and respect for the spiritual gifts of women in his day (see exposition on 1 Cor. 14:26-40) and his proclamation of the equality of men and women in Christ (see exposition on Gal. 3:26–4:7).

3:1-13 So you want to be a leader? Anyone desiring to be an "elder" or "bishop" in the church is to be commended, but he must meet rigid spiritual qualifications. He must be considered above reproach by his family and even by nonbelievers, as well as by the church. Such high standards are necessary, considering the crucial responsibilities of church leaders (see Heb. 13:17).

The Greek word used here for "elder" (also translated "bishop") is

THE CHURCH OFFICERS

ELDER

Qualifications for the Office of an Elder (1 Tim. 3:1-7)

An elder must
- be without reproach;
- be faithful to his wife;
- be self-controlled;
- live wisely;
- be respectable;
- be hospitable;
- be able to teach;
- not be a heavy drinker;
- not be violent;
- be gentle;
- be peace loving;
- not love money;
- manage his own family well;
- not be a new Christian;
- have a good reputation in the community.

DEACON

Qualifications for the Office of a Deacon (1 Tim. 3:8-13)

A deacon must
- be respected;
- have integrity;
- not be a heavy drinker;
- not be greedy for money;
- have a clear conscience;
- have had previous church responsibilities;
- have a wife who is respected and faithful;
- be faithful to his wife;
- manage his children and household.

episkopos, meaning "overseer." It is often used interchangeably with the Greek word *presbuteros* (used in Acts 20:17, 28; Titus 1:5-7).

Many Protestant scholars identify this office with that of the pastor (see Eph. 4:11), while others see it as a separate role, involving one or more leaders (see 5:17).

An elder should be "faithful to his wife" (3:2) or, in the original Greek, "a one-woman man." There are two main interpretations of this requirement:

- That an elder should not be a polygamist. This meaning is unlikely, because
  - ➤ Paul had already forbidden polygamy for all believers (see 1 Cor. 7:2; Rom. 7:1-3); such a restriction on elders would have been redundant.
  - ➤ Rome had outlawed polygamy. There is no evidence that the early church ever faced the problem.
- That an elder should not be divorced. This view seems the more likely one.

The phrase "a one-woman man" is reversed concerning widows, who should be "one-man women" (5:9).

The qualifications for deacons (3:8-13) are virtually the same as those for elders. "Deacon" is *diakonos* in Greek, meaning "servant," so presumably Paul had in mind someone who would serve under the elders, such as those selected in Acts 6. Though deacons were not required to be able to teach as were the elders (3:2), their qualifications describe men of great spiritual depth.

Though not clearly stated, we can assume that Paul viewed the offices of elder and deacon to be limited to men:

- He talked about the wives of these officers, but not about their husbands.
- His earlier denial of the authoritative teaching role to women would preclude their serving as elders.

3:14-16 *A hymn to God our Redeemer.* As Paul instructed Timothy concerning the church, he did so to preserve the gospel in all its majesty, of which he now spoke in words that may have been from a hymn (3:16). God

- "appeared in the flesh," referring to his becoming human (the Incarnation; see Isa. 7:14; 9:6; John 1:14; Gal. 4:4). This was unimaginable in the normal course of nature (see Dan. 2:11).
- was "shown to be righteous by the Spirit" (see Matt. 3:16; John 15:16).
- was "seen by angels." Christ's earthly ministry was observed by
  - ➤ elect angels (see Matt. 4:11; Luke 2:13; 22:43; 1 Pet. 1:12)
  - ➤ evil angels (see Mark 1:23-26; 5:1-13)
- was "announced to the nations," (see Matt. 28:18-20; Acts 1:8; Rom. 15:18-19).
- was "believed on in the world." Though officially rejected as Israel's Messiah, our Lord left in his wake a powerful minority group of dedicated believers (see Acts 2:41; 4:4; 9:42; 11:21; 17:4, 34; 18:8).
- was "taken up into the skies" (see Acts 1:9).

On "mystery" (3:16), see exposition on Colossians 1:24-29.

PREPARING PASTORS FOR THE GOOD FIGHT (4–6)

4:1-11 *Apostasy alert.* Paul foresaw increasing apostasy in the days ahead (4:1-5) and charged Timothy to warn people about such deviations, to avoid useless doctrinal speculations, and to stay spiritually fit (4:6-11). Asceticism

(4:3) was a key ingredient of Gnosticism (see exposition on Col. 2:4-10).

Peter, James, John, and Jude, as well as Paul, use phrases such as "last times" (4:1), "last days," or "last time" with reference to the period between Christ's ascension and his return (see 2 Tim. 3:1; Heb. 1:2; James 5:3; 1 Pet. 1:5; 2 Pet. 3:3; 1 John 2:18; Jude 1:18).

4:12-16 *Examples, exhorters.* Rather than allowing the church to perhaps look down on him because of his youth or inexperience, Timothy should be an example to them in all areas of spiritual life (4:12; see *Background*). Three key ingredients should mark his teaching of God's Word (4:13):

- "reading" (information)
- encouraging (application)
- teaching (interpretation)

Paul exhorted Timothy to faithfully develop his spiritual gift (4:14; see 1:18). What we don't use, we lose (see Heb. 2:1-3). Timothy's spiritual progress should be evident to all, so that they would want to follow him. A growing pastor means a growing church; no man can lead others where he has not gone himself. By leading the church, Timothy would "save" both himself and them (4:16)—not from eternal damnation, but from God's judgment of their stewardship (see exposition on 1 Cor. 3:10-17). They would avoid being placed on the shelf as useless vessels (see 1 Cor. 9:27).

5:1-2 *Fathers, mothers, sisters, brothers.* Fellow believers should be regarded as a close-knit spiritual family and should be treated with respect.

5:3-16 *A word about widows.* We should look out for the emotional and financial welfare of older widows, if they truly have no family to care for them. As for younger widows, it is good for them to remarry and bear children, to avoid sexual sin.

5:17-20 *Respect and support your elders.* Elders who work full-time in ministry should be highly respected and should be financially supported by their congregations. An accusation against such a leader should not be entertained lightly.

5:21-25 *Advice on leadership and health.* Paul encouraged Timothy to be impartial in his leadership and to be careful in choosing coleaders (5:21-22). Great discernment is needed in judging character (5:24-25). Paul also offered some medical advice (5:23), which should be viewed as just that and not as a license for social drinking. Apparently the gift of healing was by this time less prevalent than in the church's first days. Paul was not only unable to heal Timothy (5:23), he was also unable to heal Trophimus (see 2 Tim. 4:20) and himself (see 2 Cor. 12:7-10).

6:1-2 *Servants: Free in Christ, bound to their masters.* Though they are free in Christ, bond servants should, for testimony's sake, serve their masters diligently. If their masters were also Christians, they should not let this spiritual equality (see Gal. 3:28) lessen their respect for them as masters. On slavery, see *Philemon: Background.*

6:3-10 *Greed vs. contentment.* Paul warned against false teachers who viewed the gospel as a means of getting rich (6:3-5), and warned about the perils of wealth (6:6-10). The love of money brings only grief (6:9-10). Contentment is a more logical approach to life and brings great blessing (6:6-8).

6:11-16 *The good fight of faith.* We should flee all that is evil and aggressively pursue all that is good, living in hope of Christ's return, which will bring us eternal life.

6:17-19 *"If you're wealthy, use it well."* Christians who happen to be wealthy should be careful not to trust in their wealth, focusing instead on using it to help others, thereby "storing up their treasure" (see Matt. 6:19-21; 19:16-22).

6:20-21 *"Finally, in closing . . ."* Paul closed with another urgent exhortation for Timothy: Keep the faith that has been entrusted to you, and don't get caught up in the "so-called knowledge" many are professing—probably another allusion to Gnosticism (see exposition on 4:1-11 and on Col. 2:4-10).

PEOPLE TO REMEMBER FROM 1 TIMOTHY

TIMOTHY

Key Fact: Ministry partner and disciple of Paul, who addressed two NT letters to him.
Father: Unnamed (Acts 16:3)
Mother: Eunice
Occupation: Missionary, pastor
Total Bible References: 24
Key References: 1–6; Acts 16–20; Phil. 2:19-23; 1 Thess. 1; 2:3-4; 3:2-6; 2 Tim. 1–4; Heb. 13:23

Timothy Speaks

Thank God Mark and I arrived in time to see Paul before his death. Hopefully we were of some comfort during his final hours. I know from personal experience just how bad prison life is. But he suffered the ultimate injury, being forsaken by many of his closest friends. (Heb. 13:23; 2 Tim. 4:6, 9-11, 16)

No doubt about it, he became the spiritual father I never had. He constantly prayed for me, was aware of my tears, and showed real concern over my health. Most important, he regarded me as a man of God. (1:1; 5:23; 6:11; Acts 16:3; 2 Tim. 1:3-4)

How God used that man, in addition to my grandmother and mother, in shaping my life! But even more vital have been the Holy Scriptures I was taught from my youth. So much has happened since I joined up with Paul there in Lystra. How often have I remembered the special ordination service that followed. (4:14; Acts 16:1-3; 2 Tim. 1:5-6; 3:15)

My prayers go out to the believers in Thessalonica, Corinth, Philippi, and Berea to whom I have ministered. Of course, my greatest burden is for the saints here in Ephesus, my current post of duty. (1:3; Acts 17:14; 1 Cor. 4:17; 16:10-11; Phil. 2:19-23; 1 Thess. 3:1-2)

"Preach the word of God. Be persistent, whether the time is favorable or not." This is the challenge you gave me, beloved Paul. And this is the challenge I plan to keep! (2 Tim. 4:2)

Spiritual Lessons from Timothy

- Though burdened by poor health (5:23), Timothy was used by God to faithfully and fruitfully minister to at least five NT churches. Not even physical infirmities can keep us from serving God, if we will only trust him.
- Paul admonished Timothy in 10 key areas that apply to us as well:
  - ➤ Be a good soldier for Christ (1:18; 6:12; 2 Tim. 2:3).

- ➤ Don't neglect your spiritual gifts (4:14; 2 Tim. 1:6).
- ➤ Guard your own spiritual life (4:16).
- ➤ Denounce all sin (5:20).
- ➤ Be impartial (5:21).
- ➤ Pursue righteousness (6:11).
- ➤ Give yourself to God's Word (2 Tim. 2:2, 15; 3:14; 4:2).
- ➤ Flee sexual sin (2 Tim. 2:22).
- ➤ Be firm but gentle (2 Tim. 2:24-26).
- ➤ Bring others to Christ (2 Tim. 4:5).

Key Verses
"I have no one else like Timothy, who genuinely cares about your welfare. All the others care only for themselves and not for what matters to Jesus Christ. But you know how Timothy has proved himself. Like a son with his father, he has helped me in preaching the Good News" (Phil. 2:20-22).

2 TIMOTHY

A.D. 35
Paul's conversion

c. 51
Timothy joins Paul on 2nd journey

60–64
Paul imprisoned, released, writes 1 Timothy

c. 66–67
Paul imprisoned again, writes 2 Timothy, is martyred

BACKGROUND

After writing his first letter to Timothy, Paul left Corinth with Titus and sailed to Crete, where he left Titus to look after the church (Titus 1:5). Paul then returned to either Greece or Asia Minor, from where he wrote Titus. Then, with Trophimus and Erastus, he headed for Nicopolis, where he intended to spend the winter (Titus 3:12). He left Trophimus sick at Miletus, and left Erastus at Corinth (4:20). He returned to Troas for a short visit and was arrested, apparently at the home of Carpus, and taken to Rome. His arrest was so sudden that he didn't have time to gather his personal possessions, including books, parchments, and a cloak (4:13). In the dungeon cell, with the temperature an even 55 degrees and nothing to occupy his time, Paul needed these personal items. He wrote this letter to ask Timothy to bring them to him. However, before asking this favor, he encouraged Timothy in his ministry at Ephesus. The tone of the letter, especially 4:6-22, suggests that Paul expected to be executed very soon.

Tradition says Paul was imprisoned in Rome's Mamertine Prison, which had only two cells, one below the other, with Paul occupying the lower cell.

AUTHOR

Paul (1:1; see *Romans: Author*).

DATE

A.D. 67–68. See *1 Timothy: Date and Location.*

PURPOSE

Though a faithful and trusted disciple of Paul, Timothy seemed to lack natural courage and strength (1:7; 1 Cor. 16:11). Before making several personal requests (4:9-22), Paul therefore exhorted Timothy concerning

- faithfulness (1)
- endurance (2:1-13)
- adherence to sound doctrine (2:14-26)
- the danger of apostasy (3)
- his ministry (4:1-8)

UNIQUE FEATURES

- As Paul's final letter, written as he awaited death, 2 Timothy is very personal. Now was the time for honesty and confession. To Timothy he offered no rebuke, only exhortation. He spoke as a dying father to his son, encouraging him to keep on keeping on.
- 2 Timothy contains the Bible's most complete statement concerning its own origin and purpose (3:15-17).
- Though written some 1,500 years after the event, 2 Timothy is the only biblical mention of the names of the magicians who opposed Moses (3:8; see Exod. 7:11).

COMPARISON WITH OTHER BIBLE BOOKS

John 14–16 and 2 Peter:

- These, like 2 Timothy, are farewell discourses.

2 Thessalonians 2; 1 Timothy 4; 2 Peter 2; Jude:

- 2 Timothy 3, like these, deals with apostasy.

1 Timothy and Titus:

- All concern the care and discipleship of believers.

2 Peter and Revelation:

- Paul's final writing, like Peter's and John's, contains exhortations to study God's Word.

OUTLINE

EXHORTATIONS (1:1–4:8)
- Exhortation to faithfulness (1)
- Exhortation to endurance (2:1-13)
- Exhortation to sound doctrine (2:14-26)
- Warning against apostasy (3:1-13)
- Exhortation to faithfulness in Bible study (3:14-17)
- Exhortation to faithfulness in ministry (4:1-8)

REQUESTS AND GREETINGS (4:9-22)
- Personal requests (4:9-13)
- Warning about Alexander (4:14-15)
- Recollections and assurances (4:16-18)
- Greetings, information, benediction (4:19-22)

EXHORTATIONS (1:1–4:8)

1:1-7 *"Remember your heritage; stir up your gift."* Paul thanked God for Timothy, reminded him of his solid spiritual upbringing, and expressed confidence that Timothy was carrying on that tradition of faith (1:1-5; see Acts 16:1-3). Paul was apparently concerned, however, that Timothy, perhaps because of his youth or natural reticence (1:7; see exposition on 1 Cor. 16:5-12), was not making full use of his pastoral gift, so he encouraged him to do so (1:6-7). While Timothy's mother and grandmother had taught him spiritually, his father was apparently an unbeliever (see Acts 16:3).

1:8-12 *"Don't be ashamed, for I'm not ashamed."* The strength of Paul's faith made him proud to proclaim the gospel (1:12; see Rom. 1:16). He admonished Timothy to also be proud of the gospel and of his association with Paul, even though Paul was now in prison (1:8). Paul had committed everything—his life of service as well as his very salvation—to Christ, being fully persuaded that it was safe in his keeping (1:12).

1:13-14 *A call to loyalty.* Paul urged Timothy to be loyal to the "right teaching," that is, the correct doctrine, which Paul had taught him—a theme he would return to later (see 2:14-26; 1 Tim. 1:10-11; 6:3).

1:15-18 *Many betrayers, one befriender.* When Paul was rearrested, most of his friends from Asia, where the arrest probably took place, had deserted him (see *Background*). Onesiphorus, a happy exception, had been like a breath of fresh air, searching for and finding Paul in prison. Recalling how faithful Onesiphorus had been even in earlier days, Paul commended him to the Lord.

2:1-2 *Passing the baton of belief.* Paul urged Timothy to pass on to others the truth he had learned. Christians must do three things with God's Word: Read it, heed it, and deed it.

2:3-10 *Timothy: Soldier, athlete, and farmer.* Paul compared the endurance necessary in the Christian life to that required of soldiers, athletes, and farmers (2:3-6; compare 1 Cor. 9:24-26; Eph. 6:11-17). He reminded Timothy of Christ's resurrection, the solid historical fact on which the Christian faith is founded (2:8; see 1 Cor. 15:1-8), and for which Paul was willing to suffer all things (2:9-10). On "those God has chosen" (2:10), see exposition on 1 Peter 1:1-2.

2:11-13 *A song of secure salvation.* Quoting perhaps from an early Christian hymn (compare 1 Tim. 3:16), Paul declared that all who have died with Christ can be assured of one day living with him (see Rom. 6:4-5). Likewise our present suffering should be seen in light of the fact that we will one day reign with him in his Kingdom.

2:12-13 can seem contradictory; this is one possible interpretation:

- If we "deny" Christ, that is, if we deny him first place in our lives, he will also "deny" us, that is, we will suffer the loss of our rewards at his judgment seat (see exposition on 1 Cor. 3:10-17).
- But no matter how "unfaithful" we are, that is, no matter how much we fail him, he will remain "faithful" and will never "deny himself," that is, he will never go back on his promise to save us (see 2:19; 2 Cor. 1:19-22; Eph. 1:13-14; 1 Pet. 1:3-5).

2:14-18 *"Absorb God's precepts; avoid human philosophy."* Rather than get involved in foolish philosophical discussions as some had done, to the great detriment of their followers (2:14, 16-18), Timothy should learn to correctly interpret God's Word. The Greek for "correctly explains" (2:15) means to "cut straight." Paul may have been thinking of his work as a tentmaker, where each knife stroke on the canvas helped determine the strength of the finished tent.

2:19-26 *A consecrated container for Christ.* Amid all the problems brought on by false teaching, Timothy could be sure of God's witness in his life if he would always strive to be a "utensil God can use" (2:19-21). He could do this by maintaining personal holiness (2:22) and by relating to his opponents with humility, patience, and a readiness to stand for the truth (2:23-26). On "clean" (2:21, "sanctified," KJV), see exposition on Heb. 10:1-18.

3:1-5 *Final days, fearsome days.* Paul predicted that the last days of human history would be "difficult" and listed the kinds of sinful people who would typify those times. The Greek for *perilous* is translated "dangerous" or "exceedingly fierce" in Matthew 8:28, suggesting the severity of Satan's last-ditch efforts against Christ and humanity. On "last days" (3:1), see exposition on 1 Timothy 4:1-11.

3:6-13 *Blinding the blind, persecuting those who see.* Never themselves able to grasp the truth, these latter-day sinners will victimize others who are spiritually weak. They will resist the truth just as Pharaoh's magicians resisted Moses (3:6-9). Just as Paul had suffered greatly despite his righteousness, all those who would live for Christ will suffer, even as the enemies of God grow more deceived and more strongly opposed to the truth (3:10-13).

3:14-17 *Confirming, correcting, completely equipping.* Having been taught the OT Scriptures by his mother and grandmother (3:15; see exposition on 1:1-7), Timothy should continue to study them and to absorb as well the writings of the apostles that would become the NT. These would provide everything he needed for a successful Christian life and ministry. On the Bible's inspiration (3:16), see *Inspiration*, p. 877.

4:1-5 *A cure for itching ears?* Timothy should be prepared to proclaim the truth at every opportunity, even though many, "wanting to have their ears tickled" (4:3, NASB), would look for teachers to tell them what they wanted to hear.

4:6-8 *First the race, then the reward.* Paul evidently sensed that death was near (4:6). Yet, having "fought a good fight" (compare 1 Tim. 6:12), he was ready to leave this life and receive his reward from God. Having always seen his life as an offering to God (see Rom. 15:16; Phil. 2:17), he viewed his approaching death as completing the sacrifice. Paul had successfully "finished" his purpose in life, unlike the wicked Belshazzar, who was simply finished (see Dan. 5:26).

REQUESTS AND GREETINGS (4:9-22)

4:9-13 *"Come quickly and bring the following . . ."* Having lost several companions through either desertion or reassignment, Paul urged Timothy to come to him quickly, bringing with him some personal items he had left in Troas, possibly at the time of his second arrest (see *Background*). The "papers" or "parchments" were probably Paul's copies of the OT. Paul had seen at least four visions of Christ, had written approximately half the books that would become the NT, and had organized most of the first 50 or so Christian churches. Yet now as he awaited death he requested the Scriptures, still eager to learn from those precious pages!

Demas, now a deserter (4:10), had been Paul's faithful colleague (see Col. 4:14; Philem. 1:24). On Mark, see exposition on Acts 15:36-41. On the chronological significance of events

A MAN CALLED PAUL

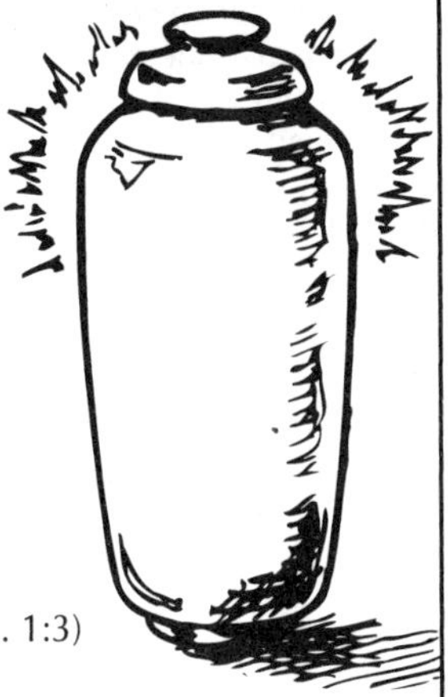

A Chosen Vessel (Acts 9:15-16)

A Missionary to the Gentiles
(Acts 13:46; 18:6; 22:21; 26:17-18; 28:28)

A Lover of Israel (Rom. 9:1-3; 10:1)

A Prolific Writer
Author of at least 13 New Testament books

A Mighty Prayer Warrior
(Acts 9:11; Col. 3:16-17; 1 Thess. 5:17; 2 Tim. 1:3)

A Miracle Worker (Acts 15:12; Rom. 15:19; 2 Cor. 12:12)

A Tactful Christian (1 Cor. 9:19-22)

A Zealous Preacher (Rom. 1:14-16; 1 Cor. 9:16)

A Respected Coworker
"Our beloved Barnabas and Paul" (Acts 15:25)

A Forgiving Coworker (2 Tim. 4-11, 16)

A Teacher (Acts 11:26; 13:1; 18:11; 19:8-10)

A Faithful Steward (1 Cor. 4:1-2; 1 Thess. 2:3, 5-6)

A Consistent Example (Gal. 4:12; Phil. 3:17; 4:9)

A Compassionate Soul Winner (Acts 20:20-21; 24:24-25; 26:26-29)

Like a Gentle Mother (1 Thess. 2:7-8)

A Lover of Scripture (2 Tim. 2:15; 3:15-17; 4:2, 13)

Chosen by God to Be an Apostle (Rom. 1:1)

A Suffering Servant
(Rom. 8:18; 1 Cor. 4:9-13; 2 Cor. 4:8-12, 16-18; 6:4-10; 11:23-28; Phil. 3:6-11; 2 Tim. 2:9)

in 4:8-22, see *Background* and *1 Timothy: Date and Location.*

4:14-18 *A forgiving and faithful Father.* Alexander had done much harm to Paul's ministry (4:14-15; see 1 Tim. 1:20). Paul had apparently been abandoned by most of his friends, yet he prayed that God would forgive them (4:16), echoing the similar prayers of Jesus (see Luke 23:34) and Stephen (see Acts 7:59-60). Yet God had been, and would be, faithful amid Paul's trials. "Saved me from certain death" (4:17) may indicate that Paul's first defense (4:16) had gone well. Nonetheless, he sensed martyrdom was near (4:6).

4:19-22 *"Come before winter."* Paul sent greetings to Priscilla and Aquila (see exposition on Acts 18:1-6) and to the family of Onesiphorus (see exposition on 1:15-18). On Trophimus's illness, see exposition on 1 Timothy 5:21-25. Cold and alone in his dungeon, Paul closed by urging Timothy to try to come before winter.

TITUS

A.D. 35
Paul's conversion

60–64
Paul imprisoned, released, visits Crete, writes Titus

c. 67
Paul martyred

BACKGROUND

Paul had visited Crete on his voyage to Rome (Acts 27:7-21) and again following his first Roman imprisonment, at which time he apparently established several churches. He left Titus behind to oversee those churches (1:5). Though the Cretan believers came out of a very different culture than the Jews, Jewish legalizers were making serious efforts to influence them. Paul wrote this letter to help Titus with that and other church-related issues.

AUTHOR

Paul (1:1; see *Romans: Author*).

DATE AND LOCATION

A.D. 62–66, after 1 Timothy, from somewhere in Greece or Asia Minor where Paul was stopping on his way to Nicopolis (3:12). See *1 Timothy: Date and Location.*

PURPOSE

- To encourage Titus to complete the task of organizing the churches in Crete (1)
- To discuss the teaching of doctrine and the conduct of ministry (2:1–3:11)
- To advise Titus of Paul's future plans and wishes (3:12-14)

UNIQUE FEATURES

- Titus shows that grace does not negate the necessity of good works:
  - ➤ The book contains classic descriptions of God's grace (2:11-14; 3:4-7).
  - ➤ But it emphasizes good works as much as James does (1:16; 2:7, 14; 3:1, 8, 14).
- In Titus, Paul quoted Epimenides, a Cretan poet (1:12; compare Acts 17:28).

COMPARISON WITH OTHER BIBLE BOOKS

2 Corinthians:

- Titus carried 2 Corinthians to the Corinthian church (2 Cor. 8:16-23); he is the recipient of this letter.

1 Timothy:

- Both emphasize church organization.

1, 2 Timothy:

- All are pastoral letters. 1, 2 Timothy are more personal; Titus is more official.

James:

- Both emphasize good works as the visible proof of saving faith (see *Unique Features*).

OUTLINE

ELDERS FOR THE CHURCH (1)
- Salutation (1:1-4)
- Appointing elders (1:5-9)
- Combating false teachers (1:10-16)

MINISTRY IN THE CHURCH (2–3)
- Teaching doctrine (2)
- The conduct of ministry (3:1-11)
- Instructions, greetings (3:12-15)

ELDERS FOR THE CHURCH (1)

1:1-4 *From Paul, God's servant, to Titus, Paul's child.* Paul greeted Titus, who like Timothy was his "child" in the faith (see exposition on 1 Tim. 1:1-2). He reminded him of the glorious gospel they both proclaimed, which God had "promised . . . before the world began" (see exposition on Eph. 1:1-6).

1:5-9 *"Select shepherds who meet the standards."* Paul had left Titus in Crete to bring order to new churches. He was to appoint godly leaders for each church. Concerning the requirements for such leaders (1:6-9), see exposition on 1 Timothy 3:1-13.

1:10-16 *"Here's why we need them."* The appointment of elders was urgent because false teachers—especially Judaizers—were trying to lead believers astray. Titus should soundly rebuke such deceivers. As the context suggests, "everything is pure to those whose hearts are pure" (1:15) refers to Mosaic dietary laws, not morals in general (see Matt. 15:11; Acts 10:15; Rom. 14:14). Paul had strong words for those who "claim they know God" but in fact do not (1:16; see 2 Tim. 3:5). Christ condemned such hypocrites as well (see Matt. 7:21-23; 23).

MINISTRY IN THE CHURCH (2–3)

2:1-10 *Tips for junior and senior saints.* Older men should be serious and sensible. Older women should be godly role models for younger women. Younger men should be self-controlled (2:1-6). The pastor himself should be an example in both walk and talk (2:7-8). Servants can elevate Christ by obeying their masters (2:9-10).

2:11-15 *What to do while awaiting that blessed hope.* Paul reminded Titus of the good news of grace, showing how grace should affect everyday life (2:11-14). He urged him to boldly declare this truth (2:15). A proper understanding of grace will produce good works and Spirit-controlled living as we await Christ's return. See exposition on Romans 1:1-7 and on Ephesians 2:1-10.

3:1-8 *Why Christians should be good citizens.* Christians should be models of good citizenship and good character (3:1-2, 8) because by God's grace and by the presence of his indwelling Holy Spirit (3:4-7) we have been saved and are being saved from our sinful, selfish human nature (3:3).

3:9-11 *Avoid both debates and debaters.* Arguments such as those promoted by the Judaizers are useless and should be avoided. Those who promote such things should be admonished not to do so. If they fail to repent, they should be excommunicated (compare exposition on the following passages: Matt. 18:15-20; 1 Cor. 5:1-8; 2 Thess. 3:6-15).

3:12-15 *"Hope to see you in Nicopolis soon!"* Paul stressed once more that God's grace should motivate good works. He told Titus he was sending someone to replace him for a while in Crete so that he could join Paul in Nicopolis.

PEOPLE TO REMEMBER FROM TITUS

TITUS

Key Fact: Ministry associate and disciple of Paul, who addressed a NT letter to him
Occupation: Missionary, pastor
Total Bible References: 12
Key References: 1–3; 2 Cor. 2:13; 7:6-7, 13-15; 8:16-23; Gal. 2:1-3; 2 Tim. 4:10

Titus Speaks

Word finally reached me here in Crete today. Paul has been martyred in Rome. I am told Luke, Mark, and Timothy were with him. How sorely we will miss him. I feel I have lost both a spiritual father and a brother. (1:4; 2 Cor. 2:13; 2 Tim. 4:6, 9, 11)

Paul encouraged me to be faithful in my ministry here in Crete. Of course I will strive to do just that. But frankly, it is a very difficult place to minister, as I must deal with both the materialistic Cretans from without and the legalistic Judaizers from within. (1:4-5, 10, 12; 3:9)

But it could be worse. What if I were called to pastor the church in Corinth? What a confused and carnal assembly of believers—though by God's grace I was able to help them a little. (2 Cor. 7:6-7, 13-15)

Lord Jesus, I thank you for Paul's incredible influence in my life. He once exhorted me to "promote the kind of living that reflects right teaching." Through your grace I have and will! (2:1)

Spiritual Lessons from Titus

- Paul told both Timothy (1 Tim. 1:3) and Titus (1:5) to remain where they were, suggesting that each of them may have desired to leave and assume a less difficult ministry elsewhere. Until unmistakably called elsewhere by God, we should bloom where we are planted.

Key Verses
"You yourself must be an example to them by doing good deeds of every kind. Let everything you do reflect the integrity and seriousness of your teaching. Let your teaching be so correct that it can't be criticized. Then those who want to argue will be ashamed because they won't have anything bad to say about us" (2:7-8).

PHILEMON

A.D. 35
Paul's conversion

54–57
Paul meets Philemon in Ephesus?

60–62
Paul imprisoned, meets Onesimus, writes Philemon

c. 67
Paul martyred

BACKGROUND

Onesimus, the slave of a Christian in Colosse named Philemon, had apparently stolen from his master and fled to Rome. There he encountered Paul, who led him to Christ (1:10, 18-19), after which Onesimus had been a great help to Paul (1:11, 13). Having asked Tychicus to deliver his letters to the Ephesians and Colossians (Eph. 6:21-22; Col. 4:7-8), Paul also asked him to return Onesimus to Philemon (Col. 4:9), along with this letter sharing the news of Onesimus's conversion and urging Philemon to forgive him and receive him as a brother in Christ.

Philemon, as a Christian, would surely have treated Onesimus well, even before his conversion. Under the Roman Empire, however, slaves had none of the rights mandated by Mosaic law (see exposition on Lev. 25:35-55). Though Paul didn't directly challenge the institution of slavery here or elsewhere (1 Cor. 7:20-24), the kind of relationship he envisioned between Philemon and Onesimus would have greatly improved the lot of any Roman slave with a Christian master (1:15-16; 1 Cor. 12:13; Gal. 3:28).

AUTHOR

Paul (1:1, 9, 19; see *Romans: Author*).

DATE AND LOCATION

A.D. 61, during Paul's house arrest in Rome (Acts 28:30-31), about the same time as Ephesians and Colossians.

RECIPIENT

Philemon was a personal note to its namesake, probably an elder in the church that met in his home at Colosse (see *Colossians: Recipients*). He was a wealthy man, known for generosity (1:7). 1:19 suggests that Philemon was converted by

Paul. Since Paul had never been to Colosse, he may have met Philemon during his extended ministry in nearby Ephesus (Acts 19).

PURPOSE

- To commend Philemon for his compassion to other believers (1:1-7)
- To commend Onesimus to Philemon and ask for his complete forgiveness and restoration (1:8-21)

UNIQUE FEATURES

- Philemon is the only totally private letter in Scripture.
- It gives a valuable glimpse into the social life of apostolic times.

COMPARISON WITH OTHER BIBLE BOOKS

1 Corinthians:

- The entire letter is a concrete example of the truth of 1 Corinthians 12:13.

Ephesians, Philippians, Colossians, and 2 Timothy:

- All were written by Paul from prison.

Ephesians and Colossians:

- These show that Christians form the body of Christ; Philemon illustrates love within the body of Christ.

Colossians:

- Except for Philemon and Apphia, everyone mentioned in Philemon is mentioned in Colossians as well (compare 1:1-2, 10, 23-24 with Col. 4:9-17).

OUTLINE

COMMENDING PHILEMON (1:1-7)
- Salutation (1:1-3)
- Commendation of Philemon (1:4-7)

INTERCEDING FOR ONESIMUS (1:8-25)
- Intercession for Onesimus (1:8-21)
- Plans for a visit (1:22)
- Greetings (1:23-25)

COMMENDING PHILEMON (1:1-7)

1:1-3 *From a prisoner to his personal friend.* Paul greeted Philemon, his "much-loved coworker," along with Apphia, Archippus, and the church that met in their house. Though Paul had never been to Colosse, he may have led Philemon to Christ (see 1:19), and we may suppose this wealthy believer had prayed for and financially invested in Paul's ministry. Apphia was probably Philemon's wife and Archippus his son. In Colossians, Paul seemed to imply that Archippus had become pastor in Colosse when Epaphras, founder of the church, went to Rome to visit Paul in prison (see Col. 4:17). At any rate, Philemon seemed to have his family well in hand (compare Josh. 24:15).

1:4-7 *Praise for a true refresher.* Paul thanked God for Philemon's love and generosity and his ministry of "refreshment" toward Paul and other believers (1:4-5, 7). He prayed for the continued effectiveness of Philemon's witness for Christ (1:6). Paul's praise may have been both an expression of respect for Philemon and an attempt to butter him up for the request that was coming (1:8-20).

INTERCEDING FOR ONESIMUS (1:8-25)

1:8-16 *"Remember your slave Onesimus? He's now your brother Onesimus!"* Paul now got to the main purpose of his letter: He asked Philemon to take back into his household Onesimus, his runaway slave (1:8). Onesimus had apparently found his way to Rome and been led to Christ by Paul (1:10). Onesimus had been a great help to Paul (1:11, 13), who had come to love him dearly (1:12-13). He appealed to Philemon to receive his former slave as a brother in Christ (1:16), urging Philemon to see God's providence even in Onesimus's disobedience, since it had resulted in his salvation (1:15-16).

Onesimus means "profitable" or "useful." Until his conversion, any resemblance between Onesimus's name and his actions was purely accidental. But now that Christ had made all things new, Philemon was invited to give Onesimus a chance to live up to his name (1:11). Though Paul, as an apostle, could have pulled rank on Philemon, he preferred to appeal to him as a friend (1:8-9). Nowhere besides this very personal letter does Paul refer to himself as "an old man" (1:9).

1:17-21 *"If for no other reason, do it for me."* Paul appealed for Onesimus on the basis of
- his friendship with Philemon (1:17)
- his willingness to reimburse Philemon for Onesimus's misdeeds (1:18-19)
- the spiritual debt Philemon owed him, as the one who had led him to Christ (1:19)

Paul's remarks about his own suffering in prison (1:9) may also have been a not-so-subtle effort to transfer to Onesimus Philemon's sympathy for Paul.

1:22-25 *"Oh, yes, could you have my room ready?"* Evidently expecting to be released from house arrest, Paul announced his hopes to visit Philemon soon. Evidence suggests he was indeed released but was later arrested again and put to death (see exposition on Acts 28:30-31; *1 Timothy: Date and Location*).

A.D. 60
Paul imprisoned in Rome

c. 67
Timothy imprisoned, released?

c. 68
Hebrews written

70
Jerusalem destroyed

HEBREWS

BACKGROUND

In the first century A.D., the practice of Judaism was sanctioned and protected by Roman law. Christianity, on the other hand, was not. Jewish Christians faced the dilemma of whether they should continue professing Christianity and risk danger or even death, or return to the safety and security of Judaism. This letter warned Christians against returning in any way to Judaism and encouraged them to go on to maturity in Christ. Luther, Zwingli, and Calvin nailed to the masthead of their movement three great principles from Hebrews:

- no sacrifice but Calvary
- no priest but Christ
- no confessional but the throne of grace

AUTHOR

Many have been suggested, including Paul, Apollos, Barnabas, Luke, Priscilla, and Silas. While cases can be made for and against each of these, the safest view is that of Origen: "Who wrote the letter, God only knows with certainty."

DATE AND LOCATION

Probably c. A.D. 68, perhaps from Italy (see 13:24):

- It was probably before the Temple's destruction in 70:
  - ➤ The Temple was apparently still in use (8:4-5; 10:11).
  - ➤ If the destruction had occurred, it would surely have been mentioned because of its interest to the readers and relevance to the book's theme.
- However, it was probably not much earlier than 70:
  - ➤ The recipients were apparently second-generation Christians who themselves had been believers for a fairly long time (see *Recipients*).
  - ➤ Timothy had just been released from prison (13:23). His imprisonment is not mentioned elsewhere in

Scripture but could have followed Paul's plea to visit him in prison, c. 67 (see 2 Tim. 4:9, 21).

RECIPIENTS

Second-generation Jewish Christians, probably living in or near Jerusalem, who had been Christians for some time (2:3-4; 5:11-14; 10:32) and had suffered persecution (12:3-4).

PURPOSE

- To show the superiority of the person and work of Christ to all aspects of Judaism (1:1–10:18)
- To encourage Christian maturity (5:11–6:3)
- To give comfort amid persecution (11:1–12:13)
- To warn about the danger and severity of divine chastisement (see *Unique Features*)

UNIQUE FEATURES

- Hebrews quotes from the OT about 100 times, from the Septuagint rather than the Hebrew text. It does more to explain OT typology than any other Bible book.
- It contains God's final recorded message to Israel before the final destruction of its Temple in A.D. 70.
- It contains five warning passages concerning the danger of abandoning the gospel and returning to the law. These warnings include exhortations and illustrations from the OT (see 2:1-4; 3:7–4:13; 5:11–6:20; 10:19-39; 12:14-29).
- It contains the famous "Hall of Faith" (11).
- Many of the key themes of Hebrews are reflected in its 13 "Let us" exhortations:
  - "Let us fear lest any of you . . . come short of [His rest]" (4:1, NKJV).
  - "Let us do our best to enter that place of rest" (4:11).
  - "Let us cling to [Jesus] and never stop trusting him" (4:14).
  - "Let us come boldly to the throne of our gracious God" (4:16).
  - "Let us stop going over the basics of Christianity again and again. Let us go on instead and become mature in our understanding" (6:1).
  - "Let us go right into the presence of God, with true hearts fully trusting him" (10:22).
  - "Without wavering, let us hold tightly to the hope we say we have" (10:23).
  - "Let us consider one another in order to stir up love and good works" (10:24, NKJV).
  - "Let us strip off every weight that slows us down, especially the sin that so easily hinders our progress" (12:1).
  - "Let us run with endurance the race that God has set before us" (12:1).
  - "Let us be thankful and please God by worshiping him with holy fear and awe" (12:28).

- ➤ "Let us go out to him outside the camp and bear the disgrace he bore" (13:13).
- ➤ "Let us continually offer our sacrifice of praise to God" (13:15).

COMPARISON WITH OTHER BIBLE BOOKS

Matthew:

- Matthew shows how Christ fulfilled OT prophecy; Hebrews shows how he fulfilled OT worship.

Luke and Acts:

See *Luke: Comparison with Other Bible Books*

John:

- Both begin by praising Jesus Christ as both Creator and Redeemer (compare 1:1-4 with John 1:1-5).

Romans:

- Romans shows the necessity of Christ; Hebrews shows the preeminence of Christ.

Colossians:

- Colossians shows the preeminence of Christ by direct statement; Hebrews shows the preeminence of Christ by striking contrasts.

OUTLINE

THE PREEMINENCE OF CHRIST (1:1–10:18)
  Christ's preeminence (1:1-4)
  His superiority to angels (1:5–2:18)
  His superiority to Moses (3:1-6)
  His Sabbath rest (3:7–4:13)
  His superior priesthood (4:14–10:18)
    His superior qualifications (4:14–5:11)
    Warning against apostasy (5:12–6:20)
    Comparison to Melchizedek (7)
    His superior sacrifice (8:1–10:18)
CHRIST'S PREEMINENCE APPLIED (10:19–13:25)
  Exhortation, warning, encouragement (10:19-39)
  Examples of faith (11)
  Exhortation to endurance in faith (12)
  Concluding exhortations (13)

THE PREEMINENCE OF CHRIST (1:1–10:18)

1:1-4 *Our Creator is also our Redeemer.* While in times past God spoke through intermediaries such as prophets (1:1) and angels (see 2:2), he has now spoken directly, through his Son, Jesus Christ, who is himself a part of the Godhead. He is both Creator and Redeemer (1:3) and as such has now resumed his rightful place at God's right hand (1:3). Compare John 1:1-5.

1:5-14 *Jesus is greater than angels.* While angels play an important role in God's plans (1:7, 14), Jesus plays a far more important role (1:5-6, 8-13) and therefore should be the focus of our worship. God addressed Christ as his divine equal (1:8-9).

2:1-4 *What if we reject him?* Considering the overwhelming greatness of Christ, we should pay very close attention to what he has said. If Israel in OT times was punished for disobeying the law, given by angels (see Acts 7:53; Gal. 3:19), how much more will we be punished for disobeying God's Word, given by his own Son? The obvious answer to 2:3 is that there is no escape, only eternal punishment, for those who reject Christ.

2:5-18 *We lost control, so he took control.* In his first recorded words to us, his creatures, God placed the world under our control (2:5-8; see Gen. 1:28). However, through sin and rebellion, we lost this lofty position (2:8; see Gen. 3:6, 17-19). But there is hope for us, for "we do see . . . Jesus" (2:9), who, by being made "lower than the angels," that is, by becoming human (2:14; compare 2:7 and 2:9), has through his death and resurrection become "a perfect leader" (2:10) and the "High Priest" who is able to completely forgive our sins (2:17-18).

With the eyes of faith we see Jesus, already crowned and reigning over the universe, fulfilling our own lost destiny:

- We were meant to rule over "all things" (2:8).
- At the present, this is far from reality (2:8). Unredeemed humans can't subdue their own sinful nature, let alone their environment.
- But Jesus will bring us "into glory," allowing us someday to help him rule the universe (2:10; see 2 Tim. 2:12; Rev. 20:4, 6; 22:5).

If I am a child of God, Jesus is not only my Creator (see John 1:3), my Redeemer (see Rev. 5:9), and my Shepherd (see John 10:11) but also my elder brother (2:11, 17; see Ps. 22:22; Rom. 8:29).

3:1-6 *Jesus is greater than Moses.* Jesus is also greater than Moses, who as giver of the law was the most revered person in Israelite history. Moses was a faithful servant in God's house, while Christ, the faithful Son, is in charge of the house.

3:7-19 *"Don't let this happen to you."* Though God led Israel out of Egypt, their constant rebellion caused him to swear that they "will never enter my place of rest," meaning that the generation that began the journey would not see Canaan (see exposition on Num. 14:10-38 and on Josh. 1:12-18). We should be careful, and remind each other daily, not to harden our hearts and miss God's eternal Sabbath rest (see exposition on 4:1-11).

4:1-11 *Enter his rest today!* God's offer of rest began far before the days of Moses (4:4), and the offer is still good today (4:1, 9-11; see Matt. 11:28). We need only accept it through faith (4:2-3, 9-10). Even the rest achieved by those who entered Canaan under Joshua was only temporary, as seen by the psalmist's reference, years later, to God's rest as something yet to come (see 3:15; 4:3, 8; Ps. 95:6-11). The word *rest* occurs repeatedly throughout 3:11–4:11:

- *Lack of faith* kept Israel from God's rest (3:11, 18; 4:11).
- *Lack of faith* will keep Christians from God's rest (4:1).
- *Faith* will give us God's rest, which involves our "finding rest" from our "labors," by which we may have tried to earn salvation (4:9-10).

4:12-13 *Truth sharper than a sword.* As we contemplate God's promise of rest, we know that we can trust his Word, for it is full of living power and can cut into our innermost thoughts, exposing us for what we really are.

4:14-16 *Meet him at the mercy seat!* Returning to the theme of Christ as our High Priest, the writer spoke at some length of the superiority of Christ's priesthood (4:14–10:18). Because Christ endured all the temptations we have endured, we can depend on him to supply all the grace we need (see 2:17-18).

5:1-11 *Priests must be compassionate and chosen.* A Jewish high priest had to be chosen by God and had to be compassionate (5:1-4). Jesus fulfilled both requirements:

- God selected him to be an eternal priest like Melchizedek, as David had predicted (5:5-6, 10; see 7; Ps. 110:4).
- While on earth, Christ showed great compassion (see Matt. 9:36; 14:14; 15:32). He learned much about our suffering through his own suffering (5:7-10).

5:12–6:3 *From milk to maturity.* The Hebrew Christians had been believers long enough to have graduated, in a spiritual sense, from seminary. Instead, they were still at a grade-school level (5:12-14; compare 1 Cor. 3:1-2). The writer encouraged them to get past the basics of the faith and explore deeper truth (6:1-3).

6:4-12 *A warning of the unthinkable?* Another stern warning: People who "taste" things related to salvation and then fall away can never be restored to repentance. Various scholars have suggested that this refers to

- *Christians who, through some horrible sin, "lose their salvation."* If this is the meaning, the passage also teaches that such people can never be saved again.
- *professed believers who have only "tasted" the things of God but never really "swallowed" them.* This seems unlikely, since the writer used "taste" earlier to denote full experience, not just experimentation (see 2:9). Nor is it likely that a mere "taster" would also be a recipient of the "gifts of the Holy Spirit" (2:4).
- *the "sin that leads to death"* (1 John 5:14-17).
- *a hypothetical case of something that, in the writer's view, could not happen.*

Though not one of these views is without its problems, 6:9-12 suggests that the author saw this scenario as hypothetical, at least for the people to whom he was writing, whose spiritual fruit had amply demonstrated their salvation.

6:13-20 *Confident in his promises.* Having declared his confidence in the faith of those to whom he was writing (see 6:9-12), the author sought to reinforce their confidence in God's promises. We can trust God to fulfill his promises to us just as he fulfilled his promises to Abraham, for God does not lie (6:13-18). The salvation God promised is as an "anchor" connecting our souls here on earth with Jesus in heaven (6:14-20). Jesus "has already gone in there for us" (6:20), describing the ancient Greek equivalent of a tugboat, which guided larger ships into shallow waters and secured their anchors within the harbor.

7:1-10 *Messiah and Melchizedek.* The author now spoke at length about Melchizedek, whom he had introduced as the prototype of Christ's priesthood (see 5:5-6, 10-11). This mysterious priest-king, of whose origin and destiny we know nothing (see exposition on Gen. 14:17-24), is a fitting type of the eternal Christ since they both, in essence, "remain a priest forever" (7:3). Melchizedek blessed Abraham, and Abraham tithed to him (see Gen. 14:18-20). Both actions show that Melchizedek was greater than Abraham (7:4-8). The entire Levitical priesthood, in essence, was tithing to Melchizedek through their ancestor Abraham (7:8-10).

7:11-28 *Jesus is greater than Aaron.* If the priesthood of Aaron and his sons could have brought perfection, why was there a need for a new priest who would be like Melchizedek (7:11; see 5:6; Ps. 110:4)? Christ was from the tribe of Judah, not from the priestly tribe of Levi (7:13-17), yet while Aaron's ministry could never perfect the people, Christ's ministry does this very thing (7:18-19). What's more, God declared with an oath that Christ's priesthood is permanent (7:20-22). The Aaronic priests died, but Jesus lives forever (7:23-25). The Aaronic priests offered up animals, but Jesus offered up himself as the perfect and eternal sacrifice for sin (7:26-28).

Jesus is both our Priest and the perfect sacrifice for our sin. This dual role can be seen in his seven final sayings from the cross. The first three demonstrate his priestly ministry (see Luke 23:34, 43; John 19:26-27), while the last four demonstrate his role as sacrifice (see Matt. 27:46; Luke 23:46; John 19:28, 30).

8:1-13 *Old vs. new: Hand vs. heart.* The earthly priests of Israel were a mere shadow of Christ, our eternal Priest in heaven, who has offered up himself (8:1-6). God's first covenant with Israel was imperfect, thus the need for a new one, as predicted by Jeremiah (8:7-13; see exposition on Jer. 31:31-34). God led Israel by the hand out of Egypt, only to see them rebel against him. Now he writes his laws on hearts, resulting in total obedience.

The Old Covenant
- was mediated by Moses (see Exod. 19)
- was conditional (see Deut. 28)
- was written on dead stones (see Exod. 32:15)
- didn't produce righteousness (8:8-9; see Rom. 3:20 and exposition on Rom. 7:7-25)

The New Covenant
- is mediated by Christ (see 9:15; John 1:17)
- is unconditional (8:9-10)
- is written on living hearts (8:10)
- does produce righteousness (8:11; see exposition on Rom. 3:21-26)

Who are the recipients of this New Covenant? There are at least four theories:
- The church has replaced Israel in God's plan and is the sole recipient of the New Covenant.
- The New Covenant is with the nation of Israel only.
- There are two New Covenants, one for Israel and the other for the church.
- There is one New Covenant, which applies in different ways to Israel and the church.

Of these four views, the third is possible, but the fourth seems most probable (see exposition on Jer. 31:31-34 and on Rom. 11:11-32).

9:1-15 *Tabernacle and sacrifices, old and new.* The OT Tabernacle and Temple had two rooms:
- the sanctuary or Holy Place (9:1-2), into which any priest could go (9:6)
- the "Holiest of All" or "Most Holy Place" (9:3-5, 25), into which only the high priest could go once a year, on the Day of Atonement (9:7; see exposition on Lev. 16:1-34)

This limited access showed that no sacrifice could totally, once for all, cleanse the hearts of the people who brought it (9:8-10). But now Christ, the perfect High Priest, has entered the perfect Tabernacle with the perfect sacrifice of his own body for sin, making eternal life possible for all who will accept that sacrifice (9:11-15).

9:16-28 *The cost of the New Covenant.* The Old and New Covenants are actually "testaments" or wills. Just as a will is not in force until the death of the one making it (9:16-17), so also both the Old (9:18-22) and the New (9:23-28) Covenants necessitated a death. The New Covenant necessitated the death of Christ himself, but this death occurred not once a year like the OT sacrifices (9:25) but one time only, making sufficient atonement for all who will accept his death on their behalf (9:28).

9:28 includes the third and seventh steps in Christ's sevenfold ministry on our behalf, as described in Hebrews:

- his incarnation (see 1:2; 2:16-17)
- his earthly ministry (see 5:7-9)
- his crucifixion (see 2:9; 7:27; 9:28)
- his resurrection (see 13:20)
- his ascension (see 4:14; 6:20)
- his heavenly intercession (see 7:25; 8:1-2; 9:12, 24)
- his second coming (9:28).

10:1-18 *Many sin reminders, one sin remover.* The fact that the Mosaic sacrifices had to be offered continually proves that they could never totally remove sin (10:1-4). The best they could do is be a continual reminder of that sin (10:3; see Rom. 3:20). But Christ's body, offered once for all, can remove all sin for all time, for those who believe (10:5-10). OT priests stood while performing their duties, for their work was never done. But Christ, having offered the perfect sacrifice once for all, is seated at God's right hand (10:11-14). With the New Covenant in place because of Christ's death, there is no more need for offerings for sin (10:15-18; see Jer. 31:31-34).

Christ's death "perfected" or sanctified, once for all, "those whom he is making holy" (10:14). Sanctification is both an accomplished fact and an ongoing process:

- All who accept Christ's death on their behalf are sanctified in his sight (see 2:11; 10:10; John 17:17, 19; 1 Cor. 1:2, 30; 6:9-11; Eph. 5:25-26; 1 Thess. 5:23).
- But sanctification is also a growth process in which we are to take an active part (see 2:11; Lev. 19:2; Rom. 6:19; 1 Thess. 4:1-7; 2 Tim. 2:21; 1 Pet. 1:15).

CHRIST'S PREEMINENCE APPLIED (10:19–13:25)

10:19-25 *Have faith, and share it!* Having shown the superiority of Christ and the salvation he offers (see 1:1–10:18), the author now invited his readers to enter fully into the reality of that salvation (10:19-23) and to encourage other believers to do the same (10:24-25). Christ's flesh represents the veil that separated us from God's presence in the Most Holy Place (10:20); therefore, when he died on the cross, that veil was literally torn asunder (see Mark 15:38).

10:26-31 *Warning the willful sinner.* For those who "deliberately continue sinning" after knowing the truth, there is "no other sacrifice that will cover these sins" (10:26), only judgment. The phrase "The Lord will judge his own people" (10:30) suggests that the author may have had believers in mind (compare exposition on the following passages: 6:4-12; 1 Pet. 4:12-19; 1 John 5:14-17).

10:32-39 *Remember your spiritual honeymoon!* To prevent apostasy and its terrible consequences, the readers are urged to recall and rekindle the joy they experienced, even amid persecution, as new believers. The KJV rendering of 10:34 suggests that the author of Hebrews had been in prison. On "a righteous person will live by faith" (10:38), see *Habakkuk: Comparison with Other Bible Books.*

11:1-3, 6 *This thing called faith.* Having climaxed his presentation of Christ our High Priest by declaring that "a righteous person will live by faith" in him (see 10:38), the author gave several real-life examples of such faith (11). Faith is the "confident assurance" or "substance" of things hoped for and the "evidence" or "proof" of things we cannot yet see. Faith is trust in the unseen, not the unknown (11:3; see 11:27). Faith is necessary for trusting God and accepting his salvation (11:6).

11:4-5, 7-40 *Examples of faith.* The author highlighted several great heroes of faith:

- Though he was the world's first murder victim, the faith of Abel "still speaks to us" today (11:4).
- Both Enoch and Noah (11:5-7) pleased God by their brave stand for truth during times of great wickedness (see Jude 1:14-15), and God rewarded them.
- The faith of Abraham and Sarah was demonstrated in many ways (11:8-19). It has been observed that Abraham obeyed God
  - ➤ when he didn't know where (11:8-10)
  - ➤ when he didn't know how (11:11-12)
  - ➤ when he didn't know when (11:13-16)
  - ➤ when he didn't know why (11:17-19)
- Isaac, Jacob, and Joseph all took actions that showed their faith in God's promises to Israel (11:20-22).
- Both Moses and his parents were people of faith (11:23-28). By faith Moses gave up the comfort of Egypt for the challenge of leading his people.
- Though the Israelites were often faithless, they were commended for their faith in crossing the Red Sea and in defeating Jericho (11:29-30).
- Rahab, the pagan prostitute who helped Israel defeat Jericho, became an ancestor of Christ and was here honored for her faith (11:31; see Matt. 1:5).
- The Hall of Faith includes countless other OT saints, many of them nameless (11:32-38), who endured the unendurable because they saw the invisible. We who have seen the fulfillment of their faith are challenged to be people of faith like them (11:39-40).

12:1-2 *Running the race, looking to the leader.* Since we have so many good examples of faith to inspire us (see 11), we should lay aside all hindrances, repent of all known sin, and run the race of faith that God has mapped out for each of us, keeping our eyes focused on Jesus, who is both the reason for our faith and our best example of faithful endurance.

The "huge crowd of witnesses" (12:1; see 11) should assure us that we are not alone in our struggles of faith. When Elijah thought he was all alone, God told him of a crowd of 7,000 "witnesses" (see 1 Kings 19:10-18).

Rather than *dromos,* a more common Greek word for "race," the writer here used *agon,* from which we get "agony." The Christian life is a serious race!

12:3-11 *It's true! He does it because he loves us!* Discipline from the Lord should be accepted joyfully, as an opportunity for growth. God's discipline of a sinning Christian does not imply condemnation but rather confirmation, demonstrating that we belong to him (12:5-10). The real question is not simply how many mistakes a Christian makes but how much he or she learns from those mistakes. The psalmist spoke of how "happy" the person is whom God disciplines (see Ps. 94:12; 119:67, 71, 75).

12:12-17 *"Be revived! Don't be like Esau!"* Those struggling in their faith should pursue holy living and brotherly love (12:12-15). Esau is a negative role model (12:16-17), selling his birthright (see Gen. 25:29-34) and losing his blessing (see Gen. 27:1-35). Esau had no interest in the spiritual benefits of the birthright and blessing. His sorrow (12:17) probably came only when he realized he would lose the material benefits as well.

12:18-29 *The mountains of bondage and blessing.* Sinai and Moses, the mountain and the man of law, were contrasted with Zion and Christ, the mountain and the Man of grace. Meeting God at Sinai was an awesome experience indeed (12:18-21), but Christ and his New Covenant are incomparably greater (12:22-24). Again came the exhortation not to turn away from the gospel, for if disobedience was punished under the law, "how terrible our danger" if we reject the gospel (12:25; compare 2:3). God's voice shook the earth at Sinai, but one day he will shake both the heavens and the earth in judgment (see Isa. 2:5–4:1). Those who accept his grace, however, receive "a kingdom that cannot be destroyed" (12:28). Realization of these truths should produce "holy fear and awe" (12:28-29).

13:1-6 *Love people, not money.* The writer concluded with various exhortations regarding personal and church life. We should be hospitable to strangers, for some, like Abraham (see Gen. 18:1-2) and Lot (see Gen. 19:1-3), have entertained angels without realizing it. We should be concerned for all who are mistreated. We should be faithful to our marriage vows. We should avoid materialism.

13:7-19 *Submit to leaders; identify with Christ alone.* We should respect and obey our spiritual leaders because of their teaching and example and because of the gravity of their responsibility for our souls (13:7, 17). We should also pray for them (13:18-19). We should avoid heresies such as those of the Judaizers (13:9-10), focusing instead on Christ and his simple, unchanging offer of salvation (13:8).

Like the true sacrificial Lamb that he was, "Jesus suffered and died outside the city gates" of Jerusalem (13:11-12). The Jewish Christian recipients of Hebrews were urged to share Christ's reproach by staying outside the gate of Judaism (see *Background*). Christians of all times, both Jewish and Gentile, should live apart from those things that occupy nonbelievers, realizing that their home is in heaven, not on earth (13:14). They should worship Christ continually in word and deed (13:15-16) and bear his reproach in whatever way he calls them to (13:13).

13:20-25 *That great Shepherd and his sheep.* Hebrews ends with the writer's prayer that God, who raised Jesus from the dead, will anoint each of us with his mighty power.

JAMES

A.D. 30?
James believes on risen Christ

45
James writes 1st NT book

49
James presides at Jerusalem Council

c. 62–63
James martyred?

c. 67
Paul martyred

BACKGROUND

James was written very early in the history of the church (see *Date and Location*) to encourage its Jewish Christian recipients during a time of suffering and to address various issues related to their faith.

AUTHOR

James, half brother of Jesus (Matt. 13:55; Gal. 1:19), who didn't believe in Jesus' deity until after his death and resurrection (John 7:5; Acts 1:14), perhaps not till Jesus personally appeared to him (1 Cor. 15:7). James became known as an apostle (Gal. 1:19) and along with Peter and John was a "pillar" of the Jerusalem church (Gal 2:9; Acts 12:17; 21:18). He presided at the Jerusalem Council in A.D. 49 (Acts 15) and, according to tradition, died a martyr's death c. 62–63.

DATE AND LOCATION

James was the earliest book of the NT canon, probably written c. A.D. 45 from Jerusalem, where James ministered. The early date (four years before Paul's first letter) is suggested by

- the absence of any mention of the Jerusalem Council (Acts 15), at which James played a key role, or of the Jewish vs. Gentile issues that led up to the council, which would have been of interest to his readers
- the fact that James, while emphasizing the importance of good works as an evidence of faith, made no attempt to reconcile that teaching with Paul's emphasis on salvation by faith alone

RECIPIENTS

The "Jewish Christians scattered among the nations" (1:1), who were James's "brothers and sisters" and had suffered persecution (1:2). These were probably Jewish Christians who, having been persecuted for their faith, had fled from Judea to various parts of the Roman Empire (Acts 8:1-4).

PURPOSE

See *Background.*

UNIQUE FEATURES

- The letter reads like sermon notes on various topics rather than a well-thought-out, logical presentation. It is saturated with the teachings of Christ, though there are no direct quotes and no mention of specific events in Christ's ministry.
- James mentions no individuals in his letter, yet his writing is warm and fatherly in tone.
- It is practical rather than doctrinal.
- It draws rich imagery from nature (1:10-11; 3:3-8, 11-12; 4:14).
- It draws spiritual lessons from OT people.

COMPARISON WITH OTHER BIBLE BOOKS

Proverbs:

- Though James is a letter, with its many wise sayings its tone is similar to that of Proverbs.

Hebrews:

- Both are written to Jewish Christians. Hebrews emphasizes doctrine; James emphasizes the deeds that grow out of doctrine.

OUTLINE

ENCOURAGEMENT AND EXHORTATION (1)
- Testings and temptations (1:1-20)
- Hearing and obeying the Word (1:21-27)

EXHORTATION AND WARNINGS (2:1–5:6)
- Showing partiality (2:1-13)
- Faith and works (2:14-26)
- Controlling the tongue (3:1-12)
- Two kinds of wisdom (3:13-18)
- Warning against worldliness (4)
- Dangers of wealth (5:1-6)

ENCOURAGEMENT AND EXHORTATION (5:7-20)
- Patience (5:7-12)
- Praying for the sick (5:13-18)
- Reclaiming the apostate (5:19-20)

ENCOURAGEMENT AND EXHORTATION (1)

1:1-4 *Persecution brings perfection?* Writing to Jewish Christians who had fled persecution, James urged them to take a positive view of their trials, focusing on the character development those trials can produce. "Trouble" or "trials" (1:2) come to test faith (1:3; see Gen. 22:1; Exod. 20:20; Deut. 8:2-3). From 1:2 we learn three things about such trials:

- They are *certain* to come. James says "when," not "if."
- They can come *suddenly;* thus we "fall" into them (KJV).

- They can come in *several* ("various," NASB) forms, such as financial, physical, spiritual, mental, or social.

1:5-8 *The wise and the wavering.* God promises wisdom to all who ask in faith, but those who are double-minded about their commitment to the Lord should not expect any significant amount of such wisdom.

1:9-11 *Fading flowers and fortunes.* From God's viewpoint, earthly poverty is a cause for pride while earthly wealth is a cause for humility, for like a flower it will eventually lose its beauty and importance, and it provides no help at all in the hour of death (see exposition on the following passages: 2:1-13; 5:1-6; Matt. 6:19-24; 1 Tim. 6:3-10; 17-19).

1:12-20 *Godly living amid persecution.* Those who successfully endure temptation will receive "the crown of life" from the Lord (1:12). Such temptations never come from God, who is himself above all such temptation. Rather, each person must accept responsibility for allowing temptation to enter his or her life and for the sin that too often follows the temptation (1:13-16). God desires only the best for us (1:17). He has given us spiritual birth through the gospel (1:18). The godly qualities we learn from him should help us in our trials (1:19-20).

1:21-27 *Hear the Word, then do it!* As best we can, we should rid our lives of sin, humbly learn from God's Word, then immediately begin practicing the things we learn. Anyone who claims to be a Christian while not obeying God's Word is only deceiving himself (1:21-25). The Christian life is characterized not so much by religious observances or experiences as by purity and love in speech and action (1:26-27).

EXHORTATION AND WARNINGS (2:1–5:6)

2:1-13 *Don't be prejudiced against the poor.* To favor the rich over the poor is both sinful (2:1-4) and illogical, since the rich people we favor may be the very ones who oppress us (2:5-8). Such partiality is just as sinful as any other infringement of God's law (2:9-11). In this as in all our moral choices, we should remember that God will judge us (2:12-13).

2:14-26 *Faith is futile without works.* Faith without works is "dead," said James (2:17, 20, 26), for faith alone will never clothe or feed the needy (2:14-16). One who claims to have faith is not necessarily any better than a demon (2:19), unless his or her faith results in good works (2:18). The faith of both Abraham and Rahab was demonstrated by the things they did (2:20-26).

Some have seen a contradiction between James and Paul:

- Paul said, "God saved you by his special favor when you believed. . . . Salvation is not a reward for the good things we have done" (Eph. 2:8-9).
- James said, "That kind of faith can't save anyone. . . . We are made right with God by what we do, not by faith alone" (2:14, 24).

However, a close reading shows James is simply saying that the kind of faith that saves (2:23-24) will be evident through the good works it produces. Even Paul, who would never suggest that we are saved *by* good works, did say that we are saved *for* good works (see Eph. 2:8-10). If faith is salvation's basis, works are its barometer.

3:1-12 *Can your tongue be tamed?* Taming the tongue is a lifelong challenge. The person who can control his or her tongue probably has total self-control—just as the person who controls the rudder controls the whole ship (3:2-4). As a small spark can destroy a whole forest, an unruly tongue can destroy many people (3:5-8). Of special concern is the person whose words routinely include both blessing and cursing (3:9-12; see Matt. 7:16-20).

The Egyptian king Amasis once sent a sacrifice to his god and requested the priest to send back the best and worst part of the animal. The priest sent back the tongue, which, he said, met both demands. It has been said that a person should control his tongue in such a way that he would not hesitate to sell his talking parrot to the town gossip!

3:13-18 *Wisdom: From serpent or Savior?* An unredeemed person may be wise, but that wisdom will probably be used for selfish purposes. The believer, by contrast, has access to a "wisdom that comes from heaven" (3:17; see 1:5) and produces things like purity, peace, love, submission, and righteousness.

4:1-10 *Sin: Its source and solution.* Our sinful desires (4:1-3) and the sinful influences of the world around us (4:4) can tempt us to abandon our faith. The indwelling Holy Spirit will give us the strength to overcome, but only if we humble ourselves (4:5-6, 10), resist the Devil (4:7), draw near to God (4:8), and truly repent (4:9). Concerning the Spirit's jealousy (4:5), see exposition on 2 Corinthians 11:1-4.

4:11-12 *Be cautious when criticizing.* To speak evil against or judge another person (without due process—see exposition on Matt. 18:15-20) is to speak evil against and judge the law itself, since the law clearly forbids such things (see exposition on Matt. 7:1-6). When we thus judge the law, we are in essence judging God, who gave the law.

4:13-17 *Who knows what a day will bring?* Human life is uncertain at best, appearing and disappearing as the morning fog. Therefore, rather than putting too much stock in future plans, our philosophy should be, I will do this or go there if God wills.

5:1-6 *A warning to the wicked wealthy.* James sternly warned those who had become wealthy at the expense of others: They should repent of their terrible greed and inhumanity, or face fiery judgment. Compare 5:3 with Luke 12:20-21. On "the day of judgment" or "last days," see exposition on 1 Timothy 4:1-11.

ENCOURAGEMENT AND EXHORTATION (5:7-20)

5:7-12 *The patience of Job.* James urged patience amid suffering, citing Job as an example. Just as God rewarded Job's patience (see Job 42:7-17), he will reward ours, "for the coming of the Lord is near" (5:8).

An honest person should not have to rely on oaths to back up his or her word (5:12; see Matt. 5:34-37).

5:13-20 *Pray, sing, be anointed and healed!* Christians should be bold in expressing their emotions before the Lord, whether that involves sorrow expressed in prayer, or joy expressed in worship (5:13). Those who are ill should not hesitate to ask for prayer. The prayer of faith will heal, and if sin is involved and confessed, God will forgive (5:14-16; see 1 John 1:9). Elijah is our model: Though he was human just like us, his prayers had amazing results (5:17-18; see 1 Kings 17:1; 18:41-46). However, it is not always God's will to heal the sick (see exposition on 1 Tim. 5:21-25). Suffering, if rightly understood and endured by the believer, can bring glory to God (see Exod. 4:11; John 9:1-3; see exposition on 2 Cor. 12:7-10). Note that healing is promised not through so-called faith healers but through elders of local churches. James also urged concern for the spiritually sick (5:19-20).

1 PETER

BACKGROUND

In the closing days of his earthly ministry, Jesus predicted that Peter would one day "strengthen" his fellow believers (Luke 22:32; see John 21:15-17). In this first of his two letters Peter did just that, encouraging Christians who were experiencing persecution (2:12; 3:16; 4:4) and who would soon experience far greater persecution as Nero, falsely blaming Christians for the fire that destroyed Rome in A.D. 64, took vengeance on believers throughout the empire.

AUTHOR

Simon Peter (1:1), one of the original 12 apostles, formerly a fisherman in Capernaum on the north shore of Galilee (John 1:40-42). Peter was one of the inner circle of three disciples, along with James and John. On key occasions he was spokesman for all the disciples (Matt. 16:16-18; John 6:68-69). After his serious failure of denying Christ (Matt. 26:69-75), he went on to become an elder and key leader in the early church (5:1; Acts 2; 10; 12; 15). According to tradition, he suffered martyrdom in Rome by being crucified upside down, c. 67–68.

DATE AND LOCATION

A.D. 63–64, just before Nero's persecutions and the death of Paul. Peter apparently wrote from "Babylon" (5:13), which could have been either the ancient city on the Euphrates, or Rome, for which Babylon was a popular code name among victims of its oppression.

RECIPIENTS

Christians, both Jewish and Gentile, scattered by persecution throughout several provinces of Asia Minor (1:1).

A.D. 26–27
Peter called, follows Christ

29
Peter's great confession

30
Peter denies Christ, repents, preaches at Pentecost

40
Peter leads Cornelius to Christ

64–65
Peter writes 1,2 Peter

67–68
Peter & Paul martyred?

PURPOSE

- To encourage and instruct Christians concerning persecution (3:13–5:11)
- To instruct concerning salvation (1:1–2:10)
- To instruct concerning subjection (2:11–3:12)
- To confirm Peter's agreement with Paul (see exposition on 2 Pet. 3:14-18)

UNIQUE FEATURES

- 1 Peter has a very polished Greek literary style.
- It emphasizes Christ's sufferings, mentioning them in every chapter.
- As one who had himself failed several times, Peter shows great tenderness in this letter.
- His rhetorical style in the letter is similar to that of his speeches in Acts.
- For its length, 1 Peter contains more OT quotations than any other NT book.

COMPARISON WITH OTHER BIBLE BOOKS

2 Corinthians:

- Both deal extensively with suffering: 2 Corinthians concerning the sufferings of Paul; 1 Peter concerning the sufferings of Christians generally.

James:

- Both were addressed to Christians scattered abroad by persecution, and both are intensely practical:
  - ➤ James, written c. 45, addressed primarily Jewish Christians.
  - ➤ 1 Peter, written some 20 years later, addressed Jews as well as the many Gentiles who had by then become believers and faced similar opposition.

OUTLINE

OUR DESTINY: SALVATION (1:1–2:10)
- Salutation (1:1-2)
- The plan of salvation (1:3-12)
- The products of salvation (1:13-25)
- The purposes of salvation (2:1-10)

OUR DUTY: SUBJECTION (2:11–3:12)
- In the world (2:11-25)
- In the home (3:1-7)
- In the church (3:8-12)

OUR DISCIPLINE: SUFFERING (3:13–4:19)
- Suffering leads to witness (3:13-17)
- Christ's mission to the "spirits in prison" (3:18-22)
- The value of suffering (4:1-6)
- Serving one another (4:7-11)
- Suffering for our faith (4:12-19)

OUR DUTY: SERVING (5)
- Serving as shepherds (5:1-4)
- Serving as soldiers (5:5-11)
- Conclusion (5:12-14)

OUR DESTINY: SALVATION (1:1–2:10)

1:1-2 *"To God's chosen people everywhere."* Those "chosen" for salvation have been chosen by the Father, made holy by the Spirit, and cleansed by the Son. The Bible never reveals the basis upon which some are chosen for salvation and others are not. We are only told that "God knew his people in advance" (Rom. 8:29) and "long ago, even before he made the world, God loved us and chose us in Christ" (Eph. 1:4). The Bible also makes it clear that, while God chooses who will be saved, we humans have a choice as well (see John 3:16; Rom. 10:13; Rev. 22:17). In one single statement, our Lord combined the doctrines of election and free will: "Those the Father has given me [election] will come to me [free will]" (John 6:37). See also exposition on Romans 9:14-29.

C. H. Spurgeon, asked how he reconciled God's election with human choice, replied, "I never have to reconcile friends!"

1:3-5 *A future we can count on!* Because of Christ's resurrection, Christians have a hope of eternal salvation that is actually a certainty, for it is "beyond the reach of change and decay." It is guaranteed and protected by God himself (see exposition on John 10:22-30).

1:6-9 *"It's rough now, but just wait!"* Christians should rejoice in their assurance of salvation, even amid earthly trials. Our goal should be to demonstrate the kind of faith that will "bring [us] much praise and glory and honor" at Christ's return (1:7). Peter spoke of four things that are "precious" (1:7, 19; 2:4, 6-7; 3:4).

1:10-12 *They didn't always understand what they wrote.* The OT prophets faithfully recorded God's promises of eternal salvation, realizing all the while that they would never see the fulfillment in their own lifetime but that they were recording those words for future generations (see Dan. 12:8-13; Matt. 13:17). In similar fashion, the elect angels, though they are not fallen and therefore do not need redemption, are intensely interested in it (1:12; compare Dan. 12:5-6). God's dealings with us are a sort of object lesson to them (see 1 Cor. 4:9; Eph. 3:10).

1:13-21 *The holy one says, "Be holy."* We should put all our hopes on our sure salvation, seeking to imitate God's holiness as we await Christ's return (1:13-17; see Lev. 11:44; 19:2; see exposition on Heb. 10:1-18). We should always remember the great price paid for our salvation: the "lifeblood of Christ, the sinless, spotless Lamb" (1:19). God has been planning our salvation from before the dawn of time (1:20-21; see exposition on Eph. 1:1-6). On "these final days" (1:20), see exposition on 1 Timothy 4:1-11.

1:22-25 *Passing glory, permanent glory, pure love.* Unredeemed human life will fade like a fallen flower, but God's glorious Word is everlasting, as are all who put their trust in it (1:23-25). As everlasting beings, we should love each other with "sincere" and holy love (1:22).

2:1-3 *Seek it for spiritual strength.* God's Word, like wholesome milk, produces spiritual growth, so we should desire it, as David did (see Ps. 19:9-10). Israel as a whole, however, had no desire for God's Word in OT times, and as Isaiah predicted (see Isa. 53:2), when Christ appeared they had no desire for him either.

2:4-8 *Stones and the Stone.* Christ is the cornerstone of our faith. We are smaller "living stones," with which he is building a "spiritual temple":

- Christ is a precious stone to those who believe in him (2:4-7; see Exod. 17:6; 1 Cor. 10:4; Eph. 2:20).

- But to those who reject him, he is a stone of destruction (2:7-8; see Dan. 2:34; Matt. 21:44; Rom. 9:32-33; 1 Cor. 1:23).

Though Israel now rejects Christ as their cornerstone, they will one day accept him as such (see Zech. 4:7).

2:9-10 *We are kings and priests!* Having been "nobodies" (see Hos. 1:10; Rom. 9:25), we are now both kings and priests:

- kings, for we'll someday rule with Christ (see 2 Tim. 2:12)
- priests, for we have direct access to God (see Eph. 2:18; Heb. 4:16)

Israel *had* a priesthood; Christians *are* a priesthood. Believer-priests offer:

- themselves (see Rom. 12:1; Phil. 2:17; 1 John 3:16)
- their substance (see Rom. 12:13; Gal. 6:6, 10; Titus 3:14)
- their service (see Heb. 13:16)
- their songs of praise (see Heb. 13:15)

OUR DUTY: SUBJECTION (2:11–3:12)

2:11-20 *Rules for royal priests.* Bearing in mind that earth is only our temporary home, we should guard against its temptations. We should maintain a good witness and let our light shine before unbelievers (2:11-12; see Matt. 5:13-16); the government (2:13-17; see Rom. 13:1-7); and our employers, even when they treat us unjustly (2:18-20; see Eph. 6:5-8).

2:21-25 *Redeemer and role model.* Jesus not only died to give us everlasting life, but by his personal example he showed us how to live that new life. Because Christ suffered without complaining (2:23), we should be willing to do the same (2:18-21). This call to suffering is the final of God's "Seven Sovereign Summonses" to believers:

- the call to salvation (see Rom. 8:30)
- the call to sonship (see 1 John 3:1)
- the call to sanctification (see 1 Thess. 5:23-24)
- the call to service (see Mark 10:43-44)
- the call to separation (see 2 Cor. 6:17-18)
- the call to subjection:
  - ➤ children to parents (see Eph. 6:1)
  - ➤ wives to husbands (see Eph. 5:22)
  - ➤ employees to employers (2:18)
  - ➤ citizens to government (2:13-14)
  - ➤ all believers to God (see Rom. 12:1-2)
- the call to suffering (2:21; see Phil. 1:29)

3:1-6 *Wisdom for wives.* Wives should submit to their husbands, as Sarah did to Abraham (3:1, 5-6). If a woman has an unbelieving husband, her submission will be a silent but effective witness to him (3:1-2). Women should focus on developing inward, rather than outward, beauty (3:3-4).

3:7 *Wisdom for husbands.* The Christian husband should understand that his wife

- is to have a special place of honor in his heart
- is physically weaker and should not be abused
- is spiritually his equal

Observance of these principles will enhance the spiritual atmosphere of the home.

3:8-12 *One big happy family.* The church should be characterized by positive, loving relationships. Righteous living brings happiness, for it brings God's favor and blessing (see Ps. 34:12-16).

OUR DISCIPLINE: SUFFERING (3:13–4:19)

3:13-17 *Persecution and witness.* We need not fear, no matter how much we are mistreated, if we are doing God's will (3:13-14). When we silently suffer for our faith, people will notice, and when that happens we should point to Christ as our source of strength.

3:18-22 *"Spirits in prison."* Christ, our example, suffered death for our sins, then was raised by the Holy Spirit (3:18). By the Spirit's power he also "preached to the spirits in prison—those who disobeyed God long ago . . . while Noah was building his boat" (3:19-20). There are at least three possible interpretations for this difficult passage:

- that, in the time between his death and resurrection, Christ took the gospel to those now dead ("in prison") who had rejected Noah's message (see 2 Pet. 2:5)
- that the preincarnate Christ was proclaiming the gospel through Noah and that those who rejected his message (everyone, that is, except Noah and his family) were now "spirits in prison"
- that these spirits were actually fallen angels who had tried to corrupt humans in Noah's day (see Gen. 5:29–6:7); if this is true, then Christ's message was one of judgment

As Peter contemplated the great Flood, he saw in it "a picture of baptism" (3:21), which "saves" us, not in and of itself, but by the power of Christ's death and resurrection (3:20-22). Water baptism is an outward symbol of our baptism by the Holy Spirit (see exposition on 1 Cor. 12:12-31).

4:1-6 *Suffering subdues sin.* We should gladly follow Christ's example of suffering (4:1), especially since suffering causes sin to lose its power over us (4:1-3). Suffering causes us to focus on the important things in life, while pleasure often distracts us from those things, giving Satan his best opportunity with us (see Eccles. 7:1-4). Of course our unbelieving friends don't understand this, so they will ridicule us for not joining in their wickedness, but God will judge them (4:4-5).

The gospel "was preached even to those who have died—so that although their bodies were punished with death, they could still live in the spirit as God does" (4:6). While the language of 4:6 is similar to that of 3:19-20, there is not necessarily a direct connection. William J. Dalton lists four possible interpretations:

- Christ, while dead, offered salvation to all who had died before his time.
- Christ, while dead, offered salvation to the just of OT times.
- The passage refers to the preaching of the gospel by the apostles and others to the spiritually dead.
- It refers to Christians who had died.

4:7-11 *Lessons for the last days.* Since we are living in the last days, we should be thoughtful people of prayer. We should show deep love for each other, be hospitable, and wisely use our spiritual gifts (see Rom. 12:6-8). The sins of others should evoke concern, not gossip (4:8; see Prov. 10:12; 1 Cor. 13:6).

4:12-19 *Share the grief; share the glory.* We should not be surprised when we suffer for our faith. Rather, we should rejoice, knowing that, if we suffer with Christ now, we will reign with him forever. For the second time Peter used the image of fire (4:12; see 1:7)—perhaps a prophetic description of the actual burning of believers by Nero in days not far ahead (see *Background*). We should be sure, however, that our suffering results from our faith and not from any wrongdoing on our part (4:15-19).

While references to believers occur frequently throughout the NT and our English translations often use the word *Christians,* the Greek word for *Christians* occurs only three times in Scripture (4:16; see Acts 11:26; 26:28).

OUR DUTY: SERVING (5)

5:1-4 *Elders should feed and lead.* Being himself an elder, Peter urged elders to serve willingly and with pure motives. They should be role models, not directors. They should have shepherds' hearts, looking to Christ the Chief Shepherd (see John 10:11, 14; compare Ps. 23) as their own role model and the one who will reward them.

5:5-7 *The way up is the way down.* Christians should humbly submit to each other, knowing that God rewards humility with his grace. We can take all our cares and concerns to God, knowing that he cares for us.

5:8-9 *Look out for that lion!* Satan, like a lion, is always looking for human prey. We should firmly resist him, encouraged by the fact that we are not alone in our suffering.

5:10-14 *From suffering to stability.* As a benediction, Peter asked that God would strengthen his readers amid their suffering. God's grace is truly with us "no matter what happens." As Christians we have received "one gracious blessing after another" (John 1:16). James says, "He gives us more grace" (James 4:6, NIV). The Scriptures speak of saving grace (see Eph. 2:8-9); serving grace (see 1 Cor. 15:9-10); sanctifying grace (see Rom. 5:17; 6:17); sacrificing grace (see 2 Cor. 8:1-9); singing grace (see Col. 3:16); speaking grace (see Col. 4:6); strengthening grace (see 2 Tim. 2:1); and suffering grace (5:10; see 2 Cor. 12:9).

Peter was sending his letter by Silas (Silvanus). He sent greetings from Mark. Both of these men were also associates of Paul. On "Babylon," see *Date and Location.*

2 PETER

BACKGROUND
In light of his imminent death (1:14-15), Peter wanted to prepare his readers for the time when he would no longer be with them. They needed to press on to spiritual maturity, beware of apostasy, and be assured of the Lord's certain coming.

AUTHOR
See *1 Peter: Author.*

DATE AND LOCATION
A.D. 64–67, shortly after 1 Peter (see *1 Peter: Date and Location*).

RECIPIENTS
See *1 Peter: Recipients.*

PURPOSE
- To remind his readers of God's provisions for salvation and spiritual maturity (1)
- To warn of the dangers of apostasy (2)
- To assure them concerning the Lord's return (3)

UNIQUE FEATURES
- The letter blends severity and tenderness, as Peter contemplated death while seeking to address urgent problems in the church.
- 2 Peter contains key passages on
  - ➤ the inspiration of Scripture (1:19-21)
  - ➤ false teachers (2)
  - ➤ the "day of the Lord" (3:10-13)
- Peter showed that he and Paul had repaired the rift between them, acknowledging Paul's letters to be on the same level as OT Scripture (3:15-16).

***A.D. 26–27* Peter called, follows Christ**

***29* Peter's great confession**

***30* Peter denies Christ, repents, preaches at Pentecost**

***40* Peter leads Cornelius to Christ**

***64–65* Peter writes 1,2 Peter**

***67–68* Peter & Paul martyred?**

COMPARISON WITH OTHER BIBLE BOOKS

John 14–16 and 2 Timothy:

- All are farewell discourses.

2 Thessalonians:

- Both concentrate on the darker side of things to come.

Jude:

- 2 Peter 2 warns of false teachers who would come; Jude warns against false teachers who were already there.

OUTLINE

GOD'S PROVISION (1)
- For Christian living (1:1-11)
- For knowledge of the truth (1:12-21)

FALSE TEACHERS (2)
- Description (2:1-3)
- Their doom, our salvation (2:4-9)
- Description (2:10-22)

CHRIST'S CERTAIN RETURN (3)
- False teachers' denial of his return (3:1-7)
- The day of the Lord (3:8-13)
- Living in light of the day of the Lord (3:14-18)

GOD'S PROVISION (1)

1:1-2 *"The same precious faith."* Describing himself as a servant and missionary, and addressing those "who share the same precious faith," Peter urged them to abound in the knowledge of Christ.

1:3-11 *Victory virtues.* Since God has made all the necessary provisions for our spiritual maturity (1:3-4), we are to try our best to incorporate godly qualities into our lives (1:5-8). Our election by God for salvation is a sure thing, but we can experience it to the full in this life only as we consistently practice godliness (1:9-11; see exposition on 1 Pet. 1:1-2).

1:12-15 *"Now, a few words before I go . . ."* Peter knew he would soon die a martyr's death, as Christ had predicted (see John 21:18-19). He was writing this second letter to help ensure that, after his death, his disciples would remain faithful to Christ. He spoke of his death as a departure (1:15; compare Luke 9:31). Moses (see Deut. 4:22) and Paul (see 2 Tim. 4:6) had similar premonitions of death.

1:16-21 *A word more sure.* The truth Peter had proclaimed was not mere hearsay; he had been an eyewitness of Christ's life and teachings (1:16) and was one of the privileged three to witness the Transfiguration (1:17-18; see Matt. 17:1-8). As memorable as that experience was, however, Peter seemed to treasure it mostly because of how it confirmed the written words of Scripture (1:19-21).

Scripture should never be interpreted lightly or out of context as a proof text. It is the inspired Word of God and should be handled with utmost care. Bible authors were "moved" by the Holy Spirit (1:21) as a sailboat is carried along by the wind. They did not go into a trance but were fully alert as God spoke to them (see *Inspiration*, p. 877).

The same Holy Spirit who originally gave the Word desires to teach it both to and through God's people today (see John 14:26; 16:13-14; 1 Cor. 2:9-16).

On "until the day dawns" (1:19), compare Malachi 4:2 and Revelation 22:16.

FALSE TEACHERS (2)

2:1-3 *False teachers past and present.* Even as God's faithful prophets were recording his Word, there were (and still are) many false prophets, some of whom deny Christ's deity. Many fall victim to them, but they will one day be judged.

2:4-9 *He saves some while judging others.* Even as God judges false teachers (2:4-8), he will surely rescue the righteous (2:9). This can be seen in the way he

- saved Noah while judging the world with water (2:5)
- saved Lot while judging Sodom with fire (2:6-8)

2:4 may refer to

- all the angels who sided with Lucifer in his great revolt (see Isa. 14:12-15; Ezek. 28:11-19; Rev. 12:3-4)
- or, more specifically, the angels who some scholars believe are described in Genesis 6:1-5 (see Jude 1:6)

It would be hard to conclude from Genesis 13–14, 19 that Lot was "righteous" (2:8); however, "the Lord knows those who are his" (2 Tim. 2:19). Through his selfish and wrong choice concerning where to live, Lot subjected himself to being distressed and sickened by Sodom's moral depravity.

2:10-16 *Just like brute beasts.* Apparently with certain false teachers in mind, Peter described them as lustful, greedy, and insolent (2:10-11). In intellect and lifestyle, they were little more than animals (2:12-14). They were like Balaam, the false prophet who was rebuked by the very donkey he was riding (see Num. 22:28-30; Jude 1:11; Rev. 2:14).

2:17-22 *Just like hogs and dogs.* Like "dried-up springs of water," these false teachers' words were empty of meaning; they enslaved immature believers (2:17-18). They promised their converts freedom while they themselves were slaves of depravity (2:19). It would be better for these false teachers to have never been born, than to have known the truth and rejected it (2:20-22).

Some see 2:20-21 as an indication that Christians can lose their salvation. However:

- The harsh language would suggest otherwise: Nowhere in the Bible does God call a believer a pig or a dog—animals despised in ancient times (2:22).
- A preponderance of other Scriptures assure the believer that salvation cannot be lost (see exposition on the following: John 10:22-30; Eph. 1:13-14; Heb. 6:4-12; 1 Pet. 1:3-5; however, see also exposition on Heb. 10:26-31).

CHRIST'S CERTAIN RETURN (3)

3:1-7 *They forget the Flood, but they'll see the fire!* Just as the prophets had warned, Peter again warned that many "scoffers" and false teachers would arise in the last days (3:1-3). Pointing to the ancient unchanging laws of nature, they would ridicule the very notion of Christ's second coming—conveniently forgetting God's other miraculous deeds, such as the Flood (3:4-6). Since God had already judged the world once, no one should doubt that he'll do it again: Just as he destroyed it with water, he will someday destroy it with fire (3:7).

3:8-13 *From mercy to meltdown to Millennium.* When will God next destroy the world? We cannot say, for our human concept of time means nothing to God, who created and controls time (3:8). The only reason God *delays* judgment is to give as many as possible the opportunity for salvation (3:9). When judgment does come, it will be final and catastrophic, with the very elements of nature melting in "fire" (3:10). In light of this certain judgment, we should live in holiness as we await the better world that will follow (3:11-13). Concerning "the day of the Lord" (3:10) and the day of God (3:12), see *Isaiah: Background* and exposition on Isaiah 2:5–4:1.

3:14-18 *"Be holy and hopeful, like Paul said."* As we look forward to Christ's return, we should live in peace and holiness and hope of salvation, as Paul also urged us to do (3:14-16). If we keep growing spiritually, we will avoid falling away from our faith (3:17-18). Note Peter's statements concerning Paul:

- He and Paul continued to be good friends following their confrontation in Antioch (see Gal. 2:11-14).
- He attested to the divine inspiration of Paul's writings.
- He admitted that some of Paul's writings were "hard to understand," and noted that some in his day (as in our day) deliberately misinterpreted those and other Scriptures. Yet with the Holy Spirit's help (see John 16:13), we can understand even Paul (3:18).

1 JOHN

BACKGROUND
Many false teachers had gone out from Ephesus to surrounding cities, teaching erroneous views about Christ. John wrote his Gospel to convince his readers that "Jesus is the Messiah" (John 20:30-31). He wrote this letter to reassure them that through Jesus they have eternal life (5:13) and can enjoy fellowship with God and with fellow believers (1:3-4).

AUTHOR
Though no author's name appears within the body of this letter or the other two letters bearing John's name in their titles, the early church fathers attributed all three to John, the beloved disciple of Christ. Their similarities in vocabulary and literary style with the Gospel of John support this view, as do the author's claims to have been an eyewitness of Christ's ministry (1:2-3; 4:14).

DATE
C. A.D. 85–95, probably sometime after the Gospel of John. See *John: Date.*

LOCATION AND RECIPIENTS
See *John: Location and Recipients.* 1 John was probably a circular letter to believers throughout the Roman province of Asia, including the seven churches of Revelation 2–3.

PURPOSE
See *Background.*

UNIQUE FEATURES
- 1 John contains no salutation or signature.
- It has no direct quotations from the OT.
- It highlights three characteristics of God:

A.D. 26–27
John called, follows Christ

31
John ministers in Samaria

49
Paul mentions John as church leader

??–??
John ministers in Ephesus?

85–95
John writes 5 NT books

98
Death of John

    - He is light (1:5).
    - He is righteous (2:29).
    - He is love (4:8, 16).
- John was known as the beloved disciple (John 13:23), but also as a "Son of Thunder" (Mark 3:17). This letter, with its gentleness and severity, justifies both names:
    - Repeatedly throughout the letter, John addressed his readers as "my dear children."
    - Yet he was adamant in warning of apostasy and in maintaining the division between the absolute light of God and the absolute darkness of the Devil and his works (1:5).
- It contains perhaps the Bible's best and most concise description of worldliness (2:15-17).

COMPARISON WITH OTHER BIBLE BOOKS

Genesis and John:

- All three begin with a beginning:
    - In Genesis, the beginning is Creation.
    - In John and 1 John, the beginning is the eternally preexistent Word.

John:

- Both contain specific statements of the author's purpose of writing (see *Background* and exposition on 1:1-4).
- 1 John supplements John in its efforts to strengthen believers in their faith.

OUTLINE

THE BASIS OF FELLOWSHIP (1:1-4)
PROOFS OF FELLOWSHIP (1:5–2:27)
- Walking in the light (1:5–2:2)
- Keeping his commandments (2:3-14)
- Not loving the world (2:15-17)
- Abiding in the truth (2:18-27)

THE FRUITS OF FELLOWSHIP (2:28–3:24)
- Eager expectation of Christ's return (2:28–3:3)
- The practice of righteousness (3:4-10)
- Love of the brethren (3:11-15)
- A clear conscience (3:16-24)

EXHORTATIONS ON FELLOWSHIP (4–5)
- Testing the spirits (4:1-6)
- Loving one another (4:7-21)
- Overcoming the world (5:1-5)
- Assurance of the Incarnation (5:6-10)
- Assurance of eternal life (5:11-13)
- Prayer (5:14-17)
- Final exhortations (5:18-21)

THE BASIS OF FELLOWSHIP (1:1-4)

1:1-4 *"I saw, heard, and touched him."* In an introduction reminiscent of the introduction to his Gospel (see exposition on John 1:1-5), John expressed his desire to write concerning Christ, the eternal Word of life, so that we his readers could have the same wonderful fellowship he had with Christ.

PROOFS OF FELLOWSHIP (1:5–2:27)

1:5-10 *Living in the light.* God is "light," or truth (1:5; see exposition on John 1:9-13), and cannot have fellowship with darkness. We cannot claim to be in fellowship with God if we continue to live in the darkness of falsehood and sin (1:6). If, however, we seek to live according to God's will, we will enjoy fellowship with other believers and continuing forgiveness from God (1:7). In this life we will never achieve sinless perfection (1:8, 10; see Phil. 3:12-14). But as we continually confess all the sins of which we are aware, we will continually experience the reality of our once-for-all forgiveness through Christ (see exposition on Eph. 1:13-14) and will be free from the stain of unrighteousness.

"Confess" (1:9) is *homologeo,* meaning "to agree with." When the Spirit points out a sin in our life, we should immediately agree with him. While the blood of Christ will cleanse us of every sin, it will not cleanse us of even one excuse.

2:1-2 *"Don't sin! But if you do . . ."* We should want to be free of sin. When we do sin, however, we can depend on Christ to defend us before God. "Sacrifice" ("propitiation," KJV) means atonement. Its Greek root is found four times in the NT: 2:2; 4:10; Romans 3:25; and Hebrews 9:5, where it is translated "place of atonement" or "mercy seat." Under the law, once a year the high priest made atonement for Israel by sprinkling blood on the lid of the Ark, known as the mercy seat (see Lev. 16:13-19). Christ's death is our place of atonement, as God's holiness is satisfied by his blood.

"If you do sin" cannot possibly mean that sinless perfection is possible in this life (see exposition on 1:5-10). Rather, it means that sin should not characterize the believer's life.

2:3-11 *Two ways to know that we know him.* We can be assured that we know God if we

- try to obey his commands and imitate Christ (2:3-6)
- love our fellow believers (2:7-11)

Through love, we can overcome the powers of darkness. The commandment to love is both old (2:7; see Matt. 22:34-40) and new (2:8; see John 13:34; 15:12).

2:12-14 *Focus on the family.* Wherever we are in the family of God, new believer or mature in our faith, we can overcome Satan through remembering our salvation and past spiritual victories and by abiding in God's Word.

2:15-17 *"Don't love . . . Do love . . ."* We should not love the evil things of this world, which will soon pass away. Rather, we should love God, who can give us eternal life. On "the lust for physical pleasure, the lust for everything we see, and pride in our possessions," see exposition on Matthew 4:1-11.

2:18-27 *Antichrists and inner anointing.* John warned about the coming "Antichrist" and the many "antichrists" who would precede him (2:18; see exposition on 4:1-6). These antichrists are apostate religious teachers who deny Christ (2:22-23), thus proving that they never knew him (2:19). The Holy Spirit, who "anoints" or resides in the believer, teaches us all spiritual truth, allowing us to distinguish between the false and the true (2:20-21;

see John 16:13). If God's Word abides in us, we will enjoy fellowship with God, will have the hope of eternal life, and will understand spiritual truth (2:24-27).

"You don't need anyone to teach you" (2:27) should be interpreted in light of passages such as Ephesians 4:11-13, which shows clearly that the Holy Spirit uses human agents to teach us.

THE FRUITS OF FELLOWSHIP (2:28–3:24)

2:28–3:3 *Confident at his coming.* If we live in such a way as to maintain fellowship with Christ, we will be confident to stand before him when he returns (2:28-29). God loves us enough to call us his children on earth (3:1-2) and to promise us glorified bodies when he returns (3:2; see Rom. 8:18-19; Phil. 3:20-21). In light of our relationship with God, we should want to be holy just as he is holy (3:3; see 1 Pet. 1:16).

3:4-9 *A simple truth: If you sin, you're a sinner.* Jesus came to save us from sin and destroy the works of Satan, the originator of sin. If our lives are characterized by continual sin, we do not know God and have not truly been saved. While every Christian will sin from time to time (see exposition on 1:5-10), a true Christian will not "keep on sinning" (3:6).

3:10-15 *Another simple truth: If you hate, you're a sinner.* Just as a Christian cannot be a habitual sinner, nor can he or she be filled with hate, as was Cain. Love is a sure mark of the true Christian (see exposition on 2:3-11; Gen. 4:1-8).

3:16-24 *Which is best: Works of love or words of love?* We should show our love by our actions, just as Christ did (3:16-18). Loving deeds give us even more assurance of our salvation (3:19, 21). If we are truly saved, even when we feel condemned God still knows and accepts us (3:20; see 2 Tim. 2:19). How wonderful to obey God and love each other, so that we can approach God with a clean conscience and receive the things we need from him (3:22-23).

EXHORTATIONS ON FELLOWSHIP (4–5)

4:1-6 *Are you dealing with the right Spirit?* We should not believe everyone claiming divine inspiration. People may claim to revere Jesus as a great teacher, but only those who acknowledge him as God in the flesh are truly Christians. All others speak by "the spirit of the Antichrist" (4:3), and we should avoid them. When such false teachers come calling, we can be confident that the Holy Spirit who indwells us is more powerful than the evil one who indwells them.

The Antichrist

- will appear during the last days (see 2:18; 4:3)
- will deny Christ's deity (see 2:22) and Christ's humanity (4:3; see 2 John 1:7)
- has had many prototypes ("antichrists") throughout history (2:18; 4:3)

While the word *Antichrist* appears only in John's letters, several other passages talk of a person many scholars identify as the Antichrist (see exposition on the following: Dan. 9:20-27; 11:36-45; 12:5-13; Zech. 11:15-17; 2 Thess. 2:1-12; Rev. 13:1-10).

4:7-21 *The bottom line: God is love.* Christians should love, for God *is* love (4:7-8) and has shown us what true love is (4:19). God demonstrated his love by sending his Son to die for our sins (4:9-10, 14; see John 3:16). We can demonstrate love in return by our concern and care for fellow believers (4:11-12). As we do so, we will gain confidence in our own salvation (4:16-18). The person who claims to love God but hates people is self-deceived (4:20-21). Christian love has been defined as unselfish concern for the welfare of another. We can love even those we don't like.

5:1-5 *"Once again, this is how we know. . . ."* If we have truly been "born again" (John 3:3), we will believe that Jesus is God's Son, and will experience ongoing victory over evil (5:4).

5:6-10 *The testimony of the Trinity.* Fulfilling the law's requirement of two or three witnesses (see Deut. 19:15), Christ's deity was confirmed by three witnesses:

- the Spirit
- the water (Christ's baptism)
- the blood (his death)

The KJV translation of 5:7 reflects some late manuscripts that add three witnesses in heaven:

- the Father (see Matt. 3:17)
- Jesus himself ("the Word," John 1:1)
- the Spirit ("the Holy Ghost")

The three heavenly witnesses "are one" (5:7, KJV). They are a "Trinity" (see exposition on Gen. 1:26-31).

There is also the witness within the believer's heart (5:9-10).

5:11-13 *The record of redemption.* God has given us eternal life through Christ, his Son (5:11-12). It was to assure us of this eternal life that John wrote this letter (5:13).

5:14-17 *Assurance when we pray.* Since we have assurance of eternal life, we can know that God will answer our prayers (5:14-15; see Matt. 7:7-11; Heb. 4:16). When we see a fellow believer sin, we should pray for him or her, unless it is a "sin that leads to death" (5:16-17), which apparently involves God's removing a carnal Christian to heaven before his or her time (see Eccles. 3:2; see exposition on Heb. 6:4-12; 10:26-31).

5:18-21 *"Once again, don't sin. . . ."* A person truly born again does not habitually sin but is kept from the power of Satan by the power of God's Word. John closed by reminding his readers once more of the deity of Christ and by warning them against idolatry.

A.D. 26–27
John called, follows Christ

31
John ministers in Samaria

2 JOHN

49
Paul mentions John as church leader

BACKGROUND

John wanted to warn a godly lady (1:1) against entertaining or encouraging false teachers traveling in her area.

AUTHOR

See *John: Author* and *1 John: Author.*

??–??
John ministers in Ephesus?

DATE AND LOCATION

C. A.D. 85–95, after 1 John and about the same time as 3 John; from Ephesus, as were John, 1 John, and 3 John.

RECIPIENTS

2 John is addressed to "the chosen lady and to her children" (1:1). Among suggested interpretations:

- a church in the vicinity of Ephesus
- Martha of Bethany (traditional view)
- a wealthy woman in the vicinity of Ephesus—the view of most conservative scholars today

85–95
John writes 5 NT books

98
Death of John

PURPOSE

- To commend and encourage a godly woman and her children for their Christian living and testimony (1:1-6)
- To warn them against entertaining or encouraging itinerant false teachers (1:7-11)

UNIQUE FEATURES

- 2 John is the only NT book specifically addressed to a woman.
- It is the only Bible book besides 1 John to use the term *antichrist* (1:7).
- It gives specific instruction concerning the believer's attitudes and actions toward false teachers.

COMPARISON WITH OTHER BIBLE BOOKS

1 John:

- 8 of 2 John's 13 verses repeat the themes of 1 John.

3 John:

- 2 John warns against entertaining false teachers; 3 John encourages entertaining true teachers.

OUTLINE

COMMENDATION, ENCOURAGEMENT (1:1-6)
WARNING (1:7-13)

COMMENDATION, ENCOURAGEMENT (1:1-6)

1:1-6 *Love and truth: They're inseparable!* John wrote to a very special but unnamed mother, commending both her and her children for their godly walk in the faith (1:1-4). In phrases reminiscent of 1 John, he encouraged her to practice Christian love and be faithful to the truth (1:5-6). We can never separate love and truth:

- Truth without love leads to legalism.
- Love without truth leads to liberalism.

Paul likewise combines the two (see Eph. 4:15).

WARNING (1:7-13)

1:7-11 *"Watch out for the wicked ones."* Faithfulness to the truth is especially important in light of the many false teachers who, though perhaps claiming to be Christians, deny Christ's humanity and are thus "antichrists" (1:7; see exposition on 1 John 4:1-6). John urged denying hospitality to such people (1:10-11).

1:12-13 *"I'll sign off now and hope to see you soon."* John had more to say to this woman but felt that a face-to-face meeting would be better and hoped such a meeting would happen soon.

3 JOHN

BACKGROUND

From his headquarters in Ephesus John sent itinerant ministers to churches in the surrounding area. Gaius entertained the apostolic delegates to his church. Diotrephes, a domineering church official, rebuked Gaius for showing them hospitality and forbade other church members from doing so, upon threat of excommunication (1:10). When they returned to Ephesus, the itinerant ministers gave a glowing report of Gaius and a scathing condemnation of Diotrephes. John wrote this letter to commend Gaius, to condemn Diotrephes, and to introduce Demetrius, the bearer of the letter.

AUTHOR

See *John: Author* and *1 John: Author.*

DATE AND LOCATION

See *2 John: Date and Location.*

RECIPIENTS

Gaius (1:1), mentioned only in this book and not to be confused with the other three NT men by that name.

PURPOSE

See *Background.*

UNIQUE FEATURES

- 3 John is very affectionate in tone. The term *dear friend* or *beloved* occurs four times (1:1, 2, 5, 11).
- It gives insight into first-century church life.

A.D. 26–27
John called, follows Christ

31
John ministers in Samaria

49
Paul mentions John as church leader

??–??
John ministers in Ephesus?

85–95
John writes 5 NT books

98
Death of John

OUTLINE

COMMENDING GAIUS (1:1-8)

1:1-8 *"The news about you has made my day!"* John had heard a thrilling report concerning the testimony of his good friend Gaius, filling the apostle with joy. He commended him especially for his hospitality to itinerant evangelists.

CONDEMNING DIOTREPHES (1:9-11)

1:9-11 *There's always one in every congregation.* John warned Gaius concerning Diotrephes, who had slandered John himself and was trying to excommunicate anyone who dared to disagree with him.

INTRODUCING DEMETRIUS (1:12-15)

1:12-15 *The tremendous testimony of Demetrius.* In sharp contrast to Diotrephes was Demetrius, whom John introduced with a threefold commendation (1:12):

- *public:* "everyone speaks highly of Demetrius"
- *scriptural:* "even truth itself"
- *personal:* "we ourselves can say the same for him"

As with the addressee of his second letter, John hoped to see Gaius soon (1:13-14).

c. A.D. 30?
Jude believes on risen Christ

c. 69?
Jude writes letter

70
Jerusalem destroyed

JUDE

BACKGROUND
Scarcely 40 years after Christ's death, many believers had become lax in doctrine and practice, and there were many false teachers preying upon them. Jude wrote to encourage Christians in their faith and to warn them of false teachers.

AUTHOR
Jude, brother of James and half brother of Jesus (1:1; Matt. 13:53-56), who like his siblings did not believe in Christ's deity until after his resurrection (John 7:5; Acts 1:14). Six other Judes are mentioned in the NT, but the fact that the author of this letter did not need to further identify either himself or James (a leader in the Jerusalem church) supports the view that he was well known as Christ's and James's brother.

DATE
Perhaps c. A.D. 69:

- 1:14-18 seems to describe the false teachers Peter had warned were coming (2 Pet. 2:1-19; 3:1-3). While Peter, writing c. 64–67, expected their arrival soon (2 Pet. 2:1), they had already arrived by the time Jude wrote (1:4).
- Jude probably wrote before Jerusalem's fall in 70, since if that event had already occurred it would have been natural for him to mention it in connection with the Exodus (1:5).
- 1:17 suggests that, though most of the apostles were gone by the time Jude wrote, many of his readers had been instructed by them.

RECIPIENTS
Christians everywhere (1:1), though reference to the OT and other Jewish writings suggests the recipients were primarily Jewish Christians.

PURPOSE

See *Background.*

UNIQUE FEATURES

- Addressed to Christians everywhere, Jude is the most general NT letter.
- It emphasizes the relationship between right believing and right living.
- It chronicles opposition to God from before time (1:6) to the end of time (1:14-15).
- It is filled with OT illustrations.
- It is the only biblical reference to
  - ➤ the dispute over Moses' body (1:9)
  - ➤ the prophecy of Enoch (1:14-15)

COMPARISON WITH OTHER BIBLE BOOKS

James:

- Both use metaphors from nature (1:10, 12-13; see *James: Unique Features*).

2 Peter:

- Jude said that the false teachers Peter prophesied would come—had indeed come.

OUTLINE

WARNING OF APOSTATES (1:1-16)
- Warning that apostates have come (1:1-4)
- God's judgment of past apostasies (1:5-7)
- Description and doom of present apostates (1:8-16)

ADVICE TO BELIEVERS (1:17-25)
- Remember the warnings of apostasy (1:17-19)
- Guard your personal fellowship with God (1:20-23)
- Praise God always (1:24-25)

WARNING OF APOSTATES (1:1-16)

1:1-4 *"Here's why I'm writing."* Writing to all believers loved and chosen by the Father and kept by the Son (1:1), Jude said that he had originally planned to write on the subject of salvation but felt led instead to address the serious problem of religious apostasy (1:3-4). The word used in verse 3 (translated "I must" or "I felt the necessity") means "to bear down upon; to compress." God literally pressured Jude to write concerning apostasy (compare 1 Cor. 9:16).

We are to "defend the truth of the Good News," which God gave "once for all time to his holy people" (1:3):

- Defending the truth involves both offense and defense, as exemplified by Nehemiah (see Neh. 4:16-18).
- Now, in postbiblical times, the truth has been given to us "once for all time" in the canon of Scripture (see *How We Got the Bible,* p. 877). We are not to add to or take from it (see Rev. 22:18-19).

1:5-7 *Three guilty groups.* God judged apostasy severely in the past, as in the cases of Israel during the Exodus, a certain group of fallen angels, and

Sodom and Gomorrah (compare 2 Pet. 2:4-8).

1:8-10 *Disrespectful animals.* The false teachers, like brute beasts, were arrogant and immoral, even slandering angels ("glorious ones"). Jude contrasted their arrogance with the humility of Michael the archangel, who was reluctant to directly accuse even Satan himself. The occasion of Michael's confrontation with Satan is not recorded in Scripture but is recorded in the extrabiblical book *The Assumption of Moses.*

1:11 *Examples from history.* Jude compared the present apostates to three historical apostates, all of whom have their counterparts today:

- Cain, who ignored God's wishes and offered a bloodless sacrifice (see Gen. 4:1-7; Heb. 11:4; 1 John 3:12). Many today, while claiming to be Christians, ignore God's Word.
- Balaam, the greedy prophet hired to curse Israel, who was reprimanded by his donkey (see Num. 22:1–25:9; Rev. 2:14). Many today make merchandise of the gospel.
- Korah, who slandered and rebelled against Moses (see Num. 16). Present-day apostates speak evil against those who speak for God.

1:12-13 *Examples from nature.* Apostates are self-serving, like clouds without rain, trees without fruit, or stars that wander and are therefore useless as guides for travelers.

1:14-16 *Even Enoch saw it coming.* Citing a prophecy by Enoch, Jude declared that God would someday judge these false teachers. Enoch predicted Christ's second coming and judgment centuries before he came the first time. Even so, his prediction of Christ's return "with thousands of his holy ones" bears a striking similarity to predictions made by Paul and John (see 1 Thess. 3:13; Rev. 19:11-14). Jude quoted Enoch's prediction from the apocryphal book of Enoch, written c. 100 B.C.

ADVICE TO BELIEVERS (1:17-25)

1:17-19 *More recent warnings of apostasy.* Moving closer to the present, Jude reminded his readers that the apostles had warned of these false teachers (see 2 Pet. 2:1). On the "last times," see exposition on 1 Timothy 4:1-11.

1:20-23 *"Strengthen yourselves, and others as well."* In the face of such erroneous and dangerous teaching, Christians should practice the twin virtues of prayer and patience, building themselves up in the faith as they await Christ's return (1:20-21). At the same time, they should look after the spiritual needs of others, from those suffering honest doubt to those on the very brink of hell (1:22-23).

1:24-25 *The Redeemer will rejoice over the redeemed!* Jude concluded with praise to Jesus, who can keep us from sin (see Rom. 16:25) and who will rejoice when he presents us faultless before God (see Col. 1:22).

REVELATION

A.D. 26–27
John called, follows Christ

31
John ministers in Samaria

49
Paul mentions John as church leader

??–??
John ministers in Ephesus?

85–95
John writes 5 NT books

98
Death of John

BACKGROUND

As the first century A.D. drew to a close, the churches of Asia Minor were endangered by two foes, persecution and heresy, with heresy being by far the greater danger. The ascended Christ directed John, the aging apostle, to address this urgent situation (1:17-19). These churches needed a renewed vision of God and a revelation of his glorious plans for their future.

It is fitting that Revelation comes last in the biblical canon, for it is the climax of all that has gone before as it foretells the ultimate fulfillment of God's efforts to redeem lost humanity.

There are two main views concerning how the prophecies of Revelation (primarily 4–22) should be interpreted. Some see these chapters as a symbolic picture of the eventual triumph of Christ and his church over Satan. Others view these prophecies more literally. The fact that so many biblical prophecies have already been fulfilled literally would suggest that this latter view has more merit.

AUTHOR

John, beloved disciple, apostle, and elder (1:1, 4, 9; 22:8). The reign of church fathers all confirm John's authorship. The similarities of vocabulary and literary style with John's other writings confirm it as well (see *John: Author*).

DATE AND LOCATION

According to tradition, c. A.D. 95–96, in the latter years of the reign of Roman emperor Domitian, who had begun persecuting Christians. John wrote from Patmos (1:9), a rocky volcanic island in the Aegean Sea, 10 miles long by 6 miles wide, to which he had probably been banished by Domitian because of his faith (1:9).

RECIPIENTS

"Seven churches" in the Roman province of Asia (1:4, 11; 2–3). Geographically, these churches (cities) were roughly in a circle, which fits the imagery of 1:12-18, where Christ is seen as surrounded by them.

PURPOSE

- To give believers a renewed vision of the risen, ascended, and ruling Lord (1)
- To call for repentance and renewal (2–3)
- To reveal God's future plans for his church (4–22)

UNIQUE FEATURES

- Revelation begins and ends with the second coming of Christ (1:7; 22:20).
- It begins and ends with the Lord Jesus at the center of things (1:13; 22:1-5).
- It contains more OT references than any other NT book.
- Numbers—especially 4, 7, 12, and 24—have a prominent role.
- Revelation pronounces blessings on
  - ➤ "all who listen to [this book] and obey what it says" (1:3)
  - ➤ "those who die in the Lord" (14:13)
  - ➤ "all who are watching for [Christ]" (16:15)
  - ➤ "those who are invited to the wedding feast of the Lamb" (19:9)
  - ➤ "those who share in the first resurrection" (20:6)
  - ➤ "those who obey the prophecy written in this scroll" (22:7)
  - ➤ "those who wash their robes so they can . . . eat the fruit from the tree of life" (22:14)

COMPARISON WITH OTHER BIBLE BOOKS

See *Genesis; Ezekiel; Daniel: Comparison with Other Bible Books.*

Daniel;

- Much of Revelation's symbolism is based on Daniel.
- John is told to reveal (22:10) what Daniel was told to conceal (Dan. 8:26; 12:8-9).

2 Thessalonians 2;

- 2 Thessalonians 2 shows the Antichrist's rise and fall; Revelation gives the details of his rise, career, and fall.

2 Peter 3;

- Both depict the end of earth and beginning of heaven:
  - ➤ 2 Peter 3 gives details on the end of earth and mentions the new heavens and earth.
  - ➤ Revelation mentions the end of earth and gives details on the new heavens and earth.

OUTLINE

John revealed the outline of his prophecy in 1:19: "Write down what you have seen—both the things that are now happening and the things that will happen later."

WHAT YOU HAVE SEEN: CHRIST IN HIS ASCENDED GLORY (1)
- Prologue (1:1-8)
- The vision (1:9-20)

THE THINGS THAT ARE NOW HAPPENING: MESSAGES TO CHURCHES (2–3)
- Ephesus (2:1-7)
- Smyrna (2:8-11)
- Pergamum (2:12-17)
- Thyatira (2:18-29)
- Sardis (3:1-6)
- Philadelphia (3:7-13)
- Laodicea (3:14-22)

THE THINGS THAT WILL HAPPEN LATER: CHRIST'S PLAN FOR THE FUTURE (4–22)
- The divine judge (4–5)
- The Tribulation (6–19)
  - Seven seals (6–8:5)
  - Seven trumpets (8:6–11)
  - The woman, child, and dragon (12)
  - The beast and false prophet (13)
  - Heavenly choir; angel evangelists (14:1-13)
  - Preview of Armageddon (14:14-20)
  - Seven bowls (15–16)
  - Babylon's doom (17–18)
  - Christ's triumph; Armageddon (19)
- Satan's imprisonment (20:1-3)
- The Millennium (20:4-6)
- Satan's final rebellion and doom (20:7-10)
- Judgment; doom of the unrighteous (20:11-15)
- New heavens and new earth (21:1–22:5)
- Conclusion (22:6-21)

WHAT YOU HAVE SEEN: CHRIST IN HIS ASCENDED GLORY (1)

1:1-4a *From the Father to the Son to an angel to John to the churches.* John wanted to impart to the seven churches of Asia a vision Christ revealed to him through angels, concerning "events that will happen soon." The "time" that is near (1:3) refers not to time as measured by clocks and calendars (Greek, *chronos*) but to *kairos*, meaning a fixed, determined season. The fixed season in view here, as prophesied by Daniel, is the time when God will sovereignly bring human history to a climax (see exposition on Dan. 9:20-27).

1:4b-8 *Our resurrected Redeemer.* John wrote in the name of God the Father and of Jesus Christ, who, having been raised from the dead, is king of all the earth (1:4-6). All Israel will one day acknowledge this Messiah whom they "pierced" (1:7; see exposition on Zech. 12:10-14). All humankind will acknowledge him as well (1:7; see exposition on Isa. 45:14-25). Compare 1:8 with 21:6; 22:13; Isaiah 41:4.

Christ's description of himself as the "Alpha and Omega" occurs only in Revelation (1:8; see 21:6; 22:13). The phrase refers to the first and last letters of the Greek alphabet. God described himself as "the First and the Last" (Isa. 44:6; 48:12).

1:9-11 *A trumpet on Patmos.* Having been exiled to Patmos for his faith (see *Date and Location),* John heard Christ's voice "like a trumpet blast," telling him to write down the things he would see in a vision and to send it to seven specific churches. John had probably been exiled by Domitian, the brother of Titus, who had destroyed Jerusalem about 25 years previously, in A.D. 70. God thus allowed one pagan ruler to destroy his earthly city, then used his brother to bring about the revealing of his heavenly city.

John was told several times to *write* what he had seen (see 1:19; 3:1; 14:13). Once, however, he was forbidden to do so (see 10:4).

1:12-18 *A glimpse of his glory.* Upon hearing the trumpet, John turned and saw the resurrected Christ, amid seven golden lampstands, holding seven stars in his hand, his face shining like the sun (1:12-16). The effect on John of this dazzling sight was nothing less than paralyzing, and he fell at Christ's feet, whereupon Christ spoke words of reassurance (1:17-18).

John had walked with Christ and enjoyed close friendship with him for three years. He had witnessed his miracles and heard his sermons. He had watched him die on the cross, had rejoiced in his resurrection, and had viewed his ascension. But that had all happened some 60 years before. Now, he was overwhelmed as he saw the Redeemer in all his blinding brightness. But John's loving Lord quickly performed that tender task the apostle had so often witnessed: He reached out and touched the one in need.

Jesus assured John, "I am the living one who died" (1:18). The real symbol of Christianity is not the cross, but the empty tomb.

Jesus has "the keys of death and the grave" (1:18). There are five keys mentioned in the NT, and our Lord carries them all. The other four are: "the keys of the Kingdom" (Matt. 16:19); "the key of knowledge" (Luke 11:52); the key of the throne of David (3:7); "the key to the bottomless pit" (20:1; see 9:1).

1:19-20 *"Write it all down, including this secret. . . ."* John was again told to write down everything he saw in the vision (see *Outline*). The Lord revealed that the seven lampstands were seven specific churches. Upon hearing this, John surely understood why Christ was dressed as he was (see 1:13): He was now our great High Priest, tending to the lampstands (representing his people) just as Aaron had tended the lampstands in the Tabernacle.

THE THINGS THAT ARE NOW HAPPENING: MESSAGES TO CHURCHES (2–3)

2:1 *To the Christians in Ephesus . . .* John was now given special messages for each of the seven churches. Ephesus was the main religious and commercial center of the Roman province of Asia, influencing both east and west—Europe and Asia. At 240 by 418 feet, its temple of Diana was the largest of all Greek temples (see *Ephesians: Background*).

2:2-7 *"You've got a lot going for you, but . . ."* The Christians in Ephesus had suffered patiently, possessed high standards, and exercised spiritual discernment, but they had forsaken their first love (2:4). Christ told them to do three things (2:5):

- *remember* the faith they had loved (give their *heads* to Christ)
- *repent* (give their *hearts* to Christ)

- *repeat* their first works (give their *hands* to Christ)

If they did these things, they would partake of the tree of life (2:7). If they failed to respond, their "lampstand" would be removed (2:5; see 1:20). God planted the "tree of life" in Eden (Gen. 2:9). When Adam and Eve sinned, this tree disappeared from human history, not to be mentioned again till 2:7 (see also 22:2, 14).

The one who "is victorious" (2:7) is anyone who truly believes in Christ (see 1 John 5:4-5). The identity of the Nicolaitans (2:6, 15) is unknown. As with his words to each of the churches, Christ began his charge to the Ephesians with, "I know all the things you do," and ended with, "Anyone who is willing to hear should listen. . . ."

2:8 *To the Christians in Smyrna . . .* 40 miles north of Ephesus, Smyrna was a seaside city of rare beauty on a trade route from India and Persia to Rome. Celebrated for its schools of science and medicine, for its handsome buildings and wide paved streets, it also boasted the temple of Bacchus, god of wine. According to tradition it was the birthplace of Homer.

2:9-11 *A moment of pain, a crown of life.* The Christians of Smyrna had been slandered and would soon be imprisoned, through the influence of their city's Jewish community. But if they were faithful, though they died they would receive eternal life. According to extrabiblical history, the Jews of Smyrna reported Christians for refusing to take part in emperor worship, thus earning John's description of them as the "synagogue of Satan" (2:9), a description shared by the Jews of Philadelphia (3:9).

Jesus warned this church that they would "be persecuted for 'ten days'" (2:10). He may have meant an actual 10-day period, or he may have been prophesying the 10 intensive periods of persecution that would eventually fall upon the church at the hands of 10 Roman emperors—during which an estimated five million saints were martyred. As a percentage of first-century world population, this would be equivalent to the martyrdom of 100 million Christians today.

2:12 *To the Christians in Pergamum . . .* Pergamum, about 80 miles north of Ephesus, was the political capital of Asia. Its famous library of 200,000 volumes was given by Mark Antony to Cleopatra. The people of Pergamum may have been the first to use parchment.

2:13-17 *"Stand firm . . . forsake false doctrine."* John described Pergamum as the location of Satan's throne (2:13). History confirms that it was given over to idolatry and emperor worship more than any other city in Asia. The church had remained loyal to Christ but was tolerating those who held to the teachings of Balaam (2:14; see Num. 22:1–25:9; Jude 1:11) and of the Nicolaitans (2:15). The choice before them was simple: Repent and enjoy eternal life, or persist in tolerating evil and invite God's anger (2:16-17).

The name Antipas (2:13) appears in no other historical record. But God knew all about this humble believer who lived and died for Christ (see John 10:3; 2 Tim. 2:19).

2:18 *To the Christians in Thyatira . . .* Thyatira, about 30 miles southeast of Pergamum, was famous for its trade unions of tanners, potters, weavers, dyers, and robe makers, each dedicated to a pagan deity. Lydia, a seller of purple dye and Paul's first European convert (see Acts 16:14), was from this city.

2:19-29 *"You're doing well, so stop tolerating Jezebel."* The believers of Thyatira were growing in faith, but they, like the believers of Pergamum, were tolerating false doctrine, namely, the

THE SEVEN CHURCHES OF REVELATION (Rev. 2:1–3:22)

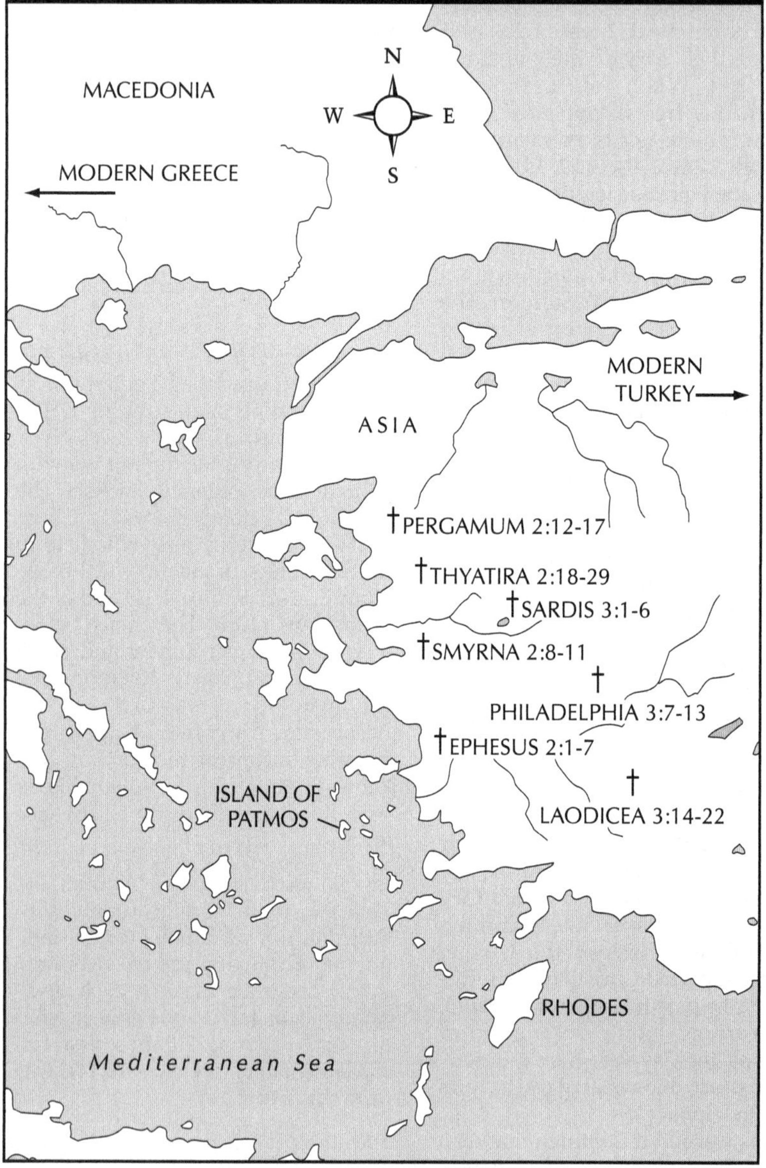

ministry of a prophetess aptly named Jezebel (see 1 Kings 16:28–19:21; 21), who was promoting immorality and idolatry. John pronounced a curse on Jezebel and her followers (2:22-23) and urged the rest of the people to remain faithful to Christ (2:24-29).

3:1 *To the Christians in Sardis . . .* Sardis, about 35 miles south of Thyatira, had been a city of wealth and importance in ancient times. Destroyed by an earthquake in A.D. 17 and rebuilt by Tiberius Caesar, it never regained its former glory but maintained its trade in carpets and woolen goods.

3:1-6 *"How sad: You're living on your reputation."* Just as their city was known mostly for its past greatness, the Christians of Sardis had a reputation for spiritual life but were actually on the verge of spiritual death. Christ's advice: Review the things you have been taught; repent and obey.

3:7 *To the Christians in Philadelphia . . .* Philadelphia was founded about 150 B.C. by Philadelphus, ruler of Pergamum, in an effort to bring Greek culture to his area. It was destroyed in 17 by the same earthquake that leveled Sardis, and like Sardis was rebuilt by Tiberius Caesar. Philadelphia had a large Jewish population and was known for its excellent wine.

3:7-13 *The open door that no one can close.* The church of Philadelphia, though poor, small, and persecuted, had remained true to Christ. It was the only one of the seven churches with which he found no fault. Rather, he promised an "open door" (3:8; compare Acts 14:27; 1 Cor. 16:9; 2 Cor. 2:12; Col. 4:3), preservation through future persecution (3:10), and a place of honor in his coming Kingdom (3:11-13). As the final and eternal King in the line of David, Christ has the power to either admit people to his eternal Kingdom or to exclude them from it (3:7; see Isa. 22:22).

3:14 *To the Christians in Laodicea . . .* Laodicea, 11 miles west of Colosse, was founded by Antiochus II, forebear of Antiochus Ephiphanes (see exposition on Dan. 11:2-20) and was named after his wife. Known as a banking center, it was immensely wealthy, graced with resplendent temples and theaters. It was noted for the manufacture of garments from black, glossy wool, and for its hot mineral springs. Perhaps because of its excellent medical school, Laodicea was also famous for its eye salve, called cellyrium.

3:15-22 *Knocking on a lukewarm door.* While the Lord said nothing bad about the church at Philadelphia, he said nothing good about the church at Laodicea. They were neither hot nor cold. They thought they had everything, just like their city, but God said they had nothing. Therefore, because they were lukewarm, God would "spit" them out of his mouth. The water from Laodicea's hot springs was palatable only if very hot. When lukewarm, it became nauseating. The Laodiceans were invited to turn from their indifference (3:19). Christ pictured himself standing at the door of their hearts, waiting for them to open it to him (3:20-22). In one famous artistic depiction of this verse, Christ is seen knocking on a door with no handle: The door of our heart can be opened only from the inside.

THE THINGS THAT WILL HAPPEN LATER: CHRIST'S PLAN FOR THE FUTURE (4–22)

4:1 *Our man in heaven.* John was apparently transported to heaven to view future events and report them to his readers. He began this new section with the words "after these things" (4:1; see *Outline*). The events of 4–5 set the stage for the Great Tribulation at the end of human history (6–19), after the church has been taken up to heaven in the Rapture (see *Isaiah: Background;* exposition on Matt. 24–25 and on 1 Thess. 4:13-18). Having been mentioned nearly 20 times in 1–3, the church now disappears from the scene until 19:7, where it reappears as the glorious bride of Christ.

4:2-5 *A throne surrounded by thrones.* John saw the glory of God the Father on his throne (4:2-3). He found the sight too overwhelming to give any physical description, other than to say that God was "as brilliant as gemstones—jasper and carnelian." Surrounding God's throne were 24 smaller thrones, on which sat 24 elders, clothed in white with golden crowns (4:4). Thunder, lightning, and voices emanated from God's throne.

Some suggest that the 24 elders, who reappear several times in John's vision, were angelic beings. Others believe they may have been a representative body of OT and NT saints (compare 21:12-14). This latter view is suggested by the fact that the Greek word for their crowns is *stephanos,* used elsewhere in the NT to describe the crowns or rewards of victorious believers (see 1 Cor. 9:25; 1 Pet. 5:4), rather than *diadema,* which describes a crown worn by royalty or, in Revelation, by supernatural beings (see 12:3; 13:1; 19:12).

Some see the "seven spirits of God" (4:5; see 1:4) as seven angels. Others view the phrase as a description of the Holy Spirit in his perfection.

4:6-11 *Off come the crowns!* Also surrounding God's throne were four "living beings," similar to those seen by Ezekiel (see Ezek. 1:10; see exposition on Ezek. 10:1-22), whose sole purpose was to proclaim God's holiness. Whenever the living creatures worshiped God, the 24 elders removed their crowns and joined in praising him for his work at Creation (4:11). Everything the Bible tells us about God falls into one of two categories:

- his work at Creation (Gen. 1–2)
- his work in redemption (Gen. 3—Rev. 22)

Having celebrated Creation, the creatures and elders would soon celebrate redemption (5:8-10). Throughout eternity the redeemed will celebrate these two aspects of God's activity.

5:1-7 *No one worthy, except . . .* God held a scroll in his right hand, secured with seven seals, that no one was able to open (5:1-4) until Christ himself stepped forward and offered to do so (5:5-7). The scroll apparently contained God's final will and testament concerning his world: the ushering in of his long-awaited Millennium (see exposition on 20:1-6 and *Isaiah: Background*). The seven seals represent seven judgments that will purify the planet in preparation for the Millennium (see 6–19). In ancient Rome, documents containing money had five seals, but only the most serious documents, those dealing with life and death, had seven seals.

Christ was announced as "the Lion of the tribe of Judah," who had "conquered" (5:5). But when John looked, instead of a conquering lion he saw "a Lamb that had been killed" (5:6). Christ had indeed conquered—through his death on Calvary! He is pictured as having seven horns, symbolic of perfect power and authority; and seven eyes, symbolizing perfect knowledge and wisdom.

5:8-10 *The new song of redemption.* As Christ took the scroll, the creatures and elders sang a second hymn of praise (compare 4:11), focusing this time on God's work of redemption. Because he was slain for our sins,

Christ is worthy to execute the judgments of the seven seals (6–19).

5:11-14 *Worthy is the Lamb!* The creatures and elders were now joined by countless thousands of angels, all proclaiming Christ's worthiness. On "the Lamb worthy is" (5:12), see exposition on Genesis 22:1-24. Even the unsaved—those "under the earth"—will praise the worthy Lamb (5:13; see exposition on Isa. 45:14-25).

6:1-2 *First seal: A man on a white horse.* When Christ opened the first seal on the scroll of Tribulation judgment, John saw a man on a white horse who will conquer, apparently without bloodshed—a picture of the Antichrist (see exposition on 13:1-10) as he subdues the world through peaceful deception (see 1 Thess. 5:3).

6:3-4 *Second seal: Bloodshed and rebellion.* When the second seal was opened, John saw a rider on a red horse, who will bring war upon the earth. The peace of the Antichrist will prove counterfeit and temporary.

6:5-6 *Third seal: Worldwide famine.* The opening of the third seal brought a rider on a black horse and scenes of worldwide famine, so bad that a loaf of bread will cost a full day's wages.

6:7-8 *Fourth seal: Two pale horses.* The fourth seal revealed two horsemen, named Death and Hades, who through various means will kill a fourth of all the world's population—destruction far greater than World War II, when an estimated 1 in 40 humans died.

6:9-11 *Fifth seal: How long? Not long!* John now saw in heaven the souls of martyred saints. They want to know when God will avenge their blood, and are assured that their vindication will come as soon as all people destined to die for their faith have done so (6:11; see Heb. 11:40). These martyrs are "under the altar" (6:9). This could signify that they have been sacrificed for their faith (compare 2 Tim. 4:6) or that they are covered by Christ's blood—both of which are true. These verses give some important clues about the present state of the dead:

- These martyred believers apparently will not take part in the Rapture, which will have already occurred (see exposition on 4:1). They are probably OT saints, who will be raised at the first resurrection, following the Tribulation (see exposition on 20:1-6 and on 1 Cor. 15:20-28).
- Yet these saints have bodies of some sort, enabling them to speak and to wear their white robes. They are fully conscious, not in some sort of soul sleep (see exposition on Luke 16:19-31).

6:12-17 *Sixth seal: Continents shake, stars fall, sinners hide.* The terrifying results of the opening of the sixth seal will cause all unsaved people, small and great, to hide in caves, calling for the rocks to crush them rather than face God's wrath. (Compare 6 with Matt. 24:3-31.)

7:1-8 *"Don't start till we've sealed his servants!"* God's angels will then prevent further devastation to the earth until they "have placed the seal of God on the foreheads of his servants" (7:3; see 14:1). These 144,000 Jews, 12,000 from each of Israel's 12 tribes (7:5-8), will evangelize the whole world, in fulfillment of Matthew 24:14.

7:9-17 *What a great crowd! What a great celebration!* John then saw a vast multitude from all nations, too numerous to count, standing before Christ's throne, rejoicing in their salvation and being ministered to by their Lord. These, he was told, are people who have found salvation during "the great tribulation" (7:14).

8:1-6 *A moment of silence, then the trumpets.* When the seventh seal was opened, there was silence for a half hour. An angel then offered incense, mixed with the prayers of God's people, and seven angels prepared to blow their trumpets, announcing further judgments. The judgment of the seventh seal encompasses those of the seven trumpets and seven bowls that follow (8–19).

8:7-13 *Four trumpets, then, "Look out for the next three!"* The first four angels blew their trumpets, bringing various devastations to the earth, including what may be a meteor (8:10-11). An eagle (8:13) then declared that the judgments brought by the next three trumpets would be far worse. These would be the three "terrors" or "woes" (8:13; see 9:12; 11:14). The cosmic signs of 8:12-13 recall the words of Amos 8:9 and of Luke 21:25.

9:1-12 *Fifth trumpet: Locusts from the bottomless pit.* As the fifth trumpet sounded, a "star that had fallen to earth," apparently a demon, unlocks the "bottomless pit," releasing demons like locusts with the sting of scorpions. For five agonizing months they will torment those without God's seal of salvation (9:4-5). Their victims will want to die, but death will elude them (9:6).

The "bottomless pit," mentioned twice in these verses, will appear again in 11:7; 17:8; and 20:1-3. Some scholars believe this abode of demons is located in the heart of our planet. The demons from the pit will be led by Apollyon, whose name means "destroyer" (9:11).

9:13-21 *Sixth trumpet: Hellish horsemen.* The sixth trumpet revealed another demonic army, this one 200 million strong, unleashed from the vicinity of the Euphrates River with the mission of killing one-third of the world's population (9:13-19). With a fourth of humanity already dead (see 6:8), this second onslaught will leave less than half of the world's population alive, yet the survivors will not repent but will only intensify their idolatry, immorality, and rebellion against God (9:20-21).

If the unbelievers of Tribulation times seem callous and unrepentant, one need only remember other historic examples of unbelief:

- the pre-Flood people, all but eight of whom were destroyed (see 1 Pet. 3:20)
- Sodom, where not even 10 were righteous (see Gen. 18:32)
- the Exodus Israelites, all but two of whom died for unbelief (see Num. 14:29-30)
- the Canaanites, destroyed for their sin (see Deut. 9:4)
- Israel, destroyed for disobedience (see 2 Kings 17:7-23; 2 Chron. 36:14-16)
- the Jewish majority that rejected Christ (see Acts 7:51-53)

Note the similarities of John's and Isaiah's contemptuous descriptions of idol worship (9:20; see exposition on Isa. 44:6-28). It has been estimated that the army of 200 million would, in human terms, occupy an area of 100 square miles. The Euphrates River valley, land of Babylon, is where evil began on earth (see Gen. 3), where false religion began (see Gen. 4:3; 11:1-9), and where false religion will meet its end (17–18).

10:1-11 *Trumpet interlude, part 1: The scroll.* There had been an interlude (see 8:1-6) between the sixth and seventh seals. Now there was an interlude (10:1–11:14) between the sixth and seventh trumpets. This interlude began with an angel bringing John a "small scroll" (10:2) and announcing that there would be no further delay before the earth felt the total and terrifying hammer of God's angry judgment—which would be heralded by the seventh trumpet (10:1-7). At the angel's command, John ate the little book, and just as the angel had predicted, it was sweet in his mouth but sour in his stomach (10:8-11). Up to this point, John had for the most part seen non-Israelites destroyed by God. From this point on, his own people would face judgment. Compare Ezekiel 2:9–3:3.

The words of the seven thunders (10:4) are the only part of the book of Revelation that remain sealed.

11:1-14 *Trumpet interlude, part 2: The two witnesses.* As the interlude continued, the angel put John to work measuring the Temple. However, he was not to measure the outer court, for it was "turned over to the nations," who will "trample the holy city for 42 months" (11:2). During those 42 months, two witnesses will prophesy on God's behalf, protected from their enemies (11:1-6). After those 42 months, when the witnesses have completed their testimony for God, the "beast" (the Antichrist—see exposition on 13:1-10) will be allowed to kill them, and all God's enemies will rejoice at their death (11:7-10). After being dead for three and half days, the two witnesses will be raised up and ascend to heaven, and a terrible earthquake will strike Jerusalem, leaving 7,000 dead (11:11-14).

The earthquake marks the end of the "second terror" (11:14; see 8:13). The third terror, which "is coming quickly," encompasses all the events associated with the seventh trumpet (11:15–19:21).

"42 months" (11:2), which is the same as "1,260 days" (11:3), refers to the second half of the Tribulation, when the Antichrist will unleash his full fury against believers (see Dan. 9:27; Matt. 24:15; 2 Thess. 2:4). This time period is also called "a time, times and half a time" (12:14; see 12:6; 13:5; Dan. 7:25; 12:7). Jesus also predicted this "age of the Gentiles" (Luke 21:24; see 11:2).

Some have suggested that the two witnesses are Elijah and Moses. Elijah is suggested because

- Malachi predicted his end-times return (see exposition on Matt. 17:10-13);
- he appeared with Moses at the Transfiguration (see Matt. 17:3);
- the prevention of rain (11:6) resembles one of Elijah's miracles (see 1 Kings 17:1).

Moses is suggested because

- he appeared with Elijah at the Transfiguration (see Matt. 17:3). It is also interesting, though perhaps coincidental, that Malachi mentioned Moses along with Elijah in the closing words of the OT (see Mal. 4:4-5);
- the turning of water to blood (11:6) resembles one of Moses' miracles (see Exod. 7:19);
- some have suggested that Satan's effort to claim Moses' body (see Jude 1:9) may have been motivated in part by his desire to prevent his appearance at the Transfiguration and as one of these two witnesses.

The beast will be unable to kill the two witnesses until they finish their divine assignment. Satan cannot touch one hair on the head of the most humble saint until God gives him specific permission (see Job 1:12; 2:6). These two, like Paul, will finish their work (see 2 Tim. 4:7).

11:15-19 *The world's kingdoms become his Kingdom!* The seventh trumpet then sounded, announcing that Christ will soon return to begin his glorious reign on earth. Many will rejoice at the coming of the Kingdom (11:16-17; see 19:6-7; 20:4-6), but the wicked will be angry, provoking God's final judgment (11:18; see 20:7-15).

11:19 suggests that an actual Temple exists in heaven (see 14:15, 17; 15:5-6, 8; 16:1, 17; Isa. 6:1-8; Heb. 8:2, 5; 9:24) and that it served as a pattern for the earthly Tabernacle and Temple (see Exod. 25:8-9, 40; 1 Chron. 28:11-12, 19). These worship centers represented God's desire to dwell with his people (see exposition on Exod. 29:43-46). As eternity begins, the Temple will no longer be needed, for God will at last be dwelling with his people (see 21:3, 22).

12:1-6 *A woman, a child, and a dragon.* John now saw in heaven a woman ready to give birth (12:1-2) as a dragon waited to devour her newborn child (12:3-4). She bore the child, he was caught up to heaven, and she fled to the wilderness, where God would protect her for 1,260 days. The child in this scenario is clearly Christ, who came to rule with a rod of iron (12:5; see Ps. 2:9). The dragon is clearly Satan (12:9). The woman is Israel, whom Satan will persecute (see 12:13) but God will protect during the last half of the Tribulation (12:6). Satan's effort to devour the infant Christ found human expression in Herod (see Matt. 2:16-18). "Caught up to God" (12:5) refers to Christ's ascension.

12:7-17 *Satan attacks; Israel takes flight.* At some future time, apparently at the midpoint in the Tribulation, Satan will suffer a major defeat (12:7-11). Then, knowing his time is short (12:12), he will persecute Israel (12:13). But God will protect Israel, and some of them will turn to Christ (12:14-17; see Zech. 13:8-9, which seems to indicate that this will involve fully a third of Israel).

Israel's "place" of refuge (12:14) is not specified, but it could be Petra, in present-day Jordan: Zechariah identifies "Azal," a place associated with Petra, as Israel's refuge (see exposition on Zech. 14:1-5); Isaiah portrayed a triumphant Christ coming from Edom (see Isa. 63:1-6), of which Petra was the capital; Edom will be spared from the Antichrist (see Dan. 11:41), perhaps so that it can protect Israel.

On Satan as "Accuser" (12:10), see exposition on Job 1:6-12.

13:1-10 *A beast from the sea.* The "beast," briefly mentioned in 11:7, is now described in detail. Empowered by Satan ("the dragon"—13:2; compare 12:9), the beast will rise from the sea, receive the adoration of unbelievers, and reign unchallenged for the final 42 months (second half) of the Tribulation (13:1-5). He will blaspheme God and fight against his people (13:6-7). This frightful and vicious individual is given various names in Scripture:

- the Antichrist (see exposition on 1 John 4:1-6)
- man of sin, lawless one, son of perdition (see exposition on 2 Thess. 2:1-12)
- little horn, wicked king, prince (see exposition on Dan. 7:15-28; 8:15-27; 9:20-27)

The "seven heads and ten horns" (13:1) may refer to the nations through which the Antichrist will rise to power, which may be a revived Roman Empire, since the most important prophetic details concerning the old Roman Empire in Daniel 2:40-44 are still unfulfilled (see exposition on Dan. 2:36-45; 7:15-28).

A significant factor in the beast's initial popularity will be his notoriety for having recovered from a mortal head wound (13:3, 12, 14).

13:11-18 *A beast from the land.* John saw another beast, this one coming out of the earth, who will promote the worldwide worship of the first beast, perform great miracles, and make it almost impossible to survive without receiving the "mark" of the beast, the number 666. This second beast is also called the "false prophet" (16:13; 19:20; 20:10).

14:1-5 *History's greatest all-male choir.* The scene now shifted back to heaven (14–15), where John saw the 144,000 (see exposition on 7:1-8), now taken up to heaven, singing a song of redemption.

14:6-13 *Three angelic evangelists.* John saw three angels proclaiming the gospel to unbelievers on earth:

- The first invites people to fear and glorify God before judgment falls (14:6-7).
- The second predicts Babylon's fall (14:8; 18).
- The third warns against worshiping the Antichrist (14:9-11).

Apparently no one responds. God will now pour out such undiluted wrath that, for believers, death will be better than life (14:13). How tragic that Christ, at Calvary, drank this cup of wrath for the very sinners now forced to drink it again.

14:14-20 *The bloodiest battle of all time.* John was then given a preview of Armageddon (compare 16:12-16; 19:17-19). Christ will return to earth triumphant (14:14; see Dan. 7:13) and, joined by two angels, will begin "harvesting" the earth with sharp sickles, resulting in a river of human blood some 200 miles long and as high as a horse's bridle. On the "grapes" of God's "wrath" (14:18-19), see 19:15; Isaiah 63:1-6; Joel 3:13.

15:1-8 *Two songs, then seven bowls of wrath.* As seven angels prepare to pour out the seven bowls of God's wrath (15:1), a great choir composed of victors over the Antichrist will sing the song of Moses, commemorating God's bringing his people out of Egypt, and the song of the Lamb, celebrating his bringing them into his millennial Kingdom (15:2-4)—the first and last songs in Scripture. Then, heaven's Temple (see exposition on 11:15-19) will be opened, and the seven angels will prepare for judgment as God's glory fills the Temple (15:5-8; see exposition on Exod. 14:19-20).

16:1-9 *Four bowls of wrath, but no repentance.* The first angel will pour out "horrible, malignant sores" on all who have worshiped the Antichrist and accepted his mark (16:1-2; see exposition on 13:11-18). The second angel will turn the sea to blood (16:3). As the third angel turns all fresh water to blood, he will acknowledge the justice of this judgment on those who have shed the blood of God's people (16:4-7). The fourth bowl will cause the sun to sear humanity with intense heat (16:8-9). Even after these plagues, no one will repent (16:9).

16:10-11 *Another bowl, and still no repentance.* As the fifth bowl brings darkness, the cumulative pain of all the plagues will become more and more unbearable, but instead of repenting, the worshipers of the Antichrist will only increase their cursing of God.

16:12-16 *An empty Euphrates: Invitation to Armageddon.* The sixth outpouring of God's wrath will dry up the Euphrates River, allowing "kings from the east" to march across and join God's other enemies for battle against him at a place called Armageddon. They will be lured there by three evil spirits. The exact location of this last great battle is unknown, though some have suggested the valley below Megiddo in Galilee. With its demise enabling Armageddon, the Euphrates will have proved to be both the cradle (see Gen. 2:14) and the grave of human civilization.

16:17-21 *Seventh bowl: The earth shakes; hail falls.* The seventh and final bowl of God's wrath on unrepentant humanity will bring history's greatest earthquake and hailstorm (16:17-21). The greatest loss of life in any earthquake so far is 830,000, on January 23, 1556, in Shensi Province, China. That will pale in comparison to the Tribulation earthquake, which will destroy every city on earth, level every mountain, and submerge every island. Meanwhile the Tribulation hailstorm will rain down 100-pound chunks of ice. Even after all this, the worshipers of the beast will continue to curse God rather than repent (16:21)—proof positive of humanity's total depravity (compare 9:20-21; 16:8-9; see Isa. 64:6; Jer. 17:9; Rom. 3:10).

17:1-18 *Mystery Babylon: The false church.* John saw a blasphemous prostitute sitting on a seven-headed, 10-horned beast, wearing costly clothes, drunk with the blood of the believers she had killed (17:1-6). She had had "immoral relations" with the "rulers of the world," which has an intoxicating effect on all people (17:2). The beast, who will cause the world to marvel because he "was alive but isn't now. And yet he will soon come up" (17:8), is the Antichrist, whose miraculous recovery will cause the world to marvel (see 13:3). He will proceed from the bottomless pit and eventually go to "eternal destruction" (17:8).

Though not explicitly stated in the text, scholars generally agree that the prostitute represents the worldwide false religion that has always existed and that the Antichrist will turn toward worship of himself during the Tribulation (see 13:8; 2 Thess. 2:4). The worldwide scope of this end-times false church is seen in 17:15, 17-18. Throughout the Bible, prostitution symbolizes spiritual apostasy (see Jer. 3:1-5; see exposition on Ezek. 16:15-43). One of the precursors of this end-times false religion of Babylon was the Tower of Babel, built on the site that would later be Babylon (see Gen. 11:1-9). On the seven heads and 10 horns, see exposition on 13:1-10.

The false church will use all its evil strength to elevate the Antichrist during the first part of the Tribulation (17:17). It will flourish and enjoy its wealth (17:15, 18). But suddenly things will change. The Antichrist will turn against the false church (17:16), probably because it has tried to control him. Throughout history, religious establishments have tried to control secular rulers; the Antichrist won't bow to such control.

18:1-24 *Babylon's fall: Grief for the greedy, joy for the godly.* The metaphor of Babylon is now extended to include godless political and economic systems. An angel announces Babylon's fall (18:1-3). Believers are warned to flee (18:4) as her judgment is pronounced (18:5-8). While the kings and merchants of the world mourn the city that made them rich (18:9-19), the saved in heaven will rejoice that their persecutor has received divine justice (18:20). An angel throws a huge boulder into the sea, symbolizing the end of this city that excelled in all worldly pursuits but persecuted God's people (18:21-24).

19:1-10 *His victory and wedding.* All heaven will celebrate Christ's victory over Babylon (19:1-6) and his marriage to his bride, the church, who is adorned in the whitest and finest of linens (19:7-9; compare Ezek. 16:1-14; Hos. 2:19-20; Eph. 5:25-33). "Hallelujah!" (19:1) occurs some two dozen times in Psalms but only here in the NT. The Holy Spirit will reserve it for this special occasion! An overexcited John tried to worship the angel showing him these things (19:10).

19:11-21 *Victory at Armageddon!* John now saw Christ return to earth with his armies, ready for the last great battle (19:11-15), already displaying his rightful title (19:16). An angel will invite scavenger birds to stand by for a great feast (19:17-18). The Antichrist and his human allies will gather at Armageddon (19:19). The Antichrist and false prophet will be captured and thrown into everlasting hell (19:20). Then all the gathered armies will be slaughtered, and the birds will have their promised feast (19:21).

20:1-6 *His 1,000-year sentence, our 1,000-year reign.* An angel will bind Satan with a chain and cast him into the bottomless pit, where he will remain for 1,000 years, after which he will be released for a while (20:1-3). All who have suffered for Christ (20:4) and all others who by God's grace qualify for the "first resurrection" (20:5-6; see Dan. 12:1-2; Luke 14:14; John 5:29; see exposition on 1 Cor. 15:20-28) will now reign with him for 1,000 years. ("Millennium" is Latin for a 1,000-year time period.)

20:7-10 *Satan's release, rebellion, and removal.* After the Millennium, Satan will be released from the bottomless pit and will make one final desperate attempt to dethrone God but will be utterly defeated and thrown forever into the lake of fire, where the Antichrist and false prophet will already be (see 19:20). Incredibly, even after enjoying the blessings of the Millennium, apparently a significant portion of humanity will support Satan in his last great rebellion (20:7-10). On "Gog and Magog" (20:8), see exposition on Ezekiel 38–39. This last great rebellion will show, once again, the total depravity of unredeemed human nature (see exposition on 16:17-21). While utopians dream of a better world, the Bible shows that our most basic problems are of a spiritual, rather than a socioeconomic, nature.

20:11-15 *A test no one will pass.* John saw the Judge of the universe seated behind his great white throne, sentencing all the unsaved to the lake of fire forever. Faith in Christ would have placed their names in the "Book of Life," and they would have been saved. The only other possible avenue of salvation was to be judged "according to what they had done" (20:12), but the Bible is clear that no one can be saved on this basis (see Rom. 3:20).

21:1-8 *The new heaven and new earth.* John now saw "a new heaven and a new earth" (21:1; see exposition on Isa. 65:17-25) and the new Jerusalem, prepared as a bride beautifully dressed for her husband (see exposition on 19:1-10). God will now dwell with his people forever and will banish all sinners, all sin, and the terrible results of sin, such as illness and death. The present heavens and earth, incurably tainted by sin, will have been destroyed by now (21:1; see exposition on 2 Pet. 3:1-13). The new heaven and earth is the place Christ is now preparing for believers (see John 14:1-4).

21:9–22:5 *That shining city among the stars.* The angel showed John the new Jerusalem in all its glory. The city will be a square, 1,500 miles on each side. If placed in America, it would reach from New York to Denver, and from Canada to Florida. Its 12 gates and 12 foundations will commemorate the 12 tribes of Israel and the 12 apostles. Its main street will be made of gold so pure that it is transparent. There will be no Temple, for the Lord himself will be its temple in that he will now be dwelling with his people (21:22; see 21:3; see exposition on 11:15-19), enjoying perfect fellowship with them (see 22:3-4).

In the new Jerusalem will be the tree of life, off-limits to people since Eden but now available for nourishment and healing (22:1-2, 14). The city's glorious light will proceed not from the sun but from the very person of God himself (21:23; 22:5). Heaven will be a place of energetic commercial and social activity, whose gates will never close (21:24-26).

The Millennium will last for 1,000 years, but the new Jerusalem will last "forever and ever" (22:5; see Dan. 7:18, 27).

22:6-9 *Themes restated, a mistake repeated.* The angel restated the purpose of the visions John had seen (compare 22:6 with 1:1). Christ once again

THE FIVE WORLDS OF THE BIBLE

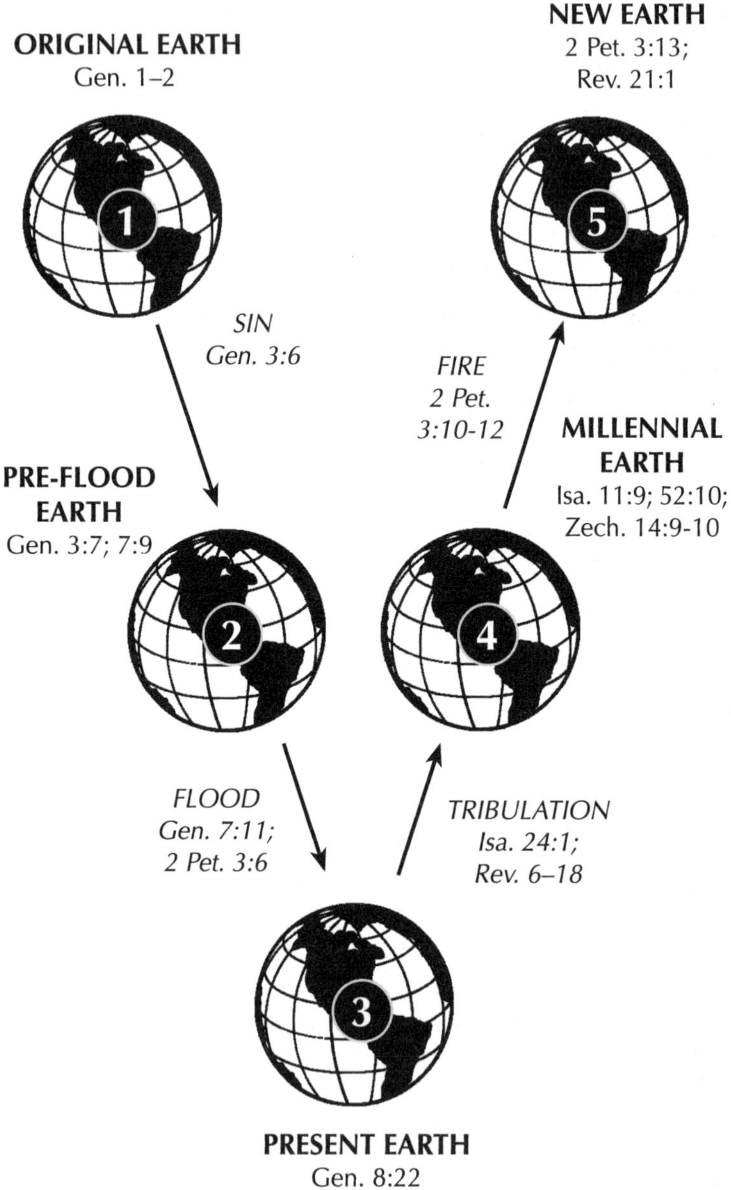

declared he was coming soon (compare 22:7 with 3:11) and pronounced a blessing on those who would keep his Word (compare 22:7 with 1:3). And John, for the second time, tried to worship his angel guide but was prohibited from doing so (22:8-9).

22:10-17 *"Keep it open! The time is near!"* The angel urged John to openly share what he had seen, for Christ's coming is near, and though sinners will probably continue in their sin, the righteous must be encouraged in their faith (22:10-11). Christ himself then promised to come soon and reward the faithful (22:12-13). John pronounced a blessing on those who obey God (22:14-15). Christ gave his final stamp of approval to John's revelation, identifying himself as the Root and Offspring of David (22:16; see 5:5; Isa. 11:1), and "the bright morning star" (22:16; see 2:28; 2 Pet. 1:19). Then the Holy Spirit extended his final invitation to lost humanity (22:17).

22:18-21 *No additions or subtractions allowed.* John ended the report of his visions with the warning not to add to or take from what had been revealed, and stipulated a severe penalty for doing so. While John intended his warning only for this one book, it unquestionably applies to the entire Bible as well (see Deut. 4:2; 12:32; Prov. 30:5-6).

Finally, one last promise from the Lord: "Yes, I am coming soon!"

PART II:

BIBLE BACKGROUNDS, LISTS, AND STUDY HELPS

THE SCRIPTURES

THE SCRIPTURES AND GOD

God the Father

Everything the Bible tells us about God can be placed under one of two categories:

- His work in *creation* (Gen. 1–2)
- His work in *redemption* (Gen. 3—Rev. 22)
  - ➤ The need for redemption (Gen. 3:1-14)
  - ➤ The promise of redemption (Gen. 3:15)
  - ➤ The preparation for redemption (Gen. 3:16—Mal. 4:6)
  - ➤ The fullness of redemption (New Testament)

God the Son

- The OT records the *preparation* for Christ.
  - ➤ That we might be aware of his coming (Luke 24:27; John 5:39)
  - ➤ That we might be assured by his coming (Rom. 15:4)
- The Gospels record the *manifestation* of Christ.
  - ➤ The fact of his birth (Matt. 1)
  - ➤ The fact of his death (Matt. 27)
  - ➤ The fact of his resurrection (Matt. 28)
  - ➤ The fact of his ascension (Luke 24)
- Acts records the *propagation* of Christ.
  - ➤ The birth of the church (Acts 2:1-13)
  - ➤ The life and mission of the church (Acts 2:14–28:31)
- The Epistles record the *interpretation* of Christ.
  - ➤ The reason for his birth (1 Tim. 1:15; Heb. 10:4-7)
  - ➤ The reason for his death (Rom. 4:25; 5:8-9; Heb. 2:14-15)
  - ➤ The reason for his resurrection (Rom. 4:25; 1 Cor. 15:20-28)
  - ➤ The reason for his ascension (Rom. 8:34; Heb. 4:14-16; 9:24)
- Revelation records the *coronation* of Christ.
  - ➤ The witnesses of the Lamb (Rev. 1–3)
  - ➤ The worship of the Lamb (Rev. 4–5)
  - ➤ The wrath of the Lamb (Rev. 6–19)
  - ➤ The wonder of the Lamb (his millennial reign) (Rev. 20)
  - ➤ The wife of the Lamb (the church) (Rev. 21–22)

God the Holy Spirit

As the third person of the Trinity (see exposition on Gen. 1:26-31), the Holy Spirit was involved with the work of the Father and Son

- From the very beginning:
  - At Creation (Gen. 1:2)
  - In OT times, temporarily empowering believers to accomplish specific tasks (see exposition on 1 Sam. 9:27–10:8)
- During Christ's earthly ministry:
  - Bringing about Christ's birth (Matt. 1:18)
  - Validating his Messiahship (Matt. 3:16)
  - Empowering his ministry (John 1:33; Acts 10:38)
  - Empowering his disciples' ministry (Luke 12:12)
- Following Christ's ascension:
  - Was promised to all believers (Matt. 3:11; John 14:16-17; Acts 1:8)
  - Baptizing and empowering disciples at Pentecost (Acts 2:4)
  - Producing awareness of sin and truth (see exposition on John 16:6-11)
  - Baptizing all believers; empowering them for righteous living and witness (see exposition on 1 Cor. 12:12-31)
  - Indwelling, guiding, giving assurance of salvation (see exposition on John 16:12-15 and on Rom. 8:5-17)
  - Helping in times of weakness (see exposition on Rom. 8:26-27)
  - Restraining the devil's power (2 Thess. 2:7)

❖ ❖ ❖

THE SCRIPTURES AND THE PEOPLE OF GOD

What the Bible does for the believer:

- Upholds (Ps. 119:116)
- Guides (Ps. 119:133)
- Produces joy (Ps. 119:162)
- Strengthens (Ps. 119:28; 1 John 2:14)
- Gives hope (Ps. 119:74, 81)
- Gives light (Ps. 119:105, 130)
- Gives understanding (Ps. 119:169)
- Shows God's will (John 7:17; 17:17)
- Builds up (Acts 20:32)
- Produces fruit (John 15:7-8)
- Convicts of sin (Heb. 4:12)
- Converts the soul (John 20:31; James 1:18; 1 Pet. 1:23)
- Cleanses the conscience (John 15:3)
- Consecrates (John 17:17)
- Corrects the wrong (2 Tim. 3:16)
- Confirms the right (John 8:31; 2 Tim. 3:16)
- Comforts the heart (Ps. 119:50, 54)

What the Bible demands from the believer:

- Read it (Deut. 31:11; Luke 4:16; Col. 3:16; Rev. 1:3)
- Heed it (Ps. 119:9; 1 Tim. 4:16)

- "Seed" it (Matt. 28:19-20)
- Desire it (1 Pet. 2:2)
- Preach it (2 Tim. 4:2)
- Correctly understand it (2 Tim. 2:15)
- Live by it (Matt. 4:4)
- Use it in spiritual warfare (Eph. 6:17)
- Suffer and even die for it (Rev. 1:9; 6:9; 20:4)

❖ ❖ ❖

CHRONOLOGY OF THE BIBLE

Date each Bible book was written

Many dates are approximate. See *Date* item for each book.

Old Testament Books (B.C.)

2000	Job
1486	Genesis
1446	Exodus
1446	Leviticus
1406	Numbers
1406	Deuteronomy
1380	Joshua
1020	Judges
1000	Ruth
?	Psalms (many written c. 975)
?	Proverbs (many written c. 950)
950	Song of Songs
935	Ecclesiastes
930	1, 2 Samuel
840	Obadiah
810	Joel
785	Jonah
750	Amos
735	Micah
720	Hosea
690	Isaiah
625	Zephaniah
620	Nahum
615	1, 2 Kings
608	Habakkuk
586	Lamentations
580	Jeremiah
570	Ezekiel
536	Daniel
520	Haggai
520	Zechariah
450	Esther
440	1, 2 Chronicles

430	Ezra
430	Nehemiah
430	Malachi

New Testament Books (A.D.)

45	James
49	Galatians
51	1 Thessalonians
51	2 Thessalonians
55	1 Corinthians
56	2 Corinthians
57	Romans
58	Mark
59	Luke
60	Acts
60	Ephesians
60	Colossians
61	Philemon
61	Philippians
63	1 Timothy
63	Titus
64	1 Peter
65	Matthew
65	2 Peter
67	2 Timothy
68	Hebrews
69	Jude
90	John
92	1 John
92	2 John
92	3 John
95	Revelation

Historical Order of Bible Books

OLD TESTAMENT
Creation and Pre-Israel History
Genesis 1–11 • Creation; the Fall; the Flood

The Patriarchs of Israel
Genesis 12–50 • Abraham to Joseph; Israel goes to Egypt

Suffering of an Early Saint
Job • (Poetry)

The Exodus and Journey to Canaan
Exodus • Israel freed from slavery, becomes nation, gets law
Leviticus • Further exposition of law
Numbers • Israel's journey to Promised Land

Deuteronomy • Moses' final exposition of law

The Conquest of Canaan
Joshua • Israel claims Promised Land

The Time of the Judges
Judges • Military leaders save Israel from enemies
Ruth • Story of an ancestor of David and Christ
1 Samuel 1–7 • Eli's ministry; early days of Samuel

The United Kingdom of Israel
1 Samuel 8–31 • Saul's reign; David's rise to power
2 Samuel • David's reign
1 Chronicles • Genealogies; Saul's death; David's reign
1 Kings 1–11 • Solomon's reign
2 Chronicles 1–9 • Solomon's reign
Psalms • Israel's book of worship
Song of Songs • Celebration of love
Ecclesiastes • Meditations on life's problems
Proverbs • Wisdom of Solomon and others

The Divided Kingdom: Judah and Israel
1 Kings 12–22 • Civil war, division of Israel and Judah
2 Kings • History and fall of Israel and Judah
2 Chronicles 10–36 • History and fall of Judah

Prophecy
Obadiah • Edom's doom; Judah's restoration
Joel • Warning all nations
Jonah • Warning Nineveh
Amos • Warning Israel; promise of Messiah
Hosea • God's love for Israel
Isaiah • Warning Israel and Judah; ministry of Messiah
Micah • Warning Judah; triumphant Messiah
Nahum • Hope for Judah; punishment for Nineveh
Zephaniah • Judgment and restoration of Judah
Habakkuk • Judgment and restoration of Judah
Jeremiah • Final warning to Judah; hope of restoration
Lamentations • Lamenting and learning from Judah's fall

The Captivity of Judah and Israel; More Prophecy
Ezekiel • Lessons of exile; promise of restoration
Daniel • God's sovereignty in spite of exile

The Return from Captivity
Ezra • Jews return from Babylon, rebuild Temple
Esther • Jews left in Babylon escape genocide
Nehemiah • Jerusalem's wall rebuilt

More Prophecy
Haggai • Encouragement to rebuild Temple
Zechariah • Encouragement to rebuild Temple
Malachi • Warning the restored Judah and Israel

NEW TESTAMENT
The Life, Death, and Resurrection of Christ
Matthew • Christ the Messiah of Israel
Mark • Christ the obedient servant
Luke • Christ the perfect man
John • Christ the Son of God

The Birth and Early Days of the Church
Acts 1:1–15:35 • Birth, early days of church; Paul's conversion, first missionary journey
James • Letter on the Christian life
Galatians • Letter about being saved by grace, not by law
Acts 15:36–18:22 • Paul's second missionary journey
1 Thessalonians • Letter of commendation and teaching; Christ's return
2 Thessalonians • Letter regarding Christ's return
Acts 18:23–21:16 • Paul's third missionary journey
1 Corinthians • Letter regarding problems in church
2 Corinthians • Letter; Paul defends his apostleship
Romans • Letter; plan of salvation explained
Acts 21:17–28:31 • Paul arrested, imprisoned in Rome
Ephesians • Plea for unity; preparation for spiritual conflict
Colossians • Preeminence of Christ
Philemon • Conversion of a runaway slave
Philippians • Commendation; exhortation
1 Timothy • Advice to a young pastor
Titus • Church organization and leadership
1 Peter • Encouragement for persecuted Christians
2 Peter • Blessings of salvation; warnings against apostasy
2 Timothy • Paul's farewell message
Hebrews • Superiority of person and work of Christ
Jude • Warning about false teachers
1 John • Fellowship with God and other believers
2 John • Commendation; warning about false teachers
3 John • Commendation; condemnation
Revelation • Prophecy about final victory of Christ and his church

Dates of Selected Bible Events

Old Testament (B.C.)
Particularly significant events are in bold type.

?	**Creation (Gen. 1:1–2:14)**
?	The Fall (Gen. 3:1-6)
?	The Flood (Gen. 6–8)

?	Tower of Babel (Gen. 11:1-9)
2090	**Call of Abraham (Gen. 12:1-4)**
2066	Sodom destroyed (Gen. 19)
2065	Birth of Isaac (Gen. 21:1-3)
2045	Abraham offers Isaac (Gen. 22:1-14)
2025	Marriage of Isaac and Rebekah (Gen. 24:67; 25:20)
2006	Birth of Esau, Jacob (Gen. 25:24-26)
1990	Death of Abraham (Gen. 25:7-8)
1929	Jacob flees to Haran (Gen. 28:10)
1922	Jacob marries Leah and Rachel (Gen. 29:18-28)
1915	Birth of Joseph (Gen. 30:22-24)
1909	Jacob returns to Canaan (Gen. 31:3, 17-18)
1898	Joseph sold, taken to Egypt (Gen. 37:28)
1885	Joseph becomes leader in Egypt (Gen. 41:41-44)
1876	Jacob's family moves to Egypt (Gen. 46:1-7)
1859	Death of Jacob (Gen. 49:33)
1805	Death of Joseph (Gen. 50:26)
1730	Israelites enslaved in Egypt (Exod. 1:8-14)
1528	Pharaoh orders death of Hebrew male babies (Exod. 1:22)
1526	Birth of Moses (Exod. 2:1-2)
1486	Moses flees to Midian (Exod. 2:15)
1446	Call of Moses (Exod. 3:1-10)
1446	**The Exodus (Exod. 12:51)**
1446	Law given at Sinai (Exod. 19:1—Num. 10:10)
1443	Kadesh-barnea rebellion (Num. 13–14)
1406	Death of Moses (Deut. 34:5-7)
1406	Israel enters Canaan (Josh. 3:17)
1399	Conquest of Canaan completed (Josh. 11:23)
1377	Othniel becomes Israel's first judge (Judg. 3:9-11)
1192	Gideon becomes judge (Judg. 6:7–8:35)
1100	Ruth and Boaz (Ruth)
1093	Call of Samuel (1 Sam. 3:1-10)
1081	Birth of Saul
1075	Samson becomes judge (Judg. 13:2–16:31)
1069	Philistines capture the Ark of the Covenant (1 Sam. 4:17; 5:1)
1068	Ark returned to Israel (1 Sam. 6)
1051	**Saul becomes Israel's first king (1 Sam. 9–10)**
1041	Birth of David
1024	First anointing of David, by Samuel (1 Sam 16:13)
1011	Death of Saul (1 Sam. 31:6)
1011	Second anointing of David, by Judah (2 Sam. 2:4)
1004	Third anointing of David by all 12 tribes (2 Sam. 5:1-3)
1004	God's covenant with David (2 Sam. 7:8-17)
1003	Jerusalem becomes capital (2 Sam. 5:6-10)
1002	David brings Ark of the Covenant to Jerusalem (2 Sam. 6:17)
1002	David and Bathsheba (2 Sam. 11–12)
971	Death of David (1 Kings 2:10)

971	Solomon becomes king (1 Kings 2:12)
960	Completion of Temple (1 Kings 6:37-38)
931	Death of Solomon (1 Kings 11:43)
931	**Israel divided: northern, southern kingdoms (1 Kings 12)**
874	Ahab becomes king—northern (1 Kings 16:29)
874	Elijah's ministry begins (1 Kings 17–22; 2 Kings 1:1–2:11)
852	Elijah taken up to heaven (2 Kings 2:11)
852	Elisha's ministry begins (2 Kings 2–13)
841	Joash survives Athaliah's purge (2 Chron. 22:10-12)
740	Call of Isaiah (Isa. 6:1-10)
722	**Fall of northern kingdom (2 Kings 17:6-23)**
701	Death angel saves Jerusalem (2 Kings 19:35-37)
640	Josiah becomes king—southern (2 Kings 22:1)
627	Call of Jeremiah (Jer. 1:2)
621	Forgotten copy of Law discovered (2 Kings 22:3-10)
612	Fall of Nineveh (Nah. 3:7)
605	Battle of Carchemish ends (Jer. 46)
605	First siege of Jerusalem; Daniel exiled (2 Kings 24:1-4; Dan. 1:1-6)
597	Second siege of Jerusalem; Ezekiel exiled (2 Kings 24:8-12; Ezek.1:1-2)
592	Ezekiel's ministry begins (Ezek. 1:1-2)
586	**Jerusalem destroyed; fall of southern kingdom (2 Kings 25:8-10)**
550	Cyrus becomes king of Persia (Isa. 45:1)
539	Handwriting on wall; Babylon falls to Persia (Dan. 5)
538	**First return of Jews to Jerusalem—Zerubbabel (Ezra 1–2; Isa. 44:28)**
536	Beginning of second Temple (Ezra 3:10)
520	Ministries of Haggai, Zechariah
516	Completion of second Temple (Ezra 6:15)
490	Battle of Marathon: Greece defeats Persian army
478	Esther becomes Xerxes' queen (Esther 2:16-17)
474	Haman's plot to exterminate Jews in Persia (Esther 3)
457	Second return of Jews—Ezra (Ezra 8:31-32)
445	Third return of Jews—Nehemiah (Neh. 1:1–2:11)
445	Nehemiah rebuilds Jerusalem's walls (Neh. 2:12–7:4)
445	Beginning of the 490 years of Daniel (Dan. 9:24-27)
430	**Malachi written; Old Testament completed**
333	Alexander defeats Persians at Issus (Dan. 8:1-7)
323	Death of Alexander; kingdom divided into four parts (Dan. 8:8; 11:4)
250	Translation of Hebrew Bible into Greek (Septuagint)
168	Antiochus Epiphanes defiles Temple (Dan. 8:9-12)
167	Revolt of Maccabees (apocryphal books of 1, 2 Maccabees)
165	Temple cleansed; Festival of Dedication instituted (John 10:22)
146	Rome destroys Carthage, becomes world power (Dan. 2:40; 7:7)
64	Pompey captures Jerusalem
40	Herod the Great becomes king of Judea
20	Herod begins expansion of Temple (John 2:20)

New Testament (B.C.)

5 Birth of John the Baptist (Luke 1:57-79)
5 Birth of Christ (Luke 2:1-20) (The birth of Christ is now believed to have occurred in the year we refer to as "5 B.C." [five years before Christ!]. The discrepancy is due to a calendar mistake that was corrected in the sixth century.)
4 Visit of wise men (Matt. 2:1-12)
4 Flight to Egypt; slaughter of infants (Matt. 2:13-18)
4 Return from Egypt to Nazareth (Matt. 2:19-23)

New Testament (A.D.)

8 Christ in Temple at age 12 (Luke 2:41-52)
26 Baptism of Christ (Matt. 3:13-17)
27 Conversion of Nicodemus (John 3)
28 Choosing of the 12 (Matt. 10:1-4)
29 Martyrdom of John the Baptist (Matt. 14:1-12)
29 Feeding of the 5,000 (John 6:1-14)
29 Lazarus resurrected (John 11:1-46)
30 Death, resurrection of Christ (Matt. 27–28)
30 Pentecost (Acts 2)
31 Death of Ananias and Sapphira (Acts 5:1-11)
32 Deacons selected (Acts 6:1-7)
34 Martyrdom of Stephen (Acts 6:8–7:60)
35 Conversion of Paul (Acts 9:1-7)
37 Paul returns to Jerusalem as believer (Acts 9:26-29; Gal. 1:18-20)
40 Conversion of Cornelius (Acts 10)
44 Martyrdom of James (son of Zebedee) the apostle (Acts 12:1-2)
47 Paul begins first missionary journey (Acts 13:1-3)
49 Paul completes first journey (Acts 14:26)
49 Jerusalem Council (Acts 15)
50 Paul begins second missionary journey (Acts 15:40)
52 Paul completes second journey (Acts 18:22)
53 Paul begins third missionary journey (Acts 18:23)
54 Nero becomes emperor
57 Paul completes third journey (Acts 21:15)
57 Paul arrested in Jerusalem (Acts 21:27-28)
59 Paul's voyage to Rome (Acts 27:1)
60 Paul imprisoned in Rome (Acts 28:16)
62 Paul freed from prison (Philem. 1:22)
64 Great fire in Rome
65 Martyrdom of Peter (2 Pet. 1:14)
66 Paul's final imprisonment (2 Tim. 1:8)
66 Jewish revolt against Rome; Christians flee Jerusalem
67 Martyrdom of Paul (2 Tim. 4:6-8)
68 Nero commits suicide
69 Vespasian becomes emperor

69 Birth of Polycarp
70 Jerusalem destroyed
73 Masada falls
79 Josephus publishes *Jewish Wars*
95 Revelation written; New Testament completed
98 Death of John the apostle

BIBLICAL COVENANTS

A covenant (Hebrew, *berith;* Greek, *diatheke*) is a promise or agreement between two parties. A covenant may be conditional or unconditional. The Bible records eight important covenants God made with humankind:

The covenant with Adam

- Before the Fall: He could remain in Eden as long as he obeyed (conditional) (Gen. 1:28; 2:15-17).
- After the Fall: God would someday send a Savior (unconditional) (Gen. 3:15).

The covenant with Noah (unconditional) (Gen. 8:21-22)

- The earth would not be destroyed by water again.
- Nature would continue in a relatively predictable course till the end of time.

The covenant with Abraham (unconditional)

- God would make Abraham the founder of a great nation (Gen. 12:2-3, 7; 13:16; 15:5).
- God would someday give Palestine forever to Abraham's seed (Gen. 13:14-15, 17; 15:18; 17:8).

The covenant with Moses and Israel (conditional)

- Israel could have the Promised Land if they obeyed (Exod. 19:3-8; Lev. 26:1-13; Deut. 28:1-14).
- Israel would forfeit all God's blessings if they disobeyed (Lev. 26:14-46; Deut. 28:15-68).

The covenant with David (unconditional)

- From David would come an everlasting kingdom (2 Sam. 7:12-16; 23:5; 2 Chron. 13:5).
- From David would come an everlasting king (2 Sam. 7:12-16; Ps. 45:6-7; Isa. 9:6-7; Heb. 1:5, 8-9).

The covenant with all repenting sinners, to save them through Christ (unconditional) (Matt. 26:28; Titus 1:1-2; Heb. 13:20-21)

The covenant with the church (unconditional)

- Christ would build his church, and all the fury of hell would not destroy it (Matt.16:18).
- He would perfect all the members of his church (Phil. 1:6; Heb. 13:20-21).

The New Covenant with Israel (unconditional) (Jer. 31:31-40; Rom. 11:26-27)

- God would eventually bring Israel back to himself.

- He would forgive and forget their sin.
- He would use them to reach and teach Gentiles.
- He would establish them in Palestine forever.

❖ ❖ ❖

BIBLICAL DISPENSATIONS

The school of Bible interpretation known as dispensationalism views the world as a household run by God. God "dispenses," or administers, the affairs of his "household world" in various stages of revelation (see exposition on Eph. 1:7-12).

The dispensation of innocence
From Creation to the Fall (Gen. 1:28–3:6)

The dispensation of conscience
From the Fall to the Flood (Gen. 4:1–8:14)

The dispensation of civil government
From the Flood to the dispersion at Babel (Gen. 8:15–11:9)

The dispensation of promise (patriarchal rule)
From Babel to Mount Sinai (Gen. 11:10—Exod. 18:27)

The dispensation of Mosaic law
From Mount Sinai to the upper room (Exod. 19—Acts 1)

The dispensation of the bride of the Lamb (the church)
From the upper room to the Rapture (Acts 2—Rev. 3)

The dispensation of the wrath of the Lamb (the Tribulation)
From the Rapture to the Second Coming (Rev. 6:1–20:3)

The dispensation of the rule of the Lamb (the Millennium)
From the Second Coming through the Great White Throne Judgment (Rev. 20:4-15)

The dispensation of the new creation of the Lamb (the world without end)
From the Great White Throne Judgment throughout all eternity (Rev. 21–22)

❖ ❖ ❖

FACTS ABOUT HEAVEN AND HELL

Heaven (The New Jerusalem)

Who will be there?

- Those who have been born again (John 3:3)
- Those who faithfully looked forward to Christ before his birth (Heb. 11:10, 16)
- The elect angels (Dan. 7:10; 1 Tim. 5:21; Heb.12:22; Rev. 5:11)

What will they experience?

- Holiness (Rev. 21:27)
- Beauty (Ps. 50:2)
- Unity (Eph. 1:10)
- Perfection (1 Cor. 13:10)

- Joy (Ps. 16:11)
- No tears (Rev. 7:17; 21:4)
- No sickness or pain (Rev. 21:4; 22:2)
- No death (Isa. 25:8; 1 Cor. 15:26; Rev. 21:4)
- No thirst or hunger (Rev. 7:16)
- No sin or judgment (Rev. 21:27; 22:3)
- No need for sun or moon (Rev. 21:23)
- No night (Rev. 21:25; 22:5)

How long will it last?
- Forever (Ps. 23:6; John 3:15; Rev. 22:5)

Hell

Who will be there?
- The devil and his angels and all unredeemed humans (Matt. 25:31-46; Rev. 20:10)

What will they experience?
- Undiluted divine wrath (Hab. 3:2; Rev. 14:9-10)
- Unquenchable fire (Matt 13:41-42; 18:8; Mark 9:43)
- Misery and pain (Rev. 14:9-11)
- Frustration and anger (Matt. 13:42; 24:51)
- Separation (Rev. 2:11; 20:6, 15)
- Memory and remorse (Luke 16:19-31)
- Unquenchable thirst (Luke 16:24-26)

How long will it last?
- Forever (Dan. 12:2; Matt. 25:46; Jude 1:7)

❖ ❖ ❖

THE LENGTH OF THE BIBLE

As seen in this list, the Bible comes from a wide variety of sources, from very long historical documents to very short personal letters.

	BOOKS	CHAPTERS	VERSES
Bible	66	1189	31,173
Old Testament	39	929	23,214
New Testament	27	260	7,959

Bible books arranged by length

	CHAPTERS	VERSES
1. Psalms	150	2,461
2. Jeremiah	52	1,364
3. Ezekiel	48	1,273
4. Genesis	50	1,533
5. Isaiah	66	1,292
6. Numbers	36	1,288
7. Exodus	40	1,213
8. Deuteronomy	34	959
9. 2 Chronicles	36	822
10. Luke	24	1,151

	CHAPTERS	VERSES
11. 1 Samuel	31	810
12. Leviticus	27	829
13. 1 Kings	22	816
14. Acts	28	1,007
15. Matthew	28	1,071
16. 2 Kings	25	710
17. 2 Samuel	24	695
18. 1 Chronicles	29	942
19. John	21	878
20. Judges	21	618
21. Joshua	24	685
22. Mark	16	678
23. Proverbs	31	915
24. Revelation	22	404
25. Daniel	12	357
26. Nehemiah	13	406
27. Job	42	1,070
28. 1 Corinthians	16	437
29. Romans	16	433
30. Ezra	10	280
31. Hebrews	13	303
32. Zechariah	14	211
33. 2 Corinthians	13	257
34. Esther	10	167
35. Ecclesiastes	12	222
36. Hosea	14	197
37. Amos	9	146
38. Lamentations	5	154
39. Micah	7	105
40. Galatians	6	149
41. Ephesians	6	155
42. Song of Songs	8	117
43. Ruth	4	84
44. 1 John	5	105
45. 1 Peter	5	105
46. James	5	108
47. 1 Timothy	6	113
48. Joel	3	73
49. Philippians	4	104
50. Colossians	4	95
51. 1 Thessalonians	5	89
52. Malachi	4	55
53. 2 Timothy	4	83
54. Zephaniah	3	53
55. 2 Peter	3	61

56. Habakkuk	3	56
57. Jonah	4	48
58. Nahum	3	47
59. Haggai	2	38
60. 2 Thessalonians	3	47
61. Titus	3	46
62. Obadiah	1	21
63. Jude	1	25
64. Philemon	1	25
65. 2 John	1	13
66. 3 John	1	15

❖ ❖ ❖

INTERDEPENDENCE OF THE OLD AND THE NEW

As any Bible student knows, the New Testament contains numerous quotations from the Old Testament. It is estimated, for instance, that more than 10 percent of Christ's recorded words are quoted from the OT. The truth and value of the OT becomes fully apparent only in the pages of the NT, and the truth and value of the NT likewise depends on the historical and prophetic foundation of the OT. These two lists will give some idea of the scope of the interdependence between the two Testaments.

Old Testament books referred to in the New Testament

OT BOOK	NT REFERENCES	NUMBER OF NT BOOKS THAT REFER TO IT
Isaiah	472	23
Psalms	454	23
Genesis	260	21
Exodus	250	19
Deuteronomy	208	21
Daniel	152	15
Ezekiel	151	17
Jeremiah	137	17
Leviticus	120	15
Numbers	100	14
Zechariah	71	14
Proverbs	66	20
1 Kings	53	9
2 Chronicles	45	14
Job	36	16
1 Samuel	35	8
Joel	34	8
Hosea	26	12
2 Samuel	26	11
2 Kings	26	6
Malachi	25	10

OT BOOK	NT REFERENCES	NUMBER OF NT BOOKS THAT REFER TO IT
Amos	23	9
1 Chronicles	23	5
Joshua	22	8
Micah	14	6
Judges	14	5
Jonah	9	4
Habakkuk	8	8
Lamentations	7	6
Haggai	7	4
Ecclesiastes	6	5
Ezra	6	3
Ruth	6	2
Nehemiah	5	4
Zephaniah	5	3
Nahum	4	4
Esther	3	2
Obadiah	1	1
Song of Songs	0	0

Number of Old Testament books each New Testament book refers to

NT BOOK	NUMBER OF OT BOOKS IT REFERS TO
Matthew	33
Revelation	32
Luke	31
John	26
Acts	25
Mark	25
Romans	23
Hebrews	21
1 Corinthians	18
James	17
1 Peter	15
2 Corinthians	14
Ephesians	13
1 Timothy	11
Galatians	10
Philippians	9
2 Thessalonians	9
1 Thessalonians	8
Jude	8
Colossians	7

NT BOOK	NUMBER OF OT BOOKS IT REFERS TO
2 Timothy	7
1 John	7
Titus	6
2 Peter	6
2 John	1
3 John	1
Philemon	0

THE SAVIOR

THE UNFOLDING REVELATION OF CHRIST

Old Testament

Many OT books speak clearly of Jesus Christ. In all OT books we see those attributes he shares with God the Father (see John 14:9). Following are the OT appearances, prophecies, and symbols of Christ.

Genesis
- Seed of the woman (3:15)
- Shiloh (49:10)

Exodus
- Passover Lamb (12:3)

Leviticus
- Anointed High Priest (8:7-12)

Numbers
- Bronze serpent (21:8-9; John 3:14-15)
- Star of Jacob (24:17)
- Scepter of Israel (24:17)

Deuteronomy
- Prophet like Moses (18:15)
- The great Rock (32:4; 1 Cor. 10:4)

Joshua
- Captain of the Lord's army (5:14)

Judges
- Angel of the Lord (2:1)

Ruth
- Family redeemer

1 Samuel
- The great judge (2:10; Ps. 96:13; 2 Tim. 4:8; Rev. 19:11)

2 Samuel
- Seed of David (7:12-13)

1 Kings
- Lord God of Israel (8:15, 25)

2 Kings
- God of the cherubim (19:15)

1 Chronicles
- God of our salvation (16:35)

2 Chronicles
- God of our ancestors (20:6)

Ezra
- Lord of heaven and earth (1:2)

Nehemiah
- Covenant-keeping God (1:5)

Esther
- God of providence

Job
- Risen and returning Redeemer (19:25)

Psalms
- Anointed Son (2:2, 12)
- Holy One (16:10)
- Good Shepherd (23:1)
- King of glory (24:7-10)

Proverbs
- Wisdom of God (8; 1 Cor. 1:24)
- Architect at Creation (8:30; John 1:1-3; Col. 1:15-17)

Ecclesiastes
- The one above the sun

Song of Songs
- Chief among 10,000 (5:10)
- Altogether lovely (5:16)

Isaiah
- Virgin-born Immanuel (7:14)
- Wonderful Counselor (9:6)
- Mighty God (9:6)
- Everlasting Father (9:6)
- Prince of Peace (9:6)
- Servant (52:13)
- Man of sorrows (53:3)

Jeremiah
- The Lord our righteousness (23:6; 33:16; Rom 10:4; 1 Cor. 1:30)

Lamentations
- Faithful and compassionate (3:22-23, 31-33)

Ezekiel
- The tender shoot (17:22)
- The one who has the right to judge (21:27)

Daniel
- The rock (2:34)
- One like a divine being (or like "the Son of God") (3:25)
- One like the Son of Man (7:13)

Hosea
- King of the resurrection (13:10-14)

Joel
- God of the battle (2:11; 3:2, 9-17)
- Giver of the Spirit (2:28-32)

Amos
- Lord God Almighty (4:13)
- Plumb line (7:7-9)

Obadiah
- Destroyer of the proud (1:8, 15)

Jonah
- Risen prophet (2:10)
- God of the second chance (3:1-2)
- Long-suffering one (4:9-11)

Micah
- God of Israel (4:1-5)
- Born in Bethlehem (5:2)
- God who pardons (7:18-20)

Nahum
- Avenging God (1:2)
- Bringer of good tidings (1:15)

Habakkuk
- Eternal (1:12)
- Pure (1:13)
- Glorious (2:14)

Zephaniah
- King of Israel (3:15)

Haggai
- Desire of all nations (2:7)

Zechariah
- My Servant (3:8)
- The Branch (3:8)

- Builder of the Temple (6:12-13)
- King of triumphal entry (9:9)
- Pierced one (12:10)
- King of the earth (14:9)

Malachi
- Sun of Righteousness (4:2)

New Testament
Matthew
- King of the Jews (2:2; 27:37)

Mark
- Servant (9:35; 10:43-44)

Luke
- Perfect man, Son of Man (2:40, 52; 9:22, 58; 22:48)

John
- Eternal God (1:1-5; 20:28, 31)

Acts
- Ascended Lord (1:9)

Romans
- The Lord, our righteousness (10:4)

1 Corinthians
- Our resurrection (15)

2 Corinthians
- God of all comfort (1:3)

Galatians
- Redeemer of those under the law (4:4-5)

Ephesians
- Head of the church (1:22; 2:19-20)
- Giver of gifts (4:7-16)

Philippians
- Supplier of every need (1:19; 4:19)
- Obedient servant (2:5-8)

Colossians
- Fullness of the Godhead (1:9; 2:9-10)

1 Thessalonians
- The coming Christ (4:13–5:11)

2 Thessalonians
- The consuming Christ (2:8)

1 Timothy
- Savior of sinners (1:15; 3:16)

2 Timothy
- Author of Scripture (3:16-17)
- Righteous and rewarding judge (4:8)

Titus
- Our great God and Savior (1:3; 2:10, 13; 3:4)

Philemon
- Payer of our debt

Hebrews
- Appointed heir of all things (1:2, 4)
- Greater than prophets or angels (1:4; 3:3)

James
- Ever-present God (4:8)
- Coming One (5:7-8)
- Great Physician (5:15)

1 Peter
- Unblemished Lamb (1:19)
- Great example (2:21-24)
- Lord of glory (3:22)
- Head Shepherd (5:4)

2 Peter
- Beloved Son (1:17)

1 John
- Word of life (1:1)
- Advocate (2:1-2)

- Sacrifice (4:10)
- Son of God (3:8, 4:15; 5:5)

2 John
- Son of the Father (1:3)

3 John
- The truth (1:4, 8)

Jude
- Preserver and only wise God (1:1, 25)

Revelation
- Alpha and Omega (1:8)
- Lion of Judah (5:5)
- Root of David (5:5)
- King of kings (19:16)
- Lord of lords (19:16)

❖ ❖ ❖

KEY EVENTS IN THE LIFE OF CHRIST: A HARMONY OF THE GOSPELS

Particularly significant events are in bold type.

	MATT.	MARK	LUKE	JOHN
TWO GENEALOGIES				
Abraham to Christ	1:1-17			
Christ to Adam			3:23-38	
TWO PREFACES				
Christ the historical person			1:1-4	
Christ the Word of God				1:1-5
THREE ANNOUNCEMENTS				
To Zacharias (birth of John)			1:5-25	
To Mary (birth of Jesus)			1:26-38	
To Joseph (Mary's purity)	1:18-25			
THREE SONGS OF PRAISE				
Of Elizabeth to Mary			1:41-45	
Of Mary to God			1:46-55	
Of Zacharias to God			1:57-79	
Birth of Christ			2:1-19	
Circumcision			2:21-24	
Dedication			2:25-38	
The wise men	2:1-12			
Flight to Egypt	2:13-23			
Boyhood in Nazareth			2:39-40, 51-52	
Temple visit, age 12			2:41-51	
Baptism	3:13-17	1:9-11	3:21-22	1:31-34
Temptation	4:1-11	1:12-13	4:1-13	
Calling first disciples	4:18-22	1:16-20	5:2-11	1:35-42
First miracle: water to wine				2:1-11
First rejection at Nazareth			4:16-30	
Sermon on the Mount	5–7			
First cleansing of Temple				2:13-17
Matthew's dinner	9:9-13	2:14-17	5:29-32	

	MATT.	MARK	LUKE	JOHN
Calling the Twelve	10:1-42	3:13-19	6:12-16	
"Woes" on Galilean cities	11:20-24	10:13-15		
Great Invitation	11:28-30			
Second rejection at Nazareth	13:53-58	6:1-6		
Death of John the Baptist	14:1-12	6:14-29		
Feeding 5,000	14:14-21	6:31-44	9:10-17	6:1-13
Walking on water	14:24-33	6:47-52		6:16-21
Peter's confession	16:13-20	8:27-30	9:18-21	
Transfiguration	17:1-9	9:2-10	9:28-36	
Blessing little children	19:13-15	10:13-16	18:15-17	
Weeping over Jerusalem			13:34-35	
Lazarus resurrected				11:1-46
Caiaphas predicts crucifixion				11:45-57
FINAL EIGHT DAYS				
SATURDAY				
Anointed by Mary	26:6-13	14:3-9		12:1-8
First Pharisee death plot				12:9-11
SUNDAY				
Triumphal Entry	21:1-11	11:1-10	19:28-38	12:12-19
Weeping over Jerusalem	23:37-39			
Weeping over Jerusalem again			19:41-44	
MONDAY				
Fig tree cursed	21:18-19	11:12-14, 20-21		
Second cleansing of Temple	21:12-13	11:15-17	19:45-46	
Greeks ask to see Christ				12:20-36
TUESDAY				
The widow's mite		12:41-44	21:1-4	
Mt. Olivet discourse	24–25	13:1-37	21:5-38	
Christ predicts his death	26:1-2			
Second Pharisee death plot	26:3-5	14:1-2	22:1-2	
WEDNESDAY				
Judas agrees to betrayal	26:14-16	14:10-11	22:3-6	
THURSDAY				
Passover events	26:17-30	14:12-26	22:7-30	13
Passover teaching				14–16
FRIDAY				
Final prediction of death	26:31-32	14:27-28		
High priestly prayer				17
Gethsemane, betrayal	26:36-56	14:32-52	22:39-53	18:1-13
Jewish religious trials				
Before Annas				18:13-14, 19-23
Before Caiaphas	26:57	14:53	22:54, 63-65	18:24
Before entire Sanhedrin	26:59-68;	15:1	22:66–23:1	

	MATT.	MARK	LUKE	JOHN
Roman political trials				
Before Pilate (first time)	27:1-2, 11-14	15:1-5	23:1-5	18:28-38
Before Herod Antipas			23:6-12	
Before Pilate (second time)	27:15-26	15:6-15	23:13-24	18:39–19:16
Delivered to be crucified	27:26	15:15	23:24-25	19:4-16
Mock trial by soldiers	27:27-31	15:16-20		19:2-3
Led away to Calvary	27:31	15:20	23:26	19:16
Death of Judas	27:3-10			
Peter's denials	26:33-35, 69-75	14:29-31, 54, 66-72	22:31-34, 54-62	13:36-38, 18:15-18, 25-27
Simon of Cyrene	27:32	15:21	23:26	
Women weeping			23:27-31	
Crucifixion	27:32-50	15:20-37	23:32-46	19:16-30
3:00 P.M. (time of death)				
God's action				
Veil of Temple torn	27:51	15:38	23:45	
Earthquake	27:51			
Graves opened	27:52-53			
The human reaction				
Centurion believes	27:54	15:39	23:47	
Crowd is confused			23:48	
Christ's followers watch from distance	27:55-56	15:40-41	23:49	
3:00 P.M. to 6:00 P.M.				
Soldier pierces Christ's side				19:31-37
Preparation for burial	27:57-58	15:42-45	23:50-52, 55-56	19:38-39
Burial	27:59-60	15:46	23:53-54	19:40-42
SATURDAY				
Sealing the tomb	27:62-66			
SUNDAY: **RESURRECTION**				
Indication of resurrection: empty tomb	28:1-7	16:1-7	24:1-12	20:1-9
Validations of resurrection: appearances of risen Savior				
First: to Mary Magdalene		16:9		20:11-18
Second: to some women	28:8-10			
Third: at Emmaus		16:12-13	24:13-35	
Fourth: to Simon Peter			24:34	
Fifth: upper room, Thomas absent			24:36-49	20:19-23
FINAL APPEARANCES, DURING 40 DAYS FROM RESURRECTION TO ASCENSION				
In the upper room, Thomas present				20:24-29

	MATT.	MARK	LUKE	JOHN
At Sea of Galilee				21:1-14
To apostles and more than 500 people	28:16-20	16:14 *(also 1 Cor. 15:6-7)*		
Ascension		16:19-20	24:50-53 *(also Acts 1:9-11)*	
POST-ASCENSION APPEARANCES				
To Stephen	*recorded in Acts 7:56*			
To Paul	*recorded in 1 Corinthians 15:8*			
To John	*recorded in Revelation 1:13*			
MIRACLES				
Calming the sea	8:23-27	4:35-41	8:22-25	
Feeding 4,000	15:32-38	8:1-9		
Feeding 5,000	14:14-21	6:31-44	9:10-17	6:1-13
Fig tree destroyed	21:18-22	11:12-14, 20-21		
Fish—first great catch			5:1-11	
Fish—second great catch				21:1-14
Fish, money in mouth	17:24-27			
Walking on water	14:24-33	6:47-52		6:16-21
Water to wine				2:1-11
HEALINGS				
Blind Bartimaeus (or, "two blind men")	20:29-34	10:46-52	18:35-43	
Blind man in Bethsaida		8:22-26		
Blind man in Jerusalem				9:1-41
Blind men, two	9:27-31			
Blind, mute demoniac	12:22		11:14	
Centurion's servant	8:5-13		7:1-10	
Deaf man, speech impediment		7:31-37		
Syro-Phoenician girl	15:21-28	7:24-30		
Demoniac		1:21-28	4:33-37	
Demoniac boy	17:14-21	9:14-29	9:37-43	
Dropsy victim			14:1-6	
Leper	8:2-4	1:40-45	5:12-14	
Lepers, 10			17:11-19	
Malchus's ear restored			22:49-51	18:10
Man crippled for 38 years				5:1-16
Maniac of Gadara	8:28-34	5:1-20	8:26-39	
Healed "many"				
First occasion	8:16-17	1:32-34	4:40-41	
Second occasion	12:15	3:7-12		
Third occasion	14:34-36	6:53-56		
Fourth occasion	15:29-31			
Mute demoniac	9:32-34			
Nobleman's son				4:46-54
Paralytic	9:2-8	2:1-12	5:17-26	

	MATT.	MARK	LUKE	JOHN
Peter's mother-in-law	8:14-15	1:29-31	4:38-39	
Withered hand	12:9-13	3:1-6	6:6-11	
Woman crippled 18 years			13:10-17	
Woman with flow of blood	9:20-22	5:25-34	8:43-48	
RESURRECTIONS				
Widow's son			7:11-17	
Jairus's daughter	9:18-19, 23-26	5:22-24, 35-43	8:41-42, 49-56	
Lazarus				11:1-46
PARABLES				
Children in marketplace	11:16-19		7:31-35	
Dragnet	13:47-50			
Faithful, evil servants	24:42-51		12:35-48	
Fig tree	24:32-35	13:28-31	21:29-33	
Fig tree, fruitless			13:6-9	
Forgiven who wouldn't forgive	18:21-35			
Forgiving debts, 50 vs. 500 denarii			7:36-50	
Friends of bridegroom	9:14-15	2:18-20	5:33-35	
Good Samaritan			10:30-37	
Growing seed		4:26-29		
Guests for banquet			14:15-24	
Hidden treasure	13:44			
House on rock	7:24-27		6:48-49	
Leaven	13:33			
Lost coin			15:8-10	
Lost sheep			15:1-7	
Mustard seed	13:31-32	4:30-32	13:18-19	
New cloth on old cloth	9:16	2:21	5:36	
New wine, old bottles	9:17	2:22	5:37-39	
Obedient, disobedient sons	21:28-32			
Pearl of great price	13:45-46			
Pharisee and tax collector			18:9-14	
Prodigal son			15:11-32	
Rich fool			12:13-21	
Rich man and Lazarus			16:19-31	
Sheep and goats	25:31-46			
Sower	13:3-9, 18-23	4:1-9, 13-20	8:4-15	
Spirits and swept house	12:43-45		11:24-26	
Subduing strong man	12:25-30	3:20-27		
Taking lower seat			14:7-14	
10 servants, 10 minas			19:11-27	
10 talents	25:14-30			
10 virgins	25:1-13			
Treasures old and new	13:52			
Unjust steward			16:1-13	
Unprofitable servants			17:7-10	

	MATT.	MARK	LUKE	JOHN
Wedding garment	22:1-14			
Wheat and tares	13:24-30, 36-43			
Wicked vinedressers	21:33-45	12:1-12	20:9-19	
Widow and weary judge			18:1-8	
Workers in vineyard	20:1-16			
SERMONS				
Abundance of Life				15–16
Bread of Life				6:22-71
Light of Life				8:12-59
Mt. Olivet discourse	24–25			
Isaiah 61 sermon			4:16-30	
Sermon on the Mount	5–7			
Shepherd of Life				10:1-39
Source of Life				5:16-47
Way, Truth, and Life				14:1-31
INFORMAL TEACHINGS				
Accountability for words	12:33-37			
Children and greatness	18:1-14	9:33-37, 42	9:46-48; 17:1-2	
Church discipline	18:15-20			
Confession and denial	10:32-33		12:8-9	
Division caused by gospel			12:49-53	
Divorce	19:3-12	10:2-12	16:18	
Faith	17:19-20; 21:18-22	9:23	17:5-6	
Fasting and feasting	9:14-15	2:18-20		
Forgiveness	18:21-22	11:25-26	17:3-4	
God's knowledge and care			12:6-7	
Hell	18:8-9	9:43-50	12:4-5	
Holy Spirit			12:11-12	
Judgment			12:2-3	
Kingdom of God			17:20-21	
Last days, Christ's return			17:22-37	
Repentance			13:1-5	
Rewards	16:27; 19:27-30	10:28-31	18:28-30	
Taking up one's cross	16:24-26	8:34-38	9:23-26; 14:25-27	
Unpardonable sin	12:31-32	3:28-30	12:10	
Vain traditions	15:1-9	7:1-13		
PRAYERS				
At baptism			3:21	
Before first preaching tour		1:35	4:42	
After healing leper			5:16	
Before choosing the Twelve			6:12	
After feeding the 5,000	14:23	6:46		6:15
Before Peter's confession			9:18	

	MATT.	MARK	LUKE	JOHN
At Transfiguration			9:28-29	
At report of Seventy	11:25-27		10:21-22	
Example for disciples	6:9-13		11:1-4	
Before raising Lazarus				11:41-42
When Greeks asked to see him				12:20-28
After leaving upper room				17:1-26
IN GETHSEMANE				
First	26:39	14:35-36	22:41-43	
Second	26:42	14:39	22:44	
Third	26:44			
WORDS FROM THE CROSS				
"Father, forgive these people, because they don't know what they are doing."			23:34	
". . . today you will be with me in paradise."			23:43	
"He is your son. . . . She is your mother."				19:26-27
"My God, my God, why have you forsaken me?"	27:46	15:34		
"I am thirsty."				19:28
"It is finished!"				19:30
"Father, I entrust my spirit into your hands!"			23:46	
JOHN THE BAPTIST				
Birth			1:57-80	
Message	3:1-12	1:1-8	3:1-19	1:19-36
Imprisonment	4:12; 14:3-5	1:14; 6:17-20	3:19-20	
Inquiry from prison	11:2-6		7:18-23	
Christ commends	11:7-19		7:24-28	
Martyrdom	14:1-12	6:14-29		
APOSTLES AND DISCIPLES				
Peter, Andrew, James, John	4:18-22	1:16-20	5:2-11	1:35-42
Philip, Nathanael				1:43-51
Matthew	9:9	2:14	5:27-28	
The Twelve	10:1-41	3:13-19	6:12-16	
The Seventy			10:1-24	
WOULD-BE DISCIPLES, WHO INSTEAD CHOSE . . .				
Comfort and security	8:19-20		9:57-58	
Family and friends	8:21-22			
PREACHING TOURS				
GALILEE				
First	4:12-17	1:14-15	4:14-15	
Second	4:23-25	1:35-39	4:42-44	
Third	9:35-38			

	MATT.	MARK	LUKE	JOHN
Fourth	11:1			
Fifth			8:1-3	
Phoenicia	15:21-28	7:24-30		
Decapolis		7:31		
Beyond Jordan				10:39-42
Perea	19:1-2	10:1		
To Jerusalem	21:1	11:1	19:28	12:12
ENCOUNTERS WITH RELIGIOUS LEADERS				
SABBATH CONTROVERSY				
Working on	12:1-8	2:23-28	6:1-5	
Healing on	12:9-14	3:1-6	6:6-11	
PHARISEES DEMAND A SIGN				
First occasion	12:38-42		11:29-32	
Second occasion	16:1-4	8:11-12		
Anointed at Simon's house			7:36-48	
Dinner at Pharisee's house			14:7-24	
Healing in Temple	21:14-17			
FINAL WEEK ENCOUNTERS, CONCERNING				
Christ's authority	21:23-27	11:27-33	20:1-8	
Tribute to Caesar	22:15-22	12:13-17	20:20-26	
Resurrection	22:23-33	12:18-27	20:27-40	
Greatest commandment	22:34-40	12:28-34		
The Messiah	22:41-46	12:35-37	20:41-44	
Christ condemns Pharisees	23:1-36	12:38-40	20:45-47	
OTHER ENCOUNTERS				
Nicodemus				3:1-21
Woman at well				4:1-42
Adulteress				8:1-11
Mary and Martha			10:38-42	
Rich young ruler	19:16-30	10:17-22	18:18-30	
Zacchaeus			19:1-10	
CHRIST'S FAMILY				
His attitude toward them	12:46-50	3:31-35	8:19-21	
Their attitude toward him				7:1-5

THE SUFFERINGS CHRIST ENDURED

Rejected by

His nation (John 1:11)
His hometown (Luke 4:28-29)
His family and friends (Mark 3:21; John 7:5)

Tempted by Satan (Luke 4:1-13)

Ridiculed because of

His hometown (John 1:46; 7:52)
His parentage (John 8:41; 9:24, 29)

Threatened by
Herod (Matt. 2:16)
His hometown (Luke 4:29)
The Jews, because of
- healing on Sabbath (Luke 6:6-11; John 5:1-16)
- his claims (John 8:58-59; 10:30-33)
- his sermons (Matt. 26:1-4; Mark 12:12; Luke 11:53-54; John 8:40)
- his miracles (John 11:47-48, 53; 12:10-11)

Homeless (Matt. 8:20)

Betrayed by a follower (John 13:21-27; 18:1-5)

Denied by a friend (Matt. 26:69-75)

Misunderstood by disciples (Matt. 15:16; 17:6-13; Mark 6:52; John 10:6; 12:16)

Forsaken by all (Matt. 26:56)

Misquoted (compare Matt. 26:61; 27:40 with John 2:19-22)

At Crucifixion
Indicted on false charges (compare Luke 23:1-2 with Matt. 22:15-21)
Illegally tried seven times (see *The Sanhedrin,* p. 866)
Mocked by
- Roman soldiers (Mark 15:16-20)
- Watching crowd (Luke 23:35)
- Chief priests (Mark 15:31)
- Two thieves (Matt. 27:44)

Tortured
- Slapped (John 18:22)
- Blindfolded (Luke 22:64)
- Spat upon (Matt. 26:67; 27:30)
- Beaten (Matt. 26:67)
- Flogged (Matt. 27:26)
- Pierced with thorns (Matt. 27:29)
- Struck on head (Matt. 27:30)

Crucified (Matt. 27)

❖ ❖ ❖

OLD TESTAMENT PROPHECIES ABOUT CHRIST

	PROPHESIED	FULFILLED
PRE-CRUCIFIXION		
Born of a woman	Gen. 3:15	Luke 2:7
Born of a virgin	Isa. 7:14	Matt. 1:22-23
Would inherit throne of David	2 Sam. 7:16; Ps. 132:11; I5 Isa. 9:6-7; 16:5; Jer. 23:5	Luke 1:31-32

	PROPHESIED	FULFILLED
His throne would be eternal	Dan. 2:44; 7:14, 27; Mic. 4:7	Luke 1:33
Would be called Immanuel	Isa. 7:14	Matt. 1:23
Would have a forerunner	Isa. 40:3-5; Mal. 3:1	Luke 1:76-78; 3:1-6
Born in Bethlehem	Mic. 5:2	Matt. 2:1, 5-6
Kings would bring gifts to him	Ps. 72:10; Isa. 60:3, 6, 9	Matt. 2:11
Would live in Egypt for a while	Hos. 11:1	Matt. 2:14-15
Children would be slaughtered in his birthplace	Jer. 31:15	Matt. 2:16-18
Would be called a Nazarene (branch = Hebrew *neser)*	Isa. 11:1	Matt. 2:23
A prophet like Moses	Deut. 18:15	John 1:45; 6:14
Zealous for God the Father	Pss. 69:9; 119:139	John 2:13-17
Filled with the Spirit	Ps. 45:7; Isa. 11:2; 61:1-2	Luke 4:18-21
Would heal many	Isa. 53:4-5	Matt. 8:16-17
Would deal gently with Gentiles	Isa. 9:1-2; 42:1-3	Matt. 4:13-16; 12:17-21
Would speak in parables	Isa. 6:9-10	Matt. 13:10-15
Rejected by his own	Ps. 69:8; Isa. 53:3	John 1:11; 7:5
Triumphal entry into Jerusalem	Zech. 9:9	Matt. 21:4-5
Children would praise him	Ps. 8:2	Matt. 21:16
The rejected cornerstone	Ps. 118:22-23	Matt. 21:42
Some would not believe his miracles	Isa. 53:1	John 12:37-38
CRUCIFIXION		
A man of sorrows	Isa. 53:3	Matt. 26:37-38
Betrayed by a friend for 30 pieces of silver	Pss. 41:9; 55:12-14; Zech. 11:12-13	Matt. 26:14-16, 21-25
His blood money would buy a potter's field	Jer. 18:1-4; 32:6-9; Zech. 11:12-13	Matt. 27:7-10
Forsaken by disciples	Zech. 13:7	Matt. 26:31, 56
Flogged, spat upon	Isa. 50:6; 53:5	Matt. 26:67; 27:26
Crucified with two thieves	Isa. 53:12	Mark 15:27-28
Would die for sins of humankind	Isa. 53:5	Matt. 27:50
Given sour wine to drink	Ps. 69:21	Matt. 27:34, 48
Hands and feet pierced	Ps. 22:16; Zech. 12:10	John 19:34, 37; 20:25-27
Garments parted and gambled for	Ps. 22:18	John 19:23-24
Surrounded and ridiculed by enemies	Ps. 22:7-8	Mark 15:29-32
Would thirst	Ps. 22:15	John 19:28

	PROPHESIED	FULFILLED
Would commit his spirit to the Father	Ps. 31:5	Luke 23:46
His bones would not be broken	Exod. 12:46; Num 9:12; Ps. 34:20	John 19:33-36
Publicly stared at while dying	Zech. 12:10	Matt. 27:39, 47
Buried with the rich	Isa. 53:9	Matt. 27:57-60
POST-CRUCIFIXION		
Would rise from the dead	Ps. 16:10	Matt. 28:2-7
Would ascend into heaven	Pss. 24:7-10; 68:18	Luke 24:51
Would one day return	*OT term the "day of the LORD" (used in Joel 2:30-31 and other passages) was applied by NT writers to the Second Coming (see 1 Thess. 5:2 and 2 Pet. 3:10)*	

❖ ❖ ❖

PREDICTIONS MADE BY CHRIST

Concerning himself

- Betrayal by Judas
  - ➤ Predicted twice in Galilee (Matt. 17:22; John 6:70-71)
  - ➤ Predicted in upper room (Matt. 26:21, 25)
- Denial by Peter
  - ➤ Predicted in upper room (John 13:37-38)
  - ➤ Predicted on way to Gethsemane (Matt. 26:34)
- Desertion of apostles (Matt. 26:31)
- Death
  - ➤ Fact of (Matt. 16:21; 17:12, 23; John 10:11, 15)
  - ➤ Place of (Matt. 20:18)
  - ➤ Method of (Matt. 20:18-19; John 3:14; 12:32)
- Resurrection
  - ➤ Fact of (John 10:17-18)
  - ➤ After three days (Matt. 12:40; 16:21; 17:23; 20:19; John 2:19)
- Post-resurrection appearance (Matt. 26:32)
- Ascension (John 7:33; 13:33; 14:28)
- Second Coming (Matt.16:27; 24:30; 26:63-64; John 14:3)

Concerning the Holy Spirit

- Fact of his ministry (Luke 24:49; John 7:37-39; 14:16)
- Its duration (John 14:16)
- Its location (John 14:17)
- Its nature regarding
  - ➤ The Savior (John 15:26; 16:14)
  - ➤ The saved (John 14:26; 16:13)
  - ➤ The sinner (John 16:8)

Concerning the church

- Its existence (Matt. 16:13-19)
- Its ministry (Matt. 28:19-20; Acts 1:8)
- Its field of service (Matt. 28:19; Acts 1:8)
- Its authority (Matt. 16:19; 18:18; John 20:23)
- Its persecution (Matt. 10:16-23, 34; John 15:18-21; 16:1-3, 33)
- Its heavenly reward (John 14:2-3)

Concerning the nation of Israel

- Its blindness (Matt. 23:37-39)
- Its rejection (Matt. 21:43)
- Its regathering (Matt. 24:31)
- Destruction of Jerusalem (Luke 19:43-44)
- Destruction of Temple (Mark 13:1-2)

Concerning the end times

- The last days (Matt. 24:32-34; Luke 17:26-30)
- The Great Tribulation (Matt. 24:21, 29; Luke 21:22-26)
- The coming of Elijah (Matt. 17:11)
- The Antichrist (Matt. 24:15; John 5:43)
- Resurrection of the dead (John 5:28-29)
- Future rewards (Matt. 10:41-42; 19:29)
- The Millennium (Matt. 8:11; 13:43; 19:28; 25:34)
- Great White Throne Judgment (Matt. 25:31-33)
- Heaven (John 14:2-3)
- Hell (Matt. 13:49-50; 18:8-9; John 5:28-29)

On other subjects

- Resurrection of Lazarus (John 11:11)
- Death of Peter (John 21:18-19)

THE SCRIPTURES AND THE SAVIOR

Both are the Word of God: The Scriptures are the written Word (Exod. 31:18) and the Savior is the Living Word (John 1:14)
Both are eternal: 1 Peter 1:23 and Hebrews 13:8
Both came from heaven: Psalm 119:89 and John 3:13
Both came to bless a lost world: Luke 11:28 and Acts 3:26
Both partook of the human and the divine: 2 Peter 1:20-21 and 1 Timothy 3:16
Both enjoyed angelic support: Acts 7:53; Galatians 3:19; Matthew 4:11; Luke 22:43
Both are faultless: Proverbs 30:5 and 1 John 3:5
Both are sources of life: Hebrews 4:12 and John 14:6
Both are sources of light: Psalm 119:130 and John 1:4, 9
Both are absolute truth: John 17:17 and John 14:6
Both provide food for the soul: Deuteronomy 8:3 and John 6:35
Both provide cleansing: John 15:3 and 1 John 1:9

Both produce fruit: Matthew 13:23 and John 15:5
Both give peace: Psalm 119:165 and John 14:27
Both are like a sword: Ephesians 6:17 and Revelation 19:15
Both are called wonderful: Psalm 119:18 and Isaiah 9:6
Both are called the power of God: Romans 1:16 and 1 Corinthians 1:24
Both successfully complete their assignments: Isaiah 55:10-11 and John 17:4; 19:30
Both must be received for salvation: John 8:31-32 and John 1:12
Both have been attacked by sinners: Jeremiah 36:27-28 and John 10:31
Both have been rejected by sinners: Mark 7:9 and Isaiah 53:3
Both will eventually judge all sinners: Romans 2:12; 3:19 and John 5:22

THE PEOPLE OF THE BIBLE

PATRIARCHS OF ISRAEL

Adam. First human being, participated in first sin (Gen. 1:26–5:5)

Noah. Builder of ship that preserved eight people during universal Flood (Gen. 5:29–10:32)

Abraham. Father of the nation of Israel (Gen. 11–25)

Isaac. Abraham's promised heir (Gen. 17:5–35:29)

Jacob. Father of 12 sons who founded 12 tribes of Israel (Gen. 25–37)

FATHERS OF ISRAEL'S 12 TRIBES

Reuben. First son of Jacob, saved Joseph from brothers' death plot (Gen. 29:32; 37:21-30)

Simeon. Second son of Jacob; with Levi, massacred Schechemites after rape of Dinah (Gen. 29:33; 34:25-26)

Levi. Third son of Jacob, ancestor of Israel's priests (Gen. 29:34; Num. 18:1-2)

Judah. Fourth son of Jacob, ancestor of Israel's kings and of Christ (Gen 29:35; 49:10; Matt. 1:2)

Dan. Fifth son of Jacob (Gen. 30:6)

Naphtali. Sixth son of Jacob (Gen. 30:8)

Gad. Seventh son of Jacob (Gen. 30:11)

Asher. Eighth son of Jacob (Gen. 30:13)

Issachar. Ninth son of Jacob (Gen. 30:18)

Zebulun. Tenth son of Jacob (Gen. 30:20)

Joseph. Eleventh and favorite son of Jacob, sold as slave by brothers, saved family from famine (Gen. 37–50)

Benjamin. Twelfth son of Jacob; Rachel died giving birth to him (Gen. 35:16-20)

JUDGES

Othniel. First judge, delivered Israel twice (Judg. 1; 3)

Shamgar. Delivered Israel by killing 600 Philistines with ox goad (Judg. 3:31)

Deborah. Prophetess, helped Barak defeat Canaanites (Judg. 4–5)

Gideon. Defeated Midianites with just 300 men (Judg. 7)
Tola. Ruled 23 years (Judg. 10:1-2)
Jair. Ruled 22 years (Judg. 10:3-5)
Jephthah. Military leader who became judge; his daughter died because of his rash vow (Judg. 10:6–12:7)
Ibzan. Ruled seven years (Judg. 12:8-9)
Elon. Ruled 10 years (Judg. 12:11)
Abdon. Ruled eight years (Judg. 12:13-14)
Samson. Last judge, notable for feats of strength and victories over Philistines (Judg. 13–16)

KINGS AND EMPERORS
(Dates sometimes overlap due to factors such as coregencies, gaps in genealogical record, or changes in calendars.)

Assyrian
Tiglath-pileser III (Pul) (745–727 B.C.). Carried Transjordanian Israelite tribes into captivity c. 733 (2 Kings 15:29; 16:7, 10)
Shalmaneser V (727–722). Son of Tiglath-pileser III; destroyed Samaria, imprisoned Hoshea (2 Kings 17:1-6; 18:9-11)
Sargon II (721–705). Another son of Tiglath-pileser III; finished sacking of Samaria (Isa. 20)
Sennacherib (705–681). Nephew of Shalmaneser. His armies were destroyed near Jerusalem by death angel in 701 (2 Kings 18–19)

Babylonian
Merodach-baladan (721–710 B.C.). Hezekiah showed his ambassadors the wealth of Judah (2 Kings 20:12-13; Isa. 39:1-2)
Nebuchadnezzar II (also called Nebuchadrezzar II) (605–562). Captured and destroyed Jerusalem; ruled while Daniel was in Babylon (2 Kings 25; Dan. 1–4)
Evil-merodach (562–560). Released the imprisoned Jehoiachin in Babylon (2 Kings 25:27)
Belshazzar (553–539). Regent in Babylon in place of his father, King Nabonidus; saw handwriting on wall (Dan. 5)

Egyptian
Unknown pharaoh. Abraham lied to him concerning Sarah (Gen. 12:14-20)
Unknown pharaoh. Made Joseph prime minister of Egypt (Gen. 41:37-45)
Thutmose I (c. 1525–1508 B.C.). Possibly king who "knew nothing about Joseph" and began persecuting Israelites (Exod. 1:8)
Thutmose III (1504–1450). Possibly king who tried to kill Moses (Exod. 2:15)
Amenhotep II (1450–1420). Possibly king during 10 plagues and Exodus (Exod. 5:1)
Unknown pharaoh. Gave Solomon his daughter as a wife (1 Kings 3:1)
Shishak (c. 945–915). Besieged Jerusalem in time of Rehoboam (1 Kings 14:25-26)
Neco II (610–595). Killed Josiah in battle, was then defeated by Babylonians at Carchemish in 605 (2 Kings 23:29-30; Jer. 46:1-2)

Hophra (589–570). Failed to save Jerusalem from Babylon in 586; deposed in 570, fulfilling Jeremiah's prophecy (Jer. 37:5-10; 44:30)

Herodian

Herod the Great (lived 73–4 B.C.). Ruthless Edomite king, given control of Judea by Rome; ruled at time of Christ's birth; killed newborns in effort to kill Jesus (Matt. 2:1-20)

Herod Archelaus. Oldest son of Herod the Great, ruled after him till A.D. 6. When Joseph, returning from Egypt, heard that Archelaus had replaced his father in Judea, he took Mary and Jesus to Galilee instead (Matt. 2:22)

Herod Philip. Son of Herod the Great; first husband of Herodias, who left him for Antipas, his half brother (Matt. 14:3)

Herod Antipas (lived 21 B.C.–A.D. 39). Youngest son of Herod the Great, took over from Archelaus; had John the Baptist killed (Matt. 14:1-11)

Herod Agrippa I (lived 10 B.C.–A.D. 44). Grandson of Herod the Great, killer of apostle James. Angel struck him dead for accepting worship (Acts 12)

Herod Agrippa II (lived A.D. 27–c. 100). Great-grandson of Herod the Great; king Paul spoke to about becoming a Christian (Acts 25:13–26:32)

Persian and Mede

Cyrus the Great (559–530 B.C.). Issued return decree for Jews (2 Chron. 36:22-23; Ezra 1; Isa. 44:28)

Darius the Mede (539?). Identity uncertain; possibly ally of Cyrus, possibly another name for Cyrus himself (Dan. 6)

Darius the Great (521–486). Son of Cyrus the Great; allowed Temple work to continue (Ezra 6)

Xerxes (Ahasuerus) (486–465). Son of Darius the Great; husband of Esther (Esther 1)

Artaxerxes (465–424). Son of Xerxes; befriended both Ezra and Nehemiah (Ezra 7:1; Neh. 2:1)

Darius III (336–331). His armies destroyed by Alexander the Great (Dan. 8)

Roman

Augustus Caesar (31 B.C.–A.D. 14). Emperor when Jesus was born (Luke 2:1)

Tiberius Caesar (A.D. 14–37 or 42). Emperor during Jesus' earthly ministry (Luke 3:1; 20:22-25)

Claudius Caesar (41–54). Emperor during Paul's ministry (Acts 11:28; 18:2)

Nero Caesar (54–68). Emperor Paul appealed to, who later probably ordered Paul's and Peter's executions (Acts 25:10-12)

Israel: United Kingdom

Saul (1051–1011 B.C.). Israel's first king; later rejected by God (1 Sam. 9–31)

David (1011–971). Saul's successor; Israel's best-loved king (1 Sam. 16—1 Kings 2)

Solomon (971–931). Son of David and Bathsheba; Israel's wisest and richest king (1 Kings 1–11)

Israel: Divided Kingdom, Northern ("Israel")

Jeroboam (931–909 B.C.). Rebelled against Solomon, built rival worship centers at Dan and Bethel (1 Kings 11:26–14:20)

Nadab (911–909). Son of Jeroboam, killed by Baasha (1 Kings 15:25-28)

Baasha (909–886). Built wall to cut off trade with Jerusalem (1 Kings 15:27–16:7)

Elah (886–885). Son of Baasha, killed by Zimri while drunk (1 Kings 16:6-14)

Zimri (885). Committed suicide after ruling for seven days (1 Kings 16:15-20)

Omri (885–873). Army commander, made king after Zimri's death, established Samaria as northern capital (1 Kings 16:15-28)

Ahab (874–853). Son of Omri, wicked husband of Jezebel, condemned by Elijah and killed in battle (1 Kings 16:28–22:40)

Ahaziah (853–852). Wicked oldest son of Ahab (1 Kings 22:40—2 Kings 1:18)

Joram (Jehoram) (852–841). Youngest son of Ahab, sent Naaman to Elisha to be healed (2 Kings 3:1–9:26)

Jehu (841–814). Army commander, known for his chariot driving and extermination of Ahab's dynasty (2 Kings 9:1–10:36)

Jehoahaz (814–798). Jehu's son, saw his army almost wiped out by Syrians (2 Kings 13:1-9)

Jehoash (Joash) (798–782). Jehoahaz's son, waged successful war against Judah, visited Elisha at his deathbed (2 Kings 13:10–14:16)

Jeroboam II (794–753). Jehoash's son, reigned during time of Jonah (2 Kings 14:23-29)

Zechariah (753–752). Jeroboam II's son, last of Jehu's dynasty, killed by Shallum (2 Kings 14:29–15:12)

Shallum (752). Reigned one month, killed by Menahem (2 Kings 15:10-15)

Menahem (752–742). One of most brutal northern kings (2 Kings 15:14-22)

Pekahiah (742–740). Son of Menahem, killed by Pekah, his army commander (2 Kings 15:22-26)

Pekah (740–732). Killed by Hoshea (2 Kings 15:27-31)

Hoshea (732–722). Northern kingdom's last king, dethroned and imprisoned by Assyrians (2 Kings 15:30; 17:1-6)

Israel: Divided Kingdom, Southern ("Judah")

Rehoboam (931–913 B.C.). Solomon's son, whose stupidity and arrogance sparked civil war (1 Kings 11:43–12:24; 14:21-31)

Abijam (Abijah) (913–911). Rehoboam's son, helped by God to defeat Jeroboam in battle (1 Kings 14:31–15:8)

Asa (911–870). Abijam's son, Judah's first godly king (1 Kings 15:8-24)

Jehoshaphat (873–848). Asa's son, godly king; built merchant fleet, made alliance with Ahab (1 Kings 22:41-50; 2 Chron. 18:1)

Jehoram (853–841). Jehoshaphat's son; married Athaliah, wicked daughter of Ahab and Jezebel (2 Kings 8:16-24)

Ahaziah (841). Son of Jehoram and Athaliah, killed by Jehu (2 Kings 8:24–9:29)

Athaliah (queen) (841–835). Assumed throne on death of her son Ahaziah; slaughtered all his children (her own grandchildren!) except for Joash, who was hidden from her (2 Kings 11:1-20)

Joash (835–796). Son of Ahaziah, sole heir of David to escape Athaliah's purge, was later murdered, but not before having a son to continue Davidic line (2 Kings 11:1–12:21)

Amaziah (796–767). Son of Joash, defeated by northern king Jehoash; killed in conspiracy (2 Kings 14:1-20)

Uzziah (Azariah) (790–740). Son of Amaziah, struck with leprosy for allowing pagan worship to continue (2 Kings 15:1-7)

Jotham (750–731). Son of Uzziah, built Temple's upper gate and fortified Jerusalem (2 Kings 15:32-38)

Ahaz (735–715). Son of Jotham, godless king, sacrificed son to pagan god (2 Kings 16)

Hezekiah (728–686). Son of Ahaz; reformer, friend of Isaiah; king when Jerusalem was saved by death angel (2 Kings 18–20)

Manasseh (695–642). Son of Hezekiah; Judah's worst king, though later converted (2 Kings 21:1-18; 2 Chron. 33:11-16)

Amon (642–640). Son of Manasseh, executed by his own household servants (2 Kings 21:19-26)

Josiah (640–609). Son of Amon, ruler when Law found in Temple; leader of national reform, slain in battle against Egypt (2 Kings 22:1–23:30)

Jehoahaz (609). Son of Josiah, ruler after his death in battle; deposed after only 90 days by Pharaoh Neco; taken to Egypt, where he died (2 Kings 23:31-33)

Jehoiakim (609–597). Josiah's son; persecuted Jeremiah and burned his scroll; carried to Babylon by Nebuchadnezzar (2 Kings 23:34–24:5; Jer. 36)

Jehoiachin (597). Jehoiakim's son; incurred special judgment from God; carried to Babylon by Nebuchadnezzar (2 Kings 24:6-16)

Zedekiah (597–586). Uncle of Jehoiachin; blinded and taken into exile in Babylon while Jerusalem and Temple were destroyed (2 Kings 24:17–25:30)

Other Kings

Abimelech. Philistine king to whom Abraham lied about Sarah (Gen. 20–21)

Abimelech. Philistine king to whom Isaac lied about Rebekah (Gen. 26)

Achish. Philistine king with whom David twice took refuge, in whose presence David feigned madness (1 Sam. 21; 27–29)

Adoni-zedek. King of Jerusalem who formed Canaanite alliance to fight Joshua (Josh. 10)

Agag. King of Amalek, defeated but spared by Saul, leading to Saul's rejection as king (1 Sam. 15)

Balak. King of Moab who summoned Balaam to curse Israelites (Num. 22–24)

Ben-hadad II. King of Aram (Syria), twice defeated by Ahab (1 Kings 20)

Bera. King of Sodom, tried to bribe Abraham (Gen. 14:2, 21-24)

Hazael (843–798). Aramean (Syrian) king, led several campaigns against Israel (1 Kings 19:15-18; 2 Kings 8–13)

Hiram (986–935). King of Tyre, furnished wood for Temple (1 Kings 5)

Jabin. King of Hazor, defeated by Joshua at Merom (Josh. 11:1-15)

Jabin. King of Hazor, defeated by Israelites in time of Deborah and Barak (Judg. 4)

Kedorlaomer. King of Elam, leader of alliance that captured Sodom while Lot lived there (Gen. 14:1-17)

Melchizedek. King of Salem, blessed Abraham, seen as type or even manifestation of Christ (Gen. 14:18-20; Heb. 5:6-10; 7:1-22)

Mesha. Moabite king who sacrificed his own son in futile effort to win battle (2 Kings 3)

Nahash. Ammonite king defeated by Saul (1 Sam. 11)

Og. Giant king of Bashan (Deut. 3:11; Josh. 13:12), whose defeat by Moses was remembered for centuries to come (Num. 21; Deut. 3; Josh 13; Ps. 135:10-11; 136:18, 20)

Rezin (c. 738). King of Aram (Syria), tried to form alliance with Judah against Assyria, then joined with Israel to invade Judah (2 Kings 15:37–16:9)

Sihon. Amorite king who refused passage to Israelites on their way to Canaan and was defeated by them (Num. 21:26-30)

Queens

Athaliah. (reigning queen, listed with kings of Judah, above)

Babylonian queen mother. Advised Belshazzar to call for Daniel (Dan. 5:10-12)

Bathsheba. Originally wife of Uriah, then David's wife and mother of Solomon (2 Sam. 11–12)

Bernice. Sister and wife of Herod Agrippa II (Acts 25:13, 23; 26:30)

Candace. Ethiopian queen who allowed her servant to visit Judea, where he was converted by Philip (Acts 8:27)

Esther. Jewish queen of Persia; saved Jews from extermination (Esther 2–10)

Herodias. Wife of Herod Philip, then of Herod Antipas; plotted John the Baptist's death (Matt. 14:1-12)

Jezebel. Wicked wife of Ahab (1 Kings 16:31—2 Kings 9:37)

Maachah. Idol-worshiping grandmother of King Asa (1 Kings 15:10; 2 Chron. 15:16)

Michal. Daughter of Saul; David's first wife, stricken barren for ridiculing his devotion (1 Sam. 18:20-29; 2 Sam. 6:20-23)

Nehushta. Mother of Jehoiachin, taken to Babylon (2 Kings 24:8-16)

Queen of Sheba. African or Arabian queen who visited Solomon (1 Kings 10:1-13)

Rizpah. Saul's wife; tried to protect bodies of her two sons and five of Saul's grandsons till David had them buried (2 Sam. 21:8-14)

Vashti. Persian queen deposed by King Xerxes (Esther 1)

NONWRITING PROPHETS

(For writing prophets, see *Bible Authors*)

Old Testament

Ahijah. Predicted Jeroboam would rule over 10 tribes after Israel's civil war (1 Kings 11:29-39)

Azariah. Prophesied to King Asa, as did his father, Oded (2 Chron. 15:1-7)

Elijah. Opposed Baal worship in time of Ahab and Jezebel (1 Kings 17—2 Kings 2)

Elisha. Successor to Elijah who performed many miracles and predicted salvation of Samaria (2 Kings 2–13)

Enoch. Prophesied before Flood concerning judgment (Gen. 5:21-24; Jude 1:14-15)

Gad. Predicted nature of judgment on David for taking census of Israel (1 Sam. 22:5; 2 Sam. 24:11-19)

Hanani. Thrown into prison by King Asa for rebuking his sin (2 Chron. 16:7-10)

Iddo. Prophesied against Jeroboam (2 Chron. 9:29; 12:15; 13:22)
Jacob. Prophesied concerning his 12 sons' descendants (Gen. 48–49)
Jehu. Rebuked Baasha and Jehoshaphat (1 Kings 16:1-13; 2 Chron. 19:1-3)
Micaiah. Predicted Ahab's death in battle with Aram (Syria) (1 Kings 22:1-28)
Nathan. Rebuked David for adultery and murder (2 Sam. 7, 12; 1 Kings 1)
Noah. Prophesied about sons' descendants (Gen. 9:24-27)
Oded. Prophesied in days of King Ahaz (2 Chron. 28:9-11)
Shemaiah. Warned King Rehoboam against war with Jeroboam (1 Kings 12:22-24)
Unnamed prophet. Explained to Israel the reason for their sufferings (Judg. 6:7-10)
Unnamed prophet. Predicted God would deliver Syrians to Ahab (1 Kings 20:13-43)
Unnamed prophet. Predicted death of Hophni and Phinehas (1 Sam. 2:27-36)
Unnamed man of God. Predicted name and reforms of King Josiah 315 years before his birth, was himself later killed by a lion for his disobedience (1 Kings 13:1-24)
Unnamed man of God. Told King Amaziah he need not depend on hired troops from northern kingdom to help him defeat Edomites (2 Chron. 25:7-16)
Uriah. Prophesied against Judah, martyred by Jehoiakim (Jer. 26:20-23)
Zechariah. Ministered to King Uzziah (2 Chron. 26:5)

New Testament
Agabus. Predicted famine and Paul's imprisonment (Acts 11:28; 21:10-11)
John the Baptist. Prophesied concerning Christ and final judgment (Matt. 3:1-12; 11:2-10)
Judas and Silas. Exhorted believers in days of Jerusalem Council (Acts 15:22, 32)
Simeon. Prophesied concerning Christ (Luke 2:25-35)
Tribulation prophets ("witnesses"). Will prophesy against Antichrist (Rev. 11:3-12)
Zechariah. Prophesied concerning his son John the Baptist (Luke 1:67-79)

❖ ❖ ❖

PROPHETESSES

Old Testament
Deborah. Also one of Israel's judges, predicted Barak's victory over Canaanites (Judg. 4:4-9)
Huldah. Prophesied following rediscovery of Law during Josiah's reign (2 Chron. 34:22-28)
Isaiah's wife. Called a prophetess, bore Isaiah two sons whose names were prophetic (Isa. 7:3; 8:3-4)
Miriam. Moses' sister, called a prophetess, led Israelite women in victory song (Exod. 15:20-21)

New Testament
Anna. Elderly widow, present at dedication of Jesus in Temple (Luke 2:36-38)
Philip's four daughters. Paul met them in Caesarea (Acts 21:8-9)

❖ ❖ ❖

FALSE PROPHETS AND PROPHETESSES

Old Testament
Ahab. Jeremiah predicted his death (Jer. 29:21)
Balaam. Hired by Balak, king of Moab, to curse Israel (Num. 22–24)

Hananiah. Tried to refute Jeremiah's 70-year prophecy, saying Babylonian captivity would last only 2 years (Jer. 28)
Noadiah. Prophesied in time of Nehemiah (Neh. 6:14)
Shemaiah. Jeremiah predicted his descendants would all die (Jer. 29:24-32)
Unnamed old prophet. His lying words to another prophet cost that other prophet his life (1 Kings 13:11-25)
Zedekiah. Jeremiah predicted his death (Jer. 29:21)
Zedekiah. Wrongly predicted Ahab would defeat Aram (Syria) (1 Kings 22:11-28)

New Testament
Elymas (Bar-Jesus). Sorcerer, confronted Paul on Cyprus (Acts 13:6-12)
False prophet during Tribulation. Will work with the Antichrist (Rev. 16:13; 19:20; 20:10)
Jezebel. False teacher in church at Thyatira (Rev. 2:20)

PRIESTS
Old Testament
Aaron. Older brother of Moses, Israel's first high priest (Exod. 4:14—Deut. 10:6; Heb. 7:11)
Abiathar. Only son of Ahimelech to escape bloodbath at Nob (1 Sam. 22:20-23)
Ahimelech. Head of priestly compound at Nob, killed by Saul along with 85 other priests for befriending David (1 Sam. 21–22)
Ahimelech. Son of Abiathar, grandson of Ahimelech (above), key advisor to David (2 Sam. 8:17)
Amariah. High priest in days of Jehoshaphat (2 Chron. 19:11)
Amaziah. Ungodly priest of Bethel, confronted Amos (Amos 7:10-17)
Azariah. High priest; confronted King Uzziah when he foolishly tried to assume priestly duties (2 Chron. 26:16-20)
Eleazar and Ithamar. Godly sons of Aaron; Eleazar became Israel's second high priest (Lev. 10:6, 16-20; Num. 20:26-28; 26–27)
Eli. Descendant of Ithamar, Samuel's mentor (1 Sam. 1–4)
Eliashib. High priest during days of Nehemiah (Neh. 3:1; 13:4-5)
Elishama and Jehoram. Teaching priests in days of Jehoshaphat (2 Chron. 17:7-9)
Ezra. Scribe, teacher, priest during rebuilding of Jerusalem's walls (Ezra 7, 10; Neh. 8, 12)
Hilkiah. High priest in time of King Josiah, found forgotten Book of Law (2 Kings 22–23)
Hophni and Phinehas. Wicked sons of Eli, slain by God (1 Sam. 2:12-34; 4:11)
Jahaziel. Assured Jehoshaphat he would be delivered from an enemy's threat (2 Chron. 20:14-19)
Jehoiada. High priest who, with wife, Jehosheba, saved Joash from Athaliah's purge (2 Kings 11–12)
Jeshua. Judah's first high priest following Babylonian captivity (Hag. 1:1; Zech. 3)
Nadab and Abihu. Wicked sons of Aaron, slain by God for offering strange fire (Lev. 10:1-2)
Pashhur. False priest; persecuted Jeremiah (Jer. 20:1-6)
Phinehas. Son of Eleazar, Israel's third high priest (Num. 25:7-13; 31:1-6)

Shelemiah. In charge of storehouses in Nehemiah's day (Neh. 13:13)
Uriah. Built foreign altar for King Ahaz (2 Kings 16:10-16)
Zadok. High priest in days of David and Solomon from whom Sadducees took their name (2 Sam. 15; 1 Kings 1; 2:35; 4:2-4)

New Testament
Ananias. President of Sanhedrin when Paul was brought before it (Acts 23:2; Acts 24:1)
Annas. Wicked high priest during time of Christ (Luke 3:2; John 18:13; Acts 4:6)
Caiaphas. Wicked high priest, son-in-law of Annas (Matt. 26:3; Luke 3:2; John 11:47-53; 18:13-14)
Sceva. Pretending Jewish priest in Ephesus whose seven sons tried to duplicate Paul's ministry (Acts 19:14)
Zechariah. Father of John the Baptist (Luke 1:5-23, 59-64)

APOSTLES

For a list of the 12 apostles who served Christ during his earthly ministry, see Matthew 10:1-4. Two others were named apostles after Christ's ascension: Matthias, to replace Judas; and Paul, to take the gospel to the Gentiles.
Andrew. Brother of Peter, fisherman from Bethsaida in Galilee (John 1:44); brought Peter to Christ (John 1:40-42)
James the son of Alphaeus. Also called James the less (Mark 15:40, KJV) or James the younger (NLT)
James the son of Zebedee. Brother of John, fishing partner of Peter and Andrew (Matt. 4:21), nicknamed "Son of Thunder" by Christ (Mark 3:17); first apostle to be martyred (Acts 12:1-2)
John. Brother of James (son of Zebedee) and a fisherman (Matt. 4:21), also called "Son of Thunder" (Mark 3:17); most prominent apostle, member of "key three" (Matt. 17:1-4), called "the disciple whom Jesus loved" (John 13:23, NIV); only apostle present at cross (John 19:26); early church leader in Jerusalem (Gal. 2:9); wrote Gospel, three letters, and Revelation
Judas Iscariot. Treasurer for apostles (John 12:6), heartless thief (John 12:4-6), betrayed Christ (Matt. 26:15-16; 26:49; John 18:2-5), returned his blood money in great remorse (Matt. 27:3-4), and hanged himself (Matt. 27:5)
Matthew (Levi). Tax collector (Luke 5:27), responded to Christ after a simple "follow me" invitation (Matt. 9:9), hosted large feast (Luke 5:27-29), wrote Gospel bearing his name
Matthias. Chosen by lot to replace Judas (Acts 1:23-26)
Nathanael (Bartholomew). Witnessed to by Philip, under a fig tree (John 1:45-46), first to call Christ the Son of God and King of Israel (John 1:49)
Paul. Former persecutor of Christians (Acts 7:58; 8:1-3; 9:1-2), converted (Acts 9:3-19), carried gospel throughout Gentile world (Acts 9:15–28:31), wrote at least 13 NT books
Peter (Simon, Cephas). Most outspoken of original 12; brother of Andrew, who brought him to Christ (John 1:41-42); made memorable public confessions concerning Christ's deity (John 6:68-69; Matt. 16:16), denied Christ three times

(John 18:15-18, 25-27); main speaker at Pentecost (Acts 2), evangelist and church leader (Acts 3–12; 15), wrote two NT letters

Philip. Brought Nathanael to Christ (John 1:43-46), was approached by Greeks wanting to see Jesus (John 12:20-22), asked Christ to "show us the Father" (John 14:8-9)

Simon the Canaanite (the Zealot). Often associated with the Zealots, a right-wing political party (Matt. 10:4)

Thaddaeus (Lebbaeus, Judas). Brother of James the less, asked Christ how he would manifest himself (John 14:22)

Thomas. Absent during Christ's first resurrection appearance (John 20:24), doubted resurrection till saw Christ in person (John 20:25-28)

❖ ❖ ❖

BIBLE AUTHORS

More than 40 people were inspired by God to write various portions of the Bible. Some wrote multiple books, others wrote as little as a single chapter. The books or portions each one authored are listed in italics at the end of the entry.

Old Testament

Agur. Biographical details unknown. *Proverbs 30*

Amos. Shepherd (Amos 1:1; 7:14-15) who became a prophet and evangelist. *Amos*

Asaph. Chief of musicians appointed by David to oversee song service in tabernacle (1 Chron. 6:39; 16:4-5; Neh. 12:46). *Psalms 50, 73–83 (Some of these psalms were probably written by his descendant and namesake.)*

Daniel. Taken captive to Babylon in 605 B.C. (2 Chron. 36:6-7; Dan. 1:1-6), served in courts of Nebuchadnezzar (Dan. 2:48) and Darius (Dan. 6:1-3). *Daniel*

David. Israel's second and greatest king (2 Sam. 5:1-5) *Psalms 3–9, 11–32, 34–41, 51–65, 68–70, 86, 101, 103, 108–110, 122, 124, 131, 133, 138–145*

Ethan. Musician in time of Solomon, known for his wisdom (1 Kings 4:31; 1 Chron. 15:19). *Psalm 89*

Ezekiel. Taken captive to Babylon in 597, ministered as a prophet to his fellow captives. *Ezekiel*

Ezra. Bible teacher, priest, scribe (Ezra 7:1-6, 10) who led the second of three returns of Jews from Persia to Jerusalem (Ezra 7:27-28). *Ezra; compiled Nehemiah from Nehemiah's memoirs; according to tradition he may have compiled 1, 2 Chronicles*

Gad and Nathan. Prophets who ministered to David (1 Sam. 22:5; 2 Sam. 7:2-3; 12:1-14; 24:11-19). Each would later write a book about David's life, and 1 Chronicles 29:29 suggests that their books may have been combined with the memoirs of Samuel to form *1, 2 Samuel.*

Habakkuk. Prophet of Judah. *Habakkuk*

Haggai. Led his people in completion of second Temple (Hag. 1:2-8). *Haggai*

Heman. Samuel's grandson, one of three key Levitical musicians in time of David (1 Chron. 6:31-33). *Psalm 88*

Hezekiah. King of Judah, saw Jerusalem saved by death angel (2 Kings 19:35); was given an additional 15 years to live (2 Kings 20:1-11). *Suggested by some as author of Psalms 120–121, 123, 125–126, 128–130, 132, 134*

Hosea. Prophet in northern kingdom during 40 years just before its fall in 722. *Hosea*

Isaiah. Prophet of Judah, called "prince of prophets." *Isaiah*

Jeremiah. Prophet of Judah, known as the weeping prophet (Jer. 9:1). *Jeremiah; Lamentations; some say he also wrote 1, 2 Kings*

Joel. Biographical details unknown. *Joel*

Jonah. Predicted restoration of part of Israel under Jeroboam II (2 Kings 14:25); later prophesied in Nineveh. *Jonah*

Joshua. Moses' successor, led Israel into Promised Land (Josh. 1–4). *Joshua*

Sons of Korah. Korah, with Dathan and Abiram, was killed by God for his rebellion against Moses (Num. 16:1-2, 31-33; 26:10-11), but some of his descendants became spiritual leaders. *Psalms 42, 44–49, 84–85, 87–88*

Lemuel. Some believe Lemuel (Prov. 31:1) was another name for Solomon; others think he could have been Hezekiah or an Ishmaelite. *Proverbs 31:1-9*

Malachi. Biographical details unknown. *Malachi*

Micah. Prophet of Judah (Jer. 26:16-19; Mic. 3:12). *Micah*

Moses. Liberator (Exod. 5–14) and lawgiver (Exod. 20—Deut. 34) of Israel. *Genesis; Exodus; Leviticus; Numbers; Deuteronomy; Psalm 90*

Nahum. Biographical details unknown. *Nahum*

Nehemiah. Led final of three Jewish returns from Persia to Jerusalem (Neh. 2:5), rebuilt its walls (Neh. 6:15). *The book of Nehemiah was based on his memoirs.*

Obadiah. Biographical details unknown. *Obadiah*

Samuel. Levite prophet (Acts 13:20) who anointed both Saul and David as king over Israel (1 Sam. 9:27–10:1; 16:13). *1 Samuel 1–24 was probably compiled from his memoirs, and Judges may have been as well.*

Solomon. Son of David and Bathsheba, Israel's third king, history's wisest man (1 Kings 3:5-12). *Proverbs 1–29; Psalms 72, 127; Song of Songs; Ecclesiastes*

Zechariah. Contemporary of Haggai. *Zechariah*

Zephaniah. Prophet of Judah. *Zephaniah*

New Testament

James. Half brother of Jesus (Matt. 13:55), an unbeliever (John 7:5) till after Resurrection (1 Cor. 15:7); pastored church at Jerusalem (Acts 15:13-21; 21:17-18). *James*

John. Disciple "whom Jesus loved" (John 13:23, NIV). *John; 1, 2, 3 John; Revelation*

Jude (Judas). Brother of James, half brother of Jesus (Matt. 13:55) *Jude*

Luke. Gentile physician (Col. 4:14), Paul's traveling companion (2 Tim. 4:11). *Luke; Acts*

Mark. Paul's missionary colleague (Acts 12:12; 13:13; 2 Tim. 4:11). *Mark*

Matthew. Tax collector who became an apostle (Matt. 10:3; Luke 5:27-29). *Matthew*

Paul. Enemy of Christians who, following his conversion (Acts 9:3-9), became apostle and missionary. Wrote nearly half of NT books. *Romans; 1, 2 Corinthians; Galatians; Ephesians; Philippians; Colossians; 1, 2 Thessalonians; 1, 2 Timothy; Titus; Philemon*

Paul, Apollos, Luke. Possible authors of *Hebrews.*

Peter. Fisherman who became unofficial spokesman for the 12 apostles. *1, 2 Peter*

❖ ❖ ❖

OTHER NOTEWORTHY PEOPLE OF THE BIBLE

Old Testament Men

Abednego. Friend of Daniel, saved from fiery furnace (Dan. 3)
Abel. Son of Adam, world's first martyr (Gen. 4:1-8)
Abimelech. Murderous son of Gideon (Judg. 8–9)
Abinadab. Israelite in whose house Ark of the Covenant was kept for 20 years after being retrieved from Philistines (1 Sam. 6:19–7:2)
Abiram. Joined Korah's rebellion against Moses and Aaron (Num. 16)
Abishai. David's nephew and soldier in army, won key battles (1 Sam. 26:5-12; 2 Sam. 10:9-19; 21:16-17)
Abner. Relative of Saul, commander of army, fought against David to preserve Saul's dynasty after his death (1 Sam. 14:47-52; 26; 2 Sam. 2–4)
Absalom. Son of David, tried to overthrow him (2 Sam. 13–19)
Achan. His disobedience caused Israelite defeat at Ai (Josh. 7)
Adonijah. Son of David, tried to steal throne from Solomon (1 Kings 1–2)
Ahithophel. David's counselor, betrayed him and joined Absalom's rebellion (2 Sam. 15–17)
Amasa. David's nephew, commanded rebel army of Absalom (2 Sam. 17–20)
Amnon. David's son, raped his half sister Tamar (2 Sam. 13)
Baruch. Jeremiah's scribe (Jer. 36; 45)
Barzillai. Gileadite, befriended David during Absalom's revolt (2 Sam. 17; 19)
Bezalel. Chief designer of tabernacle (Exod. 31:2; 35:30; 36:1-2)
Bildad. Friend and advisor to Job (Job 8; 18; 25)
Boaz. Husband of Ruth, great-grandfather of David (Ruth 2–4)
Cain. Son of Adam and Eve, history's first murderer (Gen. 4:1-17)
Caleb. One of two spies who brought good report at Kadesh-barnea (Num. 13–14)
Canaan. Son of Ham, cursed for Ham's sin against Noah (Gen. 9:18-27)
Dathan. Joined Korah's rebellion against Moses and Aaron (Num. 16)
Doeg. Saul's chief herdsman, murdered 85 priests (1 Sam. 22)
Ehud. Israelite hero, used his left-handedness to kill a Moabite king (Judg. 3)
Eliakim. Hezekiah's steward, negotiated with Sennacherib's men (2 Kings 18:18–19:7)
Eliezer. Abraham's servant, originally designated to be his heir (Gen. 15:2)
Elihu. Friend and advisor to Job (Job 32–37)
Eliphaz. Friend and advisor to Job (Job 4–5; 15; 22)
Ephraim. Younger son of Moses, received Jacob's blessing instead of the older Manasseh (Gen. 48:12-20)
Er. Son of Judah, husband of Tamar, killed by God because of his wickedness (Gen. 38:3-7)
Esau. Son of Isaac, sold birthright to Jacob (Gen. 25–28; 32–36)
Gedaliah. Israelite appointed by Nebuchadnezzar to govern Judah after he had taken most Israelites captive to Babylon (2 Kings 25:22-25)
Gehazi. Servant of Elisha (2 Kings 4–5; 8:1-6)
Goliath. Philistine giant killed by David (1 Sam. 17)
Ham. Son of Noah (Gen. 5; 9)

Haman. Highest official under Persian king Xerxes, attempted genocide of Jewish exiles (Esther 3–7)

Hur. Assistant to Moses and Aaron, helped uphold Moses' arms during battle (Exod. 17:8-14; 24:14)

Hushai. Friend of David, persuaded Absalom not to take Ahithophel's advice (2 Sam. 15:32–17:16)

Ishbosheth. Saul's son, took up fight against David when Saul died (2 Sam. 2–4)

Ishmael. Son of Abraham and Hagar (Gen. 16–17; 25)

Japheth. Son of Noah (Gen. 5:32)

Jeduthun. One of worship leaders in Temple (1 Chron. 16; 25)

Jehudi. Royal official who read Jeremiah's scroll to King Jehoiakim (Jer. 36)

Jesse. Father of David (1 Sam. 16–17)

Jethro. Father-in-law of Moses, offered timely advice (Exod. 3:1; 4:18; 18)

Joab. David's nephew, commander of army (2 Sam. 2–3; 10–14; 18–24; 1 Kings 1–2; 11:15-21)

Johanan. Judean official, fled to Egypt after fall of Jerusalem, taking Jeremiah with him (2 Kings 25:23; Jer. 40–43)

Jonadab. David's nephew, plotted with David's son Amnon against Tamar and Absalom (2 Sam. 13)

Jonathan. Son of Saul, friend of David (1 Sam. 13–23; 31)

Korah. Levite, led rebellion against Moses and Aaron (Num. 16)

Laban. Jacob's father-in-law (Gen. 29–31)

Lamech. Descendant of Cain, bragged about vengeance killing (Gen. 4:18-24)

Lamech. Father of Noah (Gen. 5:25-31)

Lot. Abraham's nephew, saved from Sodom (Gen. 11–14; 19)

Maher-shalal-hash-baz. Son of Isaiah, whose name was prophetic (Isa. 8:1-4)

Manasseh. Elder son of Moses, whose blessing Jacob gave to his younger brother, Ephraim (Gen. 48:12-20)

Manoah. Father of Samson (Judg. 13)

Mephibosheth. Crippled grandson of Saul, befriended by David (2 Sam. 4:4; 9)

Meshach. Friend of Daniel, saved from fiery furnace (Dan. 3)

Methuselah. History's oldest person (Gen. 5:25-27)

Moab. Son of Lot by his own daughter, father of Moabites (Gen. 19:37)

Mordecai. Relative and guardian of Esther (Esther)

Naaman. Leper healed by Elisha (2 Kings 5)

Nabal. Saved from David's wrath by his wife, Abigail, who after Nabal's death became David's wife (1 Sam. 25)

Naboth. Jezreelite murdered by Jezebel for refusing to sell his vineyard (1 Kings 21)

Nimrod. Grandson of Ham, builder of cities (Gen. 10:8-12)

Onan. Son of Judah, killed by God for refusing to father a child with Tamar for his dead brother Er (Gen. 38:1-10)

Potiphar. Captain of Pharaoh's guard; bought Joseph from Midianites, later imprisoned Joseph on his wife's false charges (Gen. 37:36; 39:1-20)

Sanballat. Governor of Samaria, tried to prevent Nehemiah's rebuilding of Jerusalem's walls (Neh. 2; 4)

Seth. Third son of Adam and Eve (Gen. 4:25–5:8)

Shadrach. Friend of Daniel, saved from fiery furnace (Dan. 3)

Shear-jashub. Son of Isaiah, whose name was prophetic (Isa. 7:1-9)

Sheba. Led rebellion against David after Absalom's rebellion failed (2 Sam. 20)

Shechem. Canaanite whose rape of Dinah, daughter of Jacob, led to deaths of himself and every man in his city (Gen. 34)

Shem. Son of Noah, ancestor of Israelites (Gen. 5:32)

Shimei. Taunted David during Absalom's rebellion (2 Sam. 16; 19)

Sisera. Commander of army of Hazor, defeated by Barak, killed by Jael (Judg. 4)

Tobiah. Israelite who joined Sanballat in opposition to Nehemiah's rebuilding of Jerusalem's walls (Neh. 2; 4)

Uriah. Husband of Bathsheba, murdered by David (2 Sam. 11)

Uzzah. Son of Abinadab, killed when he touched Ark of the Covenant to keep it from falling (2 Sam. 6:3-7)

Zerubbabel. Grandson of King Jehoiachin, led first return of Jews from exile back to Jerusalem, became governor of Judah (Ezra)

Zophar. Friend and advisor to Job (Job 11; 20)

Old Testament Women

Abigail. David's second wife (1 Sam. 25)

Abishag. Shunammite woman, David's nurse in his old age (1 Kings 1:1-4)

Bilhah. Handmaiden of Rachel, given to Jacob for childbearing, bore two sons (Gen. 30:3-8)

Delilah. Betrayed Samson (Judg. 16:4-20)

Dinah. Daughter of Jacob, raped by Shechem (Gen. 34)

Eve. First woman, wife of Adam, participated in first sin (Gen. 2:19–4:25)

Gomer. Unfaithful wife of Hosea; used as example of Israel's unfaithfulness to God (Hos. 1–3)

Hagar. Egyptian handmaid of Sarah, given to Abraham for childbearing, bore Ishmael (Gen. 16; 21)

Hannah. Mother of Samuel (1 Sam. 1–2)

Jael. Killed Sisera with tent peg (Judg. 4)

Jehosheba. Wife of Jehoiada the high priest, helped him save Joash, last heir of house of David, from Queen Athaliah's purge (2 Kings 11–12)

Jochebed. Mother of Moses (Exod. 2:1-10; 6:20)

Keturah. Abraham's last wife, bore six sons (Gen. 25:1-4)

Leah. Jacob's first wife, bore four sons, one daughter (Gen. 29)

Naomi. Ruth's mother-in-law (Ruth)

Rachel. Jacob's most-beloved wife, bore two sons (Gen. 29:6–35:20)

Rahab. Prostitute, helped Israel defeat Jericho (Josh. 2; 6:17-25)

Rebekah. Wife of Isaac (Gen. 24–27)

Ruth. Moabite, wife of Boaz, great-grandmother of David (Ruth)

Sarah. Abraham's first wife, bore Isaac (Gen. 11–25)

Tamar. Daughter-in-law of Judah, seduced him and bore Perez, ancestor of David and Christ (Gen. 38)

Tamar. Daughter of David and Maacah, raped by her half brother Amnon, leading indirectly to her brother Absalom's revolt (2 Sam. 13)

Zilpah. Handmaiden of Leah, given to Jacob for childbearing, bore two sons (Gen. 30:9-13)

Zipporah. Wife of Moses (Exod 2:16-22; 4:18-26; 18:1-12)

New Testament Men

Aeneas. Healed by Peter (Acts 9:32-35)

Alexander. Heretical teacher condemned by Paul (1 Tim. 1:20; 2 Tim. 4:14-15)

Ananias. Killed by God, along with his wife, Sapphira, for lying (Acts 5:1-11)

Ananias. Ministered to and baptized the newly converted Paul (Acts 9:10-18)

Apollos. Eloquent Jewish Christian preacher discipled by Priscilla and Aquila (Acts 18:24-28)

Aquila. Assisted Paul, along with his wife, Priscilla (Acts 18)

Archippus. Friend of Paul, involved in ministry (Col. 4:17; Philem. 1:2)

Aristarchus. Traveling companion of Paul (Acts 19–20; 27; Col. 4:10)

Barabbas. Jewish prisoner released in place of Christ (Mark 15)

Barnabas. Paul's partner on first missionary journey (Acts 13)

Clement. Helper of Paul (Phil. 4:3)

Cleopas. One of those to whom Christ appeared on road to Emmaus (Luke 24:18)

Cornelius. Gentile centurion converted by Peter (Acts 10)

Crispus. Ruler of synagogue in Corinth, converted by Paul (Acts 18:8)

Demas. Companion of Paul, forsook him during Paul's final imprisonment (Col. 4:14; 2 Tim. 4:10; Philem. 1:24)

Demetrius. Defender of goddess Diana, led riot against Paul in Ephesus (Acts 19:21-41)

Diotrephes. Troublemaking church leader (3 John 1:9-11)

Epaphras. Disciple of Paul, evangelized around Colosse (Col. 1:7-8; 4:12-13; Philem. 1:23)

Epaphroditus. Brought gift from Philippian church to Paul in prison in Rome (Phil. 2:25; 4:18)

Erastus. City treasurer of Corinth, helped Paul on his journeys (Acts 19:22; Rom. 16:23; 2 Tim. 4:20)

Eutychus. Fell from window while Paul preached; resurrected by Paul (Acts 20:7-12)

Felix. Roman governor convicted by Paul's preaching (Acts 23:24–24:27)

Festus. Roman governor, accused Paul of becoming "insane" from "too much study" (Acts 24:27–26:32)

Gaius. Recipient of John's last letter (3 John 1:1)

Gamaliel. Pharisee who advised fellow Pharisees to keep an open mind about Christians (Acts 5:33-41)

Hymenaeus. Heretical teacher condemned by Paul (1 Tim. 1:18-20; 2 Tim. 2:16-18)

Jason. Sheltered Paul and Silas from mob in Thessalonica (Acts 17:5-9)

Joseph of Arimathea. Helped care for Christ's body after crucifixion (John 19:38-42)

Joseph. Husband of Mary, legal father of Christ (Matt. 1:18-25)

Julius. Roman centurion, saved Paul's life during voyage to Rome (Acts 27)

Lazarus. Brother of Mary and Martha, resurrected by Christ (John 11:1-46)

Nicodemus. Pharisee who came to Christ by night, helped care for his body after crucifixion (John 3:1-21; 19:38-42)

Onesimus. Runaway slave of Philemon, converted by Paul, returned to his master (Philem.)

Onesiphorus. Paul's friend, comforted him during final imprisonment (2 Tim. 1:16; 4:19)

Philemon. Friend of Paul, recipient of letter bearing his name (Philem.)

Philip. One of first seven deacons, evangelist (Acts 8)

Pontius Pilate. Roman governor of Judea, sentenced Christ to death (Luke 3:1; 23:1-25)

Publius. Chief official of Malta, befriended Paul after his shipwreck (Acts 28:7-8)

Sergius Paulus. Governor of Cyprus, converted by Paul (Acts 13:4-12)

Silas (Silvanus). Paul's traveling companion during second missionary journey (Acts 15–16)

Simon of Cyrene. Passerby compelled to carry Christ's cross (Matt. 27:32)

Simon the leatherworker. Owner of house where Peter stayed in Joppa (Acts 9:43–10:32)

Simon the Pharisee. Rebuked by Christ during a meal in his home (Luke 7:36-50)

Simon the sorcerer. Rebuked by Peter for wanting to buy the power to impart the Holy Spirit (Acts 8:14-24)

Sosthenes. Companion of Paul, former synagogue leader in Corinth (Acts 18:17; 1 Cor. 1:1)

Stephen. One of first seven deacons, first recorded Christian martyr (Acts 6:1–7:60)

Stephanas. Convert of Paul in Corinth (1 Cor. 1:16; 16:15-17)

Tertullus. Roman prosecutor employed by Sanhedrin to present their case against Paul before Felix (Acts 24:1-9)

Timothy. Paul's disciple and coworker, recipient of two of his letters (1, 2 Tim.)

Titus. Paul's coworker, recipient of letter bearing his name (Titus)

Trophimus. Ephesian, accompanied Paul on his final trip to Jerusalem (Acts 20:4; 21:29; 2 Tim. 4:20)

Tychicus. Ephesian convert, delivered some of Paul's letters (Acts 20:4; Eph. 6:21; Col. 4:7-9; 2 Tim. 4:12; Titus 3:12)

Zacchaeus. Tax collector, climbed tree to see Christ pass by (Luke 19:1-10)

New Testament Women

Chloe. Corinthian woman, told Paul of trouble in her church (1 Cor. 1:11)

Dorcas (Tabitha). Resurrected by Peter (Acts 9:36-43)

Elizabeth. Mother of John the Baptist (Luke 1)

Eunice. Timothy's mother (Acts 16:1; 2 Tim. 1:5)

Euodia. Member of Philippian church, quarreled with Syntyche (Phil. 4:2)

Joanna. Financial supporter of Christ, one of those who discovered empty tomb (Luke 8:1-3; 24:10)

Lois. Grandmother of Timothy (2 Tim. 1:5)

Lydia. Merchant from Thyatira, converted by Paul in Philippi (Acts 16:11-40)

Martha. Sister of Lazarus and Mary, admonished by Christ about priorities (Luke 10:38-42; John 11:1-46)

Mary. Mother of Christ (Luke 1:26-56; 2:1-7)

Mary. Sister of Lazarus and Martha, commended by Christ for choosing the "one thing worth being concerned about" (Luke 10:38-42; John 11:1-46)

Mary Magdalene. Former demoniac, became follower of Christ (Luke 8:1-2), first to see him after resurrection (Matt. 27:55-56, 61; John 20:1-18)
Phoebe. Faithful helper of Paul and many others, deacon in Cenchrean church (Rom. 16:1-2)
Priscilla. Assisted Paul, along with her husband, Aquila. (Acts 18)
Rhoda. Servant who encountered Peter after his release from prison (Acts 12:13)
Salome. Mother of James and John (Matt. 20:20; 27:56, Mark 15:40; 16:1)
Sapphira. Killed by God, along with her husband, Ananias, for lying (Acts 5:1-11)
Susanna. Financial supporter of Christ (Luke 8:1-3)
Syntyche. Member of Philippian church, quarreled with Euodia (Phil. 4:2)

Old Testament Unnamed Women
Ezekiel's wife. God told Ezekiel to use her death as an object lesson for Israel (Ezek. 24:15-24)
Jephthah's daughter. Jephthah's rash vow led to her death (Judg. 11:29-40)
Job's wife. Urged her stricken husband to "curse God and die" (Job 2:9-10)
Lot's two daughters. Desire for children led them to deceive their father into committing incest with them (Gen. 19:30-38)
Lot's wife. For looking back at Sodom, became pillar of salt (Gen. 19:1-29)
Medium of Endor. Consulted by a desperate King Saul (1 Sam. 28:3-25)
Naaman's wife's servant. Israelite girl who suggested Naaman seek Elisha for healing (2 Kings 5:1-4)
Potiphar's wife. Her false accusations against Joseph led to his imprisonment (Gen. 39)
Shunammite woman. Elisha resurrected her dead son, who had been born in fulfillment of Elisha's earlier prophecy (2 Kings 4:8-37)
Widow of Zarephath. Provided for Elijah from her meager possessions; he resurrected her dead son (1 Kings 17:8-24)
Widow with only a pot of oil. Elisha increased her oil supply enough to pay all her debts (2 Kings 4:1-7)

New Testament Unnamed Men
Boy who gave his lunch to Christ. Helped feed 5,000 (John 6:1-14)
Ethiopian royal official. Converted by Philip as he read from Isaiah while traveling (Acts 8:26-40)
Philippian jailer. Converted by Paul, who had passed up the chance to escape from his jail (Acts 16:16-34)
Rich young ruler. His wealth kept him from following Christ (Matt. 19:16-22)
Roman officer at Calvary. Events surrounding crucifixion won him to Christ (Matt. 27:54)
Roman officer in Capernaum. Christ healed his servant, was impressed by his faith (Luke 7:1-10)
Shepherds at Christ's birth. Guided by angel to Bethlehem, saw Christ and spread news of his birth (Luke 2:8-20)
Teacher of religious law who commended Christ. Christ, in turn, declared him to be "not far from the Kingdom of God" (Mark 12:28-34)

Two thieves crucified with Christ. Both reviled him at first; one later repented and was promised entrance into heaven (Matt. 27:38, 44; Luke 23:39-43)

Wise men. Guided by star to Bethlehem, where they gave gifts and worshiped the newborn Christ (Matt. 2:1-12)

New Testament Unnamed Women

Herodias's daughter. Danced for Herod, then asked for head of John the Baptist (Matt. 14:1-12); identified as Salome in extrabiblical sources

Pilate's wife. Troubled by a dream, she urged Pilate to avoid the case against Jesus (Matt. 27:19)

Widow who gave two pennies. Commended by Christ for her sacrificial gift (Luke 21:1-4)

Woman caught in adultery. Forgiven by Christ in presence of self-righteous scribes and Pharisees (John 8:1-11)

Woman of Samaria. Spread news of Christ after encountering him at well (John 4:1-42)

Woman who anointed Christ at Simon's house. Christ used her sincere faith and love as example for Simon (Luke 7:36-50)

THE BIBLE'S TOP 20

The name of God the Father occurs more than 10,000 times in Scripture. The various names of Christ occur some 1,300 to 1,400 times. After that, the most frequently mentioned names in the Bible are

1. David 1,118
2. Moses 804
3. Saul 388
4. Aaron 339
5. Abraham 307
6. Solomon 297
7. Jacob 252
8. Joseph 214
9. Joshua 201
10. Peter 183
11. Paul 180
12. Joab 138
13. Jeremiah 134
    Samuel 134
14. Isaac 128
15. Hezekiah 124
16. Elijah 95
17. Ezekiel 93
18. Nebuchadnezzar 91
19. Ahab 90
    John the Baptist 90
20. Daniel 87

NATIONS AND POLITICS OF BIBLE TIMES

NATIONS OF BIBLE TIMES

Nine nations or people groups played significant roles in the history of Israel in Bible times.

Sumerians

The dispersion following the tower of Babel (Gen. 11) probably took place sometime before 3000 B.C. There is evidence of at least two people groups dating from that time in Mesopotamia, the "land between the two rivers" (the Tigris and the Euphrates). The Akkadians lived in the upper valleys, while the Sumerians occupied the lower valleys, including the city of Ur, birthplace of Abraham.

Sumerians were excellent architects and builders. Ur, for example, had a massive royal palace with huge staircases, large columns, and paneled walls covered with beautiful paintings.

The Sumerians were the earliest recorded people to write. They used pictographic symbols but later changed those symbols into conventional signs, writing on soft clay tablets with a stylus. The stylus had a triangular tip and made strokes in the shape of a wedge. This writing later became known as *cuneiform,* which means "wedge-shaped." Among the most famous Sumerian writings are *The Creation* and *The Epic of Gilgamesh,* which tells about a universal flood.

Egyptians

Protected on all sides by natural barriers and blessed by the bounty of the Nile, Egypt became one of the earliest civilizations—with nationwide dynasties dating from as early as 3300 B.C. Mizraim, a son of Noah's son Ham, is widely regarded as the ancestor of the Egyptians as well as the Philistines; Mizraim is the Hebrew word for Egypt (see Gen. 10:6, comparing NKJV and RSV).

Egypt was at the height of its power c. 1600–1100 B.C. Joseph was sold as a slave to Egypt c. 1900, with his family coming there to escape famine some 25 years later. After another hundred or so years the Egyptians began using the Israelites as forced labor on their massive royal building projects. God liberated them through the miraculous events of the Exodus in 1445. Having been freed from Egypt and established in their own homeland, the Israelites would from time to time seek alliances with Egypt against other world powers. Israel's prophets would always warn against such alliances, and subsequent events would always bear out those warnings (see *Jeremiah: Background*). Egypt's world-power status faded forever during the years of Roman dominance.

Canaanites

"Canaanite" is a general term for the people living in the Promised Land at the time Israel reclaimed it following their liberation from Egypt. Canaanites would include the Phoenicians, Philistines, Ammonites, Hittites, Jebusites, Amorites, and Hivites. Many of these peoples were the descendants of Canaan, Ham's fourth son (Gen. 9:22-27; 10:6, 15-20), and the name Canaanite may have come from him. Some believe, however, that the name came from the Greek *canaan,* meaning "blood-red." Phoenicians and other seafaring traders came to the area to secure a dye from the murex shellfish, and because of the dye's distinctive color they came to refer to the entire area as Canaan.

Early cities founded by the Canaanites included Gezer, Megiddo, Jericho, Sodom, Gomorrah, and Jerusalem. The Canaanites probably were the first people to have an alphabet; theirs consisted of 31 symbols.

The nations of Canaan were known to be the most sexually perverted, morally depraved, and bloodthirsty peoples of all ancient history. Their depravity is mentioned in the Bible (Gen. 13:13; 15:16; 18:20; 19:1-11; Num. 25:1-3; Judg. 19:14-25; 1 Kings 14:24; 15:12; 22:46; 2 Kings 23:7). It is also mentioned by Philo of Byblos, a Phoenician scholar c. 100 B.C., and in the literature of ancient Ugarit, found at Ras Shamra in 1929 (See *Ugarit,* p. 900). It was because of the depravity of the Canaanites that God gave their land back to the Jews and ordered their extermination (Deut. 7:1-5; 20:10-15; Josh. 9:24).

Philistines

Among the Canaanites, the Philistines were especially noteworthy for their interactions with Israel. The seafaring Philistines came from the island of Crete ("Caphtor," Deut. 2:23; Jer. 47:4; Amos 9:7) and settled in Canaan around 1200 B.C. They, like the Egyptians, were from the line of Ham, through his second son, Mizraim (1 Chron. 1:11-12). A warlike people, they conquered the native nations and formed a five-city league (the "Pentapolis"), consisting of Gaza, Ashdod, Askelon, Ekron, and Gath. "Palestine," often synonymous with Canaan, derives from "Philistine."

The Philistines were very religious, worshiping Dagon (the grain god), Ashtoreth (god of propagation), and Baal-zebub (god of habitation) (1 Sam. 5:2-4; 31:10; 2 Kings 1:2). Baal-zebub later became known as Beelzebub, whom Jesus called "the prince of demons" (Matt. 12:24, 27). The Philistines celebrated their victories in the temple of their idols (1 Sam. 31:9) and often carried their gods into battle (2 Sam. 5:21).

Shamgar and Samson fought the Philistines (Judg. 3:31; 13:1; 15:20). They were eventually driven back to the coast by Samuel (1 Sam. 7:12-14). Saul lost to them and was killed in the battle (1 Sam. 31). David fought them (1 Sam. 17; 2 Sam. 5). They were totally subjugated by the time of Solomon (1 Kings 4:21).

Assyrians

By about 1200 B.C. the Assyrians ruled all of Mesopotamia from their capital of Nineveh—perhaps the greatest city of antiquity. The cruelest people in ancient history, the Assyrians conquered and ruled by sheer terror. When they conquered a nation, they would carry its inhabitants back to Assyria as slaves and would make the conquered territory available for homesteading to any foreigners who desired to live there (See *Samaritans,* p. 866). The Assyrians developed the science of siege warfare, using battering rams and other equipment to destroy enemy fortifications.

Assyria began threatening Israel c. 750 and defeated the northern kingdom in 722, leading most of its people into an exile from which they would never return (2 Kings 15–17). Nineveh and its Assyrian empire fell to Babylon in 612.

Babylonians

Between the years 2000–1800 B.C., Mesopotamia was controlled by an eastern people called the Elamites, who descended from Noah's son Shem (Gen. 10:22; 14:1, 9) and who had conquered the Sumerians. The Elamites were driven out of Mesopotamia in 1760 by a people living west of the Euphrates, called Amorites. The victorious general who led this invasion was Hammurabi. Claiming he was the earthly representative of the god Marduk, Hammurabi established Babylon as his capital, beginning the Old Babylonian kingdom.

Hammurabi is known not only as the founder of the Old Babylonian Empire but also for the Code of Hammurabi, a set of some 300 laws governing all social, political, and economic aspects of Babylonian life.

After Hammurabi's death, the Old Babylonian Empire almost immediately disintegrated, and remained in pieces for nearly a thousand years until the coming of a Chaldean soldier named Nebuchadnezzar, who would establish the second Babylonian kingdom in 612 by defeating the Assyrians. In 605 he defeated the remaining challenger, Egypt, at the battle of Carchemish. Nebuchadnezzar pursued the fleeing Egyptians as far west as Jerusalem. His first visit to Jerusalem was short, for he hurried home because of the sudden death of his father, Nabopolassar.

Later that year, Nebuchadnezzar occupied Jerusalem, allowed Jehoiakim (Josiah's son) to rule as his puppet king, and took some of the Temple treasures and key royal descendants to Babylon. Among this group were Daniel and his three friends (2 Chron. 36:6-7; Dan. 1:1-6).

In 597 Nebuchadnezzar came again and took the rest of the Temple treasures to Babylon, along with King Jehoiachin (Jehoiakim's son), Ezekiel the prophet, and 10,000 princes, officers, and chief men (2 Kings 24:14-16).

In 586 Nebuchadnezzar returned once more to punish the rebellion led by Zedekiah, Judah's last king. This time the walls were broken, the Temple destroyed, and the city burned. Zedekiah's sons were killed and he himself was blinded and taken to Babylon. Babylon fell to Persia in 539.

Persians

For 217 years (550 to 333 B.C.) the Persians ruled what was at that time the most extensive empire in history. They established one of the best systems of government known until the Roman Empire, subjecting even their kings to the rule of law. The Persian king Cyrus conquered Babylon in 539 and, in fulfillment of biblical prophecy (Isa. 44:28–45:1), permitted all Jewish exiles who so desired to return to Judea (see Ezra). With the blessing of Persia's rulers the Jews were able to rebuild their Temple and capital city (see Ezra—Nehemiah). Many Jews chose, however, to remain in the Persian empire, where, in 473, they would be saved from the extermination plot of a wicked Persian prince by Queen Esther (see Esther). Persia eventually fell to Alexander the Great of Greece in 331.

Greeks

Greece had already seen its "Golden Age"—the era that produced such greats as Pericles, Herodotus, Hippocrates, Socrates, Plato, Aristotle, and Demosthenes—when Alexander the Great came to power at the age of 20, ready to carry out his father's dream of invading Persia. In 334 B.C. he crossed into Asia and defeated the Persians at Granicus. He routed them again at Issus in 333. He destroyed Tyre, spared Jerusalem, and was welcomed by Egypt, where he founded Alexandria. He crushed the Persians forever at Arbela in 331. After invading India in 327, he began planning to rebuild Babylon to its former glory. But he died in India in 323 at the age of 32. His mighty empire was divided among his four generals.

Israel was dominated by the part of Alexander's former empire centered in Egypt (ruled by the Ptolemies) until 198, at which time it came under the control of the Seleucids of Syria. In 171, the Seleucid ruler Antiochus Epiphanes began a cruel anti-Jewish crusade in which he killed tens of thousands of Jews and desecrated the Temple (see exposition on Dan. 8:15-27) before being defeated by the Jews in 165 (recounted in the apocryphal book of 1 Maccabees).

Part of the legacy of Greece was its language, which became widely spoken throughout its empire—so much so that the OT was translated into Greek c. 250.

Romans

The traditional date for the founding of Rome is April 21, 753 B.C. By 338, Rome controlled central Italy and by 150, it had displaced Greece's four successor kingdoms as the dominant world power. By 64, Rome controlled Palestine. Next came a period of civil wars and uncertainty, with the empire being saved and consolidated by Julius Caesar during the Gallic wars (58–51 B.C.). Caesar was assassinated on the Ides of March, 44 B.C., and the empire was taken over by Octavius (Augustus) Caesar. Augustus defeated the forces of Anthony and Cleopatra at Actium and made Egypt into a Roman province. The Roman Empire now entered its zenith of power and glory. It was during the rule of Augustus that Christ was born (Luke 2:1). Augustus ruled from 31 B.C. to A.D. 14 and was succeeded by Tiberius (14–37). The ministries of both John the Baptist and Christ took place during his reign (see *Matthew: Background*).

✣ ✣ ✣

POLITICAL AND RELIGIOUS PARTIES OF NEW TESTAMENT TIMES

During his ministry Christ interacted with members of various political and religious factions, much as he would have had he walked the earth in our day.

Galileans

The Galileans arose in northern Palestine, headed by Judas of Galilee, who led a rebellion against all foreign elements, advocating "Galilee for Galileans." They were the "extreme right" fanatics of their day. The anti-Roman position of the Galileans would have put them at odds with officials such as Pontius Pilate, who on one occasion felt forced to slaughter a number of them (Luke 13:1). Christ's enemies tried to identify both him and his disciples with the Galileans (Matt. 26:69; Mark 14:70; Luke 23:6).

Herodians

The Herodians were a political party who favored rule by the family of Herod. Though Jewish, they saw the rule of the Herods, under Roman oversight, as Israel's best chance for survival as a nation. They were therefore the "law and order" advocates of the day. They regarded Christ as a revolutionary fanatic and on three occasions joined the efforts of the Pharisees to silence him (Mark. 3:6; 12:13; Matt. 22:16). Christ soundly condemned them (Mark 8:15; 12:13-17).

Levites

The Levites were the descendants of Levi and were in charge of the Temple. Though quite prominent in Israelite history, they make only two appearances in the NT: The Jews sent some priests and Levites to check out the desert ministry of John the Baptist (John 1:19); Christ used them as an example of uncharitable religiosity in the parable of the Good Samaritan.

Pharisees

The Pharisees, who came to prominence c. 100 B.C. during the time of the Maccabees, were known as the champions and guardians of Israel's written and oral law. As such they became the most bitter and hateful enemies of Christ. They numbered about 6,000 in Christ's day. John the Baptist called the Pharisees a "brood of snakes" (Matt. 3:7). Christ denounced them for letting their traditions negate the power of God's Word (Matt. 15:1-9; 23:1-36). He warned his followers about their false righteousness (Matt. 5:20), false teaching (Matt. 16:11), and false humility (Luke 18:10-14).

The Pharisees in turn condemned Christ for things such as associating with sinners (Matt. 9:11; Luke 7:39; 15:2), healing on the Sabbath (Luke 6:7; 14:1-6), and allowing his disciples to work on the Sabbath (Matt. 12:1-2). They despised him because he refused to follow their traditions (Matt. 15:1-2). They sought to entrap him on various theological issues (Matt. 19:3; 22:15). They denied his miracles (John 9:15-16). And, from early in his ministry, they sought to kill him (Matt. 12:14; John 11:47-53).

Nicodemus (John 3:1) and Paul (Acts 23:6; Phil. 3:5) were Pharisees by birth and training.

Sadducees

Taking their name from Zadok, high priest during the reign of Solomon (1 Kings 2:35), the Sadducees came into prominence at about the same time as the Pharisees, a century before Christ. The Sadducees were the Jewish aristocrats of Christ's day and held most seats on the Sanhedrin. As the "insiders" of the priestly class, they accepted only the written Law and rejected the oral traditions popular with Pharisees. But both parties briefly set aside their differences to accomplish their common goal of getting rid of Christ.

John the Baptist lumped the Sadducees and Pharisees together, calling both of them a "brood of snakes" (Matt. 3:7). Christ, likewise, warned his followers to beware of the erroneous teachings of both Pharisees and Sadducees (Matt. 16:11).

The Sadducees, unlike the Pharisees, rejected the idea of resurrection and an afterlife, and on at least one occasion they tried to ridicule Christ on this point (Mark 12:18-27). Later, this difference of opinion was used by Paul to drive a wedge into the Pharisees' and Sadducees' united opposition to Christ (Acts 23:1-10).

Samaritans

When the Assyrian king Sargon II took the northern kingdom of Israel into captivity in 722 B.C., he followed the Assyrian custom by leaving only the poorest and most uneducated Israelites behind and inviting other nations to come in and homestead the land vacated by those taken captive. These newcomers brought with them their pagan religions (2 Kings 17:24-33). As the Jews left in the land intermarried with them, they came to be viewed as a separate race, neither Jew nor Gentile, and were held in contempt by Jews. (The name Samaritan comes from Samaria, the capital of the northern kingdom. In Christ's day the name referred to the entire territory between Judea and Galilee.)

The Samaritans offered to help rebuild the Temple in 536, but their offer was refused (Ezra 4:1-3). A century later, the Samaritan governor Sanballat tried to frustrate Nehemiah's rebuilding of Jerusalem's walls (Neh. 6:1-9). A complete break between the Jews and Samaritans occurred when the grandson of Eliashib the high priest married Sanballat's daughter, contrary to the statute prohibiting mixed marriages (Neh. 13:23-28). Since he refused to annul the marriage, he was promptly expelled from the priesthood and exiled. He retired to Samaria, where Sanballat built a temple for him on Mount Gerizim. This temple was destroyed by John Hyrcanus in 128 because the Samaritans had compromised with paganism under Antiochus Epiphanes IV by dedicating their temple to the Greek god Zeus.

By the time of the NT, the hatred between Jews and Samaritans had reached its zenith (John 4:9; 8:48). Christ once ordered his disciples not to enter Samaria (Matt. 10:5), though he himself ministered to Samaritans (John 4:1-42). A Samaritan was the hero in one of Christ's parables (Luke 10:30-37). When he healed 10 lepers, the only one who thanked him was a Samaritan (Luke 17:11-19).

During Christ's final days of ministry, one village of Samaritans rejected him because of his plans to go on to Jerusalem (Luke 9:51-56). Just prior to his ascension, however, Christ commanded his disciples to proclaim the gospel in Samaria (Acts 1:8).

The Sanhedrin

The Sanhedrin (the "high council," NLT) was the Jewish Supreme Court for both religious and legal matters. It may have come from the time of Moses (Num. 11:16-17) or of King Jehoshaphat (2 Chron. 19:8). It had 71 members, including: the high priest, who was president; the heads of the 24 priestly service divisions; scribes and lawyers; and elders, representing the laity. The word *Sanhedrin* comes from two Greek words: *sun* ("together with"), and *hedra* ("a sitting place"), thus referring to a group that sits in session. (*Cathedral* and *ex cathedra* have the same roots.)

Though the Jewish people trusted the Sanhedrin to render justice, when Christ stood before them prior to his crucifixion (Matt. 26:57-68; 27:1-2) the trial was unjust in several ways:

- They normally met in a semicircle with the prisoner standing in the midst, able to see them all. Jesus was blindfolded.
- Normally, two clerks were appointed—one to record the votes for acquittal, the other for conviction. In Christ's case this was not done.
- The arguments for acquittal were normally given first. There is no record of this happening in Christ's trial.
- If the vote was for acquittal, the prisoner was set free immediately; if the vote was for conviction, condemnation could not be pronounced until the following day. Christ was condemned the same day (Matt. 26:66).

Several leaders of the early church were also tried before the Sanhedrin (Acts 4:5-22; 5:21-40; 6:12-15; 22:30–23:10).

Scribes

Scribes (also called "experts in religious law"—Matt. 22:35; Luke 7:30) were the students, interpreters, and teachers of the OT Scriptures. Scribes had great power in Jewish society and were often called upon to settle disputes. They became bitter enemies of Christ, who grouped them with Pharisees, calling them both hypocrites (Matt. 23:13).

Scribes in the NT refused John's baptism (Luke 7:30); tried to entrap Jesus on the issues of adultery (John 8:3-12) and healing on the Sabbath (Luke 6:7); demanded that Jesus perform signs (Matt. 12:38); and condemned him for associating with sinners (Luke 15:2).

Christ warned his disciples about the scribes' false righteousness (Matt. 5:20) and denounced the scribes for letting their traditions negate the power of God's Word (Matt. 16:21; 21:15; 23:1-36; Mark 12:28-40).

❖ ❖ ❖

50 IMPORTANT CITIES OF BIBLE TIMES

Following the names and descriptions of each of these 50 important Bible cities is a list of noteworthy events occurring in that city.

Antioch of Pisidia. Roman colony, commercial center on road from Ephesus to Syria with large Jewish population

- Paul's first recorded sermon (Acts 13:14-52)

Antioch of Syria. Major city of Roman Empire

- Disciples first called Christians (Acts 11:19-26)
- First missionaries sent (Acts 13:1-3)

Ashdod. One of five main Philistine cities

- Their capture of Ark of the Covenant caused destruction of Philistine god Dagon (1 Sam. 5:1-8)

Athens. Capital of Greece

- Paul's Mars Hill sermon (Acts 17:15-34)

Babylon. Capital of Babylonian Empire

- Site of Tower of Babel (Gen. 11:1-9)
- Destination of Israelite captives after fall of southern kingdom (2 Kings 25)

- Where Daniel and Ezekiel lived and wrote their books (Dan. 1:1-7; Ezek. 1:1-3)

Beersheba. Southernmost city of Israel (Judg. 20:1)
- Abraham sent Hagar there to escape Sarah's wrath (Gen. 21:14)
- Abraham signed covenant with Abimelech (Gen. 21:22-34)
- Abraham lived there for a while (Gen. 22:19)
- God appeared to Isaac (Gen. 26:23-25) and to Jacob (Gen. 46:1-4)

Bethany. Village two miles east of Jerusalem
- Lazarus resurrected (John 11)
- Mary anointed Jesus' feet (John 12:1-8)
- Jesus blessed disciples before Ascension (Luke 24:50-53)

Bethel. Important center of worship before Jerusalem became capital of Israel; 10 miles north of Jerusalem
- Abraham worshiped there upon arriving in Palestine (Gen. 12:8)
- Jacob's "ladder" dream (Gen. 28:11-19)
- Jacob told to return there (Gen. 35:1-15)
- Jeroboam set up golden calf images there and at Dan (1 Kings 12:26-29)
- Elisha mocked by children (2 Kings 2:23-24)

Bethlehem. Village five miles south of Jerusalem
- Near burial place of Rachel (Gen. 35:16-19)
- Home of Boaz and Ruth (Ruth)
- Birthplace of David, site of his anointing (1 Sam. 16:4-13)
- Birthplace of Mary and Joseph (Luke 2:1-4)
- Birthplace of Jesus (Mic. 5:2; Luke 2:7; John 7:42)

Bethsaida. Village on north side of Sea of Galilee
- Jesus healed blind man (Mark 8:22-26)
- Home of Philip, Andrew, and Peter (John 1:44)

Caesarea. Roman seaport on Mediterranean, 23 miles south of Mount Carmel
- Home of Cornelius (Acts 10:1-18)
- Herod Agrippa struck down (Acts 12:19-23)
- Home of Philip and his four daughters (Acts 21:8-14)
- Paul witnessed to Felix (Acts 24:10-27) and to Agrippa (Acts 26:24-32)

Caesarea Philippi. Important Roman city on southern slope of Mount Hermon
- Peter's confession, Christ's promise to build his church (Matt. 16:13-19)

Cana. Village 10 miles west of Sea of Galilee
- Christ's first miracle—water to wine (John 2:1-11)
- Christ heals government official's son (John 4:46-54)
- Home of Nathanael (John 21:2)

Capernaum. City on northern shore of Galilee
- Main headquarters of Jesus' earthly ministry (Matt. 4:13)
- Bread of Life sermon (John 6:22-71)
- At least nine of Christ's 35 recorded miracles:
  - ➤ Centurion's servant (Matt. 8:5-13)
  - ➤ Peter's mother-in-law (Matt. 8:14-15)
  - ➤ Demoniac (Mark 1:21-27)
  - ➤ Man lowered from roof (Mark 2:1-5)
  - ➤ Woman with internal bleeding (Matt. 9:20-22)

- ➤ Jairus's daughter (Matt. 9:18-19, 23-25)
- ➤ Two blind men (Matt. 9:27-31)
- ➤ Mute demoniac (Matt. 9:32-34)
- ➤ Tax money (Matt. 17:24-27)

Colosse. City in southwestern Asia Minor
- Home of Philemon and Onesimus (Col. 4:9)
- Church received letter from Paul

Corinth. Large seaport, commercial center in southern Greece
- Home of Aquila and Priscilla (Acts 18:1-2)
- God encouraged Paul in vision (Acts 18:9-10)
- Paul spent 18 months there on second journey (Acts 18:11)
- Received two of Paul's letters

Damascus. Major political and commercial center in Syria
- Home of Abraham's servant Eliezer (Gen. 15:2)
- Elisha visited sick king (2 Kings 8:7)
- King Ahaz built pagan altar in Jerusalem after seeing similar one in Damascus (2 Kings 16:10-12)
- Paul was on way there to persecute Christians when converted to Christ (Acts 9:1-18)

Dan. Northernmost city of Israel (Judg. 20:1)
- Jeroboam set up golden calf images there and at Bethel (1 Kings 12:26-29)

Dothan. City 12 miles north of Samaria
- Joseph sold into slavery (Gen. 37:12-28)
- Syrian army struck blind (2 Kings 6:13-18)

Emmaus. Said to be about seven miles from Jerusalem (Luke 24:13), exact location unknown
- Post-resurrection appearance of Christ (Luke 24:13-31)

Endor. City near Mount Tabor
- Saul visited medium (1 Sam. 28:7-25)

Ephesus. Seaport on western coast of Asia Minor
- Paul visited on second missionary journey (Acts 18:19)
- Apollos instructed by Aquila and Priscilla (Acts 18:24-26)
- Paul met some of John the Baptist's disciples (Acts 19:1-7)
- Book-burning ceremony; confrontation with worshipers of Artemis (Acts 19:21-41)
- Church received letter from Paul

Gaza. One of five main Philistine cities, south of Joppa near Mediterranean coast
- Samson destroyed its gates (Judg. 16:1-3)
- Samson imprisoned after betrayal by Delilah (Judg. 16:21)
- Philip met Ethiopian eunuch (Acts 8:26-40)

Gerar. City near Gaza
- Abraham lied about Sarah for second time (Gen. 20)
- Isaac lied about Rebekah (Gen. 26)

Gibeon. City five miles northwest of Jerusalem
- Its citizens tricked Joshua into sparing it (Josh. 9)
- Sun stood still (Josh. 10:12-13)
- Solomon granted wisdom (1 Kings 3:4-15)

Gilgal. Area near Jericho
- Israel's first stop after crossing Jordan (Josh. 4:19)
- Saul proclaimed king (1 Sam. 11:14-15)
- Saul violated priesthood (1 Sam. 13:4-14)
- Saul lied about killing Amalekites (1 Sam. 15:10-23)

Haran. Important trade center between Nineveh and Syria, on upper tributary of Euphrates River
- Abraham got bogged down for a while after starting out for Canaan (Gen. 11:31; 12:4)
- Home of Rebekah and Jacob for 20 years—birthplace of all Jacob's sons except Benjamin (Gen. 28–29)

Hebron. City 19 miles southwest of Jerusalem
- Abraham built altar (Gen. 13:18)
- Site of Machpelah, burial place of Sarah, Abraham, Isaac, Rebekah, Jacob, and Leah (Gen. 23:2, 19; 25:9; 35:27-29; 49:30-31; 50:13)
- One of six cities of refuge (Josh. 20:7)
- David anointed king over Judah (2 Sam. 2:1-4)
- Joab killed Abner (2 Sam. 3:27)
- David anointed king over Israel (2 Sam. 5:1-5)
- Headquarters of Absalom during his rebellion (2 Sam. 15:7-10)

Jericho. City east of Jerusalem, near Dead Sea
- Home of Rahab (Josh. 2)
- "Shouted down" by Israel (Josh. 6)
- Elijah taken up to heaven (2 Kings 2:1-11)
- School of prophets (2 Kings 2:5, 15)
- Mentioned in Good Samaritan parable (Luke 10:30-37)
- Jesus healed blind Bartimaeus (Luke 18:35-43)
- Jesus met Zacchaeus (Luke 19:1-10)

Jerusalem. Capital of Israel for most of its history

IN THE OLD TESTAMENT (all dates B.C.)
- Home of Melchizedek (Gen. 14:18)
- Joshua defeated its King Adoni-zedek (Josh. 10:1-15)
- Claimed temporarily by tribe of Judah, 1380 (Judg. 1:8)
- Captured by David, 1003; made capital of his kingdom (2 Sam. 5:6-12; 6:1-19)
- Temporarily taken by Absalom (2 Sam. 16:15-16)
- Solomon built Temple, 967–960 (1 Kings 6)
- Plundered by Shishak, king of Egypt, during Rehoboam's reign, 925 (1 Kings 14:25-28)
- Plundered by Philistines and Arabs during Jehoram's reign (2 Chron. 21:16-17)
- Plundered by Arameans (Syrians) during reign of Joash, c. 800 (2 Chron. 24:23-24)
- Plundered by northern Israel during Amaziah's reign, c. 775 (2 Chron. 25:23)
- Surrounded by Sennacherib's Assyrian army during Hezekiah's reign, saved by death angel, 701 (2 Kings 18–19; 2 Chron. 32)

- Taken briefly by Pharaoh Neco, after King Josiah's death, 609 (2 Kings 23:28-37)
- Besieged by Nebuchadnezzar, 597 (2 Kings 24:10-16)
- City and Temple destroyed by Nebuchadnezzar, 586 (2 Kings 25)
- Its reconstruction began after decree of Cyrus, 536 (Ezra 1)
- Temple dedicated by Zerubbabel, 516 (Ezra 6:13-18)
- Nehemiah rebuilt walls, 445 (Neh. 6:15)
- Alexander the Great visited, 332
- Captured by Ptolemy Soter, 320
- Annexed to Egypt, 302
- Walls destroyed, Temple desecrated by Antiochus Epiphanes, 168
- Temple cleansed, rededicated by Mattathias of Hasmonean dynasty, 165
- Captured by Roman general Pompey, 64
- Walls rebuilt by Antipater (Herod the Great's father), 44
- Herod the Great began rebuilding Temple, 20

IN THE NEW TESTAMENT

- Jesus dedicated (Luke 2:21-38)
- Jesus attended Passover, age 12 (Luke 2:41-50)
- Jesus cleansed Temple (John 2:13-17)
- Jesus spoke to Nicodemus (John 3:1-21)
- Jesus forgave adulterous woman (John 8:1-11)
- For events surrounding Christ's death and resurrection, see *Key Events in the Life of Christ,* page 830
- The coming of the Holy Spirit at Pentecost (Acts 2)
- First persecution of Christians (Acts 4:1-3)
- Death of Ananias and Sapphira (Acts 5:1-11)
- Second persecution (Acts 5:17-42)
- First elders or deacons chosen (Acts 6:1-7)
- Third persecution, Stephen martyred (Acts 6:8–7:60)
- Fourth persecution (Acts 8:1-4)
- Saul returned to Jerusalem after conversion (Acts 9:26-28)
- Famine (Acts 11:27-30)
- Fifth persecution (Acts 12:1-19)
- Council on circumcision (Acts 15:1-29)
- Paul arrested, imprisoned (Acts 21–28)
- Temple and city destroyed, September 8, A.D. 70

Jezreel. City 15 miles southwest of Sea of Galilee

- Home of Naboth (1 Kings 21)
- Jezebel's death (2 Kings 9:10, 30-37)
- Jehu killed two kings: Joram (northern), and Ahaziah (southern) (2 Kings 9:16-29)

Joppa. Mediterranean seaport north of Gaza.

- Jonah boarded ship to flee from his assignment (Jonah 1:3)
- Peter resurrected Dorcas (Acts 9:36-42)
- Peter saw vision of sheet (Acts 9:43; 10:9-13)

Kiriath-jearim. City 10 miles west of Jerusalem

- Ark of the Covenant kept there 20 years (1 Sam. 6:21–7:2)

Lydda. City 11 miles southeast of Joppa
- Peter healed Aeneas (Acts 9:32-35)

Lystra. Roman military colony in south-central Asia Minor
- Paul stoned (Acts 14:19; 2 Tim. 3:11)
- Home of Timothy (Acts 16:1-4)

Mizpah. City in territory of Benjamin, north of Jerusalem
- 11 tribes declared war on Benjamin (Judg. 20:1-36)
- Israel gathered for prayer and rededication (1 Sam. 7:5-7)
- Saul introduced to Israel as first king (1 Sam. 10:17-24) Note: Saul was anointed at Ramah (1 Sam. 9:15–10:1), introduced at Mizpah, and publicly crowned at Gilgal (1 Sam. 11:14-15)

Nazareth. City 15 miles west of Sea of Galilee
- Angels announced birth of Jesus to both Mary (Luke 1:26-35) and Joseph (Matt. 1:18-25)
- Jesus grew to manhood (Luke 2:39-40)
- He preached Isaiah 61 sermon, was rejected by townspeople (Luke 4:16-30)

Nineveh. Capital of Assyria, 220 miles northwest of Baghdad on Tigris River
- Jonah sent by God to preach there (Jonah 1:2)
- Destroyed (Nah. 3:7)
- Used by Jesus as example of repentance (Matt. 12:41)

Philippi. Roman colony, commercial center in eastern Macedonia
- Three notable conversions:
  - ➤ Lydia (Acts 16:14-15)
  - ➤ Demon-possessed Greek girl (Acts 16:16-19)
  - ➤ Jailer (Acts 16:25-34)
- Church received letter from Paul

Ramah. Town in "hill country of Ephraim" (1 Sam. 1:1)
- Home of Samuel's parents (1 Sam. 1:19)
- Israel demanded a king (1 Sam. 8:4-5)
- Saul anointed king (1 Sam. 9:15–10:1)
- Samuel's headquarters (1 Sam. 15:34; 16:13)
- Samuel buried (1 Sam. 25:1)

Rome. Capital of Roman Empire
- Church received letter from Paul
- Paul imprisoned, had many opportunities to minister and evangelize (Acts 28:11-31; Phil. 1:12-14; 4:22)

Samaria. Capital of Israel's northern kingdom, 35 miles north of Jerusalem
- Built by King Omri (1 Kings 16:24)
- Elijah confronted Ahab about murder of Naboth (1 Kings 21:17-29)
- Death of Ahab (1 Kings 22:37-38)
- Ahab's ivory palace (1 Kings 22:39)
- Naaman healed of leprosy (2 Kings 5:3-14)
- Elisha led blinded Syrian soldiers there (2 Kings 6:19)
- Saved by four lepers (2 Kings 7)
- Jehu killed all Baal worshipers (2 Kings 10:17-28)
- Philip the evangelist led great revival (Acts 8:5-25)

Shechem. City 30 miles north of Jerusalem, between Mts. Gerizim and Ebal
- Jacob and family live there awhile (Gen. 33:18–35:4)
- Rape of Dinah, avenged by her brothers (Gen. 34)
- Jacob buried false household gods (Gen. 35:4)
- One of six cities of refuge (Josh. 20:7-8)
- Joshua's farewell address (Josh. 24:1-25)
- Joseph's bones buried (Josh. 24:32)
- Abimelech's headquarters (Judg. 9)
- Rehoboam crowned king (1 Kings 12:1)

Shiloh. City 19 miles north of Jerusalem
- Home of Tabernacle after conquest of Canaan (Josh. 18:1)
- Land divided among tribes (Josh. 18:2-10; 19:51; 21:1-3)
- Benjamite warriors found wives (Judg. 21:16-23)
- Hannah prayed for a son (1 Sam. 1)
- Call of Samuel (1 Sam. 3)
- Jeroboam's wife tried to trick Ahijah (1 Kings 14:1-18)

Sidon. Port on Mediterranean, 22 miles north of Tyre
- Home of Jezebel (1 Kings 16:31-33)
- Home of Canaanite woman whose daughter Jesus healed (Matt. 15:21-28)

Sodom. City in southern region of Dead Sea
- Abraham refused pact with its king (Gen. 14:21-24)
- Destroyed with fire and burning sulfur (Gen. 19)

Thessalonica. Roman city, commercial center in Macedonia
- Paul established church here (Acts 17:1-9)
- Church received two letters from Paul

Troas. Roman colony, port on Aegean Sea in northwest Asia Minor
- Paul's Macedonian vision (Acts 16:6-11)
- Eutychus resurrected (Acts 20:6-12)
- Paul left his coat (2 Tim. 4:13)

Tyre. Port on Mediterranean, north of Israel
- Home of Hiram, supplier for Solomon's Temple (1 Kings 5:1-11; 9:11-14)
- Ezekiel prophesied against it (Ezek. 26)
- Paul prayed by seashore (Acts 21:2-6)

Ur. Commercial center and seaport on Persian Gulf at mouth of Euphrates River
- Birthplace of Abraham (Gen. 11:27-28; 15:7)

CHURCHES OF NEW TESTAMENT TIMES

Antioch of Pisidia
- Begun by Paul on first journey (Acts 13:14)
- Heard Paul's first recorded sermon (Acts 13:14-41)
- Jewish reaction led Paul to begin preaching to Gentiles (Acts 13:42-51)
- Christians in Antioch were "filled with joy and with the Holy Spirit" (Acts 13:52)

Antioch of Syria
- Begun during persecution following martyrdom of Stephen (Acts 11:19)

- Had two early revivals (Acts 11:21, 24)
- Paul and Barnabas worked there (Acts 11:26), were sent out as missionaries (Acts 13:1-3)
- Disciples first called Christians (Acts 11:26)

Berea
- Founded by Paul, Silas, and Timothy (Acts 17:10-14)
- Believers commended for open-mindedness and love of Scripture (Acts 17:11)

Colosse
- Received letter from Paul (Colossians)
- Led by Epaphras (Col. 1:7)
- Apparently Onesimus was a member (Col. 4:9)

Corinth
- Founded by Paul on his second journey, with help of Priscilla and Aquila (Acts 18:1-2)
- Paul stayed there 18 months (Acts 18:11)
- Received several letters from Paul (1 Cor. 5:9; 2 Cor. 10:9-10), two of which are in the NT (1, 2 Corinthians)

Crete
- Several churches, with elders appointed by Titus (Titus 1:5)

Derbe
- Founded by Paul and Barnabas (Acts 14:20-22)

Ephesus
- Possibly founded by Aquila and Priscilla, during Paul's second journey (Acts 18:18-21)
- Paul had fruitful ministry there (Acts 19:11-41; 20:17-21)
- Received letter from Paul (Ephesians)
- Received exhortation from John (Rev. 2:1-7)

Iconium
- Paul had fruitful ministry there on first journey (Acts 14:1-6)

Jerusalem
- Begun at Pentecost, with more than 3,000 members (Acts 2:41-47)
- Saw apostles perform many miracles (Acts 2:43; 5:12-16)
- Members shared their financial resources (Acts 2:44-45; 4:32-35)
- Saw much evangelistic outreach (Acts 2:14-36; 3:11-26; 4:33; 5:42)
- Grew steadily (Acts 2:47; 4:4; 5:14; 12:24)
- Endured several persecutions (Acts 4:1-3; 5:17-42; 6:8–8:3; 12:1-19)
- Sent missionaries (Acts 8:4-5, 14; 11:22; 13:1-3; 15:22, 27)
- Apparently later compromised with Judaizers (Acts 21:18-25)

Joppa
- Peter ministered there after raising Dorcas (Acts 9:36-43)

Laodicea

- Apparently had close ties with church at Colosse (Col. 2:1; 4:13, 15-16)
- Apparently received letter from Paul (Col. 4:16)
- Received exhortation from John (Rev. 3:14-22)

Lydda

- Saw great revival after Peter healed Aeneas (Acts 9:32-35)

Lystra

- Paul and Barnabas visited on the first journey (Acts 14:8-20)

Pergamum

- Received exhortation from John (Rev. 2:12-17)

Philadelphia

- Received exhortation from John (Rev. 3:7-13)

Philippi

- Organized by Paul in Lydia's home (Acts 16:15, 40)
- Town jailer and family converted (Acts 16:25-34)
- Received letter from Paul (Philippians)
- Timothy ministered to them (Phil. 2:19)
- Helped with Paul's material needs (Phil. 4:15, 18), looked after him in prison (Phil. 2:25)

Rome

- Priscilla and Aquila ministered there, church met in their home (Rom. 16:3-5)
- Received letter from Paul (Romans)
- Their witness had spread far and wide (Rom. 1:8)
- Though Paul had not been to Rome when he wrote to them, he had many friends there (Rom. 16)

Samaria

- Apparently many churches were founded in Samaria and other Samaritan cities by Philip, Peter, and John (Acts 8:1-25)

Sardis

- Received exhortation from John (Rev. 3:1-6)

Smyrna

- Received exhortation from John (Rev. 2:8-11)

Thessalonica

- Founded by Paul and Silas on second journey (Acts 17:1-9)
- Received two letters from Paul (1, 2 Thessalonians)
- Members were effective and influential in sharing faith (1 Thess. 1:8)
- Timothy ministered there (1 Thess. 3:1-2)

Thyatira

- Received exhortation from John (Rev. 2:18-29)

Troas

- Saw Paul resurrect Eutychus (Acts 20:6-12)

Tyre

- Paul found believers there on his way to Rome (Acts 21:1-6)

HOW WE GOT THE BIBLE

While God found it expedient to speak to humankind "in many ways" in times past (Heb. 1:1), he has chosen to communicate with all people for all ages through a written record. The advantages of writing are many:

- *Precision:* One's thoughts must be somewhat precise to be put in written form.
- *Propagation:* Writing allows maximum distribution with minimal compromise of the original message.
- *Preservation:* Men die and memories fail, but the written record remains.

To better understand how we got the Bible, we will briefly consider its inspiration, composition, and canonization, as well as the faithful efforts of Bible translators down through the ages.

- *Inspiration:* How can we be sure that the Bible is God's authoritative Word?
- *Composition:* How did it come to be composed of 66 separate books, with material from some 40 authors?
- *Canonization:* How do we know that those 66 books—no more and no less—are to be received and trusted as God's Word?

INSPIRATION

- The Bible claims to be no ordinary book, but to have been inspired by God himself (2 Tim. 3:16) and communicated to us through human agents specially chosen by God (Luke 1:70; 2 Pet. 1:20-21).
- These human agents were guided by the Holy Spirit (1 Pet. 1:10-11; 2 Pet. 1:20-21).
- The content of their message is relevant for all time (Heb. 1:1-2), is vitally important for all to hear (1 Cor. 10:6, 11), and is sufficient to meet our every spiritual need (2 Tim. 3:16-17).
- Those who mishandle this divine revelation will be severely judged (Deut. 4:2; 12:32; Prov. 30:5-6; Rev. 22:18-19).

COMPOSITION

The Language of the Bible

The Old Testament was written in Hebrew, except for a few segments in Aramaic (Ezra 4:8–6:18; 7:12-26; Daniel 2:4–7:28; Jeremiah 10:11). Hebrew is a pictorial, descriptive language, rich in metaphors and symbols not found in any other language. It has also been described as a personal language, appealing more to the heart than to the mind.

The entire New Testament was written in Greek. Contrary to the OT Hebrew, Greek can be considered a language of the mind, allowing the NT writers to discuss concepts like justification, propitiation, and imputation with rabbinic precision. Greek also offered the advantage of being, at that time, a universal language.

Writing Materials Used by Bible Authors

As the Spirit of God moved upon the authors of the Bible, they recorded the messages upon whatever material was in use at the time. The following verses, while not all directly relating to the writing of the Bible itself, illustrate the various means of writing used in Bible times:

- Clay (Jer. 17:13; Ezek. 4:1)
- Stone (Exod. 24:12; 31:18; 34:1, 28; Deut. 27:2-3; Josh. 8:31-32)
- Papyrus (two layers of split papyrus reeds pressed together to form a sheet) (2 John 1:12; Rev. 5:1)
- Vellum (calfskin), parchment (lambskin), leather (cowhide) (2 Tim. 4:13)
- Metal (Exod. 28:36; Job 19:24; Matt. 22:19-20)

CANONIZATION

The 66 books accepted as part of God's inspired, written Word are often described as the "canon" of Scripture. Charles Ryrie, in his book *Basic Theology,* explains several things about the word *canon:*

1. *Its derivation.* The word comes from the Greek word *kanon,* which refers to a measuring instrument. It therefore came to mean a rule of action (this is the word rendered "rule" in Gal. 6:16 and Phil. 3:16, KJV).

2. *Its history.* In the early church the word *canon* was used to refer to the creeds. In the middle of the fourth century it came to be used of the Bible; i.e., of the list of accepted books that were acknowledged to make up the Bible.

3. *Its meaning.* Actually the word *canon* has a twofold meaning. It refers to the list of books that met certain tests or rules and thus were considered authoritative and canonical. But it also means that the collection of canonical books becomes our rule of life.

Preservation of the Canonical Books

OLD TESTAMENT

Before the Babylonian captivity, the OT books were apparently laid beside the Ark of the Covenant in the Temple (Deut. 31:24-26).

During the Babylonian captivity, they were probably carried to Babylon. Daniel 9:2 indicates that Daniel had access to them. Daniel says he was reading Jeremiah and "the writings," a reference, no doubt, to the other OT books written up to that time.

After the Babylonian captivity, the books Daniel refers to may have been taken back to Jerusalem by Ezra and kept in the newly completed Temple (see Ezra 3:10-11; 6:15-18; Neh. 8:1-8).

NEW TESTAMENT

While the OT books were kept in the Temple, the NT books, unwelcome in the Temple, were apparently cared for and circulated among the Christian community by various local churches (Col. 4:16; 1 Thess. 5:27).

Tests of Canonicity

To determine whether or not they should be a part of the Bible, books were subjected to various tests:

- *Authorship.* Was the author respected and regarded as speaking with divine authority?
- *Local church acceptance.* Had it been read by the various churches? What was their opinion of it?
- *Early church leaders' recognition.* Did the students of Christ's apostles (such as Polycarp, a disciple of John) quote from the book?
- *Content.* What did the book teach? Did it contradict other recognized books?
- *Personal edification.* Did the book inspire, convict, and edify local congregations and individual believers?

Bible Books Whose Canonicity Was Disputed

The canonicity of about a dozen books now in the Bible was at first doubted:

Disputed Old Testament books:

- *Esther,* because it makes no overt mention of God
- *Proverbs,* because of seeming self-contradictions (e.g., 26:4-5)
- *Song of Songs,* because it seemed merely a poem on human love
- *Ecclesiastes,* because some felt it taught atheism (e.g., 9:5)
- *Ezekiel,* because it seems to contradict the Mosaic law

Disputed New Testament books:

- *Hebrews,* because of uncertainty about its authorship
- *James,* because it seemed to contradict the teachings of Paul (compare James 2:20 with Eph. 2:8-9)
- *2, 3 John,* because they seemed to be purely personal letters
- *Jude,* because it refers to the uncanonical book of Enoch
- *Revelation,* because of uncertainty about the book's authorship and because of its mysterious symbols

The Apocrypha

After the OT canon had been recognized by the Jews as officially closed, and prior to the NT period, there arose a body of literature which is today commonly referred to as the Apocrypha. *Apocrypha* literally means "that which is hidden." The term refers to the 14 books which were included in the Greek Septuagint but not in the Hebrew OT. The Apocrypha is accepted by the Roman Catholic church and appears in Catholic and various other versions of the Bible.

Here is a brief survey of the apocryphal books:

- **1 Esdras** covers much of the material found in Ezra, Nehemiah, and 2 Chronicles, but also includes a fanciful story concerning three Jewish people working as servants while captive in Persia. King Darius asked each of them what was the greatest thing in the world. One said wine, another replied women, while the third said truth. When offered a reward, the man who had said "truth" suggested the king allow the Jews to rebuild the Temple in Jerusalem.
- **2 Esdras** tells of visions given to Ezra, dealing with God's government of the world and the restoration of lost Scriptures.
- **Tobit** is the story of a pious Jew who is blinded by sparrow dung and healed by an angel named Raphael, who applies a concoction of fish heart, liver, and gall to his eye.
- **Judith** tells of a beautiful and devout Jewish princess who saves Jerusalem from Nebuchadnezzar. She beguiles the enemy general through her beauty, then returns to Jerusalem with his head in her handbag!
- **Additions to the Book of Esther** try to show the hand of God in the story of Queen Esther by inserting six additional passages in which the word *God* and the subject of prayer receive frequent mention. (The word *God* does not appear in the canonical Esther.)
- **Wisdom of Solomon,** often called the "Gem of the Apocrypha," tries to teach a biblical view of righteousness in a way that would appeal to the Greek mind.
- **Ecclesiasticus,** also called "the Wisdom of Jesus the Son of Sirach," resembles Proverbs and gives detailed rules for personal conduct in civil, religious, and domestic life.
- **Letter of Jeremiah** purports to be a letter, similar to the one mentioned in Jeremiah 29, from Jeremiah to the exiles in Babylon.
- **Baruch** was supposedly written by Jeremiah's secretary, Baruch. It contains prayers and confessions of the Jews in exile, along with promises of restoration.
- **Song of the Three Young Men** adds to the book of Daniel, taking up the story right after the fiery furnace episode (Dan. 3). It contains the eloquent prayer of one of the three Hebrew men thrown in the fire. (Some treat this prayer as a separate book.)
- **Susanna** relates how the godly wife of a wealthy Jew in Babylon, falsely accused of adultery, was cleared by the wisdom of Daniel.
- **Bel and the Dragon** is also an addition to Daniel and relates the destruction of the idols Bel and the Dragon, two objects of Babylonian worship. It also tells of Daniel's rescue from the lions.
- **Prayer of Manasseh** is supposedly the confessional prayer of wicked King Manasseh of Judah after he was taken captive to Babylon (2 Chron. 33:12-13).
- **1 Maccabees** is the history of the Maccabean period (175–135 B.C.), telling of the Jews' heroic struggle for liberty.
- **2 Maccabees** covers in part the same period as 1 Maccabees but is somewhat inferior in content.

Reasons for rejecting the books of the Apocrypha include the following:

- The apocryphal books were never included in the OT canon by such recognized authorities as the Pharisees and Ezra.

- None of them were ever quoted by any NT writers.
- The great Jewish historian Josephus excluded them.
- The well-known Jewish philosopher Philo did not recognize them.
- The early church fathers excluded them.
- The Bible translator Jerome did not accept them, though the pope forced him to include them in the Latin Vulgate Bible.
- None of these 14 books claims divine inspiration; in fact, some actually disclaim it.
- Some of them teach false doctrines, such as praying for the dead.
- No apocryphal book can be found in any catalogue list of canonical books composed during the first four centuries A.D. In fact, it was not until 1546 at the Council of Trent that the Roman Catholic church officially recognized these books, basically in an attempt to strengthen certain of its doctrines that had been undermined by the Reformers.

Though excluded from the biblical canon, the books of the Apocrypha remain valuable resources on the history, religion, and culture of Bible times, especially of the intertestamental period. Another valuable source for biblical history is the collection of writings known as the Pseudepigrapha, so called because many were written under pseudonyms. These writings cover the period c. 200 years before to c. 200 years after Christ. For further information, see *The Old Testament Pseudepigrapha,* ed. James H. Charlesworth and *The New Testament Apocrypha,* ed. R. McL. Wilson.

Recognition of the Canon

The Old Testament. By 300 B.C. (at the latest) all OT books had been written, collected, revered, and recognized as official, canonical books. Many believe Ezra led the first recognition council.

The New Testament. During the Third Council of Carthage, A.D. 397, the 27 books that make up the NT as we know it were declared to be canonical. However, it must be understood that the Bible is not an authorized collection of books, but rather a collection of authorized books: The 27 NT books are not to be seen as inspired simply because the Carthage Council proclaimed them to be; rather, they proclaimed them to be inspired because it was obvious to them that they were.

Accuracy of the Canon

Can we be sure that the books of our Bible have been preserved for us in exactly the way God inspired their authors to write them?

The bad news: As every Bible student knows, none of the actual, original versions of any of the 66 books has been preserved. Our Bible today is a translation of a copy (or copies) of the original writings.

The good news: Even though the original books are lost, there is overwhelming evidence that our translated Bibles today represent amazingly accurate copies of the first manuscripts. The number of existing Hebrew and Greek Bible manuscript fragments runs literally into the thousands. There are some 5,300 NT Greek manuscripts. Years of scholarly comparison among these manuscripts have led to a consensus among scholars that the Bible as we have it today is virtually identical to the original manuscripts.

❖ ❖ ❖

TRANSLATION

Perhaps the most thrilling story in human history is the account of the earnest and sometimes agonizing efforts to translate God's precious Word into the languages of particular times and places. Literally billions of hours have gone into this effort. We shall briefly examine some of the better known fruits of all this sweat and study.

Before the time of Christ

The Dead Sea Scrolls. In 1947, in some caves near the Dead Sea, a discovery was made that would soon excite the entire religious world. This discovery was the Dead Sea Scrolls. Archaeologist William F. Albright calls this find "the most important discovery ever made concerning the Old Testament manuscripts." These scrolls were probably hidden there sometime during the second century B.C. by a Jewish religious order called the Essenes. The scrolls included fragments in Hebrew of every OT book except Esther. Especially exciting was a complete scroll of Isaiah.

This discovery was so important because, till then, the earliest available copy of Isaiah's writings dated from the ninth century A.D. Now scholars could move more than a thousand years closer to the time when the prophet actually wrote (c. 700 B.C.). When a comparison was made between the Dead Sea copy and the ninth-century copy, they were found to be almost identical, once again reassuring us that our copy of God's Word today is indeed accurate and reliable. See *The Dead Sea Scrolls,* p. 901.

The Greek Septuagint. The Septuagint is a translation of the OT Hebrew into Greek, made around 250 B.C. at the request of Jewish leaders concerned about the many Jews who had moved away from Palestine and no longer understood Hebrew. It was called the "Septuagint" (Greek for "seventy") because, according to tradition, it was translated by 70 Jewish scholars in just 70 days. The Septuagint was the Bible used in Jesus' day.

From the time of Christ to the fifth century A.D.

The Papyri. Hundreds of sheets of papyrus were found in central Egypt in 1895. Some were stuffed in mummy cases and embalmed crocodile bodies. Among the sheets was a two-by-three-inch fragment containing John 18:31-38. Carbon-14 dating has shown this to have been written around A.D. 125, making it the closest to the original of any known Bible manuscript.

The Latin Vulgate. During the fourth century A.D. it was felt that a new translation of the Bible was needed in Latin, the common language in the Western world. In 382 the scholar Jerome was appointed by Damascus, Bishop of Rome, to begin the translation. For the next 25 years Jerome worked, going right to the Hebrew and Greek. The term *vulgate* comes from the Latin word for "common," and indeed the Vulgate, though in Latin, would be the most widely recognized Bible of English-speaking Christendom until the King James Version in 1611. In 1228 Stephen Langton, archbishop of Canterbury, divided the Vulgate into chapters; in 1551 Robert Stephens divided it into verses; and around 1571 the verses were numbered. The Vulgate Bible was reputedly the first book to be printed by Johann Gutenberg, in 1455.

Codex Sinaiticus. This Greek manuscript of both Testaments dates from approximately 330. It was discovered by the German Bible scholar Konstantin von Tischendorf in the monastery of St. Catherine on Mount Sinai in 1844. While visiting the monastery he noticed vellum pages with Greek writings on them, in a wastebasket waiting to be burned—and discovered that they contained Scripture. The Codex Sinaiticus consists of 199 pages of the OT plus the entire NT. On December 24, 1933, this priceless document that came so close to being burned was sold to the British government by the Soviet Union for $510,000. It is now in the British Museum.

Codex Vaticanus, also from around 330, has been in the Vatican Library in Rome since 1481, and until the nineteenth century Roman Catholic popes had refused to allow competent Bible scholars to study it. It is thought that both this codex and the Codex Sinaiticus are among the original 50 copies ordered by Emperor Constantine shortly after he came to power in 312. It is, however, incomplete, omitting the Pastoral Epistles, Philemon, Revelation, and the last few chapters of Hebrews.

Codex Alexandrinus dates from around 450 in Egypt. It was given to the Patriarch of Alexandria in 1708, and in 1757 was transferred to the British Museum.

The Coptic Version. During the second century a new kind of language came into being that was a mixture of Greek and Egyptian and became known as Coptic. Around 350, several Bible translations were made from Greek into this emerging language.

The Ethiopic Version. We know there were Ethiopian Christians as early as Acts 8:26-39. The earliest Ethiopic translation dates from around 350. It is both readable and accurate in its verbal rendering of the Greek.

The Gothic Version: Codex Argentus. The Goths, a warlike people, lived north of the Danube River and west of the Black Sea, the area of present-day Hungary and Romania. During one of their raids into Asia Minor (present-day Turkey), they captured a young man named Ulfilos. Ulfilos was a Christian scholar, and in about 350 he translated the Scriptures into Gothic. He left out the books of Samuel and Kings for fear that they would only encourage the Goths in their warlike ways! A copy of this version, with its gold and silver letters on purple vellum, is in the University Library at Uppsala, Sweden.

The Armenian Version. In about 406 a missionary and writer named Mesrob began translating the Bible into Armenian. Some call it the most beautiful and accurate of all ancient versions.

English translations from the fifth century to the present

OLD ENGLISH PERIOD (450–1100)

There were at least 10 known translators of the Bible during this period, including a servant, two bishops, two monks, a king, two priests, an archbishop, and a hermit. Of these we will note two:

Caedmon (d. 680). This stable worker at a monastery in North England did not translate the Bible on paper but rather memorized great portions of it and sang it with his harp in short lines of beautiful Celtic-Saxon verse wherever he traveled. He sang the story of Genesis, Exodus, a part of Daniel, the doctrines of the resurrection, ascension, and the Second Coming of Christ, and of heaven and hell.

Bede (674–735). This godly monk, scholar, historian, and theologian, commonly known as "the Venerable Bede," is often called the "Father of English history."

MIDDLE ENGLISH PERIOD (1100–1500)

One name stands out from this period: **John Wycliffe** (1329–1384) has often been called the "morning star of the Reformation." He was a teacher at Oxford University, as well as a preacher, reformer, and translator. Wycliffe was the first to translate the entire Bible into the English language, doing for England what Martin Luther would later do for Germany. His was the only English Bible translation for 145 years.

MODERN ENGLISH PERIOD (1500–present)

The Tyndale Version (1525). If Wycliffe was the "morning star" of the Reformation, then William Tyndale's Bible could rightly be called the "Milky Way" of modern English Bible translations. Perhaps no other man in history did as much in translating the Word of God for the people of God as did William Tyndale. It is thought that Tyndale's NT was based on the Greek text of the scholar Erasmus (first printed in 1516) and that his OT text was taken in part from a 1488 Hebrew version. He also consulted the Latin Vulgate and Martin Luther's translation. Tyndale was martyred in 1536.

The Coverdale Version (1535). Miles Coverdale, born in 1488, was converted to Christ and developed a strong love for Scripture. He was a friend of Tyndale and later finished Tyndale's OT translation and revised his NT. It was a secondary translation, based on Latin, German, and English translations, since Coverdale was not familiar with the Greek or Hebrew.

Matthew's Version (1537) was translated by John Rogers, who used the pseudonym Thomas Matthew. Rogers, a known friend of Tyndale, felt his work would be more acceptable if this relationship were not known. Rogers was burned to death for his opposition to Roman Catholicism in 1555, during the reign of Bloody Mary. Matthew's Version was the first revision of the Tyndale Bible. Ironically, it was approved by King Henry VIII, who had hated Tyndale and his work.

The Great Bible (1539). The notes and prefaces of Tyndale's and Coverdale's translations aroused so much argument that Henry VIII authorized a new version that would include no controversial footnote material. It was called the Great Bible because of its size. In 1538 the king issued an injunction that all churches should purchase a copy of the Great Bible, making it the first English Bible "appointed to be read in all the churches." In practice, this substantial volume was usually chained to a "reading post" within a church and was therefore not as accessible to the ordinary parishioner as it might have been. The King James Version is basically a revision of the Great Bible.

The Geneva Bible (1557). During the vicious persecution of Protestants under Bloody Mary, many Reformers fled to Geneva, Switzerland, and enjoyed the protection of Geneva's great leader John Calvin. It was here that Calvin's brother-in-law, William Whittingham, produced the Geneva Bible, based on the text of the Great Bible. This translation became important for the following reasons:

- It was the first English version to divide the text into verses.
- It was the first to omit the Apocrypha.
- It was the most-beloved Bible of the common people up to that time, and went through more than 160 editions.
- It was the Bible of Shakespeare and John Bunyan.
- It was the Bible the pilgrims brought with them on the Mayflower to America in 1620.

The Bishops' Bible (1568). This version was called for because the Church of England did not use the notes in the Geneva Bible and because the Geneva Bible was undermining the authority of the Great Bible and of the bishops. The Bishop's Bible was translated by Matthew Parker, archbishop of Canterbury, and nine other bishops. It was the second "authorized version" of the church, but was never accepted by the common people. Even Queen Elizabeth ignored it. It has gone down in history as the most unsatisfactory and useless of all the old translations.

The Rheims-Douai Bible (1582) represented an attempt by the pope to win England back to the Roman fold. The translation team was headed by William Allen and Gregory Martin, two Protestant turncoats from Oxford University. The name comes from the two places where the OT and NT were produced. The Douai Version was the first Catholic English Bible and was taken almost literally from the Latin Vulgate. The footnotes in this version strongly attacked all Protestant "heresies" and defended all Roman Catholic doctrines and practices.

The King James Version (1611). One of the first tasks King James faced upon ascending his throne at the beginning of the seventeenth century was the reconciliation of the various religious parties within his kingdom. Work on the King James Version began with a request by Puritan spokesman John Reynolds of Oxford concerning the need for a new translation. James agreed almost at once. He had disliked the popular Geneva Bible because of its footnotes. He also realized that neither the Geneva, nor the Great, nor the Bishop's Bible could be held up by him as a rallying point for Christians.

The King James Version is remarkable for many reasons. It is, first of all, undoubtedly the most beautiful, beloved, and popular English translation to date. It is also probably the only translation in which no parties involved had an axe to grind. In other words, it was a national undertaking in which no one had any interest at heart, save that of producing the best possible version of the Scriptures.

The King James Version was not, however, immediately accepted by the general public. The Roman Catholics claimed it favored Protestantism. Arminians said it leaned toward Calvinism. The Puritans disliked certain words such as "bishop," "ordain," and "Easter." But after some 40 years it overtook the popular Geneva Bible.

The English Revision of the King James Version (1881–85). By the late nineteenth century, the Church of England felt that a new revision of the King James Version was needed for the following reasons:

- Changes in the meanings of some words
- The discovery of new manuscripts since 1611
- The improved science of biblical criticism

The American Revision of the King James Version (1901). The American Standard Version offered several changes and improvements over its English cousin, such as

- substitution of "demon" for "devil" (Greek, *daimon*);
- "Holy Spirit" instead of "Holy Ghost";
- "who" instead of "which" in reference to persons. (The KJV's "Our Father, which art in heaven," became, "Our Father, who art in heaven.")

A select listing from the latter half of the 20th century:

- Revised Standard Version (1952)
- Anchor Bible (1964)
- Amplified Bible (1965)
- Jerusalem Bible (1966)
- New English Bible (1970)
- New American Standard Bible (1971)
- The Living Bible (1971)
- Good News for Modern Man (1976)
- New International Version (1978)
- New King James Version (1982)
- New Century Bible (1988)
- The Message (1994)
- The New Living Translation (1996)

ARCHAEOLOGY AND THE BIBLE

The Bible does not depend on archaeological discoveries for proof of its authenticity. It claims to be the inspired word of God (see *Inspiration,* p. 877), and its internal consistency and cohesiveness backs up that claim. However, the findings of archaeologists can increase one's faith in and understanding of the Bible in several ways:

- Archaeology *confirms* and *corroborates* the biblical record historically and chronologically, often giving additional information concerning people and events of which the Bible gives only a glimpse.
- It adds helpful *color* and *clarification* to the biblical accounts of people and and events remote from us in time and culture.

Archaeological evidence is as abundant for biblical people and events as for those of secular history. The findings discussed below are only a representative sample.

22 OLD TESTAMENT FINDS

Mount Ararat

A unique coin, now on display at the Israel Museum, presents new evidence for the antiquity of the tradition associating the mountains of Ararat in Turkey with the landing place of Noah's ark, according to Yaakov Meshorer (see *Biblical Archaeology Review,* Sept./Oct., 1981). This large bronze medallion was struck 1,700 years ago at Apameia Kibotos in Asia Minor (modern Turkey) near the mountains of Ararat. The town was named for Apameia, mother of Antiochus I (280–261 B.C.). The Greek word *kibotos,* which means "ark," was added to differentiate this Apameia from two nearby towns of the same name. Its use shows that, in the third century B.C., the Jewish people of Apameia associated their town with the ark. "Kiboto"s is inscribed on the coin.

The coin depicts events of the story of Noah's ark (Gen. 6–8), the only coin known to bear biblical scenes. Three events are depicted on one side of the coin. In the center, the ark, depicted as a box with an open lid, floats on water. The heads and shoulders of Noah and his wife protrude from the ark while the lid shelters them from the rain. The side of the ark is inscribed with the three Greek letters *NOE* (Nu, Omega, Epsilon). Above the ark's lid, a dove with an olive spray in its beak is landing on the cover of the ark, symbolizing the subsidence of the Flood. The third event is shown to the right of the ark. Noah and his wife are standing with arms upraised in an attitude of grateful prayer for their salvation.

Sodom and Gomorrah

Have Sodom and Gomorrah been found? Walter E. Rast, of Valparaiso University, and R. Thomas Schaub, of Indiana University of Pennsylvania, excavated two sites near the eastern shore of the Dead Sea in Jordan and say they strongly believe these are the biblical cities destroyed by fire (see *Biblical Archaeology Review,* Sept./Oct. 1980, p. 27).

The principal site, Bab edh-Dhra, lies less than one mile east of the Lissan, a tongue-like peninsula that protrudes into the Dead Sea on the eastern shore. It was occupied during the Early Bronze Age (third millennium B.C.). Overlooking the Dead Sea from a height of 550 feet, Bab edh-Dhra was no doubt built on a bluff for defense purposes. The site consists of a town and a large cemetery. One scholar estimated that the cemetery is composed of more than 20,000 tombs in which more than 500,000 people were buried along with more than three million pottery vessels. A large rectangular structure found inside the town is thought to be a temple. The archaeologists also uncovered the remains of what they believe was the altar associated with the temple.

It is significant that there are only five sites located in the Dead Sea area, each near a flowing spring; that all five date to the same time, the Early Bronze Age; and that there is no other evidence of occupation in the area until the Roman period more than 2,000 years later. Sodom and Gomorrah had been part of a coalition of five cities that had rebelled against their overlord (Gen. 14). The five are generally referred to as the "cities of the plain" (Gen. 13:12; 19:29) and include Sodom, Gomorrah, Admah, Zeboiim, and Bella, or Zoar (Gen. 14:2). Geographical references in Genesis 14 seem to suggest that they were located in the Dead Sea area. One reference is to "Siddim Valley (that is, the valley of the Dead Sea)" (Gen. 14:3).

If Bab edh-Dhra and the four other sites are indeed the remains of the five "cities of the plain," it is also significant that the foundations of some of the buildings were buried under tons of rubble, and that beneath the rubble there is clear evidence of a fiery conflagration.

Oldest Biblical Text

In June 1986 archaeologists in Jerusalem announced the discovery of the oldest biblical text ever found. On two small silver amulets was part of the text of Numbers 6:24-26. The find was actually made about three years earlier in a dig conducted by Gabriel Barkay of Tel Aviv University, on the grounds of the Scottish Presbyterian Church across the Hinnom Valley from Mount Zion and the Old City of Jerusalem. Announcement of the find was delayed at first because the dig itself was being kept secret because it was on the site of ancient graves, and any digging around Jewish graves is sure to bring a hostile reaction. Another reason for the delayed announcement was that it had taken a long time and much tedious work to open the fragile, rolled-up amulets.

Even when the silver scrolls were opened, the text was so faint and small that it took some time to decipher. It was clear right away that it was in the most ancient Hebrew script, not at all like the script in use today, nor like that of the time of

Jesus. The script was, in fact, in keeping with the dating already assigned to the site—the First Temple period, between 960 B.C. and the time when the Temple was destroyed in 586. Barkay placed it in the century preceding that destruction, making it about 400 years older than the Dead Sea Scrolls, which had provided the oldest biblical text to date. The part of the scrolls that can be read is almost identical in content to the Hebrew text of that passage in use today.

The age of the text may prove to be a nail in the coffin of theories that the Pentateuch was not written by Moses nor even in Moses' time. Those theories generally place large portions of the first five books of the Bible in the period of Ezra, 400–500 B.C. In this debate, some of the argument revolves around the use of YHWH, the divine name of God (sometimes transliterated "Jehovah"), which was supposedly not in use before 400–500 B.C. The silver scrolls, dating from before 586, contain that name. In fact, this was the first time that the name had been found in any dig in Jerusalem.

Tel el-Qudeirat/Kadesh-barnea

Between 1976 and 1979, Rudolph Cohen began excavating at Tel el-Qudeirat, searching for the ancient Kadesh-barnea of Numbers 13–14. The springs there are the most abundant in Sinai, watering the largest oasis in northern Sinai. Cohen feels there is a strong possibility that Tel el-Qudeirat is indeed ancient Kadesh, the very spot where Moses sent the 12 Israelite men to scout out the Promised Land. In fact, the place is now officially known as Tel Kadesh-barnea.

Mount Ebal

Just prior to his death, Moses commanded that after crossing the Jordan and entering the Promised Land, the Law should be read for the congregation of Israel upon two mountains. The promised blessings for keeping the Law were to be proclaimed from Mount Gerizim, and the judgments for disobeying God's commandments were to be read from Mount Ebal (Deut. 27–28), just east of Gerizim.

The actual ceremony on Mount Ebal, in obedience to Moses' command, is described in Joshua: "Then Joshua built an altar to the LORD, the God of Israel, on Mount Ebal. He followed the instructions that Moses the LORD's servant had written in the Book of the Law: 'Make me an altar from stones that are uncut and have not been shaped with iron tools.' Then on the altar they presented burnt offerings and peace offerings to the LORD" (Josh. 8:30-31).

In 1980 Adam Zertel began excavating on Mount Ebal. This 3,000-foot-high mountain, the highest in Samaria, is located some 30 miles due north of Jerusalem. Before the initial project ended some three years later, strong evidence suggested that Zertel and his team may have uncovered the altar built by Joshua some 1,400 years before Christ. He discovered a rectangular altar once filled with alternating layers of earth, ash, and field stones. It was approximately 9 feet high, 25 feet wide, and 30 feet long, with walls 5 feet thick. Its large stones were uncut, just as prescribed in Joshua. Around the altar were the burned bones of young bulls, sheep, and goats. The altar had a ramp leading up to it, instead of steps like most pagan altars. This would correspond to Exodus 20:26, which requires a ramp rather than steps. Pottery shards found near the altar suggest a date concurrent with the time of Joshua.

Shiloh

After the conquest of Canaan, Joshua assembled the Israelites at Shiloh and erected the Tabernacle (Josh. 18:1). Shiloh was established as the religious center of Israel, a position it apparently held throughout the period of the judges. In the days of Eli and Samuel, the Ark of the Covenant was taken from Shiloh to Ebenezer, where Israel was engaged in battle with the Philistines (1 Sam. 4:1-4). Israel lost the battle, and the Philistines captured the Ark. It was taken on a "tour" through Philistine cities, bringing a plague with it at each stop. When the Philistines returned the Ark to Israel, it eventually ended up at Kiriath-jearim in the house of Abinadab (1 Sam. 7:1-2). It was never returned to Shiloh. No explanation is given as to why it was not returned to the religious center.

Shiloh (modern Seilun) was excavated by Danish archaeologists in four stages, 1926–1963. In the early 1980s, Israel Finkelstein returned there to excavate and reevaluate their findings. His excavation confirmed an earlier conclusion of the Danes, that Shiloh had been destroyed by fire around 1050 B.C. Though the Bible does not record the fact, apparently Israel's religious center was destroyed after the Ark had been taken from it, and that is why the Ark was not returned there.

Pim

From Scripture we learn that the Philistines were more technically advanced in metalworking than the Israelites (a fact confirmed by archaeology), and therefore the Israelites were compelled to have their tools and implements sharpened by the Philistines (1 Sam. 13:19-22). Yet the KJV says that the Israelites "had a file for the mattocks" and their other implements (1 Sam. 13:21), which causes one to wonder why the Israelites needed to have the Philistines sharpen their instruments.

The problem concerns the Hebrew word *pim,* which the KJV translates "file" and which for a long time defied any better translation. Now, at various sites, archaeologists have found *weights* bearing the inscription *pim.* Though the precise meaning of the term is not entirely clear, it is now recognized that *pim* represents a weight equivalent to two-thirds of a shekel. Thus the once problematic text informs us that the Israelites were paying a fee of two-thirds a shekel to have their plow points sharpened. All modern translations reflect this new understanding.

Millo

Another difficult word that archaeology has helped us understand is "Millo" (2 Sam. 5:9, KJV). The Hebrew word *millo* is not difficult, for it has to do with "filling." But Millo is something that David, Solomon, and Hezekiah were said to have built or repaired (1 Kings 9:24; 11:27; 1 Chron. 11:8; 2 Chron. 32:5). Older commentators suggested that this was perhaps a corner tower or something similar. Kathleen Kenyon's excavations at Jerusalem in the 1960s have helped a great deal. She learned that the millo was probably a series of terraces along the eastern side of the Jebusite town of Jerusalem upon which houses were built, allowing for an expansion of the residential area—a town laid out on terraces was better than one built on a steep slope. Unfortunately, however, terraces were liable to collapse. Thus the walls of the structures needed repair from time to time, as especially the NIV of 2 Chron. 32:5 affirms.

Warren's Shaft

It is commonly believed that, much earlier than Hezekiah built his tunnel to ensure Jerusalem's water supply (see *Hezekiah's Tunnel,* p. 893), someone else had a similar plan and had a shaft cut to the Gihon Spring. This shaft was discovered in 1867 by Charles Warren. It was explored again in 1909–1911 by M. B. Parker and most recently in the early 1980s by Yigael Shilo. Some scholars have suggested that this shaft is the "water tunnel" through which David's officer Joab first penetrated the city to take it from the Jebusites (2 Sam. 5:6-8; 1 Chron. 11:4-6, KJV).

The City of David

One of the most fascinating archaeological finds in recent years came in the summer of 1983 at the "City of David" (2 Sam. 5:9) dig just a few hundred yards from the southern wall of Jerusalem's Old City. 26 clay seals were unearthed, bearing the names of dozens of people who lived in Jerusalem in the time of the first Temple, 960–586 B.C. (The seals were on the floor of a building dating back to 600–800.) Some of the names of Jewish merchants and citizens mentioned in the seals may be those of people mentioned in Scripture.

Yigael Shilo and his team also came across the debris left by the Babylonians' destruction of Jerusalem. Some of the piles of rubble were reportedly nearly 10 feet high. Probing beneath the ruins, Shilo found remnants of the original Canaanite wall that had surrounded the city when young King David took Jerusalem and made it his capital. Shilo also found tools and pottery used by the people of Jerusalem in the time of David and Solomon.

Fortresses Built by Solomon

One of Solomon's first projects after securing Israel's throne was to build fortified cities in the central Negev to protect the southern flank of his kingdom (1 Kings 9:15-19). During the reign of Solomon's son Rehoboam, Shishak, ruler of Egypt, destroyed these southern strongholds (1 Kings 14:25-26; 2 Chron. 12:1-12). In the 1960s and 70s, archaeologists Rudolph Cohen, Z'ev Meshel, and others discovered 11 of Solomon's oval fortresses. Some were 406 feet in circumference, with walls 6 feet high and 6 feet thick. The architecture of the houses found in the settlements near the fortresses was of standard Israelite origin. Pottery discovered in the area suggests a 10th-century period, the time of Solomon and Rehoboam.

The Black Obelisk

When the Assyrian king Shalmaneser III made a successful campaign into Syria, he left a boastful record of his success on a 6 1/2-foot-high black sandstone pillar. The pillar was found at Calah (modern Nimrud) in 1946 by archaeologist Austen Henry Layard, and is today known as the Black Obelisk. It bears five rows of bas-relief panels on each of its four sides, with a descriptive inscription over each panel. One panel in the second row from the top shows a bearded Semite kneeling before the king while his servants standing behind him present tribute. This kneeling figure is identified by the inscription: "Tribute of Jehu, son of Omri." (Jehu was not actually the son of Omri but may have been called that because he took the kingship from the house of Omri—1 Kings 16:23-28; 2 Kings 9:1-13; 10.)

The Black Obelisk is important for several reasons. It is our only extant graphic representation of an Israelite king (or perhaps his representative). It bears another reference to Jehu's predecessor, Omri. It presents a graphic description of Israelite dress. And it supplements Scripture by telling us of Jehu paying tribute to Shalmaneser. Perhaps it was this action of Jehu that warded off an invasion by Assyria during his reign.

Ahab

Bible readers are familiar with Israel's notoriously wicked king Ahab, who reigned 874–853 B.C. (1 Kings 16:28–22:40). He is best known for his marriage to Jezebel, their worship of Baal, and their undying hatred of Elijah. Scripture records Ahab's confrontations with Ben-hadad and the Syrians, but little else is said of his foreign policy or his influence on the larger international scene. Archaeology has produced several editions of the annals of the Assyrian King Shalmaneser III (858–824). From them we learn that Shalmaneser's drive to the northwest to raid and plunder was checked by an anti-Assyrian coalition at Qarqar in northern Syria in 853. His own records tell of the 12 kings who comprised the coalition to stop him. Ahab of Israel ("A-ha-ab-bu Sir'-i-la-a-a") is identified as one of the coalition leaders (along with the kings of Damascus and Hamath), and he is credited with making a major contribution of 2,000 chariots and 10,000 foot soldiers to this successful resistance effort.

The Moabite Stone

Both Ahab and his father, Omri, are named on the Moabite Stone (sometimes called the Mesha Stele). This monument, which is probably dated between 840 and 820, was found about 13 miles east of the Dead Sea at Diban by a missionary, F. A. Klein, in 1868. Mesha, king of Moab (2 Kings 3:4), writes that Omri, king of Israel, and his son Ahab had subdued Moab because Chemosh, the national god, was angry with his land. Mesha, however, claims to have found favor with Chemosh and to have been enabled to rebel and reclaim the land lost to Israel. His rebellion against Israel and Ahab's son, Jehoram, is attested to in Scripture (2 Kings 3:5-27), but the successful outcome that he reports is fanciful and contradictory to the biblical record. It is interesting that Mesha mentions Chemosh's counterpart, Israel's God, Yahweh, in his account of the events.

Mazar's Discoveries at the Temple Mount

Since 1968, Benjamin Mazar has been directing excavation of a section of the Temple Mount, near its southwestern corner, on behalf of the Hebrew University of Jerusalem. Excavators found a huge stone on the southwest corner of the Herodian Temple Mount retaining wall. Inscribed on the stone were Hebrew words translated, "The place of the trumpeting." Doubtless this was the actual location where the priest stood when he blew the *shofar* to announce to all Jerusalem the arrival and departure of the Sabbath (Lev. 23:24; 25:9). Mazar may also have uncovered the building where Joash (835–795) was murdered by his own palace guard (2 Kings 12:20-21).

Sennacherib, Taylor Prism

Scripture reports that in the 14th year of Hezekiah (701), the Assyrian king Sennacherib (705–681) invaded Judah and marched against Jerusalem (2 Kings 18:13). Having held the city in siege and threatened Hezekiah, he retreated to

Assyria after the death angel killed 185,000 of his men (2 Kings 19:35). It was then that he recounted his version of the event on a hexagonal cylinder discovered at Kuyunjik (ancient Nineveh) in 1830 by J. E. Taylor. Sennacherib boasted of taking 46 walled cities in Judah. And concerning Hezekiah he stated, "He himself I shut up like a caged bird within Jerusalem, his royal city." What Sennacherib conveniently failed to admit was that Hezekiah remained quite safe and protected from the Assyrians inside his city, while Sennacherib's men were miraculously killed.

Hezekiah's Tunnel, Siloam

Hezekiah made preparations for Sennacherib's invasion in 701 by seeking to maintain an adequate water supply within the safety of the city walls (2 Kings 20:20; 2 Chron. 32:2-5). He had a conduit cut underground through the rock to channel water from the Gihon Spring outside the city wall to the Pool of Siloam inside the city. This channel, known as Hezekiah's Tunnel, runs a very crooked course for approximately 1,700 feet. One can visit it and even walk through it today. A six-line Hebrew inscription (called the "Siloam Inscription") was found in 1880 in the channel near the Pool of Siloam. It describes the workers cutting through the rock, beginning from both ends and meeting triumphantly at the midpoint.

The Babylonian Chronicles

As in most languages, Hebrew prepositions have a variety of possible meanings. At a time when the OT was the primary source for ancient Near Eastern history, the KJV of 2 Kings 23:29 translated the Hebrew preposition *al* as "against," although it can also mean "alongside of" or "on behalf of." Thus it appears that Pharaoh Neco went to fight "against" the king of Assyria but that Josiah interfered and was killed. The question arose, why would Josiah try to prevent someone from fighting his enemy, the king of Assyria?

From the Babylonian Chronicles we learn that the Egyptian army had come to help the Assyrian king. Thus Neco had come not "against" him but alongside of or on behalf of him. Modern translations reflect this new understanding of Josiah's interference.

The Lachish Wall

Just before threatening Jerusalem in 701, Sennacherib had laid siege to Lachish, Judah's second most important city (2 Chron. 32:9). Beginning in 1973, David Ussishkin, sponsored by Tel Aviv University and the Israel Exploration Society, unearthed a counter wall ramp, some 360 feet long, erected against the inner wall of the ancient city to support it from the expected Assyrian attack. Ussishkin also excavated the siege ramp built by the attacking Assyrians. It measures 215 feet wide at the bottom and extends to 170 feet. Several dozen arrowheads, apparently fired by the enemy toward the defenders on the wall, were found, along with some scales of Assyrian armor.

The Ridge South of the Temple Mount

In 1978 Yigael Shilo began excavating the eastern portion of the ridge south of the Temple Mount in Jerusalem. Shilo's dig has produced the most extensive information available thus far on the last years of the Judean monarchy. Several houses of the late pre-exilic period were found. Built on terraces, these structures become progressively poorer the closer in time they came to the Babylonian destruction. The most sensational find was a hoard of 50 clay seals, among them one belonging to "Gemariah the son of Shaphan"—certainly the same individual mentioned in Jeremiah 36:9-12 as scribe to King Jehoiakim. Shilo believes that the building where this seal was found may have been part of the royal chancellery.

The Nabonidus Chronicles

Until 1854 the Bible was the lone witness to a person known as Belshazzar, the Babylonian king named in Daniel 5. Greek historians claimed that the last king of Babylon, who fell to Cyrus in 539, was Nabonidus (555–539). In 1854 J. G. Taylor found several small clay cylinders bearing inscriptions in temple ruins at Ur in southern Iraq. The inscriptions contained prayers for Nabonidus and his firstborn son, Belshazzar. But then in 1882 T. G. Pinches published what is known as the Nabonidus Chronicles. From this record it was learned that Nabonidus fell into disfavor with the priests of Marduk, the patron deity at Babylon, because of his zeal for the moon god Sin. Consequently he spent many years away from Babylon in self-imposed exile at a remote oasis in Teima in Arabia. He left his son Belshazzar as regent in Babylon, which explains Belshazzar's offer to make Daniel the "third highest ruler in the kingdom" if he could interpret the handwriting on the wall (Dan. 5:16).

The Cyrus Cylinder

The Cyrus Cylinder answers doubts raised by Ezra 1:2-4. Ezra states that, in his first year after conquering Babylon, Cyrus acknowledged the Lord God of heaven, who had commanded him to build the Temple in Jerusalem and permit God's people (the Jews) to return. Scholars of the past century had serious doubts that the Persian Cyrus would pay any honor to the God of the Jews, or grant them special privileges to return to their homeland.

In the nineteenth century, Hormuzd Rassam found at Babylon a nine-inch, baked clay cylinder. Its inscription gives Cyrus's account of how Marduk had blessed his efforts to capture Babylon. Then Cyrus tells how he had made it his policy to permit all former Babylonian captives to return to their homelands and restore the temples of their national deities. In reality, Cyrus was exploiting the occasion to his advantage. He understood that happy and satisfied subjects would be loyal subjects. So Cyrus's act of benevolence was simply part of his international policy. He was, however, unwittingly fulfilling Isaiah's prophecy concerning him (Isa. 44:28–45:1), that he would be the Lord's "shepherd" and "anointed one" who would perform his pleasure.

❖ ❖ ❖

FIVE NEW TESTAMENT FINDS

Simon Peter's House

In 1968 archaeologists V. Corbo and S. Loffreda turned their attention to an octagonal-shaped building near the Capernaum synagogue. The discovery of an apse and baptistry identified the building as a church. It was dated to the middle of the fifth century A.D. It is known that a similar octagonal-shaped church in Bethlehem marks the spot where Jesus is believed to have been born. Therefore, it has been concluded that this church in Capernaum was also a memorial to something. But what?

It was discovered that the church was situated over a house, the layout of which was similar to others in Capernaum, except that it alone had plastered walls and floors. Over 100 Christian graffiti were found scratched in the plaster fragments, some of which mention Jesus as "Lord" and "Christ." Peter's name appears several times. One very indistinct inscription has been interpreted by the Franciscan archaeologists to read, "Peter, the helper of Rome," though other scholars are not so certain of this.

It does appear, though, that the house was originally built in the first century B.C. and used as a house church in the first century A.D. But why was this house selected as a meeting place for Christians? In the fourth century Christian pilgrims on visits to Capernaum claimed to have seen Peter's house. Is the octagonal-shaped church a memorial to the apostle Peter's home (Matt. 8:14; Mark 1:29)? Corbo and Loffreda think it is.

The Galilean Boat

A severe drought in Israel in 1985–1986 led to an accidental but extraordinary discovery. With the water level of the Sea of Galilee (Kinneret) extremely low, wide areas of the lake bed were exposed. In January, 1986, Moshe and Yuval Lufan were exploring the lake bed when they discovered the oval outline of a boat buried entirely in the mud. Careful removal of the mud around one section of the boat revealed that the planks of the hull were edge-joined with mortise-and-tenon joints and held in place with wooden pegs. (This was the characteristic form of construction of ancient boats found sunken in the Mediterranean Sea, dating as early as the fourteenth and fifteenth centuries B.C.) Pieces of pottery found near the boat and carbon-14 tests have led to a 120 B.C. to A.D. 40 dating of the boat.

The boat, measuring 26.5 feet long, 7.5 feet wide, and 4.5 feet deep, has generated tremendous excitement and considerable speculation. It is believed that the boat had a mast for a sail. Thus it could have been sailed and rowed, perhaps by as many as four oarsmen. A boat of this size and construction could easily have accommodated Jesus and his disciples on their many trips across the Sea (e.g., Mark 4:35-41; Matt. 9:1; 14:22-32; 15:39). This large a boat would also have been the kind necessary for net fishing. This "Kinneret Boat" represents the kind of boat referred to in the Gospels in relation to Jesus' crossing the sea, and it provides a better understanding of the sailing techniques of NT times.

The Burial Plot of Caiaphas the High Priest

During the creation of a water park in Jerusalem's Peace Forest (just south of the Dome of the Rock) in 1990, workers accidentally uncovered a burial cave. It was clearly a Jewish burial cave, as indicated by the 12 ossuaries found there. Ossuaries are limestone boxes used for storing human bones after the flesh has decomposed; such burial procedures occurred mainly at the end of the first century B.C. and in the first century A.D. Five of the ossuaries were inscribed with names, supposedly the names of those whose bones had been placed inside. The two that drew the most attention, however, were those which were inscribed with a form of the name *Qafa,* (Caiaphas). One ossuary was inscribed simply Qafa, but the other had a more complete inscription, *Yehosef bar Qayafa* (Joseph, son of Caiaphas). One is surely curious whether this is the burial plot for the high priest who presided over the trial of Jesus (Matt. 26:57; John 18:28) or at least a family member. A preliminary dating of the burial cave (by a coin found in one of the other ossuaries) suggests an early first-century A.D. burial. The biblical name Caiaphas seems definitely confirmed. However, the positive identification of the name with the NT high priest, though quite possible, remains uncertain at this date.

The Second Temple "Golden Gate"

In April 1969 archaeologist James Fleming was standing in front of the Jerusalem Golden Gate. Suddenly the rain-soaked earth gave way, and he fell into a hole eight feet deep. Disoriented but uninjured, Fleming surveyed his surroundings in the dim light that came through the hole above his head. As reported in *Biblical Archaeology Review* (Jan./Feb. 1983, p. 24), he saw an ancient wall below the Golden Gate. He comments:

> The gate itself is built into a turret that protrudes about six feet from the wall. The underground stones of the wall south of the turret were large and imposing. . . . On the eastern face of the turret wall, directly beneath the Golden Gate itself, were five wedge-shaped stones neatly set in a massive arch spanning the turret wall. Here were the remains of an earlier gate to Jerusalem, below the Golden Gate, one that apparently had never been fully documented. (p. 30)

Could the Lower Gate Fleming discovered have been the gate through which Jesus entered the Holy City (Mark 11:11)? Unfortunately, it is difficult to date this underground gate precisely. However, according to Fleming's comparison of masonry in the gate with that in other parts of the wall, a date earlier than the time of Christ, and possibly as early as the time of Solomon, is possible.

Fleming concludes:

> Perhaps the most important implication of the presence of the Lower Gate below the threshold of the Golden Gate is that this area has long been identified as a location for the eastern entrance into the Temple Mount. Many Jerusalem maps show a Temple gate due east of the Dome of the Rock in the Haram esh-Sharif. The Golden Gate, however, is located about 350 feet north of this point. We now know that the location of the present Golden Gate was determined by an earlier gate. (p. 37)

The Second Temple Rabbinical Tunnel

Since 1967 Israel's Ministry of Religious Affairs, in cooperation with its Department of Antiquities, has cleared out an ancient passage in Jerusalem that they named the Rabbinical Tunnel. Undoubtedly it dates back to the time of Christ. The tunnel runs north along the Western Wall and is more than 600 feet long. Meir Kusnetz, an American-born civil engineer, has been in charge of the project. Since 1967, more than 17,000 cubic meters of fill have been excavated. The tunnel stops just short of the northwest corner of the Temple Mount. Its starting point is in the hall under Wilson's Arch, directly to the left of the present-day men's prayer section of the Western Wall.

The finished stones inside the tunnel are still beautifully preserved, and some are of unbelievable size. For example, near the beginning of the tunnel is a gigantic chiseled limestone rock 46 feet long, 10 feet wide, and 10 feet high, weighing more than 415 tons! By comparison, the largest megalith at Stonehenge, England, is a mere 40 tons, and the rocks used by the Egyptians to build the pyramids were only 15 tons. Other similar stones weighing more than 300 tons have been uncovered in the tunnel. The massive rocks are so well cut that although there is no mortar holding them together, even a thin knife blade cannot fit between their joints!

Christ's disciples were understandably impressed by the size of these stones (Mark 13:1).

❖ ❖ ❖

EIGHT SITES PRODUCING ARCHIVES

Nineveh

Nineveh's ruins lie about 220 miles northwest of Baghdad on the east bank of the Tigris River. The first investigation of this site is credited to P. E. Botta in 1842, followed by Austen Henry Layard in 1845 and others later. It was Hormuzd Rassam, however, who in 1853 uncovered the remains of the palace of the Assyrian king Ashurbanipal (668–629 B.C.), who is mentioned in Ezra 4:10 (called "Osnappar" in some versions). Most significant, Rassam found Ashurbanipal's library. Among the tablets written in cuneiform script were two epics that have sparked a considerable amount of attention from scholars. One is the Enuma Elish, sometimes called the Babylonian Creation Epic (Pritchard, *Ancient Near Eastern Texts,* pp. 60–72, 501–503), from which scholars have seized upon the most trivial details to find parallels to the Genesis Creation account. The female deity *Ti'amat,* who personified the primeval salt seawater, was connected linguistically to the Hebrew *tehom,* "the deep" of Genesis 1:2 (KJV). This account was written on seven tablets, which were thought, perhaps, to correspond to the seven days of Genesis 1–2. Man's creation occurred in the sixth Enuma Elish tablet, just as man was created on day six of the biblical account.

However, the Babylonian theology of creation shows striking dissimilarities. The epic depicts the god Marduk's ascension to the head of the Babylonian pantheon. The account is mythological and typically polytheistic. Marduk kills the goddess Ti'amat and from her corpse lays out the cosmos. Man is created to relieve the gods of their work. Earlier views that this epic is somehow related to Genesis 1–2 have generally been abandoned.

The second epic, the Gilgamesh Epic, contains noticeable parallels to the Genesis flood. The hero receives divine warning concerning a coming flood and saves himself and his family from impending death by building a ship. The story's framework undeniably corresponds to the biblical account, although there are many differences in the details, most importantly concerning the cause of the flood: In the Gilgamesh Epic it is an arbitrary decision of the gods to eliminate irksome mankind from the earth, not the just decision of a holy God to judge sinful mankind. Despite this difference, however, it is clear that the Gilgamesh Epic and Genesis 6–8 point to the same historical event. Archaeology has shown through the recovery of this independent, extrabiblical tradition a memory of a world judged by water, though the memory is clouded by superstition and polytheism.

Amarna

Amarna is a city on the east side of the Nile River about 190 miles south of Cairo. It marks the site of Akhetaten, a city that replaced Thebes as the capital city of Amenhotep IV (also called Akhenaten, c. 1374–1358). Amarna was not recognized as an important archaeological site until a chance discovery in 1887 by a peasant woman digging in the decayed material of a building. She uncovered clay tablets inscribed with cuneiform writing.

This archive consisted of nearly 380 tablets written in Akkadian, the diplomatic language of the day. More than 350 of the tablets contained royal correspondence between the Egyptian pharaohs and rulers of the Hittites, Mitannians, Assyrians, Babylonians, and of particular interest to biblical students, Syrians and Canaanites. The biblical sites Jerusalem, Gazer, Ashkelon, Shechem, and Megiddo were represented in these letters from Canaan. These extrabiblical citations bear witness to the importance of these Palestinian cities.

The letters from Palestine portray unsettled conditions in the land. A common feature of the letters is a plea to Egypt for help against invaders, some of whom are described as Habiru. Even the ruler of Jerusalem, Abdi-hiba, who wrote six of the letters, felt threatened by these Habiru.

It has been tempting for evangelical students who date the conquest of Canaan at c.1400 B.C. to equate the Habiru with the Israelites. It is believed by many that the name Hebrew derives from Habiru. However, references to the Habiru, who were apparently a landless people, a lower class of society, and sometimes mercenary warriors, have been known to appear in texts found at Mari, Haran, Hattusha, and Ugarit, sites found over a rather large geographical area. It is possible that the Israelites (Hebrews) may have been among the invaders who were called Habiru, but it cannot be assumed that all Habiru were biblical Hebrews. It is not impossible, however, that these Amarna letters do indeed depict unsettled conditions in Canaan shortly after the conquest.

Hattusha

As late as the 19th century, scholars expressed doubts concerning the existence of the people the Bible calls Hittites (Josh. 1:4). Hattusha, a massive 400-acre site at Boghazky, Turkey, about 125 miles east of Ankara, is now known to have been the capital of the Hittite empire. The site was first examined by C. Texier in 1834. The first real excavation, however, was conducted by Hugo Winckler from 1906 to 1912. A large royal archive was unearthed, containing more than 10,000 clay tablets in an unknown language (cuneiform script). These Hittite tablets were deciphered in 1915 by Bedrich Hrozny, and as a result, a people lost in history were rediscovered and seen in their historic splendor and prominence in the ancient Near East.

Of particular interest to Bible scholars is what these tablets revealed about the characteristic Hittite treaty form. 21 reasonably well-preserved suzerainty treaties of the 14th–13th centuries B.C. display a remarkable similarity in structure to parts of Exodus, Deuteronomy, and Joshua 24. Critical scholarship has generally considered Deuteronomy to be non-Mosaic in authorship and written considerably later than the time of Moses. However, the similarities between Deuteronomy and these Hittite treaties suggest that Deuteronomy was indeed written during the time of Moses (Kenneth A. Kitchen, *The Bible in Its World,* pp. 80–83).

Nuzi

Nuzi (modern Yorghan Tepe), in northeastern Iraq, was excavated by Edward Chiera, Robert H. Pfeiffer, and R. F. S. Starr from 1925 to 1931. The 20,000 clay tablets discovered here reflect cultural customs of this city under Hurrian domination about 1500 B.C., though many of the customs undoubtedly pre-date that time. They depict the prevailing culture of northern Mesopotamia and westward, the general area where Abraham was born and where his relatives continued to live after God directed him to Canaan.

Discovery of the Nuzi documents radiated excitement because they seemed to provide evidence for historical parallels to the patriarchal narrative: sister/wife relationships (Gen. 12:13; 20:12); slave adoption (Gen. 15:4); secondary wives in cases of barrenness (Gen. 16:2); transfer of birthright (Gen. 25:33); oral blessings and deathbed pronouncements (Gen. 27:2-10); presentation of a handmaid to a new bride (Gen. 29:24, 29); shepherding contracts (Gen. 31); and ownership of household gods (Gen. 31:19, 30-39).

Initial reaction to these texts was somewhat overzealous, for scholars tended to interpret all similarities to the patriarchal narrative as direct parallels, even if it was necessary to reconstruct the biblical story to make the examples from Nuzi fit. The criticism of recent scholars has led to a rethinking and modification of early interpretations of the so-called parallels. It is safe to assert, however, that these texts have provided valuable insight into common family life and culture in northern Mesopotamia. John Walton summarizes:

> What is clear is that the patriarchs and their families were very much a part of the culture of the ancient Near East. Even if we do not identify specific parallels, the similarities between the lifestyle and culture of the patriarchs on the one hand and the lifestyle and culture in centers such as Nuzi on the other hand are patently clear. In this area . . . we see that religious practice was the main element that separated the biblical characters from their Near Eastern counterparts. (*Ancient Israelite Literature in Its Cultural Context,* p. 58)

Mari

Mari (modern Tell Hariri) lies just south of the Euphrates River in southeastern Syria. André Parrot excavated there from 1933 to 1939 and again from 1951 to 1956. The city has a rich history dating back to the third millennium B.C. In addition to a royal palace and a large ziggurat, more than 20,000 tablets were discovered in the royal archives. These texts, often mostly in Akkadian, contain diplomatic correspondence between King Zimri-lim of Mari and Hammurabi of Babylon.

As at Nuzi, these texts have supplied a wealth of helpful historical, geographical, religious, and cultural information from northwestern Mesopotamia. It is possible that Mari at one time controlled the district of Haran from which Abraham migrated. Of special interest to patriarchal studies are the names of several sites from the region of Haran. They are equivalent to Abraham's ancestors Peleg, Serug, and Nahor, who are mentioned in Genesis 11:16-29. Though these names in the Mari texts cannot be connected directly to Abraham, they do show that the names in Genesis 11 are representative of that time and place.

Another point of interest is the large quantity of texts embodying prophecy. Such literature has provided material with which to compare and contrast Israel's prophets and the content of their messages (John Walton, *Ancient Israelite Literature in Its Cultural Context,* pp. 201–214).

Ugarit

Ugarit (modern Ras Shamra) on the Syrian coast is another ancient city beyond the borders of Israel that has made a tremendous impact on biblical studies. An accidental discovery by a Syrian peasant in 1928 led to the excavations of this important commercial center by Claude F. A. Schaeffer, from 1929 to 1960. Remarkable as were the archives of Nuzi and Mari, they were almost eclipsed by the astounding collection of tablets uncovered at Ugarit. This collection contained texts written mostly in the fifteenth to the thirteenth centuries B.C. in seven different languages, including Egyptian, Sumerian, Akkadian, Hittite, and Hurrian. Most momentous was the discovery of a totally new "Canaanite" language in cuneiform script. "Ugaritic," as it was called, had close affinities to biblical Hebrew. The literature from Ugarit proved to be more closely related linguistically, culturally, and chronologically to the earliest Hebrew literature than any previously discovered literature from Mesopotamia or Egypt.

Some 350 texts from Ugarit were consequential to OT studies. Religious epics revealed the sharp contrast in Canaanite mythology and Israel's theology. Bible scholars became more fully aware of the gross sexuality, prostitution (both male and female), and moral depravity of the Canaanite fertility cult that centered in deities such as Baal and his consort Asherah. It became abundantly clear why Baal worship was repeatedly condemned in Scripture. (The term translated "groves" in the KJV, as in Deuteronomy 7:5, is translated "Asherah poles" in the NLT and NIV.)

The study of OT poetry has benefitted greatly from knowledge of Ugaritic grammar. The affinities between Ugaritic and Hebrew are numerous. Many parallels have been found between Ugaritic poetic style and the phraseology of the Psalms. Earlier proposed emendations of difficult Hebrew phrases in the Psalms have been shown to be unwarranted.

Tell Mardikh

The most recent discovery of a royal archive occurred at Tell Mardikh (modern name for the site of ancient Ebla), 30 miles south of Aleppo in Syria. Paolo Matthiae began excavations there in 1964, and in 1974 he uncovered 42 clay tablets. The next year he found thousands more, all dating to c. 2300 B.C. In addition to Sumerian, many were inscribed in a strange, previously unheard of language (now called Eblaite after its discovery site) in cuneiform script. This new language was a Semitic language with affinities to Ugaritic, and especially to Hebrew.

As in the case of earlier discovered archives, many of these tablets contained commercial texts. Others were religious or mythological texts bearing the names of a variety of deities, some of whom, such as Dagon and El, were known in Canaan. (*El* is also a Hebrew name for God.) This archive caused quite a stir initially among biblical scholars because early reports claimed that the Ebla tablet mentioned personal names such as Abram, Eber, Ishmael, Israel, Saul, and David, and the place names Nahur, Ur, Hazor, Megiddo, Lachish, Sodom, and Gomorrah. The accuracy of some of the early reports has been contested by later scholars, however, so that the significance and value of these texts to biblical studies still is not entirely known. If early translations stand, the Ebla tablets still predate Abraham by several hundred years, so no direct connection can be made between the names found at Ebla and biblical personalities.

The tablets do, however, show that the names we find in the Bible are names that were common in that area at that time. Moreover, it is likely that the Eblaite language will make its contribution to the study of biblical Hebrew just as other Semitic languages have.

The Dead Sea Scrolls

Though not part of a royal archive, an equally sensational and valuable collection of documents now known as the Dead Sea Scrolls began to emerge after a chance discovery by a Bedouin shepherd in 1947. He came upon a cave in which he found clay jars containing ancient scrolls. Subsequent investigations by archaeologists of nearly 300 caves in the region located 11 caves containing a variety of types of manuscripts: OT books, commentaries on biblical books, apocryphal and OT pseudepigraphal writings, and sectarian literature. These texts were all found in the vicinity of Qumran, a community established about 135 B.C. It is generally believed that Qumran was inhabited by a Jewish sect known as the Essenes. Apparently this community was broken up during the wars with the Romans from A.D. 66 to 70 and its library was taken for safekeeping to the dry caves in the region.

The importance of these scrolls (and thousands of fragments) can hardly be exaggerated. Neither is it possible to itemize all the significant finds. Several examples will have to suffice. Every OT book except Esther is represented by at least fragments. The entire book of Isaiah was found on one scroll. Modern critics claim two or three authors for Isaiah, with a break between chapters 39 and 40. Significantly, the Isaiah scroll has no such break. In addition, before 1947 the oldest text of Isaiah was dated about A.D. 900, but this scroll dating to c. 100 B.C. shows that over a period of about a thousand years the text of Isaiah had been preserved with remarkable accuracy.

The sectarian literature from Qumran is also valuable to NT studies, for it sheds new light on Jewish history and religious life and thought in Palestine, especially in the years just preceding the birth of Christianity.

There still remains much to be learned from these scrolls. For several decades, study of the Dead Sea materials came to a virtual standstill as the public waited for a select few scholars to translate and publish the texts assigned to them. Pressure from scholars and laymen alike have begun to speed up the process, and only time will reveal what important information is yet to be disclosed.

❖ ❖ ❖

FOR FURTHER READING ON ARCHAEOLOGY AND THE BIBLE

Blaiklock, Edward M., and R. K. Harrison, eds. *The New International Dictionary of Biblical Archaeology.* Grand Rapids, Mich.: Zondervan, 1983.

Free, Joseph P. Revised by Howard F. Vos. *Archaeology and Bible History.* Grand Rapids, Mich.: Zondervan, 1992.

Kitchen, Kenneth A. *The Bible in Its World.* Downers Grove, Ill.: InterVarsity, 1977.

Pritchard, James B. *Ancient Near Eastern Texts Relating to the Old Testament with Supplement.* Princeton, N.J.: Princeton University Press, 1969.

Schoville, Keith N. *Biblical Archaeology in Focus.* Grand Rapids, Mich.: Baker, 1978.

Thompson, J. A. *The Bible and Archaeology.* 2nd. ed. Grand Rapids, Mich.: Eerdmans, 1982.

Walton, John H. *Ancient Israelite Literature in Its Cultural Context.* Grand Rapids, Mich.: Zondervan, 1989.

Vos, Howard F. *Archaeology in Bible Lands.* Chicago: Moody, 1977.

Yamauchi, Edwin. *The Stones and the Scriptures.* Philadelphia: J. B. Lippincott, 1972.

CHARTS

ISRAEL'S CALENDAR

Month names in early Bible times came from Canaanite sources; after the Exile, Babylonian names were used. For instance, Exodus 13:4 calls the first month Abib, while Esther 3:7 calls it Nisan. Months are often referred to numerically, as the "first month," etc. (Month names in parentheses are the earlier Canaanite names.)

MONTH	HEBREW MONTH	EQUIVALENT	REFERENCE
First	(Abib) Nisan	March–April	Exod. 12:2; 13:4; Esther 3:7
Second	(Ziv) Iyyar	April–May	Exod. 16:1
Third	Sivan	May–June	Exod. 19:1; Esther 8:9
Fourth	Tammuz	June–July	2 Kings 25:3
Fifth	Ab	July–August	Num. 33:38
Sixth	Elul	August–Sept.	1 Chron. 27:9; Neh. 6:15
Seventh	(Ethanium) Tishri	Sept.–Oct.	Gen. 8:4
Eighth	(Bul) Marchesvan	Oct.–Nov.	Zech. 1:1
Ninth	Kislev	Nov.–Dec.	Ezra 10:9; Zech. 7:1
Tenth	Tebeth	Dec.–Jan.	Gen. 8:5; Esther 2:16
Eleventh	Shebat	Jan.–Feb.	Deut. 1:3; Zech. 1:7
Twelfth	Adar	Feb.–March	Esther 3:7; Ezra 6:15

ISRAEL'S SABBATHS

DAY	OCCURRENCE	REFERENCE	PURPOSE
Sabbath	Seventh day of week	Exod. 31:12-17; Lev. 23:3; Deut. 5:12-15	The people were to separate themselves from their work and focus on God in worship. This resting of mind and body maintained health and vigor.
Sabbath year	Every seventh year	Exod. 23:10-11; Lev. 25:1-7	God rests the land for one year, allowing nutrients to replenish.

Year of Jubilee	Every 50th year (after seven cycles of seven years)	Lev. 25:8-55; 27:17-24; Num. 36:4	All property was to return to original owners. It was meant to stabilize society and help the poor.

❖ ❖ ❖

ISRAEL'S FESTIVALS

DATE	NAME	REFERENCE	PURPOSE
14th of Nisan (March–April): One day	Passover	Exod. 12:1-14; Lev. 23:5; Num. 9:1-14;28:16; Deut 16:1-7; Luke 22:13-20; 1 Pet. 1:19	To remember Israel's deliverance from Egypt. Blood of lamb was shed for every household. Typifies the death of Christ, the "Passover Lamb" (1 Cor. 5:7).
15th–21st of Abib (March–April): Seven days	Festival of Unleavened Bread	Exod. 12:15-20; 13:3-10; 23:15; 34:18; Lev. 23:6-8; Num. 28:17-25; Deut. 16:3-4, 8	To remember how God brought Israel out of Egypt in haste. Bread without yeast (unleavened) was prepared and eaten. Pictured leaven as evil—to be separated from. Typifies believer's walk of separation and holiness (1 Cor. 5:8).
16th of Abib (March–April): One day	Festival of Firstfruits	Lev. 23:9-14	To acknowledge the Lord's bounty and fullness in the land he shares with his people. First barley harvest is presented as wave offering, putting God's portion first. Typifies Christ's resurrection, assures believer's resurrection (1 Cor. 15:23).
Sixth of Sivan (May–June) 50 days after Festival of Unleavened Bread: One day	Festival of Harvest (Pentecost)	Exod. 23:16; 34:22; Lev. 23:15-21; Num. 28:26-31; Deut. 16:9-12	To express thanksgiving for harvest. Typifies advent of Holy Spirit (Acts 2:4).
First of Tishri: (Sept.–Oct.): One day	New Year/ Festival of Trumpets (Rosh Hashanah)	Lev. 23:23-25; Num. 29:1-6	Precise purpose not known. Was celebrated on first day of civil year (seventh month). Typifies regathering of Israel (Matt. 24:31).

DATE	NAME	REFERENCE	PURPOSE
10th of Tishri: One day	Day of Atonement (Yom Kippur)	Lev. 16:23, 26-34; Num. 29:7-11	Tenth day of seventh month was unique day of fasting and repentance. Israel sought atonement for its sins (Lev. 16:29; 23:27; 29:7). Fellowship with God was restored. Theologically, speaks of national cleansing and of inability to make final atonement for sin.
15th–22nd of Tishri: Eight days	Festival of the Final Harvest (Shelters, Booths, Ingathering)	Exod. 23:16; 34:22; Lev. 23:33-36, 39-43; Num. 29: 12-34; Deut. 16: 13-15; Neh. 8:13-18; Zech. 14:16-19	Third of the three great annual festivals. People traveled to the central worship place and lived for a week in booths made of branches. Typifies millennial rest (Zech. 14:16; Matt. 17:4).
22nd of Tishri: One day	Holy Assembly	Lev. 23:36; Num. 29:35-38	A day of meetings, rest, and sacrifices to mark end of yearly cycle of festivals.
14th–15th of Adar: Two days	Festival of Purim	Esther 9:18-32	Reminded Israelites of deliverance from Persia in time of Esther. A day of joyous celebration with feasting and giving.

UNITS OF MONEY

(approx. U.S. weights in italics)

UNIT	EQUIVALENT	NKJV	REFERENCE
Talent (Hebrew/ Greek)	3,000 shekels; 6,000 bekas; 60 minas (*66 pounds*)	talent	Exod. 25:39; 1 Kings 20:39; Matt. 25:24 Rev. 16:21
Kesitah (Hebrew)	125 shekels *(4 pounds)*	piece of money, piece of silver	Gen. 33:19; Josh. 24:32
Mina (Hebrew/ Greek)	50 shekels; 100 bekas *(1 pound)*	mina	Luke 19:13, 16
Shekel (Hebrew)	2 bekas; 20 gerahs *(1/2 ounce)*	shekel	Gen. 24:22; Exod. 38:26; 2 Kings 7:1; Neh. 10:32; Ezek. 45:12

UNIT	EQUIVALENT	NKJV	REFERENCE
Beka (Hebrew)	half-shekel; 10 gerahs *(1/5 ounce)*	bekah	Exod. 38:26
Gerah (Hebrew)	1/20 shekel *(1/50 ounce)*	gerah	Exod. 30:13; Lev. 27:25
Drachma (Greek)	one day's wage	silver coin	Luke 15:8-10 (probably)
Denarius (Roman)	one day's wage	denarius	Matt. 18:28; 20:2, 9; Mark 6:37; 14:5
Lepton (Greek)	very small copper coin	mite	Mark 12:42

❖ ❖ ❖

UNITS OF MEASUREMENT

(approx. U.S. measurements in italics)

Length and distance

UNIT	EQUIVALENT	NKJV	REFERENCE
Roman mile	8 stadia *(9/10 mile)*	mile	Matt. 5:41
Day's journey	*(20 miles)*	day's journey	Num. 11:31; Jon. 3:4; Luke 2:44
Sabbath day's journey	6 stadia (2,000 cubits, according to rabbis) *(7/10 mile)*	Sabbath day's journey	Acts 1:12
Stadion (Greek/Roman)	1/8 Roman mile *(606 feet)*	furlong	Rev. 14:20
Rod	3 paces; 6 cubits *(9 feet)*		
Rod (in Ezekiel)	6 long cubits *(10.5 feet)*	rod; measuring rod	Ezek. 40:3-8; 41:8; 42:16-19
Pace	1/3 rod; 2 cubits *(3 feet)*	pace	2 Sam. 6:13
Cubit	1/2 pace; 2 spans *(18 inches)*	cubit	Deut. 3:11; 1 Sam. 17:4; Luke 12:25
Span	1/2 cubit *(9 inches)*	span	1 Sam. 17:4
Handbreadth	1/3 span; 4 fingers	handbreadth	1 Kings 7:26
Finger	1/4 handbreadth	finger	Jer. 52:21
Fathom	length of outstretched arms *(6 feet)*	fathom	Acts 27:28

Weight

UNIT	EQUIVALENT	NKJV	REFERENCE
Talent	60 minas; 3,000 shekels	talent	*(see "Units of Money")*
Mina	50 shekels	pound	
Shekel	2 bekas; 20 gerahs	shekel	
Beka	half-shekel; 10 gerahs	bekah	
Gerah	1/20 shekel	gerah	
Litra	*(12 ounces)*	pound	

Capacity (dry)

UNIT	EQUIVALENT	NKJV	REFERENCE
Kor (homer)	10 ephahs *(6 1/2 bushels)*	kor	1 Kings 4:22; Ezek. 45:10-11
Lethech	1/2 kor (1/2 homer) *(3 1/4 bushels)*	half-homer	Hosea 3:2
Ephah	1/10 kor (1/10 homer) *(3/4 bushel)*	measure	Lev. 19:36
Omer	1/10 ephah *(2 quarts)*	omer	Exod. 16:16-36
Kab	1/18 ephah *(1/2 pint)*	kab	2 Kings 6:25

Capacity (liquid)

UNIT	EQUIVALENT	NKJV	REFERENCE
Kor	10 baths *(60 gallons)*	kor	Ezek. 45:14
Metrete	*(10 gallons)*	firkin	John 2:6
Bath	1 ephah *(6 gallons)*	measure; bath	Ezek. 45:10-11
Hin	1/6 bath *(1 gallon)*	hin	Ezek. 45:24
Log	1/72 bath *(1/3 quart)*	log	Lev. 14:10

❖ BIBLIOGRAPHY

Bancroft, Emery. *Christian Theology.* Grand Rapids, Mich.: Zondervan, 1961.
Barnhouse, Donald. *Genesis.* Grand Rapids, Mich.: Zondervan, 1971.
Boa, Ken. *Talk through the Bible.* Nashville, Tenn.: Thomas Nelson, 1983.
Charlesworth, James H., ed. *The Old Testament Pseudepigrapha.* Garden City, N.Y.: Doubleday, 1985.
Coder, S. Maxwell. *Jude: The Acts of the Apostates.* Chicago, Moody, 1967.
Criswell, W. A. *The Bible for Today's World.* Grand Rapids, Mich.: Zondervan, 1965.
Custance, Arthur. *Genesis and Early Man.* Grand Rapids, Mich.: Zondervan, 1975.
Dalton, William J. *Christ's Proclamation to the Spirits.* Rome: Pontifical Bible Institute, 1965.
Davis, John. *Conquest and Crisis.* Grand Rapids, Mich.: Baker, 1969.
Day, G. M. *The Wonder of the Word.* Chicago: Moody, 1957.
Elwell, Walter. *Evangelical Dictionary of Theology.* Grand Rapids, Mich.: Baker, 1984.
Grounds, Vernon. *The Reason for Our Hope.* Chicago: Moody, 1945.
Halley, Henry H. *Halley's Bible Handbook.* 24th ed. Grand Rapids, Mich.: Zondervan, 1965.
Hoyt, Herman A. *The End Times.* Winona Lake, Ind.: Brethren Missionary Herald, 1978.
Kac, Arthur W. *Rebirth of the State of Israel.* Grand Rapids, Mich.: Baker, 1976.
McGee, J. Vernon. *Second Timothy.* Nashville, Tenn.: Thomas Nelson, 1983.
———. *Reveling through Revelation.* Nashville, Tenn.: Thomas Nelson, 1982.
———. *Thru the Bible with J. Vernon McGee.* Nashville, Tenn.: Thomas Nelson, 1981.
Mears, Henrietta. *What the Bible Is All About.* Ventura, Calif.: Regal, 1982.
New Scofield Reference Bible. New York: Oxford University Press, 1967.
Pentecost, J. Dwight. *Your Adversary, the Devil.* Grand Rapids, Mich.: Zondervan, 1990.
The People's Study Bible. Wheaton, Ill.: Tyndale, 1986.
Ryrie, Charles. *Basic Theology.* Wheaton, Ill.: Victor Books, 1987.
———. *Revelation.* Chicago: Moody, 1968.
———. *The Ryrie Study Bible.* Chicago: Moody, 1976.
Sauer, Erich. *Dawn of World Redemption.* Grand Rapids, Mich.: Eerdmans, 1951.
Strauss, Lehman. *God's Plan for the Future.* Grand Rapids, Mich.: Zondervan, 1965.
Strong, A. H. *Systematic Theology.* Valley Forge, Penn.: Judson, 1965.

Tenney, Merrill. *New Testament Survey*. Grand Rapids, Mich.: Eerdmans, 1985.
Unger, Merrill F. *Unger's Bible Handbook*. Chicago: Moody, 1967.
Walvoord, John. *Jesus Christ Our Lord*. Chicago: Moody, 1969.
Walvoord, John, and Roy Zuck, eds. *Bible Knowledge Commentary: New Testament*. Wheaton, Ill.: Victor Books, 1983.
———. *Bible Knowledge Commentary: Old Testament*. Wheaton, Ill.: Victor Books, 1985.
Wilson, R. McL., ed. *The New Testament Apocrypha*. Philadelphia: Westminster, 1963.
Wuest, Kenneth. *Word Studies in Philippians*. Grand Rapids, Mich.: Eerdmans, 1953.

❖ GENERAL INDEX

❖ INDEX OF "PEOPLE TO REMEMBER"

❖ MAP INDEX

❖ ILLUSTRATION INDEX